THE
EXPOSITOR'S
BIBLE
COMMENTARY

EXPOSITOR'S BIBLE COMMENTARY

in Thirteen Volumes

When complete, the Expositor's Bible Commentary will include the following volumes:

To see which titles are available, visit www.zondervan.com.

THE
EXPOSITOR'S
BIBLE
COMMENTARY

REVISED EDITION

Luke ~ Acts

Tremper Longman III & David E. Garland

General Editors

ZONDERVAN®

ZONDERVAN.com/
AUTHORTRACKER
follow your favorite authors

 ZONDERVAN®

The Expositor's Bible Commentary: Luke–Acts Vol. 10

Luke—Copyright © 2007 by Walter L. Liefeld and David W. Pao
John—Copyright © 2007 by Robert H. Mounce
Acts—Copyright © 2007 by Richard N. Longenecker

Requests for information should be addressed to:

Zondervan, *Grand Rapids, Michigan 49530*

Library of Congress Cataloging-in-Publication Data

The expositor's Bible commentary / [general editors], Tremper Longman III and David E. Garland.—Rev.
     p. cm.
    Includes bibliographical references.
    ISBN-10: 0-310-23500-6 (hardcover)
    ISBN-13: 978-0-310-23500-2
    1. Bible. N.T.—Commentaries.   I. Longman, Tremper.   II. Garland, David E.
BS2341.53.E96 2005
220.7—dc22   2005006281

Interior design by Tracey Walker

Printed in the United States of America

12 • 10 9 8 7 6 5 4 3

CONTENTS

CONTRIBUTORS TO VOLUME TEN

Luke: **Walter L. Liefeld** (Ph.D., Columbia University and Union Theological Seminary) is distinguished professor emeritus of New Testament at Trinity Evangelical Divinity School in Deerfield, Illinois.

Luke: **David W. Pao** (Ph.D., Harvard University) is associate professor of New Testament at Trinity Evangelical Divinity School in Deerfield, Illinois.

John: **Robert H. Mounce** (Ph.D., University of Aberdeen) is president emeritus of Whitworth College in Spokane, Washington.

Acts: **Richard N. Longenecker** (Ph.D., University of Edinburgh) is professor emeritus of New Testament at Wycliffe College, University of Toronto in Toronto, Canada.

General editor: **Tremper Longman III** (Ph.D., Yale University) is Robert H. Gundry professor of biblical studies at Westmont College in Santa Barbara, California.

General editor: **David E. Garland** (Ph.D., Southern Baptist Theological Seminary) is associate dean of academic affairs and William M. Hinson professor of Christian Scriptures at George W. Truett Seminary, Baylor University, in Waco, Texas.

PREFACE

Frank Gaebelein wrote the following in the preface to the original Expositor's Bible Commentary (which first appeared in 1979): "The title of this work defines its purpose. Written primarily by expositors for expositors, it aims to provide preachers, teachers, and students of the Bible with a new and comprehensive commentary on the books of the Old and New Testaments." Those volumes achieved that purpose admirably. The original EBC was exceptionally well received and had an enormous impact on the life of the church. It has served as the mainstay of countless pastors and students who could not afford an extensive library on each book of the Bible but who wanted solid guidance from scholars committed to the authority of the Holy Scriptures.

Gaebelein also wrote, "A commentary that will continue to be useful through the years should handle contemporary trends in biblical studies in such a way as to avoid becoming outdated when critical fashions change." This revision continues the EBC's exalted purpose and stands on the shoulders of the expositors of the first edition, but it seeks to maintain the usefulness of the commentary by interacting with new discoveries and academic discussions. While the primary goal of this commentary is to elucidate the text and not to provide a guide to the scholarly literature about the text, the commentators critically engage recent academic discussion and provide updated bibliographies so that pastors, teachers, and students can keep abreast of modern scholarship.

Some of the commentaries in the EBC have been revised by the original author or in conjunction with a younger colleague. In other cases, scholars have been commissioned to offer fresh commentaries because the original author had passed on or wanted to pass on the baton to the next generation of evangelical scholars. Today, with commentaries on a single book of the Old and New Testaments often extending into multiple volumes, the need for a comprehensive yet succinct commentary that guides one to the gist of the text's meaning is even more pressing. The new EBC seeks to fill this need.

The theological stance of this commentary series remains unchanged: the authors are committed to the divine inspiration, complete trustworthiness, and full authority of the Bible. The commentators have demonstrated proficiency in the biblical book that is their specialty, as well as commitment to the church and the pastoral dimension of biblical interpretation. They also represent the geographical and confessional diversity that characterized the first contributors.

The commentaries adhere to the same chief principle of grammatico-historical interpretation that drove the first edition. In the foreword to the inaugural issue of the journal *New Testament Studies* in 1954, Matthew Black warned that "the danger in the present is that theology, with its head too high in the clouds, may end by falling into the pit of an unhistorical and uncritical dogmatism. Into any new theological undertaking must be brought all that was best in the old ideal of sound learning, scrupulous attention to philology, text and history." The dangers that Black warned against over fifty years ago have not vanished. Indeed, new dangers arise in a secular, consumerist culture that finds it more acceptable to use God's name in exclamations than in prayer and that encourages insipid theologies that hang in the wind and shift to tickle the ears and to meet the latest fancy. Only a solid biblical foundation can fend off these fads.

The Bible was not written for our information but for our transformation. It is not a quarry to find stones with which to batter others but to find the rock on which to build the church. It does not invite us simply to speak of God but to hear God and to confess that his Son, Jesus Christ, is Lord to the glory of God the Father (Php 2:10). It also calls us to obey his commandments (Mt 28:20). It is not a self-interpreting text, however. Interpretation of the Holy Scriptures requires sound learning and regard for history, language, and text. Exegetes must interpret not only the primary documents but all that has a bearing, direct or indirect, on the grammar and syntax, historical context, transmission, and translation of these writings.

The translation used in this commentary remains the New International Version (North American edition), but all of the commentators work from the original languages (Hebrew and Greek) and draw on other translations when deemed useful. The format is also very similar to the original EBC, while the design is extensively updated with a view to enhanced ease of use for the reader. Each commentary section begins with an introduction (printed in a single-column format) that provides the reader with the background necessary to understand the Bible book. Almost all introductions include a short bibliography and an outline. The Bible text is divided into primary units that are often explained in an "Overview" section that precedes commentary on specific verses. The complete text of the New International Version is provided for quick reference, and an extensive "Commentary" section (printed in a double-column format) follows the reproducing of the text. When the Hebrew or Greek text is cited in the commentary section, a phonetic system of transliteration and translation is used. The "Notes" section (printed in a single-column format) provides a specialized discussion of key words or concepts, as well as helpful resource information. The original languages and their transliterations will appear in this section. Finally, on occasion, expanded thoughts can be found in a "Reflections" section (printed in a double-column format) that follows the Notes section.

One additional feature is worth mentioning. Throughout this volume, wherever specific biblical words are discussed, the Goodrick-Kohlenberger (GK) numbers have been added. These numbers, which appear in the *Strongest NIV Exhaustive Concordance* and other reference tools, are based on the numbering system developed by Edward Goodrick and John Kohlenberger III and provide a system similar but superior to the Strong's numbering system.

The editors wish to thank all of the contributors for their hard work and commitment to this project. We also deeply appreciate the labor and skill of the staff at Zondervan. It is a joy to work with them—in particular Jack Kuhatschek, Stan Gundry, Katya Covrett, and Dirk Buursma. In addition, we acknowledge with thanks the work of Connie Gundry Tappy as copy editor.

We all fervently desire that these commentaries will result not only in a deeper intellectual grasp of the Word of God but also in hearts that more profoundly love and obey the God who reveals himself to us in its pages.

David E. Garland, associate dean for academic affairs and
William M. Hinson professor of Christian Scriptures, George W.
Truett Theological Seminary at Baylor University

Tremper Longman III, Robert H. Gundry professor of biblical
studies, Westmont College

ABBREVIATIONS

Bible Texts, Versions, Etc.

ASV	American Standard Version	NEB	New English Bible
AT	*The Complete Bible: An American Translation* (NT: Goodspeed)	NET	New English Translation (www.netbible.com)
Beck	*New Testament in Language of Today*	NIV	New International Version
		NJB	New Jerusalem Bible
CEV	Contemporary English Version	NKJV	New King James Version
CSB	Christian Standard Bible	NLT	New Living Translation
ESV	English Standard Version	Norlie	*New Testament in Modern English*
GNB	Good News Bible (see also TEV)	NRSV	New Revised Standard Version
GWT	God's Word Translation	NT	New Testament
JB	Jerusalem Bible	OT	Old Testament
KJV	King James Version	Phillips	*New Testament in Modern English,* J. B. Phillips
Knox	*Holy Bible: A Translation from the Latin Vulgate*		
		REB	Revised English Bible
LXX	Septuagint (the Greek OT)	Rieu	*Penguin Bible*
MLB	Modern Language Bible	RSV	Revised Standard Version
Moffatt	*A New Translation of the Bible*	TCNT	Twentieth Century New Testament
Montgomery	*Centenary Translation of the New Testament in Modern English*		
		TEV	Today's English Version
MT	Masoretic Text of the OT	TNIV	Today's New International Version
NA²⁷	*Novum Testamentum Graece,* Nestle-Aland, 27th ed.		
		UBS⁴	*The Greek New Testament,* United Bible Societies, 4th ed.
NAB	New American Bible		
NASB	New American Standard Bible	Williams	*The New Testament in the Language of the People* (C. B. Williams)
NCV	New Century Version		

Old Testament, New Testament, Apocrypha

Ge	Genesis	Ru	Ruth
Ex	Exodus	1–2Sa	1–2 Samuel
Lev	Leviticus	1–2 Kgdms	1–2 Kingdoms (LXX)
Nu	Numbers	1–2Ki	1–2 Kings
Dt	Deuteronomy	3–4 Kgdms	3–4 Kingdoms (LXX)
Jos	Joshua	1–2Ch	1–2 Chronicles
Jdg	Judges	Ezr	Ezra

Ne	Nehemiah	Gal	Galatians
Est	Esther	Eph	Ephesians
Job	Job	Php	Philippians
Ps/Pss	Psalm/Psalms	Col	Colossians
Pr	Proverbs	1–2Th	1–2 Thessalonians
Ecc	Ecclesiastes	1–2Ti	1–2 Timothy
SS	Song of Songs	Tit	Titus
Isa	Isaiah	Phm	Philemon
Jer	Jeremiah	Heb	Hebrews
La	Lamentations	Jas	James
Eze	Ezekiel	1–2Pe	1–2 Peter
Da	Daniel	1–2–3Jn	1–2–3 John
Hos	Hosea	Jude	Jude
Joel	Joel	Rev	Revelation
Am	Amos	Add Esth	Additions to Esther
Ob	Obadiah	Add Dan	Additions to Daniel
Jnh	Jonah	Bar	Baruch
Mic	Micah	Bel	Bel and the Dragon
Na	Nahum	Ep Jer	Epistle of Jeremiah
Hab	Habakkuk	1–2 Esd	1–2 Esdras
Zep	Zephaniah	1–2 Macc	1–2 Maccabees
Hag	Haggai	3–4 Macc	3–4 Maccabees
Zec	Zechariah	Jdt	Judith
Mal	Malachi	Pr Azar	Prayer of Azariah
Mt	Matthew	Pr Man	Prayer of Manasseh
Mk	Mark	Ps 151	Psalm 151
Lk	Luke	Sir	Sirach/Ecclesiasticus
Jn	John	Sus	Susanna
Ac	Acts	Tob	Tobit
Ro	Romans	Wis	Wisdom of Solomon
1–2Co	1–2 Corinthians		

Dead Sea Scrolls and Related Texts

CD	Cairo Genizah copy of the *Damascus Document*
1QapGen	*Genesis Apocryphon* (texts from Qumran)
1QH	*Hôdāyōt* or *Thanksgiving Hymns* (texts from Qumran)
1QIsa	Isaiah (texts from Qumran)
1QM	*Milḥāmāh* or *War Scroll* (texts from Qumran)
1QpHab	Pesher Habakkuk (texts from Qumran)
1QS	*Serek hayyaḥad* or *Rule of the Community* (texts from Qumran)

1QSa	*Rule of the Congregation* (texts from Qumran)
1QpMic	*Pesher Micah* (text from Qumran)
4QpNa	*Pesher Nahum* (texts from Qumran)
4QpPs	*Pesher Psalms* (texts from Qumran)
4Q44 (4QDt^q)	*Deuteronomy* (texts from Qumran)
4Q174	*Florilegium* (texts from Qumran)
4Q243	*Pseudo-Daniel^a* (texts from Qumran)
4Q252	*Commentary on Genesis A*, formerly *Patriarchal Blessings* (texts from Qumran)
4Q394	*Miqṣat Maʿáśê ha-Torah^a* (texts from Qumran)
4Q400	*Songs of the Sabbath Sacrifice* (texts from Qumran)
4Q502	*Ritual of Marriage* (texts from Qumran)
4Q521	*Messianic Apocalypse* (texts from Qumran)
4Q525	*Beatitudes* (texts from Qumran)
11Q13	*Melchizedek* (texts from Qumran)

Other Ancient Texts

Abraham	*On the Life of Abraham* (Philo)
Ad.	*Adelphi* (Terence)
Aeth.	*Aethiopica* (Heliodorus)
Ag.	*Agamemnon* (Aeschylus)
Ag. Ap.	*Against Apion* (Josephus)
Agr.	*De Lege agraria* (Cicero)
Alc.	*Alcibiades* (Plutarch)
Alex.	*Alexander the False Prophet* (Lucian)
Amic.	*De amicitia* (Cicero)
An.	*De anima* (Tertullian)
Anab.	*Anabasis* (Xenophon)
Ann.	*Annales* (Tacitus)
Ant.	*Antigone* (Sophocles)
Ant.	*Jewish Antiquities* (Josephus)
Ant. rom.	*Antiquitates romanae* (Dionysius of Halicarnassus)
Apol.	*Apologia* (Plato, Tertullian)
1 Apol.	*First Apology* (Justin Martyr)
Apos. Con.	*Apostolic Constitutions*
Ascen. Isa.	*Ascension of Isaiah*
As. Mos.	*Assumption of Moses*
Att.	*Epistulae ad Atticum* (Cicero)
b. ʿAbod. Zar.	*ʿAbodah Zarah* (Babylonian Talmud)
2–4 Bar.	*2–4 Baruch*
b. B. Bat.	*Bava Batra* (Babylonian Talmud)
b. Ber.	*Berakhot* (Babylonian Talmud)
b. Ketub.	*Ketubbot* (Babylonian Talmud)
b. Meg.	*Megillah* (Babylonian Talmud)
b. Ned.	*Nedarim* (Babylonian Talmud)
b. Pesaḥ.	*Pesaḥim* (Babylonian Talmud)
b. Šabb.	*Šabbat* (Babylonian Talmud)
b. Sanh.	*Sanhedrin* (Babylonian Talmud)
b. Šebu.	*Shevuʾot* (Babylonian Talmud)
b. Taʿan.	*Taʿanit* (Babylonian Talmud)
Bapt.	*De baptismo* (Tertullian)
Barn.	*Barnabas*
Ben.	*De beneficiis* (Seneca)
Bibl.	*Bibliotheca* (Photius)
Bibl. hist.	*Bibliotheca historica* (Diodorus Siculus)
Bride	*Advice to the Bride and Groom* (Plutarch)
Cels.	*Contra Celsum* (Origen)
Cic.	*Cicero* (Plutarch)
Claud.	*Divus Claudius* (Suetonius)

1–2 Clem.	*1–2 Clement*	*Gen. Rab.*	*Genesis Rabbah*
Comm. Dan.	*Commentarium in Danielem* (Hippolytus)	*Geogr.*	*Geographica* (Strabo)
		Gorg.	*Gorgias* (Plato)
Comm. Jo.	*Commentarii in evangelium Joannis* (Origen)	*Haer.*	*Adversus Haereses* (Irenaeus)
		Hell.	*Hellenica* (Xenophon)
Comm. Matt.	*Commentarium in evangelium Matthaei* (Origen)	*Hist.*	*Historicus* (Polybius, Cassius Dio, Thucydides)
Corrept.	*De correptione et gratia* (Augustine)	*Hist.*	*Historiae* (Herodotus, Tacitus)
Creation	*On the Creation of the World* (Philo)	*Hist. eccl.*	*History of the Church* (Eusebius)
		Hist. Rome	*The History of Rome* (Livy)
Cyr.	*Cyropaedia* (Xenophon)	*Hom. Acts*	*Homilies on Acts* (John Chrysostom)
Decal.	*De decalogo* (Philo)		
Decl.	*Declamationes* (Quintilian)	*Hom. Col.*	*Homilies on Colossians* (John Chrysostom)
Def. orac.	*De defectu oraculorum* (Plutarch)		
Deipn.	*Deipnosophistae* (Athenaeus)	*Hom. Jo.*	*Homilies on John* (John Chrysostom)
Deut. Rab.	*Deuteronomy Rabbah*		
Dial.	*Dialogus cum Tryphone* (Justin Martyr)	*Hom. Josh.*	*Homilies on Joshua* (Origen)
		Hom. Phil.	*Homilies on Philippians* (John Chrysostom)
Diatr.	*Diatribai* (Epictetus)		
Did.	*Didache*	*Hom. Rom.*	*Homilies on Romans* (John Chrysostom)
Disc.	*Discourses* (Epictetus)		
Doctr. chr.	*De doctrina christiana* (Augustine)	*Hom. 1 Tim.*	*Homilies on 1 Timothy* (John Chrysostom)
Dom.	*Domitianus* (Suetonius)		
Ebr.	*De ebrietate* (Philo)	*Hom. 2 Tim.*	*Homilies on 2 Timothy* (John Chrysostom)
E Delph.	*De E apud Delphos* (Plutarch)		
Ench.	*Enchiridion* (Epictetus)	*Hom. Tit.*	*Homilies on Titus* (John Chrysostom)
1–2 En.	*1–2 Enoch*		
Ep.	*Epistulae morales* (Seneca)	*Hypoth.*	*Hypothetica* (Philo)
Eph.	*To the Ephesians* (Ignatius)	*Inst.*	*Institutio oratoria* (Quintilian)
Epist.	*Epistulae* (Jerome, Pliny, Hippocrates)	*Jos. Asen.*	*Joseph and Aseneth*
		Joseph	*On the Life of Joseph* (Philo)
Ep. Tra.	*Epistulae ad Trajanum* (Pliny)	*Jub.*	*Jubilees*
Eth. nic.	*Ethica nichomachea* (Aristotle)	*J.W.*	*Jewish War* (Josephus)
Exod. Rab.	*Exodus Rabbah*	*L.A.E.*	*Life of Adam and Eve*
Fam.	*Epistulae ad familiares* (Cicero)	*Leg.*	*Legum allegoriae* (Philo)
Fid. Grat.	*De fide ad Gratianum* (Ambrose)	*Legat.*	*Legatio ad Gaium* (Philo)
Flacc.	*In Flaccum* (Philo)	*Let. Aris.*	*Letter of Aristeas*
Flight	*On Flight and Finding* (Philo)	*Lev. Rab.*	*Leviticus Rabbah*
Fr. Prov.	*Fragmenta in Proverbia* (Hippolytus)	*Liv. Pro.*	*Lives of the Prophets*
		m. Bek.	*Bekhorot* (Mishnah)

m. Bik.	*Bikkurim* (Mishnah)		*Praescr.*	*De praescriptione haereticorum* (Tertullian)
m. Giṭ.	*Giṭṭin* (Mishnah)		*Princ.*	*De principiis* (Origen)
m. Mak.	*Makkot* (Mishnah)		*Prom.*	*Prometheus vinctus* (Aeschylus)
m. Mid.	*Middot* (Mishnah)		*Pss. Sol.*	*Psalms of Solomon*
m. Naz.	*Nazir* (Mishnah)		*Pud.*	*De pudicitia* (Tertullian)
m. Ned.	*Nedarim* (Mishnah)		*Pyth.*	*Pythionikai* (Pindar)
m. Nid.	*Niddah* (Mishnah)		*Pyth. orac.*	*De Pythiae oraculis* (Plutarch)
m. Pesaḥ	*Pesaḥim* (Mishnah)		*Quaest. conv.*	*Quaestionum convivialum libri IX* (Plutarch)
m. Šabb.	*Šabbat* (Mishnah)		*Quint. fratr.*	*Epistulae ad Quintum fratrem* (Cicero)
m. Sanh.	*Sanhedrin* (Mishnah)			
m. Tamid	*Tamid* (Mishnah)		*Rab. Perd.*	*Pro Rabirio Perduellionis Reo* (Cicero)
m. Ṭehar.	*Ṭeharot* (Mishnah)			
Magn.	*To the Magnesians* (Ignatius)		*Resp.*	*Respublica* (Plato)
Mand.	*Mandate* (Shepherd of Hermas)		*Rewards*	*On Rewards and Punishments* (Philo)
Marc.	*Adversus Marcionem* (Tertullian)			
Mem.	*Memorabilia* (Xenophon)		*Rhet.*	*Volumina rhetorica* (Philodemus)
Midr. Ps.	*Midrash on Psalms*		*Rom.*	*To the Romans* (Ignatius)
Migr.	*De migratione Abrahami* (Philo)		*Rosc. com.*	*Pro Roscio comoedo* (Cicero)
Mor.	*Moralia* (Plutarch)		*Sacrifices*	*On the Sacrifices of Cain and Abel* (Philo)
Moses	*On the Life of Moses* (Philo)			
Nat.	*Naturalis historia* (Pliny)		*Sat.*	*Satirae* (Horace, Juvenal)
Num. Rab.	*Numbers Rabbah*		*Sera*	*De sera numinis vindicta* (Plutarch)
Onir.	*Onirocritica* (Artemidorus)		*Serm.*	*Sermones* (Augustine)
Or.	*Orationes* (Demosthenes, Dio Chrysostom)		*Sib. Or.*	*Sibylline Oracles*
			Sim.	*Similitudes* (Shepherd of Hermas)
Paed.	*Paedagogus* (Clement of Alexandria)		*Smyrn.*	*To the Smyrnaeans* (Ignatius)
			Somn.	*De somniis* (Philo)
Peregr.	*The Passing of Peregrinus* (Lucian)		*Spec.*	*De specialibus legibus* (Philo)
Pesiq. Rab.	*Pesiqta Rabbati*		*Stat.*	*Ad populum Antiochenum de statuis* (John Chrysostom)
Pesiq. Rab Kah.	*Pesiqta of Rab Kahana*			
Phaed.	*Phaedo* (Plato)		*Strom.*	*Stromata* (Clement of Alexandria)
Phil.	*To the Philippians* (Polycarp)		*T. Ash.*	*Testament of Asher*
Phld.	*To the Philadelphians* (Ignatius)		*T. Dan*	*Testament of Dan*
Phorm.	*Phormio* (Terence)		*T. Gad*	*Testament of Gad*
Planc.	*Pro Plancio* (Cicero)		*Tg. Ps.-J.*	*Targum Pseudo-Jonathan*
Plant.	*De plantatione* (Philo)		*Theaet.*	*Theaetetus* (Plato)
Pol.	*Politica* (Aristotle)		*t. Ḥul.*	*Ḥullin* (Tosefta)
Pol.	*To Polycarp* (Ignatius)			
Posterity	*On the Posterity of Cain* (Origen)			

T. Jos.	*Testament of Joseph*	*Virt.*	*De virtutibus* (Philo)
T. Jud.	*Testament of Judah*	*Vis.*	*Visions* (Shepherd of Hermas)
T. Levi	*Testament of Levi*	*Vit. Apoll.*	*Vita Apollonii* (Philostratus)
T. Mos.	*Testament of Moses*	*Vit. beat.*	*De vita beata* (Seneca)
T. Naph.	*Testament of Naphtali*	*y. ʿAbod. Zar.*	*ʿAbodah Zarah* (Jerusalem Talmud)
Trall.	*To the Trallians* (Ignatius)		
T. Reu.	*Testament of Reuben*	*y. Ḥag*	*Ḥagigah* (Jerusalem Talmud)
Tusc.	*Tusculanae disputationes* (Cicero)	*y. Šabb.*	*Šabbat* (Jerusalem Talmud)
Verr.	*In Verrem* (Cicero)		

Journals, Periodicals, Reference Works, Series

AB	Anchor Bible	BDF	Blass, Debrunner, and Funk. *A Greek Grammar of the New Testament and Other Early Christian Literature*
ABD	*Anchor Bible Dictionary*		
ABRL	Anchor Bible Reference Library		
ABW	*Archaeology in the Biblical World*		
ACCS	Ancient Christian Commentary on Scripture	BECNT	Baker Exegetical Commentary on the New Testament
ACNT	Augsburg Commentaries on the New Testament	BETL	*Bibliotheca ephemeridum theologicarum lovaniensium*
AnBib	Analecta biblica	BGU	*Aegyptische Urkunden aus den Königlichen Staatlichen Museen zu Berlin, Griechische Urkunden*
ANF	*Ante-Nicene Fathers*		
ANRW	*Aufstieg und Niedergang der römischen Welt*		
		BI	*Biblical Illustrator*
AThR	*Anglican Theological Review*	*Bib*	*Biblica*
BA	*Biblical Archaeologist*	*BibInt*	*Biblical Interpretation*
BAGD	Bauer, Arndt, Gingrich, and Danker (2d ed.). *Greek-English Lexicon of the New Testament and Other Early Christian Literature*	BibS(N)	Biblische Studien (Neukirchen)
		BJRL	*Bulletin of the John Rylands University Library of Manchester*
		BJS	Brown Judaic Studies
BAR	*Biblical Archaeology Review*	*BR*	*Biblical Research*
BASOR	*Bulletin of the American Schools of Oriental Research*	*BRev*	*Bible Review*
		BSac	*Bibliotheca sacra*
BBR	*Bulletin for Biblical Research*	BST	The Bible Speaks Today
BDAG	Bauer, Danker, Arndt, and Gingrich (3d ed.). *Greek-English Lexicon of the New Testament and Other Early Christian Literature*	*BT*	*The Bible Translator*
		BTB	*Biblical Theology Bulletin*
		BZ	*Biblische Zeitschrift*
		BZAW	Beihefte zur Zeitschrift für die alttestamentliche Wissenschaft
BDB	Brown, Driver, and Briggs. *A Hebrew and English Lexicon of the Old Testament*	BZNW	Beihefte zur Zeitschrift für die neutestamentliche Wissenschaft

CBQ	Catholic Biblical Quarterly	GRBS	Greek, Roman, and Byzantine Studies
CGTC	Cambridge Greek Testament Commentary	HALOT	Koehler, Baumgartner, and Stamm. The Hebrew and Aramaic Lexicon of the Old Testament
CH	Church History		
ChrT	Christianity Today		
CIG	Corpus inscriptionum graecarum	HBT	Horizons in Biblical Theology
CIL	Corpus inscriptionum latinarum	Herm	Hermeneia commentary series
CJT	Canadian Journal of Theology	HNT	Handbuch zum Neuen Testament
ConBNT	Coniectanea biblica: New Testament Series	HNTC	Harper's New Testament Commentaries
ConBOT	Coniectanea biblica: Old Testament Series	Hor	Horizons
CTJ	Calvin Theological Journal	HTKNT	Herders theologischer Kommentar zum Neuen Testament
CTR	Criswell Theological Review		
DRev	Downside Review		
DukeDivR	Duke Divinity Review	HTR	Harvard Theological Review
EBC	Expositor's Bible Commentary	HTS	Harvard Theological Studies
ECC	Eerdmans Critical Commentary	HUCA	Hebrew Union College Annual
EcR	Ecumenical Review	IB	Interpreter's Bible
EDNT	Exegetical Dictionary of the New Testament	IBS	Irish Biblical Studies
		ICC	International Critical Commentary
EGT	Expositor's Greek Testament		
ESCJ	Etudes sur le christianisme et le judaisme (Studies in Christianity and Judaism)	IDB	Interpreter's Dictionary of the Bible
		IDBSup	Interpreter's Dictionary of the Bible: Supplement
ETS	Evangelical Theological Society	Int	Interpretation
EuroJTh	European Journal of Theology	ISBE	International Standard Bible Encyclopedia, 2d ed.
EvQ	Evangelical Quarterly		
ExAud	Ex auditu	IVPNTC	IVP New Testament Commentary
ExpTim	Expository Times		
FF	Foundations and Facets	JBL	Journal of Biblical Literature
FRLANT	Forschungen zur Religion und Literatur des Alten und Neuen Testaments	JBMW	Journal for Biblical Manhood and Womanhood
		JETS	Journal of the Evangelical Theological Society
GBS	Guides to Biblical Scholarship		
GNS	Good News Studies	JQR	Jewish Quarterly Review
GR	Greece and Rome	JRS	Journal of Roman Studies
Grammar	A Grammar of the Greek New Testament; in the Light of Historical Research (A. T. Robertson)	JSNT	Journal for the Study of the New Testament
		JSNTSup	JSNT Supplement Series

JSOT	*Journal for the Study of the Old Testament*	NIVSB	Zondervan NIV Study Bible
		Notes	*Notes on Translation*
JSOTSup	JSOT Supplement Series	*NovT*	*Novum Testamentum*
JSP	*Journal for the Study of the Pseudepigrapha*	NovTSup	Novum Testamentum Supplements
JSS	*Journal of Semitic Studies*	*NPNF*	*Nicene and Post-Nicene Fathers*
JTC	*Journal for Theology and the Church*	NTC	New Testament Commentary (Baker)
JTS	*Journal of Theological Studies*		
KEK	Kritisch-exegetischer Kommentar über das Neue Testament	NTD	Das Neue Testament Deutsch
		NTG	New Testament Guides
L&N	Louw and Nida. *Greek-English Lexicon of the New Testament: Based on Semantic Domains*	*NTS*	*New Testament Studies*
		NTT	New Testament Theology
		NTTS	New Testament Tools and Studies
LCC	Library of Christian Classics	*OJRS*	*Ohio Journal of Religious Studies*
LCL	Loeb Classical Library	*PEGLMBS*	*Proceedings, Eastern Great Lakes and Midwest Bible Societies*
LEC	Library of Early Christianity		
LSJ	Liddell, Scott, and Jones. *A Greek-English Lexicon*	*PEQ*	*Palestine Exploration Quarterly*
		PG	Patrologia graeca
MM	Moulton and Milligan. *The Vocabulary of the Greek Testament*	PL	Patrologia latina
		PNTC	Pillar New Testament Commentary
NAC	New American Commentary		
NBD	*New Bible Dictionary*, 2d ed.	*Presb*	*Presbyterion*
NCBC	New Century Bible Commentary	*PresR*	*Presbyterian Review*
		PRSt	*Perspectives in Religious Studies*
Neot	*Neotestamentica*	PTMS	Pittsburgh Theological Monograph Series
NewDocs	*New Documents Illustrating Early Christianity*		
		PTR	*Princeton Theological Review*
NIBC	New International Biblical Commentary	*RB*	*Revue biblique*
		RBibLit	*Review of Biblical Literature*
NICNT	New International Commentary on the New Testament	*RefJ*	*Reformed Journal*
		RelSRev	*Religious Studies Review*
NICOT	New International Commentary on the Old Testament	*ResQ*	*Restoration Quarterly*
		RevExp	*Review and Expositor*
NIDNTT	*New International Dictionary of New Testament Theology*	*RHPR*	*Revue d'histoire et de philosophie religieuses*
NIDOTTE	*New International Dictionary of Old Testament Theology and Exegesis*	*RTR*	*Reformed Theological Review*
		SBB	Stuttgarter biblische Beiträge
NIGTC	New International Greek Testament Commentary	*SBJT*	*Southern Baptist Journal of Theology*
		SBLDS	Society of Biblical Literature Dissertation Series
NIVAC	NIV Application Commentary		

SBLMS	Society of Biblical Literature Monograph Series	THKNT	Theologischer Handkommentar zum Neuen Testament
SBLSP	*Society of Biblical Literature Seminar Papers*	*ThTo*	*Theology Today*
SBT	Studies in Biblical Theology	*TJ*	*Trinity Journal*
SE	*Studia evangelica*	*TLNT*	*Theological Lexicon of the New Testament*
SEG	Supplementum epigraphicum graecum	TNTC	Tyndale New Testament Commentaries
SJT	*Scottish Journal of Theology*	TOTC	Tyndale Old Testament Commentaries
SNT	Studien zum Neuen Testament		
SNTSMS	Society for New Testament Studies Monograph Series	*TS*	*Theological Studies*
SNTSU	Studien zum Neuen Testament und seiner Umwelt	*TWOT*	*Theological Wordbook of the Old Testament*
SP	Sacra Pagina	*TynBul*	*Tyndale Bulletin*
ST	*Studia theologica*	*TZ*	*Theologische Zeitschrift*
Str-B	Strack, H. L., and P. Billerbeck, *Kommentar zum Neuen Testament aus Talmud und Midrasch*	*VE*	*Vox evangelica*
		WBC	Word Biblical Commentary
		WMANT	Wissenschaftliche Monographien zum Alten und Neuen Testament
SUNT	Studien zur Umwelt des Neuen Testaments	*WTJ*	*Westminster Theological Journal*
SVF	*Stoicorum veterum fragmenta*	WUNT	Wissenschaftliche Untersuchungen zum Neuen Testament
SwJT	*Southwestern Journal of Theology*	YCS	Yale Classical Studies
TDNT	Kittel and Friedrich. *Theological Dictionary of the New Testament*	*ZAW*	*Zeitschrift für die alttestamentliche Wissenschaft*
TDOT	Botterweck and Ringgren, *Theological Dictionary of the Old Testament*	*ZNW*	*Zeitschrift für die neutestamentliche Wissenschaft und die Kunde der älterern Kirche*
TF	*Theologische Forschung*	ZPEB	*Zondervan Pictorial Encyclopedia of the Bible*
Them	*Themelios*		
ThEv	*Theologia Evangelica*	*ZWT*	*Zeitschrift für wissenschaftliche Theologie*

General

AD	*anno Domini* (in the year of [our] Lord)	cf.	*confer*, compare
		ch(s).	chapter(s)
Aram.	Aramaic	d.	died
BC	before Christ	diss.	dissertation
ca.	*circa* (around, about, approximately)	ed(s).	editor(s), edited by, edition
		e.g.	*exempli gratia*, for example

ABBREVIATIONS

esp.	especially	n(n).	note(s)
et al.	*et alii*, and others	n.d.	no date
EV	English versions of the Bible	NS	New Series
f(f).	and the following one(s)	p(p).	page(s)
fig.	figuratively	par.	parallel (indicates textual parallels)
frg.	fragment		
Gk.	Greek	repr.	reprinted
GK	Goodrick & Kohlenberger numbering system	rev.	revised
		s.v.	*sub verbo*, under the word
Heb.	Hebrew	TR	Textus Receptus (Greek text of the KJV translation)
ibid.	*ibidem*, in the same place		
i.e.	*id est*, that is	trans.	translator, translated by
Lat.	Latin	v(v).	verse(s)
lit.	literally	vs.	versus
MS(S)	manuscript(s)		

LUKE

WALTER L. LIEFELD AND DAVID W. PAO

Introduction

Had modern methods of publishing been available in the first century, the books of Luke and Acts might have been found standing side by side in paperback editions on a bookseller's shelf. Possibly they would have been bound together in one hardback volume. Though Acts has some characteristics of the ancient novel, this need not be understood as impugning its historical value. One can picture a Gentile reader going from adventure to adventure, delighting in the story of Paul's shipwreck and learning something of the gospel as he reads the various speeches. Likewise the gospel of Luke contains narratives and sayings of Jesus cast in a variety of literary forms. No doubt among its readers would have been the "God-fearers," those Gentiles who had already been convinced of Jewish monotheism and of Jewish ethical standards.[1] They, in turn, would have interested their friends in reading Luke–Acts.

1. LITERARY GENRE

It is difficult to know with what literary genre, if any, the first-century reader would have identified the Gospels. There has been much discussion of this issue in recent years. Robert Gundry evaluated the

---

1. See, however, Max Wilcox, "The God-Fearers in Acts—A Reconsideration," *JSNT* 13 (1981): 102–22. The existence of God-fearers as a distinct category in the ancient world is confirmed by the Aphrodisias Inscription (see Joyce Reynolds and Robert Tannenbaum, *Jews and God-Fearers at Aphrodisias* [Cambridge: Cambridge Philological Society, 1987]; J. A. Overman, "The God-Fearers: Some Neglected Features," *JSNT* 32 [1988]: 17–26).

literature up to the early 1970s in "Recent Investigations into the Literary Genre 'Gospel.'"[2] In the 1980s, David E. Aune provided an excellent discussion of some of the alleged first-century parallels to the Gospels, as well as a critical evaluation of twentieth-century approaches.[3] More recently, Richard A. Burridge traced the origin of Greco-Roman biographies to classical historiographies,[4] concluding that this relationship between biographies and historiography provided the framework for the writing of Luke and Acts.[5] Moving from form to function, ancient epic literature may also provide a model considering the foundational role that the Gospels and Acts played in the identity development of the early Christian communities.[6]

2. DISTINCTIVE FEATURES

Before proceeding further it will be helpful at least to recognize some of the distinctive features of Luke's gospel, especially in comparison with other gospels. Among these are Jesus' concern for all people, especially those who were social outcasts—the poor, women, and those who were known as "sinners"; Luke's universal scope; his alteration of some of the terminology of Mark to facilitate the understanding of Luke's readers (e.g., the Greek term for "lawyer" [*nomikos*, GK *3788*] instead of the Jewish term "scribe" [*grammateus*, GK *1208*]); an emphasis on Jesus' practical teaching (see, e.g., chs. 12 and 16, which deal with finances); Luke's sense of purpose, fulfillment, and accomplishment; his sense of joy and praise for God's saving and healing work; Jesus' strong call to discipleship; Jesus' dependence on the Holy Spirit and prayer; and many examples of the power of God.

In the first century, when pagans had not only long since turned from the traditional gods but had also wrestled unsuccessfully with issues of luck and fate and had turned to the false hopes of the so-called Eastern or mystery religions, such a narrative as Luke's undoubtedly had a genuine appeal. Here was a "Savior" who actually lived and cared about people. He was among people; he was crucified and actually was raised from the dead. And Luke tells all this with a conviction and verisimilitude that brought assurance to Theophilus and continues to bring assurance in our day.

---

2. See Robert H. Gundry, "Recent Investigations into the Literary Genre 'Gospel,'" in *New Dimensions in New Testament Study*, ed. Richard N. Longenecker and Merrill C. Tenney (Grand Rapids: Zondervan, 1974), 97–114; see also Frank E. Gaebelein, "The Bible as Literature," *ZPEB* 3:944.

3. See David E. Aune, "The Problem of Genre of the Gospels: A Critique of C. H. Talbert's *What Is a Gospel?*" in *Gospel Perspectives*, ed. R. T. France and D. Wenham (Sheffield: JSOT Press, 1981), 2:9–60. See also his discussion (David E. Aune, *The New Testament in Its Literary Environment* [LEC 8; Philadelphia: Westminster, 1987], 17–76) in which he points to the varieties of biographies that can provide a context for evaluating the genre of gospel.

4. See Richard A. Burridge, *What Are the Gospels: A Comparison with Graeco-Roman Biography* (New York: Cambridge Univ. Press, 1992).

5. Loveday C. A. Alexander (*The Preface to Luke's Gospel* [SNTSMS; Cambridge: Cambridge Univ. Press, 1993]) suggests that the Lukan prologue finds its home in scientific discourse. This broad identification does not exclude history and biography, however.

6. See, e.g., Marianne P. Bonz, *The Past as Legacy: Luke–Acts and Ancient Epic* (Minneapolis: Fortress, 2000).

3. UNITY OF LUKE–ACTS

Before discussing the issue of authorship, the relationship between Luke and Acts needs to be addressed. The following facts are worth noting: (1) Both Luke and Acts are addressed to an individual named "Theophilus" (Lk 1:3; Ac 1:1); (2) Acts refers to a previous work (1:1), presumably Luke; (3) certain stylistic and structural characteristics, such as the use of chiasm and the device of focusing on particular individuals, are common to both books and point to a single author; and (4) not only do the two volumes have a number of themes in common, but some of these receive a distinctive emphasis not found elsewhere in the NT. These facts point to a common author behind the two volumes.

Two further observations force one to move beyond the hypothesis of common authorship: (1) Luke and Acts show structural and thematic parallelism, and (2) the narrative of Luke finds its proper "fulfillment" in Acts. In 1927, Henry J. Cadbury made popular the notion of a hyphenated Luke–Acts.[7] This recognition of the unity of these two Lukan volumes is affirmed by subsequent studies that have examined the theology,[8] narrative,[9] and conceptual background[10] of Luke and Acts.[11]

4. AUTHORSHIP

The author of this gospel indicated that he was a second-generation Christian who was in a position to investigate the traditions about Jesus (Lk 1:3). As for the book of Acts, the author associated himself with Paul in the well-known "we-passages" (Ac 16:10–17; 20:5–15; 21:1–18; 27:1–28:16). While the use of the first person plural in the "we-passages" certainly does not prove that Luke was the author of Acts, it does accord with other data pointing in that direction.[12] Paul mentioned Luke as a companion (Col 4:14; 2Ti 4:11; Phm 24; assuming a genuine tradition of Pauline authorship here).[13]

The tradition of the early church is consistent in attributing the third gospel to Luke.[14] Thus the Muratorian Canon (ca. AD 180) says, "The third book of the Gospel according to Luke, Luke that physician, who

---

7. See Henry J. Cadbury, *The Making of Luke–Acts* (New York: Macmillan, 1927).

8. See Ulrich Wilckens, *Die Missionsreden der Apostelgeschichte* (WMANT 5; Neukirchen: Neukirchener, 1961); Robert F. O'Toole, *The Unity of Luke's Theology: An Analysis of Luke–Acts* (GNS 9; Wilmington, Del.: Michael Glazier, 1984).

9. See Robert C. Tannehill, *The Narrative Unity of Luke–Acts: A Literary Interpretation* (FF; Philadelphia: Fortress, 1986).

10. See David W. Pao, *Acts and the Isaianic New Exodus* (Grand Rapids: Baker, 2002).

11. The dissenting voice can be found in Mikeal C. Parsons and Richard I. Pervo, *Rethinking the Unity of Luke and Acts* (Minneapolis: Fortress, 1993). Most, however, continue to find Cadbury's original thesis convincing (see, e.g., the recent collection of essays in *The Unity of Luke–Acts*, ed. J. Verheyden [BETL 142; Leuven: Leuven Univ. Press, 1999]).

12. The most extensive defense of Lukan authorship along these lines can be found in Claus-Jürgen Thornton, *Der Zeuge des Zeugen* (WUNT 56; Tübingen: Mohr, 1991), 83–367. For a negative assessment, see V. K. Robbins, "The We-Passages in Acts and Ancient Sea Voyages," *BR* 20 (1975): 5–18.

13. A major argument against the identification of the author of Luke–Acts as the companion of Paul is the apparent difference between the Lukan Paul and the one found in the Pauline epistles. Recent studies have shown, however, that the two portrayals of Paul are not only reconcilable but should be expected since they came from two different authors. See the detailed discussion in Stanley E. Porter, *The Paul of Acts: Essays in Literary Criticism, Rhetoric, and Theology* (WUNT 115; Tübingen: Mohr, 1999).

14. The oldest manuscript of the gospel ($\mathfrak{P}^{75}$) identifies Luke in the attached title.

after the ascension of Christ, when Paul had taken him with him as companion of his journey, composed in his own name on the basis of report." But even before this, the heretic Marcion (ca. AD 135) acknowledged Luke as the author of the third gospel. Irenaeus and successive writers continued this tradition of authorship.

As seen in the above quotation from the Muratorian Canon, tradition also held that Luke was a physician (cf. Col 4:14). In 1882, William Hobart attempted to prove that Luke and Acts "were written by the same person, and that the writer was a medical man."[15] His study of the alleged medical language is informed, rich, and still useful, but it does not necessarily prove his point. Henry Cadbury argued that, though the terminology cited by Hobart was used by medical writers in the ancient world, others who were by no means physicians also used it.[16] Cadbury's work does not, of course, disprove that Luke was a physician, much less that he wrote Luke and Acts; but it does weaken the linguistic evidence for the former assumption. Nevertheless, the form and content of the prologue show that the author is familiar with scientific writings of his time,[17] and his interest in traveling is also consistent with what we know of ancient medical doctors.[18]

Irenaeus (*Haer.* 3.14.1) not only attested to Luke's authorship of the gospel but also said that Luke was Paul's "inseparable" companion. While there were periods of time when Luke was not with Paul, their relationship was deep and lasting. Taking 2 Timothy 4:11 as a genuine comment of Paul, only Luke was with him during his final imprisonment. Paul's comment in Colossians 4 leads us to assume that Luke was a Gentile, because in vv. 10–11 Paul listed several friends and said, "These are the only Jews among my fellow workers for the kingdom of God." Then he mentioned "our dear friend Luke" (v. 14). This, however, falls short of a direct statement that Luke was a Gentile. Some have held that he was a Jewish Christian, even (according to an early church tradition) one of the seventy-two disciples (Lk 10:1). The Semitic elements of style in Luke, especially in chs. 1–2 and in the Jerusalem narrative in Acts (chs. 1–15), may also suggest that he was a Jewish Christian. But as we will note below, there are other possible reasons for these stylistic traits. There is a church tradition that Luke came from Antioch in Syria. It is generally accepted, not on its own authority but because of Luke's involvement with the church in Antioch. This would mean, of course, that Luke was not (as some believe) the "man of Macedonia" Paul saw in his vision at Troas (Ac 16:8–9).[19]

5. PURPOSE

Can we discern a single purpose for the gospel of Luke? The answer must be based on a consideration of the prologue to the gospel (1:1–4), the apparent purposes of Acts, the major themes and theology of the book, and its life situation.[20] The following proposals are worth weighing.

---

15. William K. Hobart, *The Medical Language of St. Luke* (1882; repr., Grand Rapids: Baker, 1954), xxix.

16. See Henry J. Cadbury, *The Style and Literary Method of Luke* (HTS 6; Cambridge, Mass.: Harvard Univ. Press), 39–72.

17. See Alexander, *Preface to Luke's Gospel.*

18. See Martin Hengel and Anna Maria Schwemer, *Paulus zwischen Damaskus und Antiochien: Die unbekannten Jahre des Apostels* (WUNT 108; Tübingen: Mohr, 1998), 18–22.

19. For more detail and a citation of scholars on each side of this question, see Joseph A. Fitzmyer, *The Gospel According to Luke* (AB 28 & 28A; Garden City, N.J.: Doubleday, 1981–85), 35–53, 59–61.

20. See Schuyler Brown, "The Role of the Prologue in Determining the Purpose of Luke–Acts," in *Perspectives on Luke–Acts*, ed. Charles H. Talbert (Edinburgh: T&T Clark, 1978), 99–111.

Evangelism

The centrality of the theme and theology of salvation and the frequent proclamation of good news, both in Luke and in Acts, make the evangelization of non-Christians a possible purpose for Luke–Acts (see "Salvation," p. 38). When evangelism is understood in a broader sense, Luke's concern for the outcasts and those outside the worshiping community of Israel highlights the significance of this agenda.

Confirmation and Assurance of the Factual Basis for Faith

This purpose is supported by the prologue (1:1–4), the historical references throughout the two books, the references to eyewitnesses (e.g., 1:2; Ac 10:39), and the apologetic value of proof from prophecy (e.g., Ac 10:43). To ground the "creeds" and "confessions" of the earliest Christians in their proper historical setting can be counted among the reasons for the writing of these two volumes; this grounding is also related to a corresponding concern for conviction and assurance within the reader. Luke 1:4 says that Luke wrote so that Theophilus might "know the certainty of the things" he had "been taught."

Continuation of Salvation History

Did Luke write simply because he sensed the need to preserve the record of the origin and growth of the early church? Few if any ancient writers wrote history simply to preserve a chronicle of events. Also, it would be difficult to explain the disproportionate space given to early events and figures in the life of the church if Luke were merely composing a historical chronicle. Many have rightly proposed that this is a "continuation of biblical history" in that it shows the validity of apostolic tradition as part of that continuity and locus of salvation truth.[21]

Identity of the Early Christian Community

Related to the above point is Luke's interest in the identity of the early Christian community. The concern with the Scriptures of Israel and the emphasis on the continuation of the acts of God within the early Christian movement may point to Luke's interest in clarifying the relationship between Israel and the church. Is the church a new entity? Are all Christians to be considered part of Israel spiritually, or is there some other way to view this new group? (See "Israel and the People of God," p. 40.)

Apologetic Treatise

One version of this purpose, which was occasionally proposed in an earlier generation, was that Luke wrote Acts as a brief for Paul's trial at Rome. The contents are too broad for this purpose, and it does not explain the gospel of Luke. A more likely proposal is that the gospel is an apologetic for Christianity as a religious sect. Jews had certain rights under the Roman Empire, and Luke may have written to

---

21. See Nils A. Dahl, *Jesus in the Memory of the Early Church* (Minneapolis: Augsburg, 1976), 87–98.

demonstrate that Christianity should also have such rights, along with Pharisaism and the other sects of Judaism.[22] At his trials, Paul tried to identify himself with Judaism, especially Pharisaism. He himself called Christianity a "sect" in Acts 24:14, a term used in the accusation against him in v. 5.

Solution to a Theological Problem

It has been common in recent years to assume that Luke was writing to explain the delay of the parousia.[23] According to this theory, the early Christians were troubled because Christ did not return immediately, as they had expected him to do; therefore, they needed both assurance and some explanation for this delay. This questionable assumption will be dealt with below (see "Eschatology," p. 41). Another possible problem relates to the death of Christ and the suffering of the apostles. Is the death of Christ inconsistent with his claim to be the Anointed One? Does the suffering of the early Christians disqualify their claim that God is with them? While such questions do not explain the inclusion of many of the stories and speeches, certain passages in Luke and Acts may well reflect an attempt to address these concerns.

Conciliation

The well-known contention of F. C. Baur and the Tübingen School was that the book of Acts was an example of the Hegelian principle of thesis, antithesis, and synthesis.[24] Baur and his group saw Peter and Paul as representing opposing parties, with Luke trying to bring the antithetical viewpoints together in a synthesis of organized, normative Christianity. That there were differences is obvious, and Luke may well have written in part to show that these differences were not irresolvable. But the process as described by the Tübingen scholars does not fit the facts and requires too long a period of time.

Defense against Heresy

During the period when Gnosticism was being proposed as a problem dealt with by several NT books, Charles H. Talbert proposed a short-lived hypothesis that Luke was written against this heresy.[25] Not only is there insufficient evidence in Luke's writings to support this hypothesis, but it also leaves unanswered the question as to why so much else is included in these books that is not relevant to the gnostic issue. Furthermore, the existence of full-blown Gnosticism during Luke's time is questionable.

---

22. Whether such rights were formally formulated in terms of *religio licita* ("legitimate religion") is subject to debate. Recent scholarship has questioned the evidence for the existence of this category in the first century, but most would affirm that certain groups did enjoy "special" rights.

23. See, in particular, Hans Conzelmann, *The Theology of St. Luke* (New York: Harper & Row), 95–234.

24. See F. C. Baur, *Paul, the Apostle of Jesus Christ: His Life and Work, His Epistles and Teachings* (1873; repr., Peabody, Mass.: Hendrickson, 2003).

25. See Charles H. Talbert, *Luke and the Gnostics* (New York: Abingdon, 1966).

Dealing with Social Problems

Recent works have made a good deal of the prominence of the theme of poverty and wealth in both Luke and Acts (cf. n. 84, p. 42). This concern was hardly large enough in comparison to other, more major matters to be considered a major purpose for Luke's writing, but it does call for a response from the reader. More appealing are the proposals of those who situate this concern within the larger theme of reversal in the Lukan corpus; this theme of reversal may then be related to other social and theological concerns.

Multiple Purposes

If none of the above qualify as the sole purpose for the writing of Luke–Acts, should we think instead in terms of primary and secondary purposes? In this case, we may take the prologue to the gospel as articulating the primary purpose not only of the gospel but, at least to an extent, of Acts as well, inasmuch as the prologue provides enough information about Jesus and his significance for those who follow him to supplement the instruction Theophilus had already received so as to confirm him in his faith. By extrapolation, we may assume that Luke wrote to bring the gospel—and the assurance of salvation that follows its acceptance—to a larger audience than the one individual, Theophilus. This certainly does not exclude subsidiary purposes, especially in the second volume (Acts). Since Luke clearly distinguishes the second volume from the first, there is no reason why he could not have accomplished his purpose mainly in the first volume and then continued the story of "all that Jesus began to do and to teach" (Ac 1:1) in the second one to accomplish yet further objectives.

If in addition to winning and establishing individual converts Luke is concerned with forwarding the Christian movement, such aims as establishing the legitimacy of that movement as the people of God, demonstrating the innocence of Jesus and Paul at their trials, clarifying the relationship of Jewish and Gentile believers to Israel, and rooting the gospel record in Jewish and secular history all have their place. It was important for Luke to deal with specific problems, whether eschatological or social, if such problems threatened to hinder the forward movement of the church. Far from producing a simplistic or fragmented work, Luke brings together all the data and addresses all the issues he believes it necessary to deal with in order to advance Christ's cause throughout the world.

6. INTENDED READERSHIP

Any conclusions as to the readership of the gospel must be drawn primarily from the prologue (1:1–4) and secondarily from conclusions about the purpose of the gospel. As to the first, see comments at 1:1–4 about Theophilus. From our brief survey of theories about Luke's purpose, it would appear that, while Luke–Acts had an appeal to the non-Christian, Luke expected and desired it to be read by Christians, especially new converts. Some of the characteristics of the gospel, such as its orientation to the secular world, its references to Judaism, and its Septuagintisms, along with the prominence of God-fearers in both books, make it plausible that Luke had those God-fearers in mind. They were Gentiles, at home in secular society but monotheistic by conviction (see n. 1, p. 21); and they were accustomed to hearing the Jewish Scriptures read in the synagogue, though they may not have been familiar with Palestinian geography and society. Like the God-fearers reached through Paul's mission (cf. the Acts narrative), they formed an ideal bridge from the synagogue to the Gentile world. It is possible, though unprovable, that Luke himself had been a God-fearer. While it is impossible to restrict Luke's readership to the God-fearers,[26] it is difficult to imagine his writing without at least having them in mind.[27]

7. LITERARY CHARACTERISTICS

James Hope Moulton called Luke "the only *littérateur* among the authors of NT books."[28] He said this mainly because of Luke's rare use of the optative mood. To Moulton, Luke was a Greek who had the "native instinct" not only to write well but also to vary his style scene by scene. While there is no uniform agreement today regarding Luke's background or the reasons for his distinctive style, his writings are generally held to be superb in both style and structure.[29]

As to the linguistic and syntactical idioms of Luke's gospel, we find a mystifying combination of literary Greek and Semitic styles. The latter includes expressions characteristic of Hebrew, Aramaic, or both, as well as Septuagintisms. Some of these characteristics can be seen in familiar KJV expressions such as "he answering said" (where the participle "answering" is redundant, e.g., 1:19; 4:12; 5:5, 22, 31), "before the face of" (e.g., 2:31), the use of the verb *egeneto* with a finite verb (familiar from the KJV's "it came to pass that . . ."), and the intensive "with desire I have desired" (22:15), to name a few. (The NIV's idiomatic renderings generally eliminate these awkward expressions.)

These characteristics occur more often in Luke 1 and 2 and in Acts 1–15 than in the rest of each book. Also there are fewer such expressions in the "we-passages," which leads Nigel Turner to suggest that these are from a diary Luke wrote earlier than he did the rest of the work and before he was exposed to Septuagintal idioms through Paul.[30]

Among the theories advanced to explain this occurrence of Hebrew and Aramaic "interference" in Luke's fine Greek style and the traces of Septuagintal influence are the following: (1) Luke was actually

---

26. The collection of essays in Richard Bauckham, ed., *The Gospels for All Christians: Rethinking the Gospel Audiences* (Grand Rapids: Eerdmans, 1998), shows that one should resist the temptation to speak too specifically of the "Lukan" community.

27. Robert Maddox (*The Purpose of Luke–Acts* [Göttingen: Vandenhoeck & Ruprecht, 1982], 187) notes that "[Luke] writes to reassure the Christians of his day that their faith in Jesus is no aberration, but the authentic goal towards which God's ancient dealings with Israel were driving."

28. James Hope Moulton, *A Grammar of New Testament Greek* (vol. 2, *Accidence and Word-Formation*; ed. J. H. Moulton and Wilbert F. Howard; Edinburgh: T&T Clark, 1929), 7.

29. See Cadbury, *Style and Literary Method of Luke*, who demonstrates the excellence of Luke's style. Among Luke's distinctive words are many with a literary flavor, medical terms (see comments on Hobart's theory, p. 24), and distinctive theological terms. The following are the major sources for word statistics: Lloyd Gaston, *Horae Synopticae Electronicae: Word Statistics of the Synoptic Gospels* (Missoula, Mont.: Scholars Press, 1973); John Caesas Hawkins, *Horae Synopticae: Contributions to the Study of the Synoptic Problem* (1909; repr., Grand Rapids: Baker, 1968); R. Morgenthaler, *Statistik des neutestamentlichen Wortschatzes* (Zürich: Gotthelf, 1973).

30. See Moulton, *Grammar* (vol. 4, *Style*; ed. Nigel Turner; Edinburgh: T&T Clark, 1976), 55, cf. 61. The most useful survey of data is by Fitzmyer, *Gospel According to Luke*, 1:107–25. For a helpful survey of scholarship on this matter, see Fred Horton, "Reflections on the Semitisms of Luke–Acts," in *Perspectives on Luke–Acts*, 1–23.

Jewish; (2) he was a Gentile but had a long exposure to Semitic idioms; (3) he was a Greek who perhaps unconsciously adopted a Septuagintal style, possibly through association with Paul; (4) he artificially assumed a Semitic style to give a ring of genuineness to certain sections of his works; and (5) at times he was using a source with a tradition that went back to a Semitic original. Though these idioms occur in some places more heavily than in others, they are found scattered throughout Luke's works.

Of these various theories, the most likely are (2), supported by Fitzmyer, or (3), supported by Turner, with (5) applying in certain parts. The idea of a Semitic source behind Luke 1–2 has received recent cautious support from S. C. Farris, based on the research of R. A. Martin.[31]

As to structure, Luke also shows literary skill. Charles H. Talbert has demonstrated Luke's ability to use the device of chiasm (a sequence of topics repeated in reverse order) as a major structural means of presenting his message; Talbert notes other examples of this in some of the finest Greek writings.[32] It is widely acknowledged that the two books attributed to Luke exhibit a unified structure (which, as noted above, is significant with regard to the issue of authorship). Henry J. Cadbury has observed two striking pairs of stylistic characteristics.[33] The first is "repetition and variation," i.e., Luke at times has obvious repetitions, such as, "the growth of a child in Luke 1:80; 2:40; 2:52," to which we could add the growth of the church under the favor of God and of people (Ac 2:47). The second pair of characteristics is "distribution and concentration." By this, Cadbury means the tendency to use a term frequently in a passage or in a sequence of passages, only to use it rarely or never elsewhere. All in all, it is evident that Luke's writings are rich in linguistic, stylistic, and structural creativity.

8. COMPOSITION AND METHODS OF READING

The first written gospel in the NT form was probably Mark. Matthew apparently had access to Mark as well as to other traditions that contained sayings of Jesus.[34] These other traditions are referred to by scholars as "Q," but whether or not that was a written collection is now impossible to determine. Scholars have been increasingly reluctant to accept the hypothesis of the relation of Matthew and Luke to the two sources of Mark and "Q," but it still seems to be, with modifications, the most satisfactory hypothesis at this time. In his reconstruction of synoptic traditions, B. H. Streeter called the other material known to Luke, beside

---

31. S. C. Farris, "On Discerning Semitic Sources in Luke 1–2," in *Gospel Perspectives*, vol. 2 (ed. France and Wenham). The Semitic character of Luke 1–2 also forms a significant step in establishing the historicity of the virgin birth in J. Gresham Machen, *The Virgin Birth of Christ* (1930; repr., Grand Rapids: Baker, 1965), 62–101. The Semitic characteristics of chs. 1–2 may also be explained by the possibility that Luke intentionally writes in "biblical Greek" to show the continuity of biblical history. See Joel B. Green, "The Problem of a Beginning: Israel's Scriptures in Luke 1–2," *BBR* 4 (1994): 61–85.

32. See Charles H. Talbert, *Literary Patterns, Theological Themes and the Genre of Luke–Acts* (SBLMS 20; Missoula, Mont.: Scholars Press, 1974).

33. See Henry J. Cadbury, "Four Features of Lucan Style," in *Studies in Luke–Acts*, ed. Leander Keck and J. Louis Martyn (New York: Abingdon, 1966), 87–102.

34. Since the synoptic problem and the proposed frameworks for its solution involve some of the same data for Matthew as for Luke, the reader should consult D. A. Carson's introduction to Matthew in volume 8 of The Expositor's Bible Commentary (Grand Rapids: Zondervan, 1984), 11–17.

Mark and "Q," by the letter "L."[35] Though this terminology is less used today, it is customary to assume that, in addition to other materials, Luke had one main, special source. The parts of the gospel unique to Luke include 1:5–2:52 (the birth and childhood narratives); 3:10–14 (John the Baptist's ethical teaching); 7:12–17 (the raising of the widow of Nain's son); a good deal of the material in 9:51–19:44; and a number of incidents in the passion narrative, along with other small sections.[36] Whether, as Streeter and others have supposed, Luke wrote an earlier gospel (which Streeter called "Proto-Luke") before he became acquainted with Mark or with the content of his first two chapters is extremely doubtful. Not to be ignored, however, is the possibility that oral traditions were also available to Luke in the writing of his gospel.

Since the publication of Hans Conzelmann's work *Die Mitte der Zeit* in 1953 (English title, *The Theology of St. Luke*), major attention has been given to the "redaction criticism" of Luke. The term comes from the German *Redaktionsgeschichte* and has to do with the analysis of the editorial work of an author as he shaped the written or oral materials that came to his hand. To some, it implies creativity to the extent of changing or slanting the materials received for the purpose of imposing the editor's theological viewpoint on that material. Such a radical handling of sources is, however, not a necessary presupposition to a redactional study of the Synoptic Gospels. There is no question that each of the gospels contributes a distinctive perspective on the life and teachings of the Lord Jesus. It is to the enrichment of our total understanding of the person and work of Christ that we thoroughly investigate these distinct contributions. Extreme caution is needed, however, lest we superimpose on the gospel the supposed conditions of the church communities at the time Luke wrote and to do this so as to alter what Jesus actually taught. The same caution applies to superimposing our own schemes of theology on the gospel (see opening paragraphs of section 12, "Themes and Theology," pp. 35–36).

In 1971, Tim Schramm showed that much of the distinctive material in Luke was due not so much to Luke's redactional activity as to his use of sources different from those available to Matthew and Mark.[37] Also, it has long been assumed that many of the differences in Luke are due to his stylistic improvements of Mark. Various scholars have analyzed individual pericopae (sections) of Luke to determine the extent of his redaction.[38] The most detailed study of the passion narrative was done in a series of studies originally published as separate monographs by Heinz Schürmann.[39] In summary, there are three main reasons why a passage in Luke may differ from parallel passages in Matthew or Mark: theology, literary style, and source material.

Those who have engaged in redaction criticism of Luke have not necessarily followed the conclusions of Conzelmann. One of the first full-scale responses was that of Helmut Flender, whose work included a

---

35. See B. H. Streeter, *The Four Gospels* (New York: Macmillan, 1930).

36. For a fuller list, a useful discussion of the entire matter of Luke's sources, and a full bibliography, see Fitzmyer, *Gospel According to Luke*, 63–106.

37. See Tim Schramm, *Der Markus-Stoff bei Lukas* (SNTSMS 15; Cambridge: Cambridge Univ. Press, 1971).

38. See, e.g., Bruce Chilton, "Announcement in Nazara: An Analysis of Luke 4:16–21," in *Gospel Perspectives* [ed. France and Wenham], 2:147–72.

39. See Heinz Schürmann, *Der Paschamahlbericht* (Münster: Aschendorff, 1953); *Der Einsetzungsbericht* (Münster: Aschendorff, 1955); *Jesu Abschiedsrede* (Münster: Aschendorff, 1957).

fascinating study of the dialectical structure of Luke–Acts that has not received complete acceptance.[40] W. C. Robinson employed a redactional approach but criticized Conzelmann and proposed a geographical scheme for Luke's theology.[41] Schuyler Brown has contributed a major study that counters some of Conzelmann's ideas. Brown debates Conzelmann's theory that between the temptation of Jesus and the betrayal of Judas, Satan was not actively opposing the ministry of Jesus; Brown answers this by reexamining the meaning of *peirasmos* ("temptation," "trial," GK *4280*) in Luke.[42]

The negative assessment Conzelmann made of Luke's knowledge of Palestinian geography and of historical matters has also been challenged by a number of writers. One of the finest assessments of Luke as both a theologian and historian was written by I. Howard Marshall.[43] Nevertheless, a good deal of skepticism about Luke's accuracy persists, and, sadly, redaction criticism is often carried out under such negative assumptions.

One of the recent approaches to the material in the Gospels is that of "structuralism," which does not pertain uniquely to Luke. Structuralism is a large, complex, and much-debated approach that seeks to understand reality—relating to sociology and a number of other disciplines, as well as to linguistics and literature—in universal terms. Scholars using it construct theoretical structural models to explain particular linguistic and literary elements, such as the roles and actions within a narrative or parable.[44]

More fruitful is a literary or narrative approach that pays attention to the text as a unified whole. In examining the role of the narrator, the development of the characters, and the unfolding of the plot, one can move beyond a radical redaction-critical approach that focuses primarily on small units of text.[45] This approach needs to be supplemented, however, by an adequate appreciation of the historical framework and basis of the text, since the narrative and the historical planes cannot be strictly separated.

A final comment on Luke's method of composition relates to the central section of the gospel (9:51–19:44). This part has no parallel in the other gospels, though some of the stories and parables within it do.

---

40. See Helmut Flender, *St. Luke: Theologian of Redemptive History* (Philadelphia: Fortress, 1967).

41. See W. C. Robinson Jr., *Der Weg des Herrn* (TF 36; Hamburg-Bergstedt: H. Reich, 1964).

42. See Schuyler Brown, *Apostasy and Perseverance in the Theology of Luke* (AnBib 36; Rome: Pontifical Biblical Institute, 1969).

43. See I. Howard Marshall, *Luke: Historian and Theologian* (3d ed.; Downers Grove, Ill.: InterVarsity, 1988).

44. The following works are useful for understanding structuralism: R. Barthes et al., *Structural Analysis and Biblical Exegesis: Interpretational Essays* (PTMS 3; Pittsburgh: Pickwick, 1974); Daniel Patte, *What Is Structural Exegesis?* (GBS; Philadelphia: Fortress, 1976); Daniel and Aline Patte, *Structural Exegesis: From Theory to Practice* (Philadelphia: Fortress, 1978); R. M. Polzin, *Biblical Structuralism: Method and Subjectivity in the Ancient Texts* (Philadelphia: Fortress, 1977); Robert W. Funk, ed., "A Structuralist Approach to the Parables," in *Semeia* 1 (1974); A. C. Thiselton, "Keeping Up With Recent Studies: II. Structuralism and Biblical Studies: Method or Ideology?" *ExpTim* 89 (1977–78): 329–35. For an introduction to the subsequent movement of poststructuralism, see Stephen D. Moore, *Poststructuralism and the New Testament: Derrida and Foucault at the Foot of the Cross* (Minneapolis: Fortress, 1994).

45. In any literary analysis of the text, the precise model with which the text is being examined needs to be noted. Needless to say, a model constructed solely on categories informed by modern English literary studies will not be entirely applicable to the ancient text. For the promises and limitations of literary criticism, see Anthony C. Thiselton, *New Horizons in Hermeneutics: The Theory and Practice of Transforming Biblical Reading* (Grand Rapids: Zondervan, 1992), 471–79.

It has long been a matter of debate whether Luke is merely following some literary or historical procedure in the composition of this section or whether he has some theological purpose in mind. The most persistent supposition is that he is consciously constructing a parallel to Deuteronomy. (For further remarks on this subject, see Overview, 9:51–19:44.)

9. TEXT

There are some textual problems in Luke that demand the attention of the exegete, though not as many as in Acts. In general, the Alexandrian tradition of the text has proved reliable, especially since the discovery in 1961 of the papyrus $\mathfrak{P}^{75}$. In some cases (e.g., Lk 22:19b–20; 24:3, 6, 12, 36, 40, 51–52), the omission of words from the Western text, which tends to add rather than omit words, was so unusual that these omissions were considered significant. Certain studies have challenged this assessment,[46] and it is a good possibility that the inclusion of the wording in question in the Alexandrian textual tradition is correct. For more, see remarks on the verses in question in the Notes portions of the commentary.[47]

10. HISTORY AND HISTORICITY

Discussion of the historical value of Luke usually proceeds along one or more of the following lines: (1) Luke's careful observation of the historical setting of his narratives; (2) the question as to whether a work so tendentious, so committed to establishing certain theological conclusions, can possibly be historically objective; (3) the authenticity and accuracy of Luke's sources; (4) his own claim to historical accuracy in his introduction; (5) problems caused by apparent errors (e.g., his reference to the census under Quirinius in 2:12; see comments at 2:12); and (6) apparent discrepancies between Luke and the other gospels.

The first of these has to do with the kind of data collected by W. M. Ramsay and by A. N. Sherwin-White.[48] Richard Cassidy calls these data "empire history," i.e., things "within the broad category of political affairs . . . [such as] the description of rulers and officials . . . the dating of specific events in relation to other events more widely known throughout the empire" and so on.[49] It is important to recognize that where Luke can be checked historically—except for the few problem texts mentioned in section 9 above—his accuracy has been validated. We should, however, acknowledge that this does not in itself guarantee Luke's accuracy in everything he relates.

Second, as indicated earlier, Luke's theological intentions should not be taken as invalidating his historical accuracy. Even so careful a scholar as Fitzmyer assumes that Luke's theological concern sets him apart from both ancient and modern historians, noting that Luke's introduction "reveals his historical concern as

---

46. See, e.g., Klyne Snodgrass, "Western Non-Interpolations," *JBL* 91 (1972): 369–79.

47. See also Gordon D. Fee, "The Textual Criticism of the New Testament," in *Biblical Criticism*, ed. R. K. Harrison et al. (Grand Rapids: Zondervan, 1978), 127–55; Fitzmyer, *Gospel According to Luke*, 128–33.

48. See, e.g., the following by W. M. Ramsay: *St. Paul the Traveller and the Roman Citizen* (New York: Putnam, 1898); *Was Christ Born in Bethlehem? The Bearing of Recent Discovery on the Trustworthiness of the New Testament* (1915; repr., Grand Rapids: Baker, 1953). See also A. N. Sherwin-White, *Roman Society and Roman Law in the New Testament* (Oxford: Clarendon, 1963).

49. Richard J. Cassidy, *Jesus, Politics, and Society: A Study of Luke's Gospel* (Maryknoll, N.Y.: Orbis, 1978), 13.

subordinate to a theological one."[50] But it does not logically follow that because historical concern is subordinate, error must result.[51] Likewise we must remember that other ancient historians were seeking to establish certain viewpoints as they wrote their histories.

Third, the matter of sources was briefly discussed in section 8, "Composition and Methods of Reading." We also addressed the question of whether Luke's use of Semitic constructions indicates Semitic source material (see section 7, "Literary Characteristics"). If it does, the presence of such sources (with the tradition handed down either in the original Semitic idiom or in Septuagintal Greek) points to an early Palestinian origin of the book. Though this does not guarantee authenticity or accuracy, it certainly increases their probability. It appears that in some instances Luke follows an even earlier tradition than does Matthew or Mark. An example is the tradition of the institution of the Lord's Supper, where the wording in Luke is close to that found in 1 Corinthians 11, which had probably been committed to writing earlier than Matthew or Mark. Apparently both Luke and Paul had access to a very early tradition.

Fourth, the terminology of Luke's prologue (1:1–4) certainly implies careful historical research. Such a claim to historical accuracy does not in itself prove accuracy. But the honesty of the writer in distinguishing himself from the eyewitnesses and the care he took to provide an orderly, accurate account cannot be overlooked. Historians in the ancient world were, contrary to what many have thought, interested in accurate reporting.[52]

Fifth, there are indeed several serious historical problems in Luke's writings, such as the reference to Quirinius (2:2) and the reference to Theudas (Ac 5:36). A few others are more easily handled. Nevertheless, as the commentary shows, there are possible solutions that obviate extreme skepticism as to Luke's historical accuracy.

Sixth, the issues involved in the apparent discrepancies between the gospels are so complex as to preclude brief discussion here. However, it must at least be said that attempts at reasonable reconciliation are often summarily dismissed as "harmonization," as though any attempt to give the benefit of the doubt to one of two parallel ancient documents were somehow unworthy. To think that one can either "prove" or "disprove" the historical value of an ancient historical work on the basis of the slight amount of information we have about the remote events it deals with is presumptuous.

11. DATE

The dating of Luke depends largely on four factors: (1) the date of Mark, and Luke's relationship to it; (2) the date of Acts; (3) the reference to the destruction of Jerusalem in ch. 21; and (4) the theological and ecclesiastical tone of Luke–Acts.

First, the date of Mark is, of course, relevant only if Luke used Mark as one of his sources. That probability is strong enough to assume here. With rare exceptions, scholars today hold that Mark was written about AD 70, probably just a few years before that date, which was marked by the destruction of Jerusalem.

---

50. Fitzmyer, *Gospel According to Luke*, 16.

51. See the strong comments on this topic by Martin Hengel, *Acts and the History of Earliest Christianity* (Philadelphia: Fortress, 1979), 59–68.

52. See A. W. Mosley, "Historical Reporting in the Ancient World," *NTS* 12 (1965–66): 10–26.

Yet there is no compelling reason why it could not have been written a few years earlier, toward AD 60. At this time it is not possible to be certain.[53]

Second, the issues surrounding the date of Acts are more complex. Presumably Luke completed his gospel before writing Acts, though this has been debated. Apart from its connection with the writing of the gospel and the implications of the theological climate of the two books, which will be discussed below, the main considerations in the dating of Acts relate to the time of Paul's imprisonment and the date of the Neronian persecution. Acts 28:30 takes leave of Paul with a reference to his two-year imprisonment at Rome, which is generally agreed to have taken place around AD 60 to 62. This provides a *terminus a quo* for the date of Acts. The fact that there is no record in Acts of the subsequent persecution under Nero in AD 65 and of Paul's death at about that time has convinced some that Luke wrote Acts before these events. There is no hint of further hostilities between the Jews and the Romans or of the climax in AD 70. On the ground of these historical matters, it is possible that Acts was written between AD 61 and 65.[54] On the other hand, for those who see the arrival of Paul and the gospel in Rome as the climax of Luke's work, the omission of the later events may not be critical to the dating of Acts.[55]

Third, Luke's reference to the destruction of Jerusalem in his version of the Olivet Discourse (21:8–36) complicates the problem of dating the gospel. Most scholars see it as a *vaticinium ex eventu*, a "prophecy" given after the event. In that case Luke would have added sufficient detail to the discourse in Mark 13, once the event had occurred, to show his readers what he thought Jesus must have intended. An obvious response to this, though not in itself conclusive, is that one cannot assume that Jesus did not include or actually could not have included Jerusalem in his prediction. Also, if Luke had adapted the prediction to the event, it is strange that he did not also modify the prediction of the accompanying apocalyptic events, including the coming of the Son of Man. These did not happen in AD 70, at least in the literal sense in which Luke probably would have understood them.[56] But the conventional apocalyptic terminology does stand in Luke 21, and the passage has very little additional detail about the destruction of Jerusalem, as might be expected had it been written after the event. Furthermore, if Jesus had, either explicitly or implicitly, referred in the Olivet Discourse to the destruction of Jerusalem, why was Luke the only one of the synoptic writers to include that specific reference, unless he were indeed writing after the event? The answer would seem to be that it is only Luke who throughout his gospel stresses Jerusalem as the city of destiny. His gospel opens with a scene in the temple in Jerusalem, Jesus is constantly pressing toward Jerusalem (see comments at 9:51), and Luke includes a lament of Jesus over the city (19:41–44). It is natural that he would pick up any tradition

---

53. See R. T. France, *The Gospel of Mark* (NIGTC; Grand Rapids: Eerdmans, 2002), 35–41.

54. A detailed discussion along these lines is presented in Colin J. Hemer, *The Book of Acts in the Setting of Hellenistic History* (WUNT 49; Tübingen: Mohr, 1989), 365–410.

55. N. T. Wright (*The New Testament and the People of God* [London: SPCK, 1992], 375) suggests that in Acts 28 Luke presents the conquest of the gospel of Jesus the Savior of the world in the capital of the Roman Empire. Daniel Marguerat (*The First Christian Historian: Writing the "Acts of the Apostles"* [SNTSMS 121; Cambridge: Cambridge Univ. Press, 2002], 40) is probably correct when he suggests that Luke omits Paul's death because of his understanding of the secondary role of the apostles as "witnesses" but not "actors" in the salvific drama.

56. See Leon Morris, *The Gospel According to St. Luke* (TNTC; Grand Rapids: Eerdmans, 1978), 23.

of Jesus' words about the fate of that city, even before the event occurred. The question of whether Jesus specifically predicted the fall of Jerusalem and whether Luke wrote ch. 21 before or after the event should, therefore, not be decided subjectively.

Fourth, another reason why many date Acts and also Luke later (even as late as the early second century) is that they believe Acts reflects a theological climate and ecclesiastical situation nonexistent in the 60s or 70s. They base their view largely on the assumption that the author of Acts shows little knowledge of the apostle Paul as the early epistles portray him and also that the author reflects a view of the church more in common with the later Pastoral Epistles and "early Catholicism."[57] See also E. Earle Ellis's discussion of this issue and his treatment of the date of Luke.[58] Among other points, Ellis sees evidences in Luke of a troublesome time such as that begun by the Neronian persecution. He prefers a date of around AD 70 for Luke. In my judgment, the only compelling reason for assigning a date much earlier than this would be the lack of allusions in Acts to the death of Paul and to the Neronian persecution. Even this conclusion is based on the assumption that Luke would have alluded to such events had he written later—though he might not have done so if those events did not contribute significantly to his historical and theological program. All things considered, then, it seems preferable to date the completion of Luke's two works somewhere in the AD 60s and 70s.

12. THEMES AND THEOLOGY

A word of caution is necessary here. Fitzmyer warned against superimposing a "thesis" about Lukan theology on the data of Luke and Acts.[59] Though his warning is directed largely against the books by Conzelmann and J. C. O'Neill,[60] it applies to other works as well and serves as a warning to all expositors. It is constantly necessary to check one's understanding of an author against the actual data in his or her work. But what constitutes evidence for biblical theology? It is one thing to exegete the propositions in the logical argument of an epistle (and even here there is much room for disagreement); it is another thing to reconstruct the theology of a narrator such as Luke. The evidence ranges from overall patterns of structure (cf. Talbert's *Literary Patterns*) to the possible significance of (e.g., the use or nonuse of) an article before the word "mountain" in Matthew or Luke. Word frequency is certainly one valuable clue. Yet it is not enough to make a simple word count and draw conclusions from it. As Lloyd Gaston has shown, it is necessary to use modern statistical methodology, such as standard deviation, to assess the significance of word counts.[61] We also need to bear in mind the source of the material under consideration. If a word appears frequently in one of Luke's special sources (assuming we know when he is using such a source), should we use this as

---

57. On this complex matter, see Leon Morris, "Luke and Early Catholicism," *WTJ* 35 (1973): 121–36; I. Howard Marshall, "'Early Catholicism' in the New Testament," in *New Dimensions in New Testament Study* (ed. Longenecker and Tenney), 217–31.

58. See E. Earle Ellis, *The Gospel of Luke* (NCBC; New York: Nelson, 1966), 44–51, 55–60.

59. Fitzmyer, *Gospel According to Luke*, 6–7.

60. See Conzelmann, *Theology of St. Luke*; J. C. O'Neill, *The Theology of Acts in Its Historical Setting* (2d ed.; London: SPCK, 1970).

61. See Gaston, *Horae Synopticae Electronicae*.

evidence for Luke's own theological viewpoint? Does the very fact he selected that source indicate that he wanted to express its theology? One would assume this to be the case and that Luke was being divinely led in weaving together his materials into a cohesive theology.

Moreover, those passages in the gospel that are of most theological weight must be taken into account, namely, not only passages that contain specific teachings but also those that contain a confluence of significant Lukan terminology. For example, Jesus' conversation with Zacchaeus (19:1–10) includes the words "today" (twice), "salvation," "save," and the name "Abraham." Such terminology is relatively frequent in Luke. Also, Zacchaeus, who was a tax collector and so was called a "sinner" by the people, exemplifies the kind of person Luke uses to show God's grace. This incident is of high significance (see comments at 19:1–10).

Jesus' preaching at Nazareth (4:16–21) exemplifies the kerygmatic (proclamation) theme in Luke and provides a programmatic statement regarding Jesus' ministry (see Overview, 4:14–30). In Luke's narrative, this passage is also situated at a significant point in the development of the plot.

While the proper use of redaction criticism in discerning the theology of a gospel's author must depend on careful comparison with parallel passages in the other gospels, the coherence of themes within a gospel is as important as a comparison of themes between the gospels. For example, the messiahship of Jesus and the kingdom of God must be recognized as important themes in Luke's theology, whether or not they appear with unusual frequency as compared with Matthew and Mark.

History and geography play an important part in Luke's theology. (We object to the criticism that this fact implies that Luke is less reliable in these areas.) Luke's "empire history" (to use Cassidy's term; see p. 32), as well as the local context of events in his gospel, demonstrates the reality and importance of salvation history in time and space. The providence of God in history has an important relation to the sequence of events in Luke–Acts.

In Luke's central section (9:51–19:44), we can discern a theological motif in the way Jesus orients his thinking and ministry toward Jerusalem, the city of destiny, which would be the scene of the passion and ascension of Christ (9:51). That Luke, in contrast to the other gospels, does not describe the actual entrance of Jesus into Jerusalem itself is significant. (See comments at 19:28–44. Other historical and geographical matters of theological importance will be treated at various points in the commentary. See also "Eschatology," p. 41, for remarks on Luke's scheme of history as understood by Conzelmann.)

The following are some of the more significant topics in Luke:

Christology

The gospel opens with a series of birth narratives alternating between Jesus and John the Baptist. Among other purposes, these narratives aim to contrast the two figures, both of whom are identified in Luke as prophets.[62] From the beginning it is apparent that Jesus is also the Son of God, born of a virgin (1:26–38). The atmosphere of chs. 1–2 is that of the OT. Jesus is presented in terms of messiahship (cf. 1:32b–33, 68–

---

62. See Paul S. Minear, *To Heal and to Reveal* (New York: Seabury, 1976), 95–96; cf. Marshall, *Luke: Historian and Theologian*, 125–28.

75). Simeon and Anna give testimony to the baby Jesus in the temple and announce that God's day of redemption has dawned, since the coming of the Savior means light to the Gentiles and glory to Israel (2:25–38). At the age of twelve, Jesus expresses his filial consciousness—his unique awareness that God is his Father (2:49).

There are hints throughout the gospel that Jesus came as a "prophet" (e.g., 4:24; 13:33; 24:19). This emphasis on the prophetic office combines the themes of glory and suffering in the life of Christ, though Luke also makes it clear that Jesus is more than a prophet. Luke (unlike Mark) effectively focuses on the messiahship of Jesus by taking the reader directly from the question of Herod—"Who, then, is this I hear such things about?" (9:9)—to the messianic act of feeding the five thousand (9:10–17), and then immediately to Peter's affirmation that Jesus is "the Christ of God" (9:20). In portraying Jesus as the Prophet, the continuation with the past is emphasized. In portraying him as the Messiah, the climax of salvation history is noted.[63]

Unlike the other gospels, Luke's narrative concludes with the ascension of Jesus. This marks both the conclusion of the gospel and the beginning of Acts and is thus pivotal in the two-volume work. Moreover, Luke makes mention of the ascension in 9:51, at the beginning of the central section of his gospel. With the ascension, Jesus came to be recognized as the Lord of all—a status that forms the basis for missions in Acts when mission work is understood in terms of the proclamation of the lordship of Christ throughout the world.

Doxology

The prominence of the ascension in Luke contributes to his "theology of glory." It has often been observed that Luke has emphasized the resurrection, ascension, and vindication of Christ (taking into account also the early chapters of Acts). The descriptive term "glory" (*doxa*, GK *1518*) is also appropriate because there is a sense of doxology—i.e., of ascribing glory to God—throughout Luke's work. Those who observe or benefit from the healing power of Christ are filled with wonder and bring glory to God (e.g., Lk 5:25–26; Ac 3:8–10; other examples of praising and blessing God in Luke are in 1:46–55, 68–79; 2:13–14, 20, 28–32; 7:16; 10:21; 18:43; 19:37–38; 24:53). Such acclamations show that in Jesus, one finds the presence of God himself.[64]

Soteriology

If Luke has a theology of glory, does it mean he lacks a theology of the cross? Not at all. It is true that the gospel as proclaimed in the first chapters of Acts does not feature the doctrine of the atonement as we

---

63. For a discussion of Jesus as Messiah within the prophetic paradigm of OT, see Mark L. Strauss, *The Davidic Messiah in Luke–Acts: The Promise and Its Fulfillment in Lukan Christology* (JSNTSup 110; Sheffield: Sheffield Academic Press, 1995).

64. For a discussion of the Lukan theology of glory in terms of the transcendence and immanence of God, see H. Douglas Buckwalter, "The Divine Saviour," in *Witness to the Gospel: The Theology of Acts*, ed. I. Howard Marshall and David Peterson (Grand Rapids: Eerdmans, 1998), 112–20.

have come to understand it from Paul. Nevertheless, the cross is central.[65] Even before the first passion prediction of Luke 9:22, there are foreshadowings of Jesus' sufferings (2:35; 5:35). Jesus is clearly moving toward the cross in 13:33. His words instituting the Last Supper must not be overlooked as evidence of his understanding of the cross (22:19–20).

Salvation

"The central theme in the writings of Luke is that Jesus offers salvation to men." This is the thesis of I. Howard Marshall.[66] This offer of salvation is not to be dissociated from the concept of salvation history that, properly understood, has a significant place in Luke and elsewhere in Scripture. It does, however, focus on the person and saving work of the Lord Jesus Christ rather than on a scheme of history (as in Conzelmann). *Sōzō* ("save," GK *5392*) occurs often in Luke (6:9; 7:50; 8:12, 36, 48, 50; 9:24; 13:23; 17:19; 18:26, 42; 19:10; 23:35, 37, 39), as does *sōtēr* ("Savior," GK *5400*; 1:47; 2:11), *sōtēria* ("salvation," GK *5401*; 1:69, 71, 77; 19:9), and *sōtērion* ("salvation," GK *5402*; 2:30; 3:6).

We observed above that one of the key passages in Luke is 19:1–10, which concludes with the statement that "the Son of Man came to seek and to save what was lost." The entire gospel of Luke pictures Jesus as reaching out to the lost in forgiveness. We see this exemplified in the beautiful story of the sinful woman (7:36–50). In the well-known parables in ch. 15, Jesus displays an attitude that contrasts with that of the Pharisees by identifying himself with the heavenly Father in rejoicing over the return of those who are lost.[67]

Holy Spirit

The prominence of the Holy Spirit in Luke–Acts has received considerable attention.[68] It is through the overshadowing spirit and power of God that Mary conceives the one who will be called the Son of God (1:35). The same Spirit would fill John the Baptist (1:15) and his mother, Elizabeth (1:41). The Spirit was on Simeon, who through the Spirit gave testimony to the Messiah (2:25–35). Jesus was full of the Spirit and was led by the Spirit at the time of his temptation (4:1). The great passage from Isaiah quoted by Jesus in the synagogue at Nazareth begins, "The Spirit of the Lord is on me" (4:18). Furthermore, Jesus promised the Holy Spirit both as an answer to prayer (11:13) and in anticipation of Pentecost (24:49; Ac 1:4). The Holy Spirit, of course, has a major place throughout Acts.

The age of the Spirit as promised by the OT prophets is now becoming a reality with the ministry of Jesus,[69] and this same Spirit is also at work in the ministry of the apostolic witnesses as they continue the

---

65. Previous scholarship on Luke's understanding of Jesus' death had focused primarily on the differences between Luke and Mark. For a positive evaluation of the third gospel on its own terms, see Peter Doble, *The Paradox of Salvation: Luke's Theology of the Cross* (SNTSMS 87; Cambridge: Cambridge Univ. Press, 1996).

66. Marshall, *Luke: Historian and Theologian*, 116.

67. See Marshall, *Luke: Historian and Theologian*, 116–44, for a fine discussion of Jesus' ministry of salvation.

68. Still useful is the survey of scholarship in François Bovon, *Luke the Theologian* (PTMS 12; Pittsburgh: Pickwick, 1987), 198–238.

69. For a helpful study on Lukan pneumatology in the light of Jewish traditions, see Max Turner, *Power from On High: The Spirit in Israel's Restoration and Witness in Luke–Acts* (Sheffield: Sheffield Academic Press, 1996).

mission of Jesus. Not only does the Spirit provide the force behind the unfolding of God's plan of salvation; the eschatological manifestation of this Spirit also signals the arrival of the climax of salvation history.

Prayer

Prayer was significant throughout Jesus' life and in the early church, but it seems to have been especially important in times of transition and crisis. Only Luke records that Jesus was praying at his baptism when the Holy Spirit descended on him (3:21). He prayed before choosing the twelve apostles (6:12). Again, only Luke records that Jesus was praying on the Mount of Transfiguration (9:29). Luke 11:1–13 and 18:1–8 contain his special teaching and parables on prayer. Other instances of Jesus' praying in Luke are 5:16; 9:18; and 11:1. The presence of accounts of prayer in critical moments in the narrative points to the nature of Jesus' ministry as one that is to be absolutely identified as the outworking of God's will and plan.[70]

Miracles

All four gospels record miracles of Christ. In Luke, as noted above, the performance of miracles often results in expressions of praise to God. The word *dynamis* ("power," GK *1539*) occurs frequently in Luke, though not significantly more so than in Matthew or Mark. It also occurs a number of times in Acts. The miracles manifest the arrival of God's kingdom (4:18–19; 7:22). Besides revealing the presence of God's power, these miracles also have ecclesiological significance, as many of them were performed on the outcasts and those outside of the worshiping community of Israel (e.g., 5:12–14; 7:1–10, 36–50; 8:26–39; 13:10–17). In Luke, these miracles function as markers that point to the formation of a true community of God through the life and ministry of Jesus.

Sense of Destiny

The word *dei* ("must," "necessary") is prominent in Luke and Acts. Jesus "had to" be in his Father's house (Lk 2:49); he "must preach the good news of the kingdom of God . . . , because that is why I was sent" (4:43); he "must suffer" (9:22; cf. Mt 16:21; Mk 8:31); he must finish the way appointed to him, the way that culminated in the cross (13:33); and it was necessary for the Son of Man to be betrayed and crucified, suffering first before entering his glory (24:7, 26, 44–47). In this way, Jesus occupies the central place in salvation history, fulfilling the plan of God.[71]

---

70. In Luke, prayer is not simply understood in an individualistic way but belongs to the "theology proper." It is related both to Christology and the development of salvation history. See David Crump, *Jesus the Intercessor: Prayer and Christology in Luke–Acts* (Grand Rapids: Baker, 1999).

71. For more, see Charles H. Cosgrove, "The Divine *Dei* in Luke–Acts: Investigations into the Lukan Understanding of God's Providence," *NovT* 26 (1984): 168–90; John T. Squires, *The Plan of God* (Cambridge: Cambridge Univ. Press, 1993). This use of the term *dei* probably originated in the wider eschatological traditions where the necessity of the fulfillment of God's plan was emphasized (cf. *TDNT* 2:23–25).

Promise and Fulfillment

God's plan in Christ was in accordance with OT promises. Though Luke does not use the fulfillment formulas of Matthew, the idea of fulfillment is in his gospel. It is especially notable in the programmatic statement in 4:16–21. The quotation of Isaiah 61:1–2, which Jesus concluded with the words "the year of the Lord's favor," became contemporary as Jesus said, "Today this scripture is fulfilled in your hearing" (4:21).[72] The theme of fulfillment also has apologetic value in Luke. "Proof from prophecy" is significant, especially in ch. 24 and in the early chapters of Acts.[73] This does not exhaust, however, the significance of Luke's allusions to OT promise. Frequently, OT material is also evoked to "explain" the significance of God's climactic act in salvation history through the work of his own Son.

Israel and the People of God

The term *laos* (GK *3295*, "people") is to be distinguished, as Paul S. Minear points out, from the more general *ochlos* (GK *4063*, "crowd").[74] In his gospel, Luke uses the former to describe believers and sympathetic Jews. Significantly, in Acts the term is also used to refer to believers among Gentiles (e.g., Ac 15:14). Whereas the crowds are sometimes hostile to Jesus, the "people" are responsive. But what happens to the Jewish people who become believers in Christ? Once they are part of the Christian church, are they separated from Israel? Or, at the other extreme, is the entire church to be considered "Israel"? Peter Richardson suggests that the term "Israel of God" (Gal 6:16) does not refer to the church itself but rather to "those within Israel to whom God will show mercy."[75] Jacob Jervell likewise refrains from applying the term "Israel" to the church as a whole.[76] He points to a group of repentant Jews who have accepted the gospel and argues that the Gentile mission grows out of the fulfillment of the biblical promises to Israel. Jervell's view is consistent with the emphasis in Acts on the conversion of great numbers of Jews, though one would not want to downplay the subsequent focus on the inclusion of the Gentiles into the people of God.[77] The thesis of Richardson and Jervell should also be qualified by the Lukan emphasis on the continuity between Israel and the church that is defined by the person of Jesus Christ. Moreover, the redefinition of Israel (with the inclusion of the Gentiles) has always been part of the restoration program proclaimed by the prophets (e.g., Isa 40–55).[78]

---

72. The significance of this in connection with the OT Year of Jubilee is noted in Robert B. Sloan Jr., *The Favorable Year of the Lord* (Austin, Tex.: Schola Press, 1977). For the wider connections between Luke–Acts and the prophetic promises, see Rebecca I. Denova, *The Things Accomplished Among Us: Prophetic Tradition in the Structural Pattern of Luke–Acts* (JSNTSup 141; Sheffield: Sheffield Academic Press, 1997).

73. Cf. Nils A. Dahl, "The Story of Abraham in Luke–Acts," in *Studies in Luke–Acts* (ed. Keck and Martyn), 139–58.

74. See Paul S. Minear, "Jesus' Audiences, According to Luke," *NovT* 16 (1974): 81–109.

75. Peter Richardson, *Israel in the Apostolic Church* (Cambridge: Cambridge Univ. Press, 1969), 82.

76. See Jacob Jervell, *Luke and the People of God: A New Look at Luke–Acts* (Minneapolis: Augsburg, 1972), 41–74.

77. The ambivalent portrayal of the Jews in Luke–Acts is rightly noted by many (see, e.g., Joseph B. Tyson, *Images of Judaism in Luke–Acts* [Columbia: Univ. of South Carolina Press, 1992]).

78. See Pao, *Acts and the Isaianic New Exodus*, 217–48.

Eschatology

The continuity of the true people of God and the mission to the Gentiles are part of the plan of God that is a major theme in Luke. The opening chapters of Luke emphasize the messianic promises, especially through the songs of Mary (1:46–55) and Zechariah (1:68–79). The ultimate fulfillment of these still lies in the future. Luke, in common with the other Synoptic Gospels, contains teachings of Jesus about his return and about the glorification of the Son of Man.[79] It has been common to picture Luke, however, as writing at a time when Christians were despairing over the return of Christ, which they had expected immediately. This "delay of the parousia" was of such major concern to Luke that he devised a scheme that divided history into three phases: (1) the OT period, (2) the life of Jesus, and (3) the period of the church. Hans Conzelmann sets forth this idea, but one of the problems is that it makes Luke distort the traditions of Jesus' sayings regarding his return by superimposing on them a concept of an extended period of the church in which life is to go on without the return of Christ.[80]

A number of studies have addressed this issue, maintaining the importance of those eschatological teachings that Luke does incorporate and that were not reinterpreted as radically as Conzelmann had thought.[81] It is possible to see stages in the fulfillment of predictions made both in the OT and by Jesus, with a partial fulfillment now and a consummation later. According to E. Earle Ellis, the problem is "not the delay of the parousia . . . but false apocalyptic speculation that has misapplied the teachings of Jesus and threatens to pervert the church's mission."[82] Thus Luke contains vivid warnings against coming judgment, an encouragement to watchfulness (e.g., 12:40), and the description of the coming of the Son of Man (17:22–37) but warns against misguided speculation (17:20–21). Faithfulness is needed during the time the Master is away (12:42–48; 19:11–27). In another response to Conzelmann that seeks to maintain the eschatological element in Luke, Eric Franklin sees the ascension and proclamation of Jesus as Lord as an eschatological climax.[83]

There are other subjects related to eschatology that cannot be discussed here. The concept of present and future stages in the fulfillment of prophecy naturally includes the idea of the kingdom of God, with its present or "inaugurated" aspects and its later consummation. Likewise, we see Luke's emphasis on the present reality of God's work in the use of the word "today" (*sēmeron*, GK *4958*), alluded to earlier. The following passages in Luke are significant: 2:11; 4:21; 5:26; 12:28; 13:32–33; 19:5, 9; 22:34, 61; 23:43. "Today" also occurs nine times in Acts.

---

79. See D. A. Carson's excursus on "Son of Man" (at Mt 8:20) in volume 8 of The Expositor's Bible Commentary, 209–13.

80. See Conzelmann, *Theology of St. Luke*; the German title *Die Mitte der Zeit* (i.e., the central point in time) reflects his theory.

81. See, e.g., I. Howard Marshall, *Eschatology and the Parables* (London: Tyndale, 1963); cf. E. Earle Ellis, *Eschatology in Luke* (Philadelphia: Fortress, 1972); A. J. Mattill Jr., *Luke and the Last Things* (Dillsboro: Western North Carolina Press, 1979); John T. Carroll, *Response to the End of History: Eschatology and Situation in Luke–Acts* (SBLDS 92; Atlanta: Scholars Press, 1988).

82. Ellis, *Eschatology in Luke*, 19.

Discipleship and the Christian in the World

This topic covers a multitude of subjects that cannot be discussed in this brief introduction but which have occasioned much attention in recent years. Only Luke contains the narrative of 9:57–62 on following Jesus and the teaching of Jesus on the cost of discipleship (14:25–35).

A major question in Lukan studies is whether Jesus requires the sacrifice of material possessions for salvation or for discipleship, or whether he just presents it as an ideal for those who are especially devoted. The first idea is not taught in Luke. The case of the rich ruler (18:18–30) is unique (see comments there). Likewise those who want to be disciples should *yield* up all their possessions but not necessarily *disperse* them (see comments at 14:33). But if this is an ideal, it is an ideal strongly taught. Luke includes Jesus' woes as well as blessings (6:24–26), which speak strongly against the wealthy. He also addresses the matter of possessions in chs. 12 and 16. In addition, Acts not only mentions but also emphasizes the sacrificial giving of the early church (2:45; 3:6; 4:32–37; 5:1–11).[84]

Scholarly attention to Jesus' social and political teachings has focused on their implications for possible political revolution.[85] Richard J. Cassidy concludes that Luke gives an accurate description of Jesus' social and political stance and that, though he rejected the use of violence, Jesus challenged the social status quo under the Roman Empire.[86] Cassidy holds that the teachings of Jesus as found in the gospel of Luke would, if carried out widely, have seriously challenged the principles of the Roman government. He bases his conclusions on Jesus' social teachings in general and on specific texts such as Luke 20:23–25, the familiar "give to Caesar what is Caesar's, and to God what is God's."

The Word of God

This is a more important theme in Luke than is generally realized. The first appearance of *logos* (GK *3364*, "word") is in 1:2: "servants of the word." Luke emphasizes the graciousness and effectiveness of Jesus' word in 4:22, 32, 36. The term is prominent in the parable of the sower (8:4–15). It is those who "hear the word, retain it, and by persevering produce a crop" (8:15) who are truly related to Jesus. We also learn from

83. See Eric Franklin, *Christ the Lord: A Study in the Purpose and Theology of Luke–Acts* (Philadelphia: Westminster, 1975).

84. A number of works address the theme of poverty and wealth in the NT. See especially Martin Hengel, *Property and Riches in the Early Church* (Philadelphia: Fortress, 1974); Luke Timothy Johnson, *The Literary Function of Possessions in Luke–Acts* (SBLDS 39; Missoula, Mont.: Scholars Press, 1977); R. J. Karris, "Poor and Rich: The Lukan *Sitz im Leben*," in *Perspectives on Luke–Acts*, 112–25; Craig L. Blomberg, *Neither Riches Nor Poverty* (Downers Grove, Ill.: InterVarsity, 2001). Regarding the understanding of the early church on biblical teachings, see L. William Countryman, *The Rich Christian in the Church of the Early Empire* (Lewiston, N.Y.: Mellen, 1980); David P. Seccombe, *Possessions and the Poor in Luke–Acts* (SNTSU B6; Linz: Fuchs, 1982).

85. See Oscar Cullmann, *The State in the New Testament* (New York: Scribner's, 1956); Cullmann, *Jesus and the Revolutionaries* (New York: Harper & Row, 1970); Martin Hengel, *Was Jesus a Revolutionist?* (Philadelphia: Fortress, 1971). For a different position, see S. G. F. Brandon, *Jesus and the Zealots* (Manchester: Manchester Univ. Press, 1967). See also John Howard Yoder, *The Politics of Jesus* (Grand Rapids: Eerdmans, 1972). For a study of Jesus as a revolutionary in the context of the social world of first-century Palestine, see Richard A. Horsley, *Jesus and the Spiral of Violence: Popular Jewish Resistance in Roman Palestine* (San Francisco: Harper & Row, 1987).

Luke that not only is the word of God in the OT fulfilled in the life of Jesus but Jesus' own words are also fulfilled (e.g., 19:32:"just as he had told them"). Thus we have the prophetic word, the authoritative word of Jesus, and the inspired word that is the gospel of Luke itself. Significantly, in the second volume of Luke's writings, the church comes to be identified as the community of "the word" (Ac 6:7; 12:24; 19:20).[87]

13. BIBLIOGRAPHY

The following is a selective list of commentaries and monographs on Luke available in English, confined for the most part to those referred to in the commentary (they will be referred to simply by the author's name [and initials only when necessary to distinguish two authors of the same surname]). In instances where the same author has written a commentary as well as (a) book(s) and/or (an) article(s), the commentary will be referred to by the author's name, and the book(s)/article(s) by the author's name and short title.

References to resources that do not appear in the bibliography will carry full bibliographic details at the first mention and thereafter a short title.

Bailey, Kenneth. *Poet and Peasant: A Literary-Cultural Approach to the Parables in Luke.* Grand Rapids: Eerdmans, 1977.
———. *Through Peasant Eyes.* Grand Rapids: Eerdmans, 1980.
Black, Matthew. *An Aramaic Approach to the Gospels and Acts.* 3d ed. Oxford: Clarendon, 1967.
Bock, Darrell L. *Luke.* 2 vols. Baker Exegetical Commentary on the New Testament. Grand Rapids: Baker, 1994–96.
Bovon, François. *Luke.* Vol. 1. Hermeneia. Philadelphia: Fortress, 2002.
Brodie, Thomas L. *Luke the Literary Interpreter: Luke–Acts as a Systematic Rewriting and Updating of the Elijah–Elisha Narrative.* Rome: Pontifical Univ. of St. Thomas Aquinas, 1987.
Brown, Raymond E. *The Birth of the Messiah: A Commentary on the Infancy Narratives in the Gospels of Matthew and Luke.* Revised edition. New York: Doubleday, 1993.
———. *The Death of the Messiah: From Gethsemane to the Grave: A Commentary on the Passion Narratives in the Four Gospels.* 2 vols. New York: Doubleday, 1994.
Brown, Schuyler. *Apostasy and Perseverance in the Theology of Luke.* Analecta biblica 36. Rome: Pontifical Biblical Institute, 1969.
Carroll, John T. *Response to the End of History: Eschatology and Situation in Luke–Acts.* Society of Biblical Literature Dissertation Series 92. Atlanta: Scholars, 1988.
Cassidy, Richard J., and Philip J. Scharper, eds. *Political Issues in Luke–Acts.* Maryknoll, N.Y.: Orbis, 1983.
Conzelmann, Hans. *The Theology of St. Luke.* Translated by Geoffrey Buswell. New York: Harper & Row, 1960.
Creed, I. M. *The Gospel According to St. Luke: A Commentary on the Third Gospel.* London: Macmillan, 1930.
Crump, David. *Jesus the Intercessor: Prayer and Christology in Luke–Acts.* Grand Rapids: Baker, 1999.
Danker, F. W. *Jesus and the New Age According to St. Luke: A Commentary on the Third Gospel.* St. Louis: Clayton, 1972.
Dillon, R. J. *From Eyewitnesses to Ministers of the Word.* Analecta biblica 82. Rome: Pontifical Biblical Institute, 1978.
Doble, Peter. *The Paradox of Salvation: Luke's Theology of the Cross.* Society for New Testament Studies Monograph Series 87. Cambridge: Cambridge Univ. Press, 1996.
Doeve, J. W. *Jewish Hermeneutics in the Synoptic Gospels and Acts.* Assen: Van Gorcum, 1954.
Ellis, E. Earle. *The Gospel of Luke.* New Century Bible Commentary. New York: Nelson, 1966.
Evans, Craig A., and James A. Sanders, *Luke and Scripture: The Function of Sacred Tradition in Luke–Acts.* Minneapolis: Fortress, 1993.

---

86. Cassidy, *Jesus, Politics, and Society.*

Fitzmyer, Joseph A. *Essays on the Semitic Background of the New Testament*. Missoula, Mont.: Scholars Press, 1974.

———. *The Gospel According to Luke*. 2 vols. Anchor Bible 28. Garden City, N.J.: Doubleday, 1981–85.

Gaston, Lloyd. *Horae Synopticae Electronicae:Word Statistics of the Synoptic Gospels*. Missoula, Mont.: Scholars Press, 1973.

Godet, Frederic. *A Commentary on the Gospel of St. Luke*. Translated by E. W. Shalders and M. D. Cusin. Edinburgh: T&T Clark, 1893.

Green, Joel B. *The Gospel of Luke*. New International Commentary on the New Testament. Grand Rapids: Eerdmans, 1998.

Hawkins, John Caesas. *Horae Synopticae: Contributions to the Study of the Synoptic Problem*. 1909. Repr., Grand Rapids: Baker, 1968.

Hendriksen, William. *Exposition of the Gospel According to Luke*. Grand Rapids: Baker, 1978.

Jeremias, Joachim. *The Parables of Jesus*. Revised edition. Translated by S. H. Hooke. New York: Scribner, 1963.

Johnson, Luke Timothy. *The Literary Function of Possessions in Luke–Acts*. Society of Biblical Literature Dissertation Series 39. Missoula, Mont.: Scholars Press, 1977.

Longenecker, Richard N. *The Christology of Early Jewish Christianity*. London: SCM, 1970.

Manson, T. W. *The Sayings of Jesus*. London: SCM, 1949.

Marshall, I. Howard. *The Gospel of Luke: A Commentary on the Greek Text*. Grand Rapids: Eerdmans, 1978.

———. *Luke: Historian and Theologian*. 3d ed. Downers Grove, Ill.: InterVarsity, 1988.

Mattill, A. J. Jr. *Luke and the Last Things*. Dillsboro: Western North Carolina Press, 1979.

Metzger, Bruce. *A Textual Commentary on the Greek New Testament*. Revised edition. Stuttgart: German Bible Society, 1994.

Minear, Paul S. *To Heal and to Reveal*. New York: Seabury, 1976.

Moessner, David P., ed. *Jesus and the Heritage of Israel: Luke's Narrative Claim upon Israel's Legacy*. Harrisburg, Pa.: Trinity International, 1999.

Morris, Leon. *The Gospel According to St. Luke*. Tyndale New Testament Commentaries. Grand Rapids: Eerdmans, 1974.

Neyrey, Jerome H., ed. *The Social World of Luke–Acts: Models for Interpretation*. Peabody, Mass.: Hendrickson, 1991.

Nolland, John. *Luke*. 3 vols. Word Biblical Commentary 35. Dallas, Tex.: Word, 1989–93.

O'Collins, Gerald, and Filberto Marconi, eds. *Luke and Acts*. Translated by Matthew J. O'Connell. New York: Paulist, 1993.

Pao, David W. *Acts and the Isaianic New Exodus*. Grand Rapids: Baker, 2002.

Plummer, Alfred. *A Critical and Exegetical Commentary on the Gospel According to St. Luke*. International Critical Commentary. 5th ed. Edinburgh: T&T Clark, 1922.

Schramm, T. *Der Markus-Stoff bei Lukas. Eine literarkritische und redaktionsgeschichtliche Untersuchung*. Society for New Testament Studies Monograph Series 15. Cambridge: Cambridge Univ. Press, 1971.

Schürmann, H. *Das Lukasevangelium*. Vols. 1–2.1. Herders Theologischer Kommentar zum Neuen Testament. Freiburg–Vienna: Herder, 1969, 1994.

Shepherd, William H. Jr. *The Narrative Function of the Holy Spirit as a Character in Luke–Acts*. Society of Biblical Literature Dissertation Series 43. Atlanta: Scholars, 1994.

Siker, Jeffrey S. *Disinheriting the Jews: Abraham in Early Christian Controversy*. Louisville, Ky.: Westminster, 1991.

Talbert, Charles H. *Literary Patterns, Theological Themes and the Genre of Luke–Acts*. Society of Biblical Literature Monograph Series 20. Missoula, Mont.: Scholars Press, 1974.

———. ed. *Perspectives on Luke–Acts*. Edinburgh: T&T Clark, 1978.

Thompson, Richard P., and Thomas E. Phillips, eds. *Literary Studies in Luke–Acts: Essays in Honor of Joseph B. Tyson*. Macon, Ga.: Mercer Univ. Press, 1998.

14. OUTLINE

I. Introduction (1:1–4)

II. Birth and Childhood Narratives (1:5–2:52)

   A. Anticipation of Two Births (1:5–56)

      1. The Birth of John the Baptist Foretold (1:5–25)

      2. The Birth of Jesus Foretold (1:26–38)

      3. Mary's Visit to Elizabeth (1:39–45)

      4. Mary's Song: The Magnificat (1:46–56)

   B. Birth Narratives (1:57–2:20)

      1. The Birth of John the Baptist (1:57–66)

      2. Zechariah's Song: The Benedictus (1:67–80)

      3. The Birth of Jesus (2:1–7)

      4. The Announcement to the Shepherds (2:8–20)

   C. Jesus' Early Years (2:21–52)

      1. Presentation of Jesus in the Temple (2:21–40)

      2. The Boy Jesus at the Temple (2:41–52)

III. Preparation for Jesus' Ministry (3:1–4:13)

   A. The Ministry of John the Baptist (3:1–20)

   B. The Baptism of Jesus (3:21–22)

   C. Jesus' Genealogy (3:23–38)

   D. The Temptation of Jesus (4:1–13)

IV. The Galilean Ministry (4:14–9:50)

   A. Initial Phase (4:14–6:16)

      1. First Approach and Rejection at Nazareth (4:14–30)

      2. Driving Out an Evil Spirit (4:31–37)

      3. Healing Many (4:38–44)

      4. Calling the First Disciples (5:1–11)

      5. The Man with Leprosy (5:12–16)

      6. Healing a Paralytic (5:17–26)

      7. Calling Levi (5:27–32)

      8. The Question about Fasting (5:33–39)

      9. Sabbath Controversies (6:1–11)

     10. Choosing the Twelve Apostles (6:12–16)

   B. Jesus' Great Sermon (6:17–49)

      1. Blessings and Woes (6:17–26)

      2. Love for Enemies (6:27–36)

      3. Judging Others (6:37–42)

      4. A Tree and Its Fruit (6:43–45)

      5. The Wise and Foolish Builders (6:46–49)

B. The Passion of the Lord (22:1–23:56)
1. The Agreement to Betray Jesus (22:1–6)
2. The Last Supper (22:7–23)
3. Teachings at the Table (22:24–38)
4. Prayer on the Mount of Olives (22:39–46)
5. Jesus' Arrest (22:47–53)
6. Peter's Denial (22:54–62)
7. The Mocking of Jesus (22:63–65)
8. Trial before the Jewish Leaders (22:66–71)
9. Trial before Pilate and Herod (23:1–25)
10. The Crucifixion (23:26–43)
11. Jesus' Death (23:44–49)
12. Jesus' Burial (23:50–56)
C. The Resurrection and Ascension (24:1–53)
1. The Resurrection (24:1–12)
2. On the Emmaus Road (24:13–35)
3. The Appearance to the Disciples (24:36–49)
4. The Ascension (24:50–53)

Text and Exposition

I. INTRODUCTION (1:1–4)

OVERVIEW

The introduction to Luke is a long, carefully constructed sentence in the tradition of the finest historical works in Greek literature. It stands in contrast to the genealogical table of Matthew, the concise opening sentence of Mark, and the theological prologue of John. It was customary among the great Greek and Hellenistic historians, including the first-century Jewish writer Josephus, to explain and justify their works in a preface. Their objective was to assure the reader that they were capable and reliable and that they had done thorough research. While such a weighty introduction does not in itself guarantee the honesty of the writer, neither should its conventional form be dismissed as merely formal pretension.

The classical literary style of the preface contrasts with the remainder of the gospel, in which Semitisms abound (cf. comments in introduction, sections 7 and 10; see Overview, 1:5–2:52).

[1]Many have undertaken to draw up an account of the things that have been fulfilled among us, [2]just as they were handed down to us by those who from the first were eyewitnesses and servants of the word. [3]Therefore, since I myself have carefully investigated everything from the beginning, it seemed good also to me to write an orderly account for you, most excellent Theophilus, [4]so that you may know the certainty of the things you have been taught.

COMMENTARY

1 The preface opens with the Greek word *epeidēper* (GK 2077, untranslated in NIV; KJV, "forasmuch as"; NASB, "inasmuch as"), a classical word used only here in the NT but found in such major authors as Thucydides, Philo, and Josephus. It stands in stylistic contrast to the colloquial *egeneto* ("there was"), which in v.5 opens the narrative. The NIV omits *epeidēper* for the sake of concise English style, adding "therefore" in v.3. This clarifies the meaning—that Luke's account was written after those of many others.

"Many have undertaken" implies that by the time Luke wrote there was considerable interest in data about Jesus and his ministry. Luke does not say that he himself actually reproduced material from any of the existing accounts, though that could be assumed from this and subsequent evidence. The choice of the word "undertaken" (*epecheireō*, GK 2217) need not mean that earlier attempts to write gospel narratives had failed (cf. MM, 250–51; Vernon K. Robbins, "The Claims of the Prologues and Greco-Roman Rhetoric," in *Jesus and the Heritage of*

Israel [ed. Moessner], 63–83). Obviously Luke would not be writing if there were no need for something further, but this does not necessarily reflect adversely on his predecessors. "To draw up an account" (*anataxasthai diēgēsin*, GK *421, 1456*) means "to write a report or narrative, relating events in an orderly way" (cf. MM, 38). The verbal form of *diēgēsis* (*diēgeomai*, GK *1455*) occurs in Luke (8:39; 9:10) and Acts (9:27; 12:17).

"Fulfilled" is a better translation of *peplērophorēmenōn* (GK *4442*) than "most surely believed" (KJV) in this context. The word and its cognate *plērophoria* (GK *4443*) can be translated "full assurance" or "assurance" when their basic reference is to the confident attitude of a person (cf. Ro 4:21; 14:5; Col 2:2; Heb 6:11; 10:22). Otherwise, and especially with reference to things rather than people, the idea of accomplishment or completion is foremost. (See "discharge all the duties" and "fully proclaimed" in 2Ti 4:5, 17.) Further, if the accomplishment of God's purposes in the life and ministry of Jesus is one of Luke's themes, it is appropriate for the preface to reflect this.

2 "Just as they were handed down" stresses the validity of the tradition of Jesus' words and deeds. The same emphasis occurs in Paul, who was careful to pass on to others what had been "handed down" to him (1Co 11:23; 15:3; cf. O. Cullmann, *The Early Church: Studies in Early Christian History and Theology* [Philadelphia: Westminster, 1956], 59–75).

Though the "eyewitnesses and servants" may have included some of the "many" (v.1), they are mostly to be distinguished from them because they were prior to them. Luke is establishing the validity of the information both he and his predecessors included in their narratives. Witnesses are important to Luke. While the concept of "witness" is not as prominent in Luke as in John (see esp. Jn 5:31–47), it is integral to Luke's historical and theological purposes.

The words "from the first" (probably meaning from the early days of Jesus' ministry) are tied to the word "eyewitnesses" as closely as grammar permits—i.e., "the from-the-first witnesses" (*hoi ap' archēs autoptai*). These were not passive observers but "servants of the word." Luke is probably referring primarily to the apostles, whose authority he upholds throughout Luke–Acts. In Acts 10:39–42, Peter speaks as one of those who were both witnesses and preachers.

"Word" (*logos*, GK *3364*) here means "the message of the gospel," especially as embodied in the words and deeds of Jesus. Ancient Greek writers often stressed the importance of matching one's words with appropriate deeds. In Acts 1:1, Luke combines the words "do" and "teach" when he describes Jesus' ministry. This is essential to the fulfillment mentioned in v.1. While all four gospels use the term *logos* (with particular significance in Jn 1:1, 14), Luke uses it surprisingly often. This is especially true in passages unique to Luke (see Gaston, 64, 76; Hawkins, 20, 43). In summary, v.2 makes a serious claim regarding Luke's careful historical research of witnesses and sources that has weighty implications for our estimation of the entire gospel.

3 The opening words in the Greek order are "it seemed good also to me" (*edoxe kamoi*). This establishes a balance and pattern of comparison between vv.1–2 and 3–4: "Many have undertaken" and "it seemed good also to me"; "to draw up an account" and "to write an orderly account"; "handed down to us" and "so that you may know."

Luke now describes his own work of investigation and writing. The word "everything" may partially explain how his work differed from that of the "many" (v.1) and also from that of Mark—namely, in its greater comprehensiveness. "From the beginning" translates *anōthen* (GK *540*), which can mean, according to the context, either "above" or "again." Here in its relation to historical research it has a temporal sense. Theologically, Luke's concern for the "beginning" of the gospel surfaces here. Luke did his research "carefully" (*akribōs*, GK *209*; lit., "accurately") and wrote an "orderly" (*kathexēs*, GK *2759*) account. We cannot determine from this preface alone whether Luke is referring to a chronological or a thematic order. He does not specifically claim to have aimed at chronological sequence. Perhaps he may have followed an order found in his sources. If so, this could explain his occasional differences from Matthew and Mark. Or he may have rearranged his sources according to another pattern. Taken alone, the prologue is not conclusive as to these possibilities. In any event, Luke intended his claim of working in an orderly way to inspire confidence in his readers.

The identity of "Theophilus" is unknown, though many suggestions have been made (cf. R. H. Anderson, "Theophilus: A Proposal," *EvQ* 69 [1997]: 195–215). The name ("friend of God") might be either a symbol or a substitute for the true name of Luke's addressee. Theophilus was, however, a proper name, and "most excellent" naturally suggests an actual person of some distinction. He may have been Luke's literary patron or publisher, after the custom of the times (cf. E. J. Goodspeed, "Some Greek Notes: I. Was Theophilus Luke's Publisher?" *JBL* 73 [1954]: 84).

4 Though it is not clear whether Theophilus was a believer, he had doubtless received some instructions in the faith. The genitive plural (*logōn*) of *logos* ("word," GK *3364*) is here translated in the NIV as "things"—a legitimate extended use. Theophilus has learned of both the words and deeds of Jesus. "Taught" (*katēchēthēs*, GK *2994*) may refer to formal church teaching (Gal 6:6), but does not necessarily do so. For some reason Theophilus needed assurance, or "certainty" (*asphaleia*, GK *854*), as to the truth of the things taught to him. Possibly he was troubled by denials of the resurrection and other historical foundations of the faith that gnostic speculation was challenging. Such are not to be countered by mere speculation but by the factual narrative Luke is about to write. His book will set forth evidences and purposes ancillary to the one he has stated in this preface.

According to the prologue, Luke's purpose in writing was to assure Theophilus of the "certainty" of the gospel tradition. His gospel can still fulfill this purpose, without excluding other purposes for Luke–Acts (cf. section 5, "Purpose," in the introduction).

NOTES

1–4 Among the many useful articles on the Lukan prologue and the method of his historical investigation, see Ned B. Stonehouse, *The Witness of Luke to Christ* (Grand Rapids: Eerdmans, 1951), 24–25, in which he especially surveys the contributions of H. J. Cadbury. Supplementary to this is Stonehouse's *Origins of the Synoptic Gospels* (Grand Rapids: Eerdmans, 1963), 113–31. This discussion continues in the works of D. J. Sneen, "An Exegesis of Luke 1:14 with Special Regard to Luke's Purpose as a Historian," *ExpTim* 83 (1971–72): 40–43; and I. I. du Plessis, "Once More: The Purpose of Luke's Prologue," *NovT* 16 (1974): 259–71. The most extensive study is found in Loveday C. A. Alexander, *The Preface to Luke's Gospel*, where scientific prose is understood as providing the appropriate context to examine Luke's preface. While Alexander may have pointed to the social location of Luke, significant parallels to prefaces in historiographical material should not be ignored (see the study by Daryl Schmidt, "Rhetorical Influences and Genre: Luke's

Preface and the Rhetoric of Hellenistic Historiography," in *Jesus and the Heritage of Israel* [ed. Moessner], 27–60).

3 The word ἀκριβῶς (*akribōs*, GK *209*) can also mean "fully" in ancient historical prefaces. See David L. Balch, "ἀκριβῶς ... γράψαι (Luke 1:3): To Write the *Full* History of God's Receiving All Nations," in *Jesus and the Heritage of Israel* (ed. Moessner), 29–50.

II. BIRTH AND CHILDHOOD NARRATIVES (1:5–2:52)

OVERVIEW

This narrative introduces a section in Luke unparalleled in the other gospels (see introduction for critical and stylistic issues). Its distinctive characteristics include (1) an atmosphere reminiscent of the OT, with a Semitic grammatical and stylistic cast; (2) an alternating focus on John the Baptist and Jesus; (3) the awesomeness of heavenly beings appearing to humans; and (4) a note of joy, especially as heard in four songs: Mary's (1:46–55), Zechariah's (1:68–79), the angels' (2:14), and Simeon's (2:29–32).

(1) The Semitic style fits the religious and historical connection Luke is establishing between the OT and NT periods. Luke does not use the fulfillment formulas Matthew uses but shows that OT promises stand behind the events he describes. He does this by giving his style and vocabulary a Septuagintal flavor. He also takes pains to ground the Christian message in Jerusalem and in its temple, the cultic center of Israel.

(2) To make this connection with the OT, Luke also uses a pattern of alternation in which attention shifts back and forth between John the Baptist and Jesus. Far from being the result of a confusion of sources, as is sometimes supposed, this alternation is a literary device to focus attention successively on each person (cf. G. N. Stanton, *Jesus of Nazareth in New Testament Preaching* [SNTSMS 27; Cambridge:

Cambridge Univ. Press, 1974], 55–56). Luke clearly identifies John as a successor to the OT prophets. Through his alternating presentations, Luke links John and Jesus, whom Luke apparently also identifies as a prophet (cf. Minear, 95–96). Since he also sees in Jesus far more than a prophet, Luke's device of alternation goes beyond comparison to contrast, with Jesus presented as "Son of the Most High" and messianic Deliverer (1:32–33, 69, 76; 2:11, 30). This same point is expressed through the structuring of the material, where the parallelism between John the Baptist and Jesus is "broken" by two episodes that highlight the superiority of Jesus (1:39–56; 2:41–52). The structure of the section then is (1a) the announcement of John's coming birth; (1b) the announcement of Jesus' coming birth; (2) Elizabeth's blessing of Mary, and Mary's praise to God; (3a) John's birth; (3b) Jesus' birth, which is acclaimed by angels in heaven and by saintly Jews in the temple; and (4) Jesus at the temple, where he reveals his wisdom and knowledge (cf. Karl Kuhn, "The Point of Step-Parallelism in Luke 1–2," *NTS* 47 [2001]: 38–49).

(3) The appearance of angels is likewise appropriate for an account that teaches that God has acted decisively in the history of his people to accomplish their salvation. Some reject this supernatural activity, attempting to explain the narratives as an accre-

tion of legends. To do so deprives the event of an effective cause. Actually, the appearance of an angel is no more remarkable than the incarnation itself.

(4) The theme of joy finds expression not only in the songs but also in the tone of the whole passage. The gospel is always "good news of great joy" (2:10). Moreover, the passage realistically includes a reminder both of the pain of sin and of the cost of our deliverance, as Simeon's allusion to the ultimate death of Mary's son (2:35) shows.

Another pattern of themes may be seen in the repetition of the phrase "Most High": (1) Jesus is the "Son of the Most High" (1:32); (2) Mary's conception by the Holy Spirit is said to be by the "power of the Most High" (1:35); and (3) John is called a "prophet of the Most High" (1:76; cf. H. H. Oliver,

"The Lucan Birth Stories and the Purpose of Luke–Acts," *NTS* 10 [1963–64]: 215–26).

While the phrases just outlined do not occur in close sequence, they should probably be taken together as relating to three major themes in Luke's gospel: (1) John is the final prophet of the OT period, the forerunner of the Messiah, and the first proclaimer of the kingdom; (2) Jesus is the unique Son of God, the true eschatological prophet and Messiah; and (3) the Holy Spirit's ministry both validates and empowers the ministry of Jesus. (The Holy Spirit is mentioned frequently in this section; see 1:15, 35, 41, 67, 80 [TNIV text note]; 2:25–27.) Other themes prominent in Luke occur in these opening narratives and will be noted in the commentary section.

A. Anticipation of Two Births (1:5–56)

1. The Birth of John the Baptist Foretold (1:5–25)

⁵In the time of Herod king of Judea there was a priest named Zechariah, who belonged to the priestly division of Abijah; his wife Elizabeth was also a descendant of Aaron. ⁶Both of them were upright in the sight of God, observing all the Lord's commandments and regulations blamelessly. ⁷But they had no children, because Elizabeth was barren; and they were both well along in years.

⁸Once when Zechariah's division was on duty and he was serving as priest before God, ⁹he was chosen by lot, according to the custom of the priesthood, to go into the temple of the Lord and burn incense. ¹⁰And when the time for the burning of incense came, all the assembled worshipers were praying outside.

¹¹Then an angel of the Lord appeared to him, standing at the right side of the altar of incense. ¹²When Zechariah saw him, he was startled and was gripped with fear. ¹³But the angel said to him: "Do not be afraid, Zechariah; your prayer has been heard. Your wife Elizabeth will bear you a son, and you are to give him the name John. ¹⁴He will be a joy and delight to you, and many will rejoice because of his birth, ¹⁵for he will be great in the sight of the Lord. He is never to take wine or other fermented drink, and he will be filled with the Holy Spirit even from birth. ¹⁶Many of the people of Israel will he bring back to the Lord their God. ¹⁷And he will go on before the Lord, in the spirit and power of Elijah, to turn

the hearts of the fathers to their children and the disobedient to the wisdom of the righteous—to make ready a people prepared for the Lord."

[18]Zechariah asked the angel, "How can I be sure of this? I am an old man and my wife is well along in years."

[19]The angel answered, "I am Gabriel. I stand in the presence of God, and I have been sent to speak to you and to tell you this good news. [20]And now you will be silent and not able to speak until the day this happens, because you did not believe my words, which will come true at their proper time."

[21]Meanwhile, the people were waiting for Zechariah and wondering why he stayed so long in the temple. [22]When he came out, he could not speak to them. They realized he had seen a vision in the temple, for he kept making signs to them but remained unable to speak.

[23]When his time of service was completed, he returned home. [24]After this his wife Elizabeth became pregnant and for five months remained in seclusion. [25]"The Lord has done this for me," she said. "In these days he has shown his favor and taken away my disgrace among the people."

COMMENTARY

5 As already mentioned, the style of this section is different from the classical style of vv.1–4. Likewise, the method of dating differs from that used later in 3:1, where Luke is interested in establishing a more precise point of historical reference. In this verse, his only concern is to locate the events in the reign of Herod (king of Judea, 37–4 BC).

Luke emphasizes the Jewish roots of Christianity by mentioning that not only was Zechariah (whose name means "God remembers") a priest, but his wife had also been born into the priestly line. (See comments at vv.8–9 for the functioning of this "priestly division.")

6 This is a description of a truly pious couple wholly devoted to God. The language of the verse "implies a religious rather than a purely ethical character" (Marshall, 53). Marshall remarks that v.6 shows that their childlessness did not imply any sin. The OT would use the Hebrew *tām* or *tāmîm* (GK

9447) to describe such a couple (translated as "blameless," Ge 6:9; Job 1:8).

7 To be childless brought sorrow and often shame. At her advanced age, Elizabeth could no longer entertain the hope of every Jewish woman to be the mother of the Messiah. While her situation and the subsequent intervention of God had its precedents in the OT (cf. Sarah, Ge 17:16–17; Hannah, 1Sa 1:5–11), no other woman had such a total reversal in fortune as to bear the forerunner of the Messiah. Quite in line with the OT narrative is the fact that the unfolding of the plan of God will not be affected by human limitation.

8–9 The "division" (cf. v.5) was one of twenty-four groups of priests divided by families and structured after the pattern of 1 Chronicles 23 and 24 (note Abijah, Zechariah's ancestor [1Ch 24:10]). The exile had interrupted the original lines of descent; thus the divisions were regrouped, most of them corresponding to the original in name only. Each of the twenty-four divisions served in the temple for one week, twice a year, as well as at the major festivals (cf. J. Jeremias, *Jerusalem in the Time of Jesus* [London: SCM, 1969], 198–207). An individual priest, however, could offer the incense at the daily sacrifice only once in his lifetime (v.9; see Notes), since there were so many priests. Thus this was the climactic moment of Zechariah's priestly career, perhaps the most dramatic moment possible for the event described to have occurred. God was breaking into the ancient routine of Jewish ritual with the word of his decisive saving act. Considering his interest in the Jewish origin of Christianity, Luke probably viewed this dramatic moment not so much as a judgment against Judaism as an appropriate and significant context for the new revelation.

10 Mention of the worshipers outside not only heightens the suspense but also prepares the reader for vv.21–22. They were probably pious Jews who loved to be near the temple when sacrifices were offered. The NIV's "assembled worshipers" obscures the important word *laos* ("people," GK *3295*; see comments at v.27).

11 The suddenness of the appearance of the angel accords with other supernatural events in Luke and elsewhere in Scripture (cf. 2:9, 13). Luke does not describe the angel, but the fact that he tells exactly where the angel appeared shows the reality of the vision. Only a heavenly being had the right to appear in the Holy Place with the priest.

12 "Startled" represents a word of deep emotion (from *tarassō*, GK *5429*) and is coupled with the descriptive phrase "gripped with fear." This is not only a natural reaction to such an appearance but is also consistent with what the gospels say about the response of the disciples and others to the presence of the supernatural (e.g., 5:8–10). Sometimes this betrays unbelief. But this is certainly not true of Mary (v.38); rather, her attitude (v.29) shows her

genuine awe and quite natural trepidation at being confronted by the heavenly visitor.

13 This is the first indication of prayer on the part of Zechariah. The word Luke uses (*deēsis*, GK *1255*) indicates a specific petition. If this was for a child (probably a son), the aorist tense in the phrase "has been heard" refers to Zechariah's lifelong prayer. Otherwise, his just-offered prayer in the temple was probably for the messianic redemption of Israel. Actually, the birth of his child was bound up with redemption in a way far beyond anything Zechariah expected. That the prayer included a petition for a son is substantiated by the further description of the child, beginning with his name. "John" (*Iōannēs*) combines in its Hebrew form the name of God with the word *ḥānan* ("to show favor to or be gracious to," GK *2858*). God did indeed answer Zechariah's prayer. That the child was named before his birth stresses God's sovereignty in choosing him to be his servant.

14–15 The description of the child's mission has a counterpart in Gabriel's words to Mary (vv.32–33). This is part of the literary device that connects and compares the roles of Jesus and John.

The "joy" (v.14) so characteristic of the day of God's salvation and so prominent in Luke came first to the parents of the forerunner, then spread to "many of the people [lit., sons] of Israel" (v.16). Also, "joy and delight" stand in contrast to Zechariah's "fear" (v.12). The child will be "great" (*megas*, GK *3489*) as the prophetic forerunner of the Messiah (v.15). "Great" also describes Jesus in v.32, though in the latter case it is absolute greatness without the qualifying "in the sight of the Lord." Later there would be those who found it hard to relinquish their devotion to John to follow Jesus. They would need to realize that while both were great, Jesus was the greater (3:16). Also, John's greatness related to the pre-messianic age (7:28). "In the sight of the Lord" indicates divine choice and approval. This expression, or its equivalent, is used frequently in Luke and Acts (see Notes).

It is difficult to identify John with a particular religious group simply by this description or the one in Mark 1:6. "He is never to take wine" suggests the Nazirite vow (Nu 6:1–12), but no mention is made of John's hair. Nazirites were to let their hair grow (Nu 6:5). Danker, 8, refers to the priests' abstinence from strong drink prior to entering the tabernacle and sees John as a priestly figure calling the people to repentance. On the other hand, the radical elements in John's appearance and behavior may exemplify his radical message of repentance. The Spirit's control ("filled with the Holy Spirit") is contrasted with the control wine can have over a person (cf. Eph 5:18). In the life of Jesus, the Spirit's ministry will be even more prominent than in John's life.

16–17 The OT prophets were repeatedly concerned with turning the erring people back to God, i.e., to repentance (v.16). In this work, none were more prominent than Elijah on Mount Carmel (1Ki 18:20–40). Luke does not here identify John as a reincarnated Elijah but qualifies his statement with the words "in the spirit and power of Elijah" (v.17). Moreover, Luke uses the language of Malachi 4:5–6 (cf. Mal 3:1) to compare John's ministry with that of Elijah. (See comments at 9:30 for further discussion of Elijah.)

"To turn the hearts of the fathers to their children" must be interpreted with reference to both the expanded form in Malachi 4:6 and the next phrase in this context (v.17). If the words are parallel to the phrase "wisdom of the righteous," then "the fathers," previously "disobedient," may be following the example of their children who are presumably listening to the message of John—"the wisdom of the righteous." Grammatically less likely but more probable, it might mean that when those who disobey heed wisdom, their Jewish ancestors would, if they knew of it, be pleased with them (cf.

Godet, 79–80). In their OT context, the words "turn the hearts" relate to averting divine wrath—a concept certainly basic in the ministry of John.

"People" (*laos*, GK *3295*) is a significant word in Luke. Thirty-five of its forty-nine occurrences in the Synoptic Gospels are in Luke (Gaston, 76; cf. Hawkins, 20–21, 45). Paul Minear ("Jesus' Audiences, According to Luke," *NovT* 16 [1974]: 82) holds that the term *laos* as used by Luke, in contrast to *ochlos* ("crowd," GK *4063*), "normally refers to Israel as the elect nation which forever retains the specific identity given to it by God." This suggestion accords with Luke's interest in the Jewish origins of Christianity, though it may be too comprehensive. Minear also comments that "it is this specific entity [people] which Luke sees as the initial and ultimate audience for all God's messengers, whether John the Baptist (Acts xiii 24) or the apostles ([Acts] iii 12f.)" (ibid., 82). The "people prepared for the Lord" ultimately includes not only these initial Jewish hearers but also those who formerly were "not a people" (1Pe 2:10), the Gentiles (see Jacob Jervell, *Luke and the People of God* [Minneapolis: Augsburg, 1972]).

18–20 Zechariah's question (v.18) seems innocent, but v.20 reveals that it was asked in doubt. In contrast, Mary's question—"How can this be?" (v.34)—arises from faith (v.45). Mary simply inquired as to the way God would work; Zechariah questioned the truth of the revelation. "How can I be sure of this?" apparently was a request for a sign. Though we are told that Zechariah was devout (v.6), his quest for confirmation was perilously close to the attitude described in 11:29. Since the gospel requires a response of faith, and since Zechariah, of all people, should have believed without question, the angel's reply (v.20) is not overly severe. The narrative gains solemnity by mentioning that Gabriel stood "in the presence of [*enōpion*, GK *1967*] God" (v.19; cf. "in the sight of" [v.15] and "before" [v.17]).

The "good news" will come to fulfillment in spite of human unbelief, but Zechariah must nevertheless bear the sign of his doubt. "Will come true" (*plērōthēsontai*, GK *4444*) means "will be fulfilled" and forms part of Luke's presentation of the fulfilled word of God.

The irony these verses present cannot be missed. Though Zechariah was presented the "good news," he was not able to speak because of his own disbelief.

21–22 The element of suspense during the unusually long time of prayer contributes to the vividness of Luke's narrative (v.21; cf. v.10). The worshipers who had been praying outside now understood, without anyone telling them, that Zechariah had seen a vision. Verse 22 reinforces the extraordinary nature of his experience and loss of speech.

24–25 As with the announcement to Mary, the word concerning Zechariah's and Elizabeth's promised son was given before his conception (v.24; cf. Joseph's experience [Mt 1:19–25]). It is characteristic of Luke to mention Elizabeth's grateful acknowledgment of the Lord's grace in removing the stigma of her childlessness (v.25).

NOTES

5–25 The literature on Luke 1 and 2 is extensive. The following are especially useful for the birth narratives: R. Brown, *Birth of the Messiah*, 235–499; I. Howard Marshall, *Luke: Historian and Theologian*, 96–102; Paul S. Minear, "Luke's Use of the Birth Stories," in *Studies in Luke–Acts*, ed. Leander Keck and J. Louis Martyn (New York: Abingdon, 1966), 111–30; H. H. Oliver, "The Lucan Birth Stories," *NTS* 10 [1963–64]: 202–26; E. W. Conrad, "The Annunciation of Birth and the Birth of the Messiah," *CBQ* 47 (1985): 656–63; Richard A. Horsley, *The Liberation of Christmas: The Infancy Narratives in Social Context* (New York: Crossroad, 1989).

6 The word ἄμεμπτοι (*amemptoi*, "blamelessly," GK *289*) does not imply sinlessness. Abraham was told to be "blameless" before the Lord (Ge 17:1 [LXX]). Paul, who affirms universal sinfulness (Ro 3:23), says he had been "faultless" as regards "legalistic righteousness" (Php 3:6).

8 The Greek ἐγένετο δὲ (*egeneto de*, "once") reflects the Hebrew idiom *wayᵉhî*, "and it came to pass," in the narrative construction. This is a common expression in Luke used in various combinations. In this form and in others, the verb γίνομαι (*ginomai*, "be," GK *1181*) is used frequently in Luke—more than in Matthew and Mark combined. Of the 107 occurrences, 31 in Luke are apparently editorial additions to his sources (Gaston, 70).

9 "According to the custom of the priesthood" could go with v.8, but the NIV is probably correct in taking it with "he was chosen by lot." "Incense" was offered in connection with the morning and evening sacrifice (*m. Tamid* 2.5; 5.2; 6.3). Marshall (*Luke: Historian and Theologian*, 54) connects the offering of incense, which symbolizes prayer in Scripture (Ps 141:2; Rev 5:8; 8:3–4), with Luke's particular interest in prayer.

13 "Prayer" here means, as noted above, a specific request. The more general word is προσευχή (*proseuchē*, GK *4666*; cf. 6:12; 19:46; 22:45).

15 Luke is the only synoptic writer to use ἐνώπιον (*enōpion*, "in the sight of," GK *1967*). He does so twenty-two times.

19 Gabriel (cf. Da 8:16; 9:21) is one of two angels named in Scripture, the other being Michael (Da 10:13, 21; 12:1; Jude 9; Rev 12:7). R. Brown (*Birth of the Messiah*, 271), noting the significance of Gabriel in Daniel and here in Luke 1, concludes: "The eschatological atmosphere evoked from Daniel is echoed in the tone of the message that follows."

The verb εὐαγγελίζω (*euangelizō*, "tell . . . good news," GK *2294*) has a special significance in Luke. Of its eleven occurrences in the Synoptics, ten are in Luke (see 2:10; 3:18; 4:8, 43; 7:22; 8:1; 9:6; 16:16; 20:1). The noun εὐαγγέλιον (*euangelion*, "good news, gospel," GK *2295*) occurs in Mark but not in Luke. The words do not always denote news that is good (*TDNT* 2:707–37; cf. Marshall, *Luke: Historian and Theologian*, 123–24), but in the context of OT prophecies the word-group points to the coming of the salvation of God. See Otto Betz, "Jesus and Isaiah 53," in *Jesus and the Suffering Servant: Isaiah 53 and Christian Origins*, ed. W. H. Bellinger and W. R. Farmer (Harrisburg, Pa.: Trinity International, 1998), 70–87.

2. The Birth of Jesus Foretold (1:26–38)

OVERVIEW

Continuing in the same style in which he has described Zechariah's encounter with the angel of the Lord, Luke now weaves deep theological meaning into his simple and delicate narrative. This section is the highest of several summits of revelation in chs. 1 and 2. The account of Jesus' nativity, beautiful and essential as it is, rests theologically on the angel Gabriel's announcement to Mary. Luke presents the theology of the incarnation in a way so holy and congruent with OT sacred history that any comparisons with pagan mythology seem utterly incongruous. Instead of the carnal union of a pagan god with a woman, producing some kind of semi-divine offspring, Luke speaks of a spiritual overshadowing by God himself that will produce the "holy one" (v.35) within Mary.

Several themes are intertwined in this passage: (1) the divine sonship of Jesus (vv.32, 35); (2) his messianic role and reign over the kingdom (vv.32–33); (3) God as the "Most High" (vv.32, 35; cf. v.76); (4) the power of the Holy Spirit (v.35); and (5) the grace of God (vv.29–30, 34–35, 38).

26In the sixth month, God sent the angel Gabriel to Nazareth, a town in Galilee, 27to a virgin pledged to be married to a man named Joseph, a descendant of David. The virgin's name was Mary. 28The angel went to her and said, "Greetings, you who are highly favored! The Lord is with you."

29Mary was greatly troubled at his words and wondered what kind of greeting this might be. 30But the angel said to her, "Do not be afraid, Mary, you have found favor with God. 31You will be with child and give birth to a son, and you are to give him the name Jesus. 32He will be great and will be called the Son of the Most High. The Lord God will give him the throne of his father David, 33and he will reign over the house of Jacob forever; his kingdom will never end."

34"How will this be," Mary asked the angel, "since I am a virgin?"

> ³⁵The angel answered, "The Holy Spirit will come upon you, and the power of the Most High will overshadow you. So the holy one to be born will be called the Son of God. ³⁶Even Elizabeth your relative is going to have a child in her old age, and she who was said to be barren is in her sixth month. ³⁷For nothing is impossible with God."
>
> ³⁸"I am the Lord's servant," Mary answered. "May it be to me as you have said." Then the angel left her.

COMMENTARY

26 The mention of Elizabeth's "sixth month" (cf. v.24) points to the pattern of alternation and establishes a link with the prophet John the Baptist (see comments at vv.5–25). The same chronological device points in v.36 to God's power over human reproduction. This theme of the direct action of God is one of the basic themes in Luke–Acts. (See v.19 in reference to the angel Gabriel.) Luke calls Nazareth a *polis* (GK *4484*), which can often be translated "city" but here describes a "town" (NIV) or "village." It was off, though not totally inaccessible from, the main trade routes. Its close proximity (three miles) to the major city of Sepphoris, a city called "the ornament of all Galilee" (Josephus, *Ant.* 18.26–28), reminds us that Nazareth was not exactly isolated from the wider cultural world. Its relatively insignificant size contrasts with Jerusalem, where Gabriel's previous appearance had taken place. John 1:46 records the contemporary Judean opinion of Nazareth.

Likewise, the region of Galilee contrasts with Judea. Surrounded as they were by Gentiles, the Galileans were not necessarily irreligious. They were, however, somewhat lax respecting such things as keeping a kosher kitchen (cf. Seán Freyne, *Galilee from Alexander the Great to Hadrian 323 B.C.E. to 135 C.E.* [Notre Dame, Ind.: Univ. of Notre Dame Press, 1980], 259–97). Though the Galileans had a reputation for pugnacity, Galilee was not a hotbed of revolutionary activity, as some have thought (ibid., 208–55).

27 The young virgin Mary contrasts with the old priest Zechariah, who was past the time for fathering children. The word "virgin" refers here to one who had not yet had sexual relations (see Notes). Mary's question in v.34 and the reference here to her being "pledged to be married" make this clear. Since betrothal often took place soon after puberty, Mary may have just entered her teens. This relationship was legally binding, but intercourse was not permitted until marriage. Only divorce or death could sever betrothal; in the latter event, the girl, though unmarried, would be considered a widow.

Luke calls Joseph "a descendant of David." Even though the genealogy in 3:23–37 is often taken as showing Mary's line, this is never stated. Neither does Luke or any other NT writer say that Mary was descended from David. Since Joseph is named here and in 3:23 and is explicitly linked with the royal line, we should probably assume that Luke considers Jesus a legitimate member of the royal line by what we today might call the right of adoption. This has an important bearing on the promise in v.32b.

28 Here Luke establishes another contrast with the preceding narrative—this time by relating Gabriel's greeting (vv.30–32) to Mary. But Zechariah had received no such greeting.

"Highly favored" renders *kecharitōmenē* (from *charitoō*, GK *5923*), which has the same root as the words for "greetings" (*chairō*, GK *5897*), and "favor" (*charis*, GK *5921*; v.30). Mary is "highly favored" because she is the recipient of God's grace. A similar combination of words occurs in Ephesians 1:6—"his glorious grace, which he has freely given [same Greek word as for "highly favored"] us." Some suggest that Luke implies a certain grace has been found in Mary's character. While this could be so, the parallel in Ephesians (the only other occurrence of the verb *charitoō* in the NT) shows that the grace in view here is that which is given to all believers apart from any merit of their own. Mary has "found favor with God" (v.30); she is a recipient of his grace (v.28), and she can therefore say, "My spirit rejoices in God my Savior" (v.47). "The Lord is with you" recalls the way the angel of the Lord addressed Gideon to assure him of God's help in the assignment he was about to receive (Jdg 6:12).

29-30 Zechariah had been "gripped with fear" (v.12) at the very appearance of the angel, but it was the angel's words—namely, his greeting (v.28)—that "greatly troubled" Mary (v.29). He responded first by assuring her that she had indeed "found favor" with God (v.30; cf. Ge 6:8, where Noah is spoken of as having "found favor" with God). God's grace, like his love, banishes fear of judgment (1Jn 4:17–18).

31 Gabriel now explains why his preliminary assurance of Mary's having found grace with God is so significant for her. The wording here is virtually identical to the "virgin" passage in Isaiah 7:14 (LXX) and to the assurance the angel of the Lord gave the fugitive Hagar (Ge 16:11 [LXX]). The word "virgin" is not, however, mentioned in the allusion to Isaiah, though Mary's question (v.34) shows she was a virgin—a fact Luke has mentioned in v.27.

The name "Jesus" ("Joshua") had been common in OT times and continued to be a popular name through the first century AD (*TDNT* 3:284–93).

Matthew 1:21 provides an explanation for giving the child a name that contains, in its Hebrew form, the word "saves" (*yāsa'*, GK 3828): "because he will save his people from their sins."

32-33 Some scholars consider it significant that, whereas in v.15 Gabriel had qualified his prophecy of the greatness of John ("he will be great in the sight of the Lord"), here his statement of the greatness of Mary's Son has no qualification whatsoever. The striking term "Son of the Most High" (v.32; cf. vv.35, 76) leads to a clear messianic affirmation—the reference to the "throne of his father David." Jesus' divine sonship is thus linked to his messiahship in accord with 2 Samuel 7:12–14 and Psalm 2:79 (cf. Ps 89:26–29). The description of Jesus' messianic destiny follows the statement of his sonship, and this sonship is related in v.35 to his divine origin. Clearly Luke sees the messianic vocation as a function of God's Son rather than seeing sonship as just an aspect of messiahship.

The OT concepts of "throne," Davidic line, "reign" (v.33), and "kingdom" are spoken of as eternal—i.e., they "will never end." Though this idea is found in Micah 4:7, it is not common in Jewish thought.

34 Unlike Zechariah, Mary does not ask for a confirmatory sign (cf. comments at v.18) but only for enlightenment on how God will accomplish this wonder. As Luke has it, the question does not relate to the remarkable person and work of her promised son but arises from the fact that she "does not know [*ou ginōskō*, GK *1182*; i.e., has not had sexual relations with] a man" (NIV, "I am a virgin"). R. Brown (*Birth of the Messiah*, 289; emphasis his) notes that "while the tense is present, it describes a state resultant from a past pattern of behavior—Mary has not known *any* man and so is a virgin."

Because she was betrothed, we may assume that Mary fully expected to have normal marital relations later. It is difficult, therefore, to know why she saw a problem in Gabriel's prediction. The text does not say that Mary had Isaiah 7:14 in mind and wondered how she, still a virgin, could conceive. Perhaps Luke's condensed account is intended to suggest (1) that Mary assumed an immediate fulfillment before marriage and (2) that the informed reader should understand the issue in terms of Isaiah 7:14, already hinted at in v.31. Marshall (*Luke: Historian and Theologian*, 69–70) lists several alternative explanations, none of which is satisfactory by itself (cf. also R. Brown, *Birth of the Messiah*, 303–9). What is clear is the fact that virginal conception is at issue in this verse. For a further discussion, see David T. Landry, "Narrative Logic in the Annunciation to Mary (Luke 1:26–38)," *JBL* 114 (1995): 65–79.

35 Once again (cf. v.15), Luke mentions the Holy Spirit, as he does six more times in his first two chapters (1:41, 67, 80 [TNIV text note]; 2:25, 26, 27). The word for "overshadow" (*episkiazō*, GK 2173) carries the sense of the holy, powerful presence of God, as in the description of the cloud that "covered" (Heb. *šākan*, GK 8905; NIV, "settled upon") the tabernacle when the tent was filled with the glory of God (Ex 40:35; cf. Ps 91:4). The word is used in all three accounts of the transfiguration to describe the overshadowing of the cloud (Mt 17:5; Mk 9:7; Lk 9:34). Likewise, in each account the voice comes out of the cloud, identifying Jesus as God's Son—a striking reminder of Luke 1:35, where the life that results from the enveloping cloud is identified as "the Son of God." The phrase "will be called the Son of God" does not mean that Jesus will later be recognized by those around him as the Son of God. To be called "Son of God" means simply that he *is* "the Son of God" (see John J. Kilgallen, "The Conception of Jesus [Luke 1:35]," *Bib* 78 [1997]: 232).

The child whose life is thus engendered by the power of God, which power is identified as the Holy Spirit, is himself called by Gabriel "the holy one." Because of this connection with the Holy Spirit, and because of the ethical meaning of "holy" in v.49, this word probably relates here to the purity of Jesus instead of to separation for a divine vocation.

36–37 The angel cites the pregnancy of Elizabeth (v.36) as further evidence of God's marvelous power and concludes with the grand affirmation of v.37—surely one of the most reassuring statements in all of Scripture. The impossibility motif further links this passage with the Abrahamic material, where the pregnancy of Sarah is also understood as a mighty act of God (cf. Ge 18:4). This impossibility motif is not limited to the birth narratives, however (cf. Walter Brueggemann, "'Impossibility' and Epistemology in the Faith Tradition of Abraham and Sarah [Ge 18:1–15]," *ZAW* 94 [1982]: 615–34).

38 Mary's exemplary attitude of servanthood recalls that of Hannah when she was praying for a son (1Sa 1:11, where the LXX also has *doulē*, "servant," GK 1527). Nothing is said about the relation of Mary's submission to her consciousness of the shame a premarital pregnancy could bring her. Her servanthood is not a cringing slavery but a submission to God that in OT times characterized genuine believers and that should characterize believers today (cf. v.48). Understandably, Mary doubtless felt empathy with Hannah's sense of being at the Lord's disposal in a part of life over which a woman before modern times had little or no control. Mary's trusting submission at this point in her life may be compared with her attitude toward her son later on (cf. Jn 2:5).

NOTES

27 The meaning of παρθένος (*parthenos*, GK *4221*) is not in doubt here, since it is amplified in v.34 (where the NIV introduces the term "virgin" to explain the text). Therefore, while it is alleged on the basis of some other literature that παρθένος, *parthenos*, occasionally had a broader meaning under special circumstances (cf. J. Massingbyrde Ford, "The Meaning of 'Virgin,'" *NTS* 12 [1966]: 293–99), the meaning here is not affected. The literature on the virgin birth includes James Orr, *The Virgin Birth of Christ* (New York: Scribner's, 1907); J. Gresham Machen, *The Virgin Birth of Christ* (1930; repr., Grand Rapids: Baker, 1965); Thomas Boslooper, *The Virgin Birth* (Philadelphia: Westminster, 1962); R. E. Brown, *The Virginal Conception and Bodily Resurrection of Jesus* (New York: Paulist, 1973); and Robert Gromacki, *The Virgin Birth: Doctrine of Deity* (Nashville: Nelson, 1974). For a discussion of what the concept of virginity itself evokes in the minds of the ancient audience, see Mary F. Foskett, *A Virgin Conceived: Mary and Classical Representations of Virginity* (Bloomington, Ind.: Indiana Univ. Press, 2002), 23–112.

28 The meaning of "greetings" (KJV, "hail") for χαῖρε (*chaire*, GK *5897*) is debated. It is the simple Greek word for a greeting. In the LXX of Zephaniah 3:14 it means "rejoice" (cf. Zec 9:9). In light of the significance of the theme of joy elsewhere in the Lukan corpus, the meaning of "rejoice" is probably intended. Some have seen a connection—significant for Roman Catholic interpreters—between Mary and the "Daughter of Zion" addressed in Zephaniah. Although an allusion to Zephaniah 3:14 is dubious, the parallel between "mighty to save" in Zephaniah 3:17 and Mary's reference to God as "Savior" and "Mighty One" in Luke 1:47, 49 may make it a remote possibility. The Latin form of the greeting is preserved in the familiar words "Ave Maria."

The phrase ὁ κύριος μετὰ σοῦ (*ho kyrios meta sou*, "the Lord is with you") is followed, in many MSS, by the words εὐλογημένη σὺ ἐν γυναιξίν (*eulogēmenē su en gynaixin*, "blessed are you among women"). This clause, familiar from the Roman Catholic "Hail Mary," is in the later MSS represented in the KJV, and is probably copied from v.42 (cf. Metzger, 108). Since it is hard to explain why Sinaiticus (א) and Vaticanus (B) omitted it if it were authentic, and since its presence in other MSS can be explained as a transfer from v.42, it is best left out. It was included in the KJV and Douay Version.

28, 30 For studies on χάρις (*charis*, "grace, favor," GK *5921*), see *TDNT* 9:372–402, and *NIDNTT* 2:115–24.

32, 35 The title ὁ ὕψιστος (*ho hypsistos*, "Most High") is found seven times in Luke, twice in Acts, and only four times elsewhere in the NT. It appears frequently in the LXX. See Marshall, *Luke: Historian and Theologian*, 67, for a defense of the Semitic rather than Hellenistic character of the term as used here. The issue affects the question of the Palestinian origin and, therefore, the authenticity of the narrative.

35 Observe that the title υἱὸς θεοῦ (*huios theou*, "Son of God") occurs in a Jewish Palestinian setting here. Formerly its use in the NT was commonly attributed to Hellenistic influence. Recent scholarship has corrected this error. Nolland, 1:51–52, further points to the juxtaposition of the two phrases ("Son of the Most High" and "Son of God") in the Qumran material (4Q243 2.1). The literature on this subject is vast. For a summary of the data, see *TDNT* 8:334–92, esp. 376–82; cf. Martin Hengel, *The Son of God: The Origin of Christology and the History of the Jewish–Hellenistic Religion* (Philadelphia: Fortress, 1976). R. Brown (*Birth of the Messiah*, 311–16) surveys the relevant data in this passage.

The syntax of τὸ γεννώμενον ἅγιον κληθήσεται υἱὸς θεοῦ (*to gennōmenon hagion klēthēsetai huios theou*, "the holy one to be born will be called the Son of God") is difficult. The alternating possibilities can be visualized as follows:

NIV: "The holy one to be born will be called   the Son of God."
RSV: "The child   to be born will be called holy, the Son of God."

The second possibility takes "holy" as a predicate adjective, rather than as a modifier of the subject. In supporting the second rendering, R. Brown (*Birth of the Messiah*, 291) cites Isaiah 4:3 and Luke 2:23 as parallels (the parallel in Lk 2:23 is not clear in the NIV, which substitutes "consecrated" for "called holy"). In both parallels, the verb καλέω (*kaleō*) follows the predicate, which is the normal order (cf. Marshall, *Luke: Historian and Theologian*, 71). If v.35 follows this pattern, "holy," not "Son of God," is in the predicate position, with "Son of God" in apposition to "holy," as in the RSV. In either case, the incarnated son is the Son of God; so the virginal conception brings into human existence one who is the Son of God.

3. Mary's Visit to Elizabeth (1:39–45)

OVERVIEW

At this point Luke deftly combines the two strands about Elizabeth and Mary. So far the narrative has not stressed Jesus' superiority to John. But now attention centers on Jesus and his mother (v.43). Even so, the pattern of alternation continues, giving John his own important place as the prophet who goes before the Lord.

³⁹At that time Mary got ready and hurried to a town in the hill country of Judea, ⁴⁰where she entered Zechariah's home and greeted Elizabeth. ⁴¹When Elizabeth heard Mary's greeting, the baby leaped in her womb, and Elizabeth was filled with the Holy Spirit. ⁴²In a loud voice she exclaimed: "Blessed are you among women, and blessed is the child you will bear! ⁴³But why am I so favored, that the mother of my Lord should come to me? ⁴⁴As soon as the sound of your greeting reached my ears, the baby in my womb leaped for joy. ⁴⁵Blessed is she who has believed that what the Lord has said to her will be accomplished!"

COMMENTARY

39–40 Mary apparently started on her journey as soon as possible (v.39). Luke does not specify the town she went to, but we can assume that it was fifty to seventy miles from Nazareth to "Zechariah's home" (v.40)—a major trip for Mary.

41–42 To speculate about how Mary's greeting caused the child to leap in Elizabeth's womb (v.41) would be to miss the unaffected beauty of this narrative in which the stirring of the unborn child becomes a joyful prelude to Elizabeth's being "filled with the Holy Spirit," who enlightened her about the identity of the child Mary was carrying (v.42).

43 Nowhere in the NT is Mary called "Mother of God." Deity is not confined to the person of Jesus (we may say, "Jesus is God," but not [all of] "God is Jesus"). She was, however, the mother of Jesus, the Messiah and Lord. In Luke, "Lord" (*kyrios*, GK *3261*) is a frequently used title (95 out of 166 occurrences in the Synoptics; so Gaston, 76). Jesus is called "Lord" two other times in the Lukan birth narratives (1:76; 2:11).

45 "Blessed" describes the happy situation of those God favors. Elizabeth gave the blessing

Zechariah's muteness prevented him from giving. See vv.68–79 for the blessing he later pronounced on the infant Jesus. Luke uses the blessing Elizabeth gave Mary to call attention to Mary's faith.

The way in which v.45 supplements v.42 is noteworthy. In v.42, Mary is called the "blessed" one because of her maternal relationship with her son Jesus. In v.45, however, Mary is recognized to be truly "blessed" because of her faith in and obedience to God. The same contrast is developed later in the Lukan material. In 8:19–21, for example, Jesus redefines family relationship in terms of one's faith in and obedience to God: "My mother and brothers are those who hear God's word and put it into practice" (v.21).

4. Mary's Song: The Magnificat (1:46–56)

OVERVIEW

This song, commonly known as "the Magnificat," has several striking features. First, it is saturated with OT concepts and phrases. Plummer, 30–31, cites twelve different OT passages the song reflects line by line in addition to Hannah's prayer in 1 Samuel 2:1–10, on which the song seems to have been modeled.

Second, assuming that the song is correctly attributed to Mary (see below), it shows her deep piety and knowledge of Scripture. Such familiarity with the OT was not at that time so unusual for a pious Jewess like Mary as to bar her from consideration as its author. Moreover, it reflects qualities suitable to the mother of the Lord.

Third, though it reveals a God who vindicates the downtrodden and ministers to the hungry (cf. 1Sa 2:1–10), it also strikes a revolutionary note. If Hannah spoke of the poor as being raised to sit with princes (1Sa 2:8), Mary sees the princes toppled

from their places of power (Lk 1:52). Yet Hannah's song is not without its elements of judgment in which the hungry and those who arrogantly oppose God are routed (1Sa 2:3, 5, 10; cf. Lk 1:51, 53). Luke conveys a strong social message to us, one that is rooted in the OT and that, with cultural adaptations, is of continued meaning.

Fourth, Mary's Magnificat markedly transcends Hannah's song. It does this through its messianic element and implies Mary's consciousness of her own exalted role as the kingdom dawns (v.48).

This song can be divided into four strophes: (1) vv.46–48 praise God for what he has done for Mary—a theme that continues into the first part of the next strophe; (2) vv.49–50 mention certain attributes of God—power, holiness, and mercy; (3) vv.51–53 show God's sovereign action in reversing certain social conditions; and finally, (4) vv.54–55 recall God's mercy to Israel.

How much of the Magnificat was originally spoken by Mary rather than composed by Luke? Apart from basic matters of inspiration and literary or critical factors, several considerations should be kept in mind. One is the creative potential of even a poorly educated girl from a rural area. Another is the ability of people in ancient times to absorb and remember the spoken word, especially the biblical word. This applies both to Mary's knowledge of OT phraseology and to her repetition of these phrases.

Further, we are not told that Mary composed the song on the spot. Even a few days of meditation during her journey would have been sufficient time for her to produce the composition, especially since she was a girl who reflected deeply (cf. 2:51).

Finally, the song may be taken as prophecy in the broad biblical sense, in which case the Holy Spirit who instructed Elizabeth (v.41) may well have led both Mary and Luke in the composition and transmission of the song.

⁴⁶And Mary said:

"My soul glorifies the Lord
⁴⁷   and my spirit rejoices in God my Savior,
⁴⁸for he has been mindful
    of the humble state of his servant.
    From now on all generations will call me blessed,
⁴⁹   for the Mighty One has done great things for me—
    holy is his name.
⁵⁰His mercy extends to those who fear him,
    from generation to generation.
⁵¹He has performed mighty deeds with his arm;
    he has scattered those who are proud in their inmost thoughts.
⁵²He has brought down rulers from their thrones
    but has lifted up the humble.
⁵³He has filled the hungry with good things
    but has sent the rich away empty.
⁵⁴He has helped his servant Israel,
    remembering to be merciful
⁵⁵to Abraham and his descendants forever,
    even as he said to our fathers."

⁵⁶Mary stayed with Elizabeth for about three months and then returned home.

COMMENTARY

46–47 The excitement of Elizabeth, who actually shouted her benediction (v.42), gives way to a restraint that is no less joyful. A synonymous parallelism like that in the Psalms characterizes vv.46b–47.

This first major song in Luke derives its name ("Magnificat") from the first word of the Latin version of the song, which translates *megalynei* (GK 3486). The NEB's translation, "Tell out . . . the greatness of the Lord," is a beautifully phrased expression of Mary's intent. The word *megalynei* literally means "enlarge." In this context, it connotes the ascription of greatness to God. The song that follows extols the mighty acts of God not only for Mary but also for God's people, Israel (cf. vv.54–55). It is in this sense that some see Mary as "Israel personified" (cf. Carroll, 43).

Mary's song begins on the note of salvation as she acknowledges her dependence on God (v.47). Her words are comparable to those of Habakkuk, who came through his trials rejoicing in God his Savior (Hab 3:18). Note that in beginning the Magnificat by praising "God my Savior," Mary answered the Roman Catholic dogma of the immaculate conception, which holds that from the moment of her conception Mary was by God's grace kept free from all taint of original sin. Only sinners need a Savior.

48 Mary's "humble state" probably refers to her lowly social position. The word does not usually convey the idea of "humiliated." For the meaning of "servant," see comments at v.38; for that of "blessed," see comments at v.45 and 6:20–23.

49 Mary is in awe of the "Mighty One," whose great power has been exercised in her life. The word "great" (*megala*, GK 3489) recalls "glorifies" (*megalynei*, GK 3486) in v.46. God's "name" is, according to the common ancient meaning, his whole reputation or character.

50 "Mercy" expresses an aspect of God's character sometimes overlooked when his power and holiness are stressed. A false dichotomy between holiness and mercy characterized some of the Pharisees (cf. Mt 23:23). "Fear" means here, as often in Scripture, a "pious reverence."

51–53 The main verbs in the next two strophes are in the aorist tense. The use of the aorist tense could be gnomic (somewhat like a proverb; e.g., v.53: "God always fills the hungry"). If not gnomic, the aorists could recall the specific times in the OT when God acted (vv.51–52). We must not, however, overlook the fact that Mary's references to the acts of God relate to the coming of the Messiah and indicate, as mentioned above, radical social reversals. Also, use of the aorist tense here could actually be predictive (as in Isa 53:19), though general in content.

54–55 Mary here recalls God's covenant. The words translated "forever" (*eis ton aiōna*, v.55) occur emphatically as the final words in the original text of the song. To avoid the impression that "to Abraham and his descendants" are indirect objects of "as he said" (as though parallel with "to our fathers"), the NIV reverses v.55a and 55b (see Notes). The sustained interest in Abraham is unique to Luke among the gospels (e.g., 1:73; 13:16, 28; 16:22–30; 19:9; cf. Siker, *Disinheriting the Jews*).

56 Luke leaves us perplexed as to whether Mary's stay of "about three months" ended before or continued after the birth of John (cf. vv.26, 36, 39). His reticence should preclude rather than stimulate needless speculation.

NOTES

46 There are several reasons—textual and contextual—for questioning the word "Mary" here. Some theorize that Elizabeth, not Mary, composed the Magnificat. Among the contextual reasons is the fact that the earlier social shame of Elizabeth's childless condition corresponds both to the situation of Hannah, whose prayer in 1 Samuel 2 is similar to this, and possibly to the description of the author of the Magnificat in v.48. The former parallel is significant, but the meaning of v.48 is equally or more appropriate to Mary. Of the contextual reasons, the strongest is the wording of v.56, which is, literally, "Mary stayed with her" (i.e., with Elizabeth; so NIV). If Mary had just sung the Magnificat, one might expect the verse to say, "She stayed with Elizabeth." Yet this is hardly conclusive.

Textually, there is only scant testimony to the reading "Elizabeth" in v.46 (cf. Metzger, 109). The editors of the UBS Greek NT considered alternate possibilities but found the evidence for the originality of "Mary" in the text "overwhelming." (For a presentation of the argument that Elizabeth was the author of the Magnificat, see Creed, 22–23.)

47 The verb ἠγαλλίασεν (ēgalliasen, "rejoices"), unlike μεγαλύνει (megalynei, "glorifies") in v.46, is in the aorist tense. It may be a Semitism (waw conversive) or just an example of an aorist used with a perfective sense, i.e., describing a present state that is the continuation of a past event (cf. Moulton, Grammar [vol. 3, Syntax; ed. Nigel Turner; Edinburgh: T&T Clark, 1963], 68–81). This may also be an example of the "dramatic aorist," in which the emotional force of the verb is highlighted (cf. Daniel B. Wallace, Greek Grammar Beyond the Basics [Grand Rapids: Zondervan, 1996], 565).

49–55 A certain militant tone in the song calls to mind some extrabiblical phraseology as well as some of the ideals of the Zealots. For a significant, even if not entirely convincing, discussion of this tone, see J. Massingbyrde Ford, "Zealotism and the Lukan Infancy Narratives," NovT 18 (1976): 281–92, especially 284ff.

49 The phrase ὁ δυνατός (ho dynatos, "the Mighty One," GK 1543) has no exact OT parallel, though God was often lauded for his power. Psalm 24:8 (23:8 [LXX]) has the word δυνατός, dynatos ("mighty"), twice, but the closest expression is in Zephaniah 3:17 [LXX]: "The LORD your God is in your midst, a victorious warrior" (lit.; NIV, "is with you, he is mighty to save").

55 The words "to our fathers" clearly go with the verb "said." The second half of the verse, beginning with "to Abraham," probably completes "remembering to be merciful" in v.54.

B. Birth Narratives (1:57–2:20)

1. The Birth of John the Baptist (1:57–66)

OVERVIEW

This section is a brief sequel to vv.5–25 and serves to introduce "the Benedictus" (vv.67–79). It pictures a rural, closely knit society in which personal experiences are shared by the community.

⁵⁷When it was time for Elizabeth to have her baby, she gave birth to a son. ⁵⁸Her neighbors and relatives heard that the Lord had shown her great mercy, and they shared her joy.

⁵⁹On the eighth day they came to circumcise the child, and they were going to name him after his father Zechariah, ⁶⁰but his mother spoke up and said, "No! He is to be called John."

> ⁶¹They said to her, "There is no one among your relatives who has that name."
> ⁶²Then they made signs to his father, to find out what he would like to name the child.
> ⁶³He asked for a writing tablet, and to everyone's astonishment he wrote, "His name is John." ⁶⁴Immediately his mouth was opened and his tongue was loosed, and he began to speak, praising God. ⁶⁵The neighbors were all filled with awe, and throughout the hill country of Judea people were talking about all these things. ⁶⁶Everyone who heard this wondered about it, asking, "What then is this child going to be?" For the Lord's hand was with him.

COMMENTARY

57–61 These verses give the impression that no one in the neighborhood knew of Elizabeth's pregnancy. Perhaps a seclusion that would have prompted suspicion in the case of a younger woman seemed normal for an older one. On one level, the "joy" (v.58) is over Elizabeth's emergence from the shadow of childlessness; on another, it accords with the messianic joy of verses 44 and 46.

Circumcision on the eighth day (v.59) was in accord with Genesis 17:9–14 (cf. Lev 12:3). Luke offers no explanation as to why the child had not been publicly named at birth. Possibly the narrative reflects the Hellenistic custom of waiting a week or so to name a newborn child. In any event, there was obviously a considerable audience for the naming at the circumcision. To choose a name after a baby's grandfather or father, especially if one of them was highly esteemed, was natural (v.61). The objection from Elizabeth (v.60) was against custom and was apparently discounted, probably because she was a woman.

62–63 Zechariah may have been deaf as well as mute, though this has not been indicated. Luke says he was "unable to speak" (v.22), but the word used (*kōphos*, GK 3273) can also mean "deaf" (as in 7:22). In any case, the relatives and neighbors made signs (v.62), to which he responded on a waxed writing tablet (v.63). The present tense in the statement "his name is John" has the ring of deliberate emphasis. The naming is significant in this context since it locates John the Baptist not only in relationship with his parents but also with God, because it was God's angel who had provided the name (cf. Bovon, 71).

64–66 When the time of his disability (v.20) was over, Zechariah's first words were words of praise (cf. Ac 2:11—"declaring the wonders of God"). Luke stresses the widespread response (v.65) to the events surrounding the birth of John, just as he later stresses the fame of Jesus (e.g., 2:52). A child whose birth was attended by such marvelous circumstances would surely have an unusual destiny (v.66).

NOTES

58 The word translated "great" is actually a verb, ἐμεγάλυνεν (*emegalynen*, GK 3486)—the same verb used in v.46, meaning to "magnify" or "make great." The idea of greatness is also repeated in v.49. For "mercy," see vv.50, 54.

59 The imperfect ἐκάλουν (*ekaloun*) could mean that they were already naming him John, or, as in the NIV, that they were trying or "were going to name him."

66 The verb ἦν (*ēn*, "was") in the clause "for the Lord's hand was with him" probably indicates that the comment was not made by the people at the time but that it is Luke's later reflection. A few Western texts omit the verb. The omission probably was a deliberate change to make the comment fit in as part of the dialogue (cf. Metzger, 109–10).

2. Zechariah's Song: The Benedictus (1:67–80)

OVERVIEW

This second major song in Luke is called "the Benedictus," the first word in the Latin version, which is a translation of the Greek *eulogētos* ("blessed," GK *2329*). The song has two main parts: (1) praise to God for messianic deliverance (vv.68–75), and (2) celebration of the significant role John the Baptist will have in this work of deliverance (vv.76–79). In both sections, there is a strong emphasis on salvation, national and personal, and on the covenant and preparation that are about to be realized in their fulfillment. There is striking use of chiasmus (a rhetorical device that entails inversion in parallel literary structures) in the first part of Zechariah's song. From the ends to the center, the following terms recur, usually in reverse order: "come" (or "visit"; vv.68, 78 [some versions have "dawn" in v.78]); "his people" (vv.68, 77); "salvation" (vv.69, 77); prophet(s) (vv.70, 76); "hand of our enemies" (vv.71, 74); father(s) (vv.72–73); "covenant" and "oath" (vv.72–73). With the words "covenant" and "oath" in juxtaposition at the center, i.e., at the end of the first and the beginning of the second sequence of the chiasm, God's faithfulness to the covenant occupies a central position theologically in the Benedictus. Once again Luke makes the connection between the Christian gospel and its OT roots. Plummer, 39, notes sixteen OT parallels in the Benedictus.

> [67] His father Zechariah was filled with the Holy Spirit and prophesied:
>
> [68] "Praise be to the Lord, the God of Israel,
>   because he has come and has redeemed his people.
> [69] He has raised up a horn of salvation for us
>   in the house of his servant David
> [70] (as he said through his holy prophets of long ago),
> [71] salvation from our enemies
>   and from the hand of all who hate us—
> [72] to show mercy to our fathers
>   and to remember his holy covenant,
> [73]   the oath he swore to our father Abraham:

74to rescue us from the hand of our enemies,
        and to enable us to serve him without fear
75   in holiness and righteousness before him all our days.

76And you, my child, will be called a prophet of the Most High;
        for you will go on before the Lord to prepare the way for him,
77to give his people the knowledge of salvation
        through the forgiveness of their sins,
78because of the tender mercy of our God,
        by which the rising sun will come to us from heaven
79to shine on those living in darkness
        and in the shadow of death,
    to guide our feet into the path of peace."

80And the child grew and became strong in spirit; and he lived in the desert until he appeared publicly to Israel.

COMMENTARY

67 Zechariah the priest now prophesies. As the Holy Spirit had filled Elizabeth (v.41), he now fills Zechariah. Observe that Zechariah's previous doubt and his discipline through loss of speech did not mean the end of his spiritual ministry. So when a believer today has submitted to God's discipline, he or she may go on in Christ's service. The emphasis on Zechariah's act of prophesying is explained by the quotation of Joel in Acts 2, where it is noted that in the last days even "old men" will experience the Spirit of prophecy (Ac 2:17–18).

The description of the song as prophecy points to the various functions of prophecy in the OT. Prophecy is not only concerned with the prediction of the future; it also functions as exhortation for God's people. At its heart is the assumption that God is the one who reveals himself through his mighty acts (cf. Nicholas Wolterstorff, *Divine Discourse: Philosophical Reflections on the Claim That God Speaks* [Cambridge: Cambridge Univ. Press, 1995]).

It is not surprising, therefore, to find Zechariah's prophecy focusing on the mighty acts of God.

68 The NIV uses "praise" to translate *eulogētos* (GK *2329*) here. The word *eulogētos* can refer both to a human being on whom God has showered his goodness (i.e., "blessed," v.42) and to God, to whom we return thanks for that goodness (i.e., "praise"; cf. Robert J. Ledogar, *Acknowledgment: Praise-verbs in the Early Greek Anaphora* [Roma: Herder, 1967]). A form of the same word occurs in v.64 (*eulogeō*, "praising"). It is as though vv.68–79 provide the content of the praise expressed in the earlier verse (v.64). "Israel" is paralleled by "his people" in vv.68, 77, carrying along the promise of v.17 (see comments there).

The action centers in two verbs: "has come" and "has redeemed." The first is from the verb *episkeptomai* (GK *2170*). In secular Greek it means simply "to look at, reflect on," or "to visit" (often in a charitable way, such as a doctor's visiting the sick; cf. Mt 25:36, 43; Jas 1:27). The element of special concern is deepened to the spiritual level in the LXX's use of the word. A particular example is that of God's "visiting" people in grace or in judgment (Ex 4:31; Zec 10:3; cf. *TDNT* 2:599–605). The idea of God's graciously "visiting" or "coming" to his people in the sense of vv.68, 78 appears also in 7:16. In these three verses, as well as in Acts 15:14, where *episkeptomai* is translated "showed concern," the word "people" also occurs. Tragically, Jerusalem did not recognize the day of her "visitation" (Lk 19:44; NIV, "the time of God's coming").

The second verb, "redeemed," represents two Greek words: *epoiēsen lytrōsin* ("accomplished redemption"). The idea of redemption runs throughout Scripture, with the exodus being the great OT example of rescue from enemies and captivity. Luke 24:21 shows the expectation Jesus' followers had that he would do a similar work of freeing God's people. Luke, though committed to the universal application of the gospel, includes these words of redemption that apply especially to Israel (see esp. v.69). This not only reflects his emphasis on the Jewish roots of Christianity; it also underlines the sociopolitical aspects of redemption foremost in the minds of Zechariah's contemporaries.

69 "Horn" is a common OT metaphor for power because of the great strength of the horned animals of the Near East. The word "salvation" describes the kind of strength Zechariah had in mind. The power of salvation resides in the Savior. Again, the messianic theme occurs—this time in an allusion to Psalm 132:17 (131:17 [LXX]), where in fulfilling the Davidic covenant God "will make a horn grow for David." The verb "raised up" (*egeirō*, GK *1586*) is not used in the LXX of Psalm 132. Here it is appropriate for stressing God's sovereignty. Later in Luke's writing, this verb will assume great importance in relation to the resurrection of Christ (24:6, 34; Ac 3:7, 15; 4:10). A possible parallel to the phrase "horn of salvation," in the context of the expectation of the future Davidic dynasty, can be

found in Jewish liturgical material of the first century. The Semitic context is again evident (cf. F. Manns, "Une prière juive reprise en Luc 1:68–69," *Ephemerides Liturgicae* 106 [1992]: 162–66). The messianic motif is further emphasized by a reference to the "house of . . . David."

70 The mention of the "holy prophets of long ago," while placed in parentheses in the NIV for clarity, is not theologically parenthetical. Like a similar reference in Hebrews 1:1, it serves to confirm the OT origin of and support for the messianic role of Jesus.

71–73 Placing v.70 in parentheses clarifies the relationship of vv.71–75 to v.69. "Salvation" (v.71) is the link. It is the first of three aspects of God's redeeming work, the others being "mercy" and the remembrance of God's "covenant" (v.72). The salvation Zechariah is speaking of is at this stage clearly political. Mercy to the "fathers" seems to mean that God has not thwarted their hopes. This mercy may be related to v.17 and Malachi 4:6. The "oath" (v.73) to Abraham in view here is recorded in Genesis 22:16–18, where the Lord promised Abraham not only that his descendants' enemies would be subdued but also that universal blessing would result from his obedience. Therefore, the salvation in view involves both political deliverance and spiritual blessing (cf. the next verses).

As noted earlier, the words "covenant" and "oath" form the central point of the chiasm (inverse repetition of terms). This has the effect of emphasizing the importance of God's covenant and God's faithfulness to it. Not only does this serve an important theme in Luke, but it also gives encouragement to us to trust the promises of God. (The connection between "covenant" and "oath" is also a common feature in the OT, especially in the Abrahamic material [Ge 17:4; 22:16–17; cf. Bovon, 74]).

74–75 The fulfillment of God's promise does not mean passivity for Israel but a new opportunity for service—negatively, service "without fear" (v.74) and, positively, "in holiness and righteousness" (v.75; cf. Mal 3:3).

76 The second part of Zechariah's hymn begins with a direct word to his son. The role of John, like that of Paul and the Lord's servants throughout history, derives its significance and greatness from God's purpose and, even more, from the greatness of the Person served. Before addressing the theme of salvation, Zechariah speaks of the "Most High" and "the Lord" John represents.

The description of John here, when compared with Isaiah 40:3 and Malachi 3:1; 4:5, clearly links him with Elijah, dispelling any doubts about the recognition of this link in Luke. Such doubts have arisen largely from Luke's omission of the conversation (cf. Mt 17:10–13; Mk 9:11–13) about Elijah following the transfiguration. There Jesus says that Elijah has "already come," i.e., the predictions about Elijah were fulfilled in John the Baptist. Also Luke's parallel to Matthew 11:12 (Lk 16:16) has seemed to some to detach John from the age of Jesus and the church. Thus some have considered it unlikely that Luke thought of John as the Elijah figure whose coming was to usher in the last days. We must keep in mind that as a physician Luke was strongly aware of corporeality. More than the other gospel writers, he stressed the physical resurrection of Jesus ("they did not find the body of the Lord Jesus" [24:3]), the reality of Jesus' ascension, and the Spirit's descent in "bodily form" like a dove (3:22) at Jesus' baptism. It would, therefore, be understandable for Luke to hold that John had indeed come "in the spirit and power of Elijah" (1:17), yet for him to avoid saying anything that might imply the reincarnation of Elijah as John. If Elijah could still appear in recognizable form, as he did at the transfiguration, Luke may have hesitated to include in his gospel anything about Elijah's apparent identification with John. Luke 1:76, though consistent with the idea that

John came in the "spirit and power of Elijah," avoids the kind of terminology about which Luke may still have had some hesitation. For more insight, see Walter Wink, *John the Baptist in the Gospel Tradition* (London: Cambridge Univ. Press, 1968), 42–45.

77 The theme of "salvation" for God's "people," expressed in political terms in v.71, now finds its spiritual identity through "forgiveness." John will go on to preach "a baptism of repentance for the forgiveness of sins" (3:3).

78–79 The NIV's "rising sun" (v.78; see Notes) has a dynamic quality that suits the word "come" (or "visit"; cf. v.68). Verse 79 uses a beautiful quotation from Isaiah 9:2 to carry forward the imagery of light (the sun; see also Isa 60:1–3) and to offer hope of peace to those who were then outside the faithful remnant of Judaism (cf. Eph 2:12).

The theme of peace is a prominent one in the Lukan writings, and most of its occurrences appear in uniquely Lukan passages (Lk 1:79; 2:14, 29; 7:50; 14:32; 19:42; 24:36). This theme points back to the OT promises in which the end-times are characterized by an eternal period of peace. See Willard M. Swartley, "Politics and Peace (*Eirēnē*) in Luke's Gospel," in *Political Issues in Luke–Acts* (ed. Cassidy and Scharper), 18–37.

80 This brief description of John's boyhood reflects Luke's interest in human beings. Later he will comment more fully on Jesus' personal developments (2:40, 52). Since the discovery of the Dead Sea Scrolls near Qumran, there has been speculation about the possibility of contact between John and the Qumran community. If his elderly parents had been unable to care for him, or if they had died in his youth, it is conceivable that John might even have lived for a time at Qumran. Taking in young men was the only way the celibate community could reproduce itself. Nevertheless, such a connection lacks supporting evidence (cf. Otto Betz, "Was John the Baptist an Essene?" *BRev* 6 [December 1990]: 18–25).

NOTES

67 Both the unity and literary history of the Benedictus are disputed, but its theology arises from the OT. The themes of the two parts (vv.68–75 and vv.76–79) are intertwined, and the concepts in each part are appropriate to Jesus and John respectively. For a discussion of the issues, see Marshall, *Luke: Historian and Theologian*, 87; Nolland, 1:83–84.

68–79 This song is so thoroughly Jewish in its orientation and theology that it would be difficult to imagine that it originated in the Hellenistic church and was adapted back into this context. The distinction between "we" and "they" is ingrained throughout—e.g., "us" in vv.69, 74, which is parallel to "his people," over against the "enemies . . . all who hate us." Only at the end does a salvation seem to extend beyond Israel, and this promise is rooted in Isaiah 60.

68 The qualification "of Israel" in describing "God" does not limit the blessings of God to the physical Israel. It recalls the God who is faithful to his covenantal promises, and ultimately the election of Israel is for the blessing of the nations. The firm grounding of this new stage of salvation history in the history of Israel is again evident.

The noun λύτρωσις (*lytrōsis*, "redemption," GK *3391*) is found only twice in Luke: here (where the NIV renders the noun as a verb for smoother English) and in Anna's prophecy about the infant Jesus (2:38). The verbal form occurs in 24:21. Luke is the only gospel to use the longer form ἀπολύτρωσις (*apolytrōsis*, GK *667*), which is of major importance in the epistles. For a discussion of redemption in the NT, see Leon Morris, *The Apostolic Preaching of the Cross* (Grand Rapids: Eerdmans, 1955), 9–59; cf. also David Hill, *Greek Words and Hebrew Meanings* (SNTSMS 5; London: Cambridge Univ. Press, 1967). Significantly, despite Luke's stress on the concept of redemption, when λύτρον (*lytron*) occurs in Matthew 20:28 and Mark 10:45, Luke omits it in his parallel of these verses. This may be because the concept is already inherent in the narrative of the Last Supper, which in the Lukan order just precedes it. Luke 22:24–27 may not, however, be a true parallel.

69 The noun σωτηρία (*sōteria*, "salvation," GK *5401*) is also mentioned in vv.71, 77; 2:30; 3:6; σωτήρ (*sōter*, "Savior") appears in 1:47; 2:11; and there are numerous occurrences of σῴζω (*sōzō*, "save"; see also Marshall, *Luke: Historian and Theologian*, 92–102; Joel B. Green, "'The Message of Salvation' in Luke–Acts," *ExAud* 5 [1989]: 21–34).

71 The use of the accusative σωτηρίαν (*sōterian*, "salvation") here is debatable. It seems to function as the object of ἐλάλησεν (*elalēsen*, "said") in v.70. Or, it could stand in apposition to κέρας (*keras*, "horn"), which is already identified in v.69 with salvation.

78 The noun ἀνατολή (*anatolē*, GK *424*) is interestingly rendered "dayspring" in the KJV, "day" in the RSV, "sunrise" in the NASB, and "rising sun" in the NIV. These renderings represent attempts to translate a word with a basically simple meaning—the rising of the sun or stars—yet one that the LXX used in translating the distinctive Hebrew messianic term ṣemaḥ, "sprout," "branch," GK *7542*; Jer 23:5; Zec 3:8; 6:12). However ἀνατολή, *anatolē*, is translated, it is important to keep this messianic aspect in mind (cf. *TDNT* 1:352–53).

80 The phrase ἐκραταιοῦτο πνεύματι (*ekrataiouto pneumati*, GK *3194, 4460*) probably means "became strong in spirit" in the sense of development of moral character, though somewhat similar wording in Ephesians 3:16 describes a strengthening by God's Spirit.

The plural form ἐν ταῖς ἐρήμοις (*en tais erēmois*, GK *2245*, "in the desert") is idiomatic. John ministered near the Jordan River, but it is not certain that he grew up in the same area. While the desert had various popular connotations (e.g., the home of demons), here it simply implies relative isolation. The genitive singular form ἀναδείξεως (*anadeixeōs*, "appeared publicly," GK *345*) is literally "until the day of his appearance" or "commissioning" (so BDAG, 62).

3. The Birth of Jesus (2:1–7)

OVERVIEW

In comparison with the complex narrative in ch. 1, the actual birth narrative of Jesus is brief. In it Luke stresses three things: (1) the political situation (to explain why Jesus' birth took place in Bethlehem); (2) the fact that Bethlehem was the town of David (to stress Jesus' messianic claim); and (3) the humble circumstances of Jesus' birth.

The mention of Caesar Augustus may not only be for historical background but also to contrast the human with the divine decrees. A mere Galilean peasant travels to Bethlehem ostensibly at the decree of the Roman emperor. Actually, it is in fulfillment of the divine King's plan, which is reflected in Luke's frequent reference to what "must" (*dei*, GK *1256*) be done.

Related to this is the understanding that all these events took place within the context of the imperial rule. This may serve as a contrast to Judas the Galilean and his movement that refused to operate within the prescribed power structure (Josephus, *Ant.* 18.4–5; cf. J. Massyngberde Ford, "Reconciliation and Forgiveness in Luke's Gospel," in *Political Issues in Luke–Acts* [ed. Cassidy and Scharper], 87). It may also be understood as an implicit challenge to the imperial power, as the imperial system is now being used to bring fulfillment to the OT promises that point to the birth of the Lord of all.

¹In those days Caesar Augustus issued a decree that a census should be taken of the entire Roman world. ²(This was the first census that took place while Quirinius was governor of Syria.) ³And everyone went to his own town to register.

⁴So Joseph also went up from the town of Nazareth in Galilee to Judea, to Bethlehem the town of David, because he belonged to the house and line of David. ⁵He went there to register with Mary, who was pledged to be married to him and was expecting a child. ⁶While they were there, the time came for the baby to be born, ⁷and she gave birth to her firstborn, a son. She wrapped him in cloths and placed him in a manger, because there was no room for them in the inn.

COMMENTARY

1 Augustus became the leader of the Roman world in 27 BC. That Luke uses the emperor's Latin title, Augustus, instead of the expected Greek *Sebastos* (GK *4935*)—a title known to Luke (cf. Ac 25:21, 25)—demands an explanation. Moreover, the transliterated form of Augustus does not appear in Greek literature prior to Luke. According to Royce L. B. Morris ("Why ΑΥΓΟΥΣΤΟΣ? A Note to Luke 2.1," *NTS* 38 [1992]: 142–44), Luke uses Augustus to avoid the sacred connotations the term *Sebastos* may evoke in the minds of his Greek audience.

In the ancient world, a "census" was usually taken by the ruling power for two reasons: (1) to provide an accurate account of the size of its military strength and (2) to update the record for taxation purposes. The oppressive nature of the imperial rule is again evoked by this mention of the census.

2 Luke clearly intends to secure the historical and chronological moorings of Jesus' birth. Ironically, it is precisely this that has led some to question Luke's accuracy.

The first census (i.e., enrollment prior to taxation) known to have occurred under the governorship of Quirinius took place later (i.e., AD 6) than is usually reckoned as the time of Jesus' birth. Reference to this census is found in both Acts 5:37 and Josephus (*Ant.* 18.26). Many have supposed that Luke confused this census of AD 6 with one he thinks was taken earlier but which lacks historical support. The most satisfactory solutions that have been proposed follow.

(1) Quirinius had a government assignment in Syria at this time and conducted a census in his official capacity. Details of this census may have been common knowledge in Luke's time but are now lost to us (cf. E. M. Blaiklock, "Quirinius," *ZPEB* 5:56). An incomplete manuscript describes the career of an officer whose name is not preserved but whose actions sound as though he might have been Quirinius. He became imperial "legate of Syria" for the "second time." While this is ambiguous, it may be a clue that Quirinius served both at the time of Jesus' birth and a few years later (cf. Mark Smith, "Of Jesus and Quirinius," *CBQ* 62 [2000]: 278–93).

(2) The word *prōtē* can be construed to mean not "first," as usually translated, but "former" or "prior." The meaning of v.2 is then, "This census was before that made when Quirinius was governor" (Nigel Turner, *Grammatical Insights into the New Testament* [Edinburgh: T&T Clark, 1965], 23–24; cf. Marshall, 104). As noted by Brook W. R. Pearson ("The Lukan Censuses, Revisited," *CBQ* 61 [1999]: 282), since "each and every aspect of the census as it is described by Luke has close parallels in other parts of the Roman Empire, we would do better to take a plausible grammatical solution which accords with the evidence rather than to ignore the evidence on the basis of shaky grammar."

(3) The existence of two "Quiriniuses" is also a possibility that must be noted. A recently discovered coin has the name "Quirinius" on it, and this coin places this Quirinius as proconsul of Syria and Cilicia during the time of Jesus' birth. Other evidence points to the popularity of this name. Thus the existence of yet another Quirinius becomes a real possibility (cf. John McRay, *Archaeology and the New Testament* [Grand Rapids: Baker, 1991], 154).

Furthermore, it is scarcely conceivable that Luke, careful researcher that he was (1:1–4), would have stressed the census—a piece of information relatively easy to verify—unless he had reasonable historical grounds for doing so. (See further F. F. Bruce, *Jesus and Christian Origins Outside the New Testament* [Grand Rapids: Eerdmans, 1974], 192–94; Marshall, *Luke: Historian and Theologian*, 98–104.)

3 It was customary to return to one's original home for such a census. The census as described in the British Museum papyrus 904, dated to AD 104, explicitly notes such a requirement. This decree allowed Mary and Joseph to return to Bethlehem, the city of David.

The phrase "everyone went to his own town" may recall a similar phrase that appears in the discussion of the Year of Jubilee in Leviticus: "each one of you is to return to his family property" (25:10). In the light of Luke's interest in the Year of Jubilee (cf. Lk 4:19), this phrase may contribute to the theme of fulfillment in Luke's eschatology (cf. G. D. Kilpatrick, "Luke 2:4–5 and Leviticus 25:10," *ZNW* 80 [1989]: 264–65).

4–5 Luke does not say how long in advance of Jesus' birth Joseph left for Bethlehem or why he took Mary with him. It is possible that he used the emperor's order as a means of removing Mary from possible gossip and emotional stress in her own village. He had already accepted her as his wife (Mt 1:24), but apparently they continued in betrothal (v.5, "pledged to be married") till after the birth. The text neither affirms nor denies the popular image of the couple's arriving in Bethlehem just as the baby was about to be born. Luke simply states that the birth took place "while they were there" (v.6). Since she had stayed three months with Elizabeth, Mary was at least three months pregnant. It is possible that they went down during her last trimester of pregnancy, when the social relationships in Nazareth would have grown more difficult. They may have stayed in a crowded room in the home of some poor relative till the birth of the baby necessitated their vacating it for privacy and more space. Any such reconstruction is, however, merely speculative.

The emphasis on the Davidic line (v.4) recalls the promises of the throne of David in 1:32, 35, and the focus on the house of David in 1:69 (cf. 1:27).

Moreover, the allusion to Micah 5:2 in reference to the expected exalted role of Bethlehem can also be heard. Green, 127, further notes the prophetic element in these verses as the "provisional nature" of Roman rule is revealed.

7 The word *katalyma* (GK *2906*), usually translated "inn," may mean a room (e.g., the "guest room" used for the Last Supper [22:11], referred to as an "upper room" in 22:12), a billet for soldiers, or any place for lodging, which would include inns (cf. L. Paul Trudinger, "'No Room in the Inn': A Note on Luke 2:7," *ExpTim* 102 [1991]: 172–73). It is not, however, the usual Greek word for an inn—*pandocheion* (GK *4106*), to which the Good Samaritan took the robbery victim (10:34). As the etymology of the word—*pan* ("all," GK *4246*) and *dechomai* ("receive," GK *1312*)—suggests, inns accepted all kinds of people, often the worst. Stories were told of discomfort and even of robberies at inns.

Luke could have painted a sordid picture, had he so desired. Instead he uses the general word for a lodging place and states the simple fact that when Mary's time came, the only available place for the little family was one usually occupied by animals. It may have been a cave, as tradition suggests, or some part of a house or inn. Even today in many places around the world farm animals and their fodder are often kept in the same building as the family quarters. The eating trough, or "manger," was ideal for use as a crib. Luke does not seem to be portraying a dismal situation with an unfeeling innkeeper as villain. Rather, he is establishing a contrast between the proper rights of the Messiah in his own "town of David" (v.4) and the very ordinary and humble circumstances of his birth. Whatever the reason, even in his birth Jesus was excluded from the normal shelter others enjoyed (cf. 9:58). This is consistent with Luke's realistic presentation of Jesus' humanity and servanthood.

NOTES

1–3 For a negative judgment on the historicity of Luke's account of the census, see R. Brown, *Birth of the Messiah*, 547–55. A call to take Luke's historical record seriously can be found in J. Lawrence, "Publius Sulpicius Quirinius and the Syrian Census," *ResQ* 34 (1992): 193–205.

7 The significance of Isaiah 66 in early Christian writings has long been recognized. This chapter is also important for Luke. In Luke 2:34, one finds a parallel to Isaiah 66:19. Jesus' response to the council in Luke 22:68 also alludes to Isaiah 66:4. Building on these parallels, J. D. M. Derrett ("Luke 2.7 Again," *NTS* 45 [1999]: 263) further suggests that Luke 2:7 alludes to Isaiah 66:1, where the reference to the place where the Lord can rest is found. This would mean that Jesus cannot be contained by that which human hands can build, and he alone is the proper object of worship. The existence of this allusion is questionable, however.

4. The Announcement to the Shepherds (2:8–20)

OVERVIEW

The pastoral scene described in this section actually conveys more theological significance than is sometimes realized. Both the words of the angel and the symbolism of what happened have theological implications.

⁸And there were shepherds living out in the fields nearby, keeping watch over their flocks at night. ⁹An angel of the Lord appeared to them, and the glory of the Lord shone around them, and they were terrified. ¹⁰But the angel said to them, "Do not be afraid. I bring you good news of great joy that will be for all the people. ¹¹Today in the town of David a Savior has been born to you; he is Christ the Lord. ¹²This will be a sign to you: You will find a baby wrapped in cloths and lying in a manger."

¹³Suddenly a great company of the heavenly host appeared with the angel, praising God and saying,

¹⁴"Glory to God in the highest,
  and on earth peace to men on whom his favor rests."

¹⁵When the angels had left them and gone into heaven, the shepherds said to one another, "Let's go to Bethlehem and see this thing that has happened, which the Lord has told us about."

¹⁶So they hurried off and found Mary and Joseph, and the baby, who was lying in the manger. ¹⁷When they had seen him, they spread the word concerning what had been told them about this child, ¹⁸and all who heard it were amazed at what the shepherds said to them. ¹⁹But Mary treasured up all these things and pondered them in her heart. ²⁰The

shepherds returned, glorifying and praising God for all the things they had heard and seen, which were just as they had been told.

COMMENTARY

8 There may be several reasons for the special role of the shepherds in the events of this unique night. Among the occupations, shepherding had a lowly place (cf. Str-B, 2:114). Shepherds were considered untrustworthy and their work made them ceremonially unclean. Thus the most obvious implication is that the gospel first came to the social outcasts of Jesus' day. This would accord with a recurring emphasis in Luke. Moreover, it may be significant that in the Lord's instructions to Nathan about giving David the covenant, the Lord reminds David, who was to become Messiah's ancestor, that he was called from the shepherd's life (2Sa 7:8). Finally, in both Testaments shepherds symbolize those who care for God's people, including the Lord himself (Ps 23:1; Isa 40:11; Jer 23:1–4; Heb 13:20; 1Pe 2:25; 5:2). The shepherds of Luke 2 may, therefore, symbolize all the ordinary people who have joyfully received the gospel and have become in various ways pastors to others.

That the shepherds were out in the fields at night does not preclude a December date, as the winter in Judea was mild. But, of course, the text says nothing about the time of year. The traditional date for the nativity was set, long after the event, to coincide with a pagan festival, thus demonstrating that the "Sol Invictus," the "Unconquerable Sun," had indeed been conquered. December 25 was widely celebrated as the date of Jesus' birth by the end of the fourth century. January 6 was also an important date in the early church, held by many as the occasion of the arrival of the Magi and known as Epiphany. (See Oscar Cullmann, "The Origin of Christmas," in *The Early Church* [Philadelphia: Westminster, 1956], 21–36; and Susan K. Roll, *Toward the Origins of Christmas* [Kampen: Kok Pharos, 1995].) Morris, 84, suggests that if the birth did take place in winter, the shepherds may have been raising sheep for sacrifice at Passover a few months later.

9 First a single angel (cf. 1:11, 26) appears; the multitude of angels does not appear till v.13. The shepherds' terror recalls that of Zechariah (1:12). It was not just the angel that terrified them but the visible manifestation of the glory of God—something neither Zechariah nor Mary had seen. This glory is a signal that God will again act on behalf of his people (9:31; cf. John J. Kilgallen, "Jesus, Savior, the Glory of Your People Israel," *Bib* 75 [1994]: 305–28). As in 1:13 and 1:30, the angel speaks reassuringly.

11 The angel's announcement includes several of the most frequently used words in Luke's gospel (see Notes)—a fact that shows the tremendous importance of the angelic pronouncement. It is a bold proclamation of the gospel at the very hour of Jesus' birth.

The constellation of christological titles here is important. Implicitly, once again, Jesus is David's son. The term "Savior" is especially important in this context when Augustus (v.1) also claimed to be the savior of the world. Likewise, "Christ the Lord" affirms the unique lordship of Christ. The arrival of a new ruler is clearly presented. Thus in this whole section Luke shares his perception of major themes that support the declaration: the time has come ("today") for the fulfillment of the prophetic expectation of Messiah's coming.

12 The "cloths" (KJV, "swaddling clothes," from the verb *sparganoō*, "to swathe," GK *5058*) would constitute a "sign." Babies were snugly wrapped in long strips of cloth, giving them warmth, protection of extremities, and a sense of security in their newborn existence. The combination of a newborn baby's wrappings and the use of the manger for a crib would be a distinctive "sign." Perhaps they also imply that in spite of seeming rejection, symbolized by the manger, the baby was the special object of his mother's care. In Ezekiel 16:1–5, Jerusalem is symbolically described as a heathen child who was neglected from birth until God rescued and cared for her. She had not been given the usual postnatal care and so was not wrapped with strips of cloth (Eze 16:4). But Jesus was not so neglected. On the other hand, the "sign" might be only the strange circumstance of the newborn child's being in the manger at all. If one moves further in the Lukan narrative, this "sign" may also point to the burial scene of Jesus, in which linen becomes yet another "sign" (cf. J. Winandy, "Le signe de la mangeoire et des langes," *NTS* 43 [1997]: 140–46).

13 "Suddenly" (*exaiphnēs*, GK *1978*), along with cognate words, often describes the unexpected nature of God's acts, especially the eschatological events. Malachi had predicted the sudden coming of the Lord to his temple (Mal 3:1). Now the angels suddenly announce his arrival at Bethlehem. The Spirit's coming at Pentecost was sudden (Ac 2:2), as was the appearance of the Lord to Saul on the road to Damascus (Ac 9:3). Mark 13:36 and 1 Thessalonians 5:3 describe the suddenness of future events.

The "heavenly host," which often meant heavenly bodies in the OT, refers here to an army or band of angels (cf. 1Ki 22:19).

14 The doxology "glory to God in the highest" is the climax of the story. Its two parts relate to heaven and earth respectively. In Luke's account of the triumphal entry, the crowds say, "Peace in heaven and glory in the highest!" (19:38). In Eph-esians 3:21, Paul ascribes glory to God, not now in the heavens but "in the church and in Christ Jesus." Verse 14b is best translated as in the NIV: "and on earth peace to men on whom his favor rests." For reasons discussed in the Notes, "good will toward men" (KJV) is inaccurate. Luke emphasizes the work of Christ on earth. (See also Jesus' own declaration that "the Son of Man has authority on earth to forgive sins" [Lk 5:24].)

The "peace" here is that which the Messiah brings (cf. 1:79). Those whom Jesus healed or forgave on the basis of their faith could "go in peace" (7:50; 8:48). This peace surpasses the Pax Romana that Augustus had promised (cf. Allen Brent, "Luke–Acts and the Imperial Cult in Asia Minor," *JTS* 48 [1997]: 411–38).

Those on whom God's "favor" (*eudokia*, GK *2306*) rests are the "little children" to whom God graciously reveals truth according to his "good pleasure" (10:21; the only other use of *eudokia* in the Gospels, except for the parallel in Mt 11:26).

15–16 Luke does not say that the angels disappeared but that they went "into heaven" (v.15), an expression typical of his attention to spatial relationships (cf. comments on the ascension at 24:51, where the same words appear in what is probably the original text; cf. Ac 1:11). The realization of God's promise ("this thing [*rhēma*] . . . , which the Lord has told us about") is expressed also in v.29: "as you have promised" (*kata to rhēma sou*, lit., "according to your word"). Luke combines the phenomena of ancient (v.15) and recent (v.29) prophetic words, thus emphasizing the connection between the old and new ages, the Jewish orientation of the gospel and the reality of the heavenly in the earthly. Both the idiomatic particle *de*, which conveys a note of urgency (BDAG, 222) expressed in the NIV's "let's go" (v.15), and the words "hurried off" (*elthan speusantes*, v.16) heighten the sense of excitement and determination that propelled the shepherds to the baby's side.

17–18 Then they "spread the word" (v.17) and became the first evangelists of the Christian era. Luke's observation (v.18) that those who heard them "were amazed" (*ethaumasan*, GK *2513*) is the first of his many comments on the enthusiastic response to the messianic proclamation. The next occurrence is when Mary and Joseph "marvel" at what Simeon says about their child (v.33). In v.47 everyone is "amazed" (*existanto*, GK *2014*) at Jesus' answers in the temple discussion. The initial reaction of the audience to Jesus' opening declaration in the synagogue of Nazareth that the prophecy of Isaiah 61 was at that moment fulfilled was amazement (4:22; cf. 8:25; 9:43; 11:14, 38; 20:26; 24:12, 41). There are also passages that use other words to describe a similar response (e.g., 4:15, 36; 5:26).

19 In contrast to the overreaction of the people, Mary (*hē de Mariam*, "Mary on the other hand") meditates on the meaning of it all (cf. v.51; cf. also Ge 37:11). Unlike her response in ch. 1 that includes a lengthy prophetic speech (vv.46–55), the events that are unfolding are moving beyond Mary's ability to comprehend (cf. Mary F. Foskett, *A Virgin Conceived* [Bloomington: Indiana Univ. Press, 2002], 135).

20 Just as the seventy-two disciples "returned [*hypestrepsan*, GK *5715*] with joy" after their preaching mission (10:17), so the shepherds "returned [*hypestrepsan*], glorifying and praising God." It is clear that in Luke this spirit of doxology is the proper response to the mighty works of God (cf. 5:25–26; 7:16; 13:13; 17:15; 18:43; 23:47; similar occurrences in Acts).

NOTES

9–11 The significant terms characteristic of Luke that occur in these verses include εὐαγγελίζομαι (*euangelizomai*, "bring good news," GK *2294* [always in the verbal form in Luke]); χαρά (*chara*, "joy," GK *5915*), which occurs more often in Luke than in Matthew and Mark combined; λαός (*laos*, "people," GK *3295*), used 35 times in Luke against 14 in Matthew and none in Mark (with Luke using it some 47 additional times in Acts); σήμερον (*sēmeron*, "today," GK *4958*), which occurs more in Luke than in Matthew and Mark combined (see comments at 4:21 for its significance in Luke); σωτήρ (*sōtēr*, "Savior," GK *5400*), used only by Luke among the Synoptics; and κύριος (*kyrios*, "Lord," GK *3261*), which occurs 95 times in Luke out of 166 in the Synoptics. The word δόξα (*doxa*, "glory," GK *1518*), which occurs in v.9 and reappears in v.14, is also distinctively Lukan. Along with the verb δοξάζω (*doxazō*, "glorify," GK *1519*), Luke uses it more than the two other Synoptics combined.

14 In the KJV, "good will" is the subject of the clause because the KJV followed the Textus Receptus, which has the nominative εὐδοκία (*eudokia*, GK *2306*). However, the oldest MSS have an added sigma (ς), indicator of the genitive case (εὐδοκίας, *eudokias*). The inadvertent omission of the small elevated half circle that was customarily used to indicate the genitive sigma is more likely than the *addition* of a sigma. On the principle that the harder reading is more likely the original one, the genitive should be assumed, since a nominative would read more smoothly. And since similar phrases describing people "of [God's] good pleasure" are now known from hymns in the Dead Sea Scrolls (1QH 8.6; 12.32–33; 17.10), there is no difficulty in accepting this reading. More recently an Aramaic text from Cave 4 with a syntactical structure even closer to Luke's has confirmed the matter (Fitzmyer, *Semitic Background*, 101–4). It is also more in accordance with the doctrine of grace than is the idea that those of "good will" are rewarded with peace (cf. Metzger, 111).

C. Jesus' Early Years (2:21–52)

1. Presentation of Jesus in the Temple (2:21–40)

OVERVIEW

It is important to understand the sequence and background of these events. According to Jewish law, a woman became ceremonially unclean at the time of giving birth to a child. On the eighth day, male infants were circumcised (cf. 1:59; Ge 17:12), after which the mother was unclean an additional thirty-three days—sixty-six if the child was female (Lev 12:1–5). At the conclusion of this period, the mother offered a sacrifice—either a lamb or, if she was poor, two doves or two young pigeons (Lev 12:6–8). In addition, the first son was to be presented to the Lord and then, so to speak, bought back with an offering (Nu 18:15; cf. 1Sa 1:24–28, where Hannah actually gives up Samuel to the Lord).

Luke, conflating the performance of these OT obligations into this single narrative, shows how Jesus was reared in conformity with them. His parents obeyed the Lord in naming him (1:31). The offering of birds instead of a lamb shows that he was born into a poor family. Perhaps this helped him identify with the poor of the land (cf. 6:20; see Robert F. O'Toole, "Luke's Position on Politics and Society in Luke–Acts," in *Political Issues in Luke–Acts* [ed. Cassidy and Scharper], 1–17).

In this passage, one also finds the Lukan interest in the city of Jerusalem. Salvation begins in Jerusalem, as the prophets have promised. But one will also find Jerusalem rejecting the Messiah. (For the ambivalent portrayal of Jerusalem in the Lukan corpus, see Mikeal C. Parsons, "The Place of Jerusalem on the Lukan Landscape: An Exercise in Symbolic Cartography," in *Literary Studies in Luke–Acts* [ed. Thompson and Phillips], 155–71.)

²¹On the eighth day, when it was time to circumcise him, he was named Jesus, the name the angel had given him before he had been conceived.

²²When the time of their purification according to the Law of Moses had been completed, Joseph and Mary took him to Jerusalem to present him to the Lord ²³(as it is written in the Law of the Lord, "Every firstborn male is to be consecrated to the Lord"), ²⁴and to offer a sacrifice in keeping with what is said in the Law of the Lord: "a pair of doves or two young pigeons."

²⁵Now there was a man in Jerusalem called Simeon, who was righteous and devout. He was waiting for the consolation of Israel, and the Holy Spirit was upon him. ²⁶It had been revealed to him by the Holy Spirit that he would not die before he had seen the Lord's Christ. ²⁷Moved by the Spirit, he went into the temple courts. When the parents brought in the child Jesus to do for him what the custom of the Law required, ²⁸Simeon took him in his arms and praised God, saying:

²⁹"Sovereign Lord, as you have promised,
    you now dismiss your servant in peace.

³⁰For my eyes have seen your salvation,
³¹   which you have prepared in the sight of all people,
³²a light for revelation to the Gentiles
          and for glory to your people Israel."

³³The child's father and mother marveled at what was said about him. ³⁴Then Simeon blessed them and said to Mary, his mother: "This child is destined to cause the falling and rising of many in Israel, and to be a sign that will be spoken against, ³⁵so that the thoughts of many hearts will be revealed. And a sword will pierce your own soul too."

³⁶There was also a prophetess, Anna, the daughter of Phanuel, of the tribe of Asher. She was very old; she had lived with her husband seven years after her marriage, ³⁷and then was a widow until she was eighty-four. She never left the temple but worshiped night and day, fasting and praying. ³⁸Coming up to them at that very moment, she gave thanks to God and spoke about the child to all who were looking forward to the redemption of Jerusalem.

³⁹When Joseph and Mary had done everything required by the Law of the Lord, they returned to Galilee to their own town of Nazareth. ⁴⁰And the child grew and became strong; he was filled with wisdom, and the grace of God was upon him.

COMMENTARY

25 In vv.25–38 Luke presents two pious figures who, under divine inspiration, testify to the significance of Jesus. Once again, Luke assures us of the credentials of Jesus as Messiah, taking care to show that each witness is an authentic representative of Judaism.

"Now" represents the attention-getting word *idou* ("behold," GK *2627*). Luke neither associates Simeon with a leading sect or party nor calls him a priest. The important thing is that he is "righteous and devout" (cf. Zechariah and Elizabeth, 1:6). He could be described as one of the believing remnant of Judaism looking forward to the messianic age in its spiritual aspect. It is appropriate that the Spirit who is the Consoler (see Notes) was upon one who awaited the consolation.

26 The same Spirit had revealed to Simeon that the Messiah ("the Lord's Christ") would come before Simeon died. This may but need not necessarily imply that he was an old man. The connection between the coming of the Messiah and the arrival of the time of consolation is made (cf. v.25).

27–28 Mary and Joseph are referred to as Jesus' "parents" (v.27) and as "the child's father and mother" (v.33). Jesus would have been considered Joseph's own son; so Luke's terminology is not inconsistent. In the genealogy, however, the particulars of the relationship had to be made more explicit (3:23). Here, as in v.38, Luke notes the providential timing, as the Spirit brings Simeon to the temple courts to be ready for the family's arrival. In this touching scene, Luke again shows the presence of Jesus, now in Simeon's arms (v.28), as an occasion of offering praise (*eulogeō*, GK *2328*) to God; actually, the word is "blessed"—the same as in v.34.

29 Simeon's psalm begins with the word *nun* ("now"), emphasizing the fact that the Messiah has indeed come (hence the Latin title Nunc Dimittis ["Now Dismiss"]). "Dismiss" (*apolyō*, GK *668*) here means "allow to die" (BDAG, 117–18; cf. Nu 20:29 [LXX]). The NIV loses the emphasis of the Greek word order because it reverses the phrases. Nevertheless, it does retain the words "in peace" in their place of final emphasis (cf. 1:79; 2:14). On "as you have promised," see comments at v.15. Note the contrast between "Sovereign Lord" and "servant." God's servant is now ready for his final order—to depart in death (cf. Ge 15:15; Nu 20:29)—because he has indeed seen the "Lord's Christ" (v.26).

30–32 Simeon does not say, however, that he has seen the Messiah but rather that his eyes have seen God's salvation. To see Jesus is to see salvation embodied in him—a theme prominent in Luke (cf. 1:69, 71, 77; 19:9, and comments). Luke's concern for the universal application of the gospel finds support in the words "in the sight of all people" (v.31). Verse 31 echoes Isaiah 52:10 and Psalm 98:3.

The parallel structure in v.32 may involve a detailed contrast as well as a larger one. That is, not only are Gentiles and Jews put in contrast, but also the same light (Isa 49:6) that brings "revelation" to pagans (cf. 1:78–79) brings "glory" to Israel (cf. 1:77). Note also "all people" (v.31) and "your people" (v.32; cf. comments on 1:77).

33–35 In spite of what they already know, Joseph and Mary are amazed at Simeon's song (v.33; cf. comments at v.17). Moreover, in it a somber note is sounded. In vivid language Simeon predicts that because of the child "many in Israel" (v.34) will be brought to moral decision, some to a point of collapse (*ptōsis*, GK *4774*; NIV, "falling") and others to what can well be called a resurrection (*anastasis*, GK *414*; NIV, "rising"). Many consider this verse as referring to the divided response of Israel—one that is repeatedly noted in Acts (Nolland, 1:121). Others believe there is but one group that falls and then rises (Marshall, 122; cf. Michael Wolter, "Israel's

Future and the Delay of the Parousia, according to Luke," in *Jesus and the Heritage of Israel* [ed. Moessner], 311).

But there will be a cost to Jesus. As the one who himself is the ultimate "sign," the visible affirmation of God's declared intentions, he will be vulnerable to the hostility of unbelievers. A negative attitude toward him, however, serves to brand the unbeliever as one who has rejected not only him but also the whole of God's revelation (v.35; cf. Jn 5:45–47). This clash will inevitably wound Jesus' mother.

36 Luke's attention to the renewal of prophecy at the coming of the messianic age continues with the introduction of Anna as a "prophetess." Zechariah had been "filled with the Holy Spirit and prophesied" (1:67). Simeon, though not called a prophet, was filled with the Spirit and also prophesied. Prophetesses functioned in both OT and NT times (Ex 15:20; Jdg 4:4; 2Ki 22:14; Ne 6:14; Isa 8:3; Ac 2:17; 21:9; 1Co 11:5). Apparently Anna could trace her genealogy; though the tribe of Asher was not outstanding (Ge 30:12–13; 35:26), Luke considered it important to show her true Jewishness. The mention of the name of the tribe may also reflect Luke's attempt to portray all Israel as anticipating the arrival of the salvation of God (cf. Richard Bauckham, "Anna of the Tribe of Asher [Luke 2:36–38]," *RB* 104 [1997]: 161–91).

37–38 Anna was a familiar figure at the temple. Possibly she lived in one of the rooms surrounding the temple precinct; or she may have, like the disciples in 24:53, centered her life there. She was the ideal widow described in 1 Timothy 5:5. Once more, Luke points out the providential timing (v.38; cf. v.27). He may be underlining the desire for the messianic deliverance of Jerusalem (cf. Isa 52:9) by describing Anna's thanksgiving with a rare verb (*anthomologeomai*, GK *469*), which occurs in a psalm lamenting the defilement of the Jerusalem temple (Ps 79:1–3 [78:1–3 LXX]). Later Luke will mention another pious Jew who had been expecting the messianic kingdom—Joseph of Arimathea (23:51).

39–40 As he continues the narrative, Luke takes another opportunity to mention the fidelity of Jesus' parents to the Jewish law (v.39). He omits mention of the flight to Egypt. It is important to Matthew, as it provides another example of fulfilled prophecy (Mt 2:13–15); but this is not so significant at this point in Luke. What is significant is that Jesus' parents were faithful to the Jewish law and that the child grew normally, as the object of God's grace (v.40; cf. v.52).

NOTES

25 The "consolation [παράκλησις, *paraklēsis*, GK *4155*] of Israel" refers to the time when, according to Isaiah 40:12, God would end Israel's time of alienation and suffering through the advent of the Messiah (cf. Isa 49:13; 57:18; 61:2). Notice also the theme of encouragement in Acts 4:36; 9:31; 13:15; 15:31. The time of the "consolation" would also be the age of the promised Holy Spirit, who himself is the one who consoles and encourages—παράκλητος (*paraklētos*, "Counselor," GK *4156*; cf. Jn 14:16; 15:26; 16:7).

30 The word for salvation, σωτήριον (*sōtērion*, GK *5402*), is in neuter form rather than the common feminine form. The use of the neuter form is most likely influenced by Isaiah 40:5 [LXX], as in the quotation in Luke 3:6.

33 Understandably, the designation ὁ πατὴρ αὐτοῦ καὶ ἡ μήτηρ (*ho patēr autou kai hē mētēr*, "his father and mother") for Joseph and Mary raises questions in the minds of believers in the virgin birth. Some early scribes doubtless felt the need for making it clear that Joseph was not Jesus' biological father. As a result, there are far too many readings and sources to cite here (see UBS[4] apparatus at 2:33; Metzger, 111–12). The NIV's rendering has strong MS support and is the natural way the family would be described.

37 "Until she was eighty-four" is the most natural way to understand ἕως ἐτῶν ὀγδοήκοντα τεσσάρων (*heōs etōn ogdoēkonta tessarōn*). E. J. Goodspeed's conclusion (*Problems of New Testament Translation* [Chicago: Univ. of Chicago Press, 1945], 79–81) is that if Luke meant "for eighty-four years" (which would make her 105 years old), he would have omitted ἕως, *heōs* ("until"), and used the accusative instead of the genitive, or used ἕως, *heōs*, with an ordinal rather than a cardinal number in the genitive. If Anna were 105 years old, she would have been the same age as Judith in the Apocrypha (Jdt 16:23; cf. J. K. Elliott, "Anna's Age [Luke 2:36–37]," *NovT* 30 [1988]: 100–102).

2. The Boy Jesus at the Temple (2:41–52)

OVERVIEW

This section provides the only account we have of Jesus' boyhood apart from apocryphal legends. The focal point is not simply his precocious wisdom, noteworthy as it was. Here Luke leads us to the real climax—Jesus' reference to God as "my Father" (v.49). This is the first instance of Jesus' "filial consciousness," his awareness that in a unique way he was the Son of God. His wisdom can in turn be understood in the light of this special relationship with his Father.

⁴¹Every year his parents went to Jerusalem for the Feast of the Passover. ⁴²When he was twelve years old, they went up to the Feast, according to the custom. ⁴³After the Feast was over, while his parents were returning home, the boy Jesus stayed behind in Jerusalem, but they were unaware of it. ⁴⁴Thinking he was in their company, they traveled on for a day. Then they began looking for him among their relatives and friends. ⁴⁵When they did not find him, they went back to Jerusalem to look for him. ⁴⁶After three days they found him in the temple courts, sitting among the teachers, listening to them and asking them questions. ⁴⁷Everyone who heard him was amazed at his understanding and his answers. ⁴⁸When his parents saw him, they were astonished. His mother said to him, "Son, why have you treated us like this? Your father and I have been anxiously searching for you."

⁴⁹"Why were you searching for me?" he asked. "Didn't you know I had to be in my Father's house?" ⁵⁰But they did not understand what he was saying to them.

⁵¹Then he went down to Nazareth with them and was obedient to them. But his mother treasured all these things in her heart. ⁵²And Jesus grew in wisdom and stature, and in favor with God and men.

COMMENTARY

41–42 Luke takes yet another opportunity to emphasize the fidelity of Jesus' family to Judaism. Adults were supposed to attend the three major feasts in Jerusalem annually—Passover, Pentecost, and Tabernacles. For many this was impossible, but an effort was made to go at least to Passover. In puberty a boy became a "son of the covenant," a custom continued in the present bar-mitzvah ceremony. It was considered helpful for a boy to attend the Jerusalem festivals for a year or two before becoming a son of the covenant so that he would realize what his new relationship involved.

43–45 Luke calls Jesus a "boy" (*pais*, GK *4090* [a term also used for servanthood], v.43) in contrast to "child" (*paidion*, GK *4086*, v.40). The exact theological significance of this choice of word should not be pressed, however.

At this intermediate age, Jesus might have been either with the women and children or with the men and older boys, if the families were grouped this way in the caravan. Each parent might have sup-

posed he was with the other (v.43). We need not assume that his parents neglected him. It was after a day of travel that they missed Jesus (v.44); another day would have been required for the trip back (v.45), and on the next day ("after three days," v.46) the successful search was made.

46–47 The questions Jesus put to the teachers were probably not merely boyish inquiries but the kind of probing questions used in ancient academies and in similar discussions. He also gave answers (v.47). Doeve, 105, suggests that Jesus engaged in a midrashic discussion of biblical texts: "Their amazement must relate to his deducing things from Scripture which they had never found before." The amazement expressed by the Jewish authorities demonstrates the unique status of Jesus.

48 Luke vividly describes the parents' emotions. The first is astonishment (cf. v.33). There is no inconsistency or lapse in Luke's attributing surprise to those who should have known best the uniqueness of Jesus' person and mission. It is one of the characteristics of Luke to observe the various responses of awe at the words and deeds of Jesus, which is also consistent with ancient narratives touching on the observation of wonders. His mother's natural concern then issues very humanly in a hint of scolding. Next she uses the word "anxiously" (the participle *odynōmenoi*, GK *3849*) to describe Joseph's and her feelings as they hunted for him. The word is unusually strong, often indicating pain or suffering (16:24–25; Ac 20:38; cf. *TDNT* 5:115). The mention of the father in this verse paves the way for the introduction of the heavenly Father in v.49.

49–50 Jesus' answer, "Why were you searching for me?" (v.49), pointedly prepares the hearer for a significant statement that is then understood as being theologically inevitable. The same pattern occurs in 24:5: "Why do you look for the living among the dead?" followed by, "He is not here; he has risen!" (24:6). In the present instance, the second part of the statement is of extraordinary significance. The importance of Jesus' use of the phrase "my Father," with its implied designation of himself as the unique Son of the Father, is heightened not only by the preceding question but also by the subsequent statement of v.50. By saying that Mary and Joseph did not understand, Luke underlines the awesome mystery of Jesus' statement of filial con-

sciousness. Here one finds a subtle contrast between the words "your father" (v.48) and "my Father" (v.49). The fact that this is the place where we find the first words coming from the mouth of Jesus is also significant. The mission of Jesus is identified as one that is aligned to the will of God and not as one fueled by human desires.

51 Immediately following this intimation of Jesus' divinity, Luke assures us also of his perfect humanity by noting his obedience to his parents. Once more Mary reflects inwardly on the significance of it all (cf. Ge 37:11). Like the boy Samuel (1Sa 2:26) and the responsible son in Proverbs 3:4, Jesus matures into a person of whom both God and people approve.

52 Jesus' growth was normal. Unlike some stories in the apocryphal gospels, Luke's account does not try to portray Jesus as exhibiting unusual powers. To say Jesus "grew in wisdom" does not detract from his deity. Even if wisdom means innate knowledge, Philippians 2:7 suggests that, as a servant, Jesus was willing to forgo the full use of his divine powers; so a normal development of knowledge is not ruled out. "Stature" (*hēlikia*, GK *2461*) is ambiguous, referring either to physical growth or, more likely, personal development, i.e., maturity. The good reputation Jesus enjoyed with other people was continued in the church (Ac 2:47).

NOTES

46 The phrase "after three days" (μετὰ ἡμέρας τρεῖς, *meta hēmeras treis*) is not an allusion to the resurrection, an event that is depicted by a different phrase in Luke. See Bovon, 112.

49 The tendency in recent versions has been to understand the Greek idiom ἐν τοῖς τοῦ πατρός μου (*en tois tou patros mou*, "in the [noun omitted] of my Father") to refer to the temple rather than to the affairs or "business" of God. The latter is not impossible (cf. 1Co 7:33; 1Ti 4:15), but the former is more appropriate to the context (cf. Ge 41:51 [LXX]; cf. also Creed, 46). Also possible is that the ambiguity is intentional. Luke may be referring to both the "matters" of the Father as well as the "house" of the Father (cf. D. D. Sylva, "The Cryptic Clause *en tois tou patros mou dei einai me* in Luke 2:49b," *ZNW* 78 [1987]: 132–40).

III. PREPARATION FOR JESUS' MINISTRY (3:1–4:13)

A. The Ministry of John the Baptist (3:1–20)

OVERVIEW

This pericope, like the foregoing, bears Palestinian Jewish characteristics in its language, themes, and setting. An example of this is vv.1–2. Here Luke not only shows classical historical precision in the dates he provides but also reflects the opening words of the OT prophets (e.g., Isa 1:1; Jer 1:1–3; Hos 1:1; Am 1:1). God's word is not simply the vehicle for timeless truth; it is a word in and to specific human circumstances. At this point in history, after a long silence, the prophetic word was again being heard.

¹In the fifteenth year of the reign of Tiberius Caesar—when Pontius Pilate was governor of Judea, Herod tetrarch of Galilee, his brother Philip tetrarch of Iturea and Traconitis, and Lysanias tetrarch of Abilene—²during the high priesthood of Annas and Caiaphas, the word of God came to John son of Zechariah in the desert. ³He went into all the country around the Jordan, preaching a baptism of repentance for the forgiveness of sins. ⁴As is written in the book of the words of Isaiah the prophet:

"A voice of one calling in the desert,
'Prepare the way for the Lord,
make straight paths for him.
⁵Every valley shall be filled in,
every mountain and hill made low.
The crooked roads shall become straight,
the rough ways smooth.
⁶And all mankind will see God's salvation.'"

⁷John said to the crowds coming out to be baptized by him, "You brood of vipers! Who warned you to flee from the coming wrath? ⁸Produce fruit in keeping with repentance. And do not begin to say to yourselves, 'We have Abraham as our father.' For I tell you that out of these stones God can raise up children for Abraham. ⁹The ax is already at the root of the trees, and every tree that does not produce good fruit will be cut down and thrown into the fire."

¹⁰"What should we do then?" the crowd asked.

¹¹John answered, "The man with two tunics should share with him who has none, and the one who has food should do the same."

¹²Tax collectors also came to be baptized. "Teacher," they asked, "what should we do?"

¹³"Don't collect any more than you are required to," he told them.

¹⁴Then some soldiers asked him, "And what should we do?"

He replied, "Don't extort money and don't accuse people falsely—be content with your pay."

¹⁵The people were waiting expectantly and were all wondering in their hearts if John might possibly be the Christ. ¹⁶John answered them all, "I baptize you with water. But one more powerful than I will come, the thongs of whose sandals I am not worthy to untie. He will baptize you with the Holy Spirit and with fire. ¹⁷His winnowing fork is in his hand to clear his threshing floor and to gather the wheat into his barn, but he will burn up the chaff with unquenchable fire." ¹⁸And with many other words John exhorted the people and preached the good news to them.

¹⁹But when John rebuked Herod the tetrarch because of Herodias, his brother's wife, and all the other evil things he had done, ²⁰Herod added this to them all: He locked John up in prison.

COMMENTARY

1 The dating provided here was more immediately useful to Luke's first-century readers than to the average reader today who does not know the period during which Luke was writing. More importantly, it locates the life and ministry of Christ within the setting of world history (cf. Ac 26:26). If the reign of Tiberius was dated from the occasion of his predecessor's death (Augustus having died on 19 August AD 14), his "fifteenth year" would be from August AD 28 to August AD 29, according to the normal Roman method of reckoning. If Luke was following the Syrian method as a native of Antioch, Tiberius's "fifteenth year" would have been from the fall of AD 27 to the fall of AD 28 (see Notes). For Luke to use the Roman method would have been in keeping with his cultural environment and appropriate for his readers.

"Herod" is Herod Antipas, son of Herod the Great who ruled Galilee and Perea from 4 BC–AD 39 (cf. Lk 3:19–20; 13:31; 23:7). Philip, like Herod Antipas, was a son of Herod the Great. He ruled a group of territories in the northeast of Palestine, namely, Iturea and Traconitis (4 BC–AD 33/34). Lysanias, unlike an earlier ruler of that same name, is unknown except through inscriptions (see Creed, 307–9). Pontius Pilate was governor (Luke uses the general term *hēgemoneuontos*, not the disputed "procurator") from AD 26–36 (cf. Jerry Vardaman, "A New Inscription Which Mentions Pilate as 'Prefect,'" *JBL* 81 [1962]: 70–71).

2 The official high priesthood of Annas had ended in AD 15, but his influence was so great, especially during the high priesthood of his son-in-law Caiaphas (AD 18–36; cf. Jn 18:13), that his name is naturally mentioned along with that of Caiaphas. With the reference to the high priests, we move from the secular world to the religious and are ready for the introduction of the prophet John, who has gone to the desert (1:80). The desert held memories for the Jews as the locale of the post-exodus wanderings of Israel. It also had eschatological associations (cf. not only Isa 40:3 but also Hos 2:14), and the sociopolitical connotations of John's activity in the desert should be noted as well (cf. Robert L. Webb, *John the Baptizer and Prophet: A Socio-Historical Study* [Sheffield: JSOT Press, 1991]). Some believed demons inhabited the desert, and it was later alleged that John had a demon (Mt 11:18). Luke's interest is not only in the coming of John (Mt 3:1; Mk 1:4, "John came") but also in the message: "the word of God came" (see Notes).

3 The impression that Luke, more than the other gospels, gives is that John had an itinerant ministry. Apparently he not only preached in the wilderness but followed the Dead Sea coast to the Jordan River and then also a distance from there. The "desert" is a barren rocky area that covers a large territory. Naturally he went where there was enough water to perform baptisms (see Jn 3:23).

John's baptism was "of repentance" (*metanoias*, GK *3567*), i.e., its chief characteristic was that it indicated sorrow for sin and a moral change on the part of those he baptized (vv.8–14). The noun *metanoia* ("repentance") appears elsewhere in Luke (3:8; 5:32; 15:7; 24:47), as does the verb *metanoeō* ("repent," GK *3566*; 10:13; 11:32; 13:3, 5; 15:7, 10; 16:30; 17:3–4). The basic idea comes from the Hebrew *šûb* ("turn" [GK 8740], i.e., from sin to God; cf. *TDNT* 4:975–1008). Repentance is an ancient prophetic theme (e.g., Eze 18:21, 30). "For [*eis*, with a view to] the forgiveness of sins" expresses the result of the repentance shown in baptism.

4–6 In its OT context, Isaiah 40:1–11 points to the arrival of the time of consolation. This eschatological tone is heightened in Malachi 3:1, where the way of the Lord is understood in a metaphorical sense. In the intertestamental period, Isaiah 40:3 became a symbol for the Jewish expectation of the end-times (e.g., *Pss. Sol.* 8.17; *T. Mos.* 10.1; *1 En.* 1:6; cf. Carl J. Davis, *The Name and Way of the Lord*

[JSNTSup 129; Sheffield: Sheffield Academic Press, 1996], 61–102). Isaiah 40:3 was also used by the community at Qumran as rationale for leading a separated life in the desert, where they believed they were preparing the way for the Lord by means of a constant reading of the law (1QS 8.12–16; 9.19–20).

For Matthew and Mark, the Isaiah passage was a clear prophecy of the ministry of John the Baptist. Luke includes more of the quotation than Matthew and Mark do. He first cites the extraordinary way in which, on the analogy of preparations made for a royal visitor, even the seemingly immovable must be removed to make way for the Lord. What needs removal is the sin of the people. Luke then concludes the Isaiah quotation with words that aptly describe his own evangelistic and theological conviction: "And all mankind will see God's salvation." Luke finds here, following the LXX, a biblical basis for his own universal concern and his central theme of salvation (cf. Morris, 95). The words concerning the appearance of God's glory (Isa 40:5) are omitted. Luke does stress the glory of God often elsewhere, beginning with 2:14; but for some reason he apparently does not think it appropriate to stress it here.

The fact that Luke includes an extended quotation from Isaiah 40 also points to the significance of that chapter for the understanding of his entire gospel. As Isaiah 40 calls attention to the arrival of salvation for God's people, the inclusion of the Gentiles, and the irresistible power of the Word, Luke carefully describes how this wider program is being fulfilled in the early Christian movement. Moreover, using the language of Isaiah 40:3, Luke later describes the church as the "Way" (Ac 9:2; 19:9, 23; 22:4; 24:14, 22; cf. Pao, 45–68).

7 The word "crowds" represents *ochlos* (GK *4063*), an assorted group of people, rather than *laos* (GK *3295*; cf. v.18). Luke does not specify who was in this group. (Mt 3:7 says they were Pharisees and

Sadducees; cf. Jn 1:19, 24.) Perhaps Luke wants to leave the first narration of a specific confrontation with the Pharisees until they have one with Jesus himself (5:17). Similarly, no mention is made of people coming from Jerusalem (cf. Mk 1:5).

John's language is strong, as was that of OT prophets who preceded him. His words (vv.7–9) are virtually identical to those in Matthew 3:7–10. Luke has, however, omitted one element and added another. Matthew's reference to John's words "Repent, for the kingdom of heaven is near" (Mt 3:2) is not found anywhere in Luke's account. Although Luke does emphasize the kingdom, he reserves its introduction for Jesus (4:43). What he adds here is a list of specific instances in which his audience ought to exhibit behavioral changes consistent with repentance.

Jesus himself used the epithet "brood of vipers" against the Pharisees (Mt 23:33). Here John uses it as a prophecy of judgment under the direction of God's Spirit. OT prophets had also spoken strongly and made similar allusions to reptiles (Isa 59:5). The question "Who warned you to flee from the coming wrath?" suggests that, while their "coming out to be baptized by him" was the proper thing to do, their motives were in question.

8–9 The language is picturesque. Two images are presented. First, a tree that does not produce fruit should be chopped down and removed to make way for one that will. Jesus speaks later about appropriate fruit (6:43–45) and also tells a parable about cutting down a barren fruit tree (13:6–9). The imagery may be intended to call to mind the figure of Israel as a fig tree or vine (cf. Isa 5:1–7). Black, 145, suggests a possible wordplay in the original Aramaic that would have included *raq* and *qar* (twice) in the words for "flee," "root," and "cut down." The second image, the ax "at the root" (v.9) symbolizes an impending radical action, the destruction of the whole tree. This imagery draws from Isaiah 10:34,

and in intertestamental traditions this verse has been understood in the context of the coming of the Messiah (cf. Richard Bauckham, "The Messianic Interpretation of Isa. 10:34 in the Dead Sea Scrolls, 2 Baruch and the Preaching of John the Baptist," *Dead Sea Discoveries* 2 [1995]: 202–16). The threat of judgment is heightened through the imagery of fire, a theme reintroduced in the reference to Jesus' ministry (vv.16–17).

The theme of Abraham's "children" (v.8) is found elsewhere (Jn 8:31–41; Ro 4:12–17; Gal 3:6–9). Mere physical descent from Abraham is not important; God can create his own children out of stones (cf. Isa 51:1–2), just as he can cause inanimate stones to praise his Son in the event that humans remain silent (Lk 19:40). One finds the continuation of Lukan interest in the redrawing of the boundaries of the people of God (cf. Siker, 108–9).

10–11 This prophetic word of judgment elicits a response, first from the crowd in general (v.10), then from the unpopular and greedy tax collectors (v.12), and finally from the soldiers (v.14). The conversations, which are unique to Luke, provide opportunity for some clear statements about social justice and responsibility. The exact relationship among these statements can be further defined, however. While it is possible that John is simply combining a series of proverbs in the form of prophetic speech (cf. Bovon, 1:122 n. 25), others have seen the three issues as a unified whole. J. D. M. Derrett ("The Baptist's Sermon: Luke 3:10–14," *Biblica et orientalia* 37 [1995]: 155–65) suggests that Exodus 23:1–13 provides a meaningful context for the discussion of sharing resources and avoiding illegal exactions and extortion.

The crowd, which is mixed, in contrast to the groups of tax collectors and soldiers (vv.12, 14), is told to share clothing and food with the needy (v.11). John is not requiring a strict communal life like that at Qumran, but rather "fruit in keeping with repentance" (v.8; cf. Gal 5:22–23). The "tunic" was the short garment (*chitōn*, GK *5945*) worn under the longer robe (*himation*, GK *2668*). One might have an extra tunic for warmth or a change of clothes (cf. 9:3: "take . . . no extra tunic"). Those who had broken the biblical law of love needed to demonstrate their repentance in this kind of sharing.

12–13 The "tax collectors" were part of a despised system (cf. 5:27; 15:1). Of the three groups, they would have been considered most in need of repentance. The chief tax collectors (*architelōnēs*, GK *803*), such as Zacchaeus (19:2), bid money for their position. Their profit came from collecting more than they paid to the Romans. The chief tax collectors hired other tax collectors to work for them. Because their work and associations rendered them ritually unclean and because they regularly extorted money, they were alienated from Jewish society and linked with "sinners." While John shows social concern, he does not advocate overthrow of the system but rather advocates a reform of the abuses. Since these abuses arose out of individual greed, a radical change in the practice of the collectors themselves was required (v.13).

14 The "soldiers" (*strateuomenoi*, GK *5129*) were probably not Roman but Jewish, assigned to internal affairs (cf. comment on "officers" at 22:4). The very nature of their work gave them opportunity to commit the sins specified. Soldiers could use threats of reprisal to extort money from the people. The soldiers' question suggests the seriousness of their moral need by means of the added words *kai hēmeis* ("even we")—"what about us?" (as the JB puts it). Here again the need of others is set over against personal greed. The second great commandment (cf. 10:27b) needs to be applied.

15–17 The question naturally came to the minds of "the people" (cf. v.18) whether such a radical prophet as John might be the Messiah. In John 1:19–25, popular opinion about him is reported in greater detail. Here John answers the unexpressed question in several ways. The Messiah is "more powerful" than he is (v.16); the Messiah is worthy of such reverence that even the task of tying his sandals is more than John feels worthy of (cf. Jn 1:27).

The Messiah will baptize, not with water in a preparatory way, as John had done, but actually "with the Holy Spirit and with fire" (v.16). These are not two separate categories of baptism. The single word "with" (*en*) combines the two (cf. Mt 3:11; Mk 1:8). The coming of the Spirit is to have the effect of fire. John uses an agricultural image to explain this. The grain is tossed in the air with a "winnowing fork" (v.17). The lighter and heavier elements are thus separated, the heavier grain falling on the "threshing floor." The "chaff," which is not the true grain, is burned up and the wheat stored in the barn.

Interpreters have discussed whether the fiery work of the Spirit is judgment or purification also. Modern readers find it difficult to understand how the concepts of the Spirit, baptism (usually associated with water), and fire relate to one another. The biblical background (e.g., Isa 44:3; Eze 36:25–27; Joel 2:28–29) and also lQS 4.20–21 show that the concept of washing and refreshing was associated with the Spirit. Fire is an ancient symbol of judgment, refinement, and purification (see Notes). We may conclude that John and his contemporaries were already acquainted with all of these nuances. The Holy Spirit was understood as being active in saving, purifying, and judging. The Spirit had definitely, but not frequently, been associated with the Messiah (Isa 11:1–2), whose coming would mean also the availability of the Spirit's ministry.

18 That John not only "exhorted" the people but also "preached the good news" shows that grace accompanies the warning to flee from judgment. The summary of John's preaching as that of "good news" points also to the inclusion of John in the time of fulfillment. It is noteworthy that here and in v.21 Luke uses the word *laos* ("people," GK *3295*; cf. v.21)—the term he specifically employs to describe not just a "crowd" (*ochlos*, GK *4063*; v.7) but also a potentially responsive group (see comments at 1:68, 77). It is this "people," who apparently stayed on to hear more of John's message, who heard the further proclamation of "good news."

19–20 "Herod" is Herod Antipas, mentioned in v.1. His brother is Philip, whose wife, Herodias, left him for Herod. Herod's marriage to her was one of many sins, and the climactic sin "added" (v.20) to this sordid series was his imprisonment of John. For John's death, see 9:7–9 and the fuller account in Mark 6:17–29. By his brief anticipation here of John's imprisonment, Luke underscores both the boldness of John and the sickness of the society he called to account. Verse 20 also indicates that John's ministry was completed before that of Jesus began. The same point is made in Peter's sermon to Cornelius (Ac 10:37–38). Charles Talbert ("The Lukan Presentation of Jesus' Ministry in Galilee," *RevExp* 64 [1967]: 490) presents this relationship between John's and Jesus' ministries as part of a comprehensive theological scheme in Luke. (See also comments on Jesus and John at v.21.)

NOTES

1 Several alternative methods of chronological reckoning have been applied to the data in this verse. Some have proposed that Luke followed a chronology used at that time in the Near East by which the reign would have been counted not from the actual date but by a regnal-year scheme. According to the Julian calendar, 19 August to 31 December AD 14 would have been the year of accession, with the first full year beginning 1 January AD 15. The fifteenth year would have been 1 January to 31 December AD 29. This calculation and that cited in the commentary above allow for an AD 33 crucifixion date, which many now think likely.

It is also possible that a Syrian system was used, according to which Tiberius's fifteenth year was 21 September AD 27 to 8 October AD 28. Still other possibilities exist (see Harold W. Hoehner, *Chronological Aspects of the Life of Christ* [Grand Rapids: Zondervan, 1977], 29–37; cf. G. Ogg, "Chronology of the New Testament," in *NBD*, 201–2). These dates must be correlated with those of Luke 3:23; John 2:20; 8:57; and other passages relating to the crucifixion, as well as those pertaining to Jesus' birth. Recent studies have also pointed to the reference to the Year of Jubilee in Luke 4:19 as a way to correlate the dating of 3:1 (cf. A. Strobel, "Plädoyer für Lukas: Zur Stimmigkeit des chronistischen Rahmens von Lk 3.1," *NTS* 41 [1995]: 466–69). For further information about Herod Antipas, see Harold W. Hoehner, *Herod Antipas* (Grand Rapids: Zondervan, 1972).

2 The noun ῥῆμα (*rhēma*, "word," GK *4839*) emphasizes the actual words spoken, whereas λόγος (*logos*, "word," GK *3364*) in Luke can be used as a broader theological term pointing to the gospel message and God's revelatory acts. Seventeen of the twenty-three occurrences of ῥῆμα, *rhēma*, in the Synoptics are in Luke (cf. Christoph Burchard, "A Note on ῥῆμα in JosAs 17:1f.; Luke 2:15, 17; Acts 10:37," *NovT* 27 [1985]: 281–95).

3 Dipping and washing ritually in water became increasingly common in the first century AD. Such lustrations were used at Qumran, both as one confessed his sins and entered the community (1QS 5.7–20) and on subsequent occasions (1QS 2.25ff.; 3.4–5). John's probable knowledge of the Qumran community, which was in the Judean desert, has led some to see a connection between his baptism and theirs. His baptism was not, however, intended for frequent repetition, nor did it link the participants with a community like theirs. Probably as early as John's day, baptism along with circumcision (for males) and the offering of a sacrifice marked the full conversion of a proselyte to Judaism. The striking difference between the baptism of Jewish proselytes and that which John practiced is that John's subjects were already Jews; for them to be baptized carried negative implications as to the sufficiency of Judaism. Josephus (*Ant.* 18.117) has a different understanding of John's baptism and perhaps sees it only as a lustration such as he knew was practiced at Qumran. In Josephus's view, John wanted people to do righteous deeds and then be baptized. This may be explained by the way Josephus is presenting his material to a Hellenistic audience. Luke, however, shows John baptizing repentant sinners, who then go on to live righteous lives.

4 The Greek αὐτοῦ (*autou*, "for him") is parallel with κυρίου (*kyriou*, "for the Lord"); Luke uses αὐτοῦ, *autou*, whereas Isaiah 40:3 [LXX] has τοῦ θεοῦ ἡμῶν (*tou theou hēmōn*, "our God"). In this way, Luke makes it easier to understand that the words "the Lord" here refer to Jesus (cf. Mt 3:3; Mk 1:3).

7 On ἀπὸ τῆς μελλούσης ὀργῆς (*apo tēs mellousēs orgēs*, "from the coming wrath"), see also Romans 2:5; 1 Thessalonians 1:10; and Revelation 6:15–17. John the Baptist will allude to this in v.9 (cf. *TDNT* 5:422–47).

16 In the clause "with the Holy Spirit and with fire," the second "with" (ἐν, *en*) was omitted in the 1973 edition of the NIV. That was technically correct, as the Greek does not repeat the word. The 1978 edition added the second "with," possibly for stylistic reasons.

17 The continuity of John the Baptist and the ministry of the Spirit is assumed in the use of this agricultural imagery. The winnowing took place during the ministry of John, while the Coming One will bring the separated piles to their destined end. See Robert L. Webb, "The Activity of John the Baptist's Expected Figure at the Threshing Floor (Matthew 3.12 = Luke 3.17)," *JSNT* 43 (1991): 103–11.

There are many relevant passages in OT, intertestamental, and NT literature on the Spirit, water, fire, purification, and judgment (e.g., Ge 19:24 [cf. Lk 17:29]; Am 7:4; Mal 3:2; *1 En.* 90:24–27; *Pss. Sol.* 15:6; 1QS 2.8; 1QpHab 2.11ff.; Mt 5:22; 13:40; 25:41; 1Pe 1:7; Rev 20:14). For the association of fire with fluidity, see Daniel 7:9–10 and 1QH 11.29–32. See also J. D. G. Dunn, *Baptism in the Holy Spirit* (London: SCM, 1970), 8–22; cf. Webb, *John the Baptizer*, 289–95.

18–20 The use of the contrastive μέν . . . δέ (*men . . . de*) clause serves to highlight the contrast between John the Baptist and Herod. While John proclaims the good news to the people, Herod added to the evil deeds that he did by putting John in prison.

19–20 Outside the canonical gospels, Josephus (*Ant.* 18.116–19) also provides an account of the death of John the Baptist. In his account, Josephus sees as the reason for John's arrest the threat to Herod Antipas's security posed by John's popularity. John's reproach of Herod's relationship with Herodias is missing. This does not contradict the canonical accounts, however, since "the Christians chose to emphasize the moral charges that [John] brought against the ruler, whereas Josephus stresses the political fears that he aroused in Herod" (Louis H. Feldman, *Josephus and Modern Scholarship [1937–1980]* [New York: Walter de Gruyter, 1984], 675).

B. The Baptism of Jesus (3:21–22)

OVERVIEW

For a comprehensive study of the events contained in these two verses, the parallels in Matthew 3:13–17; Mark 1:9–11; and John 1:32–34 should be consulted.

> [21]When all the people were being baptized, Jesus was baptized too. And as he was praying, heaven was opened [22]and the Holy Spirit descended on him in bodily form like a dove. And a voice came from heaven: "You are my Son, whom I love; with you I am well pleased."

COMMENTARY

21 As in the birth narratives, there is at Jesus' baptism a supernatural attestation. Many see in the event his "call" to his mission. His baptism comes as the climax of the baptism of "all the people" (see Notes).

Unlike Matthew and Mark, Luke does not explicitly mention who baptized Jesus. Moreover, this baptismal account follows the mention of John's imprisonment. The omission of John from this baptismal scene can be explained in a number of ways. (1) Some have pointed to the early church's embarrassment about Jesus' being baptized by John to explain Luke's intentional downplaying of the role of John (see Morton S. Enslin, "John and Jesus," *ZNW* 66 [1975]: 1–18). The significance of the role of John in Luke 1–2 makes this hypothesis unlikely, though one can indeed find the emphasis on Jesus' superiority. (2) Conzelmann, 18–27, believes that Luke intentionally limits John to the period of Israel and therefore denies his role at the beginning of Jesus' baptism. This theory is based on a misreading of Luke 16:16 and a neglect of Acts 1:22, where John's inclusion in the climax of salvation history is

recognized. (3) Appealing to Acts 18:24–19:7, some have suggested that Luke is fighting against some "Baptist" groups, and the omission of John in Luke 3:21 reflects Luke's "antibaptistic polemic" (so Richard J. Erickson, "The Jailing of John and the Baptism of Jesus," *JETS* 36 [1993]: 455–66). This reading is again problematic in light of the positive portrayal of John in Luke, especially in 3:18–20.

The best solution for the omission of John is one already provided in the text. In 3:21–22 both the baptism of Jesus and the people are placed in subordinate clauses (see Notes). The main clause appears when Luke describes the opening of the heavens and the descending of the Spirit. In other words, the baptismal scene simply provides the context for the descent of the Spirit on Jesus as he begins proclaiming the arrival of the kingdom of God. This serves as a parallel to Acts, in which the descent of the Spirit also signifies the beginning of the ministry of the apostles. Since the focus is on the descent of the Spirit, the role of John is assumed but not emphasized. Moreover, to place the imprisonment of John before Jesus' baptism is also a literary technique that

Luke frequently employs to complete his discussion of one topic before beginning another.

Jesus was baptized not because he was a sinner in need of repentance but as a way of identifying himself with those he came to save. His reasons are expressed in Matthew 3:15. This is the first of several important events in Luke that took place when Jesus prayed (cf. esp. 6:12; 9:18, 29; 22:41). Though Luke's description of the opening of the heavens is not as dramatic as Mark's (1:10), it does make clear that Jesus had a true vision of the Deity (cf. Ezekiel's vision, Eze 1:1; Stephen's, Ac 7:56; and Peter's, Ac 10:11). In contrast, the disciples on the Mount of Transfiguration were enveloped by a cloud (Lk 9:34). Though they heard God speaking, their vision was of Christ and the heavenly visitors rather than of God in heaven.

22 God had appeared in OT times through theophanies. Now the Spirit appears as a dove. Only Luke has the expression "in bodily form," giving more substance to the experience of the Spirit's presence. Luke does not say that anyone other than Jesus was aware of the Holy Spirit. Perhaps others present saw only a dove without realizing its significance. The descent of the Spirit is reminiscent of Genesis 1:2 (see Notes).

"You are my Son, whom I love" designates Jesus as the unique Son of God. The words, like those heard at the transfiguration (9:35; cf. Mt 17:5; Mk 9:7), effect a blend of OT christological passages, namely, Psalm 2:7 and Isaiah 42:1. Present scholarly opinion holds that the concept of divine sonship in Jewish thought was not only applicable to angels (Job 1:6; 2:1) and to the nation of Israel and her kings (Ex 4:22; 2Sa 7:14; Hos 11:1) but was coming into use, at least at Qumran, as a designation for the Messiah (4Q174 1.10–14). At the annunciation Jesus was designated the "Son of the Most High" (1:32; on his sonship and OT passages, see comments at 9:35 for a discussion of the wording common to both passages). Here we may simply observe that the words "love" and "well pleased" convey the idea of divine election and special relationship. Jesus has now received the Spirit and the commission. He is ready (following the temptation, 4:1–12) to begin his ministry.

NOTES

21 The infinitival phrase βαπτισθῆναι (*baptisthēnai*, "were baptized," GK 966; NIV, "were being baptized") could, because the verb is an aorist, imply antecedent action. In this case it would indicate that the baptism of the people had ended, thus distinguishing Jesus' baptism from theirs. The construction does not necessarily imply this, however.

Luke also uses an aorist, this time in participial form—βαπτισθέντος (*baptisthentos*, "was baptized")—to describe Jesus' own baptism, perhaps in contrast to the durative idea of the present participle προσευχομένου (*proseuchomenou*, "was praying," GK 4667). Jesus' baptism, like that of the people, was a single event in time; but his praying continued throughout his lifetime. The most striking aspect of Luke's use of grammar in vv.21–22 is his use of dependent clauses leading up to the affirmation, "You are my Son . . . ."

22 The significance of the dove's descent has been much discussed (cf. L. E. Keck, "The Spirit and the Dove," *NTS* 17 [1970–71]: 41–67; Marshall, *Luke: Historian and Theologian*, 151–52; and the sixteen different interpretations in W. D. Davies and Dale C. Allison Jr., *A Critical and Exegetical Commentary on the Gospel According to Saint Matthew* [ICC; Edinburgh: T&T Clark, 1988], 1:331–34). As in the case of Genesis 1:2, in this baptismal scene we have the same three elements: the Spirit of God, water, and the image of a bird implied in the verb "hovering." This interpretation is strengthened by a Messianic Vision fragment (see Dale C. Allison Jr., "The Baptism of Jesus and a New Dead Sea Scroll," *BAR* 18 [1992]: 58–60). In the context of the discussion of the end-times, one finds the hovering of the Spirit on the "poor" and the "faithful." This text seems to be able to provide the missing precedent for the eschatological use of Genesis 1:2. If the image of the dove in Luke 3:22 can be understood in this way, the eschatological tone can be heard as the period of a new creation that is in view.

Scholars have debated the relationship of the "voice ... from heaven" to the Hebrew *bat qôl*, lit., "daughter of a voice," i.e., the voice of God heard not directly but as an echo. The rabbis thought that God, having ceased to speak through prophets as in the OT, now spoke indirectly. Otto Betz (*TDNT* 9:288–90, esp. 298) shows that the voice was still considered a shared communication from God. The heavenly voice to Jesus was not identical to the *bat qôl*, being directed to one person and involving a first-person address: "You are *my* Son, whom I love" (emphasis added).

Against the view that the word υἱός (*huios*, "son") is a later substitute for an original παῖς (*pais*, "servant") under Hellenistic influence, see I. H. Marshall, "Son of God or Servant of Jehovah?—A Reconsideration of Mark 1.11," *NTS* 15 (1968–69): 326–36.

An early variant in the Western text, "This day I have begotten you," echoing Psalm 2:7 and the synoptic parallels, is not supported by the best MSS (cf. Metzger, 112–13).

C. Jesus' Genealogy (3:23–38)

OVERVIEW

Both Luke and Matthew in his gospel recognize the importance of establishing a genealogy for Jesus, in accordance with the care given to such matters in ancient Israel.

In their handling of Jesus' genealogy, the two writers differ in several ways. (1) Matthew begins his gospel with the genealogy, thereby establishing an immediate connection with the OT and with Israel. Luke waits until the significant part of the ministry of John the Baptist is completed and Jesus stands alone as the designated Son of God. A biblical precedent is provided in Exodus, where Moses' genealogy (ch. 6) is provided after his call (ch. 3; cf. William S. Kurz, *Reading Luke–Acts: Dynamics of Biblical Narrative* [Louisville, Ky.: Westminster, 1993], 24). (2)

Matthew begins with Abraham, stressing Jesus' Jewish ancestry; Luke, in reverse order, goes back to Adam, probably with the intention of stressing the identification of Jesus with the entire human race. (3) Matthew groups his names symmetrically; Luke simply lists them. (4) Both trace the lineage back through ancestral lines that diverge for a number of generations from Luke's, though both meet at the generation of David. (5) Matthew includes the names of several women (a feature one might have expected in Luke because of his understanding and respect for women).

These differences, as well as some problems of detail, have been explained in part by one or more of the following assumptions: (1) Joseph's lineage is given in Matthew, Mary's in Luke; (2) the legal line is traced in Matthew, the actual line of descent in Luke; and (3) there was a levirate marriage at one or more points in the line.

The first assumption is without solid foundation and does not seem to accord with the emphasis on Joseph in Luke 1:27. Nevertheless, Luke's narrative seems to be from Mary's point of view, whereas Matthew's is from that of Joseph (cf. J. Gresham Machen, *The Virgin Birth of Christ* [1930; repr., Grand Rapids: Baker, 1965], 202–9, 229–32). The second assumption is possible; it allows for breaks in Matthew's line, with heirship still retained. The levirate marriage assumption has been a popular option since ancient times (proposed by Africanus [third century], as cited in Eusebius, *Hist. eccl.* 1.7). The widow of a childless man could marry his brother so

that a child of the second marriage could legally be considered as the son of the deceased man in order to perpetuate his name. In a genealogy, the child could be listed under his natural or his legal father. Joseph is listed as the son of Heli in Luke but as the son of Jacob in Matthew. On the levirate marriage theory, Heli and Jacob may have been half brothers, with the same mother but fathers of different names. Perhaps Heli died and Jacob married his widow.

To all this it must be added that we possess not a poverty but a plethora of possibilities. Therefore, the lack of certainty due to incomplete information need not imply error in either genealogy. Morris, 100, observes that it is not possible to know how Luke would have handled a genealogy involving a virgin birth, and so "the case is unique."

[23]Now Jesus himself was about thirty years old when he began his ministry. He was the son, so it was thought, of Joseph,

the son of Heli, [24]the son of Matthat,
the son of Levi, the son of Melki,
the son of Jannai, the son of Joseph,
[25] the son of Mattathias, the son of Amos,
the son of Nahum, the son of Esli,
the son of Naggai, [26]the son of Maath,
the son of Mattathias, the son of Semein,
the son of Josech, the son of Joda,
[27] the son of Joanan, the son of Rhesa,
the son of Zerubbabel, the son of Shealtiel,
the son of Neri, [28]the son of Melki,
the son of Addi, the son of Cosam,
the son of Elmadam, the son of Er,
[29] the son of Joshua, the son of Eliezer,
the son of Jorim, the son of Matthat,
the son of Levi, [30]the son of Simeon,
the son of Judah, the son of Joseph,
the son of Jonam, the son of Eliakim,

³¹ the son of Melea, the son of Menna,
the son of Mattatha, the son of Nathan,
the son of David, ³²the son of Jesse,
the son of Obed, the son of Boaz,
the son of Salmon, the son of Nahshon,
³³ the son of Amminadab, the son of Ram,
the son of Hezron, the son of Perez,
the son of Judah, ³⁴the son of Jacob,
the son of Isaac, the son of Abraham,
the son of Terah, the son of Nahor,
³⁵ the son of Serug, the son of Reu,
the son of Peleg, the son of Eber,
the son of Shelah, ³⁶the son of Cainan,
the son of Arphaxad, the son of Shem,
the son of Noah, the son of Lamech,
³⁷ the son of Methuselah, the son of Enoch,
the son of Jared, the son of Mahalalel,
the son of Kenan, ³⁸the son of Enosh,
the son of Seth, the son of Adam,
the son of God.

COMMENTARY

23 The age of Jesus is given in very approximate terms. He might have been in his mid-thirties. "Thirty" is a round number and might also indicate that, like the priests who began their service at that age, he was ready to devote himself to God's work. Compare the extreme comment recorded in John 8:57.

NOTES

23 Significant studies include M. D. Johnson, *The Purpose of the Biblical Genealogies: With Special Reference to the Setting of the Genealogies of Jesus* (SNTSMS 8; rev. ed.; Cambridge: Cambridge Univ. Press, 1989); William S. Kurz, "Luke 3:23–38 and Greco-Roman and Biblical Genealogies," in *Perspectives on Luke–Acts* (ed. Talbert), 169–87; see also M. D. Johnson's article (*ISBE* 2:424–31) in which he summarizes the data (and his viewpoint that the genealogies are "probably examples of the tendency to historicize traditional motifs in the Gospel material"). For a conservative approach to this complex subject, see the concise summary in Marshall, *Luke: Historian and Theologian*, 157–66; cf. R. L. Overstreet, "Difficulties of New Testament Genealogies," *Grace Theological Journal* 2 (1981): 303–26.

REFLECTIONS

The significance of the genealogy in Luke probably lies in the emphasis on Jesus as a member of the human race, a son of Adam; in the contrast of Jesus, the obedient Second Adam (a theme implicit but not explicit in Luke), with the disobedient first Adam; and in the emphasis on Jesus as the true Son of God (cf. "Adam," v.38).

D. The Temptation of Jesus (4:1–13)

OVERVIEW

This vivid narrative contains an important blend of theological themes—the divine sonship and messiahship of Jesus, the warfare between Christ and Satan, OT theology, and principles of obedience to the divine Word.

[1]Jesus, full of the Holy Spirit, returned from the Jordan and was led by the Spirit in the desert, [2]where for forty days he was tempted by the devil. He ate nothing during those days, and at the end of them he was hungry.

[3]The devil said to him, "If you are the Son of God, tell this stone to become bread."

[4]Jesus answered, "It is written: 'Man does not live on bread alone.'"

[5]The devil led him up to a high place and showed him in an instant all the kingdoms of the world. [6]And he said to him, "I will give you all their authority and splendor, for it has been given to me, and I can give it to anyone I want to. [7]So if you worship me, it will all be yours."

[8]Jesus answered, "It is written: 'Worship the Lord your God and serve him only.'"

[9]The devil led him to Jerusalem and had him stand on the highest point of the temple. "If you are the Son of God," he said, "throw yourself down from here. [10]For it is written:

"'He will command his angels concerning you
  to guard you carefully;
[11]they will lift you up in their hands,
  so that you will not strike your foot against a stone.'"

[12]Jesus answered, "It says: 'Do not put the Lord your God to the test.'"
[13]When the devil had finished all this tempting, he left him until an opportune time.

COMMENTARY

1–2 These verses shed light on the significance of the episode. Jesus is in the "desert" (v.1) for a period of "forty days" (v.2). This probably relates to Israel's experience in the desert after the exodus. It may also allude to Moses' forty days without food on the mountain (Dt 9:9). The parallel with Israel becomes stronger if it is meant as a comparison between Israel as God's "son" (Ex 4:22–23; Hos 11:1) who failed when tested and Jesus as his unique Son who conquered temptation. God led Israel into the desert; likewise the Spirit led Jesus. In the former case, God tested his people; now God allows the devil to tempt his Son.

The focus on the Spirit's leading of Jesus here is paradigmatic for the Lukan narrative. That the power of the Spirit is with Jesus identifies him to be the unique Son of God (cf. 3:22), and after the temptation narrative Jesus is again led by the Spirit (4:14). In spite of the attempt of the evil one to "lead" him (vv.5, 9), Jesus remained faithful in his path to the cross (cf. Shepherd, 132).

It is important to distinguish among three kinds of tempting (*peirasmos*, GK *4280*). (1) Satan tempts people, i.e., lures them to do evil. God never does this; nor can he himself be tempted in this way (Jas 1:13). Further, not all temptation comes directly from Satan; often it comes from our own lower nature (Jas 1:14–15). (2) People may tempt (test) God in the sense of provoking him through unreasonable demands contrary to faith. This is what Israel did in the desert and what is probably referred to in Jesus' quotation of Deuteronomy 6:16 (see comments at v.12). (3) God tests (but does not tempt) his people, as he did in the desert (Dt 8:2). All three kinds of testing are involved in the parallels between the desert experiences of Israel and of Jesus. (On this theme, see Birger Gerhardsson, *The Testing of God's Son* [ConBNT 2; Lund: Gleerup, 1966].)

Though God already knows all about us, he reveals the thoughts and intents of our hearts through our response to him in times of trial. Thus he tested Israel in the desert to "see" whether the people would obey (Ex 16:4). In this temptation by the devil, the Lord Jesus shows the validity of what God had just said of him: "With you I am well pleased" (3:22).

We see here two other contrasts besides the one between Israel and Jesus discussed above. The first is the absolute contrast between Jesus, who is both filled and led by the Spirit (note Luke's emphasis on the Spirit), and the devil, who opposes both Jesus and the Spirit. (The unpardonable sin is called "blasphemy" against the Spirit [12:10; cf. Mt 12:31–32].) The second contrast is the one implied between Jesus as "hungry," i.e., physically empty, and yet as "full of the Spirit." Our own experience is usually the reverse.

3 The "devil" (*diabolos*, GK *1333*) has several names in biblical and other Jewish literature, notably the OT name "Satan," which is used often in the NT (*Satanas*, GK *4928*; cf., e.g., 4:8 KJV; 10:18; 11:18). He opposes God and God's servants (1Ch 21:1; Job 1:6–12; 2:1–7; Zec 3:1–2). He may seem to be ubiquitous but is not omnipresent. Sometimes he works indirectly through the evil spirits that form his domain (cf. 11:14–20). Here the devil's statement, "If you are the Son of God," picks up the declaration of Jesus' sonship in 3:22. The conditional construction does not imply doubt, but it is a logical assumption in the dialogue.

The reference to bread is conceivably an allusion to God's provision of manna for Israel during the exodus. Apparently some of Jesus' contemporaries expected that the coming Messiah would perform some such miracle of provision for them (cf. Jn 6:30). Consequently, this temptation may have been an appeal for Jesus to do a work of messianic significance. Alternatively (and more probably), his temptation may have been to satisfy his own need and gratify himself; however, bread is necessary, not evil, and is hardly an object of "the cravings of sinful man" (1Jn 2:16). Further, Jesus' temptation is not the same as the self-engendered lusting described in James 1:14–15—a fact to keep in mind when we question how Jesus could have been perfect and yet truly tempted. The issue, therefore, is not one of allurement to perverted self-gratification but a challenge to act apart from faithful dependence on God.

4 Jesus' reply is brief—a partial quotation of Deuteronomy 8:3 (found more fully in Mt 4:4). In Deuteronomy, Moses was reminding Israel that during the forty years in the desert God had led them "to humble you [i.e., Israel] and to test you in order to know what was in your heart, whether or not you would keep his commands" (Dt 8:2). The next verse (8:3) specifically refers to hunger and the provision of manna, which the Lord gave to Israel so that the people might know that human beings need not merely bread but also the sustaining word of God.

Thus while he is being "tempted" by the devil, Jesus is also proving faithful to God in contrast to Israel's response when "tested" by him. This contrast is further illustrated by the fact that all three responses of Jesus come from Deuteronomy 6–8 (see below), a passage given to Israel during their days in the wilderness. Jesus proves by his response that his heart is not divided but that he is dependent on God and obedient to his word. So he becomes our example in temptation (Heb 4:14–16; 5:8).

5 The second temptation, though of a different nature, involves similar issues. The devil takes Jesus to a "high place" (cf. "mountain" in Mt 4:8, where a parallel with Moses on Mount Nebo may be implied [Dt 32:49; 34:1–3]). "In an instant" probably shows that this part of the temptation involved a vision. It was not necessary for Jesus to see every part of the world physically for this to be an actual temptation.

6 Once again, what the devil offered was legitimate in itself. The Messiah would someday rule the whole world and possess all "authority and splendor." In this temptation the devil claims to possess the world. Jesus does not challenge the claim (cf. Jn 12:31); neither does he acknowledge it. To worship the devil in order to recapture the world, even for its good, would have meant "casting out devils by Beelzebub" (Morris, 103).

7 Had Jesus accepted the devil's offer, our salvation would have been impossible. First, Jesus would have sinned by giving worship to the devil and thus could not have offered himself as a perfect sacrifice for our sins. (The same applies to all three temptations.) Second, Scripture teaches that the Messiah should first suffer and only then "enter his glory" (24:26). Third, since the devil tried to prevent Christ's voluntary death for our sins, the implication of this second temptation was that accepting an immediate kingdom would avoid the cross.

8 The temptations deal with both the divine sonship and messiahship of Jesus—related concepts in biblical thought. But the temptations also tested his perfect manhood. This aspect of them especially interested Luke. Moreover, they show us that Jesus is our example. By quoting Deuteronomy 6:13, he responded as the perfect man—the obedient last Adam (Ro 5:19)—should respond, worshiping and serving his only God. Both of the OT texts Jesus quoted thus far (Lk 4:4, 8) are more than weapons against the devil; they apply to Jesus himself.

9–12 Luke records this temptation in the last rather than second place (cf. Mt 4:5–7). It may be that Matthew preferred to conclude with a kingdom reference. Possibly Luke wants to center on the city of Jerusalem, which Matthew does not mention by name, because of his theme of the progression of the gospel from Jerusalem to the Gentile nations. The essence of this temptation is that of presuming on God (v.12) and displaying before others one's special favor with him. In this instance, the devil quotes a passage of Scripture (Ps 91:11–12) out of context. Notice that merely using words from Scripture does not necessarily convey the will of God (v.10). Further, Satan omits the words "in all your ways" (Ps 91:11), possibly to facilitate application to an act inconsistent with the normal "ways" of the godly person.

Gerhardsson (*Testing of God's Son*, 54ff.) sees here a theme of protection (cf. Dt 1:31 with the context of Ps 91, from which the devil quotes). He sees the temple as a place of protection and finds a play on words between "wings" (Ps 91:4 [90:4 LXX], *pterygas*, GK *4763*) and "highest point" or "pinnacle" (*pterygion*, GK *4762*). But it is doubtful that Luke intended this parallel. The rabbinic tradition that the Messiah would appear on top of the temple (cf. Str-B, 1:151) may provide a background that accounts for the form of this temptation (even though the idea of jumping down is absent).

12 Again Jesus responds with Scripture, this time by quoting Deuteronomy 6:16. This quotation could be understood as applying to the devil, who "tempted" Jesus in the first sense of the word; more probably it is applied to Jesus, who thus refuses to "tempt" God in the second sense of the word, i.e., he will not repeat the sin that Israel committed in the desert by putting God to the test (see comments at vv.1–2). To do that would be to provoke God by making inappropriate demands for a divine sign to be used for display. This request for a sign would actually be an act of unbelief masquerading as extraordinary faith.

13 This verse may be considered the conclusion of this section rather than the beginning of the next (so NIV). The devil leaves only temporarily—"until an opportune time." This departure does not signify a Satan-free period during the ministry of Jesus, since his ministry is characterized by constant oppositions from the evil one (see Notes). Moreover, if the temptations noted here are understood as characteristic of ways in which Satan is attempting to prevent the plan of God from unfolding, the note of his departure points more to Satan's defeat than to the end of his activity (cf. Green, 196).

NOTES

9 The noun πτερύγιον (*pterygion*, "highest point," GK *4762*) may be the corner of the walls that encompassed the temple area. The southeastern corner was directly above a cliff, making possible a terrifying drop down to the Kidron Valley.

13 Conzelmann's view, 38, that Luke believed Satan to be inactive during Jesus' ministry imposes an artificial scheme on this gospel. Conzelmann reads too much into the first half of this verse and holds that the "opportune time" does not come until 22:3. In his book *Apostasy and Perseverance*, Schuyler Brown counters this concept by maintaining that Satan is active throughout Luke's gospel—a conclusion based on a view of the nature of temptation in Luke that differs from Conzelmann's.

IV. THE GALILEAN MINISTRY (4:14–9:50)

A. Initial Phase (4:14–6:16)

1. First Approach and Rejection at Nazareth (4:14–30)

OVERVIEW

This passage has an important place in the Lukan presentation. Not only does it mark the beginning of Jesus' ministry, but it is also the first major narrative about his ministry that is not largely paralleled in Matthew or Mark. The setting is Nazareth, the place of Jesus' childhood (v.16). A lengthy quotation from Isaiah (vv.18–19) issues in a proclamation of immediate fulfillment. Jesus also implies at the very outset of his ministry the selection of Gentiles for divine favor (vv.24–27). Observe that this event occurs in Luke much earlier than what appears to be the same occurrence later in the presentations of Matthew and Mark. Whatever the literary and historical relationship may be between this passage and Mark 6:1–6, its placement here shows that Luke considers it of prime importance and a bold introductory statement as Jesus begins his ministry in Galilee (see Notes for further discussion).

Also a pattern appears here that is unveiled more clearly later on in Luke–Acts: (1) the presentation of the gospel to Jews in their synagogues, (2) rejection, and (3) turning to the wider Gentile world (cf. Ac 13:46). Even the content of Jesus' sermon resembles that of the synagogue sermons later in Acts as Jesus focuses on his own identity, the call to evangelize, and the message of forgiveness. Therefore, the significance of Luke 4:14–30 should not be limited to the ministry of Jesus; it also serves as a theological introduction to the early Christian movement as recorded in Acts (cf. Bruce D. Chilton, "Announcement in Nazara," in *Gospel Perspectives*, ed. R. T. France and D. Wenham [Sheffield: JSOT Press, 1981], 2:147–72).

¹⁴Jesus returned to Galilee in the power of the Spirit, and news about him spread through the whole countryside. ¹⁵He taught in their synagogues, and everyone praised him.

¹⁶He went to Nazareth, where he had been brought up, and on the Sabbath day he went into the synagogue, as was his custom. And he stood up to read. ¹⁷The scroll of the prophet Isaiah was handed to him. Unrolling it, he found the place where it is written:

¹⁸"The Spirit of the Lord is on me,
  because he has anointed me
  to preach good news to the poor.
He has sent me to proclaim freedom for the prisoners
  and recovery of sight for the blind,

to release the oppressed,
19 to proclaim the year of the Lord's favor."

²⁰Then he rolled up the scroll, gave it back to the attendant and sat down. The eyes of everyone in the synagogue were fastened on him, ²¹and he began by saying to them, "Today this scripture is fulfilled in your hearing."

²²All spoke well of him and were amazed at the gracious words that came from his lips. "Isn't this Joseph's son?" they asked.

²³Jesus said to them, "Surely you will quote this proverb to me: 'Physician, heal yourself! Do here in your hometown what we have heard that you did in Capernaum.'"

²⁴"I tell you the truth," he continued, "no prophet is accepted in his hometown. ²⁵I assure you that there were many widows in Israel in Elijah's time, when the sky was shut for three and a half years and there was a severe famine throughout the land. ²⁶Yet Elijah was not sent to any of them, but to a widow in Zarephath in the region of Sidon. ²⁷And there were many in Israel with leprosy in the time of Elisha the prophet, yet not one of them was cleansed—only Naaman the Syrian."

²⁸All the people in the synagogue were furious when they heard this. ²⁹They got up, drove him out of the town, and took him to the brow of the hill on which the town was built, in order to throw him down the cliff. ³⁰But he walked right through the crowd and went on his way.

COMMENTARY

14–15 Once again, as Jesus enters a new phase of his experience, Luke mentions the special activity of the Holy Spirit (cf. 4:1). Shortly Jesus will make a significant declaration about the meaning of the Spirit's ministry in his life (v.18). So far we have seen the Spirit's activity at Jesus' conception (1:35), baptism (3:22), and temptation (4:1). The "news" that spread about Jesus and the fact that "everyone praised him" (v.15) are the first of several observations Luke makes about public response to Jesus ministry (cf. vv.22, 28, 32, 36–37).

16 By the words "where he had been brought up," Luke emphasizes that Jesus was in his hometown. He stresses Jesus' Jewish piety with a reference to his custom of attendance at synagogue. This strengthens the contrast with his rejection. Luke does not say whether Jesus had publicly read from the Scriptures before; nor does Luke say whether Jesus himself chose to read from Isaiah 61 (v.17) or whether the passage was assigned for that Sabbath (see Notes).

17 The passage was Isaiah 61:1–2, with the words "to release the oppressed" (v.18) taken from Isaiah 58:6. The variation from the usual wording may simply reflect the interpretive translation in use at that time.

18–19 The quotation has significance both as our Lord's statement of his call to his saving ministry and as Luke's affirmation of this ministry as thematic in his gospel. The various components provide categories for the organization of events in the ministry of Jesus: (1) to bring good news to the poor; (2) to proclaim release to the captives; (3) to restore sight to the blind; (4) to let the oppressed go free; and (5) to proclaim the year of the Lord's favor. Max Turner (*Power from on High* [Sheffield: Sheffield Academic Press, 1996], 250) argues that the first four phrases all point to the oppressed situation of Israel in the context of Isaiah. All five, therefore, are concerned with Israel's salvation. The literal/material reading should not be entirely eliminated, however, since the arrival of the salvation of God has its social and political manifestations (cf. Lk 7:22).

18 The "good news" Jesus was to proclaim recalls both the joyful announcement in 1:19 and the frequent use of the term elsewhere in Luke. It also builds on Isaiah 40:9; 41:27; and especially 52:7. The concerns for the "poor," like the "prisoners," the "blind," and the "oppressed," point then to Luke's (and Isaiah's) focus on the theme of reversal when those humbled ones will be blessed (see comments at 1:53; 6:20).

19 The "year of the Lord's favor" is reminiscent of the Jubilee (one year in every fifty) when debts were forgiven and slaves set free (Lev 25:8–17). It means not so much a time that is "acceptable" to people but the time in history when God in sovereign grace brings freedom from the guilt and effects of sin. The inclusion of this quotation is consistent with Luke's stress on the dawning of the new age of salvation (cf. Michael Prior, *Jesus the Liberator* [Sheffield: Sheffield Academic Press, 1996]).

The omission of the next phrase in Isaiah 61:2—"the day of vengeance of our God"—is also significant. Jesus' audience would suppose that the day of their own salvation would be the day of judgment on their pagan enemies. But the delay of judgment means that this time of the Lord's favor also benefits the Gentiles. Jesus affirms (vv.24–27) that Gentiles are also recipients of God's grace, even when Jews were not so blessed. Another possible reason for the omission of the phrase is that Luke can high-

light it "to proclaim the year of the Lord's favor." It has also been suggested that the omission of the phrase about vengeance is the cause of the hostility in v.28. But while the two may be related, Luke does not say so.

20 We now have a description of the synagogue procedure. Jesus hands back the scroll to the "attendant." In addition to other services rendered at the synagogue (including at times the teaching of children), the attendant had the sacred duty of handling the revered scroll. After this was replaced in its cabinet or ark, the reader took the customary sitting position for instructive comments on the passage. Luke now makes the first of several comments on the response of the congregation, which is at first intense attention and ultimately hostility.

21 Jesus' comment is brief but of the highest import. We do not know whether he said more than what Luke recorded. But it is not important, for the single sentence recorded is of profound significance. It announces the fulfillment of the reading from Isaiah concerning the subject of the prophecy (Jesus) and the time of God's gracious work ("today"). Since the quotation from Isaiah lacks the phrase about the day of God's wrath, it must be understood that "today" refers only to the part about God's grace.

The term "fulfilled" (*peplērōtai*, GK *4444*) is not as prominent in Luke as in Matthew. Usually it occurs with a unique Lukan meaning (see comments at 7:1). Only here and in the Emmaus conversation (24:44) does Luke use the word in relation to the fulfillment of OT prophecy, and in both cases the Matthean formula "to fulfill what was spoken" is lacking. Thus these two lone references to fulfillment stand out at the beginning and end of Jesus' public appearances and thereby emphasize the fulfillment of God's eternal purpose in the ministry of Christ.

In saying "today this scripture is fulfilled in your hearing," Jesus identifies himself as the subject of

Isaiah's prophetic word. As such he is (1) the bearer of the Spirit (v.18); (2) the eschatological prophet, the proclaimer of the "good news"; and (3) the one who brings release to the oppressed (a messianic function). His role as Suffering Servant is not specified here, but an association may be assumed on the basis of the place of Isaiah 61 among the Servant passages.

We have already observed Luke's frequent mention of the Holy Spirit in Jesus' life (see comments at 4:14). Now we see that Jesus' ministry will be uniquely marked by the presence of the Spirit as prophetically foretold.

His role as eschatological prophet is intertwined with that of John the Baptist as prophetic forerunner (for the sense in which John was a prophet and was characterized by the spirit of Elijah, see comments at 1:17; 7:24–28). Jesus, however, not John, was *the* prophet predicted in Deuteronomy 18:18 (cf. Jn 1:19–24, esp. v.21). Luke gives special attention to Jesus as a prophet in a number of ways. Among them are sayings of Jesus not found in other gospels (4:24; 13:33) and comments by others (7:16, 39; 9:8, 19; 24:19 [only in Luke]; 39; see also Ac 3:22; 7:37, 52). In the present passage the prophetic mission described by Isaiah (a mission of proclamation) is accepted by Jesus.

The prophetic role of Jesus overlaps with his role as Messiah (cf. discussion in Marshall, *Luke: Historian and Theologian*, 124–28). His ministry of deliverance is messianic in character. This assumption probably lay behind the doubts in John's mind when release from prison was not forthcoming (7:18–19).

In summary, Luke presents the quotation from Isaiah and Jesus' ensuing comments as a programmatic statement of Jesus' (and the apostles') ministry. As prophet and Messiah, he will minister to the social outcasts and needy, including Gentiles, in the power of the Spirit.

22 The audience's response to Jesus' comment on Isaiah's words has been variously interpreted. Most expositors take *emartyroun autō* ("bore him witness," GK *3455*) as implying a positive attitude toward what he had said; hence the NIV's "spoke well of him." The same verb is used in Acts 22:12 of Ananias, where the NIV has "highly respected." But J. Jeremias (*Jesus' Promise to the Nations* [SBT; London: SCM, 1958], 44–45) takes it in a negative sense, as he does the statement in v.20b, assuming that hostility against Jesus began when he did not refer to the day of God's judgment (see, however, Gabriel K. S. Shin, *Die Ausrufung des endgültigen Jubeljahres durch Jesus in Nazareth* [Bern: Lang, 1989], 197–204).

The ambiguous nature of the passage continues with *ethaumazon* ("were amazed," GK *3455*), which does not indicate clearly either favor or disfavor. The cause of the people's amazement was Jesus' "gracious words" (*hoi logoi tēs charitos*). This phrase may refer to the kind and wise manner of his speech or of what he said about the grace of God. A near parallel in Acts 14:3 suggests the latter, but there it is "word" (*ho logos*, singular, i.e., "message") of grace, which is closer to the phrase "the gospel of God's grace" in Acts 20:24. The word "grace" is also used in the sense of "power" in Luke–Acts (cf. Ac 6:8), and the reaction of the audience may therefore be caused by the power of Jesus' message (cf. John Nolland, "Words of Grace [Luke 4:22]," *Bib* 84 [1984]: 44–60).

At some point, here or shortly after, the hostility of the audience begins. Does the question, "Isn't this Joseph's son?" indicate hostility? The question does seem to express perplexity and irritation at this man who grew up in the home of a fellow Nazarene and is now making such impressive claims. The question could be colloquially rendered, "He's Joseph's son, this one, isn't he?"

23 Jesus' response is not intended to reassure his audience but rather to draw out their subconscious attitudes. The future tense in "you will quote" (*ereite*, from *legō*, GK *3306*) might refer to another occasion, especially if we assume that Jesus has not yet preached in Capernaum. Yet this incident might be the same as that recorded in Matthew 13:53–58 and Mark 6:1–6. Both gospels have made prior references to Jesus' preaching in Capernaum. Matthew 4:13 says Jesus lived there, and Mark 1:21–28 tells of his teaching and popularity there. It is not necessary, however, to go to the other gospels for support; Luke himself records an apparently extensive and popular ministry in Galilee prior to this time (4:14–15). It would be strange if this had not included Capernaum. It is, therefore, more likely that Jesus is expressing the reply he would expect the people to make in response to his message in the synagogue—namely, that they would challenge him to fulfill Isaiah's prophecy by doing miracles in the presence of those who heard him. Throughout his ministry Jesus would be challenged to do miraculous signs to prove his claims (e.g., 11:16, 29).

The distinction between the "hometown" (i.e., Nazareth) and "Capernaum" prepares for the distinction between native and foreign lands in v.24. This distinction is later widened into one between Jews and Gentiles (cf. vv.25–27).

24 "I tell you the truth" (*amēn* [GK *297*] *legō hymin*) is used six times in Luke to introduce a solemn assertion. This expression shows the authority with which Jesus spoke and is clearly an authentic word of Jesus. This introductory formula with the Greek word for "amen" appears often in Mark and even more frequently in Matthew, especially in the material unique to that gospel. Luke includes a few other quotations in which he changes the "amen" to its equivalent in idiomatic Greek, most notably in 9:27: *legō de hymin alēthōs* (GK *242*; "I tell you the truth").

Here the statement so solemnly introduced anticipates Jesus' rejection. It sees him as a prophet

and may be a variation of the saying found in Matthew 13:57 and Mark 6:4. The difference is in the sentence structure and in Luke's use of the word "accepted" (*dektos*, GK *1283*), the same adjective used in v.19 ("favor") to describe the year of the Lord. The double use of this word in this context may be intended to show that though God desires to accept the people, they do not respond by accepting the prophet who tells them of God's grace. The "proverb" (*parabolē*, GK *4130*, v.23) itself is apparently a version of a common adage making the point that whoever achieves greatness is never fully trusted back home. But here its meaning is the deeper one that Jesus stands in the line of the prophets who were rejected by their own people.

25–27 These verses are introduced by Jesus' saying, "I assure you," a phrase very similar to the "amen" formula in v.24. The examples come from 1 Kings 17:8–24 and 2 Kings 5:1–19. Observe that Jesus does not state here that the prophets Elijah and Elisha went to Gentiles because they were rejected by the Jews; rather, they went because they were sent there by God. Jesus' audience is becoming more and more enraged as they realize that they will receive no special favors from him and that he considers himself above home ties and traditions. (For the significance of Elijah and Elisha in Luke–Acts, see Brodie, *Luke the Literary Interpreter*.)

Together with v.24, these verses provide significant qualifications for the jubilant message in Isaiah 61: (1) the good news may not be acceptable to God's people (v.24); and (2) the good news will not be limited to the physical Israel (vv.25–27). Both of these themes can already be found in Isaiah.

29–30 Nazareth lay among the ridges of the southern slopes of the Galilean hills. Jesus allowed the crowds to drive him out of the town (as he later did on going to the place of crucifixion). But it was not yet his time to die, and by some unexplained means he made his way out (v.30).

NOTES

16–30 The location of this narrative in Luke has been a major problem of critical scholarship. If the similar incident recorded in Matthew 13:53–58 and Mark 6:1–6 is actually a different and later occurrence, several questions arise. Did the same sort of event take place twice? It would seem strange that Jesus would return a second time and meet a similarly incredulous response, as though no such incident had occurred before. Yet even though it may seem improbable, it is not for us to judge it impossible. Also, the wording in Matthew and Mark, including most of the dialogue portion, is almost totally different from that in Luke (note another variation in Jn 6:42).

Nevertheless, a case may be made for the same incident's description in all three of the Synoptics. If so, Luke has simply placed it earlier in his narrative. It may be, as is often suggested, that he had theological reasons for placing it early, namely, in order to show the progression of the gospel from Jewish environs to the Gentile world and Rome (at the end of Acts). Luke emphasizes this progression by featuring here the statements about the extent of God's grace to the Gentiles. On the other hand, the order may reflect Luke's care in following a source or combination of sources in which this incident did in fact stand at the beginning of Jesus' ministry. This explanation is congruous with the remarkable fact that not only Mark but even Matthew, who is so interested in the fulfillment theme, does not include the quotation from Isaiah. If Luke used a source different from those known to Matthew, the whole matter is clarified, and Luke has written "an orderly account" (1:3).

Significant studies of this crucial passage include H. Anderson, "Broadening Horizons: The Rejection at Nazareth Pericope of Luke 4:16–30 in Light of Recent Critical Trends," *Int* 18 (1964): 259–75; D. Hill, "The Rejection of Jesus at Nazareth," *NovT* 13 (1971): 161–80; Robert Sloan, *The Favorable Year of the Lord* (Austin, Tex.: Schola Press, 1977; cf. n. 59); Christopher M. Tuckett, "Luke 4:16–30, Isaiah and Q," in *Logia: Les Paroles de Jésus—The Sayings of Jesus* [ed. Delobel], 343–54; Christopher J. Schreck, "The Nazareth Pericope: Luke 4.16–30 in Recent Study," in *L'Evangile de Luc—The Gospel of Luke*, ed. Frans Neirynck (Leuven: Leuven Univ. Press, 1989), 399–471; Jeffrey S. Siker, "'First to the Gentiles': A Literary Analysis of Luke 4:16–30," *JBL* 111 (1992): 73–90. (See also the studies by Chilton and Shin, noted above.) On the Isaiah quotation itself and its use by Jesus, see J. A. Sanders, "From Isaiah 61 to Luke 4," in *Christianity, Judaism and Other Greco-Roman Cults*, ed. J. Neusner (Leiden: Brill, 1975), 1:75–106; Pao, 70–84.

16 The phrase ἀνέστη ἀναγνῶναι (*anestē anagnōnai*, "he stood up to read") shows the synagogal custom of standing to read Scripture and sitting to preach. The first reading, following the Shema—"Hear, O Israel . . . " (Dt 6:4)—and prayers, was of the passage for the day from the lectionary (selected verses of Bible readings) of the Pentateuch. The second reading was from the Prophets. The choice of the passage may have still been up to the reader in Jesus' day. For a discussion of the description of synagogal worship in Luke and our knowledge of pre–AD 70 synagogues, see R. E. Oster, "Supposed Anachronism in Luke–Acts' Use of συναγωγή," *NTS* 39 (1993): 178–208.

18 The verb ἔχρισεν (*echrisen*, "anointed"; from χρίω, *chriō*, GK *5987*) designates appointment to the messianic mission and possibly refers to Jesus' baptism (3:22–23); εὐαγγελίσασθαι (*euangelisasthai*, "preach," GK *2294*) is a significant word in Luke (already found in 1:19; 2:10; 3:18), while ἀπέσταλκεν (*apestalken*, "sent") is from ἀποστέλλω (*apostellō*, GK *690*), commonly used in relation to sending someone on a mission. It could refer, as in John 3:17 and elsewhere in John, to the Father's sending of Jesus into the world.

19 The phrase ἐνιαυτὸν κυρίου δεκτόν (*eniauton kyriou dekton*) is literally the "acceptable" (RSV) or "favorable" (NASB) "year of the Lord." The NIV both expresses the meaning here and follows the Hebrew text (cf. Isa 61:2). Luke's text follows the LXX.

20 The verb ἀτενίζω (*atenizō*, "fasten on," GK *867*), in the phrase οἱ ὀφθαλμοὶ ἦσαν ἀτενίζοντες αὐτῷ (*hoi ophthalmoi ēsan atenizontes autō*, "the eyes . . . were fastened on him"), is used once more in Luke (22:56) and ten times in Acts. It is usually found in situations of extreme emotion, e.g., of those watching the ascension of Christ (Ac 1:10), and of Stephen's looking into heaven just before his martyrdom (Ac 7:55). It also can connote hostility (Ac 13:9). In a somewhat parallel situation, the Sanhedrin "looked intently" at Stephen at the beginning of his trial, "and they saw that his face was like the face of an angel" (Ac 6:15). Here (v.20), since no hostility to Jesus has yet been expressed, we cannot take ἀτενίζοντες, *atenizontes*, as meaning more than intense anticipation of how Jesus will interpret the passage from Isaiah.

21 The NIV omits ἤρξατο λέγειν (*ērxato legein*, "began to say"). It may be "simply a case of redundant usage," but more likely "what follows is the arresting opening of a sermon, so that the use of the verb is justified" (Marshall, 184–85).

The adverb σήμερον (*sēmeron*, "today," GK *4958*) occurs relatively frequently in Luke (2:11; 5:26; 12:28; 13:32–33; 19:5, 9; 22:34, 61; 23:43) and nine times in Acts. Its use is consistent with Luke's interest in the presence of the kingdom and in the time of salvation.

23 For the ancient literary parallels to the proverb and the different readings these parallels suggest, see John Nolland, "Classical and Rabbinic Parallels to 'Physician, Heal Yourself' (Lk. IV.23)," *NovT* 21 (1979): 193–209; Sijbolt J. Noorda, "'Cure Yourself, Doctor!' (Luke 4:23): Classical Parallels to an Alleged Saying of Jesus," in J. Delobel, *Logia: Les Paroles de Jésus—The Sayings of Jesus* (BETL 59; Leuven: Leuven Univ. Press, 1982), 459–67.

2. Driving Out an Evil Spirit (4:31–37)

OVERVIEW

The incident Luke relates here about the driving out of an evil spirit is perhaps more striking than the parallel (Mk 1:21–34) because it exemplifies the liberating work described in the preceding quotation from Isaiah (vv.18–19).

> ³¹Then he went down to Capernaum, a town in Galilee, and on the Sabbath began to teach the people. ³²They were amazed at his teaching, because his message had authority.
> ³³In the synagogue there was a man possessed by a demon, an evil spirit. He cried out at the top of his voice, ³⁴"Ha! What do you want with us, Jesus of Nazareth? Have you come to destroy us? I know who you are—the Holy One of God!"

35"Be quiet!" Jesus said sternly. "Come out of him!" Then the demon threw the man down before them all and came out without injuring him.

36All the people were amazed and said to each other, "What is this teaching? With authority and power he gives orders to evil spirits and they come out!" 37And the news about him spread throughout the surrounding area.

COMMENTARY

31 Luke has already mentioned Capernaum (v.23) as a center of miraculous activity in the ministry of Jesus. Capernaum was on the northwest shore of the Sea of Galilee. Luke adds a geographical note for Gentile readers. The ruins of a later (probably third-century) synagogue may be seen today in that vicinity. The expression "went down" reflects the descent necessary from the elevated situation of Nazareth to the coastal plain.

The implication of the imperfect periphrastic *ēn didaskōn* ("was teaching") may be that it was Jesus' custom to attend the synagogue (v.33) and to teach there. Though the plural *tois sabbasin* can have a singular meaning (NIV, "on the Sabbath"), as it does in the Markan parallel (Mk 1:21), if it has a plural meaning here in Luke it would support the possibility that the imperfect implies repeated action. This would be true to the pattern Jesus had established. It is more likely, however, that the imperfect means he was "just in the process of teaching" (NIV, "began to teach") when the demon-possessed man interrupted him.

32 The reaction of the people, though comparable to that in the preceding incident (vv.20–22), differs from it in one important aspect. Now they are astonished that this teacher, who in their eyes was not even a rabbi, taught with "authority." The contrast is sharpened in Mark 1:22 by the additional words "not as the teachers of the law." The majority of rabbis would base their teaching on the chain of tradition, citing the opinions of their predecessors. By omitting this specific comparison, Luke may simply be deferring to his Gentile readers, who would perhaps not be as aware of rabbinical custom as Jewish readers. But it may also be that Luke is emphasizing the absolute authority of Jesus. In support of this possibility is Luke's use of the word "message" (*logos*, lit., "word," GK *3364*; for the importance of the "word" in Luke, see comments at 1:1–4). Keeping in mind that the parallel passage in Mark does not use "word" but says "he taught them," Luke would seem to be emphasizing the "authority" of Jesus' "word" (cf. v.36).

In the following verses, we learn that the authority of Jesus is related not only to his teaching (v.32; cf. v.22) but also to his powerful deeds (v.36). In terms of teaching, Jesus' authority surpasses that of his contemporaries as he is able to convey directly the will of God. In terms of deeds, Jesus shows that even the evil one is threatened by his presence. Jesus, the One anointed by the "Spirit of the Lord" (v.18), will now challenge the power of the "evil spirit" (v.33).

33 Demon-possession is too frequent and integral to the gospel narratives to minimize or, worse, discard it as Hellenistic superstition. This is only the first mention of it in Luke, the climax of such incidents coming in 11:14–22. Significantly, Jesus is confronted by demonic activity during his first public ministry described by Luke following the introductory sermon at Nazareth. The "good news of the kingdom of God" (v.43) Jesus was proclaiming signaled an attack on the forces of evil. Luke wants us to understand the centrality of the kingdom in Jesus' ministry and in that of his disciples. (See his unique use of the expression "kingdom of God" in such passages as 9:27, 60, 62.) A holy war is being launched and, as v.34 suggests, the demons know it. This war will be carried on by Jesus' disciples (9:1–2; 10:8–9, 17).

The man is possessed by a spirit (v.33) that is "evil" (*akathartou*, "unclean," GK *176*; so NIV text note). Though some would see in the terms "evil" and "unclean" evidence for different kinds of demons, there is little biblical support for this. In 8:2, "evil" spirits are mentioned; several verses later we read simply of a "demon" (8:27), which is said to be "unclean" (8:29, NIV text note). There seems to be no difference, and the NIV uses the same term ("evil") in both cases. An evil spirit is unclean in contrast to the holiness of God and may well cause both moral and physical filth in a possessed human (cf. R. K. Harrison, "Demon, Demoniac, Demonology," *ZPEB* 2:92).

34 The possessed man shrieks and utters an expression of "indignant surprise" (Creed, 70). The word "ha!" is followed by an idiomatic rhetorical question (*ti hēmin kai soi*, "what do you want with us?") that may be rendered, "What do we have to do with each other?" or, loosely, "Why this interference?" (Danker, 61). The demon, perhaps exemplifying James's comment that "the demons believe . . . and shudder" (Jas 2:19), senses the purpose of Jesus' presence. In keeping with the pattern in the Gospels, testimony to the truth about Christ comes from a number of different and unexpected sources.

The term "the Holy One of God" (*ho hagios tou theou*) contrasts strongly with the remark that this was an unclean demon.

35 Jesus responded sternly (see Notes) with a command to be silent. While it is possible that the command simply points to the overwhelming power of Jesus over the demons, this may also be the beginning of a pattern of prohibiting the premature proclamation of his identity. Throughout the Gospels Jesus guards the fact of his messiahship, probably (1) to prevent a misinterpretation that would draw to him revolutionary-minded dissidents seeking a leader against Rome; (2) to allow his messianic works themselves to establish his authority among true believers (cf. 7:18–23); and (3) to avoid an inappropriate self-proclamation as Messiah, especially if there was, as it now appears (cf. Longenecker, 71–74), an understanding that the true Messiah would allow others to proclaim him as such rather than doing so himself. If none of these provide the reason here, Jesus is at least maintaining his authority by silencing the enemy.

What follows is not technically an exorcism, for Jesus does not use an incantation or invoke the authority of another. Instead he speaks a simple word of command on his own authority ("Come out of him!"). Luke, always interested in the physical condition of people, observes that the demon came out violently but without hurting the man.

36 Once again, Luke notes the amazement of the people. The astonishment this time is not only at his "teaching" (*logos*, GK *3364*; see comments at v.32) and "authority" (*exousia*, GK *2026*) but also at his "power" (*dynamis*, GK *1539*).

37 Luke's theme of the spread of the gospel finds expression in the conclusion of the narrative. With this note, one finds the beginning of a period of time when Jesus' fame and popularity grow, even when a hint of opposition is never far away.

NOTES

34 The translation of ἔα (*ea*) as "ha!" (cf. Fitzmyer, 1:545) takes the word as a particle. It is also possible that the word is an imperatival form of ἐάω (*eaō*, GK *1572*), in which case the translation would be, "Let us alone!" (NRSV; cf. Green, 223).

35 The verb ἐπετίμησεν (*epetimēsen*, "said sternly," GK *2203*) is a strong word of rebuke or warning (cf. v.39; 8:24; 9:42; see Notes, v.39). Its appearance in the stories of exorcism may point to a special use of this term (cf. Howard C. Kee, "The Terminology of Mark's Exorcism Stories," *NTS* 14 [1967–68]: 232–46).

3. Healing Many (4:38–44)

³⁸Jesus left the synagogue and went to the home of Simon. Now Simon's mother-in-law was suffering from a high fever, and they asked Jesus to help her. ³⁹So he bent over her and rebuked the fever, and it left her. She got up at once and began to wait on them.

⁴⁰When the sun was setting, the people brought to Jesus all who had various kinds of sickness, and laying his hands on each one, he healed them. ⁴¹Moreover, demons came out of many people, shouting, "You are the Son of God!" But he rebuked them and would not allow them to speak, because they knew he was the Christ.

⁴²At daybreak Jesus went out to a solitary place. The people were looking for him and when they came to where he was, they tried to keep him from leaving them. ⁴³But he said, "I must preach the good news of the kingdom of God to the other towns also, because that is why I was sent." ⁴⁴And he kept on preaching in the synagogues of Judea.

COMMENTARY

38–39 Jesus' healing ministry continues in a more private setting. This account lacks the vivid detail of Mark's, but Luke stresses the miraculous by adding the word "immediately" (*parachrēma*; NIV, "at once," v.39). Luke mentions Simon Peter here without special introduction, though he has not yet described Peter's call. Probably Peter was so well known by Luke's readership that this did not seem abrupt, and the call does follow immediately. Both this passage and 1 Corinthians 9:5 inform us that Peter was married. A crisis of serious illness in the family gives occasion for Jesus to help. The fact that Jesus "rebukes" (see Notes) an impersonal fever, as

he had earlier rebuked the demon, has led some to assume that a personal evil force had caused the fever. If so, one might also suspect this in 8:24. Otherwise either the fever is simply personified in effect, through the use of a vivid verb, or Luke is emphasizing the active force of Jesus' word. The vividness of the scene continues as Jesus bends over the woman; she immediately rises and begins to serve the group.

The fact that Simon's mother-in-law "began to wait on them" immediately after she was healed may also point to her willingness to serve after her experience of grace. The presence of this theme of discipleship is strengthened by a later reference in Luke where the service of Christ becomes the model for believers: "For who is greater, the one who is at the table or the one who serves? Is it not the one who is at the table? But I am among you as one who serves" (22:27; cf. J. H. Schrock, "'I Am Among You As One Who Serves.' Jesus and Food in Luke's Gospel," *Daughters of Sarah* 19 [1993]: 20–23).

40 One of the most beautiful scenes in Scripture now follows. The crowds have apparently waited till evening, after the Sabbath was over. In the remaining hours of diminishing light they perform the labor of love they could not do on the Sabbath, namely, carrying the sick to Jesus. It is noteworthy that Jesus himself has not yet ventured out on the Sabbath to perform healings publicly. This bold action will take place later (6:1–11). Luke carefully distinguishes between those who were simply sick (v.40) and those who were demon-possessed (v.41). This warns us not to assume that the gospel writers believed all disease to be caused by demons. Luke mentions that Jesus laid his hands on the people who came to him—a detail not found in the parallel accounts (Mt 8:16; Mk 1:34). Though the laying on of hands was a common practice in ancient religious acts, here it shows that Jesus is the source of the healing power and that he had a personal concern.

41 Luke is also the only synoptic writer who says at this point that the demons called Jesus the Son of God. As already mentioned (see comments at v.34), the gospel writers show various people testifying to the identity of Christ, including even unbelievers and demons. This provides a broad base for the case the Gospels are establishing. The injunction to silence (v.35) is here amplified. This knowledge of the demons stands in ironic contrast to the ignorance of the crowds.

42–44 Shifting quickly from dusk to dawn, Luke portrays Jesus in a sharply contrasting setting. He is alone (v.42). Surprisingly Luke, in view of his special attention to prayer (cf. 5:16), does not tell us that Jesus is praying, as Mark does (1:35). Luke, however, does express with greater force than does Mark the reason for Jesus' refusal to linger at Capernaum. The difference gives us a clue to one of the dominant themes in Luke. The words "must," "kingdom of God," and "sent" (v.43) are unique to Luke's narrative at this point (see Notes). Along with "preach," these words constitute a programmatic statement of Jesus' mission and also of Luke's understanding of it. Verse 44 emphasizes the continuation of the mission, as Jesus preaches in the synagogues throughout the "land of the Jews" (NIV text note; see Notes).

Here, then, Luke has provided representative incidents from the ministry of Jesus. It is the kind of activity summarized in Acts 10:38 as "doing good and healing all who were under the power of the devil."

NOTES

38 By using the word εὐθύς (*euthys*, "immediately," GK *2317*; NIV, "as soon as"), Mark (1:29) connects this incident more closely with the synagogue incident than does Luke, but the implication in Luke is also that it occurs on the same Sabbath day. Luke's use of πυρετῷ μεγάλῳ (*pyreto megalo*, "high fever," GK *4790, 3489*) shows that he follows the ancient medical custom in distinguishing levels of fever.

39 The phrase ἐπιστὰς ἐπάνω αὐτῆς (*epistas epano autes*, lit., "standing above her") may be better understood in the light of Jewish context. J. Duncan M. Derrett ("Getting on Top of a Demon [Luke 4:39]," *EvQ* 65 [1993]: 99–109) suggests that in Jewish conceptions impurity moves vertically, and Jesus' standing above Simon's mother-in-law simply points to his encountering and defeating the disease. Whether Luke did have this particular context in mind is unclear, however.

"In [the] NT ἐπιτιμάω [epitimaō, GK 2203] has no other meaning than 'rebuke'" (Plummer, 134; see Notes, v.35). It is a "prerogative of Jesus in the Gospels . . . which declares His position as the Lord. . . . He is also Lord over the demons and bends them to do His will" (TDNT 2:625–26). This being the case, some believe that here and in Luke 8:24 (cf. Mt 8:26; Mk 4:39) there must be demonic influence behind fever and storm. In this case, one may have to distinguish the metaphorical use of language and a deeper reading that reflects the ancient understanding of reality.

The adverb παραχρῆμα (parachrēma, "at once," GK 4202) is one of Luke's favorite words, though he does not use it as frequently as Mark does εὐθύς (euthys, "at once," "without delay," GK 2317; see Notes, v.38). In Luke παραχρῆμα, parachrēma, contributes to the sense of urgency (see next note).

43 The word δεῖ (dei, "must," GK 1256) conveys a strong sense of urgency. Two-thirds of its occurrences in the Synoptics are in Luke—most of these in the material unique to this gospel and the others added by Luke as he edited his work. While the number of occurrences is not great, the proportion is statistically significant and the particular applications are striking. Among the significant examples of its use are 2:49; 13:33; 22:37; 24:7, 26 ("have to"), 44 (cf. Charles H. Cosgrove, "The Divine Dei in Luke–Acts: Investigations into the Lukan Understanding of God's Providence," NovT 26 [1984]: 168–90).

Luke's distinctive stress on the sovereign purpose of God and the relationship of that to Jesus' mission appears also in Luke's use of ἀποστέλλω (apostellō, "send," GK 690). Luke uses it only slightly more times than Mark, but it has greater significance in Luke because of the way he introduces it into the narratives. The present passage is an example of this, because where Mark 1:38 has ἐξῆλθον (exēlthon, "have come"), Luke has the stronger ἀπεστάλην (apestalēn, "was sent").

The phrase τὴν βασιλείαν τοῦ θεοῦ (tēn basileian [GK 993] tou theou, "the kingdom of God") represents a major topic in Jesus' teaching and in Luke's presentation of that teaching. Several passages summarizing Jesus' ministry and that of his disciples specify that the kingdom is the core of Jesus' message (e.g., 8:1; 9:2; cf. 9:62; 10:9; 16:16). The occurrences of the term in Matthew and the proportion of occurrences in his work are even greater than in Luke. For a full study of the kingdom in Jesus' teaching, see G. E. Ladd, *The Presence of the Future* (Grand Rapids: Eerdmans, 1974).

44 The Greek τῆς Ἰουδαίας (tēs Ioudaias, "of Judea") is a difficult reading since Luke is clearly describing Jesus' Galilean ministry. For that very reason early copyists of the NT seem to have welcomed alternative possibilities: τῆς Γαλιλαίας (tēs Galilaias, "of Galilee"), in conformity with Mark 1:39 and Matthew 4:23, and τῶν Ἰουδαίων (tōn Ioudaiōn, "of the Jews"). By using a slight paraphrase, "the land of the Jews," the text note in the NIV has conveyed what is probably Luke's intention. The word "land" is the traditional word for all of Palestine, the home of the Jews. In Luke's mind, Judea may have had the same significance. Marshall, 199, notes that it is not correct to draw a sharp distinction between "the two parts of Jesus' ministry" (i.e., Galilee and Judea), for "v.43 indicates that Jesus' ministry is directed to the Jews as a whole; the point is theological rather than geographical."

4. Calling the First Disciples (5:1–11)

OVERVIEW

This narrative is similar in certain details to Matthew 4:19–22 and Mark 1:16–20. Luke's account is much fuller, containing the unique encounter between Jesus and Peter. The climax of each account is a call to "catch men" and the obedience of the disciples. Luke lacks the specific command, "Follow me." The sequence in which this account occurs in Luke is different from that in Mark, who records the call in 1:16–20—before the incidents in Capernaum (1:21–28), which Luke put just prior to the present narrative (4:31–41).

Naturally, these similarities and differences have led scholars to different conclusions about the relationship of the two accounts and the history of the tradition behind them. In light of Luke's method of focusing on individuals as a means of their drawing attention to Jesus, we can understand the placement and character of the narrative (cf. G. N. Stanton, *Jesus of Nazareth in New Testament Preaching* [Cambridge: Cambridge Univ. Press, 1974], 20, 59). Though Jesus might have called the disciples several times (one such calling having already taken place, according to Jn 1:35–51), to attempt a harmonization by defining the Lukan narrative and that in Matthew and Mark as separate incidents is unnecessary. Luke focuses on Peter, shows the sovereignty and holiness of Jesus in a way Matthew and Mark do not, and alone mentions the total abandonment of the disciples' possessions as an act of discipleship (cf. 14:33).

The difference in placement is likewise understandable. None of the Synoptics tie the incident into a strict chronological sequence; so the placement is flexible. Luke first establishes the program of Jesus' ministry (4:16–30, 43). Now he is ready to establish the sovereign lordship of Christ in his relationship first with Peter as representative of the disciples and then with the social outcasts and "sinners" he has come to save (5:32; 19:10), such as the man with leprosy (5:12–15) and Levi also (5:27–32).

Elements of this narrative also resemble the post-resurrection story in John 21:1–14. Scholars do not agree about the relation between the traditions represented in the two passages (see Creed, 73–74; Marshall, 199–200; R. E. Brown, *The Gospel According to John XIII–XXI* [AB 29A; Garden City, N.J.: Doubleday 1970], 1089–92). Johannine issues aside, the Lukan narrative is coherent and natural in its context. Arguments for an originally post-resurrection setting for Luke's tradition are unconvincing. Moreover, as S. O. Abogunrin ("The Three Variant Accounts of Peter's Call: A Critical and Theological Examination of the Texts," *NTS* 31 [1985]: 592–93) has rightly noted, "the differences between the accounts are more striking than the similarities."

¹One day as Jesus was standing by the Lake of Gennesaret, with the people crowding around him and listening to the word of God, ²he saw at the water's edge two boats, left there by the fishermen, who were washing their nets. ³He got into one of the boats, the one belonging to Simon, and asked him to put out a little from shore. Then he sat down and taught the people from the boat.

⁴When he had finished speaking, he said to Simon, "Put out into deep water, and let down the nets for a catch."

⁵Simon answered, "Master, we've worked hard all night and haven't caught anything. But because you say so, I will let down the nets."

⁶When they had done so, they caught such a large number of fish that their nets began to break. ⁷So they signaled their partners in the other boat to come and help them, and they came and filled both boats so full that they began to sink.

⁸When Simon Peter saw this, he fell at Jesus' knees and said, "Go away from me, Lord; I am a sinful man!" ⁹For he and all his companions were astonished at the catch of fish they had taken, ¹⁰and so were James and John, the sons of Zebedee, Simon's partners.

Then Jesus said to Simon, "Don't be afraid; from now on you will catch men." ¹¹So they pulled their boats up on shore, left everything and followed him.

COMMENTARY

1 "One day" represents the simple *egeneto* ("it happened [that]"; KJV, "it came to pass"). It does not indicate a specific chronological sequence. The geographical description is more precise: "lake" is used instead of the word "sea." Luke mentions the pressure of the crowds, as he occasionally does elsewhere (8:42, 45; 19:3). Their attention is on the "word of God"—another instance of Luke's focus on the "word" (cf. 4:32, 36; "message," "teaching"). The shore of the lake provided an excellent, acoustically serviceable amphitheater.

2–3 Luke, being observant of detail, draws our attention to two boats. Next he singles out Simon as the owner of one of them (v.3). The description in v.2 along with the comment in v.5 serve to emphasize the futility of the night's work. Luke is careful to mention that Jesus again teaches—now from the boat, from which his voice would carry across the water to the crowd. Not even the next event, miraculous as it is, may in Luke's narrative be allowed to direct attention away from Jesus' teaching ministry.

The mention of Simon first reflects the primacy of this apostle in history and in the memory of the early Christians. The obedient response of Simon also symbolizes the first positive response of one who will be the leader of Jesus' disciples (cf. Bock, 1:455).

4–5 The sharp contrast between the expert-but-unsuccessful fisherman and Jesus needs no comment. Jesus' command (v.4) must have seemed unreasonable to them after their failure during the night (v.5). Peter, here called by his old name, Simon, demurs; but he does what Jesus says.

Unlike other miracles of provision, this story does not focus on God's provision for the physical needs of the people. This miracle story is transformed into a parable that Jesus uses to explain the call to the work of the kingdom (cf. Jacques Geninasca, "To Fish/To Preach: Narrative and Metaphor [Luke 5:1–11]," in *Signs and Parables* [Pittsburgh, Pa.: Pickwick, 1978], 185–222).

6–10a Luke now moves quickly to three focal points in his narrative. He first describes the gathering of the fish (v.6). This extraordinary happening is similar to that in John 21 (cf. also Jesus' uncanny ability to direct Peter to a fish with a coin in its mouth

[Mt 17:24–27]). The details of the breaking nets and loaded boats (v.7) help give the narrative the ring of truth.

Second, the miracle moves Peter (whom Luke now designates by his full name, Simon Peter, probably signifying a new stage in his relationship with Jesus), who is overcome by awe (v.9), to abase himself before Jesus (v.8). He now calls Jesus "Lord" (*kyrios*, GK *3261*), with a greater depth of meaning than the common "Sir." Peter is gripped not merely by a sense of his inferiority but of his own sinfulness (though the two cannot be strictly separated, since the reference here may not be referring to Peter's individual moral failings but to his utter unworthiness as a human being in the presence of a holy and pure God). The experience of Isaiah 6:5 comes to mind, but Peter needs no such vision; he is face-to-face with Jesus. Luke's reason for including this incident may be not only to portray the confrontation of human sinfulness with Jesus but also to show that to receive the saving grace of Christ a "sinful" (*hamartōlos*, GK *283*; see Notes) person must repent. Long before Luke speaks of the Gentiles with their gross sins and their inclusion in saving grace, we are faced with the realization that even Peter, who in Luke's time was known for his obedience to the Jewish laws, must acknowledge his place as a sinner (cf. Danker, 65). Luke mentions James and John (v.10a), but only in passing; the central figures are Jesus and Peter.

10b The third focal point in the narrative following Peter's obedience to Jesus in letting down the net is Jesus' declaration that he will "catch men" from then on. Here interpretations vary, but in view of Luke's emphasis on God's kindness in reaching out to embrace all humankind, it is more likely to signify a beneficent rather than judgmental ingathering. It presages the widening horizons of both Luke and Acts, culminating in a sense in Peter's visions symbolizing the reception of Gentiles into the church and his subsequent witness to the Gentile Cornelius (Ac 10:9–48, esp. vv.34–35).

11 After the declaration about catching people, the disciples followed Jesus. Luke's observation that they left everything, not stated in Matthew or Mark, underscores the condition of discipleship Jesus taught later on (14:33). Compare also his words to the rich ruler (18:22).

NOTES

5 All seven synoptic occurrences of ἐπιστάτης (*epistatēs*, "Master," GK *2181*) are in Luke. In all but one of these (17:13) it is the disciples who use the title. It is used instead of διδάσκαλος (*didaskalos*, "Teacher," GK *1437*) in 8:24 (cf. Mk 4:38) and 9:49 (cf. Mk 9:38), and instead of "Rabbi" in 9:33 (cf. Mk 9:5). It was a term Luke's readers understood, and it often referred to officers. The transformation of Simon's response in v.8, where Jesus is now called κύριε (*kyrie*, "Lord," GK *3261*), signals the realization of the power (if not the unique status) of Jesus.

8 The Greek ἁμαρτωλός (*hamartōlos*, "sinner," GK *283*) is one of Luke's characteristic words. Of twenty-two occurrences in the Synoptics, fifteen are in Luke, mainly in material unique to his gospel and usually assigned to the "L" source. Luke does not use the term pejoratively but compassionately, as a common term applied to those who were isolated from Jewish religious circles because of their open sin, their unacceptable occupation or lifestyle, or their paganism. Luke shows that these sinners are the objects of God's grace through the ministry of Jesus.

10 The phrase ἀπὸ τοῦ νῦν (*apo tou nyn*, "from now on") is an important indicator of transition in Luke (cf. 22:18 [NIV, "again"], 69; Ac 18:6). "You will catch" (ἔση ζωγρῶν, *esē zōgrōn*, GK *1639, 2436*) is a future periphrastic suggesting continuity of action.

5. The Man with Leprosy (5:12–16)

OVERVIEW

Luke not only presents the gospel of salvation but also supports it with signs and witnesses (though not as prominently as John does). In this section, Jesus performs a miracle that is to be a "testimony" (v.14). By such an act Jesus also challenges the Jewish system of purity as he demonstrates the need to include those who are excluded from the worshiping community of Israel (cf. Hector Avalos, *Health Care and the Rise of Christianity* [Peabody, Mass.: Hendrickson, 1999], 66–71).

> ¹²While Jesus was in one of the towns, a man came along who was covered with leprosy. When he saw Jesus, he fell with his face to the ground and begged him, "Lord, if you are willing, you can make me clean."
>
> ¹³Jesus reached out his hand and touched the man. "I am willing," he said. "Be clean!" And immediately the leprosy left him.
>
> ¹⁴Then Jesus ordered him, "Don't tell anyone, but go, show yourself to the priest and offer the sacrifices that Moses commanded for your cleansing, as a testimony to them."
>
> ¹⁵Yet the news about him spread all the more, so that crowds of people came to hear him and to be healed of their sicknesses. ¹⁶But Jesus often withdrew to lonely places and prayed.

COMMENTARY

12 Leprosy is a general term in Scripture for certain skin diseases. They were not necessarily equivalent to what we know as Hansen's disease. While their interpretation as a type of sin may have been overdrawn by some commentators, such an application is consistent with the nature of such diseases. They were repulsive and resulted in the physical, social, and psychological isolation of their victims (cf. Lev 13, esp. v.45).

Luke is once again careful to note the nature and extent of a disease ("covered with leprosy"). The assumption is that the man has some knowledge of Jesus' prior miracles. Just as Peter fell at Jesus' feet in shame at his sinfulness, this man falls face downward in shame at his uncleanness. The disease was of such a nature as to give the impression of filth, and the appeal for cleansing was appropriate to the condition. The appellation "Lord" doubtless has less meaning than it does on Peter's lips (v.8) and here means no more than "Sir." The condition "if you are willing" may express a sense of unworthiness rather than doubt as to Jesus' ability or kindness.

13 The very act of touching is significant, especially since lepers were always kept at a distance. Later Jesus touched a coffin (7:14)—an act ritually prohibited. Perhaps our contemporary society, having rediscovered the significance of touching as a means of communicating concern, can identify to an extent with Jesus' kindness in touching the leper. Such contact also symbolized the transfer of healing power (cf. being touched by a suppliant, 8:44). Jesus' "I am willing" meets the man's need of reassurance, just as his "don't be afraid" reassured Peter (v.10). Luke notes that the healing was accomplished "immediately" (*eutheōs* [GK 2311], more common in Mark).

14 The command to silence follows the pattern noted above in 4:41. Jesus wanted first to do the works of the Messiah and to fulfill his basic mission of sacrificial suffering before being publicly proclaimed as Messiah. The healing of lepers is one of the messianic signs of which the imprisoned John the Baptist was reminded (7:22). Also, as has often

been observed, the crowds could all too easily apply to Jesus their commonly held view of the Messiah as a military or political liberator.

For the cleansed leper to show himself to the priest was essential. One reason often suggested is that Jesus wanted to observe the ritual prescribed in Leviticus 14. (In 17:14 he gives the same command.) Here, however, something further is involved: the messianic act of healing was to be "as a testimony to them" (see comments at 7:21–23). Ironically, in complying with the Jewish cultic requirements Jesus is in a sense showing how he surpasses this system by making it clear that a new era has now dawned for God's people.

15–16 If the command to silence is part of a pattern in the Gospels, so is the failure to obey it. The immediate effect of the healing is Jesus' increased popularity. Though this popularity leads others to come and be healed (v.15), Jesus is forced to withdraw in order to seek quiet (v.16). Once again, Luke speaks of Jesus' habit of prayer (see Notes, 3:21). In contrast to his earlier freedom to minister in "the towns" (v.12), Jesus must now make a practice of finding solitude in deserted areas.

NOTES

12 The word ἀνήρ (*anēr*, "man," GK 467) occurs far more often in Luke than in all the other Synoptic Gospels. On leprosy, see *ABD* 4:277–82.

16 "Often" represents an imperfect periphrastic, ἦν ὑποχωρῶν (*ēn hypochōrōn*, lit., "was withdrawing"), suggesting repeated action.

6. Healing a Paralytic (5:17–26)

OVERVIEW

Jesus' activities inevitably brought him into confrontation with the religious authorities. Far from minimizing this, the Gospels actually focus on sev-

eral such occasions. (See, e.g., the Sabbath controversies in ch. 6 and the encounters in ch. 20.) Luke is especially concerned in his gospel and in Acts to clarify the original relationship between Christianity and Judaism and to show the reasons why the gospel had to break out of the confines of Judaism. Here he stresses the authority of Jesus once more. In

4:32 Jesus' teaching was authoritative; 4:36 shows his authority over demons; 5:24 shows his authority to forgive sins.

---

[17]One day as he was teaching, Pharisees and teachers of the law, who had come from every village of Galilee and from Judea and Jerusalem, were sitting there. And the power of the Lord was present for him to heal the sick. [18]Some men came carrying a paralytic on a mat and tried to take him into the house to lay him before Jesus. [19]When they could not find a way to do this because of the crowd, they went up on the roof and lowered him on his mat through the tiles into the middle of the crowd, right in front of Jesus.

[20]When Jesus saw their faith, he said, "Friend, your sins are forgiven."

[21]The Pharisees and the teachers of the law began thinking to themselves, "Who is this fellow who speaks blasphemy? Who can forgive sins but God alone?"

[22]Jesus knew what they were thinking and asked, "Why are you thinking these things in your hearts? [23]Which is easier: to say, 'Your sins are forgiven,' or to say, 'Get up and walk'? [24]But that you may know that the Son of Man has authority on earth to forgive sins...." He said to the paralyzed man, "I tell you, get up, take your mat and go home." [25]Immediately he stood up in front of them, took what he had been lying on and went home praising God. [26]Everyone was amazed and gave praise to God. They were filled with awe and said, "We have seen remarkable things today."

COMMENTARY

17 The opening words, "one day," loosely connect this narrative with the preceding ones. The implication is that Jesus was teaching over a period of some time. Luke mentions, as he often does, the teaching ministry of Jesus. The word "teach" does not occur in this context in Matthew or Mark. While this is not specifically stated, it seems that Jesus' reputation had aroused the attention of the Jewish religious authorities, who considered it important to hear what he was teaching. Whereas Mark (2:6) introduces the scribes (*grammateis*, GK 1208; NIV, "teachers of the law") almost casually later in the narrative, Luke centers attention on them immediately, even specifying that they had

come from as far away as Jerusalem. By doing this, he lays stress on the crucial nature of the religious issues to be raised. This is also Luke's first introduction of the Pharisees and "teachers of the law."

Earlier in their history, the Pharisees had helped the Jews maintain the purity of their religion by teaching how the Mosaic law and the traditions that grew up alongside it ought to be applied in daily life. Many Pharisees became rigid, imbalanced, and hypocritical (cf. comments at 11:37–54). Here Luke introduces them without any comment. The "teachers of the law" were not a religious party, as were the Pharisees, though most of the teachers were also Pharisees. In Luke's narrative they were also related to the elders (9:22) and chief priests (9:22; 19:47; 20:1; 22:2; 23:10). They were respected as having expert knowledge of the details of Jewish legal tradition and so would be expected to form an opinion about the correctness of Jesus' teaching.

As in the previous story, Luke turns from Jesus' teaching ministry to that of healing—a subject of great interest to him. These two elements, doctrine and healing power, climax this narrative. The presence of the Lord's power to heal means that God himself was there.

18 Attention now focuses on a different group— one motivated by earnestness and faith. As in the case of the leper, the paralytic is also an outcast who is not able to participate fully in the worship community of Israel. Here in Luke, Jesus again turns his attention to this outcast in an attempt to redefine ways through which one can approach God.

19 The typical flat roof could be reached by an outside stairway. Roofing materials, whether tiles (as in Luke) or mud thatch (as implied, though not stated, in Mk 2:4; see Notes) were separable without being damaged.

20 Two declarations form the focal point of this narrative, which, because it appears in the gospel in order to provide a context for a pronouncement, may be called a "pronouncement story" (without prejudice to its historicity). The first is a declaration of forgiveness, the second an affirmation of Jesus' authority to make that declaration (v.24).

The plural reference in the term "their faith" is to the four who brought the man, though we may assume from his subsequent forgiveness that he also believed. Jesus' attention to the faith of the man's helpers demonstrates the important fact that God responds to the intercession of others regarding a person in need. This does not imply, of course, that faith that trusts Jesus for salvation can ever be by proxy. Those who brought the paralytic to Jesus believed that Jesus would save him. But the para-

lytic's salvation was an intensely personal matter between Jesus and him. Indeed, we are not even told that he had faith. Jesus chose to heal him; and out of the totality of his need the paralytic looked in faith to Jesus. Perhaps when he did what Jesus asked him to do, that was his declaration of faith in Jesus.

Jesus' declaration of the forgiveness of the paralytic's sin does not imply that sin was the immediate cause of his disease. To be sure, this was commonly assumed even by Jesus' own disciples (Jn 9:2). Though correct theology sees sickness and death as part of the deterioration humankind has suffered because of universal sin, and though some specific ills may be connected with particular sins (1Co 11:29–30), the connection is not explicitly made in this context. More to the point is the Lukan understanding of salvation whereby the entire person is to be restored. This is well expressed in the programmatic statement in Luke 4:16–30.

21 In Jewish law, conviction of blasphemy, which was a capital crime penalized by stoning, had to be based on unmistakable and overt defilement of the divine name. Luke shows that Jesus, with his divine insight, probed the unvoiced thoughts of the Pharisees and teachers of the law, who were convinced that he had arrogated to himself the divine prerogative.

22–23 Without making a point of it, Luke indicates that Jesus exercises extraordinary knowledge (cf. 2:35). In a typical dialogue form of question and counterquestion, the challengers are impaled on the horns of a hypothetical dilemma (v.23; cf. 6:9; 20:3–4, 44). Obviously, while the two sentences are in one sense equally easy to say (and equally impossible to do), in another sense it is easier to say that which cannot be disproved, namely, "your sins are forgiven."

24 The structure of this sentence is broken by the redirecting of Jesus' comments from the leaders to the man. This presents no problem. The form of the sentence is virtually identical in all three Synoptic Gospels, which deliberately retain its irregular structure. Thus a focus is maintained both on Jesus' running controversy with the religious leaders and on his ministry to the paralytic.

Here is the first appearance of the term "Son of Man" in Luke (see Notes). It occurs earlier in the gospel than we might have expected and certainly before the issues of Jesus' identity and titles have been spelled out. Further, it occurs in connection with the right to pronounce forgiveness rather than with the themes of suffering and glory that characterize its specific use in the other passages where it is used. Nevertheless, the appearance of this title in a confrontation story may reflect Luke's intention to highlight the pervasiveness of the opposition to the work of the Messiah.

25–26 The healing validates the declaration of forgiveness. The fulfillment of the command to the paralyzed man is impossible—except by the power of God. To respond took an act of obedience based on faith. The man stood up "immediately" (*parachrēma* [GK *4202*] which appears ten times in Luke out of its twelve occurrences in the Synoptics). The result is the glorification of God (v.25) both by the man and by the crowd (v.26). As already observed (see comments at 2:20), to glorify God is one of Luke's important objectives. This praise is offered by the one who is the object of God's power and by the witnesses of that power.

The onlookers were "amazed" (v.26); Luke uses the same word to describe the response of the crowds to the events at Pentecost, when by God's power the disciples told of his great works (Ac 2:11–12). In this case, the people say that what they have observed is contrary to expectation (*paradoxa* [GK *4141*], from which our word "paradox" is derived; NIV, "remarkable").

The final word in both the Greek and the NIV is "today." Its use in this particular position, at the very end of the passage, strikingly recalls its occurrence as the first word uttered by Jesus after reading the Isaiah passage in Nazareth (4:21). The other gospels do not have the word in this final sentence. By including it here, Luke assures the reader that this indeed is the awaited eschatological "today."

NOTES

17 Literature on the Pharisees is vast. Among the more significant studies are W. D. Davies, *Introduction to Pharisaism* (Philadelphia: Fortress, 1954, 1967); A. Finkel, *The Pharisees and the Teacher of Nazareth* (Leiden: Brill, 1964); Anthony J. Saldarini, *Pharisees, Scribes and Sadducees in Palestinian Society* (Wilmington, Del.: Glazier, 1988). See also E. P. Sanders, *Judaism: Practice and Belief, 63 BCE—66 CE* (Philadelphia: Trinity Press International, 1992), 380–451. On the role of the Pharisees in the Lukan narrative, see John T. Carroll, "Luke's Portrayal of the Pharisees," *CBQ* 50 (1988): 604–21; Jack D. Kingsbury, "The Pharisees in Luke–Acts," in *The Four Gospels*, ed. F. van Segbroeck et al. (Leuven: Leuven Univ. Press, 1992), 2:1497–1512.

Luke thoughtfully avoids the Jewish word γραμματεύς (*grammateus*, "scribes," GK *1208*), using instead νομοδιδάσκαλοι (*nomodidaskaloi*, "legal experts," GK *3791*; NIV, "teachers of the law") for the benefit of his largely Gentile readership (see *TDNT* 1:740–42; 2:159).

19 Much discussion has centered on what is alleged to be a contradiction between Mark, who describes an action suitable to a roof made of thatch held together with mud, and Luke, who uses the word κέραμος (*keramos*, GK *3041*; cf. "ceramic"; NIV, "tile"). But it is wrong to call it a contradiction, for at most Luke is adapting the terminology in order to communicate the scene vividly to those used to tile roofs. Even so, tile was not unknown in Palestine; and Luke's terminology may be even more suitable to the specific nature of the roof than we realize.

20 "Friend" translates ἄνθρωπε (*anthrōpe*, "[O] man," GK *476*)—a surprising use by Luke of a less tender term than that used by Matthew and Mark, namely, τέκνον (*teknon*, "son," GK *5451*; Mt 9:2; Mk 2:5). For the sake of theological precision, it should be noted that Jesus does not say here that *he* forgives sins but that they *are forgiven*. The passive ἀφέωνται (*apheōntai*, "are forgiven") probably suggests that God is the source of forgiveness (cf. 7:48, where, in the only other similar pronouncement, the passive is also used). The premise was correct: only God can forgive sins, but the leaders failed to recognize who stood before them.

24 The phrase ὁ υἱὸς τοῦ ἀνθρώπου (*ho huios tou anthrōpou*, "the Son of Man") is common in the Synoptics and was certainly used often by Jesus. However, many think that its inclusion in this narrative is redactional or the result of the influence of the early church during the history of its tradition. This conclusion is partly based on the assumption that Jesus did not attach to the OT figure of the Son of Man (e.g., Da 7:13), or to himself, the authority to forgive sins. The immense concentration of study on the development of concepts about the Son of Man still leaves enough questions to prevent dogmatism here. But to forgive sins is certainly a legitimate function of an eschatological figure who is concerned with righteous judgment.

There is no textual evidence against the genuineness of this saying, nor does the literary structure of the passage in Luke or Mark require a negative judgment against its appropriation in the passage. Nor does Son of Man here mean "man" in general. It is inconsistent with the rest of the Gospels and NT literature to allow humankind the authority implied in this statement. For helpful surveys, see *TDNT* 8:400–477; I. H. Marshall, "The Synoptic Son of Man Sayings in Recent Discussion," *NTS* 12 (1965–66): 327–51. Other good resources include A. J. B. Higgins, *The Son of Man in the Teaching of Jesus* (SNTSMS 39; New York: Cambridge Univ. Press, 1980); Barnabas Lindars, *Jesus Son of Man: A Fresh Examination of the Son of Man Sayings in the Gospels in the Light of Recent Research* (Grand Rapids: Eerdmans, 1983); Darrell L. Bock, "The Son of Man in Luke 5:24," *BBR* 1 (1991): 109–21; D. R. Burkett, *The Son of Man Debate* (Cambridge: Cambridge Univ. Press, 1999).

7. Calling Levi (5:27–32)

OVERVIEW

The succession of people on whom the Lord bestows his favor continues. We have seen his grace to a demoniac, a leper, and a paralytic; now we see it given to a tax collector. So Jesus liberates those suffering from malign spirits, physical disabilities, and social disfavor. The antagonists—Pharisees and teachers of the law—who were merely named in the preceding narrative, are again on the scene. David Daube (*The New Testament and Rabbinic Judaism* [New York: Arno, 1973], 170) has discerned a pattern here (cf. 4:15–30; 5:17–26; 6:1–11; 11:14–54; 13:10–17; 20:1–8): "(1) Jesus and his disciples perform a revolutionary action, (2) the Pharisees remonstrate with him or, on occasion, merely 'marvel'—and (3) he makes a pronouncement by which they are silenced."

The fact that a "tax collector" is called to follow Jesus shows that the call narratives (see also 5:1–11) and the healing stories in this chapter are intricately related: they point to the center of Jesus' ministry to include those who are excluded and to build up a community that finds its identity in the life and ministry of Jesus.

---

²⁷After this, Jesus went out and saw a tax collector by the name of Levi sitting at his tax booth. "Follow me," Jesus said to him, ²⁸and Levi got up, left everything and followed him.

²⁹Then Levi held a great banquet for Jesus at his house, and a large crowd of tax collectors and others were eating with them. ³⁰But the Pharisees and the teachers of the law who belonged to their sect complained to his disciples, "Why do you eat and drink with tax collectors and 'sinners'?"

³¹Jesus answered them, "It is not the healthy who need a doctor, but the sick. ³²I have not come to call the righteous, but sinners to repentance."

COMMENTARY

27 Levi is identified as Matthew in Matthew 9:9. He was a "tax collector" (see Notes); as such he had incurred the dislike of those who looked on such officials as crooked and serving an unpopular government (see comments at 15:1; 19:2). Levi himself was not a "chief" tax collector, as Zacchaeus was (see Notes; also comments at 3:12); nor is it said that he, like Zacchaeus, was wealthy, but Levi was obviously treated by the Pharisees as a religious outcast.

28 The direct command of Jesus to follow him (v.27) results in Levi's immediate and total obedience—a paradigm of the kind of discipleship Jesus will later specify in detail. Luke notes both the negative aspect (leaving everything) and the positive one (following Jesus) of what Levi did (cf. 9:23–25).

29 A "banquet" in the NT symbolizes joy and often hints at the eschatological banquet, the future celebration of God's people with the patriarchs in the presence of God. In Luke, the meal setting frequently serves as the context in which the community of God's people is defined by Jesus' teaching.

These meal scenes are also understandable in the Greco-Roman context, in which banquets/symposiums defined the boundary of one's circle of association (cf. Dennis E. Smith, "Table Fellowship as a Literary Motif in the Gospel of Luke," *JBL* 106 [1987]: 613–28; see also his *From Symposium to Eucharist: The Banquet in the Early Christian World* [Minneapolis: Fortress, 2003]). In this case, Jesus is the guest of honor; but Levi does not, as might be expected, limit the guest list to his new Christian friends, the disciples of Jesus. Instead of immediately cutting off his old associates, Levi invites them into his home, probably to bring them also into contact with Jesus. Luke mentions "others," who turn out to be "sinners" (v.30) as far as the Pharisees are concerned. The joy of the participants is now opposed by the dour criticism of the religious leaders—a contrast we see running throughout the Gospels.

30 The complaint of the Pharisees, and particularly of those among them who were also scribes, is more than a superficial attempt to find fault. To join in table fellowship with irreligious "sinners" is to cast doubt on one of the essential assumptions of Pharisaic teaching. This sect was dedicated to upholding the purity of Jewish faith and life. Implicit in their teachings was strict adherence to both law and tradition, including necessary rites of purification and separation from all whose moral or ritual purity might be in question. The Galilean people had a reputation (not always deserved) for disdaining such scruples and disregarding the traditions.

The Pharisees' complaint is specifically directed to the act of eating and drinking because table fellowship implied mutual acceptance. No act, apart from participation in the actual sinful deeds of the guests, could have broken the wall of separation more dramatically. Yet the Pharisees are not yet ready to argue with Jesus himself. In the previous incident they did not even express their thoughts openly (v.21). Now they direct their question to Jesus' disciples and also (in Luke only) charge the disciples themselves, not just Jesus, with this unacceptable conduct.

31–32 It is important to recognize that Jesus not only originated proverbs and parables but also made wise use of current ones. So, citing a self-evident proverb of his day (v.31), he described his mission in terms that he would go on to amplify in the parables in ch. 15. Since none are truly "righteous" (v.32; cf. 18:19; Ro 3:23), Jesus used the word here either in a relative sense or with a touch of sarcasm. The prodigal son's older brother, for example, could rightly claim that he had not deserted his father as the prodigal had (15:29). If, therefore, Jesus meant by "righteous" those who are generally loyal or devout, v.32

means that he gave more help to those in greater need. But if, as is more likely, Jesus implied that the Pharisees only thought that they were righteous, the point is that one must first acknowledge oneself to be a sinner before he or she can truly respond to the call to repentance. Luke allows the proverb Jesus quoted to come full circle theologically by including the word "repentance," omitted in Matthew 9:13 and Mark 2:17. With this word Luke introduces a topic of major importance. While the gospel of grace and forgiveness is for everyone (2:10), repentance is a prerequisite to its reception. The tax collector in 18:13–14 met this prerequisite, but not the Pharisee (18:11–12). The Lukan theme of joy is linked with that of repentance in 15:7, 10, 22–27, 32. Repentance was previously mentioned in Luke 3:3, 8, but only in the context of John the Baptist's ministry.

Jesus' use of the proverb may contain an allusion to Ezekiel 34, where the leaders of God's people were accused of failing to take care of their flock since they had not "strengthened the weak or healed the sick or bound up the injured" (34:4; cf. Green, 248). If this allusion can be established, then Jesus is also saying that his Messianic ministry points to the disqualification of the Jewish leaders as the "shepherds" of God's people. This challenge to those in power is effectively issued in this context of table fellowship when the "traditional meal praxis" of the society is overturned (S. Scott Bartchy, "The Historical Jesus and Honor Reversal at the Table," in *The Social Setting of Jesus and the Gospels*, ed. W. Stegemann, B. J. Malina, and G. Theissen [Minneapolis: Fortress, 2002], 175–83).

NOTES

27 "Tax collector," not "publican" (KJV) is the proper translation for τελώνης (telōnēs, GK 5467). The latter comes from the Latin *publicanus*, which was normally applied to chief tax collectors (Gk.

ἀρχιτελώνης, *architelōnēs*, GK *803*), such as Zacchaeus (19:2). Levi is not further mentioned by that name in Luke but is called "Matthew" in 6:15.

30 On the connotation of the word ἁμαρτωλοί (*hamartōloi*, "sinners," GK *283*) in Jesus' day, see *TDNT* 1:327–33. For the specific use of the "sinners" as a narrative character in Luke, see also David A. Neale, *None but the Sinners: Religious Categories in the Gospel of Luke* (JSNTSup 58; Sheffield: JSOT Press, 1991).

8. The Question about Fasting (5:33–39)

OVERVIEW

In all three Synoptic Gospels the issues related to Levi's banquet lead to further questions about religious practices. From Jesus' mention of fasting and prayer, along with almsgiving as "acts of righteousness" in the Sermon on the Mount (Mt 6:1–18), we know that these practices were considered significant indications of religious devotion. In contrast to the two previous incidents (vv.21, 30), this time the leaders challenge Jesus directly.

³³They said to him, "John's disciples often fast and pray, and so do the disciples of the Pharisees, but yours go on eating and drinking." ³⁴Jesus answered, "Can you make the guests of the bridegroom fast while he is with them? ³⁵But the time will come when the bridegroom will be taken from them; in those days they will fast." ³⁶He told them this parable: "No one tears a patch from a new garment and sews it on an old one. If he does, he will have torn the new garment, and the patch from the new will not match the old. ³⁷And no one pours new wine into old wineskins. If he does, the new wine will burst the skins, the wine will run out and the wineskins will be ruined. ³⁸No, new wine must be poured into new wineskins. ³⁹And no one after drinking old wine wants the new, for he says, 'The old is better.'"

COMMENTARY

33 The question, which is stated as a fact, not a query, is cleverly expressed. First, the Pharisees and the disciples of John the Baptist, who were assumed to be particularly sympathetic to Jesus, are lined up against Jesus' disciples, who are thus made to appear out of step. Second, there is a hint that Jesus' disciples were neglecting the important duty of prayer. Again Jesus himself is not criticized directly but through his disciples. Fasting was actually only prescribed for one day in the year but was practiced as a religious exercise more often—twice a week by the Pharisees (cf. 18:12). The disciples are now criticized not only for eating with sinners but also for leading a lifestyle that seems to be in contrast to proper religious decorum.

34-35 Jesus' answer is so remarkable that many have assumed that the saying in v.35 must not be an authentic prophecy but a reflection of the church after Jesus' death. The first part of the saying is clear (v.34). Jesus compares the situation to a wedding, which naturally calls for joy (cf. Eph 5:25-33; Rev 19:6-9; there the image of the bridegroom is treated in-depth). But to think at a wedding of the possibility of the groom's death is highly unusual. The allusion is so abrupt that we cannot ignore it. Neither can we ignore the fact that Jesus anticipated his rejection and death at the hands of his enemies.

Jesus' response assumes that the audience is aware of the conditions when fasting is needed. First, fasting reflects a condition of dissatisfaction, if not grief. The presence of the time of eschatological joy eliminates the need to fast (cf. 2:10). Second, fasting can also reflect one's sense of guilt with an assumption that forgiveness is possible. When Jesus, the one who delivers the gospel of divine forgiveness (cf. 5:17-26), is present, one encounters the immediate presence of divine grace.

36 The context provides for Jesus an opportunity to state a basic principle in a series of parabolic figures. His mission involved a radical break with common religious practices. Jesus neither affirms nor denies the value of fasting, and he does not mention prayer here at all; rather, he teaches that he has not come merely to add devotional routines to those already practiced, for what he brings is not a patch but a whole new garment. Merely to "patch things up"—i.e., to have a dinner celebration in place of fasting—would fail for two reasons. First, it would ruin the rest of the new garment from which it is taken, and second, just one new patch will not help preserve the old garment but will in fact be conspicuously incongruous. The form of the saying in Luke carries the image beyond the way Matthew and Mark state it.

37-38 The second illustration has a slightly different connotation—namely, Jesus' teaching is like fermenting wine that seems almost to have inherent vigor and cannot be contained within an old rigid system. Later on, Jesus will speak of a new covenant (22:20), which is indeed new and not merely an improved extension of the old.

39 Jesus is not reversing himself and saying that his new teaching is not as good as the old that it replaces. The point emphasized is that people tend to want the old and reject the new, assuming (wrongly in this case) that the old is better. With this verse, the discrepancy between the announcement of the kingdom and its reception is again noted (cf. Arthur H. Mead, "Old and New Wine: St. Luke 5:39," *ExpTim* 99 [1988]: 234-35).

NOTES

33 Fasting in the OT is concerned more with the interaction between God and human beings than the ascetic interest in the treatment of the body. For the gospel writers, what is emphasized is the arrival of the eschatological banquet: "Jesus is a living symbol of plenty, just as the kingdom of God itself is the advent of the abundant harvest" (Mary Ann Tolbert, "Asceticism and Mark's Gospel," in *Asceticism and the New Testament*, ed. L. E. Vaage and V. L. Wimbus [New York: Routledge, 1999], 40). For a survey of the practices of fasting in the Jewish traditions, see *ABD* 2:773-76.

9. Sabbath Controversies (6:1–11)

OVERVIEW

The uneasy tension between Jesus and the Pharisees described in ch. 5 hardens into controversy over one of the main institutions of Judaism, the Sabbath. The Gospels list three Sabbath controversies. Two occur in the Synoptics and one in John 5. In each instance, Jesus allows or even stimulates the controversy, providing several types of response: (1) the Sabbath is for people's benefit (Mk 2:27); (2) the Son of Man is "Lord of the Sabbath" (v.5); (3) the Sabbath is for helpful deeds, the omission of which would be evil (v.9); and (4) the Father works even on the Sabbath and so may the Son (Jn 5:17).

Keeping the Sabbath provided an appropriate issue for debate because it (1) had roots both in the creation account and in the Ten Commandments, (2) involved every seventh day and consequently called for many decisions about what was permitted or forbidden on that day, (3) consequently became the subject of two tractates in the Mishnah (*Šabbat* and *Eruvin*), (4) afforded a public disclosure of one's observance or nonobservance of the day, and therefore (5) became one of the prominent identity markers for God's faithful people.

[1]One Sabbath Jesus was going through the grainfields, and his disciples began to pick some heads of grain, rub them in their hands and eat the kernels. [2]Some of the Pharisees asked, "Why are you doing what is unlawful on the Sabbath?"

[3]Jesus answered them, "Have you never read what David did when he and his companions were hungry? [4]He entered the house of God, and taking the consecrated bread, he ate what is lawful only for priests to eat. And he also gave some to his companions." [5]Then Jesus said to them, "The Son of Man is Lord of the Sabbath."

[6]On another Sabbath he went into the synagogue and was teaching, and a man was there whose right hand was shriveled. [7]The Pharisees and the teachers of the law were looking for a reason to accuse Jesus, so they watched him closely to see if he would heal on the Sabbath. [8]But Jesus knew what they were thinking and said to the man with the shriveled hand, "Get up and stand in front of everyone." So he got up and stood there.

[9]Then Jesus said to them, "I ask you, which is lawful on the Sabbath: to do good or to do evil, to save life or to destroy it?"

[10]He looked around at them all, and then said to the man, "Stretch out your hand." He did so, and his hand was completely restored. [11]But they were furious and began to discuss with one another what they might do to Jesus.

COMMENTARY

1-2 Luke centers attention on the disciples, though in accordance with custom their teacher was held responsible. To glean by hand (not using a sickle) in someone's field was permitted by the law (Dt 23:25). But to do this and to rub the heads of grain (a detail Luke alone includes) was considered to be threshing in the Pharisaic interpretation of the Torah. Jewish traditions, as reflected in the later Mishnah, forbid threshing (v.2) on the Sabbath (*m. Šabb.* 7:2).

3-4 Jesus' response centers in an analogy from Scripture (1Sa 21:1-6). He is not providing a specific teaching, such as would be necessary to establish a rabbinical rule (cf. W. Lane, *The Gospel According to Mark* [Grand Rapids: Eerdmans, 1974], 117). Instead he simply calls to mind an instance in which the infringement of a rule to meet human need received no condemnation (v.4). His illustration is apt because the general principle then and in his time continues to be the same and because a leader (David and David's messianic descendant) is involved along with his companions. The point is that ceremonial rites (being only means to an end) must give way to a higher moral law. Moreover, the presentation of Jesus as the authoritative guide to understanding the Scripture is an important theme for Luke.

5 Following this analogy, on which the Pharisees offer no comment, Jesus makes a statement in which for the second time in Luke he uses the phrase "Son of Man" (cf. 5:24). While some have argued that "Son of Man" simply means "man" here (so Creed, 84-85), Morris, 122, objects and asserts, "Jesus never taught that man is Lord over a divine institution." Therefore what Jesus says at this point is a claim to unique authority and takes the argument of vv.3-4 a step further. In a context where one finds allusions to the Torah, the temple, and the Davidic legacy, Jesus' claim of authority takes on added significance.

6 The second Sabbath controversy involves basically the same issue as the first—human need versus ceremonial law. This episode elaborates the meaning of Jesus as the Lord of the Sabbath. Luke presents some specific details (lacking in the parallel synoptic passages) that show this event occurred on a different Sabbath and that it was the man's "right hand" that Jesus healed. As in 4:15-16, 31-33, Jesus is teaching in the synagogue. Luke does not say that the man actually asked for healing; Jesus simply took the initiative. The hand was "shriveled," i.e., atrophied and useless.

7-8 As in 5:17, "the Pharisees and the teachers of the law" are present, scrutinizing Jesus' every action to find fault. Now, after the first Sabbath controversy, they think they have a case against him. Human reasoning tends to be evil (Ge 6:5; 8:21; Eph 5:17-18); Jesus is aware of their thoughts (v.8) and in the light of that knowledge performs the healing. He has the man stand in front of the people so that all will see what follows.

9 Jesus' question goes beyond the fact that the healing could have been postponed a day. After all, it was not a critical illness that might take a turn for the worse if not treated immediately. Had that been the case, scribal code would have permitted healing on a Sabbath. But Jesus implies in his double question that if any illness is left unattended when healing can be provided, evil is done by default. Jesus is not breaking the Sabbath—he is using it to do good to a human being in need.

The phrase "to save life" points to the deeper concern of this passage. While the context encourages the reader to think of this phrase as referring to the physical healing that was performed, this statement from the mouth of Jesus points to the primary contrast between good and evil, salvation and destruction. The (implied) objection of the Pharisees and teachers of the law is therefore taken as a way to obstruct the salvific work of God in the person Jesus.

10 Here Jesus commanded the impossible. Presumably the man exercised obedience born of faith, though Luke has not said that the man had faith or asked to be healed. Jesus healed the withered hand completely.

11 The response is violent; the opposition to Jesus mounts in a crescendo of fury more intense than that after the previous miracle. The Pharisees and the teachers of the law were threatened by the presence of unique authority in Jesus' words and deeds. So now, near the very start of Jesus' ministry, a plot against him begins to form.

NOTES

1 The phrase σαββάτῳ δευτεροπώτῳ (*sabbatō deuteropōtō*, "second-first Sabbath"), an alternative reading to σαββάτῳ (*sabbatō*, "a Sabbath"), has puzzled textual critics. First, the meaning of the variant is uncertain. There is an attractive speculation that Luke keeps a careful chronological record and that this is the second Sabbath after Jesus' major sermon (4:16; followed by 4:31 and 6:1). Marshall, 230, calls this "a solution born of despair." This reading could refer to a sequence of Sabbaths beginning with the one occurring after Passover, during the weeklong Feast of Unleavened Bread. The Sabbath in 6:1 would be the first after that feast, the second after Passover. But this also seems a strained solution, except that Leviticus 23:1–16 shows that this period, leading up to Pentecost, is carefully numbered by weeks (cf. *TDNT* 7:23 n. 183). Also Luke seems to be interested in the Sabbath along with the Jubilee (see comments at 4:19) as symbols of God's work of salvation and freedom. However, this variant reading seems to have little support (cf. UBS[4] apparatus). While it is the more difficult reading, and on that ground more likely to be the original, it may not be original. Instead, it may have arisen if the word πρώτῳ (*prōtō*, "first") had been (1) written in; (2) crossed out, with δευτέρῳ (*deuterō*, "second") substituted; and then (3) through scribal confusion reinstated along with δευτέρῳ *deuterō* (cf. Metzger, 116). This, too, seems strained; but by showing how the reading might have arisen, it at least might balance the claim that as the more difficult reading it should be accepted. The MS evidence is the least problematic factor in the decision and should probably lead to a rejection of the extra word. H. Klein, "Am ersten Sabbat: Eine Konjektur zu Lk 6:1," *ZNW* 87 (1996): 290–93, has further suggested that since the reading with the word πρώτῳ (*prōtō*, "first") may best explain the existence of other readings, the inclusion of the word πρώτῳ, *prōtō*, should be considered as original. This, again, is not the best solution in light of the lack of substantial external support.

4 Some have seen liturgical connotations behind the phrase λαβὼν ἔφαγεν καὶ ἔδωκεν (*labōn ephagen kai edōken*, "taking ... ate ... and gave"; cf. Bovon, 1:200). In the development of the narrative, however, it is the wider theme of table fellowship that resurfaces; therefore, this passage also contributes to the understanding of the community of those who submit to Jesus' unique authority.

10. Choosing the Twelve Apostles (6:12–16)

OVERVIEW

At this point in the narrative sequence, Mark (3:7–12) summarizes Jesus' ministry of healing. Luke postpones that summary to 6:17–19 as his introduction to the Sermon on the Plain. He puts the call of the disciples first, though not necessarily "in order to gain an audience for the sermon" (Marshall, 237), since a statement about a crowd of disciples and others already stood available in the Markan summary (Mk 3:7).

¹²One of those days Jesus went out to a mountainside to pray, and spent the night praying to God. ¹³When morning came, he called his disciples to him and chose twelve of them, whom he also designated apostles: ¹⁴Simon (whom he named Peter), his brother Andrew, James, John, Philip, Bartholomew, ¹⁵Matthew, Thomas, James son of Alphaeus, Simon who was called the Zealot, ¹⁶Judas son of James, and Judas Iscariot, who became a traitor.

COMMENTARY

12 Jesus spent an entire night in prayer—a sure indication that the circumstances were pressing, namely, the preceding controversy, the resultant threatening atmosphere, and the selection to be made of the twelve apostles. The second clause indicates that the first was not a routine devotional exercise.

13–16 The "disciples" up to this time were a group of followers interested in attaching themselves to Jesus the teacher. (See further on discipleship in the comments at 9:23–27; 14:25–33.) From among these followers Jesus chose the Twelve. Luke alone tells us that Jesus gave them the designation "apostles" (see Notes). That Luke does so accords with his regard for apostolic authority.

Most interpreters assume that Jesus intended the number of apostles to correspond with the number of the tribes of Israel, thereby indicating that a new people of God was coming into existence. The apostles' names appear several other times in the Gospels and Acts (Mt 10:2–4; Mk 3:16–19; Ac 1:13), with the same grouping and differing only in the form of a few names.

"Judas son of James" (v.16) apparently had, like many people, two names and is to be identified with Thaddaeus in Mark and Matthew. One of the two Simons was a "Zealot," i.e., one who had advocated revolutionary opposition to Rome (see Notes). The other Simon, Peter, is at the head of every list. Judas Iscariot (see Notes) is always last. From a promising beginning he "became a traitor." The group is not distinguished by particular abilities or position in life (cf. the principle in 1Co 1:26–29).

NOTES

12 Conzelmann, 44, believes that Luke has enlarged Mark's concept of the mountain as "the place of revelation" and that "there is no question of locating 'the' mountain." It is a mythical place to which the people "cannot come." Mountains did provide an environment that seemed very near to heaven, but it is unnecessary to assume that Luke uses mountains or any other topographical or geographical site merely symbolically (see comments at 9:28; also note at 9:28).

13 From later Jewish literature we learn that an "apostle" was a messenger who during his particular mission acted with the full authority of the one who sent him (*y. Ḥag.* 1.8). It may be anachronistic to see that particular meaning here, but there is no reason the basic concept cannot be attributed to Jesus' situation (cf. *TDNT* 1:398–447).

15 Some have argued that the Zealots as a political party did not exist during the time of Jesus (so R. A. Horsley and J. S. Hanson, *Bandits, Prophets, and Messiahs* [New York: Harper & Row, 1985], 190–243). This is not, however, the only way to read the ancient evidence (cf. Martin Hengel, *The Zealots: Investigations into the Jewish Freedom Movement in the Period from Herod I until 70 AD* [Edinburgh: T&T Clark, 1989]). Furthermore, this term may have been used in a loose way before the Jewish revolt of AD 66–73, and the focus may be placed on religious zeal (cf. C. Mézange, "Simon le Zélote était-il un revolutionaire?" *Bib* 81 [2000]: 489–506).

16 Ellis, 110, and Marshall, 240, support the option that the name Ἰσκαριωθ (*Iskariōth*, "Iscariot," GK *2696*) means the "false one," a derivation from the Aramaic *šᵉqar*, "falsehood." Other suggestions are an unlikely derivation from *sicarius* (lit., "dagger man" or "assassin") and the traditional "man of Kerioth" (cf. Jos 15:25), which still remains a possibility.

B. Jesus' Great Sermon (6:17–49)

1. Blessings and Woes (6:17–26)

OVERVIEW

The settings of this passage and of the Sermon on the Mount in Matthew 5–7 are not indisputably the same, and there is considerable difference in content. Therefore some scholars call the Lukan material "the Sermon on the Plain," with the implication that it is, in Luke's opinion, an entirely different sermon. The probability is that there was one sermon among many Jesus preached on similar themes that was something like a "keynote" address. This was a basic affirmation of the kingdom message, beginning with beatitudes and ending with a parable about builders. Within this framework, Matthew and Luke present samples or selections of Jesus' teachings that differ at points; Luke (Matthew also to a lesser extent) distributes some of the sermon's teachings, which Jesus probably repeated frequently, in other contexts in the gospel narrative. One clear example is the Lord's Prayer in Luke 11:2–4 (cf. Mt 6:9–13).

The sermon as presented in this chapter includes the "Blessings and Woes" (vv.20–26), "Love for Enemies" (vv.27–36), "Judging Others" (vv.37–42), and a final section (vv.43–49) on the test of genuineness in two parts: "A Tree and Its Fruit" and "The Wise and Foolish Builders" (following the divisions in the NIV text). However, vv.39–49 may be viewed as a unified section from a literary perspective, as this part is marked by a parabolic style.

¹⁷He went down with them and stood on a level place. A large crowd of his disciples was there and a great number of people from all over Judea, from Jerusalem, and from the coast of Tyre and Sidon, ¹⁸who had come to hear him and to be healed of their diseases. Those troubled by evil spirits were cured, ¹⁹and the people all tried to touch him, because power was coming from him and healing them all.

²⁰Looking at his disciples, he said:

"Blessed are you who are poor,
　　for yours is the kingdom of God.
²¹Blessed are you who hunger now,
　for you will be satisfied.
Blessed are you who weep now,
　　for you will laugh.
²²Blessed are you when men hate you,
　　when they exclude you and insult you
　　and reject your name as evil,
　　　　because of the Son of Man.

²³"Rejoice in that day and leap for joy, because great is your reward in heaven. For that is how their fathers treated the prophets.

²⁴"But woe to you who are rich,
　　for you have already received your comfort.
²⁵Woe to you who are well fed now,
　　for you will go hungry.
Woe to you who laugh now,
　　for you will mourn and weep.
²⁶Woe to you when all men speak well of you,
　　for that is how their fathers treated the false prophets."

COMMENTARY

17–19 The going down from the mountain to speak to the crowd may be an allusion to Moses after he received the commandments on the mountain (cf. Schürmann, 1:320). The "level place" (*epi topou pedinou* [GK *4628*]) is apparently an area on the "mountainside" mentioned in Matthew 5:1. If it were a plain, such as Jesus often used for his teaching near the sea, just the words *epi pedinou* would probably have been used (cf. Godet, 295). Luke mentions a "large crowd" of Jesus' disciples plus "a great number of people" (cf. 4:14–15 and Luke's stress on Jesus' popularity). Matthew mentions disciples in 5:1 and speaks of "crowds" only at the end of the sermon (7:28).

Though Jesus directs his comments to the disciples (v.20), he is surely conscious of his larger audience. His teachings in the sermon, especially those in Matthew 5:17–20, keep a balance between two extreme viewpoints that would have been familiar to any crowd. One is the strong legalistic "righteousness" often characteristic of the Pharisees; the other is the attitude attributed to many of the "people of the land," who knew little of the rabbinic tradition and were thought to disregard many religious practices. The emphasis in vv.18–19 on "power" and "healing" is characteristic of Luke. (For another instance of Jesus' power being drawn on by a "touch," see 8:43–46.) Luke clearly distinguishes here between those affected by demons and those whose illness was basically physical.

20–23 Luke's version of the blessings (or "beatitudes") is shorter than Matthew's and is different in some particulars. Also the beatitudes appear in negative form in the woes. Both blessings and woes are familiar forms in the OT (e.g., Ps 1, which also carries an implication of woes; Isa 5:8–23) and in Jewish traditions (e.g., Tob 13:16; 4Q525). The entire theme of reversal of fortune has already been encountered in the Magnificat (1:51–55). It is also implicit in the attention Luke gives to social and religious outcasts throughout his gospel.

20 "Blessed" (vv.20–22), as elsewhere in the NT, "refers to the distinctive religious joy which accrues to man from his share in the salvation of the Kingdom of God" (*TDNT* 4:367). "Poor" (*ptōchoi*, GK 4777) in Luke implies those who are utterly dependent on God. They are the special recipients of the "good news" Jesus came to preach (4:18). Often the economically destitute sense their need of God more than others. Whether voluntary poverty such as that practiced at Qumran is in view is not clear (cf. Ellis, 113). Marshall, 249, shows that nonviolence is implied. Matthew 5:3 specifies the spiritual poverty—i.e., recognition of one's spiritual need. To inherit "the kingdom of God" is the antithesis of poverty. Note the emphatic sense of assurance the present tense gives: "yours *is*" (emphasis mine). There may also be an element of "inaugurated eschatology" in the present tense—i.e., the presence of some aspects of the coming kingdom of God. In this case, the poor can rejoice even in the midst of their destitution because they are already able to share in some of the blessings of the kingdom.

21 "Hunger" (*peinōntes*, GK 4277) is presented in its reality without spiritualization. It may well carry the connotation of hungering "for righteousness" (Mt 5:6). Those who "weep" (*klaiontes*, GK 3081) may be those who carry the burden not only of personal grief but also of a hurting society. (The passage Jesus quoted in his synagogue sermon [4:18–19] goes on to speak of mourning giving way to gladness [Isa 61:2b–3a].) Both parts of v.21 stress the contrast between the situation "now" and the future blessing. Notice the difference in tone between Luke's "laugh" (*gelasete*, from *gelaō*, GK 1151) and Matthew's "be comforted" (*paraklēthēsontai*, from *parakaleō*, GK 4151; 5:4).

The idea of laughter is vividly carried forward in the next section on persecution (vv.23–26). Persecution is described in some detail, and the contrasting "rejoice" (*charēte*, from *chairō*, GK 5897) and "leap for joy" (*skirtēsate*, from *skirtaō*, GK 5015) stand out all the more (v.23).

22 Note the progression from hatred to exclusion (which later took the form of being banned from the synagogue) to insult (cf. 1Pe 4:14) to defamation of their name (cf. Mt 5:11). Those who share the rejection of the "Son of Man" relive the experience of the prophets (see comments at 20:9–12).

23 The promise of "reward in heaven" does not suggest that the disciples are to work for some future gain but that there will be personal vindication and appropriate recognition and blessing from the Lord. Luke emphasizes the vindication of the people of God who patiently wait for him (cf. 18:1–8 and comments). He also presents Jesus' teaching on reward for faithful servants (12:37, 42–44). What is unclear is whether these rewards refer to additional recognition in the kingdom or simply the right to participate in the kingdom itself (see v.35; cf. Craig Blomberg, "Degrees of Reward in the Kingdom of Heaven?" *JETS* 35 [1992]: 159–72).

24–26 The woes in both structure and content form a direct contrast to the blessings. This again resembles the Magnificat. "He has filled the hungry with good things but has sent the rich away empty" (1:53).

Woe comes to the "rich" (*tois plousiois*, GK *4455*), not simply because they are wealthy but (1) because the implication is that they have chosen present gratification over future blessing (v.24); (2) because rich people criticized in Luke disregard spiritual realities (e.g., 12:15–21); and (3) perhaps because, as was generally assumed, the wealthy became so at the expense of others (cf. Jas 2:6–7). The same thought runs through v.25 ("well fed"; possibly also v.26), where those who "laugh now" presumably do so at the expense of others.

26 The word "all" in the clause "when all men speak well of you" should be carefully noted, lest we distort the basic concepts of honor and praise. False prophets plagued God's people in OT times; they were a threat in Jesus' day (Mt 7:15–23), in Paul's day (Ac 13:6; cf. 20:29–30), and on into the church age (cf. *Did.* 11:5–6; 12:5). What is implicit is that Jesus himself is the true prophet and his followers are also prophets who extend the mission of Christ. To be rejected by the people becomes a sign of true prophets (cf. 4:24).

NOTES

20–23 In Second Temple Jewish literature, one finds ethical beatitudes that focus on present behavior and the apocalyptic type that point to the future when the situation of the people is reversed (see James W. Thompson, "The Background and Function of the Beatitudes in Matthew and Luke," *ResQ* 41 [1999]: 109–16; James H. Charlesworth, "The Qumran Beatitudes [4Q525] and the New Testament [Mt 5:3–11; Lk 6:20–26]," *RHPR* 80 [2000]: 13–35). While not as prominently, beatitudes also appear in Greco-Roman material. See Hans D. Betz, *The Sermon on the Mount* (Herm; Minneapolis: Fortress, 1995), 97–100.

20 Building on the spiritual aspects of the term οἱ πτωχοί (*hoi ptōchoi*, "the poor," GK *4777*), some have seen the term as referring to the people of God in general and the disciples in particular as they point to their purity before God. A parallel use can also be found in the Qumran documents, where the term was used as a self-designation (e.g., 1QM 11.9, 13; 1QH 13.13; cf. Dieter Georgi, *Remembering the Poor* [Nashville: Abingdon, 1992], 33–36).

22 In its parallel to ἕνεκα τοῦ υἱοῦ τοῦ ἀνθρώπου (*heneka tou huiou tou anthrōpou*, "because of the Son of Man"), Matthew 5:11 lacks τοῦ υἱοῦ τοῦ ἀνθρώπου, *tou huiou tou anthrōpou* ("Son of Man"), having only ἕνεκεν ἐμοῦ (*heneken emou*, "because of me"). Since Luke does not add the title "Son of

Man" where it does not appear in the tradition as he received it, its appearance here is authentic, contrary to some critical opinion (cf. Marshall, 253).

24 The verb ἀπέχετε (*apechete*, from ἀπέχω, *apechō*, GK *600*) means "have received your full payment," hence the NIV's "you have already received." This is in contrast to the blessed ones, whose full reward lies ahead (v.23).

2. Love for Enemies (6:27–36)

OVERVIEW

In place of the five antitheses of Matthew 5:21–48, Luke selects one theme (contained in two of the antitheses [Mt 5:38–42, 43–48]) and enlarges it. As might be expected from his basic concern for people, he chooses the theme of love. He does not present the teaching of Jesus over against the prevalent distortion of the OT (cf. Mt 5:43–44); instead he conveys only the positive command. The Golden Rule, which Matthew apparently postpones to use as a summary statement later in the sermon (7:12), occurs in Luke in what seems to be a natural context. Also, the conclusion in v.36 is significantly different from Matthew 5:48, each expression being eminently appropriate to its context (see below).

27"But I tell you who hear me: Love your enemies, do good to those who hate you, 28bless those who curse you, pray for those who mistreat you. 29If someone strikes you on one cheek, turn to him the other also. If someone takes your cloak, do not stop him from taking your tunic. 30Give to everyone who asks you, and if anyone takes what belongs to you, do not demand it back. 31Do to others as you would have them do to you.

32"If you love those who love you, what credit is that to you? Even 'sinners' love those who love them. 33And if you do good to those who are good to you, what credit is that to you? Even 'sinners' do that. 34And if you lend to those from whom you expect repayment, what credit is that to you? Even 'sinners' lend to 'sinners,' expecting to be repaid in full. 35But love your enemies, do good to them, and lend to them without expecting to get anything back. Then your reward will be great, and you will be sons of the Most High, because he is kind to the ungrateful and wicked. 36Be merciful, just as your Father is merciful."

COMMENTARY

27 "You who hear me" are probably those who are taking in what Jesus is saying, not casual listeners. The word "love" (*agapē*, GK *27*, in the nominal form) must be understood in its classic Christian sense of having a genuine concern for someone irrespective of his or her attractiveness or of the likelihood of any reciprocation in kind. The spirit of Jesus' words finds expression in Romans 12:14–21. Here in Luke the specifics are spelled out.

28 In the first instance, apparently no physical harm has been done; so the response also is not physical but to "bless" (*eulogeō*, GK *2328*) and to "pray" (*proseuchomai*, GK *4667*). The next situations involve action that must be met by some physical response.

29 Opinions differ as to whether when "someone strikes you on one cheek," it is (1) a mere insult (the cheek in Mt 5:39 being the right one, indicating a backhanded slap), (2) the "ritual slap on the cheek given a Christian 'heretic' in the synagogue" (Ellis, 115), or (3) "a punch to the side of the jaw," on the basis that *siagōn* (GK *4965*) means jaw, not cheek (Morris, 129, but see Notes). In any case, the injunction is directed to individuals (the form of the Greek imperatives and pronouns here is singular, not plural) who desire to live as "sons of the Most High" (v.35). Jesus is not advocating the suspension of normal civil judicial procedures. If pagan governments abandoned the protection of civil rights, the result would be an unbiblical anarchy (Ro 13:4).

"If someone takes your cloak" may refer to a street robbery (since the clothing seized is the immediately accessible outer robe [*himation*, GK *2668*]). In Matthew 5:40, the short tunic (*chitōn*, GK *5945*), which is worn underneath, is taken first, possibly in court action. Nevertheless, the implication seems to be that the person has a need or believes that he does. The teaching of the passage as a whole relates not so much to passivity in the face of evil as to concern for the other person. As ancient Greek philosophers recognized, to refrain from doing evil often means suffering evil. This was the path of the Lord Jesus (cf. 1Pe 2:20–24), who prayed for his enemies (Lk 23:34) and died for them (Ro 5:10).

30 The same spirit is expressed in this verse, where the practical application of this hyperbolic command would be to refuse to demand that which would genuinely be to the good of the other person, even at our expense. Quite consistent with Luke's interest elsewhere, the giving up of one's possession marks true discipleship.

31 The Golden Rule is now cited—not with theological comment (as in Mt 7:12) but as a practical governing principle (see Notes). With this note, the boundary between friends and enemies is broken as the universalizing understanding of the love command "radicalizes the highest demands group solidarity might impose and asks for these to be practiced in relation to the enemy" (Nolland, 1:296).

32–36 In these few verses, we do not simply have an elaboration of the Golden Rule. They provide ways through which v.31 can be understood correctly. Taking v.31 out of context can produce a reading that is based on the principle of reciprocity: one's action should be based on one's expectation of return. This reading is now qualified by three significant points: (1) we should not do good based on our expectation that we will be treated well (vv.32–35a); (2) we have to act in the light of our future hope and relationship with God (v.35b); and (3) the ultimate basis for our behavior is the nature and deeds of God (v.36). The discussion of the unconditional love for one's enemies in vv.27–30 has already prepared the readers for these qualifications. It is only with these critical qualifications that one can see the unique power of Jesus' teaching. (For the paradoxical nature of Jesus' combination of the Golden Rule and these critical qualifications, see Paul Ricoeur, "The Golden Rule: Exegetical and Theological Perplexities," *NTS* 36 [1990]: 392–97.)

32–34 We have here a remarkable series of comparisons between the courtesies of believers and those of worldly people. Even "sinners" act decently toward others when kindnesses are reciprocated. The sermon in Matthew makes three basic comparisons with unbelievers regarding the quality of their relationship (1) to God (Mt 6:7–8), (2) to people (Mt 5:46–47; cf. the present passage), and (3) to material possessions (Mt 6:32; cf. Lk 12:30).

Loving (v.32) is augmented by doing good (v.33), which in turn is expressed in lending (v.34). Marshall, 263, argues that *hina apolabōsin* [GK 655] *ta isa* ("expecting to be repaid in full," v.34) means "the reception of loans in return." One hardly makes a loan "expecting" to receive back the principal; that is assumed. Nor would a good Jew normally charge interest. Therefore, some kind of equal treatment in return seems to be implied. One should benefit the helpless as well as one's friends.

35 Believers are to be like what they really are, "sons of the Most High," and as such will have recognition. Jesus is not teaching that one earns sonship (cf. Jn 1:12–13); rather, the day will come when the world will recognize God's children (Ro 8:19, 23).

36 "Be merciful" (*ginesthe oiktirmones*, GK 3880) singles out that area of life in which, given the preceding examples, one is very likely to come short. The Pharisees tithed spices but neglected "justice, mercy and faithfulness" (Mt 23:23). The believer's righteousness must exceed theirs (Mt 5:20). It should be measured against the perfection of God himself (Mt 5:48). Since Luke omits a discussion of the Law and Pharisees, which would not be appropriate for his readership, he omits the imperative about being perfect and replaces it with one about being merciful. This accords with his emphasis on kindness to others in need (cf. 10:25–37).

NOTES

27–29 For surveys of ancient discussions on the principle of nonretaliation, see John Piper, *"Love Your Enemies": Jesus' Love Command in the Synoptic Gospels and in the Early Christian Paraenesis* (SNTSMS 38; Cambridge: Cambridge Univ. Press, 1979), 19–49; D. Gill, "Socrates and Jesus on Non-retaliation and Love of Enemies," *Hor* 18 (1991): 246–62. The uniqueness of Jesus' teaching lies in the absoluteness of Jesus' command and the theological justification for this command (v.35).

29 Though σιαγών (*siagōn*, GK 4965) meant "jaw" in earlier classical literature, it came to mean "cheek" (so NIV) in the Hellenistic period. With the omission of Matthew's δεξιάν (*dexian*, "right," GK 1288; 5:39), any allusion to a ritual slap is gone. (It would have been meaningless to his Gentile audience anyway.) So the idea of outright violence is stressed here in Luke and is heightened by his statement about yielding the cloak, which he presents as a robbery rather than a court action.

31 No claim to originality is inherent in Jesus' use of the Golden Rule. It existed in a negative form, attributed to Rabbi Hillel, to the effect that one should not do to others what he does not want to happen to himself (*b. Šabb.* 31*a*; Tob 4:15). Jesus uses and strengthens the "rule," but he also provides significant qualifications to prevent misunderstanding (see comments at vv.32–36 above). There is a change from the singular verbal form in the preceding injunctions to the plural in this general command καθὼς θέλετε . . . ποιεῖτε (*kathōs thelete . . . poieite*, "as you desire . . . do").

32–34 The word χάρις (*charis*, GK 5921) here means "favor" or "credit" (cf. μισθός, *misthos*, "reward," GK 3635, in v.35 and Mt 5:46). God will not overlook what is done for him at personal sacrifice.

34 For further discussion of the various possible interpretations of the phrase "expecting to be repaid in full," see Bovon, 1:237–38.

35 On υἱοὶ ὑψίστου (*huioi hypsistou*, "sons of the Most High"), see 1:32 and comments there.

3. Judging Others (6:37–42)

37"Do not judge, and you will not be judged. Do not condemn, and you will not be condemned. Forgive, and you will be forgiven. 38Give, and it will be given to you. A good measure, pressed down, shaken together and running over, will be poured into your lap. For with the measure you use, it will be measured to you."

39He also told them this parable: "Can a blind man lead a blind man? Will they not both fall into a pit? 40A student is not above his teacher, but everyone who is fully trained will be like his teacher.

41"Why do you look at the speck of sawdust in your brother's eye and pay no attention to the plank in your own eye? 42How can you say to your brother, 'Brother, let me take the speck out of your eye,' when you yourself fail to see the plank in your own eye? You hypocrite, first take the plank out of your eye, and then you will see clearly to remove the speck from your brother's eye."

COMMENTARY

37–38 These verses deal with the kind of mercy expected of the Lord's disciples. If the preceding imperative about being merciful refers indirectly to the lack of mercy among the Pharisees, then this one may refer to the kind of judgmental attitude that religious people, such as the Pharisees, often have. Since "do not judge" could be misunderstood as ruling out any ethical evaluation at all, it is important to note the further definition provided by the parallel "do not condemn" (*mē katadikazete*, GK 2868). In Matthew 7:6, the injunction not to "give dogs what is sacred," which obviously requires some discernment, provides the balance. Just as God will give a suitable reward to the merciful (vv.32–36), so v.37 implies that he will bring appropriate judgment on the unmerciful. The idea of suitable reward carries over in the next illustration of an overflowing measuring cup (v.38). Those who are generous (both materially [vv.27–36] and in their estimation of others [v.37]) will be abundantly repaid.

39–40 Some have found vv.39–40 difficult to relate to the context. If Jesus still has the Pharisees in mind (cf. Schürmann, 1:365–79), it is not necessary to assume that he is directly accusing them. Rather, his thought in addressing the disciples runs like this: The disciple of a rabbi dedicates himself to his master's teachings and way of life; thus he cannot be expected to be different from, or better than, his master (v.40). If the rabbi lacks a proper view of life, his student will be misled as well (v.39). The criticism and hostility already apparent in the Pharisees may unfortunately crop up in their disciples, but it must never find a place among Jesus' disciples.

This interpretation assumes that v.40 carries on the thought of v.39, in which both teacher and follower are "blind"—not a description of Jesus and his disciples. If, however, v.40 introduces a new comparison, it might mean that Jesus' disciples ought not to go beyond what they have learned from him, namely, a merciful, uncensorious spirit. In that instance v.39 could refer to the Pharisees or others.

41–42 The humorous illustration of the "speck" (*karphos*, GK *2847*) and the "plank" (*dokon*, GK *1512*) hits the mark with force when the person who casually calls the one he is criticizing "brother" (v.42) suddenly hears himself called "hypocrite" by the Lord. Danker, 89, observes, "What is criticized by Jesus is the moralist's patronizing attitude." He cites Democritus (fifth century BC): "Better it is to correct one's own faults than those of others." Jesus'

humor makes the point vividly. In the Gospels, "hypocrisy" does not merely point to the inconsistency between words and deeds; at a deeper level, it is the discrepancy between a person's inner nature and his or her outward appearances (cf. Mt 23:25–28; see Mark A. Powell, *God with Us: A Pastoral Theology of Matthew's Gospel* [Minneapolis: Fortress, 1995]). This leads to the next parable, in which consistency between one's inner nature and outward expressions is called for.

NOTES

38 The phrase εἰς τὸν κόλπον ὑμῶν (*eis ton kolpon hymōn*, "into your lap") refers to the fold of one's robe used as a pocket.

4. A Tree and Its Fruit (6:43–45)

OVERVIEW

These verses extend the discussion of "hypocrisy" in v.42, as outward expressions often reflect one's inner nature. Sincere warnings and admonitions cannot be produced by a person who has an evil heart.

> **43**"No good tree bears bad fruit, nor does a bad tree bear good fruit. **44**Each tree is recognized by its own fruit. People do not pick figs from thornbushes, or grapes from briers. **45**The good man brings good things out of the good stored up in his heart, and the evil man brings evil things out of the evil stored up in his heart. For out of the overflow of his heart his mouth speaks."

COMMENTARY

43–45 Though the mention of speech (v.45) relates this passage primarily back to v.42, the emphasis on the consistency between source and product (cf. the teaching of John the Baptist [3:7–9 and comments]) may also connect these verses back

to v.40—like teacher, like student; like tree, like fruit. The parallel passage (Mt 7:15–20) refers to false prophets—a fact that supports a link between v.43 and v.39 about a blind leader.

NOTES

45 The phrase ἐκ τοῦ ἀγαθοῦ θησαυροῦ τῆς καρδίας (*ek tou agathou thēsaurou tēs kardias*) is, literally, "out of the good treasure of the heart." The heart is a treasury in which good or evil is "stored up" (NIV). See also Matthew 15:19 and Mark 7:21, both of which verses are in contexts criticizing the Pharisees.

5. The Wise and Foolish Builders (6:46–49)

⁴⁶"Why do you call me, 'Lord, Lord,' and do not do what I say? ⁴⁷I will show you what he is like who comes to me and hears my words and puts them into practice. ⁴⁸He is like a man building a house, who dug down deep and laid the foundation on rock. When a flood came, the torrent struck that house but could not shake it, because it was well built. ⁴⁹But the one who hears my words and does not put them into practice is like a man who built a house on the ground without a foundation. The moment the torrent struck that house, it collapsed and its destruction was complete."

COMMENTARY

46–49 If Jesus' audience was relaxing in the assumption that the preceding teachings were directed only at the Pharisees and their followers, they could not dodge the direct force of this challenge. It is specifically directed to those who profess to follow Jesus (v.46). In Matthew the statement is amplified with a description of self-deception, probably at first deliberate and then habitual. Here only the basic point is made: it is not mere words or even generally ethical behavior or religious practice that mark true believers, but whether they "do" (*poieite*) what Jesus says (cf. Jas 1:22–25). The thrust of the parable is clear. Luke includes reference to "the foundation" (v.48), but he omits some of the graphic detail found in Matthew 7:24–27. Luke also omits the response of the people (cf. Mt 7:28–29).

NOTES

46 Marshall, 274, notes that "already . . . during [Jesus'] ministry, the address of Κύριε [*Kyrie*, "Lord"] was taking on a deeper significance than a mere honorific 'Sir.'"

48–49 This parable has to be understood in its proper geographical context, where the house that was built on hard sand in the summer will be destroyed when the flooding of the winter months arrives. Only houses with a foundation that reaches to the bedrock can survive. See Gordon Franz, "The Parable of the Two Builders," *ABW* 3 (1995): 6–11.

C. Ministry to Various Human Needs (7:1–9:17)

1. The Faith of the Centurion (7:1–10)

OVERVIEW

This incident has an important place in Luke's narrative. First, it marks a pivotal point in the progress of the word of the Lord from its original Jewish context to the Gentile world. The Jews' appreciation of a pious Gentile (the centurion) is an important theme in Luke, which was written partly to show the compatibility of early Christianity with Judaism. At the same time, Jesus compares the Gentile's faith more than favorably with that of the Jews, which serves Luke's desire to justify the prominence of Gentiles in the church.

Second, the incident is paralleled by the conversion of Cornelius (Ac 10), which itself marks a historic transition from a purely Jewish church to one including Gentiles. Luke is careful to speak well of each centurion and his religious concern.

Third, Luke has been careful to note those who had "faith" (*pistis*, GK *4411*), beginning with Mary (1:45) and then the four men who brought the paralyzed man to Jesus (5:20). Further, the authority of Jesus is stressed, and his "word" (v.7) is believed to have power (cf. 4:32, 36).

Finally, the connection between this story and the evocation of the Elijah–Elisha stories in the scene in the Nazareth synagogue (4:25–27) points to the significance of this story in the wider plan of God. The move to the Gentiles is embedded in the election of Israel, and this move should not be considered an accidental development of Jesus' mission (cf. Thomas Brodie, "Not Q but Elijah: The Saving of the Centurion's Servant [Luke 7:1–10] as an Internalization of the Saving of the Widow and Her Child [1 Kings 17:1–16]," *IBS* 14 [1992]: 54–71).

¹When Jesus had finished saying all this in the hearing of the people, he entered Capernaum. ²There a centurion's servant, whom his master valued highly, was sick and about to die. ³The centurion heard of Jesus and sent some elders of the Jews to him, asking him to come and heal his servant. ⁴When they came to Jesus, they pleaded earnestly with him, "This man deserves to have you do this, ⁵because he loves our nation and has built our synagogue." ⁶So Jesus went with them.

He was not far from the house when the centurion sent friends to say to him: "Lord, don't trouble yourself, for I do not deserve to have you come under my roof. ⁷That is why I did not even consider myself worthy to come to you. But say the word, and my servant will be healed. ⁸For I myself am a man under authority, with soldiers under me. I tell this one, 'Go,' and he goes; and that one, 'Come,' and he comes. I say to my servant, 'Do this,' and he does it."

⁹When Jesus heard this, he was amazed at him, and turning to the crowd following him, he said, "I tell you, I have not found such great faith even in Israel." ¹⁰Then the men who had been sent returned to the house and found the servant well.

COMMENTARY

1 The introductory words, "when Jesus had finished saying all this," provide more than just a transition from the preceding sermon. They suggest another step in the mission Jesus came to fulfill (1:1), for the word "finished" translates *eplērōsen* ("fulfilled," GK *4444*). Matthew's formula following a collection of sayings uses *etelesen* ("finished," GK *464*; e.g., 7:28). "In the hearing of the people" (*eis tas akoas tou laou*) echoes "you who hear me" (6:27) and establishes the reliability of the witnesses from Galilee who would later bear testimony to the truth about Jesus' words and deeds.

2–3 On behalf of his seriously ill "servant" (*doulos*, GK *1528*; cf. comments at v.7), the centurion "sent some elders [*presbyterous*, GK *4565*] of the Jews" (i.e., the leaders of the community) to Jesus. At this point a comparison with Matthew 8:5–13 shows a significant difference of detail. Luke, with his great interest in the character and importance of the centurion, gives us a fuller narrative than Matthew. Two groups come from the centurion to talk with Jesus on his behalf. Matthew provides a more condensed version, as is his custom, relating the words of the centurion to Jesus as though he had been there in person.

4–5 In v.4 we learn why the village elders were willing to intercede for the centurion: they were genuinely indebted to him for his generosity (v.5). The perceived honor of the centurion is grounded in his act as the benefactor of the Jews (cf. Bruce Malina and Jerome H. Neyrey, "Honor and Shame in Luke–Acts: Pivotal Values of the Mediterranean World," in *The Social World of Luke–Acts* [ed. Neyrey], 49).

6–7 It seems strange that at this point, having invited Jesus to come, the centurion now sends another group of "friends" (*philous*, GK *5813*) to stop him short of entering (v.6). They express the centurion's sense of unworthiness (v.7). Indeed, one wonders why at this point the centurion did not simply come out and speak for himself. Luke, however, apparently wishes to stress the humility of the man and possibly also his concern that Jesus might be criticized for entering a Gentile's house. Moreover, the motif of double-delegation coincides with other Lukan concerns. Theologically, the impartiality of God is implied. Sociologically, the conversion of a Gentile who is a friend of the Jews provides a model for the people of God (for a further discussion of this double-delegation motif, see Robert A. J. Gagnon, "Luke's Motives for Redaction in the Account of the Double Delegation in Luke 7:1–10," *NovT* 36 [1994]: 122–45).

8 The focal point of the section is the centurion's concept of Jesus' authority. The wording is significant: "For I myself am a man under authority" (*gar egō anthrōpos eimi hypo exousian tassomenos*). He compares Jesus' relationship to God with his own to his superiors. The position of responsibility implies "authority" (*exousia*, GK *2026*) to command others. Therefore he has faith that Jesus' authoritative "word" (*logos*, GK *3364*; v.7) will accomplish the healing.

9 Jesus is not criticizing the faith he has found among Jews but rather says that "not . . . even" (*oude*) in Israel has he found such faith. The Jews would be expected to have faith, considering their possession of God's revelation in their Scriptures (cf. Ro 3:1–2). But not all the Israelites accepted the good news (Ro 10:16); many missed the element of personal faith (Ro 10:6–13). This failure to respond to their privileges was ending in Jesus' day, and the response of the centurion stood out in welcome contrast.

10 Unlike the story in Matthew (8:13), Luke does not emphasize the explicit words of healing uttered by Jesus. Throughout the story the emphasis is on the humility of the centurion and the faith expressed through that humility.

NOTES

2 A ἑκατοντάρχης (*hekatontarchēs*, "centurion," GK *1672*) is presumably a Roman—though stationed not over Roman but Jewish soldiers—hired by the Herodian rulers to maintain their position. A centurion, though a noncommissioned officer, was comparable to an army lieutenant and was responsible for about a hundred men. A more precise definition is impossible in light of the varied functions of the different types of "centurions" in the first-century Roman world (cf. Uwe Wegner, *Der Hauptmann von Kafarnaum* [WUNT II.14; Tübingen: Mohr, 1985], 57–60).

2. Raising a Widow's Son (7:11–17)

OVERVIEW

Jesus is now about to perform the ultimate kind of miracle that will certify him as the Messiah and will be reported to John the Baptist ("the dead are raised," v.22). Luke also wants his readers to understand that while John the Baptist came in the spirit and power of Elijah, it is Jesus himself who is the great prophet of the end-time. As we shall note, this miracle significantly resembles miracles performed by Elijah and Elisha. Luke has already included a reference to the widow to whom Elijah ministered (4:25–26; cf. Craig A. Evans, "The Function of the Elijah/Elisha Narratives in Luke's Ethic of Election," in *Luke and Scripture* [ed. Evans and Sanders], 76–77).

> [11]Soon afterward, Jesus went to a town called Nain, and his disciples and a large crowd went along with him. [12]As he approached the town gate, a dead person was being carried out—the only son of his mother, and she was a widow. And a large crowd from the town was with her. [13]When the Lord saw her, his heart went out to her and he said, "Don't cry."
>
> [14]Then he went up and touched the coffin, and those carrying it stood still. He said, "Young man, I say to you, get up!" [15]The dead man sat up and began to talk, and Jesus gave him back to his mother.
>
> [16]They were all filled with awe and praised God. "A great prophet has appeared among us," they said. "God has come to help his people." [17]This news about Jesus spread throughout Judea and the surrounding country.

COMMENTARY

11 The time reference is vague. The trip to Nain would not have taken more than a day; the town lay a few miles to the southeast of Jesus' hometown, Nazareth. Nain lay on the other side of the Hill of Moreh from Shunem, where Elisha raised the son of the Shunammite woman. "Nain" may actually be an abbreviation of Shunem, and this geographical reference may strengthen the connection with the Elisha story. Luke typically notes the "large crowd" (e.g., 5:15, 29; 6:17; 8:4).

12–13 The cortege has already gone through the town and is on the way to the place of burial, which was customarily outside the town. The deceased was the "only son" (*monogenēs*, GK *3666*) of his mother (see Notes). The compassion of the Lord Jesus, and of Luke as well, goes out to the woman. She is a widow (*chēra*, GK *5939*) who, without a man in her family, would probably become destitute, unable in that society to earn a living. Our Lord's words are deeply human: "Don't cry" (*mē klaie*, v.13), but only he could say that and at the same time remove the cause of the tears. Otherwise such words would be hollow, though well-meant.

14–15 Jesus risked ritual defilement by touching the "coffin" (*sorou* [GK *5049*], a litter on which the shrouded body was laid). One can only imagine the thoughts of the pallbearers as they stopped. Jesus did what would seem useless—he spoke to a dead person. On the young man's return to life, Jesus "gave him back to his mother" (v.15), words similar to those in 1 Kings 17:23 regarding Elijah and the widow.

16–17 Once more, Luke records the response of the people, noting that they "praised" (*edoxazon*, GK *1519*; lit., "glorified") God (cf. 5:26; 18:43; 23:47). The similarities noted with Elijah and Elisha would naturally cause the people to use the word "prophet" to describe Jesus. Moreover, the connection with 1 Kings 17 is highlighted by the Targum's paraphrase of the statement in 1 Kings 17:24: "You are the prophet of the Lord" (cf. Brodie, 134–53).

The second exclamation also echoes an OT expression: "God has come to help his people" (e.g., Ru 1:6). For the significance of "come" (*episkeptomai*, GK *2170*), see comments at Luke 1:68. Equally important is the understanding of the work of Christ as the work of God himself.

17 Once again, Luke emphasizes the spread of the "news" (*logos*, GK *3364*) about Jesus.

NOTES

12 Whenever μονογενὴς υἱός (*monogenēs huios*, "the only son," GK *3666, 5626*) is used in Scripture, it is of an only son who is either in mortal danger or already dead (cf. 8:42; 9:38; see also Jdg 11:34–35; Zec 12:10; Jn 3:16; Th. C. de Kruif, "The Glory of the Only Son, John 1:14," in *Studies in John* [Leiden: Brill, 1970], 111–23). Luke shows his compassion and the beauty of God's saving grace by showing that these were precious only children even where Matthew and Mark do not have the term.

3. Jesus and John the Baptist (7:18–35)

OVERVIEW

In 3:16–17 John had described the one who would come baptizing with the Holy Spirit and with fire. Then Jesus was baptized, receiving divine approval and anointing for his work. In 4:16–21 Jesus assumed the task prophesied in Isaiah 61:1–2. Now, after a cycle of teachings and healings, the validity of his messianic calling is once more under consideration; and John the Baptist is the other central figure. Unlike the earlier portrayal of John the Baptist, however, John is depicted as one who is in doubt and one who is not able to discern the sig-nificance of Jesus' work. John's question does, how-ever, provide an occasion to clarify the identity and mission of Jesus.

[18]John's disciples told him about all these things. Calling two of them, [19]he sent them to the Lord to ask, "Are you the one who was to come, or should we expect someone else?"

[20]When the men came to Jesus, they said, "John the Baptist sent us to you to ask, 'Are you the one who was to come, or should we expect someone else?'"

[21]At that very time Jesus cured many who had diseases, sicknesses and evil spirits, and gave sight to many who were blind. [22]So he replied to the messengers, "Go back and report to John what you have seen and heard: The blind receive sight, the lame walk, those who have leprosy are cured, the deaf hear, the dead are raised, and the good news is preached to the poor. [23]Blessed is the man who does not fall away on account of me."

[24]After John's messengers left, Jesus began to speak to the crowd about John: "What did you go out into the desert to see? A reed swayed by the wind? [25]If not, what did you go out to see? A man dressed in fine clothes? No, those who wear expensive clothes and indulge in luxury are in palaces. [26]But what did you go out to see? A prophet? Yes, I tell you, and more than a prophet. [27]This is the one about whom it is written:

"'I will send my messenger ahead of you,
    who will prepare your way before you.'

[28]I tell you, among those born of women there is no one greater than John; yet the one who is least in the kingdom of God is greater than he."

[29](All the people, even the tax collectors, when they heard Jesus' words, acknowledged that God's way was right, because they had been baptized by John. [30]But the Pharisees and experts in the law rejected God's purpose for themselves, because they had not been baptized by John.)

[31]"To what, then, can I compare the people of this generation? What are they like? [32]They are like children sitting in the marketplace and calling out to each other:

"'We played the flute for you,
    and you did not dance;
we sang a dirge,
    and you did not cry.'

[33]For John the Baptist came neither eating bread nor drinking wine, and you say, 'He has a demon.' [34]The Son of Man came eating and drinking, and you say, 'Here is a glutton and a drunkard, a friend of tax collectors and "sinners."' [35]But wisdom is proved right by all her children."

COMMENTARY

18–20 "These things," i.e., the healings and presumably also the raising of the widow's son, apparently have not sufficed to convince John of Jesus' messiahship. This reluctance seems strange, considering John's role in announcing the Coming One and in baptizing Jesus.

19 There are several reasons why John needed further confirmation. He was in prison (Mt 11:2). This could lead to depression and, in turn, doubt. Further, he might wonder why, if the Messiah was to release prisoners (Isa 61:1) and if Jesus was the object of that prediction (Lk 4:18), he had not freed John. Also, though he had received reports of Jesus' ministry, John himself had apparently not witnessed spectacular messianic miracles such as he might have expected; nor had he heard Jesus claim outright that he was the Messiah. From the text of Luke, the opposition of the people may also cast doubt as to whether Jesus is indeed the approved Messiah sent from above. The fact that John still had "disciples" (v.18) does not necessarily mean he had been continuing a separate movement because of uncertainty about the Messiah. A number continued with John even after he had pointed them to Jesus.

21–22 Jesus responds by listing the messianic works (some of them just described in Luke) that he has accomplished. It was understood in those days that the true Messiah would not proclaim himself such but would first do appropriate messianic works that would lead to public acknowledgment of his identity (cf. Longenecker, 71–74). The works of Jesus echo not only Isaiah 61, quoted at Nazareth, but also other passages from Isaiah (e.g., 42:7). Isaiah 35:5–6 declares that in the messianic age those who could not see, hear, walk, or speak would be healed. While most of the activities that Jesus described here had already appeared in these OT texts, the raising of the dead was strikingly absent.

This can be explained by the understanding that Jesus' action exceeded the expectation of God's own people. More helpful is the explanation provided in the Qumran material where one could find the extension of the Isaianic portrayal of the Messianic era to include the act of raising the dead (cf. 4Q521 1.2.1–14; J. D. Tabor and M. O. Wise, "4Q521 'On Resurrection' and the Synoptic Gospel Tradition: A Preliminary Study," *JSP* 10 [1992]: 149–62). This could serve as the proper context for understanding Jesus' messianic claim here.

23 Jesus pronounces a blessing on the person who accepts his credentials rather than being trapped (*skandalizō*, GK *4997*; NIV, "fall away") because of a false evaluation of Jesus. This could point to the disparity between the popular messianic hope and the actual ministry of Jesus, who focuses on the poor and is rejected himself.

24–27 The topic now changes from the role of Jesus to that of John. Jesus asks a couple of gently ironic questions that, through obviously negative answers, stress the inflexibility and austerity of John. Jesus uses the term "prophet" (v.26) and adds the role of "messenger" (v.27) from Malachi 3:1. If John is the messenger, obviously this forcefully implies the significance of Jesus' own role. This also shows that the connection between John and Jesus lies in the fulfillment of the wider plan of God.

28 Jesus now puts John into historical perspective. John came in advance of the kingdom, which has now become a reality (16:16). As great as John was, it is greater to participate in the kingdom than to announce it. We are not to conclude from this, however, that John himself is excluded. Luke 13:28 affirms that all the prophets will be in the kingdom.

The identification of "the least" is not explicitly stated. Some have understood "the least" to be Jesus Christ himself (so Oscar Cullmann, *The Early*

Church [London: SCM, 1956], 180). Most scholars, however, have taken the term as referring to the disciples (so Bock, 1:675–76). The reference to the "kingdom of God" favors the ecclesiological reading, and the comparison points to the priority of one's status within the kingdom of God. The two readings are not mutually exclusive, however, when the focus is understood to be the arrival of the new era in salvation history: the humble will be exalted with the arrival of God's salvation, and this reversal is symbolized by the suffering and exaltation of Jesus himself (cf. Benedict T. Viviano, "The Least in the Kingdom: Matthew 11:11, Its Parallel in Luke 7:28 [Q], and Daniel 4:14," *CBQ* 62 [2000]: 41–54).

29–30 Attention now turns to the response of the people and of their leaders to John and Jesus also. Observe the contrast between the "people" (*laos*, GK *3295*; see comments at 1:17) and the hostile religious leaders. In v.24 the neutral word "crowd" is used. The "tax collectors" (*telōnai*, GK *5467*) are mentioned along with the "people" as those who stood ready to believe Jesus and thereby "acknowledged that God's way was right." Notice that the issue is not only the role of Jesus and John but also the entire counsel of God, whose "purpose [*boulēn*, GK *1087*] for themselves" (v.30) was rejected by the "Pharisees and experts in the law [*nomikou*, GK *3788*]." John's baptism was a symbol they chose to reject.

31 "This generation" is not simply a temporal reference to those who are with Jesus during his ministry; it is a phrase used in the OT texts to describe the wilderness generation that failed to remember the mighty acts of God and to be obedient to his will. The polemical tone is embedded within the mere use of the phrase (see Notes).

32 The obdurate opposition to each of God's messengers is described as childish fickleness (v.32; cf. their earlier attempt to play John against Jesus, 5:33). The children's words are those of annoyed leaders who want their friends to play "grownup" and, when the leaders play cheerful or sad music, pretend that they are at a celebration, such as a wedding, or at a funeral. They become petulant when their friends refuse to play. Jesus and John, when in confrontation with the Jewish leaders, refused to "play their game" and so are the object of their taunts.

33–34 The people not only criticize but also exaggerate the habits both of John (v.33), calling his asceticism demonic (demons having been said to inhabit the desert where John was), and Jesus (v.34), labeling as gluttony and drunkenness his normal habits of eating and drinking. The issue of judgment points to a court setting, and their act of judging points to their self-understanding as those in power of judgment. The irony is that they are simply children (cf. v.32) who are not capable of discernment (cf. W. J. Cotter, "The Parable of the Children in the Marketplace, Q [Lk] 7:31–35: An Examination of the Parable's Image and Significance," *NovT* 29 [1987]: 289–304).

35 The concluding saying probably means that those who respond to wisdom prove its correctness. These "children" of wisdom may point to the common people and sinners who responded to Jesus' message (cf. v.29), and the irony noted in the previous verse reaches its climax here as the sinners are now considered to be the wise ones. In the light of its immediate context, however, "children" points ultimately to Jesus and John the Baptist.

NOTES

19 The word κύριον (*kyrion*, "Lord") does not have convincing MS support, but the UBS Greek NT chose it because "it is not likely that copyists would have deleted the name Ἰησοῦν [*Iēsoun*, "Jesus"], and since κύριος [*kyrios*] is in accord with Lukan style" (Metzger, 119).

The phrase ὁ ἐρχόμενος (*ho erchomenos*, "he who is coming"; NIV, "the one who was to come") alludes to the coming Messiah or prophet (Jn 6:14; 11:27; cf. Da 7:13 with Hab 2:3; Heb 10:37 with Mt 3:1).

27 Danker, 97, sees a reminder here of the angel who went before the people of Israel in the desert (Ex 23:20).

30 The phrase οἱ νομικοί (*hoi nomikoi*, "experts in the law," GK *3788*) is a term used almost exclusively by Luke. It was more readily understood by his Gentile readers than γραμματεύς (*grammateus*, "scribe," GK *1208*; see Notes, 5:17).

31 For a detailed study of the phrase "this generation" in the synoptic traditions as well as in the contemporary Jewish literature, see E. Lövestam, *Jesus and "This Generation"* (Stockholm: Almqvist & Wiksell, 1995).

35 In the Matthean parallel, it is the "actions" of wisdom that are mentioned (Mt 11:19). In light of the Jewish understanding of wisdom as righteous living, the product of wisdom is the righteous acts performed by wisdom's children.

4. Anointed by a Sinful Woman (7:36–50)

OVERVIEW

The criticism Jesus has received (v.34) does not preclude Luke from setting down another example of Jesus' concern for sinners. The story contrasts a sinner and a Pharisee. It is similar to another incident (cf. Mt 26:6–13; Mk 14:3–9; Jn 12:1–8). A woman brings perfume to Jesus while he is at a banquet hosted by a Pharisee named Simon (anonymous in John). There are several differences: the other incident occurs immediately before Jesus' crucifixion, the host is a leper (Matthew and Mark), the woman pours the perfume on Jesus' head (Matthew and Mark), and the controversy centers in the cost of the perfume, not the character of the woman.

The differences are sufficient to require two traditions. Some of the similarities may be coincidental (e.g., Simon was a common name); others may be due to cross influence. In this typical Lukan scene, the banquet setting again provides the context for the definition of Jesus' followers (Evelyn R. Thibeaux, "'Known to Be a Sinner': The Narrative Rhetoric of Luke 7:36–50," *BTB* 23 [1993]: 151–60). As a literary genre, the symposium setting also draws one's attention to the dialogue prompted by the disruption of the normal course of the meal.

³⁶Now one of the Pharisees invited Jesus to have dinner with him, so he went to the Pharisee's house and reclined at the table. ³⁷When a woman who had lived a sinful life in that town learned that Jesus was eating at the Pharisee's house, she brought an alabaster jar of perfume, ³⁸and as she stood behind him at his feet weeping, she began to wet his feet with her tears. Then she wiped them with her hair, kissed them and poured perfume on them.

³⁹When the Pharisee who had invited him saw this, he said to himself, "If this man were a prophet, he would know who is touching him and what kind of woman she is—that she is a sinner."

⁴⁰Jesus answered him, "Simon, I have something to tell you."

"Tell me, teacher," he said.

⁴¹"Two men owed money to a certain moneylender. One owed him five hundred denarii, and the other fifty. ⁴²Neither of them had the money to pay him back, so he canceled the debts of both. Now which of them will love him more?"

⁴³Simon replied, "I suppose the one who had the bigger debt canceled."

"You have judged correctly," Jesus said.

⁴⁴Then he turned toward the woman and said to Simon, "Do you see this woman? I came into your house. You did not give me any water for my feet, but she wet my feet with her tears and wiped them with her hair. ⁴⁵You did not give me a kiss, but this woman, from the time I entered, has not stopped kissing my feet. ⁴⁶You did not put oil on my head, but she has poured perfume on my feet. ⁴⁷Therefore, I tell you, her many sins have been forgiven—for she loved much. But he who has been forgiven little loves little."

⁴⁸Then Jesus said to her, "Your sins are forgiven."

⁴⁹The other guests began to say among themselves, "Who is this who even forgives sins?"

⁵⁰Jesus said to the woman, "Your faith has saved you; go in peace."

COMMENTARY

36–38 Since he accepted an invitation from a Pharisee, Jesus cannot be accused of spurning the Pharisees socially. The woman took advantage of the social customs that permitted needy people to visit such a banquet to receive some of the leftovers (v.37). She came specifically to see Jesus, bringing a jar or little bottle of perfume. Since Jesus was reclining (*kateklithē*, GK *2884*) at the table according to custom (v.36), she prepared to pour the perfume on his feet (v.38)—a humble act (cf. 3:16). A flow of tears preceded the outpouring of the perfume; so she wiped his feet lovingly with her hair and, perhaps impulsively, kissed them before using the perfume. The tears should be understood as tears of remorse (so Bovon, 1:295), and the mention of tears encourages the readers to place the woman's action in its proper context.

39-40 In this masterly narrative Luke now directs attention to the Pharisee. He mulls over the matter and reaches three conclusions: (1) if Jesus were a prophet, he would know what kind of woman was anointing his feet; (2) if he knew what kind of a woman she was, he would not let her do it; and (3) since he does let her anoint his feet, he is no prophet and should not be acknowledged as such. But Jesus does let her expend the perfume on him and does not shun her. He shows that he does have unique insight into the human heart, for he knows what the Pharisee is thinking. When Jesus tells Simon his host that he has something to say to him (v.40), Simon, perhaps expecting some stock word of wisdom from his teacher-guest, replies perfunctorily, "Tell me, teacher."

41-43 The point of the incident (vv.41-42) is clear, and Simon is made to give the conclusion that will condemn him. His "I suppose" (v.43) probably implies an uneasy reluctance.

44-50 Again the woman is the focal point of the narrative. Surprisingly, Jesus first contrasts her acts of devotion with a lack of special attention on Simon's part as host (vv.44-46; see Notes). The main point is reached swiftly. Jesus can declare that her sins (of which he does not hesitate to say were "many") have been forgiven (v.47). He can affirm this (v.48) because her act of love shows her realization of forgiveness. Her love is not the basis of forgiveness; her faith is (v.50). This faith is directed to Jesus himself, as is consistent with the Lukan emphasis on faith elsewhere (e.g., Ac 15:7-11; cf. John J. Kilgallen, "A Proposal for Interpreting Luke 7:36-50," *Bib* 72 [1991]: 305-30). As in the event itself, the forgiveness was unearned, and it is this fact that elicits her love (see Notes, v.47).

As the episode ends, attention rapidly shifts from one person to the other. Simon obviously knows little of either forgiveness or love (v.47). Jesus pronounces the woman forgiven. Then he becomes the object of another discussion because he presumes to absolve her from her sins (v.49; cf. 5:21). The woman receives his pronouncement of salvation—"saved" (*sesōken*) being in the perfect tense and expressing an accomplished fact—and his benediction, "go in peace" (v.50)—traditional and common words that have true meaning only for those who have been saved by faith (8:48; 17:19; 18:42; cf. Jdg 18:6; 1Sa 1:17; 2Sa 15:9; 1Ki 22:17; Ac 16:36; Jas 2:16).

NOTES

37 The noun ἁμαρτωλός (*hamartōlos*, "sinner," GK 283; NIV, "who had lived a sinful life") is the word Luke often uses to identify a person who has a reputation for gross immorality. The woman's unbound hair (v.38) might indicate that she was a prostitute.

41 A δηνάριον (*dēnarion*, "denarius") was the approximate daily wage of a laborer.

44-46 Schürmann, 1:435-36, followed by Marshall, 312-13, holds that Simon was not actually at fault as a host, because the amenities mentioned, while customs of the day, were not necessary acts of hospitality. Bailey (*Through Peasant Eyes*, 5), on the other hand, says, "The formal greetings were clearly of crucial significance in first-century times." The contrast remains strong in either case because of the extraordinary nature of what the woman did.

47 The NIV (following UBS[4]) has a comma before and after "I tell you," making the phrase οὖ χάριν λέγω σοι (*hou charin legō soi*, "therefore, I tell you") parenthetical and thus linking "therefore" with "her many sins have been forgiven." While this is grammatically possible, the KJV, RSV, NASB, and JB are probably correct in linking the deeds of the woman (described in vv.44–46) with Jesus' response rather than with her forgiveness (e.g., JB: "for this reason I tell you"). The use of ὅτι (*hoti*, "for") here is not to show causality but evidence (see discussions in C. F. D. Moule, *An Idiom Book of New Testament Greek* [2d ed.; Cambridge: Cambridge Univ. Press, 1959], 147; M. Zerwick, *Biblical Greek* [Rome: Pontifical Biblical Institute, 1963], paragraph 422). The TEV has "the great love she has shown proves that her many sins have been forgiven."

48 The passive form of the verb ἀφέωνται (*apheōntai*, "forgiven") could be understood as a divine passive, with God being the implied subject of the act of forgiving. In the light of v.49 and the previous discussion of Jesus' authority to forgive (Lk 5:17–26), it seems best to see Jesus as the one who forgives (for further discussion, see John J. Kilgallen, "Luke 7:41–42 and Forgiveness of Sins," *ExpTim* 111 [1999]: 46–47).

5. Parable of the Sower (8:1–15)

OVERVIEW

As in Matthew 13:1–23 and Mark 4:1–20, the sequence in vv.4–15 is (1) the parable of the sower, (2) Jesus' reason for using parables, and (3) the interpretation of the parable of the sower. Each part deals with the mixed response Jesus was receiving from his audiences, a response also basic in the next two pericopae (vv.16–18; 19–21). Jesus' realism regarding the failure of people to believe his message also appears elsewhere in Luke, notably in the saying about the persistent widow and others who cry for vindication. They will receive justice quickly, but "when the Son of Man comes, will he find faith on the earth?" (18:8). Jesus explains the present parable and his reasons for using the parabolic form—both to warn those who neglect the word they hear and to encourage his disciples when that word is not fully accepted.

¹After this, Jesus traveled about from one town and village to another, proclaiming the good news of the kingdom of God. The Twelve were with him, ²and also some women who had been cured of evil spirits and diseases: Mary (called Magdalene) from whom seven demons had come out; ³Joanna the wife of Cuza, the manager of Herod's household; Susanna; and many others. These women were helping to support them out of their own means.

⁴While a large crowd was gathering and people were coming to Jesus from town after town, he told this parable: ⁵"A farmer went out to sow his seed. As he was scattering the seed, some fell along the path; it was trampled on, and the birds of the air ate it up. ⁶Some fell on rock, and when it came up, the plants withered because they had no moisture. ⁷Other seed fell among thorns, which grew up with it and choked the plants. ⁸Still other seed fell on good soil. It came up and yielded a crop, a hundred times more than was sown."

When he said this, he called out, "He who has ears to hear, let him hear."

[9]His disciples asked him what this parable meant. [10]He said, "The knowledge of the secrets of the kingdom of God has been given to you, but to others I speak in parables, so that,

"'though seeing, they may not see;
though hearing, they may not understand.'

[11]"This is the meaning of the parable: The seed is the word of God. [12]Those along the path are the ones who hear, and then the devil comes and takes away the word from their hearts, so that they may not believe and be saved. [13]Those on the rock are the ones who receive the word with joy when they hear it, but they have no root. They believe for a while, but in the time of testing they fall away. [14]The seed that fell among thorns stands for those who hear, but as they go on their way they are choked by life's worries, riches and pleasures, and they do not mature. [15]But the seed on good soil stands for those with a noble and good heart, who hear the word, retain it, and by persevering produce a crop."

COMMENTARY

1–3 The opening verses provide a summary of yet another preaching tour (cf. the previous circuit described in 4:44). Pointing back to the programmatic chapter (4), Jesus here is said to be proclaiming the "good news of the kingdom of God." In preparation for the central section of Luke's gospel (chs. 9–19), the focus on Israel (as signified by the Twelve) and the itinerant ministry of Jesus are mentioned. Luke is careful to mention "the Twelve" here, as they will serve as witnesses and authorities in the days following Jesus' ascension.

What is new is the mention of several women who not only accompany Jesus but also share in his support (vv.2–3). It was not uncommon for ancient itinerant cult leaders, fortune-tellers, and their kind to solicit the financial support of wealthy women (Lucian, *Alex.* 6; cf. 2Ti 3:6–7). In this case, however, it is in a Jewish, not a pagan, culture; and the relationship is morally pure. Some of these women, at least, had a great debt of love to

Jesus, as did the woman in the preceding incident (7:36–50). Luke does not say that Mary Magdalene had been a prostitute, as is often thought; she is not identified with the woman of 7:36–50. He does refer to her as an object of the grace and power of God in her being released from seven demons. "Joanna the wife of Cuza" is otherwise unknown, but her presence at the crucifixion (in contrast to the flight of most of the disciples) shows her faithfulness. She is the first person connected with the Herodian household to be mentioned in this gospel. Later the gospel often reached into distinguished and royal homes through the witness of Christian servants. The third woman mentioned, Susanna, is not further introduced by a description of her background.

It is noteworthy that these women were industrious, in their time truly "liberated," and helped in the support not only of Jesus but of the Twelve, to whom the word "them" (*autois*) in v.3 refers. In their service they do not simply act as patrons but also as humble servants who follow Jesus. The benefactor system is therefore significantly qualified, and one is encouraged to see these women as those who follow the example of Jesus as "the patron who serves" (cf. 22:27; Halvor Moxnes, "Patron-Client Relations and the New Community in Luke–Acts," in *The Social World of Luke–Acts* [ed. Neyrey], 263). The fact that two of these women (Mary and Joanna) reappear in the resurrection appearance account (24:10) also reflects the emphasis on the continuity of traditions. Together with the Twelve they form the community that will testify to the life and ministry of the earthly Jesus.

4 Luke begins this section with an observation on the size of the crowds (so also Mt 13:2; Mk 4:1). But whereas Matthew and Mark specify a location by the lake, Luke omits this. Instead, he adds to the comment on the crowd by speaking of those who were coming to Jesus from "town after town." The effect is to help the reader visualize a large, mixed group of people who represent the various types of "soil" in the parable.

5–8 This particular parable reflects a situation well known to the audience, and the details of the parable would have been grasped immediately by the hearers. The very fact that circumstances so familiar need still further comment before the spiritual meaning is clear underlines the paradox presented in v.10—namely, that those who see and hear do not understand.

The focal point of the parable has been variously interpreted. In none of the Gospels are the sower (v.5; NIV, "farmer") the center of attention (not even in Mark, though some have taken Mk 4:14 as directing attention to the sower). Nor is particular stress laid on the seed—certainly not as in the parable of the secretly growing seed (Mk 4:26–29). This is not to say that the seed is unimportant. On the contrary, it represents the word of God (v.11); and

the whole act of sowing the seed is proclaiming the gospel of the kingdom (cf. Mk 4:14).

What does catch attention is the variety of soils. Contrary to what a modern Western perspective might lead us to expect, the sower is not immediately concerned about the kind of soil. Since plowing followed sowing in Jesus' culture, the trampled ground where people crossed the field might later be plowed under with seed; so it is not excluded from the sowing. The same could be true of young thornbushes (v.7). Furthermore, the rocky subsoil (v.6) might not be visible at the time of sowing. The low yield from the poor soil is overshadowed by the very large yield from the good soil (v.8)—an encouragement for Jesus' disciples to realize that the ultimate greatness of the kingdom will make all of their efforts worthwhile.

9 Here in Luke the disciples' question refers only to this parable, not to Jesus' larger ministry as in Matthew 13:10 and Mark 4:10.

10 The reference to the "secrets" (*mystēria*, GK *3696*) occurs in this context in all three Synoptics. Mark 4:11 uses the singular form *mystērion*; Matthew (13:11), like Luke, includes the word "knowledge" (*gnōnai*, lit., "to know," GK *1182*). Only in this situation does *mystērion* occur in the teachings of Jesus. An immensely significant word in biblical literature, *mystērion* (lit., "mystery") is found also in extrabiblical Jewish literature. Biblical scholars, now freed from the earlier idea that NT references to a "mystery" derived from the Hellenistic mystery religions, find rich meaning in the word when examined within its Jewish context (cf. M. Bockmuehl, *Revelation and Mystery in Ancient Judaism and Pauline Christianity* [Grand Rapids: Eerdmans, 1997]). While the word occurs in the LXX only in Daniel 2, where God is praised as the one who reveals secrets (Da 2:20–23, 28–30), it appears in varied frames of reference in the NT. The basic concept of *mystērion* is that of the purpose and plan of God, which he works out phase by phase in human history and through the church. The issues of the problem of evil, suffering, and the delay of vindication will be resolved when God finally reveals his "mystery," which is "accomplished" (*etelesthē*, GK *5464*) after the "delay" (*chronos*, GK *5989*) has ended (Rev 10:6–7). The "mystery" or "secret" is only revealed by God's sovereign grace to his people. As Luke writes, "The knowledge of the secrets of the kingdom of God has been given to you."

"To others" (*tois loipois*, lit., "to the rest," GK *3370*) is not as specific as Mark's "those on the outside" (*tois exō*, GK *2032*; 4:11). The quotation from Isaiah 6:9—"though seeing . . . not understand"—shows that Jesus' teaching is in accord with the consistent principle in Scripture that those who fail to respond to a saving word from God will find that they are not only under judgment for rejecting what they have heard but that they are unable to understand further truth (cf. Jn 3:17–19 with Jn 9:39–41, which contains words similar to Isa 6:9; Ex 8:32, regarding Pharaoh, with Ex 9:12 and Ro 9:17–18; see also Ac 28:26–27, another quotation from the Isaiah passage; Mt 7:6; Lk 20:1–8; Rev 22:11). For such, the very parable that reveals truth to some hides it from them. Given this sober reality, it is all the more important that the interpretation of the present passage be in full accord both with the Greek syntax of this sentence and with the whole biblical revelation of God's character and the way he deals with unbelief (see B. Lindars, *New Testament Apologetic* [Philadelphia: Westminster, 1961], 159–67).

While "so that" (*hina*) may be understood as indicating result, it more normally indicates purpose. The thought may be that the principle of Isaiah 6:9 may be fulfilled. Reading this quotation in its OT context, one should also remember the prophetic nature of this warning. The ultimate purpose of this dire warning is, after all, based on the hope that some within the wider people of God

will repent. In this context, Luke does not include the additional difficult words from Isaiah that are found in Mark 4:12—"otherwise they might turn and be forgiven"—but instead hastens on to the interpretation of the parable in question. The fuller quotation will appear at the end of the Lukan writings, however (see Notes).

11–12 Having shown the danger of unbelief in v.10, Jesus now returns to the parable, explaining why the proclaimed "word of God" fails to bring a uniform response of faith. Luke's inclusion of the clause "so that they may not believe and be saved" (v.12; lacking in Matthew and Mark) reflects his intense concern regarding salvation. The clause is introduced by *hina* ("so that"); and here, unlike its use in v.10, there is no doubt that it expresses deliberate purpose. Note the contrast between the devil's purpose and God's purpose (cf. 2Pe 3:9).

13–14 In the next two instances (seed fallen on rock, v.13; seed fallen among thorns, v.14), there is an initial response. The superficial reception given the word may be compared to those who "believed" Jesus (Jn 8:31), only to be called children of the devil (Jn 8:44); obviously, they did not go on to true, liberating faith (Jn 8:32). Luke alone among the synoptic writers says that these people actually "believe for a while" (*pros kairon pisteuousin*, v.13; cf. Mt 13:21; Mk 4:17—"last only a short time"). It is "in the time of testing" (*en kairō peirasmou*, GK *2789, 4280*; cf. *thlipseōs ē diōgmou* ["trouble or persecution," GK *2568, 1501*], Mt 13:21; Mk 4:17) that they "fall away" (*aphistantai*, GK *923*; cf. the use of *skandalizō* ["stumble," GK *4997*] in Mt 13:21; Mk 4:17). In all three Synoptic Gospels the response is superficial and cannot endure adversity. S. Brown, 14, sees this as characteristic of Luke's concern for apostasy under external testing.

The third example (v.14) has to do not with adversity but with distractions, such as those Jesus warned against (Mt 6:19–34; Lk 11:34–36; 12:22–32;

16:13). The comment that the hearers in this example "do not mature" (*ou telesphorousin* [GK *5461*], often used of fruit; cf. *akarpos*, "unfruitful," GK *182*, in Mt 13:22; Mk 4:19) is comparable to the statements in James 2:14–26 on a "dead" (*nekra*, GK *3738*, v.17) and "useless" (*argē*, GK *734*, v.20) faith and in 2 Peter 1:8 on those who are "ineffective" (*argous*) and "unfruitful" (*akarpous*; NIV, "unproductive"). That being fruitful is not simply a matter of the quality of one's Christian life but of whether one has life at all is suggested by Jesus' parallel teaching on wealth in Matthew 6:19–34. There the "single [good] eye" (see comments at Lk 11:34) is opposed to the total darkness that envelops a divided heart (Mt 6:22–24; cf. Hos 10:1–2: "Israel was a spreading vine.... Their heart is deceitful"). The unresponsive people described in v.14 apparently lack the following essentials to true saving faith: understanding (Mt 13:23; cf. v.19), accepting the word (Mk 4:20), and retaining it (Lk 8:15).

15 Luke's stress on the character of the individual is in contrast to Matthew's reference (13:23) to "understanding" (*synieis*, GK *5317*) the word. This is in accord with Matthew's interest in comprehending the secrets of the kingdom (cf. Mt 13:11, 14–15, 19–23). The description "noble and good" (*kalē kai agathē*, GK *2819, 19*) is a Christian adaptation of an ancient Greek phrase. The word "heart" (*kardia*, GK *2840*) means the spiritual, intellectual, volitional center of a person's being, i.e., the whole person. This person is marked by singleness of purpose, unlike those of a divided heart mentioned in Hosea 10:1–2 (cf. Ps 101:2 [100:2 LXX]—*en akakia kardias*, "with blameless heart"—and 1Ch 29:17–19). Jesus' emphasis here is not so much on whether a person perseveres but on the kind of person who does persevere. The RSV's "bring forth fruit with patience" (*en hypomonē*, GK *5705*) is more literal and perhaps more accurate than the NIV's "by persevering produce a crop."

NOTES

4 Teaching in παραβολαί (*parabolai*, "parables," GK *4130*; i.e., placing things alongside others for comparison) was common among the rabbis of Jesus' day. The ancient Greeks used the literary form of parable. In the Hebrew tradition, there were a variety of figures of speech all subsumed under the word *māšāl* (GK 5442), usually translated παραβολή, *parabolē*, in the LXX. Contemporary NT scholars generally recognize that, while the parable is distinct from allegory in that the various features in the parable do not each convey a particular meaning, neither does the parable convey a simplistic ethical truth. Rather, it is an art form offering various possibilities of expression to the speaker or writer. In the NT it usually conveys a message about the kingdom of God that in its very telling by Jesus involved the hearer in a crisis of personal response.

Among the useful works on parables are Kenneth E. Bailey, *Poet and Peasant*; Craig Blomberg, *Interpreting the Parables* (Downers Grove, Ill.: InterVarsity, 1990); A. M. Hunter, *The Parables Then and Now* (Philadelphia: Westminster, 1971); J. Jeremias, *The Parables of Jesus*; A. Parker, *Painfully Clear: The Parables of Jesus* (Sheffield: Sheffield Academic, 1996); R. H. Stein, *An Introduction to the Parables of Jesus* (Philadelphia: Westminster, 1981). Other critical and literary studies include C. W. Hedrick, *Parables as Poetic Fictions: The Creative Voice of Jesus* (Peabody, Mass.: Hendrickson, 1994); B. B. Scott, *Hear Then the Parable: A Commentary on the Parables of Jesus* (Minneapolis: Fortress, 1989); Mary Ann Tolbert, *Perspectives on the Parables* (Philadelphia:

Fortress, 1979). On the parables and Luke 8:4–15, see P. B. Payne, "Metaphor as a Model for Interpretation of the Parables of Jesus with Special Reference to the Parable of the Sower" (PhD diss., Cambridge University, 1975).

5 The phrase τὸν σπόρον αὐτοῦ (*ton sporon* [GK 5078] *autou*, "his seed") is found only in Luke and is probably merely a stylistic addition, not a theological emphasis on "seed."

6–7 The verb φυέν (*phyen*, "came up," GK 5886) occurs only in Luke (also in v.8); so also συμφυεῖσαι (*symphyeisai*, "grew up with," GK 5243) in v.7.

6 The phrase διὰ τὸ μὴ ἔχειν ἰκμάδα (*dia to mē echein ikmada* [GK 2657], "because they had no moisture") replaces διὰ τὸ μὴ ἔχειν ῥίζαν (*dia to mē echein rhizan* [GK 4844], "because they had no root") in Mark 4:6. The statement is less vivid than in Mark and Matthew because Luke does not refer to the scorching heat of the sun.

8 In ancient times, a reasonable expectation of yield of cereal crops is fourfold to fivefold. A hundred-fold yield ("a hundred times more") should therefore be understood as "miraculous" (Robert K. McIver, "One Hundred-Fold Yield—Miraculous or Mundane? Matthew 13.8, 23; Mark 4.8, 20; Luke 8.8," *NTS* 40 [1994]: 606–8).

The verb ἐφώνει (*ephōnei*, "called out," from φωνέω, *phoneō*, GK 5888) is unique among the Synoptics to Luke in this parable and perhaps emphasizes the opportunity of the crowds, to whom Jesus has given special attention (v.4), to receive the teaching. The call to "hear" (ἀκουέτω, *akouetō*, GK 201) prepares for the saying in v.10 and may be derived from the quotation from Isaiah (cf. a similar exhortation in 14:35; Mt 11:15; Rev 2:7 [and in each letter to the seven churches]; 13:9; see also Gregory K. Beale, *The Book of Revelation* [NIGTC; Grand Rapids: Eerdmans, 1999], 236–39).

10 The Greek ἵνα (*hina*, "so that") can be causal, but grammarians are reluctant to acknowledge it as such in this passage or in Mark 4:12 (cf. Zerwick, *Biblical Greek*, 413; BDF, paragraph 369 [2]). Moule (*Idiom Book*, 142–43) notes this reluctance but hesitates to see this as a final (purpose) clause because of the apparent incongruity of a purpose sense here with the rest of NT thought. Others have pointed to the use of ἵνα, *hina*, to introduce a result clause in the NT, and therefore it is possible that the "unintended" result is that which is noted (cf. Daniel B. Wallace, *Greek Grammar Beyond the Basics* [Grand Rapids: Zondervan, 1996], 371). Zerwick further notes that after the parallel verse in Mark 4:12, Mark (4:33) says that Jesus spoke in parables "according as they were able to hear." In theological terms, it seems best to maintain the tension between God's foreknowledge (of one's rejection of the gospel) and human responsibility here.

That the fuller quotation appears only at the end of Luke's writings may reflect Luke's interest in emphasizing the rejection of the gospel message by God's own people. It is unclear, however, whether Luke's use of this quotation points to the closing of the gospel's door to the Jews. For a further discussion of Luke's use of Isaiah 6:9–10, see Pao, 101–9.

11–15 The interpretation of the parable has often been attributed to the early church rather than to Jesus. Jeremias, 77–79, 149–50, acceded to this view on the basis of the vocabulary and theology, which he thought were more characteristic of the primitive church than of Jesus. Birger Gerhardsson ("The Parable of the Sower and Its Interpretation," *NTS* 14 [1968]: 165–93) concluded that it is not possible to identify here a later hortatory application by the early church that is distinct from the original eschatological teaching given by Jesus. The supposition that Jesus could not have employed a multiple form of interpretation such as we have in this passage can no longer be sustained in view of the allegorical methods used by rabbis in the first century. Luke's own modifications of the tradition expand but do not alter the theological teaching in Mark (cf. I. H. Marshall, "Tradition and Theology in Luke: Luke 8:15," *TynBul* 20 [1969]: 56–75). We can conclude that the interpretation in vv.11–15 belongs to Jesus' authentic teaching.

13 The verb ἀφίστανται (*aphistantai*, "fall away," from ἀφίστημι, *aphistēmi*, GK *923*) is related to ἀποστασία (*apostasia*, GK *686*), from which our word "apostasy" is derived (cf. 1Ti 4:1; Heb 3:12, where the verbal form clearly means to depart from a biblical faith in God).

6. Parable of the Lamp (8:16–18)

OVERVIEW

This section contains three distinct sayings. The order of the sayings is the same in Mark and Luke, but Matthew places the first two in entirely different contexts. The considerable dissimilarities in wording among the gospels suggest that the sayings were repeated on many occasions and written down separately.

16"No one lights a lamp and hides it in a jar or puts it under a bed. Instead, he puts it on a stand, so that those who come in can see the light. 17For there is nothing hidden that will not be disclosed, and nothing concealed that will not be known or brought out into the open. 18Therefore consider carefully how you listen. Whoever has will be given more; whoever does not have, even what he thinks he has will be taken from him."

COMMENTARY

16–17 Here the theme is the same as that of vv.11–15—namely, that what is genuine can and will be tested for its authenticity. If what is "hidden" (v.17) is evil, this saying affirms that God's judgment on those referred to in v.10 and in vv.12–15 will be just. If what is "hidden" is good, the saying may refer to the truth of Jesus' private teachings to his disciples, which they are exhorted to proclaim publicly. More likely it indicates that God's truth, now partially hidden from those who reject it, will someday be publicly vindicated. The absurdity of lighting a lamp (v.16) only to hide it reinforces the point.

18 In Matthew 13:11 this saying relates to personal response to the proclamation of the kingdom of heaven. There the meaning is that those who accept the message of the kingdom will also be given the knowledge of the "secrets," but those who reject it will lose even the opportunity of hearing more teaching. Here Luke has the verse in a different setting, though its meaning may well be the same as in Matthew. Notice the additional word "think" in Luke: "even what he thinks he has."

7. Jesus' True Family (8:19–21)

OVERVIEW

Matthew and Mark continue with parabolic teaching at this point, but Luke turns to an incident that Matthew and Mark locate at the conclusion of the Beelzebub controversy. When Luke comes to this controversy (11:14–28) he inserts something different, though on the same theme of obedience to God's word. Here the theme of obedience appropriately continues vv.5–15.

> [19]Now Jesus' mother and brothers came to see him, but they were not able to get near him because of the crowd. [20]Someone told him, "Your mother and brothers are standing outside, wanting to see you."
>
> [21]He replied, "My mother and brothers are those who hear God's word and put it into practice."

COMMENTARY

19–21 Jesus is not, of course, dishonoring his family (vv.19–20) but honoring those who obey God (v.21). The incident Luke now gives us teaches a profound lesson about how believers may be near to the Lord Jesus as the emphasis is placed on the hearing and practicing of the word of God. Elsewhere Luke shows the place family must take in the life of one who desires to be Jesus' disciple (14:25–26).

On the ecclesiological level, this passage points to the redefinition of the people of God. Those who belong to Jesus are not limited to those who are related to him by flesh. Obedience to Jesus' words becomes the criterion for one to be included in this new community. This theme of redefinition finds its fulfillment in Luke's second volume, where the inclusion of the Gentiles is at the very center of Luke's concern. In his gospel, this theme had already appeared in the words of Elizabeth, who pointed not only to Mary's exalted role as the mother of Jesus but also as one who has believed the divine word (1:42–45).

NOTES

20 The word ἀδελφοί (adelphoi, GK 81) is most naturally translated "brothers." To render it "cousins" or "stepbrothers" on the theory that Mary remained a virgin is to strain the meaning. Moreover, even Catholic scholar Joseph Fitzmyer, 724, admits that "there is no indication in the NT itself about Mary as aie parthenos, 'ever virgin.'"

21 The phrase τὸν λόγον τοῦ θεοῦ (ton logon tou theou, "God's word") may be an alternative term Luke uses to express the idea behind "the will of God" in the parallels (Mt 12:50; Mk 3:35) in order to stress again God's "word" (cf. v.11), which is the expression of his will. In Acts, "the Word of God/the Lord" becomes one of the controlling themes in the development of the narrative (cf. Pao, 147–80).

8. Calming the Storm (8:22–25)

OVERVIEW

Luke resumes the sequence of narratives illustrating the powerful, authoritative word of Jesus (notice esp. 8:25, 29, 32, 54; cf. 4:36). Jesus exercises his power against natural forces, demons, illness, and death. Then he delegates this power to his disciples (9:1–2). Schürmann, 1:472–73, groups the incidents in 8:22–56 as a trilogy of "great miracles" that are "almost Johannine signs."

The story itself is noteworthy for its vividness and for its portrayal of the Lord Jesus as in complete control of himself and his environment. The climax comes not with the miracle itself but with the question of the disciples (v.25) concerning the identity of the Master. It is a nature miracle marking the first time in Luke that Jesus applied his power to a non-living object rather than to a person. Jesus is affirming sovereignty over storm and sea as God did in the exodus. Some have further pointed to Jesus' command over the sea storm as signifying his control over the evil and chaotic power. This is supported by the Jewish (and other ancient cultures') understanding of water as symbolizing evil forces (cf. Jon D. Levenson, *Creation and the Persistence of Evil* [New York: Harper & Row, 1988]). This would fit Luke's interest here, but he does not further develop this particular theme.

> ²²One day Jesus said to his disciples, "Let's go over to the other side of the lake." So they got into a boat and set out. ²³As they sailed, he fell asleep. A squall came down on the lake, so that the boat was being swamped, and they were in great danger.
> ²⁴The disciples went and woke him, saying, "Master, Master, we're going to drown!"
> He got up and rebuked the wind and the raging waters; the storm subsided, and all was calm. ²⁵"Where is your faith?" he asked his disciples.
> In fear and amazement they asked one another, "Who is this? He commands even the winds and the water, and they obey him."

COMMENTARY

22 Luke omits some of the details found in Mark, including a specific reference to the time of day. His words, "Let's go over to the other side of the lake," should have assured the disciples that they would indeed complete their trip across the water (as the Jews did in the exodus).

23 Luke uses vivid language, as does Mark, to describe the fury of the storm. Luke mentions the wind three times (vv.23–25). This was an intense "squall" (*lailaps anemou*, lit., "windstorm of wind"), such as characteristically swept down on the Sea of Galilee, which lies in a shallow basin rimmed by hills. Luke mentions earlier in the narrative than do Matthew and Mark that Jesus was asleep. This placement heightens the contrast between the turmoil of the storm and Jesus' peaceful rest.

24–25 The fear and unbelief of the disciples is in contrast not only to the calm of their Master but also to the endurance they themselves should have had in "the time of testing" (cf. v.13). Even so, in Luke's account Jesus does not say, "Do you still have no faith?" as in Mark 4:40, but only, "Where is your faith?" (v.25). The double "Master, Master" (v.24) expresses both respect and terror (contrast the less respectful question in Mk 4:38). The fear of being lost at sea is a common human fear and typifies the sense of helplessness in the immensity of life (cf. Ps 107:23–31). In its wider context, this miracle of Jesus would have had special meaning during the unsettling and threatening conditions the church encountered through persecutions during its early period of existence.

The question of the disciples, "Who is this?" serves to show not only their amazement but also the slowness of their apprehension of the "Master's" true identity. This question not only marks the climax of this story but is also a key question in Luke. In fact, because Luke omits a large amount of material found in Mark (6:45–8:26, which otherwise would come between vv.17 and 18 of Luke 9), he can move quickly from the next occurrence of this question (9:9) to the question at Caesarea Philippi: "Who do you say I am?" (9:20).

NOTES

24 The verb ἐπετίμησεν (*epetimēsen*, "rebuked"; from ἐπιτιμάω [*epitimaō*, GK 2203]) suggests to some interpreters that there is a demonic presence behind the storm (see comments at 4:39). On the other hand, the word may simply reflect the tendency of Semitic and other peoples to personify natural forces. In the LXX, ἐπιτιμάω (*epitimaō*, "to blame," "reprove") often expresses the "creative or destructive" work of God (*TDNT* 2:624). It would be natural for the disciples to say that these forces "obey [ὑπακούω, *hypakouō*, lit., "hearken to," GK 5634] him" (v.25).

9. Healing a Demon-possessed Man (8:26–39)

OVERVIEW

This narrative provides the strongest expression yet of the power of Jesus against the forces of evil. (A previous instance of Jesus' casting out demons [4:33–35] offered little descriptive comment.) Luke gives us far more detail than Matthew does, though not quite as much as Mark, and provides a lively, forceful picture of the destructive effects of demon-possession. Not only the power of the kingdom (11:20) but also the power of the Messiah to release the captives of the kingdom of darkness move against this demonic force. The very narrative that describes this power of Jesus grips the reader. First, there are several progressive levels of action (in both Luke and Mark) involving the demoniac, the demons, the swine, the townspeople, and finally the demoniac after his healing. Second, Luke by his literary skill has inserted part of the description of the demoniac's past life between the lines of dialogue to heighten the readers' awareness of the man's helplessness under demonic control.

²⁶They sailed to the region of the Gerasenes, which is across the lake from Galilee. ²⁷When Jesus stepped ashore, he was met by a demon-possessed man from the town. For a long time this man had not worn clothes or lived in a house, but had lived in the tombs. ²⁸When he saw Jesus, he cried out and fell at his feet, shouting at the top of his voice, "What do you want with me, Jesus, Son of the Most High God? I beg you, don't torture me!" ²⁹For Jesus had commanded the evil spirit to come out of the man. Many times it had seized him, and though he was chained hand and foot and kept under guard, he had broken his chains and had been driven by the demon into solitary places.

³⁰Jesus asked him, "What is your name?"

"Legion," he replied, because many demons had gone into him. ³¹And they begged him repeatedly not to order them to go into the Abyss.

³²A large herd of pigs was feeding there on the hillside. The demons begged Jesus to let them go into them, and he gave them permission. ³³When the demons came out of the man, they went into the pigs, and the herd rushed down the steep bank into the lake and was drowned.

³⁴When those tending the pigs saw what had happened, they ran off and reported this in the town and countryside, ³⁵and the people went out to see what had happened. When they came to Jesus, they found the man from whom the demons had gone out, sitting at Jesus' feet, dressed and in his right mind; and they were afraid. ³⁶Those who had seen it told the people how the demon-possessed man had been cured. ³⁷Then all the people of the region of the Gerasenes asked Jesus to leave them, because they were overcome with fear. So he got into the boat and left.

³⁸The man from whom the demons had gone out begged to go with him, but Jesus sent him away, saying, ³⁹"Return home and tell how much God has done for you." So the man went away and told all over town how much Jesus had done for him.

COMMENTARY

26 "They sailed" connects this episode with the previous one, suggesting the accomplishment of the goal stated in v.22. If the purpose of the trip across the lake was to liberate the demoniac (no other activity is recorded in the region of the Gerasenes), we are probably to understand the storm at sea as the deliberate attempt of evil forces to prevent Jesus' arrival, though biblical teaching is not clear on this point. The connection between the calming of the sea and the healing of the demoniac functions to underscore the sequence of Jesus' mighty works, though one cannot rule out the presence of a continuum of demonic activity.

The NIV has adopted the reading "Gerasenes" (see Notes). Luke may have added the clause at the end of v.26 simply as a geographical explanation. Yet the fact that the locale was in Gentile territory is especially important to Luke as validating the Christian mission to Gentiles. Verse 27 implies that the man was right by the shore when Jesus arrived.

27 In vv.27 and 29 we have a classic description of demon-possession. The symptoms of such possession are like those of certain psychic illnesses known today, but Luke does not confuse illness with demon-possession (cf. 4:40–41), though he does link the two when appropriate. Certain effects of demon-possession cited in this passage are (1) disregard for personal dignity (nakedness), (2) social isolation, (3) retreat to the simplest kind of shelter (caves, often containing tombs; also being used for shelter by the very poor), (4) demons' recognition of Jesus' deity, (5) demonic control of speech, (6) shouting, and (7) extraordinary strength. The basic tragedy of the demoniac lay not in mental or physical symptoms; in his case a human being was controlled by powers totally antithetical to God, his kingdom, and the kingdom blessings of "righteousness, peace and joy in the Holy Spirit" (Ro 14:17).

28 The term "Most High God" appears in the NT in an orthodox sense, as in the OT (Ge 14:18–22; Nu 24:16; Isa 14:14; Da 3:26; 4:2), and also as a general term for deity apart from worship (contrast Lk 1:32, 35, 76 with Ac 16:17). Here it is used in the latter sense. The words "fell at his feet" do not indicate worship; the plea, "I beg you, don't torture me!" (v.28), along with the dialogue in vv.30–31, makes it clear that the man's words and actions are not his own. The "torture" (from *basanizō* [GK *989*], which can indicate either physical or mental torture) is presumably that of being cast into the "Abyss" (cf. v.31) or else the advance threat of that fate. Matthew 8:29 adds "before the appointed time," i.e., the eventual judgment of Satan and his followers after his incarceration in the Abyss (Rev 20:1–3, 10; cf. *1 En.* 15–16; *Jub.* 10:8–9; *T. Levi* 18:12).

30 Jesus was not actually an exorcist, because he did not need formulas nor did he invoke the authority of another in driving out demons. His asking the demoniac's name should not simply be interpreted as an attempt to control the demons through knowing the name of their host. The question may also function as a way to describe the person's inability to know his own identity (cf. Bock, 1:773). Moreover, it is not clear whether Jesus asked the name of the man or of the demons, though the response comes from the latter. "Legion" was not normally used as a proper name. It refers to a Roman military unit consisting of thousands of soldiers (the precise number varied). Thus "Legion" implies that there were many demons. The evocation of this name may also point to the context of spiritual warfare (cf. Bovon, 1:328).

31 The word "Abyss" (*abyssos*, GK *12*) has a long history and varied meanings ranging from the idea of primeval chaos to the abode and prison of evil beings (see Notes).

32–39 The episode of the pigs, often considered a legendary accretion, is integral to the present narrative in two ways: (1) theologically, it completes the cycle just described; and (2) psychologically, it is essential for understanding the complex response of the townspeople. The report of what happened to the pigs (vv.34, 36) first triggered the people's fear, which merged into overwhelming awe on seeing the former demoniac "dressed and in his right mind" (vv.35, 37).

But what about the ethical aspect of the pigs' destruction? Obviously, the good of the man was more important than that of the pigs. Moreover, the demons themselves insisted on entering the pigs; Jesus permitted them to do this but did not actively send them there. The discussion moves inevitably from exegesis to theology and the problem of evil—why it exists and why God in his wisdom, power, and love permits evil in this world.

The narrative does not say that the demons were destroyed so that they could never again be at large. The biblical references to the Abyss connote that God may allow evil beings to go abroad from there, just as Satan, though defeated, still roams the earth (1Pe 5:8). Nevertheless, the description of the pigs' entering the lake may foreshadow the ultimate destruction of the evil power in the end of time (cf. Craig A. Evans, *Luke* [NIBC; Peabody, Mass.: Hendrickson, 1990], 135).

33 When the demons entered the pigs, they were carried "into the lake." In ancient thought, a sea or large lake was one form of the Abyss. The cosmology behind this, however, is not clear; nor is it clear that the demons, intent on carrying out their destructive work even on animals, met the fate they wanted to avoid.

38–39 Once the demons are off the scene, attention centers on the man and Jesus. Now healed and a new man (observe the contrast between vv.27–29 and 35), the former demoniac is commissioned by Jesus not to go with him as a disciple but to be a witness where he lived. Jesus has different ways for different believers to serve him (cf. Jn 21:21–22). In the wider context of Luke's writings, one may also detect an anticipation of the future Gentile mission in Acts.

NOTES

26 Γερασηνῶν (*Gerasēnōn,* "of the Gerasenes") is the preferred reading (UBS⁴) over Γεργεσηνῶν (*Gergesēnōn,* "of the Gergesenes") and Γαδαρηνῶν (*Gadarēnōn,* "of the Gadarenes"). The appearance of several names at this point in the various MSS results not only from possible phonetic confusion but also from the existence of several towns with similar names east and south of the Sea of Galilee. "Gerasenes" seems original in Luke, as in Mark, having good MS support (see Metzger, 121). Perhaps Mark had reasons unknown to us for assuming that the territory of Gerasa extended some thirty miles from the town of that name (southeast of the sea) to the place on the shore of Galilee, which with its steep slopes and modern city of Kursi (or Kersa) may have been the scene of the incident (cf. Vincent Taylor, *The Gospel According to St. Mark* [London: Macmillan, 1963], 278). Another suggestion is that there may have been another town with the name Gerasa, or a phonetically similar name, on the seacoast near modern Kursi (Kersa) and near the steep slopes (cf. C. E. B. Cranfield, *The Gospel According to St Mark* [Cambridge: Cambridge Univ. Press, 1960], 176; Marshall, 337). But it is also possible that Kursi marks the site of Gergesa rather than a second Gerasa. Origen, writing on John 6, suggested that the town was Gergesa—a suggestion reflected in some MSS.

The claim of Gadara (the modern Umm Qeis) to be the site of the miracle lies in the importance of that name in MSS of Matthew, in its location six miles from the shore of the lake, and from the possibility that the territory named after the town might have extended to the shore of Galilee. It is possible that people in the area were identified by the name of the more important city of Gerasa rather than by that of the smaller Gadara (cf. E. Smick, *Archaeology of the Jordan Valley* [Grand Rapids: Baker, 1973], 135–37; however, Smick did not deal with M. Avi-Yonah's evidence against Gadara [*The Holy Land* (Grand Rapids: Baker, 1966), 174]). Without more certain knowledge, the textual reading Γερασηνῶν, *Gerasēnōn,* should tentatively be considered correct. We must also keep in mind that all three Synoptic Gospels use a general expression, εἰς τὴν χώραν (*eis tēn chōran,* "into the region"), leaving the precise location unspecified.

29 The verb παρήγγειλεν (*parēngeilen,* "had commanded," from παραγγέλλω, *parangellō,* GK *4133*) is aorist. The twenty-fifth edition of the Nestle Greek text had the imperfect παρήγγελλεν (*parēngellen,* "was commanding")—a reading assumed by Turner (*Syntax,* 65) and Marshall, 338. However, the UBS text has the aorist, following B and $\mathfrak{P}^{75}$ among other MSS, but with no footnote and consequently no comment in Metzger's *Textual Commentary*.

31 The word ἄβυσσος (*abyssos*, "Abyss," GK *12*) is used only here in Luke (cf. Ro 10:7; Rev 9:1–3; 11:7; 17:8; 20:1–3). In the OT, the term came to be used to refer to the place of the dead (e.g., Ps 63:9), and in Second Temple Jewish traditions the Abyss is the prison for the demons (e.g., *1 En.* 10:4–6; 88:1–3). The connection between the Abyss and chaotic waters can also be found in the contemporary Jewish literature (cf. David E. Aune, *Revelation 6–16* [WBC; Nashville: Nelson, 1998], 525–26).

10. Jesus' Power to Heal and Restore Life (8:40–56)

OVERVIEW

The third part of the section on Jesus' power is composed of two intertwined stories—a pattern of alternation common to all the synoptic accounts and apparently one that goes back to the tradition (see Introduction, pp. 29–30). We must ask why the two events are so closely connected. In both, the power and compassion of Jesus are notably displayed. Also in both, we see the importance of faith. Another point of comparison may be that Jairus's daughter (vv.40–42a) was about twelve years old, while the woman (vv.42b–48) had suffered a hemorrhage for the same period of time. Perhaps we ought also to reflect on the tension created for Jesus and his disciples by the two pressing needs: prevention of impending death, and helping a pathetic woman whose illness had isolated her from normal life and relationships.

[40]Now when Jesus returned, a crowd welcomed him, for they were all expecting him. [41]Then a man named Jairus, a ruler of the synagogue, came and fell at Jesus' feet, pleading with him to come to his house [42]because his only daughter, a girl of about twelve, was dying.

As Jesus was on his way, the crowds almost crushed him. [43]And a woman was there who had been subject to bleeding for twelve years, but no one could heal her. [44]She came up behind him and touched the edge of his cloak, and immediately her bleeding stopped.

[45]"Who touched me?" Jesus asked.

When they all denied it, Peter said, "Master, the people are crowding and pressing against you."

[46]But Jesus said, "Someone touched me; I know that power has gone out from me."

[47]Then the woman, seeing that she could not go unnoticed, came trembling and fell at his feet. In the presence of all the people, she told why she had touched him and how she had been instantly healed. [48]Then he said to her, "Daughter, your faith has healed you. Go in peace."

[49]While Jesus was still speaking, someone came from the house of Jairus, the synagogue ruler. "Your daughter is dead," he said. "Don't bother the teacher any more."

⁵⁰Hearing this, Jesus said to Jairus, "Don't be afraid; just believe, and she will be healed."
⁵¹When he arrived at the house of Jairus, he did not let anyone go in with him except Peter, John and James, and the child's father and mother. ⁵²Meanwhile, all the people were wailing and mourning for her. "Stop wailing," Jesus said. "She is not dead but asleep."
⁵³They laughed at him, knowing that she was dead. ⁵⁴But he took her by the hand and said, "My child, get up!" ⁵⁵Her spirit returned, and at once she stood up. Then Jesus told them to give her something to eat. ⁵⁶Her parents were astonished, but he ordered them not to tell anyone what had happened.

COMMENTARY

40–42a The words "now when Jesus returned" (v.40) establish a continuity with the preceding episodes and alert the reader to this sequence of Jesus' mighty works. Once again Luke shows us the popularity of Jesus. The only recent event to have caused such expectation was the episode in Gerasene territory, word of which must have spread immediately. The present section now before us ends, by contrast, with Jesus' command not to speak of the girl's healing (v.56).

As a leader of the synagogue, Jairus was locally prominent (see Notes). In the extremity of his need, he humbled himself as a suppliant. Luke describes the girl as Jairus's "only" (*monogenēs*, GK 3666) daughter (v.42a). The term "only" (or "one and only," as in Jn 3:16) adds to the pathos, as it is used in Scripture to designate an only child who has died or is in mortal danger (see Notes, 7:12). The further detail, "about twelve," points out that in Jewish society she was about to become a young lady of marriageable age. This intensifies the poignancy.

42b–46 The "crowds" (*ochloi*, GK 4063), now an integral part of the narrative, cover the woman's furtive approach to Jesus. The verbs "almost crushed" (*synepnigon*, v.42b), "crowding" (*synechousin*, v.45), and "pressing against" (*apothlibousin*, v.45) bring the scene to life. Luke does not specify the nature of the

"bleeding" (v.43), which is usually taken to have been a gynecological problem. The restrictions imposed by Leviticus 15:25–33 and by Jewish custom (codified in *m. Zabim*) would have radically affected the woman's life. But her primary problem was the discomfort and embarrassment of her prolonged malady. If Luke did not mention the failure of the physicians to help the woman (v.43; cf. Mk 5:26) because he was one himself, it would be understandable. Yet the omission may be of no more significance than others (as in v.42; cf. Mk 5:23).

More serious questions are raised (1) by the woman's touching of his cloak (v.44), as though magical power could be transferred, and (2) by Jesus' awareness of the transfer of power apparently without knowledge of who had done this (vv.45–46). As to the first, the intrusion of Hellenistic ideas and superstitions may indeed have influenced her action. But Jesus did not quench the "smoldering wick" (Mt 12:20) of her faith; instead, he fanned it into flame (v.48). Elsewhere it is implied that God honored even stranger expressions of faith, presumably because imperfect knowledge did not hinder confidence in the Lord himself (cf. Ac 5:14; 19:11–12).

Regarding Jesus' awareness of the transfer of some of his power, his question (v.45) need not imply ignorance of the woman's identity but only his intention of singling her out. The dialogue (vv.45b–46) suggests that he knew only the fact that power had been transferred. (Just as Jesus was the bearer of the Spirit [see comments at 3:22], so he was the bearer of the power of God.) While at times he chose to heal people who had not expressed any faith, the reverse seems to be true here—namely, that someone with faith in him drew on his power without his conscious selection of that person. Since he bore the very power of God, and since God the Father had not assumed the voluntary human limitations the incarnate Son had, God could have extended his healing power through his Son even though Jesus may not yet have been aware of the woman's identity. "Power has gone out from me" (v.46) does not mean that Jesus' power was thereby diminished, as though it were a consumable commodity.

47 The woman had desired to go unnoticed, possibly because of the embarrassment of her illness or because of her audacity in breaking her ritual isolation to touch Jesus' cloak. Her public confession of faith may constitute the purpose for which Jesus asked, "Who touched me?" (v.45). This focus on public confession—an element missing in the synoptic parallels—reflects Luke's interest in the public recognition of Jesus' power that leads to the question of his own identity in the next chapter (cf. V. K. Robbins, "The Woman Who Touched Jesus' Garment: Socio-Rhetorical Analysis of the Synoptic Accounts," *NTS* 33 [1987]: 502–15).

48 To address an older person as "daughter" reflects the practice of Jewish teachers, but it may also function to highlight the authority of Jesus as the Messiah (cf. Bovon, 1:339). In light of the discussion of Jesus' true family in 8:19–21, this address may also point to the creation of the new family based on a person's response of faith. The one who is not allowed to worship in the temple because of her physical "impurity" can now worship and praise the Son of God. As in 7:50, the concluding bene-

diction points beyond physical healing when both "faith" and "peace" describe the experience of one who is now transformed by grace.

49–50 The episode of the sick woman delayed Jesus until word of the death of Jairus's daughter reached him (v.49). Yet the woman's healing also paved the way for Jesus' words in v.50. The note on "believing" and "healing" ties this narrative to the previous healing (cf. v.48).

51–56 It was only on particular occasions that Jesus selected Peter, James, and John alone to be with him—e.g., at the transfiguration (Mt 17:1; Mk 9:2; Lk 9:28) and in Gethsemane (Mt 26:37; Mk 14:33). The secrecy involved and the command to silence (v.56) may seem incomprehensible to some apart from the awkward theory of the "messianic secret" (see comments at 7:21–23; 9:21). In actuality Jesus often tried to avoid publicity to prevent premature or misguided declarations of his messiahship from being made. Of course, it would be hard to keep silent about the girl's restoration to active life, but the use of the word "asleep" (v.52) might have diverted the attention of the mourners and others from Jesus to the girl. While Jesus' statement, "she is . . . asleep" (*katheudei*, GK *2761*), meant that her death was not forever but only till the resurrection (cf. Jn 11:11; 1Th 4:13–14), the others probably assumed that she had, after all, only been in a coma. If they thought she was only revived, not raised from death, Jesus could thus reserve the public acknowledgment of his messiahship till the proper time. But the words "her spirit returned" (v.55) plainly imply that the child actually was dead. Because of these words, Marshall, 348, suggests that the miracle is not to be described as a resuscitation of a body but as the calling back of the girl's spirit (see Notes). The secrecy of this miracle is in contrast with the public nature of the raising of the young man from Nain (7:16–17), and it is a theme that is taken from Mark.

NOTES

41 The description of Jairus as "a ruler of the synagogue" (ἄρχων τῆς συναγωγῆς, *archōn tēs synagōgēs*) may reflect Luke's interest in highlighting the superiority of Jesus over the authorities of the Jewish institution. This reading is supported by the fact that this was primarily an honorific title (cf. P. W. Van der Horst, *Ancient Jewish Epitaphs* [Kampen: Kok, 1991], 89–90).

55 The word πνεῦμα (*pneuma*, GK *4460*) may be used in a metaphorical sense in describing the return of the "spirit" to the physical body. It can also be translated as "breath" (cf. Fitzmyer, 749) and can therefore describe the observable sign of the gift of life.

11. Sending Out the Twelve (9:1–6)

OVERVIEW

Luke describes the mission of the Twelve in less detail than does Matthew, who presents it as one of his five major discourses. Some of the instructions that appear in Matthew 10:1–10 (as well as the saying about the harvest in Mt 9:37–38) are not found here in Luke 9 but rather among the instructions to the group of seventy-two sent out by Jesus (Lk 10:1–12). There are a large number of verbal similarities among the accounts in Matthew 10, Mark 6, Luke 9, and Luke 10, along with some apparent discrepancies. The usual approach to these textual phenomena is to postulate an intertwining of traditions. There is also the possibility that Jesus gave approximately similar instructions on different occasions and that parts of these instructions were also repeated in the early church as normative guidelines. (For example, the teaching in Mt 10:10 about the worker's being worth his keep is repeated in Lk 10:7; 1Co 9:14; 1Ti 5:18; *Did.* 13:1.) What is described in these "sending" passages in the Gospels is not appointment to a permanent office but commissioning for an immediate task. The practice of sending a man on a mission empowered to act with full authority on behalf of the sender is known from the Talmud (*y. Ḥag.* 1.8). Such an appointment could therefore be repeated using words essentially similar though varying in detail. The common theme found in the biblical passages cited above and in others (e.g., 3Jn 5–7) is that the servants of Christ should go forth not seeking support from unbelievers but trusting God completely to supply their needs through his people.

¹When Jesus had called the Twelve together, he gave them power and authority to drive out all demons and to cure diseases, ²and he sent them out to preach the kingdom of God and to heal the sick. ³He told them: "Take nothing for the journey—no staff, no bag, no bread, no money, no extra tunic. ⁴Whatever house you enter, stay there until you leave that town. ⁵If people do not welcome you, shake the dust off your feet when you leave their town, as a testimony against them." ⁶So they set out and went from village to village, preaching the gospel and healing people everywhere.

COMMENTARY

1–2 The "Twelve" (*dōdeka*) receive both the "power" (*dynamis*, GK *1539*) and "authority" (*exousia*, GK *2026*) to do works of the sort Jesus has performed in the episodes Luke has thus far reported. Luke includes the word *dynamis*, which does not occur in either Matthew 10 or Mark 6. While the word *dynamis* itself is not usually prominent in Luke's vocabulary (it is absent in 9:27, but the parallel in Mk 9:1 has it), nevertheless signs and wonders are important in his books, especially in Acts. This is because Luke stresses the validation of the gospel by, among other means, the apostles' miraculous power as God's messengers. Others were claiming supernatural powers (cf. the Jewish sorcerer Bar-Jesus, or Elymas, and the itinerant Jewish exorcists in Ac 13:6–10; 19:13); so it was necessary for Jesus' disciples to have both "authority" (*exousia*) and "power" (*dynamis*). This principle appears in a different context in Luke 5:24. The connection between the casting out of demons and the coming of the kingdom is not as clear there as in 11:20; but the double mention of the ministry of healing here in 9:1–2 suggests that relationship. The authority of the Twelve extends over "all" (*panta*) demons. None are too powerful for them.

3 The instructions indicate the urgency of the task. The severely limited provisions Jesus allows the Twelve to take along may be intended to express their dependence on God alone. Without bread or money they would need to be given daily food. The forbidden "bag" (*pēra*, GK *4385*) may be the kind frequently used by itinerant philosophers and religious mendicants for begging (see Notes). The disciples are learning to trust God for food, protection, and shelter. (See comments at 22:35–38 on the apparent reverse of these instructions.)

4 The disciples should receive hospitality graciously. Hospitality was important as well as necessary in days of difficult traveling conditions and poor accommodations at inns. The disciples are not to move about from house to house, a practice that might gain them more support but would insult their hosts.

5 The disciples will also encounter those who refuse them a welcome. As a solemn symbol of judgment, the disciples are to "shake the dust" of an unresponsive town off of their feet, just as Jewish travelers might do on returning from pagan territory (Str-B 1:571). This action expressed symbolically what Jesus would say about Korazin and Bethsaida in 10:13–15. Jesus himself later wept over Jerusalem's unresponsiveness (19:41).

Elsewhere Jesus specifies the kind of person who is to have the privilege of supporting the disciples. He must be a "worthy [*axios*, GK *545*] person" (Mt 10:11), a "man of peace" (*huios eirēnēs*, lit., "son of peace," Lk 10:6). Such a person is clearly in sympathy with the message brought by Jesus' disciples.

6 Luke concludes this section with a summary of the mission of the Twelve, including another reference to preaching and healing. Their instructions had not included any limitation of scope such as in Matthew 10:5. "Everywhere" (*pantachou*) may even indicate the opposite.

NOTES

1, 2, 6 Luke uses two words for healing without a difference in meaning: θεραπεύω (*therapeuō*, GK *2543*) and ἰάομαι (*iaomai*, GK *2615*). See *NIDNTT* 2:164–69.

3 The problem of Luke's "no staff" (μήτε ῥάβδον, *mēte rhabdon*, lit., "neither a staff"; cf. Mt 10:10: μηδὲ ῥάβδον, *mēde rhabdon*, "no . . . staff") over against the apparently contradictory words in Mark 6:8 (μηδὲν . . . εἰ μὴ ῥάβδον μόνον, *mēden . . . ei mē rhabdon monon*, "nothing . . . except a staff") has several possible explanations: (1) Luke follows Q, which contains the original wording; he is not intentionally changing Mark (Marshall, *Luke: Historian and Theologian*, 352); this may well be so, but the difference remains. (2) The authors had different types of staves in mind, one for walking and the other, a club, for protection. D. A. S. Ravens ("Luke 9:7–62 and the Prophetic Role of Jesus," *NTS* 36 [1990]: 121) further suggests that the Lukan and Matthean staff points back to Moses' staff, which serves as a symbol of his miraculous power (Ex 4:2–17; 7:15–20). This reading suffers from the fact that only one Greek word is used for "staff." (3) Mark adapts his wording so as to parallel the instructions to Israel (Ex 12:11); but the difference remains. (4) Two similar-sounding Aramaic words are used, meaning "except" and "and not" respectively (M. Black, *An Aramaic Approach to the Gospels and Acts* [3d ed.; Oxford: Clarendon, 1967], 216ff.). This is attractive but improbable; it does not solve the problem for those who hold to the inerrancy of the canonical Greek text. (5) Jesus taught that the disciples were not to procure a staff if they lacked one; but this fits Matthew 10:10 better than Luke, for Matthew 10:9 uses κτάομαι (*ktaomai*, "acquire," GK *3227*), whereas Luke uses αἴρω (*airō*, "take," GK *149*). (6) Jesus meant that they were not to take an *extra* staff. This would fit the wording of each gospel, but it leaves the question of whether anyone would normally carry two staffs.

The answer probably lies near the approaches of (1), (5), and (6). Whether or not one chooses some such explanation or does not attempt a harmonization of detail, the intent in all three Synoptics is the same: travel light, trust God, accept the gracious help of pious people, and do not let a mere staff interfere with these principles.

The word πήρα (*pēra*, "bag," GK *4385*) was commonly used to designate both a leather pouch in which provisions could be carried and a wallet for collecting alms (cf. LSJ, s.v.; BDAG, 811). The latter use was so well known and such a symbol of itinerant begging preachers that it probably has that sense here.

12. Herod's Perplexity (9:7–9)

OVERVIEW

Jesus has come to the end of his great Galilean ministry. The subsequent events take place to the north and east of Galilee and culminate in the confession of Jesus' messiahship, followed by the first prediction of Jesus' passion (9:19–27). These events are related more fully in Mark 6:30–8:26 along with other episodes Luke chose not to include, perhaps (1) because of their similarity with the other examples of Jesus' ministry that Luke includes elsewhere; (2) because of the limitations of space; and (3) in order to move quickly to Peter's confession in 9:18–21. The omission of the Markan material also has the effect of removing stories that are related to the Gentiles. This may reflect Luke's interest in focusing on Jesus' mission to Israel at this point of his narrative (cf. D. A. S. Ravens, "Luke 9:7–62 and the Prophetic Role of Jesus," *NTS* 36 [1990]: 121). It is also possible that Luke used an earlier draft of Mark that lacked these parts, but this cannot be proved. Luke does include the event that is most important for his purpose—the feeding of the five thousand (9:10–17). And here, prior to that narrative, he states that Herod "was perplexed" (*diēporei*, GK *1389*, v.7) about Jesus. This is of great importance in the sequence of Luke's gospel because it introduces the question, "Who, then, is this . . . ?" (v.9; cf. Mk 6:16, where Herod answers his own question). This all-important question is picked up again in vv.18–20.

> [7]Now Herod the tetrarch heard about all that was going on. And he was perplexed, because some were saying that John had been raised from the dead, [8]others that Elijah had appeared, and still others that one of the prophets of long ago had come back to life. [9]But Herod said, "I beheaded John. Who, then, is this I hear such things about?" And he tried to see him.

COMMENTARY

7–9 The focus on Herod's perplexity appears only in Luke, and this passage is more concerned with Jesus' identity than with the fate of John the Baptist.

7 "All that was going on" (*ta ginomena panta*) probably refers to the activities of both Jesus (cf. Mt 14:1) and the disciples on their mission. In Matthew 14:2 and Mark 6:14 Herod is interested in the "powers" (*dynameis*, GK *1539*) Jesus was reputed to have. (On the identity of Herod the tetrarch, see comments at 3:1. Luke uses the proper official title.)

8 The questions of Jesus' identity and also of the reappearance of a dead prophet are reintroduced in vv.18–19 and parallels (cf. Jn 1:19–22). John the Baptist is naturally on Herod's mind (and doubtless also on his conscience). Luke makes only a brief reference to John's execution (cf. 3:19–20, described more fully in Mt 14:3–12; Mk 6:17–29). Herod was not able to see Jesus (v.9) but had his curiosity satisfied when Pilate sent Jesus to him (23:8–11).

9 The question Herod raised provides an introduction to the material that follows as Luke attempts to provide the answer by showing who Jesus is. His identity is revealed not only by his miraculous deeds (vv.10–17) and the revelation of his exalted status (vv.18–21) but is also further and fully revealed only through his journey to the cross (vv.51–56).

13. Feeding the Five Thousand (9:10–17)

OVERVIEW

The fact that this miracle is in all four gospels indicates its importance. Luke's account is sparse, straightforward, and a little shorter than Mark's, though it includes some additional words (e.g., on the kingdom, v.11). This story recalls the stories of Elijah and Elisha where one finds the multiplication of meat and oil (1Ki 17:7–16; 2Ki 4). Second Kings 4:42–44, in particular, provides numerous formal parallels to our present story: the approach of those in need, the presentation of the bread, the command of the prophet, the reaction of the servant/disciples, the reissuing of the order, the distribution of the food, and the note concerning the leftovers (see F. Bovon, "The Role of the Scriptures in the Composition of the Gospel Accounts: The Temptations of Jesus [Lk 4:1–13 par.] and the Multiplication of the Loaves [Lk 9:10–17 par.]," in *Luke and Acts*, ed. G. O'Collins and F. Marconi [New York: Paulist,

1993], 26–31). The Elijah–Elisha stories, in turn, find their roots in the exodus story, in which God's presence in the midst of his people is symbolized by the provision of food. As in these OT stories, Jesus' feeding of the crowds shows that God still remembers his people and that the time of God's abundant provision is present.

---

[10]When the apostles returned, they reported to Jesus what they had done. Then he took them with him and they withdrew by themselves to a town called Bethsaida, [11]but the crowds learned about it and followed him. He welcomed them and spoke to them about the kingdom of God, and healed those who needed healing.

[12]Late in the afternoon the Twelve came to him and said, "Send the crowd away so they can go to the surrounding villages and countryside and find food and lodging, because we are in a remote place here."

[13]He replied, "You give them something to eat."

They answered, "We have only five loaves of bread and two fish—unless we go and buy food for all this crowd." [14](About five thousand men were there.)

But he said to his disciples, "Have them sit down in groups of about fifty each." [15]The disciples did so, and everybody sat down. [16]Taking the five loaves and the two fish and looking up to heaven, he gave thanks and broke them. Then he gave them to the disciples to set before the people. [17]They all ate and were satisfied, and the disciples picked up twelve basketfuls of broken pieces that were left over.

COMMENTARY

10 The return of the disciples is the occasion for Jesus' withdrawal to Bethsaida (for the purpose of resting, according to Mk 6:31). This town was on the northeast side of the lake outside Herod's territory. Only Luke mentions its name.

11 The image of the shepherd in the parallels (Mk 6:34; cf. Mt 14:14) is here replaced by that of the Savior, who "welcomed" (*apodexamenos*, GK 622) all who came and who told them about the kingdom. Thus even a time set aside for rest becomes an opportunity to fulfill the purpose expressed in Luke 4:43. As in Matthew 14:14, Luke

mentions healings. He presents Jesus as having ministered to the total needs of people as he taught, healed, and fed those who came to him.

12–13 Each of the Synoptics records the disciples' unimaginative suggestion that the crowds be sent away to find their own food (v.12; Mt 14:15; Mk 6:36) and Jesus' response, "You give them something to eat" (v.13; Mt 14:16; Mk 6:37), putting the responsibility back on the disciples. The reference to the "remote place" (*erēmō*, lit., "wilderness," GK 2245) recalls the feeding of the people of Israel in the wilderness. The loaves (*artoi*, GK 788) were a basic food often eaten stuffed with fish (*ichthys*, GK 2716) from the Sea of Galilee. While the loaves naturally evoke the memory of the feeding with manna, the fish may also point to the quail from the sea (Nu 11:31). In Jewish exegetical traditions, the quail from the sea came to be understood as flying fish (cf. Bovon, "Role of the Scriptures," 28). The loaves and fish, therefore, recall God's provision during the exodus event.

14–17 The crowd was much greater than five thousand, since there were that many "men" (*andres*, GK 467), plus women and children (Mt 14:21).

Luke briefly summarizes the miracle, showing the orderliness of the distribution, Jesus' thanks (v.16, providing a lasting example for Christian table fellowship in the presence of God), and the adequacy of the food (v.17). Luke's description of the miracle does not direct attention to the Lord's Supper, though there are some common factors. It seems best to understand this feeding story and the Lord's Supper in the light of the OT provision stories as well as the banquet theme that appears throughout the gospel of Luke.

NOTES

16 The phrase εὐλόγησεν αὐτοὺς (*eulogēsen* [GK 2328] *autous*) could mean "he blessed them," i.e., the fish, as an act of consecration (KJV, NASB), or "he gave thanks for them," which is the sense of the NIV. The latter meaning is supported by Marshall, 362, who takes αὐτοὺς, *autous*, to be an accusative of respect rather than a direct object; so "Jesus' prayer of thanks will here be one of thanks for what God is able to do to the bread."

D. Climax of Jesus' Galilean Ministry (9:18–50)

1. Peter's Confession of Christ (9:18–20)

OVERVIEW

Luke moves directly from the miracle of multiplying the loaves and fish, which pointed to Jesus' messiahship, to Peter's confession of that messiahship. To do this, Luke omits or includes elsewhere the material in Mark 6:45–8:26 (see comments at 9:7–9).

If the priority of Mark (or Matthew) is assumed, questions regarding the historicity and literary history of this narrative properly belong to the study of those gospels (cf. Mt 16:13–20; Mk 8:27–30). However, it is important to recognize the contextual integrity of its position at this point in Luke, namely,

following Herod's question about Jesus' identity (v.9) and the feeding of the five thousand, with its messianic implications. It leads directly to the transfiguration narrative through the natural transition of v.28.

Theologically, this is the most important statement thus far in Luke. It is the first time a disciple refers to Jesus as Messiah (cf. 2:11, 26; 3:15; 4:41). Observe that immediately after Peter's great declaration, Jesus predicts his own rejection, death, and resurrection (v.22), thus shedding light on the implications of his messiahship.

¹⁸Once when Jesus was praying in private and his disciples were with him, he asked them, "Who do the crowds say I am?"

¹⁹They replied, "Some say John the Baptist; others say Elijah; and still others, that one of the prophets of long ago has come back to life."

²⁰"But what about you?" he asked. "Who do you say I am?"

Peter answered, "The Christ of God."

COMMENTARY

18–19 Luke's introduction to the dialogue between Jesus and his disciples is unique in two respects: he omits any reference to Caesarea Philippi and inserts a reference to Jesus at prayer (cf. Mt 16:13; Mk 8:27). The omission is surprising because one might have expected Luke, with his interest in the Gentile world, to show Jesus' penetration of the area of Caesarea, where extant inscriptions still show the influence of Hellenistic religion. On the contrary, Luke apparently disconnects Peter's confession from time and space in order to emphasize the link between the miraculous feeding and also Jesus' intimate fellowship with God, as exemplified in his praying. This is one of the insights Luke gives us into Jesus' prayer life (cf. 3:21; 6:12; 11:1); as in other instances, significant development in the ministry of Jesus is preceded by the act of prayer. Jesus asks for the opinion of the "crowds" (*ochloi* [GK *4063*], in place of *anthrōpoi*, "men," GK *476*, in Mt 16:13; Mk 8:27), a word Luke frequently uses to draw attention to the uncommitted masses of people who heard Jesus. The responses (v.19) echo the rumors expressed in vv.7–8.

20 "Christ" (*Christos*, GK *5986*) represents the Hebrew word for "anointed" and was first an adjective before it came to be used as a proper name. Its OT occurrences with the idea of a coming anointed King include Psalm 2:2 and Daniel 9:26. The idea, without the title, appears in such passages as Isaiah 9:6–7; 11:1–16. The additional words "of God" in Luke do not explicitly express sonship as does the longer phrase in the parallel in Matthew 16:16, but they do emphasize Jesus' divine commission.

2. The Suffering and Glory of the Son of Man (9:21–27)

²¹Jesus strictly warned them not to tell this to anyone. ²²And he said, "The Son of Man must suffer many things and be rejected by the elders, chief priests and teachers of the law, and he must be killed and on the third day be raised to life."

²³Then he said to them all: "If anyone would come after me, he must deny himself and take up his cross daily and follow me. ²⁴For whoever wants to save his life will lose it, but whoever loses his life for me will save it. ²⁵What good is it for a man to gain the whole world, and yet lose or forfeit his very self? ²⁶If anyone is ashamed of me and my words, the

Son of Man will be ashamed of him when he comes in his glory and in the glory of the Father and of the holy angels. [27]I tell you the truth, some who are standing here will not taste death before they see the kingdom of God."

COMMENTARY

21 The command "not to tell" others (see comments at 8:51–56) probably stems from two circumstances: (1) the Jewish people, chafing under the domination of Rome, were all too ready to join a messianic revolutionary; and (2) there was apparently an understanding that one should not claim messiahship for himself but should first do the works of the Messiah and then be acclaimed as such by others (cf. Longenecker, 71ff.). The idea that Mark had imposed a motif of secrecy (the so-called "messianic secret") on the tradition of Jesus' teachings is neither a necessary nor a provable hypothesis for explaining Jesus' commands to silence in Mark and the other gospels (see comments at 7:20–23; 8:56).

22 This statement is known as the "first passion prediction." Though there had been foreshadowings of a dark fate for Jesus—Simeon's prediction (2:35) and Jesus' statement about the bridegroom (5:35)—here in Jesus' words is the first explicit recitation in Luke of the sequence of events at the close of his life. Some scholars find it difficult to accept the authenticity of such a prediction. Arguments pro and con tend to revolve around subjective judgments as to what Jesus might or might not have foreseen at this point in his ministry and what may or may not have been added editorially. The entire following teaching on discipleship requires some basic understanding of the passion and, indeed, of the crucifixion, since Jesus mentions the cross (v.23). The use of the term "Son of Man" (vv.22, 26) is understandable assuming that (1) Jesus

used it frequently, (2) Jesus used it especially in connection with his passion, and (3) the occurrence of the term in Matthew 16:13 is not editorial but reflects Jesus' actual use of it in his initial question to the disciples.

The word "must" (*dei*, GK 1256) is again the way Luke refers to the necessity of the divine plan to be accomplished. The passive verb "be raised" (*egerthēnai*, GK 1586) can be considered a "divine passive" where God is understood as the implied subject. That God raised Jesus up is explicitly stated in Acts (e.g., 2:32: "God has raised this Jesus to life").

23 The person who wants to be Jesus' disciple— to "come after me" (*opisō mou erchesthai*)—can only truly be said to "follow" (*akoloutheitō*, GK 199) him when he has made and implemented a radical decision to "deny" (*arnēsasthō*, GK 766) himself. This verb functions as a polar opposite to the verb "confess" (*homologeō*, GK 3933), which has the sense of acknowledging a thing or person. We should, therefore, on the one hand "confess" Christ, i.e., acknowledge him and identify ourselves with him, but on the other hand "deny" ourselves. This means that as Christians we will not set our desires and will against the right Christ has to our lives. Furthermore, we are to recognize that we now live for the sake of Christ, not for our own sake. The next words about the daily cross explain and intensify this principle. A condemned criminal was forced to carry one bar of his cross to the place of execution. He was on the way to death. To "take up [the] cross" daily is to live each day not for self but for Christ.

The sense of the word "follow" (*akoloutheitō*) at the end of the verse has to be slightly different from the phrase "come after me" (*opisō mou erchesthai*) at the beginning of Jesus' command, unless we assume that Jesus is simply repeating what he said in this verse. The word *akoloutheitō* can refer to the act of accompanying someone on the journey (see 23:27; cf. José Caba, "From Lukan Parenesis to Johannine Christology: Luke 9:23–24 and John 12:25–26," in *Luke and Acts* [ed. O'Collins and Marconi], 52), and this would fit in the context here as Jesus was about to begin his journey to the cross. The literal journey becomes a metaphor for the disciples of Jesus.

24–26 These two statements (vv.24–25) show the futility of clinging to one's "life" (*psychē*, GK *6034*), because that, paradoxically, would result in losing the very self one wants to preserve. In contrast, the person who invests his or her life for God finds that, like the kernel of wheat planted in the ground (Jn 12:24), the "buried" life is not lost after all. Jesus next uses a "magnificent hyperbole" (Morris, 170) to emphasize his point. The world the disciple is willing to forfeit rather than lose his "very self" is, after all, to be succeeded by the new order when the Son of Man "comes in his glory" (v.26). If one seeks gain by letting the world's view of Christ make him ashamed of the Lord, he rightly draws a corresponding response from the glorified Son of Man. Mention of the fact that the glory is Christ's own, along with that of the Father and of the angels, heightens the contrast with the shame Christ experienced in the world. Moreover, this verse points to the Lukan focus on the connection between suffering and glory: the glory of Christ is manifested precisely in and through his suffering, and this becomes the basis for Luke's understanding of discipleship.

27 This is a perplexing verse. "Some who are standing here" (*tines tōn autou hestēkotōn*) may refer to the disciples as a group as opposed to the crowd, or to some of the disciples as opposed to the rest of the disciples. Marshall, 378, argues well for the former. But both are possible. Even if the larger group from whom the "some" are selected is broader than the Twelve, it does not mean that the select group includes all or even most of the Twelve.

There have been several proposals offered as to the specific experience Jesus had in mind when he said, "Some who are standing here will not taste death before they see the kingdom of God." If he meant the future consummation of a literal kingdom, he would have been mistaken, for that had not yet occurred. He may have meant Pentecost, for the coming of the Spirit brought the dynamic of the kingdom (Mk 9:1 has the word "power," *dynamis*, GK *1539*), but the imagery is not obvious. The resurrection of Jesus declared him "with power to be the Son of God" (Ro 1:4), but that event does not seem to be understood in Scripture as an expression of the kingdom as such. It is true that Pentecost and the resurrection are expressions of the same power, by which the kingdom of God proved itself over the kingdom of Satan and his demons in Jesus' casting out demons.

There is, however, another event—the transfiguration (9:28–36), which Luke is about to describe—that may contribute to our understanding of this saying. It focuses even more sharply on the kingdom. The transfiguration is, among other things, a preview of the Parousia, which is clearly connected with the reign of Christ (see comments at vv.28–36). Moreover, the specific reference to the brief interval of time between the occasion of this saying and the transfiguration—an interval made even more specific by Luke's "about eight days after Jesus said this" (v.28)—tightens the connection between the saying and that event. In 2 Peter 1:16–18, Peter mentions in connection with the transfiguration the elements of power and the coming of Jesus that are associated with the kingdom.

If Jesus was referring to the transfiguration, then the "some" who would not die before seeing the kingdom were Peter, John, and James, who saw Jesus transfigured. Moreover, the transfiguration could also be understood as paving the way for the events of the cross and the resurrection. These events, in turn, point to the realization of God's reign on earth, though the final consummation is yet to come. The fact that Jesus said they would "not taste death" before participating in an event only days away can therefore be explained by the fact that the kingdom's manifestation is not realized simply in the transfiguration event.

NOTES

21 This verse begins with ὁ δέ (*ho de*), a construction left untranslated in the NIV. This may serve as an indicator that a contrast to the previous verse is intended. The emphasis on the suffering of Christ thus serves as a contrast to the jubilant proclamation of Jesus' messiahship (cf. Helmut Flender, *St. Luke: Theologian of Redemptive History* [Philadelphia: Fortress, 1967], 31).

3. The Transfiguration (9:28–36)

OVERVIEW

This glorious transformation of the appearance of Christ is one of the most significant events between his birth and passion. In each of the Synoptic Gospels it stands as a magnificent christological statement. Both the transformation itself and the divine commentary expressed in the voice from heaven declare Jesus Christ to be the beloved Son of God. Luke emphasizes a further dimension of the event— the suffering that lay ahead of God's chosen Servant. Luke does this both through the conversation of Moses and Elijah (vv.30–31) and a slightly different wording of the message of the voice.

In addition to the main elements of the transfiguration itself and the words from heaven, the narrative contains several motifs of deep significance: the eight-day interlude (v.28), the mountain, Moses and Elijah (v.30), Jesus' impending "departure" (*exodos*, GK *2016*, v.31), the shelters (v.33), and the cloud (v.34).

Two frames of reference will help us understand these motifs. One is the exodus of the people of Israel from Egypt with the events at Mount Sinai, especially Moses' experience on the mountain (Ex 24). The other is the second coming of Christ, the "parousia" (cf. reference in v.26). These two frames of reference—one past, the other future—will help us understand the biblical imagery the events of the transfiguration episode would have brought to the minds of the disciples and all later readers familiar with Scripture.

There seems to be a pattern involving the two adjoining sections—vv.18–27 and vv.28–36. Three themes are stated and then repeated in reverse (chiastic) order. The first theme is the affirmation of Jesus' identity as the Messiah (v.20); the second is the prediction of his passion (v.22); and the third is the promise of his glory (v.26). In the transfiguration narratives the order is reversed (not only in

Luke, but also, except for the words about his "departure," in Matthew and Mark), and the three themes are portrayed dramatically. The third theme, that of Jesus' glory, is first portrayed (v.29). The pre- diction of his passion is confirmed by the conversa- tion between Moses and Elijah (v.30). The identity of Jesus is the subject of the heavenly proclamation (v.35).

> [28]About eight days after Jesus said this, he took Peter, John and James with him and went up onto a mountain to pray. [29]As he was praying, the appearance of his face changed, and his clothes became as bright as a flash of lightning. [30]Two men, Moses and Elijah, [31]appeared in glorious splendor, talking with Jesus. They spoke about his departure, which he was about to bring to fulfillment at Jerusalem. [32]Peter and his companions were very sleepy, but when they became fully awake, they saw his glory and the two men standing with him. [33]As the men were leaving Jesus, Peter said to him, "Master, it is good for us to be here. Let us put up three shelters—one for you, one for Moses and one for Elijah." (He did not know what he was saying.)
>
> [34]While he was speaking, a cloud appeared and enveloped them, and they were afraid as they entered the cloud. [35]A voice came from the cloud, saying, "This is my Son, whom I have chosen; listen to him." [36]When the voice had spoken, they found that Jesus was alone. The disciples kept this to themselves, and told no one at that time what they had seen.

COMMENTARY

28 Luke's note on the passage of time—"about eight days after Jesus said this" (*meta tous logous toutous hōsei hēmerai oktō*, lit., "after these words about eight days")—is less precise than "after six days" in Matthew and Luke. It is obviously an alternative way of indicating the passage of approximately one week; however, commentators have not agreed as to any specific reason for the different wording. Luke is, as pointed out above, more precise than the other Synoptics in linking the transfiguration with Jesus' preceding sayings by a specific reference to Jesus' "words." There may be an allusion here to the time Moses waited on Mount Sinai for the revelation of God (Ex 24:15–16). This is even more likely in Matthew and Mark, where the phrase "after six days" corresponds directly to the period Moses waited.

Peter, John, and James had been taken into Jesus' confidence elsewhere, e.g., at 8:51 and in the gar- den of Gethsemane (Mk 14:33). Luke uses the def- inite article *to* ("the") with "mountain" (see NASB; NIV has "a mountain"), from which we may infer that the original readers knew what location he had in mind. On the other hand, the construction might indicate that Luke uses "mountain" symbolically. Symbolism is not infrequent in references to moun- tains, in Matthew especially; but this does not rule out a specific geographical location. The locale of the transfiguration could have been any high moun- tain (Mk 9:2; see Notes). The article with *oros* ("mountain," GK *4001*) is normal in similar gram- matical constructions in the Gospels (except for Mt 5:14). If we think of the exodus as a frame of refer- ence, then Sinai is symbolically in mind; if the

Parousia, then the Mount of Olives may be symbolized (Zec 14:4; Ac 1:10–12). Once again, Luke mentions that Jesus is at prayer—an observation repeated in v.29 but absent from the account in Matthew 17:1–2 and Mark 9:2.

29 Luke omits the actual word "transfigured" (*metemorphōthē* [GK *3565*], used in Mt 17:2; Mk 9:2), possibly to avoid a term that might have suggested Hellenistic ideas of an epiphany, the appearance of a god. Instead, he describes the remarkable alteration of Jesus' face and the dazzling whiteness of his clothing, "as bright as a flash of lightning" (*exastraptōn*, GK *1993*). In Jewish traditions, one finds Moses and others whose appearance changed when they experienced the presence of God (e.g., Ex 34:29–30; cf. B. O. Reid, "Voices and Angels: What Were They Talking About at the Transfiguration?" *BR* 34 [1989]: 27).

30–31 Moses and Elijah also appear in this scene of supernatural glory (*en doxē*, lit., "in glory" [GK *1518*], only in Luke; NIV, "glorious splendor"); nevertheless, Luke still describes them in ordinary human terminology (*andres*, "men," GK *467*; cf. 24:4 and comments). Scholars debate the significance of Moses' and Elijah's presence. The old view that they represent the Law and the Prophets respectively does not do justice to the rich associations each name has in Jewish thought. Moses had a mountaintop experience at Sinai. His face shone (Ex 34:30; 2Co 3:7), and he was not only a lawgiver but also a prophet—indeed the prototype of Jesus (Dt 18:18). Elijah was not only a prophet but was also related to the law of Moses as symbolizing the one who would someday turn people's hearts back to the covenant (Mal 4:4–6). In Jewish thought, Elijah was an eschatological figure—one associated with the end-times. So one may say that in the transfiguration scene Moses is a typological figure who reminds us of the past (the exodus), Moses being a predecessor of the Messiah, while Elijah is an escha-

tological figure pointing to the future as a precursor of the Messiah. Each man was among the most highly respected OT figures; they had in common a distinctive experience—a strange departure from this world. Elijah was taken up to heaven in a whirlwind (2Ki 2:11), and Moses was buried by the Lord (Dt 34:6). (The disposition of Moses' body was a matter of speculation in ancient Judaism; cf. Jude 9.) In summary, it seems that the presence of Moses and Elijah on the Mount of Transfiguration draws attention first to the place of Jesus in continuing the redemptive work of God from the exodus to the future eschatological consummation; second, to the appropriateness of Jesus' association with heavenly figures; and third, to the superiority of Jesus over even these great and divinely favored heroes of Israel's past.

The conversation (v.31) is about Jesus' "departure" (*exodos*, lit., his "exodus"; GK *2016*). In 2 Peter 1:15, the term means death; but here in Luke it also recalls the redemptive work of God in the exodus from Egypt (see Notes). Jesus' coming death was one that he would deliberately accomplish (*hēn ēmellen plēroun*, "which he was about to bring to fulfillment"). Luke portrays Jesus as moving unhurriedly toward the accomplishment of his goals (e.g., 4:43; see comments there). He specifies Jerusalem as the city of destiny for Jesus (v.31; see esp. comments at 13:31–35; cf. 9:51; 18:31). Thus Luke, having knowledge of this saying (which perhaps Matthew and Mark did not), included it to reinforce Jesus' prediction of his passion in v.22.

32 The writers of the Gospels use fear and sleepiness to indicate the slowness of the disciples to understand and believe. (On this point, see in Mk 9:6 the explanation of Peter's words in v.33 and the way Mark and Luke handle the sleepiness of the disciples at Gethsemane in different ways [Mk 14:40; Lk 22:45].) It is not clear from the Greek whether they were only drowsy but managed to keep awake or whether they actually fell asleep and woke up. At the least they were far from alert during the conversation about Jesus' approaching passion; and the spectacular scene aroused them thoroughly.

33 Only Luke mentions that it was as Moses and Elijah "were leaving" (*diachōrizesthai*, present tense) that Peter made the suggestion to make three shelters. This may imply that Peter did this to keep them from going. Both Luke's parenthesis here and Mark's in 9:6 show that Peter's suggestion was highly inappropriate. His use of "Master" (*epistata*, GK *2181*; cf. 5:5) is itself appropriate (cf. "Lord" in Mt 17:4; "Rabbi" in Mk 9:5). His comment, "it is good," though banal given the grandeur of the occasion, is not entirely out of order. The idea of three shelters is the main problem. These would have been temporary shelters, such as were used at Sukkoth, the Feast of Tabernacles. Peter's proposal of three presumably equal shelters may have implied a leveling perspective that put Jesus on a par with the others. More than that, it connotes an intention to perpetuate the situation as though there were no "departure" (v.31) for Jesus to accomplish. Whether the shelters symbolize a future or present rest is not completely clear (cf. *TDNT* 7:380; Marshall, 386–87; W. Liefeld, "Theological Motifs in the Transfiguration Narrative," in *New Dimensions in New Testament Study*, ed. Richard N. Longenecker and Merrill C. Tenney [Grand Rapids: Zondervan, 1974], 174–75). What does seem clear is that Peter wanted to prolong the stay of the heavenly visitors because he still failed to grasp the significance of the passion prediction of v.22 and its confirmation in v.31.

34 As with other elements in this narrative, the cloud can carry more than one symbolic inference, among them the cloud in the wilderness after the exodus (Ex 13:21–22; 16:10; 24:16; 40:34–38). But clouds are also associated with the future coming of the Son of Man (Da 7:13; cf. Mk 14:62) and of the Messiah in intertestamental literature (*2 Bar.* 53:1–

12; *4 Ezra* 13:3), and with the two prophets in Revelation 11:12.

G. H. Boobyer (*St. Mark and the Transfiguration Story* [Edinburgh: T&T Clark, 1942]) sees in this symbolism a possible reference to the parousia. H. Riesenfeld (*Jésus transfiguré* [Copenhagen: Ejnar Munksgaard, 1947], 296) believes it relates to Jewish concepts of eschatology, especially a future enthronement of the Messiah. Isaiah 4:5 describes a cloud, reminiscent of that which showed God's *shekinah* glory in the wilderness, which will appear during a future time of rest under the Messiah. The word *shekinah* is from the Hebrew *šākan*, which is translated by the Greek *episkiazō* ("overshadow," GK *2173*) in Exodus 40:35 [LXX]. The same Greek verb is used here in v.34 ("enveloped"). But above all, the cloud symbolizes the glorious presence of God (cf. Ex 19:16). This is notably true in the passage so clearly recalled by the transfiguration (Ex 24:15–18). Matthew's use (17:5) of *phōteinē* ("bright," GK *5893*) also suggests the *shekinah* glory. Though the disciples "enter the cloud" (v.34), a sense of the transcendence of God is retained as the voice comes "from" (*ek*) the cloud (v.35).

35 The voice speaking "from the cloud" is that of God the Father himself. No indirect or mediated message, no mere echo or "daughter of a voice," as Jewish writings put it, was sufficient to identify Jesus. The awesome voice of God himself must be heard. The message expressed by the voice is so clear that any uncertainty about the meaning of some of the other aspects of this great scene become comparatively unimportant. Whether seen in relation to the exodus or to the second coming of the Son of Man, the focus throughout the transfiguration is on the supreme person and glory of the Lord Jesus Christ. And now he is expressly declared to be "[God's] Son"—a declaration similar to that spoken by the voice at Jesus' baptism (cf. 3:22; cf. also Mt 3:17; Mk 1:11). In Mark the voice addresses Jesus directly; here it addresses the three disciples. In John 12:28–30, just preceding Jesus' passion, the voice from heaven speaks for the "benefit" (v.30) of a whole crowd. In each case, the voice from heaven affirms that Jesus is the one who is sent by God and who has God's authority. These words spoken by the voice on these three occasions affirm that Jesus is the Son of God, is obedient to him, and possesses divine authority for his mission. The words "this is my Son" (*houtos estin ho huios mou*), also in Matthew and Mark, recall Psalm 2:7. "Chosen" (*eklelegmenos*, GK *1721*) for "whom I love" (Mt 17:5; Mk 9:7; KJV, "beloved") points us to Isaiah 42:1 ("my servant . . . my chosen one") and the concept of the Suffering Servant found in the broader context of Isaiah, especially 52:13–53:12.

"Listen to him" is not only a command; it is also a correction of the human tendency to substitute human opinion for divine revelation (e.g., Peter in Mt 16:22, also implied here in the transfiguration [v.33]). The words also fulfill Deuteronomy 18:15, which predicts the coming of the prophet whom God would raise up and commands, "You must listen to him." Jesus alone is the True Prophet, the Chosen Servant, and the Son of God. That Moses and Elijah had disappeared and Jesus alone is the one to whom obedience is demanded reflects the unique, exalted status of Jesus the Messiah (cf. J. Fitzmyer, "The Composition of Luke, Chapter 9," in *Perspectives on Luke–Acts* [ed. Talbert], 146).

36 All three Synoptic Gospels note that at the end of the transfiguration only Jesus was there with the disciples. So the scene ends with Jesus as the center of their attention. Luke's statement is concise and ends emphatically with the word "alone" (*monos*). Luke's comment on the silence of the disciples is shorter than Mark's treatment of the same (cf. Mk 9:9–10).

NOTES

28–36 Literature on the transfiguration includes P.-Y. Brandt, *L'identite de Jesus et l'identite de son disciple* (Göttingen: Vandenhoeck & Ruprecht, 2002); J. P. Heil, *The Transfiguration of Jesus: Narrative Meaning and Function of Mark 9:2–8, Matthew 17:1–8 and Luke 9:28–36* (Rome: Pontifical Biblical Institute, 2000); A. M. Ramsay, *The Glory of God and the Transfiguration of Christ* (London: Darton, Longman and Todd, 1967); Barbara Reid, *The Transfiguration: A Source- and Redaction-Critical Study of Luke 9:28–36* (Paris: Gabalda, 1993); M. Thrall, "Elijah and Moses in Mark's Account of the Transfiguration," *NTS* 16 (1970): 305–17; R. Wild, *His Face Shone Like the Sun: Encountering the Transformed Christ in Scripture* (New York: Alba, 1986).

28 "The mountain" (NASB; τὸ ὄρος, *to oros*) has usually been identified as either Tabor in Galilee or Hermon north of Caesarea Philippi. The former is doubtful not only because of its distance from Caesarea Philippi, where Jesus had been about a week earlier, but because shortly after that time, Josephus (*J.W.* 2.572–73; 4.54–61) mentions that a Roman fortress was there. Furthermore, though Tabor does stand out as the only mountain in its immediate area, it is not really "high" (Mk 9:2), rising only 1,929 feet. Hermon, on the other hand, is high—9,232 feet. If Jesus went all the way to the summit, the trek should have required an exhausting climb of about six hours. Also, considering Hermon's remoteness, it is difficult to imagine such a large crowd (v.37), including scribes (cf. Mk 9:14), at its base. Moreover, the return trip from Hermon would not have been, in the main, "through Galilee" (Mk 9:30). A more likely place, not mentioned in tradition, is Meron, the highest mountain within Israel itself at 3,926 feet. It is just to the northwest of the Sea of Galilee. The distance from Caesarea Philippi is moderate; privacy would have been possible in the higher levels above the city of Safed (which, at 2,790 feet, is possibly the "city on a hill" of Mt 5:14); the gathering of crowds, including scribes, would be normal on the lower slopes of the mountainside; and the subsequent short trip to Capernaum would have literally been "through Galilee" (Mk 9:30).

31 The use of the term ἔξοδος (exodos, GK *2016*) in reference to both the departure of Jesus and the foundational event in the history of Israel finds its precedence in Wisdom of Solomon 3:1–3, where the term is used to refer to God's vindication of the righteous one in the context of the wider discussion of the exodus event (see Doble, 212–13). In Luke 9:31, the "exodus" points first to the vindication of the suffering Messiah as he proceeds in the journey to the cross. This journey, in turn, becomes one that brings deliverance to God's people. See also Susan R. Garrett, "Exodus from Bondage: Luke 9:31 and Acts 12:1–24," *CBQ* 52 (1990): 656–80, who understands this exodus as a reference to the cosmic struggle between God and Satan.

4. Healing a Boy with an Evil Spirit (9:37–45)

OVERVIEW

This healing is another significant example of the power of God over demons. It also implies Jesus' strong censure of the disciples for not performing the exorcism. But it is much shorter than the account in Mark and lacks the specific comment on prayer that concludes Mark's account. Moreover, Luke omits the intervening discussion on the coming of Elijah (Mt 17:10–13; Mk 9:11–13).

[37]The next day, when they came down from the mountain, a large crowd met him. [38]A man in the crowd called out, "Teacher, I beg you to look at my son, for he is my only child. [39]A spirit seizes him and he suddenly screams; it throws him into convulsions so that he foams at the mouth. It scarcely ever leaves him and is destroying him. [40]I begged your disciples to drive it out, but they could not."

[41]"O unbelieving and perverse generation," Jesus replied, "how long shall I stay with you and put up with you? Bring your son here."

[42]Even while the boy was coming, the demon threw him to the ground in a convulsion. But Jesus rebuked the evil spirit, healed the boy and gave him back to his father. [43]And they were all amazed at the greatness of God.

While everyone was marveling at all that Jesus did, he said to his disciples, [44]"Listen carefully to what I am about to tell you: The Son of Man is going to be betrayed into the hands of men." [45]But they did not understand what this meant. It was hidden from them, so that they did not grasp it, and they were afraid to ask him about it.

COMMENTARY

37 "The next day" (*tē hexēs hēmera*) may imply that the transfiguration happened at night. If so, then that great event would have been even more striking, were that possible. The descent of Jesus and the disciples "from the mountain" meant a descent into the earthly world of illness, evil, and unbelief. The "large crowd" would be surprising if the location of the transfiguration were Mount Hermon (see Notes, v.28).

39–42 Since Luke was a physician, it is interesting that he does not identify the boy's condition as epilepsy, as Matthew 17:15 does. Clearly, Luke is more concerned with the demonic aspect of the boy's affliction (v.42). The physical manifestations were similar to those of epilepsy—a fact that has contributed to the unfortunate misunderstanding of epilepsy down through the ages. Luke alone notes the continual, debilitating oppression the boy endured (v.39). While three of the disciples were witnessing the transfiguration, the others were helpless in the face of demonic power (v.40).

43a Instead of centering attention on the efficacy of prayer in exorcism, as Matthew and Mark do, Luke concludes his account of the boy's healing by speaking of the "greatness of God." We might have expected Luke to dwell on the role of prayer, given his interest in it. He does have a saying similar to the one Matthew includes in his parallel to this narrative (Mt 17:21 text note), but it is in another context (Lk 17:6). Actually, the climax in the present story is typical of Luke, for it records the reaction of those who observe a healing by Jesus. They were "amazed" (*exeplēssonto*, GK *1742*; cf. 4:32) at the "greatness" of God. Elsewhere Luke speaks similarly of people giving glory to God (5:25; 7:16).

43b–45 This repetition of the prediction of Jesus' passion (cf. 9:22 and comments) might be considered a separate section had not Luke connected it closely with the preceding incident. This is not the case in Matthew 17:22 or Mark 9:30. Luke uses another word, *thaumazontōn* ("marveling," GK *2513*, v.43b; cf. 43a), to describe the amazed reaction of the people to the healing. The passion prediction (v.44) serves to emphasize that Jesus' ultimate purpose went beyond such miracles. This time, Jesus includes a reference to his betrayal. The failure of the people to understand (v.45), even at the very time they are marveling at the greatness of God's work through Jesus, is comparable to Peter's resistance to the first passion prediction (Mt 16:22) immediately after his great confession (Mt 16:13). The people were not granted understanding of the meaning of Jesus' words. See the comparable situation in Luke 8:10 and its parallels (see comments there). Here, however, the implication is that had they asked Jesus for help in understanding his words, they might have received it.

5. Two Cases of Rivalry (9:46–50)

OVERVIEW

This passage naturally follows the preceding two verses. The disciples did not understand Jesus' role as the Suffering Servant and so could not grasp its implications for them as his disciples. They were still thinking of the Messiah only in terms of triumph, assuming, quite naturally, that their position was important. The issue was not whether there would be rank in the kingdom but the nature and qualifications of such rank (v.46).

> [46] An argument started among the disciples as to which of them would be the greatest. [47] Jesus, knowing their thoughts, took a little child and had him stand beside him. [48] Then he said to them, "Whoever welcomes this little child in my name welcomes me; and whoever welcomes me welcomes the one who sent me. For he who is least among you all—he is the greatest."
>
> [49] "Master," said John, "we saw a man driving out demons in your name and we tried to stop him, because he is not one of us."
>
> [50] "Do not stop him," Jesus said, "for whoever is not against you is for you."

COMMENTARY

47–48 The point of Jesus' reference to the "little child" (*paidion*, GK *4086*) does not illustrate simple faith (as in Mt 18:2–4). Nor does it refer to receiving a disciple who comes in the name of Jesus (as in Mt 10:40–42). Rather, it refers to receiving for the sake of Christ a person who has no status (v.48; cf. Mt 18:5). This is consistent with Jesus' (and Luke's) concern for neglected people. The meaning, then, is that instead of seeking status for ourselves (out of pride as an associate of the Messiah), we Christians should, as Jesus did, identify ourselves with those who have no status at all, welcoming them to join us in the kingdom. To put it another way, in Matthew 10 one receives a Christian apostle as consciously receiving Christ himself, whereas here in Luke 9 by ministering to a child one ministers, without realizing it, to Christ himself.

The reference to the "least among you" points back to 7:28 and to the childlike response to the call of Jesus as one sent by God. This surrendering to Jesus' authority will result in recognition by Jesus himself in his kingdom. The Lukan theme of reversal is again evident here.

49 The next episode reveals the apostles' attitude of rivalry. The issue is not orthodoxy but association. Far from merely invoking the name of Jesus in a formula and without genuine faith (as did the seven sons of the Jewish priest Sceva, to whose formula the demon refused to respond, Ac 19:13–16), the man referred to here had actually been "driving out demons" through Jesus' name. In light of the preceding context, the issue of inclusion is highlighted here where one finds a striking contrast between Jesus' call to welcome all and the disciples' acts of exclusion.

50 This verse is proverbial in form. The man was not against Jesus. Apparently he had not yet joined the group of Jesus' disciples. Perhaps he represents those who are "on the way" to joining the body of believers and who should be welcomed rather than repulsed. In a different situation (Mt 12:30), Jesus used a reverse form of this proverb and did so without contradicting the truth set forth here in Luke.

V. TEACHING AND TRAVELS TOWARD JERUSALEM (9:51–19:44)

OVERVIEW

This extensive section has no counterpart in Matthew or Mark, though much of its material is found in other contexts in those gospels. Luke 9:51 implies that Jesus was setting out on a journey one would expect to be described in the succeeding chapters. Yet these chapters say comparatively little about Jesus' traveling from one place to another.

To be sure, we do find some clues showing that Jesus is moving toward Jerusalem: e.g., 9:52, approaching Samaria; 10:38, "on their way . . . to a village where . . . Martha opened her home" (presumably Bethany, near Jerusalem); 13:22, "Jesus went through the towns and villages . . . as he made his way to Jerusalem"; 13:32–33, "I will reach my goal. . . . no prophet can die outside Jerusalem"; 17:11, "now on his way to Jerusalem, Jesus traveled along the border between Samaria and Galilee."

Following this section, Luke further notes Jesus' words, "We are going up to Jerusalem" (18:31). Then he mentions Jesus' approach to Jericho (18:35; 19:1) and finally his arrival near Jerusalem (19:28–29). It is clear from all this that Jesus is now heading toward Jerusalem, not Galilee. However, he did not make one continuous journey from Galilee to Jerusalem. (See comments at 10:38; 17:11; see also Notes, 17:11.)

To assume that Luke intends to describe a single continuous journey involves difficult problems, including the question of Luke's knowledge of geography (raised by Conzelmann, 60–73). It is reasonable and consistent with the data to understand this section as showing that Jesus' ministry has entered a new phase and taken on some new characteristics. Jesus follows routes that bring him away from Galilee and nearer to Jerusalem than his former itineraries

did (except for visits for the feasts, as in Jn 2:13; 5:1 et al.). During this period Jesus is no longer committed to the locale of his former ministry but is looking toward Jerusalem and the cross. Much of his teaching at this time is directed to the disciples. Warnings to the rich and complacent are prominent, as well as words aimed at the Pharisees. On several occasions he actually visits Jerusalem, where he proclaims the truth about himself and enters into a controversy with those who oppose his claims.

The framing of the material within the narrative of this journey is not an artificial one but one that is (1) consistent with the nature of Jesus' ministry, which has been itinerant all along; (2) consistent with the emphasis on travel in both Luke and Acts; and (3) consistent with the fact that, while Jesus did not go directly from Galilee to Jerusalem, his mind was definitely set on the impending events he faced in that city. Even at times when he may have traveled north again, his ultimate goal was Jerusalem. This also accords with the prominence of Jerusalem in the gospel of Luke (see comments esp. at 13:33–34; 19:28, 41).

In recognizing the historicity of this journey, it is still important to discuss the theological significance of Luke's emphasis on Jesus' traveling in this central section of his gospel. It has long been recognized that while this section is a travel narrative in form, the content is less concerned with the act of journeying. This apparent discrepancy has led to many hypotheses that attempt to provide justification for the structure and focus of the included material. In terms of structure, Craig F. Evans ("The Central Section of St. Luke's Gospel," in *Studies in the Gospels*, ed. Dennis E. Nineham [Naperville, Ill.:

Allenson, 1955], 37–53) has pointed to the numerous parallels between Deuteronomy and Luke 9:51–18:14, and most striking of all is the correspondence with regard to the order of events/themes between the two works. Jesus is presented as the new Moses, and the instructions given to the disciples are to be understood in the light of their OT context.

While many have questioned the existence of a strict correspondence, the influence of Deuteronomy has been affirmed by many. David Moessner (*Lord of the Banquet: The Literary and Theological Significance of the Lukan Travel Narrative* [Minneapolis: Fortress, 1989]), in particular, has provided a sustained argument for the thematic correspondence beyond the two works. Four recurring themes in Deuteronomy have been singled out: (1) Israel is a rebellious people; (2) God sent his prophets to call for repentance; (3) Israel rejected God's prophets; and (4) as a result Israel will receive her judgments from God. These themes, Moessner claims, provide coherence to Luke's central section.

Many have further pointed to the wider parallels between Luke's travel narrative and the exodus journey of Israel. In fulfilling the role of Israel, Jesus proves to be a faithful Son of God who creates a new/true people of God. The rejection of Israel and the inclusion of the outcasts further point to the formation of an eschatological community defined by one's response to Jesus and his gospel.

In the OT prophetic material, the new exodus will center on Jerusalem when she will witness the arrival of God's salvation. Drawing on the "way" motif (cf. Isa 40:3), the journey to Jerusalem points, therefore, to the fulfillment of the promises of old. It will become clear, however, that Israel will again reject the one sent by God, and the movement away from Jerusalem in Acts may then be understood as a judgment against Israel.

While theological considerations may provide the reason for Luke's emphasis on the journey of Jesus, the historical reality of the actual move from Galilee to Jerusalem provides the ultimate basis for Luke's discussion in this section.

In addition to the studies of Evans and Moessner, significant works on Luke's central section include Bailey, *Poet and Peasant*, 79–85; Craig L. Blomberg, "Midrash, Chiasmus, and the Outline of Luke's Central Section," in *Gospel Perspectives: Studies in Midrash and Historiography*, ed. R. T. France and D. Wenham (Sheffield: JSOT Press, 1983), 3:217–59; A. Denaux, "The Delineation of the Lukan Travel Narrative within the Overall Structure of the Gospel of Luke," in *The Synoptic Gospels* (ed. C. Focant, Leuven: Leuven Univ. Press, 1993), 359–92; E. Mayer, *Die Reiseerzählung des Lukas (Lk 9:51–19:10)* (Frankfurt: Lang, 1996); J. L. Resseguie, "Point of View in the Central Section of Luke (9:51–19:44)," *JETS* 25 (1982): 41–47; W. C. Robinson Jr., "The Theological Context for Interpreting Luke's Travel Narrative (9:51ff.)," *JBL* 79 (1960): 20–31; Talbert, *Literary Patterns*, 51–56.

A. The New Direction of Jesus' Ministry (9:51–10:24)

1. Travel South through Samaria (9:51–56)

[51]As the time approached for him to be taken up to heaven, Jesus resolutely set out for Jerusalem. [52]And he sent messengers on ahead, who went into a Samaritan village to get things ready for him; [53]but the people there did not welcome him, because he was

heading for Jerusalem. ⁵⁴When the disciples James and John saw this, they asked, "Lord, do you want us to call fire down from heaven to destroy them?" ⁵⁵But Jesus turned and rebuked them, ⁵⁶and they went to another village.

COMMENTARY

51 Luke uses the transitional *egeneto de* (the Semitic "and it came to pass"), omitted by the NIV for stylistic reasons. As already observed, there is now a major change in Jesus' orientation. At this significant turning point Luke once again uses a word expressing fulfillment—*sympleroō* (GK *5230*), translated "approached" in the NIV (see Notes). God's plan is another step nearer fulfillment. The approaching goal is not only the death and resurrection but also the ascension of Christ (see Notes). In the account of the transfiguration Luke has a reference to Jesus' "exodus" (v.31; cf. v.22). But now that Jesus faces the cross, Luke mentions the exaltation that would follow his "exodus." He "resolutely set out for" (the NIV's contemporary idiom for the Semitic being "set his face toward") Jerusalem, the designated place of his passion (see Notes). We will be reminded of this destination as Jesus draws nearer to Jerusalem (19:28, 41).

52 Jesus "sent messengers on ahead." This custom is described further in the particular mission of the seventy-two disciples (10:1–16). In this instance they were not told to preach but simply to "get things ready for him"—a fact that makes the attitude of James and John (v.54) even less appropriate.

53–54 The residents of the Samaritan village reciprocated the hostile attitude of the Jews (cf. Jn 4:9). They were especially negative because Jesus was going to Jerusalem, which they refused to acknowledge as a valid center of worship (cf. Jn 4:20).

The history of the Samaritans is uncertain. Many hold that they were a mixed race since the fall of the northern kingdom of Israel. The king of Assyria deported the leaders of Israel, among them the religious teachers, and replaced them with foreigners (2Ki 17:6, 24–26). From that time on, the inhabitants of the northern kingdom received no further prophetic instruction and refused to acknowledge the continuing revelation received by the Jews in the southern kingdom. Some believe that the Samaritans known in the NT arose in the early Hellenistic period (cf. "Samaritans," *NBD*, 1062–63). The animosity between the Samaritans and the Jews developed through years, and it culminated in the destruction of the Samaritan temple on Mount Gerizim by the Jews in the second century BC. In the time of Jesus, the Samaritans were a fringe segment of the Jewish world for which Jesus, and Luke following him, had a concern. They are not mentioned unfavorably elsewhere in Luke; on the contrary, he mentions them favorably in 10:30–37 and 17:11–19. James and John may have thought that Jesus would respond as Elijah had (v.54; 2Ki 1:9–12).

55 Jesus' strong disapproval of James and John's suggestion is seen in his use of the word "rebuked" (*epetimēsen*, GK *2203*; cf. 4:35, 41; 8:24). If the Samaritans were consciously rejecting Christ by rejecting his disciples, one would have expected that v.5 would apply—a mild reaction compared to that of James and John. But Jesus' messengers were rejected merely because they were Jews going to Jerusalem, as v.53 indicates.

NOTES

51 The phrase ἐν τῷ συμπληροῦσθαι τὰς ἡμέρας (*en tō symplērousthai tas hēmeras*) literally means "as the days were [or time was] being fulfilled" rather than "as the time approached" (NIV; cf. RSV, NASB). It is true that συμπληρόω (*symplēroō*, GK *5230*) can mean "approach," and the NIV's translation does convey a sense of destiny. But in view of Luke's significant use of words of fulfillment and accomplishment (e.g., 1:1; 4:21; 9:31; 22:16; 24:44), συμπληρόω, *symplēroō*, probably continues that theme here. It would be awkward in an English translation to describe days as being "fulfilled"; but from the perspective of God's plan, that is the meaning (cf. *TDNT* 6:308–9). See also Jeremiah 25:12, where the LXX's ἐν τῷ πληρωθῆναι τὰ ἑβδομήκοντα ἔτη (*en tō plērōthēnai ta hebdomēkonta etē*) is translated "when the seventy years are fulfilled."

The word ἀναλήμψεως (*analēmpseōs*, "of his ascension," GK *378*; NIV, "taken up to heaven") can refer to Jesus' death, since the word can be so used (BDAG, 67). However, not only is there evidence in extracanonical literature for its use with reference to ascension, but also that is clearly the meaning of the verbal form (ἀναλαμβάνω, *analambanō*, GK *377*) Luke used to describe the ascension of Jesus in Acts 1:2, 11. With the use of this word, many have also pointed to allusion to the Elijah–Elisha narrative (cf. T. L. Brodie, "The Departure for Jerusalem [Luke 9:51–56] as a Rhetorical Imitation of Elijah's Departure for the Jordan [2 Kgs 1:1–2, 6]," *Bib* 70 [1989]: 96–109).

The phrase τὸ πρόσωπον ἐστήρισεν (*to prosōpon estērisen*, "set his face toward," GK *4725, 5114*; NIV, "resolutely set out") points to the prophetic use of this formula. It refers not only to the will of the prophet but also the anticipated opposition to his mission. Some have further suggested that this formula evokes the judgment motif (cf. Craig A. Evans, "'He Set His Face': Luke 9:51 Once Again," *Bib* 68 [1987]: 80–84).

54 The parallel between the disciples' suggestion and Elijah's action probably gave rise to the gloss "even as Elijah did" (NIV text note). The words were included in the KJV but are absent from such important early texts as 𝔓⁴⁵ 𝔓⁷⁵ ℵ B.

55 Some ancient texts add the following: "And he said, 'You do not know what kind of spirit you are of, for the Son of Man did not come to destroy men's lives, but to save them.'" The first part of the sentence, up to "you are of," is in the Western text D and a couple of versions. The rest is, with varying details, found in a number of texts generally lacking the stature of those MSS that omit them. Those that lack the questionable reading are 𝔓⁴⁵ 𝔓⁷⁵ ℵ A B C L W, among many others. The longer reading is in the KJV, is bracketed in the NASB, and is placed in a footnote in the RSV and NIV. Marshall, 408, after weighing arguments pro and con (including the appropriateness of the saying in the context [pro] and the weak MS evidence and likelihood that a scribe would add words that seemed appropriate [con]), concludes that in view of the "considerable doubt," the words should be either omitted or bracketed; Metzger, 125, also considers the claim to genuineness weak.

2. The Cost of Following Jesus (9:57–62)

OVERVIEW

This is the second major treatment of disciple-ship in Luke (cf. v.23). The first two conversations (vv.57–60 through the words "bury their own dead") are found in Matthew 8:18–22. It is difficult to tell whether Matthew has omitted part of the material they had in common or whether Luke has used a combination of sources. There are some differences. The order of the dialogue in v.59 is the reverse of that in Matthew 8:21–22. Also, while a saying about the kingdom would have been equally at home in Matthew or Luke, the words "you go and proclaim the kingdom of God" are lacking in Matthew but are made the central state-ment in Luke's section. The "man" of v.57 is a "teacher of the law" in Matthew 8:19.

The structure of this passage is noteworthy.

The familiar "rule of three" is employed by Luke in recording three conversations. There is an inter-change of order: in the first conversation the inquirer initiates the conversation and Jesus states the objection; in the second this is reversed; in the third the man both initiates the dialogue and raises the objection and Jesus adds a comment. (On this structure, see Johannes P. Louw, "Discourse Analy-sis and the Greek New Testament," *BT* 24 [1973]: 104–8.) Each dialogue contains some theological language: "Son of Man" (v.58), "proclaim the king-dom of God" (v.60), "service in the kingdom of God" (v.62). This shows that discipleship is not sim-ply following Jesus in one's lifestyle but also includes involvement in the important work of the kingdom.

---

[57]As they were walking along the road, a man said to him, "I will follow you wherever you go."

[58]Jesus replied, "Foxes have holes and birds of the air have nests, but the Son of Man has no place to lay his head."

[59]He said to another man, "Follow me."

But the man replied, "Lord, first let me go and bury my father."

[60]Jesus said to him, "Let the dead bury their own dead, but you go and proclaim the kingdom of God."

[61]Still another said, "I will follow you, Lord; but first let me go back and say good-by to my family."

[62]Jesus replied, "No one who puts his hand to the plow and looks back is fit for service in the kingdom of God."

COMMENTARY

57 The man uses the terminology of discipleship—"follow"—and amplifies it with a sweeping promise. Jesus' reply is in accord with his prior definition of discipleship in v.23 and constitutes a comment on the man's "wherever you go."

58 Since most men do have homes, "Son of Man" must refer specifically to Jesus. The idea of the rejection—if not actual suffering—of the Son of Man is implied in Jesus' words.

59–60 Since it was a religious, social, and family obligation to provide a suitable funeral for one's father, Jesus' refusal to permit this appears to be a striking example of the radical transfer of loyalty he demanded in 14:25–27. "The dead" who are to perform the burial are often thought to be the spiritually dead who do not follow Jesus but remain at home. Manson's understanding, 73, of this as a paradoxical saying meaning "that business must look after itself" is appealing, but it is not supported by sufficient contextual references. Others have looked for exemptions within the Jewish legal codes (cf. M. Bockmuehl, "'Let the Dead Bury Their Dead' (Matthew 8:22/Luke 9:60): Jesus and the Halakhah," *JTS* 49 [1998]: 553–81). A more helpful approach is one informed by the understanding of Jewish funerary practices (cf. B. R. McCane, "'Let the Dead Bury Their Own Dead': Secondary Burial and Matthew 8:21–22," *HTR* 83 [1990]: 31–43). In first-century Palestine, secondary burial was commonly practiced; when this "father" is dead, he will be buried in the cave. After one year, his bones will be collected and placed with the bones of his ancestors. It is possible that the request of this son is to wait for another year before following Jesus. The eschatological urgency of Jesus' mission would not be able to accommodate this delay.

61–62 Though to "say good-by" (*apotaxasthai*, GK *698*) is not at all the emotional equivalent of a funeral (cf. vv.59–60), it still represents family duty that must be forsaken for service to Jesus. Danker, 125, sees here an allusion to the call of Elisha while plowing and his request to say good-by to his family (1Ki 19:19–21, cf. Marshall, 412). A further illustration of discipleship is keeping the hand on the plow. Jeremias, 195, describes the plowman concentrating on the furrow before him, guiding the light plow with his left hand while goading the oxen with the right. Looking away would result in a crooked furrow.

NOTES

62 The word "service" is not in the Greek text but is implied by the word εὔθετος (*euthetos*, "fit," GK *2310*) and by the context.

3. Sending Out the Seventy-two (10:1–24)

OVERVIEW

Luke's account of Jesus' commissioning of the Seventy-two, while in some points similar to that of the Twelve (9:1–6) but differing from it, fits well its immediate context; and in several respects it resembles Matthew's account of the commissioning of the Twelve. It continues the procedure of sending messengers ahead during Jesus' journey (9:52). At the same time, the obedient response of the Seventy-two provides a contrast to the three men (9:57–62) whose excuses disqualified them from discipleship. The mere repetition of some travel instructions given to the Twelve does not constitute a doublet. While the question of sources is complex (see Overview, 9:1–6), the material here seems to be drawn from Q (cf. Mt 9:37–38; 10:7–16) and is properly included in this place. As noted on p. 168, the instructions prescribed by Jesus were undoubtedly repeated frequently by Jesus and in the early church.

When this passage is considered in light of the development of the Lukan story, it is possible to see it as anticipating the Gentile mission in Acts. As "the Twelve" points to the mission to Israel, the number seventy (or seventy-two) itself may represent the universal significance of Jesus' ministry. For further discussion on the ways Luke's first volume anticipates the second, see T. J. Lane, *Luke and the Gentile Mission: Gospel Anticipates Acts* (Frankfurt: Lang, 1996).

Not inconsistent with the reference to the Gentile mission is the possibility of an allusion to the seventy (or seventy-two) elders who participate in the ministry of Moses (cf. Luke Timothy Johnson, *The Gospel of Luke* [SP 3; Collegeville, Minn.: Liturgical Press, 1991], 128). The numerous Moses–Jesus parallels, especially in this central section of Luke, lend credence to this reading.

---

[1]After this the Lord appointed seventy-two others and sent them two by two ahead of him to every town and place where he was about to go. [2]He told them, "The harvest is plentiful, but the workers are few. Ask the Lord of the harvest, therefore, to send out workers into his harvest field. [3]Go! I am sending you out like lambs among wolves. [4]Do not take a purse or bag or sandals; and do not greet anyone on the road.

[5]"When you enter a house, first say, 'Peace to this house.' [6]If a man of peace is there, your peace will rest on him; if not, it will return to you. [7]Stay in that house, eating and drinking whatever they give you, for the worker deserves his wages. Do not move around from house to house.

[8]"When you enter a town and are welcomed, eat what is set before you. [9]Heal the sick who are there and tell them, 'The kingdom of God is near you.' [10]But when you enter a town and are not welcomed, go into its streets and say, [11]'Even the dust of your town that sticks to our feet we wipe off against you. Yet be sure of this: The kingdom of God is near.' [12]I tell you, it will be more bearable on that day for Sodom than for that town.

[13]"Woe to you, Korazin! Woe to you, Bethsaida! For if the miracles that were performed in you had been performed in Tyre and Sidon, they would have repented long ago, sitting in sackcloth and ashes. [14]But it will be more bearable for Tyre and Sidon at the judgment than for you. [15]And you, Capernaum, will you be lifted up to the skies? No, you will go down to the depths.

[16]"He who listens to you listens to me; he who rejects you rejects me; but he who rejects me rejects him who sent me."

> [17]The seventy-two returned with joy and said, "Lord, even the demons submit to us in your name."
>
> [18]He replied, "I saw Satan fall like lightning from heaven. [19]I have given you authority to trample on snakes and scorpions and to overcome all the power of the enemy; nothing will harm you. [20]However, do not rejoice that the spirits submit to you, but rejoice that your names are written in heaven."
>
> [21]At that time Jesus, full of joy through the Holy Spirit, said, "I praise you, Father, Lord of heaven and earth, because you have hidden these things from the wise and learned, and revealed them to little children. Yes, Father, for this was your good pleasure.
>
> [22]"All things have been committed to me by my Father. No one knows who the Son is except the Father, and no one knows who the Father is except the Son and those to whom the Son chooses to reveal him."
>
> [23]Then he turned to his disciples and said privately, "Blessed are the eyes that see what you see. [24]For I tell you that many prophets and kings wanted to see what you see but did not see it, and to hear what you hear but did not hear it."

COMMENTARY

1 "After this" (*meta de tauta*) establishes the connection we have just observed with the context. The title "Lord" (*ho kyrios*, GK *3261*) occurs only here among the various accounts of commissioning, possibly to emphasize the serious dominical aspect of the instructions—namely, that they came from the Lord Jesus himself. Not only does the commissioning of the Seventy-two lack any restriction to Jewish hearers (cf. Mt 10:5–6), but the number of missionaries sent out (see Notes) parallels the number of nations thought to exist in the world and so suggests the deliberate inclusion of Gentiles.

Sending messengers "two by two" (*ana dyo*) was common not only among the early Christians (Mk 6:7; Lk 7:18–19; Ac 13:2; 15:27, 39–40; 17:14; 19:22) but also among the Jews. It provided companionship, protection, and the double witness prescribed in Deuteronomy 17:6; 19:15 (cf. J. Jeremias, *New Testament Theology: The Proclamation of Jesus* [New York: Scribners, 1971], 235). The Seventy-two were to go everywhere Jesus was going. The extent of this mission underscores that of the church: to reach the "plentiful harvest" of v.2. It may also look toward the conclusion of the church's mission at Jesus' return (cf. Mt 10:23).

2 Though the harvest imagery in Scripture usually refers to God's intervention in history through gathering his people together (cf. Mt 13:37–43), here it applies to the urgent missionary task of the present age (cf. Mt 9:37–38; Jn 4:35).

3 The imperative "go" (*hypagete*, GK *5632*) and the untranslated exclamation *idou* ("behold," GK *2627*) anticipate the difficulties of the journey. Wolves are natural enemies of sheep. No specific enemies are pointed out; the warning is a general one. The disciples are like "lambs" (*arnas*, GK *768*)—defenseless and dependent on God alone.

4 The limitations on what the Seventy-two may take with them increases their vulnerability (see comments at 9:3; also Notes, 9:3). They must also be single-minded even to the extent of not becoming involved in time-consuming greetings (cf. 2Ki 4:29). Moreover, their lack of possessions highlights the significance of their acceptance or rejection by those to whom they will be ministering (cf. Johnson, 164).

5–6 Greetings (cf. v.4) that go beyond mere formality are to be reserved for the hosts of the Seventy-two. "Peace" (*eirēnē*, GK *1645*), so familiar in Jewish salutations, has a rich connotation here. If the host has a proper attitude toward God (v.6), he will receive the blessing of the kingdom (v.9). "Man of peace" is literally "son of peace" (*huios eirēnēs*)—an idiomatic way of expressing not only a person's character but also the destiny he is worthy of. Such a person would be open to the kingdom message. For the significance of this designation, see W. Klassen, "'A Child of Peace' (Luke 10:6) in First-Century Context," *NTS* 27 (1981): 496–97.

7 Like the Twelve (9:4), the Seventy-two are to remain with their original hosts. As the Lord's servants, they are deserving of support by the Lord's people (cf. 1Ti 5:18). For the definitive discussion of this principle of support for Christian workers, see 1 Corinthians 9:3–18, where Paul speaks (1Co 9:14) of what the Lord "commanded." Likewise, John says that Christians are obligated to support the Lord's messengers, who, unlike the other itinerant preachers of the first century, sought no help from unbelievers but trusted in God alone (3Jn 5–8).

8 It is not clear whether the messengers feared being offered food prohibited to Jews. This would have been less likely in Samaria and central Judea than elsewhere. The words may have been preserved because of their appropriateness to later situations (cf. Ac 10:9–16; 1Co 10:27).

9 Healing and the proclamation of the kingdom are linked, in accordance both with the mission of the Twelve and with the ministry of Jesus (Lk 9:1–2, 11). Though Jesus was portrayed earlier as one who preaches the kingdom of God, it is only in the central section of Luke that one begins to find his proclamation of the "nearness" of God's kingdom (see also 11:20; 17:21; cf. Robert F. O'Toole, "Some Exegetical Reflections on Luke 13:10–17," *Bib* 73 [1992]: 84–107).

10–11 These verses introduce a transition to the consequences of rejecting the message of the kingdom. In 4:18–19, Jesus' quotation of Isaiah 61:1–2 stopped short of the words "and the day of vengeance of our God." Nevertheless, that day is coming, and Luke includes such warnings of it as those in 6:24–26; 12:46–48; 16:23–24; 21:22.

12 Sodom, destroyed along with Gomorrah (Ge 19:24–29), represents the consequences of ignoring God's warning to repent (cf. Mt 10:15; 11:20–24 [almost verbally identical to the present text]; Ro 9:29 [quoting Isa 1:9]; 2Pe 2:6; Jude 7). "More bearable" (*anektoteron*, GK *445*) probably relates not so much to the degree of punishment as to the degree of culpability. If Sodom cannot escape judgment, what hope does a city that rejects the Lord Jesus have?

13–14 The probable sites of Korazin and Bethsaida are near Capernaum, at the north end of the Sea of Galilee, where Jesus concentrated his ministry. The comparison with the pagan Phoenician towns of Tyre and Sidon suggests utter rebellion against the Lord. Those ancient towns suffered drastic judgment for their proud opposition to God and his people (Isa 23:1–18; Jer 25:22; 47:4; Eze 26:1–28:23; Joel 3:4–8; Am 1:9–10).

"Sackcloth" was a coarse, black fabric worn as a sign of mourning or repentance (e.g., 1Ki 21:27). Ashes could also symbolize repentance or contrition (e.g., Job 42:6). "Sitting" (or lying) on these was one custom; another was wearing the sackcloth and putting ashes on the head (cf. Est 4:1–3, where both customs are followed).

15 Capernaum had the high privilege of hearing Jesus preach there frequently, but this privilege guaranteed neither its fame nor its survival. On the contrary, in language like that of Isaiah 14:12–15, Jesus graphically portrays Capernaum's fall to the "depths" (heōs tou hadou, lit., "to Hades"; cf. the fall of Satan in v.18; also Rev 12:10).

16 Reception or rejection of Christ's messengers shows one's attitude toward the Lord himself (cf. Christ's identification of himself with the "least" of his "brothers" in Mt 25:31–46). In the parable of the vineyard, both son and servants were rejected (Lk 20:9–17). Moreover, whoever rejects Christ also rejects Moses (Jn 5:45–47).

17 Whatever their experiences may have been, the messengers returned to Jesus filled with joy. The power of the kingdom was effective against demons, just as it was in the ministry of Christ (11:20). Exorcism must be done in the name of Christ; it is not an incantation but signifies his authority (contrast Ac 19:13–16).

18 The taunt-song describing the fall of the "king of Babylon" (Isa 14:4–11) and of the "morning star" ("Lucifer," KJV, 14:12–21), to which Luke 10:15 alludes, also relates to Revelation 12:9. When the disciples exorcise demons, the forces of evil are shaken, symbolizing the defeat of Satan himself.

19 To have "authority to trample on snakes and scorpions" relates to the victorious work of Christ, who, according to the first promise of the gospel (Ge 3:15), was to bruise (NIV, "crush") the head of the serpent, the devil. The ultimate implication of overcoming "all the power of the enemy" is to be victorious over the chief enemy, i.e., the one through whose temptation Adam and Eve fell and allowed sin to enter humanity. Therefore, Jesus' saying is far from an invitation to snake handling (cf. the instructions and context in vv.17–18 of the questionable ending of Mk 16).

20 This verse, with its call to rejoicing in the supreme blessing of assurance of heaven, is one of Jesus' great sayings. "Do not rejoice" does not exclude the disciples' taking joy in spiritual victories but rather introduces a strong and typically Semitic comparison. The idea of the names of God's faithful people as being written down in heaven is common in biblical and extrabiblical Jewish writings. In those days it was natural to refer to this through the metaphor of a book or scroll (e.g., Ex 32:32–33; Ps 69:28; Da 12:1; Mal 3:16; Rev 20:12–15).

21–22 This is a thanksgiving prayer of Jesus offered in response to God's work through the Seventy-two. The emphasis on joy combines with another subject of Luke's special interest—the Holy Spirit in the life of Christ. The apparent parallel to this passage (Mt 11:25–27) lacks the reference to joy and the Holy Spirit. Correspondingly, Luke omits the words that follow in Matthew—the invitation to those who are weary and burdened. With their allusion to the "yoke" (Mt 11:29–30) of the Jewish law, these words are not as appropriate for Luke's audience as for Matthew's.

Verses 21–22 are of great doctrinal importance because they show (1) God's sovereignty in imparting revelation, (2) the relationship between the Father and the Son, and (3) the privilege the disciples had of participating in this instance of messianic revelation and salvation.

Jesus' words relate to the "time" (hōra, lit., "hour" [GK 6052]; cf. kairos, "time" or "season" [GK 2789], in Mt 11:25) in which the power of the kingdom is revealed. Jesus himself participates in the joy that characterizes the day of God's salvation—a theme established at the beginning of Luke's gospel (e.g., 1:44). Like Mary (in the Magnificat, 1:46–47), he combines joy with thanksgiving on the occasion of God's mighty, saving work.

Jesus had already spoken about God's sovereignty in hiding and revealing divine mysteries in explaining his use of parables (8:10 and synoptic parallels; cf. 1Co 1:18–25). A remarkable thing—and one that Jesus' thanksgiving stresses—is not that the wise do not understand but that the simple do. This has to do with revelation and does not negate what Scripture teaches (e.g., in Proverbs) about the importance of study and pious wisdom. The "children" (*nēpiois*, GK *3758*) are those whose open, trusting attitude makes them receptive to God's word.

The theme of revelation appears in both v.21 and v.22—first the revelation of "things" (v.21; see Notes) and then of God himself (v.22). The knowledge God gives is "committed" (*paredothē*, lit., "delivered, handed over," GK *4140*) directly to the Son. This explains why Jesus spoke with authority (4:32) in contrast to the scribes (Mt 7:29; Mk 1:22; cf. Mt 28:18), who received their ideas through tradition passed on from rabbi to rabbi. Jesus' sayings confirm other teachings in the Synoptics and in John about the fatherhood of God and the unique sonship of Christ. While some aspects of his sonship relate to his role as the Messiah, who was designated as God's Son, the relationship expressed here is clearly personal rather than functional. The same truth is one of the major themes in John's gospel (see also Mt 24:36; Mk 13:32).

Crump, 58, suggests that this prayer provides the "inner logic" for other passages on the theme of hiddenness and revelation. The hiddenness motif will become fully developed in 19:42, where the failure of the Jewish leaders to recognize the salvation of God provides an introduction to the final chapters of the gospel. The revelation motif likewise resurfaces in 24:31, where Jesus' disciples are finally granted the gift to recognize the risen Lord.

23–24 Here Jesus congratulates the disciples privately on participating in this revelation. The woes (vv.13–15) on those whose pride will be broken are balanced by the blessings of those granted salvation. This pattern has already appeared in the Magnificat (1:52–55) and in Jesus' beatitudes and woes (6:20–26). See also 1 Corinthians 2:9–10.

NOTES

1 The reading ἑβδομήκοντα [δύο] (*hebdomēkonta [duo]*, "seventy[-two]") has strong MS support, including 𝔓⁷⁵ B D, but the number "seventy" has stronger precedence in the OT. There were seventy descendants of Jacob according to the MT of Exodus 1:5; seventy elders in the Sanhedrin (*m. Sanh.* 1.6); seventy nations in the world, and so on (cf. *TDNT* 2:634). There are fewer significant instances of the number seventy-two, if one is looking for possible precedents, though S. Jellicoe ("St Luke and the Seventy-two," *NTS* 6 [1960]: 319–21) suggests that the seventy-two translators of the LXX mentioned in the *Letter of Aristeas* may have relevance. Marshall, 415, suspects that Luke wrote that number thinking of the table of nations in the LXX of Genesis 10, which lists seventy-two rather than seventy nations. Copyists, who were more familiar with the number seventy, may have changed the text in that direction. This is a reasonable proposal that fits both the MS evidence and the background situation.

2 "The Lord of the harvest" (τοῦ κυρίου τοῦ θερισμοῦ, *tou kyriou tou therismou*) is presumably God the Father. Though Jesus is called "Lord" in v.1, his reference to the Lord of the harvest as the hearer of prayer is clearly in the third person in meaning as well as form.

4 "Sandals" (ὑποδήματα, *hypodēmata*, GK *5687*) are not mentioned in 9:3. The summary in 22:35 mentions them among prohibited equipment (see Notes, 9:3, regarding the differences among the Synoptics as to what was or was not allowed.

6 The clause ἐπαναπαήσεται ἐπ' αὐτὸν ἡ εἰρήνη ὑμῶν (*epanapaēsetai ep' auton hē eirēnē hymōn*, "your peace will rest on him") portrays peace almost as an objective, personal power. God's spoken word had this characteristic in Semitic thought. It was to leave the host if he or she was not the kind of person who would be receptive to the message of the kingdom.

9 "The kingdom of God is near you" (ἤγγικεν ἐφ' ὑμᾶς ἡ βασιλεία τοῦ θεοῦ, *ēngiken eph' hymas hē basileia* [GK *993*] *tou theou*) is one of many statements of Jesus that teach the nearness of the kingdom. It is not so clear in this passage that the kingdom has actually arrived as in 11:20, where the verb ἔφθασεν (*ephthasen*) means "has come." In the latter case, Jesus' casting out of demons was an act of kingdom power. Here (v.9) it is not clear whether the disciples actually embodied or brought the kingdom or whether they just announced it. The prepositional phrase ἐφ' ὑμᾶς, *eph' hymas*, occurs both here and in 11:20, giving rise to the question of whether a common Aramaic saying underlies both, even though the Greek verbs are difficult. While this is improbable (cf. Marshall, 422), the potential of ἐγγίζω (*engizō*, "draw near," "approach," GK *1581*) to indicate actual arrival plus the idea of proximity in the prepositional phrase are sufficient to establish the point: the hearers had adequate assurance of the coming of the kingdom to them in time and space through the arrival and ministry of Jesus' representatives.

11 On καὶ τὸν κονιορτὸν (*kai ton koniorton*, "even the dust"), see comments at 9:5.

18 Julian Hills ("Luke 10.18—Who Saw Satan Fall?" *JSNT* 46 [1992]: 25–40) argues that the subject of the act of seeing is the demons: "They [the demons] saw Satan fall." The context does not, however, encourage such rendering, though the pronoun can indeed be plural. Moreover, his reading is based on the assumption that this is Luke's creation.

21 Ταῦτα (*tauta*, "these things") is without antecedent, and various solutions have been proposed, among which are as follows: knowledge of the will of God, God's mystery, Jesus' suffering, the plan of God, and the fall of Satan (for a detailed survey, see Crump, 56–57). In the context of the mission of the Seventy-two, the powerful manifestation of the dawn of God's kingdom should at least be considered as among these "things" that are revealed.

The phrase ἠγαλλιάσατο [ἐν] τῷ πνεύματι τῷ ἁγίῳ (*ēgalliasato* [*en*] *tō pneumati tō hagiō*) presents a textual and a theological problem. In turn (as often), the theological problem may have produced the textual. The wording here (UBS[4]) may be translated "rejoiced [or exulted] in the Holy Spirit." Metzger, 128, says, "The strangeness of the expression . . . (for which there is no parallel in the Scriptures) may have led to the omission of τῷ ἁγίῳ (*tō hagiō*, "the holy") from 𝔓[45] A W Δ Ψ f[13] it[q] goth Clement *al.*" The more important MSS have ἁγίῳ, *hagiō*, and it is most likely that it is in the Spirit of God, not Jesus' human spirit, that Jesus exulted. The use of square brackets around ἐν, *en*, in the UBS text acknowledges that some significant MSS omit that word. The NIV interprets the word ἐν, *en*, as instrumental and has "full of joy through the Holy Spirit." In the theology of Luke, this clause is especially significant because of his stress on Jesus and the Holy Spirit and on joy.

B. Teachings (10:25−11:13)

1. Parable of the Good Samaritan (10:25−37)

OVERVIEW

This parable, unique to Luke, requires the utmost care in its interpretation. It must neither be over-allegorized, as it was by the early church fathers, nor reduced to a simplistic meaning hardly worthy of Jesus' teaching. Above all, it must be understood in its context, with attention to the questions of vv.25 and 29 and to Jesus' application in vv.36−37.

The dialogue that precedes the parable in Luke is similar to the one that Matthew and Mark locate in Jerusalem (Mt 22:34−40; Mk 12:28−34). It is possible that Luke incorporates the same conversation in this section of Jesus' sayings; but it is equally possible, if not more likely, that the somewhat different wording indicates a different conversation. Questions about achieving eternal life and about the essence of the law of God were common in Judaism. Totally different conversations follow the recitation of the two commandments in Mark and Luke.

The parable itself may echo the story in 2 Chronicles 28:5−15, where similar concerns and themes are present (cf. F. Scott Spencer, "2 Chronicles 28:5−15 and the Parable of the Good Samaritan," *WTJ* 46 [1984]: 317−49; Thomas E. Phillips, "Subtlety as a Literary Technique in Luke's Characterization of Jews and Judaism," in *Literary Studies in Luke−Acts* [ed. Thompson and Phillips], 313−26).

The literature on this parable is extensive and includes G. Burn, "The Parable of the Bad Exegete: A Note on Luke 10:29−37," *ExpTim* 111 (2000): 299−300; R. A. J. Gagnon, "A Second Look at Two Lukan Parables: Reflections on the Unjust Steward and the Good Samaritan," *HBT* 20 (1998): 1−11; M. Graves, "Luke 10:25−37: The Moral of the 'Good Samaritan,'" *RevExp* 94 (1997): 269−75; J. J. Kilgallen, "The Plan of the '*Nomikos*' (Luke 10.25−37)," *NTS* 42 (1996): 615−19; L. W. Mazamisa, *Beatific Comradeship: An Exegetical−Hermeneutical Study on Luke 10:25−37* (Kampen: Kok, 1987).

[25]On one occasion an expert in the law stood up to test Jesus. "Teacher," he asked, "what must I do to inherit eternal life?"

[26]"What is written in the Law?" he replied. "How do you read it?"

[27]He answered: "'Love the Lord your God with all your heart and with all your soul and with all your strength and with all your mind'; and, 'Love your neighbor as yourself.'"

[28]"You have answered correctly," Jesus replied. "Do this and you will live."

[29]But he wanted to justify himself, so he asked Jesus, "And who is my neighbor?"

[30]In reply Jesus said: "A man was going down from Jerusalem to Jericho, when he fell into the hands of robbers. They stripped him of his clothes, beat him and went away, leaving him half dead. [31]A priest happened to be going down the same road, and when he saw the man, he passed by on the other side. [32]So too, a Levite, when he came to the place

and saw him, passed by on the other side. [33]But a Samaritan, as he traveled, came where the man was; and when he saw him, he took pity on him. [34]He went to him and bandaged his wounds, pouring on oil and wine. Then he put the man on his own donkey, took him to an inn and took care of him. [35]The next day he took out two silver coins and gave them to the innkeeper.'Look after him,' he said, 'and when I return, I will reimburse you for any extra expense you may have.'

[36]"Which of these three do you think was a neighbor to the man who fell into the hands of robbers?"

[37]The expert in the law replied, "The one who had mercy on him." Jesus told him, "Go and do likewise."

COMMENTARY

25 The man's expertise lay in details of the Jewish religion. The fact that he wanted to "test" (*ekpeirazō*, GK *1733*) Jesus may, but does not necessarily, indicate hostility. He addressed Jesus as "teacher" (*didaskalos*, GK *1437*). Note his assumption of human responsibility in the attainment of eternal life, and see the similar assumption on the part of the rich ruler in 18:18. "Eternal life" (*zōēn aiōnion*, GK *2437, 173*) here means the life of the kingdom (18:18, 24-25, 29; cf. Jn 3:3, 5, 15-16, 36). This concern regarding life is seen in two stories found in later Jewish tradition in which a rabbi and a merchant respectively ask who desires life. They then quote Psalm 34:12-14 as the means of achieving it (*b. ʿAbod. Zar. 19b*; *Lev. Rab.* 16).

26 Jesus' counterquestion does not constitute an affirmation of the assumption behind the question but directs the questioner back to the Law, the commandments of the OT, which are not only his special field but also the ultimate source of religious knowledge. "How do you read it?" invites the expert's personal interpretation.

27 In Luke it is the interlocutor, not Jesus, who quotes the commandment (cf. Mt 22:37-40; Mk 12:29-31). The answer is satisfactory so far as it goes. It is based on the OT (Dt 6:5; Lev 19:18; cf. Ro 13:9); in the first century this was not an uncommon response to such a question (cf. J. I. H. McDonald, "Rhetorical Issue and Rhetorical Strategy in Luke 10:25-37 and Acts 10:11-18," in *Rhetoric and the New Testament*, ed. Stanley E. Porter and Thomas H. Olbricht [Sheffield: Sheffield Academic Press, 1993], 63). The words "as yourself" will provide the crucial means of evaluating one's love of a neighbor. The ultimate evaluation will have to be based on deeds, not words, as the parable shows. It is noteworthy that the command to love one's neighbor is not subordinated to the first commandment as strongly in Luke (where it is joined by the coordinate conjunction "and," *kai*) as it is in Matthew 22:39 and Mark 12:31, where the word "second" (*deutera*) is used. (On the command itself, see V. P. Furnish, *The Love Command in the New Testament* [Nashville: Abingdon, 1972].)

28 Jesus affirms that the man has answered correctly (*orthōs*, "rightly," "properly," GK *3981*, from which our word "orthodox" is derived). The words "do" and "live," as they appear in Leviticus 18:5, are used here in Jesus' response. This does not mean that the inquirer has grasped the full meaning of the

Law, nor does it support the idea held by many Pharisees that by keeping the Law as some kind of contract with God a person can earn eternal life (see Notes).

29 The only way this man (or any person) can "justify himself" is to limit the extent of the Law's demand and consequently limit his own responsibility. This maneuver not only fails but also has an opposite effect. Jesus will change the man's very words "who is my neighbor?" from a passive to an active sense (v.36).

30 The overallegorizing of the parable that saw the Samaritan as Christ, the inn as the church, etc., must be rejected. The characters of the story must have the same significance they had to the original hearers. The religious persons act contrary to love, though not contrary to expectation. It is made clear that the priest, at least, is pursuing his religious duty, going "down" (i.e., back) from Jerusalem (v.31). To an extent, the "Law" (vv.26–27) was being observed, but studious readers will recognize the neglect of mercy (cf. Mt 23:23; esp. the occurrence of "merciful" in Lk 6:36 in place of "perfect" in Mt 5:48). The "rule of three" is fulfilled by the appearance of a third character, but unexpectedly he is not just a layperson (in contrast to the clerical characters) but also a Samaritan (in contrast to the Jewish victim).

The distance from Jerusalem to Jericho is about seventeen miles, with a sharp descent toward the Jordan River just north of the Dead Sea. The old road, even more than the present one, curved through rugged, bleak, rocky terrain where robbers could easily hide. It was considered especially dangerous, even in a day when travel was normally full of hazards.

31–32 Priests served in the temple; their highest duty was to offer sacrifices. Levites assisted in the maintenance of the temple services and order. It has been suggested that the priest and the Levite refrained from helping the man because he appeared to be dead and they feared ritual defilement. Jeremias, 203–4, rejects this explanation on the grounds that (1) ritual purity was only significant when carrying out cultic activities; (2) the priest was going "down" (v.31), i.e., away from, Jerusalem, presumably having finished his cultic duties; (3) the Levite by implication (v.32) was probably also going away from Jerusalem; and (4) when priests and Levites were on their way to serve in the temple they traveled in groups, but these two were alone and therefore not on their way to Jerusalem. Also, the point of the story seems to require that the priest and Levite be without excuse.

The combination of "priests" and "Levites" reflects a common Jewish usage in describing Jewish leadership. Michel Gourgues ("The Priest, the Levite, and the Samaritan Revisited: A Critical Note on Luke 10:31–35," *JBL* 117 [1998]: 710–11) has noted that the trilogy "priests, Levities, people" can be found in canonical postexilic texts as well as contemporary Jewish literature. The mention of the first two categories naturally leads one to expect the third—"people" or laypersons. The appearance of the Samaritans in the next verse naturally surprises the expert in the Law, as it did the original audience.

33 "Took pity" (*esplanchnisthē*, GK *5072*) implies a deep feeling of sympathy, a striking response that stands in contrast not only to the attitude of the priest and the Levite but also to the usual feelings of hostility between Jews and Samaritans.

34–35 This pity is translated into sacrificial action. The Samaritan may have even used pieces of his own clothing to make the bandages (v.34); he used his own wine as a disinfectant and his own oil as a soothing lotion (Jeremias, 204). He put the man on "his own donkey" and paid the innkeeper out of his own pocket (v.35), with a promise to pay more if needed.

36 The NT parables aim to lead one to a decision, and Jesus' second counterquestion forces the "expert in the law" to voice his decision. Jesus in his question does not focus on the object of neighborly love (the Jewish victim) but instead on the subject of that love—the Samaritan who made himself to be a neighbor. This reversal of the "expert's" question (v.29) provides in itself the key to the meaning of the parable and to Jesus' teaching on love. Love should not be limited by its object; its extent and quality are in the control of its subject. Furthermore, love is demonstrated in action—in this case in an act of mercy. It may be costly: cloth, wine, oil, transportation, money, and sacrifice of time. There is a striking reversal of roles here. The Jewish "expert" would have thought of the Jewish victim as a good person and the Samaritan as an evil one; to a Jew there was no such person as a "good" Samaritan.

Jesus could have told the story with a Samaritan victim and a Jewish helper, but the role reversal drives the story home by shaking the hearer loose from his preconceptions.

37 The "expert" cannot avoid the thrust of the parable, though he apparently finds it impossible to say the word "Samaritan" in his reply. Jesus now refers back to the original question, "What must I do?" by saying, "Go and do likewise." Both this man and the rich ruler of 18:18–25 needed to learn that God does not bestow the life of the kingdom on those who reject the command to love. Such rejection shows that they have not truly recognized how much they need the love of God themselves. In this respect they are identified with Simon the Pharisee rather than with the woman who was forgiven much and therefore loved much (7:36–50).

NOTES

28 "You will live" (ζήση, zēsē, GK *2409*) in Leviticus 18:5 is also understood as referring to "eternal life" in contemporary Palestinian and Hellenistic Jewish documents (see esp. E. Verhoef, "[Eternal] Life and Following the Commandments: Leviticus 18:5 and Luke 10:28," in *The Scriptures in the Gospels*, ed. C. M. Tuckett [Leuven: Leuven Univ. Press, 1997], 517–77).

35 The "two silver coins," literally two denarii, could provide the needs of an individual for three weeks. It is, therefore, a generous sum of money (cf. D. E. Oakman, "The Buying Power of Two Denarii. A Comment on Luke 10:35," *Forum* 3 [1987]: 33–38).

2. The Home of Martha and Mary (10:38–42)

OVERVIEW

In 8:1–3 Luke mentioned several women who traveled with Jesus and the disciples and contributed to their support. Now he tells about a woman who entered into discipleship. Once again, Luke portrays the way Jesus transcended the prejudices of his day.

Green, 436, has rightly noted that here the contrast is not between "doing" and "listening" but between focusing on Jesus as the host and being distracted by deeds that affect one's growth in authentic faith.

38As Jesus and his disciples were on their way, he came to a village where a woman named Martha opened her home to him. 39She had a sister called Mary, who sat at the Lord's feet listening to what he said. 40But Martha was distracted by all the preparations that had to be made. She came to him and asked, "Lord, don't you care that my sister has left me to do the work by myself? Tell her to help me!"

41"Martha, Martha," the Lord answered, "you are worried and upset about many things, 42but only one thing is needed. Mary has chosen what is better, and it will not be taken away from her."

COMMENTARY

38–39 The travel theme appears in v.38 ("on their way"), but Luke refrains from mentioning that the "village" was Bethany (Jn 11:1). Possibly he wants to reserve mention of Jesus' ministry in Jerusalem and its environs till later (cf. 13:32–33; 17:11; 19:28; see comments at 9:51).

The way in which Martha is mentioned seems to give her the role of hostess (cf. Jn 12:1–2). It is Mary, however, who takes the place of a disciple by sitting at the feet of the teacher (v.39; cf. Ac 22:3, "under Gamaliel," lit., "at his feet"). It was unusual for a woman in first-century Judaism to be accepted by a teacher as a disciple. Notice that Jesus is called "Lord" (*kyrios*, GK *3261*) throughout this passage.

40 Martha was "distracted," the verb *perispaō* (GK *4352*) implying that her attention was drawn away by the burden of her duties. One can only speculate about the actual feelings she had toward her sister beyond what she said and about the personal differences between herself and Mary. Martha's concern seems to have been that she had to work alone rather than that she could not sit at Jesus' feet.

41–42 The Lord shows concern for Martha's anxiety (v.41), but the precise meaning of his saying (v.42) is partly obscured because of a textual prob-

lem (see Notes). There is no explanation of "what is better" (*tēn agathēn merida*, lit., "the good part"). Some have understood it to be the contemplative life, or placing worship over service. Manson, 264–65, believed it denotes seeking the kingdom first. This interpretation has the merit of explaining Mary's seeming neglect of household duties, which in comparison with the kingdom would have a radically diminishing demand on her. The word of the Lord has first claim. For the disciple an attitude of learning and obedience takes first place. The preceding narrative and parable establish the importance of priorities in the Christian life—i.e., heeding the commands to love God and neighbor. Martha must now learn to give the Lord and his word priority even over loving service. There are important human needs, whether of the victim in vv.30–35 or of Jesus himself. But what is most "needed" goes beyond even these.

The thoughtful reader will recognize, however, that this spiritual priority is not the same as the sterile religion of the priest and Levite in vv.31–32. In line with the emphasis of the parable of the good Samaritan is the emphasis on doing what is necessary, even when it means that one has to deviate from the expected mode of behavior.

NOTES

42 The text note indicates a textual problem here. Of the several variant readings, none of them have a clear claim to originality. Among these, the most probable choices resolve into (1) "few things are needed," (2) "one thing is needed," and (3) "few things are needed or only one." The NIV has chosen (2) for its text; the UBS Greek text gives it a "C" rating. The NIV text note has (3). Reading (1) has slim support from the MSS, but Marshall, 453, believes it is worth considering because "it is indirectly attested in the good MSS which have the conflate reading" (i.e., the one reflected in the NIV text note). Also, if "few" means "few dishes of food," Marshall says, "the change from 'few' to 'one' is comprehensible; scribes were perhaps more likely to think that Jesus would give teaching not about practical hospitality but about the one spiritual goal." In any case, the basic meaning is clear—Martha's and Mary's priorities are contrasted.

REFLECTIONS

The contrast between Martha and Mary has been variously construed. For a survey of various proposals, see W. Carter, "Getting Martha Out of the Kitchen: Luke 10:38–42 Again," *CBQ* 58 (1996): 264. A reading informed by the knowledge of the social world of Mediterranean societies helps in highlighting the striking act of Jesus in his call to women to follow him.

The following comment should be quoted in full: "Martha and Mary are known only in terms of the interior of their house, where Jesus is their guest (10:38–42). The expected place of Mary, moreover, is with Martha in the women's part of that household, the kitchen; she is not expected in the dining area, and so her presence there requires a special explanation. Jesus' remark to Martha serves to vindicate Mary's exceptional presence in space not expected of her; the story consciously upsets the native perception of how things ought to be" (Malina and Neyrey, "Honor and Shame in Luke–Acts," in *The Social World of Luke–Acts* [ed. Neyrey], 25–65).

3. Teaching on Prayer (11:1–13)

OVERVIEW

The Lord's Prayer in Luke appears in connection with Jesus' own practice and teaching on prayer. Matthew presents the prayer in a somewhat different form as part of the Sermon on the Mount (Mt 6:9–13). The prayer fits each context, and the differences indicate separate traditions. It would be difficult to prove that either Matthew or Luke had significantly changed the prayer from the form in which they knew it. The Matthean form is undoubtedly more "liturgical" in that the successive petitions are parallel, are balanced, and in Aramaic may even have rhymed at points. In Matthew 6 the prayer has petitions that may supplement or substitute for some feature of the Jewish prayers of that day. Luke offers a basic prayer to say what is characteristic of Jesus' teaching.

Helpful works on the Lord's Prayer include R. A. Guelich, *The Sermon on the Mount* (Waco, Tex.: Word, 1982), 283–97, 307–20; J. Jeremias, *The Prayers of Jesus* (Philadelphia: Fortress, 1978); W. L. Liefeld, "The Lord's Prayer," in *ISBE* 3:160–64; E. Lohmeyer, *The*

Lord's Prayer (London: Collins, 1965); A. Nicholas, *The Lord's Prayer* (Notre Dame: Univ. of Notre Dame Press, 1992); J. J. Petuchowski and M. Brocke, *The Lord's Prayer and Jewish Liturgy* (New York: Seabury, 1978); V. K. Robbins, "From Enthymeme to Theology in Luke 11:1–13," in *Literary Studies in Luke–Acts* (ed. Thompson and Phillips), 191–214; E. M. Yamauchi, "The Daily Bread Motif in Antiquity," *WTJ* 28 (1965–66): 145–56.

¹One day Jesus was praying in a certain place. When he finished, one of his disciples said to him, "Lord, teach us to pray, just as John taught his disciples."

²He said to them, "When you pray, say:

"'Father,
hallowed be your name,
your kingdom come.
³Give us each day our daily bread.
⁴Forgive us our sins,
    for we also forgive everyone who sins against us.
And lead us not into temptation.'"

⁵Then he said to them, "Suppose one of you has a friend, and he goes to him at midnight and says, 'Friend, lend me three loaves of bread, ⁶because a friend of mine on a journey has come to me, and I have nothing to set before him.'

⁷"Then the one inside answers, 'Don't bother me. The door is already locked, and my children are with me in bed. I can't get up and give you anything.' ⁸I tell you, though he will not get up and give him the bread because he is his friend, yet because of the man's boldness he will get up and give him as much as he needs.

⁹"So I say to you: Ask and it will be given to you; seek and you will find; knock and the door will be opened to you. ¹⁰For everyone who asks receives; he who seeks finds; and to him who knocks, the door will be opened.

¹¹"Which of you fathers, if your son asks for a fish, will give him a snake instead? ¹²Or if he asks for an egg, will give him a scorpion? ¹³If you then, though you are evil, know how to give good gifts to your children, how much more will your Father in heaven give the Holy Spirit to those who ask him!"

COMMENTARY

1 Once more Luke speaks of Jesus at prayer (cf. 3:21; 6:12; 9:28). His exemplary practice introduces the exemplary prayer. Since prayer inevitably expresses one's theology, the prayers of the Jewish sects in the first century were distinctive. This was true of John the Baptist. Jesus responds to the request of "one of the disciples" with a model that, while not to be thoughtlessly repeated (Mt 6:7), provides words disciples can use with the confidence that they express Jesus' own teachings. The words "when [or whenever, *hotan*] you pray" (v.2) imply frequent repetition of the actual prayer.

2 The word "Father" (*patēr*, GK *4252*) expresses the essence of Jesus' message and the effect of his atoning work on our relationship with God. Through the use of this intimate but respectful term of address, the Son of God expressed his unique relationship to God. It is very probable (so *TDNT* 1:6) that in every prayer he spoke to God, Jesus used the Aramaic word *Abba* ("dear Father," GK 10003 [cf. GK *5*]), which would naturally be translated *patēr* in the Greek text. The notable exception is the prayer of derelictfrom the cross (Mk 15:34). Through his atoning death on the cross, the Savior brought about reconciliation with God, making it possible for us to become his spiritual children through the new birth. While we cannot use the term *Abba* on an equal basis with the Son of God, there is a sense in which both he and we may address God as "dear Father" (Jn 20:17; Ro 8:14–17). (For the originality of the simple term *Abba* as a form of direct address to God by Jesus, see Joachim Jeremias, *The Lord's Prayer* [Philadelphia: Fortress, 1964], 17–21.)

The petitions (vv.2–4) are usually understood as two kinds—the first two petitions relate to God, the last three to us. The first two do have implications for our daily living, and the three that follow are also centered on God and his kingdom.

"Hallowed be your name" is an ascription of worship basic to all prayer and is found in various forms in the OT (e.g., Ps 111:9) and in ancient Jewish prayers (the *Kaddish* and the Eighteen Benedictions; see Str-B, 1:406–8). "Hallowed" (*hagiasthētō*, GK *39*) means "let [your name] be regarded as holy." It is not so much a petition as an act of worship; the speaker, by his words, exalts the holiness of God. God's people were told in the OT to keep his name holy (Lev 22:32; cf. Ps 79:9; Isa 29:23). God told Israel that because they failed to honor his name, he would do it himself so the nations would know that he was Lord (Eze 36:22–23). Reading this petition in light of Ezekiel 36, the practical implications can also be felt: we pray not simply for God's name to be exalted but that God would empower us so that our behavior will bring glory to his name. With this petition, this prayer is introduced as one that centers directly on God. The aorist tense suggests that a specific time of fulfillment is in mind. This may be the coming of the kingdom. The next clause, which is about the kingdom, also contains a verb in the aorist tense.

In the *Kaddish*, the petition for the exaltation and hallowing of God's name was immediately followed by a request that we might know the rule of God in our lives now. These requests that the glory and reign of God may be realized soon are suitable for the Lord's Prayer because Jesus came to announce and bring the "kingdom." Though its consummation is still future, in his ministry the kingdom was inaugurated in power. The form of the prayer in Luke lacks these words in Matthew: "your will be done on earth as it is in heaven" (Mt 6:10).

3 Thus far, apart from the address "*Abba*" (see above), the wording has been close to what any Jew expecting the kingdom might pray. The three petitions that follow (vv.3–4) are closely connected with the "*Abba*" and give a more distinctive character to the prayer as a whole.

The first of the three petitions relating to us is for "bread" (*artos*, GK *788*), representing food in general. In the Gospels, however, "bread" is often understood in a metaphorical sense in reference to the spiritual nourishment God provides. The parable of the "bread" that follows this prayer (vv.5–13) may support this reading, since the parable concludes with the spiritual gift from God the Father: "how much more will your Father in heaven give the Holy Spirit to those who ask him!" (v.13). This interpretation is further supported by patristic evidence where the bread is understood as Word, Wisdom of God, or Body of Christ (cf. M.-É. Boismard, "'Notre pain quotidien' [Mt 6, 11]," *RB* 102 [1995]: 371–78).

The meaning of *epiousion* (GK *2157*; NIV, "daily") is obscure (see Notes), so the context of the word becomes crucial. The petition can be paraphrased in the Greek word order as follows: "Our bread, the daily, keep giving to us each day" (the verb being in the present tense, indicating continuing, daily provision). This contrasts with Matthew 6:11—"our bread, the daily, give to us today" (the verb being in the aorist tense, indicating a simple act). "Today" in Matthew and "each day" in Luke are in an emphatic position at the end of the clause. Rather than meaning "daily," *epiousion* may mean "for tomorrow." "Tomorrow" may be literally the next day. This would be appropriate if it were an evening prayer. It could also signify the eschatological bread, i.e., God's abundant provision at the consummation of the kingdom. Thus the Matthean form is a request for that kind of bread to be given in advance—on this very day. In Luke, however, any gap between present and future (assuming the future meaning of *epiousion*) is bridged by the substitution of the present imperative "keep giving us" and by the words "each day." Thus the petition as Luke has

it would then be for the provision of this aspect of the future feast in our own lives now.

The word *epiousion* can also have a more general meaning—"sufficient" or "necessary" (cf. E. M. Yamauchi, "The Daily Bread Motif in Antiquity," *WTJ* 28 [1965–66]: 147–56). This would make a smoother reading than having two terms that mean "daily" ("each day . . . daily"). It would also fit Luke's stress on present needs, though it can also point to the necessary spiritual nourishment that comes from God. To trust God for sufficient food day by day was important to people in Jesus' time who were hired only a day at a time (cf. Mt 20:1–5). When the people of Israel were in the wilderness, they learned to trust God for manna day by day (Ex 16:4; Dt 8:16). When believers look forward to the eschaton, we survive on that which God provides.

4 "Forgive us our sins" (*aphes hēmin tas hamartias hēmōn*) uses the aorist tense, which may refer to a single declaration of forgiveness, when all accounts are settled. More likely, however, it simply describes a petition repeated as needed. The word "sins" is the familiar *hamartia* (GK *281*) rather than the Jewish idiom "debts" (*opheilēmata*, GK *4052*) in Matthew 6:12. Since the petitioner has called God "Father," he is a believer, already justified and without guilt through the death of Christ; therefore, the forgiveness he must extend to others is not the basis of his salvation but a prerequisite for daily fellowship with the Father in the sense of 1 John 1:5–10. Conversely, one who does not forgive others may actually be revealing that he has not really known God's forgiveness (cf. Lk 7:47).

"Lead us not into temptation [*eis peirasmon*, GK *4280*]" does not imply that God might otherwise entice us to do evil (Jas 1:13–15 rules this out). God does, however, allow his people to be tested as to their faithfulness (see comments at 4:1–12 and references there to Dt 6–8). The word *peirasmos* probably means "testing" rather than "temptation" (i.e., to sin), though severe testing may be the occasion for one to sin. Further, there is a coming *peirasmos* that will severely try all those who undergo it, and this petition may have reference to that. In any case, the request is clearly for the Father to keep his children from falling away in the hour of trial, with a possible allusion to the temptation and fidelity of Christ. With this petition the Lord's Prayer comes to a close, lacking, except in a variant (see Notes), the additional words in Matthew.

5–6 Jesus' teaching on prayer continues with a parable unique to Luke, the meaning of which has been variously assessed. The scene is that of a Palestinian home in which the entire family is asleep in one room—perhaps the only room in the house—and probably all on one mat. The father could not get over to the door and slide back the heavy bolt that bars it without waking up his family. In such a situation no one would be happy to respond, especially in the middle of the night. Nevertheless, the man does respond to his friend at the door (v.8), for a reason to be discussed below.

The midnight arrival of the hungry friend has usually been thought normal, because "journeys were often undertaken by night to avoid the heat of the day" (Marshall, 464). Bailey (*Poet and Peasant*, 121) maintains that, on the contrary, while this is true in desert areas, the elevation of central Palestine and Lebanon and the sea breeze along the coast made travel during the day customary. The night arrival would therefore be unusual. In either case, a host in that first-century society would be expected to provide a welcome. Rather than insult his guest with too little bread (or with a broken loaf, if it was of the large variety of that area), the host would seek out a person with a good supply, knowing who in his small town had recently baked. The visitor would have been the guest not only of the individual and his family but also of the whole

community. This placed a great responsibility on both the traveler's host and the friend he approached at midnight (see Bailey on these customs, *Poet and Peasant*, 121–33).

8 The point of the parable depends partly on the context and partly on the meaning of the word *anaideia* (GK *357*), translated "boldness" (NIV), "persistence" (NASB), or "importunity" (RSV, KJV). If *anaideia* means "persistence," the parable would seem to teach that if we persist long enough, God will finally answer our prayers. But since the larger context (especially vv.10, 13, as well as the rest of Scripture) teaches God's eagerness to hear and grant our requests, the meaning "persistence" has little in its favor. Reference is sometimes made to 18:1–8 in support of the persistence theory (but see comments there). On the other hand, this parable, with its reluctant host and persistent visitor, may present not a comparison but a contrast to the way God answers prayer. In that case, the point would be that if in human circumstances a person pressed hard enough will respond to a request, even though reluctantly, surely God will answer and do so far more graciously.

Yet another interpretation has been proposed. The word *anaideia* can mean "avoidance of shame" (Bailey, *Poet and Peasant*, 125–33; D. Catchpole, "Q and 'The Friend at Midnight,'" *JTS* 34 [1983]: 407–24). While it did come to have the meaning of "persistence," the concept of shame was linked with it in the first century. The parable would thus mean that just as the man in bed would respond so as not to incur shame (for having refused the needs of a visitor to his community), so God will always do what is honorable and consistent with his character.

9–10 In threefold poetic form, Jesus teaches that "everyone who asks" (*pas ho aitōn*)—not only the persistent—will receive from God. This saying of great assurance is preserved also in Matthew 7:7–8.

11–12 The bizarre examples in vv.11–12 reinforce the point that God will respond to our petitions only in kindness. There are two steps in the argument: (1) God is our heavenly Father (v.13) and will do no less for his children than would an earthly father; (2) God is perfect and will do "much more" than sinful man would. The parallel passage in Matthew 7:11 has the general term "good gifts."

13 Luke specifically mentions the Holy Spirit, who was promised (Ac 2:33; cf. Lk 24:49; Ac 1:4). The giving of the Spirit in response to prayer can already be found in 3:21–22 where the descent of the Spirit takes place when Jesus was praying. This promise also anticipates Acts, where one witnesses the dramatic descent of the Spirit on the believing community (cf. Shepherd, 137–40).

NOTES

3 The word ἐπιούσιον (*epiousion*, "daily," GK *2157*) may be derived from a combination of ἐπί (*epi*) used as a preposition or as a prefix with εἰμί (*eimi*, "to be, exist") or with εἶμι (*eimi*, with a circumflex accent, "to come, go"). Thus it could refer to present or future time, including the presence of something needed at the moment. The lack of exact parallel usages (beyond the Matthean and Lukan Lord's Prayer) makes it difficult for modern readers to determine the exact meaning of the word. For a survey of literature, see A. Hultgren, "The Bread Petition of the Lord's Prayer," in *Christ and His Communities*, ed. A. Hultgren and B. Hall (Cincinnati: Forward Movement, 1990), 41–54; B. M. Metzger, "How Many Times Does '*Epiousios*' Occur outside the Lord's Prayer?" *ExpTim* 69 (1957–58): 52–54.

4 Various approaches have been taken in explaining the theological implications of the final petition. These include distinguishing between testing and temptation, recovering the force of the Semitic original, understanding temptation as hardship, and holding James 1:3 in tension with this petition while recognizing the different contexts of the two sayings (see P. S. Cameron, "'Lead Us Not into Temptation,'" *ExpTim* 101 [1990]: 299–301; K. Grayston, "The Decline of Temptation—and the Lord's Prayer," *SJT* 46 [1993]: 279–95; S. E. Porter, "Matthew 6:13 and Luke 11:4: 'Lead Us Not into Temptation,'" *ExpTim* 101 [1990]: 359–62).

5 Jeremias, 157, believes that as Jesus originally told the parable it was addressed not to the visitor but to the man in bed. The words translated "suppose one of you" (τίς ἐξ ὑμῶν, *tis ex hymon*, lit., "who [or which] of you?") imply, "surely none of you would do what I am going to describe." But though the immediate transition to the third person "he" in v.5 makes for some ambiguity, the hearer of the parable is not to imagine himself as the man in bed but as the visitor.

Bailey (*Poet and Peasant*, 124–25) cites as a close parallel Luke 17:7, which he thinks helpful in determining the understood subject of the verb πορεύσεται (*poreusetai*, "goes," GK *4513*) here in v.5. If the parallel holds, the hypothetical person ("one of you") is the one who "goes" rather than the friend going to him. Thus the hearer identifies himself with the visitor, who, according to Bailey's interpretation, receives the bread not because of his own persistence but because the man in bed does not want to incur shame.

C. Growing Opposition (11:14–54)

1. Jesus and Beelzebub (11:14–28)

OVERVIEW

This event shows the real nature of the increasing opposition Jesus faced. Mark and Matthew also include it but in different contexts. Mark follows it with the parable of the sower, which illustrates the varying responses to Jesus' teaching (Mk 3:20–4:20). Matthew (like Luke) follows it with Jesus' comments on the sign of Jonah but then (unlike Luke) has the parable of the sower followed by the so-called parables of the kingdom, which also show the contrast between good and evil (Mt 12:22–13:52). In Luke, the Beelzebub controversy leads to the sign of Jonah (as in Matthew) and then on to the woes against the unbelieving religious leaders. Each of the other Synoptics also includes a comment regarding Jesus' mother together with a statement that obedience to God's word is more important than even the closest human ties to Jesus.

Whether the arrangement is due to each evangelist's plan or to the order of events in his source, every occurrence of the Beelzebub incident in the Synoptics comes at a crucial point in the narrative. The incident shows that Jesus' hearers must choose between good (Jesus, the Spirit, and God's kingdom) and evil (Satan and his demons).

The issue is nothing less than the source of Jesus' authority and power. This is especially important for Luke, who is deeply aware of the importance of the supernatural as a testimony that Jesus is the promised Messiah (cf. the apostolic testimony he records in Ac 2:22, 43; 4:30; 5:12; 10:38, as well as the miracles in the gospel itself). The climax of the passage comes in v.20, which, as we will see, links the display of God's power in the exodus and the same potential power in the kingdom of God with Jesus' successful attack on the kingdom of Satan. Though Luke continues this theme in vv.21–26, he postpones the issue of blasphemy against the Holy Spirit (located at this point in Matthew and Mark) until 12:10. This may have been the order in his source for this passage.

---

[14]Jesus was driving out a demon that was mute. When the demon left, the man who had been mute spoke, and the crowd was amazed. [15]But some of them said, "By Beelzebub, the prince of demons, he is driving out demons." [16]Others tested him by asking for a sign from heaven.

[17]Jesus knew their thoughts and said to them: "Any kingdom divided against itself will be ruined, and a house divided against itself will fall. [18]If Satan is divided against himself, how can his kingdom stand? I say this because you claim that I drive out demons by Beelzebub. [19]Now if I drive out demons by Beelzebub, by whom do your followers drive them out? So then, they will be your judges. [20]But if I drive out demons by the finger of God, then the kingdom of God has come to you.

²¹"When a strong man, fully armed, guards his own house, his possessions are safe. ²²But when someone stronger attacks and overpowers him, he takes away the armor in which the man trusted and divides up the spoils.

²³"He who is not with me is against me, and he who does not gather with me, scatters.

²⁴"When an evil spirit comes out of a man, it goes through arid places seeking rest and does not find it. Then it says, 'I will return to the house I left.' ²⁵When it arrives, it finds the house swept clean and put in order. ²⁶Then it goes and takes seven other spirits more wicked than itself, and they go in and live there. And the final condition of that man is worse than the first."

²⁷As Jesus was saying these things, a woman in the crowd called out, "Blessed is the mother who gave you birth and nursed you."

²⁸He replied, "Blessed rather are those who hear the word of God and obey it."

COMMENTARY

14–16 The setting of this account of the Beelzebub controversy is the healing of a deaf mute (*kōphos*, GK *3273*). Such a healing was among the signs of Jesus' messiahship about which he reminded John the Baptist (7:22). Once more, as in 4:36 and elsewhere, the crowds are "amazed" at Jesus' power over demons. The crowd is divided, however, between those who either opposed him outright by attributing his power to the head demon, "Beelzebub" (v.15; see Notes), or taunted him to give them an even more dramatic sign, which constitutes a "testing" or provocation (v.16). The presence of the uncertainty of the crowd's response will be further developed in Acts as a sign of the failure of Israel to accept salvation from God.

17–19 Jesus "knew their thoughts" (v.17; cf. 5:22; 7:39–47). The identification of Beelzebub with Satan (v.18) is the basis of vv.17–19. The head of any army would hardly work with the enemy against his own troops. Moreover, if demons are exorcised by the power of their own leader, how do the Jews explain the power their own exorcists (v.19; cf. Ac 19:13–14) are supposed to have (see Notes)? Jesus' illustration shows the drastic antithesis between the powers of

evil, darkness, and Satan on the one hand and the power of God, the Holy Spirit, and the kingdom of light (cf. Col 1:12–13) on the other hand.

20 When the magicians in Egypt were unable to duplicate all the miracles Moses did before the exodus, they said to Pharaoh, "This is the finger of God" (Ex 8:19). So here Jesus is affirming that the source of his power is "the finger of God," i.e., God himself—a statement Matthew specifically identifies with the Holy Spirit (Mt 12:28). If this is true, then Jesus' driving out of demons is a messianic sign and "the kingdom of God has come" (see Notes).

21–23 Here the imagery is more vivid than in Matthew and Mark, for the strong man guards his own house. Jesus' victory against Satan during his temptation may be alluded to here (v.22). In any event, we have in these verses a principal reference to Jesus' tactics in his war against Satan. The ultimate and actual means of Jesus' victory is the cross. The critical place in Jesus' ministry of his victory over Satan means that we also must take a stand for or against Jesus as the one who brings the kingdom (v.23). Whoever does not "gather" (*synagō*, GK *5251*) the sheep "scatters" (*skorpizō*, GK *5025*) them by default and thus works counter to Jesus (so Marshall, 478). In John 10:11–13, the hired hand neglects his duty and the wolf "scatters" (*skorpizō*) the flock.

24–26 "Evil spirit" (*akatharton pneuma*, GK *176, 4460*) is a Jewish term for a demon (v.24). Luke does not say that the demon has been exorcized. When it is, the Holy Spirit in the power of the kingdom will accomplish that work and will indwell the person who has been possessed. In vv.24–26 a spiritual renewal has taken place, but without the indwelling Spirit. Marshall, 479, suggests that this refers to the work of the Jewish exorcists mentioned in v.19. The evil spirit wanders through "arid places" (v.24), a description in accord with the popular idea that demons inhabited the desert. (Compare the accusation that John the Baptist, who lived in the desert, had a demon [7:33].) Some see Isaiah 13:21 and 34:14 as sources for this idea.

The demon seeks a human body, and to repossess its previous abode it enlists the aid of seven demons even worse than itself (v.26). This combination of seven plus one is reminiscent of the same grouping of spirits in the *Testament of Reuben* 2 and 3. Contrast the "seven spirits" before the throne (Rev 1:4). The demons "live" (*katoikeō*, lit., "settle down"; GK

2997) there. The same verb is used in Ephesians 3:17 of Christ's full indwelling. The parallel in Matthew 12:43–45 applies the demons' settling down directly to "this wicked generation" and thus suggests that those who repented after hearing the initial proclamation of the kingdom through John the Baptist but failed to allow Jesus to bring the power of the kingdom into their lives were the ones who were worse off than before. In the context, the point of the story is to contrast the healing power of Jesus with the destructive power of the demons. This focus on the strikingly different nature of the two missions serves as the conclusion to the illustrations of the divided kingdom (vv.17–20) and the strong man (vv.21–22) above. For further discussion, see J. J. Kilgallen, "The Return of the Unclean Spirit (Luke 11:24–26)," *Bib* 74 (1993): 45–59.

27–28 This saying is unique to Luke and provides another instance of his identification of Jesus' sayings as the "word of God" (v.28). The redefinition of God's people in reference to Jesus' ministry and teaching is again noted. It must not be taken as reflecting unfavorably on Mary, especially when Mary herself was credited not simply as the mother of Jesus but as one "who has believed that what the Lord has said to her will be accomplished" (1:45).

NOTES

15 "Beelzebub" is a difficult name to analyze. It has been compared to a similar sounding word meaning "Lord of the Flies." There are several variants of the name. "Beelzebub" (NIV) has come down through the Latin MS tradition. The form "Beelzeboul" (NIV text note) is the most common one in the Greek MSS—Βεελζεβούλ (*Beelzeboul*). Among the various etymologies suggested is that which incorporated a Hebrew word for a dwelling— *zᵉbul* (GK 2291)—which was used in Jesus' day to refer to the temple (cf. ßLloyd Gaston, "Beelzebul," *TZ* [1962]: 247–55). This would have been a parody of the one who was truly "head of the house" (Mt 10:25).

Whatever its etymology, the significance of the name is clear. The wording in v.18 suggests that Beelzeboul was another name for Satan. That Beelzeboul was more than an epithet formed for the occasion is not certain, but Jesus' response points to a known and sinister figure. It is possible, though unlikely, that this "prince of demons" is to be understood as an inferior being representing Satan's cause (cf. *ZPEB*, 1505).

19 The phrase οἱ υἱοὶ ὑμῶν (*hoi huioi hymōn*; NIV, "your followers") can also have a broader reference (e.g., "your own people"). Arguing against the consensus of modern commentators, R. Shirock ("Whose Exorcists Are They? The Referents of οἱ υἱοὶ ὑμῶν at Matthew 12.27/Luke 11.19," *JSNT* 46 [1992]: 41–51) suggests that the phrase refers to Jesus' own disciples. The function of the exorcists as judges and the understanding of exorcism as the sign for the arrival of the kingdom of God lend support to this reading. Nevertheless, it remains unclear whether the Pharisees would accept the exorcism of Jesus' disciples as authentic signs of divine acts.

20 The phrase "finger of God" appears also in Exodus 31:18 and Deuteronomy 9:10. In these instances, the intervention of God in human affairs is emphasized. For further discussion of the use of this phrase in the OT, see G. A. Klingbeil, "The *Finger of God* in the Old Testament," *ZAW* 112 (2000): 409–15.

In ἔφθασεν ἐφ' ὑμᾶς (*ephthasen eph' hymas*, "has come to you"), we have what is perhaps the strongest single affirmation in the Gospels of the presence of the kingdom. While ἐγγίζω (*engizō*, "approach," "draw near," GK *1581*) implies imminent arrival (e.g., in Mk 1:15), the verb here, from φθάνω (*phthanō*, GK *5777*), can mean not only to "arrive" but even, in the proper context, to "precede," as in 1 Thessalonians 4:15. The prepositional phrase ἐφ' ὑμᾶς, *eph' hymas*, secures the meaning that the kingdom was actually there. See G. E. Ladd, *Theology of the New Testament* (2d ed.; Grand Rapids: Eerdmans, 1993), 65–68, for a discussion of the presence of the kingdom centering on the parallel passage in Matthew 12:28.

2. The Sign of Jonah (11:29–32)

OVERVIEW

This passage gives us Jesus' response to those who were prodding him for a "sign [*sēmeion*, GK *4956*] from heaven" (v.16). The gospel of John builds on the premise that Jesus performed miracles as signs (*sēmeia*). The present passage does not stand in opposition to the meaningful use of signs but rather to the unbelief that resists the testimony already obvious in the messianic works (cf. v.14 above). The Synoptics oppose an inordinate demand for extraordinary miracles beyond those needed for a witness to Jesus' authority. An even stronger statement, though not incompatible with this, occurs in Mark 8:12.

²⁹As the crowds increased, Jesus said, "This is a wicked generation. It asks for a miraculous sign, but none will be given it except the sign of Jonah. ³⁰For as Jonah was a sign to the Ninevites, so also will the Son of Man be to this generation. ³¹The Queen of the South will rise at the judgment with the men of this generation and condemn them; for she came from the ends of the earth to listen to Solomon's wisdom, and now one greater than Solomon is here. ³²The men of Nineveh will stand up at the judgment with this generation and condemn it; for they repented at the preaching of Jonah, and now one greater than Jonah is here."

COMMENTARY

29–30 The transitional phrase "as the crowds increased" encourages the reader to understand this comment on "sign" in terms of the previous passage, especially v.16. Only Luke has the phrase, just as only Luke has the reference to a sign in v.16. The "sign" of Jonah is Jonah himself, whose presence and brief message (cf. v.32, *kērygma*, GK *3060*; NIV, "preaching"), though very minimal compared with the preaching of Jesus, triggered immediate and widespread repentance. Matthew 12:40 adds a reference to Jonah's experience in the huge fish as pointing to the duration of Jesus' entombment. This is not mentioned in Luke, and Marshall's attempt, 483, to introduce it here may be unnecessary. For Luke, the preaching of Jesus—namely, his "word"—carried its authority, especially when affirmed by the power of God in miracles (e.g., 4:32, 36). This does not mean that Jesus' resurrection as a parallel to Jonah's delivery from the fish was not the ultimate sign, but only that Luke did not have that part of the tradition.

In Jewish traditions Jonah also came to be understood as a sign of judgment. Not incompatible with the call to repentance here is the focus on the idea of judgment. As we have noted, the judgment of Israel is a prominent theme in the Lukan travel narrative. In light of the reference to "judgment" (v.31), the "sign" of Jonah may ultimately refer to the message of judgment that Jonah proclaimed to the people of Nineveh (see Notes).

31–32 The inclusion of the "Queen of the South" (the queen of Sheba) fortifies the judgment on Jesus' generation, because she traveled a great distance to hear the wisdom of Solomon (cf. 1Ki 10:1–13; 2Ch 9:1–12). A double contrast is implied in these two examples: (1) the response of the audience and (2) the greatness of the preacher. The "one greater" (v.32) than Solomon and Jonah is, of course, Jesus, unless one interprets the neuter form of the word "greater" (*pleion*) to cover the whole mission of Jesus or perhaps the kingdom (though the latter would call for the feminine form).

NOTES

29 On the meaning of σημεῖον (*sēmeion*, "sign," GK *4956*) in Scripture, see *TDNT* 7:200–61 (esp. 233–34 on Jonah); *NIDNTT* 2:626–33 (630 on Jonah, which takes the sign of Jonah to be the parousia of the Son of Man); cf. *TDNT* 8:449–50, which holds that while the parousia would be significant with respect to judgment, it comes too late to validate Jesus' ministry. But in Luke, where the emphasis on judgment is without explicit reference to Jesus' resurrection (cf. Mt 12:40), this would not be as much of a problem and does not require, as clearly as Matthew does, a sign that was observable during Jesus' ministry apart from the very preaching of the word itself.

On the tradition-history of the Jonah and sign passages, see R. A. Edwards, *The Sign of Jonah in the Theology of the Evangelists and Q* (Naperville, Ill.: Allenson, 1971). Edwards attributes not only the form of the saying but also its Christology to the early church rather than to Jesus. Recent literature includes B. N. Beck, "'You Lifted Me Up from the Pit Alive': Exegetical and Theological Trajectories from the Book of Jonah in Jewish and Christian Sources" (ThD diss., Harvard University, 2000); S. Chow, *The Sign of Jonah Reconsidered* (ConBOT 27; Stockholm: Almqvist & Wiksell, 1995); J. Swetnam, "Some Signs of Jonah," *Bib* 68 (1987): 74–79.

3. The Lamp of the Body (11:33–36)

³³"No one lights a lamp and puts it in a place where it will be hidden, or under a bowl. Instead he puts it on its stand, so that those who come in may see the light. ³⁴Your eye is the lamp of your body. When your eyes are good, your whole body also is full of light. But when they are bad, your body also is full of darkness. ³⁵See to it, then, that the light within you is not darkness. ³⁶Therefore, if your whole body is full of light, and no part of it dark, it will be completely lighted, as when the light of a lamp shines on you."

COMMENTARY

33 Hearing Jesus' message lays a responsibility on the hearer. The metaphors of light, signs, and judgment (cf. vv.29–32) are akin to what we have in John (e.g., 3:19–21; 9:39–41) and elsewhere in the NT (e.g., Ac 26:18; 2Co 6:14–15; Eph 5:5–14). Much of this passage is paralleled in Matthew 6:22–23. There the Jewish concept of the "bad eye" symbolizing covetousness provides a link with the preceding saying about treasures. In the Lukan context, there is no reference to possessions.

34–35 "Good eyes" (see Notes) admit light; bad ones do not. The implication is that the individual is responsible for receiving light. The eye is thus a "lamp" (*lychnos*) not in the sense that it emits light but that through it (subject to the individual's will) the body receives light. The real source of light is outside the body; if we think we can generate our own light, we must beware lest that inner "light" prove to be "darkness" (v.35).

36 This seemingly repetitive verse resembles in its repetitiveness and subject Ephesians 5:13–14a. Its meaning becomes clear in the light of vv.34–35. The body is only completely lighted when a lamp shines on it from the outside. The repetition of two Greek words is chiastic (in reverse order): *holon phōteinon* ("whole body is full of light") and *phōteinon holon* ("completely lighted"). The concluding *holon* is emphatic. The words are repeated to introduce an analogy that describes how the body is fully lighted: "as when [*hōs hotan*] the light of a lamp shines on you." Taking vv.34–36 together, we learn that full illumination only comes when one is willing to receive light from the lamp of God's truth.

NOTES

34 The word ἁπλοῦς (*haplous*, "healthy, sound," GK 606) can have the idea of "sincere" or "generous" (so Mt 6:22, where, as noted above, the matter of possessions has been discussed). Here it means eyes that see clearly and do not deliberately obscure reality; so the NIV's "are good."

36 The exact reference of the word ἔσται (*estai*, "will be") is subject to debate, and how the repetitive nature of this saying is understood is determined partly by how one takes this word. Most see the word in a sequential chronological way. On the other hand, Susan R. Garrett ("'Lest the Light in You Be Darkness': Luke 11:33–36 and the Question of Commitment," *JBL* 110 [1991]: 93–105) argues for an eschatological sense and that the saying is to be considered as a promise that those who are full of light will in return receive light in the final judgment. G. Nebe ("Das ἔσται in Luke 11:36—ein neuer Deutungsvorschlag," *ZNW* 83 [1992]: 108–114) suggests, however, that the ἔσται, *estai*, takes on an imperatival sense and thus one finds the call to missionary work.

4. Six Woes (11:37–54)

37When Jesus had finished speaking, a Pharisee invited him to eat with him; so he went in and reclined at the table. 38But the Pharisee, noticing that Jesus did not first wash before the meal, was surprised.

39Then the Lord said to him, "Now then, you Pharisees clean the outside of the cup and dish, but inside you are full of greed and wickedness. 40You foolish people! Did not the one who made the outside make the inside also? 41But give what is inside the dish to the poor, and everything will be clean for you.

42"Woe to you Pharisees, because you give God a tenth of your mint, rue and all other kinds of garden herbs, but you neglect justice and the love of God. You should have practiced the latter without leaving the former undone.

43"Woe to you Pharisees, because you love the most important seats in the synagogues and greetings in the marketplaces.

44"Woe to you, because you are like unmarked graves, which men walk over without knowing it."

45One of the experts in the law answered him, "Teacher, when you say these things, you insult us also."

46Jesus replied, "And you experts in the law, woe to you, because you load people down with burdens they can hardly carry, and you yourselves will not lift one finger to help them.

47"Woe to you, because you build tombs for the prophets, and it was your forefathers who killed them. 48So you testify that you approve of what your forefathers did; they killed the prophets, and you build their tombs. 49Because of this, God in his wisdom said, 'I will send them prophets and apostles, some of whom they will kill and others they will persecute.' 50Therefore this generation will be held responsible for the blood of all the prophets that has been shed since the beginning of the world, 51from the blood of Abel to the blood of Zechariah, who was killed between the altar and the sanctuary. Yes, I tell you, this generation will be held responsible for it all.

52"Woe to you experts in the law, because you have taken away the key to knowledge. You yourselves have not entered, and you have hindered those who were entering."

53When Jesus left there, the Pharisees and the teachers of the law began to oppose him fiercely and to besiege him with questions, 54waiting to catch him in something he might say.

COMMENTARY

37–38 In a way typical of his use of material, Luke puts the major discourse in the setting of a dinner (cf. 14:1–24) Jesus himself attended (cf. the similar discourses in Mt 15:1–20; 23:1–36; Mk 7:1–22). This setting naturally recalls Luke 7:36–50, in which Jesus was also invited by the Pharisees and was prompted to react to their thoughts and words. When the meal setting is understood as a significant symbol of community identity, Jesus' criticism of the Pharisees paves the way for the definition of the true people of God. Having accepted table fellowship with a Pharisee, Jesus offended his host, a proponent of ritual separation, by omitting the customary ritual washing prior to eating (v.38).

Luke's introduction lacks the details about Jewish customs found in Mark 7:1–4. The reference to Isaiah 29:13 in Mark and in the similar passage in Matthew 15:1–9 is also lacking, and the comments in vv.39–54 have their parallel not in Mark 7 and Matthew 15 but in Matthew 23:1–36, where the order is different and the comments on each indictment fuller. Luke gives us a concise selection of indictments. These point up some of the most common of the sins that characterize strict religious persons ("churchmen," as Ellis, 168–69, calls them). These include hypocrisy (vv.39–41), imbalance (v.42), ostentation (v.43), impossible demands (v.46), intolerance (vv.47–51), and exclusiveness (v.52).

39–42 For the most part, the "Pharisees"—originally a group of laypersons who sought to be separate from impure things and people and attempted to apply Mosaic law to all parts of life—had by the time of Jesus lost the heart of their religion.

In vv.41–42 Jesus offered a positive corrective that clearly shows he did not oppose strict attention to religious duties but rather the neglect of caring about people that strict religionists often fall into.

This is consistent with his teaching in 6:27–36 and 10:25–37. Seen merely from the religious point of view, to wash externally was in reality only a halfway measure. Moreover, vv.39–41 imply that in their "greed and wickedness" (v.39) the Pharisees had deprived the poor of the very food and drink that were "inside" (v.40) their own carefully washed dishes. Alternatively, "inside" also refers to their inner moral life ("you are full," v.39). Likewise, they apparently were tithing possessions that they should have shared with (or that rightfully belonged to) the needy (v.42). Marshall, 498, remarks that, though it might seem inconsistent that Jesus, while not practicing ritual washing, commended meticulous tithing, tithing was an OT principle.

44 The vivid simile in v.44 is an example of Jesus' use of irony. Though the Pharisees avoided touching a grave for fear of ritual defilement, they themselves, through their own unrecognized corruption, were defiling those who came into contact with them. In Matthew 23:27 the figure is that of "whitewashed tombs."

45–46 These verses are directed against the "experts in the law" (v.45). Many of them were Pharisees, and they were often mentioned together. Yet they were distinct groups, and Jesus addressed them separately. Their religious legalism explains v.46. They could interpret the OT and the traditions built on it in such a way as to leave little room for personal moral decisions. As "experts," they could, of course, find ways of circumventing the rules themselves.

47–48 Before and during the time of Jesus, some lavish tombs were built for royalty and others. It was all very well for the experts in the law to build new tombs for prophets long since martyred by the experts' forefathers (v.47). Yet this very act ironically symbolized approval of their forefathers' crimes against God's messengers (v.48; cf. the longer version of this saying in Mt 23:29–32). The characterization of Jewish religious leaders as killers of prophets is made explicit in Acts 7:52.

J. D. M. Derrett ("'You Build the Tombs of the Prophets' [Luke 11:47–51, Matthew 23:29–31]," *SE* 4 [1968]: 187–93) suggests that the building of tombs was a way of acknowledging guilt and was analogous to the offering of blood money to a victim's survivors by a relative of one guilty of murder.

49–51 These verses relate the grim truth behind the parable of the tenants (20:9–19; see Notes, "wisdom" [v.49] and "Zechariah" [v.51]). They also pave the way for the inclusion of Jesus among the line of prophets who were rejected by God's people.

52 Jesus directed his final woe against the experts in the law at their sin of taking away not just physical but eternal life. Those who should have opened

the meaning of the OT with their "key" not only declined to use it themselves but also prevented others from "entering" (the present participle *eiserchomenous* may be conative: "trying to enter"). The implied subject of "knowledge" is probably the kingdom of God, which people were seeking to "enter." The connection of "keys" with the "kingdom" in Matthew 16:19 comes to mind here. Jesus charged the experts in the law with dereliction of their most important duty.

53–54 Jesus' series of woes made inevitable the violent hostility against him described here. His opponents followed him out of the house and fired at him a barrage of difficult questions, such as those later used to embarrass rabbinic scholars. He had challenged those who professed to be the expert biblical teachers. They were out to defend their reputation by discrediting his (v.54).

NOTES

39 In the prevailing Jewish practices before AD 70, the distinction was made between cleanliness of the inside and the outside of utensils; therefore, Jesus' comment is particularly appropriate in this verse in his criticism of the Pharisees' paying attention to merely the external practices without noting the polluted state of their hearts. See J. Neusner, "First Cleanse the Inside," *NTS* 22 (1975–76): 486–95.

42 In its wild state, πήγανον (*pēganon*, "rue") was exempt from tithing. But Luke is referring to kitchen herbs, among which cultivated rue was subject to tithing.

49 The NIV translates ἡ σοφία τοῦ θεοῦ εἶπεν (*hē sophia tou theou eipen*, lit., "the wisdom of God said") as "God in his wisdom said." This interpretation is one way to understand this unusual introduction to a quotation that has no known source in the OT. Some believe it is from an apocryphal source. Ellis, 170–73, takes it as referring to NT prophets bringing new revelations from the risen Christ. It may embody the essence of several OT passages. Many of the prophets God sent were opposed and even persecuted (e.g., 1Ki 19:10, 14; Jer 7:25–26; Eze 2:3–8). The apostles were likewise "sent" on a mission that may be described as prophetic (Lk 6:22–23). Thus the saying applies all that God said "in his wisdom" in the OT to the NT apostles and prophets. All of the above attempts to understand this difficult saying are plausible, and others could be cited. It is not clear whether there is an allusion to wisdom in its technical sense in Proverbs and other Jewish writings known as Wisdom literature. There is no apparent reason for such an allusion, but it is otherwise difficult to explain why wisdom is introduced at all here, since nothing in the saying has a unique "wisdom" characteristic. It may simply refer to the sovereign wisdom of God in allowing evil people to continue and good people (here the prophets) to suffer.

51 Bloodguiltiness is emphasized here by the specific mention of Abel (Ge 4:8–10) and of a "Zechariah" (Mt 23:35, "Zechariah son of Berekiah") whose identity is much disputed. Some consider him to be a man whose father's name was similar to that in Matthew and who was killed in the temple precincts in AD 67–68. This assumes that the saying either did not originate in the time of Jesus' earthly ministry or was expanded later. Marshall, 506, argues that without any reference to Jesus as a martyr-prophet or to the apostles, the saying cannot be classified as a Christian addition. Also possible is the view that this is an unknown Zechariah who was killed sometime before Jesus' ministry (cf. J. M. Ross, "Which Zechariah?" *IBS* 9 [1987]: 70–73).

It is more common to identify "Zechariah" with the person mentioned in 2 Chronicles 24:20–25. In addition to that Zechariah's having been murdered in the temple precincts, the account follows a description similar to those mentioned above of the divinely "sent" prophets who were resisted (2Ch 24:19). J. Barton Payne ("Zechariah Who Perished," *Grace Journal* 8 [1967]: 33–35) points out, however, that (1) the murder must have been done in the inner court (1Ki 6:36; 2Ch 4:9), in contrast to the location mentioned in 2 Chronicles 24:20–25; (2) Jesus is speaking of prophets—a term recalling the minor prophet Zechariah rather than the son of Jehoiada the priest; (3) Jewish tradition favors the prophet; and (4) taking Josephus's order of the canon, Jesus' placing of Zechariah as last in a series could well refer to the canonical order rather than to a chronological order. Further, Matthew adds the detail that the victim was the son of Berekiah, which accords with Zechariah 1:1. The problem is more vexing for interpreters of Matthew; Luke's version lacks the reference to Berekiah; so neither of the two biblical Zechariahs mentioned above is excluded.

52 The phrase τὴν κλεῖδα τῆς γνώσεως (*tēn kleida tēs gnōseōs*, "the key to knowledge") could also be understood as an appositive: "the key that is knowledge." The parallel (Mt 23:13) has "you shut [or lock up (κλείετε, *kleiete*)] the kingdom of heaven." The construction τὰς κλεῖδας τῆς βασιλείας (*tas kleidas tēs basileias*, "the keys of the kingdom") in Matthew 16:19 is grammatically close enough to suggest that the NIV's "key to knowledge" is preferable here.

53–54 "To besiege him with questions" is perhaps the best translation of ἀποστοματίζω (*apostomatizō*, GK 694), but the meaning of the word is hard to determine. It seems to have connoted "mouthing" something one was supposed to learn and repeat. Here it could have the sense of pressing a series of questions to which certain "correct" answers must be given or else the subject is considered heretical. Questions were sometimes used in rabbinic circles of the first centuries of our era to demonstrate one's own superiority over another (a possible clue to the meaning of 1Co 14:34–35). But the meaning is not at all certain. BDAG, 122, says, "Ancient commentators interpreted it as *catch* (him) *in someth. he says*=vs. 54; then approx. *watch his utterances closely*" (italics theirs). The uncertainty led to changes in the Western text. Our problem comes from not knowing the development of an idiomatic use that may have had a brief life span.

D. Teachings on Times of Crisis and Judgment (12:1–13:35)

1. Warnings and Encouragements (12:1–12)

OVERVIEW

The crisis in Jesus' relationship with the teachers of the law at the end of ch. 11 gives rise to a series of strong statements about the eternal issues involved. Jesus' audience must choose sides. He gives promises and warnings appropriate to each hearer's circumstance. Much in these exhortations is also found in Matthew's account of Jesus' instructions to the Twelve (Mt 10:19–20, 26–33). Similar ideas occur in the Olivet Discourse (Lk 21:12–19 and parallels). These other passages suggest an applica-

tion not only to Jesus' immediate audience but also to the future church, with its martyr missionaries.

This passage is also related to 8:9–18. In ch. 12 Jesus deals with the proclamation of the Word, while in ch. 8 he focuses on the reception of the Word. In both he addresses the issue of anxiety and urges believers not to be discouraged by present threats (cf. A. J. Malherbe, "The Christianization of a *Topos* [Luke 12:13–34]," *NovT* 38 [1996]: 123–35).

[1]Meanwhile, when a crowd of many thousands had gathered, so that they were trampling on one another, Jesus began to speak first to his disciples, saying: "Be on your guard against the yeast of the Pharisees, which is hypocrisy. [2]There is nothing concealed that will not be disclosed, or hidden that will not be made known. [3]What you have said in the dark will be heard in the daylight, and what you have whispered in the ear in the inner rooms will be proclaimed from the roofs.

[4]"I tell you, my friends, do not be afraid of those who kill the body and after that can do no more. [5]But I will show you whom you should fear: Fear him who, after the killing of the body, has power to throw you into hell. Yes, I tell you, fear him. [6]Are not five sparrows sold for two pennies? Yet not one of them is forgotten by God. [7]Indeed, the very hairs of your head are all numbered. Don't be afraid; you are worth more than many sparrows.

[8]"I tell you, whoever acknowledges me before men, the Son of Man will also acknowledge him before the angels of God. [9]But he who disowns me before men will be disowned before the angels of God. [10]And everyone who speaks a word against the Son of Man will be forgiven, but anyone who blasphemes against the Holy Spirit will not be forgiven.

[11]"When you are brought before synagogues, rulers and authorities, do not worry about how you will defend yourselves or what you will say, [12]for the Holy Spirit will teach you at that time what you should say."

COMMENTARY

1 "Meanwhile" (*en hois*) specifically connects this section with the preceding one. Again Luke notes the crowds, emphasizing the size of this one by the word "thousands" (*myriadōn*, lit., "of tens of thousands"—an extremely large crowd). The same word in Acts 21:20 designates the great number of Jewish people who were believers—presumably far more than the few thousand mentioned at the beginning of Acts (e.g., 2:41, 47). The popularity of Jesus at this point is contrasted with the rejection that he and his disciples will face.

Jesus addresses the disciples "first" (*prōton*, in an emphatic position). The crowds received his words later (vv.54–59). The key word "hypocrisy" (*hypokrisis*, GK *5694*) was triggered by the charges in ch. 11. Jesus compares to the action of "yeast" (*zymēs*, GK *2434*) the insidious way this attitude can influence others.

2–3 Jesus' next words about concealment and disclosure seem at first to be a warning that what hypocrites try to cover up will be revealed. But vv.3–4 have a positive thrust. Verse 3 is much like Matthew 10:26–27, where the disciples are encouraged not to be afraid but to declare publicly what they have heard privately from Jesus. This sense also fits the similar saying in the context of the parables of the kingdom (Mk 4:22; Lk 8:17). The idea of disclosure is linked to that of acknowledgment in v.8.

4–5 "Friends" (*philois*, GK *5813*) is an expression of confidence (Jn 15:14–15) and is antithetical to the hostility of the Pharisees. Jesus does not guarantee protection from death but affirms that (1) God alone controls the final destiny of people, and they should "fear" (*phobeomai*, GK *5828*) God rather than those who can merely inflict physical death (v.5); and (2) God is intimately aware of all that befalls us.

"Hell" (*geenna*, v.5) is mentioned only here in Luke but several times in Matthew and Mark, where it is clearly a place of torment ("the fire of," Mt 5:22; cf. Mt 18:8–9; Mk 9:43–48). *Geenna* is a Greek transliteration of the Hebrew words for "Valley of Hinnom" (*gē hinnōm*), a ravine to the south and southwest of Jerusalem. Because it had been used for infant sacrifices (2Ch 28:3; 33:6), it was repulsive to the Jews. Josiah attempted to prevent its use in this way (2Ki 23:10), but apparently its reputation continued. Jeremiah labels it as a place of future judgment (Jer 7:32; 19:6). The idea of a place of punishment after death, of which this valley was an analogy, was developed in the intertestamental period. Jesus taught the reality of hell unambiguously.

6–7 Sparrows (v.6) and hairs (v.7) are so insignificant that this kind of argument (from lesser to greater) has a great effect in pointing up the supreme worth of the disciples in God's eyes. References to "hair" in the context of divine protection reappear in 21:16–19 and Acts 27:34. These references have their background in OT sayings that highlight God's sovereignty (cf. D. C. Allison, "'The Hairs of Your Head Are All Numbered,'" *ExpTim* 101 [1990]: 334–36).

8–9 Jesus underscores the seriousness of the issues by referring to the ultimate issue: whether or not one sides with him. Though he has already given the substance of this warning in his first passion prediction (9:26 and parallels), the crucial nature of the present situation called for its restatement. The reference to "the Son of Man" in the third person has led some to believe that Jesus is referring to a coming figure other than himself. But this would make Jesus a personage inferior to him. In point of fact, however, the third-person usage is consistent with Jesus' guarded use of titles. Not until his trial does he publicly combine the terms "Son of Man," "Son of God," and "Messiah" in an eschatological context.

"Acknowledge" (*homologeō*, GK *3933*) and "disown" (*arneomai*, GK *766*) are semantic polar opposites (KJV, NASB, "confess" and "deny"). The reference is apparently to a future scene when the Lord Jesus, having achieved victory and honor, acknowledges those who supported him and disowns (v.9) those who repudiated him during the present age. He does this publicly before God the Father (Mt 10:32–33) and the assembled angels.

10 The final warning in this progression relates to the "unpardonable sin." The context of this saying in Luke differs from that of Matthew and Mark, and the saying itself is separate from the Beelzebub controversy. This separation not only raises questions of tradition history beyond the scope of this commentary but also makes exegesis of the passage difficult. The separation does allow for the continued buildup of hostility between Jesus and the teachers of the law and for the sequence of warnings in 12:1–9, so that it occupies a climactic place. Nevertheless, it is difficult to determine its meaning without the contextual explanations in Matthew and Mark.

Matthew 12:33–36 and Mark 3:30 make clear that the blasphemy against the Holy Spirit is the attribution of the works of Jesus to the very prince of demons. Moreover, this oral blasphemy involves not merely careless words but the expression of an incorrigibly evil heart. This background must be kept in mind as an aid to the theological application of Luke's reference to the unpardonable sin. If dishonoring the Son of Man is such a serious matter as vv.8–9 indicate, then total rejection of God by insinuating that his "Holy" Spirit is "evil" is so much the worse. One may reject Christ and later, by God's grace, accept him; but there is no remedy for absolute and complete denial of the one holy God—Father, Son, and Holy Spirit. This is what the "blasphemy" seems to be here. Some would relate this to Hebrews 6:4–6; 10:26–31 and to apostasy, but the Scriptures lack a sufficient interconnection to make this clear. The same caution should be applied to any attempt to connect this sin with the "sin that leads to death" (1Jn 5:16).

11–12 The foregoing series of warnings and encouragements conclude with this striking contrast to the blasphemy against the Holy Spirit. Far from committing that sin of speaking against him, the believers find that the Spirit speaks through them. Observe the comparison with the mission of the Twelve and with the Olivet Discourse, especially in Matthew 10:19–20 and Luke 21:14–15. The circumstance of the Spirit's speaking through believers is not preaching but persecution, in which preparation of an adequate defense is hardly possible. The reference here to the Spirit as an active actor in the historical plane paves the way for the active role of the Spirit in Acts (cf. Shepherd, 146).

NOTES

5 "After the killing of the body, . . . throw you into hell": Unlike Matthew, who mentions the destruction of both the body and soul in hell (Mt 10:28), Luke seems to focus on the eternal punishment of the soul apart from the body. C. Milikowsky ("Which Gehenna? Retribution and Eschatology in the Synoptic Gospels and in Early Jewish Texts," *NTS* 34 [1988]: 238–49) suggests that this can be explained by the differences between Jewish and Hellenistic conceptions of the afterlife. Without arguing that Matthew and Luke are operating within different visions of "Gehenna," it seems likely that Luke is simply presenting the message with the cultural background of his audience in mind.

2. Parable of the Rich Fool (12:13–21)

OVERVIEW

Though the narrative flows smoothly with the word "crowd" (v.13) making the transition from vv.1–12, the change in topic seems abrupt. A comparison with ch. 16 shows a similar placement of controversy with Pharisees alongside teaching about worldly wealth. There the words "the Pharisees, who loved money" (v.14) serve to link the two subjects.

Chapters 12 and 16 have much in common. If Talbert (*Literary Patterns*, 51–63) is correct, they may be part of an overall pattern in which the two chapters are in a chiastic relationship. In any event, the topic of wealth is prominent in Luke's writing. In this instance Jesus turns a question into an opportunity for ministry to an individual's underlying need.

---

¹³Someone in the crowd said to him, "Teacher, tell my brother to divide the inheritance with me."

¹⁴Jesus replied, "Man, who appointed me a judge or an arbiter between you?" ¹⁵Then he said to them, "Watch out! Be on your guard against all kinds of greed; a man's life does not consist in the abundance of his possessions."

¹⁶And he told them this parable: "The ground of a certain rich man produced a good crop. ¹⁷He thought to himself, 'What shall I do? I have no place to store my crops.'

¹⁸"Then he said, 'This is what I'll do. I will tear down my barns and build bigger ones, and there I will store all my grain and my goods. ¹⁹And I'll say to myself, "You have plenty of good things laid up for many years. Take life easy; eat, drink and be merry."'

²⁰"But God said to him, 'You fool! This very night your life will be demanded from you. Then who will get what you have prepared for yourself?'

²¹"This is how it will be with anyone who stores up things for himself but is not rich toward God."

COMMENTARY

13–14 A person who recognized Jesus as a "teacher" would naturally expect him to have the ability to render a judgment in ethical matters (v.14). Rabbis were often thus consulted, and in later years some traveled from place to place to render legal decisions. Jesus' refusal to answer is not a denial of his right or ability to answer, or of his concern for social and ethical matters; rather, he turns directly to an area in which others have no right to judge (cf.

Mt 7:1), namely, the question of motivation. We are not told whether the inquirer had legal ground for his request—a point that is unimportant here.

15 The audience (*autous*, "them") is probably now the whole crowd, not just the two brothers. The issue revolves around the very nature of "life" (*zōē*, GK 2437). Greed seeks possessions, which are not to be equated with true "living." In fact, they become a substitute for the proper object of man's search and worship—God. Therefore, "greed . . . is idolatry" (Col 3:5).

16–19 Since this is a parable, not an actual incident, Jesus can heighten certain elements that illustrate his point, even to the point of having God speak directly to the rich man. The man expresses in his words (vv.17–19) the attitude Jesus discerns not only in the inquirer but also in others (cf. "anyone" in v.21). "Take life easy; eat, drink and be merry," is a well-known motto for the hedonistic life (cf. A. Malherbe, *Paul and the Popular Philosophers* [Minneapolis: Fortress, 1989], 84–85), and in a meal setting it also functions as a "negative symbol of luxury" (Dennis E. Smith, "Table Fellowship as a Literary Motif in the Gospel of Luke," *JBL* 106 [1987]: 625).

20 The word "fool" (*aphrōn*, GK *933*, v.20) is not used lightly but is used in the OT sense of one who rejects the knowledge and precepts of God as a basis for life. God addresses the man on his own pragmatic terms, dealing not with matters of the kingdom or of life beyond death but with the question of the disposition of the man's possessions. This underscores the fact that he will have to "leave it all." If we read the question, "Who will get?" with Ecclesiastes 2:18–19 in mind, there is also the irony that after years of careful management the man's possessions might be frittered away by an incompetent heir.

21 This verse, which uses the contrasting words "for himself" (*heautō*) and "toward God" (*eis theon*), ends powerfully with the participle "rich" (*ploutōn*, GK *4456*) as the final word. "Stores up things for himself" resembles Matthew 6:19: "Do not store up for yourselves treasures on earth." Both passages introduce similar encouragements about God's care (cf. vv.21–22 here with Mt 6:19, 25).

NOTES

13 The word διδάσκαλε (*didaskale*, "teacher," GK *1437*) has the same sense as "rabbi," which Luke does not use in his gospel. Formerly some thought that the term "rabbi" was anachronistic in the Gospels, as it was only later that ordination was practiced in Judaism. But now it is clear that both terms were used in an honorific sense in Jesus' day (see H. Shanks, "Is the Title 'Rabbi' Anachronistic in the Gospels?" *JQR* 53 [1963]: 343–44). Jesus' contemporaries recognized that, while he was not rabbinically trained, he was a competent teacher (Jn 7:15). Luke has already stressed the crowds' assessment of Jesus' teaching authority (4:31–32).

19–20 The NIV translates ψυχή (*psychē*, GK *6034*) in three ways—"myself," "you," and "life"—thereby showing the broad sense of the word customarily translated "soul."

3. Anxiety over Possessions (12:22–34)

OVERVIEW

This section, except for vv.32–34, is virtually identical to Matthew 6:29–33 in the Sermon on the Mount. In both, one detects the presence of Psalm 104 in the background as Jesus comments on the priority of kingdom concerns (cf. J. D. M. Derrett, "Birds of the Air and Lilies of the Field," *DRev* 105

[1987]: 181–92). As noted above at v.21 (see comments there), which forms a transition to this section, both passages are connected with sayings against "storing up" things for oneself. The passage ends (v.34) with a saying about one's "treasure" (cf. Mt 6:2–13). The Greek word for "treasure" (*thēsauros*, GK *2565*) is related to that for "store up" (*thēsaurizō*, GK *2564*). Thus the passage both introduced and concluded with a saying about "treasuring" is thereby given its theme. What was implied in the warning parable of vv.16–20 is explicitly commanded here (note the *dia touto*, "therefore," of v.22). Believers should not act as does the "pagan world" (*ta ethnē tou kosmou*, v.30), represented by the rich fool of the parable.

---

²²Then Jesus said to his disciples:"Therefore I tell you, do not worry about your life, what you will eat; or about your body, what you will wear. ²³Life is more than food, and the body more than clothes. ²⁴Consider the ravens: They do not sow or reap, they have no storeroom or barn; yet God feeds them. And how much more valuable you are than birds! ²⁵Who of you by worrying can add a single hour to his life? ²⁶Since you cannot do this very little thing, why do you worry about the rest?

²⁷"Consider how the lilies grow. They do not labor or spin. Yet I tell you, not even Solomon in all his splendor was dressed like one of these. ²⁸If that is how God clothes the grass of the field, which is here today, and tomorrow is thrown into the fire, how much more will he clothe you, O you of little faith! ²⁹And do not set your heart on what you will eat or drink; do not worry about it. ³⁰For the pagan world runs after all such things, and your Father knows that you need them. ³¹But seek his kingdom, and these things will be given to you as well.

³²"Do not be afraid, little flock, for your Father has been pleased to give you the kingdom. ³³Sell your possessions and give to the poor. Provide purses for yourselves that will not wear out, a treasure in heaven that will not be exhausted, where no thief comes near and no moth destroys. ³⁴For where your treasure is, there your heart will be also."

COMMENTARY

22–23 Having addressed the crowds in vv.1–21, Jesus turns to his disciples. The word for "life" in vv.22–23 (and cf. v.20) is *psychē* (GK *6034*), which often means "soul." Here the translation "life" is appropriate. Observe the parallelism between vv.22 and 23. A comment on food comes first in each verse, followed by one on clothing. Verse 23 provides the support for the exhortation in v.22: there is more to life than these. The exhortation "do not worry" (*mē merimnate*, GK *3534*) stands alongside the implied "do not covet" in this passage and the preceding one (cf. v.15). Actually, one can both worry and be covetous, whether he is poor or rich. "Do not worry" is the first of a series of four prohibitions. The others are "do not set your heart on" (v.29), "do not worry" (v.29), and "do not be afraid" (v.32).

24 The thrust of the comparison "how much more valuable" is similar to the argument from the lesser to the greater in vv.6–7. There the sparrows represent birds of little value; here the ravens may represent birds that were considered unclean (Lev 11:13–20, esp. v.15) and therefore unworthy of God's care. Jesus assures us that the God who cares for such birds surely will care for us.

25–26 These verses constitute still another argument from the lesser (adding inches of height or minutes of life; see Notes) to the greater (totality of life and its needs). The point here is that if it is futile to worry about small matters we cannot control, it is even more futile to worry about the large matters that lie even farther beyond our control.

27–28 Jesus gives a final example of the lesser-to-greater argument in contrasting the grandeur of Solomon, who could afford the finest clothing, with common flowers, which can do nothing toward making clothes (v.27). His second contrast is between the limited life span of flowers and the (implied) eternal life that lay before the disciples (v.28). God's meticulous and lavish care for mere perishing flowers assures us of his unfailing care for his own people. In view of this, the disciples' "little faith" is all the more shameful.

29 "Do not worry" is the third of four prohibitions (see comments at v.22). The word for "worry" here (meteōrizomai, GK 3577) differs from that in v.22 (merimnaō, GK 3534). Meteōrizomai meant in classical Greek "be raised up" or "suspended." While it came metaphorically to mean "worry," the literal meaning might be expressed by "be in suspense" or "be up in the air."

30 "The pagan world" (ta ethnē, lit., "the nations," i.e., the Gentiles; GK 1620), contrasts with believers. In Matthew's report of the Sermon on the Mount, believers are cautioned three times not to behave as the pagans do: (1) in their relation to people (5:47), (2) in their relation to God in prayer (6:7), and (3) in their relation to material possessions (6:32)—the application it has here in Luke. In

Matthew, the contrast with Gentiles is especially significant in view of the Jewish slant of that gospel. Luke 6:32, the equivalent of Matthew 5:47, has "sinners" (hamartōloi, GK 283), a Lukan term. Pagans do not have the same relation believers have with a loving, caring, providing heavenly Father. To know that God knows their needs is sufficient assurance for all believers.

31 Secure in this knowledge, Jesus' disciples can turn all their attention to the kingdom they are commanded to "seek." The contrast between the concern for one's self and the concern for God's kingdom reveals the theological nature of the examples cited: to be anxious about worldly matters reflects an "erroneous perception of the character of God" (Green, 494), who is able to provide for his people and thus frees them to turn their attention toward the concerns of their Creator.

32 "Do not be afraid" (mē phobou) introduces another contrast. The "little flock" (to mikron poimnion) that now needs to be fed and defended will one day inherit the kingdom and possess its benefits and authority. The fatherhood of God and its connection with the giving of the kingdom are themes not only characteristic of Matthew but also foundational in the Sermon on the Mount, of which this passage may have been originally a part. The encouragement not to fear is appropriate in view of the hostility of the "experts in the law," who, instead of opening the way to the kingdom and its truth (11:52), stand in the way of those who seek it.

33 With the injunction to "sell your possessions" (pōlēsate ta hyparchonta hymōn, GK 4797, 5639), we come to the concluding exhortations on the "treasure" theme. It is difficult to know whether the reason for this exhortation is to benefit the poor or to rid the disciples of encumbering possessions. While the poor are mentioned, the point of the passage as a whole seems to be the total dependence of disciples on God. The second reason, therefore, is probably primary and the first secondary in this context but still important in itself and in Luke's thought throughout his gospel.

The word "all" is neither present nor implied before the word "possessions." As we have seen, the point of Jesus' teaching on treasures is that they are not to be hoarded for one's own selfish pleasure (cf. v.21; Mt 6:19). Nevertheless, the interpreter must be careful neither to blunt Jesus' strong teaching as expressed in Luke regarding a life of abandonment and giving (cf. 6:27–36; 14:26, 33) nor to introduce teachings given to one audience into a discussion with another group. One should live on such a

modest level of subsistence that the only "purses" needed are those one needs for heavenly "treasure." By their nature, such purses are never moth-eaten or stolen.

34 This verse shows the essential thrust of Jesus' teaching. It is not the extent but the place of one's possessions that is emphasized, because it is the direction of one's "heart," heavenward or earthward, that is all-important. In the light of the discussion that follows (vv.35–48), this reference to the place of one's treasure is not simply spatial (heaven) but also temporal (future), as the disciple of Jesus is called to live a life in light of the future return of the Son of Man.

NOTES

24 This verse alludes to Psalm 147:9, where it is stated, "[The LORD] provides food for the cattle and for the young ravens when they call." The idea of not sowing or reaping may have come from Proverbs 6:7, where ancient versions have "without harvesting" instead of "without commander" (as in the MT) in reference to the ants (cf. J. F. Healey, "Models of Behavior: Matthew 6:26 [//Luke 12:24] and Proverbs 6:6–8," *JBL* 108 [1989]: 497–98). The reference to Solomon in v.27 further points to the presence of Proverbs 6.

25 The NIV's translation of ἐπὶ τὴν ἡλικίαν αὐτοῦ προσθεῖναι πῆχυν (*epi tēn hēlikian autou prostheinai pēchyn*) as "add a single hour to his life" is debatable (cf. NIV text note). The word ἡλικία, *hēlikia* (GK *2461*), can mean "age" or "bodily stature" (cf. BDAG, 435–36). The word πῆχυς, *pēchys* (GK *4388*), means "cubit," a unit of measure based on the length of a human forearm (roughly eighteen inches). It could be used to describe the extent of the ἡλικίαν, *hēlikia*, in either of its senses. The NIV takes ἡλικίαν, *hēlikian*, in the sense of "age," which fits well with the parable about the rich fool (vv.16–21), who could not add to his life. Yet the words "how the lilies grow" (v.27), suggest the idea of height. A person of normal stature would scarcely want to add another foot and a half to his height, so such an explanation seems unlikely. The meaning could, however, be that one normally grows inch by inch without giving it any thought. Even if a person thought about it, he or she could not suddenly gain eighteen inches and be fully grown. While to live on some "borrowed time" may seem important and to grow a foot and a half taller is to gain about an additional fourth of one's stature, these are both insignificant in comparison with the entire scope of one's life, especially considered in its spiritual dimension. At any rate, neither is possible; so why worry at all?

27 "The lilies" (τὰ κρίνα, *ta krina*, GK *3211*) may be some specific flower of Jesus' land, but more probably Jesus was "thinking of all the wonderful blooms that adorn the fields of Galilee" (BDAG, 567; see Morris, 214).

The clause οὐ κοπιᾷ οὐδὲ νήθει (*ou kopia oude nēthei*, "they do not labor or spin") receives a cautious "D" rating by the UBS Greek NT. The Western text has οὔτε νήθει οὔτε ὑφαίνει (*oute nēthei oute hyphainei*, "they neither spin nor weave"). Metzger, 136, says the Western reading was rejected "after much hesitation . . . as a stylistic refinement." Marshall, 528, considers this to be "over-subtle for a scribe," but he still finds the support by only one Greek MS (D) weak. It is probably best to keep the UBS's reading, as does the NIV.

4. Readiness for the Coming of the Son of Man (12:35–48)

OVERVIEW

The emphatic use of the personal pronoun "you" (*hymeis*) twice in the Greek text of vv.35–36 sets the attitude of the alert Christian in contrast to that of the pagans (v.30), who seek only the things of this present world. The word "watching" (*grēgorountas*, GK 1213, v.37) expresses the theme of this passage, and the "ignorance of the hour forms the presupposition for each of these parables" (Carroll, 55). Luke introduces "watching" earlier in his gospel than do Matthew and Mark, who use it only in the Olivet Discourse (and in the parables following in Matthew) and in the Lord's words to the disciples at Gethsemane (cf. Mt 24:42–43; 25:13; 26:38, 40–41). Luke does not use the actual verb "to watch" in either of the parallel contexts (17:26–30, 34–36; 22:45–46). Here he seems to be impressed by the connections in our Lord's teaching between warnings about future judgment. The verses following the reference to "watching" (vv.39–40) and the next section also (vv.42–46) are parallel to part of Matthew's version of the Olivet Discourse (Mt 24:43–51). They are usually considered to be from Q and interwoven with other material. The scene in vv.36–37 and the parable in v.39 point clearly to the necessity of being ready for the Son of Man (v.40).

35"Be dressed ready for service and keep your lamps burning, 36like men waiting for their master to return from a wedding banquet, so that when he comes and knocks they can immediately open the door for him. 37It will be good for those servants whose master finds them watching when he comes. I tell you the truth, he will dress himself to serve, will have them recline at the table and will come and wait on them. 38It will be good for those servants whose master finds them ready, even if he comes in the second or third watch of the night. 39But understand this: If the owner of the house had known at what hour the thief was coming, he would not have let his house be broken into. 40You also must be ready, because the Son of Man will come at an hour when you do not expect him."

41Peter asked, "Lord, are you telling this parable to us, or to everyone?"

⁴²The Lord answered, "Who then is the faithful and wise manager, whom the master puts in charge of his servants to give them their food allowance at the proper time? ⁴³It will be good for that servant whom the master finds doing so when he returns. ⁴⁴I tell you the truth, he will put him in charge of all his possessions. ⁴⁵But suppose the servant says to himself, 'My master is taking a long time in coming,' and he then begins to beat the menservants and maidservants and to eat and drink and get drunk. ⁴⁶The master of that servant will come on a day when he does not expect him and at an hour he is not aware of. He will cut him to pieces and assign him a place with the unbelievers.

⁴⁷"That servant who knows his master's will and does not get ready or does not do what his master wants will be beaten with many blows. ⁴⁸But the one who does not know and does things deserving punishment will be beaten with few blows. From everyone who has been given much, much will be demanded; and from the one who has been entrusted with much, much more will be asked."

COMMENTARY

35–36 In Jesus' time, a person "dressed ready for service" by tucking his flowing outer robe under his belt or sash. This was done to prepare for travel, fighting (Eph 6:14), or work (cf. the metaphorical use in 1Pe 1:13).

Matthew 25:1–13 also describes a time of "waiting" with burning lamps for the return of a bridegroom for his wedding. In Matthew the lamps are *lampades* (GK *3286*); here they are *lychnoi* (GK *3394*). There virgins wait for the bridegroom; here servants wait for their master (v.36).

37–38 The strong affirmation "I tell you the truth" (*amēn*) appears for the first time in Luke since 4:24. There is a striking reversal of roles as the master dresses himself to serve (cf. v.35) and waits on the servants. This contrasts with Luke 17:7–10, where a different point is being made. If the return is very late in the night or toward morning, in the "second or third watch" (the middle and last division of the night hours, according to Jewish reckoning), the alertness of the servants is even more commendable (v.38).

39 The image now changes to one of burglary. The absence of figurative or parabolic terminology (cf. "like" in v.36) may indicate that this is not a story but a recent incident known to Jesus' audience. Moreover, Jeremias, 48–49, notes that the use of the aorist tense in the story gives the impression of a straightforward narrative. It is unusual but not impossible for an evil character, such as a thief, to represent a good person (see the unjust judge [18:1–8], who stands in contrast to God). Actually, it is the story as a whole, not the individual characters in it, that provides the comparison here. More recently, it has been suggested that this imagery evokes the exodus narrative, in which God's people were given the permission to plunder the houses of the Egyptians (Ex 3:21–22; 11:2; 12:35–36), and this may be the well-known event that the audience is expected to recall (for further discussion, see Notes).

40 The concluding exhortation to "be ready," because the time of the Son of Man's coming is unknown, is similar to Matthew 24:42–44 in the Olivet Discourse, where the burglary figure is also used (cf. Mt 25:13; Mk 13:33–37). Luke's version of the Olivet Discourse lacks this saying, as well as the saying about ignorance of the day and hour, which is recorded in Matthew 24:36 and Mark 13:32. Here Luke is clearly concentrating much of the Lord's teaching on the implications of his sudden return.

41–44 Peter responds, in his accustomed role as spokesman for the apostles, with a question about the extent of their responsibility (v.41). Jesus answers, as often, with a counterquestion (v.42). Though he says elsewhere that exhortations to "watch" apply to everyone (Mk 13:37), in this case the parable that follows (vv.42–46) shows that the apostles have a special responsibility.

In the illustration the "manager" (or "steward," *oikonomos*, GK *3874*) in charge of the "servants" is a "servant" (or "slave," *doulos*, GK *1528*) himself (v.43). This was a common situation in that first-century society. The passage teaches the importance of faithfulness in doing the will of the master. Verses 42–46 emphasize the responsibility one has for those who have been placed under his leadership. Conversely, the following paragraph (vv.47–48) focuses on response to the master's command.

45–46 As in 18:7 and 19:12, the clear implication is that Jesus himself would not return immediately but that there would be an interval of waiting and serving (see Notes). The attitude of the manager in v.45 is contrary to that commanded in v.40. The word "begins" (*archō*, GK *806*, v.45) suggests that the action is interrupted by the master's unexpected return. The severe treatment of the servants may be hyperbolic, but Acts 20:29–30 warns against false leaders who ravage the congregation (cf. the warning in Mt 7:15–23). Likewise, the vivid description of the manager's punishment—"cut . . . to pieces" (*dichotomeō*, GK *1497*)—stresses the seriousness of his default of responsibility (v.46; see Notes). "A place with the unbelievers" applies to the false religious leaders alluded to rather than merely to the secular characters in the story.

47–48 If this punishment seems too severe, the explanation of God's principle of judgment now clarifies matters. The "servant" in v.47 may represent those who sin "with a high hand," committing "presumptuous sins" (Nu 15:30–31; Ps 19:13 RSV). If so, the servant who "does not know" (v.48) sins "unwittingly" and has "hidden faults" (Nu 15:27–29; Ps 19:12 RSV). In either case, there is some definite personal responsibility and therefore judgment, because the servant should have made it his business to know his master's will. All have some knowledge of God (Ro 1:20), and God judges according to individual levels of responsibility (Ro 2:12–13). The closing statement (v.48) would apply especially to the apostles and church leaders throughout the successive centuries.

NOTES

39–40 The connections between this imagery of the thief's plundering of the house and the exodus event are noted in C. H. T. Fletcher-Louis, "The Gospel Thief Saying (Luke 12.39–40 and Matthew 24.32–33) Reconsidered," in *Understanding, Studying and Reading*, ed. C. Rowland and C. H. T. Fletcher-Louis (JSNTSup 153; Sheffield: Sheffield Academic Press, 1998), 48–68. The audience's awareness of the details of the exodus story should not be doubted, and the call of Jesus to "be dressed ready for service and keep your lamps burning" also recalls Exodus 12:11 [LXX]. Moreover, the plundering motif as connected with the exodus narrative appears also in Isaiah 11:14–16. Fletcher-Louis also provides a detailed discussion of Second Temple Jewish literature in which plundering is considered an expression of God's justice (cf. *Jub.* 48:18; Philo, *Moses* 1.140–42)—a theme that can again be traced back to the exodus narrative. Therefore, the thief saying of Jesus should be understood in light of the larger narrative of Israel's past in pointing to the manifestation of the ultimate justice that comes from God.

46 "He will cut him to pieces" (διχοτομήσει αὐτόν, *dichotomēsei* [GK 1497] *auton*) seems to be such an extreme punishment that various attempts have been made to explain it. Marshall, 543, surveys some of these explanations, favoring that of O. Betz ("The Dichotomized Servant and the End of Judas Iscariot," *Revue de Qumran* 5 [1964]: 43–58). According to Betz, the original Aramaic statement was "he was cut off," i.e., from the "sons of light," as in the theology of Qumran (cf. 1QS 2.16). The words in v.46 would then express this same idea in different terms. For those who prefer a literal reading, the existence of a similar usage of this imagery in Jeremiah 34:18 has also been noted (cf. T. A. Friedrichsen, "A Note on καὶ διχοτομήσει αὐτόν [Luke 12:46 and the Parallel in Matthew 24:51]," *CBQ* 63 [2001]: 258–64).

REFLECTIONS

This passage is important in determining Luke's view of the Parousia. Many scholars have assumed that Luke modified the tradition of Jesus' teaching about his return, reducing the element of imminence to accommodate the fact that Jesus was obviously not returning as soon as expected. A more realistic view, however, is that Jesus not only taught the certainty of his return at an unexpected moment but also implied, through various instructions for his disciples, that the community of believers would continue for an unspecified time serving their Lord till his return in the indefinite future (see comments at 19:11–27; cf. E. Earle Ellis, *Eschatology in Luke* [Philadelphia: Fortress, 1972]; I. Howard Marshall, *Eschatology and the Parables* [London: Tyndale, 1963]). There are neither necessary nor substantial grounds for postulating that in the transmission of Jesus' teaching about the Parousia the audience has been changed from the crowds to the disciples, so as to make the teaching apply to the church in view of a delayed return rather than to those who need to repent in view of impending judgment (cf. Jeremias, 48).

5. Division over Jesus (12:49–53)

OVERVIEW

The Lord's teaching about preparation for his return and impending judgment (vv.35–48) leads to this paragraph about the personal crises that Jesus precipitates.

49"I have come to bring fire on the earth, and how I wish it were already kindled! 50But I have a baptism to undergo, and how distressed I am until it is completed! 51Do you think I came to bring peace on earth? No, I tell you, but division. 52From now on there will be five in one family divided against each other, three against two and two against three. 53They will be divided, father against son and son against father, mother against daughter and daughter against mother, mother-in-law against daughter-in-law and daughter-in-law against mother-in-law."

COMMENTARY

49–50 It is difficult to determine the precise meaning of "fire" (v.49) because the word can signify either judgment or purification, to say nothing of other, less probable meanings. The verses that follow v.49 may, consistently with the preceding paragraphs, connote judgment. While Jesus came to bring salvation rather than judgment (Lk 4:19; Jn 3:17), his coming also meant judgment (Jn 9:39). A comparison with earlier teaching in Luke, however, suggests that "fire" means purification as well as judgment. The ministry of John the Baptist included not only judgment (3:9, 17) but also the promise that Jesus would "baptize . . . with the Holy Spirit and with fire" (see comments and OT references at 3:16). Luke 9:51–56 shows that Jesus did not intend to bring an immediate fire of judgment on those who rejected him. Since 3:16 links fire with the Holy Spirit, it is possible that this fire was to be "kindled" by the baptism of the Spirit (Ac 2:1–4). This could only occur after Jesus' own "baptism" of death, to which he referred here (v.50). Mark 10:38 mentions baptism as a symbol of Jesus' death, along with the "cup" Jesus spoke of at Gethsemane (Lk 22:42). He felt "distressed" (*synechomai*, GK 5309) in anticipation of that. "The prospect of his sufferings was a perpetual Gethsemane" (Plummer, 334).

51–52 Though the Messiah was to "bring peace" (v.51), this was not his only mission, nor, in the political sense, his immediate one. Isaiah 11:1–9 shows that even in the final period of peace, the Messiah enabled by the Spirit will exercise judgment. Already in his earthly ministry ("from now on," v.52) there is division. The parallel to v.51 in Matthew 10:34 has "sword" (*machaira*, GK 3479) instead of "division" (*diamerismon*, GK 1375). In 22:36 Luke reports Jesus' speaking of a "sword" (*machaira*) when the crisis deepens. The expression "from now on" (*apo tou nyn*) is, apart from 2 Corinthians 5:16, unique to Luke in the NT. It is an important part of Luke's vocabulary of time (cf. esp. 5:10; 22:69; also the use of "today" in 4:21; 13:32; 19:5, 9). Luke is stressing the element of crisis, both immediately and at the Lord's return. During this time his disciples must be prepared for a break in their family relationships if others do not concur with their decision to follow Jesus (vv.52–53; cf. 14:26).

53 The wording of v.53 is probably from Micah 7:6—a verse that has a long history in Second Temple Jewish literature (cf. C. Heil, "Die Rezeption von Micha 7:6 LXX in Q und Lukas," *ZNW* 88 [1997]: 211–22).

The mention of six people in v.53 does not contradict the number "five" in v.52, since one person can have two relationships (e.g., a woman can be both a mother and a mother-in-law).

NOTES

51 The phrase ἐν τῇ γῇ (*en tē gē*, "on earth") may refer to the "land" of Israel. This meaning of γῇ, *gē* (GK *1178*), is possible (*TDNT* 1:677–78). "Peace on earth" in 2:14 has ἐπί (*epi*, "on"; so 12:49), not ἐν, *en*, as here. If this was the case, Jesus' words would refer even more clearly to the Jewish messianic expectations current in his day. "No, I tell you" (οὐχί λέγω ὑμῖν, *ouchi legō hymin*) is emphatic.

6. Interpreting the Times (12:54–59)

> ⁵⁴He said to the crowd: "When you see a cloud rising in the west, immediately you say, 'It's going to rain,' and it does. ⁵⁵And when the south wind blows, you say, 'It's going to be hot,' and it is. ⁵⁶Hypocrites! You know how to interpret the appearance of the earth and the sky. How is it that you don't know how to interpret this present time?
> ⁵⁷"Why don't you judge for yourselves what is right? ⁵⁸As you are going with your adversary to the magistrate, try hard to be reconciled to him on the way, or he may drag you off to the judge, and the judge turn you over to the officer, and the officer throw you into prison. ⁵⁹I tell you, you will not get out until you have paid the last penny."

COMMENTARY

54–56 Though the text does not explicitly link this section with the preceding one, there is a common element of crisis. The words "interpret this present time [*kairon*; season]" (v.56) imply this by comparing the observation of changing weather (vv.54–55) with God's "time" of opportunity and responsibility. This emphasis on the opportune time recurs more emphatically in 19:42–44 (cf. "on this day . . . but now . . . you did not recognize the time"). Here the word "hypocrites" (v.56) shows that the people Jesus was speaking to were not sincere in their professed inability to "interpret this present time."

57–59 Here Jesus' appeal to human judgment regarding a time of personal decision (v.57) is similar to, though not verbally identical with, Matthew 5:25–26. In human affairs, one resolves a crisis situation wisely to avoid penalty (v.58). This is a secular illustration, and v.59 should not be applied spiritually in point-for-point detail aside from its basic application of reconciliation with God before the day of judgment.

While this parable is significant for an individual when confronted by the impending judgment of God, it is also addressed to Israel as a people. In terms of context, the theme of judgment on God's people is a prominent one in Luke's central section. The address to the "crowd" (v.54) further highlights this point. This address to Israel is continued in 13:1–9 when the Jewish readers are again called to repent. For a discussion of the ecclesiological significance of this parable, see the helpful study of B. R. Kinman, "Debtor's Prison and the Future of Israel (Luke 12:57–59)," *JETS* 42 (1999): 411–25, who sees the phrase "paid the last penny" as a reference to repentance.

NOTES

54–55 "West" (δυσμῶν, *dysmōn*) is the direction of the Mediterranean, and the νότον (*noton*, "south wind") comes from the desert.

7. A Call to Repentance (13:1–9)

OVERVIEW

At this point, dialogue about the problem of human suffering, evil, and repentance introduces a parable that, like Jesus' teaching in ch. 12, deals with crisis and judgment. The fate of Israel (and Jerusalem) that was hinted at in the previous chapter now becomes the central concern. The repentance of God's people in this passage anticipates Jesus' words concerning Jerusalem in vv.31–35 (see Notes). Situated within the account of Jesus' travel to Jerusalem, this focus on Israel is ultimately tied with the concern for Israel's response to the Messiah and his ministry.

¹Now there were some present at that time who told Jesus about the Galileans whose blood Pilate had mixed with their sacrifices. ²Jesus answered, "Do you think that these Galileans were worse sinners than all the other Galileans because they suffered this way? ³I tell you, no! But unless you repent, you too will all perish. ⁴Or those eighteen who died when the tower in Siloam fell on them—do you think they were more guilty than all the others living in Jerusalem? ⁵I tell you, no! But unless you repent, you too will all perish."

⁶Then he told this parable: "A man had a fig tree, planted in his vineyard, and he went to look for fruit on it, but did not find any. ⁷So he said to the man who took care of the vineyard, 'For three years now I've been coming to look for fruit on this fig tree and haven't found any. Cut it down! Why should it use up the soil?'

⁸"'Sir,' the man replied, 'leave it alone for one more year, and I'll dig around it and fertilize it. ⁹If it bears fruit next year, fine! If not, then cut it down.'"

COMMENTARY

1 We cannot be certain as to the exact incident to which v.1 refers. The social tension made revolutionary activity in those days possible at any time. Pilate's position as governor of a troubled province far distant from Rome was precarious. Josephus (*Life*, 92) says that Galileans were especially susceptible to revolt (though see comments at 1:26). Any attack against Jews who had come to offer sacrifices was horrendous, whatever its reason. The fact that the people "told Jesus" about the event implies that he was not at Jerusalem when it happened.

2–5 Jesus refuses to attribute tragedy or accident directly to one's sin, as the Jews did (cf. Jn 9:1–3). On the contrary, he affirms the sinfulness of all people, including the Jews (v.5). "Too" (*homoiōs*, v.3; *hōsautōs*, v.5) means "similarly" or even "in the same way," showing that one who flouts God cannot count on immunity from sudden adversity. Whereas the victims of the two calamities referred to in vv.1–5 perished physically, "all" (*pantes*) who do not repent face spiritual death.

6–9 Once more, Jesus alludes to Micah 7 (see comments at 12:53), this time to Micah 7:1, with its lament over unproductive fig trees. The symbolism, like that of the vine in Isaiah 5:1–7, applies to Israel. Jesus' mention (v.6) of both a fig tree and a vineyard makes the figure doubly clear. Luke includes this parable instead of the cursing of the fig tree (found only in Mt 21:18–22; Mk 11:12–14, 20–25). Here the tree is not immediately destroyed, as it was in the cursing incident, but is given an extra year of grace (v.8) even beyond the three years its owner had already waited (v.7). Israel is accused of failing to recognize her season of opportunity (cf. 12:56; 19:41–44), and the emphasis on grace again highlights the prophetic nature of Jesus' message.

NOTES

3, 5 "No!" (οὐχί, *ouchi*) is the first word in each sentence for emphasis.

4 The tower of Siloam was probably near the Pool of Siloam in the southeastern corner of Jerusalem.

8. Healing a Woman on the Sabbath (13:10–17)

OVERVIEW

The Sabbath issue, a major cause of dissension earlier (6:1–11), now reappears. As in 6:6, and for the last time in Luke's narrative sequence, Jesus is teaching in a synagogue. This incident, like the others in this chapter, shows that in spite of the failure of the religious leaders to acknowledge the time of God's working, the kingdom is still being manifested. Moreover, the theme of repentance again takes center stage in the dispute between Jesus and the leaders of the Jews.

The Sabbath setting for this miracle of healing is noteworthy. The healing is not meant to be understood merely as yet another miracle performed by Jesus. This healing demonstrates the dawning of the kingdom that transcends the dividing wall that Jewish laws and customs had come to represent. Instead of excluding others from worshiping God, the Sabbath institution was meant to demonstrate the mercy of God (cf. J. B. Green, "Jesus and a Daughter of Abraham [Luke 13:10–17]: Test Case for a Lucan Perspective on Jesus' Miracles," *CBQ* 51 [1989]: 643–54; J. J. Kilgallen, "The Obligation to Heal [Luke 13:10–17]," *Bib* 82 [2001]: 402–9).

¹⁰On a Sabbath Jesus was teaching in one of the synagogues, ¹¹and a woman was there who had been crippled by a spirit for eighteen years. She was bent over and could not straighten up at all. ¹²When Jesus saw her, he called her forward and said to her, "Woman, you are set free from your infirmity." ¹³Then he put his hands on her, and immediately she straightened up and praised God.

¹⁴Indignant because Jesus had healed on the Sabbath, the synagogue ruler said to the people, "There are six days for work. So come and be healed on those days, not on the Sabbath."

¹⁵The Lord answered him, "You hypocrites! Doesn't each of you on the Sabbath untie his ox or donkey from the stall and lead it out to give it water? ¹⁶Then should not this woman, a daughter of Abraham, whom Satan has kept bound for eighteen long years, be set free on the Sabbath day from what bound her?"

¹⁷When he said this, all his opponents were humiliated, but the people were delighted with all the wonderful things he was doing.

COMMENTARY

10–13 "Was teaching" (*ēn didaskōn*) suggests that as Jesus was speaking, he suddenly became aware of the woman (*kai idou*, "and look!" untranslated in the NIV [v.11], with perhaps some loss of effect). As often in healing narratives, Luke mentions the seriousness and duration of the disease to highlight the greatness of the cure (v.11). The "spirit" presumably was a demon, though Luke does not specifically say the woman was demon-possessed. Any activity by a demon is ultimately Satan's responsibility (v.16; see comments at 11:14–20). The fact that Jesus touched her (v.13) has led some to conclude that she was not demon-possessed, on the ground that nowhere else in the Gospels are we told that Jesus touched a demon-possessed person. But the gospel narratives by no means record every detail of Jesus' actions. Far more important, and emphasized by Luke, is the woman's instant healing and its direct attribution to God (v.13). This, of course, shows that Jesus was truly acting with God's authority. "Praised [*edoxazen*, from *doxazō*, GK *1519*] God" reflects Luke's special interest in the glory of God (cf. 5:26). And Luke

may have used *endoxois* (GK *1902*, v.17), which sounds similar and means "wonderful things," to remind his readers of this theme of praise.

14–16 The controversy over Jesus' Sabbath activities now comes to the fore (v.14), as the synagogue ruler speaks to the people on the grounds of Exodus 20:9–10. Notice that he avoids addressing Jesus directly. There was ample evidence of rabbinic precedent for helping animals in emergencies on the Sabbath. So Jesus uses a lesser-to-greater argument to move from helping animals (v.15) to helping human beings (v.16; cf. 12:24).

"A daughter of Abraham" means a Jewess, though the physical aspect will not exhaust this reference (cf. 3:8; see Notes). In keeping with Luke's purpose, this designation highlights the priority of the Jews in the program of the gospel. This ethnic label again highlights the wider concern of this passage as Jesus addresses issues related to Israel as a whole.

17 As often, Luke gives us the crowd's reaction (cf. 4:15, 22, 32, 36–37; 5:26).

NOTES

11 The description "bent over and could not straighten up" has led to numerous attempts to identify the exact illness from which she suffered. The plausibility that she was demon-possessed will not rule out the existence of a corresponding physical condition. See J. Wilkinson, "The Case of the Bent Woman in Luke 13:10–17," *EvQ* 49 (1977): 195–205.

16 The phrase "daughter of Abraham" does not simply point to the ancestry of the woman. It points to a person who represents the ideal of Israel (as the Jewish mother of the seven martyrs did in 4 Macc 15:28–32; cf. Robert F. O'Toole, "Some Exegetical Reflections on Luke 13:10–17," *Bib* 73 [1992]: 84–107; Siker, 110–12). O'Toole also notes that in later rabbinic literature all Israel can be called "the daughter of Abraham."

9. Parables of the Mustard Seed and the Yeast (13:18–21)

OVERVIEW

These two parables are linked to the previous miracle of healing by their emphases on God's sovereignty and the reality of the dawning of God's kingdom. The sovereignty of God is reflected in the inevitable growth of the kingdom despite opposition or rejection. The reality of the presence of the kingdom is revealed through the individual acts of Jesus' ministry, and the certainty of its presence will be confirmed when the power of God's kingdom is fully manifested.

In Luke's narrative, his presentation of these two kingdom parables comes later than in Matthew and Mark. Isolated from other parables, they receive the added support of the account of the miraculous healing Luke has just described.

> ¹⁸Then Jesus asked, "What is the kingdom of God like? What shall I compare it to? ¹⁹It is like a mustard seed, which a man took and planted in his garden. It grew and became a tree, and the birds of the air perched in its branches."
>
> ²⁰Again he asked, "What shall I compare the kingdom of God to? ²¹It is like yeast that a woman took and mixed into a large amount of flour until it worked all through the dough."

COMMENTARY

18–19 In Jesus' teaching the "mustard seed" (v.19) represents that which is tiny but effective (cf. 17:6). The fully grown mustard tree may reach ten feet or so in height (cf. *ZPEB*, 4:324–25) and thus be quite large enough for birds to settle in its branches. It is not certain whether birds are mentioned as vivid detail or in accord with the occasional OT use of birds to symbolize the Gentiles (see Notes). The point of the parable is not the growth of the tree or a comparison between the seed and the tree but the power inherent in the seed. This power is implicit in the kingdom (v.18), as Jesus' healing of the woman has just demonstrated.

20–21 Likewise, the point of Jesus' simile of the yeast and the kingdom is not that yeast penetrates the dough but the inherent power—i.e., of the kingdom—that enables it to do this. This interpretation fits Mark's parable of the growing seed (Mk 4:26–29).

NOTES

19 "Birds" (πετεινά, peteina, GK 4374) are specifically mentioned in each version of the parable (Mt 13:32; Mk 4:32) and may therefore be significant in symbolizing Gentile nations (Plummer, 345, cites Eze 17:23; 31:6; Da 4:9, 18[12, 21 MT] as OT evidence for this). Bock, 2:1226, also notes that the image of birds resting in a tree symbolizes calm and shelter (cf. Jdg 9:15; Isa 51:16).

21 The word ζύμη (zymē, "leaven," GK 2434; NIV, "yeast") when used metaphorically usually symbolizes evil. This is true in both biblical and secular literature (see reference notes on Mt 13:33 in J. J. Wettstein's edition [1751–52] of the Greek NT for examples). But it is difficult without reading extraneous ideas into the text to find anything other than a positive, straightforward description of the kingdom here.

The phrase "large amount of flour" is, literally, "three measures of flour"—an amount sufficient to feed 160 people (Marshall, 561).

10. Entering the Kingdom (13:22–30)

OVERVIEW

Jesus' teaching now turns to personal responsibility, and it corresponds to the previous passages in which one finds the theme of repentance and kingdom participation. With the metaphor of the "narrow door," the issue of election is addressed, together with the division of the expected responses to the message of the Messiah. Several themes appear in this section that occur in other NT settings in Matthew and Mark (cf., in sequence, Mt 7:13–14; 25:10–12; 7:22–23; 8:11–12; 19:30; 20:16; along with Mk 10:31).

²²Then Jesus went through the towns and villages, teaching as he made his way to Jerusalem. ²³Someone asked him, "Lord, are only a few people going to be saved?"

He said to them, ²⁴"Make every effort to enter through the narrow door, because many, I tell you, will try to enter and will not be able to. ²⁵Once the owner of the house gets up and closes the door, you will stand outside knocking and pleading, 'Sir, open the door for us.'

"But he will answer, 'I don't know you or where you come from.'

²⁶"Then you will say, 'We ate and drank with you, and you taught in our streets.'
²⁷"But he will reply, 'I don't know you or where you come from. Away from me, all you evildoers!'
²⁸"There will be weeping there, and gnashing of teeth, when you see Abraham, Isaac and Jacob and all the prophets in the kingdom of God, but you yourselves thrown out. ²⁹People will come from east and west and north and south, and will take their places at the feast in the kingdom of God. ³⁰Indeed there are those who are last who will be first, and first who will be last."

COMMENTARY

22–23 Here we have one of the few specific travel references in what is sometimes called Luke's "travel section" (9:51–19:44). Nevertheless, the travel theme appears repeatedly in connection with the verb *poreuomai* and its cognates (cf. *dieporeueto*, "went," v.22; see comments at v.33). The words "made his way to Jerusalem" are especially significant because the important element is not merely travel but Jesus' orientation toward that city (cf. 9:51; 13:33–34; 17:11; 19:28, 41; see comments at 19:28). This will explain why geographical references to specifics of the travel itinerary are frequently absent, while the destination is always emphasized.

As with the question on divorce (Mt 19:3), this one about whether few or many people will be saved (v.23) was the occasion of differing opinions among the rabbis. This question is especially relevant in light of the comments on the dramatic manifestation of the kingdom in vv.18–21.

24–27 Jesus' reply emphasizes not "how many?" but "who?" The saved are those who seize their opportunity now (in the "year of the Lord's favor," 4:19). Green, 530, notes that Jesus "turns a potentially speculative dialogue on soteriology into a pointed, existential challenge." Once the time for decision has passed (v.25), attempts to gain salvation afterward (note the future "will try . . . will not be

able," v.24) will be futile. Likewise, Esau "afterward" sought his inheritance in vain (Heb 12:17).

Does the "narrow door" limit the number of people who are admitted or the opportunities a person has to enter? Verse 24 by itself suggests the former; v.25 with its reference to the closing door suggests the latter. In John 10:9, entrance to salvation is only through Jesus, who himself is the gate. The use of the third person in "but he will reply" (v.27) does not refer to anyone other than Jesus as the Son of Man (cf. Mt 7:23, "I will tell them") and simply follows the pattern of v.25.

The repetition of "I don't know you or where you come from" (v.27, cf. v.25) heightens the sense of utter rejection (cf. Mt 7:23, "I never knew you"). Familiarity with Jesus (v.26) will be of no benefit then (cf. the even stronger plea in Mt 7:22). The phrase "away from me, all you evildoers" comes from Psalm 6:8. Those who do not receive the message of Jesus will experience the same fate as those who had oppressed the psalmist.

28–29 The contrast is heightened between those inside—note the reference to Israel's patriarchs—and those outside the door, i.e., outside the kingdom (v.28). Not every Jew is expected to sit with the patriarchs at the messianic banquet or "feast in the kingdom of God" (v.29). The concept of such a feast in heaven as a celebration with the Messiah is alluded to throughout the OT and other Jewish literature over a long period of time (cf. 14:15). The tragedy would not only be that of looking at the patriarchs from the outside but also that of seeing Gentiles inside with them.

30 Verse 30 describes a total reversal of positions. Here it clearly means the exclusion from future blessings of those who thought they were first in line for them. Its thrust is stronger here than its use in different contexts in Matthew 19:30; 20:16; and Mark 10:31. This Lukan focus on eschatological reversal again functions as a prophetic call for Israel to repent. Exclusion from the kingdom will lead to "weeping . . . and gnashing of teeth"—an expression found only here in v.28 but used several times in Matthew (8:12; 22:13; 24:51; 25:30) to express the horror of future doom.

NOTES

24 "Make every effort" is ἀγωνίζομαι (*agōnizomai*, GK 76), a word often used in an athletic or military context. It does not imply working for salvation but rather earnestness in seeking it (cf. its use regarding prayer in Col 4:12). While this verse focuses on the present aspect of kingdom participation as well as individual personal responsibility, other verses in the Lukan corpus should also be noted in providing a balanced view of Luke's soteriology. For a discussion that reads this verse in the light of 16:16—a verse that focuses on the eschatological work of God—see H. Giesen, "Verantwortung des Christen in der Gegenwart und Heilsvollendung: Ethik und Eschatologie nach Luke 13:24 und 16:16," *Theologie der Gegenwart* 31 (1988): 218–28.

11. Concern over Jerusalem (13:31–35)

OVERVIEW

This is the main passage in Luke in which Jesus expresses a strong sense of destiny in his final journey to Jerusalem. Note the sense of divine purpose expressed by such characteristic Lukan words as "today" (*sēmeron*, GK 4958) and "must" (*dei*, GK 1256). The passage is peculiar to Luke and shows Luke's editorial care in making a significant transition at this point. It marks a stage in Jesus' progress to Jerusalem and prepares the reader for ch. 14 (note v.1).

> ³¹At that time some Pharisees came to Jesus and said to him, "Leave this place and go somewhere else. Herod wants to kill you."
> ³²He replied, "Go tell that fox, 'I will drive out demons and heal people today and tomorrow, and on the third day I will reach my goal.' ³³In any case, I must keep going today and tomorrow and the next day—for surely no prophet can die outside Jerusalem!

³⁴"O Jerusalem, Jerusalem, you who kill the prophets and stone those sent to you, how often I have longed to gather your children together, as a hen gathers her chicks under her wings, but you were not willing! ³⁵Look, your house is left to you desolate. I tell you, you will not see me again until you say, 'Blessed is he who comes in the name of the Lord.'"

COMMENTARY

31 The Pharisees here warn Jesus of Herod's designs on his life. Later in his gospel Luke will speak out in blaming the Jewish leaders for their drastic actions against Jesus but will minimize the role of the people in opposing him (e.g., 19:47). At this point, though Luke does not explicitly attribute an evil motive to those who warn Jesus, the failure of the Pharisees to discern the plan of God (and his Messiah) can be understood as a subtle critique of the Jewish leadership. This would fit the context where the accusations against the Jews were just issued. Moreover, this reading is consistent with the portrayal of the Pharisees elsewhere in this gospel (cf. J. D. Kingsbury, "The Pharisees in Luke–Acts," in *The Four Gospels*, ed. F. van Segbroeck et al. [Leuven: Leuven Univ. Press, 1992], 2:1497–1512). We do not know where Jesus was at that time; if he was in Herod's territory, he was obviously not near Jerusalem.

32–33 In Luke's last mention of him, Herod was troubled at the reports of Jesus' miracles. By having John the Baptist beheaded, Herod thought he had done away with prophetic opposition. But Jesus, far from being threatened by Herod, called him "that fox" (v.32). Today foxes connote cleverness; in Jesus' day they also connoted insignificance or ineptitude (cf. Ne 4:3; SS 2:15; see R. Buth, "That Small-fry Herod Antipas, or When a Fox Is Not a Fox," *Jerusalem Perspective* 40 [1993]: 7–9, 14). Either or both connotations may apply here.

Jesus' intent was to continue his ministry and manifest the power of the kingdom—"drive out demons and heal people"—but not to do this indefinitely. "Today and tomorrow" (*sēmeron kai aurion*) signifies the time of present opportunity in Jesus' ministry. That time, however, was short. Since "today and tomorrow" are not literal days, so with the "third day," which must have reminded Luke's readers of the day of Jesus' resurrection. Perhaps it was intended to do so. Verses 32 and 33 are parallel, with the idea of "three days" implicit in each. In v.32 "the third day" is followed by "I will reach my goal" (*teleioumai*, "be completed, be perfected," GK 5464). In v.33 it is followed by a reference to Jesus' death. Clearly the expressions are equivalent, and there may well be an anticipation of the profound phrase in Hebrews 2:10, "perfect through suffering." In one sense v.33 marks the completion of Jesus' mission, especially in Luke's theology (cf. 9:31). Ellis, 190, suggests that it refers to consecration to the high priestly work, since the Greek word for "perfected" is used in the LXX of Exodus 29 and Leviticus 8.

The programmatic statement of Jesus' purpose and progress continues in v.33 with two additions: the specific reference to suffering ("die") and the Greek word *dei* ("must"). Luke conveys Jesus' sense of purpose and necessity more strongly than the other Synoptics do. Well over two-thirds of the synoptic uses of *dei* are in Luke (see comments at 4:43).

Another key word that reappears here is the verb *poreuomai* ("keep going," GK *4513*; see comments on "went" at v.22). Luke emphasizes the "way" of Jesus, which led to the cross and on to glory (cf. Jn 7:35; 14:12, 28; 16:7, 28). Jesus expected to suffer as a prophet. Jeremias (*TDNT* 5:714) says that to a great extent "martyrdom was considered an integral part of the prophetic office" in those days (cf. *TDNT* 6:834–35). Stephen's speech (Ac 7:52) accords with this.

34–35 The word "Jerusalem" appears three times in a row—once at the end of v.33 and twice at the beginning of the lament (v.34). The effect is to draw the reader's attention to that city of destiny both as the place of our Lord's passion and as the pathetic, unwilling object of his love. The "house," perhaps specifically the temple (cf. Jer 12:7), which had been visited by Jesus as a boy (2:41–50), will now lose him until Psalm 118:26, quoted here ("Blessed . . .

Lord"), is fulfilled. The lament and the quotation do not appear in Matthew until after the triumphal entry (23:37–39), where Jesus includes the word "again" (*ap' arti*, v.39), apparently to make it clear that there was to be a future fulfillment of the word quoted from Psalm 118:26. The substance of the quotation is recorded by all four gospels in their respective accounts of the triumphal entry; but on that occasion the words are said not by the Jerusalemites but by Jesus' supporters. Luke specifies that they were Jesus' disciples (19:37–38). It seems likely that when Jesus returns, the disciples will also be the ones welcoming him (see Notes). Not inconsistent with this interpretation is one that sees this promise as conditional: only when the Jews repent will they be able to welcome Jesus in this way (cf. Green, 538–39). The narrative that follows shows, however, that many will not be able to meet this "condition."

NOTES

35 The identity of those who will utter the saying (taken from Ps 118:26) at Jesus' return is subject to debate. In light of the parallel accounts of the triumphal entry, the disciples are to be considered as the likely subjects who will utter these words. Even for those who affirm that all Israel will eventually welcome the Messiah, this welcome does not eliminate the probability that the one whom they welcome will in turn act as their judge (cf. 14:24; see Wolter, "Israel's Future and the Delay of the Parousia," in *Jesus and the Heritage of Israel* [ed. Moessner], 308–10).

REFLECTIONS

The concern for the fate of Israel in ch. 13 has long been recognized (cf. J. D. M. Derrett, "Fig Trees in the New Testament," *Heythrop Journal* 14 [1973]: 249–65; W. R. Telford, *The Barren Temple and the Withered Tree* [JSNTSup 1; Sheffield: JSOT Press, 1980], 224–28). R. J. Shirock ("The Growth of the Kingdom in Light of Israel's Rejection of Jesus: Structure and Theology in Luke 13:1–35," *NovT* 35

[1993]: 15–29) has extended the discussion by providing a helpful outline for this chapter that highlights the concern for the role of Israel in God's kingdom and the prophetic call for Israel to repent:

| 13:1–9 | Question: Will Israel repent and retain her place? |
| 13:10–17 | Problem: The hypocrisy of Israel's leaders |

E. Further Teaching on Urgent Issues (14:1–18:30)

1. Jesus at a Pharisee's House (14:1–14)

OVERVIEW

This passage and the following one incorporate several elements—healing, conversations, and a parable—all tied together in dinner-table conversation—a familiar ancient literary device (see Notes). The conversation, except for its opening, revolves around the response and behavior of dinner guests; this leads into the response of would-be followers of Jesus and the cost of discipleship. Again one finds that Jesus is being "carefully watched" (v.1) by the Pharisees.

[1]One Sabbath, when Jesus went to eat in the house of a prominent Pharisee, he was being carefully watched. [2]There in front of him was a man suffering from dropsy. [3]Jesus asked the Pharisees and experts in the law, "Is it lawful to heal on the Sabbath or not?" [4]But they remained silent. So taking hold of the man, he healed him and sent him away.

[5]Then he asked them, "If one of you has a son or an ox that falls into a well on the Sabbath day, will you not immediately pull him out?" [6]And they had nothing to say.

[7]When he noticed how the guests picked the places of honor at the table, he told them this parable: [8]"When someone invites you to a wedding feast, do not take the place of honor, for a person more distinguished than you may have been invited. [9]If so, the host who invited both of you will come and say to you, 'Give this man your seat.' Then, humiliated, you will have to take the least important place. [10]But when you are invited, take the lowest place, so that when your host comes, he will say to you, 'Friend, move up to a better place.' Then you will be honored in the presence of all your fellow guests. [11]For everyone who exalts himself will be humbled, and he who humbles himself will be exalted."

[12]Then Jesus said to his host, "When you give a luncheon or dinner, do not invite your friends, your brothers or relatives, or your rich neighbors; if you do, they may invite you back and so you will be repaid. [13]But when you give a banquet, invite the poor, the crippled, the lame, the blind, [14]and you will be blessed. Although they cannot repay you, you will be repaid at the resurrection of the righteous."

COMMENTARY

1 Since this is the fourth time Luke records a controversy over the Sabbath, it is obvious that this was a major issue between Jesus and the religious leaders (cf. 6:1–11; 13:10–17). The host was "prominent"—literally, one of the "ruling" (*archonton*, GK *806*) Pharisees, possibly a member of the Sanhedrin. The NIV's rendering, "he was being carefully watched," brings out the durative aspect of the imperfect periphrastic tense, which Luke uses effectively (cf. "was teaching" and "were sitting," 5:17). Luke pictures the Pharisees as watchdogs of the faith as they wait for some theological flaw to appear in Jesus' teaching (vv. 1–3; cf. 5:17; 6:7).

2 "There [*kai idou*, lit., and behold] in front of him" (cf. 13:11) draws attention to a man some commentators believe was planted there to test Jesus. That would not be improbable, but the text does not affirm it. "Dropsy," an "abnormal accumulation of serous fluid in the tissues of the body" (cf. *ZPEB*, 2:134), may have popularly been considered a curse for sin (Nu 5:11–27). In the time of Jesus, dropsy was often used as a metaphor for the vice of avarice (cf. W. Braun, *Feasting and Social Rhetoric in Luke 14* [SNTSMS 85; Cambridge: Cambridge Univ. Press, 1995]); the connection between dropsy and the desire for honor and wealth in the discussion that follows may therefore have been intentional.

3–4 As in 6:9, Jesus takes the initiative with a question designed to shift the burden of proof to the opposition. "Is it lawful" may have been intentionally ambiguous, a leading question that could be answered in terms of either OT or rabbinic "law." During the silence of the "Pharisees and experts in the law," Jesus met the man's need (v.4). The healing of his condition could have waited another day, but Jesus was concerned to establish a principle. This may be why he dismissed the man without including him further in the conversation and then turned to the Pharisees.

5–6 The phrase "if one of you" (v.5) draws Jesus' listeners into the illustration (cf. 11:5, 11; 12:25; 14:28). "Immediately" (*eutheōs*, GK *2311*) stresses the urgency of meeting the need—a pointed reference back to the man with dropsy. The principle exampled in the case of a beast is in accord not only with the OT but also with rabbinic law (cf. Str-B, 1:629; *b. Šabb.* 128*b*, though compare the forbidding of help to such an animal in the Qumran sect [CD 11:13–17]). In the face of this, the silence of Jesus' opponents was no longer by choice (e.g., v.4) but of necessity; they "had nothing to say" (*ouk ischysan antapokrithēnai*, lit., "could not respond," v.6). A dilemma also silences a group of Jewish leaders in 20:3–7 (cf. 20:26).

7–11 Jesus continued to take the initiative. In his time the guests at a formal dinner leaned on their left elbows while reclining on couches, several guests per couch. The seating was according to status. The "head of the table" was the couch at one end with other couches extending from it and facing each other like the arms of a "U." The important places, the places of "honor" (v.8), were those nearest the head couch. If an important guest came late, someone might have to be displaced to make room for him (v.9).

Jesus' practical advice (cf. Pr 25:6–7) illustrates the spiritual principle he stated in v.11. The significance of this principle—and indeed of vv.7–11—is clarified by Luke's use in the parable of the Pharisee and the tax collector (18:14). The ultimate reference of the principle is to God's final judgment. Luke follows the custom of using passive verbs ("will be humbled . . . will be exalted") to avoid direct reference to God as the real subject of this profound sentence. The same may hold for 16:9 (cf. Ellis, *Gospel of Luke*, on both passages; see comments at 15:7 for another way Luke reverently avoids the use of God's name). This practice seems strange to us, but we need to realize that in the culture of that day a name both designated and represented a person. Therefore, it was safe to refer to God obliquely by a descriptive title ("Lord"), a phrase ("the Holy One," "blessed be he"), a circumlocution ("he who sits in heaven"), or a term such as "the heavens," whereas to say the divine Name itself without proper reverence could be blasphemy.

Situated at the center of Luke's parable collection, the concluding principle that highlights the Lukan theme of reversal again points to the wider concern for Israel's place in God's eschatological kingdom (cf. Mikeal C. Parsons, "Landmarks Along the Way: The Function of the 'L' Parables in the Lukan Travel Narrative," *SwJT* 40 [1997]: 33–47).

12 Having addressed the Pharisee's guests, Jesus turns to his host. What he says resembles his words in 6:32–36 (see comments there)—in view of ultimate reward from God, doing good to those who cannot repay it. As Jesus said (6:35), believers are to do good not with the expectation of a future reward but unselfishly. Then God will remember and reward them (v.14). (Scripture distinguishes between the resurrection of the righteous and that of the wicked [Da 12:2; Ac 24:15; Rev 20:4–5].)

13 Verse 13 recalls Luke's report of Jesus' concern for the poor and oppressed (cf. 4:18; 6:20–21; 7:22), though this list is more specific than the previous ones. Johnson, 133, has rightly noted that here these categories represent the kinds of "blemishes" as noted in Leviticus 21:18. The significance of this list in this chapter is further highlighted by its reappearance in v.21 (see Notes). The inclusion of these people into the banquet therefore represents the inclusion of the outcasts who were once excluded from the worshiping community of God's people.

NOTES

1 The significance of the meal setting of Jesus' conversation here has long been recognized. Moving beyond the general recognition of table setting as providing the framework for Jesus' teaching, some have further argued that ch. 14 most clearly reflects Luke's awareness of the Hellenistic symposium genre (cf. X. de Meeûs, "Composition de *Lc.*, XIV et genre symposiaque," *Ephemerides Théologiques et Lovanienses* 37 [1961]: 847–70; Smith, "Table Fellowship as a Literary Motif," 620–21). Others have, however, seen Jesus' teaching as providing an inherent critique of the pagan banquet practices (cf. Braun, *Feasting and Social Rhetoric*; C. Osiek and D. L. Balch, *Families in the New Testament World* [Louisville, Ky.: Westminster, 1997], 206). What most can agree on is the relevance of Hellenistic literary practices in understanding the form and content of Jesus' teaching in this chapter. This is not to ignore, however, the influence of Jewish messianic banquet traditions that lie behind the various feeding stories in Luke (cf. K. Snodgrass, "Common Life with Jesus: The Parable of the Banquet in Luke 14:16–24," in *Common Life in the Early Church*, ed. J.V. Hills et al. [Harrisburg, Pa.: Trinity International, 1998], 186–201).

5 The reason some MSS read ὄνος (*onos*, "donkey," NIV text note) instead of υἱός (*huios*, "son") is probably because the combination of two animals (donkey and ox) seems more likely than that of a son and an ox. Vaticanus (B) and Alexandrinus (A), significant papyri, and other early MS witnesses have υἱός, *huios*.

13 The significance of Leviticus 21 behind vv. 13, 21 is further supported by the use of this list in Second Temple Jewish literature in the context of the cultic purity of God's people. In the Qumran literature, a similar list appears that limits those who would be allowed to participate in God's eschatological kingdom (1QSa 2.5–22; 1QM 7.4–6). J. A. Sanders ("The Ethic of Election in Luke's Great Banquet Parable," in *Luke and Scripture* [ed. Evans and Sanders], 117) notes that this Lukan list can almost be considered a direct challenge to the Qumran "member list."

2. Parable of the Great Banquet (14:15–24)

OVERVIEW

Jesus continues the figure of the banquet with a striking parable about the "feast in the kingdom of God" (v. 15)—the so-called eschatological banquet. The connection between the banquet motif and the concern for the eschatological kingdom is made explicit here. Luke 13:29–30 showed that some who expect to be present will be excluded; this passage teaches that those excluded have only themselves to blame.

¹⁵When one of those at the table with him heard this, he said to Jesus, "Blessed is the man who will eat at the feast in the kingdom of God."

¹⁶Jesus replied: "A certain man was preparing a great banquet and invited many guests. ¹⁷At the time of the banquet he sent his servant to tell those who had been invited, 'Come, for everything is now ready.'

¹⁸"But they all alike began to make excuses. The first said, 'I have just bought a field, and I must go and see it. Please excuse me.'

¹⁹"Another said, 'I have just bought five yoke of oxen, and I'm on my way to try them out. Please excuse me.'

²⁰"Still another said, 'I just got married, so I can't come.'

²¹"The servant came back and reported this to his master. Then the owner of the house became angry and ordered his servant, 'Go out quickly into the streets and alleys of the town and bring in the poor, the crippled, the blind and the lame.'

²²"'Sir,' the servant said, 'what you ordered has been done, but there is still room.'

²³"Then the master told his servant, 'Go out to the roads and country lanes and make them come in, so that my house will be full. ²⁴I tell you, not one of those men who were invited will get a taste of my banquet.'"

COMMENTARY

15 The exuberant remark seems like a boorish counterpart to Peter's "it is good for us to be here" (9:33); Manson, 129, calls it "a characteristic piece of apocalyptic piety." The concept of future celebration in the kingdom is certainly biblical (cf. Rev 19:9). Jesus does not repudiate it but rather addresses the presumption on the part of some present, perhaps including the speaker in v.1, that they would inevitably participate.

16–17 It is possible that the second invitation was simply to remind those who had already accepted the invitation that it was time to come (v.17). Morris, 233, notes that "people had no watches . . . and . . . a banquet took a long time to prepare." More likely, however, is that this curious note reflects the customs of hosting a banquet in upper-class society of ancient times (cf. Est 5:8). R. L. Rohrbaugh ("The Pre-industrial City in Luke–Acts," in *The Social World of Luke–Acts* [ed. Neyrey], 125–49) has pointed to the function of an elaborate social code in events that involve the interaction of people from various classes; the function of the double invitation is, therefore, to "allow opportunity for potential guests to find out what the festive occasion might be, who is coming, and whether all had been done appropriately in arranging the dinner" (p. 141). The willingness of the host to abandon all social codes in his subsequent invitation of the "outcasts" in v.21 thus becomes all the more striking.

18–20 The striking thing is that "all" of them declined. "Alike" (*apo mias*, a unique expression in Greek) does not mean "in the same way" but probably "with one accord" or "all at once" (Jeremias, 176).

The excuses appear to be weak. One man "must" go to see a purchased field he probably had seen before he bought it (v.18). Contrast his urgent attention to material things with Jesus' healing of a man on the Sabbath (vv.2–4). The second excuse (v.19) seems to be as worthless as the first; would anyone have bought oxen without examining them? Going "to try them out" sounds like preoccupation with a new possession rather than urgent business. In both instances, materialism got in the way of honoring an invitation already extended.

The third excuse (v.20) appears to have more validity. Only men were invited to banquets (Jeremias, 177). Yet marriage was not, especially in that society, an abrupt decision and could hardly have been an unexpected factor intervening between the first (v.16) and second (v.17) invitations. With his superb narrative art, Jesus uses these three excuses to show that just as a host may be snubbed, so God's gracious invitation may be flouted.

The exact reasons for the mention of precisely these three excuses should be further explored. Many have pointed to the OT discussion of war practices (cf. P. H. Ballard, "Reasons for Refusing the Great Supper," *JTS* 23 [1972]: 341–50; J. A. Sanders, "The Ethic of Election in Luke's Great Banquet Parable," in *Luke and Scripture* [ed. Evans and Sanders], 110). In Deuteronomy 20:5–7, in particular, a person is exempted from participating in military campaigns if he had just built a new house, planted a new vineyard, or just become engaged. With the absence of military motifs in the Lukan account and the pervasiveness of Luke's critique of the concern for material wealth throughout this gospel, it seems best not to limit the context too narrowly to one passage in Deuteronomy. On the other hand, the broader interaction with Deuteronomic election theology in Luke should be affirmed. With the dawn of the critical moment in salvation history, no excuses should be considered valid for rejecting the invitation to participate in God's kingdom.

21 The host "became angry" because the rejections were both a personal insult and a public act of bringing shame on the host. A "street" (*plateia*, GK 4423) was broader and traveled by a greater variety of people than a neighborhood road. In contrast, an "alley" (*rhymē*, GK 4860) was a small lane or side path likely to harbor the loitering outcasts of society. Those brought from these places were precisely the same unfortunates Jesus had told his host to invite in v.13 (see comments there).

22–23 With room still available (v.22), the servant is to go outside the town and search even the "country lanes" (v.23). To "make them come in" is not compulsion but "an insistent hospitality" (Manson, 130).

24 Though Jesus does not interpret the parable, it is reasonable to link it with 13:28–30 and find in it an allusion of the extension of the gospel to the Gentiles. Those who had the benefit of the original invitation are perhaps best described by Paul in Romans 9:4–5—Jews with all their heritage and spiritual advantages. "Not one" refers to the parable and should not be taken literally but understood as stressing the seriousness of the consequences of rejecting God's invitation.

NOTES

16–24 As to the similarity of this parable to the one in Matthew 22:1–10, there can be only two explanations. Either there was one original parable handed down in different forms and edited by Matthew and Luke and placed in different settings, or Jesus told similar parables on two different occasions with appropriate variations. Ellis, 194, observes that the "use of the same parabolic theme to teach different truths is frequent in rabbinical writings." Comparing Luke 15:3–7 with Matthew 18:12–14 will show this. The second alternative is reasonable and does not preclude legitimate editing. The same basic story is found in logion 64 in the *Gospel of Thomas*. For a critical analysis, see Jeremias, 63–69; Bailey, *Through Peasant Eyes*, 88–113, has a number of keen insights into the significance of this parable.

3. The Cost of Being a Disciple (14:25–35)

OVERVIEW

The serious tone of the preceding parable continues as attention now turns to those who profess allegiance to Jesus. The critique of the Jewish leadership now becomes an urge for the potential followers of Jesus to abandon all for the sake of the gospel. This call to follow Jesus is issued both to individuals and to Israel as a whole.

²⁵Large crowds were traveling with Jesus, and turning to them he said: ²⁶"If anyone comes to me and does not hate his father and mother, his wife and children, his brothers and sisters—yes, even his own life—he cannot be my disciple. ²⁷And anyone who does not carry his cross and follow me cannot be my disciple.

²⁸"Suppose one of you wants to build a tower. Will he not first sit down and estimate the cost to see if he has enough money to complete it? ²⁹For if he lays the foundation and is not able to finish it, everyone who sees it will ridicule him, ³⁰saying, 'This fellow began to build and was not able to finish.'

³¹"Or suppose a king is about to go to war against another king. Will he not first sit down and consider whether he is able with ten thousand men to oppose the one coming against him with twenty thousand? ³²If he is not able, he will send a delegation while the other is still a long way off and will ask for terms of peace. ³³In the same way, any of you who does not give up everything he has cannot be my disciple.

³⁴"Salt is good, but if it loses its saltiness, how can it be made salty again? ³⁵It is fit neither for the soil nor for the manure pile; it is thrown out.

"He who has ears to hear, let him hear."

COMMENTARY

25 With the words "large crowds," Luke again draws attention to Jesus' popularity (see comments at 4:15). These crowds formed an entourage along with Jesus' own group (cf. 8:1–3). They were "traveling"—an indication of further progress toward Jerusalem (see comment on 13:22). This address to the crowds also indicates a shift in audience as Jesus now turns from the Jewish leadership to the people.

26 "Hate" is not an absolute but a relative term. To neglect social customs pertaining to family loyalties would probably have been interpreted as "hate." Jesus is not contravening the commandment to honor one's father and mother. Moreover, he says a disciple should hate "even his own life," whereas he speaks elsewhere of loving ourselves (10:27; cf. Mt 22:39; Mk 12:31).

It is important to understand the ancient Near Eastern expression without blunting its force, and various attempts have been made to further identify the precise context in which this verse is to be understood. J. D. M. Derrett ("Hating Father and Mother [Luke 14:26; Matthew 10:37]," *DRev* 117 [1999]: 251–72) has provided a helpful survey of the various possibilities. The first points to Deuteronomy 33:9, a passage in praise of Levi for his focus on the service of the Lord. The second draws from Second Temple Jewish discussions of the life of the proselytes who left their community to join the people of Israel (cf. Philo, *Spec.* 1.51.2). The third, which Derrett favors, sees the verse as evoking the metaphor of "slavery" as the master becomes the only point of reference for the slave (cf. Dt 15:15–16). In light of the significance of Deuteronomy in Luke's writings, the first and third options are likely candidates. The use of the same general imagery in various contexts suggests, however, the prevalence of this imagery in ancient times. One should therefore assume that the audience is aware of the point of this verse without having to pinpoint the precise context to locate this imagery.

27 For the meaning of v.27, see comments at 9:23.

28–32 Jesus uses two different circumstances to illustrate his basic point: discipleship requires one to be aware of the resources available to him or her. The common interpretation of these two parables is that disciples should count the cost before following Jesus. This interpretation is problematic in the light of Luke's emphasis elsewhere that one should follow Jesus regardless of the circumstances surrounding that individual. Moreover, the second parable that suggests compromising with the enemies does not fit Jesus' teaching elsewhere (see Notes). More importantly, as T. E. Schmidt ("Burden, Barrier, Blasphemy: Wealth in Matthew 6:33, Luke 14:33, and Luke 16:15," *TJ* 9 [1988]: 181) has pointed out, this interpretation is inconsistent with the conclusion in v.33. Schmidt has rightly concluded that the point of these parables is that "reliance on one's own inadequate resources precluded discipleship."

In building towers and in waging war with a strong opponent, the inadequacy of one's resources should be noted. In following Jesus, one should likewise renounce all claims to power and resources in the presence of God. Instead of carefully "counting the cost," disciples are called to decisive and urgent actions in their carrying of Jesus' cross.

33 This is clearly a crucial verse. But does it mean that it is impossible to retain any possessions at all if one wants to be a true disciple? The key word is *apotassō* ("give up," GK *698*). When used of persons, the verb means "to take leave of or say good-bye to someone"; when used of things it means "to give up or renounce" (cf. BDAG, 123). Here, in contrast to his requirement of the rich young ruler (18:22), Jesus does not say that a disciple should sell all of his possessions and give everything away. His thought is probably that of the abandonment of things, the yielding up of the right of ownership, rather than outright disposal of material possessions. The disciple of Jesus may be given the use of things in trust as a stewardship, but they are no longer his own. The present tense implies that what Jesus requires in relation to possessions is a continual attitude of abandonment.

Walter E. Pilgrim (*Good News to the Poor* [Minneapolis: Augsburg, 1981], 101–2) sides cautiously with those who take the view that abandonment was total only for Jesus' disciples in his lifetime. He nevertheless sees this radical abandonment as speaking to the rich of Luke's day and as urging them to share their goods with their needy brothers and sisters. But the principle of stewardship makes a spirit of abandonment—i.e., the willingness to part with our goods (which are not ultimately ours anyway)—necessary today. This is consistent with the command to use our possessions wisely (cf. 16:1–12).

34–35 This saying poses two questions: Why does it occur here? and How does salt lose its saltiness? Its placement here is due to the common element it shares with the preceding instruction. Equally important is the fact that it highlights the urgency of one's response to the call of Jesus. We do not know with certainty what Jesus had in mind in speaking of salt as "losing its saltiness." The reference may be to adulteration either by impurities in the beds by the Dead Sea from which salt slabs were taken or by inert fillers introduced by unscrupulous dealers. The point is that tasteless salt is useless. While the saying is addressed to individuals, the reference to the "large crowds" (v.25) may point to a wider application. This exhortation or warning may therefore be addressed to Israel as a whole in their response to the presence of God's Messiah.

The reference to Israel is further supported by the concluding statement: the ones who have ears are called to respond when the opportunity is still present (v.35; cf. 8:8). The reappearance of this metaphor of hearing at the end of the Lukan corpus where an indictment against Israel is issued (Ac 28:26–27; cf. Isa 6:9–10) points to the urgency of this call as addressed to both individuals and to Israel as God's people.

NOTES

31–32 The problem with the traditional interpretation is well illustrated in the reading of C. L. Quarles ("The Authenticity of the Parable of the Warring King," in *Authenticating the Words of Jesus*, ed. B. Chilton and C. A. Evans [Leiden: Brill, 1999], 414), who concludes his discussion of this parable with these words: "the parable served to teach the importance and urgency of unconditional surrender to the invading king as the only means of deliverance." In the context, instead of surrendering to the enemies, disciples of Christ are called to give up all to fight the battle while relying solely on the grace and power of God.

34 On the Aramaic background of μωραίνω (*mōrainō*, "loses its saltiness," GK *3701*), see Jeremias, 168; Black, 166–67.

4. Parables of Joy (15:1–32)

OVERVIEW

This section begins what Manson, 282, has called the "Gospel of the Outcast." The large body of material in chs. 15–19 is unique to Luke and dramatically shows Jesus' concern for the social outcasts of his day (e.g., 15:1; 16:19–25; 17:11–19; 18:1–8, 9–14; 19:1–10). The twin parables (15:3–7, 8–10), along with the longer one about the lost son (vv. 11–32), depend for their interpretation on vv. 1–2. The parable of the lost son in turn completes and extends the thoughts developed in the first two, shorter parables. These stories may have been drawn from common household and pastoral experiences, though allusions to OT texts may also be present. Kenneth E. Bailey ("Psalm 23 and Luke 15: A Vision Expanded," *IBS* 12 [1990]: 54–71) notes the parallels between Psalm 23 and Luke 15: symbol of the shepherd, lost sheep, crisis, banquet, and costly love. Claus Westermann (*The Parables of Jesus in the Light of the Old Testament* [Minneapolis: Fortress, 1990], 135) points to the significance of Psalm 103:13 ("As a father has compassion on his children, so the LORD has compassion on those who fear him") and Psalm 119:176 ("I have strayed like a lost sheep"). More recently, Kenneth E. Bailey (*Jacob and the Prodigal: How Jesus Retold Israel's Story* [Downers Grove, Ill.: InterVarsity, 2003]) reads Luke 15 in the light of the story of the OT patriarch Jacob.

a. The lost sheep (15:1–7)

¹Now the tax collectors and "sinners" were all gathering around to hear him. ²But the Pharisees and the teachers of the law muttered, "This man welcomes sinners and eats with them."

³Then Jesus told them this parable: ⁴"Suppose one of you has a hundred sheep and loses one of them. Does he not leave the ninety-nine in the open country and go after the lost sheep until he finds it? ⁵And when he finds it, he joyfully puts it on his shoulders ⁶and

goes home. Then he calls his friends and neighbors together and says, 'Rejoice with me; I have found my lost sheep.' [7]I tell you that in the same way there will be more rejoicing in heaven over one sinner who repents than over ninety-nine righteous persons who do not need to repent."

COMMENTARY

1 "Tax collectors" were among those who were ostracized because their work was considered dishonest or immoral (cf. Jeremias, 132). They were also considered to be instruments of the Roman imperial power (cf. 3:12). The NIV appropriately puts "sinners" in quotation marks to show that this was not Luke's designation but the way others, i.e., the Pharisees, thought of them. For an explanation of the attitude of Pharisees to such "sinners," see comments at 5:29–30.

"All" signifies either all such persons (wherever Jesus was at the time) or, generally speaking, the large proportion of them among the crowds who usually came to hear him. The imperfect periphrastic "were gathering" (see comments at 14:1) could indicate either the process of gathering at the time of the story or the habitual coming of "sinners" throughout Jesus' ministry.

2 In OT times, it was taken for granted that God's people did not consort with sinners (cf. Ps 1), but the Pharisees extended this beyond the biblical intent. To go so far as to "welcome" them and especially to "eat" with them, implying table fellowship, was unthinkable to the Pharisees. The parables that follow show that the return of "sinners" to God should be a cause for joy to the religious leaders, as it was to God. Furthermore, "Jesus makes the claim for himself that he is acting in God's stead, that he is God's representative" (Jeremias, 132).

3 The word "parable" in its singular form is used to refer to all three parables that follow. These para-

bles should, therefore, be considered together in response to the challenge of the Pharisees and the teachers of the law.

4–5 For the phrase "suppose one of you" (v.4), see comments at 14:5. There is a parallel between the expression *tis anthrōpos ex hymōn* (lit., "what man of you") and *tis gynē* ("what woman," v.8, where the lack of the additional words "of you" may indicate that no women were present).

The situation described was a common one. One hundred sheep made up a normal-sized flock. A count was taken nightly. The "open country" was a safe place to leave the sheep ("wilderness" [KJV, RSV] is misleading), though they would have to be left in someone's care. The frightened, confused, and perhaps injured sheep would have to be carried (v.5).

It is striking to note that, in the obvious analogy to the search for the sheep (v.4), Jesus takes the initiative in seeking out lost people—a major theme in Luke (cf. 19:10). In contrast were some rabbis in the early centuries who hesitated to seek Gentile converts. But that does not invalidate Jesus' comment in Matthew 23:15 about Pharisees who were proselytizing aggressively. They were apparently trying to gain adherents to their sect rather than compassionately seeking the lost.

6 The climax of the story is not only the return of the sheep but the triumphant rejoicing in its rescue. This theme of rejoicing ties the three parables of ch. 15 together. In Luke, rejoicing and celebrating signify the witness of God's salvific acts in history. Jesus is also stressing, both by parable and direct statement (v.7), that his seeking and receiving of sinners pleases God.

7 "In heaven" (v.7) is a customary way of referring reverently to God without saying his name (cf. v.10; see comments at 14:11). The NIV's rendering, "there will be . . . rejoicing," brings out the future (*estai*, "will be"), which may include the day yet future of gathering and feasting (cf. 13:29). There are none who are truly "righteous" (cf. Ro 3:10); the "righteous persons" referred to in v.7 are devout people (cf. 1:6), or those who seem so (Mt 6:1), who have no gross, open sins of which to repent.

b. The lost coin (15:8–10)

OVERVIEW

This parable is clearly linked to the preceding one, and the opening words are comparable (see comments on "suppose" at v.4). The main characters of the two parables also complement each other. In the first parable the story centers on a shepherd (man) who works outside the house. In this second parable one finds a woman working inside a house. This corresponds to the typical role men and women played in first-century Mediterranean societies (cf. Malina and Neyrey, "Honor and Shame in Luke–Acts," in *The Social World of Luke–Acts* [ed. Neyrey], 62).

8"Or suppose a woman has ten silver coins and loses one. Does she not light a lamp, sweep the house and search carefully until she finds it? **9**And when she finds it, she calls her friends and neighbors together and says, 'Rejoice with me; I have found my lost coin.' **10**In the same way, I tell you, there is rejoicing in the presence of the angels of God over one sinner who repents."

COMMENTARY

8 The "coins" are drachmas (see NIV text note on their value). They may have formed part of the woman's headdress, which, being part of her dowry, she wore constantly (cf. Jeremias, 134; Marshall, 603). Whether or not that is the case here, the mention of ten coins implies that they were all she had. "A lamp" was needed because the house would have had at best a few small windows or only a low doorway. She would "sweep" the hard earthen floor to find the coin by the sound of its clinking.

9–10 As in v.6, the extent of joy expressed is striking (v.9). Considering the neighborly feelings in a small village, this is understandable, especially if the coin represented a tenth of the woman's savings. Moreover, Jesus' final comment (v.10) reinforces the point. "In the presence of the angels of God" is a reverential reference to God, as is "in heaven" (v.7). This parable, like that of the lost sheep, justifies Jesus' welcome of sinners (v.2).

c. The lost son (15:11–32)

OVERVIEW

The great parable of the lost son (or the merciful father) speaks even more eloquently than its predecessors to the situation set forth in vv. 1–2. The first part (vv. 11–24) conveys the same sense of joy on the finding of the lost that is present in the other two parables; in contrast, the second part deals with the sour attitude of the elder brother. Like the Pharisees, he could not comprehend the meaning of forgiveness. The positions of the two sons would, in a structural analysis, be considered binary opposites—the lost son rises and the elder brother falls in moral state. The central figure, the father, remains constant in his love for both. As in v. 2 (see comments there), by telling the story Jesus identifies himself with God in his loving attitude toward the lost. He represents God in his mission, the accomplishment of which should elicit joy from those who share the Father's compassion.

The parable is one of the world's supreme masterpieces of storytelling. Its details are vivid; they reflect actual customs and legal procedures and build up the story's emotional and spiritual impact. But the expositor must resist the tendency to allegorize the wealth of detail that gives the story its remarkable verisimilitude. The main point of the parable—that God gladly receives repentant sinners—must not be obscured.

[11]Jesus continued: "There was a man who had two sons. [12]The younger one said to his father, 'Father, give me my share of the estate.' So he divided his property between them.

[13]"Not long after that, the younger son got together all he had, set off for a distant country and there squandered his wealth in wild living. [14]After he had spent everything, there was a severe famine in that whole country, and he began to be in need. [15]So he went and hired himself out to a citizen of that country, who sent him to his fields to feed pigs. [16]He longed to fill his stomach with the pods that the pigs were eating, but no one gave him anything.

[17]"When he came to his senses, he said, 'How many of my father's hired men have food to spare, and here I am starving to death! [18]I will set out and go back to my father and say to him: Father, I have sinned against heaven and against you. [19]I am no longer worthy to be called your son; make me like one of your hired men.' [20]So he got up and went to his father.

"But while he was still a long way off, his father saw him and was filled with compassion for him; he ran to his son, threw his arms around him and kissed him.

[21]"The son said to him, 'Father, I have sinned against heaven and against you. I am no longer worthy to be called your son.'

[22]"But the father said to his servants, 'Quick! Bring the best robe and put it on him. Put a ring on his finger and sandals on his feet. [23]Bring the fattened calf and kill it. Let's have a

feast and celebrate. ²⁴For this son of mine was dead and is alive again; he was lost and is found.' So they began to celebrate.

²⁵"Meanwhile, the older son was in the field. When he came near the house, he heard music and dancing. ²⁶So he called one of the servants and asked him what was going on. ²⁷'Your brother has come,' he replied, 'and your father has killed the fattened calf because he has him back safe and sound.'

²⁸"The older brother became angry and refused to go in. So his father went out and pleaded with him. ²⁹But he answered his father, 'Look! All these years I've been slaving for you and never disobeyed your orders. Yet you never gave me even a young goat so I could celebrate with my friends. ³⁰But when this son of yours who has squandered your property with prostitutes comes home, you kill the fattened calf for him!'

³¹"'My son,' the father said, 'you are always with me, and everything I have is yours. ³²But we had to celebrate and be glad, because this brother of yours was dead and is alive again; he was lost and is found.'"

COMMENTARY

12 The "share of the estate" (see Notes) that a younger son would receive on the death of the father would be one-third, because the older (or oldest) son received two-thirds, a "double portion"—i.e., twice as much as all the other sons (Dt 21:17). If the property were given, as in this case, while the father lived, the heirs would have use of it (cf. v.31); but if they sold it, they could not normally transfer it as long as the father lived. The father also would receive any accrued interest (see Jeremias, 128–29). The son may have been asking for immediate total ownership, but the parable does not specify the exact terms of the settlement. Not to be missed is the shame brought to the father with this request from his son. The property was "divided"; so the elder son was made aware of his share (cf. v.31).

13–16 The NIV captures the vivid wording of the account, including "squandered his wealth" and "wild living" (see Notes). The wasting of all the son had in a foreign land is understood as acting against the family, whose inheritance can be traced back to

the promises of God to Abraham (cf. Bailey, *Poet and Peasant*, 167–68).

The famine made employment and food even harder than usual to get. The "distant country" was apparently outside strictly Jewish territory, and the wayward son found himself with the demeaning job of feeding pigs (v.15)—unclean animals for the Jews. He would even have eaten "pods" (v.16), which were seeds of the carob tree common around the Mediterranean and used for pigs' food. He had fallen so low and had become so insignificant that "no one gave him anything"—an indication of total neglect.

17 "Came to his senses" (*eis heauton elthōn*, lit., "came to himself") was a common idiom, which in this Jewish story may carry the Semitic idea of repentance (cf. Jeremias, 130; see Notes). Certainly repentance lies at the heart of the words the son prepared to tell his father.

18–19 The motivation for the son's return was hunger, but it was specifically to his "father" (v.18) that he wanted to return. The words "against heaven" (*eis ton ouranon* [GK *4041*]) can mean "to heaven," denoting that his sins were so many as to reach to heaven; more probably the meaning is that his sins were ultimately against God, veiled in the word "heaven" (cf. Ps 51:4). Assuming this latter meaning, we see that the parable is far more than an allegory with the father representing God, for the father and God have distinct roles. The father in the story does, of course, portray the characteristics and attitudes of a loving heavenly Father. This does not mean that God is heavenly Father to everyone (note Jn 1:12; 8:42–44). Yet the Jews knew God's loving care was like that of a father (Ps 103:13). The son knew he had no right to return as a son (v.19), having taken and squandered his inheritance. He therefore planned to earn his room and board.

20 The description of the young man's return and welcome is as vivid as that of his departure, with several notable touches. The fact that his father saw him "while he was still a long way off" has led many to assume that the father was waiting for him, perhaps daily searching the distant road, hoping for his appearance. This prompted the title of Helmut Thielicke's book of Jesus' parables, *The Waiting Father* (New York: Harper, 1959). The father's "compassion" assumes some knowledge of the son's pitiable condition, perhaps from reports. Some have pointed out that a father in that culture would not normally run as he did, which, along with his warm embrace and kissing, adds to the impact of the story. Clearly Jesus used every literary means to heighten the contrast between the father's attitude and that of the elder brother (and of the Pharisees; cf. vv.1–2).

21 The son's speech was never completed. Instead the father more than reversed the unspoken part about becoming a "hired man" (v.19) and therefore impresses his son with his overwhelming love (Nolland, 2:784–85; cf. Bailey, *Poet and Peasant*, 183).

22 The robe, ring, and sandals signified more than sonship (cf. Jeremias, 130); the robe was a ceremonial one such as a guest of honor would be given, or it could be the very robe that the father usually wears. Marshall, 610, doubts Manson's assertion that the robe was "a symbol of the New Age" (see Notes). The ring signified authority, and the sandals were those only a free man would wear.

23–24 The calf was apparently being "fattened" for some special occasion, for people in first-century Palestine did not regularly eat meat. Note the parallel between "dead" and "alive" and "lost" and "found" (v.24)—terms that also apply to one's state before and after conversion to Christ (Eph 2:1–5). As in the parables of the lost sheep and the lost coin, it was time to "celebrate." This act of celebration, in a context where one finds salvation and restoration, should be considered together with the other feeding stories in Luke that celebrate the dawning of God's kingdom.

25–27 It seems strange that the older son was not there when the celebration began. Jesus' parables, however, are a fictional way of teaching enduring truth; and we may imagine that the celebration began so quickly that the older son was not aware of it (vv.26–27). Or, more likely in view of the dialogue in vv.26–31, his absence showed his distant relationship with his family.

28–30 Verse 28 contrasts the older son with the father. The son became angry; but the father "went out," as he had for the younger brother, and "pleaded" rather than scolded. The older son's abrupt beginning—"Look!" (v.29)—betrays a disrespectful attitude toward his father. Likewise, "slaving" is hardly descriptive of a warm family relationship. "You never gave me," whether true or not, shows a long, smoldering discontent. "This son of yours" (*ho huios sou houtos*, v.30) avoids acknowledging that the prodigal is his own brother—a disclaimer the father corrects by the words "this brother of yours" (v.32). The older brother's charges include sharp criticism of both father and brother. The story has made no mention of hiring prostitutes (v.30).

31–32 The father's response is nevertheless tender: "My son" (or "child," *teknon*) is followed by words of affirmation, not weakness. "We had to celebrate" (*euphranthēnai . . . edei*, v.32) is literally, "It was necessary to celebrate"; no personal subject is mentioned. This allows the implication that the elder brother should have joined in the celebration. The words "had to" (*edei*, GK *1256*) introduce once more the necessity and urgency so prominent in Luke (see comments at 4:43).

This sense of necessity points us back to one of the main emphases of the story. While it is difficult for the younger son to acknowledge his faults, it may even be more difficult for the elder son to "repent." This elder son who considers himself to be the righteous one becomes the one who is in need of salvation. The story ends without noting the response of the elder son, and this open-ended story functions as a call for Israel to return and to enter into God's kingdom, in which the outcasts have already received the call to participate (cf. vv.1–2). The failure to do so will produce a result not foreign to those who are familiar with the Scripture of Israel: the younger son will take the place of the older one (e.g., Cain and Abel; Esau and Jacob). The three stories on the compassion of God (and Jesus) therefore function as illustrations of the love of God and his concern for both Israel and the outcasts.

NOTES

11–32 Two issues—one literary and one theological—are often raised with regard to the parable of the lost son. Because the first part of the parable revolves around the younger brother and the latter around the older (and also for other reasons), some have found the parable's literary structure complex, i.e., originally consisting of two independent stories. If so, the resultant unit is well edited; for the older son appears from the very beginning, the two parts complement each other, and the latter part fits as well as the former into the context of vv.1–2. But this view cannot be sustained (cf. Marshall, 605). In the light of vv.1–2, the contrast of the two sons is actually one of the parable's central themes.

The theological issue centers in the absence of any hint that anything more than repentance and returning to God as Father is involved in salvation. (God's fatherhood is discussed in the comments at v.18.) It must, however, be kept in mind that this is a parable and thus is intended to portray only one aspect of the gospel—God's willingness to receive "sinners" and his joy over their return. Elsewhere in Luke's presentation of Christ as Savior, the cross has its place (cf. Manson, 286; Marshall, *Luke: Historian and Theologian*, 170–75).

12 In the papyri evidence, τὸ ἐπιβάλλον μέρος (*to epiballon meros*, lit., "the share that falls upon"; NIV, "my share") is a technical phrase that refers to paternal inheritance (cf. W. Pöhlmann, *Der Verlorene Sohn und das Haus* [WUNT 68; Tübingen: Mohr, 1993], 168–69).

13 The word ἀσώτως (*asōtōs*, GK *862*)—appearing nowhere else in the NT—is translated as "wild living." The word contains the stem for salvation and may have been intentionally used by the author to talk about the younger son's lack of salvation.

16 The verb χορτασθῆναι (*chortasthēnai*, "to feed on," from χορτάζω, *chortazō*, GK *5963*) has more MS support than γεμίσαι τὴν κοιλίαν (*gemisai tēn koilian*, "to fill the stomach"). The NIV appears to have followed the latter but may simply be using a contemporary idiom to express the general idea of both verbs.

17 Whether the idea of repentance can be found within the phrase "came to his senses" has been questioned by Bailey (*Poet and Peasant*, 171–73). The subsequent physical act of returning to his father affirms, however, the existence of a repentant heart in the younger son. In a parable such as this, one should not expect the idea of repentance to be expressed explicitly in theological terms. Moreover, one may agree with G. Forbes ("Repentance and Conflict in the Parable of the Lost Son [Luke 15:11–32]," *JETS* 42 [1999]: 226) in seeing Jesus as redefining the traditional understanding of repentance here; repentance is no longer understood simply as a mental act—it is to be accompanied by an observable act. The significance of the repentance of this human character may also explain the need for the third parable, since neither sheep nor coins can illustrate the significance of human responsibility.

22 Some have seen the robe as alluding to the one Joseph wore, and this is further supported by other allusions to Joseph's story in Genesis (cf. R. D. Aus, *Weihnachtsgeschichte–Barmherziger Samariter–Verlorener Sohn* [Berlin: Institut Kirche und Judentum, 1988], 126–73). The contrast between the older brother(s) and the younger one in both stories may explain the conscious evocation of the Joseph traditions. With the absence of allusions to Joseph elsewhere in Luke, it remains uncertain whether one should read this parable primarily through this lens.

5. Parable of the Shrewd Manager (16:1–18)

OVERVIEW

Chapter 16 follows the pattern characteristic of this part of Luke, namely, a combination of parables and sayings pointing again and again to the need for decision. In this chapter, in spite of obvious diversity, one theme occurs several times. It is that of Jesus' teaching about material possessions, first in the parable of the shrewd manager, then in the comment about the Pharisees "who loved money" (v.14), and finally in the parable of the rich man and Lazarus.

The interpretation of this parable is notoriously difficult. Some have even resorted to the suggestion that the original story was lost through textual transmission (e.g., C. S. Mann, "Unjust Steward or Prudent Manager," *ExpTim* 102 [1991]: 234–35; D. M. Parrott, "The Dishonest Steward [Luke 16.1–

8a] and Luke's Special Parable Collection," *NTS* 37 [1991]: 499–515)—a position that is neither necessary nor supported by textual evidence. Prior to any overall interpretation and application of it is a series of decisions regarding vv.8–13. Several interdependent questions face the expositor: (1) Is the "master" (*kyrios*, GK *3261*) in v.8 the "master" in the parable (vv.3, 5) or the Lord Jesus? (2) Why did the "master" commend a dishonest manager?—a question that becomes more acute if the "master" is the Lord Jesus. (3) Where does the parable end—before v.8 (in which case the "master" is the Lord), in the middle of v.8 (in which case the sentence beginning "for the people" begins the comment on the parable), or at the end of v.8 (with the words "I tell you" [v.9] initiating the comment)? (4) Are vv.10–12 and 13 part of the same unit, or do they represent a separate tradition?

Discussion of these issues will help us interpret the parable. First, the "master" *may* refer to the Lord Jesus because (1) Luke normally uses *kyrios* to refer to Jesus and God; (2) the latter part of v.8 (taking it as a unity) refers to believers and unbelievers rather than to characters in the story; and (3) in 18:6 *kyrios* is used to refer to Jesus when he begins the explanation of a parable (cf. Jeremias, 46–47; Ellis, 199). On the other hand, "master" more likely refers to the rich master in the story, as (1) this would not be an unusual secular use of the word *kyrios*; (2) the term frequently appears in Jesus' parables (e.g., 12:37, 47; 14:23); (3) the religious terminology of v.8 (e.g., "people of the light") seems to refer to real people (in contrast to the characters of the secular illustration) and therefore sounds like the beginning of Jesus' explanation; (4) the real parallel to 18:6 ("the Lord said") may not be in this verse ("the master commended") but in v.9 ("I tell you"); and (5) v.8a seems to form a better conclusion to the parable than does v.7 (so Fitzmyer, *Semitic Background*, 161–84).

Second, even if the "master" of v.8 is the one in the story, the Lord Jesus seems to agree with the commendation; so we are left with the second question in either case: Why was a dishonest manager commended? The answer on the surface is "because he had acted shrewdly" (v.8). But was his shrewd act not dishonest? The text does not say that the manager's action in writing off the debts was dishonest. Rather, the word "dishonest" may be used here because it serves a double purpose. First, it refers back to his initial act of mishandling the master's funds. Yet even one who had thus acted could do something commendable. Second, it introduces a chain of words using the same root. "Dishonest" (*adikos*, GK *96*) is recalled by "worldly" (*tēs adikias*,

GK *94*) in v.9 and reappears twice in v.10 and once in v.11. Ellis, 199, suggests that *adikia* is a "technical theological expression" equivalent to a term used at Qumran describing the character of that age; when *adikia* is applied to people, it is because "they belong to this age and live according to its principles."

The reason the manager was now commended, though he had previously acted dishonestly, may be that he had at last learned how one's worldly wealth can be wisely given away to do good. Some have pointed to the existence of the Jewish practice of remission of debts in first-century Palestine in explaining the commendable acts of the manager (so T. Hoeren, "Das Gleichnis vom ungerechten Verwalter [Lukas 16.1–8a]—zugleich ein Beitrag zur Geschichte der Restschuldbefreiung," *NTS* 41 [1995]: 620–29). Along similar lines, Fitzmyer (*Semitic Background*, 175–76) suggests that the amount taken off the bills in vv.5–7 was not part of the debt owed to the master but rather represented the interest the manager himself was charging. Though this would have been contrary to Jewish law (Ex 22:25; Lev 25:36–37; Dt 15:7–8; 23:19–20), charging a poor Jew such interest (actually usury) was often rationalized. The bill would be written in terms of the commodity rather than in monetary figures, with the interest hidden in the total. By law, a master could not be held accountable for the illegal acts of an employee. So the master in the parable was in a position to view the manager's activities objectively. If this explanation is correct, the manager's transaction was not illegal. In any event, the master would lose no money if the amount forfeited was simply the interest the manager would have gained. Furthermore, such a forgiveness of debts would hardly have hurt but would probably have helped the master's own reputation; therefore, the master admires the manager's shrewdness. The manager knew his job and reputation were gone because of his previous mishandling of funds.

He needed friends, and by forgoing the customary interest, he won friends among the creditors. Jesus then uses this story to show that the "people of the light" could also accomplish much by wisely giving up some of their "worldly wealth."

This explanation follows in the main that of Fitzmyer, who draws on and expands J. D. M. Derrett, "Fresh Light on St. Luke xvi. I. The Parable of the Unjust Steward," *NTS* 7 (1960–61): 198–219. Even if some details of this view turn out to be unsatisfactory, the basic interpretation remains valid, namely, that Jesus uses the story of the manager's actions not to commend graft but to encourage the "prudent use of material wealth" (Fitzmyer, *Semitic Background*, 177; cf. D. J. Ireland, *Stewardship and the Kingdom of God* [NovTSup 70; Leiden: Brill, 1992]). The repetition of the idea of the cessation of the present scheme of things, first in v.4 ("when I lose my job here") and then in v.9 ("when it is gone"), emphasizes the need for prudent preparation for the inevitable. This interpretation may be extended to include the commendation of the act of the manager as a way to challenge an unjust economic system as he redistributes his (or his master's) wealth to the poor—a theme that is not foreign to Luke's gospel (cf. J. S. Ukpong, "The Parable of the Shrewd Manager [Luke 16:1–13]: An Essay in Inculturation Biblical Hermeneutic," *Semeia* 73 [1996]: 189–210).

Some commentators see this parable primarily as an exhortation to act decisively in time of eschato-logical crisis, just as the manager acted in his personal crisis (see C. H. Dodd, *The Parables of the Kingdom* [rev. ed.; New York: Scribner, 1961], 17). This interpretation, while possible, ignores the fact that though the theme of decision is important in Luke, here as well as in other passages (e.g., 6:17–36; 13:13–34) the prudent use of material wealth predominates.

Third, the answer to the question of where the parable ends depends partly, as has been said, on who is designated "master" in v.8. It also depends on whether the reference to "people" in v.8b is to those in the world of the story or in the religious world of Jesus' time. In the former case, the reference is part of the story; in the latter, it is part of the commentary on it. If it is commentary, is it by Jesus or by Luke? If by Luke, the opening words of v.9, "I tell you," seem an abrupt reintroduction of Jesus' words. Since v.8b seems inappropriate as part of the story, it is best to assume that the parable ends with v.7 or, more likely, with the "master's" (rich man's) commendation of the manager.

Fourth, whether or not vv.10–13 were part of the original discourse (see Notes), as they stand in the text they provide an integrated sequence of teachings structured around the ideas of dishonesty (see second discussion above) and responsibility (*pistos*, "trusted" or "trustworthy" [GK *4412*; four times], and *pisteusei*, "will trust" [GK *4409*; once], in vv.10–12).

---

¹Jesus told his disciples: "There was a rich man whose manager was accused of wasting his possessions. ²So he called him in and asked him, 'What is this I hear about you? Give an account of your management, because you cannot be manager any longer.'

³"The manager said to himself, 'What shall I do now? My master is taking away my job. I'm not strong enough to dig, and I'm ashamed to beg—⁴I know what I'll do so that, when I lose my job here, people will welcome me into their houses.'

⁵"So he called in each one of his master's debtors. He asked the first, 'How much do you owe my master?'

⁶"'Eight hundred gallons of olive oil,' he replied.

"The manager told him, 'Take your bill, sit down quickly, and make it four hundred.'

⁷"Then he asked the second, 'And how much do you owe?'

"'A thousand bushels of wheat,' he replied.

"He told him, 'Take your bill and make it eight hundred.'

⁸"The master commended the dishonest manager because he had acted shrewdly. For the people of this world are more shrewd in dealing with their own kind than are the people of the light. ⁹I tell you, use worldly wealth to gain friends for yourselves, so that when it is gone, you will be welcomed into eternal dwellings.

¹⁰"Whoever can be trusted with very little can also be trusted with much, and whoever is dishonest with very little will also be dishonest with much. ¹¹So if you have not been trustworthy in handling worldly wealth, who will trust you with true riches? ¹²And if you have not been trustworthy with someone else's property, who will give you property of your own?

¹³"No servant can serve two masters. Either he will hate the one and love the other, or he will be devoted to the one and despise the other. You cannot serve both God and Money."

¹⁴The Pharisees, who loved money, heard all this and were sneering at Jesus. ¹⁵He said to them, "You are the ones who justify yourselves in the eyes of men, but God knows your hearts. What is highly valued among men is detestable in God's sight.

¹⁶"The Law and the Prophets were proclaimed until John. Since that time, the good news of the kingdom of God is being preached, and everyone is forcing his way into it. ¹⁷It is easier for heaven and earth to disappear than for the least stroke of a pen to drop out of the Law.

¹⁸"Anyone who divorces his wife and marries another woman commits adultery, and the man who marries a divorced woman commits adultery."

COMMENTARY

1–2 "Manager" (*oikonomos*, GK *3874*; often translated "steward") is a broad term for an employee or agent entrusted with the management of funds or property. Mismanagement was possible, as in this parable, because strict accounts were not always kept. When word came from others—"What is this I hear about you?" (v.2; see Notes)—he had

to "give an account" (*apodos*, cf. Mt 12:36; Heb 13:17; 1Pe 4:5).

3–4 The manager's plight was that he had a respectable "desk job" but could do little else. To "dig" is the job of the uneducated, and to "beg" is likewise a shameful act (cf. 15:16). His decision, therefore, is made with a view to his personal security after his dismissal. The word "welcome" (*dechomai*, GK *1312*, v.4) here refers to the anticipated response of those whose debts were alleviated. A wordplay might be intended when the same word appears in 16:9 in reference to the reception into the eternal abode (so Bock, 2:1329; see comments at v.9 below).

5–7 As already noted, the bills may have been written in terms of commodities rather than cash, perhaps in order to hide the actual amount of interest. The amounts owed were large; the wheat is said to be equal to the yield of about one hundred acres (cf. Jeremias, 181). The difference in the percentage of reduction may be due to the difference in the relative value of the two commodities. The actual value of the reduction in each case has been computed to equal about five hundred denarii, or sixteen months' wages for a soldier or a day laborer.

8a The meaning of v.8a, as noted above, is not that a manager is commended for an act of dishonesty but that a dishonest manager is commended for an act of prudence. Not only do these acts reflect well on the wise manager; they also bring honor to the master who has suffered when his servant's prior actions were made public (v.2; see Notes, v.2). As such, v.8a should be considered the climax of the story (cf. B. B. Scott, "A Master's Praise—Luke 16:1–8a" *Bib* 64 [1983]: 173–88).

8b–9 The contrast between those who belong to (lit., "are sons of") this age and those who belong to "the light" (v.8b) is familiar from Qumran (1QS 1:9; 2:16; 3:13; cf. Eph 5:8). Christians do not belong to this evil age, but they can nevertheless make responsible use of "worldly wealth" (v.9; see Notes). The "friends" may not refer to any particular people but simply be part of the parable's imagery (cf. Danker, 174). Usually they have been understood as being poor people, for whom Jesus (and Luke also) had a deep concern and to whom we are here urged to give alms (cf. 12:33; see John-

son, 157). "Worldly wealth" should not be stored up for oneself (cf. 12:21), since one day it will be "gone." "You will be welcomed" echoes v.4. The future passive of the NIV is a good way of representing *dexōntai hymas* (lit., "they will receive you"), which has no expressed subject. Though if we follow the context closely the subject may be the "friends," the use of the plural may reflect the Jewish custom of referring to God obliquely.

10–13 The theme of stewardship is now discussed in terms of trustworthiness as over against dishonesty (v.10). "Worldly wealth" (v.11) appears for the second time (cf. v.9). The property here is "someone else's" (v.12)—presumably God's—in contrast to the parable's imagery in which, at least in Fitzmyer's view, the amount forgiven was the manager's own commission. Except for the word "servant," v.13 appears in precisely the same form in Matthew 6:24. The verse is equally appropriate in each context; here, however, it is connected to the context not only topically but also verbally through the use, for the third time, of *mamōnas* (cf. "worldly wealth," GK *3440*, vv.9, 11), this time translated "money" in the NIV. The addition of "servant" stresses the point that though one may have both God and money, one cannot serve them both.

14–15 "Money" (v.14) links this section (vv.14–18) with the preceding one, and this remark is consistent with Luke's portrayal of the Pharisees elsewhere. For an author who has repeatedly emphasized the danger of wealth and worldly possessions, this note should be considered as among the most serious charges laid against the Pharisees. The charge that the Pharisees do not have a proper sense of values (v.15) leads to the saying about the value of the kingdom and the Law (vv.16–17). In turn, reference to the permanence of the Law becomes the context for a specific example of a contested moral standard: divorce and remarriage (v.18).

Jewish teachers who had been influenced by Hellenistic culture were aware that philosophers often taught for fees. Rabbis in the first centuries of our era often had secular jobs. The Pharisees would not have been immune to desires for remuneration commensurate with their own sense of importance. Later on, Paul was to work at a trade so that he could say he did not "put on a mask to cover up greed" (1Th 2:5; cf. 1Co 9:12). One should not assume, however, that remuneration for service rendered exhausts this charge against the Pharisees. While we do not possess detailed information about the Pharisaic understanding of the value of worldly possessions, some have suggested that their eschatology would encourage the understanding of wealth as signs of divine favor (cf. T. E. Schmidt, "Burden, Barrier, Blasphemy," *TJ* 9 [1988]: 185). Jesus' critique, therefore, aims at the heart of such an assumption. Self-justification (v.15) is a temptation for religious people (cf. Mt 5:20; 6:1), and this saying forces the transfer of one's reference point from that which can be seen to that which cannot be observed. This provides the fundamental rationale for Jesus' concern with issues of wealth in this gospel.

16–17 The Pharisees had the truth of the "Law" of Moses (Genesis to Deuteronomy) and the "Prophets" (here representing the rest of the OT). They failed to respond not only to the good news of the kingdom but even to their own Scriptures (cf. Mk 7:8–9), whose authority continued into the present age (v.17). Verse 29 also alludes to their failure to heed the Law and the Prophets (see comments there).

For the relationship of John the Baptist to the kingdom (v.16a), see 7:28 and comments there. For the meaning of "until" and "since that time," see Notes. Verse 16 appears in slightly different form— and with the sentences reversed—in Matthew's passage about John the Baptist (Mt 11:12–13). The wording in Matthew is notoriously difficult to interpret, but the substitution in Luke (v.16b) of "being preached" (*euangelizetai*, GK *2294*) for "forcefully advancing" (*biazetai*, GK *1041*; possibly, "suffered violence") limits the meaning here. *Biazetai*, which occurs in Matthew 11:12 though not in Luke 16:16b, does occur in v.16c—"is forcing his way," a translation that takes the verb, probably correctly, to be in the middle voice (but see J. B. Cortes and F. M. Gatti, "On the Meaning of Luke 16:16," *JBL* 106 [1987]: 247–59). Matthew has "forceful men lay hold of it" (*biastai harpazousin autēn*), conveying a sense of violence not necessarily implied in Luke's "everyone is forcing his way into it" (*pas eis autēn biazetai*). This could be understood as expressing violence if one interprets it in accord with what Matthew has; otherwise it could simply express the enthusiastic drive of those determined to enter the kingdom (cf. Lk 13:24). However one interprets this difficult verse, it is clear that the Pharisees had missed what was really of value (v.15), while all around them were people whose values were in order and who were energetically seeking the kingdom (cf. Mt 13:44–46). The truth of v.17 is also expressed in the Sermon on the Mount (Mt 5:17–20).

18 This brief excerpt from Jesus' teaching on divorce and remarriage is probably included as an example of one aspect of the Law the Pharisees tended to minimize. In its immediate context, it can also function as a metaphor for the irrevocability of the Law and the Prophets (so J. J. Kilgallen, "The Purpose of Luke's Divorce Text [16:18]," *Bib* 76 [1995]: 229–38). The teaching is essentially the same as that in Matthew 5:32 (cf. Mt 19:9), except that Luke (1) omits the phrase "except for marital unfaithfulness," (2) says that the remarried man commits adultery rather than that he causes his first wife to do so, and (3) includes a comment about a man who marries a divorced woman. The absence of the Matthean exception clause can be explained by the emphases of both the intent of the permanence of marriage here as well as the absolute inviolability of the Law and the Prophets in the previous verse.

To reproduce the complete teachings on marriage and divorce, therefore, one has to consider the Matthean sayings, as well as Paul's understanding of Jesus' teachings in 1 Corinthians 7. The issue of adultery committed with the act of remarriage can be understood as implying an intent to remarry another person as the cause of the initial divorce (Bock, 2:1356–58). This reading would explain the slight difference of emphasis between the Matthean and Lukan versions. Nevertheless, the broader application may apply here, since the prior relationship between the husband and his future wife is not explicitly noted. Therefore, the person who divorces his spouse and marries another is accused of committing adultery (in a metaphorical sense) because that person violates the original commitment to his original marital partner (cf. Craig L. Blomberg, "Marriage, Divorce, Remarriage, and Celibacy: An Exegesis of Matthew 19:3–12," *TJ* NS 11 [1990]: 161–96).

NOTES

2 "What is this I hear about you?" This question implies the public awareness of the servant's actions. In an honor–shame culture, the acts of the servant undoubtedly brought shame to his master. Though one may not agree with the general conclusions of J. Kloppenborg ("The Dishonoured Master [Luke 16:1–8a]," *Bib* 70 [1989]: 474–95), he may be correct in suggesting that the subsequent acts of the servants came to be understood as acts of benefaction, acts that brought honor back to his master.

4 The use of the aorist ἔγνων (*egnōn*, "I know") rather than the present tense γινώσκω (*ginōskō*) has often been commented on. Exegetes have tended to read too much into the simple aorist and to stress too much its punctiliar aspect. Here it could imply a flash of inspiration—"I've got it!"—or, more likely, the culmination of his deliberations—"I've decided."

9 The phrase μαμωνᾶ τῆς ἀδικίας (*mamōna tēs adikias*, "worldly wealth," GK *3440, 90*; lit., "the mammon of injustice/unrighteousness") is probably a Semitic expression used idiomatically to signify money. The word ἀδικίας, *adikias*, probably carries the thought, found in the Qumran writings, of that which characterizes the godless world (Ellis, 199).

10–13 These verses appear to have been independent sayings brought together here by Luke because they share certain catchwords with the preceding verses. This is not impossible; there are no transitional words that indicate that the sayings were given on the same occasion in Jesus' ministry as the preceding. Verses 10–12 are unique to Luke and presumably come from his special source. Verse 13 is found, without the word "servant," in Matthew 6:24 and is usually ascribed to Q.

15 Schmidt ("Burden, Barrier, Blasphemy," 185) has highlighted the significance of the word βδέλυγμα (*bdelygma*, "detestable," GK *1007*) in the context of OT (i.e., LXX) polemic against idolatry (e.g., Dt 7:25–26; 1Ki 14:24; Ezr 9:11; Isa 44:19). He has further pointed to the existence of Second Temple Jewish traditions that equate lovers of money with idolaters (e.g., *T. Jud.* 18.2, 6; 19.1). This context provides the link between vv.13 and 15: one can worship either God or Money (i.e., an idol), but not both.

16 The exact meaning of the phrases μέχρι ἀπὸ πότε (*mechri apo pote*, "until") and ἀπὸ πότε (*apo pote*, "since that time") has been at the center of intense debate since the publication of the classic work of

Conzelmann, 16, 22–27, who argues for the exclusion of John the Baptist from the kingdom primarily on the basis of this verse. Most recent scholars would affirm the uniqueness of Jesus' ministry while seeing John as a transitional figure involved in both eras. For a helpful survey, see M. Bachmann, "Johannes des Täufer bei Lukas: Nachzügler oder Vorläufer," in *Wort in der Zeit*, ed. W. Haubeck and M. Bachmann (Leiden: Brill, 1964), 123–55. For a general discussion of the reception of Conzelmann's periodization of salvation history, see F. Bovon, *Luke the Theologian* (Pittsburgh, Pa.: Pickwick, 1987), 11–77.

6. The Rich Man and Lazarus (16:19–31)

OVERVIEW

The expositor's basic concern is not the nature and history of this story (see Notes) but its primary significance in its Lukan context. It is set in a series of encounters with the Pharisees (cf. 15:1–2; 16:14), and its meaning must be understood in that context. The Pharisees did not follow their own Scriptures, the "Law and the Prophets" (v.16); so they were no better than the rich man's brothers, who "have Moses and the Prophets" (v.29). The Pharisees professed belief in a future life and in future judgment; however, they did not live in conformity with that belief but rather in the pursuit of wealth (v.14), just like the rich man of the parable. Even Jesus' resurrection (possibly alluded to in v.31) would not convince them. It is implicit in the account that one's attitude toward God and his word is confirmed in this life and that it cannot be altered in the next one.

Reading this parable in the light of other, similar parables in Luke's central section, the focus on the theme of eschatological reversal can again be detected (cf. R. J. Bauckham, "The Rich Man and Lazarus: The Parable and Its Parallels," *NTS* 37 [1991]: 225–46). The one who appears to be blessed will suffer, and the one who is suffering will receive eternal blessings. Moving beyond individualistic concerns, this parable also addresses Israel as a whole in their response to the message of Jesus.

While the parable does contain a few doctrinal implications, the expositor must keep in mind that one cannot build an eschatology on it. To do so will result in an anachronism; for though Revelation 20:14 places the throwing of death and Hades into the lake of fire at the end of history (the "second death"), in this story the rich man is already in a torment of fire in his body while his brothers are still living. It should be understood as a story containing some limited eschatological ideas familiar to Jesus' audience. Thus understood, the story makes a powerful case for (1) the future reversal of the human condition (cf. 6:20–26), (2) the reality of future judgment based on one's decisions in this life, and (3) the futility of even a resurrection to persuade those who persist in rejecting God's revealed word.

---

¹⁹"There was a rich man who was dressed in purple and fine linen and lived in luxury every day. ²⁰At his gate was laid a beggar named Lazarus, covered with sores ²¹and longing to eat what fell from the rich man's table. Even the dogs came and licked his sores.

22"The time came when the beggar died and the angels carried him to Abraham's side. The rich man also died and was buried. 23In hell, where he was in torment, he looked up and saw Abraham far away, with Lazarus by his side. 24So he called to him, 'Father Abraham, have pity on me and send Lazarus to dip the tip of his finger in water and cool my tongue, because I am in agony in this fire.'

25"But Abraham replied, 'Son, remember that in your lifetime you received your good things, while Lazarus received bad things, but now he is comforted here and you are in agony. 26And besides all this, between us and you a great chasm has been fixed, so that those who want to go from here to you cannot, nor can anyone cross over from there to us.'

27"He answered, 'Then I beg you, father, send Lazarus to my father's house, 28for I have five brothers. Let him warn them, so that they will not also come to this place of torment.'

29"Abraham replied, 'They have Moses and the Prophets; let them listen to them.'

30"'No, father Abraham,' he said, 'but if someone from the dead goes to them, they will repent.'

31"He said to him, 'If they do not listen to Moses and the Prophets, they will not be convinced even if someone rises from the dead.'"

COMMENTARY

19–21 This paragraph vividly pictures the earthly state of the two men and prepares the hearer and reader for the reversal in vv.22–24. The fact that Jesus named the "beggar" (v.20) while not naming the "rich man" (v.19) may imply that one was ultimately more important. The naming of a character in the story need not lead to the conclusion some have drawn that Lazarus was a real person, though parables usually do not have named characters. Nor is there convincing evidence that this Lazarus is the same one Jesus raised from the dead (Jn 11). Admittedly, the similarity is remarkable, since both stories deal with death and resurrection (cf. v.30) and since in both instances resurrection does not convince unbelievers (see Marshall, 635; cf. D. J. Bretherton, "Lazarus of Bethany: Resurrection or Resuscitation?" *ExpTim* 104 [1993]: 169–73). Nevertheless, Lazarus was a common name—the Greek form (*Lazaros*) of the Hebrew Eleazar (*ʾelʿāzār*, "[whom]

God has helped"). It is probably used symbolically, and the repeated mention of his name may support this interpretation: the one who received no help from those around him receives deliverance from God in heaven (cf. 16:22; see D. A. S. Ravens, "Zacchaeus: The Final Part of a Lucan Triptych?" *JSNT* 41 [1991]: 19–32). Bauckham ("Rich Man and Lazarus," 244) has also observed that a person who returns from the dead in a story is often named. Tradition has given the name of "Dives," the Latin word for "rich," to the anonymous rich man (see Notes).

"Purple" (v.19) was a dyed cloth worn by the wealthy. The Roman soldiers mocked Jesus by putting a purple robe on him in the Praetorium before the crucifixion (Mk 15:17, 20). In a vivid contrast to the rich man, Jesus depicts Lazarus as neglected and subjected to insult even by "the dogs" (v.21). The fact that he is poor, hungry, and "covered with sores" may be an intentional allusion to the similar lists in 6:21; 7:22; 14:13, 21 (cf. Johnson, 142). Lazarus therefore symbolizes the "outcasts" who are so often mentioned in this gospel.

22 After the rich man dies he is "buried," but Lazarus receives no burial by those around him. He is, however, escorted by "the angels." Angelic activity is not foreign to the biblical scene (Heb 1:14), and it is not surprising to see the involvement of angels in the portrayal of the afterlife of a person. Nolland, 2:829, has pointed to similar stories in Jewish traditions where a righteous person is often escorted by the angels into the heavens. "Abraham's side" may picture reclining at a banquet, like the "feast in the kingdom of God" at which Abraham will be present (13:28–29). If so, it may contrast with vv.20–21, where the rich man sits at the table while Lazarus longs for the scraps. Otherwise it might be a symbol of reunion with Abraham and the other patriarchs at death.

23 "Hell" is "Hades" (NIV text note). In early classical literature Hades was a term for "the place of departed spirits." In the LXX it represents the Hebrew *šᵉôl*, the realm of the dead. It occurs ten times in the NT, two of them in Luke (cf. 10:15). In the NT Hades is never used of the destiny of the believer. Neither is it identified with "Gehenna" (*geenna*), which is usually connected with fiery judgment, as in Matthew 5:22, 29–30 (Luke only in 12:5). Here (v.23) Hades stands in contrast to the place and state of Lazarus's blessing. The division between the two is absolute and final (v.26).

24 "Father Abraham" expresses the normal attitude that a Jew, conscious of his heritage, would have (Jn 8:39). The use of this address also recalls the other references to Abraham in Luke, where the name itself points to the ethnic and nationalistic traditions surrounding this patriarch.

25–26 Abraham's response of "son" (*teknon*, GK 5451, v.25), like the identical term on the lips of the prodigal son's father (15:31), conveys something of the compassion God shows even to those who spurn him. The possessive pronoun in "your good things" is similar in its force to the words "for himself" in 12:21. In a masterly summary, Jesus contrasts the previous states of the rich man and Lazarus with the "now" and "here" of their situations after death. Verse 26 shows the utter and unchangeable finality of their decision.

27–31 This unchangeableness comes from hardness not only toward Jesus but also toward "Moses and the Prophets" (v.29; cf. Jn 5:46). Not even a spectacular "sign" like someone returning from the dead (vv.27, 30) can change those whose hearts are set against God's word, as the response of many to the resurrection of Jesus was to show. Verse 31 again alludes to the characterization of Jesus as a prophet who will not be received by his own (cf. 4:24). The continuity between Jesus and other messengers from God is also affirmed. This will be further developed in the speech of Stephen in Luke's second volume, in which Israel as a people is accused of persecuting God's prophets in the past and now of rejecting Jesus, "the Righteous One" (Ac 7:51–52). Significantly, these accusations are also made within the discussion of their disobedience of the law of God (cf. Ac 7:53).

NOTES

19–31 Over the years, some commentators have held that this is not a parable but a story about two men possibly known to Jesus' audience (cf. R. Summers, *Commentary on Luke* [Waco, Tex.: Word, 1972], 195). The usual reasons for supporting this interpretation are (1) the story lacks an introduction similar to the introductions to most of Jesus' parables and (2) at least one of the characters is named. At the other extreme is the view that follows a study by Hugo Gressmann (see Creed, 209–10) and assumes that the story originated in Egyptian folklore. A more recent structural approach is more concerned with the structure and contemporary symbolism of the story itself than with any extended history of tradition.

As indicated in the Overview (p. 263), to interpret the story literally introduces the difficult anachronism that the man is already being tormented by fire, even though the event of Revelation 20:14 has not yet taken place. The story can be understood as a parable that realistically portrays the fate of those who have rejected the Lord. If Luke had clearly indicated that Jesus was referring to an actual event, he would have to attempt to resolve the anachronism. But since Luke has not done so, and since the story is powerfully didactic, it seems best to interpret it as a parable. However, it is no mere story chosen for its usefulness as an illustration but rather a sober portrayal of yet unseen realities.

The expositor will do best by expounding this passage in its Lukan context, stressing those elements clearly affirmed in biblical teaching elsewhere. Issues of source or of background are not as important here as are its immediate purpose and message.

19 The vagueness of ἄνθρωπος . . . τις (*anthrōpos . . . tis*, lit., "a certain man") was intolerable for early readers, and some early "improvements" were made, such as the insertion of the name Νευης (*Neuēs*) in 𝔓75 (see Creed, 211; Marshall, 631–35).

7. Sin, Faith, Duty (17:1–10)

OVERVIEW

As the heading indicates, this unit contains various brief teachings. As with other parts in this special section of Luke, it is difficult to understand why these teachings are brought together. The introductory words, "Jesus said to his disciples," are similar to those in other places where there apparently is no attempt to establish a chronological sequence (e.g., 12:22, 54; 13:6; 16:1). This does not rule out the possibility that the parables in these instances were originally given sequentially, but they could be understood as merely marking a break from the preceding section. Yet it is also possible to see a logical connection between the end of ch. 16 and the beginning of ch. 17, if we understand the "things that cause people to sin" (v.1) to be the sins of the Pharisees, such as those mentioned in 16:14.

Some may feel that logical connections within this passage are difficult to discern, e.g., between vv.4 and 5. However, there is a common unifying theme of attitudes in the Christian community. The connections are no weaker than those that join similar teachings in Matthew 18 about care for the little ones, the problem of sin in the community, and prayer. Actually, though we expect to find material in topical rather than chronological order in Matthew (in contrast to most of Luke), in Matthew 18 the pericopae are joined by chronological indicators, while those in Luke are not. The contexts of the two passages are totally different, and here in Luke the teachings on prayer are not parallel to those on prayer in Matthew 18 but rather to those in Matthew 17:19–20 and 21:21–22. Here, as throughout the Synoptics, each gospel must be studied and interpreted in its own context.

¹Jesus said to his disciples: "Things that cause people to sin are bound to come, but woe to that person through whom they come. ²It would be better for him to be thrown into the sea with a millstone tied around his neck than for him to cause one of these little ones to sin. ³So watch yourselves.

"If your brother sins, rebuke him, and if he repents, forgive him. ⁴If he sins against you seven times in a day, and seven times comes back to you and says, 'I repent,' forgive him."

⁵The apostles said to the Lord, "Increase our faith!"

⁶He replied, "If you have faith as small as a mustard seed, you can say to this mulberry tree, 'Be uprooted and planted in the sea,' and it will obey you.

⁷"Suppose one of you had a servant plowing or looking after the sheep. Would he say to the servant when he comes in from the field, 'Come along now and sit down to eat'? ⁸Would he not rather say, 'Prepare my supper, get yourself ready and wait on me while I eat and drink; after that you may eat and drink'? ⁹Would he thank the servant because he did what he was told to do? ¹⁰So you also, when you have done everything you were told to do, should say, 'We are unworthy servants; we have only done our duty.'"

COMMENTARY

1 Jesus has been addressing the Pharisees since 16:14. Now he resumes his conversation with the disciples. The "things that cause people to sin" are the familiar *skandala* (GK *4998*; lit., "traps," but symbolically whatever causes people to fall into sin). "Woe" recalls 6:24–26.

2 A "millstone" was a stone of sufficient weight to grind grain as it was being rotated in a mill. The "little ones" would seem to be either young or new believers or people the world takes little notice of. There is no mention here of children (as in Mt 18:1–6). There is no antecedent for "these." So if the conversation stands alone, it must be taken to refer to those who were actually standing there with Jesus.

3a In the paragraph structure of the NIV, v.3a— "so watch yourselves"—is joined with the preceding saying rather than with the following (cf. RSV, NASB). Either way makes sense.

3b–4 The two members of v.3b must be given equal weight. Rebuke of the sinner and forgiveness of the penitent are both Christian duties. Verse 4 does not, of course, establish a specific number of times for forgiveness but rather shows the principle of being generous in forgiving others (cf. Mt 6:12). The number seven is merely a way to talk about the high frequency of acts of sinning and of requests for forgiveness (cf. Ps 119:164; see Bock, 2:1389). This is the only right response for those who have themselves been forgiven. The significance of the relationship among believers/disciples as a way to please God is emphasized in these sayings of Jesus.

5–6 The apostles may have felt that this kind of forgiveness would demand more faith than they had (v.5). The "mulberry tree" (v.6) in Luke corresponds to the mountain in Matthew 17:20; 21:21; and Mark 11:23. In each instance, the object is to be disposed of in the "sea" (probably Galilee). The black "mulberry tree" (KJV, "sycamine," not to be confused with "sycamore") grew quite large, to a height of some thirty-five feet, and would be difficult to uproot. The "mustard seed" is proverbially small and so serves as a suitable metaphor for the amount of faith needed to do the seemingly impossible. Jesus' answer to the request for additional faith seems to be that they should use the faith they had to petition God.

7–10 This is one of the passages in which Luke presents Jesus' teaching about the ideal of servanthood, perhaps in reaction to the Pharisees and the Jewish leadership in general that are portrayed as those who are inconstantly craving for honor and wealth. The world's idea of success is to lord it over others; Jesus' way is the reverse—namely, servanthood—which is actually the way to true greatness.

Two earlier parables on this theme occur in 12:35–37, 42–48. The circumstances Jesus describes here were normal in that society and the point obvious (see Notes). In contrast, in the parable in 12:35–37 Jesus presented a reversal of the normal procedure, with the master as doing just what 17:7 rules out. The master's extraordinary act depicted in 12:35–37 symbolizes God's grace, while the normal expectation of the master here in Luke 17 symbolizes the proper attitude of a servant. Jesus did not intend to demean servants but to make their duty clear. In this respect, the NIV's translation "unworthy" for *achreioi* (GK *945*, v.10) is an improvement over the KJV's "unprofitable."

NOTES

6 The exact significance of the metaphor of the "uprooted tree" is unclear. J. D. M. Derrett, ("Moving Mountains and Uprooting Trees," *Biblica et orientalia* 30 [1988]: 231–44), has suggested that it refers to the uprooting of the old Israel with the implied implanting of a new Israel. In the light of its immediate context and the presence of the different types of metaphors in these few verses, the presence of such allegorical references is doubtful. Moreover, the image of planting a tree in the sea is apparently meant to shock and to illustrate the striking power of faith.

9 Green, 614, has rightly pointed out that in this context "'thanks' would not refer to a verbal expression of gratitude or social politeness, but to placing the master in debt to the slave" (cf. G. W. Peterman, "'Thankless Thanks': The Epistolary Social Convention in Philippians 4:10–20," *TynBul* 42 [1991]: 261–70). In the social world of the first century, the refusal of the master to say thanks will not be interpreted as an act of rudeness. For more on the role of gratitude in the Greco-Roman system of benefaction, see David W. Pao, *Thanksgiving: An Investigation of a Pauline Theme* (Downers Grove, Ill.: InterVarsity, 2002), 165–70.

8. Ten Healed of Leprosy (17:11–19)

OVERVIEW

Not only is this narrative peculiar to Luke, but it also stresses several characteristically Lukan themes: Jerusalem is the goal of Jesus' journey (cf. 9:51; 13:33); Jesus has mercy on social outcasts; he conforms to Jewish norms by requiring that the lepers go for the required priestly declaration of health (cf. Lev 14); faith and healing should bring praise to God (cf. 18:43; Ac 3:8–9); and the grace of God extends beyond Judaism, with Samaritans receiving special attention (cf. 10:25–37). In its narrative context, this story illustrates Jesus as the Coming One, and the healing of the lepers recalls his response to the disciples of John the Baptist (7:22). The theme of gratitude also links this story with the immediately preceding verses that comment on duty and indebtedness.

This passage also recalls similar OT stories of healing. The parallels with the story of Naaman (2Ki 5:1–19) in particular cannot be missed. In both stories one finds references to leprosy and Samaria/

Samaritan, and both Naaman and the Samaritan acknowledge the work of the prophet of Israel (for other parallels, see Doble, 45). These parallels are further supported by Jesus' explicit reference to Elisha's healing of Naaman in his paradigmatic speech in the synagogue in Nazareth (Lk 4:27). The evocation of the same story in Luke 17 points again to the reception of the foreigners as Israel's response to God's prophet is less favorable (cf. 4:23–24).

> ¹¹Now on his way to Jerusalem, Jesus traveled along the border between Samaria and Galilee. ¹²As he was going into a village, ten men who had leprosy met him. They stood at a distance ¹³and called out in a loud voice, "Jesus, Master, have pity on us!"
>
> ¹⁴When he saw them, he said, "Go, show yourselves to the priests." And as they went, they were cleansed.
>
> ¹⁵One of them, when he saw he was healed, came back, praising God in a loud voice. ¹⁶He threw himself at Jesus' feet and thanked him—and he was a Samaritan.
>
> ¹⁷Jesus asked, "Were not all ten cleansed? Where are the other nine? ¹⁸Was no one found to return and give praise to God except this foreigner?" ¹⁹Then he said to him, "Rise and go; your faith has made you well."

COMMENTARY

11–13 That Luke does not mention the particular place where the healing was done implies that he did not consider the exact locale important historically or theologically. What is important is the reminder (possibly to indicate a new phase of his ministry) of Jesus' progress toward Jerusalem. The "village" (v.12) lies somewhere in the border territory between Galilee and Samaria (see Notes); so Jewish and Samaritan lepers share their common misery at its edge. The lepers maintain their proper distance, call Jesus by a term found only in Luke— "Master" (*epistata*, GK *2181*, v.13; cf. 5:5)—and ask only for pity without specifying their request.

14–19 Jesus' command (v.14) required obedi-

ence based on some faith in the reliability of the speaker (cf. Mt 12:13; Mk 3:5; Lk 6:10). On their way to the priests, the lepers are "cleansed" (*ekatharisthēsan*, GK *2751*). Jesus, however, uses the more comprehensive word "made well" (*sesōken*, GK *5392*, v.19) in speaking to the Samaritan who returned to give thanks. Though Luke does not say whether the others had faith, it need not be denied them. The stress is on the openly expressed gratitude of the Samaritan, who alone brought praise to God (vv.15–16; see Notes).

The concern with the proper object of worship is also present in this passage. As in the Johannine account of Jesus' encounter with the Samaritans (Jn

4:1–42), one finds references to the cult. Instead of simply going to the "priests" (v.14), the Samaritans recognize that the proper object of worship is the person Jesus. D. Hamm ("What the Samaritan Leper Sees: The Narrative Christology of Luke 17:11–19," *CBQ* 56 [1994]: 286) further notes the significance of the word "foreigner" (*allogenēs*, GK *254*) in v.18.

This word appears nowhere else in the NT, but it does appear in the famous inscription that warns Gentiles from entering the temple proper. In Luke 17, Jesus' ironic reference to the foreigner who finds the proper place of worship redefines the community that is called to participate in the worship of the one true God.

NOTES

11 The phrase διὰ μέσον (*dia meson*, "along the border between") is troublesome. This accusative is well attested, but the Byzantine tradition has the genitive μέσου (*mesou*; KJV, "through the midst"). Conzelmann, 68–72, considered this a theological use of geography, with Luke trying to establish a travel theme based on an allegedly distorted view of the geographical relationship of Samaria to Galilee. On Conzelmann's assumption, Luke thought that Judea was directly south of Galilee, with Samaria alongside both. On this view, Jesus was going south along this supposed north–south border. Actually, Luke does not state that Jesus made just one journey from north to south but rather suggests that he crisscrossed the area, making perhaps several trips to Jerusalem before his final stay there. In this case he might have been on his way east to Perea to turn south on the highway along the east side of the Jordan River.

This ambiguous reference may also be intentional, as Luke emphasizes the transitional nature of this period. This serves as a contrast to the clear reference to Jerusalem as the destination of his journey (cf. John T. Carroll, "Luke 17:11–19," *Int* 53 [1999]: 405).

15–16 The verbs δοξάζω (*doxazō*, "to praise," GK *1519*) and εὐχαριστέω (*eucharisteō*, "to thank," GK *2373*) in these two verses can be considered rough synonyms. In the NT, God is almost always the object of thanksgiving, and to give thanks to God is to acknowledge him to be the ultimate source of goodness (i.e., the Creator). To glorify God is likewise to confess his mighty acts in history. When both are applied to the Deity, the distinction that exists in everyday discourse dissipates (cf. Robert J. Ledogar, *Acknowledgment: Praise-verbs in the Early Greek Anaphora* [Roma: Herder, 1967]).

9. The Coming of the Kingdom of God (17:20–37)

OVERVIEW

Luke contains two major discourses about the future—the present passage and 21:5–33. Both have close parallels in Matthew 24 and Mark 13. (See comments at 21:5–33 for the interpretive and critical issues involved in a comparison with these parallels.) Luke 17 is more uniformly apocalyptic than Luke 21—i.e., no human agency appears here (in contrast to the besieging armies of 21:20); God acts directly from heaven. Also the prohibition against lingering is stronger here than in ch. 21. People on the rooftop when the Son of Man is revealed dare not take a moment to go inside their houses. But those addressed in ch. 21 are threatened by a military siege and should avoid getting caught in the city. The urgency in ch. 17 is greater, with less time to spare than in ch. 21.

---

²⁰Once, having been asked by the Pharisees when the kingdom of God would come, Jesus replied, "The kingdom of God does not come with your careful observation, ²¹nor will people say, 'Here it is,' or 'There it is,' because the kingdom of God is within you."

²²Then he said to his disciples, "The time is coming when you will long to see one of the days of the Son of Man, but you will not see it. ²³Men will tell you, 'There he is!' or 'Here he is!' Do not go running off after them. ²⁴For the Son of Man in his day will be like the lightning, which flashes and lights up the sky from one end to the other. ²⁵But first he must suffer many things and be rejected by this generation.

²⁶"Just as it was in the days of Noah, so also will it be in the days of the Son of Man. ²⁷People were eating, drinking, marrying and being given in marriage up to the day Noah entered the ark. Then the flood came and destroyed them all.

²⁸"It was the same in the days of Lot. People were eating and drinking, buying and selling, planting and building. ²⁹But the day Lot left Sodom, fire and sulfur rained down from heaven and destroyed them all.

³⁰"It will be just like this on the day the Son of Man is revealed. ³¹On that day no one who is on the roof of his house, with his goods inside, should go down to get them. Likewise, no one in the field should go back for anything. ³²Remember Lot's wife! ³³Whoever tries to keep his life will lose it, and whoever loses his life will preserve it. ³⁴I tell you, on that night two people will be in one bed; one will be taken and the other left. ³⁵Two women will be grinding grain together; one will be taken and the other left."

³⁷"Where, Lord?" they asked.

He replied, "Where there is a dead body, there the vultures will gather."

COMMENTARY

20 The Pharisees' question about the kingdom here initiates this new cycle of Jesus' teachings, which includes (1) a saying about the coming of the kingdom that is unique to Luke's gospel (vv.20–21), (2) the discourse on the coming of the Son of Man (vv.22–37), and (3) a parable of encouragement for those who wait for vindication when the Son of Man comes (18:1–8).

The time of the coming of the kingdom was important to both Pharisees and Christians, though for different reasons. By the time Luke was written, rumors were abroad that the day of the Lord had already come (2Th 2:1–2). Later, others would question whether the Lord would return at all (2Pe 3:3–4). Before this point in Luke, Jesus had made it clear that the kingdom had already come insofar as God's power was unleashed against demons (11:20). Jesus will shortly indicate by a parable that the full expression of the kingdom does not take place in the immediate future (19:11–27). The present passage is important as a further definition of the nature of the kingdom.

To the question "When?" (cf. v.37, "Where?"), Jesus says that the kingdom will not come *meta paratēreseōs* (lit., "with observation"). This may have one of three meanings, none of them excluding the others: (1) it cannot be foreseen from signs; (2) it is not an observable process; and (3) it does not come with or through the observing of rites. The second meaning accords most naturally with the most common usage of *paratērēsis* (GK *4191*) and with the context, which emphasizes suddenness, though the first meaning may fit the Pharisees' frame of reference better (see Notes).

21 The NIV's "within you" (*entos hymōn*) is a questionable translation, though it is the one preferred by the early fathers (cf. T. Holmen, "The Alternatives of the Kingdom: Encountering the Semantic Restrictions of Luke 17:20–21 [ἐντὸς ὑμῶν]," *ZNW* 87 [1996]: 204–29). Jesus would hardly tell Pharisees, most of whom (especially those who interrogated him) were unbelievers, that the kingdom was within them (cf. Marshall, 655, who considers the word "you" to be indefinite, though he also rejects the translation "within"). The NIV's text note ("among you") is surely right. The focus is on neither time nor location, however, but on the person of Jesus himself. With the life and ministry of Jesus, one can experience the kingdom of God.

Luke's presentation of the kingdom in Jesus' teaching is dynamic rather than psychological, as seen in 11:20: "But if I drive out demons by the finger of God, then the kingdom of God has come to you." The idea behind "'Here it is,' or 'There it is'" is that of the kingdom's authoritative presence. Jesus is thus saying that people are the subjects, not the timekeepers, of God's kingdom. Whether he means here that the kingdom is already present (which was true, in the sense of 11:20), or whether he used the present "is" in a vivid futuristic sense, he is emphasizing its suddenness.

22–25 In this paragraph, which begins with a saying not found in Matthew or Mark, Jesus continues the emphasis on the suddenness of the kingdom's coming. Does "one of the days" (v.22) refer back to the time of his earthly ministry or forward to his return? Does "one" mean any "one" or "the first" of a series as in Matthew 28:1 and parallels? Since Jesus now addresses his disciples, who will have reason to long for his return, and since what follows deals with that return, "one of the days" probably refers to the initiation of the reign of the coming Son of Man (see Notes). "You will not see it" implies "not yet" rather than "never." His coming will be obvious, "like the lightning" (v.24); so rumors of seeing him in various places ("here," "there," vv.21, 23) cannot be true. (For Jesus' use of the plural "days" [v.22] and the third person as referring to the Son of Man [e.g., "in his day"] and the combination of these with the passion prediction in v.25, see Notes.)

The inclusion of the passion prediction (v.25) is natural in Luke, who stresses the order of suffering before glory (cf. 24:26, 46; Ac 17:3). "This generation" may obliquely refer back to the Pharisees. Broadly it refers to Jesus' contemporaries, elsewhere called by him "unbelieving and perverse" (9:41) and "wicked" (11:29; cf. 11:31–32, 50–51).

26–29 Jesus' references to Noah (vv.26–27) and Lot (v.28) serve to illustrate the suddenness of the revelation of the Son of Man. The words "eating, drinking," etc. (vv.27–28), describe the usual round of life's activities. The NIV accurately represents the Greek use of asyndeton (a sequence of words without connectives such as "and"). This effectively gives the impression of continually repeated activities. Unexpected destruction came as a judgment on people in the times of Noah and Lot. God's sudden interruption of human affairs is part of the apocalyptic perspective on the divine ordering of history. The term "apocalyptic" (from the Greek *apokalyptō*, "reveal," GK *636*) occurs in v.30: "the Son of Man is revealed" (*apokalyptetai*). The consummation of history—indeed, of the kingdom of God itself—is realized in the revelation of the Son of Man.

30–33 As already noted, unlike the siege of Jerusalem described in ch. 21, the sudden coming of the Son of Man (v.30) leaves no time even for a quick gathering of possessions from one's home (v.31). This theme of imminence blends into a call reminiscent of ch. 12 for decision between eternal values and present possessions. The reason for returning to house or field is to salvage possessions. Lot's wife (v.32), reluctant to leave her old life, looked back to Sodom (Ge 19:26). This leads to the saying in v.33 (used elsewhere in an ethical sense) regarding discipleship (cf. Mt 10:39) but employed here with a very concrete application. Unlike 9:24, the motive here is not specified, but both verses share the common assumption: one should not be preoccupied by one's present life (i.e., possessions and circumstances) in making the decisive choice in the presence of eschatological reality.

34–36 The solemn words "I tell you" (v.34) introduce a warning that the apocalyptic moment reveals ultimate destinies. Even those closely associated (in bed and at work) are separated. "Will be taken" (*paralēmphthēsetai*, GK *4161*, vv.34–35) probably has its normal sense of being taken into fellowship (in Noah's case, into safety), rather than being taken into judgment, for which there seems to be no precedent (cf. *TDNT* 4:11–14). The one "left" (*aphethēsetai*) is thereby abandoned to judgment. The alternative interpretation, however, is possible in this context. The two illustrations reflect either simultaneous activities early in the morning (Danker, 183) or, more likely, activities selected to show that the Son of Man could come at any time, day or night.

37 The Pharisees had asked "When?" (v.20); the disciples asked "Where?" Jesus' reply seems somewhat obscure to us. The hovering "vultures" (*aetoi*, GK *108*; usually translated "eagles" but here probably meaning scavengers such as vultures [BDAG, 22]) may symbolize judgment on the spiritually dead, or they may merely represent the place of carnage. In line with the discussion above, this entire verse may also point to the inevitability of the coming of the time of judgment (cf. Fitzmyer, 1173).

NOTES

20 The word παρατήρησις (*paratērēsis*, "careful observation," GK *4191*) can also be understood more narrowly as referring to astronomical observation (cf. Carroll, 75). This will also fit the context in which signs of the sky are noted (v.24). This narrower definition can have a wider application as it refers to observable signs in general and any human attempt to locate temporally the fulfillment of God's kingdom.

21 The phrase ἐντὸς ὑμῶν (*entos hymōn*, "within you") can also mean "in your control," according to an exegetical note by C. H. Roberts ("ἐντὸς ὑμῶν," *HTR* 41 [1948]: 1–8). This would not mean that the Pharisees controlled the kingdom but that response to it was under their control. C. F. D. Moule (*An Idiom Book of New Testament Greek* [Cambridge: Cambridge Univ. Press, 1959], 83–84) provides evidence against this view.

22 The phrase μίαν τῶν ἡμερῶν (*mian tōn hēmerōn*, "one of the days") seems to combine both the singular "day" (vv.24, 30) and the plural "days" (vv.26, 28). It seems to be an echo of the "day of the Lord"—

a term denoting the occasion on which God acts mightily in history, especially the inception of the messianic age. A parallel in which both singular and plural are used with the same point of reference is Amos 8:11, 13.

24 The phrase ἐν τῇ ἡμέρα αὐτοῦ (*en tē hēmera autou*, "in his day") sharpens, by its use of the third instead of the first person, the issue as to whether Jesus spoke of himself in such sayings. A common conclusion of recent studies on the "Son of Man" is that the sayings using this designation may be grouped into those that use the phrase as a neutral (or covert) reference to the speaker, those that refer to the expected suffering of Jesus, and those that refer to the future glory of the Son of Man. Some claim that the future (apocalyptic) sayings of Jesus refer to someone else, not to him. Jeremias (*New Testament Theology*, 276), however, correctly observes that "quite apart from the absence of evidence in the sources, it is impossible that in the 'Son of Man' Jesus should have seen a future saving figure who was to be distinguished from himself. In that case, one would have to suppose that Jesus had seen himself as a forerunner, as the prophet of the Son of Man." Jesus undoubtedly saw himself, not some others, as the one who fulfilled the OT prophecies. The use of the third person is common in all three types of Son-of-Man sayings. (For a fuller bibliography, see Notes, 5:24). Both the suffering and the apocalyptic types of sayings are found in this passage (vv.24–25).

Regarding the textual evidence for "in his day," a variety of significant MSS omit it (e.g., 𝔓⁷⁵ B D). The omission could have been accidental, if a copyist's eyes mistakenly jumped from the ending of "man" (-πoυ, *pou*) to the ending of "his" (-τoυ, *tou*), the last word of the Greek phrase in question. However, the MSS cited are probably correct.

34 In the OT, the phrase "on that night" appears twice (out of a total of three occurrences) in reference to the Passover night (Ex 12:8, 12 [LXX]). Some have suggested that the "leaving behind" metaphor points further to the deliverance of the Israelites while leaving behind the Egyptians (so J. D. M. Derrett, "'On That Night,' Luke 17:34," *EvQ* 68 [1996]: 35–46). The pervasiveness of references to Passover in Luke encourages one to read Luke in the light of the foundation story of Israel, but the absence of the correspondence of details makes this reading improbable.

10. Parable of the Persistent Widow (18:1–8)

OVERVIEW

On the surface, this parable is comparable to the parable of the friend who asked for bread in the middle of the night. In this context, however, the concern is with the end of time. The disciples are called to remain steadfast as they anticipate the return of the Son of Man. Verse 8 serves, therefore, as an appropriate conclusion to the parable.

> ¹Then Jesus told his disciples a parable to show them that they should always pray and not give up. ²He said: "In a certain town there was a judge who neither feared God nor cared about men. ³And there was a widow in that town who kept coming to him with the plea, 'Grant me justice against my adversary.'

4"For some time he refused. But finally he said to himself, 'Even though I don't fear God or care about men, 5yet because this widow keeps bothering me, I will see that she gets justice, so that she won't eventually wear me out with her coming!'"

6And the Lord said, "Listen to what the unjust judge says. 7And will not God bring about justice for his chosen ones, who cry out to him day and night? Will he keep putting them off? 8I tell you, he will see that they get justice, and quickly. However, when the Son of Man comes, will he find faith on the earth?"

COMMENTARY

1 This parable begins with a note on prayer but must be interpreted with reference to the eschatological theme in ch. 17. The story is not intended to apply to prayer in general, as though one needed to pester God for every need until he reluctantly responds. The theme is that of the vindication of God's misunderstood and suffering people, as v.7 states. God's people in OT days needed to wait on God as he worked out justice with apparent slowness. "Do not . . . let my enemies triumph over me. No one whose hope is in you will ever be put to shame" (Ps 25:2–3). In the final days the martyrs wait for vindication (Rev 6:9–11). Ultimately, delay is ended and the "mystery" of God completed (Rev 10:6–7). Meanwhile we wrestle with the problem of evil and with issues of theodicy. Under these circumstances we should "always pray and not give up."

2–3 The designation "unjust judge" (*ho kritēs tēs adikias*, v.6) is similar to the idiom in 16:8, "the dishonest manager" (*ton oikonomon tēs adikias*). *Adikia* ("injustice" or "dishonesty," GK *94*) also appears in connection with wealth in the Greek of 16:9, where it has the connotation of "worldly" (cf. 16:11); therefore, we should probably understand the "judge" (v.2) to be a "man of the world," who, though crooked, prided himself on shrewd judicial decisions. The judge is typical of a local Gentile judge known throughout the Hellenistic world (cf.

Danker, 184). J. D. M. Derrett ("Law in the New Testament: The Unjust Judge," *NTS* 18 [1971–72]: 179–91) suggests that as a local secular administrative officer he would be approached by those who could not bring their cases to the high religious court. Being easily accessible and having the authority to make quick decisions, he would naturally be besieged by people such as the widow of the story.

5 The words "wear me out" (*hypōpiazē me*, GK *5708*, v.5) are difficult to translate, for they literally mean "strike under the eye," "give a black eye to" (BDAG, 1043). Commentators usually give them a figurative meaning. Derrett ("Law in the New Testament," 191) shows that they are common idiom in Eastern countries, where to have one's face blackened means to suffer shame. Probably we can also compare our American idiom "to give a black eye to," meaning "to damage one's reputation." If this is so, the story may be compared to that of the friend at midnight, where, if Bailey (*Poet and Peasant*, 125–33) is correct, the friend responds to his friend's request for fear of public shame (see comments at 11:5–13). In each parable, the reputation of the one being petitioned is at stake. Therefore, though God is not compared to a crooked judge, there is a partial basis of comparison in that God will also guard his reputation and vindicate himself.

7 "Chosen ones" (*eklektōn*, GK *1723*) is a term used throughout Scripture that is especially significant in describing those who, at the end of history, are marked out as on the victorious side (Mt 24:31; Mk 13:27; Rev 17:14). To call the disciples of Jesus the "chosen ones" is also significant when the election language of the OT is now applied to those who are included in God's kingdom. "Will he keep putting them off?" (*kai makrothymei* [GK *3428*] *ep' autois*) is one of several possible translations of these words (see Notes). The point of the verse is that God patiently listens to his elect as they pray in their continuing distress and waits for the proper time to act on their behalf. This theme is clearly present in early Christian eschatological discussions (see, e.g., Ugo Vanni, "The Apocalypse and the Gospel of Luke," in *Luke and Acts* [ed. O'Collins and Marconi], 14–15).

8 Help is on the way, and the delay will prove shorter than it seems from our perspective (see Notes). The noun "faith" (*tēn pistin*, GK *4411*) is probably to be understood here in relation to its content or quality. True believers who still wait with patient trust will seem few when the Son of Man comes (cf. vv.24–25). This may reflect the theme of perseverance that S. Brown, 45–46, sees as characteristic of Luke.

NOTES

2–8 For a representative of the older interpretation of the parable that both minimizes the eschatological reference and assumes a strong contrast between God and the judge, see Benjamin B. Warfield, "The Importunate Widow and the Alleged Failure of Faith," *ExpTim* 25 (1913–14): 69–72, 137–39. For a helpful treatment of the apocalyptic elements, see F. Bovon, "Apocalyptic Traditions in the Lukan Special Material: Reading Luke 18:1–8," *HTR* 90 (1997): 383–91, who points further to the parallels between Luke 18 and 21.

7 The question καὶ μακροθυμεῖ ἐπ᾽ αὐτοῖς (*kai makrothymei ep' autois*, "will he keep putting them off?") is very difficult to exegete. The difficulty is both lexical and syntactical. Does the verb mean to "delay," "put off," or "be patient"? What is the relationship of ἐπ᾽ αὐτοῖς, *ep' autois*, to the verb? Does the question anticipate a positive answer or, like the preceding question, a negative one? If the verb means "be patient," if ἐπ᾽ αὐτοῖς, *ep' autois*, is taken with it to mean "with them" (as in Mt 18:29; Jas 5:7), and if it calls for a positive response, the meaning is, "He will also be patient with them, won't he?" For a thorough discussion of a number of possibilities, see Marshall, 674–75.

8 "Speedily" is a translation of ἐν τάχει (*en tachei*; NIV, "quickly"), which assumes v.7 means that God will not delay his act of vindication. Others think "suddenly" is the meaning here, since a period of time has intervened (recognized especially in Luke). The other uses of this word in NT eschatological discourses favor the former interpretation. A similar expression, ταχύ (*tachy*), occurs in Revelation 22:20. The prophetic scroll is not to be sealed (cf. Da 12:4, 9), for the time of fulfillment is near (Rev 22:10).

11. Parable of the Pharisee and the Tax Collector (18:9–14)

OVERVIEW

Danker, 185, observes that whereas Paul "discusses the *process* of justification . . . Luke describes the nature of the recipients of God's verdict of approval" (emphasis his). This is true throughout

Luke's gospel, but it is in this story of "the Churchman and the Politician" (Ellis, 214) that we see the characteristics of recipients and rejecters most sharply defined. The Pharisee shows the attitude of pride and self-vindication alluded to in Matthew 23:5–7; Mark 7:6; and Philippians 3:4–6. The implication of his words is a contractual relationship with God whereby he would accept the Pharisee's merit in exchange for justification. Actually, not only this parable but also the two following stories (vv.15–17, 18–30) deal with conditions for entering the kingdom. Each stresses human inability.

In clarifying the means through which an individual can be justified, Luke again focuses on the theme of reversal. The one who had been rejected may now enter the community—a community defined not by one's ability and status but by one's relationship with the Messiah. J. H. Elliott ("Temple versus Household in Luke–Acts: A Contrast in Social Institutions," in *The Social World of Luke–Acts* [ed. Neyrey], 213) has further noted that this theme of reversal is established by three pairs of contrasts: the actors and their actions, the content of their prayers, and the locations. All three are important in this parable as well as throughout Luke's narrative.

> ⁹To some who were confident of their own righteousness and looked down on everybody else, Jesus told this parable: ¹⁰"Two men went up to the temple to pray, one a Pharisee and the other a tax collector. ¹¹The Pharisee stood up and prayed about himself: 'God, I thank you that I am not like other men—robbers, evildoers, adulterers—or even like this tax collector. ¹²I fast twice a week and give a tenth of all I get.'
>
> ¹³"But the tax collector stood at a distance. He would not even look up to heaven, but beat his breast and said, 'God, have mercy on me, a sinner.'
>
> ¹⁴"I tell you that this man, rather than the other, went home justified before God. For everyone who exalts himself will be humbled, and he who humbles himself will be exalted."

COMMENTARY

9–10 Luke does not say at whom the parable was directed (v.9) but rather describes the two men (v.10) so that the parable can be understood by his readers. The characters represent extremes, but the sketches are true to life. The audience is described as both "righteous" and "looking down on" others. This striking combination of terms reveals Jesus' own view of their claims to righteousness.

11–12 The Pharisee follows custom in praying in the temple and standing while praying. His prayer expresses the essence of Pharisaism—separation from others. This in itself was not reprehensible, because at the inception of Pharisaism there was a need for a distinctive group who would maintain a piety that stood in contrast to the encroaching pagan Hellenism. This initial good hardened into obnoxious self-righteousness on the part of many (not all) Pharisees, as seen not only in Matthew 23 and Mark 7 but in Jewish literature as well. Luke has noted the Pharisees' hostility thus far (cf. 5:17; 6:2, 7; 7:39; 11:37–54; 15:2; 16:14). Pharisees did tithe (v.12)—even their herbs (11:42). They did fast, and the practice of fasting twice a week can be traced back to the second century BC, when the identity of Israel as a people was at stake (cf. F. Bohl, "Das Fasten an Montagen und Donnerstagen," *BZ* 31 [1987]: 247–50). The problem was that this Pharisee's prayer was a farce, being created only in himself (notice the sarcastic phrase "about himself" [v.11] and the mention of God only at the beginning of his prayer).

13–14 The description speaks for itself. The tax collector, generally thought of as a greedy politician whose very business depended on knuckling under to the despised Roman government, was one of the social outcasts so prominent in Luke as recipients of God's grace (e.g., 5:12, 27; 7:34, 37; 15:1–2; 16:20). His justification was immediate (v.14) and granted by God in contrast to the fantasy of self-justification the Pharisee was futilely caught up in. Verse 14b states the principle that is further illustrated in vv.15–17.

NOTES

12 The prayer of the Pharisees that lists the good deeds accomplished by the one coming into the presence of God may reflect the liturgical practices that were based on OT prescriptions (cf. F. C. Holmgren, "The Pharisee and the Tax Collector: Luke 18:9–14 and Deuteronomy 26:1–15," *Int* 48 [1994]: 252–61). In this Lukan context, however, there is no doubt that such prayers are understood as boastful acts.

REFLECTIONS

The modern reader will probably not feel the impact of this story to the extent that a first-century reader would have. We already think of the Pharisees as hypocrites and the tax collectors as those who received the grace of God. Jesus' original hearers would have thought, on the contrary, that it was the pious Pharisee who deserved acceptance by God. Noteworthy is the emphasis Luke is placing on the theme of reversal. In light of the use of this theme elsewhere, the Pharisees may again represent the Jewish leadership in general, while the tax collectors symbolize the outcasts excluded from worshiping with those who were considered "pure."

12. The Little Children and Jesus (18:15–17)

OVERVIEW

Luke's special section has now reached its conclusion. With v.15 the narrative rejoins that of Matthew (19:13) and Mark (10:13). Jesus' words about little children provide Luke's second example of the attitude essential for receiving God's grace. In its placement in this gospel, this passage not only further explores the theme of reversal (cf. vv.13–14), but it also introduces the stories that follow, in which various characters are portrayed as either having or lacking this childlike faith. S. Fowl ("Receiving the Kingdom of God as a Child," *NTS* 39 [1993]: 153–58) has included as exemplary characters the rich ruler (18:18–25), the disciples (18:26–30), the blind man (18:35–43), and Zacchaeus (19:1–10).

> ¹⁵People were also bringing babies to Jesus to have him touch them. When the disciples saw this, they rebuked them. ¹⁶But Jesus called the children to him and said, "Let the little children come to me, and do not hinder them, for the kingdom of God belongs to such as these. ¹⁷I tell you the truth, anyone who will not receive the kingdom of God like a little child will never enter it."

COMMENTARY

15–16 It is not age per se that is in view but childlike qualities such as trust, openness, and the absence of holier-than-thou attitudes; therefore, this passage does not directly bear on the question of infant baptism. Nevertheless, v.15 shows through the use of *brephē* ("babies," GK *1100*) that Jesus had compassion even on infants too young to understand the difference between right and wrong. The ones he invites in v.16 (*paidia*, "children," GK *4086*) to come to him include a broader age spread.

Only in recent years have we begun to understand the importance of communication through touching, though the instinct has always been present in those who care about other human beings. More relevant in this context is the fact that in ancient times the act of touching often symbolized inclusion and acceptance.

13. The Rich Ruler (18:18–30)

OVERVIEW

After the parable of the Pharisee and the tax collector and the incident of the little children, the story of the rich ruler illustrates once more the need for receptiveness if one is to experience God's grace. Then, lest it be thought that this response lies within human power, Jesus makes the point that it is only by the power of God that anyone is saved (vv.25–27). The story thus emphasizes both the responsibility and the helplessness of humankind.

> ¹⁸A certain ruler asked him, "Good teacher, what must I do to inherit eternal life?"
> ¹⁹"Why do you call me good?" Jesus answered. "No one is good—except God alone. ²⁰You know the commandments: 'Do not commit adultery, do not murder, do not steal, do not give false testimony, honor your father and mother.'"
> ²¹"All these I have kept since I was a boy," he said.
> ²²When Jesus heard this, he said to him, "You still lack one thing. Sell everything you have and give to the poor, and you will have treasure in heaven. Then come, follow me."

²³When he heard this, he became very sad, because he was a man of great wealth. ²⁴Jesus looked at him and said, "How hard it is for the rich to enter the kingdom of God! ²⁵Indeed, it is easier for a camel to go through the eye of a needle than for a rich man to enter the kingdom of God."

²⁶Those who heard this asked, "Who then can be saved?"

²⁷Jesus replied, "What is impossible with men is possible with God."

²⁸Peter said to him, "We have left all we had to follow you!"

²⁹"I tell you the truth," Jesus said to them, "no one who has left home or wife or brothers or parents or children for the sake of the kingdom of God ³⁰will fail to receive many times as much in this age and, in the age to come, eternal life."

COMMENTARY

18 "Ruler" (only in Luke) is too broad a term to permit precise identification of the man's background. In the light of references to such rulers/leaders elsewhere in Luke and Acts, he may be a member of the Jewish leadership who opposes Jesus (e.g., 14:1; 23:13, 35; 24:20; Ac 3:17; 13:27; cf. H. L. Egelkraut, *Jesus' Mission to Jerusalem* [Bern: Lang, 1976], 124) or a ruler of a synagogue (e.g., 8:41; Ac 13:15; cf. Thomas E. Phillips, "Subtlety as a Literary Technique in Luke's Characterization of Jews and Judaism," in *Literary Studies in Luke–Acts* [ed. Thompson and Phillips], 320). Only Matthew says that he was young (Mt 19:20). The appellation "good teacher" is not a common one and called for comment by Jesus. "What must I do?" indicates a desire to discover whether any deed has been overlooked in qualifying for eternal life. John 3:3–15 shows that eternal life is life in the kingdom and that it is received only through the new birth.

19 Jesus replies by asking the ruler a question that has puzzled many. Whatever its ultimate meaning, the question does not constitute a denial that he himself is good. Earlier commentators hold that he is subtly urging the ruler to see that if Jesus is good, and if only God is good, then there is a clear con-clusion to be drawn as to his true identity (cf. Ambrose, *Fid. Grat.* 2.1). Others point to the desire to have the ruler focus solely on God in the carrying out of the commandments (v.20–21; cf. Fitzmyer, 1199). In the light of v.18, where Jesus was addressed as "good" according to the standard of the ruler, Jesus may also be reacting to the value/status system of the ruler (cf. Green, 655). What is clear is that Jesus' purpose in this question is to establish a standard of goodness infinitely higher than the ruler supposes it to be. In other words, he brings us close to the principle in Matthew 5:20, 48.

20–21 Jesus now addresses this standard of righteousness. The first step is a summary of several of the Ten Commandments, omitting the first few that relate to God and the final one about covetousness. The translation of the word *neotēs* (GK *3744*) as "boy" may be misleading, and in this context it refers to the age of legal and moral maturity—most likely the early teens. The man, like Paul (Php 3:6), has kept the letter of the Law (v.21). The response should probably be understood primarily in legal terms, though the man may have defined moral and spiritual perfection in legal terms (cf. Mt 19:21).

22 Jesus now moves to the heart of the tenth commandment by leading the ruler to face his attitude toward his possessions (see Notes). Paul recognized his sinfulness when he became aware of the thrust of the command against covetousness (Ro 7:7–8). In Colossians 3:5 he said that greed "is idolatry." The ruler had broken the first commandment by breaking the last. Actually, in the act of giving away his goods he would have shown himself rid of that sin, and by following Jesus he would have indicated his allegiance to God. Luke's report of this part of the conversation ("you still lack one thing") corresponds to Matthew's "if you want to be perfect" (19:21), in the same way that Luke 6:36 ("be merciful") corresponds to Matthew 5:48 ("be perfect"). In each case, the record in Matthew speaks generally of righteousness, whereas that in Luke (and also Mark) concentrates on that which is yet needed in order to produce righteous perfection.

The command to "sell everything . . . and give to the poor" is difficult to interpret as well as to apply. It goes a step further than does 14:33, where Jesus says that whoever does not "give up" (*apotassetai*, GK 698) everything he has cannot be his disciple (see comments there). Here the ruler must not only surrender all rights to his possessions but must also actually dispose of them. This does not seem to be a universal requirement; it seems rather to be designed particularly for this man so as to shatter his covetousness. According to Jesus' teaching in 6:30–31, such an act would also benefit others; his wealth should be dispensed among poor people. Even this is insufficient, however, unless the ruler truly follows Jesus. The command "come, follow me" (*deuro, akolouthei moi*) means to become a disciple.

23–25 The ruler's sorrow (*perilypos*, GK 4337; only here in Luke; NIV, "very sad") over the decision about his wealth recalls the far deeper sorrow rich people who have incurred Jesus' "woe" will experience (6:24). Only Luke mentions that Jesus looked at the man as he spoke to him about the problem of wealth (v.24). This keeps the focus on the ruler even during the transition to the next dialogue. It also limits the application of v.24 to the kind of attitude the ruler had. The vivid hyperbole about the camel (v.25) makes the point unforgettable. Various alternative interpretations of this saying have been offered (cf. Fitzmyer, 1204–5), but these attempts inevitably take away its intended shock value. It is precisely the idea of "impossibility" that is conveyed here.

26–30 If wealth is such a hindrance with respect to salvation, the situation for the rich is hopeless, as the disciples realize (v.26). Jesus' reply about God's power (v.27) provides the assurance the audience needed and evokes an enthusiastic outburst from Peter (v.28), who feels that the disciples have done what the ruler did not do. Jesus acknowledges this by assuring disciples who have "left all to follow [him]" of abundant recompense, not only in the future age but also in the present (v.30). In v.29 Luke has "for the sake of the kingdom of God" instead of "for my [name's] sake" (Mt 19:29; Mk 10:29). This again identifies Jesus with the cause of God's kingdom and ties in with v.25. (In Matthew this is accomplished by an added saying [19:28].) Luke lacks the saying about the first and the last (Mt 19:30; Mk 10:31).

NOTES

18–29 Luke is following both the Markan sequence of events and, during the first part of this pericope, the Markan wording fairly closely (cf. Mt 19:16–30, which diverges significantly from Mk 10:17–31).

22 Phillips ("Subtlety as a Literary Technique," 321) has noted that the proper antecedent of ἕν (*hen*, "one thing") is τὰς ἐντολὰς (*tas entolas*, "the commandments"), even though the neuter form for εἷς (*heis*, "one") is used. If so, the tenth commandment is alluded to, as the saying that follows confirms.

24 It is possible, though doubtful, that the original Greek text of v.24 had the words περίλυπον γενόμενον (*perilypon genomenon*, "being sorrowful," referring to the ruler). Some Western and other texts have it; UBS[4] puts it in square brackets, showing its uncertainty (see Metzger, 143). The nearly similar words in v.23, however, are original.

F. Final Approach to Jerusalem (18:31–19:44)

1. A Further Prediction of Jesus' Passion (18:31–34)

OVERVIEW

This is generally referred to as the "third passion prediction" because it is basically similar to those in 9:22 and 9:44 (found in fuller form in Mt 17:22–23; Mk 9:31). Luke, however, has preserved other sayings that predict or foreshadow Jesus' death (including up to this point 5:35; 12:50; 13:32; 17:25). Also, he does not follow this saying with the dialogue found in Mark 10:35–45 with its further allusions to Jesus' passion. Since Luke normally stresses the role of Jerusalem, it is surprising that he omits the reference to it preserved in Matthew 20:17 and Mark 10:32. This may be because Jerusalem appears in 18:31 or because Jesus had already emphasized Jerusalem as the place of his destiny (13:32–33), thereby accomplishing what Matthew and Mark do in this context.

---

³¹Jesus took the Twelve aside and told them, "We are going up to Jerusalem, and everything that is written by the prophets about the Son of Man will be fulfilled. ³²He will be handed over to the Gentiles. They will mock him, insult him, spit on him, flog him and kill him. ³³On the third day he will rise again."

³⁴The disciples did not understand any of this. Its meaning was hidden from them, and they did not know what he was talking about.

COMMENTARY

31 Once again Luke, by stressing these words of Jesus, stresses the fulfillment of prophecy (cf. the first two chapters, esp. 2:25–38; 22:37). The parallels in Matthew 20:18 and Mark 10:33 omit any reference to prophecy here. The allusions to the prophets once again point to Luke's emphasis on the continuation of salvation history. The suffering and death of Jesus are not accidents in history—they belong to the wider plan of God. The mention of the Twelve likewise focuses on the continuation of Jesus and the church. The same point is made in similar terms in Luke 24:44–49, where one also finds the mission of the church included in the prophetic plan of God.

32–34 In this prediction, Jesus for the first time mentions the Gentiles as his executors (v.32). The focus on Gentiles does not deny Jewish responsibility, however, as the reference to Jerusalem (v.31) and earlier references indicate (9:22). The note on mocking and insulting is probably an allusion to Isaiah 53. Luke attributes the ignorance of the disciples (a theme much emphasized by Mark) to what is apparently a supernatural withholding of understanding (v.34; cf. the experience of the two on the road to Emmaus, 24:16). This ignorance most likely refers to the failure of the disciples to comprehend how such actions fit into God's plan for his own Messiah (cf. 24:45).

2. Healing a Blind Beggar (18:35–43)

OVERVIEW

This incident shows that Jesus, who was on his way to the royal city of Jerusalem, was actually the "Son of David" (vv.38–39), i.e., the Messiah. It also allows Luke to point again to Jesus' concern for the needy and especially to show his healing of the blind as a messianic work (cf. 4:18). In addition, this miracle emphasizes the importance of faith and (in Luke only) the glory God receives through the ministry of Jesus (v.42). At this point, the crowd is still on the side of Jesus.

> [35]As Jesus approached Jericho, a blind man was sitting by the roadside begging. [36]When he heard the crowd going by, he asked what was happening. [37]They told him, "Jesus of Nazareth is passing by."
>
> [38]He called out, "Jesus, Son of David, have mercy on me!"
>
> [39]Those who led the way rebuked him and told him to be quiet, but he shouted all the more, "Son of David, have mercy on me!"
>
> [40]Jesus stopped and ordered the man to be brought to him. When he came near, Jesus asked him, [41]"What do you want me to do for you?"
>
> "Lord, I want to see," he replied.
>
> [42]Jesus said to him, "Receive your sight; your faith has healed you." [43]Immediately he received his sight and followed Jesus, praising God. When all the people saw it, they also praised God.

COMMENTARY

35–37 Jesus' final approach to Jerusalem is underway. Luke is establishing a very important sequence: the healing of the blind man just outside Jericho (v.35), the call of Zacchaeus in Jericho (19:1–10), and then Jesus' triumphal entry into Jerusalem, his city of destiny (19:11, 28; see comments at 19:28). Luke apparently makes reference to "the crowd" here (v.36) to explain how the blind beggar knew that something special was happening (v.37). The healing of the blind man recalls 14:21, and this passage illustrates how another outcast is included in God's kingdom by his relationship with Jesus. The mention of "Jesus of Nazareth" (v.37) points further back to Jesus' inaugural sermon in Nazareth, where he proclaimed the fulfillment of prophecies that promise the "recovery of sight for the blind" (4:18).

38–39 The description of the man's insistent calling draws attention to his faith, which was based on the messiahship of Jesus, the "Son of David." So does Jesus' question in v.41, which allows the man to voice his request. The introduction of the title "Son of David" immediately after the prediction of Jesus' resurrection (v.33) anticipates Luke's second volume, in which Jesus will be proclaimed the Davidic Messiah after his resurrection and exaltation (Ac 2:29–36). The ability of this blind man to see the true identity of Jesus is contrasted with the ignorance of the disciples (cf. v.34).

43 Only Luke speaks of the praise both the formerly blind man and the people gave to God after the miracle. This is a unique Lukan feature (5:26; 17:18; Ac 2:47; 3:9), and it reveals the true nature of Jesus' works as mighty acts of God. The public nature of the manifestation of Jesus' power and identity serves as a contrast to the coming rejection in Jerusalem.

NOTES

35 It is well known that in Matthew 20:29 and Mark 10:46 Jesus is leaving, not approaching, Jericho at this point. In Luke's concern to maintain the important thematic order described above (healing, call of Zacchaeus, approach to Jerusalem), might he have described the healing before the Jericho incident in order to prevent confusion within his own narrative? This would have been acceptable to his contemporaries, though it is troublesome to us.

If this were the case, the problem would be cleared up. Luke, contrary to his custom, does not draw attention to the crowds that followed Jesus out of Jericho but only mentions them in passing (v.36). There must be some reason for the unusual omission here, especially when the crowds are stressed in the parallel passages (Mt 20:29; Mk 10:46). If Luke were following a thematic order rather than a geographical one, so that Jesus is just entering Jericho after the healing, there would be no opportunity for the crowds to follow him out of the city, as in Matthew and Mark.

If this suggestion is inadequate, we can turn to one of the various harmonizing suggestions that have been made. It is possible that Jesus was between the remains of OT Jericho and the new city, with its large Herodian palace to the south of the old city. Thus he could be "leaving" OT Jericho (Matthew and Mark) and "approaching" the NT city (Luke) at the same time. A simpler solution is provided by S. E. Porter ("'In the Vicinity of Jericho': Luke 18:35 in the Light of Its Synoptic Parallels," *BBR* 2 [1992]: 91–104), who shows how the verb ἐγγίζω (*engizō*, "approach," GK *1581*) can be understood not simply as a verb of motion but also as one of location. Therefore, instead of "approached Jericho," the proper translation may be "in the vicinity of Jericho."

3. Zacchaeus the Tax Collector (19:1–10)

OVERVIEW

This narrative contains what may well be considered the "key verse" of Luke—19:10. The incident contains several primary Lukan features: the universal appeal of the gospel (vv.2–4); the ethical problem of wealth (v.2); the call of a "sinner" who was in social disfavor (v.7); the sense of God's present work (vv.5, 9); the feeling of urgency ("immediately," *speusas*, GK *5067*, v.5), of necessity ("must," v.5), and of joy (v.6); restitution, with goods distributed to the poor (v.8); and, above all, salvation (vv.9–10).

As in the preceding stories, this one serves to answer the question raised in 18:8: "when the Son of Man comes, will he find faith on the earth?" Reading this story in the light of its immediate context, Zacchaeus can also be understood as yet another blind man who receives healing from the salvific work of Jesus. (For a discussion of the parallels between the two stories, see M. J. Hassold, "Eyes to See: Reflections on Luke 19:1–10," *Lutheran Theological Journal* 29 [1995]: 68–73.)

1Jesus entered Jericho and was passing through. 2A man was there by the name of Zacchaeus; he was a chief tax collector and was wealthy. 3He wanted to see who Jesus was, but being a short man he could not, because of the crowd. 4So he ran ahead and climbed a sycamore-fig tree to see him, since Jesus was coming that way.

5When Jesus reached the spot, he looked up and said to him, "Zacchaeus, come down immediately. I must stay at your house today." 6So he came down at once and welcomed him gladly.

7All the people saw this and began to mutter, "He has gone to be the guest of a 'sinner.'"

8But Zacchaeus stood up and said to the Lord, "Look, Lord! Here and now I give half of my possessions to the poor, and if I have cheated anybody out of anything, I will pay back four times the amount."

9Jesus said to him, "Today salvation has come to this house, because this man, too, is a son of Abraham. 10For the Son of Man came to seek and to save what was lost."

COMMENTARY

2–3 Zacchaeus was a "chief tax collector" (*architelōnēs*, GK *803*, v.2), holding a higher office in the Roman tax system than Levi did (5:27–30). This system, under which an officer gained his income by extorting more money from the people than he had contracted to pay the Roman government, had evidently worked well for Zacchaeus. His location

in the major customs center of Jericho was ideal. Being both wealthy and a member of a generally despised group, he is a notable subject for the saving grace of God.

Observe the proximity of this story to that of the rich ruler, whose attitude toward wealth kept him from the Lord (18:18–30). The emphasis on Zacchaeus's wealth may serve as a response to the questions raised earlier in 18:26: "Who then can be saved?" The note on Zacchaeus's small stature (v.3) provides a way to emphasize his eagerness to see Jesus. In the minds of the ancient readers, this note may also point to his social and moral status (cf. M. C. Parsons, "'Short in Stature': Luke's Physical Description of Zacchaeus," *NTS* 47 [2001]: 50–57). His eagerness to see Jesus is surpassed by Jesus' personal invitation to meet with him (v.5).

5–6 Not only did Jesus want to see Zacchaeus; Jesus also had to stay with him—"I must stay at your house today" (v.5). This divine necessity is stressed in Luke (see comments at 4:43). Luke also has the word "today," with its special meaning (see comments at 4:21). The reciprocity of the divine, sovereign call and the human response is striking (v.6; cf. v.10).

7 In ch. 15 Luke provides three parables told by Jesus to answer "the Pharisees and the teachers of the law" who opposed his eating with tax collectors and "sinners" (15:1–2). Now "all the people" complain that Jesus was consorting with a "sinner." Similar criticism was made of Jesus' visit with Levi the tax collector (5:29–30). In each case, table fellowship was involved—something that had a far deeper significance than our dinner parties. (See comments at 5:29–30; 15:1 for the significance of the word "sinner" from the Pharisees' point of view.)

8 Zacchaeus's announcement sounds abrupt and is probably intended to seem so. After all, for Luke (following Jesus) the use of possessions is a major indicator of one's spiritual condition (cf. 14:33; 18:22, and comments there). The first-class conditional clause implies that Zacchaeus had "cheated" people (see Notes). "Four times the amount" was far more than what the OT specified for restitution (Lev 5:16; Nu 5:7), though it is not without precedents (2Sa 12:6; cf. B. W. Grindlay, "Zacchaeus and David," *ExpTim* 99 [1987]: 46–47). Whether or not Zacchaeus knew of these laws, his offer was unusually generous and was the sort of "fruit in keeping with repentance" earlier sought by John the Baptist (Lk 3:8).

9 Salvation did not "come to this house" because Zacchaeus finally did a good deed but because he was "a son of Abraham," which may mean because he was a believer and thus a spiritual descendant of Abraham (Ellis, 220). On the other hand, it may mean that "a Jew, even though he has become one of the 'lost sheep of the house of Israel,' is still a part of Israel; the good Shepherd must seek for such" (Marshall, 698).

10 This could well be considered the "key verse" of Luke. As noted in the Overview, the context is rich with Lukan themes and an appropriate setting for a significant verse. The verse itself expresses the heart of Jesus' ministry as presented by Luke—both Jesus' work of salvation and his quest for the lost. Luke has portrayed the "lost" throughout his gospel, from Jesus' own statements (e.g., the programmatic statement in 4:18–19) to the disdainful comments of the self-righteous (e.g., the Pharisee in 18:11 and here in v.7). Jesus has sought and found another of the "lost" in Jericho. He uses the occasion and the criticism of the people (v.7) as an opportunity to restate his mission. This entire incident is the epitome of the messianic mission described in Luke 4.

NOTES

2 The name Zacchaeus derives from the Hebrew Zaccai (cf. Ne 7:14), meaning "pure." Here the name is introduced by the words ὀνόματι καλούμενος (*onomati kaloumenos*, "by the name of"), and this phrase draws attention to the name itself. It is tempting, as D. A. S. Ravens ("Zacchaeus: The Final Part of a Lucan Triptych?" *JSNT* 41 [1991]: 19–32) does, to see the name as functioning in a symbolic way. Whether the name points to Zacchaeus's initial innocence or to his subsequent reception of grace is not clear, however.

8 This is a hotly debated verse in recent scholarship. The main issue is whether Zacchaeus had cheated and therefore was considered a sinner by Jesus. Those (e.g., Fitzmyer, 1221–22; A. C. Mitchell, "Zacchaeus Revisited," *Bib* 71 [1990]: 153–76; Mitchell, "The Use of συκοφαντεῖν [*sykophantein*] in Luke 19:8," *Bib* 72 [1991]: 546–47; Ravens, "Zacchaeus") who see Zacchaeus's statement as a defense of the false charges understand the verbs in a customary present sense, and thus Zacchaeus's statement implies that he is in the practice of helping those around him. These scholars will also point to the lack of a call to repentance and the presence of other similar characters who were considered "sinners" by the Pharisees/crowd. Others such as Dennis Hamm ("Luke 19:8 Once Again: Does Zacchaeus Defend or Resolve?" *JBL* 107 [1988]: 431–37; "What the Samaritan Leper Sees: The Narrative Christology of Luke 17:11–19," *CBQ* 56 [1994]: 273–87) have defended the traditional reading by pointing to the nature of the conditional sentence as well as to the conclusion of the story (v. 10). Moreover, the fact that Zacchaeus may not be justifiably labeled a "sinner" as tax collectors were does not exclude acts of dishonesty and the need of conversion. In its context, this story best illustrates how "even" a rich person can be saved by repenting and turning to Jesus.

4. Parable of the Ten Minas (19:11–27)

OVERVIEW

This parable fulfills four important functions: (1) it clarifies the time of the appearance of the kingdom of God; (2) it realistically portrays the coming rejection and future return of the Lord; (3) it delineates the role of a disciple in the time between the Lord's departure and his return; and (4) it makes a unique contribution at this point in Luke's narrative.

In structure this parable is very similar to the parable of the talents in Matthew 25:14–30. It has been argued, on the one hand, that both go back in tradition history to one story, and on the other hand

that there were two stories told on two different occasions in Jesus' ministry. With regard to the meaning of the story, the structural similarities seem more significant than the differences in detail. Yet while some of the differences—e.g., the number of servants mentioned, the amounts entrusted, and the conclusion (ten cities being mentioned only in Luke)—are relatively minor, the description of the main figure is not. The figure of a king who is rejected is distinctive to Luke and belongs to a deep stratum of his narrative and theology.

> [11]While they were listening to this, he went on to tell them a parable, because he was near Jerusalem and the people thought that the kingdom of God was going to appear at once. [12]He said: "A man of noble birth went to a distant country to have himself appointed king and then to return. [13]So he called ten of his servants and gave them ten minas. 'Put this money to work,' he said, 'until I come back.'

¹⁴"But his subjects hated him and sent a delegation after him to say, 'We don't want this man to be our king.'

¹⁵"He was made king, however, and returned home. Then he sent for the servants to whom he had given the money, in order to find out what they had gained with it.

¹⁶"The first one came and said, 'Sir, your mina has earned ten more.'

¹⁷"'Well done, my good servant!' his master replied. 'Because you have been trustworthy in a very small matter, take charge of ten cities.'

¹⁸"The second came and said, 'Sir, your mina has earned five more.'

¹⁹"His master answered, 'You take charge of five cities.'

²⁰"Then another servant came and said, 'Sir, here is your mina; I have kept it laid away in a piece of cloth. ²¹I was afraid of you, because you are a hard man. You take out what you did not put in and reap what you did not sow.'

²²"His master replied, 'I will judge you by your own words, you wicked servant! You knew, did you, that I am a hard man, taking out what I did not put in, and reaping what I did not sow? ²³Why then didn't you put my money on deposit, so that when I came back, I could have collected it with interest?'

²⁴"Then he said to those standing by, 'Take his mina away from him and give it to the one who has ten minas.'

²⁵"'Sir,' they said, 'he already has ten!'

²⁶"He replied, 'I tell you that to everyone who has, more will be given, but as for the one who has nothing, even what he has will be taken away. ²⁷But those enemies of mine who did not want me to be king over them—bring them here and kill them in front of me.'"

COMMENTARY

11 The parable of the ten minas is connected with the pericope about Zacchaeus by the clause "while they were listening to this." The transition can be viewed in two complementary ways: (1) Marshall, 703, referring back to Jesus' words in v.9, notes that "although salvation has come *today* . . . the End, and the coming of the Son of Man to judgment, still lie in the future" (emphasis his). (2) "Son of Man" in v.10 of the Zacchaeus incident and "kingdom of God" at the beginning of this parable are conceptually related (cf. Doeve, 128, 130, 142–43). The one who has the right to reign is precisely the same Son of Man who came to seek lost sheep (v.10).

In addition to its connection with the Zacchaeus pericope, this parable is appropriate to Luke, which in passage after passage deals with Jesus' teaching about the future in general, the present and future aspects of the kingdom, and the consummation of God's purposes in history. (On Luke's eschatology, see Introduction, p. 41) Obviously this parable teaches that Jesus predicted an interval of time between his ascension and return. For the time when the kingdom will be restored to Israel, see the beginning of Luke's second volume (Ac 1:6–7). In its location at the end of the travel narrative this parable also "corrects the assumption that Jesus' spatial proximity to Jerusalem signals the temporal proximity of the revelation of divine rule" (Wolter, "Israel's Future and the Delay of the Parousia," in *Jesus and the Heritage of Israel* [ed. Moessner], 313; see Notes).

12–14 The historical background for the parable was the visit of Archelaus, son of Herod the Great, to Rome to secure permission to reign as a so-called client king, i.e., over a territory actually subject to Rome. This petition was opposed by a delegation of Archelaus's own subjects (Josephus, *Ant.* 17.213–49, 299–320; *J.W.* 2.14–22). Similarly, Jesus has gone to the heavenly seat of authority until the time for his return. In the meantime, though his qualifications for kingship are impeccable, he has been rejected by those who should serve him as his subjects (v.14).

The money each servant received was worth at least three months' wages (NIV text note) or perhaps a little more (v.13). Their responsibility was to "put this money to work" in business, trading, or by investment.

15–19 Jesus singles out three of the ten servants as examples. The first two did well (vv.16, 18)—one so well as to receive a special commendation for being "trustworthy" (v.17). The test was "small" (i.e., on a small scale), not because the amount itself was so small but because of its relative insignificance in comparison to the cities awarded to the trustworthy servants (vv.17, 19). We need not seek any particular symbolism in the cities other than the contrast between the extraordinary responsibility of ruling them and the responsibility of simply investing the sums of money (minas).

20–23 What some have called the "rule of end stress" leads the reader to concentrate on the last of the three examples. This servant allowed his fear (justified on the basis of experience) of the nobleman's anger (v.21) to prevent him from fulfilling his responsibility of putting to work the money given to him (v.20). To be sure, its investment was risky, but he was specifically charged to take the risk of investing the money (vv.22–23). In his case, conservatism was born of fear and was wrong (cf. Thielicke, *Waiting Father*, 143–45).

24–25 The principle of taking from one who has little and giving to one who has much (v.24) strikes us today as strange and unfair (v.25). In the original setting, as similarly in the kingdom parables (Mt 13:12), whether a person has little or much depends on that person's use of opportunities to increase what he already has.

26–27 The nobleman's anger is not intended to attribute such behavior to Jesus himself; rather, it pictures the kind of response one might have expected in Jesus' day, especially from the Herodians. It also reveals the seriousness of flouting the orders of the King whom God has appointed as Judge (Jn 5:22; Ac 17:31; cf. 1Pe 1:17).

NOTES

11 The presence of both present and future aspects of kingdom manifestation leads to various interpretations of the parable's main point. Against the traditional interpretation (see comments at v.11), Luke Timothy Johnson ("The Lukan Kingship Parable [Luke 19:11–27]," *NovT* 24 [1982]: 139–59) suggests that this parable focuses on the immediate revelation of God's kingdom. Both the context and the content argue against this reading, though the tension between the now and the not yet cannot be denied (cf. L. Guy, "The Interplay of the Present and Future in the Kingdom of God [Luke 19:11–44]," *TynBul* 48 [1997]: 119–37).

5. The Triumphal Entry (19:28–44)

OVERVIEW

Luke does not mention Jesus' actual entry into Jerusalem—the triumphal entry. Instead he shows us Jesus only as "near" Jerusalem (v.11), and after the crowd's welcome he is still "approaching" Jerusalem (v.41).

The story comes to its climax not in Jesus' entering Jerusalem but in his lamenting over the city (vv.41–44); therefore, while Jesus deserves a tri-umphal entry as "king" (v.38), Luke emphasizes that he is moving instead to the place of his rejection. This continues the movement Jesus spoke of in 13:33. It does not contradict Matthew or Mark, for v.45 shows that Jesus did eventually enter the city. Luke simply omits the statement that he entered (cf. Mt 21:10; Mk 11:11) to make his theological point.

28After Jesus had said this, he went on ahead, going up to Jerusalem. 29As he approached Bethphage and Bethany at the hill called the Mount of Olives, he sent two of his disciples, saying to them, 30"Go to the village ahead of you, and as you enter it, you will find a colt tied there, which no one has ever ridden. Untie it and bring it here. 31If anyone asks you, 'Why are you untying it?' tell him, 'The Lord needs it.'"

32Those who were sent ahead went and found it just as he had told them. 33As they were untying the colt, its owners asked them, "Why are you untying the colt?"

34They replied, "The Lord needs it."

35They brought it to Jesus, threw their cloaks on the colt and put Jesus on it. 36As he went along, people spread their cloaks on the road.

37When he came near the place where the road goes down the Mount of Olives, the whole crowd of disciples began joyfully to praise God in loud voices for all the miracles they had seen:

38"Blessed is the king who comes in the name of the Lord!"

"Peace in heaven and glory in the highest!"

39Some of the Pharisees in the crowd said to Jesus, "Teacher, rebuke your disciples!"

40"I tell you," he replied, "if they keep quiet, the stones will cry out."

41As he approached Jerusalem and saw the city, he wept over it 42and said, "If you, even you, had only known on this day what would bring you peace—but now it is hidden from your eyes. 43The days will come upon you when your enemies will build an embankment against you and encircle you and hem you in on every side. 44They will dash you to the ground, you and the children within your walls. They will not leave one stone on another, because you did not recognize the time of God's coming to you."

COMMENTARY

28–29 The transition "after Jesus had said this" (v.28) links his approach to the city with the parable of the ten minas, which denies an immediate appearance of the kingdom and portrays the rejection of its ruler. Luke's mention of Bethphage and Bethany (v.29) locates where Jesus went. Bethany was, of course, important as the home of Mary, Martha, and Lazarus. The Mount of Olives had a significant place in prophecy as the place of the coming Messiah's appearance (Zec 14:4).

30–32 The incident of securing the colt (vv.30–31) "just as he had told them" (v.32) reminds us (as did 2:15, 20, 29) of the dependability of the prophetic word. The colt recalls the one ridden by the king of Zion (Zec 9:9), and the fact that "no one has ever ridden" it suggests that it is reserved for royal usage (cf. J. D. M. Derrett, "Law in the New Testament: The Palm Sunday Colt," *NovT* 13 [1971]: 241–58).

34 The phrase "the Lord needs it" is striking in that Jesus is now referring to himself as the "Lord" (*kyrios*, GK *3261*). This entrance to Jerusalem is portrayed as the entrance of the one of power. The "owners" are also called *kyrioi* by Luke (v.33), which may contrast with the one who is supreme Lord (*kyrios*) and rightful owner of all that we possess.

35–37 As does Matthew, Luke shows us the humble king as he portrays Jesus riding on the colt (see Notes). (For the custom of spreading cloaks along the path [v.36], see 2Ki 9:13.) Only Luke mentions the descent from the Mount of Olives, showing that Jesus was still outside Jerusalem (v.37). The reference to praising God for Jesus' miracles is unique to Luke (see comments at 18:43).

38 Luke omits here the expression "hosanna," which might have been strange to his Gentile readers (cf. Mt 21:9, 15; Mk 11:9, 10; Jn 12:13). He also omits the messianic quotation from Zechariah 9:9

given in Matthew 21:5 and instead stresses the messianic theme with the word "king." The word "comes" is reminiscent of the designation "the coming one" for the Messiah. Luke has already quoted v.26 of the festival song Psalm 118 in Jesus' previous lament over Jerusalem (13:35). In preexilic times, Psalm 118 functioned as an enthronement psalm (cf. J. A. Sanders, "A Hermeneutic Fabric: Psalm 118 in Luke's Entrance Narrative," in *Luke and Scripture* [ed. Evans and Sanders], 140–53); the use of this psalm in the account of Jesus' entry into Jerusalem is therefore most appropriate. In addition to using the specific word "king," Luke gives us the words about "peace," reminiscent of the angels' proclamation at the nativity (2:14) and including the identical words, "glory in the highest" (*doxa en hypsistois,* GK *1518, 5736*)—a phrase that points to the salvific acts of God. Once again he omits a "hosanna."

40 Here is another saying of Jesus found only in Luke. It is a fitting prelude to vv.41–45. Ellis, 226, suggests that the words about the stones, similar to Habakkuk 2:11, may be a link to the idea of the capitulation of Jerusalem found in the Qumran commentary on Habakkuk (1QpHab 9:6ff.). The theme of judgment is therefore present as the reference to the past points to the future destruction of Jerusalem (cf. B. R. Kinman, "'The Stones Will Cry Out' [Luke 19:40]—Joy or Judgment," *Bib* 75 [1994]: 232–35); this theme of judgment links this passage with vv.41–44.

41–44 Jesus is still outside Jerusalem (v.41) as he utters this lament, which only Luke records (see Notes). Once more, Luke focuses on Jesus' concern for the city and adds his prediction of its destruction, which is not given in 13:34. "This day" (v.42; cf. 4:21, "today," see comments there) of peace has arrived; and the city ("even you," *kai su*), whose very name means "peace," has failed to recognize it. For the meaning of "hidden," see comments at 18:34. For a further description of Jerusalem's fate, see 21:20–24. God's "coming" (*episkopē*, GK *2175*, v.44) has here the sense of a "visitation" that brings good or ill—in this case, either salvation or judgment.

NOTES

35 The use of the verb ἐπιβιβάζω (*epibibazō*, "to put on," GK *2097*) may evoke the anointment and enthronement scene of King Solomon in 1 Kings 1:33–40 [LXX]. The portrayal of Jesus as the king is highlighted by the details of this Lukan account of Jesus' entry into Jerusalem.

43–44 The uniquely Lukan connection between Jesus' entry into Jerusalem and the theme of judgment demands further examination. B. R. Kinman ("Parousia, Jesus' 'A-Triumphal' Entry, and the Fate of Jerusalem [Luke 19:28–44]," *JBL* 118 [1999]: 279–94) has convincingly shown how ancient royal customs provide the framework for the Lukan entry scene, and the harsh judgment uttered here was the result of the people's rejection of Jesus as the king. The seemingly disproportionate reaction of Jesus can therefore be understood in light of the insult the Jerusalem leaders have hurled at this king. Their failure to recognize the arrival of God's Messiah (v.44) becomes the ultimate grounds for their destruction.

VI. THE JERUSALEM MINISTRY (19:45–24:53)

A. Teaching in the Temple Area (19:45–21:38)

1. Jesus at the Temple (19:45–48)

OVERVIEW

Luke has omitted the episode of the fig tree (Mt 21:18–22; Mk 11:12–14, 20–26). At first thought this is surprising, since through the strange episode Jesus taught the efficacy of the prayer of faith—a matter of particular interest to Luke. However, Luke may have felt that the drastic overtones of the cursing of the fig tree, with its relation to the fruitlessness of Israel (symbolized by the fig tree), would be inappropriate here, perhaps because of Jesus' strong words recorded in vv.41–44.

This short account of Jesus' confrontation with the Jewish leaders in the temple area is important for two reasons: (1) It sets the stage for the climactic confrontation between the two that has been anticipated since the beginning of Jesus' ministry. (2) In providing a critique of the way the temple cult functioned, Jesus is implicitly providing a new way through which God can be worshiped. In the wider theological framework of Luke's story, the ministry of Jesus in the Jerusalem temple is the fulfillment of OT prophecies where the dawning of a new era is proclaimed to be centered in the Jerusalem area (cf. Isa 40:1–11).

⁴⁵Then he entered the temple area and began driving out those who were selling. ⁴⁶"It is written," he said to them, "'My house will be a house of prayer'; but you have made it 'a den of robbers.'"

⁴⁷Every day he was teaching at the temple. But the chief priests, the teachers of the law and the leaders among the people were trying to kill him. ⁴⁸Yet they could not find any way to do it, because all the people hung on his words.

COMMENTARY

45–46 Luke states—still without specifically saying that Jesus had entered Jerusalem (see Overview, 19:28–44)—that Jesus is now in the temple area (v.45). The cleansing of the temple lacks the vivid detail in Matthew 21:12–13 and Mark 11:15–17. Luke mentions the importance of the temple as a "house of prayer" (v.46), though he omits the reference to the nations (cf. Mk 11:17). The reference to the "house of prayer" comes from Isaiah 56:7, and "den of robbers" from Jeremiah 7:11. The evocation of Isaiah 56 points to the dawning of a new era when all will be gathered to worship the one true God. The reference to "den of robbers" may likewise point to the coming destruction of Jerusalem in the way that the sanctuary of Shiloh was destroyed (Jer 7:12, 14; cf. J. Frankovic, "Remember Shiloh!" *Jerusalem Perspective* 46–47 [1994]: 24–31).

47–48 These two verses are not in Matthew and are different in form from Mark 11:18–19. Whereas Mark mentions Jesus' "teaching" (nominal form of

didachē) at the end of his brief paragraph (11:18), Luke uses the verbal form of the same word (in a vivid periphrastic construction: *ēn didaskōn*, "was teaching"), evidently to emphasize Jesus' teaching ministry (see comments at 20:1). This is appropriate because Luke has consistently portrayed Jesus as a teacher, especially since the beginning of the central section of the gospel (9:51–19:44). He adds "the leaders among the people" (*hoi prōtoi tou laou*) to those Mark says are trying to kill Jesus, but by careful omission Luke indicates that "the people" (*laos*, GK *3295*) themselves are not hostile to him. On the contrary, they "hung on his words" (v.48). This fits with Luke's attempt to distinguish between the "people," who were responsive to Jesus, and their leaders and the "crowds" (*ochloi*, GK *4063*), who were not. This in turn forms part of Luke's attempt to show that Christianity is properly seen as a continuation of true Judaism (cf. 1:68, 77; 2:10, 31–32; see comments at 1:68; 2:30–32).

2. Jesus' Authority Questioned (20:1–8)

OVERVIEW

With this controversy Luke initiates a series of dialogues, most of which are common to all three Synoptics. They include the familiar form in which a question is answered by another question designed

to catch the interrogator in his own inconsistency. The controversies are typical examples of the kinds of challenges thrown at Jesus by the various sects and parties: "the chief priests and the teachers of the law" (v.1; cf. vv.19, 39), "the Pharisees and Herodians" (cf. Mk 12:13; Luke alone has "spies," v.20), and "the Sadducees" (v.27). Jesus also addresses the "rich" in 21:1. These dialogues sharpen the issues so that the reader sees the hostility and the theological errors of the leaders of the people.

Jesus' authority is of paramount importance, and his work as teacher and prophet (especially strong in Luke) requires validation. It is therefore appropriate that each synoptic gospel begins the controversy section with this question: "By what authority are you doing these things?" (Mt 21:23; Mk 11:28; Lk 20:2). This issue of authority also ties this episode with the previous one as Jesus' action in the temple directly challenged the authority of the temple cult.

> ¹One day as he was teaching the people in the temple courts and preaching the gospel, the chief priests and the teachers of the law, together with the elders, came up to him. ²"Tell us by what authority you are doing these things," they said. "Who gave you this authority?"
>
> ³He replied, "I will also ask you a question. Tell me, ⁴John's baptism—was it from heaven, or from men?"
>
> ⁵They discussed it among themselves and said, "If we say, 'From heaven,' he will ask, 'Why didn't you believe him?' ⁶But if we say, 'From men,' all the people will stone us, because they are persuaded that John was a prophet."
>
> ⁷So they answered, "We don't know where it was from."
>
> ⁸Jesus said, "Neither will I tell you by what authority I am doing these things."

COMMENTARY

1–2 "One day" is indefinite in contrast to Mark 11:27, which, unlike in Luke (see comments on Luke's omission of Jesus' actual entry into Jerusalem at Overview, 19:28–44), speaks of Jesus' return to Jerusalem. As in 19:47 Luke emphasizes Jesus' role as a teacher. He also mentions the "people" (*laos*, GK *3295*), who (in Luke) are always receptive to his teaching (see comments at 19:47–48). Luke further adds "preaching the gospel" (*euangelizomenou*, GK *2294*), lacking in the other Synoptics. This is consistent with Luke's significant use of that verb (though not the noun *euangelion*; see Notes). The act of "preaching the gospel" at the center of the Jerusalem cult becomes a direct challenge to the authority of the Jewish leadership.

3–8 The implication of Jesus' question is clear (vv.3–4). Jesus refused to give more light to those who refused to accept the light they had (v.8) and make a decision concerning it (vv.5–7). They refused to live according to what Minear, 3–30, 37–38, calls "Consciousness B" (an awareness of the heavenly dimension of life [v.7]) and chose instead to stay on a worldly level (Minear's "Consciousness A"). The word "heaven" is a surrogate for God in vv.3, 5.

The mention of John the Baptist is appropriate in this context, as John also preached the dawning of a new era. His baptism of repentance challenged the temple cult as it offered a way to approach God. His prediction of the one to come was also a threat to the establishment. Both John and Jesus gained the support of the people while being opposed by those in power. As the prophet John was rejected by the Jewish leadership (cf. 7:30), Jesus would likewise suffer at the hands of God's own people.

NOTES

1 Luke's use of the verb ἐυαγγελίζομαι (*euangelizomai*, "to preach the good news," GK *2294*) is significant in this context. This verb appears at critical junctures of this gospel. In the birth narrative (1:19; 2:10) and in John's ministry (3:18) it paves the way for Jesus' ministry. In 4:18 the verb appears within the Isaianic quotation of Jesus' inaugural sermon in the Nazareth synagogue, and it appears frequently in summary statements of the ministry of Jesus (4:43; 7:22; 8:1; 16:16) and his disciples (9:6). In this final appearance of the verb, salvation is now being proclaimed in Jerusalem in fulfillment of OT prophecies according to which Zion will witness the salvation of God (Isa 40:1–11). Implicit is the claim that even those who worship in the temple area need to hear and receive this good news.

3. Parable of the Tenants (20:9–19)

OVERVIEW

The refusal of the leaders to accept Jesus' authority (20:1–8) leads to this parable that not only clearly affirms that authority but also alludes to Jesus' death and subsequent vindication. The parable draws its imagery from the "Song of the Vineyard" (Isa 5:1–7), though Luke's account omits the quotation of Isaiah 5:2 found in Matthew 21:33 and Mark 12:1. Unlike the Isaianic story, in which the vineyard was destroyed, in this parable the tenants are the ones who will be judged. The details of the story vary among the Synoptics. (For a discussion of the relationship among the three accounts, see K. Snodgrass, *The Parable of the Wicked Tenants* [WUNT 27; Tübingen: Mohr, 1983], 52–71.) In Matthew and Mark, one of the servants is killed; in Luke only the son is killed. The story tends more toward allegory than Jesus' parables usually do. The vineyard may be compared to Israel on the basis of Isaiah 5. The owner represents God, the son, Jesus; the tenants correspond to the religious leaders charged with cultivating the religious life of Israel (as they acknowledge in v.19), and the servants, to the prophets.

This story also provides significant information concerning Jesus' self-consciousness as the Messiah. Unique in this story is the reference to Jesus as the Son, an understanding that he represents the climax of all prophets, and the expectation that he will suffer a violent death. In parabolic form, this story reaffirms the necessity of the suffering of the Messiah (cf. R. A. Culpepper, "Parable as Commentary: The Twice-Given Vineyard [Luke 20:9–16]," *PRSt* 26 [1999]: 161–62).

⁹He went on to tell the people this parable:"A man planted a vineyard, rented it to some farmers and went away for a long time. ¹⁰At harvest time he sent a servant to the tenants so they would give him some of the fruit of the vineyard. But the tenants beat him and sent him away empty-handed. ¹¹He sent another servant, but that one also they beat and treated shamefully and sent away empty-handed. ¹²He sent still a third, and they wounded him and threw him out.

¹³"Then the owner of the vineyard said,'What shall I do? I will send my son, whom I love; perhaps they will respect him.'

¹⁴"But when the tenants saw him, they talked the matter over.'This is the heir,' they said. 'Let's kill him, and the inheritance will be ours.' ¹⁵So they threw him out of the vineyard and killed him.

"What then will the owner of the vineyard do to them? ¹⁶He will come and kill those tenants and give the vineyard to others."When the people heard this, they said,"May this never be!"

¹⁷Jesus looked directly at them and asked,"Then what is the meaning of that which is written:

"'The stone the builders rejected
    has become the capstone'?

¹⁸Everyone who falls on that stone will be broken to pieces, but he on whom it falls will be crushed."

¹⁹The teachers of the law and the chief priests looked for a way to arrest him immediately, because they knew he had spoken this parable against them. But they were afraid of the people.

COMMENTARY

9–10 The mention of the "vineyard" evokes a long history of the use of this symbol in reference to Israel (cf. Isa 5:1–2; 27:2–3; Jer 2:21; Eze 19:10; Hos 10:1). The circumstances were not such as to provoke a violent reaction (v.9). Nothing but a sample of the fruit was requested (v.10). In the early years of a vineyard's existence, the tenants would own little if anything (cf. J. D. M. Derrett, *Law in the New Testament* [London: Longman & Todd, 1970], 296ff.). An examination of leasing practices in antiquity reveals, however, that commercial farmers were often hungry for profit. The subsequent violent treatment of the messengers and the son is then understandable (cf. C. A. Evans,"Jesus' Parable of the Tenant Farmers in Light of Lease Agreements in Antiquity," *JSP* 14 [1996]: 65–83). Moreover, the comparison between the profit-seeking farmers and the Jewish leadership is thus possible.

13 The expression "whom I love" (*agapēton*, "beloved," GK *28*) must be understood with respect to its meaning in ancient Near Eastern family relationships. In the LXX, *agapētos* was at times virtually used as a synonym for *monogenēs*, "one and only" (GK *3666*; cf. Th. C. de Kruif, "The Glory of the Only Son," in *Studies in John* [Leiden: Brill, 1970], 112ff.). The latter term did not necessarily refer to origin, as the KJV's translation "only begotten" in John 3:16 implies, but rather to the unique status of the person as a beloved only child. See Luke 7:12, in which the statement that the deceased son was her "only" (*monogenēs*) son shows the widow's desolate situation. The most relevant use in the LXX of *agapētos* is Genesis 22:2: "Take your beloved son, whom you love" (*labe ton huion sou ton agapēton, hon ēgapēsas*). This is reflected in the transfiguration account in Matthew 17:5: "This is my Son, whom I love" (*ho huios mou ho agapētos*, cf. Mk 9:7). God spoke similar words at Jesus' baptism (Mt 3:17; Lk 3:22). Luke did not include *agapētos* in his account of the transfiguration but does include it here in 20:13 (cf. Mk 12:6 [Gk.]; but cf. Mt 21:38). "What shall I do?" introduces a soliloquy similar to those in 16:3–4 and 18:4–5. Luke's amplification here (cf. Mk 12:6) adds to the pathos.

14–16 Jesus' audience was in a better position than we are to surmise what would have motivated these tenants to kill the son (see comments at vv.9–12). But we are in a better position than they to understand the meaning of the story. Certainly the vivid description of the son's murder (v.15) and the father's vengeance (v.16; cf. 19:43–44) evoked from the hearers of the parable a strong "may this never be!" (*mē genoito*; cf. the Pauline use in Ro 3:4, 6, 31 et al.). They sensed the horror of the story and its drastic applications, however imperfectly they understood its details.

17–19 The quotation (v.17) is from Psalm 118:22. (In 19:38 the same psalm was quoted.) Luke shows the point of this quotation by referring to the reaction of the people in v.16. Not only will God vindicate his Son, who is the "stone" (v.17; an important NT theme), but also those who oppose him will meet destruction (v.18). The point is tacitly acknowledged in the reaction of the leaders (v.19). This carries forward the hostile scheming against Jesus referred to in 19:47.

NOTES

13 The identification of the Messiah as the Son has a long history in Jewish traditions (see J. C. O'Neill, "The Source of the Parables of the Bridegroom and the Wicked Husbandmen," *JTS* 39 [1988]: 485, who points to 2Sa 7:14; 1Ch 17:13; Ps 89:26–29; 1QSa 2:11; 4Q174 1.11; *T. Jud.* 24.2; *T. Levi* 4.2, 4; *Jos. Asen.* 6.3, 5; 13.13; *b. Sukkah* 52*a*; see also the discussion in James Charlesworth, *Jesus within Judaism* [New York: Doubleday, 1988], 149–51).

14 The concept of "inheritance" (κληρονομία, *klēronomia*, GK *3100*) is important in the covenantal history of Israel. It is tied to the promise of the land (Ge 12; 15:7; Ex 15:17; Dt 21:23; Isa 49:8), and in later writings Israel becomes God's own inheritance (Ps 33:12; 78:62). In Luke's second volume, the word was used in reference to the ancient promises (Ac 7:5) as well as to the early Christian community (Ac 20:32; cf. Pao, 174–76). In this parable, the transfer of this "inheritance" from the hands of the Jews may be implicit in light of Luke's wider narrative.

4. Paying Taxes to Caesar (20:20-26)

OVERVIEW

Luke is blunt about the motives of the visitors; he calls them "spies" (*enkathetous*, people hired to lie in wait, GK *1588*, v.20) and speaks of their insincerity ("pretended" *hypokrinomenous*, GK *5693*, v.20; related to *hypokritēs*, "hypocrite," GK *5695*). They try to catch Jesus between two positions they considered mutually exclusive and irreconcilable. Two issues are at stake here. First, the political (or nonpolitical) nature of Jesus' message is being raised, and Jesus' answer to the question may provide an opportunity for the Jewish leadership to hand him over to the Roman authorities. Second, the unique authority of Jesus is also being questioned. In the background of these two issues is the expectation of the common people that the Messiah would free them from the oppression of foreign powers. Here is, therefore, yet another attempt of the Jewish leadership to alienate Jesus from the widespread support he receives from the crowd.

---

²⁰Keeping a close watch on him, they sent spies, who pretended to be honest. They hoped to catch Jesus in something he said so that they might hand him over to the power and authority of the governor. ²¹So the spies questioned him: "Teacher, we know that you speak and teach what is right, and that you do not show partiality but teach the way of God in accordance with the truth. ²²Is it right for us to pay taxes to Caesar or not?"

²³He saw through their duplicity and said to them, ²⁴"Show me a denarius. Whose portrait and inscription are on it?"

²⁵"Caesar's," they replied.

He said to them, "Then give to Caesar what is Caesar's, and to God what is God's."

²⁶They were unable to trap him in what he had said there in public. And astonished by his answer, they became silent.

COMMENTARY

20–22 Luke, writing for an audience to whom the distinctions between Jewish parties might be unfamiliar, does not mention the Pharisees and Herodians, as Matthew and Mark do. His readers would, however, certainly know about the various forms of heavy Roman taxation (v.22). These totaled over one-third of a person's income and included a poll tax, customs, and various indirect taxes.

24–25 On the surface, the portrait on the coin (vv.24–25) represented submission to Rome. Jesus' statement may seem ordinary to us, as we have become so used to the saying. But it was an unexpected and telling response to the question. Jesus' questioners were sure his answer would alienate either the governmental officials or the pious people and zealots who opposed foreign domination. Actually, Jesus appealed neither to those who preached revolution nor to the political compromisers. He stated a principle, not an accommodation or a compromise. This principle appears in the classic passage on Christian social ethics (Ro 13:1–7). Not only is giving what the government requires *not antithetical* to religious duty—such giving is *part of* religious duty. This even goes beyond the idea of dual citizenship.

We should not take Jesus' saying as teaching blind obedience to political authorities. First, its power lies in the fact that, while it does not explicitly state that one should challenge the power of the Romans even when their policies may conflict with areas of Jewish religious practice, it does affirm that we should give "to God what is God's." What is being taught, as throughout the OT, is that *all things* belong to God. To say that one should give "to God what is God's" is not affirming a limited claim of divine authority. Second, in the second volume of Luke's writings, examples of disobedience to civil authorities can be found (e.g., Ac 4:19, 21, 29). One should therefore not take the surface reading of v.25 out of context and turn it into a general and universal principle that affirms extreme quietism even when the Christian gospel is being compromised.

NOTES

25 This verse has been understood in various ways. Some have argued for an anti-Zealot reading, while others have detected a strong subversive tone behind the saying. Still others note the ironic nature of the saying without suggesting that it supplies a general principle. For a helpful survey of the history of interpretation and the issues involved, see C. H. Gibling, "'The Things of God' in the Question Concerning Tribute to Caesar (Lk 20:25; Mk 12:17; Mt 22:21)," *CBQ* 33 (1971): 510–27; J. D. M. Derrett, "Luke's Perspective on Tribute to Caesar," in *Political Issues in Luke–Acts* [ed. Cassidy and Scharper], 38–48.

5. The Resurrection and Marriage (20:27–40)

OVERVIEW

This controversy section continues with still another group challenging Jesus. The controversy is important for two reasons: (1) it relates to the coming resurrection of Jesus and the unique authority attached to this climactic event, and (2) it presents Jesus as the faithful interpreter of Scripture (Joel B. Green, *The Theology of the Gospel of Luke* [Cambridge: Cambridge Univ. Press, 1995], 74–75). Both themes are important in the remainder of the Lukan narrative.

²⁷Some of the Sadducees, who say there is no resurrection, came to Jesus with a question. ²⁸"Teacher," they said, "Moses wrote for us that if a man's brother dies and leaves a wife but no children, the man must marry the widow and have children for his brother. ²⁹Now there were seven brothers. The first one married a woman and died childless. ³⁰The second ³¹and then the third married her, and in the same way the seven died, leaving no children. ³²Finally, the woman died too. ³³Now then, at the resurrection whose wife will she be, since the seven were married to her?"

³⁴Jesus replied, "The people of this age marry and are given in marriage. ³⁵But those who are considered worthy of taking part in that age and in the resurrection from the dead will neither marry nor be given in marriage, ³⁶and they can no longer die; for they are like the angels. They are God's children, since they are children of the resurrection. ³⁷But in the account of the bush, even Moses showed that the dead rise, for he calls the Lord 'the God of Abraham, and the God of Isaac, and the God of Jacob.' ³⁸He is not the God of the dead, but of the living, for to him all are alive."

³⁹Some of the teachers of the law responded, "Well said, teacher!" ⁴⁰And no one dared to ask him any more questions.

COMMENTARY

27 The Sadducees, who tended to be more conservative than the Pharisees, did not accept what they considered to be theological accretions to their beliefs. The OT has little specific to say about the future state of the individual after death. Greek thought sharply divided between the soul and the body (the soul's temporary prison) and saw immortality as a quality of the soul. The Pharisees leaned toward a belief in resurrection that owed more to Greek ideas than to the OT. However, the Sadducees refused even to face the clear implications of OT teaching about the future state and were skeptical of the nature of personal future existence related to rewards or punishment.

29–33 This hypothetical case of a woman who had successively had seven husbands rests on the Jewish custom of "levirate marriage" (from the Latin *levir*, "husband's brother, brother-in-law"). It provided for the remarriage of a widow to the brother of a husband who died childless, the purpose of the remarriage being to provide descendants to carry on the deceased husband's name (Dt 25:5–6; cf. Ge 38:8). The Sadducees made this custom the basis for an argument *ad absurdum* that assumed that the idea of resurrection involved sexual reunion with one's earthly partner(s).

34–38 Jesus responded along these lines: It is not legitimate to project earthly conditions into the future state (vv.34–35). Eternal life is actually the life of the age to come (v.36). The believer already participates in that life (vv.37–38), but its full expression, involving the resurrection of the body, must wait until the new age has fully come. (Note the link in v.36 between "that age" and the "resurrection.") "Worthy" (v.35) probably has somewhat the same meaning as in Matthew 10:11, 13, where it apparently refers to a person or home honoring God and blessed by him.

Though in the new age believers do not become angels (or gods), they do share certain characteristics of angels (v.36). This may refer to the absence of the sexual aspect of marriage without denying the continuation of mutual recognition and love. The Greek syntax, however, places the comment about angels nearer to "no longer die" (v.36) than to "neither marry" (v.35; cf. Ellis, 237; Fitzmyer, 1305). Being "like the angels" means that believers will be "equal to the angels." This moves the emphasis from the issue of marriage to that of the nature of the resurrection. God's children are also "children of" (i.e., are characterized by) the resurrection. Note the repetition of the word "resurrection" and the absence of any reference to the Greek concept of "immortality." Jesus is not teaching the persistence of life but that "the dead rise" (v.37). Invoking, so to speak, the authority of Moses, whom the Sadducees revered (rejecting later oral tradition), Jesus shows that Abraham, Isaac, and Jacob are also going to "rise." Therefore their existence does not lie only in the past but in the future as well; and God is called, in contemporary terms, their God.

39–40 Jesus' answer is approved by some of the teachers of the law, who are happy to see the Sadducees lose their argument. Jesus' wisdom has silenced all of his questioners (v.40).

6. The Sonship of Christ (20:41–47)

OVERVIEW

The opponents silenced, the controversy section concludes with a rhetorical question Jesus puts to his questioners—a query designed to clarify from Scripture who the Messiah is. The interpretation of these three verses has been complicated by three factors: (1) the paradox inherent in Psalm 110; (2) the lack of an answer by Jesus to his own question, thus leaving its significance to be implied; and (3) the reluctance of some to accept the christological understanding that the interpretation of these verses demands. This section has occasioned much debate.

Among the many alternative interpretations, the most common element is the idea that Jesus was not affirming but specifically denying the apparent teaching of Psalm 110:1 on the identity of the Messiah.

For more on these issues see Marshall, 744–47; for an extended critical treatment of the place of Psalm 110 in early Christian interpretation, see D. M. Hay, *Glory at the Right Hand* (Nashville: Abingdon, 1973); D. Sänger, *Heiligkeit und Herrschaft* (Neukirchen-Vluyn: Neukirchener, 2003).

[41]Then Jesus said to them, "How is it that they say the Christ is the Son of David? [42]David himself declares in the Book of Psalms:

"'The Lord said to my Lord:
"Sit at my right hand
[43] until I make your enemies
a footstool for your feet."'

[44]David calls him 'Lord.' How then can he be his son?"

⁴⁵While all the people were listening, Jesus said to his disciples, ⁴⁶"Beware of the teachers of the law. They like to walk around in flowing robes and love to be greeted in the marketplaces and have the most important seats in the synagogues and the places of honor at banquets. ⁴⁷They devour widows' houses and for a show make lengthy prayers. Such men will be punished most severely."

COMMENTARY

41–43 The term "Christ" (v.41) is, of course, used here not as a proper name but as a title, "the Messiah." The Messiah was understood by the Jewish people to be a son (descendant or "sprout," as in 4Q174 11). If this is so, the question is, why does David, in Psalm 110:1, call his descendant his "Lord" (v.42)? In that passage "the Lord" is the translation of the LXX's *ho kyrios* (GK *3261*), which in turn represents the Hebrew *Yahweh* (GK 3378), the sacred name of God. "To my Lord" represents the same word in the LXX but *ʾādôn* (GK 123) in the Hebrew. This word conveyed a sense of dignity and was often used as a substitute for the name of God. Though the rabbis of the first Christian centuries did not interpret *ʾādôn* as referring to the Messiah, it is the only meaning that makes sense here.

44 Jesus' question is not intended to suggest that there could not be a descendant of David who was also "Lord" but that the seemingly irreconcilable statement has meaning only if this "Lord" is more than just a human descendant. Paul expressed the complete answer to the question in Romans 1:3–4, which says that Jesus was a descendant of David as to his human nature but declared Son of God by his resurrection. The Lukan clarification is provided in Acts 2:34–35, where the same psalm is used in explaining the significance of the resurrection and the exaltation of Jesus as the Lord of all.

46–47 Having responded with such authority to his opponents' controversial questions, Jesus now comments on those who sought to disprove his authority. His incisive portrayal of them here is shorter than in 11:37–52. Here he stresses their pride and ostentation, as well as accusing them of taking advantage of widows. Apparently they misused their responsibility as legal arbiters (cf. 12:13; see comments there) and betrayed the financial trust that innocent widows placed in them (cf. J. D. M. Derrett, "'Eating up the Houses of Widows': Jesus' Comment on Lawyers?" *NovT* 14 [1972]: 1–9).

7. The Widow's Offering (21:1–4)

OVERVIEW

The connection between this passage and the preceding one is that both refer to widows: the first, how teachers of the law victimized them (20:47); the second, how a poor widow set an example of acceptable giving (21:2–3). In the context of Jesus' critique of the corrupted temple cult, however, this story may serve to illustrate the point that was made in 20:47. The acceptance or even request of the sacrificial giving of the widows becomes an example of the oppressive practices of the Jewish leadership.

The futility of the widow's sacrificial giving to the temple system is highlighted by the account of the destruction of Jerusalem that follows (vv.5–38; cf. A. G. Wright, "The Widow's Mites: Praise or Lament? A Matter of Context," *CBQ* 44 [1982]: 256–65; R. S. Sugirtharajah, "The Widow's Mites Revalued," *ExpTim* 103 [1991]: 42–43). The admirable act of the poor widow then becomes an instrument of the Jewish leaders in their path to power and wealth.

> [1]As he looked up, Jesus saw the rich putting their gifts into the temple treasury. [2]He also saw a poor widow put in two very small copper coins. [3]"I tell you the truth," he said, "this poor widow has put in more than all the others. [4]All these people gave their gifts out of their wealth; but she out of her poverty put in all she had to live on."

COMMENTARY

1 The "temple treasury" (*to gazophylakion*, GK *1126*) was either a room in the temple or a "contribution box" (BDAG, 186). Marshall, 751, argues for the former (following Str-B, 2:37–45) and suggests that Jesus would have heard an announcement as to how much was being donated.

2–4 The widow's "two very small copper coins" (*lepta*—the familiar "mites") were each worth only a small fraction of a day's wage. Proportionate to her total financial worth, however, the woman's gift was far more valuable than the gifts of the wealthy (vv.3–4). The focus on her giving "out of her poverty" points also to her destitute condition as compared to the condition of those who "devour widows' houses" (20:47).

8. Signs of the End of the Age (21:5–38)

OVERVIEW

Jesus concludes his teaching ministry (apart from the Upper Room Discourse in John 14–16) with this discourse on the end-times. It is immediately followed in Luke by the conspiracy by Judas. The corresponding passages in Matthew 24 and Mark 13 are called the Olivet Discourse because, unlike in Luke, they tell us that Jesus was on the Mount of Olives when he spoke. In its narrative location, this discourse functions as the climactic pronouncement of judgment against Jerusalem (cf. Lk 13:34–35; 19:39–44).

Jesus' teachings in this discourse provide both a realistic warning about future events and a strong encouragement to persevere. They entail some notable difficulties of interpretation and literary analysis. But if the expositor concentrates on the series of exhortations in the discourse, then the supporting teachings, along with the problems of interpretation, will come into focus.

These exhortations are ninefold: (1) do not follow false leaders (v.8); (2) do not be frightened by the awesome events associated with the end-times in apocalyptic literature (vv.9–11); (3) do not worry about your legal defense when you are persecuted and face legal charges because of your Christian witness (vv.12–16); (4) when all turn against you, persevere and take a firm stand (vv.17–19); (5) flee Jerusalem when it is besieged (vv.20–24); (6) when the final apocalyptic events (the portents in heaven and on earth) do take place, take heart at your coming redemption when the Son of Man returns (vv.25–28); (7) recognize that these things point to the approach of the kingdom of God (vv.29–31); (8) be assured that throughout the apocalyptic period the Lord's words endure (vv.32–33); (9) be watchful and pray so that you will come through all of these things in a way that the Son of Man will approve of (vv.34–36).

Of these exhortations, only numbers 5–7 are affected by serious interpretive problems. These include the relationship of the destruction of Jerusalem to other future events and the literary problem of the tradition history of this pericope, specifically its relationship to Matthew 24 and Mark 13. (For more on the latter, see comments at vv.12–19; for helpful resources, see Notes.)

The exhortations can be grouped under five major topics in the discourse: (1) warnings against deception (vv.5–11); (2) encouragement during persecution (vv.12–19); (3) the destruction of Jerusalem (vv.20–24); (4) future events (vv.25–28); and (5) assurances concerning these events (vv.29–36). The problem with chronological sequence is partly alleviated by the realization that in this passage it is the starting point of the various periods that are in chronological order. Significant overlapping among the events is not ruled out (cf. Ellis, 241).

⁵Some of his disciples were remarking about how the temple was adorned with beautiful stones and with gifts dedicated to God. But Jesus said, ⁶"As for what you see here, the time will come when not one stone will be left on another; every one of them will be thrown down."

⁷"Teacher," they asked, "when will these things happen? And what will be the sign that they are about to take place?"

⁸He replied: "Watch out that you are not deceived. For many will come in my name, claiming, 'I am he,' and, 'The time is near.' Do not follow them. ⁹When you hear of wars and revolutions, do not be frightened. These things must happen first, but the end will not come right away."

¹⁰Then he said to them: "Nation will rise against nation, and kingdom against kingdom. ¹¹There will be great earthquakes, famines and pestilences in various places, and fearful events and great signs from heaven.

¹²"But before all this, they will lay hands on you and persecute you. They will deliver you to synagogues and prisons, and you will be brought before kings and governors, and all on account of my name. ¹³This will result in your being witnesses to them. ¹⁴But make up your mind not to worry beforehand how you will defend yourselves. ¹⁵For I will give you words and wisdom that none of your adversaries will be able to resist or contradict. ¹⁶You will be betrayed even by parents, brothers, relatives and friends, and they will put some of

you to death. [17]All men will hate you because of me. [18]But not a hair of your head will perish. [19]By standing firm you will gain life.

[20]"When you see Jerusalem being surrounded by armies, you will know that its desolation is near. [21]Then let those who are in Judea flee to the mountains, let those in the city get out, and let those in the country not enter the city. [22]For this is the time of punishment in fulfillment of all that has been written. [23]How dreadful it will be in those days for pregnant women and nursing mothers! There will be great distress in the land and wrath against this people. [24]They will fall by the sword and will be taken as prisoners to all the nations. Jerusalem will be trampled on by the Gentiles until the times of the Gentiles are fulfilled.

[25]"There will be signs in the sun, moon and stars. On the earth, nations will be in anguish and perplexity at the roaring and tossing of the sea. [26]Men will faint from terror, apprehensive of what is coming on the world, for the heavenly bodies will be shaken. [27]At that time they will see the Son of Man coming in a cloud with power and great glory. [28]When these things begin to take place, stand up and lift up your heads, because your redemption is drawing near."

[29]He told them this parable: "Look at the fig tree and all the trees. [30]When they sprout leaves, you can see for yourselves and know that summer is near. [31]Even so, when you see these things happening, you know that the kingdom of God is near.

[32]"I tell you the truth, this generation will certainly not pass away until all these things have happened. [33]Heaven and earth will pass away, but my words will never pass away.

[34]"Be careful, or your hearts will be weighed down with dissipation, drunkenness and the anxieties of life, and that day will close on you unexpectedly like a trap. [35]For it will come upon all those who live on the face of the whole earth. [36]Be always on the watch, and pray that you may be able to escape all that is about to happen, and that you may be able to stand before the Son of Man."

[37]Each day Jesus was teaching at the temple, and each evening he went out to spend the night on the hill called the Mount of Olives, [38]and all the people came early in the morning to hear him at the temple.

COMMENTARY

6–7 The opening of the discourse resembles, with several exceptions, those in Matthew 24 and Mark 13. Luke does not mention that Jesus himself was at the temple (though the mention of architectural details and the "gifts" shows that Jesus and his disciples were on the premises, v.5). As observed above, Luke does not mention the Mount of Olives. The Matthean part of the question—"and of the end of the age" (Mt 24:3)—is missing. For the temple to be totally destroyed was unthinkable (v.6). Its sanctuary and surrounding structure were huge, solid, and glistening—a symbol of Jewish religion and Herodian splendor. The disciples do not ask for a "sign" (v.7) because they are doubting but because they need a clue as to when the end will come.

8 The word "deceived" (*planēthēte*, GK *4414*) was frequently used in the early Christian centuries to describe the activities of heretics and false prophets (e.g., 2Jn 7; cf. Rev 2:20). Even as late as the time of Origen (died ca. 254), pretenders were making such claims as v.8 describes (Origen, *Cels.* 7.9).

9–11 Certain frightening events are typically linked in apocalyptic literature with the end-times (e.g., Isa 13:10, 13; 34:4; Eze 14:21; 32:7–8; Am 8:9; Hag 2:6; *4 Ezra* 13:30ff.; 1QH 11:29–39). Jesus is teaching that, while such things are indeed to take place as history moves toward its climax, Christians should not be terrified by them. (Luke alone has *mē ptoēthēte*, "do not be frightened," v.9.) The reason is that wars, revolutions, and natural calamities are not a signal that the end of history is to come immediately (*eutheōs*, GK *2311*; NIV, "right away"), as is commonly supposed even today. The sample summary of apocalyptic events in v.11 includes the familiar "famines and pestilences" (*limoi kai loimoi*, a literary device called paronomasia [the employment of words with similar sounds]).

12–19 In its content this section resembles Mark 13:9–13 and also the account of the sending out of the Twelve (Mt 10:17–22). Yet the actual similarities are minimal—only thirteen words or syllables (Gk.) in vv.12–16 and all of v.17. It is not certain whether Luke edited Mark or drew on a different source, or whether Jesus repeated this teaching on different occasions.

Among the differences between vv.12–19 and the passages in Matthew and Mark are: (1) Luke's omission of the preaching of the gospel to the Gentiles (Mt 10:18) and around the world (Mk 13:10), possibly because he has in mind only the period just before the destruction of the temple in AD 70 (cf. Marshall, 768); (2) a promise of wisdom in time of

persecution (v.15) in place of a reference to the Holy Spirit (cf. Mt 10:20; Mk 13:11)—an unusual omission for Luke, with his strong interest in the Holy Spirit; (3) the addition of the saying "not a hair of your head" (v.18), the idea of which had already appeared in 12:7; and (4) a change in the wording of v.19; whereas Matthew 10:22 (cf. 24:13) and Mark 13:13 have "he who stands firm to the end will be saved [*sōthēsetai*, GK *5392*]" (which encourages those who are standing firm, because God will bring rescue, cf. Lk 18:7–8), the Lukan expression is stronger: literally, "you will gain [*ktēsasthe*, GK *3227*] your lives [*tas psychas hymōn*]." The meaning is close to that of Matthew 10:39; 16:25; Mark 8:35; Luke 9:24; and 17:33, which state, with some verbal differences, that whoever loses his life for the sake of Christ will preserve it, the implication being spiritual survival. If perseverance is indeed a major concern of Luke (cf. S. Brown, *Apostasy and Perseverance*), then the particular wording of 21:19 in comparison to its parallels is significant.

20–24 The reference to Jerusalem (v.20) need not be construed as a *vaticinium ex eventu* (prophecy after the event). It is often pointed out that, were this so, Luke could have included more precise details. Furthermore, the vocabulary was already at hand and well known (cf. 2Ch 15:6; Isa 3:25–26; 8:21–22; 13:13; 29:3; Jer 20:4–5; 34:17; 52:4; Eze 4:1–4; Da 9:26–27; Hos 9:7; 14:1; Zep 1:14–15).

The description of the siege of Jerusalem, a protracted event, contrasts with the sudden events in Luke's earlier apocalyptic passage (17:22–37). There the one on the roof will not even have time to reenter his house. But here those out in the country are warned not to try to get back into the city during the siege (v.21). *Kykloumenēn* ("surrounded," GK *3241*, v.20) refers to the siege itself, not its completion; so reentry was still possible (Morris, 298).

The vivid description is painful to read. It is certainly possible to assume that Jesus' predictions incorporated two phases: (1) the events of AD 70 involving the temple and (2) those in the distant future, described in more apocalyptic terms. The latter takes us back to 17:20–37 where Jesus' words about the end-time naturally fit in with the Pharisees' question (17:20). Thus what Luke has there can now be omitted from ch. 21. In its place, using much of the same vocabulary, Luke now substitutes a prophetic oracle on Jerusalem. Among the words common to Mark 13 and Luke 21 are different forms of *erēmōsis* ("desolation," GK *2247*)—a fact suggesting that Luke edited this section from Mark. Yet the word "desolation" is a natural one for this passage even if it were not in the source (see Notes).

Luke's preservation of the saying in v.24, where *plērōthōsin* (another word for fulfillment) occurs, shows his interest in the Gentiles. Verse 24 implies that an extended period of time is needed for this fulfillment—an idea consistent with Luke's twofold emphasis on a period of waiting along with an expectation of Jesus' imminent return. It also implies an end to the period when Gentiles are prominent in God's plan (cf. Ro 11:11–27, esp. v.25, "until the full number of the Gentiles has come in").

25 The words in Matthew 24 and Mark 13 about false Christs are omitted; Luke has placed them in 17:23. Now he again takes up material from the Olivet Discourse, where Jesus speaks of apocalyptic signs of the end-time. The "roaring . . . of the sea" is reminiscent of Isaiah 17:12; in biblical prophecy the sea often symbolizes chaos or stands for a source of fear.

27–28 Daniel 7:13 is the main OT source for v.27 and the NT concept of the glorified "Son of Man." "Power," "coming," and "glory" are terms appropriate to Christ as Son of Man and King (cf. Mt 16:27–28; Mk 9:1; Lk 9:26–27; 2Pe 1:16–17). Luke omits the saying about the gathering of the elect (cf. Mt 24:31; Mk 13:27), which might have

followed v.27. Instead he has Jesus' words of encouragement in expectation of "redemption" (v.28).

29 The illustration of the fig tree, found in the parallel passages in Matthew and Mark, is clear. Luke, perhaps to avoid any thought of exclusiveness based on the fig tree's symbolizing of Israel, adds the words "and all the trees."

32 "Generation" (*genea*, GK *1155*) could refer here to a span of time or to a class or race of people. In the former sense it could mean the decades following Jesus' lifetime. (Ellis, 246, notes that in lQpHab 2:7; 7:2 it includes several lifetimes.) If this whole passage thus referred to the destruction of Jerusalem, the heavenly portents would have to be understood figuratively (so J. Marcellus Kik, *Matthew Twenty-four* [Swengal, Pa.: Bible Truth Depot, 1948]). If *genea*, still in the sense of a span of time, referred to the period of time following the initial events of the end-time, it could indicate that once the sequence began it would be brought through to conclusion without delay. This does not necessarily demand a predictable time framework beginning with some identifiable event such as would permit setting dates for the Lord's return. The references cited above in the Qumran commentary on Habakkuk preclude this. The span of time would be too great to calculate precisely. The other major alternative—"generation" as a class or race of people—would make the most sense if understood as meaning the Jewish people. The point then would be that the Jewish people would be preserved throughout the ages till the consummation of history by Jesus' return.

The usage of *genea* in the Gospels is inconclusive. It frequently refers to Jesus' contemporaries, classing them as evil and unbelieving (e.g., 9:41), but that is hardly the meaning in this discourse. *Genea* here probably means the people living in the end-time, who "will be sure that the last events have begun and will be brought to a consummation" (Marshall, 780). The next most reasonable interpretation would be that it means the Jewish race, but that is hardly the emphasis here.

33 The reference to the permanence of Jesus' words is most appropriate here. In comparison to the temporary nature of the heavens and earth, the promises of Jesus will not be left unfulfilled (cf. 16:17). Significantly, while Luke begins the main section of his story with Isaiah 40 (Lk 3:4–6), in this discourse at the end of the earthly life of Jesus the same chapter is evoked where one finds a note on the permanence of God's promises ("the grass withers and the flowers fall, but the word of our God stands forever," Isa 40:8; cf. 50:10–11). Implicit in this saying is the claim that Jesus' words are to be equated with the promises of God the Father.

34 The conclusion of the discourse again emphasizes faithfulness, with warnings not only against carousing but also against the "anxieties of life" (cf. 8:14; 12:22–26). The note on the end that "will not come right away" (v.9) is balanced by this emphasis on the suddenness of the arrival of such a day ("unexpectedly like a trap").

35–36 Universal judgment will appear, and disciples are called to be alert and faithful to the end. The call to be watchful is one that frequently appears in NT eschatological discussions (cf. E. Lövestam, *Spiritual Wakefulness in the New Testament* [Lund: Gleerup, 1963]).

37–38 Only Luke discloses that Jesus taught in the temple by day but spent each night outside Jerusalem on the Mount of Olives (v.37). It is difficult to know whether Luke mentions this to show the danger awaiting Jesus in the city or to show that Jesus dissociated himself from the city (see Overview, 19:28–44), or whether it is simply a matter-of-fact statement. He is careful to tell us, just as he did in his earlier narratives of Jesus' ministry (4:14–15, 22, 32, 37, 42; 5:19, 26, 29), how popular Jesus was. Here it is the "people" (*laos*, GK *3295*), the responsive group as distinguished from the mere "crowds" (*ochloi*, GK *4063*) and the leaders, who come to the temple to hear his teaching "early in the morning" (v.38).

NOTES

5–38 The problem of the tradition history of this pericope and the issues surrounding Luke's possible editing of Mark 13 is a complex one. A concise summary with careful judgments can be found in Marshall, 752–84 (esp. 754–58). An overlooked treatment of the relationship between Luke 17 and Luke 21 is in J. Oliver Buswell Jr., *A Systematic Theology of the Christian Religion* (Grand Rapids: Zondervan, 1963), 2:368–71; written before the widespread use of redaction criticism, this book contains some original and useful suggestions. Among the major contributions to the problem are V. Taylor, *Behind the Third Gospel* (Oxford: Clarendon, 1926), 101–25, on the possibility of a source other than Mark, and T. Schramm, *Der Markus-Stoff bei Lukas* (SNTSMS 15; Cambridge: Cambridge Univ. Press, 1971), 171–82, on the same issue. A useful survey is found in D. Wenham, "Recent Study of Mark 13," *Theological Students Fellowship Bulletin* 71 (1975): 6–15; 72 (1975): 1–9. See also Colin Brown, "The Parousia and Eschatology in the NT," in *NIDNTT* 2:901–31 (an extensive bibliography follows on 931–35).

10 The formula ἔλεγεν αὐτοῖς (*elegen autois*, "he said to them") is comparable to the one in v.8 (ὁ δὲ εἶπεν, *ho de eipen*, "and he said") except for the difference in tense. Some have considered this as a marker dividing up the various topics in this discourse. Without considering it as a formal marker, this second formula (v.10) functions to widen out the discussion into material that moves beyond the immediate concern expressed by the disciples (v.7). For a further discussion of the connection between the various sections, see V. Fusco, "Problems of Structure in Luke's Eschatological Discourse (Luke 21:7–36)," in *Luke and Acts* (ed. O'Collins and Marconi), 72–92.

20 The word ἐρήμωσις (*erēmōsis*, "desolation," GK *2247*) alludes to the references in Daniel (9:27; 11:31; 12:1) in which the desolation of the temple was described (cf. Mt 24:15; Mk 13:14). The new desolation is comparable to the sacrilege of Solomon's temple, and this desolation is likewise connected with the unfolding of the plan of God. Luke's use of the word (instead of the fuller phrase "the abomination that causes desolation" in Matthew and Mark) may also reflect similar uses of the same word in other OT passages (cf. Marshall, 772) in which it implies not simply sacrilege but also destruction.

B. The Passion of the Lord (22:1–23:56)

1. The Agreement to Betray Jesus (22:1–6)

OVERVIEW

Luke's passion narrative begins ominously with a description of Judas's plot. Only Luke says that "Satan entered Judas" (v.3). Though Conzelmann's theory that the period between Jesus' temptation and this event is free from satanic activity is wrong (ably refuted by S. Brown, 6–12), there is certainly a focus on these two times of heightened satanic opposition. Ellis, 248, observes that "in the temptation Satan entices; in the passion he threatens." Moreover, the note on satanic activity also highlights the eschatological character of the events to come.

> [1]Now the Feast of Unleavened Bread, called the Passover, was approaching, [2]and the chief priests and the teachers of the law were looking for some way to get rid of Jesus, for they were afraid of the people. [3]Then Satan entered Judas, called Iscariot, one of the Twelve. [4]And Judas went to the chief priests and the officers of the temple guard and discussed with them how he might betray Jesus. [5]They were delighted and agreed to give him money. [6]He consented, and watched for an opportunity to hand Jesus over to them when no crowd was present.

COMMENTARY

1 The "Feast of Unleavened Bread" lasted seven days (Ex 12:15–20). The Jewish dates for Passover were Nisan 14–15 (early spring). The Feast of Unleavened Bread followed it immediately and also came to be included under the Passover. The mention of the two together also serves to evoke the exodus traditions.

2 Earlier the Pharisees were prominent in opposing Jesus (see comments at 5:17). Now "the chief priests and teachers of the law" were taking the initiative against him. In that society the priests were not only religious leaders but also wielded great political power. The scribes (teachers of the law) were undoubtedly involved because their legal expertise would be useful in building a case against Jesus. Matthew, Mark, and Luke all take pains to show that "the people" (*ton laon*, GK *3295*) were a deterrent to the schemes of the leaders. The mention of "the people" takes on special significance since Jerusalem will be filled with pilgrims during this major pilgrim festival. The number of those who would have been present has been estimated to be around half a million (cf. E. P. Sanders, *Judaism: Practice and Belief 63 BCE–66 CE* [Philadelphia: Fortress, 1990], 126).

3–4 Among the Synoptics only Luke exposes Judas's plot as the work of Satan (v.3; but cf. Jn 13:2, 27), and this reference points the readers back to the end of the temptation narrative where it was said that Satan left Jesus "until an opportune time" (4:13). Moreover, Luke alone mentions the presence of the "officers of the temple guard" (v.4; cf. Ac 4:1; 5:24). It was probably their soldiers who captured Jesus (Jn 18:3). Municipalities had their own officers and so did the Jerusalem religious establishment.

5 The monetary transaction helps to reveal the motive of Judas's action. The note that the Jewish leaders "were delighted" is noteworthy since in this gospel the verb used (*chairō*, lit., "to rejoice," GK *5897*) was commonly used in describing the joyful witness of God's mighty acts. Ironically, the evil act of Judas will actually result in the accomplishment of God's climactic act in history.

6 Luke alone mentions that in betraying Jesus Judas sought to avoid the crowds.

NOTES

4 The word στρατηγοῖς (*stratēgois*, "officers of the temple guard," GK *5130*) is translated, literally, "soldiers." On soldiers in the ancient world and in Luke's writings, see *TDNT* 7:704, 709–10.

6 The verb ἐξωμολόγησεν (*exōmologēsen*, "consented," "promised," GK *2018*) is, contrary to customary usage, in the active voice, thereby apparently giving emphasis to Judas's eagerness (cf. Marshall, 789).

2. The Last Supper (22:7–23)

OVERVIEW

We now come to the climax of Luke's accounts of table fellowship, as Jesus uses the setting of the table to symbolize the significance of the sharing of his life. The source behind Luke's account seems to be similar to the one behind Paul's (1Co 11:23–26), though a significant difference in emphasis remains (see Notes). In anticipating the actual death of Jesus, this "sacrifice" can be understood as a prophetic symbolic act whereby Jesus' act initiates the series of events to come (cf. N. A. Beck, "The Last Supper as an Efficacious Symbolic Act," *JBL* 89 [1970]: 192–98; D. Wenham, "How Jesus Understood the Last Supper: A Parable in Action," *Them* 20 [1995]: 11–16). Strikingly, in this sacrifice Jesus is both the "sacrificer" and the "sacrificial victim." In theological terms, the fact that Jesus is the subject of his own fate shows that his death is not an accident in history.

7Then came the day of Unleavened Bread on which the Passover lamb had to be sacrificed. 8Jesus sent Peter and John, saying, "Go and make preparations for us to eat the Passover."

9"Where do you want us to prepare for it?" they asked.

10He replied, "As you enter the city, a man carrying a jar of water will meet you. Follow him to the house that he enters, 11and say to the owner of the house, 'The Teacher asks: Where is the guest room, where I may eat the Passover with my disciples?' 12He will show you a large upper room, all furnished. Make preparations there."

13They left and found things just as Jesus had told them. So they prepared the Passover.

14When the hour came, Jesus and his apostles reclined at the table. 15And he said to them, "I have eagerly desired to eat this Passover with you before I suffer. 16For I tell you, I will not eat it again until it finds fulfillment in the kingdom of God."

17After taking the cup, he gave thanks and said, "Take this and divide it among you. 18For I tell you I will not drink again of the fruit of the vine until the kingdom of God comes."

19And he took bread, gave thanks and broke it, and gave it to them, saying, "This is my body given for you; do this in remembrance of me."

20In the same way, after the supper he took the cup, saying, "This cup is the new covenant in my blood, which is poured out for you. 21But the hand of him who is going to betray me is with mine on the table. 22The Son of Man will go as it has been decreed, but woe to that man who betrays him." 23They began to question among themselves which of them it might be who would do this.

COMMENTARY

7 Luke now sharpens his chronology (in v.1 having only mentioned that the Passover "was approaching"). The NIV adds the word "lamb" as an implication of the text. A kid could also be used. Luke clearly states that it was the day of sacrifice—normally Nisan 14. The actual Passover meal was celebrated after sundown, when according to Jewish reckoning the next day—Nisan 15—had begun. This chronological note is important for Luke as he emphasizes the framework within which Jesus' death is to be understood.

8–9 Luke shows that Jesus initiated plans for the Passover arrangements (v.8; Mt 26:17 and Mk 14:12 mention only the disciples' question, v.9). Jesus'

instructions guaranteed privacy—indeed secrecy—perhaps to avoid his premature arrest.

10–13 These verses show Jesus' supernatural knowledge. The person Jesus asked his disciples to follow would be a man carrying a water jar. Ordinarily only women carried jars; men used leather skins for water. The "large upper room" (v.12) was on the second story under a flat roof accessible by an outside stairway. It was "furnished" with the couches for reclining at a Passover meal and with necessary utensils. Things were "just as Jesus had told them" (v.13), showing that he was far more than a "Teacher" (v.11), though that term was customary.

14–16 Sometimes, as has often been observed, Luke does not use the terminology of vicarious atonement when we might expect him to. Thus in vv.24–27, the passage describing the rivalry between the disciples and the contrasting servant role Jesus adopted, Luke does not include the "ransom saying" of Mark 10:45. Nevertheless, the strong link Luke forges with the Passover underscores the redemptive motif. In the transfiguration narrative (9:31) he has already used the Greek word *exodos* (GK *2016*; NIV, "departure"), with its redemptive connotations, to describe Jesus' approaching death. (For a helpful discussion of the theology of atonement in this Lukan passage, see F. G. Carpinelli, "'Do This as My Memorial' [Luke 22:19]: Lucan Soteriology of Atonement," *CBQ* 61 [1999]: 74–91). This passage also exhibits the strong orientation to the future that characterizes Luke's gospel.

Both of Jesus' opening statements are strongly worded. "I have eagerly desired" (v.15) represents a strong double construction with a Semitic cast—*epithymia epethymēsa* (lit., "with desire I have desired," GK *2123, 2121*). The second statement begins with an emphatic future negative: I will not eat (*ou mē phagō*, v.16; a similar construction occurs in v.18). Together the sentences convey the depth of Jesus' feelings at this time and the immense significance of what is taking place. Grammatically the statements may imply that, though he had greatly desired to do so, Jesus would not partake of the Passover (so J. Jeremias, *The Eucharistic Words of Jesus* [2d ed.; London: SCM, 1966], 207–18). Luke's placement of the saying may also imply this, since he puts it before the actual meal in contrast to Mark and Matthew, who place it after the meal (Mt 26:29; Mk 14:25). It is still likely, however, that Jesus actually did partake when, as the host at the meal, he "took" the cup and the bread (vv.17, 19–20).

The word "again" in v.16 (*apo tou nyn*, lit., "from now on") accords with this likelihood. But insofar as it represents the word *ouketi*, it might better be omitted, for the text is uncertain and probably not original here (see Notes). In any case, what Jesus would not eat till the coming of the kingdom is described simply as "it" (*auto*) and probably means the lamb rather than the meal as a whole (cf. Marshall, 796).

17–18 Unlike the other accounts of the Last Supper, Luke mentions a cup before (v.17) as well as after (v.20) the bread. That vv.19–20 are missing from some Western texts complicates this difference. If the words were not in Luke's original account there would be a difficult problem—the mention of a cup before but not after the bread. In spite of some arguments to the contrary, it seems reasonable to hold the authenticity of vv.19b–20.

Luke has apparently combined his data from various sources to describe both the Passover setting of the supper (vv.7–18) and the institution of the Lord's Supper (vv.19–20) instead of following Mark (see Notes). If so, the seeming disjunction and the problem of the two cups are understandable. The cup of v.17 may be the first of the traditional four cups taken during the Passover meal. In this case, Jesus' comments come at the beginning of that meal. This cup was followed by part of the Passover meal and the singing of Psalms 113 and 114. Alternatively, the cup of v.17 may be the third cup, mentioned both here in connection with the Passover setting and again in connection with its place in the Eucharist, on which Luke focuses (v.20).

The uncertainties of the passage should not detract from the high significance of the saying itself. The meal is a turning point. Jesus anticipated it, and he likewise anticipates the next genuine meal of its kind that he will eat sometime in the future, when the longed-for kingdom finally comes, or, in Luke's characteristic vocabulary, "finds fulfillment" (*plērōthē*, GK *4444*, v.16; the saying in v.18 has a near parallel in Mt 26:29; Mk 14:25). The believer in the present age observes the Lord's Supper "until he comes" (1Co 11:26).

19–20 As stated above, these words of institution may come from a non-Markan source. Similar wording in 1 Corinthians 11:24–25, written before AD 60, shows that it was probably an early source used by both Luke and Paul. This supports the reliability of Luke's research (1:1–4). The suffering motif is consistent with Jesus' understanding of his mission as the Suffering Servant.

The "bread" (*arton*, GK *788*, v.19) was the thin, unleavened bread used in the Passover. "Gave thanks" translates the verb *eucharisteō* (GK *2373*), the source of the beautiful word Eucharist often used to signify the Lord's Supper. Luke alone has "given for you" (*hyper hymōn didomenon* [GK *1443*]) in the saying over the bread, as well as "poured out for you" (*to hyper hymōn ekchynnomenon* [GK *1773*]) in the cup saying (v.20). The "pouring out" may be interpreted as a symbolic act that points to Jesus' own death on the cross (see, however, L. C. Boughton, "'Being Shed for You/Many': Time-Sense and Consequences in the Synoptic Cup Citations," *TynBul* 48 [1997]: 249–70, who points to the possibility of a future reference in this present passive participle).

"In remembrance of me" (v.19) directs our attention primarily to the person of Christ and not merely to the benefits we receive (of whatever nature we may understand them to be) from partaking of the bread and cup. The final cup, following the sequence of several refillings during the Passover, signifies the "new covenant" (v.20) in Jesus' blood. The disciples would have been reminded of the "blood of the covenant" (Ex 24:8), i.e., the blood

used ceremonially to confirm the covenant. The new covenant (cf. Jer 31:31–34) carried with it assurance of forgiveness through Jesus' blood shed on the cross and the inner work of the Holy Spirit in motivating us and enabling us to fulfill our covenantal responsibility.

21–22 Because this saying follows the Last Supper, one might assume that Judas was present at the institution of the Lord's Supper. Matthew 26:21–25 and Mark 14:18–21, along with John 13:21–27, indicate that Judas was there at least for the Passover, for he had dipped the bread in the dish. John 13:30 says that Judas went out immediately afterward; so apparently he was not there for the supper itself. But since John does not actually relate the events of the supper, this is only an implication. By mentioning the "hand" of Judas (v.21), Luke draws attention to his participation in the Passover (or supper), thus heightening the tragedy. Significantly, while table fellowship reflects the intimacy of the community, it is within this setting that betrayal is announced.

In each of the Synoptics, this saying about the Son of Man (v.22) includes a reference to the "man" who will betray him. The Greek word *anthrōpos* (GK *476*) thus appears twice, making a sober play on the word "man." The use of "decreed" (*hōrismenon*, GK *3988*) emphasizes divine sovereignty—a theme dominant in Luke—though this particular word occurs rarely in the NT (cf. Ac 2:23; 10:42; 17:31; cf. also Ro 1:4). Instead of "decreed," Matthew (26:24) and Mark (14:21) have "it is written" (*gegraptai*, GK *1211*). Divine sovereignty is balanced by human responsibility; so Jesus pronounces a "woe" on the betrayer. The same balance occurs in Acts 2:23.

23 Luke alone among the Gospels has v.23, which shows not only the disciples' concern but also the secrecy that still surrounded Judas's treachery.

NOTES

7–23 The composition of this passage is complex. Verses 7–13 seem to be dependent on Mark 14:12–16. Verse 14 differs from Matthew and Mark and may be from a special source. Verses 15–17 are unique to Luke, with v.18 showing some similarity to Mark 14:25. Except for the first and last phrases, vv.19–20 appear to be from a non-Markan source, possibly one also used by Paul for 1 Corinthians 11:23–26, modified in the process. If this is so, it reflects a very early form of the tradition that contains the words of institution of the Eucharist. Taken together, the verses constitute an original narrative edited by Luke from different sources.

7 It is not certain on what day of the week Jesus celebrated the Passover. Few scholars question that Jesus was crucified on a Friday. There is considerable doubt, however, as to the chronological relationship between the Passover, the Last Supper, and the crucifixion. Some infer from John 13:1; 18:28; 19:14, 31, 42 that the Passover did not occur until after Jesus was crucified. In that case the paschal lambs would have been killed in preparation for the Passover at the very time Jesus was on the cross, which would have had strong symbolic significance. But if that inference is correct, then (assuming the chronological reliability of all four gospels on this point) the Synoptics could not be describing a Passover meal as the setting for the Last Supper, in spite of all appearances that it was. Another approach interprets the Johannine texts above as being consistent with a pre-crucifixion Passover. Norval Geldenhuys has a clear discussion of this possibility (*Commentary on the Gospel of Luke* [NICNT; Grand Rapids: Eerdmans, 1951], 649–70).

Most scholars now look elsewhere for a solution. A. Jaubert (*The Date of the Last Supper* [New York: Alba], 1965) proposed that the Last Supper was held on an earlier evening in the week when sectarians such as those at Qumran (where the Dead Sea Scrolls were produced) celebrated the Passover. This would allow more time for the trial of Jesus, as well as solving the Passover chronology. But the theory conflicts with other data. Harold W. Hoehner (*Chronological Aspects of the Life of Christ* [Grand Rapids: Zondervan, 1977], 65–93) suggests that the differences between the Synoptics and John arise from differing methods of reckoning dates used by different Jewish groups. If some calculated the date from evening to evening and others from dawn to dawn, both groups could celebrate the Passover on the same date but on different days. The Judeans (and John) might have followed one method and the Galileans (and the Synoptics) the other. Whether or not any of the schemes mentioned here is correct, at least we have several plausible solutions to this chronological problem.

16 The word οὐκέτι (*ouketi*, "never again, no longer") is not in some of the most reliable MSS (e.g., B or, apparently, 𝔓⁷⁵). It may have been added by a copyist, who believed it made better sense (cf. Metzger, 147).

19–20 The phrase εἰς τὴν ἐμὴν ἀνάμνησιν (*eis tēn emēn anamnēsin*, "in remembrance of me," v.19) points to the institution of a memorial, a symbol through which Jesus' death can be remembered. The reference is primarily to the "human" remembrance of Jesus and not "God's" own act of remembering (cf. Carpinelli, "'Do This as My Memorial,'" 76–78).

The words τὸ ὑπὲρ ὑμῶν . . . ἐκχυννόμενον (*to hyper hymōn . . . ekchynnomenon*, "given for you [v.19] . . . poured out [for you, v.20]") are found in every Greek uncial MS except D. They are lacking in the

Western text and some other sources. Those who have followed the assumption that because the Western text tends to include rather than omit questionable readings, and that on those few occasions when it does omit readings it should be given special weight, apply that principle here. Also, since copyists have a tendency to include anything they believe may be genuine, any shorter reading is given strong consideration. Furthermore, the wording is similar to 1 Corinthians 11:24–25, including words unusual in Luke; so there is a suspicion that this was copied from another source, perhaps combining elements from Paul and Mark.

Arguments for the longer text include the judgment that the Western text is not to be given preference (cf. K. Snodgrass, "Western Non-Interpolations," *JBL* 91 [1972]: 369–79); the weight of all the MSS that include it make it the likely original; the probability that the source of the words is a very old tradition that Paul also followed; and the likelihood that the sequence of cup-bread-cup in the longer reading was perplexing to later copyists, who preferred readings that simplified the narrative. Preferring the shorter text is A. Vööbus, "A New Approach to the Problem of the Shorter and Longer Text in Luke," *NTS* 15 (1968–69): 457–63; preferring the longer text are Ellis, 254–56; Marshall, 799–801.

3. Teachings at the Table (22:24–38)

OVERVIEW

In ancient times table fellowship frequently provided the setting for extended discussion and conversation (cf. Dennis E. Smith, *From Symposium to Eucharist* [Minneapolis: Fortress, 2003], 47–65). In this passage the setting is especially appropriate when community identity and formation is at stake. It is in this setting that one is not surprised to find discussions on the ranks of the individual members along with other instructions related to the life of this community. The dispute of the disciples shows, however, that they, too, misunderstood the true nature of God's kingdom.

[24]Also a dispute arose among them as to which of them was considered to be greatest. [25]Jesus said to them, "The kings of the Gentiles lord it over them; and those who exercise authority over them call themselves Benefactors. [26]But you are not to be like that. Instead, the greatest among you should be like the youngest, and the one who rules like the one who serves. [27]For who is greater, the one who is at the table or the one who serves? Is it not the one who is at the table? But I am among you as one who serves. [28]You are those who have stood by me in my trials. [29]And I confer on you a kingdom, just as my Father conferred one on me, [30]so that you may eat and drink at my table in my kingdom and sit on thrones, judging the twelve tribes of Israel.

[31]"Simon, Simon, Satan has asked to sift you as wheat. [32]But I have prayed for you, Simon, that your faith may not fail. And when you have turned back, strengthen your brothers."

[33]But he replied, "Lord, I am ready to go with you to prison and to death."

³⁴Jesus answered, "I tell you, Peter, before the rooster crows today, you will deny three times that you know me."

³⁵Then Jesus asked them, "When I sent you without purse, bag or sandals, did you lack anything?"

"Nothing," they answered.

³⁶He said to them, "But now if you have a purse, take it, and also a bag; and if you don't have a sword, sell your cloak and buy one. ³⁷It is written: 'And he was numbered with the transgressors'; and I tell you that this must be fulfilled in me. Yes, what is written about me is reaching its fulfillment."

³⁸The disciples said, "See, Lord, here are two swords."

"That is enough," he replied.

COMMENTARY

24 The disciples' questions about this treachery leads immediately, in Luke's order of events, to their argument—shocking on this solemn occasion—about precedence. See also the similar grasping after status that follows the passion prediction in Matthew 20:17–28 and Mark 10:32–45. The differences among the Gospels warrant our treating Luke's account of this argument as distinct from its near parallels. The word "considered" (*dokei*, "seems," "is regarded," GK *1506*) is well chosen, since status has to do with self-perception and with how one desires to be perceived by others.

25 Jesus replies by reminding the disciples of two objectionable characteristics of secular rulers: (1) they "lord it over" (*kyrieuousin*, GK *3259*) others—an attitude against which 1 Peter 5:3 warns elders in the church, and (2) they are given the title "Benefactor" (*euergetēs*, GK *2309*), which was actually a title, not merely a description (cf. *TDNT* 2:654–55). The form of the verb "call" (*kalountai*, GK *2813*) may be middle or passive. If the former, it may imply that these Gentile rulers were not passively waiting to be called Benefactor but sought the title for themselves. In Matthew 23:7 Jesus disapproved of a similar kind of status seeking. Actually, he himself is

the true "Benefactor." In Acts 10:38 Peter uses a verbal form of the word to describe Jesus as going about "doing good" (*euergetōn*, GK *2308*).

26–27 "But you" is emphatic, with the word "you" standing at the very beginning of the clause (*hymeis de*, v.26). Jesus makes two points about true greatness, namely, (1) that one should not seek the veneration given aged people in ancient Near Eastern society but be content with the lower place younger people had (this allusion to youthfulness does not appear in Mk 10:43 and is one of the variations that point to a different setting for Luke's record of the conversation), and (2) that the one who is truly great is the one who is a servant. In v.27 Luke gives an illustration from social custom. The person sitting at a dinner table had a higher social position than the waiter, who was often a slave. This illustration recalls the example of the Lord Jesus, who washed his disciples' feet as they reclined at the table of the Last Supper (Jn 13:12–17). This reversal of social expectation reveals the true nature of God's kingdom. (For more on the relationship between the Gentile "lords" and Jesus as "Lord," see P. K. Nelson, "The Flow of Thought in Luke 22.24–27," *JSNT* 43 [1991]: 113–23.)

28 Verse 28 is not in Matthew or Mark; it shows that Jesus' trials persisted between his temptation by Satan (ch. 4) and the passion events. It also recognizes the faithfulness of the disciples during this time. The fidelity of one of them is about to be tested severely (v.31). This theme of testing and faithfulness is prominent in Luke (see S. Brown, *Apostasy and Perseverance*).

29-30 The comparison "just as" (*kathōs*) is like that which Jesus gave his disciples in the commission in John 20:21, which was comparable to the one he received from his Father. Here in Luke the picture is not just that of a commission but of a conferral similar to a testament (cf. William S. Kurz, "Luke 22:14-28 and Greco-Roman and Biblical Farewell Addresses," *JBL* 104 [1985]: 251-68). There may also be a suggestion of the new covenant referred to in v.20. The verb *diatithemai* ("confer," GK *1416*) here (v.29) is cognate to *diathēkē* ("covenant," GK *1347*) there. (For a similar promise in noncovenantal language, see 12:32.)

The idea of a messianic banquet is reflected in v.30 (cf. 13:28-30; see comments there). Matthew's parallel to this verse is preceded by a reference to the "renewal of all things" (*palingenesia*, GK *4098*) instead of to the kingdom (Mt 19:28). The parallel in Matthew speaks of twelve thrones, but Luke omits the number, possibly to avoid the problem of Judas's occupying one of them. Since Luke does specify that there are twelve tribes, the omission is not important. (On the role of the Son of Man and the saints in judgment, see Da 7:9-18.) Specific designation of the number of tribes of Israel with respect to their future role does not appear again in the NT until Revelation 7:1-8. The concern for the twelve (tribes) appears, however, in Acts 1:12-26, where one finds the extended discussion of the attempt to fill out the number "twelve" due to the betrayal and death of Judas.

31-32 Only Luke records these words to Peter, at the same time omitting Jesus' prediction of the disciples' failure and their being scattered (Mt 26:30-32; Mk 14:26-28). He also omits any reference to Jesus' postresurrection appearance in Galilee, likewise omitted in his resurrection narrative (see comments at 24:6). While Luke has stressed the faithfulness of the disciples and might not wish to mention their defection, he does refer forthrightly to Peter's coming defection, where he attributes it to the direct activity of Satan. In Matthew and Mark there is a transition from the scene of the Last Supper to the Mount of Olives before the prediction of the disciples' defection is given. In Luke, Jesus' warning to Peter comes immediately after Jesus' commendation for the disciples' faithfulness and his promise concerning the kingdom. This makes a strong contrast. The repetition of Simon's name adds weight to the warning. The metaphor of sifting implies separating what is desirable from what is undesirable. Here the thought is that Satan wants to prove that at least some of the disciples will fail under severe testing.

The first occurrence of "you" in v.31 is in the plural (*hymas*). This refers to all the disciples in contrast to Peter, who is addressed (v.32) by the singular "you" (*sou*). Notice the use of the name "Simon" for Peter, apparently characteristic of Luke or of his special source.

Jesus' prayer that Simon's faith would not fail (v.32) has occasioned discussion over whether it was or was not answered. The verbal phrase "may not fail" (*mē eklipē*, GK *1722*) probably means "may not give out" or "may not disappear completely" (as the sun in a total eclipse). If this is correct, then Jesus' prayer was certainly answered. Peter's denial, though serious and symptomatic of a low level of faith, did not mean that he had ceased within himself to believe in the Lord. Nevertheless, his denial was so contrary to his former spiritual state that he would need to "return" (*epistrephō*, GK *2188*; NIV, "turn back") to Christ. The whole experience, far from disqualifying Peter from Christian service, would actually issue in a responsibility for him to "strengthen [his] brothers."

33–34 Peter's overconfident reply (v.33) includes a reference to death found among the four gospels only here and in John 13:37. The prediction of his denial (v.34) is substantially the same in all four gospels despite some differences in detail. Luke alone specifies that in the denial Peter will say he does not even know Jesus.

35–38 This short passage is difficult to interpret. The difficulties lie in (1) the syntax of v.36 (see Notes); (2) the problem of Jesus' apparent support for using weapons, which is hard to reconcile with his word to Peter when the latter used the sword (Mt 26:52); and (3) the seeming reversal of the instructions Jesus gave the Twelve and the Seventy-two concerning their missions (9:1–3; 10:1–3). Thus there is a question as to which principle regarding the use of force is normative for the church.

It is common to solve difficulties (2) and (3) by taking Jesus' words as ironic. But if that were so, v.38b—"that is enough"—would be hard to understand; for it would seem to continue the irony when one would have expected a correction of the disciples' misunderstanding of it. Any approach to a solution must take into account the fact that later, when the disciples were armed with these swords, Jesus opposed their use (vv.49–51). Moreover, the tone of v.52 is nonmilitant. Verse 36 clearly refers

back to 10:4, the sending of the Seventy-two; both passages mention the "purse" (*ballantion*, GK *964*) and the "bag" (*pēra*, GK *4385*; cf. the sending of the Twelve in 9:1–6, where the bag is mentioned but not the purse).

Here in v.35 there seems to be an affirmation of those principles in the question, "Did you lack anything?" Yet a contrast is also clearly intended. That contrast may imply that Jesus' earlier instructions were a radical statement applicable only to disciple-ship during his lifetime. On the other hand, however, it more likely indicates not a reversal of normal rules for the church's mission but an exception in a time of crisis (cf. "but now," *alla nyn*, v.36). Jesus is not being ironic but thoroughly serious. Since he told them not to buy more swords than they had (v.38), and since two were hardly enough to defend the group, the swords may simply be a vivid symbol of impending crisis not intended for actual use. Moreover, the eschatological nature of the moment may be highlighted by this evocation of a symbol that frequently appears in apocalyptic traditions. The sword may function as a symbol of the judgment that is to come on those who oppose the work of God (cf. H. A. J. Kruger, "A Sword Over His Head or In His Hand?" in *The Scriptures in the Gospels*, ed. C. M. Tuckett [Leuven: Leuven Univ. Press, 1997], 597–604).

Verse 37a is one of several clear quotations of Isaiah 53 in the NT (cf. UBS[4] "Index of Quotations," which cites Jn 12:38; Ro 10:16; Mt 8:17; Ac 8:32–33; 1Pe 2:22). These words serve as a balance to the reference to the sword as Jesus submits to the humiliation of those who oppose him.

NOTES

36 The phrase ὁ μὴ ἔχων (*ho mē echōn*, lit., "the [person] not having"; NIV, "if you don't have") lacks a direct object. It is not clear whether we should (1) supply the same object as in the first clause ("purse"), meaning that if they lacked money they should sell their cloaks to get money for swords, or (2) supply the word "sword" from the end of the clause, where it serves as the object of the verb ἀγορασάτω (*agorasatō*, "buy," GK *60*), since a sword is the needed item. The first is more balanced grammatically, but the final command to buy a sword is the same either way.

4. Prayer on the Mount of Olives (22:39–46)

OVERVIEW

Luke's account of this prayer differs in several respects from Mark's and Matthew's: (1) Luke does not specify the location as being Gethsemane; (2) he alone includes at the beginning an exhortation to the disciples to ward off temptation by means of prayer; and (3) his account omits much of the narrative included in Mark and Matthew. Such differences raise perplexing questions about Luke's sources—questions that lie beyond the scope of this commentary, though they may bear on Luke's theology. Also, there is considerable doubt as to the genuineness of vv.43–44 (see Notes). Theologically, there has been much discussion over the purpose of Jesus' prayer. Some have proposed a meaning for the "cup" of v.42 that would avoid any inference that Jesus had difficulty facing death.

³⁹Jesus went out as usual to the Mount of Olives, and his disciples followed him. ⁴⁰On reaching the place, he said to them, "Pray that you will not fall into temptation." ⁴¹He withdrew about a stone's throw beyond them, knelt down and prayed, ⁴²"Father, if you are willing, take this cup from me; yet not my will, but yours be done." ⁴³An angel from heaven appeared to him and strengthened him. ⁴⁴And being in anguish, he prayed more earnestly, and his sweat was like drops of blood falling to the ground.

⁴⁵When he rose from prayer and went back to the disciples, he found them asleep, exhausted from sorrow. ⁴⁶"Why are you sleeping?" he asked them. "Get up and pray so that you will not fall into temptation."

COMMENTARY

39 Luke singles out Jesus by using a verbal ending in the third person singular (Mk 14:32 uses a plural ending). The NIV inserts the name "Jesus" for clarity. This reminds us of the way Luke focused attention on Jesus' initiative (see comments at 19:38). Jesus went to the Mount of Olives "as usual" (*kata to ethos*; cf. the virtually identical *kata to eiōthos*, 4:16), as mentioned in 21:37. He did not change his habits to elude Judas. Luke may have omitted the name "Gethsemane" to direct the reader's attention to the Mount of Olives. But since he did not mention the Mount of Olives as the scene of the eschatological discourse but introduced it only after the conclusion of the discourse (21:37), it may be that in both places he is simply following his practice of omitting names and other words not familiar to his wide readership. That Luke uses geographical features mainly as symbols is doubtful (see comments at 9:23).

40 While it is natural to think that the "temptation" (or "trial," *peirasmon*, GK *4280*) has something to do with that of the end-time, in view of vv.16, 18 (so Danker, 225), Marshall, 830, is probably correct that without the definite article the word does not refer to that specific time. The themes of prayer and temptation are common in Luke, so it is not surprising that only he has the saying in v.40. It is repeated in v.46, to which Matthew 26:41 and Mark 14:38 are parallel. Marshall interprets it in terms of vv.28–38.

41 Kneeling in prayer was not customary in Jesus' time (standing was the normal posture). But this scene is one of intense emotional strain (cf. Eph 3:14). Matthew and Mark say that Jesus fell to the ground (Mt 26:39; Mk 14:35).

42 It is fitting that Luke, who throughout his gospel stresses Jesus' conscious fulfillment of the purposes of God, should now emphasize Jesus' concern for the will of God. "If you are willing" (*ei boulei*, v.42) is absent from Matthew and Mark at this point, though they do have the rest of v.42.

As in Matthew 20:22 and Mark 10:38, Jesus uses the "cup" as a metaphor of his imminent passion. Some, however, have imagined that this metaphor implies that Jesus faced death with less bravery than others have faced it. (But to shrink from a painful death is not necessarily cowardice; the highest bravery may consist in being fully cognizant of impending and agonizing death and yet to embrace it voluntarily.) At any rate, it has been suggested that the cup Jesus feared was that he might die from the strain he was under before he could willingly offer himself on the cross. But this view fails to recognize that Jesus would not have been as concerned with the physical pain of his death as with the spiritual desolation of bearing our sin and its judgment on the cross (2Co 5:21; 1Pe 2:24). Moreover, in the OT the wrath of God expressed against sin was sometimes referred to by the metaphor of a "cup" (e.g., Ps 11:6, where the NIV translates *kôs* as "lot" rather than "cup"; cf. Ps 75:8; Isa 51:17; Jer 25:15–17).

43–44 These verses have some formidable textual difficulties (see Notes). Since they have a claim to genuineness and are included in most texts of the Greek NT, they require comment. Luke has already mentioned angels (v.43) many times—in the nativity narrative and elsewhere, e.g., 9:26; 12:8–9; 15:10; 16:22. So the appearance of an angel here in Gethsemane is not strange. In light of the role of the angels in Jewish traditions, the ancient audience may have read these verses as indicating "God's loving response to his servant who was suffering from unjust persecution" (R. Brown, *Death of the Messiah*, 1:188). Luke describes Jesus' agony in physical terms, as we might expect a physician to do. The sweating was apparently so profuse that it looked like blood dripping from a wound (v.44).

45–46 Luke does not dwell on the weakness of the disciples, nor does he describe in further detail Jesus' agony. Matthew and Mark refer to another prayer of Jesus and mention two more instances of the disciples' falling asleep. For Luke a single reference to each suffices, with the addition of an explanation for the disciples' sleep: exhaustion from sorrow (v.45). Luke does repeat the injunction for the disciples to "pray" lest they "fall into temptation" (v.46).

NOTES

43–44 These verses are textually uncertain. Their mention of angels and their description of Jesus' physical agony are not incompatible with Luke's perspective. Also, it is unlikely that copyists would have omitted the verses because of their supernatural element, even if they seemed an intrusion into this report of Jesus' intensely human suffering. Yet the MS support is weak. The UBS Greek NT cites "ancient and diversified witnesses," among them 𝔓75 ℵ A B, that omit the verses. Their inclusion in square brackets in the text of UBS[4] does not indicate that the committee thought them genuine but rather indicates its respect for the antiquity of the verses. Even if vv. 43–44 did not appear in the canonical Luke in early stages of the tradition, they may be authentic in their substance and message and may have conceivably been composed by Luke himself at some point.

5. Jesus' Arrest (22:47–53)

[47]While he was still speaking a crowd came up, and the man who was called Judas, one of the Twelve, was leading them. He approached Jesus to kiss him, [48]but Jesus asked him, "Judas, are you betraying the Son of Man with a kiss?"

[49]When Jesus' followers saw what was going to happen, they said, "Lord, should we strike with our swords?" [50]And one of them struck the servant of the high priest, cutting off his right ear.

[51]But Jesus answered, "No more of this!" And he touched the man's ear and healed him.

[52]Then Jesus said to the chief priests, the officers of the temple guard, and the elders, who had come for him, "Am I leading a rebellion, that you have come with swords and clubs? [53]Every day I was with you in the temple courts, and you did not lay a hand on me. But this is your hour—when darkness reigns."

COMMENTARY

47–48 Luke drops the introductory "and" (*kai*). Thus this pericope "is joined as closely as possible to the preceding one" (Marshall, 835). All the Synoptics make the point that Jesus was still speaking to his disciples when Judas and the crowd arrived. This emphasizes the sudden intrusion of Judas and the crowd into the somber scene in Gethsemane. In making the transition to Judas, Luke first refers to the crowd (not mentioned by Matthew or Mark). In Luke "the crowd" (*ochlos*, GK *4063*), in contrast to "the people" (*laos*, GK *3295*), is sometimes presented as being unfeeling, perhaps even hostile. From the crowd, attention moves to "the man who

was called Judas" (*ho legomenos Ioudas*, lit., "one called Judas"). The designation occurs only in Luke and seems to be a dramatic way of isolating Judas—holding him off at a distance for a derogatory look and comment, namely, "this Judas person." Each of the synoptic writers feels compelled to say that Judas was "one of the Twelve."

The betrayal was accomplished with a kiss. In Judas's scheme of betrayal, the kiss was the way he identified Jesus in the darkness of the night (Mk 14:44). But in the high drama of the actual situation it was cruelly hypocritical. In the Greek word order following Judas's name, three elements come together in stark succession—"with a kiss/the Son of Man/are you betraying?" (v.48).

49–51 See comments at vv.33–38 for the background to this incident. John 18:10 (but none of the Synoptics) tells us that it was Peter who drew the sword. Luke alone tells us in words a physician might use about Jesus' healing of the ear of the high priest's servant (v.51).

52 In v.52 the details regarding the makeup of the crowd—religious, political, and military leaders—are peculiar to Luke. These details may be part of his design to show that it was not the believing Jews who brought about Jesus' crucifixion but their arrogant leaders. Matthew and Mark do not bring this out until later (e.g., Mt 27:20; Mk 15:11, the

substance of which is not in Luke). Jesus' comment shows the underhanded nature of their act.

53 "This is your hour [*hōra*, GK *6052*]" sounds Johannine (e.g., Jn 12:23; 17:1 et al.), especially since it refers to the passion. But Luke also uses the word "hour" frequently, as well as other words designating a time of opportunity or destiny. The verb "reigns" represents the noun *exousia* ("power," "authority," GK *2026*). In the temptation, Satan had previously offered to Jesus *exousia* (4:6); but Jesus, who after obediently going to the cross would receive "all authority" from the Father (Mt 28:18), was willing to have Satan exercise his authority for a time under the divine plan of salvation.

NOTES

47 The Lukan account did not specify whether Judas did in fact kiss Jesus. To clarify this ambiguity, some witnesses (D 𝔓⁶⁹) have explicitly noted that Judas did accomplish his intended act.

51 The phrase ἐᾶτε ἕως τούτου (*eate heōs toutou*, "No more of this!") means literally, "Permit, or let go, up to this [point]!" It is usually taken to mean, "Stop what you are doing!" Marshall, 837, prefers understanding αὐτούς, *autous* ("them"), after ἐᾶτε, *eate*, with the meaning, "Let them [i.e., the police] have their way," as in the NEB. See, however, R. Brown, *Death of the Messiah*, 1:280.

6. Peter's Denial (22:54–62)

OVERVIEW

Throughout this and the succeeding sections, dramatic tension mounts. A contributing feature is the simultaneous action taking place in the house of the high priest with Jesus (v.54) and in the courtyard with Peter (v.55). Luke separates the two sequences of events instead of intertwining them as Matthew and Mark do. While this literary device differs from his alternation of stories about the births of Jesus and of John the Baptist (ch. 1), it does

enable the reader to follow Peter's experience and then Jesus' trial separately. Luke does not tell us anything about a night session of the trial but allows for it in v.54 (cf. vv.63–65; see Notes).

The story of Peter's denial could not have been invented. It presents a sober and utterly real picture of the prominent apostle; and along with vv.31–32, it offers a deep spiritual lesson about humility and spiritual conflict.

⁵⁴Then seizing him, they led him away and took him into the house of the high priest. Peter followed at a distance. ⁵⁵But when they had kindled a fire in the middle of the courtyard and had sat down together, Peter sat down with them. ⁵⁶A servant girl saw him seated there in the firelight. She looked closely at him and said, "This man was with him."

⁵⁷But he denied it. "Woman, I don't know him," he said.

⁵⁸A little later someone else saw him and said, "You also are one of them."

"Man, I am not!" Peter replied.

⁵⁹About an hour later another asserted, "Certainly this fellow was with him, for he is a Galilean."

⁶⁰Peter replied, "Man, I don't know what you're talking about!" Just as he was speaking, the rooster crowed. ⁶¹The Lord turned and looked straight at Peter. Then Peter remembered the word the Lord had spoken to him: "Before the rooster crows today, you will disown me three times." ⁶²And he went outside and wept bitterly.

COMMENTARY

54 A number of problems surround the account of the meeting in the high priest's house—possibly the house of Annas, father-in-law of the high priest Caiaphas (cf. Jn 18:13). But this meeting seems also to have been a trial before the entire Sanhedrin (cf. Mt 26:59; Mk 14:55).

55 Though he followed Jesus at a distance, Peter, by Luke's account, is the only disciple who, as far as we know, followed him at all (but see Jn 18:15; see comments at Lk 24:12). The fire in the courtyard was needed because the evenings were—and still are—cool in the springtime in Jerusalem.

56–57 The denial had three phases. All four gospels identify the first speaker as a "servant girl." As many have observed, the girl and what she said were relatively harmless and did not deserve such a drastic response. Peter, however, realized that many ears were listening. Peter's response is called a denial. The word "deny" (*arneomai*, GK *766*, v.57) is used in the NT as the polar opposite of the word "confess" (*homologeō*, GK *3933*). We are to confess (i.e., ack-nowledge) Christ but deny ourselves (i.e.,

disown our private interests for the sake of Christ; see comments at 9:23). Peter here does the reverse. He denies Christ in order to serve his own interests. While Peter's language may recall the language of the rabbinic ban (Str-B, 1:469; cf. "I never knew you," Mt 7:23, and, more distantly, Lk 13:25, 27), this is unlikely to have been in Peter's mind.

58 After a brief time "someone else," not described by Luke, made another charge. Notice that in none of these dialogues as reported by Luke does Jesus' name actually appear. The assumption is that the recent events in Jesus' life were already known to the group in the courtyard. Luke's description of the speakers is also limited. It is only from Peter's response that we know the second speaker was a man.

59–60 Verse 59 is typical of Luke's way of indicating the passage of time. The third speaker then makes a definite assertion; the verb translated "asserted" (*diischyrizeto*, GK *1462*) means "insist," "maintain firmly" (BDAG, 246). Peter's response is stated more mildly in Luke than in Matthew and

Mark, where he accompanies his statement with an oath. Also in v.60 Peter does not directly deny Jesus but professes ignorance of him, though this amounts to the same thing. This note, however, can be considered the climax of the three denials when the question concerning Peter's Galilean origin alludes both to Peter's response to the call to follow Jesus by the Sea of Galilee (5:1–11) and to the beginning stages of Jesus' ministry (4:14–9:50). Luke emphasizes the fulfillment of Jesus' words about the rooster crowing by indicating that the third denial was just being uttered (*parachrēma eti lalountos*, lit.,

"immediately while he was still speaking") when the rooster crowed. For the timing of the crow and the existence of roosters in first-century Jerusalem, see R. Brown, *Death of the Messiah*, 1:606–7.

61–62 In telling how the Lord looked at Peter, Luke uses the word John used (Jn 1:42) to describe the way Jesus looked at Peter when they first met—*emblepō* (GK *1838*). It "usually signifies a look of interest, love or concern" (*NIDNTT* 3:519; cf. Mk 10:21). Peter's feelings (v.62) surely need no further comment.

NOTES

54–62 Immediately after his description of how Peter and the others made a fire in the courtyard and sat around it (v.55), Luke tells us about Peter's denial (vv.56–60). Then, without a break, Luke goes on to describe how the soldiers mocked Jesus (vv.63–65), after which he gives us his account of Jesus' trial (22:66–23:25). Matthew and Mark alternate episodes from the denial and the trial. It may be that Luke (1) followed a different source or (2) arranged his material for dramatic effect in bringing Peter's denial closer to Jesus' prediction of it. While there are difficulties in reconciling the accounts of the denial in the four gospels, Luke's narrative—with its designation of the three questioners as "a servant girl," "someone else," and "another"—is consistent with the other narratives. Though John 18:25 has a plural verb for the second question, this does not pose a serious problem, because it does not exclude the possibility of one man in a group serving as spokesman.

7. The Mocking of Jesus (22:63–65)

> [63]The men who were guarding Jesus began mocking and beating him. [64]They blindfolded him and demanded, "Prophesy! Who hit you?" [65]And they said many other insulting things to him.

COMMENTARY

63–65 Marshall, 845, says that the beginning of this section is "badly linked" to the incident just preceding it. Though the accusative *auton* ("him") in the Greek text of v.63 clearly refers to Jesus (note the NIV's substitution of "Jesus" for *auton*), grammatically it should refer to the subject of v.62—Peter. Again we probably have a matter of sources. Be that as it may, the incident itself is put in a position of sharp contrast between Jesus' sufferings and Peter's attempt to avoid any identification with

Jesus. Also, the soldiers' taunting of Jesus about prophesying who hit him while he was blindfolded (v.64) contrasts with Luke's clear portrayal in his gospel of Jesus as a prophet.

In Luke's passion narrative, Jesus only suffered beating at the hands of the Jewish leaders and their officers (cf. Mk 15:15–20). This is probably intended to highlight the responsibility of the Jews in the death of Jesus.

NOTES

63 Luke is the only author who repeatedly uses the verb ἐμπαίζω (*empaizō*, "to mock," GK *1850*) in the different episodes of his passion narrative and the prediction that precedes it (18:32; 22:63; 23:11, 36). These numerous "mockings" by different groups of individuals point to the universal rejection of Jesus' claim to be Lord and Messiah.

8. Trial before the Jewish Leaders (22:66–71)

OVERVIEW

This section presents special difficulties of a literary and historical nature. Jesus' trial had several phases. Between them there is some overlapping of persons and charges. There were some irregularities in the proceedings, especially in the light of later evidence from Jewish jurisprudence. Moreover, the Synoptics are not uniform in covering all aspects of the trial; each writer makes his own choice as to what to include or omit in order to fulfill his distinctive editorial purpose (see Notes for details about these things; most do not affect the exposition itself).

⁶⁶At daybreak the council of the elders of the people, both the chief priests and teachers of the law, met together, and Jesus was led before them. ⁶⁷"If you are the Christ," they said, "tell us."

Jesus answered, "If I tell you, you will not believe me, ⁶⁸and if I asked you, you would not answer. ⁶⁹But from now on, the Son of Man will be seated at the right hand of the mighty God."

⁷⁰They all asked, "Are you then the Son of God?"

He replied, "You are right in saying I am."

⁷¹Then they said, "Why do we need any more testimony? We have heard it from his own lips."

COMMENTARY

66 Luke has already indicated that Jesus was arrested during the night (see comments at v.47) and has implied that he was confronted by the authorities while in the house of the high priest (v.64). All three Synoptics mention the early morning trial, though the substance of vv.66–71 has already been given in the account of the night trial in Matthew 26:63–65 and Mark 14:61–64. Luke summarizes the crucial exchange between Jesus and the leaders and adds a temporal note that it was becoming day. Matthew and Mark refer to the same time of day, when the religious authorities reached a decision, as "very early in the morning [*prōi*, GK 4745]" (Mk 15:1).

67–68 Luke's way of reporting the questioning separates the questions regarding messiahship (v.67) and the Son of God (v.70; cf. the Matthean and Markan passages just cited). The word "Christ" at this time had not yet become a proper name; so the question is whether Jesus was claiming to be "Messiah" (NIV text note). Jesus' answer—a simple affirmation as in Mark 14:62—is twofold. First, he says that they would not believe him even if he answered them. D. Catchpole (*The Trial of Jesus* [Leiden: Brill, 1971], 195) notes the similarity of this to Jesus' answer to a similar question in John 10:24–25. Jesus also says that were he to question them, they would not answer (v.68). The truth of this had already been demonstrated in 20:1–8.

69 The second part of Jesus' answer concerns the exaltation of the "Son of Man" (who must be identified with Jesus here or the saying is irrelevant), vindicates Jesus, and proves who he is. Luke's report differs considerably from its form in Matthew 26:64 and Mark 14:62. Significant among these differences is the phrase "from now on" (*apo tou nyn*), which Mark does not have, though he has "you will see" (*opsesthe*, GK 3972) where Luke has "will be" (*estai*).

Thus Mark stresses the future revelation of the Son of Man, whereas Luke stresses the fact that from that very time in his appearance before the council he was to be exalted. This fits with Luke's emphasis on the present reality of events that may appear in Matthew and Mark to have their main significance in the future. Here Luke is concerned with the present vindication of Jesus. Matthew combines both ideas (a fact that complicates the question of sources), though his *ap' arti* is understood by the NIV to mean "in the future" or, better, "hereafter" (KJV). In light of the references in Luke's second volume (Ac 2:33–34; 5:31; 7:55–56), the note on Jesus' exaltation also points to a link between Jesus' trial, death, resurrection, and ascension.

70 Only Luke has this question. Standing independent of and subsequent to the question about messiahship, it serves to emphasize that Jesus is himself the Son of God and is not merely called such as an honorific title because of his role as Messiah. The link between Jesus' messiahship and his sonship may also be provided by the earlier discussion on Psalm 110, where Jesus is both David's Lord (i.e., Messiah) and the Son (Lk 20:41–44; cf. J. J. Kilgallen, "Jesus' First Trial: Messiah and Son of God [Luke 22:66–71]," *Bib* 80 [1999]: 401–14). Jesus' reply—lit., "You say that I am" (*hymeis legete hoti egō eimi*)—while not a direct affirmation, was taken as such, as v.71 shows. The nature of this reply is understandable in view of Jesus' remarks in vv.67b–68. The focus on Jesus' identity will be made clear in the accusation of the Jews in 23:2.

71 Ironically, the fact that the Jews have all the evidence they need against Jesus implies that they also have all the information they need to identify him and to believe in him (J. P. Heil, "Reader-Response and the Irony of Jesus before the Sanhedrin in Luke 22:66–71," *CBQ* 51 [1989]: 271–

84). What they said in v.71 is therefore the basis for the claim that they were guilty in their conscious rejection of God's own Son and Messiah (cf. Ac 2:22–24, 36).

NOTES

66–71 The probable order of Jesus' trial appearances in the four gospels is (1) before Annas (John); (2) before Caiaphas and the Sanhedrin (Synoptics); (3) before Pilate (Synoptics, John); (4) before Herod Antipas (Luke); and (5) before Pilate (Luke). The charges before Caiaphas and the Sanhedrin were (1) threatening to destroy the temple and (2) blasphemy. The charges before Pilate were (1) subverting the Jewish nation, (2) opposing the payment of taxes to Caesar, (3) claiming to be king, and (4) taking part in sedition ("stirs up the people," 23:5).

The procedures at the Jewish trial have been frequently questioned. A brief summary of the alleged illegalities in this capital case includes the following: night session, trial on a holy day, failure to wait for a second session on the following day, definition of blasphemy, and holding the trial away from the official chambers (cf. *TDNT* 7:868). While these issues are more complex than they might appear from this summary, it appears that the items cited stand in contradiction to legal procedures noted in the Jewish Talmud.

The following solutions have been proposed: (1) *The Sanhedrin in fact acted illegally.* Few, however, would still hold that the situation was clear-cut. (2) *The Gospels are in error.* Recently, however, scholars have been treating the Gospels with more confidence as to their accuracy in recording these emotionally charged events. (3) *The legal procedures described in the Talmud were not all in effect at the time of Jesus' trial.* This is probably true to some degree and may help considerably in reconciling the Jewish and Christian positions. (4) *There were two Sanhedrins; different rules might have applied to a smaller group meeting first and the whole group meeting later.* This is at best uncertain, but some would insist instead that the Sanhedrin of Jesus' time is only an ad hoc committee that might not have had a set schedule for the various types of meetings (cf. E. P. Sanders, *Jesus and Judaism* [Philadelphia: Fortress, 1985], 312–17). (5) *The trial lasted longer than it appears, so the first three illegalities listed above did not actually occur.* The trial may have lasted longer if the Last Supper were earlier, as proposed by Jaubert and others (see Notes, vv.7–23 above). We are not yet certain enough of the facts to accept this proposal without question. (6) *The first and the last two alleged illegalities listed above do not apply to Luke. The Lukan account should be given priority, though its final editing was later than the other gospels.* It is true that the sources Luke followed were early and accurate, and it is also true that Luke's account presents fewer problems than the others. But this still leaves questions regarding the other gospels, as it assumes that they are in error.

All things considered, there are enough variables in the different accounts to preclude any blanket accusation against the historical reliability of Luke's account. For more on the problems relating to Jesus' trial, see Catchpole, *Trial of Jesus*; A. N. Sherwin-White, *Roman Society and Roman Law in the New Testament* (Oxford: Clarendon, 1963), 24–47 (both of whom take the historicity of the Lukan narrative seriously).

71 The word μαρτυρία (*martyria*, "testimony," GK *3456*) points to the significance of the wider concept of "witnessing" in this gospel and especially in Acts, where the disciples are called to be Jesus' "witnesses" (μάρτυρες, *martyres*, Ac 1:8). The testimony of the apostles is based on Jesus' testimony concerning himself.

9. Trial before Pilate and Herod (23:1–25)

OVERVIEW

The trial now moves into its Roman phase. While there had doubtless been more interrogation than the Synoptics report before Pilate declared that he found no basis for a charge against Jesus (v.4), it obviously did not take Pilate long to determine Jesus' innocence. The larger part of this section deals not with the trial as such but with the difficulty the authorities had in trying to convict an innocent man.

¹Then the whole assembly rose and led him off to Pilate. ²And they began to accuse him, saying, "We have found this man subverting our nation. He opposes payment of taxes to Caesar and claims to be Christ, a king."

³So Pilate asked Jesus, "Are you the king of the Jews?"

"Yes, it is as you say," Jesus replied.

⁴Then Pilate announced to the chief priests and the crowd, "I find no basis for a charge against this man."

⁵But they insisted, "He stirs up the people all over Judea by his teaching. He started in Galilee and has come all the way here."

⁶On hearing this, Pilate asked if the man was a Galilean. ⁷When he learned that Jesus was under Herod's jurisdiction, he sent him to Herod, who was also in Jerusalem at that time.

⁸When Herod saw Jesus, he was greatly pleased, because for a long time he had been wanting to see him. From what he had heard about him, he hoped to see him perform some miracle. ⁹He plied him with many questions, but Jesus gave him no answer. ¹⁰The chief priests and the teachers of the law were standing there, vehemently accusing him. ¹¹Then Herod and his soldiers ridiculed and mocked him. Dressing him in an elegant robe, they sent him back to Pilate. ¹²That day Herod and Pilate became friends—before this they had been enemies.

¹³Pilate called together the chief priests, the rulers and the people, ¹⁴and said to them, "You brought me this man as one who was inciting the people to rebellion. I have examined him in your presence and have found no basis for your charges against him. ¹⁵Neither has Herod, for he sent him back to us; as you can see, he has done nothing to deserve death. ¹⁶Therefore, I will punish him and then release him."

¹⁸With one voice they cried out, "Away with this man! Release Barabbas to us!" ¹⁹(Barabbas had been thrown into prison for an insurrection in the city, and for murder.)

²⁰Wanting to release Jesus, Pilate appealed to them again. ²¹But they kept shouting, "Crucify him! Crucify him!"

²²For the third time he spoke to them:"Why? What crime has this man committed? I have found in him no grounds for the death penalty. Therefore I will have him punished and then release him."

²³But with loud shouts they insistently demanded that he be crucified, and their shouts prevailed. ²⁴So Pilate decided to grant their demand. ²⁵He released the man who had been thrown into prison for insurrection and murder, the one they asked for, and surrendered Jesus to their will.

COMMENTARY

1 Verse 1 links the Jewish and Roman trials. The "whole assembly" is the Sanhedrin. Pilate was Roman governor (prefect) of the province of Judah. His name appears in an inscription found in 1961 at Caesarea, his official residence. Caesarea was a large, magnificent city boasting Roman culture, where Pilate would no doubt have preferred to be at the time of Jesus' trial were it not the Passover season, when special precautions were needed in Jerusalem against civil disturbances.

2 The Sanhedrin's accusation contains three distinct charges. The first (subverting the Jewish nation) would have been of concern to Pilate, who wanted no internal strife among the Jewish people. But it was not a matter for Roman jurisprudence. This charge reappears in vv.5 and 14, and it seems to be one emphasized by Luke. D. Schmidt ("Luke's 'Innocent' Jesus: A Scriptural Apologetic," in *Political Issues in Luke–Acts* [ed. Cassidy and Scharper], 119) has rightly pointed to the presence of OT allusions behind this text. In Exodus 5:4 Moses was accused of turning the people against Pharaoh, and in 1 Kings 18:17 Elijah was also accused of perverting Israel. In noting that Jesus is being accused of "subverting" the nation, Jesus is portrayed as the innocent prophet like Moses and Elijah.

The second (opposing payment of taxes to Caesar) and third (claiming to be king) were more to the point. Luke has already shown (20:20–26) that the second charge was untrue. The third one became the key issue. Jesus' responses to the questions asked him (22:66–71) were understood as being clearly affirmative. It is also clear that the word "Christ" ("Messiah") was deliberately used to imply to Pilate that Jesus was a political activist. The word "king," put in apposition to Messiah, implies a threat to Roman sovereignty to the point where Pilate would have to take action. (In v.5 the Sanhedrin summarized all this by insisting that Jesus was guilty of sedition.)

3 In Pilate's question, the word "you" (*su*) comes first in the Greek sentence for emphasis. Jesus' answer, like those in the Jewish trial, implies a positive answer and at the same time returns the issue to Pilate. The answer (*su legeis*, "you say") is the same in all three Synoptics and is virtually similar to Matthew's report of Jesus' answer in the Jewish trial (Mt 26:64, using the synonym *su eipas*, "you say"), which interprets the "I am" of Mark 14:62.

4 Luke's account lacks the further dialogue in Mark 15:3–5. But Luke is the only one of the Synoptic Gospels that has Pilate's declaration of Jesus' innocence. Presumably, the source containing that statement was not available to Mark or Matthew, for they would certainly have wanted to make that point. Yet the point is especially important for Luke, who seeks throughout his gospel and Acts to vindicate Christianity through the vindication of both Jesus and Paul in their appearances in court.

5 The response from the Sanhedrin is clever. It implies seditious actions by saying that the people are being "stirred up" by Jesus' (unspecified) teaching.

6–12 Only Luke has this incident. It is appropriate for his narrative; he had more interest in politics than did Matthew and Mark and has already mentioned Herod Antipas, whereas they have not (3:1; 9:7–9; 13:31). Herod had a more protracted and intimate experience with Jewish politics and religion than Pilate had. For a long time he had desired to learn more about Jesus (v.8; cf. 9:7–9). Like Pilate, Herod was probably in Jerusalem because of the Passover. For Jesus' attitude toward him, see 13:31–33. Herod's territory, as a local king under the authority of Rome, was Galilee (vv.6–7) and Perea. Verse 11 probably reflects a certain frustration on his part. He apparently had no legal accusation to make, so he vented his anger by echoing the hostility of the priests and teachers (vv.9–11). Mockery (v.11) was an unworthy aspect of the whole trial scene, repeated later on (Mk 15:17–20 par.). The robe was "elegant" (*lampros*, "bright," "gleaming," GK *3287*—a word used in both biblical and secular literature to describe clothes and other adornments, such as those of the rich man in Jas 2:2). This impetuous use of someone's fine clothes contrasts with the later scene in which the soldiers used a purple robe and other symbols to mock Jesus' claim to kingship (Mk 15:17–20).

13–16 Like v.4, this section (also unique to Luke) demonstrates Jesus' innocence (vv.13–14). Marshall, 858, observes that the presence of the people here is "strange," because elsewhere in Luke they are either friendly or neutral. Actually, Luke seems to be making a significant point by mentioning their presence. The "people" (v.13) are the *laos* (GK *3295*), as

distinguished from the "crowd" (*ochlos*, GK *4063*). Throughout his gospel Luke has been careful to distinguish these two groups. He has also been careful to show that it is not the people but their leaders who oppose Jesus. Even here the people do not take an active stand against Jesus. Summoned by Pilate, they, like the crowds in v.4, hear a declaration of Jesus' innocence (vv.14–15). The "people" appear again in v.27, when they follow Jesus to the place of crucifixion, and then in v.35, when they watch Jesus die. Once more (24:19) Luke mentions them as witnesses of Jesus' mighty works. At their first mention in Acts, Luke refers to the "people" as approving the young Jerusalem church (2:47). On the other hand, to implicate the people as a whole in this case may in turn prepare for the preaching of the gospel in Acts where the need of repentance by all was repeatedly noted.

English translations usually imply that Pilate punished Jesus (v.16) because he was innocent (e.g., NIV, "Therefore, I will punish him and then release him"). In the Greek structure, the word for "punish" may be a participle (*paideusas*, GK *4084*) for stylistic reasons, but it also throws the emphasis on the main verb "release" (*apolysō*, GK *668*). The thought is probably, "Because he is innocent, I will let him go with a light scourging [*paideusas*]." In this way Luke shows that Pilate, a Roman official, wanted to treat Jesus as fairly as possible. This would fit with one of Luke's apparent goals in writing the gospel and Acts, namely, to show that Christianity deserved to be favorably treated by Rome. The word "scourged" (*paideusas*) is different from the one used by Matthew and Mark to describe the flogging that preceded the crucifixion (*phragellōsas*, GK *5849*; Mt 27:26; Mk 15:15).

18–19 Compared with Mark 15:6–11, Luke provides only a brief statement about Barabbas and has nothing about the message from Pilate's wife mentioned in Matthew 27:19. Again the writers are apparently following different sources. While Luke does mention Barabbas's crimes, he does not explain the custom Mark refers to (15:6; see Notes, v.17). Barabbas has been romanticized, but since he was probably only an unimportant leader of a small riot, history has no record of him apart from that in the Gospels.

22 We see Luke's concern to vindicate Jesus (and Christianity) to his readers again here. He emphasizes Jesus' innocence by noting that this is the "third time" Pilate spoke on Jesus' behalf, probably counting the appeals after Jesus' return from Herod (vv.15, 20, 22). On the "punishment," see comments at v.16.

23 In vivid Greek, Luke brings the crowd's action to a climax. Though he does not refer to Pilate as washing his hands of responsibility for Jesus (cf. Mt 27:24), or to the Jews' acceptance of responsibility for Jesus' death (cf. Mt 27:25), or to Pilate's wishing to "satisfy" the people (cf. Mk 15:15), he effectively shifts attention from Pilate to the people by ending the Greek sentence, not with the verb (as in the English rendering), but with a final reference to the crowds in the words *hai phōnai autōn* ("their voices"; NIV, "their shouts").

24–25 Luke omits the incident (Mk 15:17–20) of the soldiers' mockery (see comments at vv.6–12) and proceeds directly to Pilate's action. He makes it clear in both v.24 and v.25 that Pilate acted in accord with the crowd's wishes. Having emphasized God's plan and will throughout his gospel, Luke now notes the human factor: Jesus is delivered to the "demand" (v.24) of the crowd. Acts 2:23 shows how God's purpose was fulfilled even in their decision.

NOTES

17 This verse ("Now he was obliged to release one man to them at the Feast," NIV text note) is rightly omitted from the text in the NIV. It is omitted by all the earliest manuscripts, and later scribes placed it in different parts of the story. The wording in the manuscripts that include the phrase is also slightly different. The origin can be traced back to the synoptic parallels (Mt 27:15; Mk 15:6). See Metzger, 158. For a discussion of the custom to free a prisoner during the Passover feast, see R. Brown, *Death of the Messiah*, 1:814–20.

10. The Crucifixion (23:26–43)

OVERVIEW

In their accounts of Jesus' crucifixion, the four gospels relate essentially the same series of events but with varied selection of details and Jesus' words. None of them portray the physical agony of crucifixion in the shocking details that might have been given. The stark facts are there but are presented with sober restraint. What was most important for the four evangelists was the inner reality of Jesus' atoning death and his spiritual anguish in being identified with the sins of the world. Cecil Alexander put it this way in the great hymn "There Is a Green Hill Far Away":

We may not know, we cannot tell
What pains he had to bear,
But we believe it was for us
He hung and suffered there.

²⁶As they led him away, they seized Simon from Cyrene, who was on his way in from the country, and put the cross on him and made him carry it behind Jesus. ²⁷A large number of people followed him, including women who mourned and wailed for him. ²⁸Jesus turned and said to them, "Daughters of Jerusalem, do not weep for me; weep for yourselves and for your children. ²⁹For the time will come when you will say, 'Blessed are the barren women, the wombs that never bore and the breasts that never nursed!' ³⁰Then

"'they will say to the mountains, "Fall on us!"
and to the hills, "Cover us!"'

³¹For if men do these things when the tree is green, what will happen when it is dry?"

³²Two other men, both criminals, were also led out with him to be executed. ³³When they came to the place called the Skull, there they crucified him, along with the criminals—one on his right, the other on his left. ³⁴Jesus said, "Father, forgive them, for they do not know what they are doing." And they divided up his clothes by casting lots.

³⁵The people stood watching, and the rulers even sneered at him. They said, "He saved others; let him save himself if he is the Christ of God, the Chosen One."

³⁶The soldiers also came up and mocked him. They offered him wine vinegar ³⁷and said, "If you are the king of the Jews, save yourself."

³⁸There was a written notice above him, which read: THIS IS THE KING OF THE JEWS.

³⁹One of the criminals who hung there hurled insults at him: "Aren't you the Christ? Save yourself and us!"

⁴⁰But the other criminal rebuked him. "Don't you fear God," he said, "since you are under the same sentence? ⁴¹We are punished justly, for we are getting what our deeds deserve. But this man has done nothing wrong."

⁴²Then he said, "Jesus, remember me when you come into your kingdom."

⁴³Jesus answered him, "I tell you the truth, today you will be with me in paradise."

COMMENTARY

26 After Pilate yielded to the pressure of the crowd, Jesus was led to the place of crucifixion (see Notes). Jesus was required, like others condemned to crucifixion, to carry the crossbar. The wood was heavy, and Jesus was weakened by the maltreatment. The soldiers could press civilians such as Simon into service, and the note on Simon's bearing of the cross may be intended to function as a metaphor for true discipleship (cf. 9:23; 14:27). Mark 15:21 has the word *angareuō* ("forces," GK *30*), the same word Jesus used in the famous saying about going the second mile (Mt 5:41). Cyrene is a port in North Africa.

27–31 Once more Luke gives us an incident that is neither in Matthew nor Mark. For Luke it is important because it again expresses his concern for the fate of Jerusalem (cf. 19:41–44). The terrible destruction Jesus was speaking of also reflects his prediction in 21:20–24. Jewish women (v.27) had always considered barrenness a misfortune and children a blessing (v.28). In the day of Jerusalem's destruction, however, women would have the horror of seeing their children suffer and would wish they could have been spared that agony (v.29). A person standing out in the open in Jerusalem or in the Judean hills would probably not think of mountains (v.30) as a means of destruction as much as a means of protection. Therefore, Marshall, 864, is probably right in suggesting that the words from Hosea 10:8 are a plea for protection rather than for quick death (cf. the use of the same OT text in Rev 6:15–16). Fire spreads much more rapidly through a dry forest than through a wet one; so Jesus' words in v.31 warn of a situation in the future even worse than the events surrounding his crucifixion.

The placement of this uniquely Lukan discourse at this point of the narrative serves to emphasize the eschatological nature of the events that are unfolding (cf. M. L. Soards, "Tradition, Composition, and Theology in Jesus' Speech to the 'Daughters of Jerusalem' [Luke 23:26–32]," *Bib* 68 [1987]: 221–44).

32 It is not certain why, in contrast to Matthew and Mark, Luke mentions the two criminals in advance of Jesus' conversation with them. The effect is to emphasize the humiliation of his execution and perhaps also (cf. Hendriksen, 1027) his identification with sinners in his death as well as in his life. Also possible is the allusion to Isaiah 53:12 ("was numbered with the transgressors"), especially in light of the allusion to the same verse in 22:37 (cf. Darrell L. Bock, *Proclamation from Prophecy and Pattern* [JSNTSup 12; Sheffield: Sheffield Academic Press, 1987], 145).

33–34 Luke omits the name "Golgotha," either because it would not be significant to his readers or because it was not in his source. The "place called the Skull" is located on the north side outside of the city, and it was so named because of the shape of the hill (cf. Fitzmyer, 1503). Luke's narrative is concise and effective in presenting the brutal facts. It is not surprising that he, who constantly portrayed Jesus as offering God's grace and forgiveness to sinners (e.g., 7:40–43), is the only one who records Jesus' prayer for the forgiveness of his executors (v.34; see Notes for textual and interpretive issues). Stephen followed his Lord's example and prayed for those who stoned him (Ac 7:60).

35 It is difficult to know whether the connective "and . . . even" (*de kai*, possibly "but even" or "but also") identifies the "people" (*laos*, GK *3295*) with the sneering of the rulers or whether Luke intends the reader to understand the role of the "people" still to be passive rather than hostile, while everyone else—"even" the rulers—sneered. The NIV takes it in the latter sense, which is probably correct. The word "saved" (*esōsen*, GK *5392*) does not mean that the rulers believed in the claim of Jesus to forgive people but alludes to his reputation for restoring the sick and disturbed (cf. Ps 22:8–9). The lack of understanding of those uttering the words is made clear by the fact that Jesus "saves" others precisely by not "saving" himself (9:22; 17:25; so Crump, 87). Instead of the words "king of Israel" (Mt 27:42; Mk 15:32), Luke has "Christ of God, the Chosen One," which is consistent with his frequent presentation of Jesus as a prophet chosen by God. (Compare the words "whom I have chosen," which occur only in Luke's version of the transfiguration, in 9:35; cf. Isa 42:1.)

36–37 The taunts continue. Luke places this incident earlier in his narrative than Matthew and Mark do in theirs, possibly to bring together in one place the people, rulers, and soldiers (cf. Hendriksen, 1030). Though in the other gospels the offering of wine vinegar (v.36) seems to be an act of kindness, the drink being a thirst quencher carried by soldiers, Luke connects it with their mockery of Jesus (v.37). It may have been a compassionate act done in the midst of taunts. In the light of Psalm 69:21–22 (68:21–22 [LXX]), the offering of vinegar may also be understood as an insult to the one who is suffering.

38 All four gospels contain the superscription, with John offering an explanation of the circumstances (Jn 19:19–22). The full text of the superscription may be seen by comparing all the gospels. Luke's record shows the issue as Pilate, Jesus' Roman judge, saw it. Luke reserves the word "this" (houtos) for the end of the sentence, conveying the emphatic idea "the King of the Jews, this one!"

39–43 This conversation, unique to Luke's account, reinforces two characteristics of his gospel. One (v.41) is the innocence of Jesus (see comments at v.22). The other (v.43) is the immediate ("today") realization of God's saving grace through Jesus (see comments at 4:21).

As elsewhere (e.g., with Peter in 5:1–11), Luke focuses on one person in a group. In Matthew 27:44 and Mark 15:32 both criminals insult Jesus; here this attitude is attributed to one in particular (v.39). "Hurled insults" does not express the more serious aspect of the verb eblasphēmei (GK 1059). Marshall,

871, following Beyer (TDNT 1:623), observes, "To mock Jesus by refusing to take his powers seriously is to blaspheme against him; the use of the verb represents a Christian verdict in the light of who Jesus really is." The criminal's taunt, "Aren't you the Christ?" is "bitterly sarcastic" (Morris, 328).

The other criminal (v.40) recognizes that Jesus is no mere pretender and that he will reign as king (v.42). Crump, 88, may be right in suggesting that this sudden insight serves as the answer to Jesus' prayer for forgiveness in v.34. Jesus' response (v.43) assures this criminal that he need not wait for any future event but that he would have an immediate, joyful experience of fellowship with Jesus "in paradise" (en tō paradeisō, GK 4137). This Persian word, which had been taken over into Greek, symbolizes a place of beauty and delight. It means "park" or "garden" and refers to the garden of Eden in Genesis 2:8 (LXX) and to the future bliss the garden symbolizes (Isa 51:3; cf. Rev 2:7). The word sēmeron ("today," GK 4958) in Luke can refer to the immediate future (but not necessarily the "same day," cf. Fitzmyer, 1510), but this rendering is unnecessary if "paradise" is to be understood as the temporary abode for the righteous (cf. Bock, 2:1857–58).

NOTES

26 The subject of the verb ἀπήγαγον (apēgagon, "they led away," GK 552) is unclear. In the context, it seems to refer to both the people and the Roman authorities (cf. v.13), and the emphasis is on the responsibility of all in the suffering and death of Jesus. Strictly speaking, only the Roman authorities had the power to sentence a person to death, except for circumstances that related directly to the sanctity of the temple cult (cf. Ac 7:54–60; see Martin Hengel, *Crucifixion in the Ancient World and the Folly of the Cross* [Philadelphia: Fortress, 1977], 84–85). Here in the confusion that leads to the way of crucifixion, the involvement of the crowd is undeniable, though they may lack the power to declare or carry out the death sentence.

34 The familiar words "Father, forgive them . . . doing" may not have been in the original text. While it is (with some variations) in ℵ*A C f[1.(13)] 33, among other MSS, the following are among the significant and diverse MSS that omit it: 𝔓[75] B D W Θ and some versions. Reasons for and against its genuineness are not easy to weigh. Did the idea come from Stephen's prayer in Acts 7:60; or more probably, was his prayer inspired by Jesus' prayer? Do we take it as a genuine saying of Jesus that was omitted only because later events—namely, the destruction of the temple and other misfortunes of the Jews—seemed to show that they were not forgiven? (The latter view applies the saying to the Jews rather than to the Roman soldiers.) Or did some anti-Semitic feeling cause it to be dropped? Does the fact that it so beautifully reflects what we know both of Jesus' attitude and Luke's theology and style lead us to conclude that it must be original? Or should we think that it was skillfully woven into the narrative later, since it is hard to suppose that anything so appropriate to the context would have been dropped?

Ellis, 267–68, and Marshall, 867–68, have especially fine treatments of the issue. Ellis argues that the "ignorance motif" ("they do not know") is "part of Luke's theological emphasis" and derives from the OT. Deliberate and persistent ignorance, far from being excusable, is sinful. On the other hand, G. P. Carras ("A Pentateuchal Echo in Jesus' Prayer on the Cross: Intertextuality between Numbers 15:22–31 and Luke 23:34a," in *The Scriptures in the Gospels*, ed. C. M. Tuckett [Leuven: Leuven Univ. Press, 1997], 605–16) argues that Jesus is evoking OT discussions of the possibility of atonement for inadvertent sin. Both authors speak strongly for the genuineness of the saying in its context. The UBS Greek NT editors concluded that even though they believed that it was not originally part of this context, it "bears self-evident tokens of its dominical origin" (Metzger, 154). They therefore included it, but in double square brackets. For a more recent detailed defense of the authenticity of this verse, see Crump, 79–85.

42 The phrase εἰς τὴν βασιλείαν σου (*eis tēn basileian sou*, "into your kingdom") presents a double problem—textually and interpretively. While this reading is supported by 𝔓⁷⁵ B L, ἐν τῇ βασιλείᾳ σου (*en tē basileia sou*, "in your kingdom") occurs in other significant MSS (e.g., ℵ A C K W X Δ Θ) and a number of minuscules. Also, there is uncertainty as to what either of these readings means when viewed against Luke's other passages on the kingdom. While it is questionable whether a spatial concept of the kingdom is intended by εἰς, *eis* ("into"), and the accusative, the phrase would seem, from the perspective of Luke's eschatology, to indicate that the thief expected that Jesus would in some way assume his reign immediately. See the wording of 22:69 in contrast to the parallels. The word ἐν, *en*, plus the dative would seem to refer to the return of Jesus. Put another way, does the thief speak of Jesus as leaving this world for his kingdom? The latter would accord, in the view of Marshall, 872, with a Semitism meaning "as king." With such a division of MSS and with such uncertainties, not only regarding what Luke might have written but also regarding what a thief barely acquainted with Jesus' teaching might be expected to have meant, a firm conclusion is not possible. The balance textually seems to be on the side of εἰς, *eis*, with the accusative.

11. Jesus' Death (23:44–49)

OVERVIEW

The entire gospel can be said to have been preparing for this moment in which Jesus was rejected and died on the cross. Various motifs find their climax in this short passage: eschatological themes, temple imagery, the witnessing of the people, and the innocence of Jesus. The calmness of Jesus before his death has been taken as reflecting the Lukan intention to depict Jesus as the virtuous martyr (so R. J. Miller, "Prophecy and Persecution in Luke–Acts" [PhD diss., Claremont Graduate School, 1986]; G. Sterling, *"Mors philosophi*: The Death of Jesus in Luke," *HTR* 94 [2001]: 383–401). Despite its usefulness in explaining some of Luke's emphases, this model alone is not able to explain fully the soteriological significance of his death (cf. Jerome Neyrey, *The Passion According to Luke* [New York: Paulist, 1985], 129–55).

> **44**It was now about the sixth hour, and darkness came over the whole land until the ninth hour, **45**for the sun stopped shining. And the curtain of the temple was torn in two. **46**Jesus called out with a loud voice, "Father, into your hands I commit my spirit." When he had said this, he breathed his last.
>
> **47**The centurion, seeing what had happened, praised God and said, "Surely this was a righteous man." **48**When all the people who had gathered to witness this sight saw what took place, they beat their breasts and went away. **49**But all those who knew him, including the women who had followed him from Galilee, stood at a distance, watching these things.

COMMENTARY

44 Luke refrains from giving a precise time ("about the sixth hour"; cf. "about eight days," 9:28) but does imply by the word *ēdē* ("already"; NIV, "now") that the preceding events had filled the morning. Time was less precisely noted in those days, which fact may help explain some apparent differences among the gospels. Matthew, Mark, and Luke agree that there was darkness from about the sixth hour to the ninth, i.e., from noon to three o'clock. The whole "land" (*gē*, GK *1178*) could refer to all the "land" of Israel or possibly to the local area only.

45 Luke does not say what caused the sun's light to fail (see Notes); nor does he say what significance should be given to this fact, recorded in all three Synoptics. Certainly it emphasized the somberness of the event; some believe it was to symbolize, or possibly to veil, the judgment endured on our behalf by Jesus. Hendriksen, 1035, lists a number of Scriptures that link darkness with God's judgment. More-over, darkness may also indicate the presence of the power of evil in this moment in salvation history (cf. 22:53). In any case, the eschatological nature of the events cannot be doubted (cf. Ac 2:20).

Like Matthew and Mark, Luke states that the temple curtain was "torn" apart. This curtain was doubtless the one separating the Holy Place from the inner Most Holy Place (Ex 26:31–33). It might be argued that the word refers to the curtain at the entrance to the Holy Place (Ex 26:36–37), which would have been visible to passersby. The LXX uses the same word Luke does (*katapetasma*, GK *2925*) for the curtain in each location. But in this extraordinary circumstance, which would have been accompanied by the sound of the tearing, the priests would have been aware of what had happened even if it had occurred inside the Holy Place.

Such questions cannot be settled by typology. Neither can we ignore the allusion to this in Hebrews 10:19–22, where the veil can only be the one hiding the Most Holy Place. Access to the most holy God is now open through the death of Jesus. In its immediate context, the tearing apart of the temple veil also symbolizes the end of the dominance of the temple system that prevents outsiders from entering into God's covenantal community (cf. J. B. Green, "The Demise of the Temple as 'Culture Center' in Luke–Acts: An Exploration of the Rending of the Temple Veil [Luke 23.44–49]," *RB* 101 [1994]: 495–515). The subsequent recognition of God's mighty acts by a centurion in v.47 supports this reading.

46 Normally, a person in the last stages of crucifixion would not have the strength to speak beyond a weak groan, but each synoptic gospel says that Jesus spoke with a "loud voice." Jesus' words are from Psalm 31:5 (30:6 [LXX]), which was used by the Jews as an evening prayer. To the Christian reader who knows that Jesus' death was a voluntary act, these words are most appropriate. More important, this psalm is uttered by one who is called "righteous" (Ps 31:18 [31:19 LXX]). In uttering a verse from this psalm, Jesus acts as a "righteous" man who confidently places his trust in God. The statement of the centurion that proclaims Jesus to be a "righteous man" (v.47) is therefore not the least bit surprising. (For an insightful treatment of the use of Ps 31 here, see Doble, 173–76.)

47 All three Synoptics call on the centurion as a witness to Jesus' uniqueness. The act of praising God reflects the realization of God's presence. To the modern reader, Luke's words, "a righteous man" (*anthrōpos . . . dikaios*), may seem less significant than "Son of God" in Matthew 27:54 and Mark 15:39. The emphasis in Luke is on Jesus' innocence (cf. v.22) and trust in God to the very end (see Notes); so this form of the saying is appropriate. Also, the term "Son of God" might have been misunderstood by Luke's largely Gentile readership, as it was not unusual for pagans to use such terminology with a different meaning.

48 The "people" referred to in v.48 are not the *laos* (GK *3295*), who are so significant in Luke, but the *ochloi* ("crowds," GK *4063*), a mixed group. They were deeply affected, as were Jesus' own followers, who endured their inexpressible grief standing at a distance. Their beating of their breasts can be understood as an anticipation of the full repentance expressed in the early chapters of Acts (2:41; 4:4; cf. Lk 18:13).

49 Luke's gospel does not name the women, as do all the other gospels at this point, probably because he had named some of them in 8:3. The emphasis on the fact that they "had followed him from Galilee" functions to emphasize "the continuity of the witnesses" who testify to the works of the earthly and the risen Jesus (Charles H. Talbert, "The Place of the Resurrection in the Theology of Luke," *Int* 46 [1992]: 21). All of the Synoptics say that the women stood at a distance (cf. Ps 38:11).

NOTES

45 The clause τοῦ ἡλίου ἐκλιπόντος (*tou hēliou eklipontos* [GK *1722*], "the sun stopped shining") need not mean that the sun was eclipsed. While the verb (from which our English word "eclipse" comes) can mean such, it can also mean any darkening or fading of the light. It is the same word Jesus used in his prayer for Peter's faith not to disappear (22:32). It may be that copyists used the variant ἐσκοτίσθη (*eskotisthē*, "was darkened," GK *5029*) to avoid the idea of an eclipse. 𝔓75 א B retain a form of ἐκλείπω (*ekleipō*), while A and others have ἐσκοτίσθη, *eskotisthē*.

47 To understand the word δίκαιος (*dikaios*, GK *1465*) as merely denoting "innocence" is insufficient. In a richly detailed study, Doble, 93–160, has concluded that the forensic sense does not exhaust the meaning of this word in this context. The religious sense as found throughout the OT should also be noted, as Jesus is portrayed as one who fully submits himself to the will of God. Moreover, this verse paves the way for the subsequent recognition of Jesus as the "Righteous One" (Ac 3:14).

12. Jesus' Burial (23:50–56)

OVERVIEW

The fact that not all rejected Jesus is made clear by the offer of an elite Jew to bury Jesus. The account of the burial by a recognized and respected person shows that Jesus was indeed dead. Despite the warnings against Israel, God's people were not excluded from God's plan of salvation. The careful observance of the Sabbath commandments likewise stresses the continuity between the OT and its fulfillment in the life of Jesus and the mission of the church.

⁵⁰Now there was a man named Joseph, a member of the Council, a good and upright man, ⁵¹who had not consented to their decision and action. He came from the Judean town of Arimathea and he was waiting for the kingdom of God. ⁵²Going to Pilate, he asked for Jesus' body. ⁵³Then he took it down, wrapped it in linen cloth and placed it in a tomb cut in the rock, one in which no one had yet been laid. ⁵⁴It was Preparation Day, and the Sabbath was about to begin.

⁵⁵The women who had come with Jesus from Galilee followed Joseph and saw the tomb and how his body was laid in it. ⁵⁶Then they went home and prepared spices and perfumes. But they rested on the Sabbath in obedience to the commandment.

COMMENTARY

50–51 Luke is careful to assure his readers of the credentials of the man who offered to bury Jesus. Here again Luke presents someone qualified to affirm by word or action that Jesus was a just and innocent man and that by inference the claims of Christianity are valid. He describes Joseph as *agathos kai dikaios* ("good and upright," GK *19*, *1465*). He is also a good Jew, "waiting for the kingdom of God" (v.51), and so joins others in Luke whose piety and expectation of the Messiah validates their testimony (e.g., Simeon and Anna, 2:25–38). He was a member of the Council (the Sanhedrin) but had disagreed with their decision against Jesus.

53–54 Joseph laid the body in a tomb "cut in the rock." We still see such tombs today in rocky hillsides in Israel; in fact, one was recently excavated at Tel Midras. They often have more than one chamber, with a special place for initial care of the body. The exact location of the tomb is subject to debate. Two possibilities have been proposed: (1) the Church of the Holy Sepulchre in the Old City of Jerusalem, and (2) the Garden Tomb outside the Damascus Gate. Recent studies have pointed to the relative likelihood of the former, though a certain conclusion cannot be reached (see John McRay, *Archaeology and the New Testament* [Grand Rapids: Baker, 1991], 206–17). Luke's description of the shroud does not provide enough detail to allow a comparison with the "shroud of Turin." We learn in v.54 that it was Friday (the probable meaning here of the word *paraskeuē*, GK *4187*; NIV, "Preparation Day"), and the Sabbath was about to begin at sundown.

55–56 Though Matthew and Mark mention the presence of the women at this point (Mt 27:61; Mk 15:47), they do not speak of the women's preparation of the spices in advance of Easter morning, as Luke does (v.56). He carefully notes that the women did not do this on the Sabbath, even though Jewish tradition apparently would have allowed care for the dead on a Sabbath (cf. Str-B, 2:52–53). In this way Luke stresses one more time the fidelity of Jesus and his followers to the Jewish laws.

NOTES

50 To use the same term (δίκαιος, *dikaios*, GK *1465*) that was applied to Jesus in describing Joseph is a bit surprising (see Notes, v.47). One should not assume that the word is used in precisely the same way in the two instances. In this verse, the primary meaning is "just," in contrast with the "injustice" of the other council members (cf. R. Brown, *Death of the Messiah*, 2:1227).

C. The Resurrection and Ascension (24:1–53)

OVERVIEW

Luke 24 not only presents the climactic event of the resurrection; it also includes a recapitulation of the saving mission of Jesus (vv.6–7, 19–27, 45–47). As Paul Schubert ("The Structure and Significance of Luke 24," in *Neutestamentliche Studien für Rudolf Bultmann*, ed. W. Eltester [Berlin: Töpelmann, 1954], 165–88) has shown, the stories of the empty tomb, the Emmaus journey, and the appearance to the Eleven in Luke 24 are bound together by the theme of "proof from prophecy," in which Jesus is presented as the Christ/Messiah. The ascension, with which the chapter and the book conclude, is the final goal of Jesus' earthly ministry (see comments at 9:51). It also sets the scene for the church's ministry as recorded in Acts.

1. The Resurrection (24:1–12)

OVERVIEW

The first section of the narrative, concerning events at the empty tomb, contains elements that differ from those given in Matthew and Mark. Some of these are often alleged to be discrepancies that invalidate the NT records of the resurrection as dependable history. Or they have been viewed as redactional (i.e., editorial) changes Luke made to express his own theological perspectives. It is not the purpose of the comments that follow to resolve apparent discrepancies or to deal with Luke's redaction of the resurrection narrative, except as this has clear value for the expositor. The unique features of Luke's resurrection account deserve our attention as his contribution to the reality and meaning of the event.

¹On the first day of the week, very early in the morning, the women took the spices they had prepared and went to the tomb. ²They found the stone rolled away from the tomb, ³but when they entered, they did not find the body of the Lord Jesus. ⁴While they were wondering about this, suddenly two men in clothes that gleamed like lightning stood beside them. ⁵In their fright the women bowed down with their faces to the ground, but the men said to them, "Why do you look for the living among the dead? ⁶He is not here; he has risen! Remember how he told you, while he was still with you in Galilee: ⁷'The Son of Man must be delivered into the hands of sinful men, be crucified and on the third day be raised again.'" ⁸Then they remembered his words.

⁹When they came back from the tomb, they told all these things to the Eleven and to all the others. ¹⁰It was Mary Magdalene, Joanna, Mary the mother of James, and the others with them who told this to the apostles. ¹¹But they did not believe the women, because their words seemed to them like nonsense. ¹²Peter, however, got up and ran to the tomb. Bending over, he saw the strips of linen lying by themselves, and he went away, wondering to himself what had happened.

COMMENTARY

1 All four gospels specify the first day of the week as the day when the women encountered the empty tomb. This became the day of Christian worship (cf. Ac 20:7). The change from the traditional and biblical Sabbath is in itself strong evidence of the resurrection because it shows the strength of the disciples' conviction about what happened on that day. Luke refers to the time of day by the general statement that it was "very early." This fits well with what the other gospels say, though each gospel differs from the others.

2–3 All four gospels mention the removal of the stone. While this was not, as far as the NT reports, used as an apologetic to prove the resurrection, it could not have failed to impress those who heard of it; and its inclusion here is hardly incidental. Only Luke, who has shown particular interest in physical reality—e.g., he is the only synoptic writer to use the phrase "in bodily form" (*sōmatikos*, GK *5394*) to describe the Spirit's descent on Jesus at his baptism (3:22)—specifically says that the "body" (*sōma*, GK *5393*) of Jesus was gone (v.3). The double discoveries of the removal of the stone and the disappearance of Jesus' body, connected by the word "found," provide the context for the announcement of something significant that had happened.

4–5 Here (v.4), as elsewhere (e.g., 1:29, 66; 2:19), Luke describes someone pondering a remarkable event. Luke speaks of "two men" rather than "an angel" (Mt 28:2) or "a young man" (Mk 16:5). For a writer to focus on just one person when another is also present is not unusual. (Both Mark and Luke single out one of the blind men at Jericho; see Mk 10:46; Lk 18:35; cf. Mt 20:30.) Luke's mention of two men at the tomb seems consistent with his other references to witnesses to Jesus (cf. Simeon and Anna, 2:25–38; and esp. 24:48; cf. also the prominence of witnesses in Acts). Two witnesses are the minimum number for validation (Dt 17:6; 19:15; cf. E. G. Bode, *The First Easter Morning* [Rome: Biblical Institute, 1970], 60).

That Luke understands that the two "men" were angels is evident from what he says of them in v.23. Moreover, he describes their clothes as "gleaming like lightning" (*astraptousē*, GK *848*, v.4)—terminology he applies to Jesus' clothes at his transfiguration (9:29; cf. Ac 1:10, "two men dressed in white"). Luke alone tells us that not only were the women frightened (v.5), but also that in their fear they bowed their faces to the ground. The response of fear in the presence of supernatural visitation occurs elsewhere in Luke (e.g., 1:12, 29 [though in Mary's case not at the angel but at his message]; 2:9; 9:34).

The question "Why do you look for the living among the dead?" is important for two reasons: (1) "the living" (*ton zōnta*; only in Luke) stresses the factual aspect of the resurrection Luke also refers to in Acts 2:24—"it was impossible for death to keep its hold on him"; (2) more important, this entire question may be an allusion to Isaiah 8:19. While this has been noted by some (e.g., Bock, 2:1891), it is the wider context that is important for Luke. In Luke 2:34, the mention of "the falling and rising of many in Israel" is already an allusion to Isaiah 8:14–15. The significant Messianic promises in Isaiah 9:1–7 also resurface in the Lukan prologue (Lk 1:33, 79; 2:11). In the mind of Luke, Isaiah 8–9 points to the reversal of Israel's fate when the expected Savior appears. In the reply of the two men (angels) here, one can therefore see the significance of the salvific event that had taken place as the OT promises are now fulfilled in the empty tomb.

6 What Luke gives us here is not in the other gospels: The angels show the meaning of the empty tomb by repeating the essence of the three passion predictions (9:22, 43–45; 18:31–33; cf. parallel passages in Matthew and Mark). They begin with the words "remember how he told you," which imply that what the women should have understood earlier, the resurrection has now clarified. The third prediction (18:31–33) was followed by Luke's statement that the saying was obscure, hidden from them (18:34; cf. 24:16). The resurrection is the time for revelation and understanding (see comments at v.8 below).

Some believe the reference to "Galilee" is an alteration of the saying in Matthew 28:7 and Mark 16:7. There Galilee is the place where Jesus would later meet with the disciples; here it is where Jesus had given his passion predictions. Luke obviously centers attention on Jesus' appearances in the vicinity of Jerusalem, the city of destiny in this gospel (e.g., 9:51; 13:32–35). His selective focus on

Jerusalem is not, however, a major disagreement with the other Synoptics; nor does his different use of the word "Galilee" contradict theirs.

7 Luke's frequent use of *dei* ("must," GK *1256*) and other expressions of divine purpose has already been noted throughout this commentary (e.g., 2:49; 4:43; 19:5). It occurs in the first passion prediction (9:22), as it does in the other Synoptics, but then reappears only in Luke in 13:33; 17:25; 22:37. Chapter 24 contains two more references to the inevitable sequence of Jesus' death and resurrection (vv.25–27, 44–46). Luke's stress on God's plan and providence continues throughout Acts, often with *dei* but also without it (Ac 2:23–24; see Bode, *First Easter*, 65–67). The term "sinful men" (*anthrōpōn hamartōlōn* [GK *283*]) occurs in Jesus' saying at Gethsemane about his impending betrayal (Mt 26:45; Mk 14:41)—a saying Luke does not have. The idea appears again in Acts 2:23 in the term "wicked men" (*anomōn*, GK *491*). Luke often speaks of "sinners," but usually he does so when referring to notorious people on whom Jesus had compassion. Here in contrast, the "sinners" are those who opposed him and brought about his death. Only Luke has "on the third day."

8 The theme of remembrance reappears here, and it is an important theme throughout the Lukan corpus. Significantly, this word always points to God or Jesus (Lk 1:54, 72; 16:25; 23:42; 24:6, 8; Ac 10:31; 11:16), and it is related to the theme of promise and fulfillment (cf. Maria-Luisa Rigato, "'Remember' ... Then They Remembered: Luke 24:6–8," in *Luke and Acts* [ed. O'Collins and Marconi], 93–102). In the wider biblical narrative, remembrance points back to the covenantal acts of God in history. In this context, the women were not simply called to recall a certain statement from the earthly Jesus; they were called to interpret the present event in the light of the life and significance of Jesus, the One who brings salvation history to its climax.

9–11 Luke postpones naming the women until this point (v.10), whereas Matthew and Mark name them at the beginning of their resurrection narratives. Luke has already (8:1–3) told of the women who accompanied and supported Jesus in his ministry. (He also mentions the women at prayer with the apostles in Ac 1:14.) While the witness of women was not acceptable in those days, Luke still records their testimony (v.9). The apostles in their incredulity were unable to comprehend the reality the women were trying to convey (v.11). We see this incredulity again in Peter (v.12) and in the disciples on the road to Emmaus (vv.22–24). This reluctance to believe has an important relation to the evidences for the resurrection. The disciples were not expecting that event (cf. v.25). Thus they cannot be called fit subjects for hallucination, as some would have them to be.

12 Verse 12, though omitted by the Western text (see Notes; cf. J. E. Alsup, *The Post-Resurrection Appearance Stories of the Gospel Tradition* [Stuttgart: Calver, 1975], 103), is probably authentic. It is similar but not identical to John 20:6–7. Luke does not mention the "other disciple" (Jn 20:3), probably focusing on Peter, as he did in 5:1–11 and 22:54–55. The strips of linen used in the burial bear their silent but eloquent testimony to the absence of Jesus' body.

Peter leaves, "wondering [*thaumazōn*, GK *2513*] to himself" about this. In Luke, people "wonder" about things that are hard to understand. The word does not in itself imply either belief or unbelief, though in this gospel more often than not the positive sense is implied. We conclude that, while Peter has yet to be fully convinced by his visit to the empty tomb, he is on the road to accepting the fact of the resurrection event. At this point, what he had seen did not produce a statement of belief from him, however (cf. Jn 20:8; for a further discussion of the reaction of Peter and other eyewitnesses, see Joseph Plevnik, "The Eyewitnesses of the Risen Jesus in Luke 24," *CBQ* 49 [1987]: 90–101).

NOTES

3 The MSS representing the so-called Western text omit the following: (1) v.3, τοῦ κυρίου Ἰησοῦ (*tou kyriou Iēsou*, "of the Lord Jesus"); (2) v.6, οὐκ ἔστιν ὧδε ἀλλὰ ἠγέρθη (*ouk estin hōde, alla ēgerthē*, "he is not here; he has risen"); (3) all of v.12; (4) v.36, καὶ λέγει αὐτοῖς, Εἰρήνη ὑμῖν (*kai legei autois, Eirēnē hymin,* "and said to them, 'Peace be with you'"); (5) all of v.40; (6) v.51, καὶ ἀνεφέρετο εἰς τὸν οὐρανόν (*kai anephereto eis ton ouranon,* "and was taken up into heaven"); and (7) v.52, προσκυνήσαντες αὐτόν (*proskynēsantes auton,* "worshiped him"). Because Westcott and Hort concluded that the Western text tended to add words not in the original, they thought that in the opposite circumstance—i.e., when instead of interpolating words the Western text omitted words found in other MS traditions—such omissions (or "noninterpolations") should be given much weight.

In the instances mentioned here, there has been reluctance on the part of some scholars to reject that reasoning. More recently, however, the tendency has been to examine each case on its own merits, using standard textual principles in making decisions. Verses 23 and 40 present special considerations because they are similar to John's account of the resurrection. But in these verses, as in the other instances just cited, there are sound reasons for considering each verse a part of Luke's original text (see Snodgrass, "Western Non-Interpolations," 369–79; cf. Metzger, 164–66, on each verse and on the issue of Western noninterpolations).

4 The familiar expression καὶ ἐγένετο (*kai egeneto*), properly left untranslated in the NIV, is a Semitic transitional term that generally contributes little to the meaning (cf. KJV, "and it came to pass"). Its significance relates to the reason for Luke's frequent use of Semitic idioms, and in this crucial resurrection passage it cannot be overlooked. The question is the source of Luke's information. Luke's use of Semitisms may, at least in some places, show that he is following early traditions containing Aramaic idioms. On the other hand, he may—whether using such sources directly or adapting material from Mark or non-Semitic sources—introduce Semitic terminology naturally because of his familiarity with the LXX and his desire to represent the ambience of the events he is reporting.

This passage contains a number of characteristically Lukan terms and themes, some of which we have already noted. These, along with Luke's use of Semitisms, seem to indicate a mixture of Markan material, early traditions, and original touches of Luke's own editorial skill.

2. On the Emmaus Road (24:13–35)

OVERVIEW

The Emmaus story is a literary and spiritual jewel. It is at once a moving story, a testimony to the resurrection, an explanation of the empty tomb, and an occasion for Luke to summarize several of his major themes. Despite the fact that it has to a superlative degree the ring of truth—what literary scholars call "verisimilitude"—some have considered it legendary (see Notes).

¹³Now that same day two of them were going to a village called Emmaus, about seven miles from Jerusalem. ¹⁴They were talking with each other about everything that had happened. ¹⁵As they talked and discussed these things with each other, Jesus himself came up and walked along with them; ¹⁶but they were kept from recognizing him.

¹⁷He asked them, "What are you discussing together as you walk along?"

They stood still, their faces downcast. ¹⁸One of them, named Cleopas, asked him, "Are you only a visitor to Jerusalem and do not know the things that have happened there in these days?"

¹⁹"What things?" he asked.

"About Jesus of Nazareth," they replied. "He was a prophet, powerful in word and deed before God and all the people. ²⁰The chief priests and our rulers handed him over to be sentenced to death, and they crucified him; ²¹but we had hoped that he was the one who was going to redeem Israel. And what is more, it is the third day since all this took place. ²²In addition, some of our women amazed us. They went to the tomb early this morning ²³but didn't find his body. They came and told us that they had seen a vision of angels, who said he was alive. ²⁴Then some of our companions went to the tomb and found it just as the women had said, but him they did not see."

²⁵He said to them, "How foolish you are, and how slow of heart to believe all that the prophets have spoken! ²⁶Did not the Christ have to suffer these things and then enter his glory?" ²⁷And beginning with Moses and all the Prophets, he explained to them what was said in all the Scriptures concerning himself.

²⁸As they approached the village to which they were going, Jesus acted as if he were going farther. ²⁹But they urged him strongly, "Stay with us, for it is nearly evening; the day is almost over." So he went in to stay with them.

³⁰When he was at the table with them, he took bread, gave thanks, broke it and began to give it to them. ³¹Then their eyes were opened and they recognized him, and he disappeared from their sight. ³²They asked each other, "Were not our hearts burning within us while he talked with us on the road and opened the Scriptures to us?"

³³They got up and returned at once to Jerusalem. There they found the Eleven and those with them, assembled together ³⁴and saying, "It is true! The Lord has risen and has appeared to Simon." ³⁵Then the two told what had happened on the way, and how Jesus was recognized by them when he broke the bread.

COMMENTARY

13–15 The opening words of v.13 link this story with the entire Easter event. "Now" (*kai idou*) moves the reader's attention to a new and important phase of Luke's narrative. "That same day" ties the narra-tive to Jesus' death and resurrection (cf. the sequence in 23:54, 56; 24:1). Two travelers are speaking together (vv.14–15), so a valid witness is provided. A twofold witness is necessary according to Jewish law. Furthermore, the concept of witness is, as we have seen, important to Luke. Two witnesses (Simeon and Anna) bore testimony to the Messiah's arrival (2:25–38); now the two travelers testify to a particular resurrection appearance of Jesus (24:35). The words "of them" (*ex autōn*, v.13) do not clearly identify who the two are. They are not two of the Eleven (v.9; cf. vv.18, 33). Probably they are two of the followers of Jesus who had come to Jerusalem for the Passover. So they had been among the "disciples" who lauded Jesus on his triumphal entry into the city (19:39) and were now returning home.

The fact that this story is about two disciples who were not part of the Twelve shows how the significance of the report from these eyewitnesses extends beyond that which is concerned with the leadership of the early church (cf. Mark Coleridge, "'You are Witnesses' [Luke 24:48]: Who Sees What in Luke," *Australian Biblical Review* 45 [1997]: 10). The phrase "of them," like the opening words of v.13, establishes a continuity with the foregoing events.

The fact that this event occurs when the two disciples "were going" (*ēsan poreuomenoi*, v.13) and "walked along" (*syneporeueto*, v.15) continues the travel theme prominent in Luke, especially in his unique central section (9:51–19:44) in which Jesus also reveals his own identity and mission (cf. Green, 844). That section begins as Jesus "resolutely set out" (*to prosōpon estērisen tou poreuesthai*) for Jerusalem (9:51). Now these two are leaving that same city. Shortly after the earlier journey to Jerusalem began, a man had approached Jesus regarding discipleship "as they were walking" (*poreuomenōn autōn*, 9:57). Now, after the resurrection, Jesus approaches two disheartened followers as they are walking. Acts continues the theme of the traveling of Jesus' disciples, who go from Jerusalem to Rome (Paul, in ch. 28) and ultimately to the ends of the earth as "witnesses" (1:8). As for the identity of Emmaus, this is

uncertain (see Notes). It is enough to know that it is a village near Jerusalem, and it is precisely its vicinity to the city of Jerusalem that is important.

The two were talking about events surrounding Jesus' resurrection. Between the lines of their dialogue Luke shows their bewilderment. He uses two different verbs, one of them repeated: "they were talking" (*hōmiloun*, v.14), "as they talked" (*en tō homilein*, v.15), and "discussed" (*syzētein*). So the tension mounts in preparation for Jesus' appearance. Luke introduces Jesus into the story with the emphatic "Jesus himself" (*autos Iēsous*); and his comment that Jesus "walked along with [*syneporeueto*] them" suggests to us, whether or not Luke intended it, Jesus' presence with his disciples in the church age.

16 The passive form in "were kept [*ekratounto*] from recognizing him" may be a "divine passive," i.e., a means of connoting that an action, the subject of which is not mentioned, is actually the work of God. This device introduces the structural pattern of nonrecognition and recognition, which is central in this beautiful narrative. On a historical level, the failure to recognize the risen Lord is noted elsewhere in the Gospels (e.g., Jn 21:4), and one cannot rule out the possibilities that the disciples were in a state of confusion and/or the form of the risen Lord had changed. On a theological level, the failure to comprehend fully the mystery of Christ is also a notable Lukan theme (see J. M. Dawsey, "The Unexpected Christ: The Lucan Image," *ExpTim* 98 [1987]: 296–300).

17 Still another verb describes their discussion: *antiballete* ("discussed," GK *506*) reflects the exchange of ideas (lit., "throwing back and forth"). The scene in vv.14–17 is of a persistent but rather baffled attempt to understand the meaning of this most momentous weekend in history. Luke now uses a different word for walking (*peripateō*; see comments at vv.13–15). Another mention of walking is certainly not necessary merely to convey that fact, and we may assume that there is a deliberate emphasis on that movement; therefore, it is striking that when Jesus addressed them, the two travelers stopped short and "stood still" (*estathēsan*). Their attitude at that point was gloomy, perhaps even sullen.

18 Only one of the two (Cleopas) is named, probably because he was known to at least some of Luke's readers. One tradition identifies him as an uncle of Jesus, brother of Joseph, and father of Simeon, who became a leader of the Jerusalem church (Eusebius, *Hist. eccl.* 3.11; cf. Ellis, 894). This is not the same man as Clopas (Jn 19:25), though some have considered the two names as variant spellings of the same name (so Marshall, 894; cf. Fitzmyer, 1563).

19 What follows constitutes an affirmation about the person and work of Jesus that is of great significance for our understanding of him and of Luke's perception of him. Concerning the opening words, Dillon, 114, observes that "this characterization, together with the assertion of full publicity amongst the people, contains pointed echoes of Luke's introductory summary of Jesus' ministry [in the power of the] Spirit (Luke 4:14; cf. Acts 10:38)." See comments at 4:14 on the popular response to Jesus. The statement there about his reputation and power precedes the programmatic statement about his ministry under the impetus of the Spirit in 4:18–19. Acts 10:38 is Peter's summary of Jesus' powerful, Spirit-filled ministry (cf. Ac 2:22) and includes the statement "he went around doing good." Peter then tells Cornelius, "We are witnesses of everything" (Ac 10:39), calling to mind Luke 1:2—"eyewitnesses and servants of the word." The importance of the affirmation of the two disciples here in 24:19 must not in any way be underestimated. It is integral to Luke's theology and purpose.

"He was a prophet" recalls the passage in ch. 4 just mentioned, where Jesus clearly identified himself with the prophets (4:24). While in Luke's narrative Jesus is perceived as a prophet (e.g., 7:16; cf. Minear, 102–21), the resurrection affirmed him to be more than a prophet, as the two on the Emmaus road are to learn (e.g., v.26, "the Christ . . . glory"). The word "prophet" does not appear in what Peter told Cornelius about Jesus (Ac 10:36–43). This is probably not because Cornelius was not Jewish, for Jesus was "Lord of all" (Ac 10:36), but because the word "prophet" was inadequate to comprehend all that Jesus is. Nevertheless, the term is significant in understanding the life and ministry of Jesus. This title also points to the continuation of Jesus' ministry with God's work in the past. Moreover, he is "the Prophet," the unique One who is to fulfill all the promises of the prophets of old (cf. v.25; see Ben Witherington III, *Jesus the Seer* [Peabody, Mass.: Hendrickson, 1999], 338).

Another of Luke's favorite terms is "people" (*laos*, GK *3295*), used throughout his gospel for the responsive hearers in Israel (cf. 1:17, 68, 77; 2:10, 31–32). Later Luke will use *laos* of believing Gentiles (Ac 18:10).

20–21 The "chief priests and our rulers" (v.20) stand in contrast to the "people" (v.19) as elsewhere in Luke. It was they who "handed him over" for crucifixion. In v.21 the two disciples' words "but we" (*hemeis de*, emphatic) provide still another contrast. Unlike the rulers, they "hoped" that Jesus would bring deliverance. Observe that the verb is "hoped," not "trusted" (as in the KJV); there is a big difference between trusting Jesus as our Deliverer and Savior and hoping that he will prove to be our Deliverer and Savior. The past tense of "hoped" is, under the present circumstances, a pathetic reminder of their inability to recognize Jesus or to believe the report of the empty tomb. Their expectation that he would "redeem Israel" recalls the words of Zechariah in Luke 1:68 (cf. 2:38; 21:28). In view of v.46 and the passion predictions, the term "third day" had significance to Luke's readers. What should have been the day of hope realized was for them the day of hope extinguished.

22–24 The final ("in addition," *alla kai*) incomprehensible element in the travelers' report was the news of the empty tomb (v.22). This looks back to vv.1–12. Again Luke used the word "body" (v.23, see comments at vv.2–3). The mention of "angels" shows that this is what Luke meant by "men" in v.4, which is in harmony with the other gospels. Verse 24 recalls v.12. In the last words in the report, "him they did not see," the word "him" (*auton*) is placed in an emphatic position. The empty tomb without the appearance of Jesus himself was inadequate. It ironically becomes the last sad part of their confused response to Jesus' question, "What things?" (v.19).

25–27 Jesus' response begins with a note on the ignorance of the two disciples—a theme that will reappear in the speeches of Acts (cf. Jacques Dupont, *Le discours de Milet: Testament pastoral de Paul Actes 20:18–36* [Paris: Cerf, 1962], 339). The reader of the Greek text will immediately observe the pronoun *auton* ("him") in an emphatic position in v.24 and *kai autos* ("and he"; NIV, "he") in v.25 (referring, still emphatically, to the same person, though he remains unrecognized). As Dillon, 132, notes, "The Stranger seizes the platform from the confused disciple."

Jesus, who in his transfiguration was superior to Moses and Elijah (9:28–36), now invokes Moses and the Prophets to substantiate the divine plan of his path from suffering to glory (v.27). The word "all" (v.25) is a warning not to treat the Scriptures selectively and also points to the unique position of Jesus as the One who represents the goal of salvation history. In this plan of God, one cannot ignore the role of the Messiah's suffering (v.26). "The Christ" (Messiah) did "have to" (*edei*) suffer. The verb *dei* (GK *1256*), meaning "it is necessary," is one of Luke's key words (cf. 2:49; 4:43; 13:16, 33; 15:32; 18:1; 19:5; 21:9; 22:7, 37; 24:7, 44, along with the

basic passion prediction of 9:22 that occurs also in Matthew and Mark). The future "glory" of the Christ (v.26) was mentioned in the context of the passion prediction, ascribed there to the "Son of Man" (9:26; cf. 21:27). Some have argued that "glory" here is to be understood as a substitute expression for "was raised from the dead" (cf. Dillon, 141ff.). More likely it refers to the honor anticipated in the OT for the Messiah and attributed to the Son of Man in the verses just referred to. The unexpected element in Christ's messiahship was his suffering. On the other hand, one could hardly argue that Christ's glory excludes the resurrection. Paul quoted the OT to prove the necessity of both the suffering and resurrection of the Messiah (Ac 17:2–3). In any case, the connection between glory and suffering/death as found in Scripture is a constant emphasis of Luke's (Lk 9:26, 32; 21:27; 24:26; Ac 3:13; 7:55; cf. John J. Kilgallen, "Jesus, Savior, the Glory of Your People Israel," *Bib* 75 [1994]: 305–28). "Beginning with" (v.27) probably implies that Jesus drew on all the Scriptures but principally on the Law (Genesis–Deuteronomy) and the Prophets (cf. Marshall, 897). The central subject of these OT passages is "himself."

For several reasons vv.25–27 are vitally important. With great clarity they show that the sufferings of Jesus, as well as his glory, were predicted in the OT and that all the OT Scriptures are important. They also show that the way the writers of the NT used the OT had its origin not in their own creativity but in the postresurrection teachings of Jesus, of which this passage is a paradigm. The passage also exemplifies the role of the OT in Luke's theology. Though he does not directly quote the OT Scriptures as many times as Matthew does, nevertheless, he alludes frequently to the OT, demonstrating that what God has promised must take place and employing a "proof from prophecy" apologetic for the truth of the gospel (cf. Bock, *Proclamation from*

Prophecy and Pattern). In this particular statement by Jesus, one can also find the critical hermeneutical role of the OT, when contemporary events (in the time of Jesus) have to be interpreted in the light of OT promises.

28–29 As the afternoon drew on and suppertime approached, the stranger would need food and lodging. Jesus had "acted as if" (*prosepoiēsato*, GK *4701*) he were going to continue his journey (v.28). The verb *prospoieō*, in spite of well-meaning efforts to weaken it to avoid any thought of deceit on Jesus' part, often means "pretend" (BDAG, 884). Such a gesture would, like the invitation to stay itself, be appropriate in the custom of those days. While it is probably true, as Morris, 370, says, that Jesus would have gone on had he not been invited to stay, this polite action seems intended to draw out a very strong response from Cleopas and his companion, who indeed then "urged him strongly" (*parebiasanto*, GK *4128*) to stay (v.29). In other contexts this verb can mean to force someone to do something.

Not to be missed is the invitation by the two disciples for Jesus to "stay with [them]." This invitation is a sign of hospitality, and it recalls ancient narratives on the welcoming of guests who will prove to be messengers from God (cf. Ge 18:1–10). This expression of hospitality paves the way for the understanding of the following verses when hospitality and meal fellowship take center stage.

30–32 The recognition scene is the third high point in this narrative, the first two being the long reply of Cleopas and his companion to Jesus' question and Jesus' exposition of the OT's teaching about himself. The table scene is characteristic of Luke and probably of his special source material (cf. 5:29; 7:36; 14:1, 7, 12, 15–16; 10:38–40 [less obviously]). What is remarkable is that Jesus took the role of the host by breaking the bread and giving thanks (v.30). This recalls, of course, the feeding of the five thousand (9:10–17, esp. v.16) as well as the Last

Supper (22:19). Whether an allusion to the Last Supper account is intended is not clear. While Fitzmyer, 1559, for example, considers the wordings in v.30 as "the classic Lucan way of referring to the Eucharist," the connection to the Eucharist is inconclusive: (1) the wordings may simply refer to common Jewish meal practice; (2) the reference to wine is missing; (3) the focus is on recognition and not presence; and (4) one would expect the eucharistic meal to appear in the next story of Jesus' appearance to the Eleven. In light of the emphasis on table fellowship and hospitality elsewhere in Luke, it seems best to take this as the climax of these meal scenes, of which the Last Supper plays an important part (cf. Bernard P. Robinson, "The Place of the Emmaus Story in Luke–Acts," *NTS* 30 [1984]: 481–97; Arthur A. Just Jr., *The Ongoing Feast: Table Fellowship and Eschatology at Emmaus* [Collegeville, Minn.: Liturgical Press, 1993]).

As to whether it was through the actual breaking of bread or divine intervention that the moment of truth came and the two disciples recognized Jesus, the answer must be that it was through both (see Notes). Whether the two noticed the nail scars (Luke does not say they did), Jesus' acting as host led to the recognition. At the same time, the passive verb *diēnoichthē-san* ("were opened") implies divine action (v.31), as was the case when Jesus' identity was hidden from them (v.16). This provides uniformity in the structure and theological meaning, as God is the revealer of the risen Christ. Note the repetition of Jesus' opening of "the Scriptures" (v.32) and "their minds" (v.45).

The narrative ends abruptly as Jesus disappears and Cleopas and his companion reflect on their feelings of intense inner warmth (cf. Ps 39:3; Jer 20:9; the vocabulary differs but something similar may be in mind). For a survey of interpretations of *kaiomenē* ("burning," GK *2794*), see Marshall, 898–99. The specific occasion of these feelings is the presence of the Lord and his expounding of the OT.

33-35 The words "at once" (*autē tē hōra*, lit., "in the same hour," v.33) continue the chronology of the resurrection day (see comments at v.13). The reunion with the Eleven brought assurance to all, as the two disciples fulfilled their role as witnesses (vv.34-35). The message that "the Lord has risen" provides continuity between the life of Jesus and the center of the church's proclamation. (For other parallels between these verses and the reporting scenes in Acts, see Linda M. Maloney, *"All That God Had Done with Them": The Narration of the Works of God in the Early Christianity as Described in the Acts of the Apostles* [New York: Lang, 1991], 39.) The two disciples especially spoke of recognizing Jesus when he broke bread with them (v.35; see Notes, vv.30-31).

NOTES

13-35 The historicity of this story has often been challenged (e.g., H. D. Betz, "The Origin and Nature of Christian Faith According to the Emmaus Legend," *Int* 23 [1969]: 32-46). There are, indeed, elements of the story that many find difficult to accept—not merely the inability of the two to recognize Jesus but also the very appearance of Jesus after his death. But this difficulty relates to the concept one has about the resurrection itself and the possibility of a supernatural work of God in the nonrecognition and recognition sequence.

There are also similarities to elements in other ancient narratives. We must, however, be careful about drawing conclusions from works written after the composition of Luke. Also, as Dillon, 73-74, observes, we "must not invoke such parallels prematurely, on the basis of mere resemblance, as instruments of interpretation." It is impossible to prove or disprove the historicity of a story such as this, which exists in no other literature and which, unlike the resurrection, has produced no effect capable of investigation. Apart from the consideration of alleged legendary elements (remembering that issues of form do not settle issues of historicity [cf. Marshall, 891]), such issues will be decided on the basis of the setting of the story both in the resurrection narrative and within Luke's carefully researched work, with care not to reject what one may consider, a priori, difficult to accept.

13 The location of Emmaus, "about seven miles from Jerusalem," is of minor concern to the expositor but of historical interest. Attention centers on several possible sites, but certainty is not possible currently. Two sites (Abu-Ghosh and El-Qubeibeh) are located at an approximately correct distance (one about nine miles away, the other even closer to Luke's "sixty stadia"—approximately seven miles). There is little evidence, however, that either is the site.

Another place, Motza-Illit, is only three and a half miles from Jerusalem. To identify this with the village in Luke, one has to assume that Luke's figure of sixty stadia applied to a round trip. In Jesus' day it was only a "village" (κώμη, *kōmē*, GK *3267*), precisely Luke's word. Both Josephus and the Talmud mention it, the first as Emmaus and the second as Motza. It is very possible that the Semitic sound of Ha-Motza became Ammaous or Emmaus. A Roman colony was established there later in the first century, and so it is now also known as Qaloniya or Colonia. Evidence has come to light of a Byzantine church there, indicating that the site was reverenced. This may well be the true location.

There is still another site, much better known: Imwas (in the Latrun area), known also as Nicopolis probably since AD 218. It was prominent as the place of a great victory of Judas Maccabeus in the second century BC (described in 1 Macc 3–4). The site continued to be well known throughout Christian history, and it naturally has been favored by many as the NT Emmaus. One serious problem is that it is not 60 but 160 stadia away (a problem Sinaiticus and other MSS seem to have addressed by changing the number to 160). This distance, however, seems long, though not impossible, for the two disciples to have traveled in both directions (cf. v.33). It would have meant a round trip total of almost 40 miles in one busy day, with the return trip started no later than early evening.

It is possible that there were actually two places known as Emmaus in Jesus' day: the village, hardly known, 3.5 miles or 30 stadia away, and the city, 160 stadia or about 18.5 miles away. It was perhaps the former to which the disciples went on the resurrection day. See J. Monson, *A Survey of the Geographical and Historical Setting of the Bible* (Jerusalem: Institute for Holy Land Studies, 1977), 3–4; R. M. Mackowski, "Where Is Biblical Emmaus?" *Science et esprit*

32 (1980): 93–103. For a recent discussion drawing on early textual traditions, see J. Read-Heimerdinger, "Where is Emmaus? Clues in the Text of Luke 24 in Codex Bezae," in *Studies in the Early Text of the Gospels and Acts*, ed. D. G. K. Taylor (Atlanta: Society of Biblical Literature, 1999), 229–44.

30–31 Against the majority of scholars who focus on the meal scene, Crump, 101–7, understands the "breaking" and "blessing" as referring to an act of prayer, and it is in the act of prayer that Jesus was recognized. This interpretation, which points primarily to the act of prayer as the central element of the story, is questionable in light of the mention of the table and the focus on meal scenes elsewhere in Luke. In light of the Jewish evidence Crump has gathered, however, it is not impossible that the reference to the breaking of the bread in v.35 is indeed a reference to the act of prayer before the meal. One can tentatively suggest, therefore, that while this indeed is the climax of all meals, the exact moment of recognition came when Jesus was praying.

3. The Appearance to the Disciples (24:36–49)

OVERVIEW

This is the third Easter narrative in Luke. In the first Jesus is not seen; in the second he appears to two disciples; this time he appears to the Eleven. The narrative probably goes back to an older source that also lies behind John 20:19–23. It does not have as many distinctively Lukan touches as the Emmaus story

does. The events Luke tells us of here also provide the substance for his apologetic for Jesus' bodily resurrection in Acts 1:3–4 and Peter's witness to Cornelius (Ac 10:40–43). Here it is not Jesus' resurrection as such that is being proved but the fact that the sudden visitor was indeed Jesus, present in a tangible body.

[36]While they were still talking about this, Jesus himself stood among them and said to them, "Peace be with you."

[37]They were startled and frightened, thinking they saw a ghost. [38]He said to them, "Why are you troubled, and why do doubts rise in your minds? [39]Look at my hands and my feet. It is I myself! Touch me and see; a ghost does not have flesh and bones, as you see I have."

⁴⁰When he had said this, he showed them his hands and feet. ⁴¹And while they still did not believe it because of joy and amazement, he asked them, "Do you have anything here to eat?" ⁴²They gave him a piece of broiled fish, ⁴³and he took it and ate it in their presence.

⁴⁴He said to them, "This is what I told you while I was still with you: Everything must be fulfilled that is written about me in the Law of Moses, the Prophets and the Psalms."

⁴⁵Then he opened their minds so they could understand the Scriptures. ⁴⁶He told them, "This is what is written: The Christ will suffer and rise from the dead on the third day, ⁴⁷and repentance and forgiveness of sins will be preached in his name to all nations, beginning at Jerusalem. ⁴⁸You are witnesses of these things. ⁴⁹I am going to send you what my Father has promised; but stay in the city until you have been clothed with power from on high."

COMMENTARY

36 The care with which Luke connects the events after the crucifixion chronologically (23:54, 56; 24:1, 9, 13, 33) is again apparent in the words, "While they were still talking about this." Once more Luke focuses attention on Jesus by the reflexive pronoun *autos* (i.e., "Jesus himself"; see comments at v.25). The next words, "stood among them" (*estē en mesō*), are almost identical to those in John 20:19 (*estē eis to meson*). A sudden appearance is implied (cf. the sudden disappearance in v.31), but Luke does not include the reference to closed doors found in John. "Peace be with you" may not have been in the original but may rather have been added by a copyist who knew John 20:19. Yet the words may belong to the same tradition John and Luke used (see Notes). The characteristically Semitic "peace" (Heb. *šālôm*, GK 8934) would be a striking greeting if one were expecting the more familiar Greek *chaire* (GK 5897; cf. 1:28).

37–39 Luke's gospel opened with a terrified Zechariah in the unexpected presence of an angel (1:12). Now, near its end, Luke describes the fright of the disciples at the unexpected appearance of the risen Christ (v.37). One might have thought they would not respond this way, since they had just been hearing about Jesus' appearance on the Emmaus road. But whereas in that case Jesus had walked up to Cleopas and his companion as any traveler might, this time he appeared suddenly. Equally surprising to the reader are their doubts (v.38). These are significant for any who think that the disciples were expecting the resurrection and projected their hopes into a hallucination. Jesus identified himself very emphatically (v.39): "It is I myself" (*egō eimi autos*; cf. the *egō eimi*, "I am," frequent in John). The methods of crucifixion varied slightly, but Jesus apparently had nails in his hands (the Greek word can include wrists) and feet. Seeing and touching would convince the disciples. Later on John wrote of touching Jesus, not specifically with respect to the resurrection but as an argument against Docetism (1Jn 1:1). As in vv.3, 23, where he mentioned the body of Jesus, Luke drew attention to the physical aspect of the resurrection.

The argument one sometimes hears that Jesus' appearance in "flesh and bones" here contradicts Paul's statement in 1 Corinthians 15:50 that "flesh and blood cannot inherit the kingdom of God" misses Paul's idiomatic meaning; the human body cannot develop into a resurrection body without the change only God can bring.

40–43 Verse 40 is lacking in some manuscripts, but it is more likely genuine and is certainly appropriate (see Notes). What they "did not believe" (v.41) in the midst of joy and excitement is not resurrection itself but the "corporeal nature" of the resurrection (cf. S. Brown, 79). Jesus provides further evidence of his physical presence by eating (vv.42–43). Commentators refer to instances such as Genesis 18:8 and 19:3 as examples of eating by supernatural visitors, though in these two instances the reason was not, as here, to show that they were not ghosts. According to Jewish traditions in the NT period, angels do not eat (e.g., Tob 12:19; Josephus, *Ant.* 1.197; Philo, *Abraham* 118; cf. Charles H. Talbert, "The Place of the Resurrection in the Theology of Luke," *Int* 46 [1992]: 25).

44 From time to time Luke has taken care to show that whatever the Lord has said unfailingly takes place (e.g., 2:20, last phrase; 2:26; 19:32; 22:13, 37). That implication is perhaps present in the words, "This is what I told you" (*houtoi hoi logoi mou*, lit., "these are my words," v.44). Luke has a double emphasis in these verses: that which the OT predicted (notice the words, "must be fulfilled"), and that which Jesus taught during his ministry. The clause, "while I was still with you," is a way of distinguishing between the days of Jesus' earthly ministry and his temporary postresurrection ministry before the ascension. "Everything" (*panta*, v.44) recalls "all" (*pasin*, v.25); "must" (*dei*) corresponds to "have to" (*edei*) in v.26 (see comment there); "Law . . . Prophets . . . Psalms" expands "Moses and all the Prophets" in v.27 by adding the Psalms as a major component of the third division of the OT, the so-called Writings. This combination of terms in reference to Israel's Scriptures already appeared in Second Temple Jewish literature (cf. Sirach [prologue]; 4Q394 3.17— "David," "the Law," and "the Prophets").

45 In v.31 the eyes of the two were "opened" (*diēnoichthēsan*, GK *1380*). Now Jesus has "opened" (*diēnoixen*) the disciples' minds. Again Luke emphasizes the "Scriptures." The reader of the Greek text will see this emphasis in the pattern of related words: *gegrammena* ("written," v.44) . . . *graphas* ("Scriptures," v.45) . . . *gegraptai* ("written," v.46).

46–49 This statement from the mouth of the risen Lord combines three elements: (1) the death and resurrection of Jesus, (2) preaching to the Gentiles, and (3) the promise of the Spirit. The significance of the presence of these elements in one statement is that now the age of the church is connected to the life and ministry of Jesus. As Jesus himself participates in the unfolding of God's plan of salvation, the apostles (i.e., the church) will likewise participate in this great act of salvation history (cf. Jacques Dupont, "La portée christologique de l'évangélisation des nations d'après Lc 24,47," in J. Gnilka, *Neues Testament und Kirche* [Freiburg: Herder, 1974], 126). With reference to the OT, these verses provide both a review of the gospel material and a preview for the events to come in the second volume of the Lukan corpus.

46 The formula "on the third day" (cf. v.7) goes back to the first passion prediction (9:22). For the suffering of Jesus, one can point to Isaiah 53:7–8 (cf. Ac 8:32–33). For the resurrection, see the references in Isaiah 55:3 (cf. Ac 13:34) and Psalm 16:10 (Ac 13:35).

47 Even the widespread preaching of repentance and forgiveness was predicted in the OT (cf. Ac 26:23). Jewish authorities in the first centuries of our era debated whether or not they should engage in active proselytization; and some cited OT passages, especially in Isaiah, that referred to the coming of the Gentiles to the Lord. Such Scriptures as Isaiah 42:6 and 49:6 may underlie v.47 here (cf. Ac 13:47; see Pao, 84–86). The fulfillment began in Acts 2:38: "Repent . . . for the forgiveness." Gentiles heard these words in Acts 10:43 and 17:30 (cf. Paul's commission, Ac 26:17–18). The idea of reaching the Gentiles is certainly prominent in Luke (e.g., the mission to the Seventy or Seventy-two, probably representing the nations of the world [10:1]; see comments there), and this naturally finds its continuation in Acts. The connection between the call to repentance and the mission to the nations/Gentiles represents a new way by which the people of God can be defined (Guy D. Nave Jr., *The Role and Function of Repentance in Luke–Acts* [Academia Biblica 4; Atlanta: Society of Biblical Literature, 2002], 206–24). Also, the place of Jerusalem as the base of the mission accords with Luke's constant featuring of that city (cf. Isa 2:3; 51:4).

48–49 Here Luke stresses the role of "witnesses," and he will do so again in the parallel passage in Acts 1:8. The term "witnesses" only appears twice in Luke (11:48 and 24:48), but it becomes a critical term in the narrative of Acts (e.g., 1:8, 22; 2:32; 3:15; 5:32; 10:39; 13:31; 26:16; cf. Marion L. Soards, *The Speeches in Acts* [Louisville, Ky.: Westminster, 1994], 194–200). In the OT, the people of Israel were called to be witnesses (e.g., Isa 43:10); their failure to be faithful witnesses (e.g., Isa 6:9–10) anticipates the arrival of the new age, when God will work in a new way among his people.

The pronouns *hymeis* ("you") in v.48, *egō* ("I") in v.49, and *hymeis* ("you") again as the subject of "stay" in v.49 (omitted by the NIV) are emphatic and in contrast to one another. What the Father "promised" (v.49) is the Holy Spirit (Ac 1:4–5; 2:16–17), who was indeed the promised "power" (Ac 1:8). This "power from on high" (*ex hypsous dynamin*; cf. Isa 32:15) has been known in Luke from the very beginning of his narrative. The Son of God was conceived in Mary when she was overshadowed by the "power of the Most High" (*dynamis hypsistou*, 1:35).

NOTES

36, 40 See Notes, v.3, for the textual issue in these verses.

47 In the light of the parallels between Luke 24:45–49 and Acts 1:8, the two phrases πάντα τὰ ἔθνη (*panta ta ethnē* [GK 1620], "all nations") and ἐσχάτου τῆς γῆς (*eschatou tēs gēs* [GK 1178], "the ends of the earth") should both be understood in an ethnic sense, not a geographical one. The disciples are called to minister to the Gentiles. This is confirmed by Isaiah 49:6 (LXX), where the same phrase, ἐσχάτου τῆς γῆς (*eschatou tēs gēs*, "the ends of the earth"), refers to those who do not belong to ethnic Israel. See Pao, 84–91.

4. The Ascension (24:50–53)

OVERVIEW

Of the authors of the gospels, only Luke records the ascension. This event is more than the last episode in Luke's narrative sequence or a postscript to the resurrection. He has already mentioned it in 9:51 as Jesus' ultimate goal in his great journey toward Jerusalem (see comments at 9:51). The ascension also has significance in the narrative and theology of Acts.

The brevity of the account here at the close of Luke's gospel is not the measure of Luke's estimation of its importance. This brevity may imply a telescoping of the entire narrative for the sake of closure, thus explaining why Luke did not include sufficient chronological data to indicate how much time had elapsed since resurrection day; nevertheless, his words here—though few—are weighty with theological significance and very much in character with the entire book. For a discussion of the literary and theological reasons that can explain the different emphases in the two ascension accounts in Luke 24:50–53 and Acts 1:1–11, see Mikeal C. Parsons, *The Departure of Jesus in Luke–Acts* (Sheffield: JSOT Press, 1987). Since these two reports are both from the hands of Luke, the apparent discrepancies do not cause historical difficulties.

---

[50]When he had led them out to the vicinity of Bethany, he lifted up his hands and blessed them. [51]While he was blessing them, he left them and was taken up into heaven. [52]Then they worshiped him and returned to Jerusalem with great joy. [53]And they stayed continually at the temple, praising God.

COMMENTARY

50–51 The NIV's "to the vicinity of" (v.50) translates *pros* ("toward") and guards against the supposition that they had already arrived at Bethany and so were not actually on the Mount of Olives (Ac 1:12). Bethany was on the other side of the mount to the south. Jesus' action in lifting up his hands and blessing the disciples was priestly. The word "bless" (*eulogeō*, GK *2328*) was significant at the opening of Luke. Zechariah the priest was rendered speechless in the temple, so that he was unable to pronounce the priestly blessing on the people when he came out (1:22). Such a blessing now concludes the book. Elizabeth blessed Mary and her child (1:42); Zechariah blessed God (NIV, "praising") when, on his declaration of John's name, his speech was restored (1:64); he then blessed (NIV, "praise") God again in his song (1:68); Simeon blessed (NIV, "praised") God in the temple on seeing Jesus (2:28) and then blessed his parents (2:34). This word does not appear again in Luke until Jesus blessed the bread at Emmaus (24:30). Luke immediately uses the word again in vv.51 and 53. Thus he places Jesus clearly within the spiritual setting of the temple and priesthood. As the resurrected Messiah, Jesus has the authority to bless. This imagery forms an important part of the letter to the Hebrews, which describes the high priestly intercession of Jesus after his ascension to heaven (e.g., Heb 1:3; 4:14; 6:19–20; 7:23–25; cf. Ro 8:34; Eph 1:20).

Jesus is also the prophet of God, and we are again reminded of the prophet Elijah (cf. 4:26). That prophet was "taken up" to heaven (2Ki 2:11 [LXX], *anelēmphthē* GK *377*; NIV, "went up"; observe the same verb in Acts 1:2, 11; and the cognate noun in Luke 9:51, though here in 24:51 the verb is *anephereto*, GK *429*). Luke's conclusion points to Jesus as Prophet, Priest, and Messiah.

52 Jesus is also the Son of God, and so "they worshiped him." This recalls 4:8, where Jesus, refusing to bow down to Satan, asserts that only God himself deserves to be worshiped. The claim of Jesus' deity is clear here as he becomes the object of worship (cf. Joseph Plevnik, "Eyewitnesses of the Risen Jesus," *CBQ* 49 [1987]:102).

Luke's beautiful gospel closes with the theme of "joy" restated in v.52 and with the city of Jerusalem and its temple again presented as the true home of Christianity—the origin of the Christian gospel and the Christian church (see remarks on Jerusalem throughout this commentary, e.g., 13:31–35; 19:28–44; cf. Ac 1:8).

53 Luke's theme of doxology reappears at the very end, as the disciples are last seen "blessing" (NIV, "praising") God (v.53; see Notes)—a response to Jesus' blessing of them in vv.50–51. This is both an appropriate conclusion to Luke's gospel and a reminder to us to live lives of praise as we wait for the return of the ascended Lord.

NOTES

50–53 For a study of the Jewish context of this ascension narrative, see A. W. Zwiep, *The Ascension of the Messiah in Lukan Christology* (NovTSup 87; Leiden: Brill, 1997).

51–52 See Notes, v.3, for the textual issue in these verses.

53 The Byzantine texts have αἰνοῦντες καὶ εὐλογοῦντες (*ainountes kai eulogountes*, "praising and blessing")—a reading that goes back to A f¹ f¹³ 33 and other texts. If this is a conflation, as most assume, one must choose between the highly attested εὐλογοῦντες, *eulogountes* ($\mathfrak{P}$⁷⁵ ℵ B et al.), and αἰνοῦντες, *ainountes* (supported by the Western text). Internal considerations are somewhat in balance (see Metzger, 163–64), but the external witnesses give the preference to εὐλογοῦντες, *eulogountes*. It is possible that the significant use of εὐλογέω (*eulogeō*, "bless") in vv.50–51 may have caused copyists to introduce that reading here. But if, as other considerations make likely, it is the original reading here, it fits in beautifully with Luke's choice of the verb in vv.50–51. Having been blessed by God, the disciples now bless him in return (cf. Eph 1:3 for the same reciprocity). The NIV's "praising" may be a nice compromise that represents both verbs, especially since in biblical traditions a strict distinction between "blessing" and "praising" cannot be drawn when the object of the address is God himself (cf. Robert J. Ledogar, *Acknowledgment: Praise-verbs in the Early Greek Anaphora* [Roma: Herder, 1967], 115–19, 121–24).

JOHN

ROBERT H. MOUNCE

Introduction

1. OPENING COMMENTS

Introductions in commentaries run all the way from a few brief paragraphs to book-sized excursuses. John Calvin's two-volume work has only a two-page introductory word on "The Theme of the Gospel of John." By contrast, D. A. Carson's one-volume work devotes over eighty pages to a thorough discussion of such standard issues as author, date, purpose, history of interpretation, distinctive characteristics, etc. C. K. Barrett's 143-page introduction is even broader. It includes such additional issues as the background of the gospel (non-Christian as well as Christian), the theology of the gospel, and its origin and authenticity. Thus it becomes evident that the nature and size of an introduction is determined by the purpose of the commentary and the specific audience the author has in mind.

This commentary on John has not been written with the scholarly guild of NT experts in mind. While their work has played a major role in my own preparation, the end product is intended for pastors and inquiring laypeople who are looking for a relatively simple and straightforward exposition of John's account of the life and (especially) the death and resurrection of our Lord Jesus Christ. It has been my desire to explain in understandable language what the text actually says, what it means, and its relevance for daily living. In addition—and this, perhaps, is the most important purpose—I would hope that the work will lead the serious reader to a new appreciation of the wonder and awesome grandeur of God's great redemptive plan. This is why I have kept in mind the need to reflect not only on the immediate passage but also on the larger theological landscape of which a particular verse is an integral part. While careful exegesis will reveal what God has said, Spirit-controlled reflection on the text will allow God to continue to speak in the present. History becomes present reality. Truth is transformed from theoretical dogma to existential reality. As Paul tells his young colleague Timothy, the purpose of theological instruction is that believers will be "filled with love that comes from a pure heart, a clear conscience, and sincere faith" (1 Ti 1:5 NLT).

In sum, the purpose for which I have written this commentary has less to do with preliminary issues than with a desire that the truths of John's gospel effect a change in the reader's life. My treatment of such issues as date, author, and distinguishing characteristics will be restricted to a brief survey. Other works will supply more adequate coverage for those who desire to be more thoroughly informed on introductory issues.

2. WHO WROTE THE FOURTH GOSPEL?

From the closing paragraphs of the fourth gospel we learn that the one "who testifies to these things" and "wrote them down" (21:24)—i.e., the author—was "the disciple whom Jesus loved" (21:20). He is further identified as the one who leaned back against Jesus at the Last Supper to ask who the betrayer was (cf. 13:23). Elsewhere we learn that he was one of the two disciples who, on learning from Mary Magdalene that Jesus was no longer in the tomb, rushed to the grave to verify the report (20:1–9). It was to "the disciple whom [Jesus] loved" that he committed the care of his mother (19:26–27). He was also the one who first recognized the risen Lord in Galilee following the resurrection (20:7).

But who was this one characterized in such a complimentary fashion? From the account of the miraculous catch of fish (21:1–14) we know that he was one of the seven disciples who went fishing with Peter. Since Peter, James, and John served as the inner circle of the disciples—they were chosen to be with him at the raising of Jairus's daughter (Lk 8:51), on the Mount of Transfiguration (Mt 17:1), and in the garden of Gethsemane (Mk 14:33)—it seems likely that "the disciple whom Jesus loved" would be one of the favored three. It is clear that Peter is not the one in question—the text distinguishes between the two. Since James was martyred early in the history of the church (Ac 12:2), undoubtedly before the fourth gospel was written, John is the only one of the three who remains as a candidate. Granted, this does not "prove" that it was John the apostle who wrote the gospel, but it does present a strong presumption in his favor.

The case for Johannine authorship is greatly strengthened by the external evidence. D. A. Carson writes that early testimony is "virtually unanimous" that John the son of Zebedee was the author.[1] Irenaeus (*Haer.* 3.1.2), writing in the second century, says that "John the disciple of the Lord, who leaned back on his breast, published the Gospel while he was resident at Ephesus in Asia." From the gospel itself we learn that the author was a Palestinian Jew well acquainted with the religion, land, and customs of his people. Repeatedly throughout his work he gives every indication that he was an eyewitness to the scenes he was describing.

It is objected by some that an author would not refer to himself as one "whom Jesus loved," but such a criticism reads modern social and linguistic norms into an ancient setting. The designation is not to be taken in an exclusive fashion, as though Jesus loved no one else, but as a descriptive title used of one who had enjoyed the special privilege of an unusually close relationship to his Lord.

Because the fourth gospel is so different from the Synoptics, its authenticity is sometimes called into question. Many of the major themes and events of the first three gospels are missing in John, while at the same time it includes many significant episodes not mentioned by the others. The argument is that if the Synoptics present a clear picture of Jesus, then John's portrayal can hardly be accepted. Such criticisms overlook the varying purposes for which the four gospels were written. It was not John's purpose to supplement or correct the Synoptics. His gospel is a later, more reflective presentation of major themes in Jesus' life and ministry. If it is true, as many assert, that John's gospel grew out of his preaching ministry, its various differences from the Synoptics would not come as a surprise; they would, in fact, be expected.

---

1. D. A. Carson, *The Gospel according to John* (Grand Rapids: Eerdmans, 1991), 68.

3. WHEN WAS THE FOURTH GOSPEL WRITTEN?

Traditionally, the composition of the fourth gospel has been assigned a date late in the first century. If it depends on the Synoptics (as many have held), it must be subsequent to them. It is also argued that the gospel's thoroughgoing theology would have required a considerable amount of time to develop. More recently, the traditional arguments for a late date have been countered by the view that it must have been written prior to the fall of Jerusalem in AD 70.[2] For John not to have mentioned this incredibly important event of Jewish history is held to be highly improbable. Carson suggests AD 80–85 as a reasonable date.[3]

4. WHY WAS THE FOURTH GOSPEL WRITTEN?

While some have held that the purpose of the gospel was to combat Docetism or to oppose those who retained their loyalty to John the Baptist, it is clear from the evangelist's own words that his purpose in writing was that his readers would "believe that Jesus is the Christ, the Son of God, and that by believing [they might] have life in his name" (20:31). That other purposes may have been served is not denied, but to inform the author against his own testimony as to why he wrote what he did displays an unusual degree of arrogance.

5. CLOSING COMMENTS

With these few words on authorship, date of composition, and purpose, it is now time to come to grips with the gospel itself. There is no other book in the Bible that to the same degree serves as a simple primer for new believers while at the same time continues to challenge the most learned scholars with its theological depths. More graphically, Morris describes it as "a pool in which a child may wade and an elephant can swim."[4] So at whatever level you find yourself, there lies before you a work that will not only inform you but whose full meaning and significance will always seem to lie just beyond our reach. John, the beloved apostle, presents us with his own eyewitness account of the life and times of Jesus the Christ.

6. BIBLIOGRAPHY

The following is a selective list of commentaries and monographs on John available in English, confined for the most part to those referred to in the commentary (they will be referred to simply by the author's name [and initials only when necessary to distinguish two authors of the same surname]). In instances where the same author has written a commentary as well as (a) book(s) and/or (an) article(s), the commentary will be referred to by the author's name, and the book(s)/article(s) by the author's name and short title.

References to resources that do not appear in the bibliography will carry full bibliographic details at the first mention and thereafter a short title.

---

2. Leon Morris, *The Gospel according to John* (NICNT; Grand Rapids: Eerdmans, 1971), 34.
3. Carson, *John*, 86.
4. Morris, *John*, 7.

Barclay, William. *The Gospel of John*. 2 vols. The Daily Study Bible. Philadelphia: Westminster, 1955.

Barrett, C. K. *The Gospel according to St. John*. 2d ed. Philadelphia: Westminster, 1978.

Beasley-Murray, George R. *John*. Vol. 36. Word Biblical Commentary. Waco, Tex.: Word, 1987.

Bernard, J. H. *A Critical and Exegetical Commentary on the Gospel according to St. John*. 2 vols. International Critical Commentary. Edinburgh: T&T Clark, 1928.

Borchert, Gerald L. *John 1–11*. Nashville: Broadman and Holman, 1996.

Brown, Raymond E. *The Gospel according to John*. 2 vols. Anchor Bible. Garden City, N.Y.: Doubleday, 1966, 1970.

Bruce, F. F. *The Gospel of John*. Grand Rapids: Eerdmans, 1994.

Bultmann, Rudolf. *The Gospel of John: A Commentary*. 1941. Reprint, Louisville, Ky.: Westminster, 1971.

Calvin, John. *Commentary on the Gospel according to John*. 2 vols. Grand Rapids: Eerdmans, 1949.

Carson, D. A. *The Gospel according to John*. Grand Rapids: Eerdmans, 1991.

Dodd, C. H. *The Interpretation of the Fourth Gospel*. Cambridge: Cambridge Univ. Press, 1953.

Haenchen, Ernst. *John*. 2 vols. Hermeneia. Philadelphia: Fortress, 1984.

Hendriksen, William. *Exposition of the Gospel according to John*. 2 vols. Grand Rapids: Baker, 1953–54.

Hoskyns, E. C. *The Fourth Gospel*. London: Faber & Faber, 1947.

Keener, Craig S. *The IVP Bible Background Commentary: New Testament*. Downers Grove, Ill.: InterVarsity, 1994.

Kysar, Robert. *John*. Augsburg Commentary on the New Testament. Minneapolis: Augsburg, 1986.

Lindars, Barnabas. *The Gospel of John*. New Century Bible Commentary. London: Marshall, Morgan and Scott, 1977.

Marsh, John. *The Gospel of St. John*. Pelican Gospel Commentaries. Baltimore: Penguin, 1968.

Metzger, Bruce. *A Textual Commentary on the Greek New Testament*. Revised edition. Stuttgart: German Bible Society, 1994.

Morris, Leon. *The Gospel according to John*. New International Commentary on the New Testament. Grand Rapids: Eerdmans, 1971.

Reith, George. *The Gospel according to St. John*. Edinburgh: T&T Clark, 1948.

Ryle, J. C. *Ryle's Expository Thoughts on the Gospels*. Vols. 3–4. Grand Rapids: Zondervan, 1951.

Schnackenburg, Rudolf. *The Gospel according to St. John*. 3 vols. New York: Seabury, 1968.

Tasker, R. V. G. *The Gospel according to St. John*. Tyndale NT Commentaries. 1960. Reprint, Grand Rapids: Eerdmans, 1994.

Temple, William. *Readings in St. John's Gospel*. 2 vols. London: Macmillan, 1939–40.

7. OUTLINE

I. The Coming of the Eternal Word (1:1–18)
 A. His Origin (1:1–5)
 B. His Witness (1:6–8)
 C. His Incarnation (1:9–18)

II. Jesus Begins His Public Ministry (1:19–5:47)
 A. The Testimony of John the Baptist (1:19–34)
 B. Jesus Selects His First Disciples (1:35–51)
  1. Andrew and Peter (1:35–42)
  2. Philip and Nathanael (1:43–51)
 C. Initial Ministry in Galilee and Jerusalem (2:1–25)
  1. Wedding at Cana in Galilee (2:1–11)
  2. Jesus Cleanses the Temple in Jerusalem (2:12–25)
 D. Two Early Encounters (3:1–4:45)
  1. A Jewish Rabbi Learns of New Birth (3:1–36)
   a. Encounter with Nicodemus (3:1–15)
   b. Teaching on belief and judgment (3:16–21)
   c. Further witness by John the Baptist (3:22–36)
  2. A Samaritan Woman Learns of Living Water (4:1–45)
 E. Jesus Begins His Healing Ministry (4:46–5:47)
  1. An Official's Son (4:46–54)
  2. A Paralytic at the Pool of Bethesda (5:1–18)
  3. Jesus' Claim of Divine Authority (5:19–47)

III. Jesus' Continuing Ministry and the Rise of Opposition (6:1–8:59)
 A. Jesus' Continuing Ministry (6:1–71)
  1. Jesus Feeds the Five Thousand (6:1–15)
  2. Jesus Walks on Water (6:16–21)
  3. Further Teaching (6:22–71)
   a. Bread of life (6:22–59)
   b. Eternal life (6:60–71)
 B. Opposition in Jerusalem (7:1–8:59)
  1. Conflict at the Feast of Tabernacles (7:1–52)
  2. Woman Caught in Adultery (7:53–8:11)
  3. Jesus' Teaching That Offended the Religious Leaders (8:12–59)
   a. "I am the light of the world" (8:12–30)
   b. "My truth will set you free" (8:31–38)
   c. "You are children of the devil" (8:39–47)
   d. "Before Abraham was, I am" (8:48–59)

Text and Exposition

I. THE COMING OF THE ETERNAL WORD (1:1–18)

OVERVIEW

The first eighteen verses of the gospel of John are usually referred to as the prologue—a somewhat misleading designation in that it tends to suggest that the material covered in the verses is introductory rather than substantive. But John's presentation of "the Logos" in the initial paragraphs of the gospel serves as an historical and theological summary of the entire book. It tells of Jesus' preexistence, his work in creation, his incarnation, and his rejection by the world, but also of his gift of eternal life to all who will receive him. In addition to these and other obvious parallels, there are others of a more subtle nature. The prologue is a poetic overture that combines the major theological motifs that make up the entire gospel. The view that it was an early Christian hymn (Brown, 1) is unlikely, in part because material on John the Baptist is interwoven throughout. Barrett's description, 150, of the prologue as "rhythmical prose" is accurate.

A. His Origin (1:1–5)

¹In the beginning was the Word, and the Word was with God, and the Word was God. ²He was with God in the beginning.
³Through him all things were made; without him nothing was made that has been made. ⁴In him was life, and that life was the light of men. ⁵The light shines in the darkness, but the darkness has not understood it.

COMMENTARY

1 John opens his gospel with a majestic declaration: "In the beginning was the Word." Before human history ever began, even before creation itself, "the Word already was" (NEB). The Word was not, as Arius would later claim, a created being—first in the order of creation, but nevertheless part of it.

The concept of *logos* ("word," GK *3364*) has an extensive and varied background in Greek religious and philosophical thought. As far back as Heraclitus (fifth century BC), the *logos* was understood to be the unifying principle of all things. For the Sophists, the *logos* was predominantly human reason. Philo, a prolific writer and leading citizen of the Jewish community in Alexandria, used the term more than thirteen hundred times as a mediating figure linking the transcendent God and the world (cf. *TDNT* 4:88). In general, Greek speculation viewed the *logos* as the principle of reason or order in the world (Bruce, 29).

In Hebrew thought, the word of God was a dynamic concept. God spoke and the world came into existence (Ge 1:3, 6, 9, 11, 14 et al.; Ps 33:6 ["By the word of the LORD were the heavens made"]; cf. Heb 11:3). In Proverbs 8:22–31, wisdom is personified and its role in creation is described.

While it is helpful to be aware of Greek and Semitic backgrounds, John's doctrine of the *logos* is only incidentally related. John does not begin with a metaphysical concept but with the person and work of the historical Christ. W. F. Howard (*IB*, 8:442) notes that "Jesus is not to be interpreted by Logos: Logos is intelligible only as we think of Jesus. At the same time it is true that the broad and varied usage of the term provided an excellent link to contemporary thought and allowed John the opportunity to redefine *logos* in terms of the incarnate Son of God.

Having established the eternal nature of the Word, John now proceeds to declare that the Word was both "with God" and at the same time "was God." Never has so much christological truth been compressed into such a brief statement. Contrary to the later teaching of Sabellius (a third-century Roman theologian), the Word was personally distinct from God the Father. The common use of *pros* ("with," GK *4639*) followed by the accusative expresses motion toward. In this context it pictures the Word in a face-to-face relationship with the Father. BDAG, 875, cites John 1:1 as an example of the preposition meaning "(in company) with."

Not only was the Word *with* God; the Word *was* God. Tasker, 42, notes that the unique contribution of the prologue is that "it reveals the Word of God not merely as an attribute of God, but as a distinct Person within the Godhead." The lack of an article before *theos* ("God," GK *2536*) does not allow it to be translated "divine" (as some have suggested), for the lack is simply common practice for predicate nouns. Had John wanted to say that the Word was

divine, he had at hand a perfectly good Greek term (*theios* [GK *2521*]; cf. Ac 17:29). The tendency to regard the Word as somewhat less than God gave rise to the sixteenth-century heretical movement known as Socinianism, which held that the historical Jesus was a good man but only a man. He became God after his resurrection when the Father delegated to him certain divine powers. Socinus's position laid the foundation for later Unitarian movements. All such heresies overlook the clear teaching of the fourth gospel that the Word *was* God, or, as the NEB so aptly translates, "What God was, the Word was." In essence, God and the Word are one.

2 John restates the fact that the Word was "with God in the beginning." Essential truths bear repetition! The verb *ēn* ("was," GK *1639*) has no particular temporal boundaries and should be contrasted with another verb (*egeneto*, "became," GK *1181*) in v.14. The Word as eternal Son stands outside time but in the incarnation became the historical Jesus. As in the previous verse, the preposition *pros* implies personal relationship and communication.

3 It was through the Word that all things were made. He was the active agent in creation (cf. Col 1:16–17; Heb 1:2). Not a single thing that now exists was made apart from him. The universe with all its complexity and magnificence reflects his creative involvement. Matter is not eternal. It came into being ex nihilo, out of nothing. The author of Hebrews writes that "the universe was formed at God's command" and that "what is seen was not made out of what was visible" (Heb 11:3). No better explanation of what we call objective reality exists. The human mind strenuously resists the idea of the eternality of matter—the only plausible alternative to creation ex nihilo. How much more satisfactory to embrace the truth that God the Creator carried out his task by working through his Son, the Word of God.

4 "Life" (*zōē*, GK *2437*) is one of John's favorite words. Almost half of the 134 occurrences of the word in the NT are found in his writings (thirty-six in the gospel, thirteen in his first epistle, and fifteen in Revelation). In contrast to another Greek word for life (*bios*, GK *1050*), which occurs eleven times in the NT and normally refers to everyday life, *zōē* refers most often to the supernatural life that belongs to God and that the believer now shares through faith in Christ. Life is an essential attribute of God. In the course of his gospel, John will point out that God in his relationship to the believer is both the "bread of life" (6:35) and the "light of life" (8:12). He supplies the "water of life" ("living water," 4:10), and his words are "spirit and . . . life" (6:63).

The life that was in the Son is said to be "the light of men." It enables people to see that God is at work in the world. Lindars, 86, notes that it includes "the widest range of man's intellectual apprehension of God and his purposes." Life as "the light of men" makes revelation possible. Life and light are frequently associated in the OT (e.g., Ps 36:9).

5 The light "continues to shine" (Williams) in the darkness, but the darkness is unable to grasp its meaning or to put it out. The darkness about which John writes refers to the condition of the fallen race. It is personified as an active agent over against the light of Christ. The Greek *katalambanō* (GK *2898*) means "to seize" or "to grasp." If the action implied is physical, the verse means that the darkness did not "overcome" or "extinguish" the light (so RSV). If it is understood in the sense of a grasping with the mind, it means that the darkness did not "understand"—or perhaps "accept"—the light. There is no reason to limit interpretation to one or the other. When the life, which was in the Word, manifested itself as light, the world in darkness neither accepted it (cf. v.11) nor was able to put it out (ch. 20). The Living Bible translates, "His life is the light that shines through the darkness—and the darkness can never extinguish it."

NOTES

1 Since θεός (*theos*, "God"; GK *2536*) in the clause θεὸς ἦν ὁ λόγος (*theos ēn ho logos*, lit., "God was the Word") is anarthrous, i.e., it does not have an article, some have taken it in the sense of "divine." Ernest Cadman Cowell's rule ("A Definite Rule for the Use of the Article in the Greek New Testament," *JBL* 52 [1933]: 20–21) that a predicate nominative preceding the verb need not be taken as indefinite or qualitative is helpful but not determinative. Of course, if θεός, *theos*, did have an article, we would be faced with the theological problem that "no other divine being existed outside the second person of the Trinity" (Barrett, 156). The definite article before λόγος, *logos* (GK *3364*), establishes the Word as the subject of the clause. The clause with its predicate nominative (θεός, *theos*) should be understood in the sense, "what God was, the Word was" (NEB).

3 A major question of punctuation occurs at the end of v.3. Should ὃ γέγονεν (*ho gegonen*, "that has been made," *GK 1181*) complete v.3 or be moved to v.4? The argument that it belongs with v.4 is that when the Arians began to appeal to the passage to prove that the Holy Spirit was part of the creation, the church moved it to v.3. While its location in v.4 can be argued on the basis that it was the interpretation of the earliest Fathers and that it preserves "rhythmical balance," the case for its location in v.3 is stronger. Taken together, John's frequent use of ἐν (*en*, "in," GK *1877*) at the beginning of a sentence, his frequent repetition, and the fact that "in him was life" make much better sense than the rendering "that which was created [the created universe] was life in him."

4 The word ἀνθρώπων (*anthrōpōn*, "men," GK *476*) here and quite often elsewhere should be taken in the generic sense of referring to the entire human race, not to males only. In all cases, context is the most reliable indicator of the intended meaning.

B. His Witness (1:6–8)

OVERVIEW

Suddenly the focus changes from the eternal Word to the historic beginnings of the incarnate Word. John the Baptist comes onto the stage of history to herald the arrival of the promised Messiah. Since the evangelist's account of John the Baptist occupies more than 40 percent of ch. 1, it is not surprising to find him introduced so early in the prologue. More important, however, is that the text has just spoken of the light that shines in the darkness, and now we learn that John is the one who came to "testify concerning that light" (v.7). Throughout the gospel he is identified simply as John rather than John the Baptist (as in the Synoptic Gospels). On the assumption that John the apostle is the author of the fourth gospel, this way of referring to John the Baptist would cause no confusion. Some critics assume that the prominence given to John the Baptist at this point reveals the presence and influence of a large number of followers, but this is highly unlikely (cf. J. A. T. Robinson, "Elijah, John and Jesus," *NTS* 4 [1958]: 278).

> ⁶There came a man who was sent from God; his name was John. ⁷He came as a witness to testify concerning that light, so that through him all men might believe. ⁸He himself was not the light; he came only as a witness to the light.

COMMENTARY

6 John is identified as "a man who was sent from God." His mission was divine in origin. He was commissioned and sent by God to carry out a specific role in history. Calvin, 1:14, correctly notes that "what is said about John is required in all Church teachers: they must be called by God, so that the authority of teaching may have no other basis than God alone."

7 John came as a witness, or, as Moffatt has it, "for the purpose of witnessing." The Greek *martyria* (GK *3456*), with its English cognate "martyrdom," is a reminder of how quickly witnessing can lead to rejection and death. John came to testify concerning the light (the light that continues to shine in the darkness) so that through him (i.e., through John's testimony) all people might come to believe. It is also possible to take the pronoun translated "him" as referring to the light (i.e., Jesus), but this is less likely because Jesus is normally presented as the object rather than the agent of faith. That all will come to faith through the Baptist's testimony means that in that day all who did come to faith were pointed in that direction by the witness of John.

8 The evangelist is careful to point out that the Baptist "was not the light" but came to bear witness to the light. Elsewhere in the gospel the Baptist is referred to as a "lamp" (*lychnos*, GK *3394*) that burns and shines (5:35), but he is not the "light" (*phōs* [GK 5890]). In the fourth gospel Jesus is the "light of the world" (8:12; 9:5; cf. 12:46) and we are his witnesses who take that light into a dark world. A proper understanding of our role as witnesses is crucial for effective outreach. We are the ones who bear testimony, but it is the living Christ who alone can dispel the darkness of unbelief.

C. His Incarnation (1:9–18)

⁹The true light that gives light to every man was coming into the world.

¹⁰He was in the world, and though the world was made through him, the world did not recognize him. ¹¹He came to that which was his own, but his own did not receive him. ¹²Yet to all who received him, to those who believed in his name, he gave the right to become children of God—¹³children born not of natural descent, nor of human decision or a husband's will, but born of God.

¹⁴The Word became flesh and made his dwelling among us. We have seen his glory, the glory of the One and Only, who came from the Father, full of grace and truth.

¹⁵John testifies concerning him. He cries out, saying, "This was he of whom I said, 'He who comes after me has surpassed me because he was before me.'" ¹⁶From the fullness of his grace we have all received one blessing after another. ¹⁷For the law was given through Moses; grace and truth came through Jesus Christ. ¹⁸No one has ever seen God, but God the One and Only, who is at the Father's side, has made him known.

COMMENTARY

9 Grammatically, the phrase "coming into the world" can refer either to "the true light" or to "every man." Although syntax perhaps favors the latter (in the Greek text the phrase immediately follows "every man"), the majority of translators understand that John is describing the "true light" as coming into the world.

A more important consideration (from a theological point of view) has to do with what John meant by saying that the true light "gives light to [*phōtizei*, GK *5894*] every man." A common answer is that God gives light in the sense that he has endowed the human race with reason, intelligence, and the ability to discern between right and wrong. But certainly the coming of the true light had a far more important purpose. If this were all it could accomplish, the human race would still be wandering in spiritual darkness. While light is given to every person, not all will choose to receive the light. As we will see, only those who received the light became children of God (see comments at v.12).

Marsh, 106, questions the common translation of the verb *phōtizō* as "enlightens" by asking why John would then go on in the next verse to speak of the world's unbelief. He suggests that we translate the verb in its primary meaning of "bring to light" or "shine upon," so that whether or not a person accepts the light it still "shines upon him and shows him up for what he is." Jesus is the true light in the sense of being real or genuine in contrast to that which is fanciful. The comparison is not between true lights and false lights but between the one light that is real and other lights that perhaps flicker with a bit of truth but then go out. He alone is the true light, "the genuine and ultimate self-disclosure of God to man" (Carson, 122).

10 We now learn that although the Word was in the world (which had come into being through him), it "did not recognize him." Prior to the incarnation, the Word "was [on a continuing basis; cf. the same verb in vv. 1, 2, 4, 8] in the world." Even though the world came into being through the Word, it did not "recognize" (*ginōskō*, "to know," GK *1182*, in the Semitic sense of relational knowledge) him. John uses the term "world" frequently (seventy-eight times in the gospel) and with considerable variation in meaning. In v. 10a and b, the world is the entire created universe, including humanity; in v. 10c it refers to that segment of the human race that has alienated itself from God.

11 In the incarnation the Word came to "that which was his own" (*idia*, GK *2625*, neuter) but "his own" (*idioi*, masculine) people "did not receive him." It was not lack of knowledge but the set of the will that kept his own people from welcoming him into their midst. Not to receive is to reject. The eternal Word was rejected by his own people.

12 Although his people as a nation did not accept the divine Word, some as individuals did. To all those who did receive him, he gave "the right [the authority] to become children of God." People are not by nature God's children. They *become* his children by receiving Jesus Christ. God's attitude toward all humanity is that of a father, but unless they receive

his Son they cannot become his children. John always refers to believers with the word *tekna* ("children," GK *5451*) rather than *huioi* ("sons," GK *5626*), the latter term being reserved for Jesus alone.

Those who received him are further identified as those who "believed in his name." Here we see the customary use of the verb *pisteuō* ("to believe," GK *4409*) followed by *eis* (GK *1650*) and the accusative, a construction that appears thirty-six times in John. To believe is to place one's faith "into" (*eis*) another person. Faith for John is a definitive action. By contrast, *pisteuō* with the dative case means no more than to believe that something is true. It involves the intellect but not the will. The construction John uses indicates "allegiance as well as assent" (Barrett, 164). To believe in the "name" of Jesus is to accept all that his name declares him to be.

13 Being born into the family of God is radically different from natural birth into a human family. To stress this point John uses three phrases to explain the difference. While it may be true that the three are "virtually synonymous" (Lindars, 92), the fact that all three are mentioned underlines the importance of the difference between birth into a human family and birth into the family of God.

First, the children of God are born "not of natural descent," i.e., they are not brought into this world as the result of a normal sexual union. The Greek has *ouk ex haimatōn* ("not of bloods" [GK *135*]). The plural reflects an ancient idea that children were conceived by a mingling of the blood of the parents. Second, children of God are not the result of a "human decision," i.e., bodily appetite. The Greek *thelēmatos sarkos* ("will of the flesh," GK *2525, 4922*) denotes sexual desire (*sarx* in this context does not connote evil). Third, God's children are not the result of a "husband's will." Children of God are "born of God." He is the one who initiates the process. It is distinct from human procreation both in origin and in sphere.

The question sometimes arises as to whether v.13 alludes to the virgin birth of Jesus. Many of the early church fathers (e.g., Irenaeus, Tertullian) thought that it did. It is unlikely, however, that this statement regarding the way all believers come into the family of God has any relevance for the clear teaching of Scripture on the unique birth of Jesus Christ.

14 We now come to the most concise statement in Scripture regarding the incarnation. With eloquent simplicity born of brevity, John proclaims, "The Word became flesh." The philosophical mind may have taken no exception to John's teaching on the Logos up until this point. But any idea of the Logos (the eternal Reason) entering into our human estate would run counter to the fundamental Greek axiom that the gods were detached and separate from the struggles and heartaches of humanity (see Morris's extended note, 115–26, on the Logos). By declaring that "the Word became flesh," John answered the Docetics, who, while acknowledging that Jesus of Nazareth was divine, could not bring themselves to accept the fact that he was also fully human. They would claim that he only *appeared* (*dokeō*, GK *1506*; used intransitively it means "to seem") to be a real man. Throughout history Christian orthodoxy has always maintained the full humanity of Jesus, as well as his complete deity. He is the God-man. The incarnation is the embodiment of God in human form as Christ. In becoming human Jesus did not diminish in any way what he was before. While the voluntary restrictions of becoming human led him to resist any independent expression of his divine power, he was in no way less God by becoming human. He became what we are without relinquishing what he always has been and must be.

John goes on to say that the eternal Logos (God the Son) came and lived for a while ("made his dwelling") among us. The reference is to his earthly ministry as Jesus of Nazareth. The verb *skēnoō* (GK *5012*) means "to live in a tent [*skēnē*; GK *5008*]," i.e., to take up a temporary abode. The term would call to mind the wilderness trek of Israel during which time God took up his abode in the tabernacle, or Tent of Meeting. During the time of Jesus' earthly ministry, his followers recognized in him the very presence of God. He was the *shekinah* glory, the visible expression of the glory of God. He was, as the writer of Hebrews puts it, "the radiance of God's glory and the exact representation of his being" (Heb 1:3). The glory that his followers "saw" (a weak translation of *theaomai*, "to behold," GK *2517*, from *theōria*, "an appearance or spectacle," GK *2556*) was the glory of the one and only Son. The KJV's "only begotten" incorrectly suggests that *monogenēs* (GK *3666*) is derived from *gennaō* ("to beget," GK *1164*) rather than from *ginomai* (in this context, "to be born," GK *1181*). John is saying that the Son is unique, the only one of a kind. God has as sons all who have been adopted into his family on the basis of personal faith, but Jesus is the Son of God sui generis (unique). He came from the Father, "full of grace and truth" (the phrase modifies "the Word" or "the one and only Son" rather than "glory" as some have suggested). These two great Christian terms reflect the unmerited favor of a God who, true to his essential character, gives of himself for the eternal benefit of humanity.

15 For the second time in the prologue, the evangelist refers to the ministry of John the Baptist (cf. vv.6–8). John bore witness to the Word incarnate by crying out (*krazō*, GK *3189*, used here as a technical term for prophetic speech; cf. *EDNT* 2:313) that Jesus, who came after John in point of time nevertheless took precedence over him, because Jesus existed before John. It was commonly believed in antiquity that "chronological priority meant superiority" (Morris, 108). Some take the last expression (*prōtos mou*, GK *4755, 1609*) to mean "first of me," i.e., "my superior," for *pro emou* (GK 4574, 1847) would be the normal way to say "before me" (cf. Jn 5:7; Ro 16:7; Gal 1:17). In that case John the Baptist would be saying that Jesus had surpassed him because he was superior to him ("he was ever First," TCNT). In either case the Baptist was proclaiming the absolute superiority of the eternal Word, who entered history as Jesus, God's one and only Son. The verb tenses in v.15 are noteworthy (*martyrei*, "testifies," GK 3455, present; *kekragen*, "cries out," GK 3189, perfect but used with the force of a present) and emphasize that the testimony of the Baptist continues with force into the present time.

16 Following the reference to John the Baptist in v.15, the evangelist resumes his line of thought from v.14. The one and only Son is "full of grace" (v.14), and out of his "fullness" they had all "received one blessing after another." Not only had they received grace when they came to him in faith, but their experience of the goodness of God was one of continuous blessedness. The NIV rendering of *charin anti charitos* ("one blessing after another"; lit., "grace instead of grace") makes clear the progressive blessings that come in the Christian life. Each experience of the grace of God is replaced by the next, like the manna that came fresh every morning. John's point is that at the heart of new life in Christ is a constant supply of grace. It is interesting that John uses the term "grace" only here in the prologue (vv.14, 16–17) and no place else. (Contrast the writings of Paul, who uses *charis*, GK 5921, over one hundred times in his letters.)

17 John draws a contrast between "the law," which was given "through Moses," and "grace and truth," which came "through Jesus Christ." The contrast is not intended to be taken in an absolute sense. That the God of the OT was a God of grace is clear.

The psalmist writes that God is "compassionate and gracious . . . , slow to anger, abounding in love and faithfulness" (Ps 86:15; cf. Ex 34:6). Dodd, 84, notes that "law" and "grace and truth" are not directly opposed but bear a relationship of shadow and substance. There was nothing intrinsically wrong with the law. It served a preparatory role. Hendriksen, 1:89, notes that the two things it could not supply were "grace," so the sinner could be pardoned, and "truth," the reality to which all the types point. It is in this context that for the first time John uses the full name, "Jesus Christ."

18 The prologue closes with a powerful statement regarding the superiority of the Son. While "no one has ever seen God," the Son "has made him known." In the OT, God had appeared at various times in theophanies (e.g., Ex 3:2–6; Jdg 13), but such appearances were always partial and temporary. God's statement to Moses in Exodus 33:20 ("no one may see me and live") is normative. That God in his essential being is invisible is taught in several verses (e.g., Dt 4:12; Col 1:15; 1Ti 1:17). While no one has ever seen God, the Son is said to be "at the Father's side." Tasker, 49, notes that the Greek *eis ton kolpon* ("into the bosom," GK 3146) is a "Hebrew idiom expressing the intimate relationship of child and parent, of friend and friend." Beck translates "close to the Father's heart"; Norlie has "in the intimate presence of the Father." The contrast is between the impossibility of a human being even to see the Father and the intimate relationship between Father and Son that made it possible for the Son to "interpret" the Father—he "made him known." *Exēgeomai* (GK 2007) is the Greek verb from which we derive the English word "exegete." In Hellenistic literature it was a semitechnical expression for the revealing of divine secrets. Josephus used it for the rabbinic exposition of the law.

NOTES

9 The participle ἐρχόμενον (*erchomenon*, "coming," GK *2262*) may be neuter nominative, agreeing with τὸ φῶς (*to phōs*, "the light," GK *5890*), or masculine accusative, agreeing with ἄνθρωπον (*anthrōpon*, "man," GK *476*). In favor of the latter option are (1) the fact that it leads naturally to the following verse, which speaks of the light being in the world; (2) other references to Jesus having come into the world (Jn 6:14; 9:39; etc.) and in John 12:46 the additional statement that he came into the world "as a light"; and (3) the use of the periphrastic imperfect (ἦν . . . ἐρχόμενον [*ēn . . . erchomenon*, "was coming"]), which is definitely Johannine in style.

13 The suggestion that v.13 alludes to the virgin birth of Jesus comes from a few MSS that replace the plural οἳ . . . ἐγεννήθησαν (*hoi . . . egennēthēsan*, "who were born," GK *1164*, NASB) with the corresponding ὃς . . . ἐγεννήθη (*hos . . . egennēthē*, "[he] who was born"). Although Tertullian, a late-second-century church father, insisted on the singular (and many modern scholars agree), the formidable consensus of Greek MSS makes the plural certain.

14 The word μονογενής (*monogenēs*, "only [one of its kind], unique," GK *3666*; cf. *EDNT* 2:439) occurs nine times in the NT—three times in Luke in reference either to a son (7:12; 9:38) or a daughter (8:42), and four times in John as a designation of Jesus in relation to God the Father (1:14, 18; 3:16, 18; cf. 1Jn 4:9). In Hebrews 11:7 it is used of Isaac, the child of promise, Abraham's "one and only son" who was about to be sacrificed. While believers are children of God, only Jesus is the one-of-a-kind, unique Son of God.

18 On the basis of external evidence, it is difficult to decide between ὁ μονογενὴς υἱός (*ho monogenēs huios*, "the only son," GK *3666, 5626*) and the more unusual and unexpected μονογενὴς θεός (*monogenēs theos*, "only God," GK *3666, 2536*). Metzger, 169, notes that "with the acquisition of 𝔓66 and 𝔓75, both of which read θεός, *theos*, the external support of this reading has been notably strengthened." Although υἱός, *huios*, reads more easily in the context, the more difficult θεός, *theos*, explains the origin of the other reading and is to be preferred. If μονογενής, *monogenēs*, is taken as a noun and followed by a comma, the result is a threefold description of Jesus: he is the unique one; he is God; he is the one who is in the bosom of the Father.

II. JESUS BEGINS HIS PUBLIC MINISTRY (1:19–5:47)

A. The Testimony of John the Baptist (1:19–34)

OVERVIEW

John the Baptist was a witness par excellence. This section of ch. 1 portrays him as a person with a clear understanding of his mission, genuine strength of character, and an unwavering commitment to the preeminence of the one about to appear on the scene of history. Verses 23, 26–27 give John's specific testimony, although the larger context (i.e., his denial that he himself is either the Christ or one of the prophets) should probably be included.

19Now this was John's testimony when the Jews of Jerusalem sent priests and Levites to ask him who he was. 20He did not fail to confess, but confessed freely, "I am not the Christ."

21They asked him, "Then who are you? Are you Elijah?"

He said, "I am not."

"Are you the Prophet?"

He answered, "No."

22Finally they said, "Who are you? Give us an answer to take back to those who sent us. What do you say about yourself?"

23John replied in the words of Isaiah the prophet, "I am the voice of one calling in the desert, 'Make straight the way for the Lord.'"

24Now some Pharisees who had been sent 25questioned him, "Why then do you baptize if you are not the Christ, nor Elijah, nor the Prophet?"

26"I baptize with water," John replied, "but among you stands one you do not know. 27He is the one who comes after me, the thongs of whose sandals I am not worthy to untie."

28This all happened at Bethany on the other side of the Jordan, where John was baptizing.

29The next day John saw Jesus coming toward him and said, "Look, the Lamb of God, who takes away the sin of the world! 30This is the one I meant when I said, 'A man who comes after me has surpassed me because he was before me.' 31I myself did not know him, but the reason I came baptizing with water was that he might be revealed to Israel."

32Then John gave this testimony: "I saw the Spirit come down from heaven as a dove and remain on him. 33I would not have known him, except that the one who sent me to baptize with water told me, 'The man on whom you see the Spirit come down and remain is he who will baptize with the Holy Spirit.' 34I have seen and I testify that this is the Son of God."

COMMENTARY

19 John, the author of the gospel, is fond of the word *martyria* ("testimony," "witness," "report," GK 3456). The term occurs thirty-seven times in the NT, and on thirty of those occasions the author is John. While in six of the seven occasions outside the fourth gospel *martyria* is used in a religiously neutral sense, in all but three of the thirty occurrences in John it is used in reference to Jesus and his redemptive work. For John, "testimony" is an evangelical witness to the person and work of Christ. Later we will be reminded that John selected his material and wrote his gospel specifically so that others might come to have eternal life by believing "that Jesus is the Christ, the Son of God" (20:30–31). The fourth gospel is the only gospel that intentionally identifies its purpose as evangelistic. John is concerned with witness. His later years on the island of Patmos resulted from his fidelity to "the word of God and the testimony of Jesus" (Rev 1:9).

The remarkable witness of John the Baptist caused uncertainty, if not consternation, in the minds of some of the "Jews of Jerusalem." Who was this uninhibited prophet whose message was attracting so much attention? Could he be the Messiah or perhaps one of the prophets? It was time to find out. So they "sent priests and Levites to ask him who he was." When John the evangelist speaks of the "Jews," his concern is not to stress their national identity but to identify the nation—particularly its religious leaders—as hostile to Jesus. Their understanding of the OT had led them to reject Jesus as Messiah so their attitude toward Christian believers was less than cordial.

The delegation consisted of subordinate clerics who were responsible to take back an answer to their superiors (v.22). While the Levites carried out important ritual functions in both temple and synagogue (Brown, 43, calls them "specialists in ritual purification"), they were not part of the ruling elite. Apparently the threat of a major defection on the part of the common people was not considered a likely possibility at that particular time.

20 When faced by his inquisitors, John the Baptist "did not fail to confess" that he was "not the Christ." Although the text does not supply us with the actual question, John's answer assumes that they expected a negative response. Perhaps they asked, "Surely you are not the Christ, are you?" And John confessed freely that he was not. The Greek text says that "he confessed and did not deny" (*hōmologēsen* [GK *3933*] *kai ouk ērnēsato* [GK *766*]). The two verbs stand as antonyms, and since the second is negated they help define each other. To "confess" is to "admit or concede something to be true." John "admitted" that he was not the Messiah. The parallel verb ("did not deny") stresses that he did not contradict the truthfulness of their assumption, namely, that he was not the Messiah. The statement is further strengthened by the repetition of *hōmologēsen*, translated here as "confessed freely." Brown, 42, has, "He declared without qualification."

John's confession is *egō ouk eimi ho Christos*, "I am not the Christ." One cannot help but see an implied contrast with the *egō eimi* ("I am") of Jesus that so often falls from his lips (6:35, 41; 8:12; 10:7; 11:25 et al.). Jesus *is* the Messiah; John *is not*.

21 Then who is John? The delegation from the Sanhedrin needs to take an answer back. So they ask, in effect, "What then shall we conclude?" (The NIV's "then who are you?" translates the Greek neuter interrogative as though it were masculine; the NASB has "what then?") "If you are not the Christ, then you must be Elijah." The nation of Israel would remember that Elijah did not die but was taken up alive in a whirlwind into heaven (2Ki 2:11) and that Malachi, the last of the OT prophets, had predicted that God would send "the prophet Elijah before that great and dreadful day of the LORD comes" (Mal 4:5). Is it possible that John the Baptist could be Elijah returning to announce the coming of Messiah? The return of the prophet is reflected in NT writings (Mk 8:28) and was a popular theme in rabbinic legends.

John answers the query with a firm "I am not." In another setting, Matthew records Jesus' assertion that, for those willing to accept it, John was "the Elijah who was to come" (Mt 11:14). Commentators agree that Jesus' reference is to "the spirit and power of Elijah" (Lk 1:17).

The delegation wonders of John, "If you are neither the Messiah nor his forerunner Elijah, 'Are you the Prophet?'" (The NEB has "the prophet we await.") In Deuteronomy 18:15, God promised that he would raise up a prophet like Moses to speak for him. Could Jesus be that long-awaited prophet? (For other references, see Jn 6:14; 7:20; Ac 3:22; 7:37.) Now the answer comes even more abruptly: "No." John does not conform to popular Jewish messianic expectations, though he does come as the forerunner of their Messiah.

22 Then "who are you?" they ask. "Give us an answer to take back to those who sent us." John's declaration of impending eschatological judgment would identify him in the minds of the Jewish nation as one of the figures of popular messianic expectation. But since he claimed not to be "Elijah" or "the Prophet," who can he be? "What do you say about yourself?" is a wide-open question. "Tell us about how you understand your own ministry," they are asking, in effect.

23 John answers with a quotation from the OT prophet Isaiah: "I am the voice of one calling in the desert." The Synoptics quote Isaiah 40:3 and apply the prophecy to John the Baptist (Mk 1:3 par.), but in the fourth gospel John uses it to identify himself and his mission. He is not a prominent figure but only a "voice in the wilderness." His role is simply to speak a word in behalf of the Eternal Word. This understanding of mission in terms of the quotation from Isaiah may account for the fact that John begins his career in the thinly populated area ("the desert") of Israel rather than in the city. *Boaō* ("to call, shout, cry out," GK *1066*) is a strong word. It is used of Jesus' cry of desolation on the cross (Mk 15:34).

John's message is, "Make straight the way for the Lord" (cf. Isa 40:3). When an ancient dignitary was about to visit a province of his realm, the message would go out to prepare the way by removing all obstacles from the road and making it as smooth as possible. The road that the Messiah would travel was the road into the hearts and lives of his people. Only national repentance could prepare the way for that spiritual journey, and John had come to prepare the nation for the advent of the Messiah.

24–25 The delegation from Jerusalem included "some Pharisees" who questioned John's practice of baptizing, since he had acknowledged that he was not the Christ, Elijah, or one of the prophets. They viewed baptism as an eschatological rite to be per-formed by a leader in the last days. The Pharisees (the name means "separated ones") were an important group among the Jews who insisted on fastidious obedience to the Mosaic law and to the oral tradition that had grown up around the law to adapt it to changing times. Their major concern was ethical rather than theological; thus their interest in John the Baptist and his summons to national repentance. Essentially, their question is, "Why do you baptize if you are not one of those leaders whose presence heralds the end of the age?" For John to have baptized would have violated the law if he had received no public office from God (cf. Calvin, 1:29).

26 John's response to the Pharisees was to minimize his own role ("I am only baptizing in water," AT) and to extol the one who stands among them yet whom they do not know. Later John will contrast the two baptisms (v.33, "with water . . . with the Holy Spirit"), but here he wants to focus attention on the radical distinction between his own role and that of the Christ. It is tragic that the promised Messiah could be right there with them and not be recognized (cf. v.12). Metzger, 170–71, notes that the Greek perfect (*hestēken*, GK *2705*) "conveys a special force here (something like, 'there is One who has taken his stand in your midst')." The self-inflicted blindness that accompanies religious pride makes all opposing alternatives unacceptable. They did not know him because they were expecting someone quite different. Hendriksen, 1:97, writes, "In their eagerness to expose false Messiahs, they are ignoring the true Messiah."

27 John readily admits that he is "not worthy" to perform even the menial task of untying the sandal strap of the Coming One. According to rabbinic teaching, a disciple could perform for his teacher any service that a slave would do for his master except untie his sandal (cf. *b. Ketub.* 96*a*). We admire John's humility but are fully aware that the privileged role he played is unparalleled in history (cf. Mt 11:11). Humility, someone said, is a trait so rare that when you think you've found it you've lost it. Monica Baldwin writes, "What makes humility so desirable is the marvelous thing it does to us; it creates in us a capacity for the closest possible intimacy with God" (see www.worldofquotes.com/author/Monica-Baldwin/1/index.html).

28 The encounter between John and the delegation from Jerusalem took place "at Bethany on the other side of the Jordan." This was not the Bethany near Jerusalem where Mary and Martha lived (11:1) but a village of uncertain location east of the Jordan River. Since Origen could not find a village by that name near the Jordan, he accepted a variant that translates "Bethabara." John notes that this location beyond the Jordan was "where John was baptizing." The periphrastic construction (ēn . . . baptizōn, GK 966) pictures John as carrying out his ministry on a continuing basis.

29 The next day (i.e., the day after John's encounter with the delegation from Jerusalem) John saw Jesus approaching and proclaimed him to be the Lamb provided by God to take away the sin of the world. Commentators have offered a number of suggestions concerning the background of the title "Lamb of God." The three most prominent are (1) the apocalyptic lamb (Jewish apocalyptic literature contains the image of a conquering lamb that defeats the forces of evil; this messianic warrior appears in Revelation as the Lamb who triumphs over the beast and his armies [Rev 17:14]); (2) the suffering servant (some say that the Aramaic *talya*, which lies behind the Greek *amnos* (GK *303*), can be understood as "servant" as well as "lamb" (Isa 52:7); and (3) the paschal lamb (Ex 12–13). See Brown, 58–61, for a helpful discussion of these three.

Lindars, 109, concludes that "the title is based on Isaiah 53, interpreted in the light of the Passover sacrifice." J. Jeremias (*TDNT* 1:340) notes that the description of Jesus as *amnos* expresses his patience in suffering, his sinlessness, and the efficacy of his vicarious death. He is the one who "takes away the sin of the world." Temple, 1:24, writes that John uses the singular ("sin") because there is only one sin and it is characteristic of the entire world, "the self-will which prefers 'my' way to God's—which puts 'me' in the centre where only God is in place." The Greek *airō* (GK *149*; NIV, "takes away") in this context combines the two meanings "to take up" and "to carry away" (cf. BDAG, 28–29). Whether one interprets "the sin of the world" to mean all the sin of the world (as in 1Jn 2:2) or only the sin of certain people from every nation depends on one's view of the extent of the atonement: Was it for all humanity or only the elect?

30 John now refers back to his declaration in v.15. The Coming One was greater than John because he was "before him." Although he came *after* John in point of time, he has far surpassed him in significance because he was *before* John as the preincarnate Son of God. It is Jesus' preexistence that sets him apart from all earthly mortals. No other person belongs in that category.

31 When John said that he "did not know [Jesus]," he meant that he did not know him as the Coming One. It is highly probable that they knew one another, for they were related. (In Lk 1:36 Elizabeth, John's mother, is said to be a *syngenis*, GK 5151, "kinswoman" or perhaps "cousin" of Mary the mother of Jesus.) What John did not know about Jesus prior to the Spirit's descent at the scene of the baptism was that Jesus was the promised Messiah.

32 The event described here is mentioned in all four gospels, but only in Luke (3:22) do we learn that the Spirit descended "in *bodily form* like a dove" (italics added). There could be no mistake on John's part—it was not a subjective experience—because the Spirit assumed the visible form of a dove. The dove was considered an appropriate offering for the poor (cf. Lev 12:8) and symbolized such qualities as purity, gentleness, and innocence. Temple, 1:26, notes that only the dove is said to offer its own neck to the sacrificial knife. That the Spirit remained on Jesus symbolizes the permanent nature of the divine appointment.

33 John had been told that the one on whom the Spirit descended would be the one to "baptize with the Holy Spirit." Both Matthew and Luke record John the Baptist as saying that the Coming One will baptize "with the Holy Spirit *and with fire*" (Mt 3:11; Lk 3:16, italics added). In both cases the verses that follow indicate that the baptism of fire is connected with judgment. The fourth gospel is content to mention only the endowment of the Spirit as a symbol of the new covenant (cf. Eze 3:22).

34 The testimony of John the Baptist began with v.19 and now closes with v.34. "I have seen" is the indisputable basis for "and I testify" (Phillips has, "I declare publicly before you all"). His testimony is that Jesus of Nazareth "is the Son of God." In all three synoptic accounts, the descent of the Spirit is followed by a voice from heaven declaring Jesus to be God's beloved Son in whom he is well pleased (Lk 3:22 par.). John's testimony rested on God's own declaration. Coupled with the visible descent of the Spirit, there could be no question but that Jesus was the long-awaited Messiah.

NOTES

34 While NA²⁷ adopts the reading ὁ υἱὸς τοῦ θεοῦ (*ho huios tou theou*, "the Son of God"), which certainly has stronger external support (𝔓⁶⁶·⁷⁵ ℵᶜ A B C Θ cop^bo, etc.), there exists early evidence for the variant ὁ ἐκλεκτὸς τοῦ θεοῦ (*ho eklektos tou theou*, "the Chosen One of God"; 𝔓⁵ ℵ* b e ff²* sy^s·c). Internal considerations would favor the latter because, while there would be considerable motivation for a scribe to change ἐκλεκτός, *eklektos*, to υἱός, *huios*, there would be no obvious reason to replace a favorite Johannine expression ("Son of God"; cf. 1:49; 3:18; 5:25 et al.) with a title that appears nowhere else in John. For reasons supporting ἐκλεκτός, *eklektos* (GK *1723*), see Gordon Fee, "The Textual Criticism of the New Testament," in *Biblical Criticism*, ed. R.K. Harrison et al (Grand Rapids: Zondervan, 1978), 152–53. That ἐκλεκτός, *eklektos*, was probably original is supported by a third variant that joins the two (*electus filius*, "elect Son"). Rieu translates, "that this is the Elect of God."

B. Jesus Selects His First Disciples (1:35–51)

1. Andrew and Peter (1:35–42)

³⁵The next day John was there again with two of his disciples. ³⁶When he saw Jesus passing by, he said, "Look, the Lamb of God!"

³⁷When the two disciples heard him say this, they followed Jesus. ³⁸Turning around, Jesus saw them following and asked, "What do you want?"

They said, "Rabbi" (which means Teacher), "where are you staying?"

³⁹"Come," he replied, "and you will see."

So they went and saw where he was staying, and spent that day with him. It was about the tenth hour.

⁴⁰Andrew, Simon Peter's brother, was one of the two who heard what John had said and who had followed Jesus. ⁴¹The first thing Andrew did was to find his brother Simon and tell him, "We have found the Messiah" (that is, the Christ). ⁴²And he brought him to Jesus.

Jesus looked at him and said, "You are Simon son of John. You will be called Cephas" (which, when translated, is Peter).

COMMENTARY

35–36 On "the next day" (the third day in the sequence), John the Baptist was with two of his disciples. Seeing Jesus pass by, he repeated the declaration of the previous day, "Look, the Lamb of God!" (cf. v.29). From v.40 we will learn that Andrew was one of the two disciples who were with John the Baptist. (That he had a group of followers who would be considered his disciples is clear from Mk 2:18.) Most writers are of the opinion that the other disciple was John the son of Zebedee. The verb used of John's "seeing" the Lamb of God as he passed by is *emblepō* (GK *1838*), which means "to fix one's gaze on." It portrays the intensity with which he looked at Jesus, whom he now knows to be the promised Messiah.

37 The two disciples heard their teacher's words and "followed Jesus." Their personal attachment to John was less than their allegiance to the truth he taught. He had told them of one coming whose sandals he was unworthy to loosen. Now that this Coming One had appeared, it was appropriate for the disciples to break their ties with John and follow the Christ. Eighteenth-century German theologian Johann Bengel refers to this event as "the origin of the Christian Church." From the very beginning faithful ministers have pointed others to Jesus and encouraged them to follow him. To follow Jesus means to follow him as a disciple.

38 Jesus' question should be taken in the deeper sense of, "What is it that you are searching for?" The two disciples responded by addressing him with the title "Rabbi," a translation of a Hebrew word meaning "my master," and by asking, "Where are you staying?" They were not merely curious about where he would spend the night but were hoping for an invitation to go home with him so they could have a lengthy conversation about a number of questions that had been on their hearts since hearing the Baptist proclaim that the Coming One was here.

Some writers note that the term "rabbi" was not used as a title until late in the first century. It designated one who after a fairly lengthy period of rabbinic training was ordained to the teaching ministry. In the Gospels it is applied to Jesus as an honorary designation. John regularly translates Hebrew and Aramaic words for the benefit of his non-Jewish readership (cf. 1:41, 42; 4:25; 9:7 et al.). Here he indicates that "Rabbi" means "Teacher." The Greek *methermēneuomenon* ("means," GK *3493*) is a compound participle derived from "Hermes," the messenger of the gods. Compare Acts 14:12, where Paul was called "Hermes" by the crowds in Lystra "because he was the chief speaker."

39 Jesus' straightforward answer was, "Come . . . and you will see." His invitation to those in need is always, "Come!" (e.g., Mt 11:28; Jn 4:16). It remains operative today for all who would like to know him better. Later John records Jesus' promise that whoever comes to him will never be turned away (6:37). The two disciples go with Jesus and spend the day with him. It was undoubtedly the most rewarding day of their lives. For some time they had heard the Baptist extol the virtues of the Coming One; now they were sitting in his presence and listening to what he himself had to say.

By this time it was "about the tenth hour." Assuming that the time reference is to the beginning of their stay with Jesus, it would appear that the evangelist is following the Roman custom of reckoning the hours of the day as we do from midnight and noon. The tenth hour would be 10:00 a.m. If, however, the author was following the Jewish method of reckoning time (from sunrise), it would be about 4:00 p.m. Brown, 75, records the possibility that it was four o'clock Friday afternoon (the eve of the Sabbath) and the disciples would therefore be prevented by Jewish law from any extensive travel for the next twenty-four hours.

40 The events described in vv.40–42 apparently take place on the fourth day of John's sequence, although no specific mention of the day is made. (The calling of Peter could hardly have taken place while Andrew and another disciple [John?] were in conference with Jesus on day three. The next recording of the day appears in v.43.) Verse 40 identifies Andrew as one of the two disciples who had listened to the teaching of the Baptist and then followed Jesus when he was pointed out.

41 Manuscripts reflect three variants for "first thing": (1) *prōton* (GK *4754*), Andrew's *first act* was to find Simon; (2) *prōtos* (GK *4755*), Andrew was the *first person* to make a convert; (3) *prōi* (GK *4745*), "early" in the morning. The NIV is correct in following the first alternative. To encounter Jesus and discover his true identity is to become a missionary.

There is no other option for the honest believer. Missionary work begins at home.

Although we most often refer to Andrew's brother as Peter, his original name was Simon. Since Simon is a standard Greek name (e.g., Simon Magus, Ac 8:11), it would have been better to transliterate the Hebrew name as "Symeon." He was the first to hear that Jesus was the Messiah, a truth that later became a confession (cf. Mt 16:16, "You are the Christ, the Son of the living God"). John once again translates the Hebrew term "Messiah" for his Gentile readers—"that is, the Christ." Barrett, 182, points out the remarkable sequence of names ascribed to Jesus in this section of the gospel: "Lamb of God (v.36); Rabbi (v.38); the one who was foretold by Moses and the prophets (v.45); Rabbi, Son of God, King of Israel (v.49); the Son of Man (v.51)."

42 When Andrew brought Simon to Jesus, Jesus "looked" at him (*emblepō*, "to gaze intently" [GK *1838*]; cf. v.36) and addressed him prophetically by giving him a nickname that would come to characterize him at a later point in his life, following Jesus' resurrection. Jesus always sees us in terms of what we can become, not what we are at the moment. Simon's family connection is indicated by the designation "son of John." John is probably a variant form of "Jonah," which is the correct form of his name on the basis of the transliteration of the Aramaic in Matthew 16:17 (*Simon Bariōna*, "Simon son of Jonah"). While Andrew's brother is now named Simon, he will be called "Cephas" (*Kēpha*, an Aramaic nickname meaning "rock," the equivalent nickname in Greek being *Petros*, "Peter," GK *4377*). At this point in Simon's life and throughout his three years as a disciple of Jesus, he was anything but "rocklike." Following Jesus' resurrection and continuing until Peter's martyrdom some thirty-plus years later, Peter demonstrated his true character as a steadfast apostle of the Christian faith.

2. Philip and Nathanael (1:43–51)

[43]The next day Jesus decided to leave for Galilee. Finding Philip, he said to him, "Follow me."

[44]Philip, like Andrew and Peter, was from the town of Bethsaida. [45]Philip found Nathanael and told him, "We have found the one Moses wrote about in the Law, and about whom the prophets also wrote—Jesus of Nazareth, the son of Joseph."

[46]"Nazareth! Can anything good come from there?" Nathanael asked.

"Come and see," said Philip.

[47]When Jesus saw Nathanael approaching, he said of him, "Here is a true Israelite, in whom there is nothing false."

[48]"How do you know me?" Nathanael asked.

Jesus answered, "I saw you while you were still under the fig tree before Philip called you."

[49]Then Nathanael declared, "Rabbi, you are the Son of God; you are the King of Israel."

[50]Jesus said, "You believe because I told you I saw you under the fig tree. You shall see greater things than that." [51]He then added, "I tell you the truth, you shall see heaven open, and the angels of God ascending and descending on the Son of Man."

COMMENTARY

43 The "next day" is probably day five in John's reckoning. Day four is not specifically designated but must be the day following John and Andrew's visit with Jesus when Andrew brings his brother Simon to Jesus (vv. 40–42). The Greek text does not say it was Jesus who decided to leave for Galilee, but the NIV is probably correct in making "Jesus" the subject of the sentence. Some, however, find the antecedent of the unexpressed subject of the verb ("he decided") in the previous verse and make Simon the one who found Philip. In that case we would have the interesting sequence of Andrew finding Simon (v. 41), Simon finding Philip (v. 43), and Philip finding Nathanael (v. 45). Whether it was Jesus or Simon (or Andrew; cf. Carson, 157–58) who found Philip, it was Jesus who called him to discipleship with the words, "Follow me." Jesus always calls people to himself, not to a religious point of view or even (primarily) to an exemplary way of living. Discipleship depends on a close personal relationship with Jesus as Master and Lord.

44 Galilee was the land to the west of the lake bearing the same name. In the time of Jesus it was governed by the crafty tetrarch Herod Antipas, the cunning "fox" (Lk 13:32) who married his brother's wife Herodias and had John the Baptist beheaded (Mt 14:1–11). Philip, like Andrew and Peter, was "from the town of Bethsaida." The designation is Aramaic and means "house of fishing." Since Bethsaida Julias (built by Philip the tetrarch and named in honor of the emperor's daughter) was east of the Jordan, it is suggested that there may have been two towns by that name, one in Iturea (cf. Lk 9:10) and the other in Galilee (cf. Mk 6:45). Perhaps the home of Philip and the others was a suburb of Julias on the west bank of the Jordan. In any case, the designation "Galilee" was used in a popular sense to include the territory all around the lake.

45 On arriving in Galilee Philip "found Nathanael." Temple, 1:30, writes, "As soon as [Philip] becomes a disciple he also becomes a missionary." Philip's good news was that they had found the one of whom Moses and the prophets wrote. Actually it was Jesus who found them, but the excitement of the new and crucial insight was more than adequate to account for Philip's manner of expression. Philip used the complete title for Jesus in the customary form of the day: his personal name, "Jesus"; his hometown, "of Nazareth"; and his family line, "the son of Joseph" (his legal father). The name "Nathanael" is not found in any of the lists of the disciples as recorded in the Synoptic Gospels. He is usually identified with Bartholomew, a patronymic (*Bar Talmai*) meaning "son of Talmai."

46 There is no reason to take Nathanael's surprised reaction to Philip's announcement as a "scornful question" (as Barrett, 184, does). It was commonly understood that the Messiah would come from Bethlehem (Jn 7:42) and that no prophet was to appear from Galilee (Jn 7:52). It follows that a man brought up in Nazareth, a town in Galilee, could hardly be the promised Messiah. Nazareth is not even mentioned in the OT or in the current literature of the day, Jewish or pagan. It is probably worth noting that the judgment on Galilee made by the chief priests and Pharisees was wrong—the prophet Jonah was born in Gath Hepher near Nazareth (2Ki 14:25). J. Ramsey Michaels (*John* [San Francisco: HarperSanFrancisco, 1984], 22) comments that "Nathanael's answer reflects a kind of provincialism in reverse that refuses to see glory or greatness in anything familiar or close to home." Nathanael came from the nearby town of Cana (cf. 21:2); but it is doubtful that Nathanael's response

was conditioned by intertown rivalry. Far more important was the widespread understanding that the Messiah would come from Judea.

Philip's answer was a simple "come and see" (cf. v.39). While it is true that "honest inquiry is a sovereign cure for prejudice" (Bruce, 60), the verbs denote action, not discussion. Theological debate is superfluous in the presence of actual experience. How wise it is to point honest inquirers to a personal acquaintance with Jesus rather than to burden them with a detailed explanation of nonessentials.

47 Jesus referred to Nathanael as a "true Israelite" and one in whom there was no deceit. The OT patriarch Jacob, whose name was later changed to Israel, was a deceitful man (Ge 27:36). The name Jacob means "he grasps the heel" (Ge 25:26), i.e., the one who supplanted or gained the advantage over his brother Esau, first by obtaining his birthright (Ge 25:39–34) and then by deceiving his father into giving him Esau's blessing (Ge 27). By contrast, Nathanael is a "true Israelite, in whom there is nothing false." Bruce, 60, characterizes him as one who is "all Israel and no Jacob."

48 There is considerable speculation regarding what may be intended by "I saw you under the fig tree." At times rabbis studied and taught under a fig tree. In Micah 4:4 and Zechariah 3:10, sitting under a fig tree appears to symbolize messianic peace. Moffatt translates, "under *that* fig tree" (italics added), which would strengthen the possibility that Nathanael may have undergone some profound religious experience while sitting under a specific fig tree. For Jesus to know about such an experience and where it happened would require supernatural insight and would account for what Temple, 1:32, calls an "outburst of exalted hope" from Nathanael (v.49).

49 "Son of God" and "King of Israel" are different ways of saying that Jesus is the promised Messiah. They are both messianic titles found in Psalm 2 (vv.6, 7). The first points to the deity of Jesus as well.

50–51 Nathanael's belief resulted from his awareness that Jesus had supernatural insight into his past. In the future he is to see "greater things than that." The following verse (v.51) explains what the term "greater things" includes. Along with others ("you shall [all] see"—the verb is plural), Nathanael is to see heaven standing open (*aneōgota* [GK *487*]—perfect tense) and the angels of God "ascending and descending on the Son of Man." The background is the account of Jacob's dream in Genesis (28:10–17) where a ladder (or stairway) reaches from earth to heaven with angels ascending and descending on it. What it means is that Jesus is the one who connects heaven and earth. He is the mediator between God and humanity (cf. 1 Ti 2:5), "the locus of 'traffic' that brings heaven's blessings to mankind" (Beasley-Murray, 28). The reference is not to some future point in time but to the entire period of Jesus' ministry now beginning in Judea.

The declaration is prefaced with the double "amen," a characteristic of Jesus' way of presenting an important truth. (The construction appears twenty-five times in John but not elsewhere.) The NIV translates with the rather bland "I tell you the truth." The title "Son of Man" is Jesus' self-designation. It has its roots in Daniel 7:13. Because it was somewhat obscure, it could serve as a messianic title without encouraging a popular surge of messianic fervor that would hinder Jesus' real purpose.

C. Initial Ministry in Galilee and Jerusalem (2:1–25)

OVERVIEW

John 2 opens with the narrative of a wedding in Cana of Galilee at which Jesus turns water into wine. Its inclusion in the gospel is not to record an interesting day in the life of Jesus but to set forth the miracle as a sign, that is, a wondrous deed that points beyond itself to reveal some aspect of the person of Jesus as Messiah and to evoke faith on the part of those to whom it is given. The distinctiveness of the term *sēmeion* ("sign," GK *4956*) as used by John is that it constitutes Jesus' "self-manifestation" in his works (*TDNT* 7:255). Beginning with ch. 2 and extending to the passion narrative, John's gospel is built around a sequence of seven signs (e.g., 4:46–54; 5:1–9). These are selected out of a larger number and recorded for the purpose of leading the reader to believe that Jesus is the Messiah, and by believing so to "have life in his name" (20:30–31).

1. Wedding at Cana in Galilee (2:1–11)

¹On the third day a wedding took place at Cana in Galilee. Jesus' mother was there, ²and Jesus and his disciples had also been invited to the wedding. ³When the wine was gone, Jesus' mother said to him, "They have no more wine."

⁴"Dear woman, why do you involve me?" Jesus replied, "My time has not yet come."

⁵His mother said to the servants, "Do whatever he tells you."

⁶Nearby stood six stone water jars, the kind used by the Jews for ceremonial washing, each holding from twenty to thirty gallons.

⁷Jesus said to the servants, "Fill the jars with water"; so they filled them to the brim.

⁸Then he told them, "Now draw some out and take it to the master of the banquet." They did so, ⁹and the master of the banquet tasted the water that had been turned into wine. He did not realize where it had come from, though the servants who had drawn the water knew. Then he called the bridegroom aside ¹⁰and said, "Everyone brings out the choice wine first and then the cheaper wine after the guests have had too much to drink; but you have saved the best till now."

¹¹This, the first of his miraculous signs, Jesus performed in Cana of Galilee. He thus revealed his glory, and his disciples put their faith in him.

COMMENTARY

1 The wedding took place at Cana of Galilee. This Cana (one of several) was probably the ancient but unexcavated village of Khirbet Qana, about eight miles northeast of Nazareth, not the more traditionally posited site of Kefr Kenna, some four miles outside Nazareth on the road leading north-northeast toward Tiberias. At one time Josephus was apparently quartered in Cana, as he writes, "My abode was in a village of Galilee, which is named Cana" (*Life*, 16). The wedding is mentioned only here in the NT (cf. 4:46–54; 21:2). Weddings in first-century Israel included a marriage feast that could last as long as a week (cf. Samson's seven-day marriage feast, Jdg 14:12). This banquet took place in the home of the bridegroom (cf. v.9) and, as later custom would indicate, was preceded by a procession in which the friends of the bridegroom would bring the bride to his house.

John notes that the wedding took place "on the third day." This would not be the third day of the week, because virgins were married on Wednesdays (the fourth day) and widows on Thursdays (the fifth day; cf. Keener, 268). If we consider the call of Philip

and Nathanael (1:43–51) as day five, then according to John's reckoning the wedding would fall on the eighth day. Some have seen in this an indication that Jesus' public ministry represents a new beginning, the number eight being one more than the perfect seven.

In any case, the two-day interval would allow sufficient time for Jesus and his followers to travel to Galilee. It is here that Jesus performs the first "sign," intended to lead people to faith. Interestingly, John does not refer to Jesus' mother by name. Mary appears only here and at the crucifixion scene (19:25–27). Since Jesus' disciples—presumably the five mentioned in ch. 1 who answered the call of Jesus (John, Andrew, Simon, Philip, and Nathanael)—were present at the wedding party (v.2), it would appear that the celebration was a family affair. Either bride or groom could have been a close relative. This would explain Mary's involvement in the festivities.

2 Any suggestion that the presence of the disciples caused the subsequent lack of wine is pure conjecture. After all, they were invited guests. That Jesus and his disciples would take part in wedding festivities demonstrates how different their lifestyle was from that of the monastic community of Qumran.

3 Wine was a basic commodity in the fare of the ancient world (Ge 14:18; Dt 14:26; Mt 11:19). For the supply of wine to run short at a wedding would cause severe embarrassment for the host. If Mary had some part in catering the banquet, this would help explain her reporting to Jesus that the wine had run out. Some scholars think it unlikely that she expected him to perform a miracle. Only in the apocryphal (and unreliable) gospels do we have stories of various miracles that Jesus is said to have performed during the years he was growing up in Nazareth. Mary undoubtedly went to Jesus with the problem because she knew how resourceful he had been on other occasions. It was the natural thing for the mother of such an unusual son to do. Bruce, 70, notes that "she did not know what he would do, but she knew that he would do the right thing."

On the other hand, Mary knew that her son was supernaturally conceived. He was not like others. That he had by now gathered the beginnings of a band of disciples perhaps indicated that he was about to take up his messianic work. Had not John the Baptist declared him to be the "Lamb of God" who had come to "take away the sin of the world" (1:29)? Was it not possible that now would be an appropriate time for him to perform a miracle?

4 The way in which Jesus answers his mother seems rude. A literal translation of the Greek would be, "What to me and to you, woman?" The NLT softens the response by omitting the word "woman" and the NIV by adding the word "dear" before "woman" (a solution that Carson, 170, deems "too sentimental"). The NEB paraphrases, "Your concern, mother, is not mine." That the term by which Jesus addressed his mother (*gynai*, "woman," GK *1222*) did not sound overly severe or unsympathetic in the ears of the original readers is clear from the fact that Jesus used the same expression when from the cross in reference to the beloved disciple he said to his mother, "Woman, here is your son" (19:26).

The exact nuance of Jesus' words "why do you involve me?" is not completely clear. It appears to be a Hebrew idiom, the meaning of which depends on the context. Tasker, 59–60, says that often in the OT the statement means, "Don't bother me; leave me alone," but in the present passage it should be translated, "Your concern and mine are not the same." The Jerusalem Bible has, "Woman, why turn to me?" In any case, there is no antagonism in the response. The reason that Jesus hesitated to do what his mother had asked is clear from the statement that follows: "My time has not yet come." His "hour" (*hōra*, GK *6052*) is the hour of his messianic manifestation. In the fourth gospel the full revelation of Jesus as the promised Messiah takes place in connection with his death and glorification (13:1; cf. 7:30; 8:20).

5 Mary apparently does not grasp the full intent of what her son has just said, so she instructs the servants to do whatever Jesus tells them. Jesus proceeds to perform his first miracle in spite of his assertion that his time had not yet come. We are probably to understand that this miracle, though intimating to a select few the beginning of a messianic ministry, would not be broadly recognized as such. Otherwise there would be an inconsistency between what Jesus said and what he did.

6–8 Standing nearby were six stone water jars that were used by the Jews for ceremonial cleansing (cf. the parenthetical remark in Mk 7:3–4). Brown, 100, notes that the jars were of stone rather than earthenware because the latter could become ritually contaminated. Each jar held from twenty to thirty gallons (a *metrētēs*, "measure," GK *3583*, was a liquid measure of about nine gallons). Since weddings lasted for a week and were social events to which as many guests as possible were invited, a considerable amount of wine would be required.

Jesus instructed the servants to fill the jars with water up to the brim. After they had done this they were told to "draw some out" and take it to the "master of the banquet" (either a servant who had been appointed to manage the feast or one of the guests acting as master of ceremonies). Noting that the verb *antleō* ("to draw," GK *533*) is used in 4:7, 15 of drawing water from a well, some understand that the water turned to wine was a second drawing from the well. This relieves the problem of turning such a large amount of water (perhaps as much as 120 to 180 gallons!) into wine. It could also be that only the water drawn *from the jars* (not all the water poured *into the jars*) was turned into wine. But scaling down a miracle to match our expectations is hardly ever good exegesis!

9–10 When the master of the banquet tasted the wine, he called the bridegroom over and commented that while most hosts bring out the cheaper wine after the guests have had too much to drink, in this case the best had been saved till last. There is no question but that the wine that was served would cause drunkenness if taken in excess. The Greek *methyskō* (GK *3499*) in the passive voice means "to become intoxicated" ("had too much to drink"). Speculation that Jesus was acting out a charade, pretending the water to be wine, and the steward was going along with it, is ingenious but unconvincing. Wine was a basic part of the first-century diet. Even Jesus came "eating and drinking" (obviously wine, because he was falsely charged with being a "drunkard," Mt 11:19). While drunkenness is never condoned in Scripture (cf. Eph 3:18), the use of wine (often mixed with water; the Talmud recommends three parts water to one part wine; cf. Robert Stein, "Wine-Drinking in the New Testament," *Christianity Today* 19 [June 1975]: 10) is everywhere assumed. The question of intoxicating beverages in today's society should be discussed against the background of their devastating effects on personal health and social well-being, not on whether or not the wine that Paul recommended to Timothy (1Ti 5:23) could make a person drunk.

Commenting on this miracle, C. S. Lewis (*Miracles* [New York: Macmillan, 1948], 163) writes that God does what he has always been doing—making wine. At Cana, "God, now incarnate, short circuits the process: makes wine in a moment . . . . The miracle consists in the short cut; but the event to which it leads is the usual one." William Temple, 1:37, sees in the best wine coming last an illustration of how our relationship to God becomes more and more satisfying with the passage of time: "When people meet us they find us friendly and considerate. When they come to know us they may have to put up with the less good. Our communion with God is not so. As we deepen our fellowship we may at every stage say, 'thou has kept the good wine until now.'"

11 The miracle Jesus performed here was "the first of his miraculous signs" (*sēmeia*, GK *4956*). In the NT several different words are used to depict the mighty works of Jesus. *Dynamis* (GK *1539*) is regularly used to describe an act of power or might, i.e., a miracle. A *teras* (GK *5469*) is a portent, or wonder, and in the NT is always found in conjunction with *sēmeion*, a sign. For John, miracles are *sēmeia*, which point beyond themselves. The turning of water into wine is a *sēmeion* that reveals the glory of Jesus and leads his disciples to "put their faith in him." The seven signs selected and recorded by John have as their purpose bringing people to faith in Jesus (20:30–30). The faith that John speaks of in the present context is an ever-deepening trust on the part of the disciples rather than their initial step of faith in following Jesus. The "glory" of Jesus revealed by the miracle was a momentary manifestation of his divine nature as the Son of God. The full revelation of the "Lord of glory" (1Co 2:8) is an eschatological event that awaits the day of fulfillment yet future.

NOTES

1 According to the inclusive reckoning of the NT, the "third day" would be what we would normally call "the day after tomorrow" (cf. Lk 9:22; Ac 27:19; 1Co 15:4).

3 Two Old Latin witnesses (it^e,l) explain the depletion of wine on the basis of the size of the crowd: "It happened that, because of the great crowd of those who had been invited, the wine was finished" (Metzger, 172–73).

6 In the OT ceremonial uncleanness resulted from a number of things, such as giving birth (Lev 12), skin diseases (Lev 13–14), etc. All forms of uncleanness prevented an Israelite from participating in the ritual worship of Yahweh. In the NT these Mosaic regulations were extended by tradition to include such things as ceremonial washing of the hands before eating. For a large wedding feast there would have to be a considerable quantity of water available for hand washing since the practice was to pour the water over the hands.

8 A rough translation of the Greek ἀρχιτρίκλινος (architriklinos, GK 804) would be, "chief of the banquet hall of three couches" (cf. the three components: ἀρχή, archē, "ruler," GK 794; τρεῖς, treis, "three," GK 5552; and κλίνη, klinē, "bed," "couch," GK 3109). One of the primary duties of the "master of the banquet" (the NASB's "headwaiter" is too contemporary) was to regulate the distribution of wine in order to prevent overindulgence.

REFLECTIONS

Since the miracle in Cana was a "sign" (*sēmeion*, v.11), writers have been led to discover in the specifics of the narrative a number of metaphorical references. For example, the lack of wine at the wedding feast (v.3) is said to symbolize the failure of Jewish law to meet the deeper needs of humanity. The inadequacy of the law is seen as well in the number of stone jars—six being one less than the perfect number seven (v.6). That the jars each held "twenty to thirty gallons" (v.6) is said to picture the inexhaustible supply of grace that Jesus brings. In the filling of the jars "to the brim" (v.7) we are encouraged to understand that the ceremonial observances of Judaism had run their course. That the "choice wine" (v.10) was provided by Jesus is said to indicate his superiority over the law. While these allegorical reflections are homiletically permissible, they do not lie at the heart of what was intended by identifying the miracle as a sign. What the miracle pointed to was the divine nature of Jesus, not a series of comparisons between Jewish law and the gospel.

2. Jesus Cleanses the Temple in Jerusalem (2:12–25)

¹²After this he went down to Capernaum with his mother and brothers and his disciples. There they stayed for a few days.

¹³When it was almost time for the Jewish Passover, Jesus went up to Jerusalem. ¹⁴In the temple courts he found men selling cattle, sheep and doves, and others sitting at tables

exchanging money. [15]So he made a whip out of cords, and drove all from the temple area, both sheep and cattle; he scattered the coins of the money changers and overturned their tables. [16]To those who sold doves he said, "Get these out of here! How dare you turn my Father's house into a market!"

[17]His disciples remembered that it is written: "Zeal for your house will consume me."

[18]Then the Jews demanded of him, "What miraculous sign can you show us to prove your authority to do all this?"

[19]Jesus answered them, "Destroy this temple, and I will raise it again in three days."

[20]The Jews replied, "It has taken forty-six years to build this temple, and you are going to raise it in three days?" [21]But the temple he had spoken of was his body. [22]After he was raised from the dead, his disciples recalled what he had said. Then they believed the Scripture and the words that Jesus had spoken.

[23]Now while he was in Jerusalem at the Passover Feast, many people saw the miraculous signs he was doing and believed in his name. [24]But Jesus would not entrust himself to them, for he knew all men. [25]He did not need man's testimony about man, for he knew what was in a man.

COMMENTARY

12 Following the miracle at Cana in Galilee, Jesus and his family went down to Capernaum. They "went down" in the sense that Capernaum, which lies on the northern shore of the Sea of Galilee, is lower in elevation than Cana. Capernaum (undoubtedly the ruins at *Tell Hum* west of the Jordan) was to become Jesus' headquarters in his Galilean ministry (Mt 4:13). The brothers of Jesus are listed by Matthew as "James, Joseph, Simon and Judas" (Mt 13:55). They are normally understood to be sons born to Mary and Joseph after the birth of Jesus. Those who hold to the doctrine of the perpetual virginity of Mary are forced to find another explanation. Epiphanius, a fourth-century polemicist, understood the "brothers" to be sons of Joseph by a previous marriage, that is, half brothers of Jesus, while Jerome held them to be cousins (cf. Brown, 120).

13 After a few days in Capernaum, Jesus went up to Jerusalem to celebrate the Jewish Passover. The

Passover was one of the three annual feasts that required the presence in Jerusalem of every Jewish male twelve years of age and older (Dt 16:16). Strictly speaking, Passover was the night of 14–15 Nisan. In time it became associated with the seven-day Feast of Unleavened Bread, which followed immediately. Later Judaism designated the entire period as Passover. The festival celebrated the deliverance of Israel from Egyptian bondage. The fourth gospel mentions three Passovers during the public ministry of Jesus (2:13; 6:4; 11:55; some would include 5:1 as a fourth), while the Synoptics have but one (at the time of his death). John's reference to three Passovers is the major factor in determining the length of Jesus' public ministry. If, however, the fourth gospel as we have it is an arrangement of the various homilies of John on the life and ministry of Jesus, precise chronology is less than likely.

14 Arriving in Jerusalem, Jesus went to the "temple courts." The NASB retains the Greek singular *hieron*, "temple," GK *2639*—a term that included the entire temple area with its buildings and courts. There he found men selling animals for sacrifice and exchanging foreign money so visitors could pay the temple tax. Normally booths were set up on the Mount of Olives for such necessary exchange, but for rather obvious commercial reasons the trade had been moved to the court of the Gentiles. Morris (*Reflections on the Gospel of John* [Peabody, Mass.: Hendrickson, 2000], 80) writes that "for any Gentile who came up to the temple to worship it meant that prayer had to be offered in the middle of a cattle yard and money market." The selling of animals for sacrifice was a convenience for those who came to Jerusalem from a distance. It is often said that heathen coins such as the Roman denarii and Attic drachmas were not permitted in paying the half-shekel temple tax because they bore the image of the emperor. But this overlooks the fact that the required Tyrian coins similarly bore human impressions. Tyrian coins were the acceptable currency because of their accurate weight and exceptional purity.

15 Appalled by all the commotion connected with the economic transactions going on in the temple court, Jesus took some rope and made a whip. With it he drove out the mercenaries with all their provisions. It is best to understand "all" as referring to all the merchants rather than all the animals. Barrett, 198, translates the latter phrase as an explanatory addition: "the sheep and the oxen as well." Whether the "whip" was made of rushes (from the bedding for animals) or a piece of rope (cf. Ac 27:32, the only other NT occurrence of *schoinion*, GK *5389*) it was hardly a weapon that would have frightened those who were profiting from the business. Morris (*Reflections*, 81) correctly notes that Jesus had "an ally in the consciences of the traders." They were not unaware of the impropriety of using the temple court as a place of commerce. The righteous indignation of Jesus armed with a whip was all that was necessary to put them to flight. It is noteworthy that, while Jesus overturned the tables of the money changers, scattering their coins on the ground, he did not set the doves free but told their owners to remove them from the court. (Lev 5:7 indicates that doves and pigeons were the sacrifice of the poor.) Jesus did not destroy the merchant's property but instead took appropriate action to remove both seller and merchandise from the temple court.

16 Jesus' accusation, "How dare you turn my Father's house into a market!" reveals his profound displeasure with the human propensity to desecrate what is holy. Unaware or forgetful of the biblical revelation of God as holy (cf. Isa 6:3), many believers even today attempt to worship him in ways far more appropriate in the marketplace than in the sanctuary. "How dare you turn" translates the Greek *mē poieite* (GK *3590, 4472*), which means "stop making." "My Father's house" is a clear-cut messianic claim. Jesus does not bracket himself with others in his references to God the Father. When Jesus' parents found him in the temple, the boy responded with, "Didn't you know I had to be in my Father's house?" (Lk 2:49).

John's placement of the cleansing of the temple at the beginning of Jesus' public ministry brings up the question of why the Synoptics have it at the close of his ministry. Most critical scholars tend to prefer the synoptic placement because (1) two cleansings are unlikely, and (2) John is more apt to rearrange material for theological reasons. Even notable conservative scholar F. F. Bruce, 77, writes, "It seems probable that John takes it out of its chronological sequence and places it, with programmatic intent, in the forefront of his record of Jesus' Jerusalem ministry."

Tasker, 61, on the other hand, rejects the idea that John is correcting a supposed chronological blunder on the part of the earlier writers or is deliberately altering their history for theological reasons. Along with other writers (e.g., Carson, 178) he holds that there were two cleansings, one at the beginning of Jesus' public ministry (recorded by John) and another during Holy Week (included in the Synoptic Gospels). This solution seems the most likely since in the fourth gospel it is the turning of his Father's house into a "house of merchandise" (*oikon emporiou*, GK *3875, 1866*; NIV, "market") to which Jesus objects, while in the Synoptics his major objection is the dishonesty of the sellers ("you are making it a 'den of robbers,'" Mt 21:13; Mk 11:17; Lk 19:46). Since in both cases the cleansing turned out to be temporary, there is no persuasive reason to merge the two events into one.

17-18 The dramatic removal of the traders and their merchandise from the temple precincts brought to the disciples' mind a messianic passage from the Psalms, "Zeal for your house consumes me" (Ps 69:9). Symbolic actions, such as the cleansing of the temple, found their prophetic base in OT Scripture. The reaction of the temple authorities was to question by what "authority" Jesus had purged the temple area. They requested a "miraculous sign" as proof of his authority. How strange, in that the cleansing itself was a powerful sign of Jesus' intrinsic authority. Temple, 1:40, writes, "Vain enquiry! When God speaks to either the heart or the conscience He does not first prove His right to do so."

19-20 Jesus' answer to his detractors was typically paradoxical: "Destroy this temple, and I will raise it again in three days." Such a statement would be tantamount to blasphemy to those who were responsible for the temple and its activities. It is worth observing that the word used for temple is *naos* (GK *3724*), the holy place (cf. *hieron*, GK *2639*, the entire temple complex). It should have served as a clue that Jesus was not speaking literally of material buildings. But the authorities missed the

point and asked how he could rebuild in three days a set of buildings that had taken forty-six years to erect. Herod the Great began his reign in 37 BC, and Josephus (*Ant.* 15.380) indicated that Herod had started the building of the temple in his eighteenth year. Thus forty-six years later would date this encounter to the spring of AD 27 (1 BC to AD 1 is only one year). If Jesus were born shortly before 4 BC (the date of the death of Herod the Great), he would have been about thirty years of age at the beginning of his public ministry (cf. Lk 3:23).

21-22 Jesus' statement about rebuilding the temple was remembered in a somewhat garbled fashion by the false witnesses who testified to the Sanhedrin, who were looking for evidence against Jesus by which they could put him to death (Mk 14:58). John adds the obvious interpretation that the temple of which Jesus spoke was "his body." After he was raised from the dead, his disciples remembered his prediction about raising the "temple" in three days, and they "believed the Scripture [Ps 69:9 and other prophetic teaching reflecting this event] and the words that Jesus had spoken" (specifically v.19). Note that the evangelist does not hesitate to bracket the words of Jesus with the authoritative word of the OT. This is in keeping with his view of Jesus as the promised Messiah, the one sent by the Father, who spoke only what the Father gave him to say (8:28; 12:29).

23 Many of the worshipers who had come to Jerusalem for Passover saw the miraculous signs done by Jesus and "believed in his name." That their belief was not a personal commitment is clear from Jesus' refusal to entrust himself to them (v.24). Although John uses his standard phrase for saving faith (*pisteuō eis*, "to put one's faith [GK *4409*] in or on"), Bruce, 77, labels this section "Superficial Faith." There are levels of belief in Jesus, and faith inspired by miracles is less than substantial (cf. 14:11). It is certainly not the kind of faith spoken of in 1:12 as that which grants the right to become "children of God." To believe in a person's "name" is to believe in who he is, in his person and character. Obviously the Jewish crowd would be impressed with anyone who could perform what appeared to be a miracle.

24–25 Jesus did not trust himself to those attracted by his signs because "he knew all men." He had no need of being told about anyone because "he [himself; *autos*] knew what was in a man."

In Jewish literature it is God's prerogative to know what is going on in the minds of people. Psalm 94:11 reminds us that "the LORD knows the thoughts of man." Jesus, the Son of God, had immediate and supernatural insight into the inner mus-

ings of people's minds. He understood human nature, with all its intrigue and complexity. This is reflected in conversations soon to follow—with Nicodemus (3:1–21), with the woman at Sychar (4:4–26), with the invalid at the pool of Bethesda (5:1–15). His knowledge was not simply a general understanding of human nature but a precise knowledge of the inner nature of specific persons. For example, Jesus saw Nathanael approaching and declared him to be "a true Israelite in whom there [was] nothing false," to which Nathanael replied, "How do you know me?" (1:47–48). People's hearts are open before God, and nothing can be hidden from his sight (Lk 8:17).

NOTES

19 The NET translator's note at 2:19 observes that the imperative in the clause "destroy this temple" is not a simple conditional imperative ("if you destroy") but is more like the ironical imperative found in the prophets (e.g., Am 4:4; Isa 8:9)—an imperative that carries the sense, "Go ahead and do this and see what happens."

23–24 The two occurrences of the verb πιστεύω (*pisteuō*, "to believe"; GK *4409*) in these verses are of special interest. The many people who saw Jesus' miraculous signs ἐπίτευσαν εἰς τὸ ὄνομα (*episteusan eis to onoma*, "believed in his name"), but he did not ἐπίστευεν αὐτὸν αὐτοῖς (*episteuen auton autois*, "entrust himself to them"). He did not put his trust in them because the trust they put in him was less than adequate. Their "belief" fell short of the complete commitment required by Jesus. Saving faith is considerably more than intellectual acknowledgment that Jesus was an unusual person whose ability to work the miraculous was truly outstanding.

REFLECTIONS

Some writers think that the final short paragraph of this section (vv.23–25) was intended to serve as an introduction to the account of Nicodemus in ch. 3. It is difficult, however, to see exactly how it leads into the narrative that follows. Others note that the miracles to which it refers are apparently overlooked

in 4:54, which counts the healing of the son of the Capernaum official as "the second miraculous sign that Jesus performed." The answer may lie in the fact that for literary convenience John has chosen to number specific signs rather than miraculous signs in general.

D. Two Early Encounters (3:1–4:45)

1. A Jewish Rabbi Learns of New Birth (3:1–36)

OVERVIEW

If the closing verses of ch. 2 (vv.23–25) are taken as an introduction to Jesus' interview in ch. 3, then Nicodemus is probably intended to serve as an example of those attracted by Jesus' miracles but not openly committed to following him. However, if the *de* ("now") of 3:1 introduces a contrast, then Nicodemus would be an exception to the "many" of 2:23—an honest seeker who wanted to know more about what Jesus was teaching. Although Nicodemus did not openly profess faith in Jesus at this time, his later conduct indicates that the initial interview made a profound impression on him. In ch. 7 he opposed the attempts of the Sanhedrin to condemn Jesus without a fair trial (vv.50–52). And following the crucifixion he joined Joseph of Arimathea in providing a decent burial for Jesus (19:39). Subsequent nonbiblical accounts profess to tell of his baptism, his suffering as a believer, and his final expulsion from Jerusalem.

a. Encounter with Nicodemus (3:1–15)

¹Now there was a man of the Pharisees named Nicodemus, a member of the Jewish ruling council. ²He came to Jesus at night and said, "Rabbi, we know you are a teacher who has come from God. For no one could perform the miraculous signs you are doing if God were not with him."

³In reply Jesus declared, "I tell you the truth, no one can see the kingdom of God unless he is born again."

⁴"How can a man be born when he is old?" Nicodemus asked. "Surely he cannot enter a second time into his mother's womb to be born!"

⁵Jesus answered, "I tell you the truth, no one can enter the kingdom of God unless he is born of water and the Spirit. ⁶Flesh gives birth to flesh, but the Spirit gives birth to spirit. ⁷You should not be surprised at my saying, 'You must be born again.' ⁸The wind blows wherever it pleases. You hear its sound, but you cannot tell where it comes from or where it is going. So it is with everyone born of the Spirit."

⁹"How can this be?" Nicodemus asked.

¹⁰"You are Israel's teacher," said Jesus, "and do you not understand these things? ¹¹I tell you the truth, we speak of what we know, and we testify to what we have seen, but still you people do not accept our testimony. ¹²I have spoken to you of earthly things and you do not believe; how then will you believe if I speak of heavenly things? ¹³No one has ever

gone into heaven except the one who came from heaven—the Son of Man. [14]Just as Moses lifted up the snake in the desert, so the Son of Man must be lifted up, [15]that everyone who believes in him may have eternal life.

COMMENTARY

1 Nicodemus is a Greek name that means "conqueror of the people." In rabbinic literature the name appears as Naqdimon. Some have identified Nicodemus of the fourth gospel with a wealthy man by the name of Naqdimon ben-Gorion who lived in Jerusalem, but this is uncertain. What we do know about Nicodemus is that he was a Pharisee who served as a member of the Jewish high court, the Sanhedrin. This "ruling council" of seventy was composed of priests, scribes, and lay elders from influential families. It served as a court of justice in all matters, civil and religious. That Nicodemus is referred to as "a man [*anthrōpos*] of the Pharisees" (a somewhat unusual phrase) tends to join the episode with the preceding verse (2:25), in which *anthrōpos* (GK *476*) occurs twice.

2 Why Nicodemus came "at night" is not known. Perhaps he wanted Jesus' undivided attention. If it is true that the rabbis studied and debated late into the evening, that could account for the time of Nicodemus's visit. Or possibly he was concerned about a negative reaction on the part of his fellow religionists. They would undoubtedly misunderstand his concern to hear from a nonprofessional such as Jesus regarding spiritual matters. We do know that Joseph of Arimathea concealed his allegiance to Jesus "because he feared the Jews" (19:38). In any case, it is best to avoid allegorical interpretations of why his visit was at night—interpretations such as the coming out of the darkness of religion into the light of God's immediate presence in Jesus.

Nicodemus addressed Jesus with the honorable title of "Rabbi." There is no reason to detect in this greeting a "note of conscious superiority" (Morris, *Reflections*, 88). Everything we do know about Nicodemus leads us to believe that, while his understanding may have been deficient, his attitude toward Jesus was respectful. He stands apart from the fanatics whose bigotry led them to the absurd conclusion that Jesus was demon-possessed (8:48). Nicodemus was absolutely correct in his appraisal that Jesus was a "teacher ... come from God." His reasoning was sound: unless God was with Jesus, he would not be able to do the miraculous signs he was doing.

3 It is reasonable to assume that Nicodemus had come prepared to ask Jesus much the same question as did the rich young man—"What must I do to inherit eternal life?" (Mk 10:17 par.). But even before the question can be asked Jesus provides the answer. It is prefaced with the double *amēn* ("I tell you the truth," GK *297*), which stresses the validity of what is about to be said. Unless a person is "born again" he cannot see the kingdom of God. *Anōthen* (GK *540*) is an adverb either of place ("from above," as in Mt 27:51) or of time ("again," "anew," as in Gal 4:9). In this context the former meaning is primary. To be born "from above" means to be born of God (cf. the use of *anōthen*, 3:31). However, since spiritual birth is in fact a second birth, the temporal idea of "again" is included. Unless a person is reborn from above he or she is unable to "see the kingdom of God." To *see* God's kingdom means to enter into and have a part in the final establishment of God's sovereign rule. As a Jew, Nicodemus would understand the kingdom of God as the long-awaited age to come. To "see" this kingdom would mean to experience resurrection life at the end of the age. What he did not understand was that to have a part in that kingdom required a second birth.

4 Taking the expression in its literal form, Nicodemus raised the question of how it would be possible for an old man to reenter his mother's womb and be born a second time. It is highly unlikely that Nicodemus recognized the figurative nature of Jesus' statement and was replying in the same vein—"How can we expect an elderly man who is set in all his ways to start all over again." Throughout the fourth gospel Jesus tends to speak on two levels, but a recognition of this ambiguity is missing in the responses by others. They are everywhere pictured as thinking on a single and mundane level.

5 In vv.5–8 Jesus restates and expands his earlier statement that to see the kingdom of God one must undergo a second birth (v.3). The parallel nature of these two passages indicates that to be "born again" means to be "born of water and the Spirit." Some interpret "water" as a reference to physical birth (either the embryonic fluid or the male sperm); but the verse is dealing with how one is born from above, not with natural birth. After reviewing a number of proposals, Carson, 195, opts for dropping the definite article and the capital *S* and understanding the expression as a reference to "the eschatological cleansing and renewal promised by the Old Testament prophets." However that may be, it is clear that John intended *his* readers to understand the expression as a reference to Christian baptism and the resulting gift of the Holy Spirit. The immediate background is the testimony of John the Baptist regarding baptism with water and baptism with the Holy Spirit (see 1:33). Water baptism by itself is inadequate; it must be accompanied by what it signifies—the cleansing work of the Spirit. Far from teaching a doctrine of baptismal regeneration, this verse informs us that the initiatory rite of baptism is intended to lead to a life infused by the cleansing power of the Spirit.

6–7 Jesus continues his differentiation between natural birth and spiritual birth by calling attention to the obvious fact that "flesh gives birth to flesh, but the Spirit gives birth to spirit." People live in two realms. Flesh speaks of natural birth with its physical weakness and mortality; Spirit speaks of a supernatural birth into an entirely different realm. The realm of the spiritual is radically different from the realm of the natural, and nothing short of a new birth does justice to that distinction. Although Nicodemus lived in a religious culture that taught salvation by deeds, he should not have been surprised to learn that entrance into the realm of the spirit would require a spiritual birth. That this foundational truth applies universally, and not simply to Nicodemus, is indicated by Jesus' use of the plural "you" in v.7. Not only Nicodemus, but all people everywhere must be born again if they would enter the kingdom of God.

8 Verse 8 plays on the two meanings of the Greek *pneuma* (GK *4460*). Like the Hebrew *rûaḥ* (GK 8120), it means both "wind" and "spirit." There exists an analogous relationship between the wind and the Spirit of God. The wind "blows wherever it pleases"; you can hear it, but you have no idea where it comes from or where it is going. As the wind is "invisible and mysterious, yet known in experience" (Beasley-Murray, 49), so also are those born of the Spirit—their identity, source, and destination are mysterious and beyond the ken of earthly knowledge.

9–10 Nicodemus still does not understand, wondering how all this is possible. Jesus responds, in effect, "Can it be that you, the teacher of Israel [note the Greek definite article *ho*] are unable to understand these things?" Nicodemus was a man of stature among the Jewish rabbis and could be expected to know that entrance into God's kingdom was more than simply keeping the law. The Hebrew Scriptures held a number of clues that natural descent alone does not guarantee participation in the age to come.

Bruce, 86, notes that at this point the dialogue between Jesus and Nicodemus passes into a monologue on the lips of Jesus and then almost imperceptibly into a meditation by the evangelist on the subject of the new birth. The ten plurals in vv. 11–12 ("we ... you") indicate to many a transition from a private conversation to general teaching addressed to the readers. Others see in the change the indication of a dialogue between the church and the synagogue. That the singular also occurs in both verses ("I tell you ... I have spoken ... I speak") calls for a different interpretation of the plurals. In v. 2 Nicodemus spoke for himself and others when he said, "We know you are a teacher who has come from God." Jesus now engages in a rebuttal of Nicodemus by picking up his use of "teacher" and his assertion that he "know[s]." Brown, 132, says that the use of "we" (in v. 11) is "a parody of Nicodemus's hint of arrogance." The question of where or whether the words of Jesus are taken up and become the words of the evangelist is difficult to determine.

11–12 The lack of understanding on the part of Nicodemus is contrasted with the knowledge of Jesus and those who have entered into fellowship with him via the new birth. These speak of what they "know" and "have seen." But still their testimony is not accepted (cf. 1:11). The Jewish leaders were impressed with the signs Jesus had performed, but they stopped short of accepting him. So Jesus asks the obvious question: you do not believe me when I speak of "earthly things"; why then would you believe me if I speak of "heavenly things"? "Earthly things" represent truths such as the new birth for which there is a human analogy. "Heavenly things" are truths such as the heavenly descent of the Son of Man to secure eternal salvation for all who believe (cf. vv. 13–21; 31–36)—Carson, 199,

calls them, "the splendors of the consummated kingdom, and what it means to live under such glorious, ineffable rule." The contrast is more a matter of degree than of kind. In both cases we are dealing with divine action, but the latter is more incomprehensible than the former.

13 The more profound teachings of Jesus, i.e., those truths for which there are no analogies, have their origin in heaven, and with the one exception of the Son of Man, no one has ever gone into heaven to bring back that knowledge. Direct knowledge of heavenly things requires immediate and personal contact with the heavenly realm. And *no one* (note the emphasis) from earth has ever accomplished the necessary ascent. The only exception to this, of course, is the Son of Man, the one who came from heaven.

Verse 13 is a bit awkward because it seems to suggest that the ascension has already taken place. If this section is the reflection of the evangelist, the timing would cause no problem; but if the argument is that heavenly knowledge is the result of ascending to heaven, then how could Jesus have heavenly knowledge during his earthly ministry if he had not yet ascended? The problem is avoided by E. M. Sidebottom (*The Christ of the Fourth Gospel* [London: SPCK, 1961], 120), who suggests the reading, "No one has ascended into heaven, but one has descended" (taking *ei mē*, "except," in the way it is used in Mt 12:4 and Gal 1:7). In this case John would be saying that, while no one has entered heaven to secure knowledge of heavenly things, there is one who has descended to make such knowledge available.

Jesus, who alone is qualified to reveal the mind of God, bears the title "Son of Man." This designation occurs eighty-two times in the gospels, and with one exception (Jn 12:34) it is always used by Jesus of himself. Most scholars trace the title to Daniel 7:13–14 and understand Jesus' choice of a self-designation as a way of claiming messiahship while simultaneously concealing it. By referring to himself as the Son of Man, Jesus acknowledges his humanity (cf. the Semitic use of the phrase in the Psalms) but at the same time claims a heavenly origin (cf. the Daniel passage as well as noncanonical apocalyptic literature of the day).

14 Verses 14–15 draw on the account in Numbers 21 in which Moses at God's command places a bronze snake on a pole so that the Israelites who were dying from a plague of venomous snakes might look at the bronze snake and live (Nu 21:4–9). "Just as Moses lifted up the snake," so also must the Son of Man "be lifted up." The Greek verb *hypsoō* (GK *5738*) is regularly used throughout the NT in the figurative sense "to exalt" (e.g., Mt 23:12), but in all five occurrences in John's gospel it refers to the lifting up of Jesus on the cross (cf. 8:28; 12:32, 34). Paradoxically, the crucifixion of Jesus is portrayed by John as a vital part of his exaltation. Speaking of his coming death, Jesus on a later occasion said, "Now is the Son of Man glorified and God is glorified in him" (13:31). What the secular mind would judge a humiliating defeat was from God's viewpoint a display of divine glory. In God's redemptive plan it was necessary ("the Son of Man *must* be lifted up") that Jesus die as a sacrificial offering for the sins of humanity. On the basis of this one act, believers are privileged to enter into the eternal glory of their heavenly Father. In the account in

Numbers, a bronze snake provided physical healing; in the lifting up of the Son of Man, spiritual healing replaces eternal death. As Hendriksen, 1:138, notes, "The Antitype far transcends the type."

15 Verse 15 states the purpose for which the Son of Man was lifted up—so that all who believe "may have eternal life." Eternal life is more than endless existence; it is sharing in the life of the Eternal One. In his high priestly prayer, Jesus defines eternal life as knowing the only true God and Jesus Christ whom he sent (17:3). *The New Linguistic and Exegetical Key to the Greek New Testament* ([Grand Rapids: Zondervan, 1998], 185) observes that "eternal life is the life of the age to come which is gained by faith, cannot be destroyed, and is a present possession of the one who believes." John uses the verb *pisteuō* ("to believe," GK *4409*) ninety-eight times in his gospel, but only here is it followed by the preposition *en* ("in") rather than *eis* ("into"). This suggests that "in him" should follow "eternal life" rather than the verb "believes." The frequency of the verb corresponds with John's stated intention in writing his gospel—"that you may believe that Jesus is the Christ, the Son of God, and that by believing you may have life in his name" (20:31). That eternal life is a *present* possession of the believer (clearly taught elsewhere in the gospel; cf. 3:36; 5:24) is strengthened by the use of the present active subjunctive *echē* ("may have," GK *2400*).

NOTES

2 Like the people of Jerusalem who saw Jesus' miraculous signs and believed, yet to whom Jesus would not entrust himself (2:23–25), Nicodemus also "believed" in the sense that he correctly reasoned that a person who could perform such signs must have come from God. What he failed to grasp were the profound messianic implications of the miraculous deeds.

5 The Greek phrase ἐξ ὕδατος καὶ πνεύματος (*ex hydatos kai pneumatos*, "of water and the Spirit") could be translated epexegetically to mean "water, that is, the Spirit." In Ezekiel 36:25–27 cleansing with water is connected with the gift of the Spirit, so possibly the phrase could mean "converted by the Spirit" (so Keener, 270).

Several Greek MSS (ℵ*, the minuscules 245 291 472 1009, and the lectionary *l²⁶*) plus a number of early patristic writers read τῶν οὐρανῶν (*tōn ouranōn*, "of heaven," GK *4041*) rather than τοῦ θεοῦ (*tou theou*, "of God," GK *2536*). Although it could be argued that an original τῶν οὐρανῶν, *tōn ouranōn*, was replaced with τοῦ θεοῦ, *tou theou*, in order to harmonize with the same phrase in v.3, the UBS committee was persuaded by a number of factors that the latter was more likely to be original (cf. Metzger, 174). The designation "kingdom of heaven" occurs thirty-two times in the gospel of Matthew but nowhere else in the NT. Since Matthew is the gospel of Jewish Christianity, it is understandable that a reverential circumlocution for the name of God would be used (though "kingdom of God" does occur four times in Matthew).

15 The word πιστεύω (*pisteuō*, "to believe," GK *4409*) occurs thirty-four times in the fourth gospel and except in v.15 is always followed by the preposition εἰς (*eis*, "into"). Here πιστεύω is followed by ἐν (*en*, "in"). This argues for the NASB's "so that whoever believes will *in Him* have eternal life" (italics added) rather than the NIV's "everyone who believes in him." It is strengthened by the fact that when John wishes to emphasize an adverbial phrase with ἐν, *en*, he tends to place the phrase before its verb.

b. Teaching on belief and judgment (3:16–21)

OVERVIEW

In v.10 we noted the change from singular to plural pronouns, a change suggesting that Jesus at that point began speaking in more general terms. Now we find another change. The use of present tense verbs (appropriate to direct discourse) gives way to the past tense. Consequently, most commentators think that from this point forward we have the reflections of the evangelist rather than the words of Jesus. John is seen as developing the theological import of Jesus' conversation and applying it to his readers for their understanding. In any case, we come in v.16 to the very heart of the gospel. No verse in Scripture has been more widely quoted. In briefest compass it tells us of the character of God, his redemptive act in behalf of the human race, and the role of faith that leads to the gift of eternal life. Beasley-Murray, 51, calls this passage "a confessional summary of the Gospel."

¹⁶"For God so loved the world that he gave his one and only Son, that whoever believes in him shall not perish but have eternal life. ¹⁷For God did not send his Son into the world to condemn the world, but to save the world through him. ¹⁸Whoever believes in him is not condemned, but whoever does not believe stands condemned already because he has not believed in the name of God's one and only Son. ¹⁹This is the verdict: Light has come into the world, but men loved darkness instead of light because their deeds were evil. ²⁰Everyone who does evil hates the light, and will not come into the light for fear that his deeds will be exposed. ²¹But whoever lives by the truth comes into the light, so that it may be seen plainly that what he has done has been done through God."

COMMENTARY

16 The heart of the gospel is not a philosophical observation about the character of God as love but a declaration of that redemptive love in action. "For God so loved . . . that he gave." The Greek verb is *agapaō* (GK 26). It is common to discuss three Greek words for love: *eros*, *philia* (GK 5802), and *agapē* (GK 27). The first is used of passionate desire (not found in the NT) and the second of a fondness expressed in close relationships. The third word (*agapē*) was rather weak and colorless in secular Greek, but in the NT it is infused with fresh significance and becomes the one term able to denote the highest form of love. Bible scholar A. M. Hunter highlights the significance of *agapē* by noting that while *eros* is all take and *philia* is give-and-take, *agapē* is all give.

Love must of necessity give. It has no choice if it is to remain true to its essential character. A love that centers on self is not love at all but a fraudulent caricature of real love. It is instructive to note that only here in the fourth gospel is a result clause placed in the indicative rather than the subjunctive. Brown, 134, notes that this construction stresses the reality of the result: "that he *actually* gave the only Son." The Greek *monogenēs* (GK 3666) means "of sole descent," i.e., without brothers or sisters; hence the KJV's "only-begotten" (from the Latin *unigenitus*). It is also used in the more general sense of "unique," "the only one of its kind." Jesus is the sole Son of God the Father. John refers to believers as "children of God" (*tekna*, GK 5451; 1:12; 11:52), but Jesus is the only Son (*huios*, GK 5626).

The object of God's love is "the world" (*kosmos*, GK 3180). The giving of his Son was for the salvation of the entire human race. H. Sasse concludes that the cosmos epitomizes unredeemed creation, the universe of which Jesus is the light (Jn 8:12) and to which he comes (cf. *TDNT* 3:893-94). Any attempt to restrict the word *kosmos* (GK 3180) to the elect ignores the clear use of the term throughout the NT. God gave his Son for the deliverance of all humanity (cf. 2Co 5:19). This giving extends beyond the incarnation. God gave his Son in the sense of giving unto death as an offering for sin. The universal scope of God's love would have appeared novel and quite unlikely to the Jewish reader of the first century. After all, was not Israel the recipient of God's special favor (cf. Ro 3:1-2; 9:3-5)? True; but in Christ all boundaries had been broken down (Eph 2:11-22). God's love extends to every member of the human race. He died for all (cf. Ro 5:8; 1Jn 2:2).

God's role in redemption was the giving of his Son; the role of human beings is to believe. To believe in Christ is to accept and love him (Jn 1:12; 8:42). The Greek expression *pisteuō eis* ("to believe into") carries the sense of placing one's trust into or completely on someone. Paul's teaching of believers as being "in Christ" is a theological reflection on the same expression. Those who believe in Christ escape destruction and are given "eternal life." Barrett, 216, writes that "destruction is the inevitable fate of all things and persons separated from God and concentrated upon themselves." The love of God has made it possible for people to turn from their self-destructive paths and receive from God the gift of everlasting life. This gospel comes as "good news" to all who, recognizing their plight, receive the priceless gift of God, even Jesus Christ, his Son.

17 God's purpose in sending his Son into the world was to "save the world," not to "condemn" it. Jesus came "as a light, so that no one who believes in [him] should stay in darkness" (12:46). While the purpose of light is not to cast shadows, nevertheless wherever light encounters a solid object a shadow is unavoidable. Jesus did not come to "condemn" (taking *krinō*, "to judge" [GK *3212*], in the sense of unfavorable judgment), but the very nature of his redemptive mission mandated a negative result for those who refused his offer. Those who do not believe bring judgment on themselves. Barrett, 217, writes that "the process of judgment is an inseparable concomitant of salvation." Some have noted an apparent contradiction between Jesus' statement here and his later remark in 9:39, "For judgment I have come into this world." Context demonstrates, however, that this latter statement points to the result rather than the purpose of his coming (note the construction with *eis krima* rather than *hina krinē*; cf. 12:47).

18 John now draws a clear distinction between the fate of those who believe and those who do not believe: "Whoever believes [the present participle suggests a continuing relationship of trust] is not condemned, but whoever does not believe stands condemned already." Morris, 232 n. 84, notes that the use of the perfect tense here and in the following clause (*kekritai*, "has been judged" [GK *3212*], and [*mē*] *pepisteuken*, "has [not] believed" [GK *4409*]) indicates that the unbeliever "has passed into a continuing state of condemnation because he refused to enter a continuing state of belief." There will be a final judgment (5:28–29), but it will merely ratify the judgment that the nonbeliever has already brought on himself. The reason the nonbeliever "has already received his sentence" (Williams) is that he has steadfastly refused (note the perfect tense) to place his trust in the "name" of God's one and only Son. To trust the name of someone is to place one's complete reliance on everything that name stands for. The name "Jesus" in Greek transliterates the Hebrew name "Joshua,"

which means "Yahweh is salvation." Joseph is told to name Mary's newborn son Jesus "because he will save his people from their sins" (Mt 1:21). To believe in the name of Jesus is to trust him fully for the forgiveness of sins.

19 Verses 19–21 develop the concept of judgment in terms of the contrast between light and darkness. *Krisis* (GK *3213*) denotes the process rather than the sentence of judgment. The NIV's "verdict" would have been more likely if the noun had been *krima* ("decision, condemnation," GK *3210*), since nouns ending in *-ma* tend to denote content while those ending in *-sis* reflect action. "Light" came into the world with Jesus (1:5, 9; 8:12; 9:5; 12:46), but people "loved darkness instead of light." Natural men do not rejoice at the entrance of light, "because their deeds [are] evil." Elsewhere Jesus says that "out of the heart come evil thoughts, murder, adultery, sexual immorality, theft, false testimony, slander" (Mt 15:19).

20 Those whose deeds are evil hate the light and will not come to it, lest the depraved nature of their lifestyle be exposed. Evil thrives in a world of moral darkness. Like the fish in underground caverns whose eyes have gradually disappeared, leaving only sockets, so those who live in moral darkness have lost their ability to perceive the difference between good and evil.

21 By contrast, those who live "by the truth" gladly come to the light so that it may be seen that their deeds have been done "through [i.e., in fellowship with] God." Paul writes that "the god of this age has blinded the minds of unbelievers, so that they cannot see the light of the gospel of the glory of Christ" (2Co 4:4). That blindness is removed only by a willingness to accept and live by the truth. Jesus did not come to judge, but judgment is the inevitable result of his coming. Light illuminates, but wherever it is opposed it casts shadows.

NOTES

16 While most translations understand the adverb οὕτως (*houtōs*, "so") as referring to the degree of God's love, it is more likely that it refers to the manner in which God loved the world. Thus the NET has, "For this is the way God loved the world," with the following clause explaining that it was by giving his one and only Son (cf. CSB: "For God loved the world in this way: He gave his One and Only Son . . .").

c. Further witness by John the Baptist (3:22–36)

> ²²After this, Jesus and his disciples went out into the Judean countryside, where he spent some time with them, and baptized. ²³Now John also was baptizing at Aenon near Salim, because there was plenty of water, and people were constantly coming to be baptized. ²⁴(This was before John was put in prison.) ²⁵An argument developed between some of John's disciples and a certain Jew over the matter of ceremonial washing. ²⁶They came to John and said to him, "Rabbi, that man who was with you on the other side of the Jordan—the one you testified about—well, he is baptizing, and everyone is going to him."
>
> ²⁷To this John replied, "A man can receive only what is given him from heaven. ²⁸You yourselves can testify that I said, 'I am not the Christ but am sent ahead of him.' ²⁹The bride belongs to the bridegroom. The friend who attends the bridegroom waits and listens for him, and is full of joy when he hears the bridegroom's voice. That joy is mine, and it is now complete. ³⁰He must become greater; I must become less.
>
> ³¹"The one who comes from above is above all; the one who is from the earth belongs to the earth, and speaks as one from the earth. The one who comes from heaven is above all. ³²He testifies to what he has seen and heard, but no one accepts his testimony. ³³The man who has accepted it has certified that God is truthful. ³⁴For the one whom God has sent speaks the words of God, for God gives the Spirit without limit. ³⁵The Father loves the Son and has placed everything in his hands. ³⁶Whoever believes in the Son has eternal life, but whoever rejects the Son will not see life, for God's wrath remains on him."

COMMENTARY

22 After his conversation with Nicodemus, Jesus and his disciples went out into the Judean countryside, where he remained for some time baptizing. The NIV interprets the Greek *eis tēn Ioudaian gēn* ("into the Judean land") as referring to the territory around Jerusalem rather than to Judea itself (including Jerusalem). The latter alternative (followed by the NASB, "the land of Judea") would imply that Jesus came to Judea from Galilee, but this would call for a period of time between vv.21 and 22 in which

Jesus had gone to Galilee and was now returning to Judea. It is preferable to follow the NIV.

John is the only one of the four gospels that speaks of Jesus' baptismal activity. Even here, as we learn from 4:2, Jesus himself did not baptize but relegated that assignment to his disciples. The baptizing by the disciples at this particular stage should not be understood as equivalent to the later observance as carried out by the infant church. Hendriksen, 1:146, regards it as "a transition between Johannine and Christian baptism."

23 Meanwhile John the Baptist was carrying on his ministry at Aenon near Salim. The exact location of Aenon is not known. It is clear, however, that it was on the western side of the Jordan River (earlier John baptized on the eastern side; 1:28; 3:26; 10:40). The importance of the site lies in the fact that it indicates that John had moved his ministry to the north, while leaving the area around Jerusalem to Jesus and his disciples. W. F. Albright (*The Archaeology of Palestine* [Baltimore, Md.: Penguin, 1960], 247) located Salim to the southeast of Nablus near a village called Ainun. Nearby were the sources of the Wadi Farah, which would provide "plenty of water" for baptism. Since people were "constantly coming to be baptized," an abundance of water would be required. A. T. Robertson (*Word Pictures in the New Testament* [Nashville: Broadman, 1933], 54) observes that it was "not for drinking, but for baptizing" and quotes Marcus Dods as saying, "Therefore even in summer, baptism by immersion could be continued."

24 At this point the evangelist adds a parenthetical remark, indicating that the baptismal activity of Jesus and his disciples took place "before John was put in prison." Readers of the synoptic accounts would assume that immediately following the baptism and temptation of Jesus, John was put in prison and Jesus began preaching in Galilee (cf. Mt 3:13–4:17 par.). The fourth gospel reveals that Jesus car-

ried on an earlier ministry, primarily in the south, prior to the events recorded by the synoptic writers (Jn 1:36–4:54). This ministry of Jesus (not mentioned by Matthew, Mark, or Luke) was contemporary with that of John the Baptist and provided the occasion for comparison and discomfort on the part of John's disciples.

25 A dispute arose regarding the comparative value of baptism by John the Baptist and that by Jesus. It originated with the disciples of the Baptist (the preposition *ek*, "from," "out of," suggests source) and involved a "certain Jew." One variant reads *meta Ioudaiōn* ("with Jews"), thus easing the problem of a dispute with a specific person. Without textual support, a few commentators suggest an original reading of "Jesus" or perhaps "the disciples of Jesus." This would sharpen the controversy and help build a case for a lasting schism between the two factions. In view of the following verse, which describes the ministry of Jesus on the other side of the Jordan, it seems quite probable that the report was brought to John's disciples by a specific person. The NIV's "argument" is, in this context, too strong a translation of the Greek *zētēsis* (GK *2428*; prob-ably no more than "an exchange of words," *TDNT* 2:894). The subject of the encounter was "ceremonial washing." It is unlikely that John's disciples were involved in a lengthy religio-philosophical dialogue on the various merits of Jewish purification rites. The context indicates that their concern was the growing popularity of Jesus' ministry. Baptizing, both his and theirs, would fall under the general category of *katharismos* ("ritual purification" or "cleansing," GK *2752*; cf. 2:6).

26 John's disciples come to their leader with the querulous complaint that Jesus is baptizing on the other side of the Jordan and threatens to surpass him in popularity. Their dissatisfaction with the way things are going is reflected in the generous title they assigned to their leader ("Rabbi," only here), their unwillingness to use the name of Jesus (he is "that man who was with you on the other side of the Jordan"), and their exaggerated statement that "everyone is going to him." Their pique is also seen in the veiled rebuke that John had testified about him. From the standpoint of the Baptist's loyal disciples, this new turn of events did not augur well for them or for their leader.

27–28 Characteristically, John did not share the rather myopic view of his followers. God had assigned to each person a specific role in the eternal plan. John's disciples should recall that he had freely confessed to the priests sent from Jerusalem, "I am not the Christ" (1:20). He was simply "the voice of one calling in the desert"—the forerunner of the one of such immeasurable worth that even the task of untying the thongs of his sandals was beyond him (1:23, 27). If John's disciples would only bear in mind who Jesus was, their pettiness in regard to the shifting attention of the population would vanish. Like their master, they should embrace the descent into anonymity.

29 John the Baptist now restates the relationship using the metaphor of a Jewish wedding ceremony. Jesus had spoken of himself as a bridegroom (Mk 2:19), and Paul employs the same metaphor (2Co 11:2; Eph 5:23–32). The "bride" (in this case, a collective reference to those who were coming to Jesus for baptism) belongs to the "bridegroom" (Jesus). John's role (assigned "from heaven," v.27) was to be "the friend who attends the bridegroom." According to Jewish custom, the groom's closest friend was chosen as the *shoshben* (roughly equivalent to "best man") and would make all the necessary wedding arrangements. (Some differences exist between Galilean and Judean nuptial customs, but here the metaphor is used in a general sense.) The friend waits and listens for the coming of the groom, and when he hears his voice he is filled with joy. Here the *shoshben* is pictured either as standing guard at

the bride's house waiting for the arrival of those who will escort her to the groom's house, or as waiting at the groom's house for the arrival of the bride. Once bride and bridegroom are together, the friend will hear them talking with each other and will rejoice. A more specific interpretation of the "bridegroom's voice" is that it is "the triumphant shout by which the bridegroom announced to his friends outside that he had been united to a virginal bride" (Schnackenburg, 1:416).

30 With the arrival of Jesus on the scene of history, John's joy "is now complete" (v.29). All that he had waited for has come to pass. Messiah has come. As friend of the bridegroom, he shares the joy of the marriage he has arranged. His role has not been insignificant, nor does it matter in the least that with the arrival of the groom the role of the *shoshben* comes to a close. In words that reveal the magnanimity of a truly remarkable servant of God, the Baptist states with all simplicity, "He must become greater; I must become less." Were this example followed by all contemporary ministers of the gospel, what a dramatic impact it would make on today's world!

31 Earlier I suggested that Jesus' discourse with Nicodemus probably ended with v.15 and that the following paragraph (vv.16–21) consisted of a meditation or homily by the evangelist. Here at v.31 we meet a similar construction. John the Baptist's words of commendation regarding Jesus are followed with a paragraph in which the evangelist describes the relationship between "the one who comes from above" (Jesus) and "the one who is from the earth" (John the Baptist). Although vv.31–34 may be construed in a general fashion, the contrast John has in mind is primarily between the two historical ministries.

"The one who comes from above" is described in the same verse as "the one who comes from heaven," i.e., from the very presence of God. He is "above all." The Greek *pantōn* ("all") is either masculine (in which case Jesus is portrayed as above all earthly counterparts: "the supreme ruler of the human race," Barrett, 224) or neuter (above all things). The context suggests that he is "above all" in his role as the revealer of divine truth. He is not subject to the limitations of an earthly existence but testifies to that which he "has seen and heard." John, on the other hand, "speaks as one from the earth." What he says is true, but his earthly existence limits him to the role of a prophet. In contrast, Jesus comes from the presence of the Father and provides a firsthand report of what he has seen and heard (cf. Heb 1:1–2). The Greek word for "earth" (*gē*, GK *1178*), as contrasted with *kosmos* ("world," GK *3180*), does not imply evil. Although the *gē* is "the theatre of sin" (*TDNT* 1:680), it is not sinful in itself. The point being stressed is the limiting nature of earthly existence.

32 A few writers hold that the first verb, *heōraken* ("has seen," GK *3972*, perfect tense), has to do with the existence of the Son and the second, *ēkousen* ("heard," GK *201*, aorist), to his mission. It is questionable that such a distinction can be maintained in the common Greek of the first century. Even though Jesus comes from heaven and speaks out of personal experience, "no one accepts his testimony." The same sad truth is set forth in the prologue (1:11). By nature, people believe what suits them rather than what bears the marks of authenticity. The fall of the human race resulted in darkened minds that hear selectively. It is the Holy Spirit rather than logic that opens people's minds to the truth.

33 The categorical "no one" of v.32 is modified here, which indicates that some have accepted the message. The one who receives the testimony of Jesus "has certified that God is truthful." It is reasonable to ask how a human being can certify or confirm the truthfulness of God. The Greek *sphragizō* (GK *5381*) means "to provide with a seal." Used figuratively, as it normally is, its range of meanings includes "to seal up or keep secret" (Rev 10:4),

"to mark with a seal so as to identify" (Eph.1:13), and "to certify or acknowledge" (Jn 6:27). In v.33 the evangelist is saying that those who accept the testimony of the one from above (the Son) set their seal of approval on the truthfulness of what God has said. Their certification does not make the message true; it acknowledges that it is true.

34 The testimony of the messenger ("the one whom God has sent") is absolutely reliable because "he speaks the words of God." Only one who comes from above is free of the restrictions that limit both knowledge and veracity. It is "to him [the Son]" that God "gives the Spirit without limit." In a fourth-century commentary on Leviticus 13:2, Rabbi Acha says that "the Holy Spirit rested on the prophets by measure" (*Lev. Rab.* 15.2). In contrast, the Holy Spirit came upon Jesus at his baptism and *remained* (1:32–33). The fullness of the Spirit sets Jesus apart from prophets through whom God had spoken from time to time (cf. Heb 1:1). Brown's suggestion, 161–62, that here the one giving the Spirit may be the Son is grammatically defensible but unlikely in that it unnecessarily breaks the natural flow of thought.

35 The Father gives the Spirit without limit to the Son because he "loves the Son and has placed everything in his hands." The Father's love for the Son and the delegation of authority to him is the theme of Jesus' discourse in 5:19–29. The love that exists between the members of the Trinity is the love that was displayed on Calvary and becomes the prime requisite for Christian life and fellowship (1Jn 2:8–11). The delegation of authority to the Son is clearly stated in the Synoptics, where Jesus reports that all things had been committed to him by his Father (Mt 11:27).

36 Verse 36 underscores a major truth that runs throughout the entire chapter. The destiny of every person is determined by his or her personal response to the Son. Those who put their faith in the Son receive eternal life; those who reject the Son will not see life but will endure the wrath of God (cf. 1Jn 5:12, "He who has the Son has life; he who does not have the Son of God does not have life"). The issue is clearly drawn. Worth noting is the fact that it is disobedience, not disbelief, that John sets in contrast with faith. The Greek *apeitheō* (GK *578*) means "to disobey." The verb is used regularly in the LXX of disobedience to God. Not to believe is to willfully reject. In Acts 14:2 the NIV translates the same term with "refused to believe." Saving faith involves obedience as well as believing, a point often overlooked by those for whom correct doctrine tends to eclipse the necessity of a changed life.

Whoever "rejects the Son" (refuses to believe the words he speaks and consequently rejects the obvious implications regarding who he is) "will not see life" (i.e., the eternal life given to those who believe). Instead, God's wrath remains on him. The wrath of God is not an emotional and vindictive reaction toward individuals. The rejection of divine love carries serious and necessary consequences. As G. Stählin observes, "Where mercy meets with the ungodly will of man rather than faith and gratitude, . . . love becomes wrath" (*TDNT* 5:425). That God's wrath *remains* on the disobedient indicates that those who have not accepted the Son are already under condemnation (cf. 3:18).

NOTES

26 The term ῥαββί, (*rhabbi*, "my Master," GK *4806*) is used eight times in the fourth gospel and always of Jesus, with this one exception where it is used by the disciples of John the Baptist in reference to their leader. It is an honorary title derived from the Hebrew. After the NT era it developed from its popular usage as a term of honor into a more formal title to designate those who were recognized as authoritative teachers of Jewish law.

31–32 It may be worth mentioning that the last three words of v.31 ("is above all") are omitted in several MSS (cf. Metzger, 205). In that case the preceding nominative clause would provide the subject for the following verse: "The one who comes from heaven testifies to what he has seen and heard."

36 It becomes increasingly clear from John's gospel that in one sense the great eschatological events are present even now. To believe in the Son is to *have* (ἔχει [*echei*, GK *2400*] is present tense) eternal life, while rejection of the Son has already resulted in the wrath of God remaining (μένει [*menei*, GK *3531*] is also present tense) on the unbeliever. That both judgment and eternal life are present realities has led to what is called "realized eschatology," a term often associated with the work of British scholar C. H. Dodd. The NET study note at 3:21 points out that vv.16–21 of ch. 3 provide an introduction to the "realized" eschatology of the fourth gospel.

2. A Samaritan Woman Learns of Living Water (4:1–45)

OVERVIEW

In ch. 3 John recorded Jesus' encounter with a respected member of the Jewish religious elite. Now in ch. 4 he reports another encounter, this time with a Samaritan woman of questionable morals. A contrast is certainly intended between Nicodemus, a learned and highly respected member of Jewish society, and the Samaritan woman, an unschooled common person "capable only of folk religion" (Carson, 216). Yet both needed Jesus. The personal ministry of Jesus reached out to the forgotten as well as to the favored of society.

[1]The Pharisees heard that Jesus was gaining and baptizing more disciples than John, [2]although in fact it was not Jesus who baptized, but his disciples. [3]When the Lord learned of this, he left Judea and went back once more to Galilee.

[4]Now he had to go through Samaria. [5]So he came to a town in Samaria called Sychar, near the plot of ground Jacob had given to his son Joseph. [6]Jacob's well was there, and Jesus, tired as he was from the journey, sat down by the well. It was about the sixth hour.

[7]When a Samaritan woman came to draw water, Jesus said to her, "Will you give me a drink?" [8](His disciples had gone into the town to buy food.)

[9]The Samaritan woman said to him, "You are a Jew and I am a Samaritan woman. How can you ask me for a drink?" (For Jews do not associate with Samaritans.)

[10]Jesus answered her, "If you knew the gift of God and who it is that asks you for a drink, you would have asked him and he would have given you living water."

[11]"Sir," the woman said, "you have nothing to draw with and the well is deep. Where can you get this living water? [12]Are you greater than our father Jacob, who gave us the well and drank from it himself, as did also his sons and his flocks and herds?"

[13]Jesus answered, "Everyone who drinks this water will be thirsty again, [14]but whoever drinks the water I give him will never thirst. Indeed, the water I give him will become in him a spring of water welling up to eternal life."

[15]The woman said to him, "Sir, give me this water so that I won't get thirsty and have to keep coming here to draw water."

[16]He told her, "Go, call your husband and come back."

[17]"I have no husband," she replied.

Jesus said to her, "You are right when you say you have no husband. [18]The fact is, you have had five husbands, and the man you now have is not your husband. What you have just said is quite true."

[19]"Sir," the woman said, "I can see that you are a prophet. [20]Our fathers worshiped on this mountain, but you Jews claim that the place where we must worship is in Jerusalem."

[21]Jesus declared, "Believe me, woman, a time is coming when you will worship the Father neither on this mountain nor in Jerusalem. [22]You Samaritans worship what you do not know; we worship what we do know, for salvation is from the Jews. [23]Yet a time is coming and has now come when the true worshipers will worship the Father in spirit and truth, for they are the kind of worshipers the Father seeks. [24]God is spirit, and his worshipers must worship in spirit and in truth."

²⁵The woman said, "I know that Messiah" (called Christ) "is coming. When he comes, he will explain everything to us."

²⁶Then Jesus declared, "I who speak to you am he."

²⁷Just then his disciples returned and were surprised to find him talking with a woman. But no one asked, "What do you want?" or "Why are you talking with her?"

²⁸Then, leaving her water jar, the woman went back to the town and said to the people, ²⁹"Come, see a man who told me everything I ever did. Could this be the Christ?" ³⁰They came out of the town and made their way toward him.

³¹Meanwhile his disciples urged him, "Rabbi, eat something."

³²But he said to them, "I have food to eat that you know nothing about."

³³Then his disciples said to each other, "Could someone have brought him food?"

³⁴"My food," said Jesus, "is to do the will of him who sent me and to finish his work. ³⁵Do you not say, 'Four months more and then the harvest'? I tell you, open your eyes and look at the fields! They are ripe for harvest. ³⁶Even now the reaper draws his wages, even now he harvests the crop for eternal life, so that the sower and the reaper may be glad together. ³⁷Thus the saying 'One sows and another reaps' is true. ³⁸I sent you to reap what you have not worked for. Others have done the hard work, and you have reaped the benefits of their labor."

³⁹Many of the Samaritans from that town believed in him because of the woman's testimony, "He told me everything I ever did." ⁴⁰So when the Samaritans came to him, they urged him to stay with them, and he stayed two days. ⁴¹And because of his words many more became believers.

⁴²They said to the woman, "We no longer believe just because of what you said; now we have heard for ourselves, and we know that this man really is the Savior of the world."

⁴³After the two days he left for Galilee. ⁴⁴(Now Jesus himself had pointed out that a prophet has no honor in his own country.) ⁴⁵When he arrived in Galilee, the Galileans welcomed him. They had seen all that he had done in Jerusalem at the Passover Feast, for they also had been there.

COMMENTARY

1 After the incident with Nicodemus, Jesus and his disciples had gone into the Judean countryside and spent some time baptizing those who came to Jesus (3:22). The disciples of John became increasingly jealous of the growing popularity of Jesus, who they felt was in competition with their leader (3:26). Soon the Pharisees caught wind of Jesus' growing reputation and were no doubt disturbed. When Jesus learned of this new development, he left Judea and returned to Galilee (v.3) to prevent an unnecessary schism in the larger movement of national repentance.

2–3 Verse 2 makes it clear that it was not Jesus himself who was administering the rite of baptism.

We are not told how Jesus learned of the Pharisees' knowledge of his ministry in Judea (v.3), but Jesus' insight into human nature (cf. 2:24) would alert him to the response of the religious leaders. His decision to go once more to Galilee (cf. 2:1–12) was intended to forestall any early opposition that might bring his ministry to a premature close.

4 It was a three-day trip from Jerusalem to Galilee, but only if one took the shorter route that led directly through Samaria. In order to avoid the hostility of the Samaritans, many Jews would cross over into Perea for that part of the journey (cf. Mk 10:1). The text says that Jesus "had to go through Samaria." The necessity could have been of a practical nature (i.e., he needed to take the shorter route to save time and energy) or it could have been theological (he had a divine appointment to meet a certain woman residing there). Probably it was both.

The animosity that existed between Jew and Samaritan had a long and disagreeable history. When the northern kingdom fell in 722 BC, the Assyrian conquerors carried out a mass deportation of the inhabitants (especially those of substance) and replaced them with a number of colonists from five other nations (cf. 2Ki 17:24). These colonists intermarried with the Israelites who had been allowed to remain. Some years later the exiled Jews returned to their land and were included in the larger Persian province of Samaria. Bitterness developed rapidly between the two peoples, and in time the Jews gained their independence and became a separate province. The Israelites' unwillingness to accept the Samaritans' offer of help in rebuilding the temple (Ezr 4:2–3) reflects the antagonism that existed between the two groups. Subsequently, the Samaritans set up their own center of worship on Mount Gerizim (ca. 400 BC)—a center that in 128 BC was torched by the Jewish high priest, John Hyrcanus.

5 En route through Samaria Jesus came to a town called Sychar. The exact location of Sychar has long been disputed. The two most likely spots are the ancient Shechem or the modern village of Askar. The former is about a mile and a half southeast of Nablus at the foot of Mount Gerizim and the latter a short distance to the northeast on the eastern slope of Mount Ebal. Both were near Jacob's well, though Shechem lay only a few hundred feet away and Askar about half a mile off. Some writers favoring Shechem have suggested that Sychar (read in almost all manuscripts) was a cynical corruption meaning "drunken town" or "lying town." John further identifies the location as "near the plot of ground that Jacob had given to his son Joseph" (Ge 33:19; Jos 24:32), which as Lindars, 179, notes was "the oldest part of the Holy Land to belong to the Israelites by right of purchase."

6 At Sychar was a well associated with the patriarch Jacob. Though Genesis tells of the digging of many wells, it does not mention this one. Tradition locates Jacob's well about half a mile to the east of Tell Balatah at the foot of Mount Gerizim. It is interesting that the well is called a *pēgē* ("spring" or "fountain," GK *4380*; NIV, "well") rather than a *phrear* ("dug-out well or cistern," GK *5853*) as it is in vv.11 and 12 (NIV, also "well"). Both terms are appropriate because, while it had been dug out (the shaft of the well was over 100 feet deep), it was fed by underground springs.

Jesus, tired from his journey, "sat down by the well." The fourth gospel nowhere attempts to emphasize the deity of Jesus by minimizing his humanity. Elsewhere we are reminded of his human emotions and physical needs: he loved Lazarus (11:3), he wept at Mary's sorrow (11:33–35), his heart was troubled in the upper room (12:27), and he acknowledged his thirst on the cross (19:28). Truly we have a high priest who is able to "sympathize with our weaknesses" (Heb 4:15)!

John notes that "it was about the sixth hour." In view of the identical statement in 19:24, when Jesus stood before Pilate, it seems best to follow the Jewish method of reckoning time from sunup, which would place the encounter about noon. (According to the Roman method of reckoning time from midnight and noon, the hour would be either 6:00 a.m. or 6:00 p.m.). The argument that evening was the normal time to draw water (cf. Ge 24:11) is countered by the observation that this particular woman would probably come for water at a time when other women were *not* at the well.

7–8 The Samaritan woman arrived at the well to draw water. She was not from the *city* of Samaria (which was a several-hour journey to the northwest) but was a native of the *district* of Samaria. It was probably after she had drawn the water that Jesus asked her for a drink. Similar scenes in the patriarchal narratives (Ge 24:11; 29:2; Ex 2:15) have encouraged some to question whether John might be drawing on his imagination at this point and creating the incident as an allegory to bring out a spiritual lesson. However, there is no compelling reason to question the historicity of the encounter. Verse 8 is a parenthesis, probably added to explain why it was necessary for Jesus to ask for help from the woman. Normally his disciples would have drawn the water. The town to which they went to buy food would have been Sychar.

9 The Samaritan woman is surprised that Jesus has asked her for a drink. This would involve his drinking from her water pot and, as John adds by way of explanation, "Jews do not associate with Samaritans." That the disciples had gone into town to purchase food indicates that ordinary commercial dealings between Jews and Samaritans were not out of line. The KJV's "have no dealings with" implies a degree of segregation that goes beyond what actually existed. It was at a later period that a rabbinic regulation was laid down restricting the common use of vessels by Jews and Samaritans based on the fact that Samaritan women were assumed to be ceremonially unclean from the cradle (*m. Nid.* 4:1). This uncleanness would be transferred to anything they handled, so to drink from a pitcher belonging to a Samaritan woman would automatically defile. While this specific regulation did not lie behind John's explanatory note, the general separation of Jew and Gentile in matters of ceremonial importance is everywhere acknowledged. The NEB offers the felicitous translation, "Jews and Samaritans, it should be noted, do not use vessels in common."

10 Jesus does not give the Samaritan woman a direct answer to her question but points out that if she had realized who he was, she would have asked, not for water from Jacob's well, but for living water. Like the encounter with Nicodemus, which turned on a misunderstanding of what it meant to be "born again," Jesus now speaks of a water described as "living" in contrast to water from a well. On one level, "living water" would be fresh or flowing water. But Jesus uses the term in a higher and metaphorical sense. In the OT, God identified himself as "the spring of living water" (Jer 2:13; cf. 17:13). Zechariah spoke of the day when "living water will flow out from Jerusalem" (Zec 14:8). This living water is the "gift of God," which the Samaritan woman would have received had she asked for it.

What then is this gift of God that Jesus refers to as "living water"? Many understand it as Jesus himself, but in the context of the historical encounter it would seem strange for Jesus to be offering himself to the woman. Later in John (7:38–39) Jesus speaks of "streams of living water" that will flow from within the believer and distinguishes this as "the Spirit" they are to receive. Against this background it is best to understand "living water" as the new life in the Spirit that Jesus came to give, in contrast to the old forms of Judaism represented by the water of Jacob's well.

11 The Samaritan woman continues to think of Jesus' reference to living water in the literal sense of water flowing from a spring. So she raises two objections. First, Jesus has nothing to draw with. The implement normally used for drawing water was a skin bucket held open at the mouth with several crossed sticks. Apparently nothing was provided at the well, and the woman, unlike Jesus, had brought her own. Second, the well is deep. To lower the bucket some one hundred feet to the water would take a long rope made of goat's hair. Jesus had no rope.

Three times in the encounter the Samaritan woman addresses Jesus with the title "Sir" (vv. 11, 15, 19). Although *kyrios* (GK *3261*) can carry the heightened meaning of "Lord," here it is simply a polite method of addressing a stranger.

12 In the woman's mind it is highly unlikely that Jesus could possibly provide a source of water superior to that of the well associated with the patriarch Jacob. The Samaritans traced their lineage back to Jacob via Joseph (cf. Josephus, *Ant.* 11.341). So she asks somewhat disparagingly whether Jesus held himself to be greater than their ancestor Jacob, who gave them the well. In fact, he "drank from it himself," thus lending his personal distinction to the well. What is more, the water in Jacob's well was bountiful. It provided water not only for Jacob and his sons but also for their flocks and herds. It should be noted that from the Jewish standpoint any claim by a Samaritan to "our father Jacob" would be unacceptable. The woman's question (in Greek) calls for a negative response: "Surely you are not greater than Jacob?" Bishop Ryle, 3:365, observes a bit satirically, "Dead teachers have always more authority than living ones." Though the woman regarded as highly unlikely any superiority to Jacob on the part of Jesus, her question as it turned out revealed what was in fact the truth.

13 Jesus' response to the woman's less-than-flattering question contains two great truths. First, the "water" that Jesus gives will forever quench people's spiritual thirst. Those who make it a practice of drinking (*pinōn*, GK *4403*, a present participle) the water from Jacob's well will thirst again, but those who take a single draft (*piē*, aorist subjunctive) of the "water" Jesus gives will never thirst again. There was nothing wrong with the water from Jacob's well. For a time it would quench natural thirst. The superiority of the water Jesus provides is that it satisfies once and for all a much deeper and more profound thirst—the thirst for God. "The soul's deepest thirst," writes Bruce, 105, "is for God himself, who has made us so that we can never be satisfied without him."

Jesus' initial approach to the woman was to arouse her conscience, not by condemning her lifestyle, but by offering her free of charge the only thing that could satisfy her deepest longings. Here is an important lesson in evangelism. The love of God is a magnet that draws the sinner toward life eternal. Those who flee to God out of terror of the alternative are moved by a less worthy motive. God is a gentleman whose methods are consistent with his nature.

14 The second great truth in Jesus' response is that the water he gives will become in those who receive it "a spring of water welling up to eternal life." *Hallomai* ("to well up," GK *256*) occurs only here in the fourth gospel. Elsewhere in the NT it is found only in Acts, where in both 3:8 and 14:10 it describes a lame man leaping to his feet. The water that Jesus gives is no stagnant pool! It is a gushing spring that refreshes all who partake of it. It produces the abundant life that Jesus promises in John 10:10.

15–16 The Samaritan woman is apparently unable to catch the spiritual significance of what Jesus is saying. Her thinking remains on a mundane level. She responds to Jesus' offer of living water with a rather selfish request for the water that will permanently quench her thirst and keep her from making the daily trek to the well to draw a fresh supply. Her concern is for her own benefit and personal convenience. Because the woman continues to misunderstand what Jesus is saying, he changes his approach. There will be no more discussion about living water. Instead he abruptly tells the woman to go and bring her husband back to the well. The conscience must be awakened in order to create a desire for spiritual renewal.

17–18 The atmosphere changes. To this point the woman has been quite talkative. Now she simply says, "I have no husband." Her answer was true as far as it went. Unfortunately there was more to be said. It must have come as a shock to the woman to hear Jesus, a complete stranger, give voice to what only those in her town knew. She had spoken correctly when she said she had no husband; what she had not said was that she had already had five husbands and the man she was currently living with was not her husband. Where did Jesus get such knowledge? The NT reveals that although Jesus lived out his earthly life without drawing on supernatural powers in circumstances such as the performance of miracles, as the God-man he had divine insight and knowledge into the affairs of the human heart. He knew that Nathanael was a true Israelite without guile (1:47). And he knew "all that was going to happen to him" when Judas and the soldiers arrived in the garden of Gethsemane (18:4).

It is worth noting that when the woman denied having a husband, she placed the crucial word *anēr* ("husband," GK *467*) at the end of the clause. Jesus in his response placed it first, thus adding considerable emphasis. She had no real husband because she was not married to the man with whom she was living. We do not know whether all of her "husbands" were legitimate; if they were, we know nothing about the divorces. Though according to Jewish custom a woman could not divorce a man, there were many ways in which she could goad her husband into taking the necessary legal steps. The

Mosaic law set no limit on the number of divorces, but rabbis limited the number to two or in some cases three (cf. Str-B, 2:437).

Some commentators interpret the story allegorically. The most common example is that the woman represents Samaria with its five gods brought in from the five nations (mentioned in 2Ki 17:24). The husband she was living with illegitimately at that time was the God of Israel. Another allegorical interpretation has the five husbands representing the five books of the Torah, which the Samaritan religion regarded as the extent of canonical Scripture. Beasley-Murray's remark, 61, that this approach is "not to be countenanced" is on target. The encounter was historical and should be understood as such.

19 Jesus' knowledge of the woman's marital background causes her to regard him as a prophet. Once again she addresses him as "Sir" (cf. vv.11, 15), but this time *kyrios* (GK *3261*) is beginning to move from its conventional use as a polite greeting toward the special meaning of "Lord." Although the word "prophet" lacks a definite article, some writers think that the woman may be wondering whether Jesus could possibly be *the* prophet promised in Deuteronomy 18:15–18. Since the Samaritans did not accept as canonical the Jewish prophetic books, there would be no prophet between Moses and the one they called *Taheb* (the great prophet of the coming age).

20 In any case, the Samaritan woman considers Jesus to be a person who may be able to shed some light on a pivotal question that separated Jews and Samaritans: "Where is the correct place to worship?" The common assumption that she wanted to change the subject in order to evade the implications of Jesus' remark about her immoral lifestyle may be true, but all such psychological analyses lie beyond what we may know for sure. In Deuteronomy 12:1–5 Moses stressed the importance of centralizing the place of worship but did not indicate where this was to be. The Samaritans opted for Mount Gerizim because in the Samaritan Pentateuch (Dt 27:4) Joshua is instructed to erect a shrine on that mountain. (The MT's "Mount Ebal" is usually considered original, but it can be argued that this was simply anti-Samaritan.) Sanballat, a contemporary of Nehemiah who led the opposition to the rebuilding of the walls of Jerusalem, erected the temple on Mount Gerizim in the fifth century BC. It was destroyed by John Hyrcanus toward the end of the second century BC, but the Samaritans continued to worship at the site.

On the other hand, the Jews held that the proper and only place to worship was "in Jerusalem." In 2 Chronicles 6:6 God says, "I have chosen Jerusalem for my Name to be there." The psalmist writes that God chose "Mount Zion, which he loved" (Ps 78:68). In a midrash on Psalm 91 Jerusalem is said to be the "gate of heaven" and "the open door to the hearing of prayer" (Str-B, 2:437).

21 Jesus resists being drawn into a dead-end discussion on the proper place to worship. In fact, he is about to teach that the *how* of worship is infinitely more important than the *where*. His words "believe me, woman" are not to be taken in any sense as curt or disrespectful. At the wedding in Cana of Galilee (2:4), he addressed his mother with the same term, *gynai* (GK *222*). The expression "believe me" (*pisteue moi*) is unique in the NT and serves as a stylistic alternative to the usual *amēn amēn, legō hymin* ("I tell you the truth"; NASB, twenty-five times in John's gospel [1:51; 3:3, 5, 11 et al.]). The truth he wants the woman to learn is that a time is coming when the Father will be worshiped neither on Mount Gerizim nor in Jerusalem. The worship of God is to be set free from any specific locale.

22 The Samaritans worshiped "what [they did] not know" in the sense that their religion was limited. A sacred Scripture that excluded a great deal of the rich history and instruction of the OT would

of necessity be inadequate. By contrast (the "you" and the "we" of the verse are emphatic), Jewish worship is informed by the full revelation of God in the entire OT. As even the Samaritan scriptures taught, the promised Messiah of both Jew and Samaritan would come from the tribe of Judah (Ge 49:10). It is "in Judah," the psalmist declares, that "God is known" (Ps 76:1).

23 Verse 21 spoke of a time yet future when worship would be unrelated to a place. Verse 23 repeats the clause "a time is coming" but goes on to add the all-important "and has now come." Jesus brings the future into the present by declaring that at the present time those who truly worship the Father worship him "in spirit and in truth." Some understand "spirit" as the human spirit in contrast to external ritual. Others perceive the reference to be connected with the outpouring of God's Spirit in the new age. In either case, it relates to the whole-hearted commitment of the worshiper to God as Father. Nothing short of a genuine personal relationship will meet the requirements of worship in the kingdom of God. Furthermore, this kind of worship must be in full accord with the truth as revealed in and through Jesus Christ. True worship is intimate and informed. To this significant proposition Jesus adds the uniquely Christian insight that the Father is actively seeking this kind of worshiper. In other religions people are portrayed as seeking God. In the Christian faith it is God who initiates the search for us (cf. Lk 15:1–7; Jn 3:6; 15:16).

24 It is because "God is spirit" that those who worship him must worship in spirit and in truth. That God is spirit should not be taken as a metaphysical definition of God. Although God is a spiritual being, this statement is best understood in connection with two similar ones in John's epistles. God is "spirit" in the same sense that he is "light" (1Jn 1:5) and "love" (1Jn 4:16). He relates himself to the world not only as one who brings illumination and gives himself for the benefit of the human race but also as one who carries out his purposes in the realm and through the power of the Spirit. It is precisely because God is spirit that those who would worship him must worship in spirit and in truth.

25 Not fully grasping what Jesus is saying, the woman retreats to a standard theme of Samaritan theology, namely, that when Messiah comes, he will "explain everything." The Messiah of Jewish tradition was not primarily a teacher, but this was not so for the Samaritans. Building on Deuteronomy 18:18 they viewed "Messiah" as one who would explain the mysteries of the kingdom. The woman's statement here is the fifth article of the Samaritan creed. When he comes, the *Taheb* will impart divine truth. The explanatory note "(called Christ)" was added by John for the benefit of his Gentile readers in Asia Minor.

26 Jesus' forthright acknowledgment here is the first of several "I am" statements in the fourth gospel where *egō eimi* is used without a predicate (cf. 6:20; 8:28, 58). Scholars hold varying positions concerning to what extent this may be an allusion to God's self-designation in Exodus 3:14, "I AM WHO I AM." The Greek does not have the word "he" but says literally, "I am, the one speaking to you." The comma separating the two parts of the expression suggests a rendering such as "the one speaking to you is the 'I am.'" Others think that Jesus is saying no more than "I am the Christ you speak of" (Barrett, 239). Jesus could not at this time have made such a claim in Judea, lest it encourage a political response. In Samaria it was less problematic to acknowledge openly that he was the Messiah.

27 As the disciples returned from buying food (v.8), they were shocked to find their master talking with a woman. The rabbis taught against speaking with women in public. The Mishnah (*m. ʾAbot* 1:5) warns against prolonging conversation with a woman and adds, "even with one's own wife; how much more with a neighbor's wife." It was of less concern to the disciples that Jesus was talking with a Samaritan woman than that he was talking with any woman (note the absence of any definite article before "woman"—it was *a* woman, not *the* woman!). Although the disciples were astounded to find Jesus conversing with a woman, no one dared to ask what she wanted or why he was talking with her. Grammatically, the first question ("What do you want?") could be addressed to Jesus, but it is more likely that the disciples would think that it was the woman who had made an initial request.

28–30 The arrival of the disciples brought the conversation to a close. The woman apparently left in haste, since she went away without her water jar. One writer supposes that she left her water jar so Jesus could drink from it and thus know that she had taken his words to heart (Hendriksen, 1:171). Others imagine her to be so embarrassed that in her anxiety to get away she forgot the water jar. More plausible is the suggestion that since she intended to return there was no need to take it just then.

The woman now returns to her village to tell of the remarkable man she has just met. Previously she may have avoided the people of her town, but now she speaks to them directly (v.29) and tells them to come and meet a man who "told me everything I ever did" (an understandable hyperbole in view of the dramatic effect of Jesus' words on her conscience). Then, hesitatingly, she asks the question, "Could this be the Christ?" It is difficult to know the extent to which she had understood the words of Jesus, but it is clear that their effect was sufficiently profound to turn her into a missionary to her own people. So the people left the village and were making their way (*ērchonto*, GK *2252*, is imperfect) toward Jesus at the well (v.30). S. D. Gordon (*The Sychar Revival* [Chicago: Cook, 1904], 25) observes that the disciples returned from the village with *loaves* but the woman brought *people*.

31–32 "Meanwhile" (i.e., after the woman had gone and before the villagers returned) the disciples "kept urging" (*erōtōn*, GK *2263*, is imperfect) Jesus to eat. They were genuinely concerned for his physical well-being. But Jesus answered, "I have food to eat that you know nothing about" (v.32). The contrast between *egō* ("I") and *hymeis* ("you") is pronounced.

33 The disciples discussed among themselves what Jesus meant by his response. Expecting a negative answer (the question is introduced with the Greek particle *mē*), they ask, "No one could have brought food to him, could they?" The possibility that Jesus could have by some miraculous act produced bread for himself never seems to have crossed the disciples' mind. This attests to what we find elsewhere in the Gospels about Jesus' judicious use of miracles. As Nicodemus misunderstood what Jesus was saying about new birth (3:4) and the Samaritan woman misunderstood what he meant by living water (4:15), the disciples misunderstand his reference to food. While the thinking process in each case was limited to a rather literal and mundane level, Jesus was using words and ideas in a figurative sense to impart spiritual knowledge. In each case, Jesus was using the semantic impasse to lift their minds to a higher level and to teach spiritual truth.

34 Jesus goes on to explain that his "food" consisted of (1) doing the Father's will and (2) completing the work he was sent to do. His life was controlled and directed by a well-defined purpose. It was the achievement of that purpose that brought satisfaction to his soul. He calls it "my food." We are reminded of Deuteronomy 8:3, "Man does not live on bread alone but on every word that comes from the mouth of the LORD" (quoted by Jesus during his temptation, Mt 4:4). Throughout the fourth gospel Jesus speaks of his obedience to the will of the one who sent him and of completing the work of the Father (e.g., 5:36; 6:38; 14:31; 17:4). The

author of Hebrews says that Jesus "learned obedience" from what he suffered (Heb 5:8). Peter reminds believers that we have been chosen "for obedience to Jesus Christ" (1Pe 1:2). The so-called "deeper Christian life" is simply a life of unquestioning obedience to the revealed will of God. Jesus' driving passion was to "finish" (*teleioō*, GK *5457*) God's work. Just before giving up his life on the cross he cried out, "It is finished" (note the related *tetelestai*, 19:30). Happy are those who have determined to know the will of God for their lives and to complete the specific tasks that the Father desires to carry out through them.

35 In vv.35–38 Jesus employs several well-known proverbs to communicate vital information regarding a spiritual harvest of believers. "Four months more and then the harvest" is usually taken as a rural proverb indicating the length of time from sowing until reaping. Although that particular period of time is actually closer to six months, it could be taken as the four months between the end of sowing and the beginning of harvest. (Sowing took place after the fall rains [November–December], and barley was harvested in April.) Others take the saying as a chronological reference placing Jesus' encounter with the Samaritan woman in late fall. It is better to take it as a bit of conventional wisdom that Jesus used to stress the immediacy of the spiritual harvest. It is as though Jesus had said, "Normally it takes about four months to reap a harvest, but the 'harvest' that I speak of is ready right now. Look, even now the villagers are coming our way. Open your eyes [lit., lift them up] and look at the fields [*theaomai*, GK *2517*; *EDNT*, 2:136, notes that the classical significance is perceived in the NT, "where the verb regularly connotes intensive, thorough, lingering, astonished, reflective, comprehending observation"]!" The disciples are intended to see and grasp the significance of the crowds returning to learn about the living water. Jesus' remark that the fields are "white for harvest" (NASB) undoubtedly reflects the fact that the approaching crowds were dressed in light-colored clothing.

36 Jesus continues to speak in metaphors. The point is that a spiritual harvest need not require a "four month" period of waiting. It is by nature urgent and immediate. The old ways of thinking must be abandoned so the harvest can begin. So close in time are sowing and harvest that the sower and the reaper rejoice together. Deuteronomy pictures the agricultural Feast of Tabernacles that followed harvest to be a time of joy and celebration (Dt 16:13–15).

37–38 Jesus employs another proverbial saying, "One sows and another reaps." If the opening word of the verse ("thus") refers to the previous verse, then Jesus is using it to illustrate the truth just cited regarding the joy experienced by both sower and reaper. If it refers to the following verse (the Greek reads *en gar toutō*, "in this," and can be interpreted in either direction), it illustrates the fact that the disciples were sent to reap the benefits of the work of "others." Just who the "others" are is not clear. If Jesus is speaking of the immediate situation, then he himself would be "those" who did the hard work and the disciples "those" who would reap the benefits of all who came out from the village. The "I sent you" (*apesteila*, GK *690*, is aorist) is also difficult to explain. Better to take the saying in a rather general sense and understand the "others" as all who preceded Jesus with the message of God (Moses, the OT prophets, John the Baptist), into whose benefits the disciples are now entering.

39 When the woman reached her village, she shared what she had learned from Jesus. The text records her testimony as "he told me everything I ever did," but it is reasonable to assume that she also explained as best she could about the promise of living water. Otherwise the many Samaritans who "believed in him because of the woman's testi-mony" would have had no basis for their faith other than the report of Jesus' unusual knowledge of the woman's past.

40–41 When the villagers arrived at the well, they urged Jesus to stay with them for a time—a most unusual request in view of the enmity that existed between Jews and Samaritans. Jesus acquiesced and remained there for two days. As a result, "many more" Samaritans became believers, i.e., a number of others in addition to those who went out to meet him at the well. Their belief was no longer based on what the woman had told them; they had now heard him themselves.

42 On the basis that the corresponding verbal form originally means "to babble or stammer," some have translated *lalian* ("what you said," GK *3282*) rather disparagingly as "chatter." Since "chatter" is an inadequate basis for belief, we need not consider the suggestion seriously. Personal acquaintance with Jesus had led many of the Samaritans in that village to confess that Jesus "really is the Savior of the world." In the OT, God is often portrayed as the one bringing salvation to his people. In Isaiah 43:3 God says, "For I am the LORD, your God, the Holy One of Israel, your Savior." Although Jesus is often referred to as Savior (Lk 2:11; Php 3:20; 2Ti 1:10), the title "Savior of the world" is applied to him only here and in 1 John 4:14. Some have suggested that this reluctance stems from the fact that in the secular world it was used as a technical term for a number of pagan gods. Adolf Deissmann (*Light from the Ancient East* [London: Hodder & Stoughton, 1910], 364–65) notes that it was often applied to the Roman emperor as well. That Jesus came as Savior of the world is precisely the point of John 3:17, which says that God sent his Son not to condemn the world "but to save the world through him." The redemptive work of God has no geographic, cultural, or ethnic boundaries. Jesus is *the* Savior of the world.

43–45 Jesus' journey from Judea to Galilee, which was temporarily suspended after 4:3, is now resumed. After the two-day stay with the Samaritans Jesus continued on to Galilee. The proverb "a prophet has no honor in his own country" (v.44), which Jesus used in Mark 6:4 and parallels in reference to Nazareth, doesn't seem to fit here in John. Why would Jesus be going to Galilee if there where he grew up he would be without honor? In fact, the following verse says that "the Galileans welcomed him." Apparently in this context the phrase "his own country" is not to be thought of as Galilee but instead as Judea or Jerusalem. Lindars, 201, notes that from the point of view of salvation history Jerusalem was "his own home." On his final journey to that sacred city Jesus lamented, "I must keep going today and tomorrow and the next day—for surely no prophet can die outside Jerusalem!" (Lk 13:33). Although the Galileans welcomed him, it would appear that their reception was based on what he could do for them. Those who had been in Jerusalem for the Passover Feast "had seen all that he had done" (v.45). The reference would be to the cleansing of the temple and the signs he did on that occasion (2:13–25, esp. v.23).

NOTES

6 In 1866 Major Anderson descended into this well and described it as very narrow at the top (about wide enough for a man to pass through with his arms extended straight up) but widening to about seven or eight feet. In 1935 when debris was cleaned out of the well, its depth was measured at more than 130 feet. Through time, several churches have been built over the well. Currently the walled enclosure with an unfinished church is the property of the Greek Orthodox. The Greek text says that Jesus sat ἐπὶ τῇ πηγῇ (*epi tē pēgē*, "on [or near] the well"). The well may have been encircled with a low stone wall on which Jesus would have sat, or perhaps, as 𝔓[66] says, Jesus sat "on the ground."

9 The explanatory clause "for Jews do not associate with Samaritans" is omitted in several MSS (ℵ* D it[a,b,d,e,j]), perhaps on the basis of scribal opinion that it was not literally exact and therefore should be deleted (Metzger, 177).

10 The Greek noun δωρεά, *dōrea* ("gift," GK *1561*), carries the idea of that which is freely given (cf. the adverb δωρεάν, *dōrean*, "without payment, undeserved," GK *1562*). In the NT it is not used in connection with the giving of gifts between people; rather, it is reserved for divine largesse.

12 Questions beginning with μή (*mē*) in Greek expect a negative response. For this reason the NASB's rendering ("You are not greater than our father Jacob, are You . . . ?") is preferable to the NIV's ("Are you greater than our father Jacob . . . ?"). Compare especially 7:15, 31, 35, 41, 47, 48, 51, and elsewhere throughout the gospel.

19 In the Greek and Roman world, for Jesus to possess such knowledge of the woman's marital history would certify him as a miracle worker, but in the religious world of Israel it would be recognized as the distinguishing mark of a prophet (cf. 1:47–48).

44 The view that Judea was to be considered Jesus' "own country" was proposed by the third-century theologian Origen. One contemporary approach is to consider v.44 as an addition by a later scribe who felt it necessary to explain why Jesus was so poorly received in Galilee following his initial arrival. (Lk 4:16–31 tells us that following his dramatic claim in the synagogue in Nazareth, "the people were furious" and drove him out of town with the intention of throwing him down the cliff.) Such textual relocations are an argument of the last resort. Either Judea was considered his "own country," or the saying is to be taken in reference to Galilee with the understanding that, while his immediate reception was favorable, the attitude of the people changed quickly when his claim to fulfill OT prophecy rankled their religious sensitivities.

E. Jesus Begins His Healing Ministry (4:46–5:47)

OVERVIEW

Jesus' arrival at Cana marks the beginning of what is called the greater Galilean ministry. This period in Jesus' life occupies approximately 35 percent of both Matthew and Mark. By the time the gospels were written, Cana was widely recognized as the place where Jesus had turned water into wine (2:1–11). It was there that Jesus had performed the first of his miraculous signs in Galilee, with the result that the disciples had placed their faith in him (2:11). Galilee is about to become the place where Jesus will perform his second miraculous sign.

1. An Official's Son (4:46–54)

46Once more he visited Cana in Galilee, where he had turned the water into wine. And there was a certain royal official whose son lay sick at Capernaum. 47When this man heard that Jesus had arrived in Galilee from Judea, he went to him and begged him to come and heal his son, who was close to death.

48"Unless you people see miraculous signs and wonders," Jesus told him, "you will never believe."

49The royal official said, "Sir, come down before my child dies."

50Jesus replied, "You may go. Your son will live."

The man took Jesus at his word and departed. 51While he was still on the way, his servants met him with the news that his boy was living. 52When he inquired as to the time when his son got better, they said to him, "The fever left him yesterday at the seventh hour."

53Then the father realized that this was the exact time at which Jesus had said to him, "Your son will live." So he and all his household believed.

54This was the second miraculous sign that Jesus performed, having come from Judea to Galilee.

COMMENTARY

46 At Capernaum, some twenty miles to the northeast of Cana on the shore of the Sea of Galilee, there lived "a certain royal official" whose son was sick. *Basilikos* (GK *997*) is an adjective meaning "royal" and could designate either a person of royal descent or a person who served the king in some official capacity. We can probably assume that he was a courtier of Herod Antipas, the tetrarch of Galilee from 4 BC until AD 39. Though, strictly speaking, Antipas was not a king, he was regularly referred to by that title (cf. Mk 6:14, 22).

47 We do not know the ethnic background of the official, but it is very possible that he was Jewish. The following verse (v.48) includes him with the Jewish population of Galilee. Neither do we know what specifically he had heard about Jesus that caused him to ask for a miracle of healing. Perhaps he had learned of Jesus' supernatural act of turning water to wine at Cana. Some suggest that he may have been in Jerusalem at the Passover Feast and personally witnessed some of the miraculous signs Jesus did there (cf. 2:23). In any case, he believed that Jesus could heal his son and wanted him to come to Capernaum for that purpose.

A number of writers believe that this narrative in John is an independent account of the story in Matthew and Luke (i.e., in "Q") about the centurion's son, who was also healed from a distance (Mt 8:5–13; Lk 7:1–10). Schnackenburg, 1:475, reviews the problem and concludes that "once the peculiarities of the literary genre which is involved have been noted, it will be difficult to admit that these two different events are in question." On the other hand, Morris, 288, rightly concludes that "despite the parallels, the two stories are distinct." Note that in John's account Jesus is in Cana (not in Capernaum, Lk 7:1), the person ill is a son (not a servant, Lk 7:2), he is sick with a fever (not paralysis, Mt 8:6), and the father begs Jesus to come to his home (does not object to his coming as unnecessary, Lk 7:6).

48 Jesus' response to the plea indicates the immature nature of the official's faith. Like the other Galileans, he "will never believe" (an emphatic double negative) unless he sees "miraculous signs and wonders." It is commonly noted that *terata* ("wonders," GK *5469*) occurs only here in John and that

elsewhere in the NT, as here, it is always plural and is always used in conjunction with *sēmeia* ("signs," GK *4956*). A miraculous act when viewed in terms of its effect on the bystanders is a "wonder," but when seen as calling attention to the supernatural authority of the person performing the act, it is a "sign." What Jesus is saying is that "a faith based on miracles (though not negligible—14:11) is inadequate" (Barrett, 247).

49 Not grasping for the moment Jesus' teaching, the official continues to beg (*ērōta*, GK *2263*, in v.47 is imperfect, indicating a repeated petition) Jesus to come "before my child dies." In addressing Jesus as *kyrios* (GK *3261*), he undoubtedly means more than "Sir" but certainly not "Lord" in the fuller sense of the word. Previously he spoke of his "son" (*huios*, GK *5626*), but now he speaks of his "child" (*paidion*, GK *4086*, a more affectionate term). It reflects the poignant grief of the father about to lose a dear son.

50 Jesus responds with a straightforward, "Go; your son lives" (NASB; TCNT, "is living"). The official's faith is put to the test. He is to return to Capernaum on the simple word of Jesus. Jesus will not go with him and perform some miraculous healing. He simply tells the official to take him at his word. Distance causes no problem. The trust that Jesus would elicit is not dependent on anything other than the word of the Master. Translations that take the present tense *zē* ("lives," GK *2409*) as a futuristic present, such as "your son will live" (NIV) or "your boy is going to live" (Williams), promise a return to health but do not adequately stress the unusual fact, as we will learn from vv.52–53, that *at that very moment* the fever had already gone and the boy was alive and well. The man believed what Jesus said and left. (Note the construction *pisteuō* plus the dative, which reflects a less firm religious commitment than *pisteuō eis*; Brown, 191, translates as "put his trust in.")

51–52 While he was returning home (*katabainontos*, "going down," GK *2849*; Capernaum lies 695 feet below sea level), the official's servants met him with the good news that his boy was alive. Inquiring as to the specific time his son began to get better (taking *eschen*, GK *2400*, as an ingressive aorist), he was told by the servants that the "fever left him yesterday at the seventh hour." A question arises as to why a father so distraught about his son would wait a day before returning the twenty miles to learn of his condition. A few writers adopt the Roman method of computing time, which would place the healing at 7:00 a.m. In that case, the official would be able to return home the same day, since the trip took no more than six or seven hours. But it is better to follow the Jewish method of reckoning time and place the healing at 1:00 p.m. Although the "next day" would begin at sunset, it is unlikely that had he returned immediately his servants would have spoken of the moment of healing as taking place "yesterday." Perhaps the man had other business to take care of in Cana, or since he had taken Jesus at his word he did not feel compelled to rush back to verify the promise that his son was no longer in danger of dying.

53 When the official learned from his servants that the fever left his son at the seventh hour and realized that it was "the exact time" when Jesus said his son would live, "he and all his household believed." In v.50 the man believed in the sense of taking Jesus at his word. But here in v.53 belief represents full confidence in the person of Jesus. Belief about has become commitment to. Along with his entire household, the official joined the growing number of believers who were convinced that Jesus was God's answer to life with all its difficulties.

54 John adds that this was "the second miraculous sign" Jesus had performed since he had come from Judea to Galilee. It was not the second of all the signs he would perform—in Jerusalem many people had seen "the miraculous signs he was doing and believed in his name" (2:23)—but the second sign he performed in Galilee. His first sign showed his power over the physical realm, and his disciples believed (2:1–11). By his second sign he displayed his power to heal from a distance, and the official and all his household believed (cf. Hendriksen, 1:184).

2. A Paralytic at the Pool of Bethesda (5:1–18)

OVERVIEW

John 4 began with Jesus leaving Judea for Galilee. The bulk of the chapter was devoted to his encounter with the Samaritan woman en route. Near the end of the chapter, Jesus resumed his journey to Galilee and on arriving cured the son of a royal official from Capernaum. John 5 takes place in Jerusalem, but in ch. 6 Jesus is back in Galilee once again. For this reason some scholars put ch. 6 before ch. 5 in order to join segments of the Galilean ministry without an intervening trip to Jerusalem. Since there is neither manuscript evidence for such a transposition nor any discernible reason for the traditional sequence, if ch. 6 had originally preceded ch. 5, it is better to leave the chapters as they now stand. The attempt to create chronological and geographic congruence may be well intentioned but is not necessary.

¹Some time later, Jesus went up to Jerusalem for a feast of the Jews. ²Now there is in Jerusalem near the Sheep Gate a pool, which in Aramaic is called Bethesda and which is surrounded by five covered colonnades. ³Here a great number of disabled people used to lie—the blind, the lame, the paralyzed. ⁵One who was there had been an invalid for thirty-eight years. ⁶When Jesus saw him lying there and learned that he had been in this condition for a long time, he asked him, "Do you want to get well?"

⁷"Sir," the invalid replied, "I have no one to help me into the pool when the water is stirred. While I am trying to get in, someone else goes down ahead of me."

⁸Then Jesus said to him, "Get up! Pick up your mat and walk." ⁹At once the man was cured; he picked up his mat and walked.

The day on which this took place was a Sabbath, ¹⁰and so the Jews said to the man who had been healed, "It is the Sabbath; the law forbids you to carry your mat."

¹¹But he replied, "The man who made me well said to me, 'Pick up your mat and walk.'"

¹²So they asked him, "Who is this fellow who told you to pick it up and walk?"

¹³The man who was healed had no idea who it was, for Jesus had slipped away into the crowd that was there.

¹⁴Later Jesus found him at the temple and said to him, "See, you are well again. Stop sinning or something worse may happen to you." ¹⁵The man went away and told the Jews that it was Jesus who had made him well.

¹⁶So, because Jesus was doing these things on the Sabbath, the Jews persecuted him. ¹⁷Jesus said to them, "My Father is always at his work to this very day, and I, too, am working." ¹⁸For this reason the Jews tried all the harder to kill him; not only was he breaking the Sabbath, but he was even calling God his own Father, making himself equal with God.

COMMENTARY

1 After spending some time in Galilee, John went up to Jerusalem for a feast of the Jews. There is a question as to which feast this refers to. The difficulty stems from the lack of a direct article before "feast" (*heortē*, GK *2038*, which occurs eighteen times in John but only here without an article). Manuscripts that do read *hē heortē* ("the feast") undoubtedly understood the feast to be the Passover. The three great national festivals of the Jewish people were Passover (March–April), Pentecost (fifty days later), and Tabernacles (September–October). Most schol-

ars are of the opinion that the feast referred to in the present passage is the Feast of Tabernacles, though others suggest Pentecost, Trumpets (New Year), or Purim. To know which feast John refers to would add nothing to the healing miracle Jesus is about to perform, so it is best left as an interesting item for scholarly conjecture. That it was a feast "of the Jews" is an explanatory comment added by John for the benefit of Gentile readers. Jesus "went up" to Jerusalem in that every journey to the Holy City (except from Hebron) involved an ascent.

2 We know from archaeological excavations that in the northeastern quarter of Jerusalem near the church of St. Anne there were adjacent pools, which in earlier days had a covered colonnade at each corner of the area and another on the rock ridge separating the pools—hence the "five covered colonnades" referred to in the narrative.

3 In these covered areas a number of disabled people "used to lie" (taking *katekeito*, GK *2879*, as a customary imperfect). John describes them as "the blind, the lame, the paralyzed." The last term (*xēros*, GK *3831*) means "withered" or "dried up" and described people whose bodies were withered by disease (e.g., the man with the "shriveled hand" in Mk 3:3). At the end of v.3 some MSS add the clause "and they waited for the moving of the waters." This would be to throw light on the statement in v.7 regarding the troubling of the water. The same MSS also add a v.4 (missing in the better MSS; see Notes) that expresses a popular belief about angels stirring the water and the magical healing powers of that water for the first person to enter the pool when a disturbance took place. The probable explanation for a disturbance in the twin pools is that in addition to the water that came from large reservoirs, there were probably intermittent springs that augmented the flow from time to time.

5 Beside the pool lay a man who had been an invalid for thirty-eight years—longer than many people in ancient times lived. That this same number occurs elsewhere only in Deuteronomy 2:14 (Israel wasted thirty-eight years in the desert) has encouraged allegorizers to find in the paralytic a symbol of the Jewish people of Jesus' day disabled by the lack of faith. Carson, 242–43, notes that if John intended any symbolism, it would have been the impotency of superstitious religion to transform the truly needy.

6 Jesus' question may strike the reader as rather superfluous. Why else would this man be there but to be healed by the troubled waters? Perhaps by means of the question Jesus wanted to revive the man's expectation that, in spite of so many years of disappointment, healing was still possible. Jesus "learned" of the man's condition either by observation or report. The two participles (*idōn*, GK *3972*; *gnous*, GK *1182*) are coordinate and picture Jesus as *seeing* the man and then *coming to know* of his physical condition. It is less likely that we are to understand this as an example of Jesus' supernatural insight (as in 1:47–48; 4:17). The man's pitiful condition was a clear indication that for many years he had suffered from a debilitating disease.

7 Instead of answering Jesus' question, the man explains why as yet he hasn't been healed: because there is no one there to help him when the water is stirred, someone else manages to get into the pool before he can. In view of what takes place subsequently—i.e., his shifting of the blame to Jesus for his own "violation" of Sabbath rules (v.11), his not bothering to find out who healed him (v.13), and his reporting of Jesus to the authorities (v.15)—it appears that his response to Jesus' inquiry was the reaction of a grouchy old man to a question that seemed pointless to him.

8–9 Jesus' reply is direct and powerful: "Get up! Pick up your mat and walk." The same command was given in the gospel of Mark to the paralytic who was lowered through the roof by his friends (Mk 2:9). The situations, however, are quite distinct. In the Markan incident, faith was present (Mk 2:5), but here the healing seems to be apart from any faith on the part of the disabled man. Verse 9 simply says that "at once the man was cured." He was healed by virtue of the fact that accompanying the command was the power to effect it. Bruce, 124, writes, "He received power to do what a moment earlier had been quite beyond his capacity." The man's personal involvement was minimal at best. The mat on which the paralytic had lain would have been a straw pallet easy to roll up and carry on one's shoulder. It had served its purpose and now was to be taken away. The cure was permanent. The two verbs in v.9b are worth noting. The verb ēren ("picked up," GK 149) is aorist and could be paraphrased, "he took it up at once"; periepatei ("walked," GK 4344) is present tense and suggests something like, "[and] was walking around."

The healing at the pool of Bethesda took place on a Sabbath. In the Synoptics we find a number of Sabbath healings and other activities considered by the rabbis to be unlawful on that day. All three Synoptics record Jesus' disciples picking grain on the Sabbath (Mt 12:1–8; Mk 2:23–28; Lk 6:1–5) and the Sabbath healing of the man's shriveled hand (Mt 12:9–14; Mk 3:1–6; Lk 6:6–11). Luke adds the Sabbath healing of the woman crippled by a spirit for eighteen years (Lk 13:10–17) and the Sabbath healing of a man with dropsy (Lk 14:1–6).

10 When "the Jews" (the religious authorities, not the Jewish people in general) saw the man who had been healed (tetherapeumenō, GK 2543, is perfect tense, stressing the permanence of the cure), they rebuked him for carrying his mat. According to rabbinic law this activity was considered work. The Mosaic prohibition against work on the Sabbath (Ex 31:14; Jer 17:21–27) had been detailed into thirty-nine classes of work, the final one being the carrying of a load from one place to another (m. Šabb. 7.2). Although the original intention was to protect the holiness of the Sabbath, the final result was a legalistic parody of the original prohibition.

11 Knowing that the penalty for breaking the Sabbath was death by stoning (Nu 15:32–36), the man who had been healed shifted the blame to the one who had healed him. It is difficult to know just how culpable the man was for what appears to have been an evasive tactic. It may be that he was implying that anyone who could perform such a remarkable feat possessed an authority that superseded rabbinic law.

12 The Jewish authorities responded rather dis-

dainfully by asking, "Who is this fellow who told you to pick it up and walk?" It is remarkable that those in charge of the spiritual welfare of the nation were interested only in what they considered a breach of the law and were not moved by the extraordinary healing of a man who had been a cripple for thirty-eight years. How unlike Jesus, who was moved with compassion when confronted with physical suffering!

13 The man who was healed had no idea who it was who healed him because Jesus had slipped away in the large crowd of people. We do not know whether or not he tried to identify his benefactor. The general impression we gather of the man is that he was far more interested in his newly acquired health than in the one who made it possible. The verb exeneusen ("slipped away," GK 2002) comes from a root that means "to turn the head aside," "to dodge," and the word pictures Jesus as taking advantage of the large crowd to move away unnoticed by others.

14 Some time later, Jesus found the healed man in the temple and remarked on his recovery. To this he added, "Stop sinning." The prohibition in Greek is present tense (mēketi hamartane, GK 3600, 279) and may well indicate that Jesus was referring to some sin existing in the man's life at that time. The NEB translates, "Leave your sinful ways." If you don't, then "something worse may happen to you." This "something worse" to which Jesus referred could have been the normal consequences of continuing in sin. Or it could have been the end result of a sinful life—eternal separation from God. We do know that Scripture teaches that specific sins may result in a human tragedy. Ananias and Sapphira lied about the land they sold and both were struck dead (Ac 5:1–10). Paul tells us that many in Corinth were sick (and some had died) because they had taken Communion in an unworthy manner (1Co 11:27–32). Yet we are cautioned in John 9:1–4 against assuming that every disease is the result of a specific sin. It would appear, however, that in the case of the man in question his condition was closely related to some personal sinful act or attitude.

15 The man now goes to the Jewish authorities and tells them that Jesus was the one who had made him well. Once again it is difficult to ascribe motives to the man with any degree of certainty. Some scholars see him as betraying Jesus. Others have him going to the authorities to clear up the matter, which if left unresolved could eventuate in severe punishment. Carson, 246, is probably closest when he remarks that the man was "guilty of dullness rather than treachery."

16 It was because Jesus "was doing these things [imperfect tense] on the Sabbath" that the Jewish leaders "were persecuting" (also imperfect) him. Since the healing of the man at the pool of Bethesda (vv. 1–9a) was the only Sabbath violation mentioned thus far in John, the imperfect "was doing these things" was occasioned by John's later reflections, which incorporated other such instances. The NEB has, "It was works of this kind done on the Sabbath that stirred the Jews to persecute Jesus." Augustine (*Tractates on the Gospel of John*, 21.6) noted that "they sought darkness from the Sabbath more than light from the miracle."

17 Jesus justified his activity on the Sabbath by explaining that since God the Father was continuing to work even to that very day, so also is the Son free to work. Exodus 20:11 teaches that after God had completed the creation in six days, "he rested on the seventh day." The rabbis understood, however, that God's Sabbath rest did not mean that he became idle, for without the activity of divine providence on the Sabbath all life would cease; furthermore, since only God can give life and human beings are born on the Sabbath, it follows that God must be active on the Sabbath. The third-century rabbi Hoshaiah is quoted as saying that God's rest-

ing on this day from all his works "means that he rested from work on his world; but he did not rest from work on the unrighteous and on the righteous" (*Gen. Rab.* 11.10). That God remains active in this world was perfectly acceptable to Jesus' detractors. What was not acceptable was Jesus' (implied) claim that he was God's Son and therefore shared the same privilege. While the Jews sometimes referred in worship to God as their father, they would never use the term in an individual sense as Jesus had just done.

18 For Jesus to challenge the fundamental distinction between God and human beings (God being infinite and holy, human beings being finite and sinful) was tantamount to blasphemy. While Jesus' statement would not have been taken as actual blasphemy (*m. Sanh.* 7.5 says that "the blasphemer is not culpable unless he pronounces the Name itself"), the implication was perfectly clear. He was laying claim to a special and unique relationship to God as Father that gave him the right to do whatever was appropriate for God to do. The charge that he broke the Sabbath (and in so doing was relaxing or invalidating the law; cf. *TDNT* 4:336) was serious, but not nearly as damaging as the charge that by calling God his own Father he was making himself equal with God. While in Greek thought certain outstanding individuals were considered to be godlike, such a comparison was blasphemous to the Jew. Hendriksen, 1:196, comments that for Jesus to claim for himself deity "was either the most wicked blasphemy, to be punished with death; or else, it was the most glorious truth, to be accepted by faith."

Obviously Jesus' antagonists were not about to accept such a claim, so "they tried all the harder to kill him." Opposition to truth inevitably takes the course of violence. Conviction stirs up hatred in those who hold just as strongly to an opposing belief. Historically the only recourse has been to do away with those whose convictions undermine and repudiate the conventional wisdom of the day. Yet truth has a way of vindicating itself, and in the end every knee will bow and every tongue confess the lordship of Jesus Christ (Php 2:10–11).

NOTES

1 To be able to identify the feast (whether or not it is the Jewish Passover) would help in determining the length of Jesus' ministry. John specifically mentions three Passovers (2:13; 6:4; 11:55). If the feast of 5:1 was not a Passover, then Jesus' ministry would have lasted for two to three years. If, however, 5:1 was a fourth Passover, then his ministry would have continued for an additional year.

2 Verse 2 presents two textual problems related to the name and location of the incident that follows. The first has to do with the "Sheep Gate." The Greek text does not include the word "gate." If κολυμβήθρα, *kolymbēthra* ("pool," GK *3148*), is taken in the nominative, then the sentence reads, "There is in Jerusalem near the sheep [ ] a pool, which in Aramaic is called Bethesda." In this case a word must be supplied after "sheep"; NIV has chosen "gate," but "pool" and "market" have also been suggested. However, if κολυμβήθρα, *kolymbēthra*, is taken as dative, it would qualify πρφβατικῇ, *probatikē* ("sheep," GK *4583*), and the sentence would read, "In Jerusalem, near the sheep pool, there is a [ ], which in Aramaic is called Bethesda." In both cases a word must be supplied (probably "place" in the latter rendering). Because a sheep gate is mentioned in Nehemiah (3:1; 12:39), it seems preferable to follow the NIV (and NASB) rendering and supply πύλη, *pylē* ("gate," GK *4783*).

The second problem is the preferred reading for the Aramaic designation of the location. Both the NIV and NASB have chosen "Bethesda," which has in its favor the serendipitous etymology "House of Mercy." The strongest variant is "Bethsaida," but textual critics think this is the result of assimilation to the town of Bethsaida mentioned in 1:44. Metzger, 178, notes that the UBS committee concurred that Bethzatha was the "least unsatisfactory" and gave it the classification of "D" ("a very high degree of doubt"). The reading "Bethesda" receives support from the Copper Scroll from Qumran, which refers to a pool called *bêt* ešdātayin—the dual ending suggesting the translation "the place of twin outpourings." Bruce, 122, holds that this settles fairly conclusively that "Bethesda . . . is the true form."

3b–4 The standard reasons for considering vv.3b–4 as a gloss are (1) they are not included in the earliest and best witnesses (𝔓[66] 𝔓[75] ℵ A* B C* L *pc* sy[c] co); (2) more than twenty Greek witnesses mark them as spurious; (3) they include a number of words or expressions not found elsewhere in John; and (4) there is a great amount of textual diversity among the witnesses that do include the verses. However, after reviewing the evidence, the NET text critical note at 5:3 concludes that "at this point we must acknowledge that *some* portion of vv.3b–4 may be authentic." The NASB rather curiously has a marginal note that reads, "Early mss do not contain the remainder of v 3, nor v 4," but nevertheless includes them in the text, albeit in square brackets.

14 The NET translator's note sees the translation "stop sinning" as unlikely in this case because the present tense is normally used in prohibitions involving a general condition, while the aorist is normally used in specific cases; and only when they are used opposite the normal usage would the present tense after the Greek μή (*mē*) yield the idea of stopping what is being done.

3. Jesus' Claim of Divine Authority (5:19–47)

OVERVIEW

The rest of the chapter (vv. 19–47) is an extended monologue in which Jesus expands the core truth enunciated in v.17—the essential unity and equality of Father and Son. In vv.19–23, Jesus points out that he can do only those things he sees his Father doing, that the authority to raise the dead and carry out judgment comes to him by virtue of the fact that the Father loves him, and that the great eschatological purpose of this relationship is that the Son will be honored just as the Father is honored.

We are alerted to the crucial nature of this section by the announcement used by Jesus whenever an extraordinarily important statement is about to be made: "I tell you the truth" (v.19; twenty-six times in the fourth gospel). Phillips highlights the section with the editorial subtitle "Jesus makes His tremendous claim."

> [19] Jesus gave them this answer: "I tell you the truth, the Son can do nothing by himself; he can do only what he sees his Father doing, because whatever the Father does the Son also does. [20] For the Father loves the Son and shows him all he does. Yes, to your amazement he will show him even greater things than these. [21] For just as the Father raises the dead and gives them life, even so the Son gives life to whom he is pleased to give it. [22] Moreover, the Father judges no one, but has entrusted all judgment to the Son, [23] that all may honor the Son just as they honor the Father. He who does not honor the Son does not honor the Father, who sent him.
>
> [24] "I tell you the truth, whoever hears my word and believes him who sent me has eternal life and will not be condemned; he has crossed over from death to life. [25] I tell you the truth, a time is coming and has now come when the dead will hear the voice of the Son of God and those who hear will live. [26] For as the Father has life in himself, so he has granted the Son to have life in himself. [27] And he has given him authority to judge because he is the Son of Man.
>
> [28] "Do not be amazed at this, for a time is coming when all who are in their graves will hear his voice [29] and come out—those who have done good will rise to live, and those who have done evil will rise to be condemned. [30] By myself I can do nothing; I judge only as I hear, and my judgment is just, for I seek not to please myself but him who sent me."
>
> [31] "If I testify about myself, my testimony is not valid. [32] There is another who testifies in my favor, and I know that his testimony about me is valid.
>
> [33] "You have sent to John and he has testified to the truth. [34] Not that I accept human testimony; but I mention it that you may be saved. [35] John was a lamp that burned and gave light, and you chose for a time to enjoy his light.

³⁶"I have testimony weightier than that of John. For the very work that the Father has given me to finish, and which I am doing, testifies that the Father has sent me. ³⁷And the Father who sent me has himself testified concerning me. You have never heard his voice nor seen his form, ³⁸nor does his word dwell in you, for you do not believe the one he sent. ³⁹You diligently study the Scriptures because you think that by them you possess eternal life. These are the Scriptures that testify about me, ⁴⁰yet you refuse to come to me to have life.

⁴¹"I do not accept praise from men, ⁴²but I know you. I know that you do not have the love of God in your hearts. ⁴³I have come in my Father's name, and you do not accept me; but if someone else comes in his own name, you will accept him. ⁴⁴How can you believe if you accept praise from one another, yet make no effort to obtain the praise that comes from the only God?

⁴⁵"But do not think I will accuse you before the Father. Your accuser is Moses, on whom your hopes are set. ⁴⁶If you believed Moses, you would believe me, for he wrote about me. ⁴⁷But since you do not believe what he wrote, how are you going to believe what I say?"

COMMENTARY

19 The Son can do nothing "by himself." His relationship of filial obedience prevents him from acting on his own. He does nothing unless God the Father moves him to do it. (Barrett, 259, takes *poiein aph' heautou ouden* as a common Johannine idiom meaning "to do nothing without prompting.") The Jews who saw Jesus "break the Sabbath" by healing on that sacred day would consider him a rebel (v.16), but as the Son of God he was unable to do anything that was not in perfect conformity with the will and desire of the Father. That he does "only what he sees his Father doing" does not mean that he imitates the Father. Rather, it is a way of portraying the continuous relationship that exists between Father and Son.

In vv.19–20a C. H. Dodd (*More New Testament Studies* [Manchester: Manchester Univ. Press, 1968], 30–40) finds an "embedded parable" in which Jesus reflects on his earlier days at work in his father's carpenter shop. The interpretation calls for "son" and "father" to be taken without capital letters and the definite article "*the* son" as generic (cf. "the sower," Mk 4:3). The resulting picture is that of an apprenticed son learning his father's trade. Though it is an interesting possibility, most commentators remain unconvinced, primarily because the designation "the Son" was a standard christological expression.

20 The unity of action between Father and Son is based on the fact that "the Father loves the Son." Interestingly, the verb is *phileō* (GK *5797*; used only here in John as the love of the Father for the Son) rather than the more theological *agapaō* (GK *26*). Temple, 1:112, is quick to assure the reader that "the context ensures the utmost exaltation, and the greater warmth of the more familiar word is peculiarly appropriate." This continuing love (*philei* is present tense) of the Father leads him to share with the Son every prerogative that is his. He shows him "all he does" and, in fact, will show him "even greater things" (cf. vv.21–22). What the Jews are about to learn will be "to [their] amazement." To his detractors Jesus says that when the Father shows the Son these greater things, *people like you* (the pronoun *hymeis* is emphatic) will be filled with wonder (futuristic present). The Jews were simply unprepared for the tremendous truth about to be revealed to them. Even if well-intentioned, their habit of reducing God to a set of ritual requirements severely stunted their spiritual faculties.

21 The Jews believed that to raise the dead was the sole prerogative of God. When Naaman was sent to the king of Israel to have his leprosy cured, the king tore his robes and said, "Am I God? Can I kill and bring back to life? (2Ki 5:7). The point is that God and God alone can restore life (Dt 32:39; 1Sa 2:6). The rabbinic point of view is that there are three keys that only God holds: the key of rain, the key of the womb, and the key of the resurrection of the dead (*b. Taʿan. 2a*). Jesus now announces that "just as the Father raises the dead . . . , even so the Son gives life." This is the first of two "greater things" (v.20) that will amaze them. The authority of granting life belongs equally to the Father and to the Son. The Son is not merely the Father's instrument to raise the dead, but he himself possesses the intrinsic right to give life "to whom he is pleased to give it." While the teaching that the Son "makes anyone live whom he chooses" (Moffatt) may sound arbitrary, it is nevertheless consistent with what we find elsewhere in the NT (cf. Ro 9:18). The rest of the story is found a few verses later where we learn that eternal life is given to those who hear and believe (v.24). Jesus chose one man from among the many lying beside the pool of Bethesda and "gave him life" in the sense of restoring his ability to walk. In a fuller sense he gives the life of the age to come to those he has chosen. The reference is both present and eschatological.

22 The second "greater thing" (v.20) they will learn is that the Father has "entrusted all judgment

to the Son." In the OT, God was considered to be the universal judge ("Rise up, O God, judge the earth, for all the nations are your inheritance," Ps 82:8). This responsibility is now transferred to the Son. That Jesus has been entrusted with all judgment may appear to contradict the earlier statement that "God did not send his Son into the world to condemn the world" (3:17), but note that the verse goes on to say that the *purpose* of the incarnation was to "save the world through him." God did not send the Son in order to condemn, but when the salvation he offers is rejected, the *result* is judgment. In that sense the Savior becomes the judge.

23 In v.18 the Jews had reasoned that by calling God his Father Jesus was making himself equal with God. The thrust of v.23 is that they were correct. The life-giving power of the Son and his authority to judge carry with it the obvious implication that he is to be honored along with the Father. While it is true that "an ambassador receives the honour due to the sovereign whom he represents" (Bruce, 130), in the case of Jesus the honor due him is not because he represents God but because he is God. Thus the Son receives honor equal to that given to the Father. It follows that to withhold honor from the Son is to dishonor the Father. Equality in essence (vv.17–18) and in works (vv.19–22) calls for equality in honor. This truth puts to rest permanently the heresy of considering the Son a lesser created being (so the Ebionites and the Arians of the early period of church history and the Jehovah's Witnesses of today).

24 Once again Jesus prefaces an important truth with his characteristic "I tell you the truth." As in the other locations, it does not stem from fear that the hearer might think that Jesus is not telling the truth. Rather, it is a rhetorical way of underscoring the crucial importance of the pronouncement that will follow. Jesus has just spoken of his role in judgment; now he explains how not to be condemned.

To be set free from condemnation and enter into eternal life requires that a person hear the message that Jesus brings and believe in the one who sent him. In John's language, hearing and believing are not so much two separate steps as they are a single act of obedience. Barrett, 261, notes that "*akouein* [GK 201] is used, as *shama* [GK 10725] is often used in the Old Testament, with the meaning 'to hear and do,' 'to be obedient.'" As Jesus spoke a word and an invalid who lay helpless by the pool of Bethesda rose and walked away, now he speaks a word and spiritual invalids who respond in faith rise up and enter into "eternal life."

The message that Jesus brought centers in the redemptive love of God the Father. To learn of the Father who longs for the return of the prodigal and to return in faith to that intimate relationship abandoned by Adam is to "cross over from death to life." The verb (*metabainō*, GK 3553) may be used to indicate a change of residence (BDAG, 638; cf. Lk 10:7). Jesus is saying that those who hear and believe have by that response left their former residence in the realm of death and moved to a new home in the sphere of life. The perfect tense of the verb indicates that the change of quarters has already been made. Believers are enjoying eternal life right now. This is the strongest statement of "realized eschatology" found in the NT. Those who have eternal life will "not be condemned." They will "not come into judgment" (NASB; *eis krisin* [GK 3213] *ouk erchetai* [GK 2262]) because that question has been settled forever on the cross.

25 It is undoubtedly the importance of the truth Jesus is laying down that leads him to repeat his introductory "I tell you the truth" and essentially repeat in different words what he has just said. That a "time is coming and has now come" is an idiomatic way of referring to something of importance that is happening right now (cf. 4:23; 16:32). The dead who hear his voice and live are the spiri-

tually dead (cf. Eph 2:1). Jesus is bringing eternal life to believers right now. It is not something that lies well into the future following a time of judgment. To live involves a radical transformation of one's entire existence. It should not be confused with self-initiated attempts at moral improvement. The life of which Jesus speaks is a sharing of the very life of the Eternal One.

To "hear the voice" of Jesus is more than simply to allow sound waves to fall on the ear. It means to hear with the heart and put the message into action. To hear in the biblical sense of the term necessarily involves obedience. Jesus refers to himself as the "Son of God" on only three occasions in the fourth gospel (cf. 10:36; 11:4). Since the entire section has been stressing the unity of Father and Son, the designation is especially appropriate here.

26 The reason why hearing the voice of the Son of God brings life is that the Son has "life in himself." God is the only one who possesses life inherently. It is part of who he is. The life shared by the human race is derived and dependent. Verse 26 tells us that God the Father has granted to God the Son this divine prerogative of possessing "life in himself." It was not something bestowed on the Son at his incarnation but belongs to him eternally as the second person of the Godhead.

27 In addition to "life in himself," the Father has given to the Son the "authority to judge." (Note the parallels between vv. 26 and 21 where the subject is life, and vv. 27 and 22 where Jesus speaks of judgment.) This authority is his because he is "the Son of Man." On the basis that the title in the Greek text is not preceded by a definite article (*huios anthrōpou*, GK 5626, 476), some have taken it to mean "a human being." That is, God has turned judgment over to the Son because in the incarnation he (the Son) learned by experience what it means to be a member of the human race (cf. Heb 4:15). By reading the *hoti* as *ho ti* (definite article followed by an interrogative pronoun), it is possible to understand the clause to read "to pass judgment on what man is." It is most likely, however, that the title "Son of Man" is a direct allusion to Daniel 7:13. There for the first time it was used of the Messiah. Jesus has been given the authority to judge precisely because he is God's Anointed One. The title became Jesus' favorite self-designation.

28 Here we face the question as to whether "do not be amazed at this" refers back to what has just been said or forward to what will be said. In the first case, the *hoti* (NIV, "for") is taken to mean "because," so Jesus is saying, "Don't be amazed that the Son has been given the authority to judge because he will be the agent in the coming assize." In the second case, the *hoti* is taken in the sense of "namely," so Jesus is saying, "Don't be amazed at what I am about to tell you, namely that graves will be opened and everyone will rise, either to live or to be condemned." If it is necessary to choose, the first option is probably stronger, though both what has preceded and what follows would certainly be sources of amazement.

Since the apocalyptic finale is yet future, Jesus says that the "time is coming" but does not add "and has now come" (as in v.25). When that time does come, all the dead will "hear his voice and come out" of their graves. To picture an event of such catastrophic proportion forces the imagination into overload.

29 What lies ahead is a general resurrection in which every person who has lived and died in the course of human history will come out of the grave. Earlier (in v.24) Jesus said that believers have already passed "from death to life." So for them ("those who have done good") the future holds a resurrection to life. Their "spiritual resurrection" at conversion will lead to a "bodily resurrection" into the fullness of life eternal. "Those who have done evil" will also be raised, but they will "rise to be condemned." At

the final resurrection there will be a visible separation of the wheat and the weeds (Mt 13:24–30). That judgment is based on works, what a person does, is taught throughout Scripture. In Matthew 25:31–46 the sheep (those who responded to the needs of others) inherit the kingdom, while the goats (those who failed to respond compassionately to the needs of others) are sent away to eternal punishment (cf. Ro 2:6–8). Salvation is by faith alone but not faith that is alone. Believing faith inevitably expresses itself in loving response to the practical needs of others.

30 All judgment has been entrusted to the Son, but he is unable to do anything apart from the Father. What the Son hears determines how he judges, not because he is an instrument of justice in the hands of the Father, but because the two are one. Furthermore, his decisions are just because his aim is to please not himself but the one who sent him. Since the Jews would never question the fairness of God the Father, there is no basis for judging the fairness of the Son, since he acts in perfect unanimity with the Father.

31–47 We enter now a section that runs through the end of the chapter and reads like a court scene. It is as though the Jewish leaders have demanded that Jesus produce a series of witnesses who will justify the claims he has made. So Jesus calls on God (vv.32, 37), John the Baptist (vv.33–35), the work he has done (v.36), and Scripture (vv.38–40). The concluding verses (41–47) are an indictment against the Jewish antagonists, who in the end will find themselves accused by Moses—the very one on whom they have set their hopes.

31 According to a principle set forth in Deuteronomy 19:15, an accusation must be established by the testimony of at least two or three witnesses. So Jesus acknowledges that from the standpoint of Jewish legal practice his testimony about himself "is not valid" (i.e., such evidence "cannot be accepted," Weymouth). It is obviously true that God does not lie (Tit 1:2; Heb 6:18) and the Son is one with the Father. However, in the eyes of one's accusers self-testimony will not stand. No one is allowed to serve as a witness to his own signature! Some have questioned the interpretation that in this context Jesus is discussing the circumstances under which his testimony would be acceptable in a court of law (cf. Carson, 31). Even if that were so, the Greek word *alēthēs* ("true, genuine, or honest," GK 239; BDAG, 43) is sufficiently broad to cover the general idea of validity. Every testimony that is "true" is de facto admissible. Others have noticed a formal contradiction with 8:14, where Jesus declares that his self-testimony is, in fact, valid. The two settings, however, are distinct. In ch. 8 the Pharisees are said to have no way of knowing Jesus' origin or destination (v.14b), which ignorance implies that they are therefore incapable of passing judgment on his claim to be the light of the world (v.12). Jesus' testimony stands in God's court because no further witness is necessary. Beyond that, the Son is one with the Father (v.16), so in fact there are two witnesses.

32 There is "another" (*allos*, GK 257, sometimes indicates another of the same kind, as opposed to *heteros*, GK 2283, another of a different sort) who testifies in the Son's favor and his testimony "is trustworthy" (TCNT). This one is, of course, God the Father (see v.37).

33 Further, the opponents had sent an emissary to John the Baptist to learn who he was, and John freely confessed that he was not the Messiah but his forerunner (cf. 1:19–27). The following day, upon seeing Jesus approaching, John declared, "Look, the Lamb of God, who takes away the sin of the world!" (1:29). That the second verb in v.33 is in the perfect tense (*memartyrēken*, "he has testified," GK 3455) stresses that John's witness remains as evidence. Barrett, 264, says that "the effect of the perfect tense is to present his testimony as an established datum."

34 Jesus doesn't rest his case on human testimony, but he brings it up in the hope of leading his accusers to salvation. Far from simply defending himself, he reaches out toward the ultimate good of those who oppose him (cf. Mt 5:43–48).

35 Jesus describes John as "a lamp that burned and gave light." Carson, 261, says that the Greek suggests "was ignited and gave light." It is costly to "burn" for a great cause. In John's case, his bold witness cost him his life (Mk 6:14–29). The Jewish reaction to John's ministry was one of religious excitement that lasted only a short period. The Greek *agalliaō* ("to enjoy," GK 22) is a very strong word depicting unrestrained joy (*EDNT*, 1:8, refers to it as a radiant joy that encompasses the whole person). Morris, 327, says that there may have been "light-hearted merrymaking where there should have been serious purpose" because "the Jews never did take John seriously." They had a great time listening to this eccentric prophet who roamed the desert regions, but they did not really believe what he was saying. Light must be received before it can provide genuine illumination. There is a world of difference between being acquainted with truth and allowing truth to transform and redirect the life. Only in the latter case does it accomplish its salvific mission.

36 John's witness to Jesus was important and should have turned the nation to Jesus. It didn't. But Jesus had a testimony that was "weightier than that of John." The very works that Jesus was doing bore testimony to the fact that the Father had sent him. In context it would appear that these works were miraculous deeds, such as the healing of the paralytic. At the same time they were signs pointing to his heavenly origin. Nicodemus confessed that Jesus was a teacher come from God, "for no one could perform the miraculous signs you are doing if God were not with him" (3:2). While Jesus never performed miracles in order to prove his deity, the miracles were not without evidential value. They not only strengthened faith but also witnessed to the fact that the Father had sent him on his redemptive mission. It is also possible that Jesus thought of his works in a wider sense as encompassing everything he was doing that served the purpose of revealing the nature and will of God the Father. Bultmann, 265, says it refers to "the whole of Jesus' activity as the Revealer."

37–38 As a third witness Jesus calls on "the Father . . . himself." A number of suggestions have been made as to what this testimony by the Father referred to. Some hold that it was the voice from heaven at Jesus' baptism ("You are my Son, whom I love; with you I am well pleased," Mk 1:11). Others suggest the transfiguration scene in which the same message is delivered to the disciples with the added injunction, "Listen to him" (Mt 17:5). Beasley-Murray, 78, citing support from Bultmann and Hoskyns, writes that "the Father's witness in this paragraph is *his word in the Scriptures.*" But Barrett, 267, is certainly right in finding the clue in 1 John 5:9–10, which teaches that God testified about his Son and that those who believe in the Son of God have this testimony in their heart. He concludes that "what John means is that the truth of God in Jesus is self-authenticating in the experience of the believer."

This interpretation is supported by the threefold indictment that follows. The testimony of the Father about the Son continues intact (*memartyrēken*, GK 3455, "has testified," is perfect tense), "but you have never heard his voice or seen him face to face" (CEV). Furthermore, "his word has found no home in you" (NEB). And why not? The answer is that "you do not believe the one he sent." One must believe in order actually to hear. Words falling on deaf ears communicate no actual message. To "see" God the Father in the person of his Son requires an act of believing faith. To the inquiring Philip Jesus said, "Anyone who has seen me has seen the Father"

(14:9). God's word was beyond their ability to grasp because it was not heard with the ears of faith. In all matters of the spirit, the only sequence that yields results is to "taste and see that the LORD is good" (Ps 34:8). No seeing without tasting! The testimony of the Father is the word of assurance that comes with persuasive power to all who believe. That the Jews did not see the Father in the Son or hear his voice in the message that Jesus brought does not nullify the fact that the Father does in fact continue to testify to the Son.

39 It is not as though the Jewish religionist did not "diligently study the Scriptures." The premise that the study of the holy law opens the door to life in the age to come runs throughout rabbinic literature. For example, Hillel taught that "the more study of the law, the more life" and that if a man "has gained for himself words of the law, he has gained for himself life in the age to come" (*m. ʾAbot* 2:8; see also 6:7, "Great is the law for it gives to those who practice it life in this world and in the world to come"). The Greek word translated "diligently study" (*eraunaō*, GK *2236*) corresponds to the Hebrew *dāraš* (GK 2011), the technical term for rabbinic study (cf. Str-B, 2:467). Temple, 1:117, notes that it "does not suggest spiritual penetration but meticulous analysis," and Phillips translates, "You pore over the Scriptures" (NASB, "You search the Scriptures"). There is no question that the Jews held Scripture in highest regard and studied it with infinite care. (For this reason alone it is preferable to take the verb as indicative rather than imperative— the two forms are identical. They did not need to be encouraged to study!) In fact, biblical study and exposition, along with the study of the oral Torah, "was the principal activity of rabbinic Judaism" (Barrett, 267).

40 In spite of their diligent efforts to arrive at eternal life through the painstaking study of the words of Scripture, these Jewish leaders did not come to the realization that their very own sacred book testified about Jesus. Separated from the NT witness to Jesus as the Messiah the OT is a book without an ending. It points forward but never realizes its goal. As John the Baptist pointed away from himself to Jesus (1:23–27, 29–31), so also does the OT point beyond itself to the incarnate Son. Christ is the key that unlocks the deeper meaning of the OT. Carson, 263, is right in his assertion that "what is at stake is a comprehensive hermeneutical key." Scripture bore witness to the Son, but the Jews refused to "come to [him] to have life." Temple's observation, 1:117, is all too true that "there is nothing so pathetic as devotion gone astray." Sadly, Jesus is not "heard" or "seen" (v.37) by those who opt for their own approach rather than the way of faith.

41–42 As the previous verses indicate, Jesus does not stand before the Jewish teachers looking for their praise. People intent on currying favor do not chide their audience for lack of insight! Jesus does not rely on the adulation that comes from people but seeks the praise that comes from God (v.44 implied). This is the best way to understand the strong adversative with which v.42 begins (*alla*, "but"). Jesus knows them in the sense that it is clear to him that they do not really love God (taking *tou theou* as an objective genitive). While it may well be that his knowledge of them rested on an understanding of human nature that was his by virtue of his divine sonship (cf. 2:24–25), such knowledge could also be inferred from the statement that follows in the next verse—that although he came from God the Father they rejected him. When truth is rejected, it is clear that the rebel does not love the author of truth. Barclay, 2:198, writes, "They did not really love God; they loved their own ideas about him."

43 So the proof of these opponents' lack of love for God was revealed in their unwillingness to accept the Son who came in his Father's name, i.e., as a manifestation of his essential character. However, "if someone else comes in his own name, [they] will accept [that person]." The credentials that the Jews accept are those that are generated in-house. They have their own method of evaluation. So personal prejudices carry the day, while the dynamic presence of the Son of God convinces no one. How dense is the darkness of self-deception! Commentators have come up with a number of possibilities for the identity of the "someone else": messianic pretenders in the period prior to AD 70 (cf. Josephus, *Ant.* 20.97–99, 171–72), specifically Simon Bar-Kochba, who led the final Jewish revolt about AD 132 (the famous rabbi Akiba called him "the Star of Jacob" [Nu 24:17]), or the Antichrist (commonly in the church fathers). It is better, however, to take the reference in a general sense to those who come with no credentials other than their own self-authorization.

44 Jesus asks rhetorically, "How can you believe [in me]" if in fact you are all caught in gaining praise from one another rather than seeking the praise that comes from God? The obvious answer is that they can't. A mutual admiration society is not interested in believing what does not conform to its own limited and self-centered interests. Love of self has effectively precluded love of God. Lindars, 232, is right when he observes that "the desire to be admired is the besetting sin of petty officialdom everywhere." Emotional dependence on the praise of others incapacitates a person from giving genuine praise to God. Authentic praise of God transcends the boundaries of self-concern. Those who are given to praising others of their own kind and receiving back their praise find it impossible to give glory to the one who comes from God.

45–46 Since the Jews had rejected the one who claimed to be the Son, it would be most natural for them to think that he would, if possible, "accuse [them] before the Father." Jesus puts that supposition to rest with the announcement that their chief prosecutor would be none other than Moses—the very one in whom they were placing their hopes. The figure of Moses was of supreme importance to the Jews. They regarded the great lawgiver as the mediator between God and Israel. According to the *Assumption of Moses* (12:6), Moses had been appointed to pray for their sins and make intercession for them. According to Wayne A. Meeks (*The Prophet King* [Leiden: Brill, 1967], 161), there is evidence that they expected Moses to act as their intercessor in the final judgment. What a shock to learn that Moses would serve not as their advocate but as their judge! Their hopes that he would support them in the great assize will be shattered as he steps forward to bring charges against them. If, however, they had really understood and believed what Moses had written about Jesus, they would have accepted the claims of the Son. They professed to be disciples of

Moses (9:28), but they had missed the central point of the entire OT. The statement that Moses "wrote about" Jesus does not point to some particular verse in the Pentateuch (although some see a reference to Dt 18:15, "The LORD your God will raise up for you a prophet like me from among your own brothers") but refers to the entire law of Moses, which Jesus by his redemptive ministry fulfilled.

47 Jesus closes his discourse with an unanswerable question: If you don't really believe what Moses wrote, how will you be able to believe the claims I have made? To miss the point at a lower level precludes insight at a higher level. Spiritual truth builds on faith and acceptance, not skepticism and denial. It was the nineteenth-century Swiss theologian Frédéric Godet who noted in his commentary on John that "every true disciple of Moses is on the way to becoming a Christian."

NOTES

32 Metzger, 180, notes that the Western reading (οἴδατε, *oidate*, "you [plural] know," GK *3857*) reflects the desire of the copyists to heighten the argument by forcing Jesus' opponents to admit that they knew the evidence of Jesus' witness to be true. But this would be contradicted by v.37, in which Jesus says that they have "neither heard His voice at any time nor seen His form" (NASB).

III. JESUS' CONTINUING MINISTRY AND THE RISE OF OPPOSITION (6:1–8:59)

OVERVIEW

Since ch. 4 closes with Jesus in Galilee and in ch. 5 he is in Jerusalem, some writers rearrange the text by putting ch. 6 (in which Jesus is again in Galilee) immediately after ch. 4 and placing ch. 5 between chs. 6 and 7. The rearrangement is of little help because ch. 7 opens with Jesus in Galilee, while in

ch. 5 he is in Jerusalem. There is no sequence that avoids the sudden shifts of location in the early period of Jesus' ministry. Since no manuscript evidence exists that supports the conjectured reordering, it is best to accept the text as it stands.

A. Jesus' Continuing Ministry (6:1–71)

1. Jesus Feeds the Five Thousand (6:1–15)

OVERVIEW

The account of the feeding of the five thousand is the only incident prior to the triumphal entry that is recorded in all four gospels. This is not surprising in that ch. 6 is the only chapter in John devoted to Jesus' Galilean ministry. Morris, 339, cites three ways in which the account has been understood: (1) as a "miracle" that took place in people's hearts by which they overcame their selfishness and learned to share; (2) as a sacramental meal in which each person received a tiny fragment; or (3) as something that can be described only as a miracle, "something wonderful that actually happened." The uneasiness on the part of some to accept the event as a genuine miracle is an example of the natural human tendency to deny the Creator God the authority to act within his own creation as he chooses. Beasley-Murray, 88, is surely correct in his assessment that "the feeding was not a purely natural event" and that "an act of God is assumed throughout the narrative, and underscored by the response of the crowd described in vv. 14–15."

¹Some time after this, Jesus crossed to the far shore of the Sea of Galilee (that is, the Sea of Tiberias), ²and a great crowd of people followed him because they saw the miraculous signs he had performed on the sick. ³Then Jesus went up on a mountainside and sat down with his disciples. ⁴The Jewish Passover Feast was near.

⁵When Jesus looked up and saw a great crowd coming toward him, he said to Philip, "Where shall we buy bread for these people to eat?" ⁶He asked this only to test him, for he already had in mind what he was going to do.

⁷Philip answered him, "Eight months' wages would not buy enough bread for each one to have a bite!"

⁸Another of his disciples, Andrew, Simon Peter's brother, spoke up, ⁹"Here is a boy with five small barley loaves and two small fish, but how far will they go among so many?"

¹⁰Jesus said, "Have the people sit down." There was plenty of grass in that place, and the men sat down, about five thousand of them. ¹¹Jesus then took the loaves, gave thanks, and distributed to those who were seated as much as they wanted. He did the same with the fish.

¹²When they had all had enough to eat, he said to his disciples, "Gather the pieces that are left over. Let nothing be wasted." ¹³So they gathered them and filled twelve baskets with the pieces of the five barley loaves left over by those who had eaten.

¹⁴After the people saw the miraculous sign that Jesus did, they began to say, "Surely this is the Prophet who is to come into the world." ¹⁵Jesus, knowing that they intended to come and make him king by force, withdrew again to a mountain by himself.

COMMENTARY

1 Following the events of ch. 5, Jesus crossed to the eastern side of the Sea of Galilee. (Directions were normally determined from the western side of the sea, so that when Jesus "crossed to the far shore of the sea," it would be to the eastern side.) In the OT the Sea of Galilee was known as the Sea of Kinnereth (cf. Nu 34:11; Dt 3:17 et al.). At a later time it came to be known as Lake Tiberias, after the city of the same name built by Herod Antipas about AD 20 in honor of Emperor Tiberius. From the earliest gospel we learn that Jesus and the apostles crossed over to the eastern shore to get away from the crowds for a while and rest (Mk 6:31).

2 When the crowds saw where Jesus and the apostles were heading by boat, they ran along the shore and arrived at the eastern side of the lake first (Mk 6:32–34 par.). Since John puts all three verbs in the imperfect tense, one could translate, "The crowds *were following* him because they *were seeing* the miraculous signs that he *was performing* on the sick." John's description of the situation agrees with Mark's observation that "because so many people were coming and going," Jesus and his apostles "did not even have a chance to eat" (6:31). Jesus responded with compassion to the needs of the people. He healed their sick and taught them about the kingdom of God (Mt 14:14; Lk 9:11).

3 Jesus went up on a "mountainside." Several modern translations use the term "mountain" (RSV, NASB, NKJV), but since the same Greek word is used in Revelation 17:9 for the seven *hills* of the city where the great prostitute rules (certainly Rome), it would be misleading to picture what we normally mean by the word "mountain." The place where Jesus will perform his miracle is the high plateau on the northeastern side of the Sea of Galilee (currently known as the Golan Heights). Jesus "sat down"

because that was the normal position for a rabbi when teaching.

4 Only in John is it mentioned that the "Jewish Passover Feast" was at hand. This would be the second of the three Passovers mentioned by John (cf. 2:13; 11:55).

5 From his vantage point Jesus could see the large crowd climbing up the hill. The Synoptics record that the disciples told Jesus to send the crowd away so they could find lodging and buy something to eat. Jesus responded by telling the disciples that they were to provide the food (Mk 6:35–37).

6 Jesus turns to Philip and asks where they can buy bread for the crowd. Philip would know where they could purchase supplies because he came from the nearby town of Bethsaida (cf. 1:44). Jesus didn't actually need Philip's help but was asking him "only to test him." He already knew what he intended to do. John used the verb *peirazō* (GK *4279*), which usually means "to put to the test" with a view to failure, rather than the more positive *dokimazō* ("to prove by testing," GK *1507*). By means of the question, Jesus was putting Philip's faith to the test. How would he react in such a critical situation? Would his faith in Jesus be such that he would expect his master to miraculously meet the needs of a hungry crowd?

7 Philip answers from a strictly natural perspective. Even if food could be found, it would take eight months' wages to buy enough so that each person could have "even a morsel" (Moffatt). The Greek text identifies the amount as *diakosiōn dēnariōn* ("two hundred denarii"). A denarius was considered an acceptable wage for a day's labor. It would purchase about enough for a family's daily need. The NIV's "eight months'" puts the "two hundred denarii" in general terms and evades the problem that results when the amount is translated into a specific dollar figure.

8–9 At this point, Andrew, the brother of Simon Peter, speaks up. In view of the little we know about Andrew, who upon his initial contact with Jesus went immediately to tell his brother Simon (1:35–42), we are not surprised that he was the disciple who noticed the boy and ventured, somewhat hesitantly, a possible solution. The boy is referred to with the double diminutive *paidarion* (GK 4081), which means "little boy" or as we might say, "little tyke." The barley loaves would have been flat round cakes (like pancakes) that had been baked (probably on hot stones) rather than loaves of bread as we currently use the term. The fish (*opsaria*, GK 4066, used only by John in the NT; the Synoptics have the more common *ichthys*, GK 2716) were probably dried and salted and used as a relish with the bread. Though Andrew calls attention to the lad, he appears to have little confidence that such meager supplies will do any good. He adds rhetorically, "but how far will they go among so many?" The remarkable lesson he is about to learn is that little in the hands of Jesus is always more than enough.

10 Jesus directed the disciples to have the people sit down. (Mark adds that they sat "in groups of hundreds and fifties.") Since it was Passover time (March/April), there was plenty of grass there. The NIV correctly translates *anthrōpous* (GK 476) in v.10 as "people" and *andres* (GK 467) as "men." *All* the people sat down, and the number of the men alone was about five thousand (see Mt 14:21). Some writers suggest that the total crowd may have numbered more than twenty thousand. That would be four times the seating capacity of the theater in Sepphoris, a major Galilean city. For Jesus to address such a crowd would be "no small feat" (Keener, 278). Carson, 270, writes that "in the light of v.15, where the people try to make Jesus king by force, it is easy to think that, at least in John, the specification of five

thousand *men* is a way of drawing attention to a potential guerrilla force of eager recruits willing and able to serve the right leader."

11 Jesus took the few barley cakes and fish, gave thanks, and distributed them to the people sitting on the grass. The Synoptics report that Jesus, "looking up to heaven, . . . gave thanks and broke the loaves" (Mk 6:41 par.). Note that Jesus did not "bless the bread"—he "gave thanks" for it. Note also that he *looked up to heaven* to give thanks, a welcome change to the usual "bow your head and pray."

13 "Twelve baskets" were filled with the food that was not eaten. As Temple, 1:74, says, "What was ludicrously inadequate is now ample and an abundance left over." Not only do we learn the practical lesson of not wasting food, but we also learn the spiritual lesson that however bountifully the Lord bestows his grace, there is always more than enough to go around. "He is never impoverished by the generosity of his giving" (Bruce, 145).

14–15 When the people saw the miraculous sign that Jesus performed, they reasoned that this certainly must be the prophet of whom Moses spoke. In Deuteronomy 18:15 Moses counseled the nation not to listen to those who practice sorcery but to listen to a prophet from among their own brothers whom God would raise up to speak for him. While the OT promise referred to a *series* of prophets (see Dt 18:20–22), it is the basis for a messianic expectation that received unique fulfillment in Jesus (see NIVSB note at Dt 18:15; cf. Mt 11:3). Having witnessed the supernatural power of Jesus, the crowd reckoned that if the first Moses were able to lead the children of Israel out of slavery in Egypt, a second Moses would certainly be able to remove the heavy burden of Roman control. So the people saw "the miraculous sign," i.e., they saw Jesus feed an enormous crowd with the meager provisions brought by one small boy, but they did not grasp what it meant or what it foreshadowed. They did not understand that the miracle was not simply a humanitarian response to an immediate need but that it portrayed Jesus as the supplier of people's deepest hunger. They missed the import of the sign. In fact, they completely misconstrued it by interpreting it in terms of national political advantage (v.15). So Jesus, knowing that they were about to seize him and declare him king, withdrew again to the mountain to be alone. He may have recognized in their rising enthusiasm the same temptation he had withstood earlier in his ministry (Mt 4:8–10).

NOTES

1 Of the various names applied to this body of water the most common in the NT is the Sea of Galilee. Only in Luke 5:1 is it called the Lake of Gennesaret, and only in John is it named the Sea of Tiberias (6:1; 21:1). The lake is pear shaped, some thirteen miles long and eight miles wide. It lies approximately 690 feet below sea level and has a maximum depth of about 150 feet. The hills to the east rise to around 2,000 feet.

3 The NASB translates εἰς τὸ ὄρος (*eis to oros*) literally as "on the mountain." The NIV's "on a mountainside" is preferable because in this context no specific ὄρος, *oros* ("mountain"), is intended. In the NT, ὄρος, *oros*, can be either a single mountain (as in 4:20–21) or a range (cf. *TDNT* 5:483).

8 The mention of "barley loaves" reminds us of the account in 2 Kings 4:42–44 in which the man from Baal Shalishah brought twenty loaves of barley bread to Elisha. His skepticism as to whether that amount of bread would be enough to feed one hundred men is not unlike the questions about to be raised by both Philip and his brother Andrew. As it would turn out in both cases, there was bread enough to feed the group with some left over.

2. Jesus Walks on Water (6:16–21)

> ¹⁶When evening came, his disciples went down to the lake, ¹⁷where they got into a boat and set off across the lake for Capernaum. By now it was dark, and Jesus had not yet joined them. ¹⁸A strong wind was blowing and the waters grew rough. ¹⁹When they had rowed three or three and a half miles, they saw Jesus approaching the boat, walking on the water; and they were terrified. ²⁰But he said to them, "It is I; don't be afraid." ²¹Then they were willing to take him into the boat, and immediately the boat reached the shore where they were heading.

COMMENTARY

16–17 The feeding of the five thousand had taken place "late in the afternoon" (Lk 9:12), and by now it was evening. By boat the disciples headed for Capernaum, some five miles to the west. The Synoptics stress the urgency with which Jesus sent his disciples away. Mark said he "made his disciples embark" (6:45 NEB). Then he himself dismissed the crowds and went up the mountainside to pray. It is clear that he did not want his disciples to be caught up in the excitement of the crowd, lest they lend their support to an ill-advised messianic uprising.

It was an extremely difficult crossing. The Sea of Galilee lies some six hundred feet below sea level, and when the cool air flows in to displace the warm moist air over the lake, it often produces violent squalls. The NIV's "set off across the lake" (NASB, "started to cross the sea") translates the Greek *ēr-chonto* (GK 2262) as an ingressive imperfect, but it is better taken with the conative force of the imperfect, "they were trying to cross the lake."

18 John reports that "a strong wind was blowing" and that "the waters grew rough." The difficulty of the crossing is seen in that the appearance of Jesus walking on the water takes place "during the fourth watch of the night" (Mk 6:48), between 3:00 and 6:00 a.m. This means that the disciples had been rowing for at least nine hours. When John writes that "Jesus had not yet joined them," "he is writing from the point of view of one who himself had been in that boat and now, many years later, is writing the story" (Hendriksen, 1:224).

19 The disciples had rowed only three to four miles when they saw Jesus approaching, walking on the water. With the boat plowing west through the heavy waves the disciples would be facing east as they rowed with their backs to the wind. So as Jesus approached he would be coming up toward the stern of the boat. Mark says he "was about to pass by them" when the disciples saw him and thought he was a ghost (Mk 6:49). But Jesus identified himself to them and encouraged them not to be afraid. Then "they were glad to take him into the boat" (TCNT), and immediately they reached their destination.

Strange as it may seem to the average reader, there are some who question whether we are to take the account as involving a miracle. William Barclay, 1:208–9, pictures the disciples hugging the shoreline as they rowed through the heavy waters. The journey was only a few miles, and the disciples bending over their oars were unaware that they had almost made it to their destination. Looking up, they saw Jesus *epi tēs thalassēs* [GK 2498], "by the seashore." Alarmed at first, they then heard across the waters "that well loved voice—'It is I; don't be afraid.'" They wanted him to come aboard, but they were almost at land.

While it is true that *epi tēs thalassēs* may mean "by the sea" (as in 21:1), the same phrase is used in the present setting by both synoptic writers to mean "on the lake" (Mt 14:26; Mk 6:48). This follows from Matthew's statement that "the boat was already a considerable distance from land" (Mt 14:24) and Mark's placing of the boat "in the middle of the lake" (Mk 6:47). Barrett, 281, is right when he says that "there can be little doubt that both Mark and John . . . intended to record a miracle." If Jesus were merely calling out encouragement from the safety of the nearby shore, it is difficult to imagine why the disciples would have been terrified when they saw him.

20–21 Jesus' response to the frightened disciples was "it is I; don't be afraid." *Egō eimi* has been understood in different ways. Some sense a trace of divine disclosure that reflects Psalm 77:16, 19, in which God comes "in powerful theophany to the aid of his people at the Exodus" (Beasley-Murray, 89). Others understand it as simply a form of self-identification (e.g., Carson, 275). Because the blind man in John 9:9 uses the same phrase of himself, it is more plausible to understand Jesus as simply identifying himself to the disciples. It is clear from the synoptic accounts that Jesus did get into the boat. Some have taken John's statement that the disciples "were willing to take him into the boat" to mean that they were willing but that it was not necessary because "immediately the boat reached the shore." Thus we would have yet another miracle. That Matthew places the account of Peter's attempt to walk to Jesus on the water at this point before they climb into the boat (Mt 14:28–31) argues against this interpretation. J. A. McClymont understands "immediately" to mean "that the vessel went straight to its destination, and that the remaining mile or two seemed as nothing to the astonished and rejoicing disciples" (cited in Morris, 351 n. 44).

3. Further Teaching (6:22–71)

a. Bread of life (6:22–59)

22The next day the crowd that had stayed on the opposite shore of the lake realized that only one boat had been there, and that Jesus had not entered it with his disciples, but that they had gone away alone. 23Then some boats from Tiberias landed near the place where the people had eaten the bread after the Lord had given thanks. 24Once the crowd realized that neither Jesus nor his disciples were there, they got into the boats and went to Capernaum in search of Jesus.

25When they found him on the other side of the lake, they asked him, "Rabbi, when did you get here?"

26Jesus answered, "I tell you the truth, you are looking for me, not because you saw miraculous signs but because you ate the loaves and had your fill. 27Do not work for food that spoils, but for food that endures to eternal life, which the Son of Man will give you. On him God the Father has placed his seal of approval."

28Then they asked him, "What must we do to do the works God requires?"

29Jesus answered, "The work of God is this: to believe in the one he has sent."

30So they asked him, "What miraculous sign then will you give that we may see it and believe you? What will you do? 31Our forefathers ate the manna in the desert; as it is written: 'He gave them bread from heaven to eat.'"

32Jesus said to them, "I tell you the truth, it is not Moses who has given you the bread from heaven, but it is my Father who gives you the true bread from heaven. 33For the bread of God is he who comes down from heaven and gives life to the world."

34"Sir," they said, "from now on give us this bread."

35Then Jesus declared, "I am the bread of life. He who comes to me will never go hungry, and he who believes in me will never be thirsty. 36But as I told you, you have seen me and still you do not believe. 37All that the Father gives me will come to me, and whoever comes to me I will never drive away. 38For I have come down from heaven not to do my will but to do the will of him who sent me. 39And this is the will of him who sent me, that I shall lose none of all that he has given me, but raise them up at the last day. 40For my Father's will is that everyone who looks to the Son and believes in him shall have eternal life, and I will raise him up at the last day."

⁴¹At this the Jews began to grumble about him because he said, "I am the bread that came down from heaven." ⁴²They said, "Is this not Jesus, the son of Joseph, whose father and mother we know? How can he now say, 'I came down from heaven'?"

⁴³"Stop grumbling among yourselves," Jesus answered. ⁴⁴"No one can come to me unless the Father who sent me draws him, and I will raise him up at the last day. ⁴⁵It is written in the Prophets: 'They will all be taught by God.' Everyone who listens to the Father and learns from him comes to me. ⁴⁶No one has seen the Father except the one who is from God; only he has seen the Father. ⁴⁷I tell you the truth, he who believes has everlasting life. ⁴⁸I am the bread of life. ⁴⁹Your forefathers ate the manna in the desert, yet they died. ⁵⁰But here is the bread that comes down from heaven, which a man may eat and not die. ⁵¹I am the living bread that came down from heaven. If anyone eats of this bread, he will live forever. This bread is my flesh, which I will give for the life of the world."

⁵²Then the Jews began to argue sharply among themselves, "How can this man give us his flesh to eat?"

⁵³Jesus said to them, "I tell you the truth, unless you eat the flesh of the Son of Man and drink his blood, you have no life in you. ⁵⁴Whoever eats my flesh and drinks my blood has eternal life, and I will raise him up at the last day. ⁵⁵For my flesh is real food and my blood is real drink. ⁵⁶Whoever eats my flesh and drinks my blood remains in me, and I in him. ⁵⁷Just as the living Father sent me and I live because of the Father, so the one who feeds on me will live because of me. ⁵⁸This is the bread that came down from heaven. Your forefathers ate manna and died, but he who feeds on this bread will live forever." ⁵⁹He said this while teaching in the synagogue in Capernaum.

COMMENTARY

22–25 The syntax of these verses is a bit perplexing, but the general idea is relatively clear. On the next day the crowd, which was still on the eastern side of the lake where Jesus had fed the five thousand, realized that neither Jesus nor his disciples were still there. They had seen the disciples leave in the only available boat and were aware that Jesus had gone up the mountainside to be alone, but now he too was missing. What had happened? Fortunately for them, some boats from Tiberias had come ashore nearby (v.23), perhaps blown in from the west by the storm. So they got into the boats and went to Capernaum to look for Jesus (v.24). When they found him, they asked, "Rabbi, when did you get here?" (v.25). The obvious question would have been, "*How* did you get here?" but even after the miraculous provision of food they weren't about to pursue the real significance of the sign. Better an unimportant question than to venture into a realm that for them was apparently quite uncomfortable. Anyway, their intention was to pursue the possibility of making him king, not to learn of a messianic mission that had no nationalistic relevance.

26 Jesus does not answer the question but tells the people in a straightforward fashion that their motivation for searching him out was wrong. It was not because they had grasped the true significance of the miraculous sign (the multiplication of the loaves and fish) but because they had eaten the loaves and had their fill. They saw the sign but missed its true import. What they did see in the miracle was the possibility of a leader who could benefit them in a material sense. Temple, 1:84, writes that "if what is eternal is valued chiefly as a means to any temporal result, the true order is reversed."

27 Jesus tells the crowd to change their priorities radically. They are to stop working (*ergazesthe* [GK *2237*] *mē*, present imperative plus *mē*) for the "food that spoils" and work rather for the "food that endures to eternal life." The only thing that material food can do is to sustain physical life. What matters is a person's inner spiritual life. What that requires is a "food" appropriate to life in relationship to God. Obviously it is not the *food* that remains forever but the life that it sustains.

One cannot help but notice the parallel between the two kinds of food in ch. 6 and the two kinds of water in ch. 4. The "living water" of 4:10–15 is one with the "food that endures to eternal life" of 6:28. Normal water leads again to thirst and regular food to a renewed hunger. But to drink living water is to never thirst again (4:14) and to eat the food that Jesus gives is to live forever (6:28). As Scripture says, "Man does not live on bread alone, but on every word that comes from the mouth of God" (Mt 4:4; cf. Dt 8:3).

It is the "Son of Man" who provides the food that leads to eternal life. Later we will find that he himself is the food he provides (6:53–57). He has been sealed by God the Father for that very purpose. Some call attention to the aorist *esphragisen* ("sealed," GK *5381*) and look for a specific act of sealing in the life of Jesus. Either his baptism or the subsequent descent of the Spirit is usually mentioned. The NIV understands the seal placed by God on his Son to be a "seal of approval." Brown,

261, however, writes, "Here God set His seal on the Son, not so much by way of approval, but more by way of consecration." Bruce, 150, says the Son is "the one whom God has appointed as his certified and authorized agent for the bestowal of this life-giving food." Jesus, as the life-giving Son of Man, has been set aside and consecrated for the purpose of giving himself as the food that brings eternal life.

28–29 The moment Jesus speaks of working, the Jews think of the "works" required by the law that they understood would result in eternal life. So they ask what they must do in order to "do the works God requires." Jesus' answer contradicts everything they took for granted about the way to gain right standing with God. You ask about "works" (plural) but let me tell you about the only "work" (singular) that God requires. It is "to believe in the one he has sent."

The fourth gospel is at one with Paul and his message of justification by faith alone (Ro 3:22). It is trusting in Jesus, i.e., placing one's entire confidence in the redemptive power of his death and resurrection, that fulfills the requirement of God. Faith in the Son is a "work" only in the sense that it gains God's favor. In and of itself it is without merit. It earns nothing; it merely receives the good pleasure of the Father. Our "work" is an open hand stretched out to a Father desirous to give. Barrett, 287, notes that the present (continuous) tense of *pisteuēte* ("believe," GK *4409*) is perhaps significant: it is "not an *act* of faith, but a *life* of faith." The mistaken idea that a moment of belief ensures an eternity of bliss, regardless of the way a person subsequently lives, is a heresy of gigantic proportion. Throughout Scripture the reader is reminded again and again that a faith that does not alter life is no faith at all (cf. Jas 2:14–26).

30 The response of the Jews to Jesus is genuinely amazing. They had witnessed the supernatural multiplication of a few pieces of bread so that an entire crowd of perhaps twenty thousand had all they wanted and more to spare. They had watched the only available boat leave with only the disciples aboard, yet in the morning Jesus was no longer in their area but on the other side of the lake. Still they ask "what miraculous sign" Jesus will perform so they can "see it and believe [him]." As Ryle, 3:364–65, puts it, "The plain truth is that it is want of heart, not want of evidence, that keeps people back from Christ." The desire to see in order to believe is the way of the unbeliever. The divine order is, "Taste and see that the LORD is good" (Ps 34:8). In fact, "Rigid proof would render impossible the work of God, which is to believe in Jesus" (Barrett, 288). It is worth noting that in their answer the Jews do not use the normal *pisteuō eis* ("to believe in, to put one's trust in") but follow the verb with a dative. They are challenged by Jesus to put their faith *in him*, but their response reveals that they are interested only in determining whether or not they should accept what he has to say *about himself*.

31 So the people say in effect, "Prove yourself. Your claims are greater than Moses ever made. He gave manna to the Israelites when they were wandering in the desert. What will *you* do?" It was widely believed that in the messianic age the gift of manna would be renewed. The second-century AD *2 Baruch* (*Syriac Apocalypse*) says, "The treasury of manna shall again descend from on high, and they will eat of it in those years" (29:8; see Brown, 265, for additional references). The people reason that Jesus' multiplication of bread is fine as far as it goes. But if he claims that the messianic age has actually dawned, let him supply manna, as did their forefather Moses. The source of the quotation "he gave them bread from heaven to eat" is probably Psalm 78:24: "he rained down manna for the people to eat" (cf. Ex 16:4; Ne 9:15; Ps 105:40); however, as they are about to learn, it was not Moses but God who gave them "the bread from heaven."

It is worth noting here the monograph of Peder Borgen (*Bread from Heaven* [NovTSup 10; Leiden: Brill, 1965). By studying the homiletic structure in Philo and the Palestinian *midrashim*, he arrived at some standard features of Jewish exegesis. A specific text of Scripture is cited and then quite often paraphrased. The body of the homily opens with a statement that is repeated at the end. A secondary citation is often brought in that helps develop the main commentary. Borgen points out that John 6 follows this pattern: v.31 is the main text, vv.32–33 supply a paraphrase of the text; vv.35–50 represent a homily on the text that discusses sequentially the themes of "bread," "from heaven," and "eating." The opening statement of the homily ("I am the bread of life," v.35) is repeated verbatim at the close (v.48). Carson, 287–88, agrees that "many features of [Borgen's] argument are convincing" but questions his suggestion that John used these midrashic methods to counter Docetism.

32 In accordance with the established practice of rabbinic debates, Jesus responded by correcting their misunderstanding of the passage just cited. The importance of his answer is underscored by the formulaic statement "I tell you the truth." It is "not Moses who has given you the bread from heaven," as shown by the syntax, which emphasizes *ou Mōysēs* by placing it at the beginning of the clause. Rather, it is "my Father" who gives you the true heavenly bread. Note the following: (1) While the people didn't actually say that Moses was the one who had given them "bread from heaven," in view of the human tendency to elevate the man above the message, it was important to make clear the fact that the gift of manna came from God. Moses was merely the one who conveyed God's instructions to the people (Ex 16). (2) While manna could be said to come "from heaven" in the sense that God provided it miraculously, it was not the "true bread from heaven." It satisfied physical hunger but was unable to meet the deeper spiritual hunger of the human heart. (3) The present tense *didōsin* ("is giving you," GK *1443*) anticipates the truth clearly stated a few verses later that Jesus is the true bread, which God is giving right now in the gift of his Son. Barrett, 290, writes, "God *now gives* you what Moses could only foreshadow."

33 In context, the "bread of God" is the bread supplied by God. Since the Greek word for "bread" (*artos*, GK *788*) is masculine, it could be the bread of God that "comes down from heaven." But since both the present and aorist forms of the participle are used throughout ch. 6 in reference to Jesus (vv.33, 41, 50, 51, 58), it is better to read "he who comes down." The predicate should be taken as personal rather than impersonal. He is the one who "gives life to the world." The redemptive ministry of the Son was never intended to be limited to a chosen few but reaches out to the entire human race. Morris, 364, writes, "Here is no narrow particularism but a concern for all mankind."

34 That Jesus is in fact the life-giving bread that God has sent down from heaven has not sunk into the consciousness of Jesus' listeners. They respond with some deference: "Sir, . . . from now on give us this bread." Their response is similar to that of the Samaritan woman, who took "living water" to be some sort of a constant supply of water that would keep her from getting thirsty and make the daily trip to the well unnecessary (3:15). How easily we miss the spiritual impact of Jesus' teachings in our natural haste to interpret them in terms of material satisfactions! "From now on" suggests that the people expected the bread from heaven to be given repeatedly. They understood the offer to be for a continual supply of bread.

35 We now encounter the first of the seven famous "I am" statements in the fourth gospel—"I am the bread of life." The OT background is God's response to Moses, who has asked him what to tell those who inquire concerning the name of the one who sent him. God reveals his name as "I AM WHO I AM." He chooses to be known and worshiped as "I AM" (Ex 3:14). In John 8:58 Jesus applies the name to himself ("before Abraham was born, I am!"). There is a difference of opinion, however, as to the extent to which Jesus is emphasizing his own deity in the seven "I am" statements. Though Brown, 269, says that "*ego eimi* with a predicate does not reveal Jesus' essence but reflects his dealings with men," it is difficult to escape the conclusion that when Jesus uses an "I am" statement, he intends it to be understood in a revelatory sense.

Jesus corrects their misunderstanding. He is not the *giver* of the bread—God the Father does that—he *is* the bread itself. The bread of life is the "bread that gives life" (Goodspeed). Ryle, 3:373, says that Jesus "intended to be to the soul what bread is to the body: its food." It follows that whoever comes to Jesus will "never go [away] hungry" and whoever believes in him will "never be thirsty." The parallel clauses interpret one another: coming to Jesus (see vv.37, 44, 45, 65 in ch. 6 alone) is simply another way of portraying what it means to believe. It is more than mental acquiescence; it involves the activity of the will. It is the vital response of the human person to the invitation of God. While it is true that all who believe must be "drawn" to God (6:44, 65), it is equally true that none are forced against their will to go; each must "come."

It is important to understand what Jesus means by his promise that those who come believing will never be thirsty or go hungry. It does not mean that they will no longer have any desire for spiritual things. What it does mean is well stated by Morris, 366, who says that "it rules out forever the possibility of that unsatisfied hunger." Or as Carson, 288, puts it, "It does mean there is no longer that core emptiness that the initial encounter with Jesus has met." Jesus' promise is sometimes contrasted with

Wisdom's statement in Sirach 24:21, "Those who eat of me will hunger for more, and those who drink of me will thirst for more." But the two statements are complementary rather than contradictory. Spiritual food both satisfies and creates the desire for more. What is permanently satisfied by eating the bread of life is the deep-seated hunger in the hearts of people created in the image of God. He created us for fellowship with himself, and nothing short of that intimate association will ever satisfy.

36 The Jews to whom Jesus was speaking had seen the miraculous sign (following the MSS that omit *me*; see Notes), yet they still did not believe. Temple, 1:88, remarks, "The miracle of feeding was to them a convenience rather than a revelation." One is reminded of Abraham's response to the rich man in hell who wanted someone to warn his five brothers about the place of torment: "If they do not listen to Moses and the Prophets, they will not be convinced even if someone rises from the dead" (Lk 16:31). Miracles point beyond themselves only for those who see with the eyes of faith.

37 Verses 37–40 are rich in theological truth. We learn first of the irresistible power of God's electing grace. The entire company of the elect (hence the neuter *pan*, "all," in v.37) that the Father is giving to the Son will in fact come to him. The coming by faith to the Son is the unmistakable indication that they have been chosen by God. Believers do not come *because* they are elect, nor are they elect *because* God knew ahead of time that they would come (a misunderstanding of "foreknowledge" in Ro 8:29). Divine election and believing faith are the two basic elements in salvation. We have here what J. I. Packer calls an "antimony"—two statements that, while each is absolutely true, nevertheless resist being brought together into a rational relationship. Not only will all who have been chosen come to Jesus; they will come with the assurance that he "will never drive [them] away." This phrase is normally taken as an example of "litotes," a figure of speech in which a negative is used strongly to affirm the opposite. Thus "I will never ever cast outside" means "I will welcome heartily" (Lindars, 261) or "I will certainly keep in, preserve" (Carson, 290). In either case, the promise is that to come to Jesus is in fact to be accepted and kept safely.

38 The reason believers may count on Jesus' infinite care is that he has "come down from heaven" to carry out not his own will but the will of his heavenly Father. Six times in ch. 6 alone Jesus refers to his coming "down from heaven" (vv.33, 38, 41, 50, 51, 58), a phrase that points to the ultimate source and certification of his role as the giver of life. Note also that the expression is strong evidence of the preexistence of Christ. As the NEB states, "When all things began, the Word already was" (1:1). By stressing that he "comes down from heaven," Jesus clearly establishes heaven as his eternal home. This in turn grants authority to all that he has to say. What Jesus says is to be believed because it has its origin in the presence of the one who cannot but tell the truth (cf. Nu 23:19; Tit 1:2).

39 The Son has been sent on a mission to do the will of the Father. What the Father wills is twofold. First, says Jesus, I am to "lose none of all that he has given me." The eternal security of true believers is not dependent on their own feeble hold on Jesus. They are safe because it is the Father's will that Jesus lose not a single one of them. Hendriksen, 1:235, is correct in his view that "the doctrine of *the perseverance of the saints* is taught here in unmistakable terms." For the true believer to be lost would prove that Jesus is incapable of carrying out the will of the Father. Were that true, it would follow that none of his many other promises could be relied on with any degree of certainty. The second part of the Father's will is that the Son will "raise . . . up at the last day" all those given to him. Not only are true believers kept secure during the difficult passage through life, but they are also assured that at the end they will be raised to enjoy the eternal presence of the triune God. While much of the fourth gospel teaches a "realized eschatology," it does not rule out an eschatology yet to be fulfilled. Bruce, 154, writes, "To treat John's eschatology as exclusively 'realized' is to overlook those passages where Jesus is described as raising his people up 'at the last day' (see also vv. 44, 54; 11:24; 12:48)."

40 This major unit of the "bread of life" discourse (vv. 32–40) closes with a summary statement that "everyone [note the singular *pas*, each individual believer; compare with the neuter singular *pan* in v. 37b] who looks to the Son [cf. Nu 21:9; Jn 3:14] and believes in him shall have eternal life." And as a vital part in that divine plan they will be raised "at the last day." God's plan is, in essence, quite simple; his part is to provide the basis for our salvation and to preserve to the end those he has chosen. Our role is simply to place our faith in what he says he can and will accomplish. It is to place our trust without reserve in Jesus.

41 If the unit comprising vv. 32–40 is an exposition of "he gave them bread from heaven" (see the proemial text in v. 31), then vv. 41–51 constitutes an exposition of "bread from heaven to eat." When the Jews understood Jesus to say that he would supply them with the bread from heaven, they were anxious to receive it on a continuing basis (see comments at v. 34). But his claim to *be* that bread was quite another matter. Though John does not quote Jesus (in v. 41) as saying exactly what the Jews understood him to say ("I am the bread that came down from heaven"), all the ingredients are included in the previous discourse ("I am the bread of life," v. 35; "I have come down from heaven," v. 38).

So the Jews "began to grumble" (inceptive imperfect). The Greek verb (*gongyzō*, GK *1197*) is onomatopoeic and is used in the NT primarily "with the connotation of people speaking against

God in a reprehensible way" (*EDNT* 1:256). Temple, 1:89, would soften the situation slightly; he writes that "the Lord's hearers are more bewildered than antagonized." In the LXX the term is used of the complaints of the people of Israel during their wandering in the wilderness. They grumbled about the bitter water at Marah (Ex 15:23–24), the lack of food (16:2–3), and their hardships (Nu 11:1) and danger (Nu 14:1–3; cf. 1Co 10:10).

It is a bit surprising to find Jesus engaged in a discussion with "the Jews" at this point. The last mention of those to whom he was speaking was in v. 25, where those who "found him on the other side of the lake" were Galileans who were present at the feeding of the five thousand and who had traveled across the lake in pursuit of the one who had performed the miraculous sign. Some have suggested that the Jews mentioned in v. 41 were a group from Judea who had come to find out what was going on. This is unlikely because they knew about Jesus' family (v. 42). It is better to postulate a change of locale at some point in the chapter. By the time we arrive at v. 58, Jesus will be in the synagogue at Capernaum. From this we may reason that the Jews mentioned in v. 41 were members of the local synagogue, probably leaders.

42 Offended at Jesus' statement that he had come down from heaven, they kept on murmuring to one another (the imperfect *elegon*, GK *3306*, "they said," supplies the content of their "grumbling") about what they considered a highly outrageous claim. "After all, isn't this one who is claiming to have come from heaven simply Jesus, the son of Joseph the carpenter? [The rhetorical question calls for an affirmative answer.] And don't we know his father and mother? Of course we do! Then how can he say that he came down from heaven?" From their perspective, the logic was irrefutable. Jesus was either misguided or, even worse, attempting to foist off on them a fraudulent claim of essential superiority. The lowly nature of Jesus' earthly condition presented a stumbling block to natural man (cf. Ryle, 3:382).

43–44 Jesus doesn't bother to answer the issues they raise. To allow them to set the tone and control the discussion would lead nowhere. So Jesus tells them to "stop grumbling." Their premises are wrong and their conjectures are leading them in the wrong direction. The people who "come to Jesus" are those who are drawn by the Father (v.44). The Greek word for "draw" (*helkyō*, GK *1816*) when used literally means "to draw" or "to tug" (*TDNT* 2:503; in Ac 16:19 Paul and Silas are "dragged" before the authorities). When taken figuratively (as here in Jn 6:44) it means "to compel." Barclay, 1:220, notes that "it almost always implies some kind of resistance." Morris, 371 n. 110, adds, "God brings men to Himself although by nature they prefer sin." Most commentators hold that John is speaking here of a drawing that goes far beyond moral influence; it is a drawing akin to divine election. No one is able to come to the Father unless the Father draws him or her. In connection with the restoration of Israel, God through the prophet Jeremiah says, "I have loved you with an everlasting love; I have drawn you with loving-kindness" (Jer 31:3). Interestingly, in John 12:32 Jesus says that when he is lifted up, he "will draw all men" to himself. The apparent contradiction is eased when we understand that in ch. 12 Jesus speaks of "all men without distinction" rather than "all men without exception" (Carson, 293). In his sacrificial death, Jesus will draw to himself people of every cultural, social, and ethnic background (12:32), but unless a specific person is drawn, that person cannot come to Christ (6:44). The drawing here is not the persuasive power of God's concern for all, but the irresistible attraction of his grace for the elect. The CEV translates, "No one can come to me, unless the Father who sent me makes them want to come." And those who do come will be raised to life "at the last day"—

another indication that "realized eschatology" is only part of the whole story. The Father initiates the work of grace in the human heart, and the Son brings it to completion.

45 We learn now how this drawing takes place. In the Prophets (the second division of the Hebrew Bible) we read, "All your sons will be taught by the LORD" (Isa 54:13). People are drawn through divinely revealed truth, through insight into the nature and purpose of God revealed in Jesus. We are not dealing here with some sort of personal mystical knowledge. It is the person who "listens to the Father and learns from him" that comes to Jesus. The Father has something to say, and it is to be learned. Truth received and acted on leads inevitably to Jesus. The entire redemptive process has an inner logic that the person genuinely open to the work of the Spirit cannot successfully resist.

46 Jesus alone is uniquely qualified to speak of God because he is the only person who "has seen the Father." As we listen to him and obey what he says, we are increasingly drawn to God. Without this dynamic, there may be a modicum of spiritual interest in who Jesus might be, but there is no power to lift us to the very presence of God.

47–48 Verses 47–48 restate the truth that the person who believes in Jesus has, as a present possession, "everlasting life." The present tense of the participle "he who believes" (*ho pisteuōn*, GK *4409*) stresses the continuing necessity of faith. Faith is not a onetime event that covers all exigencies of the future but an ongoing trust in God that transforms the life and conduct of the believer in the here and now. Everlasting life belongs to those who are allowing faith to become the controlling factor of their existence. "I am the bread of life," said Jesus, "and everlasting life belongs to those who receive me and make me their spiritual nourishment."

49–50 Jesus draws a stark contrast between himself as "the bread of life" and "the manna" that the

Israelites ate while in the desert. While that bread sustained them physically for a time, nevertheless they died. "The manna not only could do nothing for the soul, but was unable to preserve from death those who ate it" (Ryle, 3:393). But now, Jesus comes as the true bread from heaven, and those who eat it will "not die" (spiritually). The present active *katabainōn* (GK 2849) reflects the continuing availability of Jesus, the bread from heaven. It "keeps coming down" in that he is always near at hand to nourish and provide eternal life.

51 Jesus summarizes this section of his discourse by reaffirming that he is the "living bread" come down from heaven and that whoever "eats of this bread . . . will live forever." But now a new element is added: "This bread is my flesh." The language is sacrificial. A number of writers understand this as a reference to the Eucharist. That the regular use of *sōma* ("body," GK 5393) in connection with the Lord's Supper is replaced here with *sarx* ("flesh," GK 4922) is explained as John's following a different textual tradition. Responding to those who speak as though the word *flesh* "self-evidently marked a reference to Holy Communion," Morris, 374, says rather bluntly, "It, of course, does nothing of the sort." Bruce, 158, is correct in his view that "to give one's flesh can scarcely mean anything other than death, and the wording here points to a death which is both voluntary ('I will give') and vicarious ('for the life of the world')." The "life of the world" for which Jesus will give himself refers to the eternal fellowship with God made possible by the sacrificial death of Jesus and offered to all who will respond in faith. It is the "world" that "God so loved . . . that he gave his one and only Son" (3:16). Here we catch the vision of a wide and expansive redemptive mission in which God freely bestows his saving grace on all who place their trust in him. The same world that so desperately needs the forgiving grace of God is the very world of

people for whom eternal life is made possible through the Son.

52 Jesus' statement that his own flesh was the bread of life come down from heaven caused considerable consternation among the leaders of the synagogue. They began to "argue sharply among themselves," or as Weymouth has it, "This led to an angry debate among the Jews." *Machomai* (GK 3481) is a strong verb that, when taken literally, means "to fight" or "to battle." (*EDNT*, 1:398, says that in Ac 7:26 it is used in the sense of "hand-to-hand combat.") The Jews were seriously offended by the repugnant idea of eating flesh—even the Greco-Roman world viewed any kind of "cannibalism" with horror. And if Jesus meant to be understood as speaking figuratively, what in the world did his remark mean? Little wonder that they got embroiled in a confusing argument.

Their caustic reference to "this man" exposes their scornful attitude. Only a "man like this" would make such a scandalous claim! Lindars, 267, introduces an alternative possibility stemming from the fact that the majority of MSS omit the word "his" in v.52. In that case, the Jews, in their response to what Jesus had said, would be thinking that he had alluded to Exodus 16:8, where Moses spoke of God's supply of meat every evening. Thus the point would not be a scandalous claim but a misunderstanding of how Jesus would be able to provide yet another foodstuff. But Jesus had just spoken of "my flesh" (v.51), and in the following sentence he speaks of "the flesh of the Son of Man" (v.53). Furthermore it is doubtful that a mere misunderstanding would have led to such a serious argument.

53–54 Jesus now expands the figure and in so doing manages to become even more offensive to the Jewish listeners. He introduces the central theme of the paragraph with a conditional statement: unless you eat the flesh and drink the blood of the Son of Man, you do not have life. It is only those who eat his flesh and drink his blood who have eternal life, and they are the ones who will be raised up at the last day (v.54).

Before looking at specific items, it will serve us well to discuss the approach that understands these verses in terms of the Eucharist. Roman Catholic scholar Raymond Brown, 284, holds that while the eucharistic theme was secondary in vv.35–50, it now (vv.51–58) "comes to the fore and becomes the exclusive theme." He proposes, 287, the hypothesis that "the backbone of vv.51–58 is made up of material from the Johannine narrative of the institution of the Eucharist which originally was located in the Last Supper scene and that this material has been recast into a duplicate of the Bread of Life Discourse." It was then added to vv.35–50 when the fourth gospel was in its final redaction.

Several objections have been raised to this sacramental interpretation. Verse 54 states in an unqualified manner that it is those who eat Jesus' flesh and drink his blood who have eternal life. If taken sacramentally, this would mean that the only requirement for salvation is to partake of the Eucharist, a position at odds with NT teaching as a whole. Second, the word that Jesus uses for flesh is *sarx*, while in every NT text that uses the words of institution (Mt 26:26; Mk 14:22; Lk 22:19; 1Co 11:24) the word is *sōma* ("body"). Variation in a ritual formula would be highly unlikely. Third, the parallel relationship between v.54 and v.40 indicates that eating Jesus' flesh and drinking his blood is a metaphorical way of expressing looking to the Son and believing in him. Carson, 297, writes that this "conclusion is obvious" and quotes Augustine's famous dictum, "Believe, and you have eaten." Finally, in v.63 we will learn that the things Jesus has been telling them "are spiritual and are life" (Phillips); "the flesh confers no benefit whatever" (Weymouth). So Jesus in his "bread of life" discourse is not speaking directly of the Lord's Supper. It does not follow, however, that what he is saying has no relevance to Holy Communion. Bruce, 161, writes that Jesus "does expound the truth which the Lord's Supper conveys." Carson, 298, arrives at the same conclusion: "In short, John 6 does not directly speak of the eucharist; it does expose the true meaning of the Lord's Supper as clearly as any passage in Scripture."

Several specific items in vv.53–54 call for attention. As noted earlier (in connection with 1:51; 3:13, 14; 5:27), "Son of Man" is Jesus' favorite self-designation. It emphasizes his role as the one through whom God reveals himself to humanity. He is the "eternal contact between heaven and earth" (Barrett, 187). That both verbs in the conditional clause of v.53 ("eat," "drink") are aorist points to once-for-all actions. Eating and drinking the Son of Man is a vivid way of presenting the truth that in order to have eternal life, people must take Christ into their inner being. It is interesting that in v.54 Jesus uses a different word for eating. Instead of the more common *esthiō* (GK *2266*; or more accurately, the aorist stem *phag-*; fifteen times in the fourth gospel), Jesus chooses a word that in classical Greek was used of eating by animals. *Trōgō* (GK *5592*) means to "gnaw, nibble, munch, eat (audibly)" (BDAG, 1019). This relatively crude term presses home the literal picture that Jesus wants to stress. Some think he uses it to counter docetic attempts to spiritualize what he is saying. He wants his listeners to understand that they must assimilate him if they desire eternal life.

55 Jesus continues to expand his theme by stressing that his flesh is real food and his blood is real drink. By reading *alēthōs* (an adverb meaning "truly, indeed," GK *242*) rather than *alēthēs* (an adjective meaning "real, genuine," GK *239*), some manuscripts understand Jesus to be stressing the genuine value of his flesh and blood as food and drink rather than contrasting it with something else (so Brown,

283). Although both NA[27] and UBS[4] read the adjective, the manuscripts with the adverb make better sense.

56 "To remain" or "to abide in" is a favorite expression of John and occurs some seventy times in the Johannine literature (cf. its occurrence only three times in Matthew and twice in Luke). BDAG, 631, says that it denotes "an inward, enduring personal communion." Note here that the eating and drinking is put in the present tense, which stresses its continuing quality. Those who make a practice of eating and drinking the flesh and blood of Jesus sustain that personal relationship. This makes possible the reciprocal indwelling of Christ in the believer ("and I in him").

57 The Father is the "living Father" (a title found only here in the NT) not only because he has life in himself but because he is the source of all life. Note that Jesus speaks of a believer as "one who feeds on me." This is what it means to eat his flesh and drink his blood (stated five times in vv.51–56). Since Jesus is obviously not promoting cannibalism, one must take the words as a figurative expression for personal assimilation.

58 Jesus draws the discourse to a close with a summary statement that ties together the major points he has just made. He is "the bread that came down from heaven." Although the Israelites ate manna in the wilderness, they still died. Their manna provided physical nourishment for as long as they needed it. But whoever feeds on the bread that Jesus gives "will live forever."

59 The final verse in the section tells us that Jesus said these things (perhaps everything from v.27 on, but more likely from one of the several breaks in the discourse: vv.32, 35, 43, or 53) while teaching in the synagogue in Capernaum. Visitors to the site at Tell-Hum see the ruins of a second-century synagogue that may well have been erected on the same site as the one where Jesus has just been teaching.

NOTES

23 Although Tiberias was a leading city in the region during the time of Jesus, it is mentioned only here in the NT. There is no indication that Jesus in his earthly ministry ever visited Tiberias. Built by Herod Antipas ca. AD 18–22 (and named after the emperor Tiberius), it served as the capital of Herod's tetrarchy of Galilee and Perea. Earlier (in 4 BC) he had built his capital at Sepphoris, the second city of the region, but the new site along the western shore of the lake was more central to the two districts under his control and more closely related to the road system. During the city's construction, workmen stumbled onto an ancient burial place and the Jews withdrew to avoid ceremonial defilement. Herod then populated the city with a collection of poor people and foreigners (cf. Josephus, *Ant.* 18.2.3). The modern city lies somewhat north of the ancient site. Interestingly, the city once declared unclean became a century or so later one of the four sacred sites in Israel. The Talmud reports thirteen synagogues in Tiberias (cf. *b. Ber.* 8*a*; 30*b*).

30 The NET study note at 6:25–31 explains the request for a sign in view of the recent feeding of the five thousand by positing two different groups within the crowd. Those who had witnessed the miracle and come across the lake from Capernaum are addressed in vv.26–27, while others who had not seen the miracle are addressed in vv.30–31. However, there is no compelling reason to believe that Jesus is addressing two groups of people in vv.26–31. There is no change of audience between the "they" of v.28 and the "they" of v.30.

31 From the Jewish perspective, Jesus was simply not in the same league with Moses: Jesus fed five thousand and that only once; Moses fed an entire nation for forty years (see NIVSB note at 6:31).

35 The other "I am" statements are "I am the light of the world," 8:12; "I am the gate," 10:7; "I am the good shepherd," 10:11; "I am the resurrection and the life," 11:25; "I am the way and the truth and the life," 14:6; "I am the true vine," 15:1.

36 While only a few witnesses lack με, *me* (‎א A *pc* a b e q sy^{s.c}), it is more likely to have been added from context than removed. Even if it is retained, the emphasis would be less on Jesus himself than on the miracles he performed.

46 That v.46 refers to the Son in the third person while in both the preceding and the following verses Jesus speaks in the first person has led some to regard this verse as a parenthetical remark by the evangelist rather than as a statement by Jesus himself. The argument has merit but is not conclusive. Jesus regularly speaks of himself in the third person in the Son of Man passages (e.g., Jn 3:13; 5:27; 6:62 et al.).

b. Eternal life (6:60–71)

⁶⁰On hearing it, many of his disciples said, "This is a hard teaching. Who can accept it?" ⁶¹Aware that his disciples were grumbling about this, Jesus said to them, "Does this offend you? ⁶²What if you see the Son of Man ascend to where he was before! ⁶³The Spirit gives life; the flesh counts for nothing. The words I have spoken to you are spirit and they are life. ⁶⁴Yet there are some of you who do not believe." For Jesus had known from the beginning which of them did not believe and who would betray him. ⁶⁵He went on to say, "This is why I told you that no one can come to me unless the Father has enabled him."

⁶⁶From this time many of his disciples turned back and no longer followed him.

⁶⁷"You do not want to leave too, do you?" Jesus asked the Twelve.

⁶⁸Simon Peter answered him, "Lord, to whom shall we go? You have the words of eternal life. ⁶⁹We believe and know that you are the Holy One of God."

⁷⁰Then Jesus replied, "Have I not chosen you, the Twelve? Yet one of you is a devil!" ⁷¹(He meant Judas, the son of Simon Iscariot, who, though one of the Twelve, was later to betray him.)

COMMENTARY

60 The initial response of Jesus' followers was that what he had been saying was "a hard teaching." It was "hard" not so much because they couldn't understand it but because they found it offensive. The claims that Jesus was greater than Moses (vv.32–33), that he had come down from heaven to bring life to all who believe (vv.38–40), and that by eating his flesh and drinking his blood a person would live forever (v.54) were so far-reaching that many of those who heard found them incredible, to say the least. These assertions were difficult to accept because they were so inconceivable. It is one thing to listen to sound moral teaching and respect the teacher, but what can be said about a person who makes such grandiose claims regarding his relationship to God and the significance of his own person and ministry! Those who did not believe could arrive at only one conclusion: if Jesus were not demented, he was at least a paranoid suffering severe delusions of grandeur.

61–62 Aware that his followers (not the Twelve; see vv.67–69) were finding fault with what he had said, Jesus asks the obvious question, "Does this offend you?" The tone of this question depends on one's understanding of the following verse, which states a condition but does not supply a conclusion. "What if you see the Son of Man ascend to where he was before!"

There are at least two ways to understand Jesus' statement. (1) "If what I have said offends you, then you will really be offended when I ascend to heaven." In John's world of discourse the ascension would include the entire sequence of events beginning with the crucifixion. So if the claims he has just made bothered his listeners, how much more offensive would be his "ascension." A crucified Messiah was the most preposterous idea a Jewish person could imagine. (2) "If what I have said offends you, then when I am ascended the offense will be removed because that very event will vindicate all that I have claimed."

Interestingly, one does not need to decide between the two options, because they are not mutually exclusive. For the unbeliever the "ascension" simply increases the offense, while for the believer it removes it. The cross is a stumbling block only to those who lack the necessary faith to see in it the unfolding of God's redemptive plan.

That the Son of Man returns to "where he was before" is a clear indication of his preexistence. Jesus leaves no doubt but that as God's Son he lived in eternity past with the Father. Obviously such a claim would fall on the ears of the unbeliever as incredulous. But to those of faith it is not at all remarkable that the Savior of the world should have existed long before creation itself. Intellectual difficulties do not keep people from accepting Christ; it is the sheer stubbornness of their unbelief. The idea that God must somehow rationally explain himself to our limited understanding before we will believe in him would leave us with a God incapable of saving us. God, by definition, is above and beyond his own creation.

63 That Jesus was speaking metaphorically when he said that a person must eat his flesh and drink his blood (v.54) is now made clear. It is the Spirit who "gives life." He is the one who provides life eternal. "The flesh counts for nothing"; it is totally unable to provide spiritual sustenance. "Flesh" (*sarx*, GK *4922*) here is "the earthly part of man, man as he is by nature, his intellect remaining unilluminated by the revelation of God" (Lindars, 273). Little wonder that it cannot produce life. Life comes from hearing and absorbing the words of Jesus. His words are "spirit and . . . life." It is through his words that the Spirit communicates life to the person of faith. We are reminded of Jeremiah's testimony that when the Lord's words came, he ate them, and they were his joy and heart's delight (Jer 15:16). Even though some of Jesus' followers had listened to what he had to say, they still did not believe. There is a hearing of the ears only. To hear in such a way is to acknowledge the voice but to refuse the message. There is also a hearing of the inner person. To hear in this way is to take the next step and actually commit oneself to the message. When this happens, it is the Spirit giving life through the words of Jesus. This same phenomenon is true today. To read God's Word and find one's heart "strangely warmed" (as John Wesley put it) is to discover oneself in actual communication with the Spirit, whose role it is to illumine the believing heart.

64–65 Jesus knew that some would not believe and that one of them would betray him (v.64). He knew from the beginning (i.e., from the day they left their work and went with Jesus as he traveled the land) which ones would fall away and who his betrayer would be. Imagine the sorrow of teaching a person whom you knew would rise up against you. What unlimited patience and forgiving love! And Jesus still knows who among all those who call themselves "Christian" are in fact true believers. Even today what sorrow it must bring to the Son of God to suffer the hypocritical worship of the religious nonbeliever. Better an out and out pagan than a pseudo-Christian whose pretense serves neither God nor himself. It is for this reason (i.e., the phenomenon of unbelief) that Jesus said that no one is able to come to him apart from the enabling activity of the Father. He knew ahead of time that sinful humanity does not seek after God (see Ro 3:11). If people are to be brought to God, then God must take the initiative. He is the one who both initiates and completes the drawing of people to himself. The life, death, and resurrection of Jesus is God reaching out to do for the human race what it is totally incapable of doing for itself.

66 Here was a decisive moment in the lives of many who were still somewhat undecided about following Jesus. His insistence that he had come down from heaven as the true bread that brings life was not something that a person could accept and at the same time deny that it called for a radical reorientation of life. It is one thing to consider a theological proposition and quite another to make it a conviction. Convictions have a disturbing way of changing life. So "from this time" (or "for this reason"; *ek toutou*, can be understood either way) many of Jesus' disciples "no longer followed him." They "turned back"—both in the sense of returning to their previous occupations and also to their old religious worldview—one that had no place for

a Messiah on a cross. The moment of truth had come, and those in whose hearts faith had not actually established itself found it more comfortable to turn their backs on the only one who held the answer to the only really important issues in life. Such is the fate of the secular mind unmoved by the Spirit of truth.

67–69 So Jesus turns to the Twelve and puts his call to commitment in a question that expected a negative response: "You do not want to leave too, do you?" It was not a plaintive inquiry but a clear question regarding their allegiance. Peter, the impulsive one, speaks for the group: "Lord, to whom shall we go? There is no other one. You alone have the words that bring eternal life." Then in a messianic declaration not unlike his confession at Caesarea Philippi (Mk 8:27–30 par.), Peter exclaims, "We believe and know that you are the Holy One of God." That both verbs are in the perfect tense indicates that the Twelve had not only come to believe in him and recognize the truth of his claims but also that their faith and confidence was holding steady in this time of decision. Truth calls for commitment. It allows no place for what is false. To accept the truth is to forsake all attempts to find ultimate meaning in the vagaries of human existence.

70 The confidence of the disciples in Jesus and all he claimed to be and do is the reverse side of their having been "chosen" for the role they are to play. Divine election is not coercive but ultimately finds its counterpart in the free choice of believing individuals. "Yet," says Jesus, "one of you is a devil!" The Greek *diabolos* (GK *1333*) means "slanderer" or "false accuser." In the LXX it translated the Hebrew word for adversary (*śāṭan*, GK 8477), and this is the meaning it carries in its twelve occurrences in the Johannine literature (cf. *EDNT* 1:297). Carson, 304, suggests that in this location it should probably be taken as "the devil" rather than "a devil." Barrett, 307, comments, "Satan has made Judas his ally, a subordinate devil." In the spirit of Satan, Judas would oppose everything that Jesus stood for. Although posing as a disciple, his kiss of betrayal will reveal him for what he truly is—an adversary of Jesus.

71 John closes this section with a parenthetical remark in which he makes it clear that it was "Judas, the son of Simon Iscariot," of whom Jesus spoke.

"Iscariot" probably means "the man of Kerioth," perhaps the Judean town in the southern Negev mentioned in Joshua 15:25 (or perhaps the Kerioth in Moab, Jer 48:24). The suggestion that the term means "one of the Sicarii" (an "Assassin") is intriguing but has little support. In any case, Judas was the only one of the Twelve who was not a Galilean.

NOTES

70 The NET translator's note here provides a persuasive argument for accepting the translation "one of you is *the* devil" (italics added). The KJV regularly translates δαιμόνιον (*daimonion*, "demon," GK *1228*) as "devil" and thus creates confusion with the monadic noun διάβολος (*diabolos*, "devil," GK *1333*). In v.70 it is the one and only devil that is in view, not "a devil," i.e., one of many. The error of the KJV is repeated in many modern versions, including the NIV and NRSV. The NET note cites Daniel Wallace's conclusion: "The legacy of the KJV still lives on, then, even in places where it ought not."

B. Opposition in Jerusalem (7:1–8:59)

OVERVIEW

Following the events of ch. 6 (the feeding of the five thousand, Jesus' walking on the water en route to Capernaum, the discourse on the bread of life, and the desertion of Jesus by many of his followers), Jesus continues his ministry in Galilee (7:1). *Periepatei* ("to go about," "walk around," GK *4344*) is the "imperfect of customary action" (Barrett, 309) indicating that Jesus continued his peripatetic ministry of teaching, healing, and performing miracles wherever appropriate. Mark 7–9 describes the six-month period that falls between chs. 6 and 7 of John. There we learn of his encounter with the Syrophoenician woman, the feeding of the four thousand, the healing of a blind man at Bethsaida, Peter's great confession, the transfiguration, and the healing of a boy with an evil spirit. John's purpose is not to provide his readers with a full and complete account of all that Jesus did and said; as John later observes, such a task would fill more books than the whole world could contain (21:25). The material he did select was for the express purpose of bringing people to faith in Jesus Christ so that "by believing [they might] have life in his name" (20:31).

1. Conflict at the Feast of Tabernacles (7:1–52)

[1]After this, Jesus went around in Galilee, purposely staying away from Judea because the Jews there were waiting to take his life. [2]But when the Jewish Feast of Tabernacles was near, [3]Jesus' brothers said to him, "You ought to leave here and go to Judea, so that your disciples may see the miracles you do. [4]No one who wants to become a public figure acts in secret. Since you are doing these things, show yourself to the world." [5]For even his own brothers did not believe in him.

[6]Therefore Jesus told them, "The right time for me has not yet come; for you any time is right. [7]The world cannot hate you, but it hates me because I testify that what it does is evil. [8]You go to the Feast. I am not yet going up to this Feast, because for me the right time has not yet come." [9]Having said this, he stayed in Galilee.

[10]However, after his brothers had left for the Feast, he went also, not publicly, but in secret. [11]Now at the Feast the Jews were watching for him and asking, "Where is that man?"

[12]Among the crowds there was widespread whispering about him. Some said, "He is a good man."

Others replied, "No, he deceives the people." [13]But no one would say anything publicly about him for fear of the Jews.

[14]Not until halfway through the Feast did Jesus go up to the temple courts and begin to teach. [15]The Jews were amazed and asked, "How did this man get such learning without having studied?"

[16]Jesus answered, "My teaching is not my own. It comes from him who sent me. [17]If anyone chooses to do God's will, he will find out whether my teaching comes from God or whether I speak on my own. [18]He who speaks on his own does so to gain honor for himself, but he who works for the honor of the one who sent him is a man of truth; there is nothing false about him. [19]Has not Moses given you the law? Yet not one of you keeps the law. Why are you trying to kill me?"

[20]"You are demon-possessed," the crowd answered. "Who is trying to kill you?"

[21]Jesus said to them, "I did one miracle, and you are all astonished. [22]Yet, because Moses gave you circumcision (though actually it did not come from Moses, but from the patriarchs), you circumcise a child on the Sabbath. [23]Now if a child can be circumcised on the Sabbath so that the law of Moses may not be broken, why are you angry with me for healing the whole man on the Sabbath? [24]Stop judging by mere appearances, and make a right judgment."

[25]At that point some of the people of Jerusalem began to ask, "Isn't this the man they are trying to kill? [26]Here he is, speaking publicly, and they are not saying a word to him.

Have the authorities really concluded that he is the Christ? ²⁷But we know where this man is from; when the Christ comes, no one will know where he is from."

²⁸Then Jesus, still teaching in the temple courts, cried out, "Yes, you know me, and you know where I am from. I am not here on my own, but he who sent me is true. You do not know him, ²⁹but I know him because I am from him and he sent me."

³⁰At this they tried to seize him, but no one laid a hand on him, because his time had not yet come. ³¹Still, many in the crowd put their faith in him. They said, "When the Christ comes, will he do more miraculous signs than this man?"

³²The Pharisees heard the crowd whispering such things about him. Then the chief priests and the Pharisees sent temple guards to arrest him.

³³Jesus said, "I am with you for only a short time, and then I go to the one who sent me. ³⁴You will look for me, but you will not find me; and where I am, you cannot come."

³⁵The Jews said to one another, "Where does this man intend to go that we cannot find him? Will he go where our people live scattered among the Greeks, and teach the Greeks? ³⁶What did he mean when he said, 'You will look for me, but you will not find me,' and 'Where I am, you cannot come'?"

³⁷On the last and greatest day of the Feast, Jesus stood and said in a loud voice, "If anyone is thirsty, let him come to me and drink. ³⁸Whoever believes in me, as the Scripture has said, streams of living water will flow from within him." ³⁹By this he meant the Spirit, whom those who believed in him were later to receive. Up to that time the Spirit had not been given, since Jesus had not yet been glorified.

⁴⁰On hearing his words, some of the people said, "Surely this man is the Prophet."

⁴¹Others said, "He is the Christ."

Still others asked, "How can the Christ come from Galilee? ⁴²Does not the Scripture say that the Christ will come from David's family and from Bethlehem, the town where David lived?" ⁴³Thus the people were divided because of Jesus. ⁴⁴Some wanted to seize him, but no one laid a hand on him.

⁴⁵Finally the temple guards went back to the chief priests and Pharisees, who asked them, "Why didn't you bring him in?"

⁴⁶"No one ever spoke the way this man does," the guards declared.

⁴⁷"You mean he has deceived you also?" the Pharisees retorted. ⁴⁸"Has any of the rulers or of the Pharisees believed in him? ⁴⁹No! But this mob that knows nothing of the law—there is a curse on them."

⁵⁰Nicodemus, who had gone to Jesus earlier and who was one of their own number, asked, ⁵¹"Does our law condemn anyone without first hearing him to find out what he is doing?"

⁵²They replied, "Are you from Galilee, too? Look into it, and you will find that a prophet does not come out of Galilee."

COMMENTARY

1 Jesus chose not to go into Judea, because the Jewish authorities "were looking for a chance to kill him" (NEB). In ch. 5 we learned of the intense hostility of certain Jews against Jesus. They were eager to kill him not simply because he broke the Sabbath but specifically because he called God his Father, thus claiming equality with God (5:18). Yet, as we will learn later in the narrative, it was not the fear of death that kept Jesus from ministering in Judea. When the time was right—the divinely appointed time—Jesus would enter Jerusalem and face the scorn of the religious elite, who were irritated by the radical demands of his ethical teaching and furious at his claim to be the Son of God. It was God's will that for the time being he should continue to carry out his work in Galilee.

2 The time for the "Jewish Feast of Tabernacles" was at hand. Tabernacles was one of the three great feasts of the year that every male living within fifteen miles of Jerusalem was legally bound to attend, the other two being Passover and Pentecost. Tabernacles began on the fifteenth day of the seventh month (Tishri) and was a festival of thanksgiving for the blessings of God in the harvest (Lev 23:34–36). By then, the harvest of grapes, wine, and olives was complete, with barley and wheat having been harvested two to three months earlier. It was a time of great rejoicing in the bounty of God. Coupled with the harvest celebration was a special remembrance of God's blessings on Israel during the wilderness wanderings. It is often referred to as the "Feast of Booths" (NASB) in that during the weeklong observance the Jewish people lived in little shelters or booths made of branches and greenery.

3–5 In telling Jesus that he ought to go to Jerusalem so his disciples would see the miracles he was doing, they reasoned that to become a public figure a person must not act in secret but get into the mainstream of life and show himself to the world. Several questions meet us here. Were the brothers serious in suggesting that Jesus needed to perform his miracles in Jerusalem in order to gain a following there? Were they genuinely trying to help him accomplish what they thought he wanted to achieve, or were they ridiculing him?

The first option seems unlikely in that they had not yet come to believe in him. Earlier, along with their mother, Mary, they had come to where he was teaching and wanted to talk with him, but apparently they did not understand the nature of his mission. On that occasion Jesus responded that his real mother and brothers were people who heard God's word and put it into practice (Lk 8:19–21). In view of this relationship, it is questionable that his brothers would seriously be trying to help him fulfill his plan. The second option, followed by the NLT, says they *scoffed,* with the challenge, "Go where your followers can see your miracles." But it is hard to imagine how a group of younger brothers could turn so definitely against the one who had taken over the responsibilities of the home and family after their father, Joseph, had died. It is better to view their suggestion as intending to help their older brother while at the same time being less than convinced that he really knew what he was doing. From their point of view, it was perfectly reasonable to expect a person who wanted to carry out a public mission to go to the capital city and there display his credentials.

A second question has to do with the need of his disciples to see his miracles. Hadn't they been with him when he fed the five thousand and when he approached them at sea, walking on the stormy waves? The answer to this question lies in the identity of the "disciples" in v.3. Jesus' brothers were not referring specifically to the Twelve but generally to all who were inclined to follow his teaching. During the festival, Jerusalem would be crowded with people from everywhere throughout the land, many of whom had heard Jesus teach. In the broad sense of the term they could easily be considered his disciples. Remember that in the immediate context "disciples" must be understood in terms of the way Jesus' brothers would use it. Note also that the Greek text does not use the word "miracle" in v.3. It speaks rather of the "works" (*erga*, GK *2240*) that Jesus was doing. Miracles were a substantial part of that ministry but by no means the whole of it.

From their perspective the advice of the brothers made good sense. They reasoned that anyone who believed himself to be the Messiah should not avoid publicity but instead validate his claim by a public display of his abilities. To gather a following in Galilee was one thing, but the real test was Jerusalem and the religious hierarchy of that great city. Some have suggested that the brothers, realizing that many of Jesus' followers had defected (6:66), were encouraging him to display his power in the capital city to regain his position in their eyes. While such an idea may conceivably have passed through the minds of the unbelieving brothers, the possibility is speculative at best. In any case, the incident shows that seeing Jesus perform miracles, living in his presence, and hearing him teach is not enough to make a person a believer. It is not so much the evidence that demands a decision as it is the gift of faith that moves a person from darkness into light.

6 Jesus' response to his brothers' suggestion is that "the right time" for him had "not yet come." The Greek word *kairos* (GK *2789*) means "time" in the sense of a right or favorable time (in contrast with *chronos*, GK *5989*, which refers to time in a chronological sense). While the term occurs repeatedly in the Synoptics, it is found only here in John's gospel. The immediate reference was to that specific point in time when all the circumstances would be most favorable for Jesus to enter Jerusalem. Rather than an arrival at the beginning of the weeklong celebration of Tabernacles, some later period would be more advantageous. In a more profound sense, Jesus was awaiting the "right time" in which he would fulfill his eschatological role as Son of Man. While it was not yet the right time for Jesus to go up with his brothers to the Feast, for them any time was suitable. As unbelievers, they were living out their lives apart from any divine direction and hence were not governed by God's *kairos*. They could go to the Feast whenever they wanted—it simply didn't matter. One day was as good as the next.

7 When the brothers went up to Jerusalem they would encounter no opposition. The world cannot hate them because there is no reason why it should. They were one with the prevailing culture. For Jesus, however, the situation was dramatically different. The world hated him because he testified that "what it does is evil." The prophetic voice has always disturbed the smug self-righteousness of practicers of established religion. His "woe to you, teachers of the law and Pharisees" (Mt 23:13, 15 et al.) touched their most sensitive and vulnerable spot. Jesus' ethical demands were not an agenda for discussion but a call for radical personal change. If there is anything a hypocrite fears, it is the unmasking of his or her pretense. Little wonder that the religious leaders of Judea hated Jesus!

8–9 Jesus tells his brothers that he is not going up to the Feast because the "right time" (*kairos* again, GK *2789*) for him "has not yet come." The NIV follows the inferior textual tradition that reads *oupō* ("not yet") rather than *ou* ("not"), thus alleviating the apparent inconsistency with v.10 in which Jesus *does* go to Jerusalem. It is better to follow the shorter text (so NASB) and understand Jesus as saying no more than he will not be going up to the Feast at that specific time (i.e., with his brothers). He is simply turning down their request—not promising that he will not go to the Feast a bit later when the time is right. Having turned down the advice of his brothers, Jesus remains for a time in Galilee.

10 After his brothers left for the Feast, Jesus also went up to Jerusalem—"not publicly, but in secret." Normally, large groups from the various towns went to the feasts in large caravans. At the age of twelve Jesus had gone up to the Feast of the Passover. He remained in Jerusalem and was not missed for an entire day (Lk 2:42–44). To go up *secretly* means no more than to go up privately apart from the larger group that had already made the journey from Galilee to Jerusalem. Lindars, 285, calls attention to the fact that Jesus needed to continue his work "in secret"—i.e., "without making an open claim to be the Messiah, but allowing the conclusion to arise from the implications of his ministry." One should not picture Jesus furtively slipping into the capital city to spy out what was going on. He simply appeared there without fanfare when the Feast was underway. The religious authorities were well aware of his ministry in Galilee and were on the lookout for him at the festival. They reasoned that he would certainly be there and that perhaps this would offer them the best chance to have him taken into custody and killed (cf. 5:18; 7:1).

11 It is clear that "the Jews" were the Jewish religious leaders in Jerusalem, not the general Jewish population (designated "the crowds" in v.12). They kept asking (*elegon*, GK *3306*, is imperfect), "Where is that man?" The demonstrative pronoun reflects a decidedly hostile attitude. *That* man—that one who has been going about Galilee claiming to be the Son of God—where is he?

12 Meanwhile among the crowds (the "simple-minded, true-hearted Israelites," Ryle 3:439) there was "widespread whispering" about him. The Greek word *gongysmos* (GK *1198*) normally indicates discontent (as in 6:41 where the verbal form is used—

"began to grumble"; also 6:61), but here the context indicates what Phillips aptly calls "an undercurrent of discussion." Some called him "a good man," saying, in effect, "The truths he teaches are positive and helpful. His life is beyond criticism. He is a good man." Others had a decidedly different opinion, seeing him as one who "deceives the people" (NASB, "leads the people astray"). This was a serious accusation. To mislead the masses was understood by some as a capital offense. A tradition preserved in the Babylonian Talmud says that Jesus was executed because he was a deceiver and had led Israel astray (*b. Sanh.* 43*a*).

13 Though there was much subdued and private discussion about Jesus, no one said anything publicly. The crowds were intimidated by the religious authorities and afraid to speak out or take sides in the matter. Fear of reprisal had silenced public debate of the issue.

14 Jesus waited until the Feast was well underway before he went up to Jerusalem. All we know for certain is that this was the "right time" for him to show up (cf. vv.6, 8). Some have conjectured that he waited several days until the initial excitement of Tabernacles had subsided so that his followers would not be as apt to put on a demonstration such as took place some six months later at the triumphal entry. Such a display would meet with serious consequences from the Jewish hierarchy, especially if the Feast took place shortly after the massacre of the Galileans in the temple courts (cf. Lk 13:1). When Jesus arrived in Jerusalem, he went to the outer court of the temple, where he began to teach. The crowd that gathered was undoubtedly comprised of both those who wanted to learn and others who were offended. Hendriksen, 2:9, suggests that the more receptive listeners were later joined by hostile leaders.

15 In any case, the Jews "were amazed" and asked the rhetorical question, "How did this man get such learning without having studied?" Jesus' grasp of sacred learning and the persuasive power with which he spoke surprised them. After all, he had not attended their rabbinic schools. It may have been his skill as a teacher that bothered his opponents the most. Professional jealousy is as old as the human race. While their manner of teaching labored under the burden of rabbinic tradition and precedent, his was direct and convincing (cf. Mk 1:22).

16 Critics of Jesus reasoned that, since he had not studied under an acknowledged rabbinic master, he must be setting forth his own ideas. "Not so," Jesus responded: "My teaching is not my own. It comes from him who sent me." The rabbinic approach was to substantiate every statement by demonstrating its congruence with previously accepted judgments. If Jesus had said that he was self-taught, he would have been discredited at once. Morris, 405, notes that "the age did not prize originality." But Jesus' teaching was not his own. Neither did it grow out of Jewish oral tradition. What he taught came from God. As the works he did came from the Father (5:36), so also did his teaching (7:16). Far from being an arrogant advocate of novel ideas, he was a humble and submissive exponent of truth that came directly from God.

17 The reason Jesus' critics did not recognize that his teaching came from God was that they were not living in accordance with the will of God, evidenced most immediately by their desire to kill him in spite of Moses' clear teaching against murder. Verse 17 states unambiguously that the person who chooses to do the will of God will in fact be able to discern that Jesus' teaching does not come from him but from God. Only those who actually *do* the will of God are given the capacity to know this. There is no way of testing the validity of Jesus' words from outside a relationship of faith. One must "taste" before "seeing" that the Lord is good (Ps 34:8). To know for certain that Jesus' teaching comes from God one must be committed to doing what God desires. The inescapable requirement for understanding the claims of Jesus is faith. In a slightly broader sense, it is equally true that "the perception of truth depends on the practice of virtue" (cited in Ryle, 3:448–49).

18 Jesus now strengthens his case for accepting his teaching as coming from God. He points out that those who speak on their own do so for personal benefit. When people promote their own ideas, one can be sure that the ego is involved. The desire to convince others leads to a biased presentation that cannot be taken at face value. But Jesus is not trying to win favor in the eyes of others. His desire is that "the one who sent [him]" receive "honor." It follows that, since he works for the honor of God, he is "a man of truth," and "there is nothing false about him." These words came as a stinging rebuke to the religious leaders of the day. They were consumed by the desire to gain recognition, even if it required the manipulation of what they knew to be true.

19 Jesus asks rhetorically, "Has not Moses given you the law?" "You recognize the Mosaic law as coming directly from God," declares Jesus, in effect. "Yet not one of you keeps the law." It is becoming clear why they did not realize that Jesus' teaching was not his own but came from God. They were incapacitated to recognize its divine origin because they were living in disobedience to God's will as explicitly stated in the writings of Moses. Jesus' brings the point home clearly and sharply: "Why are you trying to kill me?" "Your desire to take my life," he is saying, "directly contradicts the teaching of Moses against murder. It proves you are disobedient and therefore unable to understand that my teaching is from God."

20 The response of the crowds, unaware of the intentions of the Jewish leaders, was that Jesus must be "demon-possessed." They ask incredulously,

"Who is trying to kill you?" reasoning that anyone who would make such a statement must be paranoid at the least. Phillips translates, "You must be mad!" In NT times, insanity was often linked with demon-possession. The Gerasene demoniac who lived among the tombs, cut himself with stones, and cried out night and day returned to his "right mind" only after Jesus had cast out his evil spirits (Mk 5:15). And later in the fourth gospel when Jesus describes himself as the good shepherd who lays down his life for the sheep, many say, "He is demon-possessed and raving mad" (10:20). Borchert, 284, writes that "categorizing people is a time-honored way of refusing to take them seriously."

21–24 Undeterred by the crowd's response, Jesus continues his case against the establishment. He had done only one miracle in Jerusalem, and that was on the Sabbath. They are still astonished that he would dare to tell someone on the Sabbath to "pick up [his] mat and walk" (5:8). Yet they constantly "broke" the law of Moses by circumcising infants whose eighth day after birth fell on the Sabbath (v.22). How then could they be angry with him for making a person entirely well on the Sabbath (v.23)? They should stop judging superficially and be fair (v.24).

21 The miracle to which Jesus refers is undoubtedly the healing of the lame man at the pool of Bethesda (5:1–15). Jesus' opponents paid little attention to the fact that a man lame for thirty-eight years was cured and able to walk again. What "astonished" them—and they were still bothered by it (*thaumazete* [GK *2513*] in v.21 is present tense)—was the audacity of Jesus in performing this "work" on the Sabbath. The man had been waiting a third of a century; couldn't he wait another day? And so they "persecuted [Jesus]" (5:16). Did not the law say that "whoever does any work on the Sabbath day must be put to death" (Ex 31:15)? Yet they themselves regularly circumcised every male child born

on the Sabbath (the eight days being inclusive). The law regarding circumcision was given to them by Moses (Lev 12:3), but the covenant predated the ordinance and went back to the time of Abraham (Ge 17:10; cf. 21:4). Thus circumcision took precedence over the regulation regarding work on the Sabbath. The conclusion is inescapable—if they are free to circumcise on the Sabbath, on what basis could they object to Jesus making a man completely well on the Sabbath. Their "work" had to do with but one single part of the body, while Jesus made "a man's whole body well" (RSV). Rabbi Eleazar later made the same point, i.e., if circumcision, which concerns only one of man's 248 members, overrides the Sabbath, how much more must his whole body (if in danger of death) override the Sabbath (*b. Yoma* 85*b*).

23 The Jews circumcised on the Sabbath "so that the law of Moses may not be broken." Though circumcision on the Sabbath appears to break the law, it actually has the opposite effect. It fulfills that to which the law can only point. Morris, 409, comments, "Had [the Jews] understood the implications of the Mosaic provision for circumcision on the Sabbath they would have seen that deeds of mercy such as He had just done were not merely permissible but obligatory." At best, the law is but a gracious indicator of how people should direct their lives in order to conform to the righteous character of their Creator. When Jesus healed the lame man at Bethesda, he was fulfilling a righteous obligation for which the law could only suggest a series of dos and don'ts. Acts of mercy take precedence over the functional nature of law. The latter serves the interests of the former. In Jesus' words, "The Sabbath was made for man, not man for the Sabbath" (Mk 2:27).

24 The paragraph closes with Jesus' charge that they "stop judging by mere appearances." The present imperative with the negative (*mē krinete*) stresses that they should stop doing what they are now doing. Instead they are to "make a right judgment." Here the imperative is also present, indicating the need to judge fairly on a continuing basis. Their judgment of Jesus' act on the Sabbath was superficial. Never mind the circumstances—he was breaking the law, and that was that. A fair judgment would have gone deeper and recognized that he *was* fulfilling the moral responsibility for which the law existed. Criticism is normally irresponsible. It would rather condemn the other than find out the purpose and motivation for the person's actions. While people "look at the outward appearance," the Lord "looks at the heart" (1Sa 16:7).

25–26 Earlier (in vv.11–12), John wrote of the varying opinions among the crowds concerning the person of Jesus. Some said he was a good man; others said he deceived the people. Following Jesus' teaching regarding the origin of his message and his defense for healing on the Sabbath (vv.14–24), we again hear from those who were listening to what he had to say. This time it is "some of the people of Jerusalem"—i.e., residents of the city as over against worshipers who had come there for the Feast. They say concerning Jesus, "Isn't this the man they are trying to kill?" They cannot understand why he is allowed to continue "speaking publicly." In this context *parrēsia laleō* ("to speak openly/boldly," GK 4244, 3281) means to speak "without fear of the Jews" (*EDNT* 3:46). And the authorities have done nothing to silence him—"they have not a word to say to him" (NEB). So they ask themselves if it is possible that the religious leaders have changed their mind about Jesus. Perhaps they have been given additional information that has led them to think differently. Perhaps they have decided that he is the Messiah after all.

27 No sooner had the idea crossed their minds than it was dismissed: "There is *no* way Jesus could be the Messiah. Doesn't popular theology teach that no one will know where the Messiah comes from? Well, everyone knows that Jesus is from Nazareth." A widely held opinion in the time of Jesus was that the Messiah would come into the world and remain hidden until the divinely appointed time for his public disclosure. Barclay, 1:243, quotes the rabbinic saying, "Three things come wholly unexpectedly, the Messiah, a godsend, and a scorpion." It was no secret that Jesus grew up in Nazareth, and it was from there that he launched his public ministry. That alone in the eyes of the people would disqualify him from being the Messiah.

The fact that slightly later in the narrative (v.42) some of those in the crowd point out that "the Christ will come . . . from Bethlehem" seems to be at odds with the view concerning the Messiah's origin just expressed. Apparently there was more than one idea regarding the origin of the expected Messiah. Popular theology often deviates from Scripture. That the Messiah would suddenly appear from someplace where he had been waiting for his public manifestation ruled out any possibility that a carpenter's son from Nazareth (even if he had been born in Bethlehem) could be the Messiah.

28 At this point "Jesus . . . cried out, 'Yes, you know me, and you know where I am from.'" Some writers take this response as no more than an acknowledgment that the crowd knew who he was as a person and where he had grown up. The verb "cried out" (*krazō*, GK 3189), however, is a much stronger expression than one would expect for such a mundane utterance. In the fourth gospel the verb is always used in connection with an authoritative and prophetic declaration (e.g., John the Baptist's testimony about Jesus [1:15] and Jesus' testimony regarding himself [7:37; 12:44]). It is much more likely that Jesus was responding with irony to the crowd's confident assertion that they knew where he came from. "So you think you know me and where I am from, do you?" Their concept of his origin was earthbound. They regarded him as no more than an itinerant preacher from Galilee. What they did not know was that his true origin was inseparably entwined with the eternal nature of God the Father. They needed to grasp the fact that Jesus was not among them on his own initiative. He had been sent by God, and the one who sent him was "true," i.e., "real," in the sense that God "really is the one who sent Jesus" (Carson, 318).

29 These people did not "know him" (i.e., God), because all true knowledge is based on a relationship. In spite of their much learning, the Jewish religionists had not come to a personal knowledge of God. But Jesus knows the Father because he is "from him" and was sent by him. Divine origin and heavenly mission are tremendous claims. From the standpoint of the authorities, such claims are the very reason Jesus should be done away with. Sabbath-breaking can be forgiven, but claims such as these constitute blasphemy, the ultimate sin (cf. 5:18). Yet if such claims are true, then it follows that Jesus is who he said he was, the very Son of God. If they are not true, then he is either a terrible sinner or a misguided fool. The same decision faced by the Jews meets today's reader as well. Wherever the gospel is proclaimed, people must decide whether to believe that Jesus is who he says he is or to reject his claims as sheer nonsense. There is no middle ground.

30 This was too much for some in the crowd. They "tried to seize [Jesus]" in the sense that they were anxious and ready to lay hold of him (*ezētoun*, GK *2426*, is a conative imperfect), but no one was able to lay a hand on him. This attempt to arrest him was different from the more formal attempt in vv.32 and 45. It was the response of that part of the crowd that was incensed at what he was saying about himself and his mission. But they were not able to carry out their intentions, because "his time had not yet come." That would be the hour (*hōra*, GK *6052*), still six months away, when Jesus would be arrested, tried, and crucified (cf. 8:20; 12:23, 27; 13:1; 17:1). Until then, the evil designs of his antagonists could not be realized. As Borchert, 286, says, "His hour was certainly not decided by mob hysteria. His time was in the hand of God."

31 While some of the crowd wanted to have Jesus arrested, many "put their faith in him." Whether or not their confidence in him constituted a saving faith we really do not know. If those here who were said to believe are the same as the Jews mentioned in 8:31, there is the possibility that they became disciples of Jesus, though the narrative that follows puts a large question mark over that possibility. Their decision that Jesus must be the Messiah was based on the miracles he had done. They reasoned that it would be highly unlikely that when the Christ came he would do more miraculous signs than Jesus had done. Therefore he must be the Messiah. While faith based on signs is not encouraged (2:23–24), it is not to be ignored (10:38). Apparently an expectation had arisen that when the Messiah appeared, he would as a second Moses perform miracles as his predecessor had done. Even as the prophets gave proof by performing miracles that their message was from God, so also would the eschatological prophet validate his role by similar signs. The same argument appears in Jesus' answer to the emissaries from John the Baptist, who came asking whether he was the Coming One or whether they should expect another. Jesus sent them back to John with the message that "the blind receive sight, the lame walk" (Mt 11:5). His miracles were compelling evidence that he was in fact the Coming One.

32 Though the religious authorities had judged Jesus to be an impostor worthy of death (5:18; cf. 6:19), some in the crowd were beginning to conclude that he was the Messiah. Obviously some action had to be taken. So the Pharisees, who had become aware of the rising tide of opinion about

Jesus, together with the chief priests sent temple guards to take Jesus into custody. The Pharisees, who were the minority party of the Sanhedrin, were those most likely to know what the populace was thinking. The Sadducees were the ruling elite, and it was from among their number that the high priest was chosen. Because Rome had taken over the responsibility of assigning ecclesiastical rank, a number of priests had rotated in and out of office and consequently bore the honorary title of "chief priest" (hence the plural). While the temple guards had as their primary function the maintenance of order in the temple precincts, they often served the interests of the Sanhedrin in a much broader scope. The guards were sent to arrest Jesus, but only at a time when it would not create an uproar. Since the city was filled with messianic enthusiasts, hasty action on the part of the Jews could result in unnecessary publicity. That the Sadducees and Pharisees were together in this scheme illustrates the dictum that "common enemies make strange bedfellows" (Carson, 319; cf. Mk 14:1). While their theologies differed at vital points, their common concern about the challenge to their power and reputation united them.

33 The outcome of the temple guards' encounter with Jesus is not described by John, though we learn later that they returned to the chief priests and Pharisees with nothing but cautious admiration for Jesus and for what he was teaching (vv. 45–46). Jesus continues the thread of discourse from vv. 28–29 by telling his listeners in the temple court that he would be with them for only a short time and then he would return to the one who sent him. The earlier question about his origin (v. 27) gives way to that of his departure (v. 35). The "short time" of which he spoke turned out to be six months—the period between Tabernacles (October) and Passover (April). Death for Jesus did not mark the end but the renewal of a unique face-to-face fellowship with the Father laid aside at the incarnation. In the beginning he was "with God" (*pros ton theon*, 1:1), but he became flesh and "made his dwelling among us" (*eskēnōsen en hēmin*, 1:14). Death cannot be an enemy if it leads to glory.

34 Jesus informed his listeners that they would not find him, because where he is they could not come. Jesus may have said "where I am" rather than "where I will be" in order to stress his continuing place of honor "close to the Father's heart" (1:18; Beck). It is theologically accurate to say with Augustine that "Christ was ever in that place to which he would return." The verb (*eimi*, "I am") is a gnomic present expressing a timeless fact.

35–36 True to form, the Jews misunderstood what Jesus was saying. Still thinking in one dimension (cf. 7:28), they asked scornfully, "Where does this man intend to go that we cannot find him?" The use of the personal pronoun *hēmeis* ("we") suggests that, try as he might, "Jesus can go nowhere that *we Jews* can't get to him. He can't possibly think [the particle *mē* requires a negative response] that by going to some foreign country where he can continue his teaching among the Greeks that he will escape us." It is interesting that what the authorities said in derision will in time prove to be prophetic of the outreach of the early church. They most certainly did go to the Diaspora, and the message of Jesus they taught was taken to Gentiles throughout the known world. It is ironic that the very ones who would prevent the spread of Jesus' message by putting him to death were the agents used by God to make it happen.

37–39 Since the Feast of Tabernacles was a time of thanksgiving for the annual harvest, it is understandable that some recognition be given to the importance of adequate rainfall (note the connection in Zec 14:16–19). By NT times, the well-known water-pouring rite had become an important part of the Feast. At dawn on each of the first six days, a procession led by the high priest went to the Pool of Siloam and returned with a golden flagon of water, which was then poured out in the temple before the Lord. On the seventh day, the ceremony was repeated seven times.

37 It was on this "last and greatest day of the Feast" that Jesus stood and announced that whoever was thirsty should "come to [him] and drink." Borchert, 290, calls this "a magnificent model of contextual preaching and teaching." Since the seven-day feast was followed on the day afterward by a "sacred assembly" (Lev 23:36), some writers think that it was on this eighth day that Jesus made his proclamation. But since the water-pouring rite reached its high point on the seventh day (and was not repeated again), it would be highly unlikely that John was referring to the eighth day as the "greatest day of the Feast."

Jesus' invitation to the thirsty recalls Isaiah's famous summons to the exiles, "Come, all you who are thirsty, come to the waters" (Isa 55:1). Spiritual thirst can only be quenched at the springs provided by God. Jesus is saying that those who long for spiritual satisfaction must come to him and drink of all he has to offer. He calls out his invitation in a "loud voice" (note the use of the verb *krazō*, GK *3189*, as in v.28). His prophetic announcement is that he alone is the one who is able to supply the water of life.

38 Jesus adds that, as Scripture has said, "streams of living water will flow" from those who believe in him. Since no specific OT verse can be found to match the quote, it would appear that Jesus is drawing on certain OT passages (e.g., Isa 44:3; 58:11; Joel 3:18) that employ the symbolism of water in speaking of the blessings of God on his people.

At this point we encounter a question of punctuation that has engendered much discussion. Those who favor what is called the "christological [or Western] interpretation" connect the final two words of v.37 (in the Greek text) with what follows, resulting in a rough chiasm.

> If anyone is thirsty, let him come to me;
> And let him drink, whoever believes in me.

The important point in this arrangement of clauses is that it allows the remainder of v.38 to be a parenthetical remark by the author. Those who come to Jesus will be able to quench their thirst because, "as the Scripture has said, streams of living water will flow from within him"—i.e., from Jesus.

Of the several difficulties facing this option the most important is that the opening words of v.39 are regularly used by John in reference to Jesus' teaching. So if Jesus is the one speaking in v.38, he could not be referring to himself when he said "from within *him*" (see Gordon Fee, "Once More—John 7:37–39," *ExpTim* [1978]: 116–18). In v.39 John goes on to explain that the "living water" which was to flow from the believer's innermost being (the *koilia*, "belly," GK *3120*, having been regarded as the seat of the emotions) is to be understood as a reference to the Spirit. Those who believe in Jesus will receive the Spirit, but that can happen only after Jesus is glorified.

39 On an earlier occasion Jesus told the Samaritan woman that the water he would give to her would become a "spring of water welling up to eternal life" (4:14). The abundant life that Jesus gives is a spring bursting with spiritual vitality. It is the vibrant reality of the Spirit's presence that transforms all of life and leads to eternal life. Those who are willing to forgo the fleeting pleasures of an earthbound existence and respond affirmatively to Jesus' invitation find their deepest longings fully satisfied by the Spirit. To drink at the fountain of eternal life is to experience the fullness of the Spirit.

40 Jesus' claim to be able to supply the spiritually thirsty with streams of living water made a considerable impression on the crowd. Some of them were convinced that he was "the Prophet" come in ful-fillment of Deuteronomy 18:15. Though the prom-ise there anticipates a series of prophets like Moses (cf. the context, and esp. vv. 20–22), it was generally held that a single eschatological prophet was to be expected. When the people heard the teaching of Jesus, some were convinced and exclaimed, "With-out doubt this man is the Prophet" (Montgomery). Earlier, on the occasion of the feeding of the five thousand, the people arrived at the same conclusion (6:14). Now the offer of streams of living water renews the same conviction. Had not the first Moses brought down bread from heaven (Ex 16) and caused water to flow from a rock (Ex 17)? Certainly this man who can feed a hungry multitude with a few small loaves of bread and now offers living water to quench the thirsty is in fact the second Moses.

41 "Not so," said others. "He is the Christ." It may seem strange to us that the crowd distinguished between the Prophet and the Christ. Are they not the same? In the first century, however, there existed varying messianic expectations. The promised Prophet and the Messiah were viewed by some as distinct. Qumran literature (1QS 9:11) speaks of a prophet and two Messiahs—a priestly Messiah of Aaron and a royal or Davidic Messiah of Israel.

42 Still others enter the debate, questioning how Jesus could possibly be the Christ since Scripture clearly taught that the Messiah would come from David's family, and specifically from the town of Bethlehem, where David lived. "How can the Christ come from Galilee?" they ask incredulously. It is sad that those who knew what Scripture taught regarding the family line and birthplace of the Mes-siah could not understand that the Messiah they professed to be waiting for was standing in their presence. It is interesting that Jesus did not come to his own defense by pointing out that he *was* from the family of David (Ro 1:3) and that he *had* in fact

been born in Bethlehem (Lk 2:4–7). But the real-ization and acceptance of Jesus as the long-awaited Messiah is a matter of faith and comes by way of revelation (cf. Mt 16:16), not by public debate. Those who first read John's account could see the irony of the situation. The very argument the crowd employed to deny that Jesus could be the Christ supported the opposite conclusion. His family line was Davidic, and Bethlehem was his birthplace!

43 So the people "were divided because of him." What was true then continues to be the case today. People confronted with the revelation of God in Christ do not have the luxury of remaining neutral. As Jesus taught, he came not to bring peace on earth but division (Lk 12:51).

44 Some of the crowd, rushing to judgment, wanted to take him into custody right then and there, but no one was able to lay a hand on him. His hour had not yet come, and until that time divine restraint kept the crowd at bay.

45 Earlier (v. 32) we learned that the temple guards were sent to arrest Jesus. A few verses later John recorded an encounter that took place on the last day of the Feast (vv. 37–44). Now we read that the temple guards returned to the Jewish leaders empty-handed. Since all these events apparently happened over several days, we are safe in inferring that the mission of the guards was not so much to move in and arrest Jesus on the spot as it was to watch for a favorable time when he could be taken without creating a disturbance among the people. The NIV's "finally" translates the Greek *oun*, better represented by the NASB's "therefore," which maintains the normal inferential force of the parti-cle. No one was able to lay a hand on him, and *there-fore* the temple guards returned without having arrested Jesus. That a single article in Greek governs both the "chief priests" and the "Pharisees" supports the impression that these two rather antagonistic groups had been brought together by their shared opposition to Jesus. The "chief priests" (*archiereis*, GK 797) were those members of the Sanhedrin who belonged to high priestly families (cf. BDAG, 139), the ruling elite. The "Pharisees" were those who took with all seriousness the assumed obligation to put into practice everything the scribes said that the law and the entire corpus of oral tradition taught about being a pious Israelite. The two groups had little in common in either theology or lifestyle; yet, as we said earlier, a common enemy makes strange bedfellows.

46 In answer to the leaders' frustration at the failure to arrest Jesus, the guards declared, "No one ever spoke the way this man does." The adverb *houtōs* ("in this manner," "thus," "so") stresses the manner in which Jesus spoke, but not to the exclusion of what he said. At the close of the Sermon on the Mount we read that those who heard Jesus teach were amazed "because he taught as one who had authority, and not as their teachers of the law" (Mt 7:29; cf. Lk 4:22).

Since the stress appears to lie on the last word in the sentence (*anthrōpos*, "man," GK 476, in the Greek text), the guards may have declared more than they realized—that the speech of Jesus was not the speech of a mere *man*. It was an awareness of the supernatural authority with which Jesus spoke that prevented the guards from carrying out their assignment. They were not accustomed to hearing one whose message carried the authority of heaven. Beasley-Murray, 119, notes that "two thousand years later, with the cultures of the whole world available to us, it remains true: 'No man has ever spoken like this man.'"

47 The Pharisees' question here stems not from a desire to learn but is a derisive ad hominem intended to humiliate the officers. The Greek expects a negative answer, so the retort of the Pharisees could be paraphrased, "It isn't possible, is it, that in addition to that ignorant mob he has deceived you as well?" It

is worth noting that the religious leaders mocked the temple police not so much because they had failed to arrest Jesus but because they should have known better than to have fallen for his line. They were not ordinary soldiers without a clue as to the real issue involved, but Levites who had undergone a certain amount of religious training.

48–49 Now comes what the religious leaders thought was the clinching argument, the coup de grace—"Has any of the rulers or of the Pharisees believed in him?" "Obviously," they conclude, "study of the law makes a person wise and pious! Since *we* haven't believed in him, the question is closed. He cannot be who he claims to be, and his teachings are deceptive."

The opinion of the religious authorities that Jesus could not be the Messiah because *they* had not accepted him demonstrates the power of pride to blind a person to the truth. Not only does pride conceal truth, but it also regularly issues in a low regard for the opinions of others. So the Pharisees with arrogant disdain speak of the ignorant "mob that knows nothing of the law" and are "damned anyway" (Phillips). The common people—the people of the land, as they were called—had never been schooled in the intricacies of the law and could not be expected to live as pious Israelites. Those who did not commit themselves to keeping everything that the Pharisees held the law and oral tradition to teach were considered to be under the curse of God (cf. Dt 27:15–26). This attitude toward the common person permeated Judaism. Even the extremely tolerant Rabbi Hillel held that "no member of the common people is pious" (*m. ʾAbot* 2:5). Less complimentary was the School of Rabbi Meir, who said in effect that one could not distinguish the "people of the land" from animals (see Str-B, 3:486).

50–51 Nicodemus now raises a point of order. This is the same Nicodemus who earlier had come to Jesus reasoning that the miraculous signs Jesus had been doing indicated that God was with him (3:2). John writes that Nicodemus was "one of their own number," i.e., a ruling member of the Sanhedrin. While he was one of them in terms of his official capacity, he was anything but one of them in his concern that Jesus not be condemned without a hearing. The question he asks expects a negative response and contains a mild rebuke. "Our law does not condemn a man without first learning what he's doing, does it?" The obvious response is, "No." A rabbinic rule (*Exod. Rab.* 21:3) states that "unless a mortal hears the pleas that a man can put forward, he is not able to give judgment." All civilized legal practice allows the accused the right to present and defend his actions. The Roman procurator Festus, in discussing the apostle Paul's case with King Agrippa, said, "It is not the Roman custom to hand over any man before he has faced his accusers" (Ac 25:16).

52 One would think that such a sane reminder would have given the others pause to reflect on their hasty conclusion. Such was not the case. Instead they turn on Nicodemus with derision. "Are you from Galilee, too?" they taunt. Unable to contradict the truth of what he had said, their only recourse was to turn on him as a person. Ad hominem arguments have always been the last resort

of the desperate. Then, in a visceral rejoinder that involved them in an obvious error, they challenged Nicodemus to study the evidence and find for himself that "a prophet does not come out of Galilee." Such, however, was not the case. Second Kings 14:25 identifies Jonah as "the prophet from Gath Hepher" (about three miles north of Nazareth). Depending on how one draws the borders, no less a prophet than Elijah came from "Galilee"—Gilead lay east of the Jordan (1Ki 17:1). According to Rabbi Eliezer (*b. Sukkah* 27*b*), there was not a single tribe in Israel from which a prophet had not come. To alleviate the problem of the Pharisees' obvious mistake some call attention to the readings in two Bodmer papyri ($\mathfrak{P}^{66}$ and $\mathfrak{P}^{75}$) that include a definite article, thus reading "the Prophet"—i.e., the prophet-like-Moses promised in Deuteronomy 18:15. It is better, however, to understand the mistake of the religious rulers as resulting from their extreme frustration. Their plot to arrest Jesus had failed, and even the temple guards sent to arrest him returned with an appreciation for the authority with which he taught. Anger had blinded the Pharisees to the extent that in their desire to discredit Jesus they had fallen into the error of denying what they knew to be true.

NOTES

3 The fourth-century Latin theologian Helvidius provides the typical explanation of who the brothers of Jesus were: the natural sons of Joseph and Mary after the birth of Jesus. Opposing Helvidius, the eminent biblical scholar Jerome held that the brothers of Jesus were actually his cousins (sons of another Mary, who was the wife of Alphaeus and the sister of the virgin Mary). Epiphanius, a fourth-century polemicist, believed that they were children of Joseph by a former marriage. These latter explanations arose as a result of the doctrine of the perpetual virginity of Mary, asserted by Hilary of Poitiers in the fourth century and explicitly taught as a doctrine of the church from the fifth century onward.

7 In John the Greek κόσμος (*kosmos,* "world," GK *3180*), when used in an ethical sense, refers to the mass of mankind aligned in deadly hostility to Jesus and his teachings. Although it exists for the present time under the power and influence of Satan, "the ruler of this world" (12:31; 14:30; 16:11), it falls within the redemptive purpose of God (1:29; 3:16–17).

9 The NASB follows 𝔓⁷⁵ B D¹ T Θ (et al.) by reading αὐτοῖς (*autois*, "to them") rather than the more difficult but preferable αὐτός (*autos*, "he"), which is supported by 𝔓⁶⁶ ℵ D* W *f* ¹ 565 (et al.) and followed by the NIV.

12 The Greek πλανάω (*planaō*, GK *4414*), which means "to lead astray, cause to wander," is the word from which the English word "planet" is derived. A planet is a "wandering star."

20 In contrast to the Greek understanding of demons as sometimes benevolent, the NT always considers demons to be malicious. They are pictured as taking control and possessing human beings. Among the many indications of demon-possession are insanity (Jn 10:20), seizures (Mk 1:26), and self-destructive behavior (Mt 17:15). While the Gospels tend to differentiate rather carefully between sickness and demon-possession (e.g., Lk 13:32), there is one case in which the sickness seems to have a demonic cause (Lk 13:10–17). Apart from the Gospels and Acts, the word δαιμόνιον (*daimonion*, "demon," GK *1228*) occurs only nine times (sixty-three times in the NT).

21–22 NA²⁷ places διὰ τοῦτο, *dia touto* ("because of this"), as the first two words of v.22. The problem is that the following words do not provide the reason. One must ask, "Because of what?" Granted that John normally places διὰ τοῦτο, *dia touto*, at the beginning of a sentence (e.g., 1:31; 5:16, 18 et al.), it still makes better sense to connect it with the preceding sentence—"and you are all astonished because of this" (so Bruce, 177).

37–38 The NET translator's note argues for the Western interpretation (so-called because of the patristic support of Justin, Hippolytus, Tertullian, and Irenaeus) and notes (1) the fact that 𝔓⁶⁶ puts a full stop after πινέτω (*pinetō*, "let him drink," GK *4403*), (2) the lack of Johannine parallels that make the believer the source of living water, and (3) the scriptural quotation in v.38 that links a targumic rendering of Psalm 78:15–16 with Jesus (he is the rock from which water is brought forth; cf. Maarten J. J. Menken's article, "The Origin of the Old Testament Quotation in John 7:38," *NovT* 38 [1996]: 160–75). The Western interpretation is adopted by a number of modern scholars, including Beasley-Murray, Dodd, and Jeremias.

2. Woman Caught in Adultery (7:53–8:11)

OVERVIEW

The last verse of ch. 7 and the first eleven verses of ch. 8 record an event that occurs nowhere else in Scripture. In fact, it should probably not be included in the fourth gospel either, since it is absent from virtually all the early Greek manuscripts. Scholarly opinion, however, judges that, while it is not part of the authentic material of John's gospel, it may well have happened. The episode could have been added by a copyist at a slightly later time when there was less danger that it could be misinterpreted as countenancing promiscuity.

7:53Then each went to his own home.

8:1But Jesus went to the Mount of Olives. 2At dawn he appeared again in the temple courts, where all the people gathered around him, and he sat down to teach them. 3The teachers of the law and the Pharisees brought in a woman caught in adultery. They made her stand before the group 4and said to Jesus, "Teacher, this woman was caught in the act of adultery. 5In the Law Moses commanded us to stone such women. Now what do you say?" 6They were using this question as a trap, in order to have a basis for accusing him.

But Jesus bent down and started to write on the ground with his finger. 7When they kept on questioning him, he straightened up and said to them, "If any one of you is without sin, let him be the first to throw a stone at her." 8Again he stooped down and wrote on the ground.

9At this, those who heard began to go away one at a time, the older ones first, until only Jesus was left, with the woman still standing there. 10Jesus straightened up and asked her, "Woman, where are they? Has no one condemned you?"

11"No one, sir," she said.

"Then neither do I condemn you," Jesus declared. "Go now and leave your life of sin."

COMMENTARY

8:1–2 Because 7:53 speaks of people going to their "own home(s)" while Jesus "went to the Mount of Olives" (8:1; though Jesus was not present at the meeting described in 7:45–52), it has been proposed that the story of the woman taken in adultery was at one time attached to some other narrative. Whatever the case may be, it was Jesus' custom when in Jerusalem to spend the evenings on the Mount of Olives (cf. Lk 21:37) or with his friends just over the mountain to the east in Bethany (cf. Mk 11:11, 19–20). Early the next morning he entered the outer court of the temple, where scribes often met with their students, and began to teach the people gathering around him.

3 As Jesus was teaching, some scribes and Pharisees arrived with a woman who had been caught in adultery and made her stand before the group. Apparently her accusers had caught her while actually engaged in the act and had brought her directly to Jesus. That the entire affair was trumped-up is

clear from the fact that the man involved was not apprehended. It takes two to commit adultery! According to Mosaic law, both parties would be guilty and subject to the death penalty (cf. Lev 20:10; Dt 22:22).

While scribes (NIV, "teachers of the law") and Pharisees are regularly mentioned together in the Synoptic Gospels, this is the only occurrence in the fourth gospel. Scribes were the recognized experts in the Mosaic law; the Pharisees were those who had devoted their entire lives to observing even the most minuscule part of the law. Some but by no means all of the scribes were also Pharisees.

4–5 The accusers pose to Jesus a question designed to get him in trouble, regardless of his answer. "Teacher," they say, "this woman was caught in the act of adultery. In the Law Moses commanded us to stone such women. Now what do you say?" From Ezekiel 16:38–40 it is clear that stoning was the prescribed manner for carrying out the death penalty in cases of adultery (cf. Dt 22:23–24). Leviticus 20:10 calls for the death of both parties committing adultery but does not indicate the method. (At a later time the penalty was to be carried out by strangulation; cf. *b. Sanh.* 52*b*; 84*b*; 107*a*.) While there is no sure way of knowing whether the woman in John 8 was married or unmarried, the term "adultery" (*moicheia*, GK *3657*) implies the former.

6 The purpose of the question in v.5 was not to fulfill the demands of justice but to trap Jesus into saying something that could be used as a basis for an accusation against him. For Jesus to answer that the woman should be stoned would run counter to his recognized concern for "tax collectors and 'sinners'" (Mk 2:15). It would portray him as severe, if not vindictive. What's more, it could put him in jeopardy with the Romans, who did not allow the Jews to carry out the death penalty (Jn 18:31). On the other hand, for Jesus to say that the woman should not be stoned would be to contradict the Law of Moses. That would provide the Sanhedrin with a charge they could use in discrediting him in the eyes of the people. In either case, the accusers thought they had Jesus on the horns of a dilemma from which he could not remove himself without serious damage.

Instead of answering their question, Jesus bent down and began to write on the ground with his finger. Exactly what he wrote no one knows. Since the verb (*katagraphō*, GK *2863*), which occurs only here in the NT, means "to draw figures" as well as "to write down" (BDAG, 516; in classical Greek, "to mark" or "to scratch deeply"), it may be that Jesus was simply passing the time in order to give the accusers opportunity to reflect on what they were doing. Those who conjecture that Jesus actually wrote some words suggest such possibilities as the decision that he would then announce; a passage of Scripture such as Exodus 23:1b, 7; or some symbolic word of doom as in Daniel 5:24. Eager to get the upper hand in a verbal exchange they thought they

were sure to win, the scribes and Pharisees continued to press home their question: "This is what the Law of Moses says—so what do *you* say?"

7 Jesus does not deny that the woman's offense is worthy of the punishment decreed by the Law of Moses. What he does question is the moral competency of her accusers to carry out the penalty. In effect he says, "Go ahead and administer the proper penalty, but only if you have never committed the same offense." If we understand "without sin" in a general sense as referring to any sin at all, then it is even more evident that none of them would be able to initiate the punishment. That the accuser must be the one to cast the first stone is the clear teaching of Deuteronomy 13:9 and 17:7.

9 Obviously, these religious leaders had not expected Jesus to respond as he did. Gradually they caught on to the full import of what he had said and began to slip away one at a time, beginning with the older men, until only Jesus and the woman were left. The KJV's interpretative addition "being convicted by their own conscience" is based on inferior textual evidence. It was less their conscience than their embarrassment at being outmaneuvered that prompted them to leave the scene. Jesus' answer left them at a loss as to what to do or say next. The only option remaining was a tactical retreat. Carson, 336, says, "Those who had come to shame Jesus now leave in shame." The NIV circumvents the problem of how the woman could be "in the midst" (*en mesō*) when no one else remained by translating the phrase with "still standing there." Hendriksen, 2:39, is probably right in surmising that only the scribes and Pharisees had gone, leaving the rest of the crowd intact—thus she could still be "in the midst." There was no reason why those who were not involved in the charge against the woman should leave.

10 When those who had brought the charge had left, Jesus straightened up and asked the woman where her accusers were. Rhetorically, Jesus asked, "Has no one condemned you?"—or to put it in another way, "They didn't carry out their sentence, did they?" Lindars, 312, notes that *katakrinō* (GK 2891) means "give a judicial sentence" and in this case "indicates a decision to carry out the penalty required by the law." For obvious reasons the Jewish authorities had not carried out the penalty.

11 Jesus is not saying that the woman's act of adultery is not worthy of condemnation but that he doesn't intend to press charges. In no way does he condone her sin. Neither does he offer her divine forgiveness for what she has done. He simply tells her to "go, and never sin again" (Montgomery). We would hope that the guilty woman repented of her sin, but the text is silent about that. And of course there is room in the kingdom for every kind of sinner (including the adulteress) who turns from sin and embraces by faith the Lord Jesus.

NOTES

7:53–8:11 For a convenient summary of both the external and internal evidence in favor of excluding this unit, see the NET text critical note at 7:53. After reviewing the external evidence and concluding that "practically all of the earliest and best manuscripts we possess omit the pericope," it goes on to state and essentially refute the several arguments from internal evidence that would tend to support its inclusion. The question of whether the pericope should be regarded as authentic tradition is left open. "It could well be that it is ancient and may indeed represent an unusual instance where such a tradition survived outside of the bounds of the canonical literature." (See also Metzger, 187–89, for the textual evidence and the committee's reasons for including the pericope in the UBS Greek NT, albeit enclosed within double square brackets.)

3 Since adultery is a violation of the divinely instituted rite of marriage, it was strongly prohibited in the OT. A bride found not to be a virgin was to be stoned (Dt 22:13–21); a man who violated an unmarried woman was required to marry her (Ex 22:16); a priest's daughter who becomes a prostitute was to be burned (Lev 21:9); adultery ("voluntary sexual intercourse between a married person and someone other than his or her lawful spouse" [dictionary definition]) violates both the seventh and tenth commandments and carries the penalty of stoning. It remains an open question, however, whether or how often the penalty was carried out. In Hosea 3:1 the prophet is told by God to "go, show your love to your wife again, though she is loved by another and is an adulteress" (see also the account of David and Bathsheba in 2Sa 11).

8 Several witnesses (U 700 et al.) add ἑνὸς ἑκάστου αὐτῶν τὰς ἁμαρτίας (*henos hekastou autōn tas hamartias*, "the sins of every one of them") at the end of the sentence. Metzger, 190, suggests that the motive may have been "to satisfy pious curiosity concerning what it was that Jesus wrote upon the ground."

3. Jesus' Teaching That Offended the Religious Leaders (8:12–59)

a. "I am the light of the world" (8:12–30)

[12]When Jesus spoke again to the people, he said, "I am the light of the world. Whoever follows me will never walk in darkness, but will have the light of life."

¹³The Pharisees challenged him, "Here you are, appearing as your own witness; your testimony is not valid."

¹⁴Jesus answered, "Even if I testify on my own behalf, my testimony is valid, for I know where I came from and where I am going. But you have no idea where I come from or where I am going. ¹⁵You judge by human standards; I pass judgment on no one. ¹⁶But if I do judge, my decisions are right, because I am not alone. I stand with the Father, who sent me. ¹⁷In your own Law it is written that the testimony of two men is valid. ¹⁸I am one who testifies for myself; my other witness is the Father, who sent me."

¹⁹Then they asked him, "Where is your father?"

"You do not know me or my Father," Jesus replied. "If you knew me, you would know my Father also." ²⁰He spoke these words while teaching in the temple area near the place where the offerings were put. Yet no one seized him, because his time had not yet come.

²¹Once more Jesus said to them, "I am going away, and you will look for me, and you will die in your sin. Where I go, you cannot come."

²²This made the Jews ask, "Will he kill himself? Is that why he says, 'Where I go, you cannot come'?"

²³But he continued, "You are from below; I am from above. You are of this world; I am not of this world. ²⁴I told you that you would die in your sins; if you do not believe that I am the one I claim to be, you will indeed die in your sins."

²⁵"Who are you?" they asked.

"Just what I have been claiming all along," Jesus replied. ²⁶"I have much to say in judgment of you. But he who sent me is reliable, and what I have heard from him I tell the world."

²⁷They did not understand that he was telling them about his Father. ²⁸So Jesus said, "When you have lifted up the Son of Man, then you will know that I am the one I claim to be and that I do nothing on my own but speak just what the Father has taught me. ²⁹The one who sent me is with me; he has not left me alone, for I always do what pleases him." ³⁰Even as he spoke, many put their faith in him.

COMMENTARY

12 On the basis that the section on the woman caught in adultery (7:53–8:11) is not part of the Johannine corpus, it would appear that the audience to whom Jesus speaks in v.12 are the Pharisees. (The NIV's "the people" is an arbitrary interpretation of the Greek *autois*, "them"; NASB, "to them".) That the very next verse speaks of the Pharisees supports this connection. In fact, it is interesting that while the crowd (*ochlos*, GK 4063) is mentioned eight times in ch. 7, the designation does not occur again until 11:42 (NIV, "people"). In ch. 8 Jesus deals exclusively with his Jewish adversaries.

Apparently the Feast of Tabernacles is over and the crowds have returned to their homes. This observation has significance for the context of Jesus' famous revelatory declaration, "I am the light of the world." It is customary to point out that during the festival four huge lamps in the court of the women were lit and illuminated the entire temple precincts. It was a time of enthusiastic celebration, with men dancing all night, holding torches and singing (*m. Sukkah* 5:1–4). The celebration of light reminded the worshipers of Israel's wilderness journey, when they were led at night by a pillar of fire (Ex 13:21; Ne 9:12). Supposedly it was during this time of celebration that Jesus declared himself to be the "light of the world." However, if the festival were already past, this particular background would no longer be an option.

So what is the conceptual background of Jesus' declaration? The OT is rich in its many uses of "light" as a metaphor for spiritual illumination and life. "The LORD is my light and my salvation," sang the psalmist (Ps 27:1). "Your word is a lamp to my feet and a light for my path" (Ps 119:105). The prophet Isaiah promised Israel that in the coming age the Lord himself would be their "everlasting light" (Isa 60:19; cf. Rev 22:5). While in the OT, light and darkness are not portrayed as set over against one another as principles of good and evil (as they are in John), this dualism is prevalent in the Dead Sea Scrolls, in which the Essenes ("the sons of light") are guided by a good spirit ("the prince of lights") but opposed by an evil spirit ("the angel of darkness" [1QS 3.20–21]).

In Greek thought, darkness was often associated with ignorance and death, while light symbolized life and happiness. It would appear from the universal recognition of light as a metaphor for what is good (in contrast with darkness, which stands for evil) that Jesus' claim to be "the light of the world" would not require a specific contextual background in order to be understood. It may well be that something as simple as the rising of the sun as he spoke

gave rise to this the second of his great "I am" statements. In any case, Jesus goes on to promise that those who follow him need never "walk in darkness." As the Israelites were led unerringly throughout the night by the pillar of fire, so also can the NT believer escape the darkness of this evil world by following the person and teachings of Jesus Christ. To follow him means to obey him. Christians need walk no longer in the darkness of sin. The light, which is life in Christ, will guide them to the Promised Land.

13 The Pharisees were painfully aware that Jesus' claim to be the light of the world must be discredited. So using Jesus' own words in 5:31, they exclaim, "Here you are [a felicitous translation by the NIV of the emphatic *sy* (you)], appearing as your own witness." It is clear from certain texts (e.g., Nu 35:30; Dt 17:6; 19:15) that the testimony of one person only is not enough to establish a matter. They say that since what Jesus is claiming about himself is nothing but his own opinion, "[his] testimony is not valid" (in the sense that it is insufficient to carry the day in a court of law). Jesus' detractors are not saying that what he claims about himself is necessarily false (though they undoubtedly thought it was) but only that it cannot be verified.

14 Jesus' rejoinder is that, even though he is bearing witness to himself, his testimony *is* nevertheless valid. There are other factors to be taken into consideration beyond the mere technicality they have raised. His testimony is valid because he knows two things about himself of which they haven't the slightest idea: he knows (1) his origin ("where I came from") and (2) his destiny ("where I am going"). He is "from the Father" (1:14; 16:28) and will return "to the Father" (13:1; 14:12). Bruce, 189, adds that "meanwhile, by an eternal 'coinherence,' he is in the Father and the Father in him." Thus Jesus is uniquely qualified to bear testimony and what he says is by definition true and valid. He alone has the full knowledge necessary to judge the truth of the claims he makes.

15 The Pharisees, on the other hand, have no idea where he comes from or where he is going, i.e., they do not recognize him for who he truly is—the very Son of God. Their judgment is superficial because it is based on human standards. Limited in scope, it must necessarily be less than adequate. In apparent contradiction to 9:39 ("For judgment I have come into this world"), Jesus adds, "I pass judgment on no one." Two points need clarification. First, the verb *krinō* ("to judge," GK *3212*) can be used in the sense of "to make an informed decision" as well as in the sense of "to condemn." Both nuances are present in the immediate context—the latter in v.15 and the former in v.16. The judgment of Jesus by the Pharisees, based as it was on human standards, was heavy with censure. In contrast, Jesus passes judgment on no one (the Greek is simply *ou krinō oudena*, "I judge no one").

The second point is related. While it is true that Jesus came to save the world, not to condemn it (3:17), it is also true that people are necessarily judged by their response to him. He came as the light of the world; those who are evil try to escape the light, while those who live by the truth come to the light (3:19–21). Every norm serves to judge what deviates from it. The incarnation is the supreme expression of God's redemptive love for the world, but coincidentally it results in "judgment" for those who reject it.

16–18 If Jesus does judge (in the sense of making an informed decision), his judgments are trustworthy because he is not alone in his decision—standing with him is the Father, who sent him. While the truth of what Jesus says does not depend on a validating witness (cf. v.14), for the moment he allows his case to be considered by the standard practice of the synagogue. Deuteronomy 17:6 taught that "a matter must be established by the tes-

timony of two or three witnesses." Jesus calls this "your own Law" in the sense that it is the law that they accept as authoritative and therefore would consider determinative and binding. The two witnesses are Jesus himself and the Father who sent him (cf. 5:37). So even the formal requirements of the law have been met. According to the Jews' own regulations, the testimony of Jesus (that he has come as "the light of the world" and that those who follow him "will never walk in darkness, but will have the light of life") is trustworthy and valid.

19 Even on his opponents' terms Jesus has proven his case, no question about it. Since the Pharisees are logically stalemated, the only thing left for them is to resort to ridicule. Derisively they ask, "And where is this 'father' of yours?" (Brown, 342). In essence, they declare, "You're living in a fantasy world. Your claim to have a 'father' who can serve as another witness reveals a serious mental disorder."

Grieved by their failure to understand the spiritual import of what he has just been saying, Jesus, perhaps reluctantly, acknowledges that the Jewish religious leaders haven't the slightest clue as to who he really is and that by rejecting him they show that they are unacquainted with his Father as well. It all comes down to this: "If you knew me, you would know my Father also." The ultimate revelation of the Father is made by the Son (1:18). To deny the Son's witness is to remain in darkness in regard to the Father. Some six months later, on the eve of his crucifixion, Jesus will tell Philip, "Anyone who has seen me has seen the Father" (14:9). Since the Pharisees don't know Jesus, they can't know the Father. This relationship between the Father and the Son rules out the persistent claim that all paths lead to God.

20 John tells us that Jesus spoke these words while he was teaching in the temple precincts near the place where offerings were collected. This could not be "in the treasury" itself (KJV); rather, it happens in the court of the women, where thirteen large "shofar chests" were placed to receive offerings (cf. Mk 12:41–42). Each chest was shaped like a trumpet and bore an inscription on the side that indicated the purpose for which the money would be used. By saying that "no one seized [Jesus]," John indicates that there were those who either had tried to lay hold of him or wanted very much to do so. But it was not yet God's time. Jesus' adversaries were unable to take him into custody because "his time had not yet come" (cf. 2:4; 7:6, 8, 30; 13:1; 17:1).

21 In the previous section (vv.12–20) Jesus taught about his origin, his destiny, and his relationship to the Father. These themes are now developed more fully. Once again, Jesus tells the people that he is going away and that they are unable to come there (cf. 7:33–34). When he says, "you will look for me," it could mean that when he is gone they will continue to look for the Messiah (the one they did not recognize Jesus to be), but more likely it means that their understanding of who he really is will come too late. They will search for him, but to no avail. Repeating the earlier statement (in 7:33–34), he now adds, "and you will die in your sin." Their sin (note that the word is singular) is their rejection of Jesus. Unbelief is the essential *sin* that expresses itself in all sorts of *sins* (cf. the plural in v.24). Since they have chosen not to believe what Jesus taught about himself, they will die in their sinful state of rejection. A basic OT principle is that each person will die "for his own sin" (Dt 24:16). To die *in* one's sin is to die *for* one's sin (cf. Eze 3:18–20).

22 One would think that this stern pronouncement by Jesus would have caused men who were religious to reflect on the possibility that what he said might be true. Instead, they try to escape the truth by resorting to mockery. They ask in derision, "You're not going to kill yourself, are you? [the question in Greek expects a negative answer]. If we can't go where you are going you must have suicide in mind."

While the OT does not discuss suicide, it is quite clear that the average Jew considered it a repulsive way to end one's life. The Jewish historian Josephus (*J. W.* 3.375) says that when there has been a suicide the body should not be given a public funeral. They reasoned that if Jesus killed himself, he would go to the lowest region of Hades. Obviously the religious Jew could not follow him there! Earlier (in 7:35) they speculated that if they could not find Jesus, it would be because he had gone to the Diaspora to teach the Greeks. Here they postulate something much more serious, namely, suicide.

23 Paying no attention to what his adversaries had said, Jesus continued his discourse by pointing out the radical distinction between them and him. *They* are "from below"; *he* is "from above." The prepositions, being emphatic, serve to make the contrast as definite as possible. What he says is not to be taken in a spatial or geographic sense but has to do with spheres of existence. They are "of this world," i.e., they belong to "this fallen moral order in conscious rebellion against its creator" (Carson, 342). In sharp contrast, he is "not of this world." While he came to this world on a redemptive mission (3:16–17), he in no way shares in its fallen nature or its perspective on life. He is in the world but not of the world (17:14, 16).

24 Once again, Jesus reminds his listeners that they will die in their sins if they do not believe that he is the one he claims to be. The NIV translates the familiar *egō eimi* (lit., "I am") with "I am the one I claim to be" (NASB, "I am He"). The phrase and its background have occasioned a great deal of debate. One suggestion is that Jesus' claim echoes Exodus 3:14, where in response to Moses' request God gives his name as "I AM WHO I AM"—the one whose character is dependable and faithful and who desires the full trust of his people (see NIVSB note at Ex 3:14). But if this Exodus passage had served as the background for Jesus' claim, we would have expected *ho ōn* (as in the LXX) instead of *egō eimi*.

It is more likely that the source of Jesus' self-designation is to be found in the expression "I am he" in Isaiah 40–55 (specifically 41:4; 43:10, 13, 25; 46:4; 48:12; 51:12), which is consistently translated in the LXX by *egō eimi*. Lindars, 320–21, makes the point that in the Isaiah passages Yahweh is the one who saves his people, and on the lips of Jesus in a parallel situation we should fill out the saying with, "I am the one through whom salvation is accomplished." The critical point is that the name carries a divine affirmation. By referring to himself as "I am [he]," Jesus lays claim to deity—a claim that is either true or blasphemous in the extreme. "Not to believe what I say about myself," says Jesus, "is to die in your sins." The issue is clear: people's response to Jesus and his claim to be God determines their ultimate destiny. One cannot come face-to-face with truth and remain neutral; hence the division regarding Jesus (7:12; 8:40–41).

25 The response of the opponents ("who are you?") was not a polite request regarding his identity. It was a caustic "you, who are you to be saying such things?" (The pronoun is "scornfully emphatic" says Morris, 448, quoting Plummer.) Jesus' reply is certainly the most difficult "sentence" in the Greek text of John. Literally it says, "At the beginning what also I am saying to you." There are two ways of construing the sentence. One is to make it a question. In this case *tēn archēn* is taken to mean "at all" and *hoti* is "why." This yields something like, "Why should I speak to you at all?" The Pharisees had rejected Jesus and turned to ridicule, so he asks what reason there is for him to continue discussing the matter with them. He says in effect, "You have decided against me, so any further debate would be a waste of time." The problem with this approach is that in the following verse Jesus says that he has "much to say" to them.

The other approach is to take Jesus' words as an affirmation. In this case, *tēn archēn* (an adverbial accusative, as above) is taken to mean "at first," and *hoti* is understood as two words, *ho* and *ti* (as in NA[27]). Supplying *egō eimi* results in the answer, "I am just what I told you at the beginning," or, "I am from the beginning what I tell you" (so Barrett, 343). 𝔓[66] inserts *eipon hymin* ("I told you") at the beginning of the sentence, thus yielding, "I told you at the beginning what I am also telling you [now]." This makes good sense, but the added words are not found in any other manuscript. The evidence is stronger for the sentence to be taken as an exclamation rather than a question. Jesus is stressing that his testimony has not changed. What he told them at the beginning about himself is what he is still telling them. He claimed that he is "the bread of life" (6:35), that he has come down from heaven to do the will of God (6:38), that by eating his flesh and drinking his blood a person may gain eternal life (6:54), that those who come to him and drink will have streams of living water flowing from within (7:37–38), and that he is "the light of the world" (8:12). All such statements point to the same conclusion—that he is in fact the Son of God sent to bring a fallen human race back into fellowship with the Father. The testimony has been clear from the very beginning.

26 Jesus continues by noting that he has a number of judgments he could make against these people, but that God, who is reliable, is the one who tells him what he is to say. Jesus is unwilling to say anything beyond what the Father tells him to say. By failing to recognize Jesus for who he is, the religious leaders bring condemnation on themselves. More could be said, but only if the Father should prompt Jesus to speak.

27 John adds that the opponents did not recognize the import of what Jesus had just been telling them. In v.25 their "who are you, to be talking to us like this?" indicated they did not grasp the essential fact that God was his Father. The original reading of Codex Sinaiticus (and several Western witnesses) has *ton theon* ("God"), which translates, "He was telling them that God was [his] Father." This, undoubtedly, is the meaning of John's aside in v.27.

28 While the religious elite did not at the moment recognize the heavenly origin of Jesus and his unique relationship to the Father, the time would come when they would know who he really is. "You will know," says Jesus, "that I am the one I claim to be" (*egō eimi*), i.e., the one bringing salvation not as a messenger but as God incarnate. The title is not a philosophical statement about his eternal existence but a straightforward declaration that he has come from God, his Father, on a redemptive mission for the lost.

They will recognize Jesus for who he is when they have "lifted up the Son of Man." This use of the title "Son of Man" is consistent with the Synoptics, where it carries a double application to Jesus' heavenly origin and his humble life on earth. We first encountered the expression "lifted up" in 3:14, where Jesus taught that "just as Moses lifted up the snake in the desert, so the Son of Man must be lifted up" (cf. 12:32, 34). Lindars, 322, calls it "John's technical expression for the Passion of Jesus as the manifestation of the divine glory." For Jesus, the cross was the occasion of his glorification, in spite of its shame and humiliation. When the hour comes "for the Son of Man to be glorified" (12:23), he will be "lifted up from the earth" and "draw all men to [himself]" (12:32).

It is best to put a full stop after "claim to be" and take the subsequent clauses as a separate sentence in which Jesus repeats what he said on earlier occasions (5:30; 7:16)—he does nothing on his own but speaks only what the Father has taught him.

29 While it is true that Jesus has been sent from the Father, it is equally true that the Father is with him. The sending of the Son does not involve separation from the Father. Jesus has not been "left . . . alone" because he always does what pleases the Father (cf. 6:38). Obedience ensures the blessing of God. Those who live lives marked by obedience find that God is always present. Only disobedience forces the Father to withdraw from conscious fellowship with the believer.

30 John records that "even as [Jesus spoke], many put their faith in him." Earlier, at another feast (Passover), Jesus performed miraculous signs, and many people "believed in his name" (2:23). It appears, however, that such faith was not authentic (cf. 2:24–25). One wonders whether the faith of those who believed as a result of his discourse at the Feast of Tabernacles was any different. Ryle, 3:537, wisely says, "The extent to which men may be intellectually convinced of the truth of religion and know their duty, while their hearts are unrenewed and they continue in sin, is one of the most painful phenomena in the history of human nature."

b. "My truth will set you free" (8:31–38)

³¹To the Jews who had believed him, Jesus said, "If you hold to my teaching, you are really my disciples. ³²Then you will know the truth, and the truth will set you free."
³³They answered him, "We are Abraham's descendants and have never been slaves of anyone. How can you say that we shall be set free?"

³⁴Jesus replied, "I tell you the truth, everyone who sins is a slave to sin. ³⁵Now a slave has no permanent place in the family, but a son belongs to it forever. ³⁶So if the Son sets you free, you will be free indeed. ³⁷I know you are Abraham's descendants. Yet you are ready to kill me, because you have no room for my word. ³⁸I am telling you what I have seen in the Father's presence, and you do what you have heard from your father."

COMMENTARY

31 Jesus continues by pointing out to the believing Jews that, although they had descended from Abraham, they were still in bondage to sin (vv.32–33). Obviously this poses a problem: How could those who were continuing in sin be at the same time genuine disciples of Jesus? Some, holding that *pisteuō eis* ("to put one's faith into") in v.30 refers to genuine faith, conclude that *pisteuō* plus the dative ("to believe") in v.31 refers to a different group whose faith was spurious in the sense that it fell short of what is required to be a genuine follower of Jesus. That this distinction does not hold is clear from the use of the former construction in 2:23 of those with questionable faith and the latter construction in 5:24 where eternal life is promised to those who believe. Others propose that vv.30–31 refer to genuine believers, but from that point on the narrative speaks of Jewish opponents to the Christian faith in *John's* day. Carson, 347, is undoubtedly right in saying that such historical reconstruction "comports well with certain scholarly fads but is little based on exegesis."

The simplest answer is that as the paragraph continues Jesus is directing his remarks to those whose "faith" was far more cerebral than personal and life changing. They had mentally acquiesced to the idea that Jesus had been sent from God, but they were not prepared to respond to the ethical and moral consequences of that truth. So Jesus points out that only if they "hold [*menō*, GK *3531*] to [his] teach-

ing" (NEB, "dwell within the revelation I have brought") will they prove truly to be his disciples. *Menō* ("remain," "continue," "stand firm") is a favorite Johannine term that occurs forty times in his gospel and an additional twenty-three times in his epistles. Here it denotes a determined resolve to live out in daily life the full scope of Jesus' teaching. It is only those in whom the words of Jesus become incarnate who are in fact his disciples. Nowhere in the Gospels will you find the demands of faith watered down, so as to leave the feeling that Jesus' major concern for his followers is that they become pleasant people. The radical demands of the NT have as their goal the spiritual transformation of sinful people into the image of Jesus Christ—a demanding challenge that cannot countenance anything less than full commitment. "Live in my word," says Jesus in effect. "Let what I say control your every action, and you will show that you really are my disciples."

32 Against this background of wholehearted commitment to Jesus' teachings, obedient Christians will "know the truth," and this very truth "will set them free." The truth of which Jesus speaks is not the truth of rational discourse, an intellectual attainment, but the truth of *relationship*. It is the revelatory truth of knowing Jesus for who he is. It is the truth that liberates people from the bondage of sin and sets them free to become the kind of people their Creator intended them to be. Judaism held that a person is made free by studying the law (*m. ʾAbot* 3:5), but John maintains that those very Scriptures (the OT) testify to Jesus (5:39) and that Jesus himself is the truth (14:6) that liberates. To know the truth is not merely to understand what it affirms but to commit oneself personally to the one who is the truth. It is interesting that truth by its very nature cannot appeal to something outside itself for verification. It is self-validating. It would be beside the point, then, for Jesus, who is the truth, to provide a secondary witness in support of his claim to be who he says he is. Truth stands alone. Those who have by faith established a personal relationship with Jesus are not at all in the dark as to who he is—they recognize him as the truth, and this revelatory experience sets them free from the bondage of sin.

33 Jesus' claim that by obeying his teaching they will come to know the truth and consequently be set free strikes his Jewish audience as preposterous. From their standpoint, they *already* possess the truth. Are they not descendants of Abraham and heirs of the covenantal blessings that flow from this relationship? And since they are certain that they do have the truth, does it not follow that in no sense could they be in bondage? "We have never been slaves of anyone," they confidently assert. Undoubtedly they are not referring to political freedom. Their national history had been one long account of living under foreign dominance. First it was Egypt, then Assyria, Babylon, Media-Persia, Greece, Syria, and—at that particular time—Rome. What they are claiming is that, based on their favored position as the people of God, they cannot be held to be slaves of anything or anyone. Those who possess the truth, specifically religious truth, have no need of being set free. They are not slaves.

34 But Jesus solemnly (note the *amēn amēn* [GK 297]; NIV, "I tell you the truth") lays down the axiom that "everyone who sins is a slave to sin." The verb tense (present continuous) indicates that he is speaking of those who continue in sin, those who spend their days living in sin. Jesus' words are very much like those of Paul in Romans 6:12–23, where sin is pictured as an enslaving power that ultimately brings about death. Sin enslaves all who live in it, and the slavery it engenders is evidence of the reality of its presence.

35 Jesus goes on to point out that while a servant has no permanent place in the family, a son "belongs to [the family] forever." Jesus is pointing out the authority vested in the Son to liberate those who are in bondage to sin.

36 True freedom is not the option of doing whatever you might want to do, but the privilege of opting to do what is right. Jesus is the Son who opens the door to real freedom. So "if the Son sets you free, you will be free indeed." Note that in v.32 it was the "truth" that sets a person free; here it is the Son. The Son *is* that truth which releases the sinner from the bondage of sin. He not only speaks the truth; he is the truth.

37 Jesus acknowledges that in terms of national heritage his antagonists are indeed descended from Abraham. But they are not true spiritual descendants of the patriarch—made clear from the fact that they are "ready to kill [him]." His word has found no place in their hearts, and consequently they have decided to put him away for good (cf. 5:18; 7:1). Their conduct demonstrates that they are not Abraham's spiritual descendants; what's more, it shows that they are deserting the teaching of Jesus. Whatever the nature of their "faith" (vv.30–31), it falls tragically short of what is required to become a child of God.

38 What Jesus has been teaching (about himself and his relationship to the Father) is nothing but what he has "seen in the Father's presence." *His* knowledge of the truth is firsthand and experiential. In contrast, *they* are doing what they have "heard from [their] father"—who, as we will soon learn, is none other than the devil (v.44).

It is instructive to note the parallels in v.38:

"I" (Jesus)	"you" (the Jews);
what he has seen	what they do;
his Father	their father.

Everything these people are and do stands in stark contrast to Jesus and his redemptive mission. Little wonder that they denounced his teaching and turned to what they considered to be the ultimate solution.

NOTES

32 G. W. Bromiley (*ISBE* 4:926–28) distinguishes between truth as presented in the Bible (*ʾĕmet*, GK 622, in the OT; ἀλήθεια *alētheia*, GK *237*, in the NT) and several kinds of secular truth. Biblical truth should not be confused with the eternal truths of philosophical abstraction, because apart from the knowledge of God, human beings, flawed by sin, can evolve only approximate ideas of truth. Neither should it be confused with the truth of science, for the latter is necessarily restricted to a narrower field. Not even ecclesiastical truth (dogma) may be identified with the truth of Scripture, for, as helpful as dogma may be, "the truth of God cannot be finally reduced to an intellectualized dogmatic confession which can be handed down by ordinary processes of communication" (*ISBE* 4:927).

35 The Greek word οἰκία (*oikia*, GK *3864*) can refer either to a house as a building or to those who live in the house, i.e., "household" or "family" (NIV chooses "family"; NASB adopts the more literal "house"). It occurs five times in the gospel of John, twice with the meaning of a literal house (11:31; 12:3) and three times with the extended meaning of "household" (4:53; 8:35; 14:2). In the latter sense, it includes not only the immediate family but also relatives and servants living under the same roof. In Philippians 4:22, "those who belong to Caesar's household" included all who served in the court of the emperor, both slave and free, from wherever they may have come (cf. *EDNT* 2:495).

c. "You are children of the devil" (8:39–47)

[39]"Abraham is our father," they answered.

"If you were Abraham's children," said Jesus, "then you would do the things Abraham did. [40]As it is, you are determined to kill me, a man who has told you the truth that I heard from God. Abraham did not do such things. [41]You are doing the things your own father does."

"We are not illegitimate children," they protested. "The only Father we have is God himself."

[42]Jesus said to them, "If God were your Father, you would love me, for I came from God and now am here. I have not come on my own; but he sent me. [43]Why is my language not clear to you? Because you are unable to hear what I say. [44]You belong to your father, the devil, and you want to carry out your father's desire. He was a murderer from the beginning, not holding to the truth, for there is no truth in him. When he lies, he speaks his native language, for he is a liar and the father of lies. [45]Yet because I tell the truth, you do

not believe me! ⁴⁶Can any of you prove me guilty of sin? If I am telling the truth, why don't you believe me? ⁴⁷He who belongs to God hears what God says. The reason you do not hear is that you do not belong to God."

COMMENTARY

39 Earlier in the encounter, the Jews claimed to be descendants of Abraham (v.33). Now by calling Abraham their father, they are claiming to be his children. This latter assertion is of greater moment in that it implies a close and spiritual relationship. Jesus acknowledges that in one sense they *had* descended from Abraham (they were his *sperma*, lit., "seed," GK *5065*, v.37), but he is unwilling to concede that they are therefore his children (*tekna*, GK *5451*, v.39). The NIV follows variants that make Jesus' response a contrary-to-fact conditional sentence. "If you were Abraham's children, . . . then you would do the things Abraham did." The clear implication is that their conduct belies their assertion that they are the spiritual descendants of the patriarch. While Abraham received the messengers of God with proper decorum (Ge 18:1–8) and rejoiced when looking forward to the coming of the Christ (Jn 8:56), the attitude of Jesus' opponents is exactly the opposite—they are trying to kill him (v.37). If they were truly the children of Abraham, they would extend to him the same consideration their "father" had.

Some scholars take Jesus' statement as ironic. NA²⁷ has the first verb in the present tense (*este*, "you are") and the second in the imperfect (*epoieite*, "you were doing"). In this case, the meaning of the sentence is something like, "Since you are Abraham's children, what you have been doing [i.e., trying to kill me] must be what Abraham would have done." It is obvious that Abraham would not be trying to take Jesus' life, so it follows that their claim to be his children is a sham. However, no matter which way the sentence is taken, the result is essentially the same.

40–41 That Jesus' opponents were determined to kill him (though his only "crime" was to tell them what he heard from God) demonstrates how irrational and vicious was their reaction to truth incarnate. Leaders trained by the best minds of Israel conduct themselves as demented riffraff when confronted with the claims of truth and justice. So much for the power of intellect in dealing with issues of a spiritual nature! It is certain that Abraham would not have done what they were trying to do. Nor would any true child of Abraham. What they are doing, says Jesus, is what "[their] own father does" (v.41). While Jesus doesn't actually name their real spiritual father until v.44, they understand where he is headed.

To obscure the real point at issue they resort to personal slander and taunt Jesus with the accusation, "We are not illegitimate children" (v.41; NASB, "born of fornication"). When losing the argument, resort to *argumentum ad hominem*! Some understand the reference to illegitimacy as an allusion to certain irregularities connected with Jesus' birth. There is some (though later) evidence of Jewish slander against Jesus that claimed he was born out of wedlock (cf. *Acts of Pilate*, 2:3; Origen, *Cels.*, 1:28). Others take it as anticipating their indictment of Jesus in v.48 as "a Samaritan and demon-possessed." There is some evidence of a legend that Satan seduced Eve and that their son, Cain, became the father of the

Jews rather than Seth (cf. Louis Ginzberg, *Legends of the Bible* [Philadelphia: Jewish Publication Society, 1956], 54). In that case, the Pharisees would be denying in the strongest possible terms that they belonged to this particular illegitimate family line. Or it may be that they were affirming in OT terms that they were members of the true religion, and not apostate. Whatever their denial of illegitimacy refers to, one thing they believe to be absolutely certain: God himself is their only Father. Not only is Abraham the physical progenitor of their race, God himself is their true and only spiritual father. Not even for a moment do they consider that there might be some truth in what Jesus has been saying. His argument that conduct reveals origin goes unheeded. Their answer to all such issues is to affirm repeatedly what they have already decided to believe about themselves. No one is so blind as the person convinced of his or her own spiritual superiority.

42 The simple truth is that if God were the father of those who were opposing Jesus, they would love (instead of oppose) him. The reason is obvious—he "came from God" and now is present in their midst. To know God as Father is to love the Son who was sent by him. As John put it in his first epistle, "Everyone who loves the father loves his child as well" (1Jn 5:1). The failure of the Jews to welcome Jesus with gladness reveals the tragic fact that God is not their father.

43 Jesus asks why his "language" (*lalia*, GK *3282*, is "audible speech" in contrast to *logos*, GK *3364*, v.43b, which refers to his message, the content of what he is saying) is "not clear" to them. The words he uses should be perfectly comprehensible. He then answers his own question: they don't understand because "[they] are unable to hear" what he is saying. Since Jesus' language is clearly comprehensible, the problem must lie in a different area. The truth is that they are so blinded by their preconceptions that they are unable to hear and grasp the essential truth he is laying before them. Comprehension depends on being spiritually open to the truth. Their failure to understand stemmed from their misguided certainty that what Jesus had to say was wrong because of who they had already decided him to be.

In passing, it is interesting that the CEV takes v.43b not as answering v.43a but as an additional question: "Can't you stand to hear what I am saying?" The suggestion is not without merit, because the Greek text begins with *hoti* ("because") and requires the reader to fill in some appropriate words. (The NIV's rendering is an incomplete sentence.) If the CEV is right, v.43b essentially repeats the question rather than providing an answer to it.

44 At this point Jesus states unequivocally what up till now he has only alluded to: "You belong to your father, the devil." The issue is clear-cut, as Jesus says in effect, "Not Abraham but the devil is your true father. He has been a murderer from the beginning, and it is *his* malicious desires that you are intent on carrying out. He robbed Adam and Eve of their immortality and brought death to the entire human race [cf. Ro 5:12]. No wonder you want to kill me. Not only that, but your father, the devil, abandoned the truth. He questioned the susceptible Eve as to whether God had really prohibited eating fruit from the tree and assured her that if she did she would not die [Ge 3:1–4; cf. 2:17]." Lying comes naturally to the devil because "there is no truth in him .... He is a liar and the father of lies" (cf. Ac 5:3).

45 It is important to note that for Jesus the devil is not some personification of evil but actually exists and is engaged in all sorts of deceitful and destructive practices. His control of the minds and actions of the Jewish leaders is so extensive that it can be truthfully said that he is their father. In contrast, Jesus tells the truth, and it is for this very reason that they do not believe him. They have drunk so deeply at the wells of falsehood that they are unable to even recognize the truth. Error has become truth, resulting in a dramatic reversal in which all genuine truth is necessarily judged to be erroneous. When darkness becomes light, all light is darkness.

46 That this denunciation of his opponents is absolutely true is supported by what Morris, 465, calls Jesus' "staggering assertion of sinlessness"— "Can any of you prove me guilty of sin?" "Is there anyone anywhere," Jesus is asking, "who can demonstrate that I have done anything wrong? If not, it follows that, since I am telling the truth, you should believe me. You who are supposedly committed to the truth ought to accept what I have to say."

47 As certain as night follows day, the person who belongs to God will gladly listen to what God has to say. The reason that Jesus' adversaries do not hear and obey his message is that they "do not belong to God." These assertions made by Jesus are tremendous in their scope. He has claimed in the presence of the religious leaders of the day that he has come from God, that he is without sin and can be trusted absolutely, and that—in spite of all their pretensions—they do not belong to God but have as their father the devil. Obviously such devastating challenges cannot go unanswered.

NOTES

41 While μοιχεία (*moicheia*, GK *3657*) in v.3 refers to adultery in the sense of illicit sexual relations between two people, at least one of whom is married, πορνεία (*porneia*, GK *4518*; used here in the phrase ἐκ πορνείας . . . γεγεννήμεθα, *ek porneias . . . gegennēmetha*, "are [not] illegitimate children") is a broader term referring to "various kinds of 'unsanctioned sexual intercourse'" (BDAG, 854). The latter term is used literally in reference to prostitution, unchastity, and fornication, and figuratively of apostasy from God. Since the relationship between God and his people was viewed as a marriage bond, any breaking of that bond would be harlotry.

44 The NASB's "you are of *your* father the devil" comes closer to reflecting the Greek preposition ἐκ (*ek*), which stresses the idea of source or origin. To "belong to . . . the devil" (NIV) is much weaker than to "have one's origin in the devil". The NET has "from your father the devil," but this lacks the strong emphasis of the Greek preposition.

d. "Before Abraham was, I am" (8:48–59)

48The Jews answered him, "Aren't we right in saying that you are a Samaritan and demon-possessed?"

49"I am not possessed by a demon," said Jesus, "but I honor my Father and you dishonor me. **50**I am not seeking glory for myself; but there is one who seeks it, and he is the judge. **51**I tell you the truth, if anyone keeps my word, he will never see death."

52At this the Jews exclaimed, "Now we know that you are demon-possessed! Abraham died and so did the prophets, yet you say that if anyone keeps your word, he will never taste death. ⁵³Are you greater than our father Abraham? He died, and so did the prophets. Who do you think you are?"

⁵⁴Jesus replied, "If I glorify myself, my glory means nothing. My Father, whom you claim as your God, is the one who glorifies me. ⁵⁵Though you do not know him, I know him. If I said I did not, I would be a liar like you, but I do know him and keep his word. ⁵⁶Your father Abraham rejoiced at the thought of seeing my day; he saw it and was glad."

⁵⁷"You are not yet fifty years old," the Jews said to him, "and you have seen Abraham!"

⁵⁸"I tell you the truth," Jesus answered, "before Abraham was born, I am!" ⁵⁹At this, they picked up stones to stone him, but Jesus hid himself, slipping away from the temple grounds.

COMMENTARY

48 It is clear that the religious rulers could not allow Jesus to stand there in the temple courts and charge them with being children of the devil. So they countered by declaring that he, not they, was the one who wasn't a genuine member of the Jewish race. Calling for an affirmative response, they ask whether it is true that he is a "Samaritan and demon-possessed." Relations between the Jews and Samaritans had long been bitter and disrespectful. To tell a Jew that he was a Samaritan was the lowest kind of insult. The Samaritans were a mixed race, considered apostate, and at least at a later date often connected with magic and the demonic. Origen (*Cels.*, 6:11) tells us about Dosistheus, a prophet in Samaria who claimed to be the son of God and was considered mad by the Jews. Since in the following verse Jesus responds to the charge of being demon-possessed but not to being a Samaritan, we may infer that the two were considered essentially the same.

49 Far from being possessed by a demon, Jesus by his words and actions is bringing honor to his Father. The accusations made by the Jews are 180 degrees off target. They do not recognize that what Jesus has been telling them is in fact a message from

God himself. To charge that this message comes from one possessed by an evil spirit shows how hopelessly blind they were to spiritual reality. While Jesus honors the Father, they dishonor Jesus and consequently God too. Jesus continually brings honor to God by carrying out his will; they continually dishonor (both *timō*, GK *5506*, and *atimazete*, GK *869*, are present tense) both the Son and the Father by not accepting the message.

50–51 Jesus does not seek glory for himself but leaves it to the Father, who as judge (the one competent to decide all things with fairness) wants him to have it. Verse 51 begins with a double "amen," indicating its special importance. Astounding as it must have sounded to his adversaries, Jesus declares, "If anyone keeps my word, he will never see death." As he said earlier, to hear his word and to believe in the one who sent him is to have passed over from death to life (5:24; cf. 6:47; 11:26). He is the one who has the words that give life (6:63, 68).

52–53 The people misunderstood Jesus' remark about never seeing death to mean that he was claiming that he would never die. This confirmed them in their opinion that Jesus was demon-possessed. Death had been the common experience of every person in the long history of humankind. Even Abraham, the "friend of God" (Isa 41:8; Jas 2:23), and the prophets died. To "taste death" and to "see death" (v.51) are Hebraic expressions for dying. How could believing what this untutored Galilean had to say prevent a person from dying? Obviously he is mad. And he surely would be, except for the fact that what he said is true. There is no middle ground: Jesus is either the Son of God or a raving lunatic. The decision as to which he is falls on every individual, and the eternal fate of every human being hangs on that crucial decision.

From the perspective of the Jews, Jesus was placing himself on a higher level than Abraham. Even Abraham, the great patriarch and father of the Jewish race, shared with the prophets and everyone else the common experience of death. So they ask, "What sort of a person are you claiming to be?" Once again, the Jews miss the point. Jesus isn't setting himself up at all; he is carrying out his mission in complete subjection to the will of his Father. Their failure to grasp who Jesus really is has led to a complete misunderstanding of what he is about. The same confusion is understandable in the case of the Samaritan woman (4:12), but hardly with the religious elite of Israel.

54 Jesus doesn't answer their derisive question but explains that were he to glorify himself, it would amount to nothing. Those who claim honor for themselves are quickly understood as self-serving, and their words are hollow. No, the One who is glorifying him is none other than his Father, the very One they claim as their God. The glory of which Jesus speaks is the glory of the incarnation, brought into focus in the death and resurrection of the Son of God.

55 Jesus levels against the Jews the accusation that they "do not know [God]." This is a terrible indictment against learned religionists! In contrast (the use of the personal pronoun and its location in the sen-

tence lend considerable emphasis), Jesus *does* know him. Some writers call attention to the two verbs in v.55a used for "to know," pointing out that the Jews had not come to recognize him (*egnōkate*, perfect active indicative of *ginōskō*, GK *1182*) but that Jesus knew him intuitively and directly (*oida*, GK *3857*; so Hendriksen, 2:64). But others assert that there is probably no distinction between the two at this point (so Bruce, 204).

Note how closely Jesus links personal knowledge and obedience ("I do know him and keep his word"). The two cannot be separated. Jesus knows the Father not only because he is eternally coexistent with him but also because he obeys him. It is precisely because he lived a life of obedience to the Father that he knows him. If Jesus were to deny that he knew the Father, he "would be a liar," just like his adversaries. It is helpful to keep in mind the actual setting in which Jesus carries on this interchange. He is in an outer court of the temple, in the time following the Feast of Tabernacles, and speaking to a group of highly religious Jews whose reputations for piety depend on public opinion. To confront them in public and pronounce them liars is to put his life in severe jeopardy.

56 Jesus continues his discourse by pointing out that, in contrast to the hostility of the Jews toward him, "Abraham rejoiced at the thought of seeing my [Jesus'] day." This remark has occasioned much speculation. Did Abraham actually see the day in which Jesus lived? Some rabbis argued that Abraham was given a vision of his descendants. Rabbi Akiba (*Gen. Rab.* 44:22–28) held that Abraham was privileged to preview the coming ages. But Jesus doesn't say that Abraham actually *saw* his day, only that he rejoiced in anticipation of seeing it. Others interpret the saying in terms of certain events, such as the birth of Isaac, whose name means "he laughs" (Ge 17:19), or the time when Abraham told Isaac that "God himself" would "provide the lamb" for sacrifice (Ge 22:8). It was through Isaac that the Messiah would eventually come, so it was to this great event that these incidents pointed. However, in the final clause of v.56 Jesus said of Abraham, "he saw [my day] and was glad." In some sense, Abraham actually saw the day of Jesus. A few writers suggest that since Abraham was alive in paradise at that time (Lk 16:19–31), it was from there that he saw Jesus' day. But that all three verbs in the verse are in the aorist tense points to something that *had* happened, not something that was happening.

A related question has to do with whether "my day" is to be taken as the period of Jesus' earthly ministry or as the eschatological day of his parousia. Barrett's answer, 352, provides the most plausible resolution: "It is idle to ask whether by Jesus' 'day' John intended his ministry or the coming glory of the Son of man. He meant that the work of salvation, potentially complete in Abraham, was actually complete in Jesus." It is in this sense that Abraham rejoiced at the thought of seeing Jesus' day and, seeing it, was glad.

57 Once again, the Jews misunderstand what Jesus was actually saying and "in the inaccuracy born of irritation" (Temple, 1:149) misquote what had been said. They protest that Jesus is not yet fifty years old, so how could he have possibly seen the patriarch Abraham! They chose to pretend that Jesus was claiming to be a contemporary of Abraham (and only a madman would do that!). "Fifty years" is not intended to suggest the actual age of Jesus but was the normal age at which a Levite would stop working (cf. Nu 4:2–3; 8:24–25).

58 Jesus' answer (an unqualified "before Abraham was born, I am!") is prefaced by a double "amen." Earlier he had used the famous *egō eimi* ("I am") to establish his identity as the one coming to bring salvation (cf. vv.24, 28). "I am" became "I am he." Here *egō eimi* should be taken absolutely. Certainly it reflects Exodus 3:14, where God reveals his name as

"I AM WHO I AM" and instructs Moses to tell the Israelites that "I AM" has sent him. Barrett, 352, is again on target in taking the verse to mean, "Before Abraham came into being, I eternally was, as now I am, and ever continue to be." What Jesus is claiming is eternal existence. He knows of Abraham's delight in contemplating the future because there is no period of time in which Jesus did not exist. Not only was he before Abraham, but he now is and will forever be.

59 That the Jews understood Jesus' statement as implying deity is clear from the fact that they "picked up stones to stone him." For an itinerant Galilean teacher to claim divine prerogatives was blasphemous in their eyes. Leviticus 24:16 states unequivocally that "anyone who blasphemes the name of the LORD must be put to death," with the execution being carried out by stoning. In Jesus' case, a handy supply of stones would have been readily available, since the temple was still in the process of being built. No thought was given to the need of a trial by law. The Jews were so infuriated by what Jesus claimed for himself that they picked up stones to do away with this troublemaker once and for all. Although the Romans did not allow the Jews to carry out capital punishment (cf. 18:31), they could probably have carried out a stoning like this without undue opposition from their overlords.

In any case, Jesus' critics were so enraged that they didn't even think of possible consequences. They wanted to lynch Jesus but were unsuccessful because his time had not yet come (cf. 7:6, 8). Jesus "hid himself, slipping away from the temple grounds." Rieu translates, "made his way out of the Temple unobserved." To what extent this may have involved supernatural protection is not known. Because of the active hostility of the Jews, it would appear that God intervened in some way so as to make his escape possible (cf. Lk 4:29–30).

NOTES

59 In Scripture, stoning was a form of ritual execution carried out by the assembled community. Deuteronomy 17:6–7 requires two or more witnesses, who must then be the first to cast stones at the accused. The OT lists a number of offenses that are to be punished by stoning, ranging all the way from blaspheming the divine name (Lev 24:14) to sacrificing a child to Molech (Lev 20:2) to gathering sticks on the Sabbath (Nu 15:32–36).

IV. THE CLOSING DAYS OF JESUS' PUBLIC MINISTRY (9:1–12:50)

A. Jesus Heals a Man Born Blind (9:1–41)

OVERVIEW

John gives us no indication of the amount of time that may have lapsed between the events of ch. 8 and the healing of the man born blind in ch. 9. All we know is that this healing miracle took place between the Feast of Tabernacles (7:14) and the Feast of Dedication (10:22) some two months later.

¹As he went along, he saw a man blind from birth. ²His disciples asked him, "Rabbi, who sinned, this man or his parents, that he was born blind?"

³"Neither this man nor his parents sinned," said Jesus, "but this happened so that the work of God might be displayed in his life. ⁴As long as it is day, we must do the work of him who sent me. Night is coming, when no one can work. ⁵While I am in the world, I am the light of the world."

⁶Having said this, he spit on the ground, made some mud with the saliva, and put it on the man's eyes. ⁷"Go," he told him, "wash in the Pool of Siloam" (this word means Sent). So the man went and washed, and came home seeing.

⁸His neighbors and those who had formerly seen him begging asked, "Isn't this the same man who used to sit and beg?" ⁹Some claimed that he was.

Others said, "No, he only looks like him."

But he himself insisted, "I am the man."

¹⁰"How then were your eyes opened?" they demanded.

¹¹He replied, "The man they call Jesus made some mud and put it on my eyes. He told me to go to Siloam and wash. So I went and washed, and then I could see."

¹²"Where is this man?" they asked him.

"I don't know," he said.

¹³They brought to the Pharisees the man who had been blind. ¹⁴Now the day on which Jesus had made the mud and opened the man's eyes was a Sabbath. ¹⁵Therefore the Pharisees also asked him how he had received his sight. "He put mud on my eyes," the man replied, "and I washed, and now I see."

¹⁶Some of the Pharisees said, "This man is not from God, for he does not keep the Sabbath."

But others asked, "How can a sinner do such miraculous signs?" So they were divided.

¹⁷Finally they turned again to the blind man, "What have you to say about him? It was your eyes he opened."

The man replied, "He is a prophet."

¹⁸The Jews still did not believe that he had been blind and had received his sight until they sent for the man's parents. ¹⁹"Is this your son?" they asked. "Is this the one you say was born blind? How is it that now he can see?"

²⁰"We know he is our son," the parents answered, "and we know he was born blind. ²¹But how he can see now, or who opened his eyes, we don't know. Ask him. He is of age; he will speak for himself." ²²His parents said this because they were afraid of the Jews, for already the Jews had decided that anyone who acknowledged that Jesus was the Christ would be put out of the synagogue. ²³That was why his parents said, "He is of age; ask him."

²⁴A second time they summoned the man who had been blind. "Give glory to God," they said. "We know this man is a sinner."

²⁵He replied, "Whether he is a sinner or not, I don't know. One thing I do know. I was blind but now I see!"

²⁶Then they asked him, "What did he do to you? How did he open your eyes?"

²⁷He answered, "I have told you already and you did not listen. Why do you want to hear it again? Do you want to become his disciples, too?"

²⁸Then they hurled insults at him and said, "You are this fellow's disciple! We are disciples of Moses! ²⁹We know that God spoke to Moses, but as for this fellow, we don't even know where he comes from."

³⁰The man answered, "Now that is remarkable! You don't know where he comes from, yet he opened my eyes. ³¹We know that God does not listen to sinners. He listens to the godly man who does his will. ³²Nobody has ever heard of opening the eyes of a man born blind. ³³If this man were not from God, he could do nothing."

³⁴To this they replied, "You were steeped in sin at birth; how dare you lecture us!" And they threw him out.

³⁵Jesus heard that they had thrown him out, and when he found him, he said, "Do you believe in the Son of Man?"

³⁶"Who is he, sir?" the man asked. "Tell me so that I may believe in him."

³⁷Jesus said, "You have now seen him; in fact, he is the one speaking with you."

³⁸Then the man said, "Lord, I believe," and he worshiped him.

³⁹Jesus said, "For judgment I have come into this world, so that the blind will see and those who see will become blind."

⁴⁰Some Pharisees who were with him heard him say this and asked, "What? Are we blind too?"

⁴¹Jesus said, "If you were blind, you would not be guilty of sin; but now that you claim you can see, your guilt remains."

COMMENTARY

1 As Jesus was walking along, he "saw a man blind from birth." Seeing this man who could not see and who supported himself by begging (v.8) moved Jesus to act compassionately and restore his sight. It is worth noting that in this situation it was Jesus who took the initiative.

2 The disciples (last mentioned in 7:3) ask Jesus whose sin was responsible for the man's blindness—his own or his parents'. Reflecting the "primitive and crude conception of divine justice" that "regards every calamity as a punishment for some sin" (Temple, 1:154), the disciples reasoned that the man's blindness must be the result either of his own or his parents' sin. Since the man was born blind, it would appear that he could hardly be at fault for his lack of sight. However, some rabbis apparently thought that an infant could sin while still in the mother's womb and that such sinning could account for inherited defects. The account of Esau and Jacob struggling while still in Rebekah's womb (Ge 25:21–22) was understood by some as an attempt by the older to kill the younger (thus effecting sin in the womb; cf. Str-B, 2:527–29). On the other hand, it was clearly stated in the Decalogue that children are punished for the sin of the fathers (Ex 20:5; Dt 5:9).

While it is certainly true that in a specific case sin may be punished with a physical malady (e.g., Miriam was struck with leprosy for her sin against Moses; Nu 12:1–12; also 1Co 11:30), it does not follow that all illness is the result of some specific sin (Paul had a "thorn in the flesh" to keep him from being conceited; 2Co 12:7; cf. Gal 4:13). The disciples' understanding didn't go beyond that of Job's friends who were sure that "every person's suffering is indicative of the measure of his guilt in the eyes of God" (NIVSB, introduction to Job). To their way of thinking, obviously the man was blind because either he or his parents had sinned. The general principle was laid down by Rabbi Ammi: "There is no death without sin, and there is no suffering without iniquity" (*b. Šabb.* 55a).

3 Jesus answered their query not by denying that sin is sometimes punished with physical infirmity but by pointing out that in this specific case it was not a factor. The NEB translates, "It is not that this man or his parents sinned." The man was congenitally blind "so that [introducing a purpose clause] the work of God might be displayed in his life." It is not as though God decided that this particular individual should be blind from birth so that he would have the opportunity to show how great a work he could perform. It is rather that he overruled the misfortune so that both the man and those who would see the miracle would come to realize that Jesus was "the light of the world" (v.5).

4 Using the universal symbols of light and darkness, Jesus says that as long as daylight lasts, it is crucial that he and his disciples continue to do the work of the one who sent him. Night is coming, and no one can work when darkness falls. The day of which Jesus speaks represents the years of his life on earth, and the coming night the time of his departure from this world. Obviously we are dealing with an aphorism and should not understand Jesus as saying that, once he left this world, Christian ministry was over.

Some copyists, troubled by the plural pronoun "we" (*hēmas*) with which the Greek text of v.4 begins, substituted the singular "I" (*eme*), thus restricting to Jesus alone the work that God had sent him to do (so KJV, NKJV). While it is true that the redemptive work of the cross was carried out solely by Jesus, it does not follow that believers have no share in the task of taking the message to the world. In a larger sense, it is perfectly true that *we*, along with Jesus, must do the work of the one who sent *him*.

5 In 8:12 Jesus stated the same truth ("I am the light of the world") as a general principle; here he applies it to a specific incident. A man born blind is about to receive his sight. And so it is with everyone in a spiritual sense. We are all "born blind" and come to receive sight when touched by the one who is the light of the world. Jesus, the very Son of God (who dwells in "unapproachable light," 1 Ti 6:16) is he who brings the light of salvation to all who turn to him in faith.

6 In two other places in the Gospels Jesus is said to have used saliva in connection with a healing. In Mark 7 Jesus touched the deaf and mute man's tongue with his saliva (v.33), and in Mark 8 he moistened the eyes of the blind man at Bethsaida with saliva (v.23). People in the ancient world regarded saliva as possessing curative powers. In the Hellenistic world it was frequently used in magical rites and for that very reason came to be forbidden in the Jewish community.

7 The blind man followed Jesus' instructions by going to the Pool of Siloam and washing. We are reminded of Elisha sending Naaman to wash in the Jordan for his leprosy (2 Ki 5:10–14), though in that case Naaman resisted following the prophet's orders and had to be persuaded by his servants to do as he was told. Not so the blind man of John 9—he went to the pool, washed, and received his sight. Note the close connection between obedience and experiencing the transforming power of God at work. Had the blind man not obeyed he would have continued in his blindness. So it is with spiritual blindness. To resist the instructions of the One who came to give spiritual sight is to continue in the darkness of unbelief.

The Pool of Siloam is located just inside the southeastern section of the city wall. Water flowed through a tunnel built by Hezekiah from the Gihon spring, outside the wall, to the Pool of Siloam. In this way a supply of water was guaranteed in case the city came under attack. John explains that the word "Siloam" means "Sent." Applied originally to the aqueduct that brought the water, the name (Siloam) became transferred to the pool itself. As the water was "sent" to the pool within the city walls, so also was Jesus sent to bring refreshment and healing to the spiritually thirsty. Chrysostom, the fourth-century bishop of Constantinople, referred to Jesus as the Sent One, "the spiritual Siloam" (*Hom. Jo.* 57).

8 When the man who was born blind returned home able to see, his neighbors and others who knew him only as a blind beggar questioned whether he was that same man. Apparently there was a noticeable difference in his countenance. Now that his sight was restored, the one who used to sit at the street corner and beg suddenly experienced a new and wonderful world. No wonder his friends found it difficult to believe that he was the same man. To experience the power of the kingdom of God and for the first time to see the eternal plan of

God for life both now and in the age to come effects a radical change in the life of the new believer.

9–10 Abraham Lincoln once said that "after forty every man is responsible for his own face." More often than we are willing to admit, faces reflect the inner state of the soul. So some who were there said that he really was the blind beggar, while others held that he only looked like him. But he insisted that he was the same man whom they were accustomed to seeing as a blind beggar. Their question "How then were your eyes opened?" was not so much a procedural one as it was the natural reaction to a miracle: "How can it be that you are now able to see?"

11 The blind man tells his story in simple fashion: "The man they call Jesus" did it. It is interesting to follow the change in perspective that will take place as the narrative continues. Here he is simply "the man they call Jesus." In v.17 he is "a prophet." Finally he is "a man . . . from God" (v.33). It is the dawning realization of what has happened to him that leads the blind man to conclude that Jesus is "the godly man who does [the Father's] will" (v.31). Honest contemplation of the life and work of Jesus will lead the unbiased person to acknowledge that Jesus is who he says he is. It has always been the case that rational thought does not hinder belief in Jesus as the Son of God. This conclusion is the natural and normal outcome of any fair-minded appraisal of the facts. Those who are unable to believe begin with the assumption that such a conclusion is unthinkable.

13–34 The Pharisees' investigation of the healing took place in three steps. First they interviewed the blind man himself (vv.13–17), then they took up the matter with the man's parents (vv.18–23), and finally they interrogated the blind man a second time (vv.24–34). The Jewish authorities were frustrated by the whole affair and in the end excommunicated the very one who had experienced the healing power of Jesus.

13 The text does not say who brought the blind man to the Pharisees, but it may well have been the neighbors of the blind man and those accustomed to seeing him on the street as a beggar (v.8). Since the restoration of his sight was obviously a miracle, the most appropriate group to provide a theological explanation would be the Pharisees. The Sadducees were primarily concerned with the exercise of authority and would not have been interested in an issue of (in their opinion) such minor religious significance. Interestingly, the Sadducees are not mentioned at all in the fourth gospel. That John does not mention any "scribes" as part of the examining body may be explained by the fact that by the time he wrote his gospel all the scribes were of Pharisaic persuasion. (The single reference to "scribes" in John is in the questionable section on the woman caught in adultery; see 8:3.)

14–15 John records that the day on which Jesus had made mud and performed the healing miracle was a Sabbath. This posed a serious problem for the Pharisees in that such "work" violated the Sabbath. While it was true that healing was permitted if a person's life were in danger, in the case of the man born blind no such urgency existed. Among the thirty-nine works not allowed on the Sabbath was kneading (*m. Šabb.* 7:2), and the mixing of dirt and spittle fell into that category. So in a somewhat formal inquiry the council asked the man to explain how he had received his sight. In contrast to the question in v.10, this request has to do with the procedure involved. The blind man responded in a straightforward manner—"he put mud on my eyes, I washed, and now I am seeing." (Note the two aorists followed by a present tense.)

16 The person and work of Jesus inevitably give rise to division. His claims about himself put people in a position in which they must either accept or deny what he is saying. So it has always been and always will be. In this setting the Pharisees must come to some conclusion about him and his power to heal. Some of the Pharisees reasoned that since he violated the Sabbath he could not be from God. But another group reasoned that since Jesus had done "such miraculous signs," there was no way he could be a sinner.

The approach of the first group was theoretical. They did not stop to consider that their major premise might be flawed. Their understanding of what was not allowed on the Sabbath was the product of oral tradition. While their logic was sound, they were prevented from arriving at a satisfactory conclusion because they began with a faulty premise. The second and more open-minded group reasoned inductively from the fact of the healing itself. While biblical evidence does not support their premise that the ungodly cannot perform the miraculous (Dt 13:1–2; cf. Rev 13:13–15), they nevertheless arrived at the truth. So a division developed between the two groups (cf. 7:37; 10:19). Adolf Schlatter held that the division followed the tendencies attributed to the schools of Shammai, who tended to argue from first principles, and Hillel, who tended to pay attention to the established facts (cf. Bruce, 213).

17 It may have been members of this second group who turned to the blind man and asked for his opinion about Jesus. After all, he was the one whose eyes had been opened. Who could be better qualified to make a judgment about the one who had performed the healing? The answer of the blind man is forthright and honest: "He is a prophet" (cf. the remark of the Samaritan woman, 4:19). Temple, 1:599, cites the early writer Chemnitius as saying, "You will often find more solid theological piety among tailors and shoemakers than among cardinals, bishops, and abbots."

18 The Jewish leaders refused to believe the testimony of the man whose sight Jesus had restored. That he could now see was obvious, but had a genuine miracle been performed? Perhaps for all these years he had only pretended to be blind in order to make a living. Or perhaps he only looked like the blind beggar and was now trying to pass himself off as someone whose sight had been restored in order to gain a following for Jesus. These questions could be settled by the man's parents, so to them the Jews went for an answer.

19 The leaders asked two (or perhaps three) questions. First, "Is this man your son?" In effect, they say, "We need to know, and you as parents are in a position to verify that he is your son and that he was born blind." The Greek text continues the main clause of the sentence with a dependent clause: "who you say was born blind." The NIV turns this clause into a separate question and asks, "Is this the one you say was born blind?" Williams may be closest to the intended meaning with his interpretive, "Is this your son, and do you affirm that he was born blind?" Their final question is, "How does it happen, then, that he is no longer blind but able to see?"

What they were really struggling to find was a rational explanation for what appeared to be a miracle. Those who approach a situation with their minds made up must somehow find an explanation for evidence that points in another direction. Since it is the truth that sets a person free (8:32), all deception is a form of bondage. The authorities were enslaved to their preconceived opinions of Jesus and his claims. He could not be the Messiah, because he didn't measure up to what they had in mind.

20–21 The parents answer the first question(s) but not the last one, thus avoiding involvement in what they correctly understood to be a risky situation. "He is our son—that we know," they answered. "And we also know he was born blind." They were willing to affirm that much but unwilling to speculate as to how it was that he received his sight. "How he can see now or who opened his eyes, we don't know." It would appear that at this point they were not telling the entire truth. Certainly a person blind from birth who was made to see would have shared such a remarkable event with his own family. So the parents tell their inquisitors to ask their son. "After all, he is of age and able to speak for himself." To be "of age" undoubtedly meant that he had passed his thirteenth birthday and was legally responsible.

22–23 The reason for the parents' thoughtless evasion of the issue is that they were afraid of the Jewish leaders. So they thrust the responsibility onto their son, who until this point had been blind and had suffered the disgrace of having to beg for a living. One marvels that fear is capable of silencing the parent of a son who has had the misfortune not only of being blind from birth but also of having suffered the disgrace of mendicancy.

The leaders had already decided that anyone who acknowledged that "Jesus is the Christ" would be expelled from the synagogue. Many understand this as a confessional statement and hold that it is not historical but belongs to the time when the gospel was being written. Barrett's evaluation, 361, is often quoted: "That the synagogue had already at that time applied a test of Christian heresy is unthinkable." Supporting this argument is the fact that the adjective *aposynagōgos* ("put out of the synagogue," GK *697*) occurs only in John (9:22; 12:42; 16:2) and is therefore considered to be of later usage. Lindars, 347, excuses the anachronism on the basis that "John speaks of the cost of discipleship in terms of the conditions with which his readers were familiar."

It should be noted, however, that the statement need not be considered as the equivalent of the later Pauline confession "Jesus is Lord" (e.g., Ro 10:9). To acknowledge Jesus as *Christos* ("Christ," GK *5986*) was simply to affirm that he was "the Messiah." At Caesarea Philippi Peter had confessed, "You

are the Christ, the Son of the living God" (Mt 16:16; cf. Lk 12:8; Jn 9:35). Phillips moves entirely away from any confessional note by translating, "who admitted that Christ had done this thing." So the evidence is far too weak to maintain that the verse is anachronistic and fails to provide an accurate picture of the historical situation. The excommunication threatened by the authorities could have been permanent exclusion from the Jewish community but more likely was temporary suspension of religious privilege. In any case, it was sufficiently serious so as to cause the parents of the blind man to stay clear of any entanglement and shift the responsibility back onto their son.

24 The testimony of the blind man's parents was of no help to the Pharisees. They had hoped to learn that the man had not been born blind, but his parents had testified to the fact of his congenital blindness. The Pharisees were frustrated even further by the parents' unwillingness to go on record as to who had opened their son's eyes or how it had happened. So (the *oun*, "therefore," omitted from the NIV, is important) they turn a second time to the blind man himself. Since the only other explanation open to them—that Jesus was who he said he was—was unacceptable, they reasoned that the blind man must be hiding something that would explain the apparent healing. Their charge, "Give glory to God," is usually taken as the "equivalent of a Jewish oath" (Borchert, 321) that called on the man to own up and tell the truth. Following the rout at Jericho, Achan, who had hidden some of the spoils of battle under his tent, is told by Joshua to "give glory to the LORD" and reveal what he had done (Jos 7:19; cf. Jer 13:16, 1 Esd 9:8).

Since it is contextually difficult to relate the statement (interpreted as a Jewish oath) with the remark that follows, some have taken it to mean, "Give glory to God, not to this man Jesus." In this case the reason is clear: "we know this man is a sinner." The religious elite had already decided the case in their own minds and were pressing the man to conform to their evaluation. The "we" here is emphatic: "we, the recognized authorities in matters such as these, have decided that he is a sinner." And according to their interpretation of the law, Jesus was technically a sinner, since he had broken the Sabbath by working (read "healing") on that day.

25 The blind man refused to get entangled in the theological question of whether or not the miracle rendered Jesus a sinner; rather, he gives a straightforward declaration regarding his own experience: "I don't know whether or not he is a sinner; that is for you to decide. The one thing I do know is that I was blind but now I see!" Such evidence is beyond disputation.

This affirmation has been adopted by millions of believers who, while not certain about how the miraculous transformation in their lives took place, nevertheless know that once they were blind (without spiritual sight) but now are able to see (to understand the presence and power of the redeeming Christ). The fact that God has entered their lives is the central reality of their new life in Christ. No amount of theological obfuscation can undermine the strong confidence that comes from personal experience.

26–27 Hoping to trap the blind man in some inconsistency, the Pharisees ask him to repeat his story, saying in effect, "Tell us how he opened your eyes." The ruse does not work, and the man, now a bit weary from the repeated questioning, begins to counterattack. He answers that he has already told them what happened and they were unwilling to accept his account. Then, in what amounts to a satirical taunt, he asks why they want to hear it all again. "It couldn't be, could it," he asks, "that you want to become his disciple?" The question is asked in such a way as to expect a negative response. Bruce, 217, refers to the exchange as displaying "a hitherto unsuspected capacity for ironical repartee" on the part of the blind man.

28–29 At this point the Pharisees drop all pretense of impartiality. They take recourse to the only stratagem available to those who have come out second best in a debate—an abusive ad hominem. "We are disciples of Moses," they say, "and we know that God spoke to him; but as for this fellow [a derogatory reference], we don't know where he came from or who gave him any authority. We belong to Moses, but you have taken sides with this lawbreaker." Their answer was the equivalent of the childish taunt, "My dad is better than your dad."

The Greek articles (*sy*, "you," and *hēmeis*, "we") in v.28 mark a strong contrast. "*You* are a disciple of that man, but *we* belong to Moses. We know it was to Moses that God gave the law (Ex 33:11; Nu 12:6–8), but we don't know where this Jesus came from and therefore who it was that authorized him to speak." The comparison was meant to show how inferior were the credentials of Jesus in comparison with those of Moses. How ironic that they failed to understand it was this same Moses who spoke of the coming Redeemer (cf. Jn 5:45–47). That Isaiah had spoken of the restoration of sight to the blind as one of the signs of the messianic age (Isa 29:18; 35:5; 42:7) simply escaped them.

30–31 The Pharisees' resort to insults was meant to put the blind beggar in his place for good, but it accomplished just the opposite. Now with even greater boldness he chides them with a logical argument that begins with God's unwillingness to answer the prayers of sinners and leads irresistibly to the conclusion that Jesus is in fact "from God." "What a remarkable thing!" he says in effect. "You say you have no idea as to where he came from, and yet he has opened my eyes so that I can see. How can that be? We know that God doesn't listen to sinners but only to the one who is devout and does his will" (cf. NEB). Obviously Jesus is not denying that the sinner's penitent prayer for forgiveness goes unanswered. He is simply reflecting the common biblical teaching that those who persist in wickedness will not be heard even when they pray (Isa 1:15; cf. 1Jn 3:21–22).

32–33 The argument continues: No one has ever heard of the restoration of sight in a person who was "born blind." References to the healing of blindness in the OT are rare. God opened the eyes of the Arameans who had been blinded as a result of Elisha's prayers (2Ki 6:8–20; cf. Tob 2:10; 11:10–13), but in no case do we hear of a person born blind whose sight was restored. The conclusion is obvious: "If [Jesus] were not from God, he could do nothing." Though stated in a negative fashion, what we have is a clear confession on the part of the blind beggar that Jesus came "from God."

34 It was obvious by now that the "power brokers of religion" (Borchert, 323) had lost the argument to the blind beggar. When all else fails, resort to personal abuse. So the Pharisees, hot with anger, blurted out, "You were steeped in sin at birth." That the man was blind *from birth* was to the Jewish authorities strong evidence that God was punishing him for some sin. It would be a terrible disgrace to allow a man such as that to instruct the religious leaders of the nation. His disreputable position in society was viewed as undermining the validity of any testimony he might give. "How dare you lecture us!" Never mind that the man who had lived his entire life in darkness is now able to see; God simply doesn't work through anyone cursed by the plague of blindness—so they reasoned.

So they "threw him out." This is often understood as an official excommunication from the synagogue (so rendered in a number of contemporary translations, such as Goodspeed, NEB, NLT et al.). The problem is that only the Sanhedrin had the authority to excommunicate. Unless this particular group of interrogators was acting in an official capacity, it would be better to understand their action as a rude dismissal from their gathering. Temple, 1:159, calls it a "contemptuous expulsion from the Court." While the questioning by the Pharisees would undoubtedly lead to a full excommunication from the synagogue, it is not clear at this point whether or not that particular step has been taken. The entire episode illustrates the truth of 1:5 that "the light shines in the darkness, but the darkness has not understood it." Jesus, the light of the world, remains a mystery to those who are blinded by unbelief.

35 When the word came that the blind man had been "excommunicated" by the Pharisees, Jesus set out to find him. This illustrates one of the most profound truths of the Christian faith: it is God who pursues the needy, and not the other way around. The initiative in salvation is his, not ours. We do not seek God (Ro 3:11); he seeks us (Lk 19:10).

On finding the man cured of blindness, Jesus asks, "Do *you* [the pronoun is emphatic] believe in the Son of Man?" While the unbelief of the religious elite was a settled matter beyond discussion, the belief of the blind man was open for instruction. The designation "Son of Man" is of special interest. While it is often used in connection with judgment (as in vv.39–41), here its primary thrust is that of Jesus as the incarnate revelation of God's glory (cf. 3:13–14; 12:23; 13:31).

36 In asking, "Who is he?" the blind man is not asking about the meaning of the title, as if to say, "Who are you talking about when you say 'Son of Man?'" but is asking Jesus to identify the one who is the Son of Man. "Tell me so that I may believe in him" he adds. The blind man realizes that the one of whom Jesus speaks is the one responsible for the miracle that gave him his sight. He wants to know who this person is so that he can honor him by showing that he is fully worthy of his trust.

37 Jesus stands before the man and identifies himself as the one who has brought him his sight.

The man has seen him with eyes of faith (he obeyed the word of Jesus, went to the Pool of Siloam, and washed; v.7) and in fact is speaking with the very one who granted his sight. Note that the first verb is in the perfect tense (*heōrakas*, "have seen," GK *3972*) and the second in the present (*lalōn*, "is speaking," GK *3281*). The only other occasion on which Jesus so unambiguously declared his messiahship was his open confession to the Samaritan woman (4:26).

38 When Jesus revealed himself as the messianic Son of Man, the blind man responded, "Lord, I believe." In v.36 the vocative *kyrie* (GK *3261*) was correctly translated as a polite reference ("sir"). By v.38, however, a major theological step has been taken. When the man said, "*Kyrie*, I believe," it could only mean that he viewed Jesus as one worthy of his personal trust and obedience, hence "Lord." The contemporary ecclesiastical world contains no small group of followers who respect Jesus and regard him worthy of the title "sir." However, it is only when *kyrie* becomes a personal confession of "Jesus is Lord" that one moves from the kingdom of darkness into the kingdom of light. Having confessed his allegiance to Jesus as Lord, the blind man "worshiped him." While some think that the man's spiritual state was still in the incipient stage of growth (and therefore understand his worship as little more than an appropriate display of respect), it is far more probable, in view of the fuller connotations of "Lord," that the man actually knelt before Jesus in a true act of worship. (*Proskyneō*, GK *4686*, means "to fall down and worship," "to prostrate oneself before.")

39 The concluding verses of ch. 9 bring into focus the theological truth that lies behind the coming to faith of the blind beggar and the determined unbelief of the Pharisees. Jesus states that as a result of his coming into the world "the blind will see and those who see will become blind." The physical restoration of sight in the case of the blind man illustrates the truth that, though born in spiritual darkness, those who believe in the power of Jesus Christ to open the eyes of the soul are given the gift of spiritual sight. By the same token, those who profess a clear vision of the ways of God while at the same time denying by their lifestyle its transforming effect will ultimately find that they are blind. Bultmann, 341, calls this the "paradox of revelation." It is in this sense that Jesus can say that "for judgment [he has] come into this world." The statement is not at odds with 12:47, where he said he came *not to judge* the world but to save it. The ultimate purpose of his coming is to bring salvation, but its inevitable corollary is a separation between those who accept him and those who refuse (cf. 3:17–18).

40 Apparently some Pharisees were still with Jesus when he made this enigmatic statement. They ask somewhat incredulously, "Certainly *we* are not blind, are we?" The essential point that Jesus was making simply escaped them. Surely Jesus could not be talking about them when he said that those who see will become blind. Such is the blindness of those who are unable to follow the simplest argument when its logical conclusion runs counter to their preconceptions! They simply do not get it.

41 Jesus concludes by pointing out that if his opponents were really blind (incapable of understanding), they would not be guilty of sin, but since they claim to see, their guilt remains. The first part of the sentence does not imply that ignorance excuses guilt but that the blindness that "cries out for illumination" (Carson, 378) will not be guilty of the sin of unbelief. Rather, that kind of blindness leads to spiritual sight. On the other hand, the confident assurance that they can see (when the evidence points to a different conclusion) has resulted in a condition of continuing guilt. This kind of blindness is incurable and is what Jesus elsewhere refers to as "an eternal sin" (Mk 3:29; cf. the "sin that leads to death," 1Jn 5:16).

NOTES

2 Various diseases of the eye (including blindness) were extremely common in the ancient world. The Papyrus Ebers (1500 BC) lists a number of eye diseases and about a hundred prescriptions for treatment (cf. *ISBE* 1:525). In Israel and Egypt the most widespread form was probably a purulent inflammation of the eye. Eye disease was spread by flies that carried the discharge from one person to another. In keeping with OT tradition (Dt 28:28 lists blindness among the curses for disobedience), eastern culture in the first century AD regarded blindness as divine punishment for sin.

3 It is possible that ἵνα, *hina*, may introduce a result clause rather than a purpose clause, in which case the sentence would be saying that the man was born blind with the result that the works of God are to be displayed in him. This is supported by a similar use of ἵνα, *hina*, in the final clause of the preceding verse.

8 As cities began to grow so also did the practice of begging. In the OT, begging is associated with wickedness and slothfulness. The psalmist reminds us that never in his life has he seen "the righteous forsaken or his descendants begging bread" (Ps 37:25 NASB); and the writer of Proverbs notes that the sluggard doesn't plow at the proper time, "so he begs during the harvest and has nothing" (Pr 20:4 NASB). The Jewish distaste for begging is reflected in the apocryphal book of Sirach (composed about 180 BC by a Palestinian Jew), where the writer warns, "My son, do not lead the life of a beggar; it is better to die than to beg" (40:28). In the NT period, begging was apparently widespread (examples include the blind beggar Bartimaeus, Mk 10:46; the lame man begging at the gate of the temple, Ac 3:2), primarily due to the lack of an adequate system for extended care for those in need.

17 In calling Jesus "a prophet," the man born blind ascribed to him the highest honor he could think of. Although Jewish teachers of Jesus' day believed that prophecy had come to an end, the term was used rather widely in a perhaps more general sense. John the Baptist was considered a prophet—Matthew 14:5 records that Herod would have liked to put him to death but "he was afraid of the people, because they considered him a prophet (cf. Mt 21:26)—and so was Jesus (Mt 21:11, "The crowds answered, 'This is Jesus, the prophet from Nazareth in Galilee'"). Prophecy in the NT seems to have taken two forms—either incoherent and ecstatic or coherent and rational. The former is prominent in Acts (e.g., Agabus in 11:28; the daughters of Philip, 21:9 et al.), while the latter is found in 1 Corinthians 12 and 14. In the early church, prophets ranked second only to apostles, though their utterances had to be tested (1Th 5:20–21).

21 The TR places the words αὐτὸν ἐρωτήσατε (*auton erōtēsate*, "ask him") after ἡλικίαν ἔχει (*hēlikian echei*, "he is of age"), perhaps to match the similar sequence in v.23. Later translations follow the better MS tradition reflected in 𝔓⁶⁶ ℵ² B (D) L Θ Ψ *f*¹ 33 *pc* lat bo.

22 From the Jewish standpoint, the purpose of "excommunication" was to protect the traditional teachings of Judaism. Those who deviated from the norm must be "put out of the synagogue" in order to preserve the sanctity of Jewish teaching and tradition. The passage in Matthew 18:15–17 provides a procedure used by the Christian community (perhaps modeled after Jewish practice) for dealing with a recalcitrant sinner. He must first be approached in private. If that doesn't produce the desired result, several brothers are to confront him. If he still resists correction, he is to be taken before the church, and only after this proves unfruitful is he to be put out of the believing community ("treat him as you would a pagan or a tax collector," v.17).

35 A few MSS pose the question, "Do you believe in τὸν υἱὸν τοῦ θεοῦ [*ton huion tou theou*, the son of God]?" rather than "τὸν υἱὸν τοῦ ἀνθρώπου [*ton huion tou anthrōpou*, the Son of Man]," but "the external support for ἀνθρώπου [*anthrōpou*] . . . is so weighty . . . that the Committee regarded the reading adopted for the text as virtually certain" (Metzger, 194). In support of the text, NA[27] lists 𝔓[66.75] ℵ B D W *pc* sy[s] co.

38 The verb προσκυνέω (*proskyneō*, "to worship") occurs eleven times in the fourth gospel. In six of the seven verses God is the object of worship. Only here is προσκυνέω, *proskyneō*, used in connection with Jesus. The NET study note at v.38 calls this "extremely significant" and concludes that the act of worship on the part of the man born blind is "the climax of the entire story."

B. Further Teaching Heightens Opposition (10:1–42)

OVERVIEW

Some have argued for various rearrangements of the text of ch. 10 (e.g., placing vv.19–29 immediately after 9:41), but it is best to take the narrative as it stands. Chapter 9 closed with a word of judgment directed against the Pharisees for their blindness. Chapter 10 continues in the same vein with a parable identifying the Pharisees as false leaders of Israel who have gotten into the fold by fraudulent means. Continuity is confirmed by the fact that the double "amen" with which ch. 10 opens never occurs in John at the beginning of a discourse.

While shepherd imagery is common throughout the OT, it is Ezekiel 34 that provides the best single background for Jesus' discourse on the good shepherd (other important OT passages are Isa 56:9–12; Jer 23:1–4; Zec 11; in the NT, see Mk 6:34; Lk 15:1–7; 1Pe 2:25; 5:2–4). Ezekiel 34 begins with a castigation of the shepherds of Israel, who "only take care of themselves" and allow the sheep to be scattered (vv.2–6); it closes with a declaration by the Sovereign Lord that the nation of Israel is his flock, the sheep of his pasture, and that he is their God (v.31).

1. "I Am the Good Shepherd" (10:1–21)

OVERVIEW

In the first section of the discourse (vv.1–5), Jesus contrasts the actions of a false shepherd with those of a true shepherd. The former gains access to the sheep by climbing over the wall, while the latter calls his sheep out of the fold. They follow him because they know his voice. In these verses

Jesus builds a case in general terms against the religious leaders of Israel who have forced themselves on the people. They are contrasted with a true shepherd, who because he genuinely cares for the sheep needs only to call them by name and they follow him.

¹"I tell you the truth, the man who does not enter the sheep pen by the gate, but climbs in by some other way, is a thief and a robber. ²The man who enters by the gate is the shepherd of his sheep. ³The watchman opens the gate for him, and the sheep listen to his voice. He calls his own sheep by name and leads them out. ⁴When he has brought out all his own, he goes on ahead of them, and his sheep follow him because they know his voice. ⁵But they will never follow a stranger; in fact, they will run away from him because they do not recognize a stranger's voice." ⁶Jesus used this figure of speech, but they did not understand what he was telling them.

⁷Therefore Jesus said again, "I tell you the truth, I am the gate for the sheep. ⁸All who ever came before me were thieves and robbers, but the sheep did not listen to them. ⁹I am the gate; whoever enters through me will be saved. He will come in and go out, and find pasture. ¹⁰The thief comes only to steal and kill and destroy; I have come that they may have life, and have it to the full.

¹¹"I am the good shepherd. The good shepherd lays down his life for the sheep. ¹²The hired hand is not the shepherd who owns the sheep. So when he sees the wolf coming, he abandons the sheep and runs away. Then the wolf attacks the flock and scatters it. ¹³The man runs away because he is a hired hand and cares nothing for the sheep.

¹⁴"I am the good shepherd; I know my sheep and my sheep know me—¹⁵just as the Father knows me and I know the Father—and I lay down my life for the sheep. ¹⁶I have other sheep that are not of this sheep pen. I must bring them also. They too will listen to my voice, and there shall be one flock and one shepherd. ¹⁷The reason my Father loves me is that I lay down my life—only to take it up again. ¹⁸No one takes it from me, but I lay it down of my own accord. I have authority to lay it down and authority to take it up again. This command I received from my Father."

¹⁹At these words the Jews were again divided. ²⁰Many of them said, "He is demon-possessed and raving mad. Why listen to him?"

²¹But others said, "These are not the sayings of a man possessed by a demon. Can a demon open the eyes of the blind?"

COMMENTARY

1 "I tell you the truth" is the NIV's translation of the frequent (25 times in John) and important *amēn amēn* (KJV, "verily, verily"; NASB, "truly, truly"). It is used by Jesus to call attention to the fact that what he is about to say is especially significant. In the immediate context it emphasizes the obvious truth that any person who would climb over the wall of the sheep pen instead of entering through the gate is a thief and robber.

In Jesus' day, sheep were put into an enclosed area during the night for protection. The sheep pen was probably an outer courtyard in front of the house, surrounded by a stone wall on top of which briars were placed to provide a measure of safety. It was not uncommon for several flocks to share a single sheep pen. Jesus is making the point that a person who would gain entrance to the fold by climbing over the wall rather than going through the gate is unquestionably "a thief and a robber." The first term (*kleptēs*, GK *3095*) carries the idea of deception, and the second (*lēstēs*, GK *3334*) of seizing by force. Here they are not intended to be taken as denoting two distinct types of false leaders but are joined to give a general impression.

2 In contrast to this kind of person, the man who enters the enclosure through the door is a genuine shepherd. The very fact that he has nothing to hide (entering through the gate) proves that he is a true shepherd. That the Greek text has no definite article before *poimēn* ("shepherd," GK *4478*) indicates the sentence is to be taken in a general sense. Jesus is merely reminding his listeners that real shepherds do not need to approach their flocks surreptitiously.

3 For this kind of a shepherd (*toutō*, "this one," standing first in the sentence receives the emphasis) the watchman opens the gate, and the sheep recognize his voice. He calls them by name and brings them out. Ancient shepherds usually had certain names for favorite sheep (e.g., "long ears," "white nose," Bernard, 2:350), though some writers note that calling a sheep "by name" may mean "personally" or "individually" (see the NEB translation of *kat' onoma*, "one by one," 3Jn 15). In any case, they recognize his voice and follow him out of the sheep pen. From this portrayal of the close relationship between shepherd and sheep, Temple, 1:167, draws the important lesson that all true pastoral work is achieved through personal acquaintance.

4–5 Eastern shepherds lead their sheep—they do not follow behind—and with the help of dogs direct them where they should go. This is a profound lesson in leadership. No effective leader tries to make people go where he himself has not already gone. By definition, leaders lead! Contemporary leaders must inspire and lead their followers by providing the model—by moving out in the direction they want others to go (even though by such action they run the risk of finding themselves all alone).

To "know [the] voice" of the shepherd is to trust him to the point of fully believing all he says. Without personal confidence there is no authentic leadership. So sheep will not follow a stranger—in fact, they will "run away"—because they do not recognize his voice. True believers have a measure of spiritual discernment that alerts them to false teachers. When questionable doctrine is laid before them, they instinctively recognize it for what it is. The voice of truth can never be successfully imitated by the voice of error. Sheep who know the shepherd are not led astray.

6 The narrative form in which Jesus has just spoken is designated by John as a *paroimia* (GK *4231*), a "figure of speech." The term (which occurs five times in the NT) generally means "proverb" or "maxim" (as in 2Pe 2:22, "a dog returns to its vomit"), but in its four occurrences in John it denotes a "veiled saying" (BDAG, 629) the meaning of which is not obvious but whose spiritual truth becomes clearer to those who probe more deeply (cf. Morris, 504). In spite of the fact that Jesus used imagery intended to help his listeners understand, they did not grasp the meaning of what he was saying to them. Nothing blinds the eyes so much as pride in one's position. From their perspective they were the authentic guardians of religious truth and Jesus was merely an itinerant teacher without proper credentials. The certainty that one knows locks out the possibility of being wrong. Blinded by the pride of office, they were unable to understand that Jesus was classifying *them* as thieves and robbers.

7 The "therefore" with which this verse begins continues the illustration. In the verses that follow, Jesus does not expand what he has just said, namely, that the religious leaders fail to understand what he is telling them, but he develops the shepherd and sheep figure of speech along further lines. Central to this section is the contrast between the "hired hand" (v.12), whose allegiance is to himself (not to the sheep), and the "good shepherd" (vv. 11, 14), who is willing to lay down his life for his sheep.

Once again we hear the double "amen," this time stressing the fact that Jesus is "the gate for the sheep." Since John's readers would be anticipating what will soon be stated, namely, that Jesus is "the good shepherd" (v.11), it would come as a surprise to hear him refer to himself as a "gate." R.A.Torrey resolves this problem by maintaining that the Aramaic word for "shepherd" was misread as "gate" and then incorrectly translated into Greek; however, this suggestion runs into trouble two verses later when Jesus again says that he is the gate and that those who enter through him will be saved (a difficult concept if "shepherd" was intended!). Another approach is to cite a practice, said to be common among ancient shepherds, in which the shepherd sleeps in the gateway in order to protect the flock (in that sense he would be a "gate").

It is simpler to take the text as it stands and understand Jesus as presenting himself as both gate and shepherd. John's manner of expression, especially where he is using figurative language, certainly allows this much flexibility (cf.Rev 17:9–10, where the seven heads of the beast are both seven hills and seven kings). John Chrysostom says of Jesus, "When he brings us to the Father he calls himself a Door, when he takes care of us, a Shepherd" (cited in Hoskyns, 373).

8 In what appears to be a blanket statement, Jesus designates "all who ever came before him" as "thieves and robbers." It is clear that Jesus is not speaking of the great patriarchs and leaders of the OT era. Moses, Isaiah, and others could hardly be categorized in such a pejorative way. Jesus is referring to the religious establishment of his own day—

eisin (GK *1639*) is present tense, "are" (NASB), not "were" (NIV)—and to all the preceding "authorities" who were cut from the same bolt of cloth. The sheep didn't listen to them because they were strangers. Their voices were not the voices of authentic shepherds.

9 When Jesus declares that he is "the gate" and that those who enter the fold through him "will be saved," the immediate reference is to the safety of the flock that follows Jesus as shepherd. But in a fuller sense it speaks of all who will receive eternal life through faith in him. They will come in and go out and find pasture—i.e., in their relationship to Jesus they will find both safety and nourishment.

10 Using vivid language, Jesus says that the Jewish establishment (the "thief") has as its purpose "to steal and kill and destroy." But this is not true of Jesus the shepherd—he has come so that his followers "may have life, and have it to the full." The former are life denying, while Jesus is life affirming. The life that Jesus came to provide is not physical but spiritual. Yet that which is spiritual naturally overflows into every aspect of physical existence. Life embraces all that it means to be alive in this world and firmly attached by faith to the living Lord. Fullness of life is the reward of faith. It is by trusting Jesus and forgetting self that real life—physical and spiritual—breaks into one's consciousness like the dawning of a new day (cf. Mk 8:35 par.).

11 Jesus now gets around to identifying himself as "the good shepherd." The adjective is *kalos* (GK *2819*), which means "good" in the sense of "beautiful" or "excellent." In the context of his sacrificial life and death, the term stresses the beauty of what he did for those who by faith have entered his fold. His goodness as a shepherd is clearly seen in the fact that he "lays down his life for the sheep." That the verb is present tense (*tithēsin*, GK *5502*; also in vv.15, 17, 18) suggests that Jesus is speaking primarily of his entire life (not simply his death) as sacrificial. The incarnation in its entirety was an act of unbelievable condescension. The eternal Son laid down his life by becoming a man and living among us. Because he was a *good* shepherd, his life and death as the ideal leader of the flock is a model beautiful to behold.

Attention is often drawn to the preposition *hyper* ("for") in the phrase "for the sheep." In such passages as Mark 14:24; Luke 22:19–20; and Romans 5:6–8, it has definite sacrificial overtones. It was *on behalf of* the sheep, for their benefit, that the good shepherd laid down his life. Commentators have pointed out that the death of a Palestinian shepherd meant disaster for the sheep, but the death of the good shepherd meant life for his sheep. Hendriksen, 2:111, finds limited atonement in this passage, but building a theological edifice on a figure of speech is risky, to say the least.

12 Jesus has presented himself as the good shepherd who lays down his life for the sheep, in contrast to the hired hand who abandons the sheep "when he sees the wolf coming." Hendriksen, 2:111–12, is probably right when he argues for the KJV's "hireling" rather than "hired worker/worker" in that the former term has certain unsavory connotations.

13 The hireling is said to run away in the face of danger because he "cares nothing for the sheep." After all, he doesn't own the sheep! But the good shepherd would never desert his charge in times of danger. Instead, he willingly sacrifices himself for their benefit. The background for this contrast may well be Zechariah 11:4–17, where the prophet, as a type of the messianic Shepherd-King, is set over against "the worthless shepherd" who deserts the flock. The true test of integrity is conduct in the face of potential personal loss. Only those who genuinely care for others stand their ground when threatened with personal disadvantage.

14–15 Again Jesus declares that he is "the shepherd," i.e., "the good one" (the repetition of the arti-

cle places the adjective in apposition). Consequently, his sheep know him. The verb *ginōskō* ("to know," GK *1182*) occurs four times in vv. 14–15: Jesus *knows* his sheep and his sheep *know* him, the Father *knows* Jesus and Jesus *knows* the Father. Of the 222 occurrences of the verb in the NT, 82 are found in the Johannine literature (57 in the fourth gospel alone). While the Greeks held that knowledge of God was attainable by philosophical-theological contemplation of the divine reality, the Hebrews viewed knowledge as the result of entering into a personal relationship with God. The relationship between shepherd and sheep is like that between Father and Son. They *know* one another in the fullest sense of the word. Three times in a span of eight verses Jesus stresses that, as the good shepherd, he lays down his life for his sheep (vv. 11, 15, 17). It is the willingness of the shepherd to put his own welfare aside and to give himself without reservation for the benefit of his flock that defines what it means to be a *good* shepherd. This "goodness" is the self-emptying concern for others that was modeled by Jesus in his life and death. It is the expected lifestyle of all who bear his name. Whether or not we are in the family of God is evident by the degree of family likeness we bear.

16 Jesus the good shepherd has drawn his first sheep from the "sheep pen" of Israel. But he has other sheep that do not belong to that fold. They are the Gentiles who will come to believe in him through the missionary outreach of the early church. The obligation of Israel to serve as a beacon light for the nations (Isa 49:6) is transferred by Jesus to his own ministry. God's redemptive activity reaches out to include those of every tribe, people, and nation (Ac 10:34–35; Rev 5:9). These "other sheep" must be brought into the one flock as well.

The church of Jesus Christ is composed of converts not only from the Jewish nation but also from among the Gentiles. The Gentiles are the wild olive branches that have been grafted into the tree of which the Jews are the natural branches (Ro 11:17–21). The result is "one flock" (not "one fold," as the KJV, influenced by the Vulgate, has it). There are many ecclesiastical "folds" but only one "flock." Designations such as Presbyterian, Methodist, and Baptist may be convenient ways to classify believers on the basis of such secondary concerns as church governance and modes of worship, but the truth is that Christians are one glorious collection of all sorts of people who by faith in Jesus Christ have been adopted into the family of God. There is one flock precisely because there is but one Good Shepherd. One flock is all one shepherd can handle, so all who belong to him are in this one flock.

17 This verse seems to say that the Father loves Jesus *because* Jesus lays down his life. But certainly the love of the Father for the Son is not contingent on the willingness of the Son to give up his life. It is much more probable that Jesus is saying that his willingness to give his life is the *result* of the Father's love for him. God's love for the Son does not depend on what the Son does, but what the Son does is the result of the Father's love.

18 Jesus lays down his life in order to "take it up again." It is theologically important to see that no one takes Jesus' life from him. Even on the cross Jesus is not the helpless victim of the Jewish opposition or Roman authority. When with a loud voice he calls out, "Father, into your hands I commit my spirit" (Lk 23:46), he is giving up his life voluntarily. The "authority" to lay it down and take it up was given to him by the Father. The great sacrifice of the good shepherd cannot be minimized by suggesting that his life was torn from him by his ene-mies. No, it was by his own volition that he laid down his life for the sheep.

19–20 The words of Jesus once again caused a division among the Jews (cf. 6:52; 7:43; 9:16). Context suggests that by "the Jews" John is referring to all who heard Jesus, the crowd as well as their leaders. Many of them said that he was possessed by a demon and out of his mind (a single charge, not two; see comments at 7:20). "If that is so," they reasoned, "why should we pay any attention to him?" Others concluded that what Jesus was saying could not be the words of a man possessed by a demon; after all, there's no way that a demon could open the eyes of the blind. Those who thought Jesus was possessed by a demon began with their own preconceived ideas of what could and what could not be done on the Sabbath. Since Jesus has healed on the Sabbath, it follows that he is a sinner and, worse than that, a man possessed by a demon, a raving lunatic.

21 The other group began with the undeniable reality of a miracle performed in their presence. Now anyone who can open the eyes of a man born blind cannot be demon-possessed because such an act lies outside the scope of what a demon can do.

The logic of each position is unassailable; it is the starting point of each that leads to diametrically opposing conclusions. And so it is with faith. Arbitrarily to limit the power and activity of God is to skew the results. To begin with the reality of transformed lives is to argue the validity of the one who invites our confidence. The psalmist says, "Taste and see" (34:8), not "Think it through from whatever presupposition you may choose, and then perhaps you will want to taste."

NOTES

6 The noun παροιμία (*paroimia*, GK *4231*) does not occur in the Synoptics, but much the same idea is represented there by the more common παραβολή (*parabolē*, "parable," GK *4130*)—48 times in Matthew through Luke. A parable is "a relatively short narrative with a symbolic meaning" (L&N, 33:15). Parable was Jesus' primary method of teaching. It allowed the listener to "discover" truth that he did not know by seeing it in terms of something he did know. Like all effective learning, parable moves from the known to the unknown.

7 The NASB translates ἡ θύρα τῶν προβάτων (*hē thyra tōn probatōn*) literally as "the door of the sheep." The awkwardness of the Greek expression caused some early MSS (𝔓⁷⁵ sa ac mf) to substitute ὁ ποιμήν (*ho poimēn*, "the shepherd," GK *4478*) for ἡ θύρα (*hē thyra*, "the door," GK *2598*).

8 What appears to be a categorical denial of the validity of all who ever came before Jesus is eased by a number of MSS that omit πρὸ ἐμοῦ (*pro emou*, "before me"), and several omit πάντες (*pantes*, "all"). See Metzger, 197–98, for the variants. The UBS committee left both expressions in the text but enclosed πρὸ ἐμοῦ in square brackets.

18 The NASB translates, "no one has taken it away from me," following the Greek ἦρεν (*ēren*, "has taken," GK *149*), which is found in 𝔓⁴⁵ ℵ* B syᵖ. Though this reading is early and strong, it represents only a single textual type (Egyptian). For that reason the UBS committee chose αἴρει (*airei*, "takes"), supported by 𝔓⁶⁶ *rell* (cf. Metzger, 196–97).

20 The NIV's "raving mad" is probably too strong a translation for μαίνεται (*mainetai*, GK *3419*) in this context. It suggests that Jesus was angry, while the charge was that he was out of his mind. The NASB's "insane" is better. The word μαίνομαι, *mainomai*, occurs in three other places in the NT: it expresses the reaction of those in the house of Mary when they were told by Rhoda that Peter was at the door (Ac 12:15); the response of Festus on hearing Paul's witness to King Agrippa (Ac 26:24–25); and what unbelievers would say were they to enter the church when everyone was speaking in tongues (1Co 14:23).

2. "I and the Father Are One" (10:22–42)

OVERVIEW

The next event recorded by John was an encounter between Jesus and his Jewish adversaries that took place at the Feast of Dedication in Jerusalem. This celebration was not one of the religious festivals required by the OT but was of recent origin. In 167 BC the Syrian despot Antiochus Epiphanes took over Jerusalem and embarked on a campaign to Hellenize Judea by force. His most atrocious act was the desecration of Israel's sacred altar by erecting a pagan shrine on top of it—the "abomination that causes desolation" spoken of in Daniel 9:27 (cf. Mt 24:15). The blatant offense incited a revolt, and three years later (164 BC) under the leadership of Judas Maccabeus the temple was recaptured. An eight-day Feast of Dedication (Hanukkah) was held, beginning on 25 Kislev of that year (cf.

1 Macc 4:36–59), and has been observed ever since. This joyful celebration was also called the Feast of Lights, for legend had it that when the priests reentered the temple, they found a small cruse of consecrated oil that provided just enough fuel to kindle the menorah for one day, but it miraculously burned for eight days. During the festival, lamps and candles in homes throughout the city burned brightly.

---

²²Then came the Feast of Dedication at Jerusalem. It was winter, ²³and Jesus was in the temple area walking in Solomon's Colonnade. ²⁴The Jews gathered around him, saying, "How long will you keep us in suspense? If you are the Christ, tell us plainly."

²⁵Jesus answered, "I did tell you, but you do not believe. The miracles I do in my Father's name speak for me, ²⁶but you do not believe because you are not my sheep. ²⁷My sheep listen to my voice; I know them, and they follow me. ²⁸I give them eternal life, and they shall never perish; no one can snatch them out of my hand. ²⁹My Father, who has given them to me, is greater than all; no one can snatch them out of my Father's hand. ³⁰I and the Father are one."

³¹Again the Jews picked up stones to stone him, ³²but Jesus said to them, "I have shown you many great miracles from the Father. For which of these do you stone me?"

³³"We are not stoning you for any of these," replied the Jews, "but for blasphemy, because you, a mere man, claim to be God."

³⁴Jesus answered them, "Is it not written in your Law, 'I have said you are gods'? ³⁵If he called them 'gods,' to whom the word of God came—and the Scripture cannot be broken—³⁶what about the one whom the Father set apart as his very own and sent into the world? Why then do you accuse me of blasphemy because I said, 'I am God's Son'? ³⁷Do not believe me unless I do what my Father does. ³⁸But if I do it, even though you do not believe me, believe the miracles, that you may know and understand that the Father is in me, and I in the Father." ³⁹Again they tried to seize him, but he escaped their grasp.

⁴⁰Then Jesus went back across the Jordan to the place where John had been baptizing in the early days. Here he stayed ⁴¹and many people came to him. They said, "Though John never performed a miraculous sign, all that John said about this man was true." ⁴²And in that place many believed in Jesus.

COMMENTARY

22–23 John notes that it was winter and Jesus was walking back and forth in a roofed colonnade that ran along the eastern side of the temple enclosure. While the reference to winter could be no more than an explanation as to why Jesus was in a sheltered area, some have understood it as reflecting the spiritual condition of the Jewish leaders (cf. "it was night," 13:30). Their icy spirits and frozen response to Jesus presented a winter landscape of frigid immobility.

The name attached to this oldest remaining portico, Solomon's Colonnade, was in memory of Solomon, the builder of the first temple. It was there that Peter spoke to the people who gathered after the healing of the crippled beggar (Ac 3:11) and where the early believers used to meet (Ac 5:12).

24 There in the colonnade the Jews "gathered around him" (the verb *kykloō*, GK *3240*, means "to encircle," perhaps with hostile intent; "closed in on him" [Phillips]) to ask, "How long will you keep us in suspense?" This NIV rendition implies a relatively friendly group of Jews wondering how much longer until Jesus reveals whether he is the Messiah. While the following statement, "If you are the Messiah, say so plainly" (NEB), seems to support this reading, there is evidence that supports a different translation of the difficult Greek idiom (lit., "How long do you lift up our soul?"). Barrett, 380, suggests, "How long will you provoke us to anger." The entire encounter with the Jewish leaders has been so distinctly hostile that the Jews now ask rather irritably, "How much longer will you persist in provoking us to anger?" This reading of the text fits the context better. "If you are the Christ," they say, "tell us plainly." Jesus' opponents would like to force him out into the open and get from him a clear admission that he claimed to be the promised Messiah—providing them with an indisputable basis for bringing charges against him.

25 "I did tell you," answered Jesus, "but you do not believe" (better, "continue not to believe"—note the aorist tense, *eipon*, GK *3306*, followed by the present, *pisteuete*, GK *4409*). One might ask, "And *when* did that happen?" Although Jesus had confessed to the Samaritan woman that he was in fact the Messiah (4:26; cf. 9:35–37), so far he had not openly made that claim in Jerusalem. The reason is obvious. For the Jews of that day the title carried all sorts of military and nationalistic associations. To play into their hands as that sort of a Messiah would undoubtedly lead to a political rebellion counterproductive to Jesus' real mission as the suffering Messiah.

So although Jesus had never openly declared his messiahship, there can be no question that the miraculous deeds he had done by his Father's authority (i.e., "in my Father's name") proved him to be the Christ. To name but a few, he had just healed a man born blind (9:1–7), healed a lame man at the pool of Bethesda (5:2–9), fed the five thousand (6:5–13), and walked on water (6:16–21). In addition to the miracles, there were the many statements that pointed to his messiahship. If the Jews had viewed him through the eyes of faith, they would have understood the messianic implications of such statements as, "I am the bread of life" (6:35); "If anyone is thirsty, let him come to me and drink" (7:37); "before Abraham was born, I am" (8:58); and "I am the good shepherd" (10:11). Such words and works speak plainly to those whose ears have been opened to hear. Bruce, 231, comments, "Where the heart of the spectator [is] insensitive, each successive work [serves] but to harden it the more."

26 Ample proof existed that Jesus was the Messiah, but to understand and accept that fact as reality is not simply a matter of logic. The reason the Jews did not believe was that they didn't belong to his flock. "I did tell you," said Jesus in effect, "but you persisted in unbelief because you are not my sheep. Each sheep recognizes the voice of its own master." Jesus is not suggesting for a moment that their inability to hear was excusable; he is merely explaining why they failed to recognize him for who he is.

27 Three things are true of Jesus' flock: they listen to his voice, they are known by him, and they habitually follow (present tense) him.

28 As a result Jesus gives them eternal life. While it is common to point out that "eternal life" is more qualitative (it is "the life of the Eternal One") than quantitative, here the second feature is emphasized by the clause that follows, "and they shall never perish." "They have," as Jesus said in 5:24, "crossed over from death to life." And this life, which is the life of the Eternal One, is a life that never ends. "When we've been there ten thousand years," writes the hymnist, "bright shining as the sun, we've no less days to sing God's praise than when we'd first begun."

There is no portion of Scripture that has brought greater comfort to those who are troubled that God might somehow relinquish his hold on them and they perish than these words of Jesus: "No one can snatch them out of my hand." The preservation of the sheep is the task of the shepherd; it is up to him to keep them safe. And one can be absolutely positive that the *good* shepherd will never let any of his sheep wander beyond his care. The salvation that we received in response to our faith is a salvation that cannot be lost, because it is safeguarded and guaranteed by none other than Jesus Christ himself. Morris, 521, writes, "Our continuance in eternal life depends not on our feeble hold on Christ, but on His firm grip on us."

29 Lest the Son's power to preserve be called into question, Jesus adds that his Father, whose power is unmatched, joins him in protecting the flock, and "no one can snatch them out of [God's] hand." He and his Father are one in their determination that no believer should ever perish.

The Greek text here has at least five combinations of the variants for "who" and "greater." The NIV follows the Byzantine tradition, which takes both words as masculine; thus "My Father, who [*hos*] has given them to me, is greater [*meizōn*] than all." A more likely transcriptional development has the neuter *ho* ("that which") and the masculine *meizōn*, which results in, "My Father, in regard to what he has given me, is greater than all." While the Father is obviously "greater than all" in an unqualified sense, the point of the immediate reference is that, when it comes to the care and protection of the flock, the Father is absolutely unmatched.

30 This verse has received a great deal of attention from exegetes and theologians. In context it

seems to refer primarily to the fact that the Father and Son are one in purpose and action. When it comes to preserving the life of the believing flock, they are one in their desire and ability to safeguard every believer. But the verse must mean more than that. It is highly unlikely that the Jews would pick up stones to attack Jesus if all he were saying was that what he was doing was in perfect accord with the will of God. Others could easily make that claim.

It is often noted that the text uses the neuter *hen* ("one [thing]"), rather than the masculine *heis* ("one [person]"). The latter reading would lead to the unorthodox position that Jesus and his Father are one person. Rather, the neuter *hen* means they "belong to the same category" (Lindars, 30). The christological controversies that took place several centuries later would draw heavily on this cryptic statement. It has often been noted that the word "one" refutes the claim of Arianism, which denied unity of essence between Father and Son, and that the plural verb "are" refutes the view of Sabellianism, which denied the diversity of persons.

31–32 The Jews once again "picked up stones to stone [Jesus]" (see 8:59; cf. 5:18). They were not at all hindered by the fact that there had been no trial or that the power to execute prisoners had been denied them. Their intense hatred overruled common sense and standard practice. But before they could actually carry out their evil intention, Jesus reminded them of the great miracles he had done by his Father's power. The works are said to be *kala* ("beautiful," GK *2819*), the same adjective used of the *good* shepherd (vv. 11, 14). His works displayed the graciousness and goodness of the one who performed them; it could be no other way. Then Jesus asked his opponents very pointedly, "For which of these do you stone me?" or to put it another way, "What was it that I did that was so heinous as to deserve death?"

33 "It was not for anything you did that we are stoning you," Jesus' opponents answer, "but for blasphemy. It is because you, a mere man, claim to be God." Now the truth is out. It was because Jesus' words and actions were understood as a claim to deity that he must be put to death. While later Jewish ruling held a person guilty of blasphemy only when the sacred name of God (the tetragrammaton) was actually pronounced (*m. Sanh.* 7:5), it was Jesus' claim of a special relationship with the Father that his opponents were considering the ultimate sacrilege. Leviticus 24:13 prescribes death by stoning as the appropriate punishment for blasphemy.

While the Jews were correct in their understanding that by his words and works Jesus was claiming divine status, they were terribly wrong in their assumption that he was simply a mere man. If they had accepted the obvious truth that his miraculous works indicated divine origin, they might have reconsidered their unfounded opinion. But religious prejudice blinds the minds of even the most highly trained professionals. With dogged persistence they pursued their one central goal, namely, that Jesus be stoned—the reason being his claim to be God.

34–36 Jesus points out to the Jews that in their own Law, which cannot be broken, certain people were called "gods." How then can they say that the one who was sent into the world by God is guilty of blasphemy when he calls himself God's Son. While the term "Law" formally designates the first five books of the Bible, here it serves as an inclusive term for the entire OT. The expression "your Law" may have had the polemic force of "the Law, which even you acknowledge." The argument is secured by the fact that "Scripture cannot be broken." The breadth of meaning assigned to the term "god" in Scripture cannot be ignored simply because it doesn't suit one's immediate purpose. "It is *your* Law," says Jesus, "and you are well aware that it cannot be set aside or shown to be in error."

The statement to which Jesus refers comes from Psalm 82. The psalmist writes, "I said, 'You are "gods"; you are all sons of the Most High'" (v.6). But to whom was he speaking? Some have suggested angelic beings who have abused their power over the nations. The contrast in John, however, is not between God and angels but between God and "a mere man" (v.33). Others, stressing the context in Psalm 82, conclude that the psalmist was speaking to the corrupt judges of Israel, but the fact that they are those, writes John, "to whom the word of God came" (v.35) identifies them rather clearly as Israel at the time of the giving of the Law. Thus Jesus is saying that if the Israelites were called "gods," then there can be no real objection when he refers to himself as "God's Son" (v.36). The argument holds, even if they would not accept the fact that he was appointed by the Father and sent into the world.

37–38 Jesus confronts his Jewish listeners with a challenge: "If I am not acting as my Father would" (NASB), then "do not believe me"—the simple dative (*moi*) denotes credence, not personal faith. "But if I am acting as my Father would, even though you don't trust me, at least except the evidence of my deeds." While miracles were never intended to make people believe, they do provide strong evidence that the one able to perform the miracle is telling the truth. The argument runs like this: "The works that I do are the kinds of things my Father does, and if you can't accept that, then at least believe that the miracles I do substantiate my claims. Those who accept the evidence of the miracles come to know and understand the mutual indwelling of the Father and the Son." (The verbs are aorist, "come to know," and present, "grow in that knowledge.") What Jesus referred to in v.30 ("I and the Father are one") is spelled out in v.38b ("the Father is in me, and I in the Father").

39 Such claims were too much for Jesus' opponents. Again they tried to seize him, but he escaped from their grasp. John probably intends his readers to understand a miraculous escape such as took place when the people at Nazareth planned to throw Jesus down from a cliff outside the city (Lk 4:28–30).

40 The last three verses of ch. 10 record Jesus' "strategic retreat" (Carson, 400) back across the Jordan to the place where John the Baptist ministered at an earlier time. In 1:28 we learned that John did his baptizing "at Bethany on the other side of the Jordan." The only other Bethany we know of was the village of Lazarus and his sisters that lay a short distance southeast of Jerusalem on the road to Jericho (11:18). The "Bethany" to which Jesus now withdraws was probably the rural area known as Batanea, which lay to the northeast across the Jordan in the tetrarchy of Philip, a son of Herod the Great. There John the Baptist remained in relative seclusion.

41 It was not long until people began to come to Jesus. Unlike the religious elite in Jerusalem, these less sophisticated country people were open-minded. Remembering what John the Baptist had taught concerning the one who was to come, they confessed that, although John never performed a miraculous sign (a critical credential for a prophet), everything he said about Jesus was true.

42 The result was that there in the countryside, where the Baptist had faithfully ministered, "many believed in Jesus." Here in contrast to v.38, where *pisteuō* ("to believe") is followed by the simple dative and refers to mental assent, we have the standard *pisteuō eis*, which means "to put one's trust in" someone.

NOTES

28 The Greek construction οὐ μὴ ἀπόλωνται (*ou mē apolōntai*, "they shall never perish," GK 660) is a very strong negation. The two negatives (οὐ, *ou,* and μὴ, *mē*) strengthen each other. Commenting on this passage, Buist Fanning writes, "It would have been enough to have *ou* with a future indicative verb here, but Jesus is more emphatic. The subjunctive combination strongly denies even the possibility that any of Jesus' sheep would perish: 'they will certainly not perish,' 'they will by no means perish,' is the sense of Jesus' assertion" (cited in William D. Mounce, *Basics of Biblical Greek Grammar* [2d ed., Grand Rapids: Zondervan, 2003], 288).

34 The NET study note here holds that the quotation from Psalm 82:6 was understood in rabbinic circles as an attack on the unjust judges and that Jesus was arguing from the lesser to the greater: if OT judges could be called "gods" because they were vehicles of the word of God, Jesus deserves much more to be called God because he is the Word incarnate.

35 "And the Scripture cannot be broken" is strong attestation to the absolute truth of divine revelation (cf. Mt 5:18; 2Ti 3:16). While Jesus' affirmation refers to the OT Scriptures, the same approval is extended to the NT, which details the life and ministry of Jesus supplemented by the Spirit-inspired apostolic writings.

REFLECTIONS

John's presentation of the public ministry of Jesus began and ended with a reference to the witness of John the Baptist (1:19–10:42). From this point on, the narrative increasingly reflects the coming sacrifice of the good shepherd, who in fulfillment of his messianic mission will lay down his life for his sheep.

C. The Miracle at Bethany (11:1–57)

OVERVIEW

The account of the raising of Lazarus plays a significant role in the fourth gospel. It sets into motion the final series of events that culminate in Jesus' crucifixion. When the Pharisees heard that Jesus had raised a man from the dead—and that in plain view in a neighboring town close by the capital—they reasoned that if they allowed him to go on performing miraculous signs, two things were bound to happen: first, everyone would come to believe in him, and second, the Romans would destroy their temple and deprive them of their limited right to rule (cf. 11:48). "So from that day on they plotted to take his life" (11:53). Since this miracle is so central in John, it seems right to ask why it is not mentioned in any of the three Synoptic Gospels.

Some scholars deny that the event ever happened. Others hold that an original parable (Lazarus and the rich man, Lk 16:19–31) underwent a process that finally resulted in the present "historical" account. Still others, while acknowledging that something probably did take place, hold that there is no way to work back through the process that created the account to the original "event." Some see John as a literary artist who, fusing together material about Mary and Martha with an otherwise unknown tradition about a man raised from the dead by Jesus, created an allegory of the passion, death, and resurrection of Jesus—and thus we have no hope of recovering the truth of what actually happened.

While this is not the place for an extended discussion of the reliability of the text and the historical probability of miracles, several brief comments are in order. There is little question but that John believed that the story he was narrating actually took place. The specific and repeated mention of names and places ties the account to the real world. Furthermore, speculative explanations of the origin of the account are simply not plausible. That the Synoptics do not include the raising of Lazarus is tempered by the fact that they, as well as the fourth gospel, selected their material from a much larger source. As John reminds us, if everything Jesus did had been written down, not even the whole world would have room for that many books (21:25)! Nor was it out of any reluctance on the part of the synoptic writers to record a miraculous raising of the dead that accounts for the omission—consider the raising of Jairus's daughter (Mt 9:23–26; Mk 5:35–43; Lk 8:49–56) and of the widow's son at Nain (Lk 7:11–17).

The raising of Lazarus is not the only miracle left out of the Synoptics. The two healing miracles that John records as taking place in Jerusalem are likewise missing—the healing of the lame man at Bethesda (5:1–9) and the restoration of sight for the man born blind (9:1–7). Morris's comment, 532 n. 1, is apropos: "It is to be noted that the kind of critic who rejects the historicity of this story because it is not in the Synoptics is usually not ready to accept what is there, the feeding of the multitude, for example."

1. Lazarus Dies (11:1–16)

¹Now a man named Lazarus was sick. He was from Bethany, the village of Mary and her sister Martha. ²This Mary, whose brother Lazarus now lay sick, was the same one who poured perfume on the Lord and wiped his feet with her hair. ³So the sisters sent word to Jesus, "Lord, the one you love is sick."

⁴When he heard this, Jesus said, "This sickness will not end in death. No, it is for God's glory so that God's Son may be glorified through it." ⁵Jesus loved Martha and her sister and Lazarus. ⁶Yet when he heard that Lazarus was sick, he stayed where he was two more days.

⁷Then he said to his disciples, "Let us go back to Judea."

⁸"But Rabbi," they said, "a short while ago the Jews tried to stone you, and yet you are going back there?"

⁹Jesus answered, "Are there not twelve hours of daylight? A man who walks by day will not stumble, for he sees by this world's light. ¹⁰It is when he walks by night that he stumbles, for he has no light."

¹¹After he had said this, he went on to tell them, "Our friend Lazarus has fallen asleep; but I am going there to wake him up."

¹²His disciples replied, "Lord, if he sleeps, he will get better." ¹³Jesus had been speaking of his death, but his disciples thought he meant natural sleep.

¹⁴So then he told them plainly, "Lazarus is dead, ¹⁵and for your sake I am glad I was not there, so that you may believe. But let us go to him."

¹⁶Then Thomas (called Didymus) said to the rest of the disciples, "Let us also go, that we may die with him."

COMMENTARY

1 As the chapter opens, we learn of a man by the name of Lazarus who lived in the town of Bethany. "Lazarus" is a shortened form of the Hebrew name "Eleazar," which means "whom God helps." Apart from this account in ch. 11 and scattered references in the following chapter (thirteen in all), the name occurs only in Luke 16, where a beggar by the same name lay at the gate of a rich man (vv.20–27).

The Bethany mentioned by John is not the area to which Jesus withdrew as recorded in 10:40–42 (cf. 1:28) but a village (currently called el-'Azariyeh, a name derived from "Lazarus") lying some two miles southeast of Jerusalem on the road to Jericho. John identifies it as the village of Mary and her sister, Martha. In the only reference to the two sisters outside John, the names are reversed (Lk 10:38–42), apparently because in that context Martha, the older of the two, is portrayed as the one who is in charge of the home. It was Martha who was distracted by the obligations of hospitality, while Mary sat at Jesus' feet in rapt attention.

2 In a parenthetical sentence, John identifies Mary, the sister of Lazarus, as the one who poured perfume on the Lord and dried his feet with her hair. Since John does not record this event until the following chapter (12:1–8), some regard the verse as an early gloss. The story is included in both Matthew (26:6–13) and Mark (14:3–9), but they do not provide the name of the woman who anointed Jesus with expensive perfume. It is John who identifies her as Mary.

3 Lazarus had fallen sick, so his sisters sent word to their friend Jesus. It is worth noting that all they felt they needed to do was to let Jesus know that the one he loved was sick. They do not beg him to come and restore their brother to good health; it is enough to let him know about his good friend Lazarus's illness. Certainly this reveals an unusually close relationship between Jesus and the family at Bethany. Such confidence in Jesus undoubtedly resulted from many hours of close personal friendship. We cannot help but wish for a fuller account of the many things they must have discussed around the table. While *kyrie* ("Lord," GK *3261*) is a common Greek expression that could mean no more than "sir," it is hard not to believe that on the lips of those so close to Jesus it must have carried overtones of deity.

4 When the news of Lazarus's illness reached Jesus, he responded by declaring that the sickness would "not end in death." He did not mean by this that Lazarus would not die. Nor is his point that although Lazarus would die, he would not remain in death. Jesus is saying that the purpose of the sickness is not death but the glory of God. Bruce, 240, writes that "this illness is not so much one that will terminate in death as one which will demonstrate the glory of God." When the Father receives glory, the Son is also glorified. Both Father and Son are to receive honor and praise as a result of the events set in motion by the illness of Lazarus.

5–6 Perhaps it was because Jesus didn't go immediately to Bethany but waited a few days that John felt it necessary to add that Jesus loved Martha and her sister and Lazarus. It was important for John's readers to understand that the delay on Jesus' part did not indicate a lack of affection for the family. In fact, the specific mention of each person stresses his love for each one individually. The Greek word for "loved" (*ēgapa*, GK *26*) is a customary imperfect stressing a continuing state. Berkeley translates, "was a dear friend to." So Jesus, "though He had heard that Lazarus was ill" (Norlie), stayed where he was for two more days.

Pulling together the references to time will help us understand Jesus' actions. Jesus was across the Jordan in the place where John had been baptizing in the early days (10:20). From 1:28 we identified that locale as Batanea, some 150 kilometers northeast of Jerusalem. Lazarus was still alive when Jesus received word of his friend's illness (11:3–4). Sometime during the two-day wait, but before Jesus left for Bethany, Lazarus died (v.11). When Jesus arrived in Bethany, he found that Lazarus had already been in the tomb for four days (v.17). This would have allowed Jesus adequate time to make the relatively long journey from Batanea to Bethany.

The question as to why Jesus waited two days before going to Bethany must still be answered. One would think that the illness of a dear friend would have moved him to go to his aid without delay. Some have suggested that Jesus waited so that people would understand that Lazarus had really died and that his return to life could not be explained as resuscitation from a coma. Others refer to a popular Jewish belief that the soul lingered near the body for three days after death and that only after that could there be no hope of resuscitation (cf. Str-B, 2:544). While one cannot be certain as to why Jesus delayed his departure, the most probable answer is that his progress toward Jerusalem and his coming death were self-determined. When his brothers urged him to go up to Jerusalem for the Feast of Tabernacles, he refused, for the right time had not yet come (7:1–6). So also now, when informed that Lazarus was ill, he waited because he, not others, would determine when the time was right.

7–8 After the two days had passed, Jesus told his disciples that it was time to return to Judea. The decision was met with surprise and protest: "Rabbi, just a short time ago the Jews were trying to stone you. You're not going back there again, are you?" This is the last time in John's gospel that the disciples refer to Jesus as "Rabbi," the accepted manner of addressing a teacher. From that point on, his relationship with them was far greater than that of teacher—he was to become their Master and Lord.

9–10 Jesus' answer to the disciples' question must be understood on two levels. It is quite obvious that there are "twelve hours of daylight" and that people "will not stumble" if they walk during the day, but when night comes and there is no longer light, they *will* stumble. But what does this simple observation teach on a deeper level? The disciples have just expressed their fear that if Jesus returns to Jerusalem, he will be put to death by the same people who tried to stone him. Jesus answers that he has not yet finished his own twelve hours of "daylight," and until that determined period of time is complete, he will walk in safety. The precautionary measure they suggest will not lengthen his ministry, nor will the opposition of his enemies bring it to a premature close. It is those who try to walk at night who stumble.

Jesus is the light of the world, and until his mission is accomplished, that light cannot be extinguished. Note here a second application. The disciples also have their twelve hours of daylight; during this time, they are to carry out the tasks assigned to them. They labor illumined by the one who is the light of the world. It is those without the light who will stumble because they are trying to walk in darkness. There is no light in them.

11 Jesus tells his disciples that Lazarus has fallen asleep and that he intends to go to Bethany and "wake him up." The verb *koimaō* ("to fall asleep," GK *3121*) occurs eighteen times in the NT, four times in a literal sense (Mt 28:13; Lk 22:45; Jn 11:12; Ac 12:6), but elsewhere as a euphemism for death. Jesus refers to Lazarus as "our friend." While the term reflects the close personal relationship between Jesus (along with the disciples) and the family at Bethany, it may also have been a common way of referring to another Christian believer.

12–13 The disciples thought that Jesus was talking about Lazarus being asleep in a literal sense and so reply that if that is the case, then "he will get better." Since the verb is a future passive of *sōzō* ("to save," GK *5392*), some think John meant that believers who were now asleep in death would be saved (cf. Barrett, 393). While Jesus often speaks on more than one level, finding nuggets of theological truth at every turn is to confuse exegesis with homiletics. The disciples understood in a straightforward manner what Jesus had said. It is difficult to see how John, in recording their response, could have been adding to their words a second level of meaning. How would we know? John then adds the explanatory note that Jesus had been speaking of Lazarus's death but the disciples thought he was speaking of literal sleep.

14–15 Jesus now says plainly, "Lazarus is dead." Such knowledge on the part of Jesus about the condition of a man many miles away can be understood only in terms of supernatural enlightenment. It was certainly more than an informed guess that such a serious illness would by that time have resulted in death. Jesus adds that for the disciples' sake he is glad that he was not there in Bethany. Had he been there he may have taken action sooner and restored Lazarus to health before he actually died. Jesus' arrival to bring Lazarus back from the grave will be for this purpose: "so that [the disciples] may believe."

Jesus was not speaking of initial faith but of the growth and maturing of the faith of his followers. While faith begins with a first step of commitment to the Lord, in another sense it is a progressive relationship. Faith grows as experience continues to verify the trustworthiness of the one in whom we have placed our trust. It is said that experience is the best teacher, and in no other realm is this more true than in our relationship to Jesus Christ. It is in this sense that Paul cries out, "I want to know Christ and the power of his resurrection" (Php 3:10).

16 In response to Jesus' call, "Let us go to him," it is Thomas who says to the rest of the disciples, "Let us also go, that we may die with him." (Interestingly, apart from a single reference [6:68], Peter is not mentioned in the fourth gospel between his being chosen as a disciple [1:42–44] and the footwashing episode in the final week of Jesus' earthly ministry [13:6–38].) The name "Thomas" comes from an Aramaic word meaning "the twin." John's parenthetical statement "called Didymus" (*Didymos* meaning "twin," GK *1441*) is repeated in 20:24 and 21:22. There is some evidence that "Thomas" may have been a title rather than a personal name and that his real name may have been Judas. Less probable is the claim that he was a twin of Jesus, a theory probably motivated by gnostic theology.

While Thomas is usually portrayed as the great doubter, on this occasion his willingness to accompany Jesus all the way to death reflects not doubt but "raw devotion and courage" (Carson, 410). The others may well have abandoned Jesus in view of the danger awaiting them in Jerusalem, but it was Thomas who encouraged them to forsake the security of their refuge "across the Jordan" and go with Jesus into danger, even though it could cost them their lives.

NOTES

5 That John can speak of Jesus' love for Lazarus and his sisters using the verb ἀγαπάω (*agapaō*, GK *26*) while employing a different verb in the same context (φιλέω, *phileō*, GK *5797*, v.3) demonstrates that their semantic ranges overlap and that it is therefore unwise to distinguish sharply between the two words for "love" (as is often done in the post-resurrection account in 21:15–17).

9 Obviously not every day of the year has twelve hours of daylight. The length of sunlight in Israel varies from fourteen hours and twelve minutes to twelve hours and nine minutes, depending on the time of year.

2. The Grief of Martha and Mary (11:17–37)

¹⁷On his arrival, Jesus found that Lazarus had already been in the tomb for four days. ¹⁸Bethany was less than two miles from Jerusalem, ¹⁹and many Jews had come to Martha and Mary to comfort them in the loss of their brother. ²⁰When Martha heard that Jesus was coming, she went out to meet him, but Mary stayed at home.

²¹"Lord," Martha said to Jesus, "if you had been here, my brother would not have died. ²²But I know that even now God will give you whatever you ask." ²³Jesus said to her, "Your brother will rise again."

²⁴Martha answered, "I know he will rise again in the resurrection at the last day."

²⁵Jesus said to her, "I am the resurrection and the life. He who believes in me will live, even though he dies; ²⁶and whoever lives and believes in me will never die. Do you believe this?"

²⁷"Yes, Lord," she told him, "I believe that you are the Christ, the Son of God, who was to come into the world."

²⁸And after she had said this, she went back and called her sister Mary aside. "The Teacher is here," she said, "and is asking for you." ²⁹When Mary heard this, she got up quickly and went to him. ³⁰Now Jesus had not yet entered the village, but was still at the place where Martha had met him. ³¹When the Jews who had been with Mary in the house, comforting her, noticed how quickly she got up and went out, they followed her, supposing she was going to the tomb to mourn there.

³²When Mary reached the place where Jesus was and saw him, she fell at his feet and said, "Lord, if you had been here, my brother would not have died."

³³When Jesus saw her weeping, and the Jews who had come along with her also weeping, he was deeply moved in spirit and troubled. ³⁴"Where have you laid him?" he asked.

"Come and see, Lord," they replied.

³⁵Jesus wept.

³⁶Then the Jews said, "See how he loved him!"

³⁷But some of them said, "Could not he who opened the eyes of the blind man have kept this man from dying?"

COMMENTARY

17 When Jesus arrived at Bethany, Lazarus had already been in the tomb for four days. In the warm climate of Israel, death and burial would normally take place the same day. Deuteronomy 21:23 prescribes burial on the same day for the guilty person put to death by impalement. According to rabbinic belief, the soul of a person who has died hovers over the corpse for three days, because it desires to reenter the body. But on the fourth day, when the face of the dead person begins to change in appearance, the soul leaves (cf. *Lev. Rab.* 18.1). Since Lazarus had been dead for four days, it would be indisputable that he had really died. A return to life after being

in the tomb for that length of time would require a miracle of God.

18 The town of Bethany, the home of Lazarus and his sisters, was less than two miles from Jerusalem. The Greek text says that the distance between Bethany and the capital was *stadiōn dekapente* ("fifteen stadia"), so the village would lie approximately 1.7 miles outside Jerusalem on the road leading down to Jericho.

19 Following the death of Lazarus there would have been an extended time of mourning. Not only would the family grieve over his death, but professional mourners would also take part in the prescribed ritual, which lasted for at least seven days. Since Jerusalem was so close, many Jews were able to come and offer comfort. Those who came were not the hostile leaders intent on plotting the death of Jesus, but friends of Lazarus and his sisters who had come to mourn their loss. John's point in mentioning "many Jews" is that those who came to pay their respects constituted a large group and would provide a considerable body of witnesses for the coming resurrection of Lazarus.

20 When Martha heard that Jesus was approaching Bethany, she went out to meet him. But Mary remained sitting (*ekathezeto*, GK *2767*, is imperfect) at home. It was customary for those who were mourning to remain in the house while friends would come and sit with them in a silence broken occasionally with sobs of grief (cf. Job 2:8, 13; Eze 8:14). The picture of Mary and Martha in the fourth gospel accords well with the way they are portrayed in Luke 10:38–42. There Martha busies herself with the obligations of hospitality, but Mary sits at Jesus' feet to learn while the opportunity presents itself. In the story recounted by Luke, it is Mary who is commended for having "chosen what is better" (10:42), but in John's narrative a number of scholars think that Martha comes out better. Her response to Jesus' arrival is to go out to meet him without delay. Furthermore, in v.27 she gives voice to a magnificent confession.

21 It would be easy to interpret Martha's words here as a complaint against Jesus' late arrival. "We sent you word that Lazarus was sick, so where have you been for the last four or five days?" But that kind of response would have been inconsistent with the sisters' relationship to Jesus, not only as a dear friend but also in the heightened sense of "Lord." Martha's words were not a rebuke but a genuine expression of sorrow mingled with the confidence that, had Jesus been there, he could have prevented the death of their brother.

22 Martha goes on to say that, even though Lazarus is now dead, she is confident that God would give to Jesus anything that he would ask of him. Martha doesn't specifically ask Jesus to pray that Lazarus will be raised from the dead, though this is certainly implied in the way she poses the remark. Some would question Martha's apparent confidence, calling attention to her reluctance at the tomb when Jesus asked to have the stone removed (v.39). It is better to understand that Martha, in a general sense, believed Jesus could restore her brother to life, but that at the moment when it was about to happen, her faith gave way to the reality that a body dead for four days had already begun to decompose.

23–24 Jesus doesn't get involved in a theoretical discussion of the possibility that Lazarus could be brought back from the grave but simply tells Martha in the plainest way possible that her brother will rise again. Martha understands his words in reference to the widely accepted Pharisaic belief that the dead would be raised to life at the last day. (Only the Sadducees denied the possibility of resurrection; cf. Mk 12:18; Ac 23:8.) "I know," she says, "he will rise again in the resurrection at the last day." But this was not what Jesus had in mind. He was not speaking of something that would take place in the distant future. Those who had gathered to mourn were about to see Lazarus rise again right before their eyes.

25–26 Pharisaic doctrine was not necessarily wrong; it was simply inadequate. Not only was Jesus able to raise the dead; he was himself, as John records the words of Jesus, "the resurrection and the life" (the fifth of the seven great "I am" statements). What Jesus means by this prophetic announcement is not simply that he is able to restore life by resurrecting people from the dead but that he himself is that resurrection and life. While, as Temple, 1:181, remarks, "there is a forcing of language to express an unutterable thought," we are nevertheless called on to see Jesus as possessing eternal life in such a way that to believe in him is to share with him the resurrected life of the new age. As Paul would put it, those who are "in Christ" are one with him in the experience of a quality of life both divine and eternal (see, e.g., Ro 8:1; 1 Co 15:22; 2Co 5:17; Eph 1:3).

In the two following clauses (vv.25b–26a) Jesus explains what he means by (1) the resurrection and (2) the life. The clauses are parallel but not synonymous, the second advancing on the first. The person who believes in him will come to life (spiritually) even though that person will die (physically). This is the true meaning of resurrection—it forever frees the believer from final death. The raising of Lazarus serves as an illustration in the realm of natural life of a truth that is essentially spiritual and belongs to a higher sphere of reality. The second clause explains "life." Whoever comes to life (spiritually) by believing in me (Hendriksen, 2:150, calls living and believing "a kind of hendiadys: living by faith") will never die (spiritually). While resurrection counters the dread enemy death, eternal life is the glorious result of sharing the destiny of the Resurrected One.

So Jesus puts the question to Martha: "Do you believe this?" Not, "Do you believe that I can raise your brother from death even now before the general resurrection at the end of time?" but, "Do you believe that by faith in me a person is raised to a new level of life that is spiritual and that there is no end [death] to this glorious relationship?" In other words, "Do you really believe in me in terms of the higher truths I have taught about myself and my mission?"

27 Martha's answer comes back as one of the most complete confessions recorded in the NT. Andrew told his brother, Simon Peter, that he had met "the Messiah" (1:41), Nathanael declared that Jesus was "the Son of God" (1:49), and Philip spoke of Jesus as "the one Moses wrote about" (1:45; cf. 1:27, 30); but it was Martha who combined them all into one magnificent confession that Jesus was "the Christ, the Son of God, who was to come into the world." The perfect tense of "believe" (pepisteuka, GK 4409) reflects what Bruce, 245, calls "a settled attitude of soul." Martha has come to the firm belief that Jesus is the Messiah, that he is the very Son of God, and that he is the fulfillment of Jewish expectations. Even though Lazarus lies dead in the grave, her confidence in who Jesus is and what he can do is not diminished even the slightest. Sorrow fills her heart because her brother is dead, but faith reigns supreme in her confidence that, with Jesus at hand, all is well.

28 Martha leaves Jesus on the outskirts of Bethany and returns home, where she takes her sister Mary aside to tell her that the Teacher has arrived and is asking for her. Martha speaks to her sister "in secret" or "privately" (lathra, GK 3277; NIV, "aside") in the hope that Mary can slip away unnoticed by the friends who have come to mourn. She wants her to have a few minutes alone with Jesus. The reference to Jesus as "Teacher" is a bit unusual because rabbis would not teach women (cf. 4:27). It reflects the fact that Jesus spoke his message freely to all who would listen—to women as well as to men.

29–31 Mary responded immediately to the summons. She got up quickly and went to Jesus, who was still in the place where Martha had met him. Since in Jesus' day burial grounds were outside the town, it seems reasonable to picture Jesus as waiting there where he would soon perform a miracle rather than going into town to the home of Martha and Mary. When the mourners saw Mary leave the house so quickly, they assumed she would be going out to the tomb. So they followed her there.

One wonders why the mourners did not leave when Martha went out to meet Jesus. Could it be that they were naturally attracted by the emotional warmth of Mary but somewhat put off by her take-charge sister Martha? A winsome personality draws more friends than does any number of more aggressive types.

32 Mary's response to seeing Jesus was to fall at his feet. Lindars, 397, thinks that her reaction was one "of supplication, rather than of worship," but that is unlikely because no request is made. Instead, she speaks to Jesus using the very same words as Martha (cf. v.21). She did not, however, repeat what her sister had said about God granting to Jesus whatever he might ask (see v.22). Undoubtedly the sisters had lamented on repeated occasions that if only Jesus had been there, Lazarus would not have died. So it was natural for the women to express themselves in this way when they first encountered Jesus. Mary's "[throwing] herself at his feet" (TCNT) is consistent with what we know of her from the episode in Mark 14:3–9 (cf. Jn 12:2–8), where she anointed Jesus with expensive perfume. (The account in Lk 7:36–50 appears to be a similar event but actually took place much earlier in Jesus' ministry.)

33–34 So with Mary at Jesus' feet, weeping and surrounded by her many friends who were also weeping and wailing (*klaiō*, GK *3081*, refers to a loud, unrestrained form of weeping especially appropriate in times of sorrow for the dead), John writes that Jesus was "deeply moved in spirit and troubled." This expression has engendered considerable debate. Following the lead of Martin Luther, German scholars have emphasized the primary meaning of *embrimaomai* ("to snort" with indignation, GK *1839*) and have understood Jesus as reacting in anger at the disorderly and intemperate scene he encountered. (*EDNT*, 1:442, says he became "indignant," "furious.") If this interpretation is correct, we must ask why Jesus responded as he did. Some suggest that his frustration resulted from the

fact that such a tumult was forcing him to perform a miracle, which would lead to a premature arrest. But certainly Jesus was not boxed in to such a limited course of action. Besides, anger in such a situation runs counter to what we know of Jesus elsewhere in the Gospels. If Jesus actually was angry, then it would seem to stem from the mourners' failure to grasp the truth that their sorrow was irreconcilable with faith in the one who is "the resurrection and the life" (v.25).

The majority of English translators have understood that while *embrimaomai* in this context may well have indicated an outburst of indignation, the term is sufficiently comprehensive to include compassion as well. The expression "in spirit" (also "in himself," *en heauto*, v.38) is said to be a "Semitism for expressing the internal impact of the emotions" (Brown, 425). Phillips translates, "He was deeply moved and visibly distressed." Lindars, 399, concludes, "We are thus driven back to the classic interpretation of this verse as a testimony to the human feeling of Jesus, who shares with all men in their pain and distress." Jesus asks very simply, "Where have you laid him?" to which Mary and the others answer, "Come and see, Lord"—a strange sequel if Jesus is still in a fit of anger!

35 In the shortest verse in the Bible, we learn that "Jesus wept." Note here that John uses a different word for the tears of Jesus than for the weeping of Mary and those with her. While *klaiō* (GK *3081*) is used of loud weeping or wailing (v.33), *dakryō* (GK *1233*) refers to a more restrained breaking out in tears. *Dakryō* occurs only here in the NT, though the cognate *dakryon*, "a tear," appears ten times. We read of Jesus' tears in two other places in the NT: Luke records Jesus' weeping over Jerusalem as he approached it for the last time (Lk 19:41), and the author of Hebrews reminds us that during the days of his life on earth, Jesus "offered up prayers and petitions with loud cries and tears" (Heb 5:7).

The reason for Jesus' tears in the Lazarus story was not grief over Lazarus's death—that would bracket him with those "who have no hope" (1Th 4:13). Nor was it simply an expression of love and concern for the sisters and their friends. Jesus wept because of the havoc wrought on the world by sin and death. To the one who came to bring life, death was a stark reminder of the continuing cosmic struggle between God and Satan for the souls of men and women. As long as death reigned, the kingdom of God was not yet finally and completely established.

36 The Jews failed to understand the real cause of Jesus' tears. They said, "See how he loved him!"—an observation true enough, but one that fell far short of the real reason for Jesus' tears. He wept over the sad state of a people too blind to see that in him there is life eternal and that by faith in him death is transformed into a gateway to eternal bliss. It was the tragic state of their spiritual blindness that caused him pain and brought tears to his eyes.

37 While some of the mourners were impressed by Jesus' tears, others were more critical of him. Convinced of the astuteness of their insight, they questioned why a person who could open the eyes of a blind man had not kept his good friend from dying. They implied that since Jesus *could* have come and prevented Lazarus's death, there must have been some other (and more sinister) reason for his failure to do so.

NOTES

19 The single article τήν (*tēn*) before Μάρθαν καὶ Μαριάμ (*Marthan kai Mariam*, "Martha and Mary") is changed to τὰς περί (*tas peri*) in 𝔓⁴⁵ᵛⁱᵈ A C³ Θ Ψ 0250 et al.—a change that would indicate the Jews came not so much to Martha and Mary but to their household. The shorter text, however, is to be preferred and is supported by such MSS as 𝔓⁶⁶.⁷⁵ᵛⁱᵈ ℵ B C* L W and others. The article serves both names and binds them together as one.

25 The phrase καὶ ἡ ζωή (*kai hē zōē*, "and the life") is omitted by the early Greek papyrus 𝔓⁴⁵, two versional witnesses, and several early church fathers. This short text is suitable to the context, and the addition could easily have been made by a copyist; but the UBS committee retained the words on the basis of their age, weight, and diversification of witnesses (cf. Metzger, 199). It is interesting that while ἀνάστασις (*anastasis*, "resurrection," GK *414*) is found only once in John's gospel outside the present passage (6:39), ζωή (*zōē*, "life," GK *2437*) occurs thirty-six times.

27 Martha's affirmation of faith is strengthened by the addition of the first person personal pronoun ἐγώ (*egō*, "I"). Coupled with the perfect tense πεπίστευκα (*pepiskteuka*, "have believed"), it results in the strongest possible personal testimony of faith. While Martha is often criticized for what is regarded as paying unnecessary attention to the details of hospitality (vis-à-vis Mary's desire to learn at the Master's feet), her ringing testimony to her conviction that Jesus is the Christ, the Son of God, is a clear indication of her perceptive mind and believing heart.

33 If ἐνεβριμήσατο (*enebrimēsato*, GK *1839*) is taken more in the sense of anger, then it is certain that Jesus' "anger" was directed at death itself and at the one who holds the power of death.

35 Bruce, 246, takes ἐδάκρυσεν (*edakrysen*, GK *1233*) as an ingressive aorist and translates "burst into tears."

3. Jesus Raises Lazarus (11:38–44)

³⁸Jesus, once more deeply moved, came to the tomb. It was a cave with a stone laid across the entrance. ³⁹"Take away the stone," he said.

"But, Lord," said Martha, the sister of the dead man, "by this time there is a bad odor, for he has been there four days."

⁴⁰Then Jesus said, "Did I not tell you that if you believed, you would see the glory of God?"

⁴¹So they took away the stone. Then Jesus looked up and said, "Father, I thank you that you have heard me. ⁴²I knew that you always hear me, but I said this for the benefit of the people standing here, that they may believe that you sent me."

⁴³When he had said this, Jesus called in a loud voice, "Lazarus, come out!" ⁴⁴The dead man came out, his hands and feet wrapped with strips of linen, and a cloth around his face. Jesus said to them, "Take off the grave clothes and let him go."

COMMENTARY

38 When Jesus arrived at the tomb, his response to the situation was the same as it had been when he saw Mary and her friends mourning. He was "once more shaken with emotion" (Rieu). The tomb was a cave with a stone laid across the entrance. The Jews normally buried their dead in caves hewn out of the rocks. For private burials the vertical tomb was more common. That Lazarus was in this kind of tomb is favored by two observations: (1) the preposition *epi* ("across," GK *2093*)—the stone that covered the opening of the tomb would be laid "over" or "across" the opening, and (2) the verb in v.39, *airō* (GK *149*), which in this verse means "to lift up, move from one place to another" (BDAG, 24). Other tombs were cut horizontally into the rocks. In the walls of the main chamber were carved a number of vaults. The traditional site of the tomb of Lazarus dates back to the fourth century and is currently occupied by a mosque.

39 Jesus orders the stone that covers the mouth of the tomb to be taken away. Martha, who has joined the group by now, is quick to raise an objec-tion. Lazarus has been in the tomb for four days, and "by this time there is a bad odor," she protests. This assumes that the body was not embalmed. Some have seen a contradiction with v.44, which says that the body had been bound with strips of linen. But this does not necessarily mean that it had been embalmed. In Jewish circles, the practice of wrapping aromatic spices next to the body was to counteract the odors of decomposition, not to embalm. It has also been suggested by some that the reason Jesus wanted to have the tomb opened was not in order to prepare for the raising of Lazarus from the dead, but so that he could take a last look at his dear friend. That, however, would put Jesus in the same group with those who grieved without hope—a position inconsistent with the reality that Jesus is himself the resurrection and the life. Since Jesus was on the verge of restoring Lazarus to life, it would be pointless to "take a last look" at him in the grave.

40 So Jesus reminds Martha that if she would only believe, she would see the glory of God, i.e., "the wonder of what God can do" (Phillips). While she knew that Lazarus would be raised from the dead (v.23), that God would be glorified as a result (v.4), and that she had acknowledged the deity and the messianic mission of Jesus (v.27), still, bodies in a grave for four days are not only dead but have begun to deteriorate! It is one thing for faith to express itself in bold affirmation when it is in the form of a creed, but the stark reality of life has a way of eroding its assurance. Certainly Jesus is the Son of God who came into the world (v.27) and can receive from God whatever he asks (v.22), but, after all, Lazarus is dead and buried. The genuineness of a person's faith is seen in how it reacts to the actual crises of life.

41–42 So at Jesus' command (v.39) they took away the stone and Jesus raised his eyes (a few MSS add "up to heaven"), a characteristic preface to prayer (cf. Lk 18:13). God is addressed as "Father," not "our Father," because while Christian believers share a common relationship to God as Father, God is "Father" to the Son in a unique sense.

It is noteworthy that John does not record a prayer in which Jesus asks that Lazarus be raised from the dead. Instead he thanks God for having heard him. Apparently Jesus has been in prayer all along, asking his Father to perform a mighty miracle. With typical insight Temple, 1:184, comments, "There was no one moment of prayer. He lived prayer." Jesus "explains" to the Father that, though *he* has always known that his prayers are heard (note the *egō*, "I"), he said what he did for the benefit of the people there. The contrast is further strengthened by the strong adversative *alla* ("but"). He wanted them to know that the imminent resurrection of Lazarus was the result of prayer. His purpose was that they "may come to believe" (taking *pisteusōsin* as an ingressive aorist).

43–44 Then Jesus "raised his voice in a great cry" (NEB), "Lazarus, come out!" And as a prelude to that great day when the dead will hear the same life-giving shout and come from the tombs of this earth, Lazarus came out of the grave—"hands and feet wrapped with strips of linen, and a cloth around his face." We need not question how a man wrapped so tightly with grave clothes could walk. If God can raise the dead, he can take care of all such incidentals. We are not told how the body was wrapped. If each leg was wrapped separately, walking would have been quite possible.

Jesus then ordered that the grave clothes be taken off and that Lazarus be set free. Temple's homiletical point, 1:185, is that as the wrappings of the grave held Lazarus fast, "so old habits may cling about us when the sin itself is eradicated. If we are truly to be alive, we must be freed from these also."

NOTES

38 See v.33 for the other occurrence of ἐμβριμάομαι (*embrimaomai*) in John.

A μνημεῖον (*mnēmeion*, GK *3646*) is first of all a monument built to someone who has died (L&N, 7:76; as in Mt 23:29) and then a grave (the far more frequent usage).

43 Taking δεῦρο (*deuro*, GK *1306*) as an adverb of place yields the succinct command, "Here! Outside!" (Morris, 561 n. 83).

44 The word σουδάριον (*soudarion*, GK *5051*) is a Latin loanword (*sudarium*, "a cloth used to wipe perspiration from the face"). In Luke 19:20 it was the piece of cloth in which the third servant kept the money entrusted to him. Here in John 11:44 (and also in 20:7) it refers to a piece of cloth placed over the face (or around the head) of the corpse. In Acts 19:12 the σουδάριον, *soudarion* is best understood as a handkerchief.

4. Reaction by Jewish Authorities (11:45–57)

OVERVIEW

In the verses that follow, we read of the far-reaching results of the miracle of raising Lazarus from the dead. Some, when they saw what Jesus had done, "put their faith in him" (v.45). Others went to the Pharisees to report the miracle (v.46), and their act led to the plot that ended in the crucifixion of Jesus.

⁴⁵Therefore many of the Jews who had come to visit Mary, and had seen what Jesus did, put their faith in him. ⁴⁶But some of them went to the Pharisees and told them what Jesus had done. ⁴⁷Then the chief priests and the Pharisees called a meeting of the Sanhedrin.

"What are we accomplishing?" they asked. "Here is this man performing many miraculous signs. ⁴⁸If we let him go on like this, everyone will believe in him, and then the Romans will come and take away both our place and our nation."

⁴⁹Then one of them, named Caiaphas, who was high priest that year, spoke up, "You know nothing at all! ⁵⁰You do not realize that it is better for you that one man die for the people than that the whole nation perish."

⁵¹He did not say this on his own, but as high priest that year he prophesied that Jesus would die for the Jewish nation, ⁵²and not only for that nation but also for the scattered children of God, to bring them together and make them one. ⁵³So from that day on they plotted to take his life.

⁵⁴Therefore Jesus no longer moved about publicly among the Jews. Instead he withdrew to a region near the desert, to a village called Ephraim, where he stayed with his disciples.

⁵⁵When it was almost time for the Jewish Passover, many went up from the country to Jerusalem for their ceremonial cleansing before the Passover. ⁵⁶They kept looking for Jesus, and as they stood in the temple area they asked one another, "What do you think? Isn't he coming to the Feast at all?" ⁵⁷But the chief priests and Pharisees had given orders that if anyone found out where Jesus was, he should report it so that they might arrest him.

COMMENTARY

45 The raising of Lazarus was not without its immediate effect. John writes that when those who had come to mourn saw what Jesus had done, they "put their faith in him." John's "therefore" establishes a strong causal relationship between the raising of Lazarus and the consequent coming to faith of those who saw it happen. While faith based on the miraculous may not be a strong faith, it certainly is a beginning and is far better than no faith at all. The people's "seeing" involved far more than natural vision. Brown, 439, notes that the verb *theaomai* ("to see," GK *2517*) "often connotes perceptive vision." It wasn't the mere sight of a dead man being raised that brought about faith, but a true insight into what was really taking place.

One may ask why the text says that the Jews "had come to visit Mary" and omit any reference to Martha? One reasonable answer is that Mary, being the more emotional of the two, would have been in greater need of comfort and solace. It is also true that Martha, with her more dominant personality, would be less likely to gain the sympathy of others. Both sisters had met Jesus just outside Bethany and greeted him with the same words, but while Mary's plight brought tears to Jesus' eyes (v.35), Martha received a lesson in theology (vv.20–26).

46 Those who saw *and believed* are now contrasted with those who only saw the unusual event. This second group went to the Pharisees and reported what Jesus had done—not out of a desire to see their leaders come to faith but out of the suspicion that any man who could work such wonders must pose a serious threat to the tenuous relationship between the Jewish nation and their Roman overlords. As one might expect, the result of a miracle once again created a division (9:16; cf. 7:43). Everyone saw exactly the same thing: in response to Jesus' command, Lazarus, already dead for four days, had come out of the tomb alive. Those predisposed to believe accepted what they saw and gave God the glory; others rejected what they saw and resorted to a plot to get rid of the person who had such unusual power. Based on each group's predispositions, both responses were rational and appropriate. To repeat a figure of speech, the sheep that belong to Jesus recognize the voice of their shepherd (cf. 10:2–5).

47 On learning that Lazarus has been raised from the dead, the ruling priests and the Pharisees call a meeting of the Sanhedrin. Apparently this was an official meeting (however, see the NET translator's note that argues, on the basis of the anarthrous *synedrion* ["Sanhedrin," GK *5284*], that it was prob-

ably an informal meeting) in that Caiaphas, who was president of the Sanhedrin by virtue of his role as high priest, appeared to be in charge (vv.49–52). The plural designation "chief priests" is understood by Bruce, 250, to include "the high priest, the captain of the temple and the members of the leading priestly family."

Though much of our knowledge of the Sanhedrin comes from a later time, and therefore may not reflect the actual circumstances at the time of Jesus, it is safe to say that this judicial body of seventy-one dealt with matters of justice within the boundaries set by the Romans and was the final court of appeal for questions related to Mosaic law. It reflected primarily the Sadducean point of view. From this point forward in John we hear of the Pharisees on only three occasions (12:19, 42; 18:3), the opposition to Jesus issuing in his death being led by the chief priests.

The question "What are we accomplishing?" posed by the chief priests and Pharisees is not immediately clear. Barrett, 405, suggests that the question mark be placed after the first clause of the Greek text (*ti poioumen*) rather than at the end of the verse, which would result in a question asking, "What are we *now* doing?"—the implied answer being, "Nothing. We ought to be doing something about it but we're not, because this man is performing miracles." This rendition is superior to taking the question as a deliberative subjective, "What are we to do?" The NIV's "What are we accomplishing?" follows the former alternative, as does the NASB's "What are we doing?"

48 The members of the Sanhedrin were at an impasse. It cannot be denied that Jesus had performed many miraculous signs, the most recent and certainly the most startling being the raising to life of a dead man. If they allowed him to continue, he would quickly gain a following as a messianic leader and they, the ruling elite of the Jewish nation, would lose their favored position in Jewish life and society. As the NIV puts it, "the Romans would come and take away both our place and our nation." While "our place" (*ton topon*, GK *5536*) is normally taken as referring to the temple (see NIV text note), it is better understood as portraying the favored position in society enjoyed by the religious leaders. Of the religious leadership, Carson, 421, writes, "They are prompted less by dispassionate concern for the well-being of the nation than for their own positions of power and prestige."

49–50 Caiaphas had been appointed high priest in AD 18 and served in that capacity until he was deposed some eighteen years later. He was the son-in-law of the powerful Annas, who had been high priest until AD 15. (The intervening three years saw a quick succession of three other high priests.) While the high priest was theoretically appointed for life (Nu 35:25), such was not the case during Roman occupation. The Romans saw to it that no high priest who failed to serve their own political purposes would continue in office; they replaced such priests with individuals more amenable to Roman desires. John's reference to Caiaphas as high priest that year—as though the appointment were an annual affair, as was so often the case in the Graeco-Roman world—does not indicate any lack of knowledge on John's part about the region's customs. The expression means no more than "in that fateful/memorable year."

With the rudeness traditionally assigned to the Sadducees (cf. Josephus, *J.W.* 1.266) Caiaphas addresses the assembly: "You know nothing at all." The added personal pronoun *hymeis* puts the stress on "you"; Barclay translates, "You are witless creatures."

Caiaphas's cynical solution to the problem of Jesus, the worker of miracles, was pure utilitarianism—"You don't seem to grasp the fact that it is in our interest that one man die rather than the entire nation be destroyed." In other words, the welfare of Israel rests on our willingness to do what is necessary to preserve it—i.e., to put this man Jesus to death." The power of the human mind to rationalize a course of action, no matter how devious, is marvelous to behold. Better to kill a single person than to let an entire nation perish. Sounds reasonable, but it makes the fatal mistake of disregarding the rights of the individual. All socialist doctrine fails at its basic premise—i.e., that the good of the masses is to be preferred over the good of the individual. History has shown the vacuity of this deceptive doctrine. It is only when the rights of the individual are protected that the welfare of the group is enhanced.

51 While Caiaphas was promoting the cynical idea that the greatest amount of benefit would accrue to the greatest number of people by the murder of the one unfortunate, unwittingly he was summarizing the gospel (cf. Temple, 1:187). His words were far more profound than he ever intended. Acting as high priest, he had just prophesied that the death of Jesus would serve to bring together and make one "the Jewish nation" and "the scattered children of God" (v.52). What he intended was that by killing Jesus, political Israel would be preserved. What he actually said (and that at a deeper level) was that by his death Jesus would guarantee spiritual life to Jew and Gentile alike who came to him by faith. That Caiaphas did not speak "on his own" does not mean that he had no control over what he was saying. The thought and the words chosen to express the idea were strictly his own. What was beyond his control was that these very words, cynical as they were, could also carry an important message on a different level.

52–53 Since "the scattered children of God" refers to Gentiles who were yet to hear and respond to the gospel, it is sometimes asked how they could be designated "children of God" prior to regeneration. Such is the predestinarian nature of the fourth gospel. Jesus had already spoken in the same way of "other sheep" that would hear his voice and follow him (1:3–5; cf. 6:37). The Gentiles are currently scattered, but they will be brought together with believing Jews and made one body. This, of course, enraged the authorities, who from that day plotted to take Jesus' life (v.53).

54 Jesus then went to a village called Ephraim. The location is probably to be identified as the OT Ephron (2Ch 13:19)—the modern et-Taiyibeh, which lies about thirteen miles north-northeast of Jerusalem and some four miles northeast of Bethel. It was far enough from the capital to provide sanctuary but close enough to allow Jesus to return for the final week.

55 As the Feast of Passover approached, many Jews went up to Jerusalem from the surrounding country. Passover was one of the three great pilgrim feasts. John records a first Passover in AD 28, some forty-six years after Herod began to rebuild the temple in Jerusalem (2:20). A second Passover is mentioned in 6:4, and this is now the third (11:55). It is for this reason that most scholars accept as a time span for the public ministry of Jesus a period of slightly over two years.

56–57 Many people arrived early in Jerusalem in order to fulfill the requirements of ceremonial cleansing (cf. Ex 19:10–15; Nu 9:9–14). They were on the lookout for Jesus and wondering whether or not he would come to the Feast. They questioned one another as to whether he would show up. By this time the chief priests had issued orders that anyone who knew where Jesus was should report it to the officials so that they might arrest him.

NOTES

49 Tasker, 142 n. 49, notes that the pronoun ἐκεῖνος (ekeinos, "that") is a favorite of John and that while not always emphatic, it would appear to be so in this location. It stresses the truth that this was *annus mirabilis*, the year of man's redemption. In the parallel phrase in v.51, ἐκεῖνου, *ekeinou*, is omitted from 𝔓⁶⁶ and D, while the entire phrase is left out by 𝔓⁴⁵ e 1 sy^s.

55 From the very beginning Israel was to be a holy nation (Lev 20:26). Their moral separation from sin was to be expressed outwardly by separation from objects considered to be unclean. Israelites who had come into contact with that which was unclean were required to separate themselves from the congregation for a period of time and then be reinstated after certain purification rites were observed. At times a sacrifice was required. In preparation for the Jewish Passover, it was essential that everyone taking part in the festival undergo purification.

57 That John used the pluperfect δεδώκεισαν (*dedōkeisan*, "had given," GK *1443*) rather than the aorist ἔδωκαν (*edokan*) may reflect the continuing nature of the command. The order was to remain in force until Jesus was in fact located.

REFLECTIONS

As this chapter draws to an end, an air of expectancy hangs over the city as those who had encountered Jesus or knew anything about him wait to see what will happen. The stage is set for the most dramatic and far-reaching event of Jesus' earthly ministry. He had come to give his life "for the people" (v.50), and that moment was rapidly approaching. Angels must have held their breath in anticipation as Jesus prepared for the triumphal entry and what would follow. The redemptive invasion of God into human history is about to draw to a close with the events leading to the crucifixion of the Lamb of God and his triumphant resurrection after three days. As John the Baptist cried out at the beginning of Jesus' public ministry, "Look, the Lamb of God, who takes away the sin of the world!" (1:29).

D. Final Days before the Passion (12:1–50)

OVERVIEW

With ch. 12 Jesus' public ministry is brought to a close. In ch. 13 Jesus celebrates the Passover with his disciples in the upper room and from this point on directs his attention to his small band of followers. The three following chapters contain teachings on the return of Jesus; the power of prayer and the promise of the coming Counselor (ch. 14); the relationship of the believer to Jesus, to one another, and to the world (ch. 15); and the work of the Holy Spirit and the joy of the coming age (ch. 16). Chapter 17 provides us with the great high priestly prayer of Jesus, and chs. 18–20 tell the tragic yet triumphant story of his arrest, trial, crucifixion, resurrection, and reunion with the disciples.

The fourth gospel has been called the passion of Jesus Christ with an extended introduction. None of the Synoptic Gospels devote such a large percentage of their narrative to Jesus' final week on earth. Chapter 12 serves as a bridge between the public ministry of Jesus and the crucial final week of his life in which he carries out to the very end the purpose for which he came.

1. Mary Anoints the Feet of Jesus (12:1–11)

OVERVIEW

The relationship of John's account of the anointing at Bethany to similar accounts in the Synoptics (Mt 26:6–13 = Mk 14:3–9; and Lk 7:36–50) has received a great deal of attention. While there are both differences and similarities in the accounts, it is hard not to conclude that Matthew and Mark are writing about the same incident, while Luke appears to be reporting a similar but different incident. The crux of the problem is that while in Matthew and Mark the expensive perfume is poured on the *head* of Jesus, John pictures Mary pouring it on his *feet* and wiping it with her hair. This last item seems to reflect Luke's account, in which the woman wipes her tears from the feet of Jesus with her hair and then pours perfume on them. There is very little additional evidence, however, that would lead us to identify Mary of Bethany with the sinful woman of Luke's account. While John's incident takes place late in Jesus' ministry, Luke's story comes quite early in Jesus' Galilean ministry. Carson, 426–27, wisely calls on the reader to "inject a small dose of historical imagination before resorting too quickly to the critic's knife" and concludes that "it is reasonable to suppose that what actually happened was comprehensive enough to generate the accounts of both John and Matthew/Mark, including the divergences that initially seem so odd."

¹Six days before the Passover, Jesus arrived at Bethany, where Lazarus lived, whom Jesus had raised from the dead. ²Here a dinner was given in Jesus' honor. Martha served, while Lazarus was among those reclining at the table with him. ³Then Mary took about a pint of pure nard, an expensive perfume; she poured it on Jesus' feet and wiped his feet with her hair. And the house was filled with the fragrance of the perfume.

⁴But one of his disciples, Judas Iscariot, who was later to betray him, objected, ⁵"Why wasn't this perfume sold and the money given to the poor? It was worth a year's wages." ⁶He did not say this because he cared about the poor but because he was a thief; as keeper of the money bag, he used to help himself to what was put into it.

⁷"Leave her alone," Jesus replied. "It was intended that she should save this perfume for the day of my burial. ⁸You will always have the poor among you, but you will not always have me."

⁹Meanwhile a large crowd of Jews found out that Jesus was there and came, not only because of him but also to see Lazarus, whom he had raised from the dead. ¹⁰So the chief priests made plans to kill Lazarus as well, ¹¹for on account of him many of the Jews were going over to Jesus and putting their faith in him.

COMMENTARY

1 The scene described here took place several weeks after the raising of Lazarus. Specifically it was six days before the Passover when Jesus arrived at Bethany, the home of Lazarus. We may assume from the context that Jesus came to Bethany from the desert area northeast of Jerusalem to which he had retreated due to the Jewish plot to take his life (11:53–54). If John places the Passover that year on Friday (the fifteenth day of Nisan), then six days prior would be Saturday (beginning at sundown on Friday evening).

2 The dinner that was given to honor Jesus would have taken place on Saturday evening. (Friday evening was the beginning of the Sabbath and Martha would not be serving at that time.) The Greek word translated "dinner" (*deipnon*; GK *1270*) refers to the main meal of the day and in this case would have fallen in the evening after the close of the Passover. Some writers connect it with the *hab-*

dalah, the service that separates the Sabbath from the rest of the week. It would appear that the meal was provided by Lazarus and his sisters, though the parallel account in Matthew/Mark places it in the home of Simon the Leper (Mt 26:6; Mk 14:3). Some have suggested that this Simon may have been the father of Lazarus and the real owner of the home. Carson, 428, calls the hypothesis "attractive" but "completely without supporting evidence."

The portrayal of Martha as one who "was serving" (*diēkonei*, GK *1354*, is imperfect) is markedly consistent with what we learn of her temperament in Luke 10:38–42, where she is distracted with the obligations of hospitality, while her sister Mary sits at Jesus' feet in rapt attention to all he was saying. John notes that Lazarus was reclining at the table with Jesus.

3 Mary now pours pure nard on the feet of Jesus and wipes them with her hair. The Greek *litra* (the

Roman pound) was about twelve ounces. Nard was a very expensive and fragrant oil extracted from the nard plant, which grew in the mountains of northern India. The meaning of the Greek word *pistikos* (GK *4410*; NIV, "pure") is disputed. While it may be derived from *pistos* ("faithful," hence "pure," GK *4412*), it has also been traced to *pinō* ("to drink," GK *4403*; thus a reference to it being in liquid form) and to *pistakia* ("pistaschio tree"). Thankfully, the etymology is not theologically significant! The important point is that Mary anoints Jesus with expensive perfume in a gesture of humility and devotion.

The account in Matthew/Mark places the anointing in the village of Bethany and adds that it took place in the house of Simon the Leper. Neither Synoptic account provides the name of the woman who anointed Jesus, but both have her pouring the expensive perfume on Jesus' head rather than on his feet, as John has it. This latter point provides the only substantial difference between the accounts. Calvin, 2:11, solves the problem by indicating that the reference to feet means "the whole body . . . down to the feet." That she wipes his feet with her hair is reminiscent of an earlier incident in Luke in which a woman of questionable repute wept at Jesus' feet and wiped them with her hair (7:38). Temple, 1:189, is one who holds to a single incident in all four gospels and writes that Mary "re-enacts the earlier scene when she was still 'a woman in the city, a sinner.'" Obviously it would be unwise to claim that the Mary of Bethany could not have come from such a sordid past. After all, did not Jesus say that he came not "to invite virtuous people, but to call sinners to repentance" (Lk 5:32 NEB)? And was he not derided as "a friend of the worst sort of sinners" (Lk 7:34 NLT)? On the other hand, there are substantial textual reasons that argue against the equation of the sinful woman in Luke with Mary of Bethany as recorded by the other gospel writers.

4 It is informative to note how quick are all four of the gospel writers to point out that it was Judas Iscariot who betrayed their Master. In his account of the commissioning of the Twelve, Matthew records that it was Judas "who betrayed [Jesus]" (Mt 10:4). The same words are used by Mark in his narrative of the choosing of the Twelve (Mk 3:19). In the parallel account in Luke, Judas is named as the one "who became a traitor" (Lk 6:16). Here in John he is the one "who was later to betray [Jesus]." The memory of the despicable act lived on in infamy.

5 The perfume is said to be worth "a year's wages" (*triakosiōn dēnariōn*, lit., "three hundred denarii"). Since the average daily wage of a working person was one denarius, the value of the ointment so freely poured out by Mary was exceedingly great. It is suggested that either Mary and her family were very well-to-do and could afford to purchase the pure nard or it had been passed down to her as a family heirloom. In today's currency, its value would have been about $30,000.

6 One has to wonder why Judas, of all the disciples, was allowed to be the keeper of the money bag. Though looking back, John could properly designate Judas "a thief," at the time there was apparently no reason to doubt his integrity. While such knowledge was available to Jesus as the Son of God, it is like the Lord to give his followers the opportunity to prove or disprove their loyalty. Life is the arena in which we demonstrate by our conduct the reality of our commitment to God. Judas simply proved openly what he had always been secretly.

John explains that Judas's concern was not for the poor but had to do with the fact that he was in charge of the money bag and that "he used to help himself" to its contents. The proceeds from the sale of such expensive perfume would enhance his own position while at the same time appearing to be an act of wise benevolence on his part.

The "money bag" (*glōssokomon*, GK *1186*) was originally a case for the "tongue" (*glōssa*, GK *1185*) or mouthpiece of a flute. Later the term came to be used more generally for any kind of case or container. The Greek verb in the final clause of v.6 (*bastazō*, "to pick up" or "carry away," GK *1002*) has the nuance of "lifting" in the sense of stealing. Lindars, 418, calls it "a colloquial expression for pilfering the contents."

7 Jesus' response to the point made by Judas (that the perfume should have been sold and the money given to the poor) has been understood in various ways. When the Greek text is taken as it stands, Jesus' answer is that Mary is to be left alone so that (*hoti* is the crucial word) she might keep the perfume till the day of his burial. But this means that some (or all?) of the nard should be saved for the forthcoming burial, and it is reasonable to conclude that once the alabaster jar (Mk 14:3) had been broken the contents would spill out. Sensing the difficulty, some MSS omit the *hina* and read a perfect tense *tetēreken* ("she has kept it," GK *5498*), rather than the aorist, thus meaning that Mary had *already done* what would normally be done at the burial. The problem here is that a bit later Nicodemus will prepare the body of Jesus for burial in accordance with Jewish burial customs (19:39–40). The most satisfactory solution is to take Jesus' response elliptically and supply a clause following the interjection: Leave her alone. [The reason why she didn't sell the pure nard was] so that (*hoti*) she might keep it for my burial. The NIV's "it was intended that she should save this perfume for the day of my burial" adopts this interpretation of the verse.

8 Jesus reminds the disciples that they would always have the poor among them but they would not always have him. The designation "the poor" was not a personal or derogatory statement but a common expression among the people. Jesus was not saying that those who are economically less fortunate should be left to their misery. The opportunity to respond in practical ways to the needs of the poor will continue indefinitely into the future. Jesus, however, will not continue to be with them, so it is important to meet his need while there is still time. Hendriksen, 2:180, makes the interesting comment that by implication Jesus "is saying to the church of all the ages that the care of the poor is its responsibility and privilege." The nature of life is such that while the poor will always need the loving care of the believing church, there are certain critical periods when something of a more timely nature must take priority. The building of a sanctuary for worship could be one such example.

9–11 While Jesus was still at Bethany a large crowd of Jews arrived. Not only did they want to see Jesus but they also wanted to meet this man Lazarus whom Jesus had raised from the dead. The crowd was probably comprised of people from throughout the countryside who had come to Jerusalem early for ceremonial cleansing prior to the Passover (11:55). The attention being given to Lazarus made the chief priests realize that in addition to killing Jesus (11:53) it would be necessary to kill Lazarus too. It was because of Lazarus that many of the Jews "were falling away [from the Jewish faith] and believing in Jesus" (Rieu). He was a major embarrassment to the Sadducean religious hierarchy. Not only did a man brought back from the dead contradict one of their basic tenets (i.e., that there is no resurrection; Mk 12:18 par.), but further that man's very presence was enough to cause a number of the Jewish people to place their faith in Jesus. Such an influence must be squelched before any more damage is done to the chief priests' reputation and privileged position.

NOTES

2 Keener, 294, observes that people in Jesus' day normally "sat" at meals but "reclined" on couches for special meals, such as feasts or banquets. It is more likely that it was the women and the children who sat, while the men reclined on couches with wooden frames that were padded with mattresses and cushions. Leaning on their left elbow allowed them to eat with their right hand. A dinner given in honor of Jesus would include appropriate washing of the hands, the blessing, several courses of appetizing dishes, and a special portion for the guest.

2. Jesus' "Triumphal Entry" into Jerusalem (12:12–19)

¹²The next day the great crowd that had come for the Feast heard that Jesus was on his way to Jerusalem. ¹³They took palm branches and went out to meet him, shouting,

"Hosanna!"
"Blessed is he who comes in the name of the Lord!"
"Blessed is the King of Israel!"

¹⁴Jesus found a young donkey and sat upon it, as it is written,

¹⁵"Do not be afraid, O Daughter of Zion;
see, your king is coming,
seated on a donkey's colt."

¹⁶At first his disciples did not understand all this. Only after Jesus was glorified did they realize that these things had been written about him and that they had done these things to him. ¹⁷Now the crowd that was with him when he called Lazarus from the tomb and raised him from the dead continued to spread the word. ¹⁸Many people, because they had heard that he had given this miraculous sign, went out to meet him. ¹⁹So the Pharisees said to one another, "See, this is getting us nowhere. Look how the whole world has gone after him!"

COMMENTARY

12–13 If the dinner that Martha served was on Saturday evening following the Sabbath (vv. 1–2), then "the next day" would be Sunday of Passion Week. At that time a "great crowd" of pilgrims who had come early to Jerusalem for the necessary purification heard that Jesus was on his way to the city, took up palm branches, and went out to meet him. While Josephus's observation (*J. W.* 6:422–25) that on one occasion 2.7 million worshipers had come to Jerusalem for Passover is probably inflated, there is no doubt that during religious festivals the city was jammed with visitors. The crowd undoubtedly contained many who had heard him speak and work miracles in Galilee. Perhaps now he would step forward, take on the mantle of leadership, and guide the nation to a brighter future!

It is difficult to overemphasize the impact the raising of Lazarus had on the people who had come to Jerusalem. In their minds, anyone who could raise the dead was certainly qualified to free the Jewish nation from the yoke of Rome and restore national sovereignty. So the crowd poured out through the east gate on that Sunday morning, ready with their palm branches to declare him king. Since palm branches were used in connection with the Feast of Tabernacles but not Passover, it is held by some that the account of the triumphal entry has been transferred to the latter festival. Such a transposition is hardly necessary, since from the times of the Maccabees palm branches had served as a national symbol.

As Jesus approached, the crowd began to shout (*ekraugazon*, GK *3189*, is ingressive imperfect), "Hosanna! Blessed is he who comes in the name of the Lord!" While the origin and meaning of "Hosanna" are uncertain, most scholars understand the term as a transliteration of the Hebrew expression that appears in Psalm 118:25 as a cry to the Lord for salvation—"Save, we pray!" or "Save now!" It would appear that the original significance was lost through liturgical usage and that by NT times it had become primarily a shout of joy or welcome (cf. *ISBE* 2:761). In the NT it is found six times, always in connection with Jesus' triumphal entry into Jerusalem. On the lips of the pilgrims (and the children in the temple, Mt 21:15), it is understood as announcing that all the Jewish messianic expectations are being fulfilled in Jesus.

The greeting is followed by a declaration of blessedness on the one who comes in the name of the Lord. That the people understood "Hosanna" in a messianic sense follows from their adding to the psalm itself the words "blessed is the King of Israel." This one who comes in the name of the Lord—i.e., with the authority of Yahweh—is Israel's king, the long-awaited Messiah.

14–15 The messiah whom the crowd was acclaiming was not, however, the kind of messiah who was entering the city. Instead of riding triumphantly on a horse, the symbol of warfare (cf. Ps 33:17; Pr 21:31), King-Messiah came in on a young donkey, a lowly animal associated with missions of peace. Zechariah 9:9 (cited in part in v.15) described the coming of Zion's king in terms that would never have satisfied the messianic enthusiasm of this crowd that went to meet Jesus. The OT prophet depicted Zion's king as righteous, gentle, bringing salvation, proclaiming peace, and riding on a donkey. Jesus' triumphal entry was an acted parable in which he declared himself Messiah—not the kind of national savior they were looking for, but one who fulfilled the prophetic expectations of Zechariah 9:9–13. That the crowd came to understand that Jesus had no intention of satisfying their nationalistic expectations is supported by the fact that within a week many of the same group were calling out in a blind rage for his crucifixion (19:15).

16 Only at a later time, after Jesus had been glorified and the Holy Spirit had been given to lead the disciples into all truth (16:13), did the disciples fully comprehend what Jesus was doing when he rode into Jerusalem on a donkey. By fulfilling Zechariah's prophecy, Jesus had established himself as the true Messiah of OT expectation. That the crowd greeted Jesus as Messiah while at the same time the disciples failed to understand what was going on poses no real problem. When the crowds heard that Jesus was on his way to Jerusalem, they felt sure that their own nationalistic expectations were about to be realized. But his entry into the city on a donkey, an animal of peace, quickly dampened their enthusiasm. As for the disciples, their failure was in not grasping the full significance of what Jesus was doing. It was only later—when they had received the Spirit of truth—that they came to understand that "these things [Zechariah's prophecy] had been written about him" and why his entrance into the city had been met with such excitement by the crowd (taking "they had done these things to him" in a passive sense to mean "what had been done to him").

17–18 The crowd that was with Jesus when he raised Lazarus continued to talk about what they had seen (*emartyrei*, GK *3455*, "spread the word," is a continuous imperfect). No one else had ever performed such a miracle, and the story spread rapidly. To be fully convinced that God acts in this world results in a witness that cannot be silenced. The crowd of v.17 is not identical with the crowd of v.12. Obviously many of the earlier group were in the later crowd as well. But along with them were others to whom they had told the miraculous story of the raising of Lazarus. And these were anxious to see the one who had raised a man from the dead.

19 All of this troubled the Pharisees greatly. In effect, those who were more extreme in their opposition to Jesus said to those who were willing to wait and learn, "See, this is getting us nowhere. The way we've been handling the situation thus far is ineffective. Look at the crowd of pilgrims rushing out to greet that pretender! They are shouting Hosannas and waving palm branches as he approaches. This has got to stop. The whole world [an understandable exaggeration] is running after him."

NOTES

13 The palm tree has played an important role in the history of Israel and the surrounding countries. In *Genesis Rabbah* 15 it is identified as the "tree of life" (cf. Ge 2:9). Its image is found in sacred architecture of the day as well as on Jewish coins. Its fruit was part of the standard diet, its fronds were made into mats and baskets, and its bark was twisted into rope. In Psalm 92:12 the righteous are said to "flourish like a palm tree." Palm branches were used at the Feast of Tabernacles, and in Revelation 7:9 the great multitude stands before the Lamb with palm branches in their hands.

The NIV repeats the words "blessed is" in the final clause of the sentence although the Greek is [καί] (*kai*, "and") rather than εὐλογημένος (*eulogēmenos*, "blessed," GK *2328*). The NASB understands the καί, *kai*, in an ascensive sense and translates, "even the King of Israel" (so also ASV, RSV; the NRSV has a dash followed by "the King of Israel").

14 This is the only occurrence of ὀνάριον (*onarion*, "young donkey," GK *3942*) in the NT. The usual word for the colt of a donkey is πῶλος (*pōlos*, GK *4798*); all but one of its twelve occurrences are found in the Synoptic Gospels. Known for its strength and surefootedness, the donkey was a general utility animal in the ancient world. Young donkeys were not ridden for the first three years of their lives.

17 The reading ὅτε (*hote*, "when") is superior to the variant ὅτι (*hoti*, "because") because it is supported by better external testimony and because the latter appears to be an attempt to clarify the account (cf. Metzger, 202).

3. Greeks Come to See Jesus (12:20–26)

²⁰Now there were some Greeks among those who went up to worship at the Feast. ²¹They came to Philip, who was from Bethsaida in Galilee, with a request. "Sir," they said, "we would like to see Jesus." ²²Philip went to tell Andrew; Andrew and Philip in turn told Jesus.

²³Jesus replied, "The hour has come for the Son of Man to be glorified. ²⁴I tell you the truth, unless a kernel of wheat falls to the ground and dies, it remains only a single seed. But if it dies, it produces many seeds. ²⁵The man who loves his life will lose it, while the man who hates his life in this world will keep it for eternal life. ²⁶Whoever serves me must follow me; and where I am, my servant also will be. My Father will honor the one who serves me."

COMMENTARY

20 In contrast to the Pharisees, who were increasingly upset with the growing popularity of Jesus, a group of Gentiles wanted to learn more about this man who had raised Lazarus from the dead. They are designated as *Hellēnes* ("Greeks"), not *Hellēnistai* ("Hellenists," or Greek-speaking Jews; cf. Ac 6:1). The term is not to be limited to those who were Greek ethnically but refers to everyone of non-Jewish birth. The phrase "Jews and Greeks" occurs eight times in the NT (e.g., Ac 19:10; 1Co 1:24). The Greeks who approached Jesus were God-fearing Gentiles like Cornelius in Acts 10 and the centurion in Luke 7:1–10.

In Jesus' day there were a number of non-Jewish people who were attracted to the lofty morality and monotheism of Judaism. They often attended the religious festivals of the Jews but were not allowed any closer to the temple than the court of the Gentiles. While attracted to Judaism, these God-fearers stopped short of becoming proselytes because that would have required them to be circumcised. We are not told why these Greeks wanted to see Jesus, but we may reasonably conclude that they were drawn to him because while he worshiped within the Jewish religion, he questioned the authority of its religious leaders and appeared to be quite open to the Gentile world.

21 The Greeks wanted to "see Jesus," i.e., to spend some time talking with him. We are not sure why they approached Philip rather than one of the other disciples, but it could have been because Philip is a Greek name. In addition, Philip came from Bethsaida, which lay well within the reach of the Greek cities of the Decapolis. It could be that these Greeks were from that area and may have had some previous contact with Philip. The intensity of their desire to talk with Jesus is reflected in the use of the imperfect *ērōtōn* ("they kept asking," GK *2263*).

22 Philip is faced with the problem of knowing whether or not Jesus would at that time welcome an interview with some Gentiles. Beyond that, if such a meeting were to take place in the temple area, would that not strengthen the opposition of the religious leaders to Jesus? So Philip turns to his friend Andrew, and together they take the request to Jesus.

23 Jesus seems to ignore the specific request of the Greeks and "replies" by laying down the principle that life always comes through death. It will be through his own death and resurrection that he will be glorified. Then when he is "lifted up," he will draw people to himself (v.32). Indirectly, then, he does answer the request of the Greeks who wanted to see him. The answer to their deeper concern in talking with him is that his "hour has [now] come," and based on the events about to unfold, salvation will be extended to all who believe, regardless of race or nationality. Until this point, his "hour" (the climactic point in his redemptive ministry) has always been in the future (2:4; 4:21, 23; 7:30; 8:20). But now at last his hour *has come* (the perfect tense, *elēlythen*, GK *2262*, stresses that it has come to stay).

It is the hour "for the Son of Man to be glorified." The title "Son of Man" is Jesus' self-designation. It derives from Daniel 7:13–14, where in a vision the prophet sees "one like a son of man" to whom the Ancient of Days gives universal power and sovereignty. The title is distinctly messianic. In the Synoptic Gospels it is normally found in passages that speak either of Jesus' suffering or of his coming glory. Here in John the two concepts are joined. His hour of suffering (the crucifixion) is, at the same time, the ultimate manifestation of his glory.

24–25 Jesus lays down the fundamental principle that life comes through death. In the agricultural world it is obvious that unless a kernel of wheat falls to the ground and dies, it remains what it is—a single kernel. But if it dies, it produces "many seeds," i.e., many other kernels of wheat. It is only through the death of one that the life of many can be achieved. This principle is then applied in v.25. If someone loves his life, he will lose it, but if in this world he hates his life, he will keep it forever (cf. Mt 16:24–25; Mk 8:34–35; Lk 9:23–24 for parallel statements).

The paradoxical truth of life through death operates in the world of personal conduct as well. The person who "loves his life" is guilty of placing his own welfare above that of the kingdom of God. Such a person has failed to seek as the highest priority the kingdom and the righteousness that it requires (Mt 6:33). That person will lose the very life he is trying to save. The verb (*apollymi*, GK *660*) often means "to destroy" (Jn 10:10; 1Co 1:19) and carries this nuance here, where it is set over against "keep" or "preserve." Thus, Jesus is saying that self-love leads to self-destruction. Noting that the verb is in the present tense, Morris, 593, suggests the translation, "The man who loves his life is destroying it right now." Strange as it may seem to the secular mind, to focus on immediate personal benefit ensures the loss of the very thing being pursued.

On the other hand, the person who "hates his life" (a rather vivid Semitic way of expressing preference; cf. Lk 14:26) will preserve it "so as to live eternally" (Knox). Life comes through death not only in horticulture but also in human experience. It is those who lose themselves in the cause of Christ and his kingdom that find both here in this life and in eternity the fulfillment they so deeply desire. It is by giving that one receives. Those who live solely for themselves are caught in a vicious cycle of self-destruction. While the immediate application of this principle is to the imminent death of Jesus the Son of Man, it applies equally to all those who bear his name.

26 The perfect relationship that existed between Father and Son, reflected in the Son doing only that which he saw the Father doing (5:19), is now extended to the believer. Whoever serves the Son must follow him. To follow Jesus means to live the same kind of self-giving life that he lived, i.e., to lose oneself in God's great redemptive cause. The charge is not so much to imitate Jesus as it is to live one's life controlled by the same sense of eternal values that found their perfect expression in him.

When Jesus said, "Where I am, my servant also will be," he was not speaking geographically. The road that Jesus trod led to death on a cross. The true servant of Jesus is also on a road marked by death to self. To serve Jesus one must be where he is. And as Jesus and the believer travel the same road of self-denial, they will together be honored by the Father. The essential point is that Jesus and his followers are one in their obedience to the Father and have together embarked on the road of obedience to his will.

NOTES

25 Taking ἀπόλλυμι (*apollymi*, GK 660) in the sense of "destroy" the NET translates, "The one who loves his life destroys it." The NET's translator's note points out that this understanding of ἀπόλλυμι, *apollymi*, contrasts with φυλάξει (*phylaxei*, "keeps" or "guards," GK 5875) in the second half of the verse. The word ἀπόλλυμι, *apollymi*, occurs ten times in the fourth gospel: the NASB translates it six times as "perish," three times as "lose," and once as "destroy."

4. Jesus Predicts His Death (12:27–36)

27"Now my heart is troubled, and what shall I say? 'Father, save me from this hour'? No, it was for this very reason I came to this hour. 28Father, glorify your name!"

Then a voice came from heaven, "I have glorified it, and will glorify it again." 29The crowd that was there and heard it said it had thundered; others said an angel had spoken to him.

30Jesus said, "This voice was for your benefit, not mine. 31Now is the time for judgment on this world; now the prince of this world will be driven out. 32But I, when I am lifted up from the earth, will draw all men to myself." 33He said this to show the kind of death he was going to die.

34The crowd spoke up, "We have heard from the Law that the Christ will remain forever, so how can you say, 'The Son of Man must be lifted up'? Who is this 'Son of Man'?"

35Then Jesus told them, "You are going to have the light just a little while longer. Walk while you have the light, before darkness overtakes you. The man who walks in the dark does not know where he is going. 36Put your trust in the light while you have it, so that you may become sons of light." When he had finished speaking, Jesus left and hid himself from them.

COMMENTARY

27–28a At this point Jesus seems to be speaking primarily to himself. First he acknowledges that his "heart is troubled." The Greek verb (*tarassō*, GK 5429) used figuratively means "to cause acute emotional distress or turbulence" (L&N, 25.244). It is used in 11:33 of Jesus' reaction to Mary's weeping at the loss of her brother and in 13:21 of his mood in the upper room when he acknowledged that one of his own disciples would betray him.

In this state of emotional unrest Jesus asks himself what should be his response to the events about to unfold. One's interpretation of the answer depends on whether the second sentence of v.27 is taken as a genuine prayer for deliverance (as in the

Gethsemane scene, Mt 26:39 par.) or as a hypothetical possibility that is then dismissed. In the first case a full stop follows "Father, save me from this hour." The alternative interpretation places a question mark at the same point: "Shall I say, 'Father save me from this hour'?" This second interpretation appears to be overly cerebral in the context of acute emotional distress. Jesus would be weighing in a somewhat logical fashion the two options, only to choose the one that seemed to make the most sense in view of the purpose for which he had come to that crucial moment. It is better to take his utterance as a genuine prayer that he need not go through the terrible experience of separation from the Father. Since the fourth gospel does not recount the agony of Jesus in Gethsemane, this prayer reflects his natural abhorrence to all that death on the cross involved.

In the same way that Jesus in Gethsemane responded to his own prayer for deliverance ("Yet not as I will, but as you will," Mt 26:39), he now answers himself with a firm "No, it was for this very reason I came to this hour." The reason, of course, was to bring salvation to the human race. Unable to save themselves, people are totally dependent on the work of the only One to have emerged victorious over sin and Satan. "Father, glorify your name. Father, carry out your redemptive plan and bring eternal praise to your holy name. May your character as Savior be recognized and honored by all."

28b Now for the third time in the life of Jesus a voice from heaven is heard (cf. the temptation scene, Mt 3:17; the transfiguration, Mk 9:7). It is the very voice of God declaring that he has already glorified his name and will glorify it again. For those who viewed Jesus' life and ministry (especially his powerful signs) through the eyes of faith, the glory of God had already been manifested. And once again, in the death and exaltation of the Son the Father will bring glory to his name.

29 Many in the crowd who had heard the voice said that it had thundered. They heard the sound but did not understand the message. Others were of the opinion that an angel had spoken to Jesus. In Scripture thunder is often connected with the voice of God (Job 26:14; Rev 14:2).

30 Jesus tells the crowd that the voice from heaven was not for his benefit but for theirs. It has been asked how that could be, since the crowd did not understand what was said. But even though they could not understand the message, it would be clear to those with any degree of spiritual sensitivity that the heavenly voice must have heralded something of great and eternal significance. It would suggest to them that in the sequence of events now underway, God was bringing his redemptive plan to its climax. Jesus himself needed no such indicator.

31 The "prince of this world" is a Johannine term for Satan (cf. 14:30; 16:11). His time had come, and in the cross and resurrection he would meet his ultimate defeat (cf. Rev 12). From this point on he is a defeated foe (Col 2:13–15). Satan may have been the prince of the world, but his kingdom is about to come tumbling down.

32 In striking contrast to the defeat of Satan, Jesus is to be "lifted up"—a double reference to both his crucifixion and his exaltation. The cross is not a symbol of defeat but a symbol of victory. The world's appraisal of critical issues is distorted by its faulty understanding of reality. Jesus' dying on a cross appeared to the secular mind as the ultimate defeat, but to the eye of faith it was a glorious victory. Dark as it may have appeared, it was but the first step that would lead to a glorious resurrection and a triumphant ascension.

When Jesus is lifted up, he "will draw all men to [himself]." His love displayed on the cross will draw people to himself like a great spiritual magnet. People come to Jesus as they are drawn by the winsome power of the Spirit; by nature they choose to go their own way (Ro 3:11). By "all men," John means "all" not in the absolute sense of the term but "all without distinction"—people from every race and nation. No longer will God work primarily within the Jewish nation, but following the resurrection the universal message of salvation will reach out to all who believe, regardless of ethnic background. And this is the real answer to the inquiry of the Greeks who came to see Jesus (vv.20–21). God chose to initiate his work within the Jewish race, but with the cross and resurrection the good news of salvation reaches out to all.

33 Then, so there will be no misunderstanding, Jesus explains his being lifted up as "the kind of death he was going to die." The origin of crucifixion has been traced to the Phoenicians, from whom it passed to many other nations. Not only was it excruciatingly painful; it was designed also to publicly humiliate the victim in the most degrading way possible.

34 When Jesus spoke of being "lifted up," the crowd understood his words as a reference to death by crucifixion. But the very idea of a Messiah dying on the cross was for them unthinkable. They point out that the Law says that "the Christ will remain forever." Apparently by "the Law" they were referring to the entire Hebrew Bible insofar as it is difficult to find any passage in the Pentateuch supporting that idea. However, Psalm 110 says of the messianic King-Priest, "You are a priest forever, in the order of Melchizedek" (v.4; cf. Ps 89:36–37; Isa 9:7). Since the Messiah will continue forever, they ask Jesus what he means. "Who is this Son of Man? What kind of person is he? Is he someone other than the Messiah?"

35–36 Jesus' answer is that the light will be with them only a little while longer. Soon the darkness will come and overtake them, but they are to walk while they still have the light. The light-darkness contrast is one of the more prominent figures of speech in the fourth gospel (cf. 1:4–9; 3:19–20; 8:12). "Put your trust in the light," says Jesus, "so that you may become sons of light."

The period of light is, of course, the time of Jesus' presence with them, which will soon be over. With his ascension to heaven, the ultimate source of light will be gone. Thus Jesus urges the crowd to take advantage of the short time remaining before he will go to the cross and no longer be with them to explain his words and actions.

This encounter in John 12 marks the end of Jesus' public ministry. His days of travel and of speaking to large crowds throughout the land are over. His time has come; withdrawing from a preaching ministry, he focuses on the critical events that lie ahead. When the text says that "he hid himself from them," we are not to picture Jesus going into hiding but instead as staying out of the center of attention and all the activity connected with the Passover.

NOTES

28 Instead of δόξασόν σου τὸ ὄνομα (*doxason sou to onoma*, "glorify your name"), some witnesses (L X *f* 1.13 33 1241 *pc* vg mss sy hmg bo) have δόξασόν σου τὸν υἱόν (*doxason sou ton huion*, "glorify your Son"). The copyists were undoubtedly influenced by the opening words of Jesus' high priestly prayer in ch. 17.

32 The reading πάντα (*panta*, "everyone, all things, all") has strong external support (𝔓66 ℵ* et al.), but because it is ambiguous the UBS committee favored the masculine plural reading πάντας, *pantas* (cf. Metzger, 202). Hence both the NIV and the NASB translate, "will draw all men to myself."

35 The expression "son of light" would mean to a Semitic audience that the person in question is characterized by light. In Acts 4:36 the author tells us that the name "Barnabas" means "Son of Encouragement" (the distinguishing feature about Barnabas being his ability and eagerness to encourage).

36 The verb tenses here are instructive: "put your trust" (πιστεύετε, *pisteuete*, GK *4409*; present tense, suggesting a continuous belief) in the light so that "you may become" (γένησθε, *genēsthe*, GK *1181*; aorist tense, suggesting a specific point in time) sons of light.

5. The People Respond in Unbelief (12:37–43)

OVERVIEW

Having reached the close of Jesus' public ministry, he devotes himself from this point on to his own disciples to prepare them for his departure and their role in spreading the good news. The final verses of ch. 12 deal with the widespread failure of the Jews to believe in him. The verses correspond to a similar section in the prologue, in which Jesus spoke of the failure on the part of his own people to receive him (1:10–13). In both cases he is rejected, though in each case there are some who believe (1:12–13; 12:42).

> ³⁷Even after Jesus had done all these miraculous signs in their presence, they still would not believe in him. ³⁸This was to fulfill the word of Isaiah the prophet:
>
> "Lord, who has believed our message
>   and to whom has the arm of the Lord been revealed?"
>
> ³⁹For this reason they could not believe, because, as Isaiah says elsewhere:
>
> ⁴⁰"He has blinded their eyes
>   and deadened their hearts,
> so they can neither see with their eyes,
>   nor understand with their hearts,
>   nor turn—and I would heal them."
>
> ⁴¹Isaiah said this because he saw Jesus' glory and spoke about him.
> ⁴²Yet at the same time many even among the leaders believed in him. But because of the Pharisees they would not confess their faith for fear they would be put out of the synagogue; ⁴³for they loved praise from men more than praise from God.

COMMENTARY

37 Verse 37 summarizes the first half of this final section (vv.37–43). Though Jesus had done many miracles in their presence, the Jews "would not believe in him." Unbelief is rarely swayed by the evidence; it takes faith to handle the evidence in a fair manner. Not even the signs that Jesus performed in the presence of Jewish leaders could move them to accept his claims that he was more than a mere man.

Unbelief doggedly persists in its passion to disregard the facts and the obvious implications of supernatural intervention. The imperfect tense (*episteuon*, GK 4409) describes a continuing unwillingness to believe.

38 John writes that the unbelief of the Jews "was to fulfill the word of Isaiah the prophet." While acknowledging that the conjunction *hina* may denote result rather than purpose (see 9:2, where the disciples ask whether the blind man or his parents sinned, "with the result that" [*hina*] he was born blind), it would appear from v. 39 that in this setting it has telic force—the purpose of their unbelief was to fulfill Isaiah's prophecy. It should be kept in mind, however, that purpose and consequence often cannot be clearly differentiated. Jewish unbelief was more than the incidental fulfillment of prophecy; the prophecy in some sense necessitated the unbelief. The prophecy in question is Isaiah 53:1 (also quoted in Ro 10:16). The obvious answer to the prophet's question, "Lord, who has believed our message?" is "very few." Even the miraculous signs Jesus performed failed to awaken faith in the hearts of many of the Jewish people.

39–40 "For this reason" looks forward to a second quotation from Isaiah. The reason why the Jews "could not believe" (Gk. *ouk ēdynanto pisteuein*, "were unable to believe") was that God had "blinded their eyes and deadened their hearts" (see Isa 6:10). Beasley-Murray, 216, points out that while this sounds like "naked predestinarianism," such was not intended, nor was the quotation understood in that way. Language like this had a long history in biblical thought. For example, while in Exodus 4:21 the Lord says that he would harden the heart of Pharaoh, we learn from Exodus 8:15, 32 that Pharaoh hardened his own heart. God's decision to blind the eyes of unbelieving Israel is inseparably entwined with their own decision not to believe. As Barrett, 431, puts it, "Divine predestination works through human moral choices, for which men are morally responsible." God does not harden the hearts of people against their will, but his action is a necessary part of the consequences that flow from their decisions.

41 John records that Isaiah said what he did "because he saw Jesus' glory." The glory of God that filled the temple in Isaiah 6:1–4 is taken by John as the glory of the preincarnate Logos. In recounting his vision, the prophet was speaking about the Christ who would come.

42 While unbelief was the normal response of Jews to Jesus' claims, there were at the same time many who believed. Some of them came from the ranks of leadership in Judaism. John may have been thinking of people such as Nicodemus (3:1–21) or Joseph of Arimathea (Lk 23:50–54). Sadly, they would not confess their faith for fear of being put out of the synagogue. They were intimidated by the Pharisees into remaining quiet about their commitment. Lest the contemporary believer look with disdain on such hesitancy, it would be wise to search one's own heart to discover how often lips remain sealed for fear of displeasing someone in the secular world.

43 The reason for not confessing their faith is that "they loved praise from men more than praise from God." How devious is the human heart that it cares more for what people say than it does for God's approval. In the arena of personal witness, the average "believer" yields more quickly to the approval of others than to the "well done" of the Master (Mt 25:21). Can such timidity contribute anything to the work of God in this world?

NOTES

38 The expression ὁ βραχίων κυρίου (*ho brachiōn kyriou*, "the arm of the Lord") is a Hebrew idiom for "God's mighty power/strength." In the LXX of Isaiah 51:9 we hear the prophet telling Jerusalem to wake up and ἔνδυσαι τὴν ἰσχὺν τοῦ βραχίονός σου (*endysai ten ischyn tou brachionos sou*, lit., "put on the strength of your arm." (The NIV, following the MT, has, "Clothe yourself with strength, O arm of the Lord").

41 The reading ὅτε (*hote*, "when"), followed by the KJV, is inferior to ὅτι (*hoti*, "because"), found in all current versions. The reading ὅτι, *hoti*, is found in 𝔓⁶⁶, ⁷⁵ ℵ A B L Θ Ψ *f*¹ 33 et al. Although it was the glory of Yahweh that Isaiah saw, John quotes the prophet as speaking of the glory that would be revealed in Christ. Father and Son are one in essence (cf. 10:30; 17:22).

42 The Greek verb ὁμολογέω (*homologeō*, "confess," GK *3933*) occurs twenty-six times in the NT, and the breadth of its semantic range is seen in that in addition to the normal "confess," the NASB supplies a number of various alternatives depending on context: "declare" (Mt 7:23), "promise" (Mt 14:7), "assure" (Ac 7:17), "acknowledge" (Ac 23:8; 2Jn 1:7), "admit" (Ac 24:14), "profess" (Tit 1:16), and "give thanks" (Heb 13:15). In the present verse, in which ὡμολόγουν, *hōmologoun*, has no direct object, the NIV has supplied "their faith" and the NASB "Him."

6. Jesus' "Summary Statement" (12:44–50)

⁴⁴Then Jesus cried out, "When a man believes in me, he does not believe in me only, but in the one who sent me. ⁴⁵When he looks at me, he sees the one who sent me. ⁴⁶I have come into the world as a light, so that no one who believes in me should stay in darkness.

⁴⁷"As for the person who hears my words but does not keep them, I do not judge him. For I did not come to judge the world, but to save it. ⁴⁸There is a judge for the one who rejects me and does not accept my words; that very word which I spoke will condemn him at the last day. ⁴⁹For I did not speak of my own accord, but the Father who sent me commanded me what to say and how to say it. ⁵⁰I know that his command leads to eternal life. So whatever I say is just what the Father has told me to say."

COMMENTARY

44–46 Verses 44–50 are usually described as a summary of the main themes in Jesus' ministry to the world rather than as one last appeal on the part of Jesus before he withdraws from public ministry. The second option is favored by the opening line,

"Then Jesus cried out." It appears that Jesus is giving the unbelieving Jews one more chance. It is the content of the paragraph, however, that supports the view that this is the evangelist's concise overview of the major themes from Jesus' public ministry:

- those who believe in Jesus believe in the one who sent him, i.e., to believe in the Son is to believe in the Father;
- to see Jesus is to see God (the two are inseparable); later theological reflection declared that the Father and Son are two persons but one in essence;
- Jesus came into the world as a light so that those who believed would no longer have to walk in darkness.

47–48 Jesus' purpose in coming into this world was to save it, not to judge it. Yet there will be judgment. The very words that Jesus has spoken will on the last day condemn those who have not responded in faith to his message.

49–50 What Jesus said did not originate with him but with the Father. He was the one who told the Son what to say. The words of God lead to eternal life, and we may know for certain that what Jesus says is exactly what God has told him to say.

V. THE UPPER ROOM DISCOURSE (13:1–17:26)

OVERVIEW

John 13–17 is commonly called "the Upper Room Discourse." Whether Jesus left the upper room before or after speaking the words recorded in chs. 15–17 is not clear. In 14:31 he says, "Come now; let us leave." Yet not until three chapters later in the narrative (18:1) does John record that when Jesus finished praying, he left with his disciples and crossed the Kidron Valley. In either case, chs. 13–17 comprise those special truths Jesus wanted his disciples to understand and carry with them in view of his imminent death and departure. They are, in a sense, Jesus' "last will and testament." The truths are rich in spiritual insight and were especially important for the followers of Jesus at that critical juncture. He would soon be gone, and his redemptive mission and message would be left in their care.

A. The Setting (13:1–38)

OVERVIEW

Chapter 13 marks the beginning of the final period in Jesus' life here on earth. The previous chapter chronicled the events that took place during the six days that preceded Passover (12:1). It was a time of constant exposure to crowds of people. Six times in ch. 12 John calls attention to "the crowd." (In v.9 it is described as "large" and in v.12 as "great.") When Jesus entered Jerusalem and the crowds welcomed him with shouts of "Hosanna! Blessed is he who comes in the name of the Lord!" (v.13), the Pharisees declared, "Look how the whole world has gone after him!" (v.19).

It had been a busy week. Just before the triumphal entry, Jesus had dined with his friends in Bethany and Mary had anointed his feet with fragrant and expensive perfume. Greeks attending the festival had come to Philip requesting an opportunity to speak with Jesus. He spoke of the necessity of his death (12:24), the drawing power of his resurrection (v.32), and the judgment to come on those who refuse his teaching (v.48). He marveled that, after all he had done in their presence, "they still would not believe in him" (v.37). Now as the end approaches, Jesus turns from the crowds to give his full attention to a small group of loyal followers.

1. Jesus Washes His Disciples' Feet (13:1–17)

[1]It was just before the Passover Feast. Jesus knew that the time had come for him to leave this world and go to the Father. Having loved his own who were in the world, he now showed them the full extent of his love.

[2]The evening meal was being served, and the devil had already prompted Judas Iscariot, son of Simon, to betray Jesus. [3]Jesus knew that the Father had put all things under his power, and that he had come from God and was returning to God; [4]so he got up from the meal, took off his outer clothing, and wrapped a towel around his waist. [5]After that, he poured water into a basin and began to wash his disciples' feet, drying them with the towel that was wrapped around him.

[6]He came to Simon Peter, who said to him, "Lord, are you going to wash my feet?"

[7]Jesus replied, "You do not realize now what I am doing, but later you will understand."

[8]"No," said Peter, "you shall never wash my feet."

Jesus answered, "Unless I wash you, you have no part with me."

[9]"Then, Lord," Simon Peter replied, "not just my feet but my hands and my head as well!"

[10]Jesus answered, "A person who has had a bath needs only to wash his feet; his whole body is clean. And you are clean, though not every one of you." [11]For he knew who was going to betray him, and that was why he said not every one was clean.

[12]When he had finished washing their feet, he put on his clothes and returned to his place. "Do you understand what I have done for you?" he asked them. [13]"You call me 'Teacher' and 'Lord,' and rightly so, for that is what I am. [14]Now that I, your Lord and Teacher, have washed your feet, you also should wash one another's feet. [15]I have set you an example that you should do as I have done for you. [16]I tell you the truth, no servant is greater than his master, nor is a messenger greater than the one who sent him. [17]Now that you know these things, you will be blessed if you do them."

COMMENTARY

1 John places the events of the evening just before the Passover Feast. The question of whether the Last Supper was a Passover Feast (Mk 14:12 par.) or a meal on the previous day that had Passover characteristics is discussed at great length in more critical commentaries. Carson, 457, after working through the issue, concludes, "Jesus and his disciples did indeed eat a Passover meal on Thursday, the beginning of 15 Nisan." Passover was a sacred festival commemorating the deliverance of the Israelites from Egyptian bondage (Ex 12). It took its name from the "passing over" of the angel of death and the sparing of all the firstborn among the Israelites. At the time of the Passover, devout Jews came to Jerusalem from all over the inhabited world to join in that most sacred and holy festival.

Jerusalem was an exciting place during Passover. Religious emotions ran high. Friends from different areas would meet in the crowded streets and excitedly exchange stories of home and family. But for Jesus, his time had come, and only this one last evening remained for him to spend with his disciples. At an earlier point in his ministry, the Pharisees had tried to seize Jesus but were unable to do so because "his time had not yet come" (7:30; cf. 8:20). But now "the hour has come for the Son of Man to be glorified" (12:23; cf. 17:1). This was the hour toward which, in the eternal plan of God, all history had moved with inexorable pace. It was the hour in which the redemptive love of God would reveal itself as voluntary suffering for the unworthy. A Savior crucified by those he came to save is paradoxical only to those who have not grasped the fact that God wins his victories through suffering, not by an outward demonstration of power or might. In the great throne room scene of Revelation 4–5, the Lion of the tribe of Judah turns out to be a Lamb, who is worthy to open the seals of the scroll because he has been slain and with his blood has purchased human beings for God (Rev 5:5–6, 9).

Specifically, it was the time for Jesus to "leave this world and go to the Father." For the believer, death is not the end but the beginning. It is a departure from the realm of evil (cf. Gal 1:4) and a going home to the Father. Since Jesus is the "firstborn from among the dead" (Col 1:18), we may logically expect that as his death was a journey to the Father so also will be ours. All ideas of soul-sleep are for-

eign to NT teaching. Neither is the "soul" entrapped along the way in some place of physical punishment. Paul said it clearly: "Absent from the body . . . present with the Lord" (2Co 5:8 KJV). What a remarkable way to complete what we call life! Death has been robbed of its terror and made the passage to our eternal home. Waiting for us is the One whose love bridged the gulf created by our sin. We are the prodigals returning home, and he is the Father who rushes out to meet us. This world has been a place of hostility and heartache. Death is the entrance into joy eternal and inexpressible.

The text says that Jesus "knew" that his time had come. This was more than mere premonition; it was a clear understanding of what must necessarily take place in the dark days that lay ahead. As the Lamb of God whose blood would be shed for the sins of the world, he knew not only what would happen but also that the critical time had arrived. Jesus was not trapped into a sequence of events that unexpectedly led to the cross. With full knowledge of what the future held, he moved steadily through his years of public ministry to a destiny ordained by the Father and known by the Son. This foreknowledge makes his sacrifice all the more remarkable.

Though his disciples had often failed to grasp the full meaning of his words and had demonstrated by their behavior an inadequate commitment to his ethical demands, he "loved his own" and would now show them "the full extent of his love." In the prologue to his gospel John notes that the Word came to "his own creation," (ta idia is neuter plural), but "his own people" (hoi idioi is masculine plural) did not receive him (1:11–12). Those referred to in ch. 13 as "his own" comprise a much smaller group. To belong to Jesus—to be "his own"—requires far more than to find oneself somewhat unintentionally within an ethnic or religious organization. It requires separation from the prevailing world system and allegiance to a kingdom that belongs to another world. As Paul puts it, the Christian has his citizenship "in heaven" (Php 3:20). "My kingdom," said Jesus, "is not of this world" (Jn 18:36). Elsewhere believers are called "a people that are his very own" (Tit 2:14, drawing on Moses' reference to the Israelites as God's "treasured possession," Ex 19:5). To be called God's own is a reward given to those few who by faith have committed themselves to the reality of a universal kingdom yet undisclosed. As Jesus, misunderstood and rejected, moved among people, so also do his current followers find themselves at odds with much of contemporary wisdom and culture.

Throughout his entire ministry Jesus had loved his own. He bore with their lack of spiritual understanding and put up with their all-too-human reactions. When they failed to understand his teachings, he found other ways to communicate what he wanted them to learn. He loved his disciples. And now he was about to show them "the full extent of his love." The expression may mean either that he loved them utterly and completely or that he loved them to the end, i.e., to his death. It is better in this case not to separate the two ideas, for because the love of Jesus was of the highest degree, it would consequently carry through to the very end. A bit later he will remind his disciples that "no one has greater love than this, to lay down one's life for one's friends" (15:13 NRSV). One of the most remarkable things about Jesus from a human point of view is that there is no disparity between his words and his life. What he taught he lived.

2 In NT times, the evening meal was an important event. It brought together family (and often friends too) in a relaxed and pleasant setting. The gospels record a number of occasions when Jesus was a guest at a meal. He performed his first miracle while attending a wedding feast at Cana (2:1–11). At Matthew's house he ate with "tax collectors and 'sinners'" (Mt 9:10). In Jericho he was the guest of Zaccheus (Lk 19:5–10). The beautiful recognition scene in Emmaus took place as Jesus sat at table with two disciples and broke bread (Lk 24:30–32). How fitting that on the eve of his departure he should share a final meal with his disciples.

John begins his narrative of those final hours with the jarring reminder that the devil had already "prompted Judas . . . to betray Jesus." Later, in v.27, we read that after Judas took the bread, "Satan entered into him." While it may be that this represents a progression from demonic influence to demonic possession, another reading of the Greek text here suggests the translation, "The devil had already made up his mind that Judas should betray him." The synoptic accounts all place Judas's bargain with the chief priests before the Last Supper (Mk 14:10–11 par.). Judas had entered into a Faustian bargain with Satan, who from that time on directed his activity. Calvin, 2:56, comments that "all the wickedness which men do is incited by Satan; but the more revolting and execrable the crime, the more should we see in it the rage of the devil." More will be said of Judas when John records Jesus' announcement of betrayal and the departure of Satan's pawn (see comments at vv.21, 27–28).

3 Verse 1 taught that Jesus knew his time had come to leave the world and go to the Father. Verse 3 expands the idea by noting that he also knew he had come from God and was returning to God. The question as to when Jesus first realized his heavenly origin is impossible to answer. We know that at the age of twelve, when he lingered in the temple to question the religious teachers, he was aware that he was in his "Father's house" (Lk 2:49). As Jesus entered his public ministry, the devil attempted to sow the seeds of doubt by challenging, "If you are the Son of God . . ." (Lk 4:3, 9). At that time Jesus knew full well that he had come from God.

We can only conjecture what that knowledge of divine origin entailed. Undoubtedly it was far more than an undefined awareness of preincarnate existence, yet how specific it was is impossible to know. In his incarnate state, Jesus had experienced a veiling of certain divine attributes (cf. Mk 13:32). The beauty of his earthly life stems from the fact that even though he was truly God, he lived among us as the perfect man. Knowing that he had "come from God" must, as the end approached, have increasingly heightened his longing to "return to God," even though that return involved the shame and cruelty of a public execution. Since no two human beings have ever known the joys of a perfect father-son relationship, none of us can grasp fully the infinite beauty of that intimate association. Jesus had come from God; yet in one sense he had never left him. Now he returns to God and at the same time never really leaves us. Such is the mystery of the divine presence, the continuing fulfillment of his name "Immanuel—which means 'God with us'" (Mt 1:23).

4–5 During the meal Jesus rose from the table and poured water into a basin. He then began to wash his disciples' feet and dried them with a towel. Ancient roads were dusty, and the sandals people wore made foot washing a common courtesy. The task was normally performed by a servant (cf. 1Sa 25:41; Lk 7:44; 1Ti 5:10), but none were present in the upper room. Any one of the disciples would undoubtedly have been willing to wash Jesus' feet, but to offer the same service to another disciple would have been an admission of inferiority. Luke reports that there was a dispute among them as to which was considered the greatest (Lk 22:24–27). This was hardly the time to play the role of a servant!

Meals were eaten at a low table, with guests in a semi-reclining position. It appears that Jesus removed not simply his outer garment (*ta himatia*, "the garments," GK *2668*, is plural, as in 19:23–24; cf. the singular in 19:2, 5), but stripped down to a loincloth—the garb of a servant. The Greek verb

translated "took off" (*tithēmi*, GK *5502*, v.4) is used in ch. 10, where Jesus explains that he is the good shepherd who "lays down his life for the sheep" (10:11, 15, 17). This could serve to strengthen the view that the foot-washing episode is to be understood as an enacted parable of Jesus' imminent death. It is often noted that John does not include the Last Supper in his narrative of Jesus' final days and that the Synoptics omit the foot washing. The reason could well be that both incidents serve the same purpose. Both are graphic illustrations of Jesus' role as the Suffering Servant who "did not come to be served, but to serve" (Mk 10:45; cf. Php 2:6–8). To take the foot washing as no more than an example of humble service overlooks the deeper significance that stems from the redemptive context of the passion narrative.

The towel Jesus used would be long enough to go around his waist, with enough left free to dry the disciples' feet. Foot washing was normally performed by pouring water over the feet and catching the runoff in a basin. What a sense of mingled shame and embarrassment must have welled up within the hearts of the disciples as Jesus knelt before each one and carried out the humble task of a servant. They were too proud to serve one another, but they were hardly ready to be served in this way by their Master. Temple, 2:210, notes that humility does not begin with providing service but with the readiness to receive it. The disciples' pride kept them from entering into a genuine understanding of and appreciation for the remarkable event they were privileged to witness.

6 The sequence of events suggests that Peter was not the first disciple whose feet were washed by Jesus, and v.12 appears to imply that he was not the last. The conjunction *oun* ("therefore," omitted from the NIV but rendered "then" by the KJV and "so" by the NASB) creates a sense of expectancy. What will happen when Jesus comes to Peter? When that moment arrived, Peter was unable to contain himself. In astonishment he asked, "Lord, are you going to wash my feet?" The unusual position of the two pronouns (*sy mou*) adds an emphasis not easily translated. A reasonable paraphrase might be, "Lord, could it possibly be that *you* intend to wash *my* feet?" (emphasis added). It was not so much a question as a reaction. In similar fashion, John the Baptist, when approached by Jesus, had exclaimed, "I need to be baptized by you, and do you come to me?" (Mt 3:14).

At times Peter is portrayed rather negatively as an impetuous disciple insensitive to what would be appropriate in a given situation. But on this occasion it was Peter's wholehearted commitment to his Master, along with his sense of the incongruity between lordship and humble service, that led him to react as he did. The other disciples undoubtedly felt the same way but were not given to speaking out. Peter's response is a clear indication that enthusiasm and devotion can coexist with less than an adequate understanding of how God works.

7 Jesus answered Peter's question and placed the same emphasis on the pronouns, saying in effect, "What *I* am doing now *you* do not yet know. Later, however, you will understand; after the resurrection you will discern the deeper meaning of the foot washing [cf. 2:22; 12:16]." The Holy Spirit will come and will "teach [them] all things and will remind [them] of everything [Jesus] . . . said to [them]" (14:26; cf. 16:13).

The foot washing had a significance beyond the literal act itself. Later the disciples would see the more profound lesson here, namely, that humble service for others is the appropriate lifestyle for the believer. There is also a broad spiritual principle: "[God's] ways [are] higher than [our] ways and [his] thoughts than [our] thoughts" (Isa 55:9). There are many things God does that we simply cannot at the present understand. It is not our role to fathom the mind of God but to allow him the freedom to do what he wishes. Peter's intention was to prevent what he could not grasp, and in so doing he revealed more pride than humility. Our lack of understanding should call forth trust. Faith inevitably precedes knowledge. One of the great joys of eternity will be to enter into a more profound understanding of who God is and why he did what he did in history. Until then, we "see through a glass darkly" (KJV), while knowing that when we see him face-to-face, "we shall understand as completely as we are understood" (1Co 13:12 MLB).

8 Peter's response is remarkably strong. The Greek double negative *ou mē* has the force of an oath and is strengthened even further by *eis ton aiōna*, "unto the age, forever." You most certainly shall "never [ever] wash my feet"—once again the pronoun is emphatic. Peter's resistance stemmed from his failure to understand what the act of washing the disciples' feet symbolized. He could not understand that Jesus by his coming death would stoop as the Suffering Servant to minister to the critical need of the human race. By his death he would cleanse all those who would allow him to "wash their feet." By objecting, Peter typified all those who are confident of their ability to cleanse themselves. His refusal illustrates the human tendency to trust one's own sense of what is right rather than to accept with humility the gift of God. Calvin, 2:57, writes, "Until a man renounces his liberty of judging the works of God, however he may strive to honor God, pride will be always latent under the semblance of humility."

To Peter's emphatic refusal Jesus replied, "Unless I wash you, you have no part with me." The word translated "part" (*meros*, GK *3538*) is used in the Greek OT (LXX) to describe an inheritance (cf. Pr 17:2). Eschatologically it came to mean "an eternal reward." Here John uses the term to mean "fellowship with Christ." Jesus is saying that purification (from sin) is the unconditional requirement for sharing in the life of Christ, both now and in the age to come. As is so often the case, John would remind us that the words of Jesus may be understood on more than one level. Peter had been thinking of the foot-washing episode as no more than a customary practice in ancient Israel, while Jesus had moved ahead to a new level and was teaching about the spiritual significance of his imminent death.

9 Peter's reversal was as dramatic as his refusal: "Not just my feet but my hands and my head as well!" The idea of forfeiting communion with his Master was more than he could bear. "Wash not only my feet, but pour the water all over me. Nothing could be so terrible as to be separated from you!" Whatever else may be said about Peter, it cannot be said that he lacked fervor for his Lord.

10 Verse 10 teaches an important lesson about the difference between justification and sanctification. The person who has had a bath is the one who has been cleansed of sin by the redemptive sacrifice of Jesus. This is justification. The perfect participle *ho leloumenos* ("the person who has had a bath"—the bathed one, GK *3374*) suggests an action in the past, the effect of which continues in the present. There is no need to bathe again. Once a person has received the cleansing benefit of Jesus' sacrifice, there can be no reason why the process should be repeated. On the other hand, the cleansed person now needs only to "wash his feet." This is sanctification. Believers, through continued contact with the uncleanness of a world separated from God and prone to act out of their old nature, need to be continually cleansed from their daily contact with sin. This is why we pray, "Forgive us our debts," and, "deliver us from the evil one" (Mt 6:12, 13).

11 In the sense of divine forgiveness the disciples were clean, though "not every one of [them]." The reference was to Judas, who would soon betray Jesus. The other disciples knew only that there was a traitor in their midst; they did not know who he was. The specific reference by Jesus to one who was not clean was intended to pierce the conscience of Judas and provide him one more opportunity to forsake his treacherous intent and be forgiven. (The present participle *ton paradidonta*, "the betraying one," GK *4140*, suggests that the betrayal was already underway.) Though the disciples had traveled with Jesus throughout his public ministry, there was one who had effectively resisted the cleansing influence of such an intimate relationship. Is it not likewise highly probable that the contemporary church has among its adherents those who have never experienced the cleansing power of Jesus' death? As in the case of Judas, the day will surely come when the faithful will be separated from those whose "commitment" is based on personal advantage.

12–17 Having discussed in vv. 7–11 the theological significance of the foot washing (note that had Peter not objected to having his feet washed we may not have learned from Jesus the deeper parabolic meaning of what was taking place), we will now learn the practical meaning of the foot washing.

12 When Jesus had finished washing the disciples' feet, he put on the clothes he had laid aside and resumed his place at the table. To encourage his disciples to reflect on what had just happened he asked, "Do you understand what I have done for you?" Some writers note that *ginōskete* ("understand," GK *1182*) may be taken as an imperative ("Understand what I have done for you!"), but in either case the meaning is essentially the same. Jesus taught not only by word but also by actions. It is important to reflect on what he did as well as what he said. The verses that follow (vv. 13–17) contain Jesus' explanation of the practical implications of the foot washing.

13 The basic premise of Jesus' argument is that the disciples acknowledged him to be their Teacher and Lord. The order is significant. The disciples came to know Jesus first as Teacher (equivalent to Rabbi, the title normally used by Jewish students when addressing their master) and later as Lord. They had been with him in public ministry for almost two years before he asked, "Who do you say that I am?" and Peter answered, "You are the Christ, the Son of the living God" (Mt 16:15–16). While it is true that the day will come when every tongue will confess that "Jesus Christ is Lord" (Php 2:11), during his earthly ministry Jesus did not demand the obedience appropriate to lordship from those who had not come to know him first as Teacher. The disciples, however, were correct in acknowledging him as Teacher and Lord because, as Jesus said, "That is what I am." He was not simply one who had taught them; more important, he was their Lord.

14 This point is stressed by Jesus' reversal of the order in which he uses the titles here: "Now that I, your Lord and Teacher, have washed your feet, you also should wash one another's feet." The goal of a servant is to become like his master. The priorities and practices of the greater must of necessity become those of the lesser. Since the Lord of the disciples had washed their feet, it was incumbent on them to extend the same humble service to one another. Jesus had set an example so that they would do as he had done for them.

15 The question inevitably arises: Did Jesus intend that the church incorporate foot washing into its worship and ritual? At various times certain segments of the church have answered in the affirmative. The *pedilavium* was a foot-washing ceremony performed on Maundy Thursday in which an ecclesiastical superior washed, dried, and kissed the right foot of someone chosen for the occasion. Earlier commentaries refer to the practice as "ceremonial comedy" (Luther) or a "burlesque on the command of the Lord" (Reith). Verse 15 does not say that the disciples should do *what* Jesus had done but *as* he had done. It is the spirit of the act that is to be followed. The example Jesus set reflects an all-inclusive attitude toward others. It should not be limited simply to the act of washing another person's feet.

16 It was pride that kept the disciples from serving one another. Their concern was to establish superiority of rank (cf. Lk 22:24–27). And it is pride that prevents the church today from demonstrating as fully as it ought the power of Christian love. H. L. Mencken (*A Book of Burlesques* [New York: John Lane, 1916]) once defined an archbishop as a "Christian ecclesiastic of a rank superior to that attained by Christ." By taking the role of a servant and washing his disciples' feet, Jesus established once and for all the model for Christian love. It was crucial for his followers to learn that whoever wanted to be great must become a servant, and whoever wanted to be first must be slave of all (Mk 10:43–44). The only kind of leadership Jesus taught was servant-leadership.

17 Jesus concludes his words on foot washing by emphasizing the need for knowledge to be put into practice: "Now that you know these things, you will be blessed if you do them." The construction of the sentence in Greek implies that they do know these things (i.e., what he has just taught about foot washing), but whether or not they will put them into practice is less certain. Only if they actually do them will they be blessed (*makarios*, GK *3421*, the word used repeatedly in the Beatitudes of Mt 5:3–11). Throughout his ministry Jesus emphasized the necessity of doing God's will (Mt 7:21, 24; Mk 3:35). Knowledge of what is right has no value unless it changes conduct; in fact, to know what ought to be done and not to do it is sin (cf. Jas 4:17). The blessedness that comes from doing what is right is not so much a gift bestowed as it is that state of well-being resulting from the conduct itself. To be blessed is not to receive some extrinsic reward for good behavior but to enjoy the natural consequence of living in harmony with truth revealed.

NOTES

2 The NASB follows the reading δεῖπνου γινομένου (*deipnou ginomenou*) and translates "during supper" (GK *1270, 1181*; NIV, "The evening meal was being served"). This reading is found in ℵ* B L W Ψ 0124 1241 *pc* d r¹. The aorist (δεῖπνου γενομένου, *deipnou genomenou*) is found in 𝔓⁶⁶ ℵ² A D Θ *f* ¹·¹³ 33 and is followed by the KJV, which translates, "supper being ended." While the latter is more difficult in view of vv.4, 26, which detail items taking place during the dinner and therefore would tend to explain why a copyist would change to the present tense, the superiority of the MS evidence led the UBS committee to adopt the former reading. A minority of the committee preferred δεῖπνου γενομένου, *deipnou genomenou*, taken in the sense of an ingressive aorist, which would yield, "supper having been served" (cf. Metzger, 203).

Manuscripts vary with regard to both "Judas" and "Iscariot" and the location of the name in the sentence. In John 6:71 and 13:26 he is called "Judas the son of Simon Iscariot," while in 12:4 he is simply "Judas Iscariot." In the present verse (13:2) both the NIV and NASB refer to him as Judas Iscariot, [the] son of Simon. In the Synoptics he is always referred to as Judas Iscariot (Mt 10:4; 26:14; Lk 22:3). "Iscariot" has been traced to a number of sources. If the reference is to the town of Kerioth (in southern Israel?), he would be the "man from Kerioth." If the name is derived from the Aramaic root meaning "liar," then Judas would be "the Liar" (a reference to the betrayal). Others refer to the Latin *sicarius* ("dagger man"), which would identify him as one of the Zealots. Other suggestions are the "carrier of the *scortea*" (a leather bag for money) and the "man from Sychar."

10 Commentators often discuss whether the phrase "except for the feet" (NRSV) should be included in the text, since MSS vary in that regard. The shorter text (lit., "the one having been bathed does not have a need to wash") has the advantage of strengthening the point Jesus made in v.8. The longer text (which adds "except for the feet") has better MS support and adds the point about daily cleansing from contact with sin.

The background is the ancient custom of bathing before going out to a banquet but needing the feet to be washed on arrival due to the dust accumulated en route. Sacramentalists tend to see in these two acts baptism and penance (or the Lord's Supper). It is far more likely that they represent the initial cleansing of justification followed by the daily process of sanctification. One minister has on the door leading from his study into the sanctuary the words, "Are your feet clean?"

REFLECTIONS

How is it possible for people, who by nature seek their own advantage, to serve the interests and welfare of others? The only answer is to be set free from enslavement to oneself. Obviously, a deliverance of this magnitude poses a serious problem. Freedom from self-interest cannot be achieved by drawing on one's own resources. We need help from outside. Though the death of Jesus has provided not only forgiveness but also the power to live for others, very few have taken a firm hold of that power and allowed it to accomplish through their lives the self-forgetful service for others that God intended. Our deliverance is incomplete. Like the disciples, we often fail to show on a day-to-day basis what it means to be servants of one another.

2. The Coming Betrayal (13:18–30)

OVERVIEW

The prophet Isaiah described the coming messianic king as "a man of sorrows, and familiar with suffering" (Isa 53:3). During his public ministry Jesus had experienced sorrow of every sort. The unbelief of the Jewish nation as well as the hostility of the religious establishment caused him profound personal disappointment and pain. At one point he cried out, "O Jerusalem, Jerusalem, you who kill the prophets and stone those sent to you, how often I have longed to gather your children together, as a hen gathers her chicks under her wings, but you were not willing!" (Lk 13:34). A far deeper wound, however, was about to be inflicted by one of the Twelve. To be betrayed by a friend is the most devastating wound of all.

[18]"I am not referring to all of you; I know those I have chosen. But this is to fulfill the scripture: 'He who shares my bread has lifted up his heel against me.'

[19]"I am telling you now before it happens, so that when it does happen you will believe that I am He. [20]I tell you the truth, whoever accepts anyone I send accepts me; and whoever accepts me accepts the one who sent me."

[21]After he had said this, Jesus was troubled in spirit and testified, "I tell you the truth, one of you is going to betray me."

[22]His disciples stared at one another, at a loss to know which of them he meant. [23]One of them, the disciple whom Jesus loved, was reclining next to him. [24]Simon Peter motioned to this disciple and said, "Ask him which one he means."

[25]Leaning back against Jesus, he asked him, "Lord, who is it?"

[26]Jesus answered, "It is the one to whom I will give this piece of bread when I have dipped it in the dish." Then, dipping the piece of bread, he gave it to Judas Iscariot, son of Simon. [27]As soon as Judas took the bread, Satan entered into him.

"What you are about to do, do quickly," Jesus told him, [28]but no one at the meal understood why Jesus said this to him. [29]Since Judas had charge of the money, some thought Jesus was telling him to buy what was needed for the Feast, or to give something to the poor. [30]As soon as Judas had taken the bread, he went out. And it was night.

COMMENTARY

18 Judas's treachery must have made a marked impression on John. In 6:71 he added a parenthesis to call to the reader's attention that the "devil" of whom Jesus spoke was Judas. In 12:4 he identified Judas Iscariot as the one "who was later to betray him." Already in ch. 13 Judas has been referred to twice (vv.2, 10–11). Now in v.18 Jesus says that what is about to happen is "to fulfill the scripture." Not for a moment are we to assume that Judas was somehow trapped by divine necessity and left with no other option but to betray Jesus. To play the traitor was his own decision. The "scripture" that was fulfilled by his treacherous act is Psalm 41:9: "Even my close friend, whom I trusted, he who shared my bread, has lifted up his heel against me." To "share a person's bread" was to pledge loyalty to the person. The act reflects an intimate relationship of trust and fidelity. To "lift up the heel against" someone is a metaphor for violent opposition. It pictures a horse lifting its hoof in readiness to kick. Judas, who has posed as a faithful companion, is about to strike out in revenge. (Some have seen in the metaphor a reference to the shaking off of dust from one's feet [see Lk 9:5], while others find an allusion to Genesis 3:15. A literal translation of the Hebrew expression is "has made his heel great against me.")

In speaking as he does, Jesus is not referring to all of his disciples. "I know," he says, "those I have chosen." Some writers resist including Judas in the group of those who are said to have been chosen. They understand the choosing of the Eleven in the Pauline sense of God's gracious choice unto redemption. One way to alleviate the difficulty is to translate *tinas* ("those") as "the kind of men" (Barclay, 2:142). In this case, Jesus would be saying only that he knew what kind of men he had chosen—a statement implying that the betrayal by Judas would come as no surprise. It is better to take the word in a more general sense and understand the passage in the light of Jesus' earlier response to Peter: "Have I not chosen you, the Twelve? Yet one of you is a devil!" (6:70). Israel had been chosen by God, yet many of them betrayed their calling. Judas was chosen as a disciple but failed to remain loyal.

19 Jesus warned his disciples ahead of time of the coming betrayal so that when it did happen they would believe in him. The text reads, "that I am he." The meaning both here and in 8:24 is, "I am the one I claim to be." In both cases the Greek is *egō eimi*, "I am," with no expressed predicate. The *egō eimi* formula ultimately rests on the "I AM WHO I AM" of Exodus 3:14, "I AM" being the name by which God reveals himself in history (cf. Dt 32:39; Isa 43:10). Jesus knows ahead of time that he will be betrayed and that his betrayer will be one who "shares [his] bread." By telling his disciples beforehand, he intends that when it does happen their faith will be strengthened.

20 Verse 20 records a saying of Jesus that occurs elsewhere in the Gospels in various contexts (Mk 9:37; Lk 10:16). To accept those sent out by Jesus is to accept Jesus, and to accept him is to accept the one who sent him. Very shortly Jesus will tell his disciples, "As the Father has sent me, I am sending you" (20:21). Betrayal and death will bring confusion and discouragement, but resurrection and the knowledge that Jesus was fully aware of what would happen will result in renewed faith and the courage to carry out the commission. The point is emphasized by the doubled *amēn amēn* (NASB, "truly, truly"). It was important for the disciples to understand that as Jesus was sent by God, so also were they sent by him. Those who accept the disciples will at the same time be accepting both the Son and the Father. Apostleship carries with it the awesome privilege of divine companionship. To accept the messenger of God is to accept God as well.

21 Jesus had just indicated that one who shared his bread would lift up his heel against him (v.18). John records that after Jesus said this, he was deeply "troubled." The same word (*etarachthē*, GK 5429) was used of Jesus' response to Mary, who had fallen at his feet mourning the death of her brother Lazarus (11:33; Jesus was "troubled"). It is interesting that the gospel of John, which dwells most often on the deity of Jesus, is also the one that portrays in the most graphic ways his complete humanity.

Jesus is deeply troubled by the knowledge that one of his own disciples is about to betray him. Three years of close association has failed to win Judas's affection and loyalty. To make matters even worse, this lack of fidelity has been masked by a hypocrisy undetected by the other disciples. To know full well the deceitfulness of a "friend" and yet to bear with it till the very last out of compassion for the faithless one reveals a remarkable degree of restraint. Stoicism taught that a wise man meets all of life with equanimity. Perfect composure is the goal of life. Jesus was not a Stoic. His responses to life were fully human, and as such he revealed the nature of God as compassionately concerned with human frailty. He is a high priest who is "touched with the feeling of our infirmities" (Heb 4:15 KJV).

Jesus testified that one of his disciples would betray him. Until then, there had been no specific indication that a member of the band of disciples would be involved in what was about to happen. They had learned that not every one of them was "clean" (v.10) and that in some way the prophecy that one of them would "lift up his heel against" Jesus would be fulfilled (v.18). But the announcement that one of their very own would actually betray their Master must have struck them like a thunderbolt. The word "testify" (*martyreō*, GK *3455*; cf. the English "martyr") coupled with the double *amēn* emphasizes the supreme importance of the announcement. Incredible as it might seem, the betrayer was one of *them*. But how could anyone who had listened to the gracious teachings of Jesus and shared the intimacy of the group of disciples now turn and betray his Master?

22 The stunned disciples looked at one another, at a loss to know which of them Jesus meant. Apparently Judas had masked his duplicity so effectively that not one of them suspected him. Jesus had taught that the weeds and the wheat grow together and are not separated until the harvest, at which time the "sons of the evil one" are pulled up and burned (Mt 13:38). Even among the chosen Twelve was a "weed" sown by the devil (cf. Mt 13:39). The ability of a deceiver to feign loyalty while plotting high treason and to go unnoticed is a stark reminder of the shallowness of human perception. But while people may be easily deceived, there is no way to hide from God. From the beginning Jesus knew who the traitor would be. Calvin, 2:65, remarks that we should sometimes not point out the ungodly until God has dragged them into the light: wickedness needs to be ripe for discovery. In any case, Jesus allowed the presence of Judas until the very last.

23–24 To understand more accurately the exchange about to take place one needs to picture the way the group was arranged around the tables. Leonardo da Vinci's "The Last Supper," which pictures the disciples seated along one side of a long table, is misleading. In ancient times, the guests at special feasts would recline so that each would be resting on his left elbow supported by a cushion, with his feet pointing away from the table. In the upper room there were probably three tables arranged in a horseshoe fashion. Jesus and two of his disciples would be reclining at the center table. The place on Jesus' right would be reserved for a close friend, while the place on his left would go to the special guest.

It appears that John was the disciple who was seated on Jesus' right. Verse 25 says that he leaned back against Jesus to ask a question (a natural motion if he were on Jesus' right). The case for Judas being to the left of Jesus rests on the ease with which Jesus would hand him the bread after dipping it in the dish (v.26). It would also be consistent with the view that Jesus was offering his betrayer one more chance to abandon his wicked plan and seek forgiveness. It appears that Peter was not at the head table, because when he wanted to discover who the betrayer would be, he had to catch John's attention and ask him to relay the question (v.24). Apparently Peter enjoyed no special role among the disciples at this time.

I take the position that "the disciple whom Jesus loved" (v.23) was John the disciple and author of the fourth gospel (the same designation is found in 19:26; 20:2; 21:7, 20). Others have conjectured Lazarus or the rich young ruler, but it is highly unlikely that anyone except Jesus and the Twelve would have been present on that special occasion. The argument that John would not refer to himself in such a favorable way overlooks the nature of Oriental expression. In addition, everything we know about John leads us to believe that love was the most prominent characteristic of both his life and his teaching.

25–26 John, "leaning back against Jesus," asked him who the betrayer would be. If John was in fact sitting to the right of Jesus, this movement would not call attention to Peter's question and Jesus' answer. It helps explain why no one understood the significance of the special morsel given to Judas or what it meant when Judas left their presence (in v.29). Jesus identified the betrayer as the one to whom he would give the "piece of bread" (or meat; *psōmion* simply means "fragment" or "morsel," GK *6040*) after it had been dipped in a broth (perhaps the haroseth sauce of dates, raisins, and sour wine). To offer a special morsel was one of the ways a host could honor a distin-

guished guest. Every possible opportunity was given to Judas to turn from his wicked plan. On this special occasion he was given the place of honor and acknowledged by a distinct act of respect. Had there remained in him even a shred of integrity he would have surrendered to the love of his Master and turned from his treacherous scheme.

27–28 Instead Judas took the morsel, and immediately Satan entered into him. Earlier we learned that the devil "prompted" Judas to betray Jesus (v.2). Here it says that he "entered into him." The choice of verbs indicates a progression of influence or control. Satan's approach is subtle. What begins with a carefully designed suggestion ends in complete control. The sly question put to Eve was, "Did God really say . . . ?" (Ge 3:1). Satan achieves his objectives in our lives by gradually redirecting our affections away from God. As we are led astray by his cunning, his influence over us continues to increase. Unless checked by renewed obedience to the divine will, this line of progression leads to complete control by the adversary. Paul warns us against being deceived by Satan's cunning (2Co 11:3) and tells us to put on the full armor of God in order to "stand against the devil's schemes" (Eph 6:11).

It must have been with great heaviness of heart that Jesus said to Judas, "What you are about to do, do quickly." The words were not intended to prod Judas into moving ahead with his nefarious plan but should be taken as the sentence pronounced on a guilty man already condemned by his actions. The die has been cast. Satan entered into Judas, and the point of no return was passed. A parallel is found in Romans, where God is repeatedly said to have "given over" those who had willfully turned their backs on him (Ro 1:24, 26, 28).

No one at the table knew why Jesus said what he did. Some thought that he was telling Judas, who was in charge of the common purse, to go out and buy what was needed for the Feast; others thought that he wanted Judas to give something to the poor. What is truly amazing is that not one of the disciples suspected Judas of any sort of wrongdoing. He had masked his hypocrisy from his closest friends. How cunning are the ways of the deceitful! That he was the one charged with managing the meager resources of the group of disciples would indicate their confidence in his ability and integrity. Instead of being faithful to his charge, he was plotting the overthrow of his Master. There is a profound lesson here for those who are unaware of the deceitfulness of sin. Human nature is marred by duplicity and guile. The problem is less in detecting it in others as it is in recognizing it in ourselves. Thankfully, God's gracious forgiveness is available for those who request it.

29 "The Feast" would be the Feast of Unleavened Bread, which began at Passover and lasted for seven days. Reference to "the poor" reflects the Jewish practice of giving to the needy on the night of Passover. It is instructive to note that the possession and handling of money is not without its peculiar snares. Agur wisely said, "Give me neither poverty nor riches . . . . Otherwise, I may have too much and disown you" (Pr 30:8–9).

30 John records that "it was night" when Judas left the upper room. The observation is more than a reference to literal darkness. To turn one's back on the light of the world (cf. 8:12) is to enter the darkness of eternal night. It is because people's deeds are evil that they love darkness instead of light (3:19). Judas rejected the summons to light and chose the path of darkness. It is a frightful thing to be given the responsibility of determining one's own destiny.

NOTES

18 Textual evidence favors the reading μετ᾽ ἐμοῦ (*met emou*, "with me"; 𝔓⁶⁶ ℵ A D W Θ Ψ *f*¹·¹³ 33 lat sy bo; Eus Epiph); however, most modern translations (e.g., NIV, NASB, NRSV [but not NKJV]) read μου τὸν ἄρτον (*mou ton arton*, "my bread") as it is in the Hebrew of Psalm 41:9. The USB committee thinks that the former may have been an assimilation to Mark 14:18.

This is the first of four occasions on which John uses the formula ἵνα ἡ γραφὴ πληρωθῇ (*hina hē graphē plērōthē*, lit., "in order that the scripture may be fulfilled"). The others are in 17:12 and 19:24, 36. A similar fulfillment formula is found seven times in Matthew (ἵνα πληρωθῇ, *hina plērōthē*), with the agent through whom the fulfillment takes place always being a prophet (1:22; 2:15; 4:14; 12:17; 21:4; 26:56). The phrase is found once in Mark (14:49) but not at all in Luke.

19 The aorist subjunctive πιστεύσητε (*pisteusēte*, GK *4409*) suggests a coming to full faith. The present subjunctive πιστεύητε (*pisteuēte*), found in a few texts, would indicate a continuing faith.

27 In the NT, the Greek σατανᾶς (*satanas*, "Satan," GK *4928*) occurs thirty-six times; he is also referred to as διάβολος (*diabolos*, "the devil, the accuser," GK *1333*) approximately the same number of times. Other names are "the tempter," "the enemy," "the god of this age," "the ruler of the kingdom of the air," "the one who deceives," "the dragon," "the ancient serpent," "the father of lies," and "the evil one" (cf. *ISBE* 4:342). Although a clever and powerful foe, he was defeated on the cross. Yet even as a defeated foe he continues his attack on believers in an attempt to thwart the redemptive work of Christ. At the second advent he will be destroyed in the lake of fire, along with all his demonic cohorts and those who have surrendered to the deceptive and malevolent power of the beast (Rev 20:10).

3. Love, the New Commandment (13:31–35)

> **31**When he was gone, Jesus said, "Now is the Son of Man glorified and God is glorified in him. **32**If God is glorified in him, God will glorify the Son in himself, and will glorify him at once.
>
> **33**"My children, I will be with you only a little longer. You will look for me, and just as I told the Jews, so I tell you now: Where I am going, you cannot come.
>
> **34**"A new command I give you: Love one another. As I have loved you, so you must love one another. **35**By this all men will know that you are my disciples, if you love one another."

COMMENTARY

31 As soon as Judas leaves the upper room, Jesus cries out, "Now is the Son of Man glorified" (Moffatt translates, "Now at last the Son of man is glorified"). The presence of a traitor among the chosen Twelve, especially at the farewell banquet, must have been a great sorrow for Jesus. Now that he had gone there is a special tenderness in the words and actions of Jesus (in v.33 he calls his companions *teknia* [a nursery term for "[little] children," GK *5448*], the only time Jesus ever uses this affectionate term for his disciples).

It is regularly noted that in v.31 the verb "glorified" (*edoxasthē*, GK *1519*) occurs both times in the aorist (i.e., past) tense. A literal reading seems to say that the glorification of the Son of Man had already taken place. Not only would such a statement be less than clear; it would also make awkward the temporal word "now." The aorist tense is used because once the betrayer had gone out and the chain of events that would lead from crucifixion through resurrection and on to ascension were set in motion, the outcome was so certain that it could be stated as already having been accomplished.

It is one of the great theological insights of John's gospel that the glory of God is seen most clearly in the cross. God is love, and his glory is what most vividly displays this love. Thus the cross, the ultimate expression of God's love, is the focus of God's glory.

It is not simply the Son of Man who is glorified, but God also is glorified—the Father is glorified in the Son. We are reminded of the truth of 1:18 that the Son, "who is at the Father's side, has made him known." By word and action, Jesus taught that the Father is love, and nowhere is this clearer than in Jesus' passion.

32 As v.31 spoke of the glory of the Son (and the Father) in the cross and resurrection, v.32 speaks of the glory that will come to the Son following the ascension: "God will glorify the Son in himself," i.e., in the eternal glory that belongs to the Father. And this will take place at once. It has been properly noted that this saying enunciates the great spiritual principle that "those who glorify God shall be glorified by God" (cited in Ryle, 4:272). God is debtor to no one. His design is that redemption will issue in praise and that in eternity the redeemed will in some way share in the glory ascribed to Jesus.

33 The time has come for Jesus to tell his band of followers that soon he will be leaving them. As noted, the expression "my [little] children" reveals a special tenderness, and if the experience in the upper room is taken as a Passover meal, this designation would be especially suitable, since on that occasion parents explained to their children the meaning of the Hebrews' deliverance from Egypt (Ex 12:26–27; 13:8). Jesus will be with his disciples "only a little longer" (a prophetic expression indicating the shortness of time before God brings deliverance; cf. Isa 10:25; Jer 51:33). They will look for him, but where he is going they cannot come. On a previous occasion, he said the same thing to the Jews, but in that case, after "you will look for me," he added, "but you will not find me" (7:34). Such will not be the case with the disciples, because in a very real sense he will remain with them, even though bodily he will be absent. They will find him constantly present in the person of the Holy Spirit.

34 Jesus delivers to his disciples a new commandment: "love one another." In the Vulgate (the Latin translation, which since the sixteenth century has been the official version of the Roman Catholic Church), "new command" is translated *mandatum novum*, from which is derived the name Maundy Thursday, the anniversary of the Last Supper. The commandment is not new in the sense that it was formerly unknown. Leviticus 19:18 reads, "Love your neighbor as yourself." The newness of the command lay in the meaning given to love by the life and teachings of Jesus. It was to be a covenantal love, distinguished from even the noblest forms of human love by the fact that it was "spontaneous and unmotivated" (Brown, 614). God's love does not question the worthiness of the recipient but gladly gives of itself in humble service.

35 Jesus' charge to his disciples is crystal clear: They are to love one another as he has loved them. His life defines the meaning of love. Love is the evidence of discipleship. It is the one quality that provides indisputable evidence that a person is a genuine disciple of Jesus—all people will know that they are his disciples "if [they] love one another." The third-century apologist Tertullian (*Apol.* 39.7) noted that the pagans said of the early Christians, "See, how they love one another!" and added, "How ready they are to die for one another!" The concern and care exercised by members of the early church for each other made a definite impact on pagan culture. Little wonder that the Christian faith spread so rapidly throughout the ancient world! It has always been true that love is the mightiest force in the world. If contemporary Christianity is weak and ineffectual, it is not because of opposition from outside but because we who call ourselves "Christians" have forgotten the mandate to love one another even as Jesus loved his own.

NOTES

31 The verb ἐδοξάσθη (*edoxasthē*, GK *1519*) falls in a category that Daniel Wallace (*Greek Grammar Beyond the Basics* [Grand Rapids: Zondervan, 1996], 564) calls "proleptic aorist."

Because ch. 14 closed with the words "come now; let us leave," and this exit doesn't seem to take place until ch. 18, some writers think that chs. 15 and 16 should be inserted after "Jesus said" in 13:31. There is no MS evidence or support from early writers that would encourage us to accept the conjecture. One structural observation worth noting is that while elsewhere in the fourth gospel "signs" are followed by discourses that bring out their meaning, here the discourse (chs. 13–17) precedes the final sign (the cross and empty tomb).

32 The initial clause in v.32 (εἰ ὁ θεὸς ἐδοξάσθη ἐν αὐτῷ, *ei ho theos edoxasthē en autō*, "if God is glorified in him") is omitted in 𝔓⁶⁶ ℵ* B C* D L W 1 et al. Although the shorter reading is normally accepted as more likely to be valid, the absence of the clause can be accounted for by (1) a copyist's skipping from the ἐν αὐτῷ, *en autō*, at the end of the previous verse to the ἐν αὐτῷ, *en autō*, at the end of the clause in question (homoioteleuton), and (2) a decision to remove what appears to be redundant (cf. Metzger, 205–6).

4. Peter's Denial Foretold (13:36–38)

³⁶Simon Peter asked him, "Lord, where are you going?" Jesus replied, "Where I am going, you cannot follow now, but you will follow later." ³⁷Peter asked, "Lord, why can't I follow you now? I will lay down my life for you." ³⁸Then Jesus answered, "Will you really lay down your life for me? I tell you the truth, before the rooster crows, you will disown me three times!"

COMMENTARY

36 It would appear that what Jesus said about the new command didn't register with Simon Peter. He was still pondering Jesus' earlier statement about his leaving them and going to a place where they could not come. How could that be? They had been with him now for some three years and had accompanied him throughout Galilee and Judea. So he asked, "Lord, where are you going?" But geography was not the issue. "Where I am going," responded Jesus, "you cannot follow now, but you will follow later." The "place" where Jesus was about to go was death on a cross. Peter was not yet ready for that kind of commitment. First there would be the tragic denial and then a restoration and recommissioning to service; this in turn would lead to a life of active witness culminating in a martyr's death (cf. the prediction in 21:18–19). Tradition has it that at his request Peter was crucified in a head-down position. In the second century apocryphal *Acts of Peter* (35), the same question ("Where are you going?" Latin, *Quo vadis?*) was asked of Jesus by Peter, who was fleeing the danger of martyrdom in Rome. On learning that Jesus was going into Rome to be crucified again—in Peter's place—Peter returned to the city to surrender his life.

37–38 Convinced that he could meet any test that might arise, Peter asked, perhaps not without a bit of irritation, "Lord, why can't I follow you now? I will lay down my life for you." Bold words from a man certain of his own ability to remain faithful in testing. But Jesus knew Peter better than Peter knew himself. With a note "both of irony and of being resigned to human weakness" (Brown, 608), Jesus answered, "Will you really lay down your life for me?" The self-assurance of Peter over against the compassionate knowledge of Jesus reflects the relationship on a larger scale between Jesus and every person.

Not only will Peter not lay down his life for Jesus at this time, but before the rooster crows, he will disown his Master three times. According to Roman custom, cockcrow was the third of the four night watches and fell between midnight and 3:00 a.m. (cf. Mk 13:35). What a shocking effect this prophetic statement of Jesus must have had on Peter. Though other disciples speak freely in subsequent chapters (Thomas in 14:5; Philip in 14:8; Judas in 14:22), we hear not another word from Peter until ch. 18 (v.10). Peter had suddenly come face-to-face with the naked truth about himself, and it left him speechless.

B. Jesus' Final Words for His Disciples (14:1–16:33)

1. The Way, the Truth, and the Life (14:1–14)

OVERVIEW

It is important to remember that the chapter divisions in the Bible are not the work of the original writers. (The fourth-century AD Codex Vaticanus, which contains the oldest system we know about for dividing the NT, separates the fourth gospel into fifty units.) What we label as ch. 14 continues the previous "chapter" without any necessary break. The admonition "do not let your hearts be troubled" must be read in the context of Jesus' announcement of his imminent death (13:31–33) and his prediction of Peter's betrayal (13:38).

[1]"Do not let your hearts be troubled. Trust in God; trust also in me. [2]In my Father's house are many rooms; if it were not so, I would have told you. I am going there to prepare a place for you. [3]And if I go and prepare a place for you, I will come back and take you to be with me that you also may be where I am. [4]You know the way to the place where I am going."

[5]Thomas said to him, "Lord, we don't know where you are going, so how can we know the way?"

[6]Jesus answered, "I am the way and the truth and the life. No one comes to the Father except through me. [7]If you really knew me, you would know my Father as well. From now on, you do know him and have seen him."

[8]Philip said, "Lord, show us the Father and that will be enough for us."

[9]Jesus answered: "Don't you know me, Philip, even after I have been among you such a long time? Anyone who has seen me has seen the Father. How can you say, 'Show us the Father'? [10]Don't you believe that I am in the Father, and that the Father is in me? The words I say to you are not just my own. Rather, it is the Father, living in me, who is doing his work. [11]Believe me when I say that I am in the Father and the Father is in me; or at least believe on the evidence of the miracles themselves. [12]I tell you the truth, anyone who has faith in me will do what I have been doing. He will do even greater things than these, because I am going to the Father. [13]And I will do whatever you ask in my name, so that the Son may bring glory to the Father. [14]You may ask me for anything in my name, and I will do it."

COMMENTARY

1 Having left their homes and occupations to follow the Master, the disciples are now faced with what appears to be complete failure. The noble cause to which they had given themselves for the past three years seems about to crumble. How reassuring, then, would be the words of Jesus, "Set your troubled hearts at rest" (NEB; the present imperative may suggest "stop being troubled"). The verb (*tarassō*, GK *5429*) means "stir up," "unsettle," "throw into confusion." In 11:33 it depicted Jesus' reaction when he encountered the sorrowing Mary, in 12:27 when he anticipated death, and in 13:21 when he predicted his betrayal.

As members of the Jewish community, the disciples would know from their own religious tradition that God would never abandon them. Throughout history he had responded to the needs of his people and protected them in times of distress. Jesus is saying to his disciples, "You *do* trust in God; therefore trust also in me [*pisteuete*, "trust," GK *4409*, can be taken as indicative or imperative in either clause]. Have I not yet convinced you that I and my Father are one [10:30; cf. 17:21–23]? If the Father is worthy of your trust, so also is the Son." In light of this, then, Jesus urges, "You must not let yourselves be distressed" (Phillips).

2 The reason the disciples are able to set their hearts at rest is that, although he will leave them for a time, Jesus will return. While he is gone, he will be preparing a place for them in his Father's house, i.e., where God is, in heaven. "Many rooms" is a way of saying "enough room for everyone." The KJV's "mansions" (stemming from Tyndale) is misleading. In Old English the word meant "dwelling place" without any special reference to a palatial mansion. Some writers take the Greek *monai* ("rooms," GK *3665*) as representing an Aramaic term meaning "shelters along the road" where a traveler could spend the night. Temple, 2:226, calls them "wayside caravanserais" and pictures Jesus as "our spiritual dragoman, who treads the way of faith before us." While it is comforting to think of "resting places" as stages in our spiritual growth and of Jesus as the One who goes ahead to prepare each place and lead us there (cf. Temple, 2:227–28), it is better to take *monē* as related to *menō* ("to abide," GK *3531*), a basic verb that occurs frequently in John. The "many rooms" are in the Father's house, not along the road that leads there.

Since the place Jesus is preparing for his disciples is in heaven, it is difficult to say with any precision what this may entail. Speculations about "celestial palaces" miss the point. To be in the Father's house is to be with him; everything else will pale by comparison. Marsh, 501, holds that the actual preparation of the permanent dwelling places was accomplished "not after the death on the cross, but in it and by it"—an interesting thought, though by saying that Jesus is "going there" (i.e., to his Father's house) in order to prepare a place, the text puts the preparation subsequent to the ascension.

3 Jesus' return for his disciples is as certain as his departure: "I go" and "I will come back." It is somewhat difficult to determine whether at this point Jesus is speaking of his post-resurrection appearances or his return at the end of the age. In the first case, it is not clear in what sense he would then take his disciples to be with him; in the second case, it is difficult to understand how the second advent would fulfill the apparent immediacy of the promise. Some have solved the ambiguity by holding that Jesus is speaking at this point of his "return" in the person of the Holy Spirit. Perhaps it is best to understand the passage as blending all three suggested interpretations: in the resurrection Jesus comes back from the dead, in the current age he lives among us by the Spirit, and at the consummation he will come again for his own.

The promise Jesus makes to his followers is that on his return he will take them to be with him so that they also may be where he is. The deepest longing of the human heart is to be in the presence of God. In the book of Revelation, John portrays the essence of eternal bliss in the words, "They shall see his face" (Rev 22:4). When the new Jerusalem descends from heaven, then will be fulfilled the glorious promise, "Now the dwelling of God is with men, and he will live with them. They will be his people, and God himself will be with them and be their God" (Rev 21:3). There is no greater joy than the presence of God—which is why those who now live in vital relationship with him experience the greatest satisfactions life has to offer.

4–5 Jesus tells his disciples that they "know the way to the place where [he] is going," but Thomas questions both *where* Jesus is going and therefore *the way* that would take them there. While the question posed by Thomas is in a certain sense rational, it reveals an inability to grasp spiritual truth. True, if they don't know where Jesus is going, they cannot know the way. But Thomas should have known that Jesus was speaking spiritually rather than geographically. The disciples had been told by Jesus that he would be crucified and would return to his Father (cf. 12:7–8, 23–24, 27, 32, 46–47). Their understanding of that truth, however, was limited by the narrow scope of their imagination. They were unable to grasp the fact that for Jesus to "go away" could signify something other than merely geographical separation.

6 Unwittingly, the mundane question by Thomas led to one of the most far-reaching and provocative statements ever made by Jesus. For Thomas, the way to an unknown destination cannot be known. Jesus answers, "I am the way." Jesus is not one who shows the way but the one who himself *is* the way. He is the way—the only way—to the Father, for "no one comes to the Father except through [him]." The particularism of Jesus' teaching has caused many to stumble. The mind-set of secular society regards such exclusive claims as intolerant. Certainly there are other paths that lead to God. Not so! To accept Jesus Christ involves accepting all that he said, even though open support of his claims may cause a bit of embarrassment when brought up in certain circles of contemporary society.

Jesus is the only way to God because he is also "the truth." Note that each of the three nouns (way, truth, life) is preceded by a definite article. "Truth" and "life" do not modify "way," as though Jesus were saying, "I am the real and living way" (Moffatt). He *is* the truth. Ultimate truth is not a series of propositions to be grasped by the intellect but a person to be received and therefore knowable only by means of a personal relationship. Others have made true statements, but only Jesus perfectly embodies truth itself. He *is* the truth. And he is also "the life." Eternal life is to know Jesus Christ (17:3; cf. 1Jn 1:2; 5:20). Apart from him is darkness and death.

Barclay, 2:157, mentions that in this sublime statement Jesus took three of the great basic conceptions of Jewish religion and made the tremendous claim that in him all three found their full realization. The fifteenth-century Augustinian priest Thomas à Kempis (*The Imitation of Christ* [1441; repr., Grand Rapids: Zondervan, 1983], 208) joined the three as follows: "Without the way, there is no going; without the truth, there is no knowing; without the life, there is no living."

7 Jesus recognized that the ideas held by the disciples about him were less than adequate, so he added, "If you really knew me, you would know my Father as well." Throughout his ministry, Jesus had taught his followers that he had come to do the will of his Father and to carry out what the Father had planned. So perfect was the correspondence between the life of Jesus and the will of God that to know Jesus was to know his Father too. As a perfect Son, Jesus revealed with total accuracy the person of the Father. Anticipating the events about to take place, Jesus can say, "From now on, you do know him and have seen him."

8 The disciples were unable to grasp the meaning of Jesus' statement that from that point on it could be said that they had seen the Father. Their Jewish background had taught them that no one could see God and live (Ex 33:20; Jn 1:18; 6:46). Philip's petition, "Lord, show us the Father," was a request for a theophany such as came to Abraham at the oaks of Mamre (Ge 18:1), to Moses in the burning bush (Ex 3), and to Elijah in the cave at Horeb (1Ki 19:9–14). Philip was asking for some sort of visible manifestation of God, but Jesus had come to reveal the nature and character of God.

Philip was convinced that if they could see the Father, "that [would] be enough." The longing of the heart for God is beautifully set forth in the opening lines of Psalm 42: "As the deer pants for streams of water, so my soul pants for you, O God." What Philip had not yet learned was that in the person of Jesus, God had answered the deepest longing of the human heart. It is in Jesus that the Father presents himself to us. To know the Son is to know the Father. To see the Son is to see the Father.

9 Jesus' poignant answer reveals disappointment more than rebuke: "Don't you know me, Philip, even after I have been among you such a long time?" It seems reasonable to expect that after some three years of close association, Philip (and the others) would have come to a better understanding of who Jesus really was. But such is the ineptitude and dullness of human insight with regard to spiritual matters. By nature we are creatures prone to forget our Creator. Our minds operate in such a way as to exclude God, if possible. So Jesus restates the central truth that "anyone who has seen me has seen the Father." Morris, 643, calls this statement "staggering in its simplicity and its profundity." Jesus' claim to be one with God leaves no alternative but to accept it as true or dismiss it as the ravings of a madman.

10 The major premise running through these verses is that the Father and Son are in one another (vv.10, 11, 20; cf. 10:38; 17:21). The precise nature of this unity is beyond our ability to comprehend. It is more than a simple relationship yet less than identity. The Godhead, while remaining three per-

sons, is one in essence. The words of Jesus are the work of the Father. Jesus does not speak on his own (cf. 7:16; 8:28 et al.) but maintains that in whatever he does and says, it is the Father living in him who is doing his work through him. In fact, no one has ever been able to do the work of God. Our role, like that of Jesus, is to live in such unity with the Father that whatever we do will be God doing his work through us. The pretensions of humankind would always have it otherwise. While wanting God's help, we still want to be in charge of and receive the credit for doing his work.

11 Jesus challenges the disciples (from v.10 on the plural is used) that if they cannot believe the essential mutuality of Father and Son on the basis of his own statement, then they ought to believe on the evidence of the miracles themselves. Better a faith based on miracles than no faith at all. John the Baptist had sent messengers to ask Jesus whether he was the one who was to come or whether they should look for another. They were told to go back and report what they heard and saw, that "the blind receive sight" and "the lame walk" (Mt 11:2–5). While miracles were never intended to coerce belief, they do perform the valuable function of supporting faith. It would be better to accept Jesus at his word; if faith cannot rise to the challenge, however, then let it be energized by considering the undeniable acts of God in redemptive history.

12 Verses 12–14 have been called the "Magna Carta of primitive Christianity." The effective power of a sovereign God is placed in the hands of believers, who exercise it through prayer offered in the name of the Son. The double *amēn* ("I tell you the truth") calls attention to an utterance of unusual importance. The remarkable truth is that those who have faith in Jesus will do not only what he has been doing but "even greater things than these." We tend to understand this statement in reference to the miracles of Jesus, and the apostles of the early church did in fact perform a number of miracles (cf. Ac 4:30). However, the "greater works" (KJV) that the disciples will do will be the mighty miracles of regeneration about to take place as a result of their proclamation of the gospel. On the day of Pentecost alone, about three thousand people accepted their message and were added to the church (Ac 2:41). Jesus was limited in time and space, but his body, the church, would soon be spread throughout the entire known world and take with them the message of salvation through faith in Christ.

Our fixation on the visibly miraculous may well be due to "the scantiness of our knowledge or the vulgarity of our taste" rather than the intrinsic marvel of what takes place (Temple, 2:235). Conversion is the miracle of miracles in that it requires nothing less than the supernatural involvement of God himself in the inner reaches of the human soul. Physical healings and miracles of nature take place on a level much easier to grasp.

It is crucially important to note that these greater works will be done because Jesus is "going to the Father." Very shortly he will explain that, following his ascension, another Counselor will come to be with them forever (vv. 16–17, 26). The power to perform greater works will result from this coming of the Holy Spirit. It has nothing to do with the ability of the messenger. In every case it is God at work through the presence and power of his Spirit. Nothing has changed since the day Jesus spoke these important words. The miracle of regeneration continues to take place wherever present-day disciples trust in God's way to bring people to faith. Apart from his Spirit, the church is powerless to effect spiritual transformation.

13 Jesus gives his followers the incredible promise that he will do whatever they ask "in [his] name" (*en tō onomati mou*, used seven times in the discourse that follows: 14:13, 14, 26; 15:16; 16:23, 24, 26). The name of Jesus speaks of his essential character. To pray in his name is to pray for those things that correspond to the nature and will of Jesus. Such prayers are always answered. When we voice the desires of the Son, we pray for what is already his will but awaits our request. When we pray in his name (i.e., in a way congruent with his character), we pray as his representatives. The Father will not deny the requests of his dearly beloved Son. The purpose of answered prayer is that "the Son may bring glory to the Father." Ultimately all praise and honor belong to him. This is why Jesus taught us to pray, "Let your name [i.e., your character] be honored . . . on earth as it is in heaven" (Mt 6:9–10).

14 The verse strengthens by repetition what has just been said: whatever is asked in Jesus' name he will do. Note that prayer may be addressed to the Son as well as to the Father ("You may ask *me*"). Though God reveals himself in Scripture as triune, and though certain functions seem to be assigned quite appropriately to each member of the Godhead, there is at the same time a significant degree of overlap.

NOTES

1 The interpretation of v. 1b adopted above takes the first πιστεύετε (*pisteuete*, GK 4409) as indicative and the second as imperative. Since both can be indicative or imperative in either location (plus the fact that the first may be taken as a question), a rather confusing number of possibilities are available. Jesus is about to be rejected by the nation's leaders as the promised Messiah, and this event will expose the disciples' faith to an extreme test. So he encourages them that since they do believe in God they are also to maintain their belief in him, regardless of his coming rejection and death.

2 The second half of v.2 is ambiguous. The NIV follows a shorter text that omits the Greek conjunction ὅτι, *hoti* ("that," "because"), and by inserting a period creates an additional sentence ("if it were not so, I would have told you. I am going there to prepare a place for you"). The problem with the rendering is that it is more likely that the ὅτι, *hoti*, was dropped from the text (to simplify the passage) than that it was added. A second possibility is to take the clause "if it were not so, I would have told you" as a parenthesis and connect the final clause with the earlier part of the verse while taking *hoti* in the sense of "for." Opting for a different solution, Carson, 490, writes that the parenthesis is "somewhat awkward" and the logic of the connection "a bit stilted." Although we have no prior record of Jesus' teaching about going on ahead into heaven to prepare a place for the disciples, it would appear that it is preferable to follow the lead of the NRSV and take the unit under consideration as a question ("If it were not so, would I have told you that I go to prepare a place for you?").

4 Thomas's two-part statement/question in v.5 probably accounts for the copyist's longer reading in v.4 (καὶ τὴν ὁδὸν οἴδατε, *kai tēn hodon oidate*, lit., "and the way you know"), which is followed by the KJV and the NKJV. The NASB has, "And you know the way where I am going," which is slightly less clear than the NIV's "the way to the place where I am going."

6 For the other "I am" statements in John, see 6:35, "I am the light of the world"; 10:7, "I am the gate"; 10:11, "I am the good shepherd"; 11:25, "I am the resurrection and the life"; and 15:1, "I am the true vine."

7 NA[27] reads the perfect ἐγνώκατε (*egnōkate*, GK *1182*) followed by the future γνώσεσθε (*gnōsesthe*), which construction yields, "If you have known me, you will know my Father." The NASB follows the MS tradition that reads the pluperfect ἐγνώκειτε (*egnōkeite*) in both places: "If you had known Me, you would have known My Father also." The first option states a promise; the second is a condition contrary to fact. The NIV adopts the latter and places the statement in the English present: "If you really knew me, you would know my Father as well."

14 Verse 14 is omitted by various witnesses (such as X *f*[1] 565 *pc* vg[ms] sy[s]), probably because the eye of the copyist moved from ἐάν, *ean*, at the beginning of v.14 to the same word at the beginning of v.15. (Λ* omits the last seven words of v.13 as well, skipping from ποιήσω [*poiēsō*, GK *4472*] there to the ποιήσω, *poiēsō*, at the end of v.14.) Metzger, 208, also mentions as reasons for the omission the similarity with v.13a and the possible contradiction with 16:23.

2. The Promise of the Holy Spirit (14:15–31)

OVERVIEW

We come now to the first of five passages in the Upper Room Discourse that provide instruction on the person and work of the Holy Spirit (vv.16–17).

Bruce, 302, notes that here the Spirit functions as helper, in 14:26 as interpreter, in 15:26 as witness, in 16:4b–11 as prosecutor, and in 16:12–15 as revealer.

15"If you love me, you will obey what I command. 16And I will ask the Father, and he will give you another Counselor to be with you forever—17the Spirit of truth. The world cannot accept him, because it neither sees him nor knows him. But you know him, for he lives with you and will be in you. 18I will not leave you as orphans; I will come to you. 19Before long, the world will not see me anymore, but you will see me. Because I live, you also will live. 20On that day you will realize that I am in my Father, and you are in me, and I am in you. 21Whoever has my commands and obeys them, he is the one who loves me. He who loves me will be loved by my Father, and I too will love him and show myself to him."

22Then Judas (not Judas Iscariot) said, "But, Lord, why do you intend to show yourself to us and not to the world?"

23Jesus replied, "If anyone loves me, he will obey my teaching. My Father will love him, and we will come to him and make our home with him. 24He who does not love me will not obey my teaching. These words you hear are not my own; they belong to the Father who sent me.

25"All this I have spoken while still with you. 26But the Counselor, the Holy Spirit, whom the Father will send in my name, will teach you all things and will remind you of everything I have said to you. 27Peace I leave with you; my peace I give you. I do not give to you as the world gives. Do not let your hearts be troubled and do not be afraid.

28"You heard me say, 'I am going away and I am coming back to you.' If you loved me, you would be glad that I am going to the Father, for the Father is greater than I. 29I have told you now before it happens, so that when it does happen you will believe. 30I will not speak with you much longer, for the prince of this world is coming. He has no hold on me, 31but the world must learn that I love the Father and that I do exactly what my Father has commanded me.

"Come now; let us leave."

COMMENTARY

16 Jesus says that he will ask the Father, who in response will provide the disciples with "another Counselor." The Greek *paraklētos* (GK 4156) is difficult to translate. "Comforter" (KJV) is misleading because the meaning of the English word has changed since Wycliffe's day when it was first used. ("Comforter" stems from the Latin *fortis*, which means "brave"). "Advocate" is closer, since literally a *paraklētos* is "one called alongside" (from the verb *kaleō*, GK 2813, and the preposition *para*) to help,

especially in a legal sense. The problem with "Counselor" (NIV) is that it suggests advice rather than active assistance. Phillips translates *allon paraklēton* with, "someone else to stand by you," and Knox has, "another to befriend you."

It is often noted that the one to come will be *another* Counselor. Although the distinction should not be pressed, the use of *allos* rather than *heteros* could indicate "another of the same kind" rather than "another of a different kind." The implication that Jesus' ministry will be continued by another Counselor (thus defining in part the role of Jesus) should cause no problem. As an Advocate, Jesus prayed that Simon's faith would not fail (Lk 22:23), argued that the disciples had a right to pick grain on the Sabbath (Mk 3:23–28), and came to the aid of the man healed of blindness who had been excommunicated by the religious authorities (Jn 9). In Romans 8:34 Paul refers to the advocacy role of the resurrected Jesus ("at the right hand of God and is also interceding for us"), and the author of Hebrews writes of Jesus as the heavenly priest who lives forever and is therefore able "to intercede" for those who "come to God through him" (Heb 7:25). Jesus is telling his band of disciples that, when he has returned to the Father, another Counselor will be sent to stand in his place by their side and give them help and encouragement.

17 The coming Counselor is called "the Spirit of truth." Earlier Jesus had stated that he himself was "the truth" (14:6), so we are not surprised to learn that the one who will take his place will be eminently qualified to communicate the truth. (See especially 16:12–15 for this role.) Truth is perfect correspondence with reality. For this reason, God's Spirit, the Spirit of truth, is the most reliable means of divine revelation. Since God is person, it follows that his most compelling revelation must be through another person.

Though Jesus will soon leave his disciples to return to the Father, the Spirit of truth will be with them forever. Once given to believers, he will never be taken away. The NT era, which extends from Pentecost to the second advent, is peculiarly the age of the Spirit. He is Christ's continuing presence working in and through the church until God's redemptive work is complete. How sad that the church so often forgets its source of truth and power. Samuel Taylor Coleridge (*Aids to Reflection* [1825; repr., Princeton, N.J.: Princeton Univ. Press,

1993], xxv) remarked that the one who "begins by loving Christianity better than truth, will proceed by loving his own sect or church better than Christianity, and end in loving himself better than all."

The world (i.e., society organized apart from God) "cannot accept [*lambanō*, GK 3284, may mean to receive someone in the sense of recognizing that person's authority; cf. 1:12; 13:20]" the Spirit because "He is known only by the experience of faith" (Calvin, 2:83). In anticipation of the Spirit's coming, Jesus can tell his disciples, "You know him, for he lives with you and will be in you." His presence in their lives will be self-authenticating. Rational argument will never convince a person of spiritual truth—it must be experienced to be known. Ultimate truth may be defended by rational discourse but never established in that way. Scripture is clear that the world through its wisdom does not know God (1Co 1:18–2:16). Truth is known and recognized when the Spirit of truth indwells the believing heart. In spiritual matters, faith precedes knowledge.

18 In view of Jesus' imminent departure, how comforting must have been his promise, "I will not leave you as orphans." The word *orphanos* ("left without parents," GK 4003) is used figuratively to mean "abandoned" or "unprotected" (cf. Jas 1:27). Jesus had worked patiently with his disciples to bring them fully to trust in him and prepare them to be the first to enter a hostile world with the message of God's redeeming love. He will not abandon them at this or any other point along the way.

A second promise quickly follows the first: "I will come to you." This promise is usually held to refer to (1) the Parousia, (2) the postresurrection appearances of Jesus, or (3) his coming as the Spirit into the lives of believers. Favoring the first option is the reference to the Parousia in v.3 and the designation in v.20 of "that day" (taken as a semitechnical term for the Jewish period preceding God's final intervention). This interpretation is not likely, however, because they were to see him "before long" (v.19), yet after two thousand years the Parousia is still in the future. Further, when v.19 is taken in a strictly eschatological sense, Jesus' statement, "the world will not see me," contradicts his teaching in Matthew that "all the nations of the earth . . . will see the Son of Man coming" (Mt 24:30).

A better case can be made for the position that the coming of Jesus promised in v.18 is fulfilled in his postresurrection appearances. We know that he did return following the resurrection and met on numerous occasions with his disciples. While there is nothing that weighs heavily against this interpretation, it is more probable that in this instance Jesus is referring primarily to his "coming" in the person of the Holy Spirit to indwell and empower his disciples as they take up the arduous task of world evangelization. Consider that (1) the focus of the immediately preceding verses is the coming of the Spirit of truth, (2) v.23 speaks of the "coming" of the Father and the Son to make their home with those who love and obey Jesus' teaching, and (3) several phrases in the paragraph are best understood in a spiritual sense ("you will see me [with the eyes of faith]," v.19; "you are in me, and I am in you," v.20).

Perhaps it is not necessary to decide between the second two alternatives since, as Dodd, 395, has observed, the distinction between the various phases of Jesus' return in the fourth gospel is a "vanishing" one. This is neither to deny the reality of the resurrection nor to undermine confidence in the second advent; it is simply to draw attention to the fact that Christ "comes" at various times and in various ways. In part it corresponds with Paul's declaration that "the Lord is the Spirit" (2Co 3:17).

19–20 In a short time the world will not see Jesus any longer—he is going to the Father—but the disciples "will still see [him]" (TCNT) because they see with the eyes of faith. "Blessed are the pure in heart," said Jesus, "for they will see God" (Mt 5:8). His victory over death and the grave results in eternal life for those who believe. On that day (the "day" that stretches from Pentecost till Jesus' return), all who follow him will come to realize the mutual indwelling of the believer, the glorified Jesus, and the Father.

21 In v.15 love was presented as the motivating cause of obedience; now in v.21 obedience becomes the test of love. The one who has the commands of Jesus (has received them and made them his own) and obeys them (puts them into daily practice) is the one who loves Jesus. The instructions of our Lord were given not to make us better theologians but better people. It would be better to remain uninstructed than to hear a command and fail to obey it. Ryle, 4:311, correctly says that "passive impressions which do not lead to action, gradually deaden and paralyze the heart." To know carries the obligation to obey. Obedience is the proof of love.

Jesus promises a special reward to the one who "loves" him. (That *agapōn*, GK *26*, in v.21 is present tense suggests a continuing relationship of love.) Not only will such a person be loved by both the Father and the Son, but Jesus will "show [himself]" to him or her as well. *Emphanizō* ("to make visible," GK *1872*) is used here in the figurative sense of self-revelation through the Spirit. It is the high privilege of the one who loves the Son to experience in a unique way the reality of his presence and gain a fuller understanding of who he is. God reveals himself in the context of love. Apathy or disobedience makes it impossible to encounter God in any meaningful way. It was to Mary Magdalene, whose love expressed itself in service and sorrow, that the risen Jesus first appeared (20:10–18). It has always been true that apart from love, the things most worth knowing can never be learned.

22 Once again, Jesus is interrupted by one of the disciples (Thomas in v.5; Philip in v.8; Judas in v.22).

In each case the question or statement begins with the acknowledgment that Jesus is "Lord," and in each case the interruption serves to prepare the way for Jesus to teach a spiritual truth of great importance. Judas, further identified as "not Judas Iscariot," is "Judas son of James" (Lk 6:16; Ac 1:13), sometimes identified with Thaddaeus (Mk 3:18) or Lebbaeus (certain MSS at Mt 10:3). Judas takes Jesus' statement about "showing himself" in a physical sense and wonders why the coming manifestation will be to the disciples only and not to the world. Had not Jesus taught that "all the nations of the earth . . . will see the Son of Man coming on the clouds of the sky" (Mt 24:30)? The disciples regularly heard the words of Jesus on a level as free from ambiguity as possible. Their penchant for seeking the obvious often prevented them from grasping the spiritual meaning of Jesus' teaching. Is there not a danger that we still tend to limit the word of God to its most obvious meaning and fail to plumb its depths for what theologians call *sensus plenior* ("the fuller sense")?

23 Jesus gives no direct answer to Judas's question but encourages him to understand the promise in terms of the abiding presence of the Father and Son in the life of the obedient believer. Once again, he joins love and obedience (cf. vv.15, 21). The reward for those whose love is real and therefore issues in obedience is, "My Father will love him, and we will come to him and make our home with him" (*monē*, "home," GK 3665, occurs only here and in v.2 in the NT). The reality of God's presence in the daily experience of those who truly believe cannot be emphasized too strongly. While eternal life is life without end, it is (perhaps even more important) a quality of life that stems from the presence of the Eternal One. The Pauline mystery, "Christ in you, the hope of glory" (Col 1:27), is firmly based in Jesus' teaching of the indwelling of Father, Son, and Holy Spirit.

24 Those who do not love Jesus will not do what he says. The seriousness of this neglect lies in the fact that Jesus' words are not his own but "belong to the Father who sent [him]." To disobey God himself is a matter of grave concern, and the words of Jesus *are* the words of God. The Messenger speaks the will of the One who sent him. It is worth noting that a claim such as this must be taken either as authentic or as the rambling of an irresponsible dreamer. To deny Jesus the honor of one who speaks the very words of God is to conclude that he is not at all who he claims to be. There is no acceptable middle ground.

25 The departure of Jesus to the Father will bring to a close the time during which he has been able to instruct his disciples in the essential truths of the coming kingdom. The use of the perfect tense, "I have spoken" (*lelalēka*, GK 3281), suggests a certain finality to what has been taught. "All this" refers to all that Jesus has taught thus far during his final evening with the Twelve.

26 The instruction of the disciples, however, will not cease. The Father will send the Holy Spirit to remind them of all that Jesus has said and help them understand the full meaning of his teaching. Apart from this teaching role of the Spirit, there never could have been a reliable gospel or, for that matter, a NT at all. As Peter put it, "Men spoke from God as they were carried along by the Holy Spirit" (2Pe 1:21).

The Counselor who is to be sent by the Father is the Holy Spirit. (Only here in John is the title in Greek given in its fullest form: *to pneuma to hagion*, GK 4460, 51). For the early Christians the title would emphasize the holiness of the Spirit rather than his might and power. In his vision of the exalted Lord, Isaiah saw the seraphs as they circled the throne and called out, "Holy, holy, holy [*hagios*, LXX] is the LORD Almighty" (Isa 6:3). As God is holy so also is his Spirit. Jesus says that the Holy

Spirit will be sent by the Father "in [his] name," i.e., his task will be in accord with the character of Jesus.

If we take the last two clauses of v.26 as synonymous parallelism (so Brown, 651), the teaching work of the Spirit will be to "remind" the disciples of all that Jesus taught. It will not consist of new revelations. The Spirit will take the words of Jesus and make them known (cf. 16:13–15). He will help the disciples grasp the full meaning of what Jesus was teaching while he was with them in person. It is one thing to understand a statement as being true; it is something quite different to grasp the full meaning and significance of that truth. The Holy Spirit's teaching ministry belongs in the latter category.

Calvin, 2:88, calls the Spirit "the inward Teacher (*interior magister*)" and points out that God has two ways of teaching: first, the words that fall on our ears, and second, the inward action of the Spirit. It is still the case that biblical truth may be heard and understood without its more profound meaning laying hold of the mind and heart of the listener. Theology as an academic discipline is not the same as truth about God understood from the heart. Obviously, the "all things" taught by the Spirit does not include matters irrelevant to God's purpose in sending Jesus to be our Savior.

27 On the eve of his departure from the world, Jesus bestowed on his disciples the legacy of peace. In that day *eirēnē* ("peace," GK *1645*) was used as both a greeting (Ro 1:7) and a farewell (Mk 5:34). The Greeks thought of peace in essentially negative terms, namely, the absence of hostility. In Hebrew thought, however, peace also designated a positive sense of well-being. The LXX regularly uses *eirēnē* to translate the well-known Hebrew *šalôm* (GK 8934). Jesus further identifies peace as "my peace," the total well-being that results from a perfect relationship to God. It was *his* peace because he would purchase it by his own death and grant it as a gift to those who would accept it. Peace is a blessing that involves all the positive benefits flowing from Jesus' victory over sin and death. Like all spiritual blessings, it cannot be earned but must come as a part of the free gift of salvation.

The peace of Jesus differs from the peace that the world gives. That "peace" depends largely on circumstances, which by definition are in a state of constant flux. Tasker, 168, lists as examples of the world's peace temporary freedom from distraction and anxiety, the peace of momentary flight from all that is unpleasant, and the peace of false security. They all fall woefully short of the rich blessings of God's personal presence in the life of the believer.

The peace Jesus provides is the peace of sins forgiven and of reconciliation to God. It is a peace that "transcends all understanding" (Php 4:7). Therefore, even though Jesus will soon depart, the disciples need not be "troubled" or "afraid." (Knox translates the latter verb, *deiliaō*, GK *1262*, with "to play the coward"; Berkeley has "to be intimidated.") For the early Christians fear was incompatible with faith. Though opposition was strong, they should not be alarmed. Paul writes that not being frightened by the opposition is a sign to the opposers of their coming destruction (Php 1:28).

28 That Jesus is "going away" and "coming back" is the dominant theme of the entire chapter. Since Jesus is going to the Father, his disciples should have been filled with gladness. His departure is reason for rejoicing in that it marks the completion of his redemptive work on earth. Had the disciples been able to grasp what that would mean for the redemption of the human race they would have been overjoyed. Jesus' statement that "if they loved [him], they would be glad" should not be taken to mean that the disciples had no love at all for their Master. It was simply a vivid way of pointing out how partial was their understanding of what was happening and how incomplete was their love for him. In spite of the suffering Jesus was about to undergo, he could speak of his death in terms of a journey back to his Father. As such, it was a cause for rejoicing. The author of Hebrews reminds us that Jesus "for the joy set before him endured the cross" (Heb 12:2).

Jesus' statement that "the Father is greater than I" was used by the Arians to argue that Christ was subordinate to the Father, created but not eternal, and therefore inferior. Arianism was strongly opposed by Athanasius and rejected at the first council at Nicea in AD 325. The Athanasian Creed says that Christ is "equal to the Father as touching His Godhead, and inferior to the Father as touching His manhood." Others have argued that the Son is "inferior" in the sense that sonship implies subordination of some sort. The problem with all such metaphysical solutions is that they remove the statement from its context.

Jesus has said that his followers should have been glad that he was going to the Father *because* (*hoti*) "the Father is greater than [he.]" The last clause supplies the reason why his departure should bring joy. Interpretations that treat ontological relationships within the Godhead do not explain why there is cause for gladness. Calvin, 2:90, is certainly on the mark when he writes that Jesus was drawing a comparison "between His present state and the heavenly glory to which he was shortly to be received." In that the eternal state is infinitely more glorious than the incarnate, Jesus' departure to that realm should elicit rejoicing on the part of his followers. In any case, the statement that the Father is "greater" than the Son must be understood in the light of Jesus' clear teaching in 10:30: "I and the Father are one."

29 Jesus' purpose in telling his disciples ahead of time about what would happen is that, when it did take place, they would believe. In this context, believing means trusting in a personal sense. His departure to the Father and subsequent return is not intended to provide irrefutable proof of the superiority of the Christian faith but to encourage the disciples to place their complete trust in God.

30 The end is fast approaching. Within a short time, Judas and a detachment of soldiers, along with some religious leaders, will come to take him into custody (18:3). For Jesus, however, it is the devil who comes. People are simply the tools used by the evil one to carry out his diabolical schemes (cf. 1Jn 5:19, "the whole world is under the control of the evil one"). Satan is the "prince of this world," not in the sense that the world belongs to him or that he has any rightful claim to it, but only because God has allowed him on a temporary basis to exercise his tyranny here. The hymn "This Is My Father's World" gives expression to a theology more in line with the eternal purposes of God.

Although the arrival of the prince of this world will lead to the crucifixion, Jesus can say, "He has no hold on me." A more literal translation of *en emoi ouk exei ouden* would be "in me he has nothing." Since Jesus is without sin, the devil has no way to make an accusation against him that will hold. The clause should be taken in a legal context. Lindars, 484, writes, "From this point of view the Passion is not thought of as a struggle in which Jesus emerges as the victor, but as a court of law in which his innocence is proved."

31 It is important that the world learn of Jesus' love for the Father. This cannot be accomplished through rhetoric but only through action. While it is everywhere implied in the NT, only here do we find the specific statement that Jesus loves the Father. It is remarkable that in John 14 God is referred to as "Father" twenty-three times. The nature of God is most adequately portrayed by a metaphor taken from family life. Were God not Father, death would not be a family reunion. Jesus' love for the Father is explained by the coordinate clause, "I do exactly what my Father has commanded me." (The "and" that separates the two clauses of v.31 is epexegetical and should be translated, "that is.") The world will learn of his love by what he is about to do.

The final words of the chapter, "Come now; let us leave," have caused commentators a bit of trouble, because it is not until three chapters later that Jesus actually leaves with his disciples and crosses the Kidron Valley (18:1). Some have thought that the discourses comprising chs. 15 and 16 (and perhaps 17) were spoken along the way to Gethsemane. Others picture Jesus as continuing his teaching during the interval between the announcement of departure in 14:31 and the time when they actually left the upper room.

It is possible, however, that the final sentence should be understood on a different level. It has been noted that in normal Greek usage *agōmen* ("Let us leave," GK *72*), may imply, "Let us go to meet the advancing army" (cf. Dodd, 406–9). Furthermore, if we take the final clause as integrally related to what has preceded rather than as a somewhat out-of-place directive, then another solution appears likely. In the final verses of ch. 14, Jesus is saying, "The prince of this world is coming and he has no claim on me; yet to prove to the world my love for the Father and my willingness to do whatever he commands, let us arise and march forth to meet him." In any case, Jesus' departure to that realm should elicit rejoicing on the part of his followers.

NOTES

15 Manuscripts vary with regard to the tense and mood of the verb in the main clause of v.15. The NIV chooses the future τηρήσετε, *tērēsete* (GK *5498*), and translates, "you will obey what I command." Other translations chose the aorist imperative τηρήσατε, *tērēsate* ("keep my commandments"), while a few read the aorist subjunctive τηρήσητε, *tērēsēte*. (Brown has, "If you love me and keep my commandments.")

The first option is probably to be preferred, though the thrust of the verse is not to present a test for love but to stress that obedience stems from devotion. If we love Jesus, we will do what he commands. The obedience of a true disciple is not grudging acquiescence but the spontaneous and joyful response to an opportunity to please the Lord. Love necessarily results in a desire to please. Love is neither a sentiment nor an emotion but a relationship most convincingly authenticated by a life of obedience.

16 Thirty of the eighty-four occurrences of the emphatic κἀγώ (*kagō*, GK *2743*; "and I") are found in the fourth gospel. By comparison it occurs eight times in Matthew and six times in Luke, but not at all in Mark. Clearly, John favors the emphasis it places on the conjunction καί (*kai*, "and") when the subject of the clause is first person singular. Morris, 648 n. 40, suggests as a translation, "no less than I."

17 Apart from this one verse, the Spirit is regularly referred to throughout the fourth gospel with masculine pronouns (15:26; 16:7, 8, 13, 14). Here ὅ (*ho*) and αὐτό (*auto*) are neuter because πνεῦμα (*pneuma*, "spirit," GK *4460*) is neuter.

NA[27] has the present tense μένει (*menei*, "remains," GK *3531*) and the future tense ἔσται (*estai*, "will be"). The present μένει, *menei*, is much more probable than the future μενεῖ, *menei* (read by a few MSS), and helps to account for the present ἐστιν (*estin*), which is found in 𝔓[66*] B D* W 1. 565 *pc* it. The Spirit of truth is living *with them*, but he will take his permanent residence *in them* only after Pentecost.

3. Vital Relationships (15:1–16:4a)

OVERVIEW

Chapter 14 provided a fairly orderly presentation of the theme of Jesus' departure to the Father. The unifying theme of ch. 15 is less clear. Lindars, 486, says that the chapter seems to have been composed by bringing together several homilies preached by John on various occasions for the purpose of creating a supplementary discourse that would serve as a further exposition of 13:31–38.

There is, however, a genuine continuity that runs throughout the chapter. The first eight verses treat the relationship between the believer and Jesus; vv.9–17 speak of the relationship believers are to sustain toward one another; and vv.18–27 explain the relationship the believer will have with a hostile world. It is therefore unnecessary to conjecture various origins for supposedly separate segments. Note that the first two sections are so closely related that texts and translations differ on whether the paragraph break should be at v.9 or at v.12.

a. With the Vine—abide (15:1–11)

OVERVIEW

In ch. 14 Jesus promised not to leave his disciples as orphans (14:18). He would come again. Father and Son will make their home in the heart of the believer (14:23), and the Holy Spirit will come as Counselor and Teacher (14:26).

This new relationship between Jesus and the believer is expressed succinctly and powerfully by the analogy of the vine and the branches (15:1–8). It would be difficult to find another figure of speech that could portray the intimacy of the relationship so winsomely yet so powerfully. As a devotional classic it is unique.

[1]"I am the true vine, and my Father is the gardener. [2]He cuts off every branch in me that bears no fruit, while every branch that does bear fruit he prunes so that it will be even more fruitful. [3]You are already clean because of the word I have spoken to you. [4]Remain in me, and I will remain in you. No branch can bear fruit by itself; it must remain in the vine. Neither can you bear fruit unless you remain in me.

[5]"I am the vine; you are the branches. If a man remains in me and I in him, he will bear much fruit; apart from me you can do nothing. [6]If anyone does not remain in me, he is like a branch that is thrown away and withers; such branches are picked up, thrown into the fire and burned. [7]If you remain in me and my words remain in you, ask whatever you wish, and it will be given you. [8]This is to my Father's glory, that you bear much fruit, showing yourselves to be my disciples."

9"As the Father has loved me, so have I loved you. Now remain in my love. 10If you obey my commands, you will remain in my love, just as I have obeyed my Father's commands and remain in his love. 11I have told you this so that my joy may be in you and that your joy may be complete."

COMMENTARY

1 What was it that prompted Jesus' opening words, "I am the true vine"? Scholars who believe that the disciples left the upper room at the close of ch. 14 and were passing by the temple on the way to the garden of Gethsemane have suggested the famous golden vine, which adorned the principal gate of the temple. Others assume a eucharistic background and call attention to the "fruit of the vine" spoken of by Jesus in each of the synoptic accounts of the Last Supper (Mk 14:25 par.).

It is much more plausible that behind the figure lay the many OT references to Israel as a vine. In Psalm 80 Israel is a "vine out of Egypt" (v.8) that "took root and filled the land" (v.9) but now is "cut down" and "burned with fire" (v.16). The prophet Isaiah pictured Israel as "the vineyard of the LORD" (Isa 5:7), which "yielded only bad fruit" (5:2). Jeremiah called Israel a "corrupt, wild vine" (Jer 2:21), and Ezekiel referred to the people living in Jerusalem as a charred and useless vine (Eze 15:2–5). In the OT, wherever Israel is symbolized as a vine it is always depicted as decadent and corrupt. It is against this background that Jesus says he is the "true [i.e., "genuine" or "real"] vine." The same adjective (alēthinos, GK 240) was used earlier to describe Jesus as the "true bread from heaven" (6:32). In contrast to Israel, the vine of God that failed to produce the expected fruit, Jesus comes to them as the "true vine."

Jesus is the vine, and his Father is the gardener or "vinedresser" (RSV). Geōrgos (GK 1177) is a general term for "farmer," but here the context calls for

one who works the vineyard. Viticulture reaches back to the origins of civilization in the Near East—Noah planted a vineyard following the flood (Ge 9:20). Israel, with its bright sunshine and heavy dew in late summer, was particularly well suited for growing grapevines. Though the vines were planted in rows eight to ten feet apart, their rapid and luxuriant growth required extensive pruning.

2 Jesus says that his Father "cuts off every branch . . . that bears no fruit." He also "trims clean" (Knox) those that do bear fruit. Some writers find here a reference to the two kinds of pruning practiced in ancient times. In early spring (February or March) the dead wood unable to bear fruit was cut away. Later, when the blossoms had become ripening grapes (August), the little shoots that had appeared were cut away so that the main fruitbearing branches would receive all the nourishment. There is an interesting play on words in v.2 between airei ("cuts off," GK 149) and kathairei ("trims clean," "prunes," GK 2748), especially since katharoi ("clean," GK 2754) is used in the following verse.

The question of the identity of these nonfruitbearing branches is often posed. Some understand a reference to the Jewish nation (cf. Ro 11:17–24); others see a reference to apostate Christians (since Jesus says that the branches to be cut off are "in me"). It is better to understand the cutting out of dead wood as a vivid way of saying that where there is no life, there is no vital connection with the vine. Branches that produce no fruit are worthless and need to be cleared away. The fruit produced by a good branch is likeness to Christ. Paul identifies the fruit of the Spirit as "love, joy, peace, patience, kindness, goodness, faithfulness, gentleness and self-control" (Gal 5:22–23).

Branches that do bear fruit Jesus prunes. Since *kathairō* (lit., "to make clean") may be understood in both the figurative sense of moral purification and the more literal sense of pruning, it serves well the dual reference of the analogy. Branches are pruned so they will become more fruitful. God's "pruning" is his gracious way of directing the flow of spiritual energy in order that his plans for our lives will be realized. While pruning is painful, it serves the necessary purpose of removing those branches that would otherwise absorb our time and energy in unproductive pursuits. The well-trimmed branch is, as hymnist Elizabeth Clephane puts it, "content to let the world go by, to know no gain nor loss." Temple, 2:256–57, offers the important insight that the world doesn't understand the suffering of the innocent because it begins with the crude notion of justice as consisting in a correlation of pain and guilt; but pain is evil only in a secondary sense, and for the believer there is an "ennobling pain" we should welcome because it increases our capacity to bear fruit. Thus James can say that we should "consider it pure joy" when we "face trials of many kinds" (Jas 1:2).

3 Jesus tells his disciples that they are "already clean," i.e., the pruning *has* taken place (cf. the identical phrase, *hymeis katharoi este*, in 13:10). The instrument for cleansing is the word Jesus had spoken to them. Jesus' *logos* (singular "word," GK *3364*) is his teaching in its entirety (cf. *rhēmata*, "individual utterances," GK *4839*, in v.7). The cleansing power of the word of God is taught throughout Scripture. In answer to the question, "How can a young man keep his way pure?" the psalmist replies, "By living according to [God's] word" (Ps 119:9). Paul writes that the church is cleansed "by the indwelling of the word of God" (W. J. Conybeare's translation of Eph 5:26 in *The Epistles of Paul* [Grand Rapids: Zondervan, 1958]). It is impossible to expose oneself prayerfully and systematically to the word of God and fail to experience its cleansing power. God's word is truth (Jn 17:17), and truth brings to light duplicitous conduct as well as theological error. Those who desire moral cleansing will respond with humility and gratitude to the purifying influence of truth.

4 The central focus of Jesus' teaching in this opening paragraph is found here: "Remain in me, and I will remain in you." Since a verb must be supplied in the Greek text for the second clause, the NIV adds, "will remain." Moffatt has, "as I remain in you." Morris, 670, favors taking the second clause as a continuation of the command in the first clause and translates, "and see that I abide in you." A more satisfactory approach is to allow the ambiguous relationship between the clauses to remain and to see in the sentence as a whole the dual condition that we as believers are to bring into being. Jesus is setting before us the prospect of the mutual indwelling of Jesus and those who will abide in him. So central is this mutual indwelling to what it means to be a Christian that Temple, 2:258, can say, "Whatever leads to this is good; whatever hinders this is bad; whatever does not bear on this is futile."

The verb "remain" occurs ten times in the first eleven verses of ch. 15. For a branch to bear fruit it must share the life of the vine. Likewise, for believers to bear fruit they must remain in Christ. All spiritual power for living out the Christian life comes from God. There is only one way for a believer to receive this power, namely, to remain in unbroken fellowship with the source of power. Paul pictures the relationship in terms of a spiritual death and resurrection: "I have been crucified with Christ and I no longer live, but Christ lives in me" (Gal 2:20).

5 Thus far in the allegory it has been assumed that the branches are to be understood as the disciples. Here this identity is confirmed: "I am the vine; you are the branches." Jesus does not say that he is the stem and we are the branches. As vine he is both stem and branches. We are included in him (cf. the analogous figure of Christ as the whole body [1Co 12:12] while at the same time its head [Eph 4:15]). The life of the branch is the life of the vine. The branch has no life of its own. For this reason it must remain in the vine.

Jesus promises that if we as branches remain in him (and he in us), we will "bear much fruit." The life of the believer who abides in Christ cannot help but be productive. Fruit is the necessary result of maintaining a vital relationship with the vine. "Apart from me," says Jesus, "you can do nothing." Cut off from the source of life, the branch will wither and die. Cut off from Christ by an unwillingness to abide, the professing Christian will be unable to produce fruit or, for that matter, do anything of spiritual consequence.

6 Branches separated from the vine wither and are good for nothing but to be burned. If a person does not remain in Christ, he or she shares the fate of the withered branch, which is "picked up, thrown into the fire and burned." The present article before "fire" favors a reference to the well-known fire of eschatological punishment. The two Greek verbs translated "thrown away" and "withers" are both in the aorist (past) tense. This unexpected and abrupt change of tense implies that the penalty for failing to abide is immediate and final. Although the grammar is awkward, the meaning is clear: to have severed the life-giving relationship with Christ is to have been cast out to be burned (cf. Mt 3:10). The penalty and the separation are simultaneous.

Some have used v.6 to claim that people can lose their salvation. Since the branches are "in [Christ]" (vv.2, 6), and if they do not remain in him, they are burned in fire (v.6), it would seem that believers who fail to maintain a vital relationship with Christ will suffer the flames of eternal punishment. Theological questions of this magnitude, however, must never be decided on the basis of secondary elements in an allegory. The nature and extent of eternal punishment should be determined by less figurative passages found elsewhere in Scripture.

7 In vv.4 and 5 it was Jesus who would abide in the believer, while in v.7 it is "[his] words." To meditate on the words of Jesus is to be in communion with him. His sayings are not mere words on a piece of paper but the occasion for a genuine encounter with the living Christ. When we open ourselves to the words of Jesus, we discover that we are in dialogue with Jesus himself. Such is the mystery of the word of God (Heb 4:12; cf. Ro 1:16).

One of the most far-reaching benefits of abiding in Christ is answered prayer. Those who maintain a vital relationship with Christ may "ask whatever [they] wish, and it will be given [them]." Most manuscripts have the future indicative *aitēsesthe* ("you will ask," GK *160*), yet most translators prefer the aorist imperative *aitēsasthe* ("ask"). A few have the infinitive, which would yield, "whatever you wish to ask will be done." The prayers of Christians who abide in Christ are answered because "whatever [they] wish" turns out to be what he would like to see happen. The fruit that we bear is the direct result of God's activity released by our prayers. Prayer has always been the primary ingredient in any significant advance of God's kingdom on earth. Mary, queen of Scots, once said that she feared the prayers of John Knox more than an army of twenty thousand men. God's purposes in history are realized when believers, through fellowship with him, come to understand his will and then by prayer release him to act redemptively in the world.

8 An abundance of fruit indicates a healthy vine. When the "fruit of the Spirit" is abundantly present in the lives of Christians, God is glorified. The last clause of v.8 is difficult. Some manuscripts understand the clause as dependent on *hina* and read the aorist subjunctive *genēsthe* ("that you become," GK *1181*). In this case the latter clause is coordinate with the preceding *pherēte* ("that you bear," GK *5770*) and makes the point that the Father is glorified not only by their bearing much fruit but also by their continuing as disciples. Other manuscripts read the future *genēsesthe* ("you will be"), which makes the clause somewhat independent and sees the bearing of fruit as the evidence of their discipleship (NIV, "showing yourselves to be my disciples"; NASB, "that you bear much fruit, and *so* prove to be My disciples"). In Greek the expression "much fruit" (in both v.5 and v.8) is *karpos polys* (GK *2843, 4498*). It has been suggested that Polycarp, bishop of Smyrna, who was burned at the stake for his allegiance to Jesus, got his name from these verses in John 15.

9–10 The measure of the Father's love for the Son is the measure of the Son's love for the disciples. Since the Son lived a life of perfect obedience and spoke only what the Father told him to speak (8:28; 12:50), it is not surprising that the Father's love for the Son would be duplicated in the love of the Son for his disciples. The responsibility of the disciples is to "remain in [his] love" (cf. the parallel in Jude 21, "Keep yourselves in God's love").

How this is accomplished is clearly set forth in the following sentence: "If you obey my commands, you will remain in my love" (v.10). Love for God is defined in 1 John 5:3 as "obeying his commands." The model for Christian obedience is the obedience of the Son ("just as I have obeyed my Father's commands"). Christian ethics are integrally related to the person and conduct of Jesus himself. Obedience should not be thought of as simply compliance with a set of regulations but as wholehearted commitment to a way of life springing from and expressing the very nature of God. Obedience is not

burdensome. Jesus said, "My yoke is easy and my burden is light" (Mt 11:32). Satan wants to make us think of obedience as restrictive and palpably unfair (cf. Ge 3:1–5); in actuality, obedience frees us to become everything that someday we will rejoice to be. In the meantime we will find that the enjoyment of each day is determined by our willingness to allow our lives to be directed by the express will of God.

11 Jesus has a twofold purpose for telling his disciples "these things" (the NIV's "this" overlooks the plural *tauta* and tends to restrict the reference to what was said in v.10). His first purpose is "that my joy may be in you." This could mean the joy that comes to Jesus as a result of the obedience of his disciples; but more likely it means the joy that he already possesses, the "joy of unbroken communion" (Temple, 2:265) or the "joy of doing the Father's will" (Reith, 105). Joy springs from obedience and love. To "my peace" (14:27) and "my love" (15:10) Jesus now adds "my joy" (Bruce, 311). Up to this point in the gospel, the word "joy" was used only in 3:29. From this point on, in the Upper Room Discourse alone it occurs seven times (15:11; 16:20–24; 17:13). Paradoxical as it may seem, it is on the very eve of Jesus' crucifixion that he emphasizes joy so strongly.

Jesus' second purpose is "that [their] joy may be complete"—a purpose not realized apart from the first. A causative relationship exists between the presence of the joy that is Jesus' and the bringing to completeness of the joy of the disciples. The life of the disciple is not an imitation of Christ but the result of Christ in that life. Insofar as being a Christian calls for a supernatural life, every attempt to duplicate it apart from Christ himself is doomed to failure. Our joy is his joy in us. It is not the result of pleasant circumstances but of wholehearted obedience. Morris, 674, notes that "to be halfhearted is to get the worst of both worlds."

NOTES

2 In an attempt to avoid the difficulty of what appears to be the meaning here, i.e., that non-fruitbearing branches (believers?) are cut off from the vine (lose their salvation?), some have pointed out that the Greek αἴρω (*airō*, GK *149*) may mean "to lift up," which in this context could mean to "prop up" (a weak branch) so it can bear more fruit. Though αἴρω, *airō*, means "to pick up" in verses such as 8:59 (Jesus' opponents "picked up" stones to throw at him), it is used more often by John in the sense of "to take away" (cf. 11:39; 16:22 et al.). The suggestion also meets the considerable obstacle posed by the fact that such branches are "thrown into the fire and burned" (v.6).

8 The UBS committee finally chose the aorist subjunctive γένησθε (*genēsthe*) on the basis of the age and diversity of the external support (P⁶⁶ᵛⁱᵈ B D L X Θ Π 0250 *f*¹ 565 1079 et al.; cf. Metzger, 209). The future indicative γενήσεσθε (*genēsesthe*) is read by ℵ A and the majority of the Byzantine MSS.

b. With one another—love (15:12–17)

OVERVIEW

In John 13:34, Jesus gave his disciples a "new command"—they were to love one another. Verses 12–17 of ch. 15 now expand that theme. This section begins and ends with the injunction to "love each other." With this step the "triad of love" is complete: the Father loves the Son (v.9), the Son loves the disciples (v.9), the disciples love each other (v.12). As Jesus is the paradigm for obedience (v.10), so also is he the paradigm for love (v.12: "as I have loved you").

> ¹²"My command is this: Love each other as I have loved you. ¹³Greater love has no one than this, that he lay down his life for his friends. ¹⁴You are my friends if you do what I command. ¹⁵I no longer call you servants, because a servant does not know his master's business. Instead, I have called you friends, for everything that I learned from my Father I have made known to you. ¹⁶You did not choose me, but I chose you and appointed you to go and bear fruit—fruit that will last. Then the Father will give you whatever you ask in my name. ¹⁷This is my command: Love each other."

COMMENTARY

12 It is worth noting that the aorist tense (*ēgapēsa*, GK *26*, "loved") is used to call attention to the love of Jesus as demonstrated once and for all on the cross, while the present tense (*agapate*) is used to stress the continuous relationship of love that should exist between believers.

13 The ultimate proof of love is the willingness to sacrifice one's life for a friend. In a very few hours this rather general statement will be infused with new and heightened significance. Jesus' love for his own will be incontrovertibly demonstrated by his death on the cross. His willingness to sacrifice his life for his followers validates his claim to be the good shepherd who "lays down his life for the sheep" (10:11). Some have questioned whether dying for friends is the greatest proof of love, since Paul argues that the greatness of God's love is seen in the death of Christ for sinners rather than for the righteous (Ro 5:6–7). The context in John answers this query. Jesus is with friends, and there is no greater way for a person to prove his or her love for a friend than to die for that friend.

14 The disciples will prove their friendship by their willingness to do what Jesus commands. While this does not mean that Jesus offers a conditional friendship, it does indicate that friendship is a reciprocal relationship. The disciples do not earn Jesus' friendship by their obedience; they give evidence that such a friendship does in fact exist. Kysar, 240, notes that the definition of Jesus' friends as those he loves so dearly that he will sacrifice himself in death for them "bursts the normal boundaries of our everyday use of the word friends."

15 Jesus is able to call his disciples "friends" rather than servants because he has taken them fully into his confidence and shared with them everything that he has learned from his Father. "Everything that I have learned" should be taken in the general sense of all that is appropriate for their spiritual welfare at that time. It does not conflict with Jesus' statement in 16:12 that there is more to be said but they are not yet ready for it.

Jesus no longer calls his disciples servants, "because a servant does not know his master's business." The high regard for freedom among the Greeks led them to scorn slavery. In the Jewish community, however, the designation *doulos* ("servant," "slave," GK *1528*) could connote honor or

respect. In Judges 2:8 [LXX] Joshua is called a *doulos kyriou* (cf. the reference to Abraham, Ps 105:42, and to David, Ps 89:3). As Jesus uses the term here, the servant is simply one who has not been taken into his master's confidence. The servant's responsibility is to obey without questioning.

That Jesus "no longer" calls his disciples servants does not imply that until this point he regarded them as such. The purpose of the statement is to stress the point that now (in contrast to some former period) they have been brought to an understanding of the Father's purpose in sending the Son. As friends they share the secret of the incarnation. In times of difficulty, when we may be tempted to think that God has removed himself from us and concealed his plans, it is good to remember that we are still friends of Jesus and as such have access to insights unavailable to the unbeliever.

In ancient days there were in the royal court select groups known as "friends of the king." These exclusive cliques enjoyed free access to the throne room and maintained an intimate relationship with the king. Of all the OT patriarchs, only Abraham is called "[God's] friend" (Isa 41:8). In Genesis 18:17 God asks, "Shall I hide from Abraham what I am about to do?" That the expected answer is a strong "no" is reflected in the LXX, which understands the "question" as a strongly negative statement ("I will never ever hide from Abraham my servant what I will do"). God shares his plans with his friends!

16 It was common practice for a disciple to choose the rabbi under whom he wished to study. Not so in the case of Jesus' disciples: "You did not choose me, but I chose you." In spiritual matters the initiative is always God's. Our activity is a response to his prior action. The election spoken of here was not to eternal life but to fruit bearing. They were chosen and appointed to "go and bear fruit." Even Calvin, 2:102, says that this verse "does not treat of the common election of believers" but "of that special election by which He appointed His disciples to the office of preaching the Gospel." Appointment to the apostolic office was first of all a mandate to go as an emissary of Jesus. Second, it involved bearing fruit—in context, the conversion of those who hear the message (cf. 4:36). If the fruit of v.16 were the same as the fruit of vv.2–5 (the inner graces and outer conduct resulting from the presence of the Spirit in the life of the Christian), there would be no particular reason why the disciples should "go."

We typically think of prayer as a prerequisite for bearing fruit. The final clause of v.16 reverses the order (unless the two *hina* clauses are to be taken as coordinate—an unlikely case, since we were not chosen so that our prayers would be answered). Jesus says that fruit bearing prompts the Father to "give you whatever you ask in my name" (cf. Mt 7:7).

Bearing fruit indicates that the believer has responded to the charge to "go" and carry out this divinely ordained mission. A life of obedience allows the Father to answer the requests we make as representatives of his Son. The ministry of believers extends in time the ministry of Jesus.

17 The paragraph closes as it began with the command to "love each other" (cf. v.12). The more intimate our friendship with Jesus the greater will be our love for one another. As the spokes on a wheel converge as they near the hub, so also are the bonds of Christian love strengthened as believers move ever closer in fellowship with the one who is perfect love. The word "this" (*tauta*) at the beginning of the verse is plural in Greek. The sentence seems to say that all Jesus has taught can be summarized in the one command that we love each other.

NOTES

13 The term "friend(s)" (φίλος, *philos*, GK *5813*) occurs six times in the fourth gospel. In 3:29 John the Baptist speaks of the "friend who attends the bridegroom," and in 19:12 the Jews tell Pilate that if he releases Jesus he is no "friend of Caesar." In the other four cases it is Jesus who is speaking. Talking with his disciples he refers to Lazarus as "our friend" (11:11). The remaining three occurrences are found here in vv.13–15. It is easy to understand how it would be John, "the beloved disciple," who would call attention to what it means to be a friend of the Lord. Of the sixteen occurrences of the term in the Synoptics, only once is it used in connection with the relationship between Jesus and his disciples (Lk 12:4).

14 When a pronoun is the subject of a clause or a sentence, it is included in the verb itself. When the text includes the pronoun as well, the intent is to provide emphasis. Here ὑμεῖς (*hymeis*, "you") and ἐγώ (*egō*, "I") perform this function: *You*, not the world at large, are my friends in that you will carry out the things that *I*, not someone else, have commanded.

c. With the world—rejection (15:18–16:4a)

OVERVIEW

The third section of John 15 deals with the relationship between the disciple and the world. In the NT, the word *kosmos* ("world," GK *3180*) stands for the human system that opposes God's purpose (cf. *TDNT* 3:893, "the world is the epitome of unredeemed creation"). While the synoptic writers use *kosmos* only fifteen times, it is found almost eighty times in the fourth gospel (six times in 6:18–19 alone). Verse 17 closed with the admonition that the disciples love one another. They are to be known

for their love. The world, on the other hand, is known for its hatred—first for Jesus and then for those who follow him.

18"If the world hates you, keep in mind that it hated me first. 19If you belonged to the world, it would love you as its own. As it is, you do not belong to the world, but I have chosen you out of the world. That is why the world hates you. 20Remember the words I spoke to you: 'No servant is greater than his master.' If they persecuted me, they will persecute you also. If they obeyed my teaching, they will obey yours also. 21They will treat you this way because of my name, for they do not know the One who sent me. 22If I had not come and spoken to them, they would not be guilty of sin. Now, however, they have no excuse for their sin. 23He who hates me hates my Father as well. 24If I had not done among them what no one else did, they would not be guilty of sin. But now they have seen these miracles, and yet they have hated both me and my Father. 25But this is to fulfill what is written in their Law: 'They hated me without reason.'

26"When the Counselor comes, whom I will send to you from the Father, the Spirit of truth who goes out from the Father, he will testify about me. 27And you also must testify, for you have been with me from the beginning.

16:1"All this I have told you so that you will not go astray. 2They will put you out of the synagogue; in fact, a time is coming when anyone who kills you will think he is offering a service to God. 3They will do such things because they have not known the Father or me. 4I have told you this, so that when the time comes you will remember that I warned you."

COMMENTARY

18 "If the world hates you" is a conditional clause that assumes the premise to be true. The world *does* hate the disciple. Lindars speaks of a Semitic use of the love/hate antithesis in which the words lack emotional intensity (493) and "merely express contrasting attitudes" (429). But if "to hate" means no more than "to prefer less," then it is difficult to see how such a mild emotion could drive people to crucify Jesus. The history of martyrdom is a graphic portrayal of the world's intense hostility toward those who took their Christian faith with all seriousness. Wherever and whenever the church has

spoken with conviction against the injustices in society, it has experienced the wrath of those who benefit from the status quo.

Barclay, 2:184, suggests that the name "Christian" was hated because followers of Christ were rumored to be insurrectionists, cannibals, incendiaries, flagrantly immoral people, and those who tried to divide families. Fraudulent and misinformed charges such as these were in fact leveled at the primitive church, but the actual cause for their being hated was that Christians advocated a set of values that were fundamentally opposed to those of the pagan world.

There is nothing quite as upsetting as to have one's essential value-orientation called into question. Christians were an ethical burr under the saddle of secular society. Hatred was the result. Speaking of the world's hatred of God, and of man for God's sake, Reith, 2:107, says rather poetically that the wave that began to rise with the murder of Abel by his brother Cain gathered through the ages until it "broke in fury on the cross, and we are struggling in its broken waters." When we find ourselves overlooked or opposed by contemporary ideology, we must remember Jesus' words: "it hated me first." Hatred for the believer is hatred for the One whose life is being lived out through the believer. It is persecution based on association. It is "enduring what still needs to be endured of Christ's sorrows" (Col 1:24 Beck).

19 In contrast to the simple condition of v.18, "if you belonged to the world" of v.19 is a contrary-to-fact conditional clause. If it were true (and of course it isn't) that the disciples belonged to this world, then it would love them as its own. It is impossible for the world not to love its own minions. Such love is self-love, and the *kosmos* is not about to deny itself the mindless adulation of self-approval. The disciple, however, does not belong to this world but has been chosen "out of the world." The action of Jesus in choosing is emphasized by the presence of the personal pronoun *egō* ("I"). He himself is the one who has selected out his followers from among those who live without regard for God in the world. To be chosen out of the world does not imply some sort of other-worldly pietism—it simply designates believers as a group that have been removed from the secular mind-set of society and given the new perspective of God's plan for the human race. Temple, 2:272, notes that the antagonism of the world against Christians stems from the fact that those who began *in* the world have separated themselves *from* the world. He writes that the world "would not hate angels for being

angelic; but it does hate men for being Christians. It grudges them their new character; it is tormented by their peace; it is infuriated by their joy." "That is why the world hates you," says Jesus, because "I have chosen you out of the world."

20 In vv.20–25 Jesus speaks of the reaction of the world, first to what he has said and then to what he has done. In v.20 he reminds the disciples of his words, "No servant is greater than his master." It is interesting that earlier (in 13:16) this proverbial statement was applied in context to strengthen the admonition for humble service. Since Jesus (the Master) washed the feet of the disciples (the servants), in the same way they ought to serve one another. The same statement is used here to emphasize that "if they persecuted me [the Master], they will persecute you [the servants] also." If all the words of Jesus had been recorded (cf. 21:25!), we would undoubtedly discover that the same proverbial statement had been applied in other situations as well. This serves to remind us, as translation expert Eugene Nida used to say, that "words [and phrases] bleed their meaning from the context."

21 Whatever happens to the disciples happens because of their relationship to Jesus. Whatever the world did to Jesus it will also do to those who bear his name. Jesus had warned his followers that they would be persecuted (Mt 10:16–25). At the end of his ministry the apostle Paul had ample reason to write, "Everyone who wants to live a godly life in Christ Jesus will be persecuted" (2Ti 3:12; cf. 2Co 11:23–27). Christians need to be sure, however, that any persecution that comes their way is the result of their close association with Jesus and not due to personal idiosyncrasies that unnecessarily offend.

Jesus states the ultimate reason for persecution: the world does "not know the One who sent me." Willful ignorance of God leads to violent opposition. The spirit of rebellion, which has marked the human race from the beginning, relentlessly opposes anything that unmasks its true identity as malignantly antithetical to all God is and all he stands for.

22–23 Jesus can say that if he had not come and spoken to his opponents, they would not be guilty of sin. In the presence of Jesus, there is no neutral ground. His claims call for decision. While his purpose in coming was to "save his people from their sins" (Mt 1:21), the inescapable consequence of that coming for those who refused him was the revelation of their sinfulness and an intensification of their guilt. Their prior condition was not one of immunity from sin in general (Ro 1:20 judges the entire world to be "without excuse") but one in which they were exempt from the sin of rejecting the clear revelation of God in the incarnate Christ. Truth must be acknowledged. It would be better not to know than to know and refuse. The sin of darkness is the rejection of light.

Had Jesus not come, the world would not have been responsible for refusing him. "Now [Brown, 688, says *nyn* combined with *de* means "in reality"], however, they have no excuse for their sin." The die has been cast, and the result cannot be altered. To refuse Jesus is to hate him, and "he who hates me," says Jesus, "hates my Father as well" (v.23).

24 Had Jesus not come and spoken to the world, it would have had no sin to answer for (v.22); in v.24, had he not "done among them what no one else did," they would have been blameless. Not only Jesus' words but also his mighty works leave people without excuse for their sin. Although the miracles of Jesus were never intended to force a person to believe— after all, faith by definition is a free response—they do serve to encourage and support belief. In 14:11 Jesus chided his disciples that if they couldn't believe on the basis of what he said, then "at least believe on the evidence of the miracles themselves" (cf. 5:36).

It is no longer possible for the world to plead innocent because "they have seen these miracles, and yet they have hated both [Jesus] and [his] Father."

Both verbs are perfect in tense (*heōrakasin*, GK *3972*; *memisēkasin*, GK *3631*) and thus connote a permanent state. There can be no denying that they witnessed the truth of God revealed in Christ. The result of that exposure to revelation continues. So also does their hatred for the Father and for the Son who came to reveal him. The world is unalterably opposed to God. Their guilty conscience will not allow them the freedom to disregard completely a loyalty they sense they still owe to their Creator. Their hatred gives expression to the frustration of not being able to escape totally from the constraints of conscience. Exposure to truth simply heightens their antagonism to what they know to be right.

25 Ironically, the world's hatred fulfills "what is written in their Law: 'They hated me without reason.'" The quotation gives expression to a thought clearly set forth in the psalms (35:19; 69:4; 109:3). Strictly defined, the Law comprised the first five books of the OT; it was often used, however, to refer to Scripture in general. Jesus calls it "their Law" not to praise his opponents but to point out that their antagonism toward him is foretold in their own authoritative Scriptures. They are condemned by their own Law.

It is incredible that created beings should hate their Creator. He has done nothing to merit their hostility. The hatred of the world for God is understandable only on the basis of the tragic fall of humanity from its original place of honor. Created for fellowship with God, Adam bought into Satan's lie that God's plans were restrictive and that by an act of disobedience he could discover true freedom. The spiritual, intellectual, and psychological distortion resulting from sin has convinced people that God seeks to undermine what little fulfillment they know and wants to make them captive and dependent again. No wonder the world hates God! And how sad that this very hatred separates the world from the only remedy that can cure its malignancy.

26 Once again, Jesus refers to "the Counselor," whom he will send to the disciples from the Father (cf. 14:16). The Counselor is described as the "Spirit of truth" (cf. 14:17) who "goes out from the Father." On the basis of this clause the Eastern church argued for the eternal procession of the Spirit from the Father alone. The Western church, following the Council of Nicea in AD 325, added to the Nicene Creed what is known as the "*filioque* clause" ("and from the Son") in order to safeguard the vital truth that the Son is consubstantial with the Father; it became the main doctrinal issue in the rupture between East and West in 1054 (see Walter A. Elwell, ed., *Evangelical Dictionary of Theology* [Grand Rapids: Baker, 1984], 415). The text in John, however, is not dealing with the internal relationships of the Trinity. To go out from the Father means nothing more than to be sent from him. The different expressions are literary, not theological.

27 Jesus declares that the mission of the Counselor is to "testify about [him]" (v.26; cf. Jn 16:13–15), and he immediately adds, "And you also must testify." This juxtaposition suggests that the testifying of the disciples is not something in addition to the witness of the Counselor but the means by which the Counselor carries out his mission.

We are reminded of the synoptic teaching that when the disciples are put on trial, they are not to worry about what they should say because the Holy Spirit will be speaking through them (Mk 13:11). This same ministry of the Spirit will take place in our every witness concerning Jesus (but should never be thought of as an effortless method of sermon preparation!).

The disciples were enabled to testify because they had been with Jesus "from the beginning," i.e., since the beginning of his ministry (Hoskyns, 482, has, "since their conversion"; cf. Ac 1:21–22). The primary function of the apostle is to bear witness to Jesus. While humanitarian deeds are appropriate expressions of God's love for the world, the critical need of the human race is to know who Jesus is and what he has accomplished for their redemption.

16:1 Jesus' teaching on the theme of persecution began at 15:18 and is brought to a close at 16:4a. Unfortunately, the chapter division tends to separate the last four verses of the discussion from what has preceded. Jesus has told his disciples to expect the hatred of the world, with all the persecution that accompanies it, "so that you will not go astray." He makes it perfectly clear that if they follow him, they will inevitably incur the hostility of the world (cf. the predictions of persecution, Mt 10:17–25). It would not be long until faithfulness to Jesus would require nothing less than the willingness to lay down one's life as a martyr. There is a brand of popular Christianity that caters to people's natural desire for wealth and success. It teaches that God wants his followers to be "healthy, wealthy, and wise." All such travesties of biblical truth misconstrue the doctrine of grace and conveniently overlook the crucial fact that to live like Jesus is to be treated like Jesus.

The "all this" to which Jesus refers (the pronoun is plural, *tauta*, "these things") is the teaching on persecution beginning at 15:18, not simply the reference to the coming of the Spirit of truth mentioned in 15:26–27. His concern is that the disciples will not "go astray." The Greek word is *skandalizō*, GK *4997*, from which we get the expression "to scandalize," i.e., "to shock by something disgraceful." In context it means, "to offend so as to fall away." The etymology of the term suggests a certain unexpectedness. (The cognate noun *skandalon* was a trap laid for an enemy, and the *skandalēthron* was the bait stick, which when touched allowed the trap to close suddenly.)

More often than not, our loyalty to Jesus is tested in crises that arise without warning. We are more apt to fail in the unexpected trials of daily life than in some great test of loyalty for which we have been preparing over the years. Peter "stumbled" at the accusation of the high priest's maid that he had been with the Nazarene Jesus (Mk 14:66–68). Jesus taught his followers about the coming persecution so that when it did come, they would be less likely to compromise their faith and fall away. Earlier Jesus had pronounced a blessing on "the man who does not fall away on account of me" (Mt 11:6).

2 Until the Edict of Milan was issued in AD 313, when the emperors Constantine and Licinius granted religious tolerance to Christians, those who professed Christian faith suffered great persecution under Rome. Haenchen, 2:142, writes, "Christians were the non-conformists par excellence in antiquity and they had to pay for that." The persecution to which Jesus refers here, however, had its origin in the opposition to the Christian faith that arose within Judaism ("They will put you out of the synagogue").

It is difficult for us to understand how profoundly disturbing excommunication would have been to a first-century Jewish Christian. John 12:42 reports that many of the leaders who heard Jesus speak "believed in him," but "because of the Pharisees they would not confess their faith for fear they would be put out of the synagogue" (cf. 9:22). Wherever a specific religious commitment is the primary force providing the cohesive element within society, deviation from that commitment is a matter of utmost concern.

Jesus' call to follow him was revolutionary. From the standpoint of the leaders of Judaism, it brought into question the validity of their religious tradition. Their only recourse was to punish by excommunication. It is quite possible that some forms of current Christianity have also elevated their "tradition" to a point where faithfulness to the clear teachings of Jesus is deemed as sufficient reason for removal from the circles of influence. The most severe persecution has always come as the result of religious deviation.

Jesus says that the religious leaders who will carry out the coming persecution will be so certain that what they are doing is pleasing to God that "anyone who kills you will think he is offering a service to God." Acts 7:57–60 records the stoning of Stephen, who was "guilty" of preaching a sermon that did not please the chief priest and his cohorts. Paul was present on that occasion (v.58) and later, in his defense before Agrippa, details his own persecution of the church (Ac 26:9–11). It should be noted that earnestness in religion has nothing to do with correctness of faith. If that were so, the persecution of Christians, to say nothing of the crucifixion of Jesus, would stand as a persuasive example of self-validating religion.

The word for "service" (*latreia*, GK *3301*) denotes the idea of worship (Ro 9:4; Heb 9:6) as well as the more general concept of service to God (Ro 12:1). Knox translates this to read that anyone who kills a disciple "will claim that he is performing an act of worship to God." An ancient midrash on Numbers 25:13 reads, "Whoever sheds the blood of the godless is as one who offers a sacrifice" (*Num. Rab.* 21.4). Persecution is never more intense than where violence is given a religious sanction. Historically, holy wars have been the least holy. Temple, 2:277, remarks that it is the religious conscientiousness of the persecutor that makes him so relentless.

3 The reason the early church will suffer such persecution is that the persecutors have not known either Jesus or the Father. Had they really known the One whom they professed to worship, they would have recoiled from such blasphemous conduct.

4a In 13:19 and 14:29 Jesus told his disciples that he had taught them certain things ahead of time so that when those things came to pass, they would believe. He now says that his teaching on the coming persecution will serve to forewarn them, so that when it does happen, they will remember his words of caution. The pronoun *egō* ("I") is emphatic and stresses the importance Jesus places on his own testimony to the band of disciples.

NOTES

22 The expression "to have sin" (the verb ἔχω, *echō*, plus the noun ἁμαρτία, *hamartia*; NIV, "be guilty of sin") is found only in the Johannine material in the NT (9:41; 15:22, 24; 19:11; 1Jn 1:8). Morris, 681 n. 53, notes that it "implies that the sin in question remains like a personal possession with the person who commits it."

24 The NASB understands the latter part of v.24 as saying that the object of the "seeing" as well as the "hating" refers to the Father in addition to the Son ("but now they have both seen and hated Me and My Father as well"). While such an understanding of the first "both . . . and" construction is grammatically possible, it is ruled out by the obvious fact that the world has not "seen" the Father. While the disciples may be said to have "seen" the Father by virtue of having seen the Son (14:9), this cannot be said of those who hate the Father. The NIV more accurately has the world seeing the miracles performed by Jesus and hating both the Father and the Son.

26 The masculine demonstrative pronoun ἐκεῖνος (*ekeinos*) refers back to ὁ παράκλητος (*ho paraklētos*, "the Counselor," GK *4156*), though the intervening clause, being closer, might suggest that the antecedent would be "the Spirit of truth." This is unlikely because the expression is modified by a relative pronoun (ὅ, *ho*) that is neuter. The neuter is determined by the case of its antecedent, τὸ πνεῦμα (*to pneuma*, "the Spirit," GK *4460*).

16:3 Jesus' oneness with the Father is implied by his assertion that those who will persecute the disciples have not known either the Father or the Son. To know the Son is to know the Father. Ignorance of the one implies ignorance of the other (cf. 8:19).

4. The Work of the Holy Spirit (16:4b–15)

OVERVIEW

Much of Jesus' teaching in ch. 16 is indirect and difficult to understand with complete clarity. The disciples seem to be confused about what he is saying to them. In vv.12–13 Jesus indicated that there was more that he wanted to teach them, but until the Spirit came they would be unable to bear it. The inadequacy of the disciples is reflected in the diffi-culty presented by the chapter as a whole. Ryle, 4:409, notes that "nowhere in Scripture . . . do commentators appear to me to contribute so little light to the text as in their interpretation of this chapter." While the situation may not be quite so bleak, it is true that many of the statements in the chapter continue to receive a less-than-satisfactory explanation.

4b"I did not tell you this at first because I was with you.

5"Now I am going to him who sent me, yet none of you asks me, 'Where are you going?' 6Because I have said these things, you are filled with grief. 7But I tell you the truth: It is for your good that I am going away. Unless I go away, the Counselor will not come to you; but if I go, I will send him to you. 8When he comes, he will convict the world of guilt in regard to sin and righteousness and judgment: 9in regard to sin, because men do not believe in me; 10in regard to righteousness, because I am going to the Father, where you can see me no longer; 11and in regard to judgment, because the prince of this world now stands condemned.

12"I have much more to say to you, more than you can now bear. 13But when he, the Spirit of truth, comes, he will guide you into all truth. He will not speak on his own; he will speak only what he hears, and he will tell you what is yet to come. 14He will bring glory to me by taking from what is mine and making it known to you. 15All that belongs to the Father is mine. That is why I said the Spirit will take from what is mine and make it known to you."

COMMENTARY

4b The argument for taking the second sentence in v.4 with the verse that follows rests on the comparison of "at first" in v.4b and "now" in v.5. At first (lit., "from [the] beginning," i.e., "from the beginning of their association with him") Jesus did not tell his disciples about the inevitability of persecution; but now he is returning to the Father, and the hatred that is about to nail him to the cross will very shortly be redirected at those who take up his mission. As long as Jesus was with his followers, the world focused its hostility on him. Once he is gone it will be a different story.

In Revelation 12 the great red dragon, thwarted in his attempt to devour the male child (vv.4–6) and enraged by his failure to drown the woman (vv.15–16), goes off "to make war against the rest of her offspring—those who keep God's commandments and hold to the testimony of Jesus" (v.17). The persecution of the church has its origin in the cosmic struggle between God and Satan. The virulence of the world's opposition to Jesus is mute testimony to the truthfulness of his claims. Idiots (and Jesus would be one if his claims were untrue) are endured, not crucified.

5 "Now" marks the crowning moment in Jesus' life. All the years of his incarnate life pointed toward this great redemptive denouement, which from God's perspective found its greatest joy in the return of the Son to his heavenly home. The disciples, however, were thinking not of what the return would mean to Jesus but of how it would affect them. Concern for self precluded their full participation in the central drama of redemptive history. Sin inevitably carries with it its own penalty. It creates spiritual dwarfs where there might have been spiritual giants.

There is a note of rebuke in Jesus' words, "I am going to him who sent me, yet none of you asks me, 'Where are you going?'" Barrett, 405, says it is "both necessary and justifiable to emphasize the present tense *erōta* ["is asking," GK *2263*]." The sense is that Jesus is returning to his Father, and not one of them seems to care enough to inquire any further.

It is sometimes questioned how Jesus could say that no one asked where he was going when just a few hours before, Peter had asked that very question (13:36; cf. Thomas's statement in 14:5). The contradiction, however, is only formal since in each case the purpose for asking is distinct. Peter's question has less to do with Jesus' destination than with its consequences for the disciples. The question they *failed to ask* points up their lack of concern with what was about to take place in the affairs of their Master. Self-interest was the controlling motivation in each case: first it prompted Peter to ask, then it kept them all from asking.

6 Little wonder that the disciples are "filled with grief" (see vv.20–22). The penalty for self-concern is not only to miss out on what God is doing in the world but also to suffer the grief that accompanies isolation from the common good. The remedy for grief, says Calvin, 2:15, is Christ, absent from the body but sitting at the right hand of God to protect believers by his power.

7 Verses 7–14 contain the fourth of the Paraclete sections of the Upper Room Discourse. The disciples were filled with grief (v.6), but Jesus assured them it was to their advantage that he go away; otherwise the Counselor would not come. By going to the Father, Jesus will be enabled to send the One "who is to befriend [them]" (Knox). Ryle, 4:376, notes that "the universal presence of the Holy Ghost in the Church, is better than the visible bodily presence of Christ with the Church."

It would have been extremely difficult for the disciples to grasp that the departure of Jesus from their midst would usher in a time during which his "replacement" would serve God's purposes more effectively. The truth is more readily seen when we compare the weakness of the disciples just before the crucifixion ("everyone deserted him and fled," Mk 14:50) with their boldness after the Holy Spirit had come upon them ("the apostles left the San-hedrin, rejoicing because they had been counted worthy of suffering disgrace for the Name," Ac 5:41). Throughout history the church has surged ahead whenever it has recognized the appropriate role and mission of the Spirit in the task of world evangelism. Too often we are immobilized by the absence of the Son rather than invigorated by the presence of the Spirit. As was the case with the disciples, human discouragement blinds us to God's glorious provision.

8–11 At the Counselor's coming, he will prove the world wrong about sin and righteousness and judgment. This basic statement is expanded and made more specific in vv.9–11. While the general import is relatively clear, considerable difference of opinion exists with regard to the specific interpretation of the various parts of the passage. One's approach will depend on an interpretation of (1) the verb *elenchō* ("prove," GK *1794*; NIV, "convict . . . of guilt"), (2) the preposition *peri* ("about"; six times in vv.8–11; NIV, "of, in regard to"), and (3) the conjunction *hoti* ("because"; three times in vv.9–11).

The verb *elenchō* means "bring to light," "convict," "reprove." When taken with the accusative of person, it means, "to show someone his sin and summon him to repentance," whether privately as in Matthew 18:15 or congregationally as in 1 Timothy 5:20 (*TDNT* 2:474). It has the juridical sense of cross-examination for the purpose of providing evidence that proves guilt. Jesus declares that the Counselor (the *paraklētos*, GK *4156*, who is called alongside to provide assistance) will prove the world wrong about sin, righteousness, and judgment. Note the close relationship among the three. The world's sin reveals how inadequate is its understanding of righteousness and how certain will be its judgment. Reith, 111, says that "sin is the world's state as it is; righteousness as it ought to be; and judgment as it must and shall be that righteousness may obtain."

A common interpretation understands vv.8–11 as describing the work of the Holy Spirit in convicting sinners and bringing them to faith in Jesus. While this has been a major activity of the Spirit throughout history, these verses point to a different work of the Spirit in which he convicts the world of how wrong it has been in rejecting Jesus. The heavenly prosecutor will prove that the world is guilty for its rejection of Jesus and its distorted ideas of righteousness and judgment.

Brown, 712, holds that the proof of the world's guilt was directed not to the world but to the disciples. He pictures in the minds of the disciples a courtroom scene in which a "rerun of the trial of Jesus" takes place and "the Paraclete makes the truth emerge for the disciples to see." But a straightforward reading of the text would indicate that it is the *world*, not the disciples, that is proven wrong.

9 In vv.9–11 the preposition *peri* ("about") is used to point out the areas about which the world is wrong and the conjunction *hoti* ("because") to elaborate further. The Counselor puts aside his role as defender and becomes prosecutor. He will prove the world wrong on three crucial points. First, worldly people are wrong with regard to sin. They regarded Jesus as a sinner (9:24) and themselves as righteous (cf. Lk 18:9). Their sin consisted in their unwillingness to believe in Jesus (taking *hoti* in an explanatory rather than a causative sense). The root of sin is humanity's desire to live in isolation from God. By refusing to respond in faith to the incarnate Son, they have committed themselves to a flawed view of the nature of sin.

10 Second, worldly people are wrong with regard to righteousness. They considered Jesus worthy of death, but he will be vindicated by his return to the Father. In this context the Greek *dikaiosynē* (GK *1466*; only here in the fourth gospel) means "justice." The world's idea of justice was to put Jesus to death for his supposedly blasphemous claims to

be the Son of God. But God's idea of justice is different. He raised Jesus from the dead and welcomed him back to his preincarnate state of eternal glory (cf. Ac 2:22–24).

11 Third, worldly people are wrong with regard to judgment. The fact that "the prince of this world now stands condemned" is irrefutable proof that sin has been judged and found guilty. Judgment does exist because Satan's power has been overthrown by the cross and empty grave. In condemning Jesus, the world brought judgment on itself.

12 Jesus turns from discussing the work of the Spirit in relation to the world and speaks again (cf. 14:26; 15:26) of the Spirit's part in equipping the disciples to carry out their role in the difficult days that lie ahead. The choice of the verb *bastazō* (GK *1002*; NIV, "bear") in this context is somewhat unusual in that it normally means "to lift up" or "to carry away." Some think that Jesus is referring to the disciples' ability to understand what he was saying. For example, in Mark 4:33 Jesus speaks to the Twelve in parables "as much as they could understand" (cf. 1Co 3:2, where Paul gives the church "milk" rather than "meat" because they were "not yet ready for it"). While it is true that a teacher cannot communicate more than his students can absorb, it would seem that in this case the verb "to bear" should be taken in a somewhat more literal sense. Until the Spirit came, the Twelve would be unable to lift up and carry the full responsibilities of discipleship. They would be unable "to live out the implications of the revelation" (Morris, 699). The hostility that would shortly nail Jesus to a cross would before many days turn against those who were loyal to him and advocated his cause. To bear up in the coming crisis the disciples needed to wait in Jerusalem for the arrival of the Spirit and the power he would provide (Ac 1:4, 8).

13 Though Jesus was unable to tell them more right then, they would learn what he wanted them to know when the Spirit of truth came. This is the fourth time in the discourse that the emphatic demonstrative pronoun *ekeinos* ("that one," "he") is used (14:26; 15:26; 16:8, 13), and it will occur again in the following verse (16:14). That the masculine pronoun is used in direct juxtaposition to the neuter *to pneuma* ("the Spirit," GK 4460) is strong evidence that the evangelist understood the Spirit as a person rather than an abstract force.

The Spirit's role is to "guide [the disciples] into all truth." The verb *hodēgeō* (GK 3842) is frequently used in the LXX of the guidance and instruction of God (e.g., "He guides the humble in what is right," Ps 25:9). The context indicates that the Spirit will continue the revelatory work of Jesus. He is the one who will now become the disciples' guide and lead them "into all truth." Sadly, this phrase has often been taken as a validation for all sorts of contemporary truth claims. But the words of Jesus that immediately follow define "all truth" in a less than universal sense. It is not new truth but "the truth that is in Jesus" (Eph 4:21) that will be the focus of the Spirit's revelatory work.

The Spirit "will not speak on his own" (RSV, "on his own authority") but "only what he hears." On a number of occasions Jesus made this same claim about himself (8:26–28; 12:49; 14:10). As the Son spoke only what he heard from the Father, so will the Spirit limit his teaching ministry to "whatever he is told" (Moffatt). We are not to expect new (in the sense of additional) truth from the Spirit but a fuller understanding and appreciation of truth already known. As Paul put it, we have received the Spirit so that "we may get an insight into the blessings God has graciously given us" (1Co 2:12 Williams).

Not only will the Spirit speak what he hears, but he will also "tell you what is yet to come." The verb *anangellō* (GK 334) in earlier Greek meant "to carry back a report." Brown, 708, notes that in the context the prefix *ana* suggests repetition and the verb carries

the classical meaning of saying over again what has already been said. This would strengthen the case for the Spirit's work as drawing out the implications of and deepening insight into the truth already proclaimed by Jesus. But what is it that is "yet to come"? Calvin, 2:120, thought the reference was to "the future state of [Jesus'] kingdom, which the apostles saw soon after His resurrection but were then quite unable to comprehend." Others see a reference to the gift of prophecy that before long would be exercised in the early church (Ac 21:10–12; cf. 1Co 12:10). More often, it is taken either as the final eschatological events that bring history to a close or as the unique events that would shortly come to pass (the death and resurrection of Jesus). The second option is supported by the subject under consideration in vv.16–24 and is in keeping with the understanding of *anangellō* as discussed above.

14 The role of the Spirit is to "bring glory" to the Son. He will do so by drawing on the riches of Christ ("from what is mine") and revealing his glory to the disciples. The full significance of spiritual truth cannot be grasped apart from the illuminating work of the Spirit. As a prerequisite this requires prayerful reflection on the works and words of Jesus. The result is a deeper appreciation of Jesus and a new sense of wonder concerning his person and work. In this way the Spirit brings praise and honor to the Son. As the Son glorified the Father by completing the work he was sent to do (17:4), so will the Spirit bring glory to the Son by his work of divine illumination.

15 Jesus declares that all that the Father has belongs to him as well (cf. 17:10). The point is not to prove that Jesus is coequal with the Father but to assert that the revelatory work of the Spirit will not be hampered by less-than-complete access to the source of all truth. Whatever knowledge is appropriate for us to know will be made clear by the Spirit.

NOTES

7–8 In OT thought, God is sometimes pictured as an advocate for Israel. In connection with the predicted fall of Babylon, God says to Israel through the prophet Jeremiah, "I will be your lawyer to plead your case, and I will avenge you" (Jer 51:36 NLT). Many believed that in the final days, when Israel had prevailed over her enemies, God would establish a great tribunal in which he would carry out his judgment against the nations. Jesus says that when he has gone away, he will send the Counselor, who will act as prosecutor of the world with its faulty ideas about sin, righteousness, and judgment.

8 BDAG, 315, lists four meanings for ἐλέγχω (*elenchō*): (1) "to scrutinize or examine carefully"; (2) "to bring a person to the point of recognizing wrongdoing"; (3) "to express strong disapproval of someone's action"; and (4) "to penalize for wrongdoing." BDAG places the verse under consideration in the second category with the glosses, "convict, convince."

10 The NET has an extended translator's note at v.10 on the meaning of δικαιοσύνη (*dikaiosyne*; NIV, "righteousness") in which it argues against the rather common understanding of the word as forensic justification (as in Morris, 698–99) and concludes that in this context it refers to Jesus' vindication.

13 Greek MSS differ as to whether the phrase should read "into [εἰς, *eis*] all truth" or "in [ἐν, *en*] all truth." The former would suggest being led into a full understanding of all truth, while the latter would imply protection against straying from the path of truth. Ἐν, *En*, has slightly stronger MS support, but as Joseph Sanders (*A Commentary on the Gospel of St. John* [HNTC; New York: Harper & Row, 1968], 353 n. 6) notes, εἰς, *eis*, may have been original but removed because it was found to be theologically dangerous.

The future indicative ἀκούσει (*akousei*, "he will hear," GK *201*) is to be preferred over the present ἀκούει (*akouei*, "he hears"), which according to Metzger, 210, is "a dogmatic improvement, introduced to suggest the eternal relationship of the Holy Spirit with the Father." The MS support is strong, and it best accounts for the alternate readings.

14 The centrality of Jesus in the revelatory process is heightened by the emphatic ἐμέ (*eme*, "me") both in form and position in the clause. One might translate, "I [Jesus] am the one that he [the Father] will glorify."

5. Jesus' Return and the Joy of the Disciples (16:16–33)

¹⁶"In a little while you will see me no more, and then after a little while you will see me." ¹⁷Some of his disciples said to one another, "What does he mean by saying, 'In a little while you will see me no more, and then after a little while you will see me,' and 'Because I am going to the Father'?" ¹⁸They kept asking, "What does he mean by 'a little while'? We don't understand what he is saying."

¹⁹Jesus saw that they wanted to ask him about this, so he said to them, "Are you asking one another what I meant when I said, 'In a little while you will see me no more, and then after a little while you will see me'? ²⁰I tell you the truth, you will weep and mourn while

the world rejoices. You will grieve, but your grief will turn to joy. [21]A woman giving birth to a child has pain because her time has come; but when her baby is born she forgets the anguish because of her joy that a child is born into the world. [22]So with you: Now is your time of grief, but I will see you again and you will rejoice, and no one will take away your joy. [23]In that day you will no longer ask me anything. I tell you the truth, my Father will give you whatever you ask in my name. [24]Until now you have not asked for anything in my name. Ask and you will receive, and your joy will be complete."

[25]"Though I have been speaking figuratively, a time is coming when I will no longer use this kind of language but will tell you plainly about my Father. [26]In that day you will ask in my name. I am not saying that I will ask the Father on your behalf. [27]No, the Father himself loves you because you have loved me and have believed that I came from God. [28]I came from the Father and entered the world; now I am leaving the world and going back to the Father."

[29]Then Jesus' disciples said, "Now you are speaking clearly and without figures of speech. [30]Now we can see that you know all things and that you do not even need to have anyone ask you questions. This makes us believe that you came from God."

[31]"You believe at last!" Jesus answered. [32]"But a time is coming, and has come, when you will be scattered, each to his own home. You will leave me all alone. Yet I am not alone, for my Father is with me.

[33]"I have told you these things, so that in me you may have peace. In this world you will have trouble. But take heart! I have overcome the world."

COMMENTARY

16 Not only did this verse puzzle the disciples (see vv. 17–18), but even after Jesus' explanation in vv. 19–28 commentators are still less than certain as to its precise meaning. The crux of the problem is the period of time indicated by the double reference to "a little while." Tasker, 183, understands a single period of time viewed from a double perspective: the disciples do not see Jesus because he is in the grave, but they will see him following the resurrection. The NIV's translation of *kai palin mikron* with "and then after a little while" obscures the possibility that *palin* may not carry a temporal meaning but be better rendered rhetorically with "moreover" or "on the other hand."

It is better to understand the repetition of the phrase as indicating two different periods of time. The first "little while" refers to the interval until the crucifixion and burial. At that time, said Jesus, "you will see me no more." The second "little while," after which "you will see me," may refer to the interval prior to (1) the resurrection, (2) the coming of the Spirit, or (3) Jesus' second coming. Some think that the first alternative leaves insufficient time for "you will see me no more." A number of writers understand "you will see me" in a spiritual sense. Temple, 2:295, writes, "After a short interval of desolation, they will *see* Him with the direct spiritual vision which brings full personal knowledge and communion." The change of verbs between clauses from *theōreite* ("you gaze at," GK *2555*) to *opsesthe* ("you will see," or "you will perceive," GK *3972*) is thought by some to refer to deeper spiritual insight. If Jesus' answer in the verses that follow refers to the subsequent life of the church (rather than the immediate experience of the disciples only), then it would seem that the interval reaches out until the promised return of Christ Jesus at the end of history (cf. 14:3). The third option is preferable.

17 For the first time since Judas asked a question in 14:22 the discourse of Jesus is interrupted. The disciples are perplexed by what he means about their not seeing him after a little while and then seeing him after a little while. It is worth noting that while Jesus said they would "no longer" (*ouketi*) see him, they repeat it as "not" (*ou*) seeing him (a nuance obscured by the NIV, with its translation of "no more" in both places). They also add the clause, "Because I am going to the Father." (The two ideas are found together in v.10.)

18 The disciples' confusion is underscored by the testimony here indicating that they "kept asking" (the imperfect *elegon*, GK *3306*, being iterative). "We don't understand what he is saying" is a confession that a number of commentators have also made.

19 The disciples continued to discuss what Jesus could have meant by the "little while." Jesus could not help but notice their desire for an explanation, so he asked them whether that was what they wanted to know. The Greek *ginōskō* (GK *1182*; the form is *egnō*) is translated by the KJV with its primary meaning of "to know" (NIV, "Jesus saw"), which has led some commentators to question whether Jesus' knowledge at this point should be taken as supernatural. The context, however, would suggest that Jesus, simply by observing his disciples, would know what was troubling them. Reith, 115, notes that "their desire would be written in their faces."

20–21 Jesus had the habit of responding to questions in a less-than-direct way. In fact, in this case he never did tell them what he meant by "a little while." Instead, he used the illustration of a woman giving birth (v.21) to teach that although the sorrow they were about to experience would be intense, it would soon give way to joy (v.20). Their real need was not intellectual enlightenment but spiritual preparation.

20 Following the solemn *amēn amēn* (NIV, "I tell you the truth"), Jesus contrasts the disciples' distress with the rejoicing of the world. "You [*hymeis* is emphatic] will weep and mourn" but "the world shall rejoice" (KJV). Weeping and mourning (*klaiō*, GK *3081*, is used in John only in connection with death: 11:31, 33; 20:11, 13, 15) combine the deep sorrow connected with death and the outward expression of that sorrow. Loud wailing was a regular part of the death and burial ritual in the Near East.

We are reminded of the scene from Revelation 11 when after the death of the two witnesses, "the inhabitants of the earth will gloat over them and will celebrate by sending each other gifts" (Rev 11:10). Whenever the prophetic voice is for the moment silenced, the enemies of God rejoice. It would seem that the "little while" of John 16:16 represents every period of time during which the world appears to have overcome God's redemptive work in the world (e.g., the three days Jesus was in the grave, as well as the entire period leading up to Jesus' victorious return).

The sorrow the disciples will experience when Jesus is taken away will be difficult to bear but it will not be permanent: "You will grieve, but your grief will turn to joy." The crucifixion was a shocking experience for those who had left everything to follow Jesus. He had been their constant companion, and they had come to rely on him for all their needs. Suddenly he would be gone and their vision for the future shattered. Not yet understanding what rising from the dead would mean, they remained bewildered and afraid. How different it would have been if they had actually believed the promise of Jesus that their grief would be turned into joy. It is significant that Jesus does not speak of sorrow being replaced by joy but of sorrow being *transformed* into joy.

21 The sequence of sorrow and joy is illustrated by childbirth. A woman giving birth experiences great pain but when the child is born the suffering is forgotten. The anguish of travail gives way to the joy of birth. In the OT, the plight of Israel is often described by the metaphor of childbirth. Isaiah 26:17 reads, "As a woman with child and about to give birth writhes and cries out in her pain, so were we in your presence, O LORD" (cf. Isa 66:7–14; Hos 13:12–13). Against this backdrop, many writers find in Jesus' words a deeper reference to the "birth pangs of the Messiah"—a standard Jewish apocalyptic teaching regarding the period of severe trouble that will precede the final consummation. Others consider it unlikely that the passage holds any allusion to the rabbinical teaching about "Messianic birth-pangs" (so Bruce, 322).

22 Jesus now applies the illustration to the lot of the disciples. This will be their time of grief, but Jesus will see them again, which will lead to rejoicing. The Christian does not reject sorrow and pain but understands it as part of the human experience in a world that has turned its back on God. Grief is to be accepted and endured but always with the confidence that it is no more than a passing stage (cf. Ro 8:18–25).

In v.16 Jesus had said that after a little while they would see him. Now he promises, "I will see you again." To see Jesus is to be seen by him. The change stresses the reciprocal nature of the coming relationship. At that time, "you will rejoice, and no one will take away your joy." Like the joy accompanying the birth of a child, so will be the disciples' joy in

restored fellowship with their Master. Temple, 2:296, writes that Paul's "glorious outburst" in Romans 8:35–39 is "no more than a symphony on the theme propounded before the event by the Lord Himself."

23 In the coming day ("that day," i.e., the day of joy; see vv.22, 24) the disciples will have no need to ask Jesus about (or for) anything. The interpretation of v.23 hinges on the meaning of the two verbs in the Greek text, both of which are translated in the NIV with "ask." The primary meaning of *erōtaō* (GK *2263*; used in the first sentence) is "to ask a question," while *aiteō* (GK *160*) in religious contexts (as in the second sentence) normally means "to ask in prayer." If this distinction is maintained, then the first part of the verse is saying that in the coming days the disciples will find it unnecessary to pose such questions as, "What does 'a little while' mean?" (vv.17–19). Brown, 722–23, favors this alternative and notes that (1) the verse uses two different verbs of interrogation, (2) the lines are separated by the solemn double "amen," and (3) the context is one of understanding rather than petition (cf. vv.26, 30).

The other approach is to understand the entire verse in connection with prayer. In the coming day the disciples will no longer ask Jesus for anything but will direct their prayers to God in Jesus' name. The first verb (*erōtaō*) is often used of asking for some special benefit (cf. Jesus' prayer, 17:17), and in the LXX it serves to translate the same Hebrew word as the second verb (*aiteō*) does. If all of v.23 deals with prayer, then the point is that with the coming of the Spirit ("in that day") a new relationship will be in place that will allow believers to go directly to the Father in Jesus' name.

24 As faithful members of Jewish society, the disciples were accustomed to offering daily prayers. Until that time, they had always prayed to God the Father, but now Jesus is introducing something new. Henceforth they are to pray to God "in [Jesus'] name." Their requests will be answered because they carry the authority of the name (or character) of Jesus. The prayers God answers are those that promote his redemptive purposes in the world. To pray in the name of Jesus is to pray as a representative of the one who entered the created universe to reveal the will and purpose of the Father.

So now the disciples are to ask (the present tense, *aiteite*, suggests "keep on asking"; cf. Mt 7:7–8) and "[they] will receive." Prayer is perhaps the most highly regarded but the least employed of all the spiritual disciplines. Yet its demands on faith are not great. All it requires is a willingness to open ourselves before God and allow him to respond to our needs. The NIV's "and your joy will be complete" overlooks the important Greek conjunction *hina* ("in order that"). The prayers of the disciples will be answered *so that* their joy "may be overflowing" (Phillips). Morris, 708, notes that joy cannot be made complete in any other way. Joy is the inevitable consequence of contact with God. It is a dead giveaway that we belong to him. Life may have its full measure of pleasant experiences, but only the presence of God can meet the deepest needs of the human heart and result in a joy that, like the peace of God, "transcends all understanding" (Php 4:7).

25 Jesus says that though he has been "speaking figuratively," the time will come when he will speak "plainly." The Greek *paroimia* ("proverb"; NASB, "figurative language," GK *4231*) occurs four times in the NT. In 2 Peter 2:2 it denotes a maxim or byword, but in John 10:6; 16:25, 29 it refers to "'hidden, obscure speech' which stands in need of interpretation" (*TDNT* 5:856). In Mark 4:11 the disciples are identified as those who know the secret of the kingdom and are contrasted with outsiders, for whom everything is "in parables" (*parabolais*, GK *4130*). In John the contrast is between the ambiguous nature of Jesus' teaching during his earthly ministry and the clarity that will follow the resurrection

and the advent of the Spirit. Calvin, 2:126, notes that the obscurity did not lie so much in the teaching as in the minds of the disciples. While this is true, it would be a bit demanding to expect from the disciples a depth of insight that not even post-Pentecost believers seem to possess.

Jesus speaks of a time when he will speak plainly. The disciples understand this time to have come (cf. v.29), yet Jesus appears to be speaking of his post-resurrection ministry (cf. Lk 24:45–47; Ac 1:3). This same ministry is continued by the Spirit, who in fulfillment of divine promise comes to "guide [believers] into all truth" (v.13). Lindars, 511, understands the promise as referring to the spiritual relationship that will exist after the resurrection and the direct knowledge resulting from the mutual indwelling established at that time.

Jesus' teaching will be, as it has always been, "about [his] Father." He came to reveal the Father (cf. 1:18; 14:9), and the future will involve no change of focus. In the incarnation Jesus took the stage of history and portrayed by word and action the loving nature of God. As the author of Hebrews puts it, Jesus is "the radiance of God's glory and the exact representation of his being" (Heb 1:3). Or, as Paul writes, "He is the image of the invisible God" (Col 1:15).

26–27 In the coming age (following the resurrection) the disciples will make their requests in the name of Jesus, but they must not regard him as an intermediary who encourages a reluctant God to answer their prayers. Jesus will not have to ask the Father "on [their] behalf" because the Father himself, of his own accord (taking *autos* in the classical sense), loves them. There is no need for Jesus to intervene and persuade the Father to answer the prayers of believers. Both access and authority are given to the believer. The worn-out and unbiblical concept of an angry God whose continuing displeasure is only partially alleviated by a gentle Jesus has made prayer difficult and unpleasant for those who still live under the misconception. The great truth symbolized by the rending of the curtain of the temple (Mt 27:51) is that by the death of Jesus entry into the presence of God himself has been provided for all who believe.

That Jesus need not take the prayers of the disciples to the Father does not contradict the teaching elsewhere that he remains our intercessor before God (Ro 8:34; Heb 7:25). One has to do with our status and the other with his role in intercessory prayer.

God the Father hears and answers the prayers made in Jesus' name on the basis of love. In speaking of the Father's love (in v.27), Jesus uses a term that reflects the affection connected with natural relationships (*phileō*, GK *5797*) rather than the verb that regularly denotes the universal and self-giving love of God (*agapaō*, GK *26*). Temple, 2:299, suggests the translation, "The Father himself is friendly to you because ye have been my friends."

Saying that God loves "because [they] have loved" does not make divine love contingent on human response (cf. 1Jn 4:19). Rather, it suggests that the relationship requires our active involvement. The use of the perfect tense in "have loved" and "have believed" stresses a continuing characteristic of life. The Christian life is not a moment of belief but a lifetime of believing. While it begins at a specific point in time, it cannot remain there.

28 Verse 28 summarizes Johannine theology in two sets of balanced clauses: Jesus "came from the Father [his origin] and entered the world [his incarnation]"; he is now "leaving the world [his death and resurrection] and going back to the Father [his ascension]."

29–30 Jesus' comment leads the disciples to exclaim that now, at last, Jesus is "speaking clearly and without figures of speech." They are confident that they *now* (repeated and emphatic in v.30)

understand. They regard Jesus' supernatural insight as conclusive evidence of his divine origin. In Jewish thought, the ability to answer questions yet unasked is an indication of the divine (cf. Mt 6:8). This (i.e., Jesus' complete knowledge and his ability to anticipate questions) is what has brought the disciples to believe that he came from God.

31 Grammatically, Jesus' response may be taken as a declaration or as a question. The first option is followed by the NIV ("You believe at last!") and the second by the NRSV ("Do you now believe?"). In either case a certain amount of irony is involved.

32 Jesus does not deny the reality of their faith but questions whether it is adequate for the time about to come, when they "will be scattered each to his own home." The reference to scattering alludes to the oracle in Zechariah 13:7–9, which is quoted in both Mark (14:27) and Matthew (26:31) in connection with Jesus' prediction of the failure of the disciples to stand by him in his time of trial ("I will strike the shepherd, and the sheep will be scattered"). Their theology was correct ("you came from God," v.30), but it was not yet matched by personal commitment ("you will be scattered," v.32). On the other hand, Jesus' love for his disciples was not dependent on their fidelity. He loved them as they were. Barclay, 2:203, notes that if we idolize an individual and think of that person as faultless, we are doomed to disappointment. Instead, we must love people as they really are.

The disciples will desert their Lord and return "each to his own home" (or "to his own occupation"—the Greek is indefinite). They will leave Jesus alone, yet he will not really be alone. With full confidence he can say, "My Father is with me." It is said that this verse brought great comfort to the martyr John Huss during his lonely imprisonment preceding his death at the stake in 1415. Some commentators think that John at this point is correcting a false understanding of the "cry of dereliction" in

Matthew 27:46 ("My God, my God, why have you forsaken me?"), but the conjecture is unwarranted. The Father was always with the Son throughout his earthly life, even though in that moment of ultimate mystery the Son's awareness of the Father's presence was momentarily obscured.

33 Jesus concludes the discourse proper by encouraging his disciples with a reminder that he has told them "these things" (all the promises in the preceding chapters) so that in him they "may have peace." Peace in the biblical sense is more than tranquility. It is the *šalôm* (GK 8934) of God, the sense of complete well-being that characterizes the life lived in accordance with the design of God. Peace comes from acting on the promises of God. The close relationship between prayer (vv.23–24) and peace (v.33) is reflected in Paul's words to the Philippian church: "In everything, by prayer and petition, with thanksgiving, present your requests to God. And the peace of God, which transcends all understanding, will guard your hearts and your minds in Christ Jesus" (Php 4:6–7).

In this world the followers of Jesus are destined to have trouble. (*Thlipsis*, GK *2568*, is commonly used in the NT for the persecutions of the church; see, e.g., 2Co 8:2; 1Th 1:6.) But "take heart!" says Jesus, "I have overcome the world." There is solid reason for joyful confidence. The world will do its worst to me, yet I will come through victoriously. The victory that I will win will be yours as well. The verb "to overcome" (used only here in John's gospel) is a military term and denotes victory in warfare. The perfect tense (*nenikēka*, GK *3771*) emphasizes the abiding nature of that victory. The strong adversative *alla* ("but") suggests that something is to follow for which the circumstances have not prepared us (cf. Morris, 714 n. 80).

The chapter closes with a strong contrast. In this world the disciples will have trouble, but in Christ they will have peace. Believers were never intended to be exempt from sorrow or difficulty in this world. We are, however, expected to be at peace because by faith we have been brought into an inseparable union with Jesus Christ and share his victory over sin and Satan. "Cheer up," is the Living Bible's translation. The enemies of God are defeated, and before long that victory will be universally proclaimed (cf. Php 2:9–11).

NOTES

20 The strong contrastive conjunction in the final clause (ἀλλά, *alla*, "but"), in contrast with the milder conjunction in the previous clause (δέ, *de*, "but"), suggests that the joy of the believer after the present sorrow will come somewhat unexpectedly, while the contrast between the current sorrow of the believer and the rejoicing of the world is to be expected.

23 Manuscripts differ in the placement of the phrase "in my name." If it comes after the verb "give," then the point is that what God gives in answer to prayer is given in the name of his Son. Some writers prefer this placement on the basis that it is the more difficult reading and thus would explain the scribal alteration to an easier text. (Variants in the Greek text are often due to a difficult reading being changed to a simpler one.) The UBS Greek text places the phrase between the verbs "ask" and "give" and thus supports the more common idea of praying in the name of Jesus. This reading is to be favored in that its external support is more diversified and the context is one of prayer, which elsewhere is linked by John with the name of Jesus (cf. Metzger, 211).

27 At the end of this verse, the ASV, RSV, and NASB all read τοῦ πατρός (*tou patros*, "the Father," GK *4252*) following B C* D L X *pc* (ff²) co. Most modern versions (e.g., NIV, NRSV, NIV, NKJV, NET, NLT) read τοῦ θεοῦ (*tou theou*, "God"). The former was probably due to assimilation to the first clause of the following verse. It is not the filial relationship of Jesus to the Father but the divine origin of the Son that is emphasized in the verse.

C. Jesus' High Priestly Prayer (17:1–26)

OVERVIEW

In chs. 13–16 Jesus has been teaching his disciples those truths that would be especially important in view of his impending death. Last words reveal priorities and fundamental concerns (cf. Jacob's last words to his sons in Ge 49). Jesus now draws to a close this most intimate gathering by turning to his Father in prayer in the presence of the disciples.

Chapter 17 has traditionally been called "the high priestly prayer" of Jesus. (The specific title is attributed to sixteenth-century theologian David Chytraeus.) If the designation is accurate and Jesus is acting in the role of a high priest, then the verses that follow picture him more as a priest engaged in intercession than as a priest about to offer sacrifice. Even though in v.19 he consecrates himself for the coming sacrifice in which he is both priest and vic-

tim (in the LXX the same verb is used of consecrating priests, Ex 28:41), his role as intercessor is more dominant throughout the chapter (vv.9, 11, 15, 17, 20–21, 23).

Chapter 17, perhaps more than any other section of the fourth gospel, reveals the strong bonds of unity and mutual love between Father and Son. Nowhere is the relationship more clear than in vv.21–23, which speak of "complete unity" and of being one "as we are one." The chapter is also the longest of all of our Lord's recorded prayers. It is not to be identified with Jesus' prayer in the garden of Gethsemane (recorded in the Synoptics but not in John). The chapter divides into three sections: Jesus' prayer for himself (vv.1–5), for his disciples (vv.6–19), and for those who will come to believe (vv.20–26).

1. Jesus Prays for Himself (17:1–5)

¹After Jesus said this, he looked toward heaven and prayed:

"Father, the time has come. Glorify your Son, that your Son may glorify you. ²For you granted him authority over all people that he might give eternal life to all those you have given him. ³Now this is eternal life: that they may know you, the only true God, and Jesus Christ, whom you have sent. ⁴I have brought you glory on earth by completing the work you gave me to do. ⁵And now, Father, glorify me in your presence with the glory I had with you before the world began."

COMMENTARY

1 When Jesus had finished his final words of instruction and admonition to the disciples, he looked toward heaven and prayed. Although Haenchen, 2:150, correctly notes that the text refers to "speaking" (*eipein*, GK *3306*) rather than "praying" (*proseuchesthai*, GK *4667*), there is no question that the chapter is to be regarded as a prayer. In biblical times it was customary to lift up one's eyes in prayer (Ps 123:1, "I lift up my eyes to you"). Jesus prayed in this way at the tomb of Lazarus (Jn 11:41) and when he healed a deaf man (Mk 7:34). In the parable of the Pharisee and the tax collector, the latter "would not even look up to heaven" (Lk 18:13). Many contemporary Christians in the Western world do not feel comfortable praying in this way. It is almost universally accepted that we are to shut our eyes when we pray—a practice that is without biblical warrant. Praying with our eyes open allows God to meet us as a real person who is both counselor and friend rather than as some mysterious potentate. Obviously, God is infinite mystery, but it is also true that he is to be addressed in prayer as "Father." In fact, he is referred to by that family title over 120 times in John's gospel alone. Behind the Greek *patēr* is the Aramaic *abba* (GK 10003), which denotes "childlike intimacy and trust" (*TDNT* 1:2).

At the wedding feast in Cana, Jesus told his mother, who had reported that the wine had run out, "My time has not yet come" (2:4). Throughout the gospel we hear of an hour (NIV, "time") that is to come (4:21; 5:28; 7:30; 8:20). That hour is the time of Jesus' great sacrifice of himself on the cross for the redemption of the human race. Now that it has arrived, Jesus prays, "Glorify your Son, that your Son may glorify you [the Father]." The verb "to glorify" as used in the NT tends to mean more than simply "to extol" or "to praise." It carries the spe-

cial biblical sense of "sharing in the divine glory." Jesus asks to be glorified not out of any desire for self-aggrandizement but so that he in turn might glorify the Father. His prayer is that God will sustain him in his obedience as it moves him irresistibly onward to the cross, so that by his death he will be able to exhibit the boundless love of the Father. Jesus' primary concern is that his sacrifice brings honor and praise to God. It is difficult to grasp how the cross could possibly glorify God. Temple, 2:308, remarks that "the Cross is the glory of God because self-sacrifice is the expression of love." The way we glorify God is to obey him. Jesus' life of perfect obedience is the ultimate expression of honor to God.

2 Jesus' request to be glorified is based on the fact (taking *kathōs* in the causal sense of "since") that God has granted him authority to give eternal life to those he has received from the Father. In Daniel 7:13–14 the Ancient of Days gives "authority, glory and sovereign power" to the "one like a son of man." This universal sovereignty becomes the basis for the Great Commission in Matthew 28:18.

The verb "to give" (*didōmi*, GK *1443*) is found seventeen times in this single prayer (seventy-six times in the gospel). Morris, 718 n. 6, cites Edwin Abbott's remark that "what '*grace*' is in the Pauline Epistles, '*giving*' is in the Fourth Gospel." It is the nature of God to give, because giving is the primary expression of love (cf. 3:16). Note the predestinarian emphasis in the fact that eternal life is given to those whom the Father has given to the Son. We recognize here what Phillips calls "the controlling hand" of God (see his translation of Ro 9:22).

3 Verse 3 may well be an explanatory comment by the author of the gospel. The designation of the Father as "the only true God" occurs only here in John, and would it not seem strange for Jesus to refer to himself in the third person as "Jesus Christ"? In any case, the verse is parenthetical and defines the nature of "eternal life." Eternal life consists in knowing the only true God and Jesus Christ. Knowledge in the biblical sense means far more than intellectual comprehension; it involves a profound personal relationship. The present subjunctive (*ginōskōsin*, GK 1182) suggests that here the verb should be taken in the sense of "learning to know." It presents knowledge as a growing experience. It is instructive to note that in Scripture the verb "to know" may serve as a euphemism for sexual relations (cf. Ge 4:1 [LXX]; Lk 1:34). To know *about* God is one thing; it is something quite different to *know* God. The apostle Paul writes that he considers everything a loss compared to the "surpassing greatness of knowing Christ Jesus" (Php 3:8).

"Only" (*monos*, GK 3668) and "true" (*alēthinos*, GK 240) are attributes ascribed to God elsewhere in Scripture (Isa 37:20 [LXX]; Ex 34:6 [LXX]). They set him apart from all false deities. He is *sui generis*, one of a kind. That God the Father is said to be the "only true God" has led some to think that in some way Jesus must be less than God. But here Jesus is speaking as the Son sent into the world by the Father to secure eternal salvation for those who believe. In a world replete with objects of worship and false deities, the Son affirms that the God who sent him on this mission is "the only true God." He doesn't find it necessary to insert a qualification regarding his own relationship to the Father. Notice the emphasis throughout the chapter on being sent (vv.8, 18, 21, 23, 25).

4 Lindars, 520, notes that in vv. 4–5 there are two stages in the Son's mission of revealing the glory of God. First, there is his work on earth. By completing the work he was given to do, he brought glory to God on earth. In speaking of a work completed, Jesus was, of course, including the cross and the resurrection, which in point of time were yet future. God is glorified by obedience. We bring glory to God by allowing him to move our lives into conformity with his nature as revealed in Christ Jesus. Some today seem to believe that God is honored by solemn and elaborate ritual, while others would praise him by a paroxysm of religious fervor. Jesus brought glory to God by completing the work he was given to do.

5 A second stage in revealing the glory of God will be the glorification of the Son when he returns to the place he enjoyed before the world began. The preexistence of the Son is clearly taught throughout the fourth gospel. John's prologue begins with the assertion that "when all things began, the Word already was" (NEB). In 8:58 Jesus exclaimed, "Before Abraham was born, I am!" (see also 12:28 and Paul's word in Php 2:6).

Jesus anticipates his return to the presence of the Father because it sets the stage for the outpouring of the Holy Spirit (16:7) and the founding and expansion of the early church (Ac 1:4; 2:1–4). It is by bringing men and women to faith in Jesus that the redemptive mission of the Son is carried out in time. When the church is obedient to its mandate to "go and make disciples of all nations" (Mt 28:19), glory and praise is brought to God.

NOTES

1 The Greek οὐρανός (*ouranos*, GK 4041) may refer either to the sky (the OT "firmament"; cf. Ge 1:6–8; Pss 19:1; 150:1) or to heaven in the sense of God's transcendent abode (cf. Mt 3:17; 2Co 5:1). Seventy of the 123 occurrences of οὐρανός, *ouranos*, in the NT are found in the Johannine corpus, with all but eighteen in the book of Revelation.

2 The Greek πάσης σαρκός (*pasēs sarkos*, "all flesh," GK *4922*) is understood here in its traditional sense by the NIV ("all people") and the early NASB ("everyone in all the earth"; the updated NASB has gone to the more literal "all flesh"). The word σάρξ (*sarx*) occurs somewhat infrequently in the fourth gospel (thirteen times) and does not, as in Paul, "characterize human beings as subject to the power of sin" (*EDNT* 3:232).

4 On the "completing" or accomplishing (cf. NASB) of Jesus' redemptive work, see the same verb, τελέω (*teleō*, GK *5464*), in 19:30, where it is used in the perfect tense to emphasize both the completion of the work and its continuing effects.

2. Jesus Prays for His Disciples (17:6–19)

> ⁶"I have revealed you to those whom you gave me out of the world. They were yours; you gave them to me and they have obeyed your word. ⁷Now they know that everything you have given me comes from you. ⁸For I gave them the words you gave me and they accepted them. They knew with certainty that I came from you, and they believed that you sent me. ⁹I pray for them. I am not praying for the world, but for those you have given me, for they are yours. ¹⁰All I have is yours, and all you have is mine. And glory has come to me through them. ¹¹I will remain in the world no longer, but they are still in the world, and I am coming to you. Holy Father, protect them by the power of your name—the name you gave me—so that they may be one as we are one. ¹²While I was with them, I protected them and kept them safe by that name you gave me. None has been lost except the one doomed to destruction so that Scripture would be fulfilled.
>
> ¹³"I am coming to you now, but I say these things while I am still in the world, so that they may have the full measure of my joy within them. ¹⁴I have given them your word and the world has hated them, for they are not of the world any more than I am of the world. ¹⁵My prayer is not that you take them out of the world but that you protect them from the evil one. ¹⁶They are not of the world, even as I am not of it. ¹⁷Sanctify them by the truth; your word is truth. ¹⁸As you sent me into the world, I have sent them into the world. ¹⁹For them I sanctify myself, that they too may be truly sanctified."

COMMENTARY

6 "I have revealed you to those whom you gave me out of the world" summarizes Jesus' ministry on earth. It is another way of saying, "I have brought you glory on earth by completing the work you gave me to do." God is glorified as his character is revealed and made plain. The NIV obscures the fact that it is God's *name* (*onoma*, GK *3950*) that is revealed by Jesus. For Jesus to reveal the name of the Father means for him to enable his followers to see what the real nature of God is like. Williams translates, "made your very self known."

It is important to note that the disciples belonged to the Father before they were given to the Son. Jesus prays, "They were yours; you gave them to me." To understand this as meaning only that they belonged to God in the sense of being God-fearing Israelites before they came to Jesus is not enough. We know little about their religious condition before they decided to follow Jesus. Better to take the statement as an indication that God had from the beginning predestined them to be his children. It is comforting for believers to know that even before they responded to the gospel they belonged to God and that he was the one who gave them to his Son.

While God had taken the initiative (cf. 6:44, "No one can come to me unless the Father who sent me draws him"), his disciples were not passive recipients. So Jesus adds, "They have obeyed your word." Had they not obeyed, they would have been neither chosen nor given. The verb used here for the obedience of the disciples (*tēreō*, GK *5498*) is also used by Jesus in vv. 11, 12, and 15 as he prays for their protection. They keep his word, and God keeps (protects) them.

7–8 Now that Jesus has revealed to the disciples what God is really like, they are able to grasp the fact that God is the source of everything that has been given to the Son. Jesus gave them the words he had received from the Father, and they accepted them. A contrast is probably intended between the "word" (*logos*, GK *3364*) in v.6 and the "words" (*rhēmata*, GK *4839*) in v.8. The former refers to the divine message as a whole, and the latter calls attention to the individual sayings of Jesus. The disciples were convinced that Jesus had come to them from God, and they believed that God had in fact sent him.

That knowledge and faith occur in parallel clauses (v.8b) reminds us that the two are by no means separate and unrelated activities. Calvin, 2:743, said that "nothing can be known aright of God but by faith" and "in faith there is such certainty that it is justly called knowledge." Modern

thought tends to restrict knowledge to what may be verified by scientific methodology and relegates faith to the sphere of the unprovable. The result is a reductionistic approach to reality that excludes from intelligent discussion all the genuinely important issues of life. The disciples "knew with certainty" and therefore "believed." As theologian and apologist Edward J. Carnell often said, "Faith is the resting of the mind in the sufficiency of the evidence." The disciples accepted the words of Jesus, knew with certainty that he was from God, and believed in his redemptive mission.

9 Jesus prays not for the world but for those whom God has given him out of the world (cf. v.6). He specifically says, "I am not praying for the world"—a statement that has caused some concern because it seems inconsistent with the fact that "God so loved the world that he gave his one and only Son" (3:16). But Jesus is not talking here about the world in the sense of individual people for whom he is about to die. In John's gospel, "the world" usually designates human society organized apart from God. He could not pray for this kind of world in the same way he would pray for his disciples because it was bitterly antagonistic to all he came to do. The only hope for the world is to cease being the world. That Jesus did, in fact, pray for the salvation of *individuals* in the world is clear from vv. 21 and 23, where he asks the Father that the world might believe that he had been sent by God. (See Mt 5:24 and Lk 23:34 for examples of Jesus' prayerful concern for those who were not his own.)

In v.6 Jesus said that his disciples belonged to the Father before they were given to the Son. Now he says that they still belong to the Father ("they are yours"). The unity of Father and Son is such that distinctions in the Godhead tend to blur and responsibilities overlap. It is worth noting that the Greek text of v.9 begins with a strong emphasis on the personal pronoun (*egō*)—"*I* pray for them." The

Lord himself takes the initiative and offers his prayers to the Father on behalf of those entrusted to his care. Their safety is of crucial importance because from a human standpoint the salvation of the world depended on their security. The Greek verb for prayer throughout ch. 17 (vv.9, 15, 20) is *erōtaō* (GK *2263*), which etymologically carries the idea of inquiry rather than the stronger idea of petition.

10 That the pronominal adjectives in the first two clauses are neuter (*ema* and *sa*) seems to extend divine ownership beyond persons to include all creation. The disciples would not have been surprised when Jesus said to the Father, "All I have is yours," but the claim that followed ("all you have is mine") must have struck them as remarkable, to say the least. No sane man would dare to pretend he was co-owner with God of everything that exists. That would be the sole prerogative of the eternal Son, by and for whom all things were created (Col 1:16). That Jesus made such claims leaves us with the alternatives posed by C. S. Lewis ("What Are We to Make of Jesus Christ?" in *God in the Dock* [Grand Rapids: Eerdmans, 1970], 157–58)—either he was who he said he was, or he was "a megalomanic, compared with whom Hitler was the most sane and humble of men . . . a complete lunatic."

Jesus then declares, "And glory has come to me through them." Since the Greek *autois* ("them") can be either neuter or masculine, it is difficult to know whether the intended antecedent was "all I have/all you have" or "those you have given me" (v.9, i.e., the disciples). It is probably better to take the first part of v.10 as a parenthetical remark and allow what follows to complete the thought about the disciples. When Jesus speaks of glory having come to him through the disciples, he may be placing himself ahead in time and commenting on what would happen in the early period of the expanding church. Or it may be no more than a way of saying

with certainty that this is what will happen. Carson, 561, remarks that "the extent to which Jesus has been glorified in the lives of his disciples is still pathetically slim compared with what will yet be." God's perspective is never limited by considerations of time. He is the One who "inhabits eternity" (Isa 57:15 NKJV)—the "Alpha and the Omega . . . who is, and who was, and who is to come" (Rev 1:8).

11 The time for parting was near. Jesus was about to go back to the Father. Being "in the world" was far more than a geographic reference. It involved sharing the limitations of the human experience. When Jesus entered the world, he not only came to where we are but also placed himself within the restrictions of life as we know it. His incarnation was complete. Of Jesus, the author of Hebrews says, "He had to be made like his brothers in every way" (2:17)—he "shared in [our] humanity" (2:14) and was "tempted in every way, just as we are" (4:15). Earlier John spoke of Jesus as *going* to God (16:10, 17, 28).

Now, addressing God directly, he speaks of coming back to the Father. There is no way that we, with the imperfections and limitations of our humanity, can ever gain an adequate understanding of the incredible joy associated with the Son's return to the Father. If God "so loved" prodigals such as you and me, what joy must he have experienced when his "one and only Son" returned as the conquering Lamb!

Jesus returns to the Father, but the disciples are still in the world. Being "in the world" involves bearing the hostility of the world (cf. 15:18–25). Satan is no more willing for believers to escape his displeasure than he was to allow Jesus to live out his life without opposition. This being the case, Jesus prays to the Father, "Protect them by the power of your name." The NIV represents an interpretation of the Greek text (which says only, "Keep them in your name") that takes "in your name" in the sense of "by the power of your name." Some commentators understand the reference to the "name" in the light of the tendency in Judaism to avoid the sacred tetragrammaton, YHWH. In that case, Jesus would be asking the Father to protect the disciples by the power contained in the unspeakable "name" of God. More likely the "name" refers to the embodiment of God's character and power. Weymouth's translation ("keep them true to Thy name") is interesting but does not fit the context as well. In any case, the world in which the disciples lived and from which they would need to be protected was not the physical world but the world of sinful contamination. Elsewhere it is described as consisting of "the cravings of sinful man, the lust of his eyes and the boasting of what he has and does" (1Jn 2:16). Opposition to the believer arises both from without and from within.

Jesus addresses God with a title used only here in the NT: "Holy Father" (though cf. 1Pe 1:15–16; Rev 4:8; 6:10). Morris, 726–27, thinks the reason the title is not used more often is that the people of the OT had so thoroughly emphasized God's holiness, over against the nation's tendency to presume on his tender love and care, that God was often thought of as lofty and remote. The title may have been suggested by its verbal association with the sanctification of both the disciples and Jesus in vv.17 and 19—*hagiazō* ("to set apart for sacred use," GK *39*) comes from the same root as *hagios* ("holy," GK *41*). In any case, it suggests both that God exists in another and higher realm (he is absolutely and uniquely "Holy") and that at the same time he is present and available (he is "Father").

12 When Jesus was with the disciples, he had "protected them and kept them safe." (*Phylassō* [GK *5875*] was used in Hellenistic Greek for guard duty, and the cognate noun, *phylakē* [GK *5871*], was a common word for "prison.") He accomplished this by the name (i.e., by the power that resided in the character of God) the Father had given him. Jesus accomplished no works of wonder during his incarnate state by virtue of any power residing in him as a divine being. His reliance was totally on God the Father working through the agency of the Holy Spirit.

All the disciples except "the one doomed to destruction" were kept safe. The play on words in the Greek text can be seen in the paraphrase, "No one was destroyed [*apōleto*, GK *660*] except the one destined for destruction [*apōleias*, GK *724*]." The designation "son of perdition" (KJV) is found elsewhere in the NT only in 2 Thessalonians 2:3, where it is used of "the man of sin," i.e., the Antichrist. Judas was not predestined to destruction but chose the course of action that led to it. It was with his full consent, not against his will, that he ended up where he did. A life of disobedience and deception leads steadily on toward the predetermined end of destruction. Actions determine destiny. Scripture was "fulfilled" in the sense that God's principles are carried out in the consequences that inevitably flow from actions taken. To live like a "lost" person is ultimately to be lost. God does not coerce people to accept his grace and live according to his commands. There are no automatons in the kingdom of God.

13 Jesus once again says to the Father that he is coming to him (cf. v.11—note the direct address). If "these things" refers to the various requests in Jesus' prayer, then it probably follows that the prayer was spoken out loud and within the hearing of the disciples. The expression could refer, however, not simply to Jesus' prayer but to all he had shared with the group of disciples during their last evening together.

One purpose of the prayer was that his followers might have "the full measure of [his] joy within [them]." The joy that Jesus experienced was essentially the profound satisfaction that inevitably accompanies perfect obedience (cf. 3:29; 15:11). The fact that obedience would lead to the ultimate act of self-sacrifice is inconsequential. Joy is the experience of complete union with the redemptive purposes of God in history. For Jesus it was the cross. For us it may not be a wooden cross, but it will be death to self and whatever this may involve in our specific circumstances. Jesus prays that the joy he has found in obedience to the Father will be shared by all who follow his example. This joy finds its completion in the eternal state, when we will see him face-to-face. Bultmann, 388, notes that in rabbinic writings fullness of joy is an eschatological concept.

14 The "word" Jesus gave to his disciples included all that Jesus had taught during his earthly ministry. His teaching was nothing less than the very word of God. The world's reaction to those who heard and accepted the message was one of hatred. There may be some significance in the fact that the *giving* of Jesus in v.14 is in the perfect tense (*dedōka*, GK *1443*), while the *hatred* of the world is in the aorist (*emisēsen*, GK *3631*). God's message continues forever, while the hatred of the world is terminated in time.

The followers of Jesus are hated because they are "not of the world," even as Jesus was not of the world (repeated in v.16). To be "of the world" means to share the basic outlook of the world, i.e., hostility toward God (cf. 8:23). The disciples are not of the world in the sense that they have been born from above (3:1–8). Their allegiance is no longer to this world but to God and his kingdom. For this very reason, they receive the same treatment from the enemies of God. The hostility of the world toward God is also taught elsewhere in Scripture. James declares that "friendship with the world is hatred toward God" (Jas 4:4), and Paul regards the present age as "evil" (Gal 1:4). Those who take their stand with God must be prepared to experience the wrath of a godless society. Brown, 764, comments

that "passages such as those we have found in John have a message for an era that becomes naively optimistic about changing the world or even about affirming its values without change."

15 In the OT we find that Moses, Elijah, and Jonah all prayed that they might die (Nu 11:15; 1Ki 19:4; Jnh 4:3, 8)—better to be taken "out of the world," so they thought, than to suffer any longer for what appears to be a lost cause. But God does not remove his servants from the world; it is the specific arena of their ministry. The message of redemption serves no purpose apart from those who need to hear it. It is less important that we "hear the old, old story" yet again than it is that we share it with those who have never heard. While a hostile world may not be the most receptive audience, they are the ones who need to hear the message.

Jesus prays that his disciples be protected "from the evil one." *Tou ponērou* (GK *4505*) could be taken as neuter and translated "evil" (so KJV), but it is better to take it as masculine and translate "the evil one" (cf. 1Jn 2:13; 3:12; 5:18). To be protected *ek* ("out of") the evil one assumes that believers are in danger of falling into the grasp of Satan. One of contemporary Christianity's most serious failings is that it seems to proceed oblivious to Satan's opposition to God's work in the world. While believers regularly recite the Lord's Prayer with its petition to "deliver us from the evil one" (Mt 6:13), life seems to go on as though all such phrases are just nostalgic reminders of an earlier period in which people believed in demonic beings.

17 Because the disciples are about to begin their ministry, Jesus prays that God will "sanctify them." In the LXX, the Greek *hagiazō* ("sanctify," "consecrate") is used for the setting apart of both people (Ex 28:41) and things (Ex 28:38) for sacred use. By that act of consecration, a person was brought into the sphere of the sacred and dedicated to the service of God.

The sanctification of which Jesus speaks is brought about "by the truth"—not truth in a general sense but truth that has come by divine revelation ("your word is truth"). Earlier Jesus had told his disciples, "You are already clean because of the word I have spoken to you" (15:3). It is the word of God that cleanses believers and sets them apart for effective work in the "present evil age" (Gal 1:4). What God has spoken through his prophets is absolutely trustworthy (cf. 2Sa 7:28; 1Ki 17:24). Sadly, the famine of which Amos spoke—"a famine of hearing the words of the LORD" (Am 8:11)—is still with us in the modern world. In far too many pulpits, current spokespersons are giving their best psychological insights but failing to bring "a word from the beyond." Hungry parishioners are deprived of God's word and offered as a substitute people's best thoughts disguised in quasi-religious terms. To *do* the work of God one needs to *use* the word of God. It is the word of God that is "the sword of the Spirit" (Eph 6:17). Nothing else will accomplish the task.

18 The disciples are sent into the world in the same way that Jesus was sent into the world ("as you sent me . . . , I have sent them"). The mission Jesus began is to be completed by his followers. While they play a somewhat different role, their purpose in going into the world is the same as his, i.e., to reclaim for their rightful owner those who have turned their backs on God. God's purpose in sending his Son was not to condemn but to save the world (3:17). This same message of hope constitutes the foundational truth of the apostolic proclamation.

19 In order that the disciples may be truly sanctified, Jesus says, "For them I sanctify myself." In this act of consecration he is both priest and victim (cf. Heb 9:12–14). Lindars, 528–29, says, "the preposition *hyper* ["for" or "in behalf of"] unmistakably introduces a sacrificial connotation." It is Jesus' sacrifice on the cross that ultimately leads to holiness on the part of his people. Titus 2:14 says that he gave himself for us (*hyper hēmōn*) "to purify for himself a people that are his very own" (cf. Eph 5:26; 1Pe 2:24). God's redemptive work is not complete until all who come to him become like him. Redemption is the re-creation of a family likeness in all who enter the human race and thereby suffer the devastating effects of Adam's tragic choice.

NOTES

9 It is interesting that in this chapter, which records the high priestly prayer of Jesus, only one of the various Greek verbs for prayer is found. The word ἐρωτάω (*erōtaō*, GK *2263*) is the common verb for asking and is found sixty-three times in the NT, most often in connection with a simple question or request. Jesus uses it three times in his prayer (vv.9, 15, 20). The NIV's "he looked toward heaven and prayed" (v.1) translates εἶπεν (*eipen*, "he said," GK *3306*, as the NASB has it).

11 Seven times in ch. 17 Jesus prays for his followers using the Greek connective ἵνα ὦσιν (*hina ōsin*, "so that they might be") introducing a purpose/result clause (vv.11, 19, 21 [twice], 22, 23, 24). Four times the prayer is for unity, which according to Jesus' prayer is God's method of evangelism ("so that the world may believe that you have sent me," v.21; "to let the world know that you sent me and have loved them even as you have loved me," v.23).

3. Jesus Prays for All Believers (17:20–26)

[20]"My prayer is not for them alone. I pray also for those who will believe in me through their message, [21]that all of them may be one, Father, just as you are in me and I am in you. May they also be in us so that the world may believe that you have sent me. [22]I have given them the glory that you gave me, that they may be one as we are one: [23]I in them and you in me. May they be brought to complete unity to let the world know that you sent me and have loved them even as you have loved me.

[24]"Father, I want those you have given me to be with me where I am, and to see my glory, the glory you have given me because you loved me before the creation of the world.

[25]"Righteous Father, though the world does not know you, I know you, and they know that you have sent me. [26]I have made you known to them, and will continue to make you known in order that the love you have for me may be in them and that I myself may be in them."

COMMENTARY

20 Jesus now extends the scope of his prayer to include all "who will believe in me." It is encouraging to realize that we in the twenty-first century who have placed our faith in Jesus are beneficiaries of this remarkable prayer. His prayer was for everyone who down through the centuries would respond to him in faith. Jesus foresaw a continuing community of the faithful, extending from his own band of disciples through each succeeding generation until the time when he would come again. From a human standpoint, this would depend on the willingness of each generation to continue Jesus' ministry to the world. It is "through their message" that people come to faith (cf. Ro 10:17). Temple, 2:326, notes, "Wherever there is a true disciple, there are others whom he has won or is winning." It is encouraging to know that as we share the message with others, Jesus is praying for them. Our evangelistic efforts do not depend on our own piety or persuasiveness.

21 Jesus' ultimate purpose in praying for those who will believe is that "all of them may be one." This statement is often used in ecumenical discussions as the basis for encouraging ecclesiastical union. The unity for which Jesus prays, however, is analogous to that of the Father and the Son ("just as you are in me and I am in you")—a unity in which the members do not lose their identity. Unity does not require uniformity. The true secret of Christian unity is for believers to be one with each other by virtue of being one with the Father and the Son. This is a supernatural unity that expresses itself in love. It is more than a mystical union, because it results in the world seeing the results and being brought to believing faith ("so that the world may believe that you have sent me").

Granted, the church today seems more often to be in disarray. It is more natural for people to be divided than to stand together as one. Calvin, 2:147, says that "the ruin of the human race is that, alienated from God, it is also broken and scattered in itself." Church divisions result in great injury to the cause of Jesus Christ. They waste time, absorb energy, and give the world a ready-made excuse for unbelief. Unity in the church will not come as a result of committees assigned to the task but by a renewal of personal fellowship with the Lord so profound as to be comparable to the union between the Father and the Son. The Christian life is a supernatural experience made possible by remaining in constant contact with the source of all spiritual power. The world will never be impressed by the numerical size or the self-declared importance of the church but only by seeing the unity of its members who live in love and serve the common goal of pointing others to faith. While unity itself has no power to convert, it opens the channels through which God's redemptive love flows out with a unique ability to heal and restore.

22 The glory the Father gave to the Son has been given by the Son to his followers. This glory is the radiant presence of God. As God was at work in and through his Son, so also will he now complete his redemptive task through those who by faith are one with him. The glory of God is manifested in the lives of the faithful. The promise of Immanuel—"God with us" (Mt 1:23)—is fulfilled in the lives and ministry of believers. As Jesus' true glory was the cross, so will our glory be experienced in lowly service for others.

The purpose for which glory is given is that believers may be one as Father and Son are one. The relationship within the Godhead is the model for Christian unity. Through the prophet Jeremiah, God promised his people that he would give them "singleness of heart and action" (Jer 32:39). If the glory of God is the splendor and power of God's presence, then the unity God desires will come as we grasp the incredible truth that God has taken up his abode in the lives of his children. To be one with God is to

be one with all others who call him Father. It is his glory, his presence, that makes the difference.

23 The union that links Father, Son, and believer ("I in them and you in me") has as its purpose that the followers of Jesus "be brought to complete unity." The perfect passive participle *teteleiōmenoi* ("perfected," GK *5464*) used periphrastically indicates a permanent state. That this perfected or completed unity does have an effect on the world reveals that Jesus is not speaking of some eschatological reality but of a condition intended to prevail at the present time. Sadly, the current condition of the church falls tragically short of God's expectations. Verse 21 indicated that the unity of believers would lead the world to believe that the Father had sent the Son; in v.23 Jesus repeats the point and adds as a second purpose of Christian unity that it will lead the world to know that God has loved them even as he has loved Jesus. Brown, 772, comments, "The standard of comparison is breathtaking but logical . . . . God loves these children as He loves His Son." It would seem that love is incapable of existing in various degrees. If love is "selfless concern in action on behalf of the other," then God's love is not parceled out in degrees, depending on the worth or condition of the one loved.

24 Verses 24–26 serve as a general conclusion to the entire prayer. For the fifth time in the prayer, Jesus addresses God as "Father." Some think that by using the verb "I want" (*thelō*, GK *2527*) instead of "I pray" (*erōtaō*, vv.9, 15, 20), Jesus is informing God of his will rather than making a request. (Brown, 772, says "he majestically expresses his will.") Whether the change in verbs can bear this interpretation is questionable. In any case, Jesus is not insisting on his will over against that of the Father (cf. Mk 14:36).

His desire is that those whom the Father has given him be with him where he is. Going to the Father will separate him from his followers, but the time is coming when once again they will be united forever. Verse 24 is primarily eschatological. In that day they will "see [his] glory." It is a glory that stems from the eternal love of the Father for the Son. It is a splendor the Son enjoyed before the creation of the world (cf. v.5; Mt 25:34). As we delight to share with loved ones the sights and sounds of places they have never seen, so Jesus looks forward to that eternal day when he will be able to share with us the glory that has been his from eternity past.

25 Only here is God addressed as "Righteous Father" (cf. v.20, "Holy Father"). Attention is called to his righteousness (or justice), because standing before him are two groups: the world, and those who acknowledge the divine origin of Jesus. The syntax of v.25 has led some to take the middle clause ("I know you") as a parenthesis, which then sets the other two clauses in sharper contrast ("the world does not know you," but "they know that you have sent me"). The NIV translates all three aorist verbs as present to emphasize the continuing nature of people's response to Jesus' claims.

26 Once again Jesus says to the Father, "I have made you known to them" (cf. v.6). The Greek text says, "I have made known to them your name." A major role of the incarnate Jesus was to reveal the character of God to the world. In ch. 1 John wrote, "No one has ever seen God, but God the One and Only, who is at the Father's side, has made him known" (1:18). Apart from knowing God there is no basis for knowing anything else. Jesus will continue to make God known through the work of the Paraclete (14:26; 16:13) as well as through the close personal union referred to in the prayer.

The purpose of such revelation is that the Father's love for his Son might also be in the disciples. The Greek *en autois* ("in them," used twice in v.26) can mean either "within them" individually or "among them" corporately. There is no reason that it should be limited to either one. The love of God in the lives of individual believers will also be a love that exists among them.

Not only will God's love be in them, but Jesus himself will also be in them. At the root of the redemptive work of God is relationship. The relationship of the triune God carries over to his saving work on behalf of the world. It is because God dwells in and among his people through the agency of his Son and Spirit that the message of his love is transmitted to each succeeding generation. History will give way to eternity as the believing multitudes are swept up into the eternal glory of Father and Son. In the end, as in the beginning, perfect love will express itself in perfect fellowship. The discord of sin will be forever removed, and the church eternal will live in joyous unity to the everlasting glory of God.

NOTES

20 A quick survey of the standard NT translations shows indecision as to whether the present participle πιστευόντων (*pisteuontōn*, GK 4409) is referring to those who at that time heard the apostles' word and believed, or whether it should be taken in a future sense and include all those who would someday hear the message and believe. The NASB, ASV, RSV, and NET take it as referring to converts to the apostles' message in that day; the KJV, NIV, NKJV, NRSV, and ESV understand it in a future sense, applicable even today.

VI. THE LAMB OF GOD IS SLAIN (18:1–19:42)

OVERVIEW

John 18 brings us to the final series of events that mark the close of Jesus' earthly life. The account in chs. 18 and 19 is typically called the "passion narrative"—a designation that reflects the sufferings of Jesus during the last dark hours before his death. The centrality of the death and resurrection of Jesus in the gospel narrative is emphasized by the description of the fourth gospel as the passion story with an extended introduction.

It is often mentioned that John's narrative differs to some extent from what we have in the Synoptics.

For example, in his account of Gethsemane John says nothing of Jesus' agony in the garden (Lk 22:40–46), of the kiss by Judas (Mt 26:49), or of the flight of the disciples (Mk 14:50). He adds a reference to the reaction of the soldiers sent to arrest Jesus (Jn 18:6). While all four gospel writers follow the same general sequence, each tells the story in his own way and selects those details that help to make a specific emphasis. John stresses Jesus' command of the situation and the sovereign control of God in the events taking place.

A. The Betrayal and Arrest of Jesus (18:1–11)

¹When he had finished praying, Jesus left with his disciples and crossed the Kidron Valley. On the other side there was an olive grove, and he and his disciples went into it.

²Now Judas, who betrayed him, knew the place, because Jesus had often met there with his disciples. ³So Judas came to the grove, guiding a detachment of soldiers and some officials from the chief priests and Pharisees. They were carrying torches, lanterns and weapons.

⁴Jesus, knowing all that was going to happen to him, went out and asked them, "Who is it you want?"

⁵"Jesus of Nazareth," they replied.

"I am he," Jesus said. (And Judas the traitor was standing there with them.) ⁶When Jesus said, "I am he," they drew back and fell to the ground.

⁷Again he asked them, "Who is it you want?"

And they said, "Jesus of Nazareth."

⁸"I told you that I am he," Jesus answered. "If you are looking for me, then let these men go." ⁹This happened so that the words he had spoken would be fulfilled: "I have not lost one of those you gave me."

¹⁰Then Simon Peter, who had a sword, drew it and struck the high priest's servant, cutting off his right ear. (The servant's name was Malchus.)

¹¹Jesus commanded Peter, "Put your sword away! Shall I not drink the cup the Father has given me?"

COMMENTARY

1 The NIV takes the *tauta* ("these things") of the Greek text as referring to the prayer in ch. 17 and translates, "When he had finished praying." It is possible, however, that the reference is wider and includes all the teaching from ch. 13 on. In any case, Jesus and his disciples departed and crossed the Kidron Valley. If the teaching in chs. 15–17 was given by Jesus *after* he had left the upper room (cf. 14:31, "Come now; let us leave"), then ch. 18 marks his departure from the city. Otherwise v.1 refers to his leaving the upper room. It was Jewish custom that Passover evening should be spent in Jerusalem. To accommodate the large crowds it was necessary to extend the boundaries of the city to include nearby villages. For Jesus and his disciples to spend the night across the Kidron Valley in a sheltered garden would have satisfied this expectation.

The Kidron Valley runs south along the eastern side of the plateau of Jerusalem and joins the Valley of Hinnom as it continues southeast to the Dead Sea. Except during the period of heavy winter rains, it is a deep, dry wadi. The Greek *cheimarrou tou Kedrōn* means "the winter-flowing Kidron" (Brown, 806; NASB, "ravine of the Kidron"). Beyond the Kidron to the east is the Mount of Olives, on whose lower slopes is an olive grove the Synoptics designate as Gethsemane (Mk 14:32). The owner of the grove is not known to us, though some have conjectured that it may have belonged to the parents of the young man mentioned (autobiographically?) only in Mark (14:51–52) who escaped the grasp of the soldiers and ran away naked.

2 Judas is about to show the Jewish authorities not which one in the group is Jesus but where Jesus can be found and arrested without exciting a mob reaction. At the very time when the disciples were asleep in the garden, those bent on evil were busily engaged with their clandestine plans. We pray, "Deliver us from the evil one" (Mt 6:13) but so often fail to realize how real and present is the one who is determined to do us harm. Some have compared the victorious struggle of Jesus in the garden with the failure of the first Adam in another garden (Ge 3).

3 Judas arrives with a "detachment of soldiers" (NASB, "*Roman* cohort). A *speira* (GK *5061*) was the Greek equivalent of the Latin cohort, the tenth part of a legion, and therefore normally about six hundred men. The term was also used for a smaller group of approximately two hundred (the maniple). In either case, it was large enough to warrant the presence of a *chiliarchos*, a "commander" (cf. v.12) of a thousand (GK *5941*). Along with the detachment of Roman soldiers from the fortress of Antonia came "officials from the chief priests and Pharisees" (temple police). The surprisingly large size of the group leads Barclay, 223, to comment, "What a compliment to the power of Jesus!" It would appear that Pilate placed so many soldiers at the disposal of the priestly aristocracy because he feared the danger of a popular uprising. At times of religious festivals the nationalistic spirit of a people dominated by a foreign power would be running high.

That Jewish authorities had taken the initiative in the capture of Jesus is clear from the fact that he was taken to the high priest (vv.12–13), not immediately to Pilate. Some have wondered why it would be necessary for the captors to carry torches and lanterns, since Passover always took place during full moon. It may have been cloudy or, more likely, they may have expected that Jesus would hide in some dark corner of the garden.

4 Throughout John's presentation of the events leading up to the crucifixion is a strong emphasis on Jesus' complete control of the situation. As the soldiers and temple police approached the garden, Jesus did not try to escape by retreating into the shadows; rather, he went out to meet them. We are probably to understand that he went out of the *garden* rather than out of the *darkness* into the light of the torches. While the first Adam hid in the garden, the Second Adam presented himself boldly to his adversaries.

After the feeding of the five thousand, the people would have by force made him king, so Jesus withdrew into the hills by himself (6:15). Now his opponents come to take him by force to the cross, and he steps forward to offer himself. Jesus is not arrested against his will. He is not taken captive, but "knowing all that was going to happen to him," he asks, somewhat rhetorically, who it is that they want. Jesus' foreknowledge has been seen throughout the gospel (cf. 2:25; 6:64; 13:1, 3; 16:19). That he was fully aware of all that the next few hours would hold makes his obedience all the more remarkable. He went to the cross not as a victim but as a willing sacrifice. His life and death were fully intentional, and we are the ones who receive the reward of his obedience.

John does not record the kiss of Judas (cf. Mk 14:44–45), but it may have taken place just before Jesus asked, "Who is it you want?" With Jesus stepping forward to meet the armed mob, there would be no need to identify him from among the band of disciples. The kiss was a normal greeting between teacher and student. For Judas to have carried through with such a hypocritical act in that context was beneath contempt.

5 The soldiers declare that it is "Jesus of Nazareth" whom they wish to take into custody. Jesus responds, "I am he." The Greek (*egō eimi*) reflects the LXX rendering of the pivotal self-description of God in Exodus 3:14, where Moses is instructed by God to tell the Israelites that "I AM has sent me to you" (cf. the seven occurrences of *egō eimi* in John; "I am the bread of life" [6:35], etc.). For those familiar with the Greek Bible, Jesus' answer would probably have been understood as a claim to deity. Standing by with those who had come to arrest Jesus was Judas the traitor, or as it may be translated, "Judas, who was in the act of betraying him." It is difficult to overstress the poignancy of the scene. There in the garden Judas took his stand against the very one he professed to follow for the preceding three years. His betrayal of Jesus reveals how desperately wicked is the human heart. Such a shameful act violates even the most minimal standards of basic decency.

6 Jesus' complete control of the situation is seen in John's report (omitted in the Synoptics) that the soldiers "drew back and fell to the ground." Representative of earlier commentators is Reith, 131, who writes, "Before the calm courage of conscious innocence, force and hostility have often been quelled." Contemporary writings are more apt to question the historicity of the account. Lindars, 541, writes, "It can scarcely be regarded as an historically reliable detail. . . . It is John's way of expressing the theological fact that Jesus is above all earthly power." Haenchen, 2:165, questions where John got the "tradition" and decides that Christian scribalism had taken OT references from the "suffering pious" tradition and referred them to Jesus' passion.

Discussions of this sort reflect differing hermeneutical approaches to Scripture. If "John" were an editor working with various strands of tradition, then conjecture about what actually happened would be appropriate. If, on the other hand, he was an eyewitness of the event and wrote under the inspiration of the Holy Spirit, we should take the text at face value. The latter alternative is followed in this commentary. It is unnecessary to explain the scene as one in which those in front recoiled and caused everyone behind to stumble and fall (cf. Morris, 743–45). Similar reactions to the divine presence are found in Daniel 10:9 and Acts 9:4.

7–8 Once again Jesus asks who it is they want, and the answer is the same—"Jesus of Nazareth."

Jesus replies, "I told you that I am he." His unique-ness is emphasized by the repetition of *egō eimi* (lit., "I am") in vv.5, 6, and 8. Jesus' concern for the well-being of the disciples is clearly discerned in his request that they be allowed to go free.

9 John records that this happened in order to ful-fill the words spoken by Jesus (in 17:12), "I have not lost one of those you gave me." That Judas is not mentioned as an exception (as in 17:12 but not in 6:39) may indicate that by this time he had identi-fied completely with the enemy and in so doing revealed that he had never been "given" to Jesus by the Father. Another explanation is that Jesus did everything in his power to save Judas, but Judas acted deliberately as a free moral agent and chose a course of action that brought the inevitable conse-quences. Thus *Jesus* did not lose Judas; Judas was lost as a result of his own deliberate choice.

Some have questioned the difference between the spiritual protection for which Jesus prayed in 17:11–12 and the physical protection for which he now asks. Calvin, 2:155, wisely notes that in this precarious situation Jesus was not concerned merely for the bodily life of the disciples but wanted to spare them for the time being with an eye to their eternal salvation.

10 Although this event is recorded in all four gospels, only John tells us that the disciple in question was "Simon Peter" and that the servant was named "Malchus" (probably from the Semitic root *m-l-k*; cf. Heb. *melek*, "king," GK 4889). Peter's sword was undoubtedly a dagger or long knife rather than a full-length sword (*machaira*, GK 3479, rather than *rhom-phaia*, GK 4855). It is often mentioned that it was illegal to carry a sword on Passover night, but Lindars, 543, notes that *m. Šabb.* 6.4 explicitly permits it on the grounds that a man's weapons are "his adorn-ments." It has also been suggested that, since the slit-ting of a man's ear would disqualify him from priestly office (cf. David Daube, "Three Notes Having to Do with Johanan ben Zaccai," *JTS* NS 11 [1960]: 61), Peter's act was intended as a public insult. More prob-ably, Peter simply lashed out at the nearest person in the group that had come to take Jesus. That he severed the *right* ear could suggest that Peter was left-handed. There is certainly no reason to accept the conjecture that Peter was a cowardly right-hander who struck from behind. It is also better to take the diminutive *ōtarion* ("ear," GK 6064) as equivalent to *ous* ("ear," GK 4044; cf. Lk 22:50) and understand that the dam-age was done to the entire outer ear rather than the earlobe only. (For the latter, see Brown, 812.)

11 In the OT, the "cup" was often associated with the wrath of God (cf. Isa 51:17, 22; Jer 49:12). To "drink the cup" given by the Father was to accept the righteous retribution of a holy God—to experience the punishment for sin that must neces-sarily follow if the universe created by God is to be considered moral. God's purposes are not achieved by thoughtless reactions. Zeal uninformed by knowledge leads a person to play the fool more often than not.

NOTES

1 L&N, 1:52, says that χείμαρρος (*cheimarros*, GK 5929) refers to "a ravine or narrow valley in which a stream flows during the rainy season, but which is normally dry during the dry season—'ravine, wadi.'" BDAG, 1082, identifies it as "a stream of water that flows abundantly in the winter." They gloss, "winter tor-rent, ravine."

The word κῆπος (*kēpos*, GK 3057) refers to "a field used for the cultivation of herbs, fruits, flowers, or vegetables—'garden, orchard'" (L&N, 1.97). The NIV calls it an "olive grove" here and in 18:26 but reverts to "garden" in the three other occurrences in the NT (Lk 13:19; 19:41 [twice]). The NASB uses "garden" in all five places.

3 The NASB's "lanterns and torches" is to be preferred to the NIV's "torches and lanterns." While in earlier times φανός (*phanos*, GK 5749) referred to a torch, by NT times it was used of a type of outdoor lamp or lantern in which a small fire was protected in some way from the wind and rain. A λαμπάς (*lampas*, GK 3286) was a bundle of sticks lit and carried as a torch (cf. BDAG, 585).

B. Jesus' Trial and Peter's Denial (18:12–27)

¹²Then the detachment of soldiers with its commander and the Jewish officials arrested Jesus. They bound him ¹³and brought him first to Annas, who was the father-in-law of Caiaphas, the high priest that year. ¹⁴Caiaphas was the one who had advised the Jews that it would be good if one man died for the people.

¹⁵Simon Peter and another disciple were following Jesus. Because this disciple was known to the high priest, he went with Jesus into the high priest's courtyard, ¹⁶but Peter had to wait outside at the door. The other disciple, who was known to the high priest, came back, spoke to the girl on duty there and brought Peter in.

¹⁷"You are not one of his disciples, are you?" the girl at the door asked Peter.

He replied, "I am not."

¹⁸It was cold, and the servants and officials stood around a fire they had made to keep warm. Peter also was standing with them, warming himself.

¹⁹Meanwhile, the high priest questioned Jesus about his disciples and his teaching.

²⁰"I have spoken openly to the world," Jesus replied. "I always taught in synagogues or at the temple, where all the Jews come together. I said nothing in secret. ²¹Why question me? Ask those who heard me. Surely they know what I said."

²²When Jesus said this, one of the officials nearby struck him in the face. "Is this the way you answer the high priest?" he demanded.

²³"If I said something wrong," Jesus replied, "testify as to what is wrong. But if I spoke the truth, why did you strike me?" ²⁴Then Annas sent him, still bound, to Caiaphas the high priest.

²⁵As Simon Peter stood warming himself, he was asked, "You are not one of his disciples, are you?"

He denied it, saying, "I am not."

²⁶One of the high priest's servants, a relative of the man whose ear Peter had cut off, challenged him, "Didn't I see you with him in the olive grove?" ²⁷Again Peter denied it, and at that moment a rooster began to crow.

COMMENTARY

13 According to John's narrative, the just-arrested Jesus is taken first to Annas, who questions him (vv.13, 19–23), and then to Caiaphas (v.24), who sends him to Pilate for sentencing (vv.28–40). When this account is compared with the Synoptics several problems arise (see Notes). The major issue is that, according to the Synoptics, Caiaphas the high priest is the one who conducts the trial (cf. Mt 26:57–68), while in John Jesus is not sent to Caiaphas till after the questioning in vv.19–23.

The crafty nature of Annas and his practice of demanding exorbitant prices for sacrificial animals sold on the temple grounds are well known. The shops in the temple were called "the Bazaars of Annas." A passage from the Talmud reads as follows: "Woe is me because of the house of Ḥanin [family of Annas], woe is me because of their whisperings [their secret conclaves to devise oppressive measures]" (b. Pesaḥ. 57a). That Jesus should first be taken to the one who was in control of the ecclesiastical power structure is not surprising. Annas would take personal delight in seeing the one who had attacked his vested interests by cleansing the temple now bound and being brought to "justice."

13–14 Caiaphas, who was the high priest "that year"—i.e., that "fateful" or "notorious" year—was the one who had advised the Sanhedrin that it would be better for one man to die, even though innocent, than to place the entire nation in jeopardy (cf. 11:47–52). Ironically, the Jewish leaders would shortly send Jesus to his death, and within a generation the nation would be destroyed.

15–18 It is difficult to reconstruct everything that took place in the dark hours following Jesus' arrest. We know from Matthew 26:56 that "all the disciples deserted him and fled" (responses mentioned also by Mark but omitted by Luke and John). We can only conjecture that as Peter was running for his life, he suddenly realized how cowardly was his flight. We can picture him suddenly stopping and, after a moment's hesitation, retracing his path back to the scene of Jesus' arrest. Now he finds himself following Jesus, not as a disciple and faithful companion, but as a confused defector who cannot but follow along on the outskirts of the hostile crowd.

15 With Peter was another disciple, one who would shortly provide him access into the courtyard of the high priest. A good case can be made that "the other disciple" (v.16) was John the son of Zebedee. The same expression (but without the definite article) is used four times in ch. 20 of the one who ran to the tomb with Peter (20:2, 3, 4, 8)—undoubtedly John. Other suggestions for the identity of the other disciple include Nicodemus, Joseph of Arimathea, some member of the Sanhedrin who was a secret believer (cf. 12:42), or the owner of the house where Jesus and his disciples had celebrated their final meal together. Of these possibilities, the strongest by far is that the other disciple was John, the author of the fourth gospel.

The question arises, How could a Galilean fisherman be known to the high priest? While to be "known" could imply considerable familiarity (a close friend or even a relative), it could also indicate no more than a nodding acquaintance. We know that John's father was a fisherman with a business sufficiently large enough to employ hired men (Mk 1:20). It would not have been unusual for John to have been the one who brought Galilean salt fish to the court of the high priest during the time he worked for his father. A different though less satisfactory explanation builds on the fact that on John's mother's side, he was of priestly descent. (Salome, John's mother, was the sister of the Virgin Mary, who was related to Elizabeth, "a descendant of Aaron," Lk 1:5). Many writers think this verse in Luke is the basis for the statement by Polycrates (a second-century bishop of Ephesus) that John was by birth a priest and wore the *petalon*, a gold band inscribed with two Hebrew words signifying "HOLY TO THE LORD" and worn across the forehead (cf. Ex 28:36).

The "courtyard" into which the other disciple entered was an open atrium in the center of the palace building where the high priest lived. There is much to commend the suggestion that this may have been a common courtyard connecting two separate wings of the same palace in which Annas and Caiaphas lived, each in his own private quarters. This would be the courtyard through which Jesus would have passed as he was transferred from Annas to Caiaphas.

16 When the other disciple entered the courtyard, Peter was left waiting outside at the door. Some have suggested that the door was shut by divine providence and that Peter should have accepted it as such. In any case, the other disciple returned, spoke to the girl on duty, and secured entrance for Peter. That the doorkeeper was a woman (*tē thyrōrō*, GK *2601*; NIV, "girl on duty") would strengthen the case for the interrogation to have taken place at the private quarters of the high priest. Carson, 582, notes that "only men held such assignments in the temple precincts" (women porters are found at 2Sa 4:6 [LXX] and Ac 12:13). One can only wonder how often a well-intentioned kindness places another person in jeopardy. Had Peter not entered the courtyard, he would not have fallen into the trap that awaited him.

17 It is difficult to know the exact nuance of the question asked by the girl at the gate. Direct questions in Greek that begin with the interrogative particle *mē* ("not") normally expect a negative response; however, the inclusion here of *kai sy* ("also you") suggests that the expected answer may be positive. Lindars, 549, remarks that it implies "cautious assertion" and so constitutes a challenge. The question contains no necessary hostility. The maid may simply have been expressing surprise that not only the other disciple whom she knew but also a second companion of Jesus had followed the captors right to the house of the high priest. Bruce, 345, translates, "Oh no, not another!"

The question unwittingly invited a devious answer. Peter, who had boasted of his loyalty when he should have been humble (13:37) and was asleep in the garden when he should have been awake and in prayer (Mk 14:37), was not ready for the moment of testing. He quickly asserted that he was not one of Jesus' disciples. The suggestion that Peter's *ouk eimi* ("not I") here and in v.25 is to be understood over against the *egō eimi* ("I am") of Jesus in vv.5 and 8 reads too much into the text. Just a short time before, Jesus had told his sleepy disciple, "Watch and pray so that you will not fall into temptation" (Mk 14:38). Failing to heed the warning, Peter had now stumbled into a situation in which a simple question by a servant girl led him to deny his Lord. Temple, 2:343, writes that "we all know with what fatal ease we accept a position prepared for us if it is presented suddenly and offers a refuge from many troubles."

Note that what Peter denied was not his faith in Jesus but his relationship to him. How often today does that relationship go unexpressed and thus constitute one form of denial! The church carries out its mission when followers of Jesus do not hesitate to confess openly their allegiance to Jesus. Calvin's comment, 2:159, is all too true of many believers in almost every age: "Our courage is such that it fails of its own accord when there is no enemy."

18 The evening was cold, and the attendants (*hypēretai*, "officials," GK *5677*; cf. v.12) of the synagogue who had taken part in the capture of Jesus, along with the servants of the high priest, stood around a fire to keep warm. Once inside the gate, Peter moves into the circle around the fire and warms himself there. One falsehood leads inevitably to the next. Now he had to continue the charade and conceal his real character by pretending he was one of the group who had taken Jesus captive. Sin progressively binds the sinner, and every failure makes it increasingly difficult to reverse the trend. Peter's denials are a stark reminder of how absolutely dependent we are on the grace and power of God to overcome the deceptive assaults of sin.

19–24 John follows his account of Peter's first denial with the interrogation of Jesus by Annas (vv. 19–24). This is then followed by Peter's second and third denials (vv. 25–27). The arrangement invites a comparison between two "trials"—that of Jesus before a powerful high priest and that of Peter before servants of the high priest. Although improperly questioned and physically abused, Jesus conducts himself with dignity and propriety. By contrast, Peter's bravado disappears at the first relatively innocent query by a household servant. Such is the weakness of human nature.

19 The "high priest" here is Annas (see v. 24). Although at that time he was not serving as the official high priest (appointed by the Romans during this period), he would continue to carry the title as a courtesy. It is best to take the questioning before Annas as an informal session for the purpose of gaining evidence that could be used before the Sanhedrin to secure a verdict. Kysar, 272–73, points out that all three essential elements of the synoptic accounts of the religious trial (the witnesses against Jesus, the question of his messianic claim, and the charge of blasphemy) are missing in John. This observation supports the view that while John records the session before Annas, he passes over the trial before Caiaphas as recorded in the Synoptics (Mt 26:57–68 par.). It does not, however, relieve Annas of the illegality of interrogating Jesus to gain incriminating evidence. According to Jewish law, the accused was not required to testify against himself.

The high priest asks first about Jesus' disciples and then about his teaching. The order is significant. Knowing that sedition would be the charge most likely to move Pilate to action, Annas seeks to discover evidence about the size of Jesus' following and the extent of their activities. Such evidence would lend credibility to the charge he intended to level. Jesus must be made to appear as a revolutionary threat to Pilate's administration (cf. 19:12).

20 Rather than answering the questions raised by Annas, Jesus challenged the legitimacy of the interrogation. In order to establish a charge, Jewish law required witnesses. Jesus had conducted his ministry in public. Nothing had been done secretly or behind closed doors. If Annas needed witnesses, they would not be hard to find. He should ask those who had heard Jesus' public discourses; they would know everything that had been said. It is contrary to established legal practices to trap a person into providing evidence against himself. That Jesus had "spoken openly" (*parrēsia*, GK *4244*) to the world means that he had delivered his message boldly and without ambiguity (cf. 11:14, where Jesus tells his disciples "plainly" that Lazarus has died). John records only one instance in which Jesus taught in a synagogue but mentions several occasions when he taught in the temple precincts (cf. 6:59 with 7:14, 28; 8:20; 10:23).

Jesus' statement that he said "nothing in secret" was not a denial that he taught his disciples privately. It was only to say that he did not have two kinds of teaching—a private revolutionary brand for his followers and a public presentation designed to allay any suspicion that might arise. Nor does it conflict with other sayings, such as Matthew 10:27 ("What I tell you in the dark, speak in the daylight"), in which the context is quite distinct.

21–22 Jesus' demeanor before Annas reveals no trace of fear or timidity. Although he is the one being questioned, it is clear he is the one in control.

To his inquisitor Jesus says, "Why question me? Ask those who heard me. Surely they know what I said." In other words, "Why are you not following legal practice? Bring in witnesses, and let them tell you what I have been teaching. I am willing to stand trial if proper procedures are followed." Surprised by Jesus' straightforward and candid response, one of the attendants reached out and struck him in the face. The Greek *rhapisma* (lit., "a blow with a club," GK 4825) had come to mean "a slap in the face." It was insulting as well as painful. We can only conjecture that the abusive reaction of the attendant was motivated more by a desire to curry favor with the high priest than to redress a wrong. Exodus 22:28 taught, "Do not blaspheme God or curse the ruler of your people," but of course Jesus had done neither.

23 To the pompous demand that he not address the high priest with such effrontery, Jesus responds by calling into account the rude conduct of his antagonist. If he was guilty of having said something wrong (i.e., inadmissible in court), then let someone "testify to it" (Goodspeed), or "produce some evidence of it" (Brown, 827). But if what he said was true, then why was he slapped? Jesus is insisting on fair and legal treatment. The "trial" had thus far violated acceptable Jewish practice both in its method of questioning and in its willingness to allow personal abuse.

During his public ministry Jesus had taught that if someone strikes you on one cheek, you should turn the other to him also (Mt 5:39). Why then on this occasion didn't he follow his own teaching? The answer is that Jesus' sayings are not intended to be taken as unlimited in application. While retaliation for personal injury is not the appropriate response of a Christian in the majority of cases, there may be times when the failure to take a stand against injustice would violate some higher principle. In Acts 23:2–5 Paul apologized for calling the high priest a "whitewashed wall," but he hadn't realized that it was the high priest who was ordering others to strike him on the mouth. The situations are quite distinct.

24 Having made no progress with Jesus, Annas sends him to Caiaphas the high priest. As mentioned earlier, v.24 need not be relocated to the middle or the end of v.13. Nor should the aorist *apesteilen* ("sent," GK 690) be translated as a pluperfect ("had sent"). According to Bruce, 347, this tense is ruled out by the conjunction *oun* ("then"). It is best to take v.24 as it stands and understand it as noting that after the informal hearing before Annas, Jesus was sent to Caiaphas, who lived in another wing of the palace.

The poignant scene recorded by Luke in which Jesus turned and looked straight at Peter (22:61) may well have happened as Jesus was being taken across the courtyard for the next stage of his trial. Whether or not Jesus had been unbound during his questioning we do not know (the NIV has "still bound"). In either case, he was delivered bound to Caiaphas, as he had been to Annas (vv.12–13).

25 Peter continues to linger, warming himself by the fire. The imperfect *ēn* ("was") with the two perfect participles, *hestōs* and *thermainomenos* ("standing" and "warming," GK 2705, 2548), stresses this point. It is tragic that at the very time Jesus is standing before his accusers, Peter is found in the company of those who had taken his Master captive. Once again he was asked whether he was one of Jesus' disciples. There is some difficulty in the fact that while Matthew says that another girl asks the question (Mt 26:71), Mark implies it was the same girl (Mk 14:69), and Luke indicates it was a man (Lk 22:58). John has "they asked" (*eipon*, GK 3306), which the NIV translates as "he was asked." It would appear that the question arose among those around the fire and that, once asked, it was repeated by others as it was being directed to Peter. John's use of the plural ("they") may reflect rather accurately that the question was being pressed by a number of those whose interest about this stranger in their midst had now been aroused.

The conversation around the fire had to do with the one they had just seized in the garden of Gethsemane. The form of the question calls for a "No," but once again (as in v.17) there is in the query the suspicion that Peter *is* one of Jesus' disciples. The translation, "[Surely] you are not one of *his* disciples, are you?" reflects their surprise that one of Jesus' followers, having fled from the garden, would be so foolish as to risk entering the court of the high priest. This time Peter denies any association and says bluntly, "I am not." Calvin, 2:162, notes that "this is how Satan carries wretched men away when he has dislodged them." Once a lie has been told, it is easier to add to it yet another untruth than to correct the situation by telling the truth as it should have been told in the beginning. Sin binds the human spirit with cords that can be broken only by confession and a genuine return to truthfulness. The joy of the Christian life is often restored only by returning to that moment of untruthfulness and openly acknowledging that the intervening months or years have been marred by hypocrisy. How many lives have been rendered powerless by an unwillingness to repent and humbly endure the consequences!

26 A bit later ("about an hour," Lk 22:59) one of the high priest's servants challenged Peter with the question, "Didn't I see you with him in the olive grove?" This time in the Greek the form of the question (which begins with the negative *ouk* rather than the *mē* of the first two questions) expects an affirmative response. A "yes" is easier to anticipate when the question is translated, "I saw you with him in the olive grove, did I not?" This particular servant was a relative of the man whose ear Peter had cut off and would therefore have paid close attention to which of the disciples had offended the family honor. That the light from the charcoal fire (see *anthrakia* in 18:18) would have been quite similar to the illumination in the garden would have helped the servant recognize Peter on this later occasion. John's awareness that the servant's name was Malchus (v.10) and that this last questioner was one of his relatives reveals a rather precise knowledge of the household of the high priest.

27 For the third time Peter denied any association with Jesus, and at that very moment a rooster began to crow. Thus was fulfilled the prediction of Jesus in the upper room just a few hours earlier, "Before the rooster crows, you will disown me three times!" (13:38). In the NT era, the cock had the habit of crowing with such clocklike regularity that the four watches of the night were named Late, Midnight, Cockcrow (3:00 a.m.), and Early (cf. Mk 13:35, where the third division is named *alektorophōnia*, "cockcrowing," GK *231*; NIV, "when the rooster crows").

NOTES

12–14 Sensing the difficulty (see comments at v.13), copyists rearranged the verses in several ways. The fourth-century Sinaitic Syriac version places them in the following order: 13, 24, 14–15, 19–23, 16–18, 25–27. In addition to getting Jesus to Caiaphas before Annas's interrogation (vv.19–23), this reordering brings together into one sequence the three denials of Peter (vv.15–18, 25–27). A simpler rearrangement is followed by two twelfth-century MSS, one of which copies v.24 into the middle of v.13 (after πρῶτον, *prōton*), while the other places v.24 after v.13. Most scholars view the rearrangements simply as scribal attempts to improve the sequence.

One way to alleviate the problem is to take v.24 as a "deferred footnote," as though John, reflecting on what he has just written and aware of the misunderstanding it could cause, points out that he should have mentioned earlier that Jesus had been sent on to Caiaphas. The KJV follows this line of thought in its translation of v.24: "Now Annas had sent him bound unto Caiaphas the high priest." It may be better, however, to take the text as it stands and understand vv.19–23 as a preliminary questioning by Annas (the powerful former high priest), with the more formal trial conducted by Caiaphas (and recorded in the Synoptics; cf. Mt 26:57–68) being omitted by John. A comparison of the two interrogations shows them to be quite distinct—Annas asks about Jesus' teaching, while Caiaphas conducts a trial, complete with false witnesses and an official sentence.

That Annas would be called "the high priest" (v.19) presents no particular problem. We know that Annas served in that role from AD 6–15 and was succeeded by five sons in addition to Caiaphas, his son-in-law (cf. Josephus, *Ant.* 20.198). According to the OT, appointment to the office of high priest was for life (Nu 35:25). Thus, the deposition of Annas by the Roman procurator Valerius Gratus in AD 15 would not have been recognized by orthodox Jews. (Lk 3:2 speaks of "the high priesthood of Annas and Caiaphas"; cf. also the plural, "chief priests," in Jn 18:35 and the designation of Annas as "high priest" in Ac 4:6.) It is also quite possible that Annas lived in the same palace with his son-in-law and that the sending of Jesus to Caiaphas in v.24 need not have been to another house somewhere else in the city. This would provide some help in understanding why Peter's denials are interwoven in both interrogations as recorded in John and in the Synoptics.

15 The NASB's straightforward translation ("Simon Peter was following Jesus") is expanded by the NET to read, "Simon Peter . . . followed them as they brought Jesus to Annas." The NET's translator's note explains that "direct objects were often omitted in Greek when clear from the context." While this is certainly true of the Greek language, the additional words illustrate two different approaches to translation. Fidelity to the specific words of the original calls for "formal equivalence," while commitment to clarity and understanding in the receptor language is called "dynamic equivalence." Neither philosophy is intrinsically superior to the other; the question has to do with the purpose of the translation and the audience for whom it is intended. For the person who prizes readability and is concerned in a broader way with what the author had to say (rather than the words he used to say it), the dynamic equivalent is more suitable. For the person who is more concerned with an accurate translation of the actual words of the ancient text and accepts the challenge to determine the probable intention of the author, a formal equivalent translation is to be preferred.

16 The noun θυρωρός (*thyrōros*, "doorkeeper," "gatekeeper," GK *2601*) may be used in reference to a person of either sex. In 10:3 the "doorkeeper" (NASB; NIV, "watchman") is masculine (ὁ θυρωρός, *ho thyrōros*), while in 18:18 the "doorkeeper" (NASB; NIV, "girl on duty") is feminine (τῇ θυρωρῷ, *tē thyrōrō*).

18 The NASB correctly identifies the "fire" (NIV) as a "charcoal fire." The Greek word is ἀνθρακία (*anthrakia*, GK *471*) and refers to a pile of burning charcoal. L&N, 2.6, notes that it fits the context well, since "a charcoal fire provides a maximum of heat with a minimum of smoke." The word is found only in John (here and in 21:9), though the masculine noun ἄνθραξ (*anthrax*, "charcoal," GK *472*) is used by Paul in Romans 12:20 in quoting the proverbial statement of Proverbs 25:22, "you will heap burning coals on his head."

20 The noun παρρησία (*parrēsia*, "outspokenness," "frankness," GK *4244*; NIV, "openly") here carries the idea of "openness to the public" (BDAG, 781, paragraph 2). It inevitably involves a measure of courage. L&N, 25:158, states that the noun refers to "a state of boldness and confidence, sometimes implying intimidating circumstances."

22 Barclay (*The New Testament: A Translation by William Barclay* [Louisville: Westminster, 1999], 291) has the guard who slapped Jesus across the face exclaim, "How dare you answer the High Priest like that?" It is difficult to determine whether the question arose from the widespread expectation that leaders whom God had appointed be shown proper reverence (cf. Ex 22:28), or whether the reaction of the guard was simply motivated by personal considerations.

23 Barclay M. Newman and Eugene A. Nida (*A Translator's Handbook on the Gospel of John* [New York: United Bible Societies, 1980], 529) hold that Jesus' response is directed toward the high priest, not the official who struck him. They argue that the guard would not be the one to give evidence against Jesus and that it would be unlikely he would have slapped Jesus unless prompted by the high priest. Thus Jesus' question is understood as directed to the high priest: "Why did you cause the guard to slap me?"

27 Some hold that the ἀλεκτοροφωνία (*alektorophōnia*, "cockcrow"; in the NT only in Mk 13:35) was a specific reference to the Roman *gallicinium*, a technical term for the trumpet call that signaled the end of the third watch at 3:00 a.m.

C. Jesus Appears before Pilate (18:28–19:16a)

OVERVIEW

John does not describe Jesus' trial before the religious leader Caiaphas but moves quickly to the Roman phase of the trial (with Pilate). In 18:28–19:16a, Jesus is taken inside the official residence of the governor and then back out to his Jewish accusers at least six separate times. During this exchange, we see Pilate change from a relatively disinterested government official to a frightened functionary afraid of what the populace might do to his political future if he failed to cave in to their desires. Such is the character of those who live by expediency rather than conviction. Sadly, the nature of political life militates against judgments that are based on what is right in favor of what seems to promote the minimum social disturbance.

²⁸Then the Jews led Jesus from Caiaphas to the palace of the Roman governor. By now it was early morning, and to avoid ceremonial uncleanness the Jews did not enter the palace; they wanted to be able to eat the Passover. ²⁹So Pilate came out to them and asked, "What charges are you bringing against this man?"

³⁰"If he were not a criminal," they replied, "we would not have handed him over to you."

³¹Pilate said, "Take him yourselves and judge him by your own law."

"But we have no right to execute anyone," the Jews objected. ³²This happened so that the words Jesus had spoken indicating the kind of death he was going to die would be fulfilled.

³³Pilate then went back inside the palace, summoned Jesus and asked him, "Are you the king of the Jews?"

³⁴"Is that your own idea," Jesus asked, "or did others talk to you about me?"

³⁵"Am I a Jew?" Pilate replied. "It was your people and your chief priests who handed you over to me. What is it you have done?"

³⁶Jesus said, "My kingdom is not of this world. If it were, my servants would fight to prevent my arrest by the Jews. But now my kingdom is from another place."

³⁷"You are a king, then!" said Pilate.

Jesus answered, "You are right in saying I am a king. In fact, for this reason I was born, and for this I came into the world, to testify to the truth. Everyone on the side of truth listens to me."

³⁸"What is truth?" Pilate asked. With this he went out again to the Jews and said, "I find no basis for a charge against him. ³⁹But it is your custom for me to release to you one prisoner at the time of the Passover. Do you want me to release 'the king of the Jews'?"

⁴⁰They shouted back, "No, not him! Give us Barabbas!" Now Barabbas had taken part in a rebellion.

¹⁹:¹Then Pilate took Jesus and had him flogged. ²The soldiers twisted together a crown of thorns and put it on his head. They clothed him in a purple robe ³and went up to him again and again, saying, "Hail, king of the Jews!" And they struck him in the face.

⁴Once more Pilate came out and said to the Jews, "Look, I am bringing him out to you to let you know that I find no basis for a charge against him." ⁵When Jesus came out wearing the crown of thorns and the purple robe, Pilate said to them, "Here is the man!"

⁶As soon as the chief priests and their officials saw him, they shouted, "Crucify! Crucify!"

But Pilate answered, "You take him and crucify him. As for me, I find no basis for a charge against him."

⁷The Jews insisted, "We have a law, and according to that law he must die, because he claimed to be the Son of God."

⁸When Pilate heard this, he was even more afraid, ⁹and he went back inside the palace. "Where do you come from?" he asked Jesus, but Jesus gave him no answer. ¹⁰"Do you refuse to speak to me?" Pilate said. "Don't you realize I have power either to free you or to crucify you?"

¹¹Jesus answered, "You would have no power over me if it were not given to you from above. Therefore the one who handed me over to you is guilty of a greater sin."

¹²From then on, Pilate tried to set Jesus free, but the Jews kept shouting, "If you let this man go, you are no friend of Caesar. Anyone who claims to be a king opposes Caesar."

> [13]When Pilate heard this, he brought Jesus out and sat down on the judge's seat at a place known as the Stone Pavement (which in Aramaic is Gabbatha). [14]It was the day of Preparation of Passover Week, about the sixth hour.
>
> "Here is your king," Pilate said to the Jews.
>
> [15]But they shouted, "Take him away! Take him away! Crucify him!"
>
> "Shall I crucify your king?" Pilate asked.
>
> "We have no king but Caesar," the chief priests answered.
>
> [16a]Finally Pilate handed him over to them to be crucified.

COMMENTARY

28 From the house of Caiaphas, Jesus was led to the palace of the Roman governor. The Praetorium was the official residence of the Roman administrator. Originally it was the name given to the commander's headquarters in the center of a military camp. The Roman governor of Judea maintained his primary residence in Caesarea on the seacoast (cf. Ac 23:33–35), but in times when the national fervor of an occupied people could run high he would come with his soldiers to Jerusalem and stay in the Praetorium. His residence in Jerusalem was either in Herod's palace on the western wall or, more probably, in the Fortress of Antonia (a Hasmonean castle rebuilt by Herod the Great), located north of the temple area. The case for the latter is strengthened by the discovery of the "Stone Pavement" (*lithostrōtos*, GK *3346*, 19:13) under an adjacent convent, as well as the longstanding tradition that the Via Dolorosa began at the same location.

The transfer of Jesus to the Praetorium took place in the "early morning." In a technical sense, *prōi* ("early") stood for the fourth watch of the night (3:00–6:00 a.m.; cf. Mk 13:35), but here it is used in the more general sense of early in the morning. Mark 15:1 and parallels cite a morning meeting of the Sanhedrin. This would lend the appearance of legality to their decision, because Jewish law pro-

hibited verdicts involving the death sentence from being made at night.

The Jews did not enter the Roman garrison because to do so would have rendered them ceremonially unclean and kept them from eating the Passover. The dwelling places of the Gentiles were considered unclean for various reasons, such as the presence of yeast or the possibility that aborted fetuses had been discarded down the drains (cf. Str-B, 2:839). Although some types of ceremonial uncleanness lasted only until sundown and could be removed by means of a bath, others—especially those involving contact with a dead body—lasted for seven days. In any case, the Jews did not want to be defiled by entering the court of Pilate and run the risk of missing out on the Passover. Concern for ceremonial purity took precedence over the demands of moral integrity. Calvin, 2:163, notes that hypocrisy "is careful to cultivate ceremonies, but securely neglects the most important things." It has always been the choice of religious people to elevate their self-serving concern for ceremonial rigor over the basic and fundamental laws of justice and human rights.

If we follow the chronology of the Synoptics, which places the major Passover meal on the previous evening, the Passover referred to in v.28 would have been another of the meals eaten during the seven-day Feast of the Passover.

29–30 Since the Jews would not enter the Praetorium, Pilate went out to them to ask what accusations they were bringing against their prisoner. Pilate was the fifth Roman prefect of Judea (AD 26–36); an inscription from Caesarea designates him as *praefectus*. In the Roman provincial system, peaceful provinces were placed under the jurisdiction of the senate, while more unruly provinces requiring the presence of Roman troops were governed by procurators, who were responsible to the emperor. Josephus (*J.W.* 2.169–74; 175–77; *Ant.* 18.87) writes of three separate incidents in which Pilate unwisely aroused the hostility of the Jewish nation. After being recalled to Rome and convicted for his slaughter of the Samaritans, he committed suicide (cf. Eusebius, *Hist. eccl.* 2.7).

Pilate's question as to what charges the Jewish authorities were bringing indicated that he intended to conduct a regular trial rather than simply to pronounce the death sentence on a man already condemned by these people. This must have come as a considerable surprise to the Jews. After all, had not Pilate supplied them with a detachment of Roman soldiers when they went by night to arrest Jesus? Their disdainful response (v.30) was that if he were not a criminal, they would not have handed him over. The Jews wanted no further trial because they knew full well that they had no charge against him sustainable in a court of Roman law. *Houtos* ("this man") in the Greek text is spoken with contempt. That he was being delivered to Pilate was intended to imply that Jesus was in fact guilty of a serious offense against Rome.

31 Pilate's response is that the people should try him according to their own law. But that wouldn't do, because ever since AD 6, when Judea became a Roman province, the Jews had been denied the right to carry out the death sentence. Pilate undoubtedly enjoyed reminding them of their vassal status. That they had "no right to execute anyone" is true but creates a bit of a problem. Just a short time after the crucifixion, the Jews would put Stephen to death by stoning (Ac 7:57–60). Josephus (*Ant.* 20.200) reports the stoning of James the brother of Jesus, as well as the inscription on the wall separating the inner court of the temple that promised death for any Gentile who ventured past the barrier (cf. *J.W.* 6.126). And later Jewish law allowed execution by a number of methods—burning, stoning, strangling, and beheading. It would appear that while the Romans retained the power of the sword, the Jews were able, under certain circumstances, to take the law into their own hands without fear of reprisal.

32 According to Deuteronomy 21:23, to be hung on a tree was to bear the curse of God. Twice in Peter's sermons as recorded in Acts, he reminded his audience that the Jews killed Jesus by hanging him on a tree (Ac 5:30; 10:39). Since Jesus had predicted his own death by crucifixion (Mt 20:19; 26:2) and specifically referred to it as being "lifted up" (Jn 12:32–33; cf. 3:14; 8:28), his transfer to the Romans was necessary so that what he had said about the kind of death he would die "would be fulfilled." The most common charge leveled against Jesus during his earthly ministry was blasphemy, the penalty for which was death by stoning (Lev 24:16). The sovereign will of God was being carried out, even in the specific way in which Jesus would be put to death.

33 At this point, Pilate withdrew from the clamor of the Jewish officials, who were seeking an official sanction for their determination that Jesus be put to death, and reentered the Praetorium. Pilate summoned Jesus and asked him, "Are you the king of the Jews?" Luke records the specific charge the Jews had brought to Pilate against Jesus, namely, that he forbade the paying of tribute to Caesar and had claimed that he himself was a king (Lk 23:2).

The charge of messiahship was a subtle maneuver in that Jesus' spiritual kingship over Israel could be made to appear as rebellion against the imperial power of Rome. The Roman provincial system allowed for no "kings" among the captured peoples. Pilate's "Are you the king of the Jews?" was probably not a routine question to determine the truthfulness of the Jewish charge, but the puzzled reaction of a Roman authority to what must have seemed to have been a preposterous claim—"Are *you* [the pronoun is emphatic in the Greek text] the king of the Jews?"

34 Jesus responded by asking whether Pilate had brought the question up on his own initiative or whether it had been prompted by others. The difference is crucial. Had the question originated with Pilate, the answer would be no, for Jesus was not a political king. Had the question been suggested to him by the Jewish officials, the answer would be yes, because against that background he certainly *was* the messianic king of Israel. It could be that Jesus was appealing to Pilate's conscience and reminding him of his responsibility to decide the case on its merits apart from the subtle misrepresentation by the high priest and his accomplices.

35 Pilate's reply, "Am I a Jew?" calls for a negative response, as made clear in a translation such as, "Certainly you do not take me for a Jew, do you?" The implication is that he has no involvement or special interest in whatever the Jews intended regarding Jesus. He is his own man. After all, it was Jesus' own people who turned him over, and therefore he *must* have done something wrong. How simple (and at this moment helpful) it was to distance himself from any involvement in the issue.

36 The very fact that Jesus allowed himself to be handed over to Pilate is proof that his "kingdom" was not a political kingdom. If it had been, his servants would even then be fighting (note the imperfect tense of *ēgōnizonto*, GK 76) for his release. In contrasting his kingdom with the kingdoms of this world, Jesus asserts, "My kingdom is from another place." Brown, 536, notes that the metaphor is "spatial rather than temporal." Jesus' kingdom is of a different order. Unlike the kingdoms of this world, it is not based on earthly power. It is a kingdom that is spiritual and internal, in contrast to those that are external and physical (cf. Lk 17:21). Earlier in his ministry, when the crowds intended to make him a king by force, Jesus withdrew to be alone (Jn 6:15). Temple, 2:206, writes, "Precisely because [Jesus' kingdom] was not *of this world* it did not need the backing of physical force." Since God's kingdom is a kingdom of love, it can never defend itself by force. To do so would be to betray its essential nature.

Jesus uses the same term for his "servants" as is used elsewhere in ch. 18 for the temple police (*hypēretēs*, GK 5677; vv.3, 12, 18, 22). A deliberate contrast may be intended. Jesus' "servants" could be his followers, though the reference is more likely to angelic hosts (cf. the "twelve legions of angels," Mt 26:53).

37 Pilate's response may be taken as a statement ("You are a king, then!") or as a question ("So you are a king?"; NASB, NRSV). The exact nuance is difficult to determine, but Pilate seems to be saying that Jesus' claim to a kingdom, even though this kingdom is not of this world, makes Jesus a "king" after all. Pilate is not making a formal declaration as much as he is suggesting a conclusion in which he invites Jesus to concur—So you are a king after all; is that not true? (Lindars, 559, says that when the particle *oukoun* is accented on the second syllable it loses its negative force and becomes inferential.)

Jesus does not give a direct answer. It was Pilate, not Jesus, who had used the term "king." Nevertheless, he was not incorrect in doing so. Jesus neither refuses the title nor accepts it in the way Pilate meant it. For Pilate, "king" is a political term; for

Jesus it means something quite distinct. Jesus is king in the sense that he entered this world "to testify to the truth." A spiritual kingship deals with spiritual matters. If truth is to reign, the king will be the one who proclaims that truth. Note the strong contrast between "*you* say" and "for this reason *I* was born." (The Greek pronouns *sy* and *egō* stand at the beginning of the two respective clauses.) "Born" and "came into the world" both refer to the ministry of Jesus on earth. The purpose of the incarnation is to testify to the truth. Earlier Jesus said that he came into the world "for judgment" (9:39). The revelation of truth has the effect of judging in the sense that those who refuse the truth place themselves outside the scope of God's redemptive work, while those who accept the truth are forgiven. The reason so many resist the truth is that it carries with it the power of condemnation.

"Everyone on the side of truth," declares Jesus, "listens to me." To understand and accept truth is to recognize further truth when it comes (*EDNT*, 1:53, notes that in this verse *akouō*, GK *201*, is to be understood "in the sense of an obedient listening"). To refuse the truth is to forfeit the moral sensitivity necessary to distinguish between truth and error. Since truth has a moral claim, the denial of truth leads to moral blindness.

38 Pilate's "What is truth?" was not a genuine question but a brusque dismissal of the case. Pilate had learned enough to know that Jesus was no threat to the Roman state. In his essay *Of Truth*, Francis Bacon speaks of "jesting Pilate," who having posed the question would not stay for an answer. It is doubtful, however, that Pilate was in a jesting mood. Nor should he be portrayed as a philosopher who was wistfully posing the unanswerable question. The interview had led him to a conclusion that Jesus was innocent of the charges that had been leveled against him. Thus Pilate went out again to the Jews and reported, "I find no basis

for a charge against him." (Note the two other declarations of Jesus' innocence in 19:4, 6.)

39 If Pilate had simply left it at that, he would have gone down in history as a man of principle. Such was not the case. Pilate, searching for a middle ground that would satisfy the Jews' desire for Jesus' death while at the same time freeing himself from the responsibility of condemning an innocent man, suggests that Jesus be set free in accordance with the Jewish custom of releasing a prisoner at the time of Passover. In his overriding concern for his own problem, he failed to grasp the incongruity of regarding Jesus as both innocent and a prisoner at the same time. So he asks, hopefully, "Do you want me to release 'the king of the Jews'?"

40 The people took Pilate up on his offer but demanded a different prisoner. The Greek adverb *palin* (translated "back" in the NIV and NET), taken in the sense of "again" (NASB), would indicate that by this time the crowd was definitely getting out of hand. The name "Barabbas" comes either from the Aramaic *bar-abba* ("son of the father") or *bar-rabban* ("son of the teacher"). In either case, it is a patronymic.

The choice had to be made between a revolutionary insurgent (*lēstēs*, GK *3334*; NIV, "had taken part in a rebellion") and the teacher of Galilee. The angry mob shouted in blind fury for the death of the teacher. Moral choices are rarely rational; they are the product of people's passions. If those passions are evil, the resulting choices will inevitably be wrong.

19:1 Pilate's offer of a choice between Barabbas and Jesus had not turned out as he had planned. The crowd called for the release of the notorious Barabbas rather than the innocent Jesus. What could be done to satisfy the intense antagonism of the Jewish authorities toward Jesus that would, at the same time, fall short of satisfying their desire that he be put to death? It occurred to Pilate that having Jesus flogged might cause the Jews to change their minds and, out of compassion, no longer demand an execution.

Both Matthew and Mark place the flogging and the mocking by the soldiers as the last events prior to Jesus' taking up his cross and setting out on the road to Golgotha (Mt 27:26–31; Mk 15:15–20). Luke has no reference to flogging but notes that Jesus was mocked by the soldiers when he appeared before Herod (Lk 23:11). This has led some to conclude that John rearranged the events. Some think that there may have been two floggings. However, since apart from the clamor for Jesus' crucifixion—which would have been a continuing part of the entire episode— the materials in John 19:4–15 are peculiar to the fourth gospel, there is no reason to understand them as anything other than John's more complete account of the same trial. Luke alone has the appearance before Herod (23:6–16), and only Matthew includes the warning by Pilate's wife (27:19) as well as Pilate's washing of his hands before the crowd (27:24).

Though John uses the regular Greek verb for flogging (*mastigoō*, GK *3463*; cf. the use by Matthew and Luke of *phragelloō*, GK *5849*, a loanword from the Latin *fragelloo*, "to scourge"), it would appear from context that Pilate's intention was to teach Jesus a lesson rather than to torture him as part of the preparation for crucifixion. (Compare in Lk 23:16, 22 the milder word *paideuō*, GK *4084*, "to chastise"; NIV, "punish.") This latter form of scourging was brutal in the extreme. (Roman law prescribed various grades of flogging; see A. N. Sherwin-White, *Roman Society and Roman Law in the New Testament* [Oxford: Clarendon, 1963], 27– 28.) The victim was stripped, bound to a post or stretched on a frame, and beaten with leather whips in whose thongs were embedded pieces of bone or metal. The early-fourth-century "father of church history" Eusebius (*Hist. eccl.* 4.15.4) says that scourging sometimes tore open men's bodies so that "the hidden contents of the recesses of their bodies, their entrails and organs, were exposed to sight." That Simon of Cyrene was compelled to carry Jesus' cross argues for the more severe scourging.

2 In addition to flogging Jesus, the soldiers amused themselves by engaging in mock worship of their captive. They made a crown of thorns and placed it on his head. This "crowning" has often appeared in Christian art, usually depicted with a crown of thorns pressed inward on Jesus' head, thus causing both a flow of blood and great pain. In an important article by H. St. J. Hart ("The Crown of Thorns in John 19:2–5," *JTS* NS 3 [1952]: 66–75), the case is made for a crown that caricatured the "radiate" crown of Oriental god-kings in which the outwardly turned spikes depicted the sun and its rays. In this case, the purpose of the crown would not be to inflict pain but to mock. The traditional crown, however, would serve both purposes. To complement the kingly attire, a "purple robe" (*himation porphyroun*, GK *2668, 4528*; Mt 27:28 has *chlamyda*, GK *5948*, "robe," a short military cloak often worn by horsemen) was placed around Jesus' shoulders. Since purple dye was rare and expensive, the color purple was associated with royalty.

3 The soldiers continually approached Jesus as though to pay him homage, only suddenly to change their demeanor and strike him in the face. As they approached the "newly crowned king," they would say with mock solemnity, "Hail, king of the Jews!" The entire incident reflects the words of the Suffering Servant, "I offered my back to those who beat me, my cheeks to those who pulled out my beard; I did not hide my face from mocking and spitting" (Isa 50:6). Such was the humiliation of the Son of God at the hands of men whose consciences were hardened by the brutality of their trade. Even so, their ruthless handling of the gentle Jesus was infinitely less heinous than the carefully planned treachery of the religious leaders who perpetrated the capture and crucifixion of their Messiah.

4 Pilate once again came out from the Praetorium to stand before the angry mob. His plan was to appeal to the compassion of the Jewish leaders by presenting Jesus as a helpless and harmless peasant who already had been properly humiliated by the cruel flogging and mockery of Roman soldiers. "Certainly," reasoned Pilate, "these punishments would satisfy their desire for revenge." With a flair for the dramatic he announced that he was about to bring Jesus out. For the second time (cf. 18:38) he declared, "I find no basis for a charge against him."

5 Jesus emerges into the bright light of the morning "wearing the crown of thorns and the purple robe." Though it is probably more conjecture than exegesis to discuss the precise nuance of Pilate's declaration, a good case can be made from the context that what he said was something like, "Here he is, poor fellow! Isn't it ridiculous to consider this hapless creature as holding any pretensions to kingship?" While Pilate may have spoken with feigned contempt, John and others across the centuries have understood "the man" quite differently. Morris, 793, writes that "John intends 'the man' to evoke memories of Jesus' favorite self-designation." Tasker, 208, says that as Christians reread these famous words, they see in them "humanity at its best, the suffering Servant in whom God delights." Others discern an allusion to Zechariah 6:12 ("Here is the man whose name is the Branch"). In the Latin Bible the phrase is translated *Ecce homo*, which has provided the name for the famous arch that marks the starting place of the Via Dolorosa.

6 The spectacle of a humiliated Jesus fails to stir any feelings of compassion in the hearts of the chief priests and officials. Instead, they cry out, "Crucify! Crucify!" (Weymouth has, "To the cross! To the cross!") The chief priests leave no time for the possibility of a sympathetic response from the common people; rather, they take the initiative in moving quickly to force the execution. Ryle, 4:530, notes

that "it is a painful fact that in every age, none have been such hard, cruel, unfeeling, and bloody-minded persecutors of God's saints, as the ministers of religion." More out of exasperation than in accordance with some unknown regulation that would allow the plaintiffs to carry out a sentence, Pilate tells the Jews to take Jesus and crucify him themselves. As far as he is concerned, there is nothing with which the prisoner can be justifiably charged—a *third* declaration of innocence (cf. 18:38; 19:4). The Jews pay no attention to Pilate's suggestion. It was never intended to be taken seriously. Their dogged insistence that Jesus be put to death had pushed Pilate to the limit of his endurance, and his barbed retort displayed nothing but a sense of profound frustration.

7 The first accusation had failed, so a new basis for the charge against Jesus had to be presented. Since it was Pilate's responsibility to respect and, whenever necessary, to enforce the religious law of the Jews, the new accusation was that Jesus must be put to death because he was guilty of blasphemy—"he claimed to be the Son of God." Leviticus 24:16 states the law of blasphemy ("anyone who blasphemes the name of the LORD must be put to death") and prescribes stoning as the appropriate method of executing the offender. For Jesus to claim that God was his Father was to claim equality with God (5:18), a capital offense that should be punished without delay (cf. 11:31–39). The emphatic "we" in the Greek text (*hymeis* at the beginning of the clause) suggests that although Jesus may not have committed a crime worthy of death according to Roman law, *we* (the Jews) have a law, "and according to that law he must die."

8 That Jesus claimed to be the Son of God filled Pilate with a new fear ("he was even more afraid"; BAGD, 489, lists *mallon* ["more"] in John 18:9 under the meaning, "now more than ever"). Until this point we have not been told that Pilate was afraid, but we may reasonably assume that during the interrogation he had experienced a growing awareness that the prisoner before him was making claims that set him apart from all ordinary men. The mythology of Greece and Rome contained many stories about gods or their offspring coming to earth in human disguise. Temple, 2:361, notes that "like most heathen cynics, [Pilate had] a superstitious dread of the supernatural." Describing Pilate's predicament, Haenchen, 2:182, writes, "If Jesus is not only politically innocent, but if he really is a divine being clothed in the form of a man, might one not get caught in indescribable guilt by making the wrong move against him?"

9 So Pilate retreats into the palace and turns to his prisoner with the anxious question, "Where do you come from?" While some have suggested that Pilate was asking a geographical question, perhaps so he could escape his predicament by referring Jesus to some other government official (cf. the account of Jesus before Herod, Lk 23:6–16), his real concern was to learn whether the claim to supernatural status was indeed true. To know where Jesus comes from is the most important thing any person can learn. If he is, as he says, "from above" (v.11), then the incarnation is a fact and his words become of ultimate importance. If he is not from above, he may be wise, but in the final analysis he shares the limitations of all other members of the human race.

"Jesus gave him no answer"—the time had passed for a discussion of Jesus' heavenly origin. Had Pilate followed through earlier when Jesus spoke of truth (18:37–38), he may have learned what he wanted to know. But that was not the time, especially since Pilate was asking not in order to benefit from the truth but in order to escape his dilemma. The silence of Jesus demonstrates that God does not force himself on people or rush to the rescue of those who turn to him out of self-centered concern. That God gives people up is clearly taught in Romans 1:24, 26, 28. Jesus' silence is not simply an act of personal

refuge but serves as a statement of God's unwillingness to prolong forever his offer of help.

10 It is inconceivable to Pilate that Jesus will not speak to *him* (the Greek *emoi* is emphatic), the only person who can help Jesus at this point. Irritated and upset, he reacts with a display of authority: "Don't you realize I have power either to free you or to crucify you?" Deep in his heart, Pilate knew this was an idle boast. While theoretically he had the power, in fact he did not. An overriding concern for his own political future had removed any real possibility that he would free Jesus. He was captive to his own priorities, in bondage to his own self-centeredness. How thin is the disguise of so many of our declarations of personal freedom! Yet, the responsibility for dealing justly with Jesus did fall squarely on Pilate's shoulders, and he was fully aware of what the outcome ought to be.

11 In his final words to Pilate, Jesus reminds him that the power that is his as provincial governor has been given to him "from above"—i.e., by God. Otherwise he would have no power over Jesus. The classic statement regarding civil government as ordained by God and acting on his behalf is found in Romans 13:1–7. Barrett, 543, points out that *dedomenon* ("given," GK *1443*) is neuter and does not agree with *exousian* ("power," GK *2026*), which is feminine. A proper paraphrase would be, "You would not have any power over me at all had not God granted that you should have authority."

Jesus then declares, "Therefore [i.e., since *you* are acting in the capacity of a civil judge whose office has been ordained by God] the one who handed me over to you is guilty of a greater sin." Pilate was guilty for acquiescing in the murderous designs of the Jewish ecclesiastics, but their guilt was greater because, while he had acted against his will, they had acted with deliberate and evil intent. As Calvin, 2:174, says, they were less excusable in that they forced "a divinely appointed ruler to serve their passions."

"The one who handed me over" was Caiaphas, acting on behalf of the Jewish religious aristocracy. Though the expression is often used of Judas (cf. *ho paradidous auton*, lit., "the one who handed him over," in 18:2, 5), he could not have been the one in question here, because he had handed Jesus over to the Jews, not to Pilate.

12 Pilate was genuinely frightened. He could not dispute the fact that the authority he exercised had been delegated to him. Neither would his conscience allow him to escape the guilt of condemning an innocent man, especially one who could well be a god in human form. For this reason (*ek toutou*—better than "from then on"), Pilate "kept on trying to set Him free" (Williams; Brown, 879, takes *ezētei*, "was seeking," GK *2426* [NIV, "tried"], as a conative imperfect implying a series of attempts that were shouted down).

It was time for the Jews to set forth their most persuasive argument, namely, that a provincial governor who would release a prisoner claiming to be a king would without question be guilty of treason against the emperor: "If you let this man go, you are no friend of Caesar." Caesar was originally a proper name but became a title used by emperors after the time of Julius Caesar (cf. the German *kaiser* and the Russian *czar*). While *amicus Caesaris* ("friend of Caesar") was not used as an official title until the time of Vespasian (AD 69–79), the point being made was more than enough to convince Pilate that not to condemn Jesus would be political suicide. The Jews had played their trump card, and the outcome was decided. Pilate had no intention of opposing Caesar! His record in office had already placed his future in jeopardy.

13 So Pilate brought Jesus out and "sat down on the judge's seat." The verb *kathizō* (GK *2767*) should be understood here as intransitive ("to sit down") rather than transitive ("to cause to sit down"). It is surprising that a number of translators have chosen the second alternative (e.g., Goodspeed, who has

"had him sit in the judge's seat"), because the setting was far too serious for Pilate to have resorted to such frivolous horseplay. Bruce, 364, calls it a "curiosity of translation and exegesis." A Roman judge would never conduct himself in such a manner, though both the *Gospel of Peter* (7) and Justin's *Apologia* (35) have Pilate placing Jesus on the seat of judgment. Tradition has a way of embellishing a narrative to convey an idea more forcefully.

The judge's seat was a raised platform from which Roman magistrates rendered judgment on legal matters. In that the Greek *bēma* (GK *1037*) without the article is found only here in the NT, some have conjectured that Pilate was using a temporary judgment seat. Julius Caesar is said to have carried with him a portable mosaic pavement that served as an official place from which to deliver judgments.

Pilate was holding court at a place known as the "Stone Pavement" (*lithostrōtos*, GK *3346*, means "paved with blocks of stone"). A substantial area paved with large blocks of stone has been discovered beneath the Ecce Homo arch and the adjoining convent of Our Lady of Zion. Some have identified this as the place where Pilate delivered sentence, especially since Josephus reports that this part of the Fortress of Antonia was covered with a stone pavement. This identification is less than certain because both the building in question and the pavement belong to the second century. The Aramaic name for the place is Gabbatha, a word of uncertain origin. BDAG, 185–86, cites C. Torrey, who holds that it represents a stone pavement in the form of a platter (from the Latin *gabata*). In any case, it is another name (in Aramaic) for the same place, not a translation of the Greek *lithostrōtos*.

14 John notes that the sentencing of Jesus took place on "the day of Preparation of Passover Week," or Friday of Passover Week. There is an apparent problem between the Synoptics' portrayal of the Last Supper as a Passover meal (cf. Mk 14:12 and the narrative that follows) and John's account, which seems to place the crucifixion at the very hour when the Passover lambs were being slain, thus placing the Last Supper *before* the Passover. Morris, 785, finds the most probable solution in a confusion between the calendar Jesus was following and the one used by the temple authorities (for other solutions, see Morris's additional note, 774–86).

John adds that the sentencing of Jesus took place at "about the sixth hour." Here we seem to run into trouble with Mark's indication that Jesus was crucified at "the third hour" (Mk 15:25). The most probable explanations for this problem are that (1) a confusion of the Greek numerals for "3" and "6" occurred (so Barrett, 545); (2) while Mark followed the Palestinian method of counting hours from sunrise (the "third hour" thus being 9:00 a.m.), John followed the custom in use in Asia Minor by starting the counting from midnight (the "sixth hour" being 6:00 a.m.); or (3) both texts are no more than approximations intending to indicate something like "midmorning" (see Morris, 801, who says that "late morning would suit both expressions"; cf. Carson, 605).

Addressing the mob from his official dais, Pilate declares, not without a note of ridicule, "Here is your king," or as Kysar, 284, paraphrases, "This is the closest you will ever come to having a King." The entire affair had been a tragic masquerade in which hidden motives and concealed intentions forced otherwise rational men to act in ways unheard-of in the history of judicial proceedings.

15 In response to Pilate's granting of their desire, the Jewish authorities shout, "Take him away! Take him away! Crucify him!" The demonstrative pronoun *ekeinoi* ("those people"; NIV, "they") emphasizes the separation between Jesus and his antagonists. Pilate asks with "mock astonishment" (Reith, 144), "Shall I crucify your king?"—a question calculated more to anger the Jews than to seek instruction. Greek syntax inverts the normal sequence of words and yields the translation, "Your king, shall I crucify him [or must I crucify him]?"

The response is without precedent in Jewish history: "We have no king but Caesar." It was a denial of their basic religious belief that God alone was their supreme ruler (cf. Jdg 8:23; 1Sa 8:7). Barrett, 546, writes, "In denying all claims to kingship save that of the Roman Emperor Israel abdicated its own unique position under the immediate sovereignty of God." From another perspective, however, the denial marked no real turning point, because by their actions they were demonstrating that they had already separated themselves from the God of Israel.

16a So now at last, Pilate hands Jesus over to be crucified. "To them" refers to the soldiers, or, if taken as a dative of advantage, it means "to satisfy [the Jews]" (so NEB).

NOTES

33 We do not know whether the interview between Pilate and Jesus was carried on in Aramaic or Greek, but it would seem quite likely that, since no interpreter is mentioned and since it would be unlikely for a Roman governor to learn Aramaic, the conversation was carried on in Greek, the language in which it was recorded (cf. Morris, 768).

34 Jesus' answer (ἀπὸ σεαυτοῦ σὺ τοῦτο λέγεις, *apo seautou sy touto legeis*, lit., "from yourself are you saying this") is variously translated as, "Is that your own idea?" (NIV), "Are you saying this on your own initiative?" (NASB), and "Are you speaking for yourself about this?" (NKJV). The personal pronoun σύ (*sy*, "you") is emphatic.

36 Newman and Nida (*Translator's Handbook on the Gospel of John*, 570) suggest, "My kingly authority does not have its origin in this world," for the well-known, "My kingdom is not of this world."

38 John is specifically the gospel of "truth." Of the thirty-two occurrences of ἀλήθεια (*alētheia*, "truth," GK *237*) in the Gospels, twenty-five are in John; correspondingly, all but two of the sixteen occurrences in the Gospels of the adjective ἀληθής (*alēthēs*, "true," GK *239*) are in John.

40 In certain early MSS of Matthew 27:16–17, Barabbas's first name is given as "Jesus" ("a notorious prisoner, called Jesus Barabbas. . . .Which one do you want me to release to you: Jesus Barabbas, or Jesus who is called Christ?").While few translations (e.g., NEB) follow this reading, the UBS committee thought it should be included within square brackets (cf. Metzger, 67–68).

The word λῃστής (*lēstēs*, GK *3334*) often refers to no more than a common thief (as in Mk 11:17 of those who had turned the temple into a σπήλαιον λῃστῶν [*spēlaion lēstōn*, "den of robbers"]), but in this instance the term probably indicates a revolutionary. The root meaning of the word is "to seize as prey," so λῃστής, *lēstēs*, could be used with reference to a soldier, who had an implicit right to plunder, but it usually carried the negative sense of the misuse of force to seize what belongs to another (cf. *TDNT* 4:257–58). *TLNT*, 2:389–90, comments that "a *lēstēs* is a brigand who uses violence" and "carries out armed theft and pillage."

19:1 Horst Balz (*EDNT* 2:395–96) holds that the flogging of Jesus corresponds to the Roman punishment *verberatio*, which accompanied the penalty of death, especially by crucifixion. He does, however, acknowledge that in this passage "a separate punishment may be in view, perhaps in the sense of a torturing, in order to coerce a confession." *TDNT* (abridged, 571) holds that the scourging of Jesus here was the far more severe punishment that preceded execution.

The Greek verb μαστιγόω (*mastigoō*, "whip," "flog," "scourge," GK *3463*) should be taken in a causative sense.

2 A contemporary example of the "radiate corona" is the crown on the head of the Statue of Liberty, which has stood in New York Harbor since 1886.

The color of the robe, according to Matthew 27:28, was κόκκινος (*kokkinos*, "scarlet," GK *3132*) rather than πορφυροῦς (*porphyrous*, "purple," GK *4528*). It is sometimes argued that the soldiers would have no ready access to a purple robe, because clothing of that hue was expensive and worn by the upper classes. On the other hand, the "scarlet robe" designated by Matthew was inexpensive and readily available. In any case, the ancients did not designate colors with such prescription, and a "scarlet" robe would serve quite adequately as a "purple" robe with which to mock Jesus as King of the Jews.

3 Taking the imperfect ἤρχοντο (*ērchonto*, GK *2262*) as iterative understands the soldiers as coming up to Jesus "again and again" to taunt him. The NASB interprets the imperfect as inceptive: "they *began* to come up to Him."

The customary salutation for the Roman emperor was "Ave (Hail), Caesar!" (Keener, 310). "Hail, King of the Jews!" on the lips of the soldiers was intentional mockery.

6 The word κραυγάζω (*kraugazō*, GK *3198*) is a strong verb meaning, "to utter a loud sound, ordinarily of harsh texture," with context indicating the nature of the sound (e.g., the grunting of hungry swine or the excited screaming of the human voice; BDAG, 565).

12 The NASB translates ἐκ τούτου (*ek toutou*) in a causal sense ("as a result"), which is preferable to taking it as temporal (so NIV, "from then on").

D. The Passion of Jesus (19:16b–37)

OVERVIEW

It is difficult to comment on the crucifixion narrative because incidental remarks on the text (the stock and trade of the exegete) have a way of making the event itself seem less important. Students of the Bible should consult commentaries for historical and grammatical detail but not allow such preparatory work to become a substitute for serious theological reflection.

1. His Crucifixion (19:16b–27)

16bSo the soldiers took charge of Jesus. 17Carrying his own cross, he went out to the place of the Skull (which in Aramaic is called Golgotha). 18Here they crucified him, and with him two others—one on each side and Jesus in the middle.

19Pilate had a notice prepared and fastened to the cross. It read: JESUS OF NAZARETH, THE KING OF THE JEWS. 20Many of the Jews read this sign, for the place where Jesus was crucified was near the city, and the sign was written in Aramaic, Latin and Greek. 21The chief priests of the Jews protested to Pilate, "Do not write 'The King of the Jews,' but that this man claimed to be king of the Jews."

22Pilate answered, "What I have written, I have written."

23When the soldiers crucified Jesus, they took his clothes, dividing them into four shares, one for each of them, with the undergarment remaining. This garment was seamless, woven in one piece from top to bottom.

24"Let's not tear it," they said to one another. "Let's decide by lot who will get it."

This happened that the scripture might be fulfilled which said,

"They divided my garments among them
  and cast lots for my clothing."

So this is what the soldiers did.

25Near the cross of Jesus stood his mother, his mother's sister, Mary the wife of Clopas, and Mary Magdalene. 26When Jesus saw his mother there, and the disciple whom he loved standing nearby, he said to his mother, "Dear woman, here is your son," 27and to the disciple, "Here is your mother." From that time on, this disciple took her into his home.

COMMENTARY

16b–17 Pilate delivered Jesus into the hands of the soldiers (the implied subject of *paralambanō*, "to take charge of," GK *4161*), who then carried out the sentence. Jesus was forced to carry the cross (undoubtedly the *patibulum*, or crossbeam) out of the city to the place of execution. According to Mosaic law, the death penalty was to be enacted outside the city (Lev 24:14; Dt 17:5; cf. Heb 13:12). John writes that Jesus went out "carrying his own cross," while the Synoptics record that a passerby, Simon of Cyrene, was compelled to carry it (Mk 15:21 par.). The obvious explanation is that Jesus, in his weakened condition, carried his cross as far as he could, and at that point it was taken up by Simon. Catholic tradition has Simon assuming Jesus' burden at the fifth Station of the Cross on the Via Dolorosa. Early church fathers saw the OT account of Isaac's carrying the wood on which he himself was to be sacrificed (Ge 22:6) as a type of Jesus' carrying his own cross.

The place of execution was called "the place of the Skull." (The designation "Calvary" in Lk 23:33 [KJV] is based on the Vulgate's *locus calvaria*.) In Aramaic it was called Golgotha. The name is held to come from the skulls of executed criminals that lay scattered around, or because the place of execution was on a skull-shaped hill. The first option is doubtful because Jewish ceremonial laws regarded corpses as unclean and dead bodies would not be left lying in the open. The second option is less than certain because nowhere in Scripture does it say that Golgotha was a hill. However, references to the women watching "from a distance" (Mt 27:55 par.) could suggest a high area.

Since the Romans used crucifixion in part for its value as a deterrent, Golgotha would be a public place near Jerusalem where everyone could see what happened to those who opposed civil authority. Tradition from the time of Constantine has located Golgotha within the existing Church of the Holy Sepulcher. Because this site lies inside the present city walls (and because Jesus was crucified outside the city [Heb 13:12–13]), it would appear that the traditional site is an incorrect identification. However, excavations in 1963 indicate that the Church of the Holy Sepulcher lay *outside* the line of the second north wall of Jesus' day. An alternative possibility is "Gordon's Calvary," the *el-zahira* hill outside the Damascus gate.

18 Jesus was crucified with two others—"one on each side and Jesus in the middle." The synoptic writers tell us that the other victims were "robbers" (Mt 27:38 par.), and Luke tells of the one who turned in faith to Jesus (Lk 23:38–43). The scene reminds us of what the prophet Isaiah wrote about the Suffering Servant: "He poured out his life unto death, and was numbered with the transgressors" (Isa 53:12). The crucified Jesus hanging between two thieves, one impenitent and the other penitent, is a dramatic portrayal of the fact that Jesus divided humanity in his death as he did (and still does!) in his life. We, like Jesus' fellow victims of crucifixion, cannot escape the cross; we can only decide on which cross we wish to die.

19 The placard placed on the cross over the head of Jesus (see Mt 27:37; Lk 23:38) was inscribed with the words "JESUS OF NAZARETH, THE KING OF THE JEWS." Comparison with the Synoptics reveals that while the wording is different in each case, the central assertion ("THE KING OF THE JEWS") occurs in each. *Titulus* (the Latin word transliterated *titlos*, GK *5518*, in Greek and rendered "title" in English; NIV, "notice"; NASB, "inscription") was a technical term for the placard on which the crimes of the condemned person were written. It may have been hung from the neck of Jesus as he carried his cross through the streets of Jerusalem on the way to Golgotha. The NIV says that Pilate "had a notice prepared," though a literal rendering of the Greek text would indicate that Pilate himself did the writing. Morris, 807, detects "a certain grim revenge" on the part of Pilate.

20 Of the four gospel writers, only John notes that the inscription was written in the three major languages of the day: Aramaic, the everyday language of the Jewish people; Latin, the official language of the Roman authorities; and Greek, the common language of the civilized world. By writing the charge in this way, all would be able to read it. John draws attention to the three languages to emphasize that the kingship of the crucified Jesus was universal. Jesus was crucified "near the city," so many of the Jews would have read the sign.

21 Pilate intended the inscription as "a calculated insult" (Bruce, 368), and it accomplished its purpose. The chief priests repeatedly asked him (the imperfect *elegon*, "were saying," GK *3306*, suggests continued asking; NIV, "protested") to change it to, "This man claimed to be king of the Jews." The idea that a dying criminal should even be considered their king was a national insult and totally unacceptable. Beyond that, if they let the title stand, it could be interpreted as an admission of revolutionary intent. Brown, 902, takes the Greek of "do not write" (present imperative with *mē*) as forbidding the continuity of an act and translates, "Do not leave it written." The expression "the chief priests of the Jews" occurs only here and perhaps intends a contrast with "THE KING OF THE JEWS."

22 One would expect Pilate to yield to the request, as he had done in the past to the demands of the Jews. Not so. A streak of stubbornness surfaced, and he answered their request with an inflexible, "What I have written, I have written." Barclay, 2:252, notes, "It is one of the paradoxical things in life that we can be stubborn about things which do not matter and weak about things of supreme importance." It is less paradoxical, however, when we understand that stubbornness is more an indication of weakness than it is of strength. Pilate was a weak man because his life was ruled by expediency rather than principle. This final tough stance was no more than a feeble attempt to regain the moral ground he had forfeited by condemning an innocent man.

23–24 It was customary for soldiers assigned to the execution to divide up the personal belongings of the victim (cf. Sherwin-White, *Roman Society and Roman Law*, 46). Since Jesus' clothing was divided into "four shares, one for each of them," it appears that only four soldiers were assigned to the crucifixion. This contrasts quite markedly with the six hundred who came to the garden to arrest Jesus (18:3). However, once Jesus had been condemned and was on the way to the cross, any danger of a national uprising prompted by him would have subsided. In ancient days, men normally wore two main articles of clothing: the *himation* (the outer robe or cloak, GK *2668*) and the *chitōn* (the inner garment, GK *5945*). The NIV translates the plural (*himatia*) as "clothes" (NASB, "outer garments").

It is sometimes suggested that the Jew wore five articles of apparel (shoes, turban, girdle, tunic, and outer robe; cf. Barclay, 2:253) and that the soldiers cast lots to determine which item went to each person. It is better to understand the soldiers as tearing the cloak into four pieces (probably along the seams) and then casting lots for the undergarment. They did not want to ruin the seamless inner garment, which was woven in one piece from top to bottom and therefore of some value. (A seamless garment would avoid having joined together two forbidden materials and could therefore be purchased by a Jew.) "Let's not tear it" (v.24) suggests that the soldiers may have already divided the outer robe by tearing it.

The seamless robe has often been treated symbolically as a way of indicating that Jesus is a high priest, whose tunic was also described in similar language (cf. Josephus, *Ant.* 3.161), or as an indication of the unity of the church. Such applications are homiletically permissible but are not intended by the text itself.

John adds (v.24) that the dividing of Jesus' garments fulfilled the scripture, which said, "They divided my garments among them and cast lots for my clothing" (see Ps 22:18). Marsh, 615, notes that in the original setting "garments" and "clothing" were identical terms, which John in turn itemizes in detail so that his readers cannot escape the rightness of his application of the prophecy. But such flexibility in the interpretation of prophetic utterance is not at all unusual. NT authors, writing under the inspiration of the Holy Spirit, were led to apply messianic prophecies with a great deal of freedom.

25 John identifies several of the women standing near the cross. (Luke mentions the women but doesn't name them). By taking "his mother's sister" to be further described as "Mary the wife of Clopas," it is possible to count a total of three women. It is more likely, however, that the references designate two different women. By comparing the three accounts (cf. Mt 27:55–56; Mk 15:40), we are able to identify four women: (1) the mother of Jesus; (2) his mother's sister, or Salome the mother of Zebedee's sons; (3) Mary the wife of Clopas, who is the mother of James the younger and Joses; and (4) Mary of Magdala.

It is in keeping with what we know of John to leave unmentioned the name of his mother. Mary Magdalene is included in all four gospel accounts of the crucifixion and resurrection, but elsewhere she appears only in Luke 8:2–3. Magdala was a village on the western shore of the Sea of Galilee, not far from Tiberias. It is interesting that Mary the mother of Jesus is not mentioned in either of the synoptic accounts of this scene. Reith, 147, writing at the end of the nineteenth century, concludes that "the Mariolatry of the Church of Rome has no sanction in them at least."

The reserve with which John describes the crucifixion scene is remarkable. The women standing near the cross are simply named. No mention is made of the obvious grief they must have suffered as they saw their Lord stripped, nailed to the cross, exposed to public humiliation, and experiencing the excruciating pain of crucifixion. Some have questioned the difference between John's account, in which the women are standing "near the cross," and that of the Synoptics, which have them watching "from a distance." A reasonable answer is that they did watch the initial proceedings from a distance but moved closer once Jesus had been hoisted into the air. As some of the crowd lost interest and left as soon as the victim had been nailed in place, the women who "had followed Jesus from Galilee to care for his needs" (Mt 27:55) would move closer to provide the comfort of their presence during his hour of greatest need.

26 It was there at the foot of the cross that Simeon's prophecy to Mary was finding fulfillment: "A sword will pierce your own soul too" (Lk 2:35). Seeing his mother and the disciple whom he loved (i.e., John; cf. 13:23), Jesus says to his mother, "Dear woman, here is your son." Some have suggested that Jesus used the term "woman" rather than "mother" in order not to deepen her sorrow. But as before, when he spoke to Mary in a similar way at the wedding in Cana (2:4), the term "woman" does not connote a brusque and distant relationship but is a form of polite address.

27 To John Jesus says, "Here is your mother." Jesus did not entrust his mother to the care of his own brothers because apparently they did not as yet believe in him (cf. 7:5). Early in his public ministry, Jesus distinguished between his natural and spiritual mother and brothers (Mk 3:31–35). Tasker, 210–11, notes that part of the high priestly work of Jesus was "to create a new fellowship of the redeemed" and that "beneath the cross Christian fellowship is born." The bonds of Christian love surpass all natural barriers and bring into one great family all who love and follow Jesus.

Some commentators picture Jesus as instructing John to take his mother from the scene immediately so as to protect her from additional exposure to the shame and agony of the cross. It is more natural, however, to understand the expression "from that time on" in a more general sense as referring to the period of time following the crucifixion. The translation "into his home" (NASB, "into his own *household*") is interpretive (the Greek *eis ta idia*, lit., "unto his own things," is ambiguous). Most writers think it quite unlikely that John would have had a house in Jerusalem.

NOTES

20 The sequence "Aramaic, Latin and Greek" has strong support in the MSS; however, A Dˢ Θ *f*¹ lat sy place Ἑλληνιστί (*Hellēnisti*, GK *1822*) before Ῥωμαιστί (*Rhōmaisti*, GK *4872*), apparently to have the languages in geographical order from east to west (cf. Metzger, 217).

REFLECTIONS

The Roman orator Cicero (*Verr.* 5.64) called crucifixion "the cruelest and foulest of punishments." It is thought to have originated with the Persians and was later adopted by other peoples, such as the Carthaginians and Romans. With few exceptions it was used only for the execution of slaves, foreigners, and robbers. Crosses were of several sorts: a single stake; the Saint Andrew's cross, shaped like the letter X; the Saint Anthony's cross, resembling a capital T; and the more familiar *crux immissa*, with the crossbeam a bit lower. Both tradition and the fact that the placard was nailed "above his head" (Mt 27:37) would indicate that the cross on which Jesus died was the *crux immissa*.

After being sentenced and flogged, the victim was made to carry the crossbeam to the place of execu-tion. On the ground his arms were outstretched and tied (or, less commonly, nailed) to the beam, which was then hoisted into position and fastened to the upright stake already in place. A small wooden peg (*sedile*) placed part way up the stake supported some of the weight of the body. The feet were then brought together and nailed to the upright.

Crucifixion was a barbaric and viciously cruel form of execution. It was also the ultimate humiliation. The naked and bloody body of the victim was hung in full view of all who passed by so they could watch the torment of a slow and painful death. First-century Roman writer Quintilian (*Decl.* 274) advocated erecting crosses at the busiest intersections of the city, since crucifixion was a most effective way of discouraging crime and sedition.

2. His Death (19:28–37)

²⁸Later, knowing that all was now completed, and so that the Scripture would be fulfilled, Jesus said, "I am thirsty." ²⁹A jar of wine vinegar was there, so they soaked a sponge in it, put the sponge on a stalk of the hyssop plant, and lifted it to Jesus' lips. ³⁰When he had received the drink, Jesus said, "It is finished." With that, he bowed his head and gave up his spirit.

³¹Now it was the day of Preparation, and the next day was to be a special Sabbath. Because the Jews did not want the bodies left on the crosses during the Sabbath, they asked Pilate to have the legs broken and the bodies taken down. ³²The soldiers therefore came and broke the legs of the first man who had been crucified with Jesus, and then those of the other. ³³But when they came to Jesus and found that he was already dead, they did not break his legs. ³⁴Instead, one of the soldiers pierced Jesus' side with a spear, bringing a sudden flow of blood and water. ³⁵The man who saw it has given testimony, and his testimony is true. He knows that he tells the truth, and he testifies so that you also may believe. ³⁶These things happened so that the scripture would be fulfilled: "Not one of his bones will be broken," ³⁷and, as another scripture says, "They will look on the one they have pierced."

COMMENTARY

28 The synoptic writers, rather than John, tell us of the darkness that came over the entire land from noon until 3:00 p.m. (Mt 27:45 par.). During that terrible hour, Jesus cried out in agony of soul, "My God, my God, why have you forsaken me?" (Mk 15:34). John simply reports that "later," as the fearful ordeal was drawing to a close, Jesus said, "I am thirsty." This was "so that the Scripture would be fulfilled." If we understand John's statement in reference to the utterance itself, then Psalm 22:15 ("my tongue sticks to the roof of my mouth") would be the Scripture he had in mind. If the reference is to the actions that follow, then Psalm 69:21 ("they . . . gave me vinegar for my thirst") is more likely. The thirst motif appears in each passage, though Jesus quotes neither Scripture verbatim. Tasker, 211, suggests that if Jesus' thirst were a spiritual thirst to return to the Father, then John may

have had in mind Psalm 42:2 ("my soul thirsts for God").

29 The end has come, and Jesus has one great final statement to make. So that all could hear and understand what he had to say, it was necessary that his parched mouth be moistened. Nearby was a "jar of wine vinegar," perhaps for the use of the soldiers who were on duty during the execution. The sponge would serve well to get wine to the mouth of the victim. The sponge soaked with wine was lifted to Jesus' lips "on a stalk of the hyssop plant." Hyssop was a small plant quite adequate for its ceremonial use in sprinkling (of water, Nu 19:18; of blood, Ex 12:22), but some have thought it insufficiently stiff to have supported a wine-soaked sponge. Perhaps for this reason the eleventh-century scribe responsible for cursive 476 changed *hyssōpō* ("hyssop," GK *5727*) to *hyssō* ("on a javelin," GK

5726). A number of modern translations have adopted this variant (e.g., NEB, "so they . . . fixed it on a javelin"), though the *hyssos* (Lat. *pilum*) was used only by legionary troops at that time, and such troops were not deployed in Judea until AD 66 (cf. Metzger, 217–18). Since the cross raised its victim only a few feet off the ground, several short stalks of hyssop tied together would be stiff enough to raise the sponge to Jesus' mouth. Theologically, the hyssop calls attention to Jesus as the perfect Passover sacrifice.

30 Now that his mouth had been moistened with the wine vinegar, Jesus exclaimed, "It is finished." This English sentence translates but one word in Greek: *tetelestai* (GK *5464*). The verb means "to bring to an end," either in the sense of completion or accomplishment. In the first case, Jesus would be saying that his earthly life and mission was now over; in the second, that he had fully accomplished the work he had come to do. It is more likely that the words are to be taken in the second sense. That he was dying was obvious. That by his voluntary death on the cross he had brought to completion the redemptive purpose of the incarnation is a theological utterance of profound significance. Reith, 150, notes that "death is not only the termination of life, it is the completion of it."

It is important to note that Jesus does not die as a victim of his oppressors; rather, he remains in charge of his life until the very end. John records his death with active verbs: he received, he spoke, he bowed his head, and he gave up his spirit. Some have called attention to the fact that the same phrase was used by Jesus when he said that, while foxes have holes and birds have nests, the Son of Man has no place "to lay his head" (*tēn kephalēn klinē*; Mt 8:20; Lk 8:58). The resting place for his head that he lacked on earth was found on a Roman cross.

Brown, 910, says that Augustine's interpretation of Jesus' going to sleep rather than being in the agony of death is "a rather imaginative interpretation of the evidence." Everything about the narrative underscores the suffering and humiliation of a public execution. This does not imply, however, that the last moments of Jesus' life were out of his control and that his life was taken from him rather than freely given up. Tasker, 211–12, is closer to the truth when he refers to the bowing of the head as Jesus' final act of submission to the will of the Father. The "spirit" that Jesus gave up was not the issuing of the Holy Spirit in consequence of his work completed (cf. 16:5–16), but his own life.

31 John carefully notes that Jesus' death took place on "the day of Preparation." In the religious vocabulary of Judaism, this term had become a technical designation for Friday, the day on which preparations were made for the Sabbath, which began that evening at sundown. Since in that year Passover fell on the seventh day of the week, the following Sabbath would be a "special Sabbath." According to Jewish law, any person guilty of a capital offense was put to death and his body hung on a tree (Dt 21:22). However, the body was not to remain overnight in public view but be buried the same day. Otherwise the land would be defiled. Barclay, 2:260, quotes the Mishnah as saying, "Everyone who allows the dead to remain overnight transgresses a positive commandment." By contrast, the Romans normally left their victims hanging on the cross until they died and the vultures and wild animals had completed their grisly work. Such a display would serve to warn others who might be contemplating some act of rebellion against the realm.

The Jewish desire that the presence of dead bodies not defile their religious observances led them to go to Pilate and ask that the legs of the victims be broken and the bodies taken down. The *crurifragium*, or leg breaking, was itself a brutal form of punishment. In connection with crucifixion, its purpose was to smash the bones of the legs so they could no longer help bear the weight of the body. Not only would the resulting strain on the arms increase pain and make breathing incredibly difficult, but the additional hemorrhaging would ensure a certain and painful death. Recent excavations in Israel unearthed a first-century victim of crucifixion who had had both legs broken.

32–33 Soldiers carrying out the wishes of the Jews came first to the two criminals crucified alongside Jesus. Apparently the *crurifragium* was carried out with a heavy mallet. Why they went first to the two criminals is best left to conjecture. Perhaps Matthew's observation that when Jesus died, "the centurion and those with him . . . were terrified" (Mt 27:54) provides the most plausible explanation. When the soldiers came to Jesus, they found that he was already dead; therefore, there was no need to break his legs. The psalmist declared that the Lord protects the bones of the righteous man and that "not one of them will be broken" (Ps 34:20).

34 One of the soldiers then pierced Jesus' side with a spear. There is a question as to whether in this context the verb *nyssō* ("to pierce," GK *3817*) describes an exploratory prod (to see whether Jesus had already died) or a severe thrust (to make sure he would die). That the "piercing" left a large wound is reasonable in light of Jesus' subsequent invitation to Thomas to reach out his hand and put it into his side (20:27). Immediately there was a sudden flow of blood and water. Since the body of a dead man does not bleed, it would appear that Jesus' heart had ruptured and the coagulated blood had mingled with the watery serum in the pericardium (the sac surrounding the heart). The order of the words ("blood and water") would accurately describe the flow of the heavier blood followed by the lighter serum.

A symbolic meaning is often seen in the account. For many, blood and water represent the two sacraments (though Lindars, 587, acknowledges that,

since water is generally a symbol of the Spirit, "a sacramental interpretation is not absolutely required"). Others see a reference to justification and sanctification. Calvin, 2:186, writes, "By these words he means that Christ brought with Him the true atonement and true washing." But John's primary intention in recording this detail was to refute the docetic teaching that Jesus was not a real man and therefore did not really die (cf. 1Jn 4:1–3).

35 If v.35 is taken as an interpolation by those responsible for publishing the gospel, then "the man who saw it" (the flow of blood and water) and "has given testimony" would be the beloved disciple (cf. v.26; 21:24). He would also be the one who "knows that he tells the truth" and "testifies so that you also may believe." If John himself is the writer, then the eyewitness would be someone else—someone whom he regarded as absolutely reliable. It is also possible (but less likely) that throughout the verse John is speaking rhetorically of himself in the third person (cf. 9:37, where Jesus, referring to himself, says, "he is the one speaking with you"). Others have thought that *ekeinos* ("that one"; NIV, "he") may refer to the risen Lord, since in 1 John the demonstrative pronoun used as a personal pronoun regularly refers to Jesus. Such a reference to Jesus in this context would be quite abrupt and therefore unlikely. In any case, the event is stressed because the writer wants his readers to know beyond the shadow of a doubt that Jesus was a real man with a real body.

36 John again calls attention to the fact that what was happening was in fulfillment of Scripture (cf. vv.24, 28, 37). The statement that "not one of his bones will be broken" stems from Exodus 12:46 and Numbers 9:12, where the Israelites were given instructions regarding the Passover lamb. John is saying that the crucified Jesus has given his life as the perfect Lamb of God. He is the fulfillment of the OT promise of a Lamb whose death will atone for the sins of the world (cf. 1:29; 1Jn 2:2). The reference in Psalm 34:20 to the righteous man whose bones will not be broken underscores God's protective care. Even in death, Jesus was not separated from the loving care of his Father.

37 John adds one more reference to OT Scripture—Zechariah 12:10, "They will look on the one they have pierced." While the piercing is symbolic in Zechariah, it is literal in the case of Jesus. As Zechariah looked ahead to the coming repentance of Jerusalem, so also does John look ahead to the

hour when Jesus will hang on the cross, pierced by the spear of a Roman soldier. Zechariah's statement is also used by John in the first chapter of the book of Revelation, where the context is the second coming of Christ (Rev 1:7). The world can never understand how a messiah whose earthly destiny was a cross could ever turn out to be the Sovereign of the universe. In God's plan, however, the road to glory passes through the valley of humiliation. Those who walk with Jesus must share first of all his denial of personal privilege; only later do we share his glory.

NOTES

29 The Greek ὄξος (oxos, "sour wine, wine vinegar," GK 3954) was the Roman posca, a favorite drink of the lower ranks of society. It would relieve thirst more effectively than plain water would (cf. BDAG, 715).

32 The verb κατάγνυμι (katagnymi, GK 2862) means "to break or to shatter a rigid object" (L&N, 19.35). Three of its four occurrences in the NT are in vv.31–33 of the present narrative; the other is in Matthew 12:20, where regarding Jesus Isaiah is quoted: "a bruised reed he will not break."

34 The λόγχη (lonchē, GK 3365) was a "long weapon with sharpened end used for piercing by thrusting or as a projectile by hurling" (L&N, 6.34). Here, however, it probably referred to the iron point or "spearhead" (cf. BDAG, 601).

E. The Burial of Jesus (19:38–42)

[38]Later, Joseph of Arimathea asked Pilate for the body of Jesus. Now Joseph was a disciple of Jesus, but secretly because he feared the Jews. With Pilate's permission, he came and took the body away. [39]He was accompanied by Nicodemus, the man who earlier had visited Jesus at night. Nicodemus brought a mixture of myrrh and aloes, about seventy-five pounds. [40]Taking Jesus' body, the two of them wrapped it, with the spices, in strips of linen. This was in accordance with Jewish burial customs. [41]At the place where Jesus was crucified, there was a garden, and in the garden a new tomb, in which no one had ever been laid. [42]Because it was the Jewish day of Preparation and since the tomb was nearby, they laid Jesus there.

COMMENTARY

38 It was common practice for the family or friends of a person who had been crucified to buy the body and provide it with an honorable burial. Otherwise it would be left at the cruel mercies of birds of prey and wild beasts or thrown as refuse into a common pit with other criminals. From a human standpoint, that is what would have happened to the body of Jesus had not Joseph of Arimathea taken the initiative and secured the body with Pilate's permission. John tells us that Joseph was a disciple of Jesus (cf. Mt 27:57), and Mark notes that he was "a prominent member of the Council" (15:43). Luke adds that Joseph "had not consented to [the Sanhedrin's] decision and action" (23:51).

Joseph had not previously acknowledged his allegiance to Jesus. Although a disciple, he was one secretly because he feared the Jews (cf. 7:13). In this situation, however, he could not bear the prospect of Jesus' body being dishonored. Apparently he was a wealthy man, and because he had connections with the religious and civic authorities he was able to secure the body (perhaps at some cost!). It was with Pilate's permission that he came and took the body of Jesus. It was necessary to secure permission because in some cases friends might want to secure the body as soon as possible in the hope of reviving it.

39 Joseph was accompanied by Nicodemus, who is identified by John as "the man who earlier had visited Jesus at night" (cf. 3:1–2). Nicodemus is mentioned three other times in the fourth gospel but not at all in the Synoptics. The third reference was in 7:50–52, where he gently rebuked the Sanhedrin by asking whether their law condemned a person without first giving him the chance to explain his actions. That he brought a mixture of myrrh and aloes, "about seventy-five pounds," would indicate that he, as well as Joseph, was a man of considerable means. Lindars, 592, thinks that seventy-five pounds is "obviously an exaggeration," but note the large quantities of spices used in the burial of King Asa (2Ch 16:14) and Herod the Great (Josephus, *Ant.* 17.199). Myrrh was a fragrant resin, and aloe the aromatic, quick-drying sap of a tree. In powdered form they were mixed and sprinkled in the sheets that wound the corpse. The purpose of the spices was to counteract the unpleasant odor of the decomposing body.

It is worth noting that until this point Joseph and Nicodemus had maintained secrecy regarding their relationship to Jesus. But now that the other disciples who had followed Jesus had openly deserted him, the two secret disciples came into the open and offered help. The depth of one's commitment is clearly seen in crisis situations. Actions reveal the state of the soul. Calvin, 2:189, notes that, while there are times when it is not wrong to fear the enemies of the gospel, "when the confession of faith is withheld from fear it shows weakness of faith."

40 The body of Jesus was wrapped with spices in "strips of linen." John uses the word *othonion* (the plural meaning "thin strips of linen cloth," GK 3856), while the Synoptics have *sindōn* ("linen sheet," "shroud," GK 4984). Brown, 191, finds a twofold problem with the use of *othonion* in the sense of thin strips or bandages: (1) disagreement with the Synoptics, and (2) Roman Catholic acceptance of the authenticity of the Holy Shroud of Turin. The first objection is answered if the body was first wrapped in linen strips and then covered with a shroud. The second is only as strong as the degree to which the interpreter chooses to regard tradition. The Jewish custom of burial is contrasted with that of the Egyptians, who removed the internal organs, and the Romans, who cremated the bodies of the dead.

41 Because the fall of the first Adam took place in a garden (Ge 3), it is fitting that the redemption of the human race by the second Adam (cf. Ro 5:12–19) takes place in a garden as well: "At the place where Jesus was crucified, there was a garden." The *Gospel of Peter* (24) tells us that the garden belonged to Joseph, and Matthew 27:60 says that the tomb in which Joseph placed the body of Jesus was "his own new tomb that he had cut out of the rock." The emperor Constantine removed Hadrian's temple of Venus to build his Church of the Resurrection on what he believed was the exact location of Jesus' tomb. Since the Crusades this has been the location of the Church of the Holy Sepulcher. Bruce, 380, notes that the garden tomb gives a more general picture, though it belongs to a style two or three centuries later.

42 Since it was the "Jewish day of Preparation" and Sabbath was approaching, it was necessary to bury the body as quickly as possible. Joseph's tomb was nearby and provided an immediate solution to the problem. We do not know whether they intended to leave it there indefinitely. In any case, the resurrection made that decision unnecessary.

NOTES

38 Though Arimathea is mentioned in all four gospels (in connection with Joseph), its location is not known for certain. It may have been a small village in the hill country some twenty miles northwest of Jerusalem (see NIVSB note at Mt 27:57; cf. *ISBE* 1:290). It is often associated with Ramathaim, mentioned in 1 Samuel 1:1.

VII. THE RESURRECTION OF THE LAMB WHO WAS SLAIN (20:1–29)

A. Peter and John at the Empty Tomb (20:1–9)

¹Early on the first day of the week, while it was still dark, Mary Magdalene went to the tomb and saw that the stone had been removed from the entrance. ²So she came running to Simon Peter and the other disciple, the one Jesus loved, and said, "They have taken the Lord out of the tomb, and we don't know where they have put him!"

³So Peter and the other disciple started for the tomb. ⁴Both were running, but the other disciple outran Peter and reached the tomb first. ⁵He bent over and looked in at the strips of linen lying there but did not go in. ⁶Then Simon Peter, who was behind him, arrived and went into the tomb. He saw the strips of linen lying there, ⁷as well as the burial cloth that had been around Jesus' head. The cloth was folded up by itself, separate from the linen. ⁸Finally the other disciple, who had reached the tomb first, also went inside. He saw and believed. ⁹(They still did not understand from Scripture that Jesus had to rise from the dead.)

COMMENTARY

1 The burial on Friday had been hurried. Luke notes that the women who had come with Jesus from Galilee went home and prepared spices and perfumes "but . . . rested on the Sabbath" (Lk 23:55–56). Now, early on the first day of the week, they return to the tomb to complete their work. John identifies only Mary Magdalene, but the plural in v.2 ("we don't know") reveals the presence of others.

Mary arrived at the tomb while it was still dark. This seems to conflict with Mark's account, which reports that the women went to the tomb "just after sunrise" (Mk 16:2). A plausible answer is that Mary had hurried on ahead of the women and arrived somewhat earlier. Her strong affection for Jesus would get her to the tomb as quickly as possible. It is interesting that Mary of Magdala is mentioned only once in the Gospels apart from the crucifixion and empty tomb, yet she becomes the first person to see the risen Lord. In Luke 8:2 Mary is identified as one from whom seven demons had been expelled. Ryle, 4:611, notes that "those who love Christ most are those who have received most benefit from Him." It was not to the priests and religious officials that Jesus first appeared, but to a woman who in the eyes of the world was insignificant and without any kind of merit. God's priorities are decidedly different from those held by society, both then and now.

On arriving, Mary saw that the stone had been removed from the entrance. The Greek *ērmenon* ("had been removed") is a participial form of a verb that means "to lift up or remove" (*airō*, GK *149*) and in this context (where it is followed by *ek*, "out of") suggests a sudden act involving the exercise of force. Since the burial place was a "new tomb" (Mt 27:60; cf. Lk 27:53) perhaps not totally finished, the stone may have been more square than round, thus accounting for the somewhat unexpected verb.

Note, however, that Mark 15:46 says the stone was "rolled" (*proskyliō*, GK *4685*) against the entrance of the tomb.

2 Mary leaves the garden scene and runs to Simon Peter and the other disciple. Repetition of the preposition *pros* ("to Simon Peter and to the other disciple") leads some to infer that because of his denial Peter had left the company of the disciples and had to be found by Mary. The Synoptics include additional narrative not recorded in John regarding the women's encounter with angels at the tomb. That differences exist between the gospel accounts testifies to their validity as "spontaneous evidence of witnesses" rather than "the stereotyped repetition of an official story" (Morris, 828). Had Mary remained at the tomb, she would have heard from the angel that Jesus had risen (Mt 28:6), but in her haste to inform the disciples of the missing body she left before the events recorded in the other gospels took place. Since the robbing of tombs was a common crime in those days, it was natural for Mary to jump to the conclusion that the body of Jesus had been stolen.

3–5 Peter and John ("the other disciple, the one Jesus loved," v.2) left immediately and started running to the tomb. John, who may have been younger (though this is not stated), outran Peter and arrived first. Rather than rushing into the tomb, John stopped at the entrance, bent down, and "peeped in" (*parakyptō*, GK *4160*, v.5). Temple, 2:378, says that "a sacred awe of the Lord's burial place holds him outside." Not so Peter. Arriving at the tomb, he entered without hesitation. Natural temperaments are not changed by conversion.

6–7 Once inside, Peter saw lying in place the linen cloths in which Jesus' body had been wrapped. It is certainly possible that the body could have risen directly through the wrappings, but the text does not specifically say so. That the cloth wound around Jesus' head was "folded up by itself" argues against that manner of departure. It would also indicate that the exit had been orderly—hardly the case if the grave had been robbed.

8 In a few moments, John (who had arrived at the tomb but hesitated to enter it) joined Peter inside. While Peter surveyed the graveclothes, John "saw and believed." Morris, 833 n. 17, notes that *theōrei* ("saw," GK *2555*) in v.6 probably denotes a "more prolonged scrutiny" than does *blepei* (GK *1063*) in vv.1 ("saw") and 5 ("looked in"). What did John believe? Certainly more than the obvious fact that the body of Jesus was no longer there. He saw with the eyes of faith and arrived quickly at the conclusion that Jesus had been raised from the dead. This insight of faith made him the forerunner of all who would be declared "blessed" for believing prior to seeing (cf. v.29).

9 Verse 9 is a parenthesis indicating that the disciples at that time were not aware of the Scriptures that taught the resurrection of Jesus. It did not take long, however, for the first apostles to understand the testimony of Scripture. In his great sermon on the day of Pentecost, Peter pointed out that the affirmation in Psalm 16:10, "You will not abandon me to the grave, nor will you let your Holy One see decay," is a prediction of the resurrection of Jesus Christ (Ac 2:27, 31). Belief in the resurrection preceded the resurrection itself.

NOTES

1 Because "the first day of the week" is commonly thought of as Monday (Sunday being a part of the weekend), several modern translations specify the day as "Sunday" (e.g., NEB, NLT, TEV).

7 The σουδάριον (*soudarion*, GK *5051*) was "a small piece of cloth used as a towel, napkin, or face cloth" (L&N, 6.159). It is a Latin loanword that occurs four times in the NT: in Luke 19:20 of the "piece of cloth" in which the wicked servant kept the mina rather than investing it; in John 11:44 of the "cloth" around the face of Lazarus as he came out of the tomb; in Acts 19:12 of the "handkerchiefs" that had touched Paul and were taken to bring healing to the sick; and in the current verse of the "burial cloth" (NASB, "face-cloth") that had been around Jesus' head. Brown, 986, suggests that it may have been tied under the chin and across the top of the head to keep the mouth of the corpse from falling open.

B. Jesus Appears to Mary Magdalene (20:10–18)

¹⁰Then the disciples went back to their homes, ¹¹but Mary stood outside the tomb crying. As she wept, she bent over to look into the tomb ¹²and saw two angels in white, seated where Jesus' body had been, one at the head and the other at the foot.

¹³They asked her, "Woman, why are you crying?"

"They have taken my Lord away," she said, "and I don't know where they have put him."

¹⁴At this, she turned around and saw Jesus standing there, but she did not realize that it was Jesus.

¹⁵"Woman," he said, "why are you crying? Who is it you are looking for?"

> Thinking he was the gardener, she said, "Sir, if you have carried him away, tell me where you have put him, and I will get him."
>
> [16] Jesus said to her, "Mary."
>
> She turned toward him and cried out in Aramaic, "Rabboni!" (which means Teacher).
>
> [17] Jesus said, "Do not hold on to me, for I have not yet returned to the Father. Go instead to my brothers and tell them, 'I am returning to my Father and your Father, to my God and your God.'"
>
> [18] Mary Magdalene went to the disciples with the news: "I have seen the Lord!" And she told them that he had said these things to her.

COMMENTARY

10–12 The disciples returned to their homes, but Mary remained outside the tomb weeping. The word used here (*klaiō*, GK *3081*) indicates loud lamentation rather than quiet tears. The same word was used of the professional wailing at the tomb of Lazarus (11:33). Standing there weeping, she stooped down and looked into the tomb. Perhaps she had been mistaken and the body was still there. But instead of seeing Jesus, she saw two angels dressed in white (v.12). They were seated one at the head and the other at the foot of the place where the body of Jesus had lain. Some call attention to the position of the two golden cherubs who faced each other from the two ends of the cover of the ark (Ex 25:20). Jesus had died between two criminals (Lk 23:33), but his burial place was between two angels. Augustine's allegory that the position of the two angels signified the preaching of the gospel throughout the entire world (from east to west) is dismissed by Calvin (2:196).

Some have called attention to the fact that according to Luke's account, the women encounter two *men* rather than two angels (24:4). It is worth noting, however, that later in ch. 24, we learn of the women's report to the disciples that they had seen "a vision of *angels*, who said [Jesus] was alive" (Lk 24:23, italics added). Coupled with the observation that the "men" were dressed in "clothes that gleamed like lightning" (v.4), it would be overly literalistic to insist that in this setting "men" and "angels" were two different order of beings.

13 To the angels' question regarding her weeping Mary answers, "They have taken my Lord away, . . . and I don't know where they have put him." Obviously someone had gotten there ahead of her and removed the body. If Mary does not seem frightened in the presence of angels, it should be remembered that she was in a state of emotional shock from discovering an empty tomb. Further, as a devout Jew she would have held a strong belief in the involvement of angels in the daily affairs of life. There is nothing harsh in the salutation, "Woman" (cf. 2:4).

14 At this point, Mary turned and saw Jesus standing there but she did not recognize him. What caused her to turn from the two angels and look behind her? The most plausible answer is that the sudden appearance of Jesus behind Mary was reflected in the faces of the angels, so it was natural for her to turn to see what was happening.

Mary's failure to recognize Jesus is not answered satisfactorily by holding that her eyes were filled with tears or that it was not yet broad daylight. The risen Christ did not always reveal himself as he had been before his resurrection. Sometime later, Jesus appeared to his disciples while they were fishing, but they "did not realize that it was Jesus" (21:4). When he joined the two disciples on the road to Emmaus, their eyes had to be "opened" before they recognized him (Lk 24:31). Mary's inability to recognize the presence of her Lord, though he was right there at that very moment, is illustrative of the common experience of all too many believers in our day. May God open our eyes as he opened the eyes of Elisha's servant at Dothan (2Ki 6:17) to see that we have not been abandoned to the enemy but that God surrounds us with his protective love.

15 Jesus asked Mary why she was crying and who (not what) it was she was looking for. Mary, assuming the one speaking to her was the gardener (since the setting was a garden; cf. 19:41), asked that if he were the one who had taken Jesus away, would he tell her where he had put the body so that she could get it (and, it would appear, bring Jesus' body back and place it in the tomb!). Little did it matter that the load would have been much too heavy for her to carry. Love overlooks such trivial details. The threefold repetition of "him" in v.15 is worthy of note. Mary's entire world at that moment had no room for anything but her Master.

16 Now we come to one of the most dramatic encounters recorded in Scripture. Jesus says but one word: "Mary." Tasker, 225, writes, "In the deepest experiences of life, particularly in the reunion of those who have meant much to one another, words are wont to be few." On hearing her name, Mary suddenly realized that it could be none other than Jesus. She had seen him placed in the tomb as a lifeless corpse. But now he spoke. He was alive! We know from John 10 that when the good shepherd calls his sheep, they "know his voice" (v. 4; cf. vv.1–18). Mary belonged to his flock. Turning to him, she cried out, "Rabboni!" an Aramaic title explained by John as meaning, "Teacher." "Rabboni" is a heightened form of "Rabbi," reflecting both affection and

highest regard. A more accurate rendering of the term would be, "My Master" (NEB).

Calvin, 2:198, notes that in Mary we have an image of our calling. True knowledge of Jesus is when he intimately invites us to himself, not with the voice that falls indiscriminately on the ears of everyone, but with the voice with which he calls the sheep the Father has given to him.

It is sometimes asked why Mary is said to have turned to Jesus when just two verses before she had already turned to him, thinking he was the gardener. The scene is not difficult to imagine. After having first turned to see the one she thought was the gardener, she undoubtedly had turned back toward the tomb in disappointment and sorrow.

17 Jesus' response to Mary, especially as translated by the KJV ("touch me not"), has caused some difficulty because in v.27 Jesus invites Thomas to reach out and feel the wounds in his hands and side (for other occasions, see Mt 28:10; Lk 24:39). Lindars, 607, cites J. H. Bernard's conjecture that the original words were "fear not" (*mē ptoou*, GK *4765*), which were corrupted to the present reading (*mē mou haptou*, GK *721*). Such speculation is unnecessary since a far more reasonable explanation is at hand. The present imperative (in this case, *haptou*) with the negative (*mē*) often means to stop doing something rather than to refrain from doing it. The NIV translates, "Do not hold on to me" (NASB, "Stop clinging to Me"). Mary is not stopped short in her tracks with a warning not to touch Jesus but is told that there is no necessity for her clinging to him as though he would suddenly vanish. He explains, "I have not yet returned to the Father." The word for "return" (KJV, "ascend") is in the perfect tense and implies in this context that Jesus had not yet completed his ascension.

Rather than hold on selfishly to Jesus, Mary is to go to Jesus' "brothers" (a new and affectionate title for the disciples) with the glad news that he will be returning to the Father. Reith, 2:160, summarizes the point: "Cling not selfishly to me, but go to impart this gladness of yours to others." The obligation to tell others is more important than the natural desire to display affection. The purpose of Jesus' resurrection was not so that he could return to this world in triumph but so that he could return to God, having completed his redemptive ministry on behalf of humanity.

The forty-day interval between Jesus' resurrection and ascension was for the benefit of his followers. It established the "necessary continuity between the earthly Jesus and the glorified Christ" (Marsh, 637). The words "I am returning" portray the ascension of Jesus as an event that stretched from his resurrection forward. The actual ascension was simply the outward and physical culmination of the process. While the final ascension was in one sense a separation from his followers, in another sense it inaugurated a new era of continuing fellowship. During the days of his earthly life, Jesus was only available if one went where he was; now he is wherever we are!

The distinction between "my Father" and "your Father" and between "my God" and "your God" calls attention to the fact that while the disciples were the "brothers" of Jesus, their relationship to God the Father was not the same as his. Jesus did not say that he was returning to "our Father and our God."

18 Mary of Magdala complied with Jesus' instructions and went to tell the disciples of her remarkable encounter with the risen Lord. Love demonstrates itself in the completeness of one's obedience. Mary loved much and therefore obeyed without question.

NOTES

13 The KJV, ASV, RSV, NASB, and NKJV all take ὅτι (*hoti*) in a causal sense (rather than recitative) and translate, "Because they have taken away my Lord." This interpretation assumes an unexpressed prior clause, "I am weeping . . ."

15 The noun κηπουρός (*kēpouros*, "gardener," GK *3058*), one who tends or takes care of the κῆπος (*kēpos*, "garden," GK *3057*), occurs only here in the NT (see Nicolas Wyatt, "Supposing Him to Be the Gardener," *ZNW* 81 [1990]: 21–38). Keener, 317, notes that "gardeners were at the bottom of the social scale" and the one to whom Mary spoke would have been looking after the grounds, not taking care of the tomb itself.

C. Jesus Appears to His Disciples (20:19–23)

¹⁹On the evening of that first day of the week, when the disciples were together, with the doors locked for fear of the Jews, Jesus came and stood among them and said, "Peace be with you!" ²⁰After he said this, he showed them his hands and side. The disciples were overjoyed when they saw the Lord.

²¹Again Jesus said, "Peace be with you! As the Father has sent me, I am sending you." ²²And with that he breathed on them and said, "Receive the Holy Spirit. ²³If you forgive anyone his sins, they are forgiven; if you do not forgive them, they are not forgiven."

COMMENTARY

19 The next appearance of Jesus recorded in the fourth gospel took place on the evening of resurrection Sunday. At this point, John is not using the normal Jewish reckoning of time, because the "evening" of the first day of the week would have been Saturday night (since each new day began with sundown of the previous day). "That first day of the week" refers to the same first day with which the chapter begins. The disciples were gathered (probably in the upper room) because they had heard from four reliable sources (Mary Magdalene, the women returning from the tomb, Peter, and the disciples on the road to Emmaus) that Jesus had risen from the dead. He was no longer in the grave but had returned to life and was somewhere in the vicinity. The parallel account in Luke 24 indicates that the term "disciples" should be taken in a wider sense than the Twelve as we commonly know them. (Verse 33 indicates that the disciples on the road to Emmaus returned to Jerusalem, where they found "the Eleven and those with them.")

The group had met behind locked doors for fear of the Jews. The story was circulating that the disciples had stolen the body of Jesus while the guards were sleeping (Mt 28:13–15). There was reason to believe that some sort of retaliation would be taken. The apocryphal *Gospel of Peter* (26) tells of a search for the disciples on the ground that they had attempted to set fire to the temple. The plural "doors" most likely refers to the outer door leading into the house and the door of the specific room where they had gathered (rather than two doors to the same room).

Suddenly Jesus stands among them. Whether one understands Jesus as having caused the doors to open (cf. Ac 17:26) or simply to have passed through the closed doors, the appearance involves a miracle. Though his greeting was the usual Hebrew salutation, "Peace be with you!" (cf. 1Sa 25:6), the disciples could not but remember his promise made a short time before: "Peace I leave with you; my peace I give you" (14:27). They may have expected a strong rebuke from the one they had deserted, but they received instead his forgiveness and blessing. Such is the grace of our Lord!

20 Jesus then showed the disciples his hands and side. It is possible that the nails were driven through the wrists; both the Hebrew and the Greek word for "hand" may include the arm (cf. Mt 4:6). The wounds inflicted by the crucifixion would prove beyond doubt that the one who stood before them alive was their earthly Master. (In 1968, the skeleton of a crucified man was found in Israel with a nail driven through his ankle bones.) How poignant the scene as Jesus extends his nail-pierced hands to his own to convince them of his victory over the grave! How gracious that those same hands remain outstretched to sinners today as a symbol of his love for all for whom he died! While Calvin, 2:203, held that for anyone to infer that Christ still has a wounded side and hands would be "ridiculous," Revelation 5:6 pictures the glorified Jesus as "a Lamb, looking as if it had been slain." It would be better to leave that issue unanswered!

21 The disciples are "overjoyed" when they grasp that the one standing before them is, in reality, the Lord. Morris, 845 n. 49, notes that the aorist (*echarēsan*, GK *5897*) may point to the sudden joy that came over them when they realized it was Jesus. Jesus repeats his greeting (cf. v.19) and adds, "As the Father has sent me, I am sending you" (cf. 17:18). The mission of the church grows out of the mission of Christ. It is a continuation of what God purposed when he sent his Son on the mission of redemption. As he went, so also do we go. His mission determines the mission of the church and provides it with direction and motivation.

22 This verse has been taken in various ways. Some connect it with the ancient belief that the breath of a holy man had special power; others think that it reflects an early method of Christian ordination. Since the words "on them" do not occur in the Greek text, it is possible to translate, "He expelled a deep breath" (Hugh Schonfield, *The Original New Testament* [1958; repr., New York: Harper & Row, 1985]). It is better to take the incident as a special empowerment of the Holy Spirit for the mission to which the disciples have just been assigned. (The lack of an article before *pneuma*, GK 4460, stresses the quality rather than the person of the Spirit.) The Greek *emphysaō* ("to breathe on," GK 1874) occurs only here in the NT,

though it is used in the LXX in Genesis 2:7 (God "breathed into [man's] nostrils the breath of life, and the man became a living being") and Ezekiel 37:1-14 (the "dry bones" account). God's breath is the beginning of all life. Without his Spirit, his mission cannot be accomplished. A special infilling of the Holy Spirit is still the primary requirement for effective ministry.

23 The disciples are told that if they "forgive anyone his sins, they are forgiven" and if they "do not forgive them, they are not forgiven." It is clear from Mark 2:7 that no one but God can forgive sins. Bruce, 392, notes that the two passives (translated "they are forgiven" and "they are not forgiven") express divine agency and that the preacher's role is declaratory. It has never been the role of the minister or priest to forgive sins; they can only announce the fact that sins have been forgiven. When the message is accepted, forgiveness is granted; when it is refused, forgiveness is withheld.

NOTES

21 The ASV, NASB, NET, and NKJV take οὖν (*oun*) as inferential and translate "therefore" or "so." The RSV, NRSV, NIV, and NLT take it as transitional and supply no English equivalent. The KJV has "then."

Though two different verbs are used for "sending" (ἀποστέλλω, *apostellō*, GK 690, for the Father's sending of the Son; πέμπω, *pempō*, GK 4287, for Jesus' sending of his disciples), the meaning is the same.

23 The perfect passive indicative (ἀφέωνται, *apheōntai*, GK 904]) has strong external support (ℵ² A D (L) 050 *f* [1,13] 33[vid] 565 et al.) and the variants ἀφίενται (*aphientai*, present) and ἀφεθήσεται (*aphethēsetai*, future) are regarded by the UBS committee as "scribal simplifications which weaken the sense" (Metzger, 219). Some would interpret the perfect tense to mean that God's forgiveness is granted prior to the forgiveness extended by Jesus' disciples, but this fails to understand that "in a conditional sentence the perfect tense is used with essentially the same meaning as the present and the future, except that it emphasizes the continuous character of the action" (Newman and Nida, *Translator's Handbook on the Gospel of John*, 615-16). The NASB falls prey to this error: "If you forgive the sins of any, *their sins* have been forgiven them."

D. The Confession by Thomas (20:24–29)

OVERVIEW

We once again meet Thomas, one of the twelve disciples. In the Synoptics his name occurs only in the listing of the Twelve (Mt 10:3 par.), but John refers to him on four occasions (11:16; 14:5; 20:24; 21:2). Thomas's reluctance to accept the report of the others that Jesus is alive has earned him the title "Doubting Thomas." Opinions vary as to whether the name is accurate or does him a disservice. The two earlier references along with the current episode suggest that he was a devoted follower of Jesus but suffered from a somewhat gloomy out-look on the future. For reasons not quite clear, Calvin, 2:209, has some strong words to say of him—he was "downright obstinate"; his stupidity was "astonishing and monstrous"; he was "proud and insulting towards Christ." Such a strong reaction is hardly justified from the fragmentary account of him in Scripture. A man of such questionable character could hardly have gained the respect of early tradition, which reports that he evangelized Parthia, went to Persia, and founded Christianity in India.

> ²⁴Now Thomas (called Didymus), one of the Twelve, was not with the disciples when Jesus came. ²⁵So the other disciples told him, "We have seen the Lord!"
> But he said to them, "Unless I see the nail marks in his hands and put my finger where the nails were, and put my hand into his side, I will not believe it."
> ²⁶A week later his disciples were in the house again, and Thomas was with them. Though the doors were locked, Jesus came and stood among them and said, "Peace be with you!" ²⁷Then he said to Thomas, "Put your finger here; see my hands. Reach out your hand and put it into my side. Stop doubting and believe."
> ²⁸Thomas said to him, "My Lord and my God!"
> ²⁹Then Jesus told him, "Because you have seen me, you have believed; blessed are those who have not seen and yet have believed."

COMMENTARY

24 Thomas ("called Didymus," which means "twin") was absent from the gathering when Jesus had appeared in the midst of the disciples. No reason is given. Perhaps he wanted to be alone during this time of deep sorrow. Barclay, 2:275, reports that King George the Fifth had as one of his rules of life that if he must suffer, he wanted to be left alone to suffer like a well-bred animal.

25 When told by the others that they had seen the Lord (the imperfect *elegon*, GK *3306*, implying repeated affirmations), Thomas was adamant in his refusal to believe; unless he could see (and touch) the nail marks in Jesus' hands and the wound on Jesus' side, he would not believe. The nonnegotiable "unless" is an emphatic double negative in Greek. It is difficult to understand why Thomas was so resolved not to believe. To reject so strongly the testimony of ten close friends is not easy to justify. Temple, 2:390, explains "such vigour of unbelief" as "a strong urge to believe, held down by common sense and its habitual dread of disillusionment." Perhaps Thomas thought the others had experienced a common vision, and he wanted to be certain that when he reached out to touch the body, his hand would come in contact with genuine flesh. In any case, his skepticism cost him a week of doubt and wondering while the others were rejoicing in the truth of Jesus' resurrection. The failure to believe carries its own penalty.

26-27 "A week later" (Gk. "eight days," taken inclusively) Thomas was back with the other disciples when Jesus appeared behind locked doors as he had on Easter evening. Using Thomas's own words, Jesus invites the hesitant disciple to reach out and touch his hands and to put his hand into his side (v.27). How would the risen Lord know what Thomas had said unless he had been present at the time of the disciple's ultimatum?

"Stop doubting and believe," said Jesus. Thomas had started down the road to unbelief. *Apistos* ("faithless," GK *603*), which occurs only here in John, is used elsewhere in the NT to designate unbelievers (cf. 1Co 7:12-15; 1Ti 5:8). He is to stop going in the direction he has headed (implied by the present imperative in a prohibition) and show himself faithful (*ginomai*, GK *1181*, may carry this nuance; cf. BDAG, 199 #7). The admonition is strong but entirely appropriate in the situation. There is a time for both patient reasoning and direct orders.

28 Thomas responds, "My Lord and my God!" Though the words are in the nominative case, many commentators understand them as vocative. This yields a direct address to the Lord. It is probably better to take them as nominative and translate, "It is my Lord and my God!" In either case, Thomas is expressing his new faith in language that goes beyond anything that had been used by his fellow disciples (cf. Bruce, 394). The two designations are not intended to distinguish between two different ways in which Thomas knew Jesus (as "Lord" before the crucifixion and as "God" following the resurrection). The combination "Lord and God" would be familiar to any reader of the Greek OT, where it regularly translates the Hebrew *Yahweh Elohim*. Parallels are found in pagan sources as well (cf. the imperial title ascribed to Domitian, *Dominus et Deus noster*; cf. Suetonius, *Dom.*, 13).

29 The first clause of v.29 may be a statement (so KJV, NIV) or a question (so NET, RSV). The latter is perhaps better: "Because you have seen me, have you believed?" Then comes the contrast: "Blessed are those who have not seen and yet have believed." The entire Christian church from the ascension onward is comprised of those who have believed without seeing. If physical seeing were necessary to convince people of the reality of the resurrection, the church would have faltered within the first year of its life.

NOTES

25 Though the Greek τὸν τύπον τῶν ἥλων (*ton typon tōn hēlōn*) is twice repeated (in NA²⁷), both the NIV and NASB follow the variant τὸν τόπον, *ton topon*, in the second location and translate the two phrases with: "nail marks . . . where the nails were"; "the imprint of the nails . . . the place of the nails." Most other current versions maintain the same translation for the two occurrences of τὸν τύπον τῶν ἥλων, *ton typon tōn hēlōn*: NET, "the wounds from the nails"; NRSV, "the mark of the nails; NKJV, "the print of the nails."

The NASB's "I will not believe" leaves the impression that unless Thomas was able to see and feel the wounds, he would not believe in Jesus at all. The NIV has "I will not believe it," thus narrowing the scope to refer to the resurrection itself. Although "it" is not in the Greek, it should be added since direct objects are often omitted in Greek when the context clearly defines what is intended. Both the NET and NLT supply "it."

29 Some translations take πιστεύσαντες (*pisteusantes, GK 4409*) as a gnomic aorist, thus making it equivalent to an English present tense (RSV, "and yet believe"; TEV, "those who believe"). It is more likely that Jesus is referring to those who "[had] come to believe" (NRSV) without the benefit of having as yet seen him risen from the dead.

VIII. CONCLUDING REMARKS (20:30–21:25)

A. Why John Wrote the Gospel (20:30–31)

> [30] Jesus did many other miraculous signs in the presence of his disciples, which are not recorded in this book. [31] But these are written that you may believe that Jesus is the Christ, the Son of God, and that by believing you may have life in his name.

COMMENTARY

30 If ch. 21 is taken as an epilogue, then vv. 30–31 of ch. 20 comprise the original ending of the gospel. Serving as a summary statement, they declare that not all the miracles done by Jesus were recorded in the gospel. Those that were recorded advance the goal of bringing people to faith in Christ in order that they might receive eternal life (v. 31). John has been selective in his approach because there is no need to cite every last miracle to elicit the response of faith. The "miraculous signs" to which John refers are the many remarkable deeds performed by Jesus during his earthly ministry. They may include additional, unrecorded appearances of the resurrected Lord as well.

31 The gospels were never intended to be taken as biographies of Jesus. John's gospel is a carefully constructed narrative of significant words and works of Jesus for the purpose of bringing about faith in Christ. They were written "that you may believe."

Manuscript testimony is rather equally divided between *pisteuēte* (present subjunctive) and *pisteusēte* (aorist subjunctive), two forms of the verb "to believe" (GK 4409). The present yields, "that you may go on believing," indicating that the gospel was directed primarily to believers with the hope that their faith would grow and be strengthened; the aorist translates, "that you may come to believe," in which case the target audience would be nonbelievers. Since faith is not a static state, both emphases may be involved; neither tense in and of itself may convey the entire meaning. Certainly the gospel of John has been used by the Holy Spirit down through the ages to bring men and women to faith in Christ; equally it has strengthened the faith of believers and led them to an ever-increasing trust in their Savior and Lord. On this basis, "life in his name" encompasses not only life eternal but also the transformed life here and now.

NOTES

31 NA[27] places the sigma in square brackets (πιστεύ[σ]ητε, *pisteusēte*) in order to represent both readings. The NET's lengthy study note here reviews the arguments for both readings and then concludes that it is probably best to say that "the evangelist wrote with a dual purpose: (1) to witness to unbelievers concerning Jesus . . . and (2) to strengthen the faith of believers." Morris, however, 855 n.82, noting that the present tense πιστεύετε (*pisteuete*) has strong MS support and that the aorist would normally be expected in a sentence like this, concludes that "the present has transcriptional probability and it is likely to be correct."

B. Jesus Appears Again in Galilee (21:1–14)

OVERVIEW

The final verse of ch. 20 sounded very much like the end of John's gospel. In summary fashion he reported that many of the miraculous signs done by Jesus had been included in his gospel so that readers might believe that Jesus is the Christ and have life in his name (20:31). But now follows another chapter, which at least for some scholars seems to be an addition written either by a different author or by the same author at a later time.

A major reason for the additional material is said to have been the desire to correct a misunderstanding about the time of Jesus' return ("Didn't he say he would return before John died?" cf. 21:20–23). Arguments supporting the integrity of ch. 21 include: (1) the large number of Johannine idioms, (2) the absence of any break in style, and (3) the lack of any indication that the gospel ever circulated without this last section. Morris, 859, confesses "to being a little mystified by the certainty of those who regard it as self-evident that this last chapter is a late addition."

[1]Afterward Jesus appeared again to his disciples, by the Sea of Tiberias. It happened this way: [2]Simon Peter, Thomas (called Didymus), Nathanael from Cana in Galilee, the sons of Zebedee, and two other disciples were together. [3]"I'm going out to fish," Simon Peter told them, and they said, "We'll go with you." So they went out and got into the boat, but that night they caught nothing.

[4]Early in the morning, Jesus stood on the shore, but the disciples did not realize that it was Jesus.

[5]He called out to them, "Friends, haven't you any fish?"

"No," they answered.

[6]He said, "Throw your net on the right side of the boat and you will find some." When they did, they were unable to haul the net in because of the large number of fish.

[7]Then the disciple whom Jesus loved said to Peter, "It is the Lord!" As soon as Simon Peter heard him say, "It is the Lord," he wrapped his outer garment around him (for he had

taken it off) and jumped into the water. [8]The other disciples followed in the boat, towing the net full of fish, for they were not far from shore, about a hundred yards. [9]When they landed, they saw a fire of burning coals there with fish on it, and some bread.

[10]Jesus said to them, "Bring some of the fish you have just caught."

[11]Simon Peter climbed aboard and dragged the net ashore. It was full of large fish, 153, but even with so many the net was not torn. [12]Jesus said to them, "Come and have breakfast." None of the disciples dared ask him, "Who are you?" They knew it was the Lord. [13]Jesus came, took the bread and gave it to them, and did the same with the fish. [14]This was now the third time Jesus appeared to his disciples after he was raised from the dead.

COMMENTARY

1 Chapter 20 begins with an indefinite time reference: "afterward." There is no indication as to when the incident that follows took place. All we know is that Jesus appeared again to his disciples. (In v.14 we will learn that it was his "third" appearance to the disciples as a group following the resurrection.) The encounter took place by the Sea of Tiberias. This appears to be the official name of the sea (after the Roman emperor Tiberius), though it was commonly called the Sea of Galilee. (In Lk 5:1 it is referred to as the "Lake of Gennesaret.")

2–3 Seven of the disciples were together at the lake. We are not told anything about the other four (or more, if the "two other disciples" were those on the road to Emmaus rather than two of the original twelve; see Lk 24:13–35). Peter announces that he is "going out to fish" (v.3). It is interesting that in spite of his disowning of Jesus on the eve of the crucifixion, Peter seems not to have lost his ability to serve as leader. "We'll go with you," echo the others, and so the fishing expedition begins.

Peter is sometimes criticized for returning so quickly to his old line of work (Mk 1:16). But was he in fact returning to his former career as a fisherman? Is it not more likely that Peter was simply choosing to use his time profitably rather than to remain idle? The disciples "got into the boat"—the definite article may indicate a specific boat, perhaps the one they formerly used in their trade—and shoved off from shore to begin their work. But "that night they caught nothing." Apparently it was customary in Galilee to fish during the night so that the catch would be fresh for market in the morning.

4 It must have been discouraging to work all night long and have nothing to show for it. As the day was dawning, Jesus "stood on the shore." The text does not say that he arrived at the shore but that he stood there. It may be that the author wants us to understand that Jesus appeared there quite suddenly, much as he did behind closed doors following his resurrection (cf. 20:19). The disciples, however, did not recognize that the one standing on the shore was Jesus. Perhaps a combination of the distance (about a hundred yards, according to v.8) and the dim light of early morning kept the disciples from identifying Jesus. On the other hand, it is quite probable that Jesus kept them from recognizing him. Remember that Mary Magdalene took the risen Jesus to be a gardener (20:15), and the disciples on the road to Emmaus did not recognize him until "their eyes were opened" (Lk 24:31).

5 Jesus called out to the disciples and asked about their catch. The way the question is put in Greek (with the negative particle *mē*) normally expects a negative answer ("You haven't caught anything, have you?"), but it may be better to take the statement as a cautious assertion (some conjecture *mēti*, rather than *mē ti*, and translate, "Surely you have a bit to eat?"). The greeting *paidia* ("friends," GK *4086*) is the diminutive plural form of the word for "child." BDAG, 749, notes that it is used figuratively "as a form of familiar address on the part of a respected pers., who feels himself on terms of fatherly intimacy w. those whom he addresses." Outside the NT, the word for fish used by Jesus (*prosphagion*, GK *4709*) "normally referred to some type of relish eaten with bread, but in Jn 21:5 (the only occurrence in the NT) the reference is to the flesh of fish" (L&N 5.17).

The disciples' response to Jesus' inquiry was an abrupt no. They had toiled all night and had nothing to show for it. Calvin, 2:216, writes, "If we always succeeded when we put our hand to any labour, scarcely anyone would attribute the reward of his work to God's blessing, but all would boast of their own industry and shake hands with themselves." The night of work without results would serve to underscore the power of Jesus in what he was about to do.

6 Responding to Jesus' instruction to cast the net on the right side of the boat, the men landed such a large catch that they were unable to hoist the net over the side and dump its load into the boat. This seems to be the meaning of "haul the net in," because v.10 reports that they towed the loaded net to shore behind the boat. Whether or not this catch should be considered a miracle depends on one's definition of "miracle." Some think that a person on the shore would be able to see a large shoal of fish hidden from the view of those in the boat. However, the size of the catch and the dimness of the morning light favor viewing the incident as a genuine miracle. In either case, it is described with considerable restraint.

7 It was John, "the disciple whom Jesus loved," who first recognized the man standing on the shore. It was not that he had better eyesight but that he

had keener insight. Who else but Jesus could have directed them to such a miraculous catch of fish? So he turned to Peter and exclaimed, "It is the Lord!"

Scholars differ as to whether the text intends to portray Peter as putting on his outer garment or only tucking it up under his belt. Taken literally, the Greek text says that he was "naked" (*gymnos*, GK *1218*); however, the word can mean—and in this context undoubtedly does mean—"to be lightly clad" (NASB, "he was stripped for work"). The "outer garment" would be a short fisherman's coat. If Peter put the coat on, it would seem that he was working in nothing more than a loincloth.

Here the question is why a person would put a garment on if he wanted to swim to shore. One answer is that in the Jewish culture the exchange of greetings was a religious act not to be carried out unless both parties were properly clothed. On the other hand, if Peter was wearing the coat while working and then tucked it up under his belt, it could have been that he had nothing on under it and therefore would not have taken it off to swim (or wade) to shore. The same verb (*diazōnnymi*, "to tie around, put on," GK *1346*) is used in 13:4 to describe Jesus' tying of a towel around himself in order to wash the disciples' feet. The latter option becomes more plausible if we picture Peter wading to shore rather than swimming. The northwestern portion of the Sea of Galilee is relatively shallow for some distance out from the shore.

8 In any case, it was Peter, the impetuous one, who threw caution to the wind to get to Jesus without delay. Temple, 2:229, remarks that Peter had "the stains of recent disloyalty" on his conscience and more than the others needed personal assurance of forgiveness. The other disciples, towing behind them the net full of fish, followed in the boat. They were not far from shore—only about a hundred yards (two hundred cubits, a cubit being approximately the length of a man's arm).

9 When the other disciples arrived at shore, they found a fire burning, with a fish being roasted along with some bread. It is interesting that the narrative uses three different Greek words for fish: *prosphagion* (GK *4709*) in v.5, the more common *ichthys* (GK *2716*) in v.6, and *opsarion* (usually a small fish, GK *4066*) in v.9.

10 Jesus asks the disciples to bring him some of the fish they have just caught. It would seem that he wished to add them to the one fish (*opsarion* in v.9 being singular) already on the fire; yet in v.13 he provides breakfast for the disciples by giving them bread and "the fish" (once again singular).

11 Peter climbed aboard the boat and dragged the net full of fish to the shore. We are probably to understand that Peter was the one supervising the work rather than doing it all by himself (though Bruce, 401, accepts the latter position and notes that hauling up the net single-handedly was a tribute to the physical strength of "the big fisherman."

The net was full of large fish, 153 in number, yet it was not torn. Numbers have a strange fascination for biblical scholars, so there is no shortage of suggestions regarding the symbolic meaning of 153. Jerome reported that, according to Greek zoologists, there were 153 different kinds of fish in the world (thus indicating, perhaps, the wide range of converts that would be brought in by the net of the gospel). Others note that 153 is the sum of the numerical values of *Simōn* (76) and *ichthys* (77). It is also the triangular number of 17, i.e., the total of all the numbers from 1 through 17. Seventeen is then thought to represent the law (10) and grace (7), so that 153 would refer to all who come to Jesus either by law or grace. The simplest answer is to take 153 as the actual number of fish that were caught. Even today, fishermen remember the details of all their largest hauls!

12 Jesus invited the disciples to have breakfast with him, but not one of them ventured to question him as to who he was: "they knew it was the Lord." Apparently there was a certain mysterious quality about the encounter, and the disciples, while convinced that he was the Lord, for some reason didn't raise any questions. It was common in those days to have two meals per day. The first was the *ariston* ("breakfast," GK *756*), normally eaten before the day's work began. As a rule, the major meal of the day was the *deipnon* (GK *1270*; cf. Mk 6:21; Jn 12:2).

13–14 Jesus took the bread and gave it to the disciples; he then did the same with the fish. Many commentators see in the actions of Jesus a reference to the Eucharist. John closes the incident by noting that this was "the third time" that Jesus appeared to his disciples following the resurrection (v.14). Jesus had also appeared to Mary Magdalene and to others (including the disciples on the road to Emmaus), but John is not concerned with what was recorded in the other gospels or with Jesus' appearances to individuals. His reckoning has to do solely with his own narrative and with the larger group of disciples (20:19–23, 26–29).

NOTES

2 The name Σίμων Πέτρος (*Simōn Petros*) is typically Johannine. It is used once by each of the other gospel writers and fifteen times by John.

5 The word παιδία (*paidia*) is translated "children" by the KJV, ASV, RSV, NASB, NKJV, NRSV, Goodspeed; "friends" by the NIV, JB, NEB, NLT; "young men" by the TEV; and "lads" by Moffatt, Phillips, Williams. While it is not easy to ascertain the degree of familiarity that would be appropriate in the setting, the more colloquial "lads" is probably the closest approximation.

8 In vv.3 and 6 the boat is a πλοῖον (*ploion*, GK *4450*), while in v.8 the diminutive πλοιάριον (*ploiar-ion*, GK *4449*) is used. That both terms are used of the same vessel would indicate that the latter has tended to lose its diminutive force.

REFLECTIONS

This passage (21:1–14) is often discussed in terms of the spiritual lessons it teaches. From it we learn that (1) Christian leaders are to be fishers of people; (2) unless the Lord directs our activity, we will labor without results; (3) when the net of the gospel is drawn in, it will be filled to overflowing with people from every tribe and nation; and (4) believers are looking forward to the marriage supper of the Lamb, when we will share an eternal feast with the Lord. Scripture often lends itself to homiletical application without specifically teaching the point that is being made. As long as we do not insist that the Bible means what it means to us rather than what it meant to the writer, we are on safe ground.

C. Jesus, Peter, and John (21:15–23)

¹⁵When they had finished eating, Jesus said to Simon Peter, "Simon son of John, do you truly love me more than these?"

"Yes, Lord," he said, "you know that I love you."

Jesus said, "Feed my lambs."

¹⁶Again Jesus said, "Simon son of John, do you truly love me?"

He answered, "Yes, Lord, you know that I love you."

Jesus said, "Take care of my sheep."

¹⁷The third time he said to him, "Simon son of John, do you love me?"

Peter was hurt because Jesus asked him the third time, "Do you love me?" He said, "Lord, you know all things; you know that I love you."

¹⁸Jesus said, "Feed my sheep. I tell you the truth, when you were younger you dressed yourself and went where you wanted; but when you are old you will stretch out your hands, and someone else will dress you and lead you where you do not want to go." ¹⁹Jesus said this to indicate the kind of death by which Peter would glorify God. Then he said to him, "Follow me!"

²⁰Peter turned and saw that the disciple whom Jesus loved was following them. (This was the one who had leaned back against Jesus at the supper and had said, "Lord, who is going to betray you?") ²¹When Peter saw him, he asked, "Lord, what about him?"

²²Jesus answered, "If I want him to remain alive until I return, what is that to you? You must follow me." ²³Because of this, the rumor spread among the brothers that this disciple would not die. But Jesus did not say that he would not die; he only said, "If I want him to remain alive until I return, what is that to you?"

COMMENTARY

15–17 After breakfast, Jesus turned to Peter and asked, "Simon son of John, do you truly love me more than these?" The phrase "more than these" most likely means "more than these other disciples" rather than "more than these things" (the fishing gear and all that it stood for). Since the pronoun *toutōn* ("these") is both masculine and neuter, either reference is possible. On the eve of the crucifixion, Peter had declared his loyalty: "Even if all fall away on account of you, I never will" (Mt 26:33). Perhaps Jesus is reminding him in a gentle way that actions rather than words are the ultimate expression of love.

Some commentators think that in the ensuing dialogue between Jesus and Peter it is significant that two different words for love are used. Jesus twice asks, "Do you truly love [*agapaō*, GK *26*] me?" to which Peter answers, "Yes, Lord, you know that I love [*phileō*, GK *5797*] you." When he poses the question for the third time, Jesus resorts to Peter's word, which is then used yet again by the disciple. Unfortunately, those who see a distinction between the verbs as used in this context are at odds as to what the difference signifies.

Some think that Jesus is using the more noble word for love while Peter responds with a less exacting term (TCNT translates, "You know that I am your friend"). Then in posing the question for the third time, Jesus drops to the level of Peter's word and asks whether even that is true. Others understand the exchange as Peter's declaring of a warm and affectionate love in response to Jesus' use of a word for love that may connote a certain aloofness. When Peter twice affirms his affectionate devotion for Jesus, the Lord rises to Peter's choice of words and asks, "Do you really love me like that?"

Ancient commentators took the two words for love as essentially synonymous and understood the variation as stylistic. Many twentieth-century scholars (especially British scholars) insisted that while the meanings of the two verbs overlap, they are by no means exactly synonymous (see Hendriksen, 2:494–500, for a discussion supporting this point of view). Contemporary writers acknowledge the lexicographical differences but believe that John varied his words not to express fine shades of distinction but for purposes of style and syntax. Several arguments support this position: (1) Both *agapaō* and *phileō* are used somewhat at random in the LXX for the same Hebrew word; (2) the common view that *agapaō* is a higher kind of love does not fit in 2 Timothy 4:10, where the deserter Demas is said to have "loved [*agapēsas*] this world"; (3) the two verbs are used interchangeably within the fourth gospel (cf. 19:26 with 20:2; 14:23 with 16:27).

If the only variation in the narrative were the two words for love, an interpreter might be more inclined to see in them a difference in meaning. But such is not the case. John also uses two different words for taking care of the flock (*boskō*, "to feed," GK *1081*, and *poimainō*, "to shepherd," GK *4477*), two words (or three, following some MSS) for the flock itself (*arnia*, "lambs," GK *768*, and *probatia*, "little sheep," GK *4584*), and two words for "know" (*oida*, GK *3857*, and *ginōskō*, GK *1182*). To press the differences between the synonyms for love establishes a hermeneutic that should be applied to the other synonyms as well. This, however, would lead to an unnatural and overly subtle interpretation of the entire encounter. It is preferable to see the differences as stylistic. (I do admit, though, that it is difficult to resist Temple's suggestion, 2:406–7, that the Lord's questions follow a declining scale and the commissioning follows an ascending scale.)

Jesus' charge to Peter ("feed my lambs") underscores the basic responsibility of those who minister in the local church as pastors and teachers. Sadly, the business of the church and the felt needs of a congregation tend to usurp a pastor's time and energy. As a result, the flock goes hungry and problems multiply exponentially. Jesus has commissioned the clergy to be pastors, not livestock herders. The measure of ministers' love for Jesus is clearly demonstrated by their willingness to feed those entrusted to their care.

16 The second question repeats the first, except that the qualifying phrase "more than these" is omitted. Peter's answer is an exact duplication of his first response. Jesus then instructs Peter to "take care of my sheep." *Poimainō* ("herd," "tend," "look after") is a broad term indicating the full responsibilities of a shepherd for his flock.

17 When Jesus asks the question for the third time ("Simon son of John, do you love me?"), Peter is distressed, not because Jesus adopts the word for love that Peter has been using, but because the same question has been asked three times. The reason for the threefold repetition arises from Peter's threefold disowning of Jesus (18:17, 25, 27). Three times Peter repudiated his relationship with Jesus; three times he is called on to reaffirm his love.

Twice Peter had answered, "You know that I love you" (vv. 15, 16). Now, ashamed that he must repeat himself yet again, he says, "Lord, you know all things; you know that I love you." Lindars, 635, notes that if in v.17 there is a distinction in the two words used for "know," then *oidas* would indicate knowing as a fact and *ginōskeis* would be knowing in a feeling and intimate way. Some texts read *probata* ("sheep") rather than *probatia* ("little sheep") in v.17 and understand the Lord as committing to Peter's care the lambs (*arnia*, v.15), the young sheep (v.16), and then the entire flock (v.17). Unless our understanding of John's use of synonyms is incorrect, interpretations of this sort go beyond what is written.

18 Here again we see the characteristic Johannine double *amēn* (NIV, "I tell you the truth," GK *297*). It serves to prepare the listener for a truth of

unusual importance. For Peter it was an indication of the manner of his death (cf. v.19). Many writers see a proverbial saying behind the text as it appears in John. Bultmann, 713, suggests, "In youth a man is free to go where he will; in old age a man must let himself be taken where he does not will," but Haenchen, 2:226, notes that it is incomprehensible why anyone would lead a helpless old person where he or she did not want to go.

The proverb had to do with death (that's where a person doesn't want to go) rather than the helplessness of old age. If martyrdom is the thrust of the original proverb, then the addition of the clause, "you will stretch out your hands," would serve to indicate the specific kind of death that awaited Peter. Tertullian (*Scorpiace* 13), writing in the early third century, reported that Peter was crucified in Rome under Nero, and a century later Eusebius (*Hist. eccl.* 3.1) added that Peter at his own request was crucified head downward (cf. the second-century apocryphal *Acts of Peter* 37–38). Most scholars consider the details of Peter's martyrdom as embellishments, though they agree that in all probability he was put to death by crucifixion.

19 John notes that Jesus said what he did "to indicate the kind of death by which Peter would glorify God." Martyrdom is not defeat but victory. As the Father was glorified by the death of the Son (17:4), so will the martyrdom of Peter bring glory to God. Peter's love for his Master resulted not only in a commission to serve but also in the opportunity to die. Love inevitably involves not only responsibility but also sacrifice.

20 Apparently Jesus had taken Peter aside from the others for the discussion recorded in vv.15–19. Now Peter turns and sees "the disciple whom Jesus loved . . . following them." John is further described as the one who in the upper room leaned back on Jesus to ask about the one who would betray the Lord (cf. 13:25).

21 Seeing John following them, Peter asked, "Lord, what about him?" It was a natural curiosity on Peter's part to know what would happen to another of the Lord's disciples. Having just learned of his own martyrdom, he would wonder about the fate of his companions.

22 Jesus responded by saying that even if John should remain until he came again (the parousia), what concern would that be to Peter? His responsibility was to follow Jesus. Each person has his own calling. For Peter, the man of action, following Jesus meant a life of caring for Jesus' sheep; for John, the man of thought, it was a life of testifying to the truth as revealed in the man, Christ Jesus (cf. Tasker, 231). One follower may sacrifice his life on a cross while another may complete his years in relative peace, but both are equally the followers of Jesus Christ. Curiosity about the future is a human trait. We should be glad that God withholds from us what the future has in store. To know what tomorrow holds and be unable to alter it would be an insufferable burden. To know that God holds the future is a source of great comfort.

23 Jesus' hypothetical statement about John's remaining alive until Jesus should return was misunderstood by some. The rumor spread that John would not die, but John corrected it by explaining what Jesus said to Peter, namely, that if Jesus wanted John to remain alive until he returned, what would that be to Peter?

Over the years there have grown a number of traditions to the effect that the beloved disciple never did really die. One is that down through the centuries he has been wandering throughout the world. Another is that he is only asleep in his grave at Ephesus and that the movement of the ground above the tomb is caused by his breathing. The human mind has an incredible ability to create evidence in support of what it has already decided to believe.

NOTES

15 In an extended translator's note, the NET offers three alternatives for the interpretation of τούτων (*toutōn*, "these") in Jesus' question to Peter, "Do you truly love me more than these?": (1) "these things," i.e., "the boats, nets, and fishing gear nearby"; (2) "the other disciples," meaning, "Do you love me more than you love these other disciples?"; and (3) "the other disciples," meaning, "Do you love me more than these other disciples do?" The NET note argues (correctly, I believe) that the third alternative is to be preferred.

19 That the first sentence of v. 19 is an explanatory comment by the gospel writer is made clear by placing it in parenthesis, as in the NRSV, NAB, TEV, NET, Moffatt, and others. In v. 20 the NIV correctly identifies the writer's comment by placing it in parenthesis (contra NASB).

The phrase ἀκολούθει μοι (*akolouthei moi*) in this context means to "follow me in death." In 1:43 the same expression means "to follow Jesus as a disciple" (cf. 8:12; 10:27, the two other occasions in John where the verb ἀκολουθέω, *akoloutheō*, GK *199*, is followed by the pronoun μοι, *moi*).

23 The noun ἀδελφοί (*adelphoi*, "brothers," GK *81*) refers not merely to the immediate disciples of Jesus (as it does in 20:17) but to the larger body of believers associated with the apostle John and his ministry (see Brown, 1110).

D. Testimonies by John and Others (21:24–25)

OVERVIEW

One's interpretation of the last two verses of the fourth gospel depends on a prior decision regarding its authorship. Since "the disciple who testifies to these things" is spoken of in the third person, it would seem that the one making this statement would not be that disciple. On the other hand, if v.24 has been added by another person, the gospel would have closed with v.23, a "curious if not impossible way to end a Gospel," according to Morris, 879. In the immediately preceding verses, John has been writing a narrative in which he was one of the participants. Would it not be quite natural for him to point out that this same disciple is the one who is now testifying to what happened?

It may be that "these things" is intended to refer not only to the final chapter but to the entire gospel as well. This same disciple also wrote them down. Taken in this way, we have a claim to authorship on the part of the disciple whom Jesus loved. Bruce, 409, writes that in v.24 we have "a plain statement that the beloved disciple is the real author of the Gospel."

[24]This is the disciple who testifies to these things and who wrote them down. We know that his testimony is true.
[25]Jesus did many other things as well. If every one of them were written down, I suppose that even the whole world would not have room for the books that would be written.

COMMENTARY

24 There is no way of knowing who it was that attested the reliability of the author by saying, "We know that his testimony is true." It could have been a group of elders from the church at Ephesus. They knew that his testimony was true, not because they were eyewitnesses of the events proclaimed, but because the truth had validated itself in their personal experience. They had come to experience and realize the "self-authenticating quality of eternal truth" (Bruce, 410).

25 This verse repeats a theme from 20:30–31 but expands it with considerable hyperbole. If all the things that Jesus did had been written down, there would not be enough room in the whole world to contain the books. The opinion of Lindars, 642, that this is "an exaggerated literary conceit" assigns the author a somewhat tarnished motive. Better to allow the writers of Scripture the same literary freedom that we assign to all other writers. Hyperbole is an exaggeration for the sake of emphasis, not a moral fault.

NOTES

25 Instead of the aorist infinitive χωρῆσαι (chōrēsai, GK 6003), א¹ B C* read the unusual χωρήσειν (chōrēsein), which could be either a true future infinitive or an aorist infinitive formed by placing a present ending on an aorist stem (cf. J. H. Moulton, *A Grammar of New Testament Greek* [Edinburgh: T&T Clark, 1929], 2:216).

ACTS

RICHARD N. LONGENECKER

Introduction

"The Acts of the Apostles" is the name given to the second part of a two-volume work traditionally identified as having been written by Luke, a companion of the apostle Paul. Originally the two volumes were not only written together but also circulated together as two parts of one complete writing. During the late first or early second century, however, Luke's first volume became associated with the gospels of Matthew, Mark, and John, thereby forming the four gospels, and Luke's second volume was left to go its own way.

It was sometime in the second century, it seems, that Luke's second volume received its present title, with the word "acts" (*praxeis*, GK *4552*) evidently meant to suggest both advances of the gospel and heroic exploits by the apostles. The reference to "the apostles," however, is somewhat misleading, for the work deals almost exclusively with Peter and Paul and the persons and events associated with their ministries. Next to nothing is said about the ministries of any of the other existing original disciples of Jesus, who, as the author of Luke-Acts tells us in Luke 6:13, were also "designated apostles." Acts is the third longest of the NT writings, being about one-tenth shorter than its companion volume, Luke (the longest NT book), and almost exactly the length of Matthew. Together, Luke-Acts comprises almost 30 percent of the material in the NT, exceeding both the Pauline and the Johannine writings in size.

It is said that James Denney, the Scottish NT scholar, on being asked by a student to recommend a good "life of Christ," looked quizzically at the questioner and replied, "Have you read the one by Luke?"[1] The

---

1. Cited in A. M. Hunter, *Introducing the New Testament* (London: SCM, 1957), 48.

point is apt because too often we favor modern syntheses over primary sources. The issue is heightened when we ask about a "history of the early church." For Luke, while acknowledging the existence of other gospels in the preface of his gospel, makes no allusion to the existence of anything like his Acts. In the NT we have only his account of the early church. If we did not have Acts—or if Acts were proven basically unreliable—we would know nothing of the earliest days of the Christian movement except for some scattered bits of data gathered from the letters of Paul or inferred by looking back from later developments.

To attempt to study Christianity apart from Acts, therefore, is to proceed *ignotum per ignotius* (i.e., explaining "the unknown by the unknown"), for information about the early church gained from Paul's letters often lacks a historical context. Henry Cadbury has spoken of "the extraordinary darkness which comes over us as students of history when rather abruptly this guide leaves us with Paul a prisoner in Rome."[2] There is nothing, in fact, to replace Acts. If one or two of our canonical gospels had been lost, we would be much poorer, but we would still have the others. Acts, however, stands alone.

It is of utmost importance, therefore, to ask some searching questions about Acts. But before doing so, we must know something of how the issues have been treated in the past so that we may learn how to frame our questions in the light of our current knowledge. What follows, therefore, is first a brief history of the criticism of Acts during the past 150 years in order to learn what questions ought to be asked and what steps others have taken toward answering them. Then we will consider the nature of historical writing in antiquity and the relation of proclamation to the writing of history in Acts, so that we may learn how to frame the questions in a manner appropriate to the material at hand. From such a background, the more traditional issues having to do with the purpose or purposes of the writing, its sources, the formation of its narrative, the composition of its speeches, the structure of the work, its date, its author, and its text-critical issues can be treated with greater precision.

1. HISTORY OF CRITICISM

Criticism of the book of Acts during the past century and a half has progressed through various phases, taken various forms, and focused on various issues.

Tübingen and Responses

The nineteenth century was largely dominated by the Tübingen school of German critics and their "tendency criticism," which was based on an Hegelian understanding of the course of early Christian history. In 1831 F. C. Baur proposed that early Christianity developed from a conflict between Peter, who expressed the faith of the earliest believers and was in continuity with Jesus himself, and Paul, who epitomized a later Christian viewpoint, with Acts being a second-century endeavor to work out a synthesis between the original thesis of Peter and the antithesis of Paul.[3] For Baur, the conciliatory nature of Acts

---

2. Henry J. Cadbury, *The Book of Acts in History* (London: Black, 1955), 3.

3. See F. C. Baur, "Die Christuspartei in der korinthischen Gemeinde, der Gegensatz des petrinischen und paulinischen Christentums in der ältesten Kirche," *Tübinger Zeitschrift für Theologie* 4 (1831): 61–206; see also his *Paul the Apostle of Jesus Christ: His Life and Works, His Epistles and Teachings* (1845; repr., Peabody, Mass.: Hendrickson, 2003).

clearly indicates that the work is a later synthesis, perhaps written between AD 110 and 130, and that the Paul who wrote the *Hauptbriefe*—Romans, 1–2 Corinthians, and Galatians—could not possibly be the same Paul of Acts. According to Baur, Paul in his own letters is the champion of Christian freedom, whereas in Acts he is portrayed as compromising his convictions by repeatedly yielding to Jewish scruples. Furthermore, Baur argued that a close study of Acts shows that the text abounds in the kind of historical errors expected of an author who wrote some time after the events related and who was trying to impose a fictitious sense of uniformity and an aura of tranquility on an earlier, more turbulent time.

Baur himself wrote no commentary on Acts. But his thesis, as set out in his various writings, about how to understand the course of early Christian history was followed, in the main, by such writers as David Strauss, Bruno Bauer, and Albrecht Ritschl. In particular, Eduard Zeller, Baur's closest disciple and son-in-law, undertook a full-scale investigation of the narrative of Acts, arguing from its perceived conciliatory purpose for its tendentious, nonhistorical, and mythical character.[4]

Not everyone was enamored with the Tübingen treatment of the NT materials generally and of Acts in particular. W. C. van Manen of Leiden, the leading representative of the "Radical Dutch" school, criticized Baur for not going far enough in applying his principles—which, he believed, ultimately negated the authenticity of the entire NT (and Bruno Bauer to some extent echoed van Manen's criticism). On the other hand, most scholars came to believe that it was not just Baur's application of his principles but his principles of criticism themselves that were ill-founded and ran roughshod over the evidence. By 1914, in fact, when the nineteenth-century world of thought finally came to an end, the vast majority of scholars had rejected his views.

Of great importance in bringing about a more positive attitude toward the reliability of Acts during the latter part of the nineteenth century were the works of J. B. Lightfoot, Theodor Zahn, William M. Ramsay, and Adolf Harnack—four scholars very different in their interests, temperaments, and theological stances, but whose work, in concert, tended to support the historicity of Acts. Lightfoot objected strongly to Baur's assertion that a conciliatory purpose in Acts reflects seriously on the credibility of the account. "Such a purpose," Lightfoot insisted, "is at least as likely to have been entertained by a writer, if the two Apostles were essentially united, as if they were not. The truth or falsehood of the account must be determined on other grounds."[5] Moreover, both Lightfoot and Zahn, in separate studies of the apostolic fathers, demonstrated that the historical evidence does not support Baur's tendency criticism on a point that was considered by Baur himself to be crucial to his reconstruction of early Christianity, namely, with regard to the origin of the Clementine and Ignatian writings.[6] Such a demonstration proved to be a crushing blow for the Tübingen view of Acts. For if Baur's understanding of the writings of Clement of Rome and Ignatius of Antioch could not be supported, such a dialectical approach could not be legitimately used as the basis for a proper understanding of the course of early Christian history as found in the NT, particularly in Acts.

---

4. See E. Zeller, *The Contents and Origin of the Acts of the Apostles, Critically Investigated* (1854; trans. J. Dare; 2 vols., repr., London: Williams & Norgate, 1875–1876).

5. J. B. Lightfoot, *The Epistle to the Galatians* (London: Macmillan, 1865), 359.

6. Cf. J. B. Lightfoot, *The Apostolic Fathers* (5 vols.; London: Macmillan, 1869–1885); see also his *Essays on the Work Entitled "Supernatural Religion"* (London: Macmillan, 1889); Theodor Zahn, *Ignatius von Antiochien* (Gotha: Perthes, 1873).

In addition, Ramsay's investigations of the historical and geographical details in Acts,[7] coupled with various literary- and source-critical studies that culminated in the work of Harnack,[8] tended to confirm in most minds at the turn of the twentieth century the basic reliability of Acts. What doubts remained focused on the portrayals of the character and activities of Paul in Acts. For where the Paul of Acts could be compared with the Paul of his own letters, there seemed to be a number of serious discrepancies. Harnack, it appears, was able to quiet most of the doubts in his day by insisting that the apostle must be seen more broadly than he had usually been understood. But though there remained a nagging suspicion about Luke's portrayals of Paul in Acts, it could not displace the general confidence in Acts engendered by the research and writings of Lightfoot, Zahn, Ramsay, and Harnack.

Source Criticism

The end of the nineteenth century witnessed a growing concern regarding the question of Luke's literary dependence that erupted into a vigorous debate in the first quarter of the twentieth century. Was Luke's second volume based on an earlier source or sources (whether written or oral) that can still be identified through various linguistic features and stylistic alterations in the text? Or are we to consider Acts a free composition in the manner of certain ancient historians, with the recognizable Semitic flavor of chs. 1–15 being the result of the author's modeling his language, consciously or unconsciously, on the LXX?

The period began with Bernhard Weiss's survey (1886) of the evidence for the use of sources in the composition of Acts.[9] Many believed that the next twenty years of source-critical discussion reached their apex in Adolf Harnack's argument for (1) multiple written sources underlying the first half of Acts, with resultant doublets in the narrative, and (2) primarily personal sources (chiefly verbal accounts and Luke's own travel journal) for the second half. The debate, however, veered to an extreme position in C. C. Torrey's argument that the Semitic flavor of chs. 1–15 was the result of Luke's use of a single Aramaic source for these chapters—an Aramaic source that he translated rather mechanically into Greek.

Attempting to correct Torrey's view, Henry Cadbury, F. J. Foakes-Jackson, and Kirsopp Lake combined the linguistic arguments for an Aramaic substructure for Acts 1–15 with an acceptance of multiple underlying sources and the acknowledgment that some of the apparently Semitic features of the narrative may be explained along the lines of Septuagintal influence.[10] J. de Zwaan and W. K. L. Clarke departed further from Torrey in viewing the so-called "Semitisms" more as "Septuagintisms," though they did not entirely deny the possibility of some Semitic source materials behind the narrative here and there.[11] In

---

7. Cf. William M. Ramsay, *The Church in the Roman Empire before AD 170* (London: Hodder & Stoughton, 1893); *St. Paul the Traveller and the Roman Citizen* (London: Hodder & Stoughton, 1897); *The Bearing of Recent Discovery on the Trustworthiness of the New Testament* (London: Hodder & Stoughton, 1915).

8. Cf. A. Harnack, *Luke the Physician* (London: Williams & Norgate, 1907); *The Acts of the Apostles* (London: Williams & Norgate, 1909); *The Date of the Acts and of the Synoptic Gospels* (London: Williams & Norgate, 1911).

9. Bernhard Weiss, *Lehrbuch der Einleitung in das Neue Testament* (Berlin: Reimer, 1886), 569–84.

10. Henry J. Cadbury, F. J. Foakes-Jackson, and Kirsopp Lake, "The Composition and Purpose of Acts," in *The Beginnings of Christianity*, ed. F. J. Foakes-Jackson and K. Lake (1922; repr., Grand Rapids: Baker, 1979), 2:9–10, 129–30, 145.

11. Ibid., 2:30–105.

1923, taking a stance diametrically opposed to that of Torrey, Martin Dibelius argued that a Septuagintal styling on the part of the author of Acts is fully sufficient to explain the Semitic flavor of the narrative, which has led so many to postulate the presence of Aramaic sources.[12] Generally speaking, those scholars who argued for Semitic source materials underlying the first half of Acts also stressed the author's faithfulness to his sources and the basic reliability of the record, whereas those who explained the Semitic flavor as a Septuagintal styling usually laid emphasis on the creative ability of the writer to archaize his presentation—often, in fact, tending to view Acts as quite a free composition without any demonstrable historical authenticity.

The New Hermeneutic, Form Criticism, and Redaction Criticism

Contemporary critical studies of Acts are heavily influenced by the "new hermeneutic," "form criticism," and the embryonic "redaction criticism" of Rudolf Bultmann, Karl Schmidt, and Martin Dibelius. While the basic approach of these scholars was set out in 1919 in separate programmatic studies on the Gospels,[13] it was in a series of articles that appeared from 1923 until his death in 1947 that Martin Dibelius applied the methodology to Acts.[14] In his earliest treatments of Acts, which drew on Eduard Norden's analysis of literary structures,[15] Dibelius focused his attention on the individual units of material in Acts (the "form critical" method). Later, however, he began to deal more with the personal contribution of the author in the presentation of his materials (the "redaction critical" method). This approach gained wide general acceptance through the writings of Bultmann,[16] and it has been crystallized with respect to Acts by the works of Hans Conzelmann and Ernst Haenchen.[17]

What the new hermeneutic asserts is that so-called historical writings tell us more about the authors who wrote them than they do about the events they purport to relate. What form criticism attempts to do (at least as Bultmann and Dibelius used it) is to retrace the situation in the life of a particular writer and his church that gave rise to the fabrication of the units of material he incorporates. This it does by analyzing the literary forms and their proposed developments. And what redaction criticism aims at is to discover a profile of the author as he reveals himself in his editorial activity of fitting together the various units of material at his disposal in order to construct his portrayal; thus redaction criticism is almost entirely occupied with the author's theological concerns—concerns that spring from his own personal situation and can be detected primarily in the seams and structures of his composition. Accompanying this method, there

---

12. See Martin Dibelius, *Studies in the Acts of the Apostles* (London: SCM, 1956), 1–25.

13. See Rudolf Bultmann, *The History of the Synoptic Tradition*, trans. John Marsh (1919; repr., Peabody, Mass.: Hendrickson, 2000); Karl L. Schmidt, *Der Rahmen der Geschichte Jesu* (Berlin: Reimer, 1919); Martin Dibelius, *From Tradition to Gospel* (1919; repr., Cambridge: James Clarke, 1934).

14. These articles have been incorporated into his *Studies in the Acts of the Apostles*.

15. See Eduard Norden, *Agnostos Theos* (Leipzig: Teubner, 1913).

16. Principally through his *Theology of the New Testament*, trans. K. Grobel (2 vols.; London: SCM, 1952), which first appeared in German in 1948 and 1951.

17. See Hans Conzelmann, *The Theology of St. Luke* (New York: Harper & Row, 1961); Ernst Haenchen, *The Acts of the Apostles* (Philadelphia: Westminster, 1971).

is often a disavowal of the relevance of the historical trustworthiness of the composition studied and a diminished concern regarding its sources.

When applied to Acts, such an approach usually works from two basic postulates: (1) that Acts must be judged either as Christian proclamation or as a historical treatise, and if proclamation, which it obviously is, it cannot be taken seriously as history; and (2) that the futuristic hopes of the earliest believers precluded any real historical interest, so that when the author of Acts begins to take himself seriously as a historian, he only shows how far removed he was from the original faith and from the events he claims to be presenting.[18] The kerygmatic nature of Acts, therefore, prohibits our asking whether the sermonic illustrations in it are really authentic, and its stance as a historical narration only shows how far removed from the actual situation the work really is.

Literary criticism, according to this view, has demonstrated that Acts is historically quite inaccurate and preserves, at best, only a few names from earliest Christian times.[19] Form criticism has shown that the work must be seen as a late first- or early second-century writing, whose author was engaged in historicizing the primitive eschatological message of the earliest believers in Jesus, thereby attempting to quell a disillusionment that was arising because of the delay of the Parousia and to counter the threat of Gnosticism. So in chs. 1–15 the author must be judged as producing an edifying piece of religious propaganda rather than anything that could be called history. Sources are at a minimum. The narrative and speeches reflect more the author's own interests than those of the early church. And the pseudo-Semitic flavor of the writing only serves to evidence something of its fabricated nature. Moreover, what is true for the first half of the work carries over into the rest, since, if anything, the author was consistent in the way he wrote.

This is not to say that modern critics of the type described here have lost interest in Acts or ceased to consider it important for the study of early Christianity. That is hardly the case! A great deal of scholarly research has been and is being done on Acts by those most influenced by Bultmann and Dibelius. Nevertheless, there is a widespread confidence in contemporary scholarly circles that Acts provides its readers with historical information primarily for the postapostolic period of the church and cannot be used (except inferentially) for anything earlier. Ernst Haenchen, who is probably the most important Bultmannian commentator on Acts, offers the following counsel: "To him who knows how to read between the lines and to hear what is left unsaid, the book of Acts gives rich information about what is commonly called 'the postapostolic age.'"[20]

Issues of Importance for Today

Our survey of the criticism of Acts during the past two centuries has been brief. Much more could be said, for there have been many significant crosscurrents and eddies in the flow of contemporary critical

---

18. See Conzelmann, *Theology of St. Luke*, 12–15, 210–11; Haenchen, *Acts of the Apostles*, 90–110.

19. See Ernst Haenchen, "The Book of Acts as Source Material for the History of Early Christianity," in *Studies in Luke-Acts*, ed. K. E. Keck and J. L. Martyn (1966; repr., Philadelphia: Fortress, 1980), 258–78.

20. Ibid., 261.

thought.[21] I have provided only an overview of the course of criticism—attempting only to highlight certain issues of continuing importance for any treatment of Acts today.

Chief among these issues is the question of the kerygmatic nature of the work and its significance for the author's treatment of history. Such a consideration of Acts requires an understanding of both what Luke was attempting to do in his presentation and the nature of historical writing in antiquity. Equally important is the question of Luke's eschatology and how it varied from that of early Christianity and affected his portrayal of early Christianity. But though such queries stand at the forefront of every critical study of Acts, the more traditional matters regarding sources, narrative, speeches, structures, date, and author continue to be important, as do such topics as the conciliatory nature of Acts and the relation of the Paul of Acts to the Paul revealed in his own letters. All of these matters, together with a number of others, will be treated in what follows, both in the introduction sections and in the commentary.

2. HISTORICAL WRITING IN ANTIQUITY

Ancient historiography reached its zenith shortly after the NT period in the writings of the Greek biographer Plutarch (ca. AD 46–120) and the Roman historians Tacitus (ca. AD 55–120) and Suetonius (ca. AD 69–122). These writers drew on traditional techniques that reached back to and were developed from the fifth-century BC Greek historian Thucydides and his *History of the Peloponnesian War*.

Capturing the Ethos

Underlying in antiquity all truly historical writing, as opposed to a mere chronicling of events, was the conviction that the actions and words of distinctive people in their respective periods represent more adequately the situation than any comments by the historian himself—that the "ethos" (*ethos*, GK *1621*) of a particular time is best conveyed through portrayals of the "acts" (*praxeis*, GK *4552*) of its participants.[22] The Greek historian and essayist Xenophon (ca. 430–357 BC), for example, at the beginning of his *Memorabilia*, writes regarding Socrates, his teacher and hero: "In order to support my opinion that he benefited his companions, alike by actions that revealed his own character and by his own conversations, I will set down what I recall of these" (1.3.1).[23]

The "acts" of the subjects, understood in terms of both their actions and their words, were the building blocks for the historians and biographers of antiquity. But while the Greek word *praxeis* ("acts") suggests movement and exploits, what these historians and biographers were primarily interested in were illuminating vignettes that gave insight into the *ethos* of a period or a person's character. Plutarch, for example, in pairing forty-six famous Greeks and Romans in his *Parallel Lives*, states the following in commencing his portrayal of Alexander the Great:

---

21. For important histories of the criticism of Acts, see Jacques Dupont, *The Sources of Acts* (New York: Herder and Herder, 1964); W. W. Gasque, *A History of the Criticism of the Acts of the Apostles* (1975; repr., Peabody, Mass.: Hendrickson, 1989); C. J. Hemer, *The Book of Acts in the Setting of Hellenistic History* (WUNT 49; Tübingen: Mohr, 1989).

22. See G. N. Stanton, *Jesus of Nazareth in New Testament Preaching* (Cambridge: Cambridge Univ. Press, 1974), 122.

23. See also *Agesilaus* 1.6, where Xenophon eulogizes his friend. This same emphasis is found in Isocrates (ca. 436–338 BC), *Evagoras* 76.

It is not always in the most illustrious deeds that men's virtues or vices may be best discerned, but often an action of small note, a short saying or a jest, will distinguish a person's real character more than the greatest sieges or the most important battles. Therefore, as painters in their portraits labor the likeness in the face, and particularly about the eyes, in which the peculiar turn of mind most appears, and run over the rest with a more careless hand, so we must be permitted to strike off the features of the soul in order to give a real likeness of these great men—leaving to others the circumstantial detail of their labors and achievements.

Life of Alexander 1.2.

The historians and biographers of antiquity were interested in what might be called "indirect character portrayals," which they did by means of setting out selected actions and words of their subjects. And in the selection of those actions and words, they were more interested in representative vignettes that expressed the ethos of the period than in merely chronicling exploits.

Grouping by Categories (Per Species)

In writing their histories and biographies, the ancients frequently grouped their materials *per species*, without always specifying chronological relationships. The third-century BC biographer Satyrus's *Life of Euripides*, which is the only extant work from the peripatetic school of biographical writing, contains "only one section which can in any way be called chronological; yet there is a clear tendency towards an orderly grouping of material, at least under broad captions."[24] Likewise Plutarch makes no endeavor in his *Parallel Lives* to be precise chronologically but repeatedly uses such vague expressions as "about this time" or "some time after this." He sets out, of course, various military campaigns in roughly successive order; nonetheless, his basic method is to group his material under various categories.

Of the Roman historians, only Tacitus uses a chronological framework in marking off the various stages of Agricola's career. In his *Lives of the Emperors*, Suetonius quite naturally works chronologically in presenting first one emperor and then another. Yet, when treating each individual emperor, only when dealing with Julius Caesar (the first in his series) does he hold himself to a portrayal based strictly on chronology; more commonly he groups his portrayals under such topics as "conduct," "business," "family," "attitude toward society," and "friends." In fact, in his portrayal of Augustus, he explains his method in this manner: "Having given as it were a summary of [his] life, I shall now take up its various phases one by one, not in chronological order, but by classes [*per species*], in order to make the account clearer and more intelligible" (*Divus Augustus* 9).

Factual Accuracy among the Historians

There has been much discussion about the attitude of ancient historians and biographers toward factual accuracy. For many years, Henry Cadbury's dicta reigned almost supreme in NT circles: (1) "Instead of accuracy, the purpose of ancient historians tended to make the form the chief point of emphasis,"[25] and (2)

24. Stanton, *Jesus of Nazareth*, 120.
25. Cadbury, Foakes-Jackson, and Lake, "Composition and Purpose of Acts," in *The Beginnings of Christianity*, 2:13.

"from Thucydides downwards, speeches reported by the historians are confessedly pure imagination."[26] But that Cadbury's views were extreme has been demonstrated by A. W. Mosley in a study of the intent and practice of such writers as Dionysius (ca. 430–367 BC), Polybius (ca. 204–120 BC), Cicero (ca. 106–43 BC), and Josephus (ca. AD 37–100).[27] The ancients, according to Mosley's analysis, did indeed ask the question, Did it happen in this way? And while some may have been slovenly and uninformed in their reporting, others "tried to be as accurate as possible and to get information from eyewitnesses."[28]

Furthermore, T. F. Glasson has pointed out that those who cite Thucydides' words, "I have used language in accordance with what I thought the speakers in each case would have been most likely to say"—as though this settles the matter in favor of the thoroughly imaginative character of the Thucydidean speeches—are somewhat unfair to what he was actually saying. For the immediate context of Thucydides' statement is as follows:

> With reference to the speeches in this history, some were delivered before the war began, others while it was going on. It was hard to record the exact words spoken, both in cases where I was myself present and where I used the reports of others. But I have used language in accordance with what I thought the speakers in each case would have been most likely to say, adhering as closely as possible to the general sense of what was actually spoken.
>
> Thucydides, *Hist.* 1.22

From this Glasson has aptly observed, "He [Thucydides] does not claim to reproduce the precise words like a stenographer, but in writing the speeches he keeps as closely as possible to 'the general sense of *what was actually spoken.*' . . . This is a very different matter from the imaginative composing of speeches suitable to the occasion."[29]

Contrary to many conclusions about historical writing in antiquity, I maintain that the ancients were, in fact, interested in what actually happened. Nevertheless, it must also be insisted that history, as opposed to the mere formulation of chronicles, was written by the ancients for moral, ethical, and polemical purposes and not just to inform or entertain. This was true for the Greek biographer Plutarch and the whole tradition of biographical writing that he represents, for the Roman historians Tacitus and Suetonius in their portraits of the emperors and their times, and for the Jewish historian Josephus in his presentations of Jewish history and thought before a Roman audience. And it is true for Luke's Acts of the Apostles as well, wherein, like the historiography of the OT, there is a setting out of the redemptive activity of God in various historical events, which are selected and interpreted in accord with a particular perspective.

3. KERYGMA AND HISTORY IN ACTS

While earlier generations fixed their attention first on the Pauline letters and then on the Johannine corpus, a primary focus of scholarly attention today is on the Lukan writings—the third gospel and the book of Acts. And prominent among contemporary issues is the relation of kerygma and history in Acts. If Acts

---

26. Ibid.

27. See A. W. Mosley, "Historical Reporting in the Ancient World," *NTS* 12 (1965): 10–26.

28. Ibid., 26.

29. T. F. Glasson, "The Speeches in Acts and Thucydides," *ExpTim* 76 (1965): 165 (italics his).

is to be understood as proclamation, can it also be considered history? And if Acts presents itself as history, can it really represent the original proclamation of the earliest Christians?

Acts as Proclamation

Modern theology, often in reaction to earlier "positivistic" treatments of historical materials, has stressed the fact that Acts is really Christian proclamation and not just a simple reproduction of what actually happened, apart from any interpretation or bias. And this understanding of the nature of Acts is important and helpful, as far as it goes. Certainly Luke did not write for literary recognition or only to add to human knowledge. Rather, he wrote, as he tells us in the prologue to his two-volume work, to proclaim the certainty of what his addressee, Theophilus, had been taught (Lk 1:1–4).

Some, however, have taken the fact that Acts is Christian proclamation, and not just a record of what happened, to an unwarranted extreme, and so have effected a divorce between "kerygma" and "history." As a result, many have felt constrained to choose between the subjectivism of a "demythologized" reading of Acts or the sterility of a mere historicism. But interpretation and bias are inherent in every historical writing, for history, as distinct from chronicle, is the interplay between selected events and their interpretation. "All history at whatever level," as H. E. W. Turner has noted, "involves construction on the part of the historian, but this does not imply that he is condemned to mere imaginative 'doodling' in the sands of time."[30] The question is not whether the historian has an interpretation of the data being put forward, but whether, given the fact of a bias, proper care and exactness has been exercised so as not to falsify that data or distort their significance in the interests of a particular thesis.

Acts as Kerygmatic History

Indeed, the author of Acts has his own interests, his own theological viewpoints, and his own purposes in writing—and to a considerable extent these have affected his selection, arrangement, and shaping of each of the units of material he incorporates. But to argue that his narrative must, therefore, be viewed as historically suspect is a non sequitur. The question as to whether the event or the kerygma is decisive for faith in Acts—and for that matter throughout the NT—must never be answered in the form of an alternative.[31] The record contains an intermeshing of events (for which historicity is asserted) and the significance of those events (for which inspiration is assumed). Both the events themselves and their interpreted significance are vital for an understanding of God's mighty acts by his Spirit through his church. "Acts, like the Gospels," as Gregory Dix has insisted, "is written throughout with a strong sense of the *sacredness* of the concrete facts it narrates, because the author believes that it is through what actually happened that the 'Counsel of God' was manifested and fulfilled."[32]

---

30. H. E. W. Turner, *Historicity and the Gospels* (London: Mowbray, 1963), 18.

31. See Oscar Cullmann, *Salvation in History* (New York: Harper & Row, 1967), 89–90.

32. Gregory Dix, *Jew and Greek* (London: Dacre, 1953), 39 (italics his).

Furthermore, every history is to some extent refractive. For the passage of time between an event and how it was originally understood on the one hand, and the historian's record of that event in the light of his later interests and perspectives on the other, always modify immediate perceptions and initial responses—if not regarding the content itself, at least the historian's appreciation of the significances and implications involved. This is true no matter how homogeneous has been the development of understanding between an original and a later perception. And this is true for Acts, written as it was from the perspective of the resurrection faith and coming to birth in the context of the theology that resulted from that faith.

It is indisputable that Luke's theology was more developed at the time of writing than it could ever have been at the time of the events he relates. To this extent the new hermeneutic, form criticism, and redaction criticism are certainly correct. But it does not necessarily follow that Luke had little interest in reproducing the details and nuances of an earlier situation. And even where events are reported from the perspective of a fuller theology and a broader understanding of how they fit together, it must be always realized that the NT authors—Luke included—were convinced, as Bo Reicke argued, that such a presentation of the facts "was more empiric and historic, more adequate, correct and true than the immediate picture had been."[33]

Kerygma, History, and Eschatology

With regard to the question of whether Acts in purporting to be a historical treatise shows itself to be quite removed from early Christian convictions, and therefore unable to represent faithfully early Christian proclamation, we must consider the issue of the nature of early Christian eschatological thought. Those who answer the above question in the affirmative assume that the eschatology of the earliest believers was so entirely "futuristic" that they gave no thought to formulating their convictions into some kind of basic system of theology, structuring their communal experiences, extending their outreach through some kind of mission, or writing down their history for others more geographically distant or chronologically removed. In fact, most of those who hold this point of view assume that the experiences of the earliest believers and their expectation of Jesus' imminent return left them with no interest in or time for the matters just mentioned. Moreover, all that Acts reflects with respect to Christology, ecclesiology, a theology of mission, and the writing of church history only shows how far removed its author really was from the life and thought of the earliest Christians—i.e., how far removed he was from their emphasis on Jesus' second "coming" or "presence" (Gk. *parousia*, GK *4242*). Thus, it is argued, with the Parousia being no longer primary or vital to him, its delay caused Luke (1) to restructure his own Christian faith into a form that can be identified as "early Catholicism" and (2) to recast the proclamation and convictions of the earliest believers into a form that would support his own views.

Futuristic hopes were certainly strong among the earliest believers, and we must never deny that they were. But this fact should not be taken to mean that "realized eschatology" could not have coexisted with "futuristic eschatology"—i.e., that an understanding of eschatology as in some sense fulfilled could only

---

33. Bo Reicke, "Incarnation and Exaltation: The Historic Jesus and the Kerygmatic Christ," *Int* 16 (1962): 159.

have arisen after the abandonment of a futuristic orientation. Undoubtedly there was much uncertainty and perplexity in the early church because of the delay of the Parousia. But if we understand (as I do) the faith of the earliest Christians to be best characterized by the expression "inaugurated eschatology," then we must judge that their lives and thoughts were focused more on a person than a program. And while that person's return was delayed, his work for them and his presence with them provided the essential basis for their Christian experience. W. C. van Unnik has made this apt observation:

> I cannot help confessing that the exegetical basis for many statements in the modern approach to Luke-Acts is often far from convincing, at least highly dubious in my judgment. . . . Has the delay of the *parousia* really wrought that havoc that it is sometimes supposed to have done, or did the early Christians react differently from the way modern scholars would have done? In the light of the history of early Christianity this effect of the *Parousieverzögerung* is highly overrated. The faith of the early Christians did not rest on a date but on the work of Christ.[34]

4. PURPOSES IN WRITING

Basic to every evaluation of Acts is the question of the purpose(s) of its author. Tendency criticism argued that the nature of Acts can be explained entirely on the basis of a conciliatory purpose and that the extent of its presentation can be explained by the fact that its author was unwilling to say more. All forms of redaction criticism, ancient or modern, also begin with the insistence that to have a profile of an author from his writing is to possess the most important key to the nature of his work.

While all agree with the necessity of evaluating Acts as to the purpose(s) for which it was written, scholars differ with regard to the exact nature of the purpose(s). The Tübingen school focused on the *conciliatory* purpose of Acts. At the end of the nineteenth century, however, most were prepared to view its *apologetic* purpose as dominant. Influenced by William M. Ramsay and Adolf Harnack, many during the first half of the twentieth century considered Luke's purposes to be primarily *historical* and *didactic*. And since the middle of the twentieth century Luke's *kerygmatic* purpose has been emphasized—almost to the exclusion of all others. In what follows, I will set out more precisely what can be said about Luke's purpose(s) and show something of the nature of the supporting evidence.

Kerygmatic Purpose

Luke himself states that his purpose in writing his two-volume work was "so that you may know the certainty of the things you have been taught" (Lk 1:4). The "most excellent Theophilus" (Lk 1:3; cf. Ac 1:1) to whom Luke addressed his work seems to have been a man who, though receptive to the gospel and perhaps even convinced by its claims, continued to have many questions about Christianity. From the way Luke writes to him, we may surmise that Theophilus was concerned about how the Christian faith related to Jesus' ministry, to Jews and the world of Judaism, to the lifestyles of certain scrupulous Jewish Christians, to the more universalistic outlook of Gentiles, and to the sanctions of Roman law. Also it seems that he was

---

34. W. C. van Unnik, "Luke-Acts, a Storm Center in Contemporary Scholarship," in *Studies in Luke-Acts* (ed. Keck and Martyn), 28.

interested in how the Christian gospel had been received and what success it had met with in the various centers of influence known to him in the eastern part of the empire, from Jerusalem to Rome.

Certainly when receiving his first instruction in the gospel, Theophilus had been told of Jesus' death and resurrection. But apparently the full significance and many of the implications of Jesus' death and resurrection were not clear to him—and, it seems, a number of references to persons and events associated with Jesus' ministry baffled him. Likewise, the subsequent experiences of the early church seem to have been somewhat vague to him. The advent and activity of the Holy Spirit, the early ministries of the disciples, the conversion of Paul and his relation to the Jerusalem apostles, and the nature and extent of Paul's ministry (and perhaps even more) were all subjects about which Theophilus had questions. So Luke writes to deal with his friend's uncertainties, as well as the queries of others like him who would read Luke's account.

Acts, therefore, like many other works both ancient and modern, was probably written with multiple purposes in view. And primary among the reasons for its composition was undoubtedly a *kerygmatic* or *proclamatory* purpose. For it proclaims the continued confrontation of men and women by "the word of God" through the church. Furthermore, it shows (1) how that word—"the gospel"—is related to the course of redemptive history, (2) how it has interacted with secular history, (3) how it is universal in character, (4) how it has been freed from the Jewish law, and (5) how behind its proclamation stands the power and activity of the Holy Spirit.

In his first volume Luke portrayed how men and women were confronted by "the word of God" in the earthly ministry of Jesus (cf. Lk 5:1; 8:11, 21; 11:28). In Acts he seeks to demonstrate how men and women continued to be confronted by that same "word" or message through the ministry of the church (cf. 4:29, 31; 6:2, 4, 7; 8:4, 14, 25; 10:36; 11:1, 19; 12:24; 13:7, 44, 46, 48–49; 14:25; 15:35–36; 16:6, 32; 17:11, 13; 18:5, 11; 19:10). The expression "the word of God" is for Luke, as Ernst Haenchen has rightly observed, "the clamp which fastens the two eras together and justifies, indeed demands, the continuation of the first book (depicting the life of Jesus as a time of salvation) in a second; for the salvation which has appeared must be preached to all peoples, and the very portrayal of this mission will serve the awakening of belief, and hence the attainment of that salvation."[35]

Haenchen, of course, along with Bultmannians in general and Hans Conzelmann in particular, thinks that Luke's stress on "the word of God" as being the message of salvation in Jesus is a secondary and somewhat erroneous concept of salvation history, which was entirely Luke's own creation and introduced by him to solve the embarrassing problem of the delay of the Parousia. Others, however (myself included), view it as primary and rooted inextricably in the confessions of the earliest believers and the consciousness of Jesus himself. But be that as it may, for Luke the message of salvation in Jesus proclaimed by the church was in direct continuity with the ministry and teaching of Jesus. That is why he wrote a sequel to his gospel, thereby making explicit what was presupposed in the earliest Christian preaching.

Furthermore, this proclamation is firmly fixed in the context of world history. It began with the miraculous births of John the Baptist and then Jesus, which took place "in the time of Herod king of Judea" (Lk 1:5) and during the reign of Caesar Augustus, "while Quirinius was governor of Syria" (2:1–2). It focuses

---

35. Haenchen, *Acts of the Apostles*, 98.

on a ministry that commenced "in the fifteenth year of the reign of Tiberius Caesar—when Pontius Pilate was governor of Judea, Herod tetrarch of Galilee, his brother Philip tetrarch of Iturea and Traconitis, and Lysanias tetrarch of Abilene—during the high priesthood of Annas and Caiaphas" (3:1–2). It culminated under the inquisitions and judgments of Pilate and Herod Antipas (23:1–25). And it spread throughout the Roman world principally during the reign of the emperor Claudius (Ac 11:28; 18:2) when Gallio was proconsul of Achaia (18:12–17), when Felix and Festus ruled in Judea and Ananias was the high priest in Jerusalem (chs. 24–25), and between the times of the Jewish kings Herod Agrippa I (12:1–23) and Herod Agrippa II (25:13–26:32).

In addition, this message regarding salvation in Jesus permeated the Jewish homeland and was received with a measure of acceptance in the main centers of the eastern part of the Roman Empire—finally entering even Rome itself, the capital city of the empire, and proclaimed there "without hindrance" (*akōlytōs*, GK *219*, which is the final word of Luke's two-volume work). It is a universal message. It began at Jerusalem, the Jewish capital city, and spread "to the ends of the earth" (as promised by Jesus himself, Ac 1:8), and so includes all kinds of people. It is a message that under the Spirit's direction, by means of a process that can be depicted in its various stages, freed itself finally and inevitably from the shackles of Jewish legalism and a Jewish lifestyle. It is a proclamation that affected the lives of many through the power and activity of the Holy Spirit—that selfsame Spirit who came on Jesus at his baptism and through whom he accomplished his mission.

Apologetic Purpose

There is also inherent throughout the presentation of Acts an *apologetic* purpose. For its author seeks to demonstrate that Christianity is not a political threat to the empire, as its Jewish opponents asserted. Rather, it is the culmination of Israel's hope and the true daughter of the Jewish religion—and therefore it should be treated by the Roman authorities as a "legal religion" (*religio licita*) along with Judaism.

Roman law, for entirely pragmatic reasons, identified certain religions as *licita*, or legal and permitted, and others as *illicita*, or illegal and forbidden. Those accepted as legal had been dominant in various areas and among certain ethnic groups, and so could serve to reinforce the Pax Romana. Those forbidden were the minority faiths, which tended to fracture loyalties and splinter peoples—and so deserved in Rome's eyes harsh treatment. Judaism was considered a *religio licita* both in Palestine and throughout the Diaspora simply because of (1) its refusal to be taken as anything else and (2) the troubles it caused Rome when attempts were made to amalgamate it with other religions.

Christianity, however, had its problems with respect to legality as it moved out into the empire, even though it had been born within Judaism. Its founder had been crucified as a messianic pretender in Jerusalem, its separate identity as "Christian" had been asserted by others in its mission to Antioch of Syria (Ac 11:26), and Jews within the Diaspora were insisting that it had no right to imperial protection since it was sectarian.

Acts acknowledges the fact of such accusations. At Philippi the charge brought against Paul and Silas is that they were disturbing the peace "by advocating customs unlawful for us Romans to accept or practice" (16:21). At Thessalonica the charge is one of "defying Caesar's decrees, saying that there is another king, one called

Jesus" (17:7). And at Corinth it is that of "persuading the people to worship God in ways contrary to the law" (18:13). Furthermore, at Paul's trials, as portrayed later in Acts, the Jews charge him with being a sectarian who stirs up riots within the Jewish communities and so deserves to be tried under Roman law (24:5–9).

Luke also takes pains to point out that, despite differences between the Christian message and that of Judaism, the charge *religio illicita* against Jesus or his followers had never been accepted by any well-informed Roman official. In his gospel he lays stress on the fact that from the perspective of Roman law the crucifixion of Jesus was a gross miscarriage of justice—highlighting, in particular, Pilate's repeated protestations of Jesus' innocence (Lk 23:4, 14–16, 20, 22) and the Roman centurion's affirmation, "Surely this was a righteous man" (23:47; *dikaio*, GK *1465*, means both "righteous" and "innocent"). And in Acts he speaks of a number of Roman officials who acknowledged that there was no basis for the accusation *religio illicita* being brought against Paul and his coworkers. In Paphos, the proconsul of Cyprus, Sergius Paulus, "an intelligent man," was converted to Christianity (Ac 13:6–12). In Philippi, the magistrates apologized to Paul and Silas for illegally beating and imprisoning them (16:35–39). In Corinth, the proconsul of Achaia, Gallio, judged Paul and Silas guiltless of any offense against Roman law, viewing the Jews' dispute with them as an intramural matter (18:12–17). In Ephesus, some of the officials of the province were Paul's friends, and the city clerk absolved him of the charge of sacrilege (19:31, 35–41). In Judea, the governors Felix and Festus found Paul innocent of the charges against him (24:1–25:12), with Herod Agrippa II agreeing that "this man is not doing anything that deserves death or imprisonment" and saying further that "this man could have been set free if he had not appealed to Caesar" (26:31, 32).

It may be that the manner in which Luke closes Acts in 28:30–31—with statements about Paul's residing "for two whole years . . . in his own rented house," being free to welcome "all who came to see him," and preaching and teaching "boldly and without hindrance"—was meant to suggest that even at Rome no formal accusations were made against Paul, either by a delegation from Jerusalem or by the leaders of the Jewish community there, and that therefore the apostle was set free. But these latter matters are not certain and must be discussed later.

It seems evident that Luke had an apologetic purpose in writing Acts. But to speak of an apologetic purpose entails asking to whom that apology was directed, and the answer is not clear. At the close of the nineteenth century many viewed Acts as something of a trial document sent to a Roman magistrate named Theophilus and meant eventually for the eyes of the emperor. C. K. Barrett may have overreacted against this idea when he insisted that "it was not addressed to the Emperor, with the intention of proving the political harmlessness of Christianity in general and of Paul in particular; a few passages might be construed to serve this purpose, but to suggest that the book as a whole should be taken in this way is absurd. No Roman official would ever have filtered out so much of what to him would be theological and ecclesiastical rubbish in order to reach so tiny a grain of relevant apology."[36] Granted that no Roman official would have done so, this does not mean, however, that Luke could not have written with such an intent—much as the later apologists did, even though they seldom, if ever, received the hearing they desired. Still, the view of Acts as a trial document much overstates the case and ignores other emphases in the book.

---

36. C. K. Barrett, *Luke the Historian in Recent Study* (1961; repr., Philadelphia: Fortress, 1970), 63.

On the other hand, we need not conclude that if the work is not a trial document, then its apologetic must have been addressed only to those already in the church—either to Jewish Christians at Rome, urging them to be more conciliatory toward Gentiles since various Roman officials had a favorable attitude toward the early Christian mission (so Eduard Zeller[37]), or to Christians with a gnostic bent, arguing that an appreciation of the Christian faith cannot be restricted only to the initiated (so C. K. Barrett[38]). Instead, it is better to conclude that while Acts as an apology had Theophilus primarily in view because of his concern regarding Christianity's legal status in the empire, it was also meant for other Gentiles, whether they were Christians or not.

Conciliatory Purpose

A third purpose for writing Acts seems to have been, as F. C. Baur, Eduard Zeller, and others long ago asserted, a *conciliatory* purpose—though the Tübingen scholars much overstated this purpose and drew illegitimate implications from it. Acts presents the careers of Peter (chs. 1–12) and Paul (chs. 13–28) in strikingly parallel fashion. (For a detailed presentation of the parallelism, see Overview at 2:42–12:24.) Furthermore, Acts presents Paul as conceding both primacy in the church to Peter and primacy of apostleship to the Twelve, as based on their earthly companionship with Jesus, whereas Peter and the Jerusalem apostles, in turn, concede to Paul another mode of apostolic authority and acknowledge Peter's initiative in a law-free outreach to Gentiles.[39] Luke is a master at setting up his material in balanced form, as we will see later in discussing the structure of Acts. Moreover, to quote again J. B. Lightfoot's famous dictum on the Tübingen formulation of the conciliatory purpose, "Such a purpose is at least as likely to have been entertained by a writer, if the two Apostles were essentially united, as if they were not. The truth or falsehood of the account must be determined on other grounds."[40]

Paul's own letters, in fact, indicate quite clearly that at Jerusalem some were pitting Peter and the Jerusalem apostles against Paul because they preferred Peter. And even in Paul's churches similar party factions arose, with some saying, "I follow Paul"; others, "I follow Apollos"; others, "I follow Cephas"; and still others, "I follow Christ" (1Co 1:12). It is not too hard to imagine that Luke, when writing Acts, well knew of continuing sentiments within various churches that set the ministries of Peter and Paul in opposition to one another. So while he necessarily had to portray their differences, he also, it seems, felt the need to highlight features of continuity and points of comparison between them—and to do it, wherever possible, by means of structural parallelisms and similarities of detail.

Catechetical Purpose

Finally, Luke may well have written Acts with a *catechetical* purpose also in mind. Ancient tractates and letters were often circulated widely, even though addressed only to one person or group. Josephus, for exam-

---

37. See his *Contents and Origin of the Acts of the Apostles.*
38. See his *Luke the Historian in Recent Study.*
39. See Baur, *Paul Apostle of Jesus Christ*, 6, 88–89.
40. Lightfoot, *Galatians*, 359.

ple, in his *Against Apion*, addresses one whom he called "most excellent Epaphroditus" (prologue to vol. 1) and "my most esteemed Epaphroditus" (prologue to vol. 2). Yet he fully expected that his defense of the Jewish religion against various forms of Greek speculation would be widely circulated and read, which it was. Epaphroditus, to whom Josephus addressed his two volumes, may have been a grammarian who wrote on Homer, possessed a large library, and became Josephus's patron. But while he undoubtedly received *Against Apion* from Josephus's own hand, the work was meant to instruct many more readers than Epaphroditus himself. And in a much less formal way, Paul's letters were also meant to be read widely, as we see from his instruction to the Colossians: "After this letter has been read to you, see that it is also read in the church of the Laodiceans and that you in turn read the letter from Laodicea" (Col 4:16).

So, too, Luke probably wrote his treatise to Theophilus with the expectation that, in addition to its kerygmatic, apologetic, and conciliatory purposes, it could also be used within the churches for instructional purposes to show how Christianity moved out from its origins in Palestine to become a movement of God's Spirit in the Roman Empire. Thus Luke portrays in dramatic vignettes drawn from the early church's history (1) the essence of early Christian preaching; (2) the activity of the Holy Spirit in energizing, applying, and spreading that message; (3) the gospel's power and transforming quality; (4) its type of adherents, together with their sacrifices and triumphs; and (5) the entrance of Christianity into the city of Rome itself. Undoubtedly, as its author surely intended, such a catechetical purpose would meet a vital need among congregations only recently founded. Also, such instructional material would help draw together spiritually the scattered believers in diverse areas of the Roman Empire. And while Luke could hardly have visualized anything beyond the needs of the churches of his day, his writing continues to do just that today.

5. SOURCES

Questions about the sources that Luke used in writing Acts are more easily raised than answered. Such question need to be asked in two ways, for the first part of Acts has a definitely Semitic cast, whereas the second half has a Greek cast similar to the Greek cast of the prologue to Luke-Acts (cf. Lk 1:1–4). Most discussions of the sources of Acts, therefore, are concerned with source-critical issues for chs. 1–15 and form-critical issues for chs. 16–28. And because of the respective nature of materials, I will follow this procedure as well.

Sources and Doublets in Chapters 1–15

The identification of sources underlying the presentation of Acts 1–15 was viewed during the first decades of the twentieth century with great optimism. Of the various proposed analyses of the text, Adolf Harnack's may be taken as representative and most important.[41] Harnack discerned in Acts (1) a Jerusalem-Antiochene source behind 11:19–30 and 12:25–15:35, which has considerable historical value for at least the material from 13:4 on; (2) a Jerusalem-Caesarean source underlying 3:1–5:16; 8:5–40; 9:29–11:18; and 12:1–24 that was in written form for chs. 3–4 and 12 (though perhaps transmitted orally for the rest) and that in its "Recension A" provides "the more intelligible history of the outpouring of the Holy Spirit and

---

41. See Harnack, *Acts of the Apostles*, 162–202.

its consequences" as now appears in 3:1–5:16; (3) a "Recension B" of the Jerusalem-Caesarean source, which provides rather confused material as now found in 2:1–47 and 5:17–42, thereby setting up a number of doublets in the finished text; (4) a separate source in 6:1–8:4, which has to do with the martyrdom of Stephen, is related to the Jerusalem-Antiochean source, and includes an interpolated reference to Paul at the end; (5) a separate source in 9:1–28, which deals with the conversion of Saul; and (6) legendary material in ch. 1. Harnack doubted that the usual literary clues of vocabulary, style, and historical blunders could be used to differentiate one source from another. He insisted that Luke has so reworked his sources as to impose his own personal stamp throughout the finished product. But he did believe that one could group the material according to the persons and places depicted, with the doublets furnishing particularly useful indicators of the presence of source material involved.

Most obvious among the doublets of Acts 1–15, Harnack believed, were the two arrests of the apostles and their two appearances before the Jewish Sanhedrin in 4:1–22 and 5:17–40, which he claimed were simply two versions of the same event. In 1937, however, Joachim Jeremias showed that, far from being repetitious and therefore artificial in their dual inclusion, the two narratives actually reflect with remarkable accuracy a significant point in Jewish jurisprudence and complement each other.[42] For Jewish law, as Jeremias pointed out, held that a person must be aware of the consequences of his or her crime before being punished for it. This meant that in noncapital cases the common people had to be given a legal admonition before witnesses and could only be punished for an offense when they relapsed into the same crime after due warning. Thus Acts 4:1–22 presents the Sanhedrin as viewing the apostles as being "unschooled, ordinary men" (v.13), and so gave them a legal warning not to speak anymore in the name of Jesus (v.17), whereas Acts 5:17–40 says that the Sanhedrin reminded the apostles of its first warning (v.28) and turned them over to be flogged because they had persisted in their sectarian ways (v.40).

With this demonstration of the correlation of these two accounts, which has been convincing to most scholars today,[43] Jeremias effectively set aside what Harnack thought to be the clearest and surest instance of a doublet resulting from Luke's use of parallel source materials. And with Jeremias's demonstration, most attempts to support a thesis of parallel sources underlying the narrative of Acts 1–15 have come to an end—though, of course, doublets in Acts are still being proposed by literary critics on the basis of Luke's interpolations into his primary source materials (e.g., 11:27–30 and 15:1–33, as Jeremias himself argued), but not on the basis of supposed parallel sources.

Semitisms and/or Septuagintisms in Chapters 1–15

Though most scholars today no longer argue for parallel source materials used by Luke in his writing of Acts, the possibility remains that some basic source or sources, whether written or oral, underlie the substructure of the first half of the book. The probability of such source materials depends largely on how one

---

42. See Joachim Jeremias, "Untersuchungen zum Quellenproblem der Apostelgeschichte," *ZNW* 36 (1937): 205–21, esp. 208–13.

43. Bo Reicke, however, in *Glauben und Leben der Urgemeinde* (Zürich: Zwingli, 1957), 108–10, continues to speak of one Sanhedrin trial portrayed in two parallel forms, based on the symmetry he discovers between 2:42–4:31 and 4:32–5:42.

evaluates the markedly Semitic cast and coloring of chs. 1–15. It also depends on the question of whether Semitic features are to be seen as a translation phenomenon, as a result of underlying sources, or as the product of Luke's imitation, whether consciously or unconsciously, of the language of the LXX (i.e., "Septuagintisms")—or in some way attributed to a combination of these factors. Precise answers to such questions on a strictly linguistic basis are, as Matthew Black has rightly warned, "only very rarely possible."[44] Nonetheless, some things can and should be said to the issue.

Through linguistic analysis, Matthew Black and Max Wilcox concluded that while certain Semitic features in the text of Acts may be understood as "Septuagintisms," there are also a number of "hard-core Semitisms" in chs. 1–15 that cannot be explained except on some theory of Aramaic (perhaps also Hebrew) sources underlying the composition.[45] And Raymond Martin, on the basis of a series of studies of such unconscious syntactical traits as the frequency and positioning of conjunctions, prepositions, and articles, has argued that, while certain phrases and idioms in Acts reflect Septuagintal influence, "there are, however, a number of Semitic syntactical features particularly which are more common in the first half of Acts, *indeed in certain subsections* of the first part of Acts. This phenomenon is difficult, if not impossible, to explain on the basis of conscious or unconscious influence of the Septuagint on the writer, and most naturally to be explained as the result of Semitic sources underlying these subsections."[46] Martin identifies these subsections as being "16 sections which clearly do go back to written Semitic sources (1:15–26; 2:1–4; 4:23–31; 5:17–26; 5:27–32; 5:33–42; 6:1–7; 6:8–15; 7:9–16; 7:17–22; 7:30–43; 9:10–19a; 11:1–18; 13:16b–25; 13:26–41; 14:8–20) and 6 others which probably go back to Semitic sources (2:29–36; 2:37–42; 7:1–8; 7:44–50; 9:19b–22; 9:32–35)."[47]

This is not to suggest that such Semitic features in the first half of Acts must be viewed as merely the result of translation, as C. C. Torrey asserted in proposing his "unified Aramaic source" theory, or as Martin (along with Paul Winter and W. F. Albright[48]) tended to think has resulted through Luke's use of multiple, complementary sources. Nor does the recognition of Semitic features imply our ability to identify the nature or extent of the sources. Matthew Black was undoubtedly right in speaking of Luke's use of sources as being more literary than slavishly literal,[49] and Nigel Turner should probably be heeded in his insistence that we consider Lukan source material in more an ultimate than an immediate sense.[50] But the presence,

---

44. Matthew Black, "Second Thoughts—X: The Semitic Element in the New Testament," *ExpTim* 77 (1965): 20.

45. Contra Wilcox, see J. A. Emerton's review article (*JSS* 13 [1968]: 282–97).

46. Raymond A. Martin, "Syntactical Evidence of Aramaic Sources in Acts I–XV," *NTS* 11 (1964): 38–39 (italics his).

47. See Raymond A. Martin, *Syntactical Evidences of Semitic Sources in Greek Documents* (Missoula, Mont.: Scholars Press, 1974), 2–3.

48. See Paul Winter, "Some Observations on the Language in the Birth and Infancy Stories of the Third Gospel," *NTS* 1 (1955): 111–21; "The Proto-Source of Luke 1," *NovT* 1 (1956): 184–99; W. F. Albright, *New Horizons in Biblical Research* (London: Oxford Univ. Press, 1966), 50.

49. See Matthew Black, *An Aramaic Approach to the Gospels and Acts* (3d ed.; Oxford: Clarendon, 1967), 274–75. Foakes-Jackson and Lake (*Beginnings of Christianity*, 2:133) argued, "The truth seems to be that although there is a *prima facie* probability for the use of written sources in Acts, and especially for Aramaic sources in the earlier chapters, the writer wrote too well to allow us to distinguish with certainty either the boundaries of his sources or the extent of his own editorial work."

50. See Nigel Turner, "The Relation of Luke I and II to Hebraic Sources," *NTS* 2 (1956): 102.

character, and distribution of such "hard-core Semitisms" have much to say against the view that Luke was merely archaizing his presentation by using language drawn from the Septuagint. And though H. F. D. Sparks eloquently argued for the Septuagintal nature of Luke's material, and therefore its archaized nature,[51] it yet remains true, as Matthew Black continued to insist, that the fact "that such primitive elements have been preserved is 'a rather strong indication of the general authenticity' of the first fifteen chapters of the Acts of the Apostles."[52]

"We" Sections of Chapters 16–28

As for source materials that may underlie the writing of Acts 16–28, attention has always been directed to four sections in the narrative where the writer uses the first person pronoun "we"—in 16:10–17 (travel to and evangelization of Philippi); 20:5–15 (ministry in Troas and travel to Miletus); 21:1–18 (journey from Miletus to Jerusalem); and 27:1–28:16 (journey from Caesarea to Rome).[53]

The use of the pronoun "we" in these sections has been explained in four ways: (1) the editor of Acts, working from an earlier "travel document" or "diary," either accidentally or carelessly let the pronoun stand without noting that he was quoting directly; (2) the author of Acts designedly let the pronoun from his source materials stand in his finished product, thereby attempting to gain greater acceptance for his work by passing himself off as one of Paul's companions; (3) the author used "we" as a kind of "last-minute embellishment" or "stylistic device," apart from any necessary source materials, in order to give the narrative the appearance of a "fellow-traveler's account"; and (4) the author had, from time to time, been a companion of Paul during his travels, and he discreetly indicated this by using "we" in those places in the narrative where he tells of events at which he himself had been present.[54]

Linguistically, the "we" sections of the latter half of Acts are inextricably bound up with the whole of Luke-Acts, thus suggesting that they cannot be explained simply on the basis of the author's use of sources but must be related more directly to the evangelist himself. Furthermore, there are striking similarities between these "we" sections and the more readily identifiable editorial materials in Luke-Acts with respect to vocabulary, syntax, style, manner of presentation—even, in fact, with respect to what is neglected (i.e., similarities that do not appear in Luke's gospel when dependent on the narrative of Mark or the sayings of Q, or that do not appear in the first part of Acts where Semitic sources seem to have been used).[55] In addition, in these "we" sections a greater fullness of detail appears in the portrayals of Paul's missionary activities, whereas elsewhere in the narration of Paul's ministry the accounts are briefer. Evidence of this kind seems to require one of two conclusions: either (1) that the author of Acts was exceedingly skillful in cre-

---

51. H. F. D. Sparks, "The Semitisms of the Acts," *JTS* (NS) 1 (1950): 16–28; cf. his "The Semitisms of St. Luke's Gospel," *JTS* 44 (1943): 129–38. See also Haenchen, *Acts of the Apostles*, 73–77.

52. Black, "Second Thoughts—X," 22, quoting Max Wilcox, *The Semitisms of Acts* (Oxford: Clarendon), 181.

53. Or three "we" sections if the Miletus discourse of 20:17–38 is understood as offering no opportunity for the first person plural pronoun, and so 20:5–21:18 is viewed as a single unit.

54. On numbers 1, 2, and 4, see the summary in J. C. Hawkins, *Horae Synopticae* (Oxford: Clarendon, 1899), 182–83. On number 3, see Haenchen, *Acts of the Apostles*, 85, whose descriptive phrases are quoted.

55. See Harnack, *Luke the Physician*, 26–120; *Acts of the Apostles*, 49–263.

ating the impression of presenting for his readers eyewitness reports, or (2) that these sections must be judged as based on firsthand observation. Of the two, most constructive critics today prefer the latter.

To hold that the "we" sections are firsthand accounts on the part of the author himself is supported by what the prologue to Luke-Acts (Lk 1:1–4) reveals about him. Jacques Dupont rightly insists that "a careful study of the prologue shows that the writer is presenting himself as a contemporary and eyewitness of a part of the facts he recounts, and this statement indicates the importance that should be attributed to the passages he writes in the first person."[56] On the other hand, the main argument against accepting the "we" sections as firsthand observations is that no companion of Paul would have so grossly misrepresented the apostle's character and ministry. Luke 1:1–4 and its testimony regarding authorship will be discussed in the commentary. The portrayal of Paul in Acts will be dealt with in what immediately follows. Here it is sufficient to say that on the basis of literary and form-critical considerations alone, the "we" sections of the second half of Acts give every indication of being a firsthand report of the author of Acts.

Sermons, Discourse, and Defenses of Chapters 16–28

Much of what remains in chs. 16–28 is made up of three missionary sermons of Paul, one pastoral discourse, and five speeches of defense.[57] Each of the missionary sermons—one at Antioch of Pisidia (13:16–41), another at Lystra (14:15–17), and a third at Athens (17:22–31)—has its own form, its own manner of presentation, and its own type of argument. The first is very Jewish, the second more pedestrian, and the third quite philosophical. The pastoral discourse to the Ephesian elders at Miletus (20:17–38) also has its own form and content, being similar to the canonical Pauline letters. Each of Paul's speeches in his own defense—the first before a Jerusalem crowd (22:3–21); the second before the Sanhedrin (23:1–6); the third before the governor Felix (24:10–21); the fourth before the governor Festus (25:8–11); the fifth before king Herod Agrippa (26:2–29)—has its own distinctive styling and mode of argumentation, being largely dependent on the audience and situation addressed. One may argue that all of this variety of presentation and fitting of sermonic material to the situation shows the creative genius of the author. It is, however, much more probable that such features indicate that Luke was responsibly using various sources at his disposal for his accounts of Paul's sermons and defenses, even though his thorough reworking of those sources may prevent us from identifying or re-creating them.

"They" Sections of Chapters 16–28

Though there have been many attempts to reconstruct the sources underlying the "they" sections of the narrative in Acts 16–28—and though we may gain the impression from the narrative that its author had access to various source materials and documents—Luke's literary ability, coupled with his liberty in handling his materials, seems to have been too great and too extensive to enable us to identify with any certainty

---

56. Dupont, *Sources of Acts*, 102.
57. Also included is Paul's address to the Jewish leaders at Rome (28:25–28), though Luke gives only the final words and not a précis of that address.

the presence, extent, or nature of his sources. The writer of Acts was truly an author, not just a compiler or editor. The recognition of Semitic source materials underlying the first half of Acts and of eyewitness reports embodied in the second half, with various other source materials undoubtedly used elsewhere, certainly increases the general level of our confidence in the historical worth of the presentation. Ultimately, however, Acts must be judged as a finished literary product and not just on the basis of its sources, even granting that its sources were historically respectable.

6. NARRATIVE

Probably the most extensive attack mounted against the historical reliability of Acts was that by Eduard Zeller in the mid-nineteenth century.[58] Beginning with the position of his father-in-law, F. C. Baur, on the conciliatory purpose of Acts, Zeller undertook an exhaustive examination of the narrative of Acts. He disparaged its historical trustworthiness because of its supposed factual blunders, its inclusion of the miraculous, and its portrayal of Paul. At the end of the nineteenth century, however, the tendency criticism of Baur and Zeller was considered by most scholars to be unfounded; consequently, a Tübingen approach to understanding the early church generally and Acts in particular fell out of favor. But though the superstructure of Tübingen collapsed, the debris remained, with many of its building blocks being reused in the scholarly study of Acts today.

Issues of Perspective, Readjustments, and History

Modern critics still fault Acts for historical blunders, its inclusion of the miraculous, and its portrayal of Paul. They also commonly assert (1) that its kerygmatic purpose preempts any real interest in historical veracity, (2) that it readjusts early Christian proclamation to meet the problem of eschatological disillusionment (also, perhaps, to counter a rising Gnosticism, though this is more hotly debated), and (3) that its narrative is incomplete and fails to deal with many of the historically significant issues of the day. But though objections to the historical reliability of Acts appear formidable, much can be said to put matters in a fairer perspective.

I have already discussed Luke's purposes in writing Acts and argued that the work does reflect both a kerygmatic purpose and a conciliatory intent. But from such observations I have not drawn the same implications others have. Likewise, I have argued that, though some early believers in Jesus may well have been disillusioned by the delay of the Parousia or "coming" of Jesus, the faith of the earliest Christians was not in a program but in a person. Whatever "readjustments" are to be found in Luke-Acts, therefore, must be seen not merely as the product of its author's creative genius but as a recapturing of the essential convictions of the early church. Moreover, while recognizing that many take the impossibility of the miraculous as an axiom of historical criticism, I regard such a stance as a product of personal skepticism and a certain philosophical outlook rather than one of historical investigation and careful research. The primary issues that need to be dealt with here have to do with the portrayal of Paul in Acts and Luke's manner of treating historical details.

---

58. See Zeller, *Contents and Origin of the Acts of the Apostles.*

The Portrayal of Paul in Acts

In the opinion of many, the weightiest argument against the authenticity of Acts is that "the Paul of the Acts is manifestly quite a different person from the Paul of the Epistles."[59] As Adolf Hausrath, a nineteenth-century church historian from Heidelberg, once insisted:

> One could as well believe that Luther, in his old age, made a pilgrimage to Einsiedeln, walking on peas, or that Calvin on his death bed vowed a golden robe to the Holy Mother of God, as that the author of Romans and Galatians stood for seven days in the outer court of the Temple, and subjected himself to all the manipulations with which rabbinic ingenuity had surrounded the vow, and allowed all the liturgical nonsense of that age to be transacted for him by unbelieving priests and Levites.[60]

Many today, while not quite as colorful, agree with Hausrath because they believe that the author of Acts grossly misrepresented Paul in depicting his activities and portraying his theology. So they judge Luke's description of the relation between Paul and the Jerusalem church to be, as Barrett expressed it, "a happier one than the facts warrant."[61]

Lightfoot and Harnack, however, were notable dissenters from this type of criticism; they insisted that the split between the Paul of Acts and the Paul of the apostle's own letters is more a scholar's construction than a fact of history.[62] In my *Paul, Apostle of Liberty*, I have argued for an understanding of Paul's background and teaching that would allow for a more adequate appreciation of his practices as portrayed in Acts, and in my *The Christology of Early Jewish Christianity* for a better understanding of the basic convictions of the earliest Jewish believers in Jesus.[63]

Undoubtedly there are differences between the Paul of his own letters and the Paul of his "biographer," and early Jewish Christianity and Pauline Christianity should be seen as distinguishable entities. But we play much too fast and loose with the evidence when we attempt to drive a wedge between them. Paul, writing as an evangelist and pastor to his converts, affirms the essentials of his message within a context of personal humility, whereas Luke writes as a historian and admirer of the apostle with a sense for the historical unfolding of the gospel and a desire to highlight the heroic. While we must ask for a body of agreement in the respective portrayals, we cannot reasonably call for an identity of details or a uniformity of viewpoints.

The situation is somewhat comparable to Plutarch's treatment of the members of the Roman family Gracchus in his *Parallel Lives* and Appian's depiction of these same leaders in his *Civil Wars*. While both wrote in the second century AD, Plutarch was interested in the Gracchi primarily as statesmen, whereas Appian was interested in them as generals. The differing interests drastically affected each writer's selection and shaping of the material, as well as the impact of each man's work. Yet there is a large body of agreement between Plutarch's and Appian's treatment. As G. E. Underhill observed:

---

59. Baur, *Paul Apostle of Jesus Christ*, 11.

60. Cited in W. M. MacGregor, *Christian Freedom* (London: Hodder & Stoughton, 1914), 71.

61. Barrett, *Luke the Historian*, 74.

62. See Lightfoot, *Galatians*, 347–48; Harnack, *Date of the Acts and of the Synoptic Gospels*, 67–89.

63. See my *Paul, Apostle of Liberty* (1964; repr., Vancouver, B.C.: Regent College Publishing, 2003), 211–63; *The Christology of Early Jewish Christianity* (1970; repr., Vancouver, B.C.: Regent College Publishing, 2001).

It is not wonderful therefore that, starting from such very different points of view, and with such arbitrary methods of selecting and arranging their materials, Plutarch and Appian should have written two very different accounts of the Gracchi and their doings. The wonder is rather that they should agree so well as they do. Thus to attempt to pronounce in general terms which is to be preferred before the other, is almost an idle task: the better course is to compare the two narratives in detail, and to discuss the value of each part separately.[64]

So "it is not wonderful" that Luke portrays Paul as a great miracle worker, whereas Paul himself laid claim to "the things that mark an apostle—signs, wonders and miracles" (2Co 12:12) only when forced to assert his apostleship; or that Luke thought of his hero as an outstanding orator, whereas Paul acknowledged that some were saying that "in person he is unimpressive and his speaking amounts to nothing" (2Co 10:10); or that Luke should depict Paul's apostleship as related to and in continuity with that of the Jerusalem apostles, whereas Paul himself insisted that his apostleship was in a real sense unique.[65] If we really believe in redaction criticism, we must allow various portrayals to be influenced by the respective purposes of authors at the time of writing. Real life is broader than the precision of mathematical equations, though those who fault Acts for its portrait of Paul seem often to forget that.

Luke's Treatment of Historical Details

As for Luke's treatment of historical details in Acts, almost all of Zeller's identifications of supposed historical discrepancies have been effectively countered by the research of William M. Ramsay. Therefore we seldom hear of Eduard Zeller today. On the other hand, Ramsay became so impressed with the historical trustworthiness of Acts and the "true historic sense" of its author that at times he seems to argue that Luke wrote only as a pure historian without any other purpose than to inform his readers.[66] And because in his later writings he tended to minimize Luke's kerygmatic concerns, deny any redactional treatment in his presentation, and focus only on the historicity of Acts' depictions, Ramsay has often been neglected by contemporary biblical scholars.

But Ramsay's basic point was well made: that on matters of geography, history, Roman law, and provincial administration, as well as various Greco-Roman customs, Acts is an extremely reliable guide to the situation of the mid-first century AD. Likewise, his insistence that "a writer who proves to be exact and correct

---

64. G. E. Underhill, *Plutarch's Lives of the Gracchi* (Oxford: Clarendon, 1892), xix.

65. I am interacting here with Haenchen's three claimed "discrepancies" between "the 'Lucan' Paul and the Paul of the epistles" (see his *Acts of the Apostles*, 113–15).

66. Ramsay (*St. Paul the Traveller*, 20–21) makes this observation: "It is rare to find a narrative so simple and so little forced as that of 'Acts.' It is a mere uncoloured recital of the important facts in the briefest possible terms. The narrator's individuality and his personal feelings and preferences are almost wholly suppressed. He is entirely absorbed in his work; and he writes with the single aim to state the facts as he has learned them. It would be difficult in the whole range of literature to find a work where there is less attempt at pointing a moral or drawing a lesson from the facts. The narrator is persuaded that the facts themselves in their barest form are a perfect lesson and a complete instruction, and he feels that it would be an impertinence and even an impiety to intrude his individual views into the narrative."

in one point will show the same qualities in other matters"[67] is a legitimate inference from his more limited area of investigation and deserves general credence.

There still remain, however, a number of historical problems in Acts that seem to go beyond any ready explanation and beyond what scholars believe to have been the situation in the first century. Most notorious of these is the reference to the Jewish revolutionaries Theudas and Judas the Galilean in Gamaliel's speech as given in 5:36–37:

> Some time ago Theudas appeared, claiming to be somebody, and about four hundred men rallied to him. He was killed, all his followers were dispersed, and it all came to nothing. After him, Judas the Galilean appeared in the days of the census and led a band of people in revolt. He too was killed, and all his followers were scattered.

The major historical blunders in this passage appear to be (1) its disagreement with Josephus as to the chronological order of these rebellions, for Josephus depicts that of Judas as having taken place first in about AD 6 (*Ant.* 18.4–10), with the rebellion of Theudas coming later in about AD 44 (*Ant.* 20.97–98); and more seriously, (2) its making Gamaliel in about AD 34 refer to an uprising of Theudas that did not occur until a decade or so later. Nineteenth-century critics were quick to highlight this latter problem and usually explained it as a result of Luke's confused dependence on the historian Josephus. They argued that the writer of Acts (1) had confused Josephus's later reminiscence of Judas's revolt (*Ant.* 20.102) with the earlier actual revolt and (2) had forgotten some sixty years or more after the event—if, indeed, he ever knew—that Gamaliel's speech preceded Theudas's rebellion by a decade or so and did not follow it.

The arguments for Luke's dependence on Josephus have been virtually demolished by the literary and historical analyses of such scholars as Emil Schürer and Henry St.John Thackeray.[68] It may be that the Theudas of Gamaliel's reference was one of the many insurgent leaders who arose in Palestine at the time of Herod the Great's death in 4 BC, and not the Theudas who led the Jewish uprising of AD 44. And it may be that Gamaliel's examples of Jewish insurrectionists refer to a Theudas of about 4 BC and to Judas the Galilean of AD 6, whereas Josephus focused on Judas of AD 6 and another Theudas of AD 44. The problem with Acts 5:36–37, therefore, could be a product of our own ignorance as to the referents of Luke and Josephus, respectively, and not a disagreement between the accounts of the two writers.

Werner Georg Kümmel has enumerated a number of factors relating to what he saw as an incomplete selection and treatment of material in Acts, which incompleteness convinced him that the author lacked a real historical interest. So he discredited the historical worth of what is presented on the ground that "we do not learn the historically significant things about [Paul]."[69] Such an objection, however, may tell us only that Kümmel's view of what was significant in apostolic history differed from Luke's view of what was significant—which is a matter of very little importance when judging the historical reliability of Luke's account. As H. E. W. Turner aptly pointed out:

---

67. Ramsay, *Bearing of Recent Discovery on the Trustworthiness of the New Testament*, 80.

68. Schürer concluded, "Either Luke had not read Josephus, or he had forgotten all about what he had read" ("Lucas und Josephus," *ZWT* 19 [1876]: 582); cf. H. St.J. Thackerary, *Selections from Josephus* (New York: Doran, 1919), 194.

69. Werner Georg Kümmel, *Introduction to the New Testament* (London: SCM, 1965), 116–17.

The fact that a number of questions which we should wish to put to the documents are unanswerable does not by itself cast doubt on their veracity as historical documents. It may merely imply that we are selecting the wrong criteria to get the best out of our subject-matter or framing the wrong questions to put to our sources. However legitimate its methods and aims, criticism can easily and imperceptibly turn into hypercriticism and become in the process as ham-fisted as literalism.[70]

And W. C. van Unnik made this observation:

Would it not be wise to be somewhat more moderate in the questions we ask of Luke? Because he was not omniscient on all events of the apostolic age, it does not follow that he was unreliable in what he does tell us, or that he is a pious but untrustworthy preacher. We must grant him the liberty of not being interested in all matters that interest us.[71]

Luke, it is true, varies considerably from modern historians. He does not cite authorities or strive for completeness. Nor does he interact with competing viewpoints. He presents his material in dramatic vignettes, which "present not so much a single picture as a series of glimpses."[72] He is more concerned with ethos and indirect character portrayals than with matters of cause and effect. He is more interested in portraying episodes of the gospel's advance than in detailing resultant implications. And what he does tell us often leaves us baffled and searching for the thesis that will unify the whole. But because he has presented his material in a unique manner, is uninterested in many of the issues that preoccupy modern historians, and uses his narrative to proclaim the continuing activity of the ascended Christ in the world through his Spirit in the church, we do not have to relegate Luke's Acts to the historically unreliable. In Luke's view—which, it seems, was also the stance of many other reputable historians and biographers of his day—this unique presentation was the only way his narrative could compel interest and achieve its purposes.

7. SPEECHES

The tone for the scholarly study of the speeches of Acts was set in 1922 by Henry Cadbury in his discussion of the writing of history in Greek and Jewish traditions:

To suppose that the writers were trying to present the speeches as actually spoken, or that their readers thought so, is unfair to the morality of one and to the intelligence of the other. From Thucydides downwards, speeches reported by the historians are confessedly pure imagination. They belong to the final literary stage. If they have any nucleus of fact behind them it would be the merest outline in the *hypomnemata* ["the remembrances," GK *5704*].[73]

---

70. Turner, *Historicity and the Gospels*, 1–2.

71. Van Unnik, "Luke-Acts," in *Studies in Luke-Acts* (ed. Keck and Martyn), 29. He goes on to say, "I am sure that if the same tests to which Luke has often been subjected were applied to historians of our times, e.g., about World War II, they would not stand the test. It would be very wholesome to many a NT scholar to read a good many sources of secular history—and not only theological books. Then it would appear that sometimes a single story may be really significant for a great development, and that summaries as such are not a sign of lack of information."

72. Foakes-Jackson and Lake, *Beginnings of Christianity*, 1:301.

73. Henry J. Cadbury, "The Greek and Jewish Traditions of Writing History," in *Beginnings of Christianity*, 2:13.

A number of studies presented during the last half of the twentieth century in support of Cadbury's claim have argued (1) that Luke, as a Greek historian, indeed followed the Thucydidean model; (2) that the speeches of Acts fit too neatly into their redactional contexts for the material to be drawn from the primitive church; and (3) that the vocabulary and theology of the speeches are those of Luke himself (as determined by comparison with his editorial activity elsewhere in Luke-Acts), and so the content cannot be viewed as being representative of the earliest Christian preachers.[74] Yet critical opinion regarding the sermons and addresses of Acts has not moved in only one direction, and many have come to believe that such judgments are extreme.

Theological Content and Vocabulary

As already noted (p. 673), ancient historians did ask questions regarding what really happened and sought to be as accurate as possible. I pointed out from the example of Thucydides (*Hist.* 1.22) that even though verbatim reporting was disclaimed, the desire was to adhere "as closely as possible to the general sense of what was actually spoken."

As for the similarities of structure between particular speeches and the narrative and other speeches of Acts, this may be freely acknowledged without denigrating the content. To an extent, of course, all the sermons, addresses, and speeches in Acts are paraphrastic. Certainly their original delivery contained much more detail of argumentation and more illustrative material than Luke has included—as poor Eutychus could undoubtedly testify with regard to Paul's extended sermon at Troas (20:7–12)! Stenographic reports they are not, and probably few ever so considered them. They have been reworked, as is required in any précis—in accord with the style of the narrative. But recognition of speeches that are compatible with the narrative in which they are found should not be interpreted as inaccurate reporting or a lack of traditional source material. After all, a single author is responsible for the literary form of the whole.

Comparing Luke's gospel with that of Matthew, it is clear that Luke did not invent sayings for Jesus. On the contrary, he seems to have been more literal in transmitting the words of Jesus than in recounting the events of his life. C. F. Evans believed that such a comparison was fallacious since the discourses of Jesus and the sermons of various apostolic men in Acts are two entirely different literary genres, the one composed of independent *logia*, the other displaying more rounded and carefully constructed units.[75] Martin Dibelius insisted that the comparison should not be taken as presumptive evidence for a similarity of treatment by Luke in Acts:

> For when he wrote the Gospel, Luke had to fit in with a tradition which already had its own stamp upon it, so that he had not the same literary freedom as when he composed the Acts of the Apostles. On the other hand, unless we are completely deceived, he was the first to employ the material available for the Acts

---

74. See Dibelius, *Studies in the Acts of the Apostles*, 138–85; P. Vielhauer, "On the 'Paulinism' of Acts," in *Studies in Luke-Acts* (ed. Keck and Martyn), 33–50; E. Schweizer, "Concerning the Speeches in Acts," in *Studies in Luke-Acts* (ed. Keck and Martyn), 208–16; U. Wilckens and P. Schubert, "The Final Cycle of Speeches in the Book of Acts," *JBL* 87 (1968): 1–16.

75. See C. F. Evans, "The Kerygma," *JTS* 7 (1956): 27.

of the Apostles, and so was able to develop the book according to the point of view of an historian writing literature.[76]

Yet even though we have no comparable "Matthew" for Acts, and though the literary genre of the discourses in Luke and the speeches in Acts differ, there is no prima facie reason why Luke's handling of material in the latter should be assumed to differ widely from his treatment in the former. And though his respect for the speakers depicted in Acts never rivaled his veneration for the person and work of Jesus as portrayed in his gospel, it is difficult to believe that such a difference would have appreciably affected the desire for accuracy of content, if not also of word, that he evidences in his gospel. We must, therefore, continue to insist on a presumption in favor of a similarity of treatment in Luke's recording of the words of Jesus and his recording of the addresses of Peter, Stephen, Philip, James, and Paul—with such a presumption engendering confidence in the reliability of the content of the speeches in Acts, even though those speeches have been reworked by Luke into their present précis form.

That Luke actually strove for accuracy of content in presenting the speeches—or at least did not impose his own theology on them and so pervert their original character—has been aptly argued by Herman Ridderbos and C. F. D. Moule.[77] Ridderbos pointed to the lack of developed theology in the speeches of Peter as a mark of reliable historiography rather than of inventive genius. And Moule convincingly insisted that, in spite of frequent claims to the contrary, the Christology of Acts is not uniform, either between the speakers themselves or between them and Luke—i.e., that there are a "number of seemingly undesigned coincidences and subtle nuances," which indicate a retention of the essential nature of the content.[78]

Text-Forms of the Biblical Quotations in Chapters 1–15

The problem as to why the early Christian leaders are portrayed in Acts 1–15 as quoting, in the main, from the Septuagint (LXX) when their sermons and addresses assumedly had their origins in an Aramaic-speaking community is a difficulty without ready solution. Many have asserted that this phenomenon of Greek biblical citations in material credited to Aramaic-speaking preachers lies heavily against the authenticity of the speeches. But both the observation and the implication often drawn fail to take into account several pertinent factors.

In the first place, while the quotations of Acts are fairly representative of the LXX in general, the LXX alone is not sufficient to explain all their textual features. Jan de Waard has pointed out that the quotations in 3:22–23 (Dt 18:15, 18–19); 7:43 (Am 5:26–27); 13:41 (Hab 1:5); and 15:16 (Am 9:11) are prime examples of where "certain New Testament writings show affinities to the Dead Sea Scrolls as regards the Old Testament text."[79] Likewise, it is possible that Luke assimilated to the text Aramaic or more Hebraic type

---

76. Dibelius, *Studies in the Acts of the Apostles*, 185.

77. Herman N. Ridderbos, *The Speeches of Peter in the Acts of the Apostles* (London: Tyndale, 1962); C. F. D. Moule, "The Christology of Acts," in *Studies in Luke-Acts* (ed. Keck and Martyn), 159–85.

78. Moule, "Christology of Acts," 181–82.

79. Jan de Waard, *A Comparative Study of the Old Testament Text in the Dead Sea Scrolls and in the New Testament* (Leiden: Brill, 1965), 78.

text-forms that were "familiar to those for whom he wrote."[80] And Max Wilcox has shown that while the biblical quotations in Acts 1–15 are strongly Septuagintal, the allusions—because they are less capable of exact identification and thus less subject to special treatment—seem to have escaped a process of assimilation and retain more of their original Semitic cast.[81] Perhaps, as Wilcox goes on to argue, some credit for the Septuagintal features of the biblical quotations in chs. 1–15 should also be given to a Greek *testimonia* collection of OT passages that was circulating within the church during the time of Luke's composition.[82]

It seems that we are faced with at least two issues regarding the text-form of the quotations in the first fifteen chapters of Acts: (1) the variety of biblical versions in the first century, and (2) Luke's assimilation for the sake of his Greek-speaking readers. In addition, the possible presence of a Greek *testimonia* collection adds a further complication. Until additional evidence is available, we are well advised to leave questions regarding textual sources and deviations in early Christian preaching somewhat open. We may suspect that the answer to our problem lies in one or more of the suggestions above, and we may be able to build a reasonable case in defense of a particular thesis. But all we really know is that the biblical quotations in Acts are dominantly Septuagintal, with a few parallels to the biblical texts at Qumran. But none of this necessarily impinges on or supports authenticity.

8. STRUCTURE

The Acts of the Apostles was originally written as the second part of a two-volume work, and its relation to Luke's gospel must be constantly kept in mind if we are to understand the work. As Henry Cadbury long ago insisted, "Their unity is a fundamental and illuminating axiom. . . . They are not merely two independent writings from the same pen; they are a single continuous work. Acts is neither an appendix nor an afterthought. It is probably an integral part of the author's original plan and purpose."[83] The prologue to the two-volume work (Lk 1:1–4) suggests, in fact, that the author's intention was to write "an account of the things that have been fulfilled among us"—things that stretched from the birth of John the Baptist to the entrance of the good news into Rome.[84] And his use of the emphatic verb "began" (*ērxato*, GK *806*) as he commences his second volume (Ac 1:1) sets up the parallel between "all that Jesus *began* to do and to teach" (italics mine) as recorded in his gospel and what he *continued* to do and to teach through his church as shown in Acts.

Parallel Phenomena in the Gospel and Acts

Luke alone of the evangelists seems to have viewed the history of the advance of the gospel as of comparable importance to the life, death, and resurrection of Jesus—and to have understood, it seems, Jesus'

---

80. C. C. Torrey, *The Composition and Date of Acts* (HTS; Cambridge, Mass.: Harvard Univ. Press, 1916), 58.

81. Wilcox, *Semitisms of Acts*, 20–55.

82. Ibid., 181–82.

83. Henry J. Cadbury, *The Making of Luke-Acts* (1927; repr., London: SPCK, 1961), 8–9.

84. See Henry J. Cadbury, "The Knowledge Claimed in Luke's Preface," *The Expositor* 24 (1922): 401–20; "Commentary on the Preface of Luke," in *Beginnings of Christianity*, 2:489–510; *Making of Luke-Acts*, 344–48, 358–59.

accomplishment of redemption and the extension of that redemption through the activity of the church as being part and parcel of the same climactic movement in the drama of salvation. In fact, Luke seems to have taken pains to construct his second volume with an eye to the first by setting up numerous parallels in the portrayal of events in the two volumes and repeatedly stressing features in the second that fulfill anticipations expressed in the first. For example, the geographical movement of Jesus in the gospel from Galilee to Jerusalem is paralleled in Acts by the geographical advance of the gospel from Jerusalem to Rome. The importance of the Holy Spirit in the birth narratives, in the Spirit's descent on Jesus at his baptism, and in the Spirit's constant undergirding of his ministry (cf. Jesus' declaration of this fact found only in Lk 4:18–19) is paralleled in Acts by the Spirit's coming on the disciples at Pentecost and the repeated emphasis on the Spirit as the source of the church's power and progress.

Similarly, Luke's stress in Acts on the special significance of the apostles, the centrality of Jesus Christ in the early apostolic preaching, and the universal dimensions of that preaching finds roots in his gospel in such unique ways as calling the disciples "apostles" (Lk 6:13) and extending the quotation of Isaiah 40:3 to include the universalistic statements of vv.4–5 (Lk 3:5–6), as well as inferentially at many other places. Further instances of such parallel phenomena are much too numerous to mention here; they will be dealt with in the commentary itself. Often the parallelism is so subtly presented that it could be easily overlooked unless one studies Acts with Luke's gospel constantly in mind. This structural parallelism and tying in of details between the two volumes runs throughout Luke's writings—not crudely or woodenly but often very subtly and skillfully. We do well to watch for it.[85] As Arnold Ehrhardt has pointed out, "St. Luke is far too good a writer and too honest an historian to labour this parallelism; but the structural similarity is close enough to deserve our careful attention."[86]

Acts as the Completion of the Gospel

Acts, however, is not simply a parallel to Luke's gospel that ends at Rome as the gospel ended at Jerusalem. If it were, it would be the less important part of Luke's two volumes—something like a shadow of the original. Rather, Acts is important in its own right as the logical and geographical completion of Jesus' journey to Jerusalem. Indeed none of the apostolic figures of Acts are portrayed as paralleling the life, death, and resurrection of Jesus. This may be why Luke had no interest in closing Acts with an account of Paul's death. If he knew of it, he evidently did not consider it appropriate to include it. And if it had not occurred when he was writing Acts, he felt no compulsion to wait for it before completing the book.

Luke presents the apostolic ministry as the necessary extension of the redemption effected by Jesus. He seems to have viewed both the accomplishment of salvation (as portrayed in his gospel) and the spread of the good news (as presented in Acts) as inseparable units in the climactic activity of God's redemption of mankind—a perspective probably picked up from Paul (cf. Ro 8:17; Php 3:10–11; Col 1:24). So for Luke,

---

85. For detailed lists of parallels between Luke's gospel and Acts, see C. H. Talbert, *Literary Patterns, Theological Themes, and the Genre of Luke-Acts* (Missoula, Mont.: Scholars Press, 1974), 15–23, 58–65.

86. Arnold Ehrhardt, *The Acts of the Apostles: Ten Lectures* (Manchester: Manchester Univ. Press, 1969), 13.

as John O'Neill observed, "the full significance of the central happenings at Jerusalem is not worked out in history until Paul has reached Rome."[87]

A Structural Analysis of Acts

Various proposals regarding the structure of Acts have been offered. Some have seen it structured according to its underlying sources, others simply according to the topics treated. What is required in any structural analysis, however, is a thesis that takes into account both the parallel features in Luke's gospel and the structural phenomena in Acts.

Four features, in particular, need to be kept in mind regarding the structure of Luke's gospel:

1. It begins with an introductory section of distinctly Lukan cast, which deals with Jesus' birth and youth (1:1–2:52), before taking up the narrative that the evangelist holds in common with Mark and Matthew.
2. The Nazareth pericope (4:14–30) serves as the thesis or thematic paragraph for all that Luke presents in his two volumes, with most of what follows in these volumes being an explication of the themes contained in that thesis paragraph.[88]
3. In his portrayals of Jesus' ministry, Luke follows an essentially geographical outline, which portrays Jesus' Galilean ministry (4:14–9:50), then depicts his ministry in the regions of Perea and Judea (9:51–19:28), and finally concludes at Jerusalem (19:29–24:53).
4. Luke deliberately sets up a number of parallels between Jesus' ministry in Galilee and his ministry in Perea and Judea.[89]

By way of comparison, five structural phenomena of Acts need also to be highlighted:

1. It begins, like the gospel, with an introductory section of distinctly Lukan cast, which deals with the constitutive events of the Christian mission (1:1–2:41) before setting out the advances of the gospel "in Jerusalem, and in all Judea and Samaria, and to the ends of the earth" (1:8).
2. This introductory section is followed by what appears to be a thematic statement (2:42–47), which, while often viewed as a summary of what precedes, probably serves as the thesis paragraph for what follows.
3. In his presentations of the advances of the Christian mission, Luke follows an essentially geographical outline, which moves from Jerusalem (2:42–6:7), through Judea and Samaria

---

87. J. C. O'Neill, *The Theology of Acts in Its Historical Setting* (1961; rev. ed., London: SPCK, 1970), 6.

88. Many scholars have noted the importance of the Nazareth pericope for Luke's structure. Here are some representative comments: "a frontispiece to the Ministry" (W. Manson, *The Gospel of Luke* [London: Hodder & Stoughton, 1930], 41); "a main pillar of [Luke's] whole structure" (Conzelman, *Theology of St. Luke*, 29 n. 4); "the foundation stone of his gospel" (J. Sanders, "From Isaiah 61 to Luke 4," in *Christianity, Judaism, and Other Greco-Roman Cults*, Part I, ed. J. Sanders [Leiden: Brill, 1975], 104); "the rest of the Gospel is simply the working out of this programme" (G. B. Caird, *The Gospel of St. Luke* [New York: Harper, 1968], 86).

89. For detailed lists of parallels within Luke's gospel, see Talbert, *Literary Patterns*, 26–29, 39–56.

(6:8–9:31), on into Palestine-Syria (9:32–12:24), then to the Gentiles in the eastern part of the Roman Empire (12:25–19:20), and finally culminates in Paul's defenses and the entrance of the gospel into Rome (19:21–28:31).

4. Luke deliberately sets up a number of parallels between the ministry of Peter in the first half of Acts and the ministry of Paul in the last half.[90]

5. Luke includes six summary statements or "progress reports" (6:7; 9:31; 12:24; 16:5; 19:20; 28:31), each of which seems to conclude its own "panel" of material.[91]

Taking into account both sets of structural features, we may conclude that Luke developed his material in Acts along the following lines:

Introduction: The Constitutive Events of the Christian Mission (1:1–2:41)
    Part I: The Christian Mission to the Jewish World (2:42–12:24)
        Panel 1—The Earliest Days of the Church at Jerusalem (2:42–6:7)
        Summary Statement: "So the word of God spread. The number of disciples in Jerusalem increased rapidly, and a large number of priests became obedient to the faith" (6:7).
        Panel 2—Critical Events in the Lives of Three Pivotal Figures (6:8–9:31)
        Summary Statement: "Then the church throughout Judea, Galilee and Samaria enjoyed a time of peace. It was strengthened; and encouraged by the Holy Spirit, it grew in numbers, living in the fear of the Lord" (9:31).
        Panel 3—Advances of the Gospel in Palestine-Syria (9:32–12:24)
        Summary Statement: "But the word of God continued to increase and spread" (12:24).
    Part II: The Christian Mission to the Gentile World (12:25–28:31)
        Panel 4—The First Missionary Journey and the Jerusalem Council (12:25–16:5)
        Summary Statement: "So the churches were strengthened in the faith and grew daily in numbers" (16:5).
        Panel 5—Wide Outreach through Two Missionary Journeys (16:6–19:20)
        Summary Statement: "In this way the word of the Lord spread widely and grew in power" (19:20).
        Panel 6—To Jerusalem and from There to Rome (19:21–28:31)
        Summary Statement: "Boldly and without hindrance he preached the kingdom of God and taught about the Lord Jesus Christ" (28:31).

Implications for the Ending of Acts

Laying out the structure of Acts in this way highlights not only the parallelism that exists between Luke's second volume and his first volume, but also the parallelism built into Acts in its portrayal of the ministry of Peter in chs. 1–12 and the ministry of Paul in chs. 13–28. Likewise, accepting such a structure for Acts

---

90. See ibid.

91. See C. H. Turner, "The Chronology of the New Testament," in *A Dictionary of the Bible*, ed. James Hastings (Edinburgh: T&T Clark, 1898), 1:421 (though Turner's first panel includes all of 1:1–2:41).

provides us with a cogent explanation for one of the most difficult questions about Luke's second volume: Why does it end as it does? The reader is left at 28:30–31 with Paul a prisoner for two years in his own rented quarters at Rome, where "boldly and without hindrance he preached the kingdom of God and taught about the Lord Jesus Christ." But it has seemed strange to many that we are told no more. Various explanations have been proposed for this abrupt ending.

One common explanation is that Luke was prevented by his own death from writing more. Another is that he really intended to write a trilogy—with the third volume dedicated to Paul's ministry in the western part of the empire, as his second volume had treated Paul's ministry in the eastern part, and with the inclusion of an account of the apostle's martyrdom—but for some reason he never completed it. Those who propose this explanation usually point to the classical distinction between the word *prōtos* used in Acts 1:1, which meant the "first" of a series and could suggest the intention of more than two volumes, and the comparative *proteros*, which signified the "former" of two events or occurrences. Furthermore, they often cite Paul's intention as expressed in Romans 15:23–24, 28 of carrying on a ministry beyond Rome that would extend to Spain (cf. *1 Clem.* 5). But the classical distinction between "first" (*prōtos*) and "former" (*proteros*) seems not to have been continued in the period of Koine Greek, and there are reasons to believe that Paul's hope for a ministry beyond Rome in the western part of the empire never materialized.

Another explanation for the abrupt ending has been advanced by those who see Acts as a trial document that was written to be presented before the imperial authorities at Paul's trial at Rome. They have suggested that Luke stopped where he did because there he rested his case, and with the condemnation of his client he had no desire to complete the document by telling of Paul's execution. Others have insisted that Acts ends where it does because Luke, writing about AD 62, knew nothing more about Paul—i.e., as has been often argued, "the narrative had caught up with the events." Still others have proposed that in saying that Paul resided "for two whole years" at Rome without any formal charge being laid against him, Luke was obliquely implying that Paul was not brought to trial, but that in accordance with Roman law his case was dismissed—which, it is argued, would be an appropriate ending actually highlighting the fact that all the accusations against Paul had come to nothing.

Each proposal has some merit, and each can be argued in a more-or-less convincing fashion. Some can be joined with others in common argument. But Luke was not writing a biography of Paul, even though he included many biographical details about him. Rather, Luke was showing how the good news of humanity's redemption had begun in Jerusalem, swept through all of Palestine, gone into Asia Minor, proceeded throughout Macedonia and Achaia, and finally entered Rome, the capital of the empire. When Paul's goal was reached, his story was told. So Luke ended where he did because his purpose in writing was completed. The gospel Jesus effected in his ministry from Galilee to Jerusalem had reached its culmination in its extension from Jerusalem to Rome. And with that victory accomplished, Luke felt free to lay down his pen.

9. DATE

I have delayed discussing the date of Acts until after dealing with the book's structure, for the question of date has often been connected with a particular explanation for the ending of Acts. F. C. Baur, like many today, saw no correlation. But at the end of the nineteenth century and during the first part of the twentieth century, many explained the abrupt ending by the maxim "the narrative has caught up with the events." So they concluded that Acts was written shortly after the last event mentioned. Adolf Harnack led the way in establishing this position, and a number of more recent commentators have taken a similar stance (e.g., Alfred Wikenhauser and F. F. Bruce). Much that Harnack and his successors said about an early date for Acts is still valuable and important. But if we cannot give the same explanation as Harnack for the ending, we cannot equate the issues of its ending and its date in the same manner. To date Acts by its ending is, in fact, a non sequitur simply because it fails to take into account Luke's purpose in writing the book.

Generally Proposed Dates

Broadly speaking, scholars today are divided into three camps with respect to the date of Acts: (1) those who argue for the composition of the book somewhere around AD 115 to 130, (2) those who hold to a date somewhere between AD 80 and 95, and (3) those who hold to a date prior to AD 70. An early second-century date has often been argued on the basis of the work's apparent "early Catholicism"—i.e., its supposed recasting of futuristic eschatology and Spirit-controlled enthusiasm into matters having to do with Christology, ecclesiology, realized eschatology, and missionary outreach—and its "anti-Gnosticism." But these are issues that are hotly debated and, even if true, could have taken place earlier than the second century.

John O'Neill has taken the lead in arguing for Acts as having been written between AD 115 and 130. He begins with the thesis that "the only way now left to solve the problem about the date of Acts is to decide where its theological affinities lie."[92] He then finds the closest parallels to the theology of Acts in the writings of Justin Martyr, particularly his *First Apology*, and so argues for an early second-century date for Acts on the basis "that Luke and Justin Martyr held common theological positions without being dependent on each other, and that Luke-Acts was completed in time for Luke to be used by Marcion."[93]

There is much in O'Neill's paralleling of the writings of Luke and Justin Martyr that is of interest. But as William Barclay once said about O'Neill's view, "Of the ingenuity and of the scholarship with which it is supported there is no question; but it has failed to gain general acceptance, if for no other reason, because an easier explanation of the facts is that Justin knew Acts."[94] Furthermore, to attribute to an early second-century writer the fabrication of the earlier part of Paul's story and then to view such a writer as hesitating to produce an account of Paul's experiences in Rome is hard to imagine. "It is certain," as Arnold Ehrhardt pointed out, "that the mind of the early second-century Church, which produced a great number of apocryphal Acts of various Apostles, did not work in this way."[95]

Most scholars today date Acts somewhere between AD 80 and 95. They reason that Acts cannot have been written before the fall of Jerusalem, because the third gospel cannot have been written before that date and the third gospel is earlier than Acts. On the other hand, Acts cannot have been written after AD 95,

92. O'Neill, *Theology of Acts in Its Historical Setting*, 1.
93. Ibid., 21–22.
94. William Barclay, *The Gospels and Acts* (London: SCM, 1976), 2:256.
95. Ehrhardt, *Acts of the Apostles*, 3.

because the case for a member of Paul's missionary team having written the "we" sections is strong. Yet it must have been written sometime after Paul's death, for Paul might have objected to certain things Acts describes him as having said and done. Furthermore, Acts must have been written before Paul's letters were gathered into some kind of recognizable collection, for the book says nothing about its hero as a correspondent. The terminus a quo, therefore, is set by the references to the fall of Jerusalem in Luke 19:43–44 and 21:20–24, which require the gospel to have been written after AD 70, and by the general sequence of synoptic relationships epitomized by the revision of Mark 13:14–20 in Luke 21:20–24, which also seems to point to a date after AD 70. The terminus ad quem is set sometime after Paul's death but before the collection of the Pauline letters—a collection that seems to have been known in at least rudimentary form by Clement of Rome, who wrote *1 Clement* about AD 96—a work that quotes extensively from our canonical 1 Corinthians and shows an awareness of a number of other canonical Pauline letters.

An Early Date Hypothesis

Nevertheless, Acts contains a number of features that point to a date earlier than AD 70 for its composition. Four features need here to be highlighted. The first, and probably most important, has to do with *the portrayal of the situation of the Jews* in Acts, for they are represented as being a spiritual and political power who had influence with the Roman courts and whose damaging testimony against Christians had to be countered. But how could the Jews act as Luke depicts them acting *after* their destruction as a nation in the war of AD 66–70? And why would Luke *after* that time want to argue before a Gentile audience that Christianity should be accepted as a *religio licita* because of its relation to Judaism? True, Vespasian and Titus waged war against the Jews of Palestine, and particularly against their Zealot leadership, without mounting a general persecution against Diaspora Jews or imposing official restrictions on them. Yet in the eyes of the Roman world, Palestinian Judaism was largely defunct after AD 70, and Diaspora Judaism undoubtedly came under something of a cloud as a result.

Luke's apologetic, however, is built on the premises (1) that Jewish leaders throughout the Diaspora—and particularly the Jewish authorities at Jerusalem—are at the time an important voice before Roman courts of law, even the imperial court at Rome; and (2) that Judaism, both at Jerusalem and throughout the Diaspora, is accepted by Rome as a *religio licita*. Apart from such assumptions, Luke's apologetic makes no sense at all. Yet this was hardly the case at any time between AD 80 and 95, though it came to be the case to some extent through the efforts of Rabbi Akiba between AD 110 and 130.[96] Acceptance of Judaism by Rome as a *religio licita*, however, was the situation prior to the outbreak of hostilities and the disastrous conflagration that followed in AD 66–70.

---

96. Rabbi Akiba ben Joseph was the leading Jewish rabbi during AD 110–135. His Mishnah was the forerunner to that of Rabbi Judah the Prince (AD 150–185); and under his leadership, relations with Rome were stabilized for almost two decades. Under pressure from the Zealots, however, he proclaimed Simeon ben Kosiba (who was called by his followers bar Kochba, "Son of the Star") to be Messiah and sided with him against Rome. In AD 135 he was one of ten prominent rabbis put to death by Rome.

A second feature in Acts that argues for an early composition is *the estimation of Roman justice* that is implicit in the work. Acts expresses a generally hopeful outlook regarding Christianity's recognition by the Roman authorities and acceptance within the Gentile world, which could hardly have been the case after Nero's persecution of Christians that began in AD 65. If Luke had known of the martyrdom of Paul and Peter under Nero at Rome (cf. *1 Clem.* 5)—as well as the martyrdom of many other Christians—then, as D. Plooij long ago pointed out, "the last word of Acts [*akōlytōs*, "without hindrance," GK 219], which surely not without significance stands in its prominent place as the crown of the narrative, would be not only meaningless, but *in its tendency* nearly equal to a lie."[97] The attitude of Acts toward Roman power and justice is more like that of Paul in Romans 13:1–7, which was written before Nero's persecutions, than that of John the Seer in Revelation 17:1–6, which was written during the last years of the first century.

A third feature of note is *the archaic nature of the language* in Acts, a feature that says something about the book's date by suggesting either that its author wrote before circumstances and expressions had changed or that he was extremely ingenious in historicizing. As noted above, William M. Ramsay documented Luke's surprising accuracy in geographical, political, and territorial details. Regarding the regional boundary between Phrygian Iconium and the Lycaonian cities of Lystra and Derbe (cf. 14:6), for example, he has shown that such "was accurate at no other time except between 37 and 72 AD."[98] And Adolf Harnack has shown that the language of Acts appears to be the language of the earliest days of the church, particularly with regard to the titles ascribed to Jesus, the designations used for Christians, and the manner of speaking about the church.[99] It is possible, of course, to credit all of these features to the ingenuity and genius of Luke. But they are better explained, I believe, by the hypothesis of an early date for the writing of Acts.

Finally, there is the surprising fact that *Acts reflects no knowledge of Paul's letters*, either in what is said or what is assumed on the part of its readers. Two examples may be cited, both of which are drawn from letters undoubtedly written before Acts, no matter how early we date it: (1) there is no integration of Paul's statements in Galatians 1 and 2 regarding his personal contacts with the Jerusalem apostles and his visits described in Acts 9, 11, and 15; and (2) there is no correlation between the experiences referred to in 2 Corinthians (esp. chs. 1–2, 11–12) and Paul's missionary journeys recorded in Acts. These phenomena may, of course, be interpreted as evidence for the personal aloofness and the chronological distance of the author of Acts from his hero, and so used to support a late date for the work. On the other hand, they may be used in support of an early date—i.e., for Acts having been written before the significance of the Pauline correspondence was appreciated and by a companion who was not actually with Paul (to judge by the distribution of the "we" sections in Acts) when he wrote the particular letters in question.

To sum up, there is much to be said in support of an early date for Acts. According to this view, the terminus a quo would be the writing of Luke's gospel (which, it may be reasonably assumed, precedes Acts, and which in turn rests on the publication of Mark's gospel and at least the knowledge that Matthew had also written a gospel). It would also be after Paul's two-year imprisonment at Rome (probably during 61–63),

97. D. Plooij, "Again: The Work of St. Luke," *The Expositor* 13 (1917): 121 (italics his).

98. Ramsay, *St. Paul the Traveller*, 110–13.

99. See Harnack, *Date of the Acts and of the Synoptic Gospels*, 103–14.

which is referred to in Acts 28:30. The terminus ad quem would be the outbreak of hostilities between the Jewish Zealots and the Roman Tenth Legion in AD 66 and the start of the Neronian persecutions at Rome in AD 65. And all of this, I believe, suggests about AD 64 for the composition of Acts.

The major objections to such a date are (1) that it places the development of the synoptic tradition too early and (2) that it treats the Olivet Discourse of Mark 13; Matthew 24–25; and Luke 21 (together with Lk 17:22–37; 19:43–44) as predictive prophecy. But the nature of the development of the synoptic tradition and the dates to be assigned to that development continue to be matters of dispute. We may, for instance, believe (as I do) in the commonly accepted theory of synoptic relationships—i.e., in Markan priority and the existence of a Sayings or Logia source (Q), in the literary dependence of Matthew and Luke on Mark's narrative, and in the literary dependence of Matthew and Luke on a common Sayings or Logia (Q) source— and still question the validity of a set of dates for the Synoptic Gospels that are later than the destruction of Jerusalem. Furthermore, the dates ascribed to the Synoptic Gospels and Acts depend largely on one's view of the origin of the material making up the Olivet Discourse. And ultimately the dating of the Olivet Discourse comes down to the question of the possibility (or impossibility) of genuine predictive prophecy on the lips of Jesus during his earthly ministry—which is a possibility that I affirm.

10. AUTHOR

Since the question of authorship depends largely on how one views a number of other matters, my treatment of the subject has been reserved for the latter part of this introduction—though I have repeatedly spoken of "Luke" as having written the third gospel and Acts. But now that many of these other matters have been considered, the question of authorship arises naturally and logically.

Two Observations of Importance

Two observations from Acts itself have traditionally governed the discussion of authorship. The first is that linguistically, stylistically, and structurally, the gospel of Luke and the Acts of the Apostles are so closely related that they have to be assigned to the same author. This has been so extensively demonstrated by linguistic studies that it need not be elaborated here. Equally important, however, are the structural parallels between the two volumes and the comprehensive plan maintained throughout them. All this necessitates that, for both critical and interpretative purposes, Luke-Acts must be considered a single, unified work composed in two volumes. Hardly anyone today would dispute this basic observation regarding language, style, and structure.

A further observation pertinent to the question of authorship is that Luke-Acts claims to have been written by one who reports firsthand some of the events he records. In the prologue to his two-volume work (Lk 1:1–4), the author's use of the expression "among us" (en hēmin) should probably be taken to imply his contemporary status with some of the events he purposes to narrate, even though he disavows being an eyewitness "from the first." And his insistence that "I myself have carefully investigated [parēkolouthēkoti] everything from the beginning" suggests more than just historical knowledge of the events depicted. As Jacques Dupont observed, "The verb parakoloutheō [GK 4158] is, in point of fact, very appropriate for expressing the distinction between information received at second hand and that coming from the writer's personal presence at the events."[100] More particularly, however, the use of the first person plural in Acts 16:10–17; 20:5–15; 21:1–18; and 27:1–28:16 appears to be a deliberate endeavor to indicate that the writer was a traveling companion of Paul on certain of his missionary journeys. This leaves us with a plain choice: either to accept the suggestion made by the book itself as true or to reject it in favor of some other explanation.[101]

Having dated the composition of Acts about AD 64, there is little reason to dispute the implications of its "we" passages. In fact, accepting the author as a traveling companion of Paul during some of his missionary journeys explains quite adequately two rather peculiar features about the plan of Acts: (1) the disproportion of the work as a whole, with more than three-fifths of its space being devoted to Paul, and (2) the disproportion that appears in its portrayal of Paul, with the apostle's first mission being narrated with great brevity whereas certain parts of his second and third missionary journeys, his five defenses, and his journey to Rome are described much more fully. No writer who was a stranger to apostolic times or who worked entirely from sources would have devoted so much space to the latter part of Paul's ministry. His work would undoubtedly have been more symmetrically planned.

Lukan Authorship

Traditionally, the author of the third gospel has been identified as Luke, the companion of Paul mentioned in Colossians 4:14; 2 Timothy 4:11; and Philemon 24. Nor has tradition ever considered any author other than Luke. His authorship was accepted by Marcion (ca. AD 135), included in the Anti-Marcionite Prologue to the Third Gospel (ca. AD 170), and taken for granted by the compiler of the Muratorian Canon (ca. AD 180–200). And in the ancient manuscripts of the four gospels the heading "According to Luke" (*KATA LOUKAN*) is always found for the third gospel.

The situation regarding Acts is not quite the same. Indications of its use in the early second century are scarce. Marcion, for example, did not use Acts and seems not to have known of it, even though he knew and used Luke's gospel. And while the ancient manuscripts of Acts bear the title "The Acts of the Apostles," they do not name its author. Nevertheless, with Luke-Acts being originally one work in two volumes, which at some point during the latter part of the first century or very early in the second century began to circulate as two separate works, what is said regarding the one as to authorship must apply equally well to the other. Of lesser unanimity within the early church was the tradition that Luke was a native of Antioch of Syria, which is the claim made in the opening words of the Anti-Marcionite Prologue to the Third Gospel and repeated by Eusebius (*Hist. eccl.* 3.4) and Jerome (*On Illustrious Men* 7; preface to *Commentary on Matthew*).

In support of the traditional ascription, we need not insist that the author of Luke-Acts necessarily used a vocabulary that was special to the medical profession of his day or expressed interests that were overtly those of a doctor, thereby confirming the description of Luke in Colossians 4:14 as "our dear friend, . . . the doctor." In 1882 William K. Hobart proposed such a view based on a comparison of the language of

---

100. Dupont, *Sources of Acts*, 106 (see the entire section, 101–12).
101. See Arnold Ehrhardt, "The Construction and Purpose of the Acts of the Apostles," *ST* 12 (1958): 45–79.

Luke-Acts with that of such Greek medical writers as Hippocrates (ca. 460–377 BC) and Aretaeus, Galen, and Dioscorides, who lived during the first and second centuries AD.[102] Many scholars at the end of the nineteenth century and the beginning of the twentieth century followed him—particularly Adolf Harnack, who was so influential in propagating that thesis. In 1919, however, Henry Cadbury demonstrated, in the publication of his Harvard doctoral thesis, that the majority of the medical words identified by Hobart in Luke-Acts can be found with about the same frequency in such ancient writers as Josephus (AD 37–100) and Lucian of Samosata (ca. AD 120–200), who were not physicians.[103] Cadbury followed that work with a series of studies arguing that the supposed medical terminology of Luke-Acts was used widely in the ancient world—even among, as he called them, "horse-doctors."[104]

The gibe has frequently been made that Cadbury won his doctorate by taking Luke's away from him. All Cadbury did, however, was demonstrate that one cannot prove from the linguistic data that the author of Acts was a physician. The reference to Luke in Colossians 4:14 may be using the term "doctor" more in the sense of a "caregiver" who knew something of what we would today call "first aid." Thus while the language of Luke-Acts does not require us to believe that its author was a trained medical doctor, it puts no obstacle in the way of believing that Luke, who may have been loosely called "the doctor" by Paul, was the author of Acts.

What we can say positively is that the tradition that Luke wrote the third gospel and Acts goes back at least to the early second century, that it was unanimously accepted within the church, and that it would be very strange were it not true. If some early writer in the church was trying to pawn off Luke-Acts as the work of someone close to Paul in order to invest it with authority, why did he not attribute it to Paul himself—or at least to Timothy or Titus—both of whom were better known than Luke? Why, indeed, ascribe it to an individual who played no major part in the advance of the gospel and whose name appears only three times in the NT? To be sure, attempts have been made to set the tradition of Lukan authorship aside. But none of them are convincing. There are no compelling reasons to reject the church's unanimous tradition that Luke, who was Paul's "doctor"-friend and appears to have been a Gentile (Col 4:10–15), was the author of Acts.

11. TEXT

Before dealing with the exegesis of the text, some attention must be given to text-critical issues—to what is called "establishing" the text. While the manuscript evidence in support of the text of Acts is impressive, attesting to the carefulness of scribes during the centuries before Gutenberg's invention of the printing press in the fifteenth century, the task of establishing the Greek text of Acts is more complicated and acute than for any other NT writing.

---

102. See William K. Hobart, *The Medical Language of St. Luke* (London: Longmans, Green, 1882).

103. See Henry J. Cadbury, *The Style and Literary Method of Luke* (2 vols.; Cambridge, Mass.: Harvard Univ. Press, 1920); see esp. vol 1: *The Diction of Luke and Acts.*

104. See Henry J. Cadbury, "Lexical Notes on Luke-Acts, II—Recent Arguments for Medical Language," *JBL* 45 (1926): 190–209; "Lexical Notes on Luke-Acts, V—Luke and the Horse-Doctors," *JBL* 52 (1933): 55–65.

The Manuscript Evidence

There are basically three "families" or types of Greek texts for Acts. The first is the Alexandrian text (the "Neutral" text). It was prominent in Alexandria, hence its name, but it was also used in churches throughout the eastern part of the Roman Empire. The second type is the group of Greco-Latin texts called the Western text, which likely originated in the middle of the second century and was used dominantly in western portions of the empire. The third is the Byzantine text, also called the "Syrian" or "Antiochene" text because it is thought to have originated in the late third century at Antioch of Syria. This family of texts is sometimes known as the "Koine" ("common") text—or the "Majority Text"—because, being represented by some later uncial manuscripts and the great body of minuscule manuscripts from the ninth through the fifteenth centuries, it is numerically most common. It is frequently called the "Received Text," since it is generally comparable to the "Textus Receptus" of the Dutch religious humanist Desiderius Erasmus (1469–1536), whose text-critical work had a profound effect on Martin Luther (1483–1546) and all the Protestant Reformers of the sixteenth century, as well as on all the translations that culminated in the King James Version of 1611.

The Alexandrian text of Acts appears chiefly in the major uncial manuscripts ℵ (Codex Sinaiticus; fourth century) and B (Codex Vaticanus; fourth century), as well as in A (Codex Alexandrinus; fifth century), whose text is Byzantine in the Gospels but Alexandrian in Acts and the Pauline letters, and C (Codex Ephraemi Rescriptus; fifth century), whose text is generally Alexandrian but contains other mixed readings. It is also found in $\mathfrak{P}^{45}$ (Chester Beatty I; third century), $\mathfrak{P}^{50}$ (fourth and fifth centuries), and $\mathfrak{P}^{74}$ (Bodmer; seventh century); in most of the Coptic versions; and in quotations of Acts by Clement of Alexandria (ca. 150–215) and Origen (185–254).

The Western text of Acts appears mainly in the bilingual uncial manuscript D (Codex Bezae Cantabrigiensis), which dates from the fifth century. But that D had roots in an earlier period is evidenced by the fact that this type of text is also represented by (1) papyrus manuscripts $\mathfrak{P}^{29}$ (third century, on portions from chs. 4–6), $\mathfrak{P}^{38}$ (ca. 300, on portions from chs. 18 and 19), and $\mathfrak{P}^{48}$ (late third century, on portions from ch. 23); (2) citations of Acts that appear in the writings of such Latin Fathers as Tertullian (ca. 145–220), Cyprian (d. 258), and Augustine (354–430); (3) the commentary on Acts by Ephraem of Syria (303–373); and (4) a few recensions of early Coptic, Latin, and Syriac versions (e.g., Coptic G67, manuscript "h" of the African Vetus Latina, and the Syriac Harclean version with asterisks in the margins).

The Byzantine text of Acts appears in several uncials (H L P 049), all of which are ninth-century codices, as well as in the bulk of the minuscule manuscripts, which date from the ninth to the fifteenth centuries.

Evaluating the Evidence

While there are some differences between the Alexandrian and Byzantine texts, the major problem regarding the text of Acts has to do with relationships between the Alexandrian and Western texts. The question is this: Which of these two textual traditions is more original? The Western text of Acts, which sometimes has a smoother reading and sometimes a rougher reading than the Alexandrian text, is overall about 10 percent longer than the Alexandrian text. In particular, it differs from the Alexandrian text in such matters as (1) its frequent additional details that serve to fill out the picture given in the narrative; (2) its constant substitution of wordy paraphrases for simple sentences; and (3) its coloring of the text in various literary, psychological, and theological ways—all the while omitting some words and statements given in the Alexandrian text.[105] In 1581 Theodore Beza, who was John Calvin's friend, gave what became known as Codex D to the library of Cambridge University (thus its name Bezae Cantabrigiensis). Though it was known to contain a longer text of Acts than any other biblical manuscript, it was not published until 1793.

At first both the longer text of Codex D and the shorter, then extant texts were ascribed to Luke. The longer version was seen as having been written first and subsequently shortened and polished by Luke himself, with that latter version being the one sent to Theophilus. This view has had numerous defenders, including such notable scholars as J. B. Lightfoot, Friedrich Blass, Theodor Zahn, Eberhard Nestle, J. M. Wilson, and A. J. Wensinck. It has recently and most ably been revived, in somewhat revised form, by M.-E. Boismard and A. Lamouille, who argue that (1) Luke wrote a first edition of Acts, which finds echoes in the Western text; (2) later he thoroughly revised both the style and the content of his first edition to produce a second edition, which is now extinct; and (3) still later he fused those two editions into a single edition, which is what we now have, in the main, in the Alexandrian text.[106] Most text critics, however, have argued for the relationship between the Alexandrian and Western texts being the other way around: either (1) that the short form was the earliest form and that it was Luke himself who expanded it into the longer form (so George Salmon), or, as more commonly proposed, (2) that the longer text is the result of revisions and interpolations, whether haphazard or deliberate, which were made to Luke's original text by others during the first and second Christian centuries (so B. F. Westcott, F. J. A. Hort, Frederick G. Kenyon, Martin Dibelius, James Hardy Ropes, Eldon J. Epp, Bruce M. Metzger).[107]

The vast majority of text critics today are unwilling to ascribe the Western text of Acts to Luke. Its longer readings and alternative wordings seem to stem from a piety, outlook, and theological stance that differed somewhat from Luke's; its more substantive variant readings appear to have been inserted to correct various historical, biographical, or geographical details; and some of its minor deviations must be viewed simply as the product of scribal error. Joseph Fitzmyer aptly summarizes current scholarly opinion: "The thrust of the modern debate inclines one toward regarding the differences as a development from the shorter to the longer text, whether that be by haphazard interpolations or deliberate alterations, made later than the time of Luke himself, so that eventually a definite 'Western main redaction' emerged."[108]

---

105. For a history and convenient reproduction of the Western text, see the work of James H. Ropes in *Beginnings of Christianity* (vol. 3: *The Text of Acts*), ccxv–ccxlix; 1–255 (comparing Codex Vaticanus and Codex Bezae).

106. See M.-E. Boismard and A. Lamouille, *Le texte occidental des Acts des Apôtres: Reconstitution et Réhabilitation* (2 vols; Paris: Editions Recherche sur les Civilisations, 1984). See also M.-E. Boismard, "The Text of Acts: A Problem of Literary Criticism?" in *New Testament Textual Criticism: Its Significance for Exegesis*, ed. E. J. Epp and G. Fee (Oxford: Clarendon, 1981), 147–57.

107. Cf. Frederick G. Kenyon, "The Western Text in the Gospels and Acts," *Proceedings of the British Academy* 24 (1938): 287–315; Eldon J. Epp, *The Theological Tendency of Codex Bezae Cantabrigiensis in Acts* (SNTSMS 3; Cambridge: Cambridge Univ. Press, 1966), 1–21; K. Aland and B. Aland, *The Text of the New Testament* (Grand Rapids: Eerdmans, 1987), 95, 156–59.

108. Joseph A. Fitzmyer, *The Acts of the Apostles* (AB; New York: Doubleday, 1998), 72.

What follows in our exegesis will be a basic reliance on the Alexandrian text of Acts (Westcott and Hort call this the "Neutral" text). Some variant readings of the Byzantine and Western texts may merit a degree of consideration. In a few cases such readings will be argued to be probable rather than just possible. A mild form of "eclectic textual criticism" will be espoused, and variant readings from the Byzantine and Western traditions will be referred to in the commentary and the notes when considered important.

12. BIBLIOGRAPHY

The following is a selective list of commentaries and monographs on Acts available in English, confined for the most part to those referred to in the commentary (they will be referred to simply by the author's name, and initials only when necessary to distinguish two authors of the same surname). In instances where the same author has written a commentary as well as (a) book(s) and/or (an) article(s), the commentary will be referred to by the author's name, and the book(s)/article(s) by the author's name and short title.

References to resources that do not appear in the bibliography will carry full bibliographic details at the first mention and thereafter a short title.

For fuller listings, see *New Testament Abstracts*, published three times a year, which gives classified and annotated lists of commentaries, monographs, and articles in the field of NT studies from over 400 journals, commencing with materials published in 1956 and continuing to the present.

Barrett, C. Kingsley. *Luke the Historian in Recent Study*. London: Epworth, 1961. Repr., Philadelphia: Fortress, 1970.

Baur, Ferdinand Christian. *Paul Apostle of Jesus Christ: His Life and Works, His Epistles and Teachings*. 2 vols. Translated by E. Zeller. London: Williams & Norgate, 1846. Repr., Peabody, Mass.: Hendrickson, 2003.

Bruce, Frederick F. *The Book of the Acts: The English Text with Introduction, Exposition and Notes*. New International Commentary on the New Testament. Grand Rapids: Eerdmans, 1954. Repr., 1988.

Burkitt, F. Crawford. *Christian Beginnings*. London: University of London Press, 1924.

Cadbury, Henry J. *The Book of Acts in History*. London: Black, 1955.

De Waard, Jan. *A Comparative Study of the Old Testament Text in the Dead Sea Scrolls and in the New Testament*. Leiden: Brill, 1965.

Dibelius, Martin. *Studies in the Acts of the Apostles*. Translated by M. Ling. London: SCM, 1956.

Dix, Gregory. *Jew and Greek: A Study in the Primitive Church*. London: Dacre, 1953.

Dodd, C. H. *The Apostolic Preaching and Its Developments*. London: Hodder & Stoughton, 1936. Repr., New York: Harper, 1964.

Dupont, Jacques. *The Sources of Acts: The Present Position*. Translated by K. Pond. New York: Herder and Herder, 1964.

Ehrhardt, Arnold. *The Acts of the Apostles: Ten Lectures*. Manchester: Manchester Univ. Press, 1969.

Filson, Floyd V. *Three Crucial Decades: Studies in the Book of Acts*. Richmond, Va.: John Knox Press, 1963.

Fitzmyer, Joseph A. *The Acts of the Apostles: A New Translation with Introduction and Commentary*. Anchor Bible 31 (NS). New York: Doubleday, 1998.

Foakes-Jackson, F. J., and Kirsopp Lake, eds. *The Beginnings of Christianity: The Acts of the Apostles*. 5 vols. London: Macmillan, 1920–1933. Repr., Grand Rapids: Baker, 1979.

Haenchen, Ernst. *The Acts of the Apostles: A Commentary*. Translated by B. Noble et al. Philadelphia: Westminster, 1971.

Harnack, Adolf. *The Acts of the Apostles*. Crown Theological Library 27. Translated by J. R. Wilkinson. London: Williams & Norgate, 1909.

———. *Luke the Physician: The Author of the Third Gospel and the Acts of the Apostles*. Translated by J. R. Wilkinson. London: Williams & Norgate, 1907.

———. *The Date of the Acts and of the Synoptic Gospels*. Translated by J. R. Wilkinson. London: Williams & Norgate, 1911.

Jeremias, Joachim. *Jerusalem in the Time of Jesus*. Translated by F. H. and C. H. Cave. Philadelphia: Fortress, 1969.

Keck, Leander E., and J. Louis Martyn, eds. *Studies in Luke-Acts*. Nashville: Abingdon, 1966. Repr., Philadelphia: Fortress, 1980.

Lake, Kirsopp, and Henry J. Cadbury. "Acts of the Apostles: English Translation and Commentary." In *The Beginnings of Christianity: The Acts of the Apostles*. 5 vols. (See particularly vol. 4. 1–350.) Edited by F. J. Foakes-Jackson and K. Lake. London: Macmillan, 1920–33. Repr., Grand Rapids: Baker, 1979.

Longenecker, Richard N. *Paul, Apostle of Liberty*. New York: Harper & Row, 1964. Repr., Grand Rapids: Baker, 1976; Vancouver, B.C.: Regent College Publishing, 1993.

———. *Biblical Exegesis in the Apostolic Period*. Grand Rapids: Eerdmans, 1975. 2d ed., 1999.

———. *The Christology of Early Jewish Christianity*. Studies in Biblical Theology 2/17. London: SCM, 1970. Repr., Grand Rapids: Baker, 1981; Vancouver, B.C.: Regent College Publishing, 2001.

Martin, Raymond A. *Syntactical Evidence of Semitic Sources in Greek Documents*. Missoula, Mont.: Scholars Press, 1974.

Metzger, Bruce M. *A Textual Commentary on the Greek New Testament*. New York: United Bible Societies, 1971. Second Edition, 1994 (almost all references to Metzger are from this edition).

Munck, Johannes. *The Acts of the Apostles*. Anchor Bible 31. Garden City, N.Y.: Doubleday, 1967.

Ramsay, William M. *St. Paul the Traveller and the Roman Citizen*. London: Hodder & Stoughton, 1897.

———. *The Cities of St. Paul: Their Influence on His Life and Thought*. London: Hodder & Stoughton, 1907.

———. *The Bearing of Recent Discovery on the Trustworthiness of the New Testament*. London: Hodder & Stoughton, 1915.

Schürer, Emil. *A History of the Jewish People in the Time of Jesus Christ*. 5 vols. New York: Scribner's, 1896.

Simon, Marcel. *St. Stephen and the Hellenists in the Primitive Church*. London: Longmans, Green, 1958.

Stanton, Graham N. *Jesus of Nazareth in New Testament Preaching*. Cambridge: Cambridge Univ. Press, 1974.

Torrey, Charles C. *The Composition and Date of Acts*. Harvard Theological Studies 1. Cambridge, Mass.: Harvard Univ. Press, 1916.

Weiss, Johannes. *The History of Primitive Christianity*. Edited by F. C. Grant. New York: Wilson-Erickson, 1937. Repr. as *Earliest Christianity: A History of the Period AD 30–150*. 2 vols., with new introduction by F. C. Grant. Gloucester, Mass.: Smith, 1970.

Williams, Charles S. C. *A Commentary on the Acts of the Apostles*. Harper New Testament Commentary. New York: Harper, 1958. 2d ed., 1969.

13. OUTLINE

I. Resumptive Preface (1:1–5)

II. Introduction: The Constitutive Events of the Christian Mission (1:6–2:41)

   A. The Mandate to Witness (1:6–8)

   B. The Ascension (1:9–11)

   C. The Full Complement of Apostles (1:12–26)

     1. In the Upper Room (1:12–14)

     2. Matthias Chosen to Replace Judas Iscariot (1:15–26)

   D. The Coming of the Holy Spirit (2:1–41)

     1. The Miracle of Pentecost (2:1–13)

     2. Peter's Sermon at Pentecost (2:14–41)

       a. The *apologia* (2:14–21)

       b. The *kerygma* (2:22–36)

       c. A call to repentance and a promise of blessing (2:37–41)

III. Part I: The Christian Mission to the Jewish World (2:42–12:24)

   Panel 1—The Earliest Days of the Church at Jerusalem (2:42–6:7)

   A. Thesis Paragraph on the State of the Early Church (2:42–47)

   B. A Crippled Beggar Healed (3:1–26)

     1. The Healing (3:1–10)

     2. Peter's Sermon in Solomon's Colonnade (3:11–26)

   C. Peter and John before the Sanhedrin (4:1–31)

     1. The Arrest of Peter and John (4:1–7)

     2. Peter's Defense and Witness (4:8–12)

     3. The Apostles Warned and Released (4:13–22)

     4. The Church's Praise and Petition (4:23–31)

   D. Christian Concern Expressed in Sharing (4:32–5:11)

     1. Believers Share Their Possessions (4:32–35)

     2. The Generosity of Barnabas (4:36–37)

     3. The Deceit of Ananias and Sapphira (5:1–11)

   E. The Apostles Again before the Sanhedrin (5:12–42)

     1. Miraculous Signs and Wonders (5:12–16)

     2. The Arrest and Trial of the Apostles (5:17–33)

     3. Gamaliel's Wise Counsel of Moderation (5:34–40)

     4. The Apostles' Rejoicing and Continued Ministry (5:41–42)

   F. The Hellenists' Presence and Problem in the Church (6:1–6)

   G. *Summary Statement:* "So the word of God spread. The number of disciples in Jerusalem increased rapidly, and a large number of priests became obedient to the faith" (6:7).

   Panel 2—Critical Events in the Lives of Three Pivotal Figures (6:8–9:31)

F. Rome at Last (28:17–30)
  1. Meetings with the Jewish Leaders (28:17–28)
  2. Continued Ministry for Two Years (28:30)
G. *Summary Statement:* "Boldly and without hindrance he preached the kingdom of God and taught about the Lord Jesus Christ" (28:31).

14. MAP

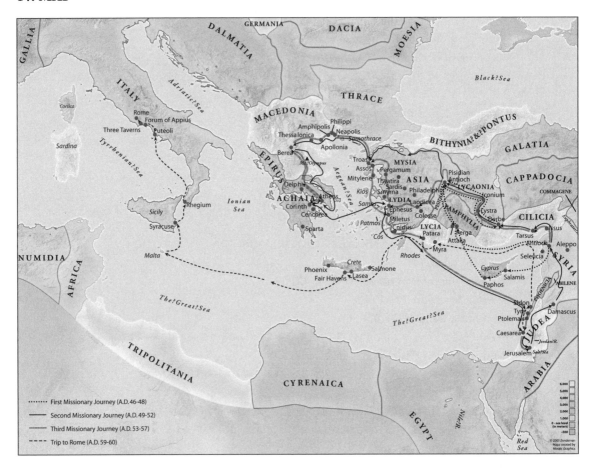

Text and Exposition

I. RESUMPTIVE PREFACE (1:1–5)

OVERVIEW

The prologue to Luke's two volumes is really Luke 1:1–4. Here, however, Luke begins his second volume with what may be called a "resumptive preface" that (1) links together the two volumes and (2) anticipates the features he wants to stress as being constitutive for the Christian mission.

> ¹In my former book, Theophilus, I wrote about all that Jesus began to do and to teach ²until the day he was taken up to heaven, after giving instructions through the Holy Spirit to the apostles he had chosen. ³After his suffering, he showed himself to these men and gave many convincing proofs that he was alive. He appeared to them over a period of forty days and spoke about the kingdom of God. ⁴On one occasion, while he was eating with them, he gave them this command: "Do not leave Jerusalem, but wait for the gift my Father promised, which you have heard me speak about. ⁵For John baptized with water, but in a few days you will be baptized with the Holy Spirit."

COMMENTARY

1 Luke calls his gospel "my former book" (*ton prōton logon*). The Greek article *ton* specifies an antecedent writing, and the suffix of the verb translated "I wrote" (*epoiēsamēn*, GK *4472*) calls for the possessive "my." The word *logos* (GK *3364*), usually translated "word" or "message" in the NT, is used here in the technical sense of a section of a work that covers more than one papyrus roll. The occurrence of the adjective *prōtos* ("first"; NIV, "former"), rather than its comparative *proteros* ("former," GK *4728*), need not imply that Luke intended his gospel to be the first in a series of three or more treatises, as Theodor Zahn and William M. Ramsay have supposed. While the classical usage of *proteros* as "former," as contrasted with "latter," is maintained by Josephus in the preface to Book 2 of his *Against Apion*—and also appears in the Pauline letters (cf. Gal 4:13; Eph 4:22; 1Ti 1:13)—Luke never uses *proteros*, which was rare in the nonliterary papyri of the day. Just as today we use "first" for "former" even when speaking about only two things, Luke should probably be understood as using *prōtos* as a comparative (cf. Ac 7:12) and without any implication that his work was intended to go beyond the two volumes.

The appearance of the article "the" (*ho*) with the name "Jesus" (*Iēsous*, GK *2652*)—which is the first occurrence of "Jesus" in Acts and so, according to Greek standards, would not call for an article—probably stems from the original union of Luke's two volumes and thus functions to bring to the reader's mind the content of his gospel. The scribes

713

of codices B and D, which are the only two manuscripts of Acts that omit the article, probably chose to omit it since (1) in their time the third gospel and Acts were treated as separate compositions, and (2) the first occurrence of a name or proper noun in a Greek writing did not require an article.

Luke says that the subject of his first volume is "*all* that Jesus began to do and to teach" up to his ascension. Throughout his two volumes Luke uses "all" (*pas*) as a general expression, which the context in each case must define. So we cannot assume he meant his gospel to be any more exhaustive than his Acts. In a number of places in the NT the terms "all" (*pas/pantes*) and "many" (*polloi*) are used interchangeably (e.g., Mk 1:32–34 // Mt 8:16; Mk 10:45 // Mt 20:28 [cf. 1Ti 2:6]; Mk 3:10 // Mt 12:15; Ro 5:12–21), with the context determining the precise nuance.

"To do" (*poieō*, GK 4472) and "to teach" (*didaskō*, GK 1438) describe the nature of the third gospel, combining as it does Mark's narrative about what Jesus did and material from the "Sayings" source or "Q" (*Quelle*, which means "source" in German) about what Jesus taught. The verb "began" (*ērxato*, GK 806), while used as something of a redundant auxiliary verb elsewhere in Acts (cf. 2:4; 11:4, 15; 18:26; 24:2; 27:35), probably appears here for emphasis, much as it does in 11:15. As such, it serves to highlight Luke's intent to show in Acts what Jesus *continued* to do and to teach through his church, just as in his gospel he had previously presented "all that Jesus *began* to do and to teach."

Acts, like the third gospel, is addressed to Theophilus, who is called "most excellent Theophilus" (*kratiste Theophile*) in Luke 1:3. The adjective *kratistos* (GK 3196) is used elsewhere in Acts when addressing the Roman governors Felix and Festus (cf. 23:26; 24:3; 26:25). This has suggested to some that the word should be seen as an honorific title for a highly placed Roman official. But it

was often also used as a form of polite address, which is probably how Luke used it of Theophilus. Origen (AD 185–254), and many others after him, treated the name Theophilus etymologically (i.e., *theos* + *philos* = "Friend of God" or "Loved by God") and so have understood "Theophilus" as a symbolic designation for an anonymous person or a class of people. Such a supposition is precarious. Theophilus occurs as a proper name at least three centuries before Luke, and the practice of dedicating books to distinguished persons was common in his day.

2 The Greek of v.2 is awkward, chiefly because of the unnatural separation of "he was taken up" (*anelēmphthē*, GK 377) at the end of the verse from "until the day" (*achri hēs hēmeras*, GK 2465) at its beginning, and because it separates "[whom] he had chosen" (*hous exelexato*, GK 1721) from "the apostles" (*tois apostolois*, GK 693). But the awkwardness was evidently intentional. Through such a word order Luke has, in effect, highlighted four important introductory matters in his first two chapters and signaled his priorities throughout the rest of his presentation in Acts.

By placing the adverbial participle *enteilamenos* ("after giving instructions," GK 1948) up front in the sentence, Luke lays emphasis on Jesus' mandate to witness. The instructions he has in mind are undoubtedly those already set out in Luke 24:48–49 as the climax of Jesus' earthly teaching: "You are witnesses of these things. I am going to send you what my Father has promised; but stay in the city until you have been clothed with power from on high." In slightly revised form, Luke quotes these instructions in Acts 1:4–5 and develops them in 1:6–8 as the theme of Acts. Apparently Luke also wanted to show through the word order of v.2 that (1) Jesus' mandate to witness (2) was given to the apostles, (3) who acted through the power of the Holy Spirit, (4) whose coming was a direct result of our Lord's ascension. Each of these four factors— the mandate to witness, the apostles, the Holy Spirit, and the ascended Lord—is a major emphasis that runs throughout Acts, and each receives special attention in chs. 1 and 2.

3 Having stated the relation of his present volume to its predecessor and shown his interest in the four factors named above—which, as will be noted, comprise the constitutive elements of the Christian mission—Luke turns back to the time before Jesus' ascension. He will reiterate and expand certain features in Jesus' ministry that are crucial to the advance of the gospel as presented in Acts. In view of v.2, this is slightly redundant. But Luke wants to be very explicit. Like the confessional material and Paul's comments in 1 Corinthians 15:5–7, Luke's emphasis is on the living Christ, who "after his suffering . . . showed himself . . . alive" and demonstrated his resurrection by "many convincing proofs." The expression "many convincing proofs" doubtless has in mind such things as the events of Luke 24:13–52. "Over a period of forty days" implies that during that time the risen Lord showed himself at intervals, not continuously. When he did so, he "spoke about the kingdom of God."

The theme of "the kingdom of God" (*hē basileia* [GK *993*] *tou theou*) is a common one in the OT and NT. It refers primarily to God's sovereign rule in human life and the affairs of history, and secondarily to the realm where that rule takes place. God's sovereignty is universal (cf. Ps 103:19). But it was specially manifested in the life of the nation Israel and among Jesus' disciples; it is expressed progressively in the church and through the lives of Christians; and it will be fully revealed throughout eternity. In the Gospels the kingdom is presented as having been inaugurated in time and space by Jesus' presence and ministry (cf. Mk 1:15: "The time has come. . . .The kingdom of God is near. Repent and believe the good news!"—with the expression "the

kingdom of heaven" being Matthew's reverential form of the same idea adapted to Jewish sensibilities). In Acts "the kingdom of God" usually appears as a convenient way of summarizing the content of the earliest Christian preaching (cf. 8:12; 19:8; 20:25; 28:23, 31). And in this proclamation by the early Christians Jesus is explicitly identified as the subject (cf. 8:12; 28:23, 31).

We may infer that Jesus' teaching during those "forty days" dealt, in essence, with (1) the validation and nature of his messiahship, (2) the interpretation of the OT from the perspective of his resurrection, and (3) the responsibility of his disciples to bear witness to what had happened among them in fulfillment of Israel's hope. This is what Luke 24:25–27, 44–49 reveal as the content of Jesus' post-resurrection teaching, and this is what Acts elaborates in what follows.

4 In vv.4–5 Luke parallels his emphasis on the living Christ by stressing the coming and baptism of the Holy Spirit as being essential to the advance of the gospel. Luke gives us an individualized scene (so NIV's inserted connective, "on one occasion") of Jesus and his disciples eating together at the time when he commanded them not to leave Jerusalem but to wait for the coming of the Holy Spirit, who had been promised by God the Father and spoken of by Jesus. The command not to leave Jerusalem is a repetition of the one in Luke 24:49, with *Hierosolyma* (GK *2642*), the hellenized name for Jerusalem, being used. This breaks the usual pattern in Acts, where *Ierousalēm* (GK *2647*) appears exclusively in chs. 1–7 (cf. 1:8, 12, 19; 2:5, 14; 4:5, 16; 5:16, 28; 6:7) and is always on the lips of those whose native tongue was Aramaic. "The gift my Father promised" also repeats Luke 24:49 and is defined in v.5: "You will be baptized with the Holy Spirit." It is a promise Jesus made on behalf of the Father. Its tradition has been incorporated in John's gospel (cf. Jn 14:16–21, 26; 15:26–27; 16:7–15).

5 The statement "you will be baptized with the Holy Spirit" appears to come from Mark 1:8, with parallels in Matthew 3:11 and Luke 3:16 (which add "and with fire"), where it is part of John the Baptist's message. One might take v.5 as an explanatory comment on Luke's part, but its parallel in Acts 11:16, where it is given as a statement of Jesus, suggests that here too it should be understood as a word of Jesus. It may be that the transferal of the *logion* ("saying") from the Baptist to the lips of Jesus occurred in the early church before Luke wrote Acts. But this seems doubtful, for the saying is commonly attributed to John the Baptist in the synoptic tradition (including Luke's gospel). The ascription of the statement to Jesus, therefore, is probably Luke's own doing. This need not be considered strange, particularly for an author who can quote the same *logion* of Jesus in two such diverse forms and in two so closely connected passages as Luke 24:49 and Acts 1:4.

The Spirit is the dynamo of all that Luke presents regarding God's working in and through his church. As in Luke's first volume, so in his second volume: there are only a few places in Acts where the Spirit's activity and influence are not in some way evident. "Thus," as Fitzmyer, 193, aptly reminds us, "Acts presents the sequel to the Jesus-story of the Lucan Gospel and stresses the continuity between what was begun in the earthly ministry of Jesus and the Christian church, initiated by the risen Christ's instruction of the apostles through the Holy Spirit."

NOTES

1 Cf. *Ag. Ap.* 1.1, where Josephus's patron Epaphroditus is addressed as κράτιστε ἀνδρῶν Ἐπαφρόδιτε (*kratiste andrōn Epaphrodite*, "most excellent of men Epaphroditus"), and *Ag. Ap.* 2.1, where he is addressed as τιμιώτατέ μοι Ἐπαφρόδιτε (*timiōtate moi Epaphrodite*, "my most esteemed Epaphroditus"), with the expressions evidently used interchangeably as terms of polite address.

2 On the stylistic difficulties, which several forms of the Western text attempted to smooth out but which are "inherent in the narrative itself," see Metzger, 273–77.

3 For the idea of "continuously throughout the period," the accusative without a preposition would have been used rather than δι᾽ ἡμερῶν τεσσεράκοντα (*di' hēmerōn tesserakonta*, "over forty days"). This is the only place in the NT where the length of Jesus' postresurrection ministry is mentioned.

Acts 14:22 clearly has only a futuristic sense of "the kingdom of God" in view. In all other passages in Acts beyond 1:3, however, while a future aspect may also be involved, Luke uses "the kingdom of God" in evangelistic settings as a shorthand way of speaking about the entire Christian proclamation that focuses in the work and person of Jesus (cf. Stanton, 17–18).

4 The temporal adverbial participle συναλιζόμενος (*synalizomenos*, GK *5259*), which is supported by all the uncial MSS (except possibly D), builds on the noun ἅλς (*hals*, "salt," GK *265*) and means "while eating [salt] together with someone"—or more generally, "while eating with someone." The rendering "while spending the night with" or "staying with" (NRSV; see NASB text note), understanding the "a" (alpha) as long rather than short, has often been conjectured but remains unproven. Luke speaks of Jesus' eating with his disciples during these forty days (Lk 24:42–43; Ac 10:41). The word is used for the evening meal in the Pseudo-Clementine *Homilies* 13:4 and *Recognitions* 7:2.

The name Ἰερουσαλήμ (Ierousalēm, "Jerusalem"), the Hebraic name that has sacred connotations, occurs in the NT seventy-six times, while Ἱεροσόλυμα (Hierosolyma, "Jerusalem"), the secular designation for the city—used more by non-Jewish writers and by Jews addressing a Greek-speaking audience—occurs in the NT sixty-three times. The authors of Hebrews and Revelation always use Ierousalēm, for they are speaking of the heavenly and eschatological city. Mark and John, however, never use the more sacred form. Luke usually reworks Mark's Hierosolyma to Ierousalēm in his gospel (using Hierosolyma only four times and Ierousalēm twenty-six times) and continues to use Ierousalēm in Acts 1–7. From Acts 8 on he uses both forms without much distinction: Ierousalēm occurs thirty-nine times throughout Acts, and Hierosolyma occurs twenty-five times. Here, however, we have the exception to the usual pattern found in Acts 1–7.

II. INTRODUCTION: THE CONSTITUTIVE EVENTS OF THE CHRISTIAN MISSION (1:6–2:41)

OVERVIEW

The structural parallelism between Luke's gospel and his Acts is immediately seen in the comparative size of the two volumes and the time spans they cover. Each would have filled an almost equal-sized papyrus roll, and each covers approximately thirty-three years—though, of course, the gospel is somewhat longer and more controlled by existing traditions within the church. The parallelism is also evident in the plan and purpose of the opening chapters of each volume. Luke 1:5–2:52 (i.e., after the prologue of 1:1–4) is essentially a preparation for 3:1–4:13, and together these sections constitute material introductory to the narrative of Jesus' ministry that begins with the pericope of 4:14–30. So, too, Acts 1:6–26 (i.e., after its preface of 1:1–5) serves to prepare for 2:1–41, and together these sections comprise an introduction to the ministry of the church that commences with the thesis paragraph 2:42–47 and continues by means of a series of illustrative vignettes beginning at 3:1.

A. The Mandate to Witness (1:6–8)

OVERVIEW

Though 1:6–8 is usually treated either as the last part of the preface (1:1–8) or as an introduction to the ascension narrative (1:6–11), in reality it serves as the theme of Acts and sets the stage for all that follows: "You will be my witnesses in Jerusalem, and in all Judea and Samaria, and to the ends of the earth" (v.8). The concept of "witness" is so prominent in Acts (the word in its various forms appears some thirty-nine times) that everything else in the book should probably be seen as subsumed under it—even the primitive kerygma, which, at least since C. H. Dodd's *The Apostolic Preaching and Its Developments* (1936), many have thought to be the leading theme of Acts. So as Luke begins his second volume he highlights this witness theme and insists it comes from the mandate of Jesus himself.

⁶So when they met together, they asked him, "Lord, are you at this time going to restore the kingdom to Israel?"

⁷He said to them: "It is not for you to know the times or dates the Father has set by his own authority. ⁸But you will receive power when the Holy Spirit comes on you; and you will be my witnesses in Jerusalem, and in all Judea and Samaria, and to the ends of the earth."

COMMENTARY

6 The expression *men oun* (NIV, "so") is a favorite connective of Luke's used sometimes, as here, in beginning a new pericope (e.g., 8:4; 11:19; 12:5), at other times in conclusions (e.g., 2:41; 5:41; 8:25; 9:31; 16:5), and frequently within a narrative to tie its various parts together. The question the disciples asked reflects the embers of a once-blazing hope for a political theocracy in which they would be leaders (cf. Mk 9:33–34; 10:35–41; Lk 22:24). Now the embers are fanned by Jesus' talk of the coming Holy Spirit. In Jewish expectations, the restoration of Israel's fortunes would be marked by the renewed activity of God's Spirit, which had been withheld since the last of the prophets. But though his words about the Spirit's coming rekindled in the disciples their old nationalistic hopes, Jesus had something else in mind.

7 Jesus' answer to his disciples' misguided question is not a denial of a place for the nation of Israel in God's future purposes. Paul speaks in Romans 9–11 not only of a remnant within Israel responding to God but also of the nation of Israel still being involved in some way in God's redemptive program (11:15–16) and being "saved" in the future (11:25–29). Luke's presentation of Jesus' words here is not in opposition to that. Jesus' answer does, however, stress that the disciples were to revise their thinking about the divine program, leave to God the matters that are his concern, and take up the things entrusted to them.

Jesus' insistence that "it is not for you to know" echoes his teaching in Matthew 24:36 and Mark 13:32, which Luke did not include in his gospel either in 17:22–37 or 21:5–36—evidently preferring to hold that aspect of Jesus' eschatological message for this place in Acts. The "times" (*chronoi*, GK 5989) and "dates" (*kairoi*, GK 2789; i.e., specific "dates" or "periods") refer, it seems, to (1) the character of the ages preceding the final consummation of God's redemptive program and (2) the particular, critical stages of these ages as they draw to a climax (cf. 1Th 5:1). These "the Father has set by his own authority" and are not to be the subject of speculation by believers—sadly, a teaching that has all too often been disregarded.

8 The mandate to witness that stands as the theme for the whole of Acts is here explicitly set out. It comes as a direct commission from Jesus himself—in fact, as Jesus' last word before his ascension and, therefore, as a mandate that is final and conclusive. All that follows in Acts is shown to be the result of Jesus' own intent and the fulfillment of his express word.

This commission lays an obligation on all Christians and comes as a gift with a promise. It concerns a person, a power, and a program—the person of Jesus, on whose authority the church acts and who is the object of its witness; the power of the Holy Spirit, which is the sine qua non for the mission; and a program that begins at Jerusalem, moves out to "all Judea and Samaria," and extends "to the ends of the earth." The Christian church, according to Acts, (1) is a missionary church that responds obediently to Jesus' commission, (2) acts on Jesus' behalf in the extension of his ministry, (3) focuses its proclamation of the kingdom of God in its witness to Jesus, (4) is guided and empowered by the very same Spirit that directed and supported Jesus' ministry, and (5) follows a program whose guidelines for outreach have been set by Jesus himself.

Whereas the geographical movement of Luke's gospel was from Galilee through Perea to Jerusalem, in Acts the movement is from Jerusalem through "Judea and Samaria" and on to Rome. The joining of Judea and Samaria by one article in the Greek (*en pasē tē Ioudaia kai Samareia*, "in all Judea and Samaria") suggests a single geographical area that can be designated by its two ethnological divisions.

And the fact that neither Galilee nor Perea is included in 1:8 as a place to be evangelized (even though 9:31 speaks in summary fashion of a growing church in "Judea, Galilee and Samaria") is probably because Luke has already shown in his gospel how Jesus had earlier evangelized those areas. So here Jesus' mandate to witness not only gives us the theme of Acts but also a basic table of contents by its threefold reference to "Jerusalem," "all Judea and Samaria," and "the ends of the earth." To be sure, Luke's development is fuller and subtler than its succinct form here. Nevertheless, in what follows he shows through a series of vignettes how the mission of the church in its witness to Jesus fared at Jerusalem (2:42–8:3), throughout Judea and Samaria (8:4–12:24), and as it progressed until it finally reached the imperial capital city of Rome (12:25–28:31).

NOTES

6 The other instances of μὲν οὖν (*men oun*, "so," "then") in Acts are 1:18; 2:41; 5:41; 8:4, 25; 9:31; 11:19; 12:5; 13:4; 14:3; 15:3, 30; 16:5; 17:12, 17, 30; 19:32, 38; 23:18, 22, 31; 25:4, 11; 26:4, 9; 28:5. Where Luke worked more from written sources (the first half of Acts), he used, it seems, μὲν οὖν, *men oun*, in his redactional introductions and conclusions to tie the units of material together. Where he wrote more on the basis of verbal reports and personal reminiscences (the second half of Acts), he used the expression within his narrative to connect the various parts of the account.

7 The expression ἐν τῇ ἰδίᾳ εξουσίᾳ (*en tē idia exousia*, "by his own authority") is best understood as an instrumental use of the dative, not a locative.

8 Luke's stress on the importance of the Spirit in the ministry of Jesus and in the mission of the church can readily, though somewhat mechanically, be seen by noting the comparative frequency of πνεῦμα (*pneuma*, "spirit," GK 4460) in the Gospels and Acts: nineteen times in Matthew, twenty-three times in Mark, thirty-six times in Luke, twenty-four times in John, and seventy times in Acts—though, admittedly, some of these occurrences refer to the human spirit (e.g., Ac 17:16) or even to unclean spirits (e.g., Lk 4:33; 6:18).

The preposition ἐν (*en*, "in") before both "Jerusalem" and "Judea and Samaria" is typical of Semitic style and so is carried on in the Alexandrian text. Its omission before "Judea and Samaria" in Byzantine and Western texts was probably because later Greek scribes felt its repetition to be unidiomatic.

B. The Ascension (1:9–11)

OVERVIEW

Luke next speaks of the second constitutive factor of the Christian mission: the church's ascended Lord. The Greek of v.2 includes this as a fourth element in its logical listing of constitutive factors, but here Luke is proceeding more chronologically. So he speaks of the ascension of Jesus before mentioning the full complement of apostles and the coming of the Holy Spirit. The ascension has earlier been referred to in Luke 24:50–51 and Acts 1:2. Many have questioned the appropriateness of three references to it, but each occurrence has its own purpose in Luke's writing.

Here the important thing is that attention is focused on (1) the fact of Jesus' ascension and entrance "into heaven" (*eis ton ouranon* [GK *4041*]), which is an expression repeated four times in vv.10–11, and (2) the angel's message that rebukes the disciples for their lack of understanding and assures them of their Lord's return. There is no explanation of how the ascension occurred or of the psychological state of the disciples—features so common to legendary development. Nor are there any apocalyptic details like those in Luke 17:22–37 (also perhaps Lk 21) as to when that return might be expected. "The story," as Haenchen, 151, has observed, "is unsentimental, almost uncannily austere." Luke's point is that the missionary activity of the early church rested not only on Jesus' mandate but also on his living presence in heaven and the sure promise of his return.

Many modern scholars have asserted that looking for the Parousia invariably paralyzes missionary activity and inhibits Christian social action by diverting attention away from present needs to the "sweet by-and-by," and so it must be postulated that the early church only turned to missions when it had to renounce its futuristic eschatology. Nevertheless, in Acts 1:9–11 Luke insists that Christian mission must be based on the ascended and living Lord, who directs his church from heaven and who will return to consummate what he has begun. Thus, rather than the missionary enterprise being a stopgap measure substituted by subapostolic Christian theologians for the unrealized hope of the kingdom of God, Luke's position is, as Oscar Cullmann ("Eschatology and Mission in the New Testament," in *The Background of the New Testament and Its Eschatology*, ed. W. D. Davies and D. Daube [Cambridge: Cambridge Univ. Press, 1964], 409) aptly expressed it, "that 'missions' are an essential element in the eschatological divine plan of salvation. The missionary work of the Church is the eschatological foretaste of the Kingdom of God, and the Biblical hope of the 'end' constitutes the keenest incentive to action."

[9]After he said this, he was taken up before their very eyes, and a cloud hid him from their sight.

[10]They were looking intently up into the sky as he was going, when suddenly two men dressed in white stood beside them. [11]"Men of Galilee," they said, "why do you stand here looking into the sky? This same Jesus, who has been taken from you into heaven, will come back in the same way you have seen him go into heaven."

COMMENTARY

9 In speaking of Jesus' ascension, Luke uses the single Greek verb *epērthē* ("he was taken up," GK 2048). He tells us very little else about the ascension except that it occurred after Jesus had given his mandate to witness and while the disciples were watching. Not even the place where the ascension occurred is mentioned in v.9, though in v.12 Luke says it took place on the Mount of Olives. More important for Luke than a description of Jesus' ascension was its significance, and this he gives us in saying that "a cloud hid him from their sight."

The cloud is undoubtedly meant to symbolize the *shekinah*—the visible manifestation of the divine presence and glory. Such a cloud hovered above the tabernacle in the wilderness as a visible token of the glory of God that dwelt within the tabernacle (cf. Ex 40:34). Such a cloud also enveloped Jesus and three of his disciples on the Mount of Transfiguration as a visible sign of God's presence and approval of his Son (cf. Mk 9:7 par.). And something very similar is presented here: Jesus as the ascended Lord is enveloped by the *shekinah* cloud, the visible manifestation of God's presence, glory, and approval.

10 Luke describes the disciples as "looking intently up into the sky as he was going." The word translated "to look intently" (*atenizō*, GK 867) is a favorite of Luke's, who uses it in twelve of its fourteen NT occurrences mainly, it seems, for dramatic effect. So it is probably illegitimate to read too much into *atenizō* with regard to the psychological state of the disciples. Some of them might have expected the cloud to dissipate and leave their Lord standing with them alone, as on the Mount of Transfiguration. Or perhaps they thought he would return momentarily. Some might have been in an attitude of worship. Probably most of them, however, were simply awestruck by the sight. But they were soon challenged by the message of the two angels "dressed in white."

11 The angels' message was twofold: (1) that the Jesus whom the disciples had known has now a heavenly existence (note the double use in this verse of the phrase "into heaven," which tends to lay emphasis on the idea), and (2) that the Jesus whom they had known would return "in the same way" as they saw him go into heaven. The use of the intensive demonstrative pronoun *houtos* ("this same") speaks of the identity between the ascended Jesus and the Jesus yet to come, while the expression *hon tropon* ("in the same way") refers to his being enveloped at his future coming, as at his ascension, in the *shekinah* cloud of divine presence and glory. See Jesus' description of his Parousia in the Olivet Discourse (Mt 24:30; Mk 13:26; cf. Lk 21:27) and his reply to Caiaphas at his trial (Mt 26:64; Mk 14:62).

NOTES

9 The Western text (D, and as represented by the Syriac Sahidic version and Augustine) has the cloud envelop Jesus while he is still standing on the ground, thereby making a more exact parallel with the depictions of the transfiguration narratives (cf. Mt 17:5; Mk 9:7; Lk 9:34).

10 On the use of ἀτενίζω (*atenizō*, "look intently" or "gaze"), see Luke 4:20; 22:56; Acts 3:4, 12; 6:15; 7:55; 10:4; 11:6; 13:9; 14:9; 23:1 (cf. 2Co 3:7, 13; 3 Macc 2:26; Josephus, *J.W.* 5.517).

On the white garb of heavenly beings, see Matthew 28:3; Mark 16:5; Luke 24:4; John 20:12 (cf. 2 Macc 11:8; also Jesus' transfigured appearance in Mt 17:2; Mk 9:3; Lk 9:29)—though, of course, others also wore white as a sign of holiness (cf. 1QpMic 8–10; CD 6:2–11; 7:9–20, where "Lebanon" stands for the communal council since *laben* means "white," and the council dressed in white).

11 The third of the four occurrences of the phrase εἰς τὸν οὐρανόν (*eis ton ouranon*, "into the heaven") in vv.10–11 is omitted by Codex Bezae (D), a few minuscules (33 242 326), and several Old Latin recensions. But as Metzger, 245, points out, it is "more likely that the words were accidentally omitted than deliberately inserted in a context which was already liberally supplied with instances of the same phrase."

C. The Full Complement of Apostles (1:12–26)

OVERVIEW

Luke's third factor underlying the rise and expansion of the early Christian mission is the centrality of the apostles and their ministry. His interest in the apostles was evident in ch. 6 of his gospel, where in reporting Jesus' choosing of his twelve disciples he alone among the evangelists adds, "whom he also designated apostles" (Lk 6:13). Now he resumes that interest by telling how under God's direction the apostolic band regained its full number after the defection of Judas Iscariot.

Structurally, there is an intermingling of early source material and Luke's editorial comments, with the seams between the two being more obvious than in many other passages in Acts. These early materials and the evangelist's own comments are combined as follows: (1) the basic Christian tradition regarding the selection of Matthias, which is set out in two places (vv.15–17, 21–26); (2) Luke's introduction to the entire pericope (vv.12–14); (3) the evangelist's short comment at the end of v.15; and (4) his longer and particularly obvious comment in vv.18–19. Luke's writing in Acts is usually so artistic as to make it almost impossible to separate his editorial comments from his source material. Here, however, the different strands are apparent.

1. In the Upper Room (1:12–14)

[12]Then they returned to Jerusalem from the hill called the Mount of Olives, a Sabbath day's walk from the city. [13]When they arrived, they went upstairs to the room where they were staying. Those present were Peter, John, James and Andrew; Philip and Thomas, Bartholomew and Matthew; James son of Alphaeus and Simon the Zealot, and Judas son of James. [14]They all joined together constantly in prayer, along with the women and Mary the mother of Jesus, and with his brothers.

COMMENTARY

12 The disciples had been instructed by Jesus to "stay in the city [of Jerusalem] until you have been clothed with power from on high" (Lk 24:49). They were "not [to] leave Jerusalem, but wait for the gift my Father promised" (Ac 1:4) and begin their witness "at Jerusalem" (Lk 24:47; Ac 1:8). So they returned to Jerusalem from the Mount of Olives, a distance Luke speaks of as being "a Sabbath day's walk from the city." The Mishnah tells us that travel on the Sabbath was limited to two thousand cubits (*m. Soṭah* 5:3), which would have been about eleven hundred meters (see NIV text note). We may therefore estimate that their journey from the place of the ascension back to Jerusalem was a bit over a kilometer, or about 3/4 mile.

13 Upper rooms in Palestinian cities were usually the choicest rooms because they were above the tumult of the crowded streets and beyond the prying eyes of passersby. For the wealthy, the upper room was the living room. Sometimes upper rooms were rented out. Often they served as places of assembly, study, and prayer (cf. Str-B, 2.594).

On their return to Jerusalem, the disciples "went upstairs to the [upper] room where they were staying." The use of the definite article in speaking of "the [upper] room" (*to hyperōon*; NASB, "the upper room," GK *5673*) and the emphatic place these words have at the beginning of the clause suggest that the room was well known to the early Christians. Perhaps it was the room where Jesus and his disciples kept the Passover just before his crucifixion (Mk 14:12–16 par.), or perhaps the room where he appeared to some of them after he rose from the dead (Lk 24:33–43; cf. Jn 20:19, 26). Or, though this is even more inferential, it may have been a room in the house of Mary, John Mark's mother, where the church later met (Ac 12:12).

Luke has already listed the names of the Twelve in his gospel (cf. Lk 6:14–16). Now he lists them again, though of course without Judas Iscariot. This is another instance of parallelism in Luke's writings. Here, however, the list points to the incompleteness of the apostolic band and sets the stage for the account of its rectification through the choosing of Matthias. All this prepares for the coming of the Holy Spirit and the beginning of the apostolic ministry. In obedience to their Lord and in anticipation of what is to follow, the apostles have returned to Jerusalem, only now they lack the full complement needed for their witness within the Jewish community.

14 In addition to the Eleven, there were also present in the upper room "the women and Mary the mother of Jesus, and . . . his brothers." They fill out the nucleus of the early church and are to be included in the apostolic witness. Reference to "the women" undoubtedly has in mind those mentioned in Luke's gospel (8:2–3; 23:49; 23:55–24:10)—the women who followed Jesus throughout his ministry, even to his death, and contributed out of their personal incomes to support him and his followers.

Codex Bezae (D) reads "their wives and children" (*tais gynaixin kai teknois*, paralleling Ac 21:5), presumably those of the apostles, and so minimizes the independent activity of women in the early church. But Luke's mention of "the women" fully accords with the attitude toward women portrayed in his gospel, which attitude in turn reflects the consciousness within the early church of the implications of the gospel's proclamation. So the Western text must be viewed as unnecessarily restrictive.

The reference to "Mary the mother of Jesus" continues Luke's interest in Mary begun in ch. 1 of his gospel, though this is the last occasion where she is recorded as being involved in the redemptive history of the NT. The reference to Jesus'"brothers" (*adelphoi*, GK *81*) is particularly interesting, for Mark 3:21–35 shows that during his ministry they thought him to be "out of his mind," perhaps even demon-possessed, and John 7:2–10 presupposes their disbelief. Paul, however, recounts an appearance of the risen Christ to James (cf. 1Co 15:7), and we may infer that Joses (or Joseph), Judas (or Jude), and Simon (cf. Mt 13:55–56; Mk 6:3) likewise came to believe in Jesus and attached themselves to the congregation of early Christians. These all are depicted as being assiduous in prayer, with the articular expression "the prayer" (*tē proseuchē*, GK *4666*) suggesting an appointed service in the Jewish practice of prayer (cf. Ac 2:42; 6:4). There must also have been others who were at various times with the Eleven, the women, Mary, and Jesus' brothers in that upper room, for Acts 1:15 speaks of the total number of believers at the selection of Matthias as being "about a hundred and twenty."

NOTES

13 The listing of disciples in Luke 6:14–16 is generally in line with Matthew 10:2–4 and Mark 3:16–19, though with two notable exceptions: (1) Luke identifies the tenth in his listing as Σίμωνα τὸν καλούμενον Ζηλωτὴν (*Simōna ton kaloumenon Zēlōtēn*, "Simon who was called the Zealot"), whereas Matthew and Mark speak of the eleventh in their listings as Σίμωνα τὸν Καναναῖον (*Simōna ton Kananaion*, "Simon the Cananaean" [see NASB text note]; and (2) Luke lists Ἰούδαν Ἰακώβου (*Ioudan Iakōbou*, "Judas son of James") as the eleventh. Matthew and Mark do not mention a Judas other than Judas Iscariot, and they refer to a Thaddaeus (or, variously in other MS traditions, to a "Lebbaeus," or a "Lebbaeus called Thaddaeus," or a "Thaddaeus called Labbaeus") as the tenth disciple. But as H.-C. Hahn (*NIDNTT* 3.1167) observed, "*Kananaios* may translate Aram. *qan'an*, zealot," which Matthew and Mark simply transliterated as "Cananean" and Luke translated by the Greek term ζηλωτής, *zēlōtēs*, which means "zealot." And the words Θαδδαῖος (*Thaddaios*) and Λεββαῖος (*Lebbaios*) convey nuances of "breast" or "heart," which may have been used as epithets or nicknames in early Christian tradition. C. E. B. Cranfield (*The Gospel According to St. Mark* [Cambridge: Cambridge Univ. Press, 1963], 132) is probably right in saying, "Possibly Judas is the correct name, and Thaddaeus or Lebbaeus an additional name or nickname."

The reference in John 14:22 to a disciple named "Judas (not Judas Iscariot)" tends to support Luke's reference to another who was called "Judas son of James" (Lk 6:16). The variations in the ordering of the Synoptic Gospels with respect to the placing of Andrew (fourth in Mark; second in Matthew and Luke), of Matthew and Thomas (seventh and eighth respectively in Mark and Luke; eighth and seventh in Matthew), and of Thaddaeus/James and Simon (tenth and eleventh respectively in Mark and Matthew; eleventh and tenth in Luke) seem inconsequential and follow no discernible pattern. They probably result only from personal preference in passing on the traditions, as do Luke's variations of order in Acts 1:13 from that already given by him in Luke 6:14–16.

14 The reference to τοῖς ἀδελφοῖς αυτου (*tois adelphois autou*, "his brothers") is most naturally taken as referring to uterine brothers of Jesus. In defense of the doctrine of the perpetual virginity of Mary, it was early argued that "his brothers" were either half brothers of Jesus (the sons of Joseph by an earlier marriage) or his first cousins (the sons of Alphaeus by Mary of Clopas, who was the sister of Mary the mother of Jesus, as inferred, erroneously it seems, from Jn 19:25).

Codices B C³ and E, together with most minuscules, have the preposition σύν (*syn*, "with") before τοῖς ἀδελφοῖς αὐτοῦ (*tois adelphois autou*, "his brothers"), which is incorporated by the Textus Receptus and translated by the KJV. But since the preposition seems to separate Jesus from his brothers, it is, as Metzger, 246–47, observes, "suspect as a scribal addition made in the interest of supporting the perpetual virginity of Mary."

2. Matthias Chosen to Replace Judas Iscariot (1:15–26)

[15]In those days Peter stood up among the believers (a group numbering about a hundred and twenty) [16]and said, "Brothers, the Scripture had to be fulfilled which the Holy Spirit spoke long ago through the mouth of David concerning Judas, who served as guide for those who arrested Jesus—[17]he was one of our number and shared in this ministry."

[18](With the reward he got for his wickedness, Judas bought a field; there he fell headlong, his body burst open and all his intestines spilled out. [19]Everyone in Jerusalem heard about this, so they called that field in their language Akeldama, that is, Field of Blood.)

[20]"For," said Peter, "it is written in the book of Psalms,

"'May his place be deserted;
   let there be no one to dwell in it,'

and,

"'May another take his place of leadership.'

[21]Therefore it is necessary to choose one of the men who have been with us the whole time the Lord Jesus went in and out among us, [22]beginning from John's baptism to the time when Jesus was taken up from us. For one of these must become a witness with us of his resurrection."

[23]So they proposed two men: Joseph called Barsabbas (also known as Justus) and Matthias. [24]Then they prayed, "Lord, you know everyone's heart. Show us which of these two you have chosen [25]to take over this apostolic ministry, which Judas left to go where he belongs." [26]Then they cast lots, and the lot fell to Matthias; so he was added to the eleven apostles.

COMMENTARY

15 "In those days" (*en tais hēmerais tautais*) marks the beginning of a self-contained unit of traditional material (cf. 6:1; 11:27)—a unit Luke ties to his introduction in vv.12–14 by the simple Greek connective *kai* ("and"). In keeping with his character portrayal of Peter throughout the third gospel, Luke here presents Peter as taking the lead among the apostles. The Western text has him standing among and speaking to "the disciples" (*tōn mathētōn*, GK 3412), and the probable reading of 𝔓⁷⁴ has him among "the apostles" (*tōn apostolōn*, GK 693). Both readings seem to be later attempts to clarify a possible confusion between "the brothers" of v.14 and those of v.15. But "disciples" (*mathētēs*) does not appear anywhere else in the first five chapters of Acts. And the better-attested reading here is "among the brothers" (*en mesō tōn adelphōn*; cf. also the use of *adelphoi*, "brothers," in the salutation of v.16), with "brothers" in Luke's source material of v.15 used as a religious idiom and "brothers" in v.14 of his own introduction referring to a blood relationship. Luke evidently did not anticipate any possible confusion. So the NIV and NRSV rightly translate "brothers" in v.15 as "believers" to bring out the religious nuance, for much the same reason that later Greek texts read "disciples" and "apostles."

16–17 The Greek literally reads "men, brothers" (*andres adelphoi*; NIV, "brothers"; NASB, "brethren"), which corresponds to nothing we know in the rabbinic literature that stems from the Pharisaic schools or the nonconformist writings of either Second Temple Judaism or the Dead Sea Scrolls. Outside Acts, it appears only in 4 Maccabees 8:19. On the ground of its use in Acts, where it is attributed to Peter (1:16; 2:29; 15:7), to the people of Jerusalem (2:37), to Stephen (7:2), to the synagogue rulers at Antioch of Pisidia (13:15), to James (15:13), and to Paul (13:26, 38; 22:1; 23:1, 6; 28:17)—and always in the context of a gathering of Jews—we may assume that it represents a type of formal address found within first-century synagogues (cf. 13:15, 26, 38) and among Jewish congregations generally.

Peter's words in v.16, and again later in v.21, speak of the necessity of Scripture being fulfilled in relation to Judas's defection and the choice of another to replace him. In Luke's writings, the verb *edei* ("it is necessary" or "one must") is used to stress the idea of compulsion that is inherent in the divine

plan—a stress usually accompanied by an emphasis on human inability to comprehend God's workings. At times, that divine necessity is explained in terms of the fulfillment of Scripture (e.g., Lk 22:37; 24:26, 44). More often, however, it is not (e.g., Lk 2:49; 4:43; 9:22; 13:16, 33; 17:25; 19:5; 24:7). This suggests that the concept of divine necessity is broader than just the explicit fulfillment of Scripture—though it may contain a specific biblical fulfillment, together with some such introductory formula as "it is written."

Here in vv.16 and 21 divine necessity is connected directly with the fulfillment of Scripture, "which the Holy Spirit spoke long ago through the mouth of David concerning Judas." Nonetheless, in neither case (and particularly not in v.21) should we say that the necessity concerns only a prophecy or certain prophecies of Scripture. The understanding expressed here is rather (1) that God is doing something necessarily involved in his divine plan; (2) that the disciples' lack of comprehension of God's plan is profound, especially with respect to Judas who "was one of our number and shared in this ministry" yet also "served as guide for those who arrested Jesus"; and (3) that an explicit way of understanding what has been going on under divine direction is through a Christian understanding of two canonical psalms that speak of false companions and wicked men generally—and which by means of the then widely common exegetical rule *qal waḥomer* ("light to heavy," or *a minore ad majorem*) could also be applied to the false disciple and wicked man par excellence, Judas Iscariot.

18–19 Luke now adds a parenthesis concerning the awful fate of Judas. Luke's use of his stylistic connective *men oun* (NASB, "now"; omitted in the NIV since it is almost untranslatable here) shows that he is adding to the tradition he has received (cf. v.6). Evidently his purpose is to emphasize the awfulness of Judas's fate, and so to suggest a basis for the disciples' perplexity in trying to comprehend the plan of God.

The difficulty of reconciling vv.18–19 with Matthew 27:3–10 is well known. Often it is considered the most intractable contradiction in the NT. The problem chiefly concerns how Judas died. But it also involves questions about who bought the field and why it was called "Field of Blood." These latter matters are perhaps not too difficult. Probably the common explanation suffices: the chief priests bought the potter's field in Judas's name with the thirty silver coins belonging to him, and local Jerusalemites (particularly Christians) nicknamed it "Field of Blood" because it had been purchased with "blood money."

The major question as to how Judas died, however, is not so easily answered. Could he have "hanged himself" (Mt 27:5)? Or was it that "he fell headlong, his body burst open and all his intestines spilled out" (Ac 1:18)? We may never know the answer. Augustine may have been right in saying that both were true. But though the precise solution seems imponderable, the problem is not very different from many other differences among the evangelists in presenting the words and activity of Jesus in their respective gospels. Nor is it very different from Luke's various portrayals of the apostolic sermons and events in Acts—as, for example, his three somewhat diverse reports of the conversion of Paul in Acts 9, 22, and 26.

If we really believe that each writer wrote from the standpoint of his own purposes to the specific interests and appreciation of his audience (as redaction criticism rightly holds), it is not difficult to believe that in the context of Matthew's fulfillment theme it was sufficient for him and his readers to portray Judas's awful end with the terse expression "he hanged himself" (*apēgxato*, GK *551*). After all, suicide itself was heinous for Jews. But that would hardly suffice for Luke, for his addressee Theophilus,

and for others in the Gentile world who would read Luke's account. For Gentiles under Stoic influence generally looked on suicide as morally neutral. Luke, however, wanted to highlight the awfulness of Judas's situation in a way that would grip his readers. So, it seems, he took the liberty of breaking into his received tradition (note again his use of the editorial connective *men oun*) in order to spell out the gory details of Judas's suicide—details he had probably gathered from some other source, whether written or oral. In so detailing Judas's gory demise, Luke's purpose, it may be conjectured, was to emphasize for his readers the divine necessity of all that happened.

20 The OT passages Luke uses to support the divine necessity manifest in Judas's defection and replacement are Psalms 69:25 (MT = 69:26) and 109:8. These psalms speak of false companions and wicked men who have become enemies of God's servant. Further, they lament his condition and give us his prayers for deliverance and desire for retribution. C. H. Dodd (*According to the Scriptures* [London: Nisbet, 1952], 61–108) has shown that Psalm 69 was one of the major blocks of OT material used within the early church on the topic of "the Servant of the Lord and the Righteous Sufferer" and applied to Jesus the Christ, the Servant and Righteous Sufferer par excellence. Psalm 69:4 is quoted in John 15:25 ("hated me without reason") as a lament of Jesus applied to himself; the first half of v.9 is quoted in John 2:17 ("Zeal for your house will consume me") as recalled by the disciples at the cleansing of the temple; the last half of v.9 is quoted by Paul in Romans 15:3 ("The insults of those who insult you have fallen on me") as characterizing Jesus' ministry; and Psalm 69:22–23 is quoted in Romans 11:9–10 ("May their table become a snare and a trap, a stumbling block and a retribution for them. May their eyes be darkened so they cannot see, and their backs be bent forever") as describing Israel's present condition. Judging by the frequency and variety of usage in the NT, therefore, the Christian use of Psalm 69 from the earliest days of the church is well established. So here in v.20 we have another example of the Christian use of this block of messianic material, to which, on the exegetical principle of analogous subject (i.e., Hillel's sixth exegetical rule: *kĕyôṣēʾ bô bĕmāqôm aḥēr*, "as found in another place"), Peter added the ominous words of Psalm 109:8: "May another take his place of leadership."

We need not insist that the early Christians believed that the primary reference of these two psalms was to Judas, as though no one could have understood them prior to his betrayal of Jesus. What they seem to be saying is that just as the psalmist's portrayals of "the Servant of the Lord and the Righteous Sufferer" can—on the basis of the Semitic concept of corporate solidarity—be applied to God's Messiah, Jesus, the Servant and Righteous Sufferer par excellence, so the retribution spoken of as coming on false companions and wicked men in general is especially applicable to Judas, who above all other men was false. So Peter quotes Psalm 69:25 in a Christian context and applies it to Judas's defection. In itself, of course, this verse gives no justification for replacing Judas—in fact, it even opposes it. Therefore Peter goes on to cite Psalm 109:8 on the Jewish exegetical principle of analogous subject in order to defend the legitimacy of replacing a member of the apostolic band.

21–22 The divine necessity for filling Judas's place was supported by Psalm 109:8, which was interpreted from a Christian perspective in line with the Semitic concept of corporate solidarity (see comments at v.20). The twelvefold witness of twelve apostles was required if early Jewish Christianity was to represent itself to the Jewish nation as the culmination of Israel's hope and the true people of Israel's Messiah. The "remnant theology" of Second Temple Judaism made it mandatory that any group claiming to be "the righteous remnant" of the nation—i.e., one having responsibility for calling the nation to repentance and permeating it for God's glory—must represent itself as the true Israel, not only in its proclamation but also in its symbolism. The Qumran covenanters thought it necessary to have twelve leaders heading up their community, with three—either from within the group of twelve or in addition to it—forming an inner circle of authority (cf. 1QS 8.11). This was an evident parallel to the twelve tribes of Israel, with a developing stress on final authority resting with a smaller body of two or three.

Likewise, Jesus predicted that "at the renewal of all things" his disciples will "sit on twelve thrones, judging the twelve tribes of Israel" (Mt 19:28; cf. Lk 22:30). And John the Seer pictured the consummation of God's redemption as a "Holy City, Jerusalem, coming down out of heaven from God," having twelve gates with "the names of the twelve tribes of Israel" written on them and twelve foundations with "the names of the twelve apostles of the Lamb" written on them (Rev 21:10, 12, 14). It was, then, for just such a reason that the early church found itself required to replace the defector Judas so as to have a full complement of twelve in its apostolic ranks.

For anyone to succeed Judas among the apostles, the first qualification laid down by Peter is that he must "have been with us the whole time the Lord Jesus went in and out among us, beginning from John's baptism to the time when Jesus was taken up from us." The phrase "went in and out among us" is a Semitic idiom for familiar and unhindered association (cf. Dt 31:2; 2Sa 3:25; Ps 121:8; Ac 9:28). The length of time designated for this association was from John's baptism to Jesus' ascension. Perhaps not all the remaining eleven original disciples themselves could claim association with Jesus from the days of John the Baptist. John 1:35–51 suggests that only about half could. But they evidently wanted to make quite sure that there would be no deficiency on this first point.

The second qualification was that of having been a witness to Jesus' resurrection. So the candidate must be both a guarantor of the gospel tradition because he had been a companion of the earthly Jesus, and a witness to the resurrection because he had been personally met by the risen Lord. It is from vv.21–22 that we can derive a strict definition of the term "apostle"—one that determines much of what Luke presents in the remainder of Acts (though in that second volume he also uses "apostle" more broadly). An apostle, then, was not an ecclesiastical functionary. Nor was he just a recipient of the apostolic faith or even a bearer of the apostolic message. He was, first and foremost, (1) a guarantor of the gospel tradition and (2) a witness to the reality of Jesus' resurrection.

23 The two men proposed were (1) Joseph, who was called by Aramaic-speaking Jews "Barsabbas" (meaning "Son of the Sabbath") presumably because he was born on the Sabbath, and who was also known by his Roman cognomen Justus, and (2) Matthias, which is a shortened form of Mattathias. Perhaps more of their associates were also considered, as v.21 ("one of the men who have been with us") seems to suggest. But only two of them had the necessary qualifications.

24–25 It was not enough, however, to possess the external qualifications the other apostles had. Judas's successor must also be appointed by the same Lord who appointed the original Eleven. Likewise, though the church could not represent itself as the righteous remnant of Israel with one apostle lacking, it could hardly symbolize its consciousness as being the true Israel of God with one apostle too many. Therefore, prayer was offered to the Lord for his selection of only one from among the two candidates.

It is not clear linguistically whether the vocative "Lord" addresses God the Father or Jesus in the prayer. Contextually, however, it is most natural to understand the same referent for the title here as in v.21: "the Lord Jesus." Furthermore, the parallel seems to be consciously drawn by Luke in his use of the same verb *eklegomai* ("choose," GK *1721*) for those selected by Jesus in Acts 1:2 and for this man who was to be selected by "the Lord" to replace Judas. And if it was important for them to have the qualifications given in vv.21–22, it was at least as important for them all to have been appointed by the same Lord.

The Greek wording *tēs diakonias tautēs kai apostolēs* probably constitutes a hendiadys—two connotative words connected by a conjunction that are used to express a single complex idea, which is normally set out by an adjective and a substantive noun—with the definite article "the" (*tēs*) tying the two elements together. It is best translated as "this apostolic ministry." The phrase "to go where he belongs" (or "to go to his own place") is likely a euphemism for "to go to hell" (cf. Str-B, 4.2.1097–98), which shows the awfulness of Judas's fate spiritually (cf. vv.18–19).

26 After determining qualifications and praying, the apostles "cast lots, and the lot fell to Matthias." The Greek literally reads, "They gave lots to them" (*edōkan klērous autois*)—a Hebrew idiom for "casting" or "throwing" down various kinds of marked objects in order to determine God's will. The practice was common within Israel and the ancient world generally and is probably best illustrated by Proverbs 16:33: "The lot is cast into the lap, but its every decision is from the LORD." So by the appointment of Christ himself, the full complement of apostles was restored and the church was ready for the coming of the Holy Spirit and the beginning of its mission.

NOTES

15 Luke's habit is to qualify his numerical data by the particles ὡς (*hōs*) and ὡσεί (*hōsei*), which both mean "about" (cf. Ac 2:41; 4:4; 5:7, 36; 10:3; 13:18, 20; 19:7, 34). Paul says in 1 Corinthians 15:6 that on one occasion Jesus appeared to over five hundred of his followers at one time. This suggests a larger pre-Pentecost nucleus in the church than Acts 1:15 indicates. But the appearance that Paul reports was probably in Galilee, with most of those referred to remaining in Galilee, whereas the number "about a hundred and twenty" given here should probably be taken as referring only to the Jerusalem contingent of early believers.

16 The Western text (D, and as reflected in the Old Latin Gigas, the Vulgate, and Irenaeus) has the third person singular present δεῖ (*dei*, "it is necessary" or "one must") rather than the third person imperfect ἔδει (*edei*, "it is necessary" or "one must") of the Alexandrian text (ℵ A B C E etc.), thus suggesting that the Western scribe failed to understand that two things are spoken of in vv.16–21: (1) the death of Judas and (2) the appointment of his successor. The verb δεῶ (*deō*, "necessary, must") in Luke's two volumes always requires consideration of the context of the statement or the predicate of the sentence (or both) in order to provide the specification. Here, of course, that specification is provided by the predicates "the Scripture had to be fulfilled" (v.16) and "it is written" (v.20), though the context suggests not exclusively by these predicates.

20 On the major blocks of OT material used in the early church as "the substructure of all Christian theology," see Dodd, *According to the Scriptures*, 61–108. Together with Psalm 69, Dodd has identified principally Isaiah 42:1–44:5; 49:1–13; 50:4–11; 52:13–21; and Psalms 22, 24, and 118 as "Scriptures of the Servant of the Lord and the Righteous Sufferer" used christologically in the NT. For further discussion of Jewish exegetical procedures and the NT's use of Scripture from a christocentric perspective and in accord with standard Jewish exegetical practices, see my *Biblical Exegesis in the Apostolic Period*.

21 The Western text (D, and as represented by the Syriac Harclean version and recensions of the Syriac and Ethiopic versions, as well as Augustine) add Χριστός (*Christos*, "Christ") after ὁ κύριος Ἰησοῦς (*ho kyrios Iēsous*, "the Lord Jesus")—which is a pious accretion rather typical of the Western text.

23 The Western text (D, and as represented by the Old Latin Gigas version and Augustine), in reading "he proposed" (ἔστησεν, *estēsen*, GK *2705*), has Peter as the one who set forward the two candidates to succeed Judas—a monarchical emphasis found elsewhere in the Western textual tradition. The better-attested Alexandrian text (ℵ A B C E Ψ etc.) has "they proposed" (ἔστησαν, *estēsan*), most likely meaning that the whole body of eleven apostles together proposed the two candidates. Internally as well, the plural suffix "they" is supported by the three occurrences of the pronoun "us" with reference to the apostles in vv.21–22.

This Joseph Barsabbas is to be distinguished from the Judas Barsabbas of 15:22 and the Jesus called Justus of Colossians 4:11; likewise from the Joseph Barnabas of 4:36 (though D and some minor texts have Βαρνάβαν, *Barnaban*, at 1:23). Having a Gentile name (whether Greek or Roman) along with a Hebrew name and a Hebrew nickname was quite common in the Jewish world (cf. 12:12; 13:9).

24 The expression προσευξάμενοι εἶπαν (*proseuxamenoi eipan*, "praying, they said") is like the LXX locution ἀποκριθεὶς εἶπεν (*apokritheis eipen*, "answering, he said"), which occurs thirty-eight times in

Luke's gospel and seven times in Acts. The aorist participle expresses action simultaneous with that of the main verb.

26 On the Day of Atonement, Aaron chose by lot a scapegoat to bear the sins of the people in the wilderness (Lev 16:7–10, 21–22). After the conquest, Palestine was divided by casting lots (Jos 14:2; 18:6; 1Ch 6:54–80); Jonathan's breaking of Saul's hasty vow was discovered by lot (1Sa 14:41–42); and the service of the Jerusalem temple was regulated by the casting of lots (Ne 10:34). Perhaps the Urim and Thummim (Ex 28:30; Dt 33:8; Ezr 2:63) were also used at times in this manner, with the stones being placed on the ephod of the high priest and the priest then picking up one or the other blindly in order to determine the divine will. In the NT we read of soldiers at the cross of Jesus casting lots for his clothing (Mt 27:35) and here in Acts of using lots to determine the Lord's will about Judas's successor. While lots are not mentioned elsewhere in the NT, their use may have continued for a time.

Τῶν ἕνδεκα (tōn hendeka, "the Eleven") is attested by all known Greek MSS except D, which has τῶν δώδεκα (tōn dōdeka, "the Twelve"). The Armenian catena, Georgian version, and Augustine rather pedantically read, "he was counted among the eleven apostles as the twelfth."

REFLECTIONS

The pericope about the selection of Matthias has a number of significant implications. In the first place, it shows the necessity of a hermeneutical method that can distinguish between normative principles and cultural practices in the progressive revelation of the Bible. We are exhorted to "search the Scriptures" and to "know what is the will of the Lord"—exhortations that are normative for all Christians. But the early church's midrashic exegesis and practice of casting lots were methods for interpreting Scripture and ascertaining God's will that were used at that time, and we need not be necessarily bound by them today.

Second, the pericope suggests that Christian decisions regarding vocation involve a number of factors: (1) the evaluation of qualifications, (2) earnest prayer, and (3) appointment by Christ himself. Each of these factors may be somewhat culturally related, and so perhaps diverse in different situations. Nonetheless, each of them is normative in any seeking of guidance, and by God's grace their significance becomes clear to those who seek divine direction.

Furthermore, it should be noted that it was Judas's defection and not simply the fact of his death that required his replacement. While the NT lays great stress on the apostolic message and faith—and, further, while Luke stresses the importance of the apostles' role—the pericope gives no justification for the theological necessity of an apostolic succession of office, as is sometimes claimed for it. According to vv.21–22, the task of the twelve apostles was unique: they were to be (1) guarantors of the gospel tradition because of their companionship with Jesus in his earthly ministry and (2) witnesses to the reality of his resurrection because they had seen the risen Christ. Such criteria cannot be transmitted from generation to generation. Thus when James the son of Zebedee was executed by Herod Agrippa in AD 44 (cf. 12:1–2), the church took no action to replace him. He had faithfully functioned as a guarantor of the gospel tradition and a witness to the reality of Jesus' resurrection for some fifteen years. And now as the church was growing, that ministry was not to be repeated.

Finally, and contrary to an often-heard claim that the apostles were wrong in selecting Matthias and should have awaited God's choice of Paul to fill the vacancy, it should be pointed out (1) that Paul had not been with Jesus during his earthly ministry—in fact, he frequently acknowledged his dependence on others with respect to the gospel tradition (cf., e.g., 1Co 15:3–5); (2) that the necessity of having exactly twelve apostles in the early church sprang largely from the need for Jewish Christians ministering within the Jewish nation to maintain this symbolic number—and while Paul could appreci-ate this need, he did not feel its necessity for his Gentile ministry; and (3) that Paul himself recog-nized the special nature of his apostleship—that it was in line with the apostleship of the Twelve but that it also rested on a somewhat different base (cf. his reference to himself as an apostle "abnormally born" in 1Co 15:7–8). Paul's background, ministry, and call were in many ways different from those of the Twelve. So while he insisted on the equality of his apostleship with that of the other apostles, he never interpreted that equality in terms of either opposition or identity.

D. The Coming of the Holy Spirit (2:1–41)

OVERVIEW

Luke's fourth constitutive factor undergirding the expansion of the early Christian mission is the coming of the Holy Spirit on believers who had assembled in Jerusalem on the day of Pentecost. To this the other three factors have pointed. Now Luke gives us an extended account of the event, which includes the baptism of the Spirit on the day of Pentecost and Peter's sermon to the multitude and which welds these separate incidents into a unified whole.

Though all four gospels include the preaching of John the Baptist, only Matthew and Luke have pre-served the Baptist's distinction between his baptism with water and the baptism to be conferred by the One to come, the "one more powerful" than he was (Mt 3:11; Lk 3:16). And Luke alone connects the Baptist's prophecy of a baptism "with the Holy Spirit and with fire" (Mt 3:11; Lk 3:16) with the miracle at Pentecost (cf. Ac 1:5; 11:16). In so doing, Luke sets out a parallelism between John's baptism of Jesus in the Jordan and the Spirit's baptism of believers assembled in Jerusalem on the day of Pentecost, with each of these events seen as the final constitutive fac-tor for all that follows in their respective accounts: first in the ministry of Jesus (cf. Luke's gospel) and then in the mission of the early church (cf. Acts).

1. The Miracle of Pentecost (2:1–13)

¹When the day of Pentecost came, they were all together in one place. ²Suddenly a sound like the blowing of a violent wind came from heaven and filled the whole house where they were sitting. ³They saw what seemed to be tongues of fire that separated and came to rest on each of them. ⁴All of them were filled with the Holy Spirit and began to speak in other tongues as the Spirit enabled them.

⁵Now there were staying in Jerusalem God-fearing Jews from every nation under heaven. ⁶When they heard this sound, a crowd came together in bewilderment, because each one heard them speaking in his own language. ⁷Utterly amazed, they asked: "Are not all these men who are speaking Galileans? ⁸Then how is it that each of us hears them in his own native language? ⁹Parthians, Medes and Elamites; residents of Mesopotamia, Judea and Cappadocia, Pontus and Asia, ¹⁰Phrygia and Pamphylia, Egypt and the parts of Libya near Cyrene; visitors from Rome ¹¹(both Jews and converts to Judaism); Cretans and Arabs we hear them declaring the wonders of God in our own tongues!" ¹²Amazed and perplexed, they asked one another, "What does this mean?"

¹³Some, however, made fun of them and said, "They have had too much wine."

COMMENTARY

1 Luke describes the miracle of the coming of the Holy Spirit, with its accompanying signs, in four short verses remarkable for their nuances. The miracle occurred on the festival known in Second Temple Judaism as Pentecost (*Pentēkostē*, "fiftieth"), which, according to Leviticus 23:15–16 (cf. Dt 16:9–12; Josephus, *Ant.* 3.252; Str-B, 2.597–602), was to be celebrated on the "day after the seventh Sabbath"—hence on the fiftieth day after Passover. It was originally the festival of the firstfruits of the grain harvest (Ex 23:16; Lev 23:17–22; Nu 28:26–31). It was called the "Feast of Weeks" because it came after a period of seven weeks of harvesting, which began with the offering of the first barley sheaf during the Passover celebration and ended with the wheat harvest. By the time of the first Christian century, however, it was considered the anniversary of the giving of the Mosaic law on Mount Sinai (as deduced from the chronological note at Ex 19:1) and as a time for the annual renewal of the Mosaic covenant (cf. *Jub.* 6:17; *b. Pesaḥ. 68b*). It was, therefore, viewed as one of the three great pilgrim festivals of Judaism, along with Passover preceding it and Tabernacles some four months later.

No one who had been a companion of the apostle Paul—or even a distant admirer (should Luke's authorship of Acts be denied)—could have failed to have been impressed by the fact that it was on the Jewish festival of Pentecost that the Spirit came so dramatically on the early believers at Jerusalem. It is this significance that Luke emphasizes as he begins his Pentecost narrative: that whereas Pentecost was for Judaism the day of the giving of the Law, for Christians it is the day of the coming of the Holy Spirit. So for Luke the coming of the Spirit on the early Christians at Pentecost is not only a parallel to the Spirit's coming on Jesus at his baptism; it is also both in continuity with and in contrast to the Law.

To be sure, Luke does not draw out from this a portrayal of Jesus as either the giver of a new Torah or himself the embodiment of such a Torah, though if either Matthew or John had written Acts they might have done something like that. Rather, by paralleling Jesus' baptism with the experience of Jesus' early followers at Pentecost, Luke is showing that the mission of the Christian church—as was also the ministry of Jesus—is dependent on the coming of the Holy Spirit. And by his stress on Pentecost as the day when the miracle took place, he is also suggesting (1) that the Spirit's coming was in continuity with God's purposes in giving the Law, and yet (2) that the Spirit's coming signals the essential difference between the Jewish faith and commitment to Jesus. For whereas Judaism is Torah-centered and Torah-directed, Christianity is Christ-centered and Spirit-directed—all of which sounds very much like Paul.

As to just where the believers were when they experienced the coming of the Spirit, Luke is vague. His emphasis is on the "when" and not at all on the "where" of the event. So all he tells us is that "they were all together in one place," which he refers to in the following verse as "the house" (*ton oikon*, GK 3875).

Many have taken "the house" to be a reference to the Jerusalem temple because (1) *oikos* was at times used to refer to the temple (cf. Isa 6:4 [LXX]; Ac 7:47; Josephus, *Ant.* 8.65–75); (2) Luke's gospel closes with the statement that Jesus' disciples "stayed continually at the temple, praising God" (Lk 24:53); and (3) in the temple precincts they would have had the best opportunity to address a large crowd. Apart from this doubtful instance in Acts 2 and Stephen's speech in Acts 7, however, Luke elsewhere always refers to the temple by the expression *to hieron* (GK 2639; twenty-two times); and where *ho oikos* is occasionally used by others of the Jerusalem temple, it is always in a context that leaves no doubt as to what is meant. Furthermore, the articular intensive pronoun *to auto* ("in one place") is best interpreted as referring to its antecedent in 1:12–26, "the [upper] room" (*to hyperōon*, GK 5673). It is therefore likely that Luke meant us to picture that same upper room as the setting for the miracle of the Spirit's coming and the place from where the disciples first went out to proclaim the gospel.

2 There is nothing necessarily sensory about the Holy Spirit. Yet God in his providence often accompanies his Spirit's working by visible and audible signs, with these signs being particularly manifest at certain crisis periods in redemptive history. This he does to assure his own people of his presence. These assurances are usually given within the appreciation of his people—though not always, it seems, in terms of their expectations.

In vv.2–4, three signs of the Spirit's presence are reported to have appeared, with each of them—wind, fire, and inspired speech—being considered in Jewish tradition to be a sign of God's presence. Wind as a sign of God's Spirit is rooted linguistically in the fact that both the Hebrew word *rûaḥ* (GK 8120) and the Greek word *pneuma* (GK 4460) mean either "wind" or "spirit," depending on the context. This dual meaning allows for a rather free association of the two ideas (cf. Jn 3:8).

Ezekiel had prophesied of the breath of God blowing over the dry bones in the valley of his vision and filling them with new life (Eze 37:9–14), and it was this wind of God's Spirit that Judaism looked forward to as ushering in the final messianic age. Thus Luke tells us that as a sign of the Spirit's coming on the early followers of Jesus, there was "a sound like the blowing of a violent wind." Just why Luke emphasized the "sound" (*ēchos*, GK 2492) of the blowing of the "wind" (*pnoēs*, GK 4466) is difficult to say. Perhaps it was because he wanted in v.6 to refer back to "this sound" (*tēs phōnēs* [GK 5889] *tautēs*). Perhaps also he wanted to retain the parallel with the Pentecost tradition of the giving of the Law, for in certain sectors of Judaism the events connected with the giving of the Law were couched in terms of God's having caused a "sound" to arise on Mount Sinai, with this "sound" then being changed into a "fire" that all could perceive as a "language" (cf. Philo, *Decal.* 33). But whatever his rationale, Luke's main point is that this "sound like the blowing of a violent wind" that "came from heaven" and "filled the whole house" symbolized to all present—in a manner well within their appreciation—the presence of God's Spirit among them in a way more intimate, personal, and powerful than they had ever before experienced.

3 Fire was a well-known symbol of the divine presence among first-century Jews. Their Scriptures recounted stories of the burning bush (Ex 3:2–5), the pillar of fire that guided Israel by night through the wilderness (Ex 13:21), the consuming fire on Mount Sinai (Ex 24:17), and the fire that hovered over the wilderness tabernacle (Ex 40:38). The apocalyptic book of 1 Enoch, in fact, depicts God's heavenly court as "surrounded by tongues of fire" (14:8–25; cf. 71:5). John the Baptist is reported as having explicitly linked the coming of the Spirit with fire in his prophecy that the Messiah would baptize "with the Holy Spirit and with fire" (Mt 3:11; Lk 3:16). The "tongues of fire" (*glōssai* [GK 1185] *hōsei pyros* [GK 4786]) here are probably not to be equated with the "other tongues" (*heterais glōssais*) of v.4, but should be taken as simply visible representations of the overshadowing presence of the Spirit of God given in the context of the appreciation of those there gathered.

Also significant is Luke's statement that these tokens of the Spirit's presence "separated and came to rest on each of them." This seems to suggest that, though under the old covenant the divine presence rested on Israel as a corporate entity and on many of its leaders for special purposes, under the new covenant, as established by Jesus and inaugurated at Pentecost, the Spirit now rests on each believer individually. In other words, though the corporate and individual aspects of redemption cannot actually be separated, the emphasis in the proclamation of redemption from Pentecost onward is on the personal relationship of God with the believer through the Spirit, with all corporate relationships resulting from this.

4 In OT times, prophetic utterances were regularly associated with the Spirit's coming on partic-

ular persons for special purposes (cf., e.g., Eldad and Medad in Nu 11:26–29; also Saul in 1Sa 10:6–12). In Judaism, however, the belief arose that with the passing of the last of the writing prophets in the early postexilic period the spirit of prophecy had ceased in Israel, and that since then God spoke to his people only through the Torah as interpreted by the teachers (cf. such passages as the prologue to Sirach and ch. 1 of *m. ʾAbot*). But Judaism also expected that with the coming of the messianic age there would be a special outpouring of God's Spirit, which would be in fulfillment of Ezekiel 37, and that prophecy would once again flourish. And this is exactly what Luke portrays as having taken place at Pentecost among the followers of Jesus: "All of them were filled with the Holy Spirit and began to speak in other tongues as the Spirit enabled them."

The "tongues" here are often identified with ecstatic utterances of the sort that Paul discusses in 1 Corinthians 12–14. This identification is made largely because (1) in both instances (Ac 2; 1Co 12–14) the expression "other tongues" (*heterais glōssais*; *heteroglōssois* [GK 2280]; NIV, "strange tongues," 1Co 14:21) is used, and (2) because the verb translated "enabled" or "gave utterance" (*apophthengomai*, GK 710) is frequently used in other Greek literature in connection with ecstatics—whether of the givers of oracles (cf. Diodorus of Sicily, *Bibl. hist.* 16.27.1; Plutarch, *Pyth. orac.* 23) or of the interpreters of oracles (cf. Mic 5:12; Zec 10:2). But the words spoken at Pentecost under the Spirit's direction were immediately recognized by the hearers as being languages then current, while at Corinth no one could understand what was said until someone present received a gift of interpretation. Furthermore, the verb *apophthengomai* used by Luke in Acts (its only three NT occurrences) appears in contexts that stress clarity of speech and understanding: (1) here in 2:4; (2) in 2:14, in Peter's address to the crowd at Pentecost; and (3) in 26:25, in Paul's defense before Agrippa II, where it is explicitly contrasted with *mainomai* (GK *3419*), which means babblings stemming from madness over which the speaker has no control. The tongues of 2:4, therefore, are probably best viewed as "languages" and so to be understood in accord with Philo's reference (*Decal.* 33) to understandable language as one of the three signs of God's presence in the giving of the Law at Mount Sinai.

The coming of the Holy Spirit at Pentecost was of utmost significance for the early church, both theologically and practically. As to the question of whether Pentecost was the birthday of the Christian church, a great deal depends on what one means by "church" (*ekklēsia*, GK *1711*). Amid a variety of uses, the word appears in the NT for both "the body of Christ" (i.e., people who have been redeemed throughout all the ages) and "an instrument of service" (i.e., new-covenant people who are distinguished from the nation of Israel and appointed by God for his redemptive purposes). Of the first (the church as the body of Christ), it can hardly be said that it had its beginning *only* at Pentecost. What can be said, however, and what Luke seems to be stressing in reporting that the tongues of fire separated and came to rest on *each* believer individually, is (1) that the relationship of the Spirit to the members of the body of Christ became much more intimate and personal at Pentecost, in fulfillment of Jesus' promise (Jn 14:17) that the Spirit who "lives with you [*par' hēmin menei*] . . . will be in you [*en hēmin estai*]," and (2) that at Pentecost a new model of divine redemption was established as characteristic for life in the new covenant—one that, while incorporating both individual and corporate redemption, begins with the former in order to include the latter.

With regard to the church as an instrument of service called into being by God to take up the mission formerly entrusted to Israel, Luke is certainly

presenting the coming of the Spirit at Pentecost as the church's birthday. Thus he parallels the Spirit's coming on Jesus at his baptism with the Spirit's coming on the earliest believers at Pentecost, for neither Jesus' ministry nor the mission of the early church would have been possible apart from the Spirit's empowering. So also he emphasizes Jesus' explicit command to the disciples to stay in Jerusalem until they were empowered from on high by the Spirit (Lk 24:49; Ac 1:4–5, 8).

5 Certain "God-fearing Jews" residing in Jerusalem from many parts of the Diaspora, together with a number of Jews and proselytes who had returned to Jerusalem as pilgrims for the Pentecost festival, were "in bewilderment," "utterly amazed," and "perplexed" by the miraculous coming of the Spirit (vv.6, 7, 12). Others, however, mocked (v.13).

Codex Sinaiticus (ℵ) omits the word "Jews" (*Ioudaioi*), and some have considered the omission a serious one, particularly because of the importance of this uncial MS as external evidence in establishing the text. But the word Luke uses for "God-fearers" (*eulabeis*, GK *2327*) is used in the NT only of Jews (cf. Lk 2:25; Ac 8:2; 22:12). It never connotes elsewhere in the NT a Gentile convert to Judaism (*prosēlytos*, "proselyte," GK *4670*), a near convert (so-called Proselyte of the Gate; *sebomenos*, "worshiper," GK *4933*), or a devout Gentile (which is often implied by *phoboumenos*, "fearer" [GK *5828*], or *eusebēs*, "godly" [GK *2356*]). It is, therefore, highly unlikely that even if *Ioudaioi* were omitted from the text, there would be ground for arguing that Luke had Gentiles in view here. Furthermore, contrary to many who have assumed that the Jews mentioned here were pilgrims to Jerusalem coming for the Pentecost festival, it is more probable that they were residents of Jerusalem who had returned from Diaspora lands (i.e., "from every nation under heaven") at some earlier time to settle down in the homeland. That is how Luke here uses *katoikountes* ("staying"), a participial form of *katoikeō* (GK *2997*)—which appears elsewhere in Acts (cf. 1:20; 7:2, 4, 48; 9:22; 11:29; 13:27; 17:24, 26; 22:12), in contrast to the verb *epidēmeō* (GK *2111*) used as a participle in v.10 in the sense of "being a stranger or visitor in town."

6 What drew the crowd and caused its bewilderment? Commentators differ as to whether it was the sound of the wind or the disciples' speaking in various languages. But if we break the sentence with some kind of punctuation after *to plēthos* ("the crowd," GK *4436*), rather than (as is usually done) after *synechythē* ("bewilderment," GK *5177*), the text then can be seen to set up two coordinate sentences with two separate yet complementary ideas: "When they heard this sound, a crowd came together. And they were bewildered because each one heard them speaking in his own language." On this reading, *tēs phōnēs tautēs* ("this sound") refers back to the *ēchos* ("sound") of v.2 and conjures up a picture of people rushing to the source of the noise to see what was going on. When they get there, they become bewildered by hearing Galileans speaking in their own native languages. The verb for "hear" (*ēkouon*, GK *201*), which seems to be the better reading, is in the imperfect tense, suggesting that their hearing took place over a period of time—perhaps first in the upper room itself, then in adjacent lanes and courtyards, and finally in the temple precincts.

7–8 Galileans had difficulty pronouncing the Hebrew gutturals and were in the habit of swallowing syllables when they spoke, and so were looked down on by residents of Jerusalem as being provincial (cf. Mk 14:70). The disciples who were speaking were Galileans. Thus it bewildered those who heard them, for they could not by themselves have learned so many different languages.

9–11 Why these fifteen countries and no others are named—and why they are cited in this particular order—are questions without ready solutions. It has frequently been argued that Luke was probably drawing on some ancient astrological treatise that correlated the then-known nations of the world with the twelve signs of the zodiac, such as the fourth-century AD Egyptian Paulus Alexandrinus did in his *Rudiments of Astrology*. This explanation, however, requires pruning Luke's list of fifteen down to twelve (i.e., deleting "Judea" as the fifth in the listing and "Cretans and Arabs" at the end, though all three are well attested in the MSS) and making certain adjustments in the order. Such astrological and historical listings of nations, however, were common in the ancient world, and Luke may only be using a current literary convention to illustrate his more prosaic statement of v.5: "from every nation under heaven." As was probably customary, the list includes both ancient kingdoms and current political entities, moving generally from east to west and in its middle section naming first the northern and then the southern lands.

The appearance of "Judea" in the listing is admittedly strange because (1) it hardly ranks being sandwiched between Mesopotamia to the east and Cappadocia to the north; (2) as an adjective used as a noun, it is "corrupt" without an article when used substantively; and (3) it involves the curious anomaly of inhabitants of Judea being amazed to hear the apostles speak in their own language. Suggested solutions to this problem have been legion. Perhaps the most cogent one involves viewing "Judea" here in a wider prophetic sense, wherein the reference is to "the land of the Jews" that was held to stretch from the Euphrates River to the Egyptian border. This would explain its sequence in the listing and the omission of Syria from the list. Furthermore, it would allow for a variety of dialects different from the one native to the residents of Jerusalem. The inclusion of "Cretans and Arabs" probably refers to seafaring peoples and Nabatean Arabs, whose kingdom traditionally extended from the Euphrates River to the Red Sea.

Each of the areas and countries named had a considerable Jewish population within its borders (cf. Str-B, 2.606–14). Some Jews had returned to Jerusalem to take up residence there (cf. the comment on *katoikountes*, "staying," in v.5). One group, however, is singled out as being religious pilgrims to the city (cf. the substantive participle *hoi epidēmountes*, "those who were visitors," of v.10). They are identified as being Jews and proselytes to Judaism "from Rome." Undoubtedly there were other festival pilgrims in the crowd, just as there must have been other Diaspora Jews in attendance who were residents of Jerusalem. But Luke's interest in Acts is in the gospel reaching out even to Rome, capital of the empire. So he singles out this pilgrim contingent for special mention. It may be that some of these "visitors from Rome" returned to Rome and formed the nucleus of the church in that city. Ambrosiaster, a fourth-century Latin father, speaks of the church at Rome as having been founded "according to the Jewish rite, without seeing any sign of mighty works or any of the apostles" (cf. P. A. Ballerini, ed., *S. Ambrosii Opera* [Rome: Mediolani, 1877], 3:373–74).

12–13 The miraculous is not self-authenticating. Nor does it inevitably and uniformly convince. There must also be the preparation of the heart and the proclamation of the gospel for miracles to accomplish their full purpose. This was true even for the miracle of the Spirit's coming at Pentecost. The Greek of v.12 indicates that "all" of the "God-fearing Jews" (v.5), whose attention had been arrested by the signs at Pentecost and whose own religious heritage gave them at least some appreciation of them, were amazed and asked, "What does this mean?" Others, however, being spiritually insensitive, only mocked, attributing such phenomena to drunkenness. All this prepares the reader for Peter's sermon, which is the initial proclamation of the gospel message to a prepared people.

NOTES

1 The preposition ἐν (*en*, "in"; NIV, "when") with the articular infinitive is a favorite Lukan construction used particularly to express the idea of time (cf. Ac 8:6; 11:15; 19:1). It occurs thirty-two times in Luke's gospel (only three times in Matthew's; twice in Mark's) and seven times in Acts. An exact parallel to the phrase ἐν τῷ συμπληροῦσθαι (*en tō symplērousthai*; lit., "in the approaching of") is to be found in Luke 9:51.

4 For rabbinic references to the cessation of prophecy in Israel in the early postexilic period and its return in the messianic age, see P. Schäfer, *Die Vorstellung vom heiligen Geist in der rabbinischen Literatur* (München: Kösel, 1972), 89–115, 143–46 (though on the continuance of the Spirit's activity, see also 116–34, 147–49).

5 Most MSS read ἐν Ἰερουσαλήμ (*en Ierousalēm*, "in Jerusalem"), though a few, including ℵ and A, read εἰς Ἰερουσαλήμ (*eis Ierousalēm*, "into Jerusalem"). Metzger, 290 (corrected ed., 1975), comments, "The construction of εἰς [*eis*] with verbs of rest (such as ἦσαν [*ēsan*] in this verse) is a Hellenistic construction that occurs in all New Testament authors except Matthew, and in Acts most frequently of all (so Blass-Debrunner-Funk, section 205; see, e.g., Ac 7.12; 8.40; 9.21; 12.19; 19.22; 21.13; 23.11 *bis*). The question here is whether Luke wrote εἰς [*eis*] which was later replaced in almost all MSS with ἐν [*en*], in accord with classical usage, or whether he wrote ἐν [*en*] which scribes altered to εἰς [*eis*], in accord with increasingly popular usage. On the basis of what is obviously Lukan usage (see Lk 4.23, 44; 21.37 as well as the passages in Acts already mentioned), a majority of the Committee preferred the reading εἰς [*eis*]."

6 The third person plural imperfect verb ἤκουον (*ēkouon*, "they were hearing," GK *201*), which appears in A, D, E, Chrysostom, and most minuscules, seems to be the original reading. The third person singular ἤκουεν (*ēkouen*, "he was hearing"), which appears in C, a few minuscules, and some translations, is probably an attempted correction of the plural imperfect verb; while the third person singular aorist ἤκουσεν (*ēkousen*, "he heard"), which is found in ℵ and B, and the third person plural aorist ἤκουσαν (*ēkousan*, "they heard"), which appears in some minuscules, likely arose from harmonization with adjacent verbs in the aorist tense.

7 The phrase ἐξίσταντο καὶ ἐθαύμαζον (*existanto kai ethaumazon*, "utterly amazed") is probably a hendiadys (i.e., one idea expressed by two independent words connected by the conjunction "and"), as is ἐξίσταντο καὶ διηπόρουν (*existanto kai diēporoun*, "amazed and perplexed," v.12).

9 The first to postulate Luke's dependence on some ancient astrological treatise was S. Weinstock, "The Geographical Catalogue in Acts II, 9–11," *JRS* 38 (1948): 43–46, though he credits F. C. Burkitt's notes on an article by F. Cumont (1909) as his inspiration. Metzger credits J. Halévy (1906) as the first to note relations here between Luke and Paulus Alexandrinus, though Halévy explained it differently. For a balanced evaluation of the problem, see Bruce M. Metzger, "Ancient Astrological Geography and Acts 2:9–11," in *Apostolic History and the Gospel*, ed. W. W. Gasque and R. P. Martin (Grand Rapids: Eerdmans, 1970), 123–33.

12 The Western text (D, and as represented by the Syriac Harclean version and Augustine) adds ἐπὶ τῷ γεγονότι (*epi tō gegonoti*, "concerning what had taken place") after ἄλλον (*allon*), which is a typical Western expansion.

13 This is the only occurrence of γλεῦκος (*gleukos*, "sweet wine," GK *1183*) in the NT. Since there would not have been new wine by the time of Pentecost, some think of this as wine sweetened with honey (Str-B, 2.614). Others postulate a method for keeping wine from fermenting (cf. Foakes-Jackson and Lake, *Beginnings of Christianity*, 4.20). All of this, however, has little relevance here, for the apostles were accused of being drunk.

2. Peter's Sermon at Pentecost (2:14–41)

OVERVIEW

Peter's sermon at Pentecost consists of (1) an *apologia* ("formal justification") for the occurrence of the phenomena (vv.14–21), (2) a *kērygma* ("proclamation") of the apostolic message in its most elemental form (vv.22–36), and (3) a call to repentance with a promise of blessing (vv.37–41). The sermon is headed by a brief introductory statement and followed by two summary sentences dealing with Peter's further preaching and the people's response. It was probably delivered in the outer court of the temple. And while the verb *apophthengomai* ("addressed") in v.14 is the same as in v.4, we should understand that Peter spoke in the local vernacular—whether some form of Aramaic or Koine Greek—and not in a foreign language, for *apophthengomai* relates more to the inspired nature of the message than its mode.

a. The apologia (2:14–21)

¹⁴Then Peter stood up with the Eleven, raised his voice and addressed the crowd: "Fellow Jews and all of you who live in Jerusalem, let me explain this to you; listen carefully to what I say. ¹⁵These men are not drunk, as you suppose. It's only nine in the morning! ¹⁶No, this is what was spoken by the prophet Joel:

¹⁷"'In the last days, God says,
　I will pour out my Spirit on all people.
Your sons and daughters will prophesy,
　your young men will see visions,
　your old men will dream dreams.
¹⁸Even on my servants, both men and women,
　I will pour out my Spirit in those days,
　and they will prophesy.
¹⁹I will show wonders in the heaven above
　and signs on the earth below,
　blood and fire and billows of smoke.
²⁰The sun will be turned to darkness
　and the moon to blood
　before the coming of the great and glorious day of the Lord.
²¹And everyone who calls on the name of the Lord will be saved.'"

COMMENTARY

14 The *apologia* of Peter's sermon is addressed to "fellow Jews and all . . . who live in Jerusalem." Later in the *kerygma* section these two groups are combined under the captions "men of Israel" (v.22) and "brothers" (v.29), for it was natural for them to be classed together. But here Peter apparently wanted to include particularly those who had been most bewildered by the multiplicity of the languages spoken. While undoubtedly many of the native-born Jews were awed by what they had seen and heard, it was probably those from the Diaspora who most appreciated the incongruity of the situation and called for an explanation.

15 Peter begins negatively by arguing that the apostles could not be drunk, for it was only "nine

in the morning" (lit., "the third hour of the day"). Such an argument was probably more telling in antiquity than today.

16–21 Positively, Peter explains the phenomena taking place among the early Christians at Pentecost as being the fulfillment of Joel 2:28–32 (MT = 3:1–5). His use of the Joel passage is in line with what, since the discovery of the Dead Sea Scrolls, we call a "pesher" treatment of Scripture (from Heb. *pešer*, "interpretation"), which emphasizes only fulfillment without attempting to exegete the details of the biblical prophecy it "interprets." So Peter introduces the passage with the typically pesher introductory formula "this is that" (*touto estin to*; NIV, "this is what"). The note of fulfillment is heightened by the alteration of the MT's and the LXX's simple "afterwards" (*ʾaḥarê kēn; meta tauta*) to "in the last days" (*en tais eschatais hēmerais*, v.17) and by interrupting the quotation to highlight the restoration of prophecy by inserting the words "and they will prophesy" (v.18). The solemnity and importance of the words are emphasized by the addition of "God says" (v.17) at the beginning of the quotation.

The way Peter uses Joel 2:28–32 is of great significance (1) for an appreciation of early Christian exegetical practices and doctrinal commitments and (2) as a pattern for our own treatment of the OT. For Peter, what Joel said is what God says. And while what God says may have been somewhat enigmatic when first uttered, when seen from the perspective of eschatological fulfillment a great deal of what was unclear is clarified. Thus Peter can proclaim from the perspective of the Messiah's resurrection and living presence with his people (1) that "this" that he and the infant church were experiencing in the outpouring of God's Spirit "is that" prophesied by Joel; (2) that these are "the last days" of God's redemptive program; and (3) that the validation of all this is the return of prophecy. In other words, he is proclaiming that this is the time for the fulfillment of OT prophecy and that these are the long-awaited "last days" of the divine redemptive program. He is also suggesting by his inclusion of the prophet's call for response that through the apostles' proclamation there will go out from Jerusalem a prophetic message of salvation and a call for repentance.

Debates arise between proponents of "realized eschatology" and "inaugurated eschatology" on the one hand, and between amillennialists (including postmillennialists) and premillennialists on the other, about how Peter and the early Christians understood the more spectacular physical signs of Joel's prophecy (i.e., "blood and fire and billows of smoke," "the sun will be turned to darkness and the moon to blood"). Realized eschatologists and amillennialists usually take Peter's inclusion of such physical imagery in a spiritual way and find in what happened at Pentecost the spiritual fulfillment of Joel's prophecy—i.e., a fulfillment not necessarily tied to any natural phenomena. This passage, they suggest, offers an interpretative key to the understanding of similar portrayals of natural phenomena and apocalyptic imagery in the OT. Some realized eschatologists and amillennialists, desiring to retain more than just the symbolic, suggest that these signs should be understood as having actually taken place in the natural world "during the early afternoon of the day of our Lord's crucifixion," when "the sun turned into darkness" and "the paschal full moon . . . appeared blood-red in the sky in consequence of that preternatural gloom" (F. F. Bruce, 69).

On the other hand, certain features in Peter's sermon show his reason for citing Joel's prophecy: his introductory formula "this is that," his changing of "afterward" (Joel 2:28) to "in the last days," his addition of "God says" at the beginning of the quotation, and his interruption of the quotation to insert "and they will prophesy." Peter quotes the entire prophecy in Joel 2:28–32 because of its traditional messianic significance and because its final sentence ("And everyone who calls on the name of the Lord will be saved") leads logically to the *kerygma* section of his sermon. He might not, however, have known exactly what to make of the more physical and spectacular elements of Joel's prophecy, though he probably expected them to take place in some way in the very near future. So his emphasis was on the inauguration of the messianic age ("the last days")—an emphasis we should take as being essential to his preaching but beyond which we are not compelled to go.

God has inaugurated, Peter proclaims, the long-awaited "last days" here and now, and we know this because of the reinstitution of prophecy. Other signs, to be sure, were part of Joel's vision, but Peter does not stress them. His emphasis is entirely on prophecy as the sign of the inauguration of the last days. Even though he might have had his own expectations about what else might happen with the fulfillment of prophecy, Peter leaves all that to God.

NOTES

14 Codex Bezae (D) has it that Peter stood "with the twelve apostles" (σὺν τοῖς δέκα ἀποστόλοις, *syn tois deka apostolois*) rather than, as strongly attested in the better MSS, "with the Eleven" (σὺν τοῖς ἕνδεκα, *syn tois hendeka*), thus suggesting either that Bezae's source was disregarded by its translators or that they were ignorant of the election of Matthias.

The compound ἄνδρες Ἰουδαῖοι (*andres Ioudaioi*, lit., "men, Jews"; NIV, "fellow Jews"; NASB, "men of Judea") is comparable to Luke's frequently used ἄνδρες ἀδελφοί (*andres adelphoi*, lit., "men, brothers") of 1:16 (see comments there). Cf. also ἄνδρες Ἰσραηλῖται (*andres Israēlitai*, lit., "men, Israelites"; NIV, "men of Israel") of 2:22.

16 On pesher interpretation at Qumran and in the NT, see my *Biblical Exegesis in the Apostolic Period*, 24–30.

The name of the prophet Joel is omitted in the Western text (D, and as represented in recensions of the Old Latin), Ephraem of Syria's commentary on Acts, and such Latin fathers as Irenaeus, Hilary, Gregory, and Augustine (*Epistulae* 199.23). This is probably because subsequent introductory formulas to quotations from the Minor Prophets in Acts (7:42; 13:40; 15:15) also omit the prophets' names.

17–21 The quotation of Joel 2:28–32 is preserved in two forms: as represented by Codex Vaticanus (B) and as represented by Codex Bezae (D). B agrees almost exactly with the text of the LXX, whereas D evidences a number of changes from the LXX—changes that often reflect an anti-Jewish bias and Gentile interests (cf. E. J. Epp, *The Theological Tendency of Codex Bezae Cantabrigiensis in Acts* [SNTSMS 3; Cambridge: Cambridge Univ. Press, 1966]). Assuming the originality of B and that modifications were introduced by the Western reviser of D, the textual variations from the MT and LXX are rather insignificant and probably without theological importance: (1) the rearrangement of clauses in v.17, so that "your young men will see visions" precedes "your old men will dream dreams," and (2) the addition in v.19 of the words "above," "signs," and "below."

b. The kerygma (2:22–36)

OVERVIEW

Dodd, 21–24, has identified six themes that appear repeatedly in Peter's sermons in Acts 2–4:

1. "The age of fulfillment has dawned."
2. "'This has taken place through the ministry, death and resurrection of Jesus, of which a brief account is given, with proof from the Scriptures."
3. "By virtue of the resurrection, Jesus has been exalted at the right hand of God, as Messianic head of the new Israel."

4. "The Holy Spirit in the Church is the sign of Christ's present power and glory."

5. "The Messianic Age will shortly reach its consummation in the return of Christ."

6. "The *kerygma* always closes with an appeal for repentance, the offer of forgiveness and of the Holy Spirit, and the promise of 'salvation,' that is, of 'the life of the Age to Come,' to those who enter the elect community."

With the exception of the return of Christ (which appears in these early sermons only at 3:20–21), all of these themes come to the fore in Peter's Pentecost sermon: the note of fulfillment explicitly in the *apologia* section and inferentially throughout; the appeal for repentance and the promise of blessing at the close of the sermon; and the remaining themes in what can be designated as the *kerygma* section proper, which focuses on Jesus of Nazareth as humanity's Lord and Israel's promised Messiah.

Despite its denial by certain scholars, it yet remains true to say that Peter's sermons of Acts 2–4 "represent the *kerygma* of the Church at Jerusalem at an early period" (Dodd, 21). They are not verbatim reports, and hardly anyone has so taken them. But though they have been styled and shaped by Luke in accordance with his own purposes, they are not simply reproductions of his own theology or that of his spiritual mentor, Paul. Rather, they exhibit Semitic features and primitive characteristics that show that they come from a period earlier than the writing of Acts and stem from the earliest Christian congregation at Jerusalem. Moreover, though many have thought otherwise, the early church was interested in the life and character of Jesus—not for merely biographical reasons, but to fill out the content of its preaching—since the focus of the apostolic proclamation was on Jesus of Nazareth, humanity's Lord and Israel's Messiah (cf. Stanton, *Jesus of Nazareth in New Testament Preaching*). Thus Peter in his Pentecost sermon includes a brief sketch of the ministry, death, and resurrection of Jesus.

The early preaching of the church regarding Jesus was principally functional in nature rather than speculative or philosophical, and it stressed ultimate causality more than secondary causes or means. One cannot, of course, speak of "what" happened redemptively without also raising questions regarding "who" and "how." Questions relating to ontology (the nature of being) and speculations about why and how things happened are inevitably bound up in the declaration of the "thatness" of divine redemption and seem to have come very soon to the fore in the thinking of the early church. Yet in presenting the earliest preaching of the apostles at Jerusalem, it is significant that Luke did not attempt to put such nuances into their mouths. Instead, he presents Peter as proclaiming "Jesus of Nazareth," "a man accredited," "handed over," put "to death," but raised "from the dead." Peter also proclaimed God as the true author of Jesus' miracles, the ultimate agent in Jesus' death, and the primary cause for Jesus' resurrection. There is, to be sure, some allusion to means in the statement "and you, with the help of wicked men, put him to death by nailing him to the cross" (v.23b). And there may be some ontological insight into who Jesus actually was in the statement "because it was impossible for death to keep its hold on him" (v.24b). Indeed, vv.25–35 explain this "impossibility," not only in terms of what Scripture has foretold, but also in terms of who this Holy One was. Yet the emphasis in Peter's proclamation of Jesus—as also in his concluding declaration (v.36) and his call to repentance (v.38)—is strongly functional, apart from any definite philosophical speculation and with only minimal attention to the way in which God's purpose in Christ was carried out.

22"Men of Israel, listen to this: Jesus of Nazareth was a man accredited by God to you by miracles, wonders and signs, which God did among you through him, as you yourselves know. 23This man was handed over to you by God's set purpose and foreknowledge; and you, with the help of wicked men, put him to death by nailing him to the cross. 24But God raised him from the dead, freeing him from the agony of death, because it was impossible for death to keep its hold on him. 25David said about him:

"'I saw the Lord always before me.
    Because he is at my right hand,
    I will not be shaken.
26Therefore my heart is glad and my tongue rejoices;
    my body also will live in hope,
27because you will not abandon me to the grave,
    nor will you let your Holy One see decay.
28You have made known to me the paths of life;
    you will fill me with joy in your presence.'

29"Brothers, I can tell you confidently that the patriarch David died and was buried, and his tomb is here to this day. 30But he was a prophet and knew that God had promised him on oath that he would place one of his descendants on his throne. 31Seeing what was ahead, he spoke of the resurrection of the Christ, that he was not abandoned to the grave, nor did his body see decay. 32God has raised this Jesus to life, and we are all witnesses of the fact. 33Exalted to the right hand of God, he has received from the Father the promised Holy Spirit and has poured out what you now see and hear. 34For David did not ascend to heaven, and yet he said,

"'The Lord said to my Lord:
    "Sit at my right hand
35until I make your enemies
    a footstool for your feet."'

36"Therefore, let all Israel be assured of this: God has made this Jesus, whom you crucified, both Lord and Christ."

COMMENTARY

22 Peter begins the *kerygma* or proclamation section of his sermon with an inclusive form of address—"Men of Israel"—which he parallels with the synonymous vocative "brothers" (v.29; see Notes, v.14). His topic concerns "Jesus of Nazareth," a title used of Jesus throughout Luke's writings (cf. Lk 18:37; Ac 3:6; 4:10; 6:14; 10:38; 22:8; 26:9) and one by which the early Christians themselves were sometimes called (cf. Ac 24:5). The ministry of Jesus is characterized by "miracles, wonders and signs" that God did among the people through Jesus. The compound expression "wonders and signs" (*terata kai sēmeia*, GK *5469, 4956*) appears often in various Greek writers, in the LXX, and in the NT itself (e.g., Ac 2:43; 4:30; 5:12; 6:8; 7:36; 14:3; 15:12; cf. 2:19), though the threefold "miracles, wonders and signs" is somewhat rare (cf. 2Co 12:12b, where the order is reversed).

23 The death of Jesus is presented as resulting from the interplay of divine necessity and human freedom. Nowhere in the NT is the paradox of a Christian understanding of history put more sharply than in this earliest proclamation of the death of Jesus the Messiah: God's purpose and foreknowledge stand as the necessary factors behind whatever happens; yet whatever happens occurs through the instrumentality of wicked men expressing their own human freedom. It is a paradox without ready solution. To deny it, however, is to go counter to the plain teaching of Scripture (both OT and NT) and to ignore the testimony of personal experience. "With the help of wicked men" points to the Roman authorities who carried out what had been instigated by the Jewish authorities. Gentiles are frequently referred to in Jewish writings as "wicked" (e.g., *Jub.* 23:23–24) and "lawless" (e.g., *Pss. Sol.* 17:11, 18; cf. 1Co 9:21), either because of their actual sins or simply because they did not possess the Mosaic law.

24 The resurrection of Jesus is attributed directly to God, apart from any action of men or even Jesus himself, just as elsewhere in the NT it is so attributed in quotations from early Christian hymns and catechisms (e.g., 1Co 15:4; Php 2:9). The imagery is of "death pangs" (*ōdinas tou thanatou*; NIV, "the agony of death"; GK *6047, 2505*) and their awful clutches (cf. 2Sa 22:6; Pss 18:4–6; 116:3), from which God set Jesus free "because it was impossible for death to keep its hold on him."

25–35 Peter quotes from Psalms 16:8–11 (LXX) and 110:1 in support of what he has just said about

Jesus in v.24. The quotations are brought together according to the second of the midrashic exegetical rules attributed by antiquity to Rabbi Hillel—i.e., the rule *gezerah shawah*, or "verbal analogy," which states that where the same words appear in two passages, the same considerations apply to both. Both quotations have "at my right hand," and so are treated together (cf. v.33). In addition, both quotations are used in pesher fashion (see comments at v.16), for it is a pesher understanding that evokes the introductory statement "David said about him" (v.25) and applies the words wholly to Jesus.

During the period of early Judaism, Psalms 16 and 110 were considered by Jewish interpreters to be somewhat enigmatic and so were variously understood. There was no problem with the confidence expressed in Psalm 16:8–9, 11, which was appropriate for the psalmist to whom God's love had been pledged and who had experienced God's covenant-keeping loving-kindness. But how could the psalmist have expected God to keep him from the grave and from undergoing decay, as in v.10? And Psalm 110 was even more difficult, for who is "my Lord" to whom "the Lord" has said, "Sit at my right hand until I make your enemies a footstool for your feet" (v.34)? Some early rabbis linked the psalm with Abraham, who as the father of the nation Israel was its Lord; others with the Torah, which was given as humanity's Lord; some with David; and some even with Hezekiah. But there is no clearly attested messianic understanding of Psalm 110 in rabbinic literature until about AD 260 (cf. Str-B, 4.452–60; D. M. Hay, *Glory at the Right Hand: Psalm 110 in Early Christianity* [New York: Abingdon, 1973], 19–33).

Nevertheless, Jesus is reported in all the Synoptic Gospels as having interpreted Psalm 110:1 as a messianic passage and applying it to himself (Mk 12:35–37 par.). And it was probably Jesus' own treatment of Psalm 110:1 that (1) furnished the exegetical key for the early Christians' understanding of their risen Lord, (2) served as the pattern for their interpretation of similar enigmatic OT passages (e.g., 2Sa 7:6–16 with Ps 2:7, and Isa 55:3 with Ps 16:10 in Paul's Antioch address of Ac 13:16–41), and (3) anchored all other passages as could be brought together on a "verbal analogy" basis (e.g., the catena of passages in Heb 1:5–13).

Therefore, working from Psalm 110:1 as an accepted messianic passage and viewing Psalm 16:8–11 as having a similar reference on the basis of the hermeneutical rule of "verbal analogy," Peter proclaims that Psalm 16:10 ("you will not abandon me to the grave, nor will you let your Holy One see decay") refers to Israel's promised Messiah and no other. It is an argument based on the exegetical precedent set by Jesus, inspired by the church's postresurrection perspective, and worked out along the lines of commonly accepted midrashic principles of the day. Furthermore, Peter insists, David could not have been speaking about himself, since he did indeed die, was buried, and suffered decay—as the presence of his tomb in the city eloquently testified (v.29). Nor did he ascend to heaven. Therefore, Peter asserts, David must have been prophesying about the resurrection of the Messiah in Psalm 16:10 and about his exaltation in Psalm 110:1. With God's raising of Jesus from the dead, these formerly enigmatic passages are now clarified and the pouring out of the Spirit explained.

36 With the proclamation of Jesus as Lord and Messiah, Peter reaches the climax and conclusion of his sermon. His initial "therefore" highlights the fact that God's resurrection and exaltation of Jesus accredits him as humanity's Lord and Israel's Messiah. So Peter calls on "all Israel" (lit., "all the house [*oikos*, GK 3875] of Israel") to know with certainty that "God has made this Jesus, whom you crucified, both Lord and Christ."

In certain quarters it has become commonplace to assert that the church did not proclaim Jesus as Lord and Christ until *after* the resurrection—or, as many prefer to express it, until after the rise within the church of "the Easter faith." The implication is that only later were such names as "Lord" and "Christ" attached to Jesus' memory, but Jesus himself did not think along these lines. And this verse is often cited in support of such a view. But it is more in line with the evidence to say that Jesus was acknowledged and proclaimed Lord and Christ not just after his resurrection but also *because of* his resurrection.

In Jewish thought, no one had the right to the title Messiah until he accomplished the work of the Messiah—in fact, in all of life, accomplishment must precede acclamation. During his earthly ministry, as portrayed in all the Gospels, Jesus was distinctly reluctant to accept such titular acclaim. This was probably because (1) his understanding of messiahship had to do with suffering, and (2) his concept of lordship had to do with vindication and exaltation by God. But now that Jesus had accomplished his messianic mission, was raised by God, and has been exalted "at his right hand," the titles Lord and Christ are legitimately his. And these themes of function and accomplishment as being the basis for any titular acclaim are recurring features in the christological statements found elsewhere in the NT (cf. Ro 1:4; Php 2:9–11; Heb 2:14; 1Jn 5:6).

The verb *epoiēsen* (GK 4472, "he made") has sometimes been taken as implying an adoptionist Christology, as though Jesus became ontologically what he was not before. But in functional contexts *epoiēsen* has the sense of "appointed" (cf. 1Sa 12:6 [LXX]; 1Ki 12:31 [LXX]; Mk 3:14; Heb 3:2), and it is in just such a context that it is used here. Peter is not proclaiming an adoptionist Christology. Rather, he is proclaiming a functional Christology with ontological overtones. It is a functional Christology that emphasizes two vitally important points: (1) that the resurrection of Jesus from the dead is God's open declaration that the messianic work has been accomplished and that Jesus now has the full right to assume the messianic title, and (2) that the exaltation of Jesus is the proclamation of his lordship, which God calls all to acknowledge.

In the twelve instances in Acts where "Christ" appears singly (2:31, 36; 3:18; 4:26; 8:5; 9:22; 17:3a; 26:23; also 3:20; 5:42; 18:5, 28, where "Christ" is in apposition to "Jesus" but still appears singly), it is used as a title (usually articular in form, except here and at 3:20) but not as a name. And in every instance where it appears as a title, it is in an address to a Jewish audience. (Only 8:5 and 26:23 are possible exceptions, though both the Samaritans and Agrippa II possessed something of a Jewish background and understanding.) Even where the combination "Jesus Christ" or "Christ Jesus" appears, the original appellative idea is still reflected in the usage.

Apparently, therefore, the messiahship of Jesus was the distinctive feature of the church's witness within Jewish circles, since Jesus' messiahship signifies his fulfillment of Israel's hopes and his culmination of God's redemptive purposes.

The title "Lord" was also proclaimed christologically in Jewish circles, with evident intent to apply to Jesus all that was said of God in the OT (cf. the christological use of Isa 45:23 in Php 2:10). But "Lord" came to have particular relevance to the church's witness to Gentiles, just as "Messiah" was more relevant to the Jewish world. So Luke in Acts reports the proclamation of Jesus "the Christ" to Jewish audiences, both in Palestine and among the Diaspora, whereas Paul in his letters to Gentile churches generally uses "Christ" as a proper name and proclaims Christ Jesus "the Lord."

NOTES

22 On the critical issues involved in these early sermons, see Introduction, pp. 691–93. For a defense of the thesis that the early church was interested in the life and character of Jesus and that the primary (though not the only) *Sitz im Leben* of that interest was the missionary preaching of the church, see Stanton, *Jesus of Nazareth in New Testament Preaching*.

It is now widely accepted as being both linguistically and historically probable that the term Ναζωραῖος (*Nazōraios*) means "an inhabitant of Nazareth" (cf. G. F. Moore, "Nazarene and Nazareth," in *Beginnings of Christianity* [ed. Foakes-Jackson and Lake], 1:426–32; W. F. Albright, "The Names 'Nazareth' and 'Nazoraean,'" *JBL* 65 [1946]: 397–401). There is no difference in intent between "Jesus from Nazareth" (Ἰησοῦν τὸν ἀπὸ Ναζωραῖον, *Iēsoun ton apo Nazōraion*) and "Jesus the Nazarene" (Ἰησοῦν τὸν Ναζωραῖον, *Iēsoun ton Nazōraion*), either here or elsewhere in Luke-Acts. And what is true here is also true, at least in part, for the much disputed appearance of Ναζωραῖος (*Nazōraios*) in Matthew 2:23.

24 The Western text (D, and as reflected in recensions of the Old Latin, Vulgate, Syriac, and Coptic versions, in Ephraem's commentary on Acts, and by such church fathers as Polycarp, Irenaeus, and Augustine) has "pangs of Hades" (ὠδῖνας ᾅδου, *ōdinas hadou*) rather than "pangs of death" (ὠδῖνας θανάτου, *ōdinas thanatou*), probably to conform with the expression "into Hades" (εἰς ᾅδην, *eis hadēn*) of 2:27 and 31 (NIV, "the grave"; NASB, "Hades"). But "pangs of death" and "pangs of Hades" were used interchangeably in the biblical tradition (cf. 2Sa 22:6 and Ps 114:3 vs. Ps 17:6 [LXX]), and there is solid early manuscript support for the former.

25 Only Luke among the synoptic evangelists has omitted the "cry of dereliction" from the cross, "My God, my God, why have you forsaken me?" (Mt 27:46; Mk 15:34), and only Luke has included the more filial final word, "Father, into your hands I commit my spirit" (Lk 23:46). Both the omission and the inclusion are in line with the quotation of Psalm 16:8 here: "I saw the Lord always [διὰ παντός, dia pantos] before me. Because he is at my right hand, I will not be shaken."

25–28 The LXX of Psalm 16:8–11 (15:8–11) has "I saw" (προωρώμην, proōrōmēn) for the MT's "I have set" (šiwwîtî); "my tongue" (ἡ γλῶσσά μου, hē glōssa mou) for "my glory" (k^ebôdî); "in hope" (ἐπ᾽ ἐλπίδι, ep' elpidi) for "in safety" (lābetah); and "destruction" or "decay" (διαφθοράν, diaphthoran) for "pit" (šahat).

34–35 On midrashic interpretation among the rabbis and in the NT, see my *Biblical Exegesis in the Apostolic Period* (2d ed.), 18–24. On Jesus' use of Psalm 110:1 as setting a paradigm for his followers and the church, see ibid. 57–62.

36 The expression "all the house of Israel" (πᾶς οἶκος Ἰσραήλ, pas oikos Israēl; NIV, "all Israel"; NASB, "all the house of Israel") occurs only here in the NT, though it was common in the liturgical prayers of ancient Judaism; cf. also Ezekiel 37:11.

The adverb ἀσφαλῶς (asphalōs, GK *857*; NIV, "be assured"), which means "beyond a doubt" or "assuredly," stands first in the sentence for emphasis.

On the christological title "Messiah" and its implications, see my *Christology of Early Jewish Christianity*, 63–119; on "Lord" and its attendant features, see ibid. 120–47.

c. A call to repentance and a promise of blessing (2:37–41)

> ³⁷When the people heard this, they were cut to the heart and said to Peter and the other apostles, "Brothers, what shall we do?"
>
> ³⁸Peter replied, "Repent and be baptized, every one of you, in the name of Jesus Christ for the forgiveness of your sins. And you will receive the gift of the Holy Spirit. ³⁹The promise is for you and your children and for all who are far off—for all whom the Lord our God will call."
>
> ⁴⁰With many other words he warned them; and he pleaded with them, "Save yourselves from this corrupt generation." ⁴¹Those who accepted his message were baptized, and about three thousand were added to their number that day.

COMMENTARY

37 Peter's preaching had been effective. The people were "cut to the heart" at the awful realization that in crucifying their long-awaited Messiah they had rejected their only hope of salvation. So in deep anguish they cried out, "Brothers, what shall we do?"

Luke uses the verb *katanyssomai* ("pierced, stabbed, cut to the heart," GK *2920*) to describe their feelings. The word may have been drawn from Psalm 109:16. It connotes a sharp pain associated with anxiety and remorse. In 1:20 Luke had used

Psalm 109:8 (108:8 [LXX]) to describe not only wicked men who oppose God's servant but also the wicked man Judas Iscariot. Now Luke apparently reaches back to that same psalm (v.16) to pick up the vivid phrase for those who stand with God's servant in opposing wicked men: "those who have been cut to the heart" (*kateugēsan tēn kardian*)—i.e., those who are "humble of heart" because they realize their need and are open to God's working (in contrast to those whom Luke describes by the verb *diapriō*, GK *1391*, "cut to the quick" in the sense of being infuriated, in Ac 5:33; 7:54). In fact, the way the men address the apostles ("brothers"; lit., "men, brothers"), shows that their hearts had already been won over.

Codex Bezae (D) and some of its Western associates (Old Latin, Coptic Bohairic version, Hippolytus, Augustine) omit "others" (*loipous*) in "the other apostles," thereby distinguishing Peter from the apostles. But Luke's stress is on the supremacy of the apostles in the church, not on the supremacy of Peter alone. While in both his gospel and Acts he portrays Peter as taking leadership among the apostles, nowhere does Luke suggest anything more than that Peter was the natural leader and spokesman of the Twelve.

38 Peter's answer to the people's anguished cry presents interpreters with a set of complex theological problems that have often been treated only as grist for differing theological mills. But Peter's words came to his hearers as the best news they had ever heard—far better, indeed, than they deserved or could have hoped for. And these words remain today as the best of good news and should be read as the proclamation of that news, not just as data for contemporary theological discussions.

Peter calls on his hearers to "repent" (*metanoeō*, GK *3566*). The term implies a complete change of heart and confession of sin. With this call he couples the call to "be baptized" (*baptisthētō*, GK *966*),

thereby linking both repentance and baptism with the forgiveness of sins. So far this sounds familiar, for John the Baptist had proclaimed a "baptism of repentance for the forgiveness of sins" (Mk 1:4), and Jesus made repentance central in his preaching (cf. Mt 4:17; Mk 1:15) and baptized (cf. Jn 3:22; 4:1–2). Furthermore, Judaism also had repentance at the core of its message and emphasized baptism (at least for proselytes). But while there is much that appears traditional in Peter's exhortation, there is also much that is new and distinctive—in three ways in particular.

One distinctive feature in his preaching is that Peter calls on "every one" of his audience to repent and be baptized. Jews thought corporately and generally viewed the rite of baptism as appropriate only for proselytes (though some sects within Judaism baptized Jews). But like John the Baptist (cf. Mt 3:9–10)—and probably Jesus, though in distinction to Judaism generally—Peter called for an individual response on the part of his hearers. So he set aside family and corporate relationships as having any final, saving significance and stressed the response of the person individually, without, however, denying the value of corporate relationships but placing them in a "new covenant" perspective.

A second feature is that Peter identifies the repentance and baptism he is speaking about as being specifically Christian in that it is done "in the name of Jesus Christ" (*epi tō onomati Iēsou Christou*). The expression was probably not at this time a liturgical formula. It appears variously in Acts with the prepositions *epi* ("on") as here (though there are variations in the textual tradition), *en* ("in") as in 10:48, and *eis* ("into") as in 8:16 and 19:5. What it means, it seems, is that in repenting and being baptized a person calls on the name of Jesus (cf. 22:16) and thereby avows his or her intention to be committed to and identified with Jesus.

A third feature in Peter's preaching is the relation of the gift of the Holy Spirit to repentance and baptism. "The gift of the Holy Spirit" is another way of describing what the disciples had experienced in "the coming of the Holy Spirit," which Jesus called "the baptism of the Holy Spirit" (cf. 1:4-5, 8). All three expressions are connected with God's promise to his people and used interchangeably in Acts 1 and 2.

We must, however, distinguish between "the gift" of the Holy Spirit and what Paul called "the spiritual gifts" (*ta pneumatika*, GK *4461*, 1Co 12:1; 14:1) of that selfsame Spirit. "The gift" is the Spirit himself, given to minister the saving benefits of Christ's redemption to the believer, while "the spiritual gifts" are those spiritual abilities that the Spirit gives variously to believers "for the common good" and sovereignly, "just as he determines" (1Co 12:7, 11). Peter's promise of "the gift of the Holy Spirit" is the result of repentance and baptism. This primary gift includes a variety of spiritual gifts for the advancement of the gospel and the welfare of God's people. But first of all, it has to do with what God's Spirit does for every Christian in applying and working out the benefits of Christ's redemptive work.

In dealing with the various elements in this passage, some interpreters have stressed the command to be baptized so as to link the forgiveness of sins exclusively with baptism. But it runs contrary to all biblical religion to assume that outward rites have any value apart from true repentance and an inward change. The Jewish mind could not divorce inward spirituality from its outward expression. And wherever the Christian gospel was proclaimed in a Jewish milieu, the rite of baptism was taken for granted as being inevitably involved (cf. 2:41; 8:12, 36-38; 9:18; 10:47-48; 18:8; 19:5; see Heb 10:22; 1Pe 3:18-21). But Peter's sermon in Solomon's Colonnade (3:12-26) stresses only repentance and turning to God "so that your sins may be wiped out" (v.19) and makes no mention of baptism. This shows that for Luke, and probably also for Peter, while baptism

with water was the expected symbol for conversion, it was not the indispensable criterion for salvation.

A few commentators have set Peter's words in v.38 in opposition to those of John the Baptist in Mark (1:8 par.) and those of Jesus (Ac 1:5), where the baptism of the Holy Spirit is distinguished from John's baptism and appears to supersede it. But neither the Baptist's prophecy nor Jesus' promise necessarily implies that the baptism of the Spirit would set aside water baptism. Certainly the early church did not take it that way. They continued to practice water baptism as the external symbol by which those who believed the gospel, repented of their sins, and acknowledged Jesus as their Lord publicly bore witness to their new life, which had been received through the baptism of the Holy Spirit. In line, then, with the Baptist's prophecy and Jesus' promise, baptism with the Holy Spirit is distinguished from baptism with water. But baptism with the Holy Spirit did not replace baptism with water. Rather, the latter was given a richer significance because of the saving work of Christ and the coming of the Spirit.

A difficult problem arises when we try to correlate Peter's words here with the accounts of the Spirit's baptism in 8:15-17 (at Samaria), 10:44-46 (in the home of Cornelius), and 19:6 (at Ephesus). In v.38 the baptism of the Spirit is portrayed as the logical outcome of repentance and water baptism; in 8:15-17; 10:44-46; and 19:6, however, it appears to be temporally separated from conversion and water baptism—either following them, as at Samaria and Ephesus, or preceding them, as with Cornelius. Sacramentalists take this as a biblical basis for separating baptism and confirmation, and charismatics see it as justification for viewing the baptism of the Spirit as a second work of grace after conversion.

Lest too much be made of this difference theologically, we should first take into account the historical situation of vv.37-41 and attempt to understand matters more circumstantially. Assuming that Luke shared Paul's view of the indissoluble connection between conversion, water baptism, and the baptism of the Holy Spirit (cf. Ro 8:9; 1Co 6:11), we may ask, What if the Pentecost experience, particularly in regard to the sequence and temporal relations of conversion, water baptism, and Holy Spirit baptism, had been fully present in each of these latter three instances?

What would have been the situation with respect to the Samaritans (8:4–8, 14–17), who had been converted through the instrumentality of Philip, one of the Hellenists expelled from Jerusalem at the time of Stephen's martyrdom? Samaritans had always been considered second-class citizens by the Jews of Jerusalem, who kept them at arm's length. What, then, if it had been the apostles residing at Jerusalem who had been the missionaries to Samaria? Probably they would have been rebuffed, just as they were earlier when the Samaritans associated them with the city of Jerusalem (cf. Lk 9:51–56). But God providentially used Philip, who himself had been rebuffed at Jerusalem (though for different reasons), to bring them the gospel. The Samaritans received him and believed his message.

But what if the Spirit had come on the Samaritan believers at their baptism by Philip? Undoubtedly, whatever feelings some of the Christians at Jerusalem had against Philip and the Hellenists would have rubbed off on the Samaritan believers and they would have been doubly under suspicion. But God providentially withheld the gift of the Holy Spirit until Peter and John—two leading apostles who would have been accepted by both the new converts of Samaria and the established congregation at Jerusalem—laid their hands on the Samaritans. Thus in this first advance of the gospel outside Jerusalem, God worked in ways conducive both to the reception of the good news in Samaria and the acceptance of these new converts at Jerusalem—ways that promoted both the outreach of the gospel and the unity of the church.

Or take the conversion of Cornelius (10:24–48). What if, in Peter's ministry to this Gentile, the order of events Peter had set down after his sermon at Pentecost had occurred (2:38): (1) repentance, (2) baptism, (3) forgiveness of sins, and (4) reception of the gift of the Holy Spirit? Some at Jerusalem might have accused Peter of manipulating the occasion for his own ends, as his lengthy defense before the Jerusalem congregation in 11:1–18 takes pains to deny. But God in his providence gave the gift of his Spirit, coupled with such signs as would convince both Peter and his possible critics at Jerusalem, even *before* Cornelius's baptism, so that all would attribute his conversion entirely to God rather than allow their prejudices to make Cornelius a second-class Christian.

As for the incident recorded in 19:1–4, this, along with the other two passages just mentioned, will be dealt with later in addressing those accounts. Enough, however, has been said here to suggest that we should understand Peter's preaching at Pentecost as being theologically normative for the relation in Acts of (1) conversion, (2) water baptism, and (3) the baptism of the Holy Spirit—with the situations at Samaria, in the home of Cornelius, and among the twelve whom Paul met at Ephesus (which is something of a case all to itself) to be more historically conditioned and circumstantially understood.

39 The "promise" that Peter speaks about includes both the forgiveness of sins and the gift of the Holy Spirit. Both are logically and indissolubly united in applying Christ's redemptive work to the believer. They were only separated chronologically, it seems, for what could be called circumstantial reasons. This promise, Peter declares, is not only for his immediate hearers ("for you") but also for succeeding generations ("for your children") and for all in distant places ("for all who are far off"). It is a promise, Peter concludes, that is sure, for it has been given by God and is based on the prophetic word of Joel 2:32: "And everyone who calls on the name of the LORD will be saved" (cf. Ac 2:21)

Some interpreters see in the expression "for all who are far off" (*pasin tois eis makran*) a temporal reference to future Jewish generations, thereby paralleling the phrase "for your children" (*tois teknois hymōn*). But *makran* ("far off") is not used temporally in the LXX or anywhere else in the NT, and so it is probably better to interpret it here more spatially than temporally. A spatial interpretation, however, raises the question of whether *makran* refers exclusively to Jews of the Diaspora or should be seen also to include Gentiles. That two OT remnant passages are alluded to here (Isa 57:19, "Peace, peace, to those far and near," and Joel 2:32) has led some commentators to assume that *makran* refers to Jews of the Diaspora. On the other hand, the use of Luke's report of Paul's defense at Jerusalem (22:21; cf. Eph 2:13) has led other commentators to argue that *makran* refers also to Gentiles.

This is probably one of those situations where a narrator (e.g., Luke) has read into what a speaker said more than was originally there, and so implied that the speaker spoke better than he knew. It seems difficult to believe that Peter himself thought beyond the perspective of Jewish remnant theology. Just as he could hardly have visualized anything beyond the next generation, so he could hardly have conceived of anything spatially beyond God's call to a scattered but repentant Jewish remnant. But Luke's desire is to show how an originally Jewish gospel penetrated the Gentile world so extensively that it came to enter the capital of the Roman Empire "without hindrance" (cf. 28:31). Very likely, therefore, in recounting Peter's words here in Acts, Luke

meant them to be read as having Gentiles ultimately in mind—whatever Peter may have been thinking at the time. So we may conclude that Luke here used *makran* in the same sense as he did in 22:21.

40 Two summary statements conclude Luke's report of Peter's Pentecost sermon. The first has to do with Peter's further words (v.40); the second indicates the extent of the people's response (v.41).

The earnestness of Peter's words is connoted by the intensive use of prepositions in the verbs *diamarturomai* ("charge," "warn," "adjure," GK *1371*) and *parakaleō* ("plead," GK *4151*), which tend to strengthen the usual verbs for "witness" (*martyreō*, GK *3455*) and "call" (*kaleō*, GK *2813*). And Peter's characterization of "this age" as a "corrupt generation" is paralleled by Jesus' words in Matthew's gospel (16:4; 17:17) and Paul's words in Philippians (2:15). We have here the vision of an evangelist, a vision that is all too often lost as the gospel is acclimated to the world and the world to the church.

41 Jews generally looked on baptism as a rite only for Gentile converts (i.e., proselytes), not for those born Jews. It symbolized the break with one's Gentile past and the washing away of defilement. So when Jews accepted baptism in the name of Jesus, it was traumatic and significant for them in a way that we in our mildly christianized culture have difficulty understanding. Nonetheless, as a result of Peter's preaching, "about" three thousand of them took the revolutionary step of baptism. And thus, Luke tells us, the congregation of believers in Jesus came into being at Jerusalem—a congregation that was made up of the original 120 followers of Jesus (cf. 1:15) and that was progressively augmented (as the imperfect form of the verb *prostithēmi*, "added to," GK *4707*, seems to suggest) by about three thousand others.

NOTES

37 On ἄνδρες ἀδελφοί (*andres adelphoi*, "men, brothers"; NIV, "brothers") as a fraternal Jewish form of address, see comments at 1:16 (see also Notes, 2:14).

The Western text (D, minuscule 241, and as represented by recensions of the Old Latin and Coptic versions, as well as Hippolytus and Augustine) omits λοιπούς (*loipous*, "others"), thereby reading not "Peter and the other apostles" but "Peter and the apostles." This may have been accidental—or, more likely, was intended to elevate Peter above the apostles.

The Western text (D, minuscule 241, etc.) also (1) has τί οὖν ποιήσομεν (*ti oun poiēsomen*, "What then will we do?"), which adds a "then" and changes the subjunctive to an indicative; (2) reads τῇ καρδίᾳ (*tē kardia*, "in the heart"), as in the LXX at Psalm 109:16 [MT = 108:16], which changes the accusative to a dative; and (3) adds ὑποδείξατε ἡμῖν (*hypodeixate hēmin*, "show us") after ἄνδρες ἀδελφοί (*andres adelphoi*, "men, brothers"). These are all rather typical Western adjustments and expansions.

38–41 Some interpreters note that there is no mention in this passage, in either the report of Peter's preaching (vv.38–40) or the summary of the people's response (v.41), of any speaking in tongues, as at Pentecost (v.4), or of the laying on of hands, as at Samaria (8:17). From this lack, various implications have been drawn. In a Jewish context, however, it would not have been surprising if both occurred. One would probably be justified in being surprised only had it been said that they had *not* occurred. Nevertheless, that they are not mentioned implies, as with the omission of baptism in 3:19, that speaking in tongues and the laying on of hands were not considered prerequisites for the reception of the Spirit.

38 The prepositions ἐπί (*epi*, "on") and ἐν (*en*, "in") were frequently interchanged in Koine Greek and are used in that way in Acts (cf. 10:48), which practice probably accounts for the variations in the MS evidence (esp. between B and D). Likewise, εἰς (*eis*, "into") in 8:16 and 19:5 should probably be interpreted synonomously (cf. 7:4, 12; 19:22).

In Jewish thought, God's renewal of his people by his Spirit and a symbolic cleansing with water go hand in hand (cf. Eze 36:25–27; 1QS 4.20–21).

41 On the use of μὲν οὖν (*men oun*; NASB, "so then"; omitted in NIV) as a favorite Lukan connective, see comments at 1:6. Elsewhere in Acts it appears in concluding statements at 5:41; 8:25; 9:31; and 16:5.

Haenchen, 188–89, 215, objects to the numbers "three thousand" here at 2:41 and "five thousand" at 4:4. He argues that it would have been impossible to be heard by such crowds without a microphone and that Jerusalem had only twenty-five or thirty thousand residents total at the time. In agreement with Martin Dibelius (quoting from Dibelius's *Studies in Acts*, 124), he writes (p. 189), "It is far more probable that the little flock of Christians led 'a quiet, even in the Jewish sense "devout" life in Jerusalem. It was a modest existence, and nothing but the triumphant conviction of the faithful betrayed that from this flock was to go forth a movement which would transform the world.'" Acoustical tests in Israel, however, have shown that such features as sound reflection and low ambient noise levels would have allowed biblical preachers to address large audiences, at least in certain locations (cf. B. C. Crisler, "The Acoustics and Crowd Capacity of Natural Theaters in Palestine," *BA* 39 [1976]: 128–41). Furthermore, the imperfect verb προσετίθει (*prosetithei*, "added") suggests something of a process as a result of Peter's preaching, not necessarily a large crowd of three thousand who heard and responded en masse. And the five thousand of 4:4 should probably be understood as the total number (cf. 6:7; 16:5), not five thousand at another time in addition to the three thousand, with those additional two thousand converts also probably being added through a process inaugurated by the miracle and preaching recorded in ch. 3.

Estimates of the number of inhabitants in Jerusalem during the first Christian century are interesting but highly inferential, as debates between J. Jeremias, E. Stauffer, and E. Bammel, based on the number of people who could get into the temple precincts during festival periods, have clearly shown. Ultimately, however, Dibelius and Haenchen are asking us to take their word over against Luke's as to how the church prospered in its earliest days, although it was Luke's version that was accepted by the church within a century of the time itself.

III. PART I: THE CHRISTIAN MISSION TO THE JEWISH WORLD (2:42–12:24)

OVERVIEW

Luke set out the theme of Acts in Jesus' words, "You will be my witnesses in Jerusalem, and in all Judea and Samaria, and to the ends of the earth" (1:8). Behind these words stands Deuteronomy 19:15, with its requirement that every matter be established by two or three witnesses (cf. A. A. Trites, *The New Testament Concept of Witness* [Cambridge: Cambridge Univ. Press, 1977], esp. 128–53). In his gospel, Luke frequently highlighted such matters as (1) the witness of the Scriptures coupled with the ministry of Jesus and the witness of the Spirit, (2) the pairings of the disciples in their journeys on behalf of Jesus (cf. 10:1), and (3) the two angels at the tomb (cf. 24:4, whereas Mt 28:2–5 and Mk 16:5 have only one). In his organization of the common tradition in his gospel he set up a number of parallels between Jesus' ministry in Galilee (4:14–9:50) and his ministry in the regions of Perea and Judea (9:51–19:27). So in Acts, Luke continues his pairings of apostolic men in their ministries: Peter and John in 3:1, 3–4, 11; 4:13, 19; 8:14; Barnabas and Saul in 11:25–26; 12:25; 13:2; Paul and Barnabas in

13:43, 46, 50; 15:2, 12, 22, 35; Judas and Silas in 15:32; Barnabas and Mark in 15:39; Paul and Silas in 15:40; 16:19, 25; 17:4, 10; and Silas and Timothy in 17:14–15; 18:5.

Luke also sets up a number of parallels between the ministry of Peter in the first half of Acts and the ministry of Paul in the last half: both heal a lame man (3:2–8; 14:8–10); both do miracles at some distance (5:15; 19:12); both exorcise evil spirits (5:16; 16:18); both defeat sorcerers (8:18–24; 13:6–11); both raise the dead (9:36–43; 20:9–12); both defend themselves against Jewish authorities (4:8–12; 5:27–32; 22:3–21; 23:1–6; 28:25–28); both receive heavenly visions (10:9–16; 16:9); both are involved in bestowing the Holy Spirit on new converts (8:14–17; 19:1–7); and both are miraculously released from prison (5:19; 12:7–11; 16:25–27). More important, both proclaim the same message and even use to some extent the same set of proof texts (e.g., Ps 16:10; cf. 2:27; 13:35).

It is from Jesus' declaration about the apostles' witness as given in 1:8 that Luke derives the framework for his narrative of Acts. Thus he goes on to portray first of all the mission of the Jerusalem apostles and their colleagues within the Jewish world, and then the mission of Paul and his companions within the Gentile world. He sets out all this in six panels or blocks of material—three of them dealing with the mission to Jews and three with the mission to Gentiles.

PANEL 1—THE EARLIEST DAYS OF THE CHURCH AT JERUSALEM (2:42–6:7)

OVERVIEW

Acts 2:42–6:7, which is the first of Luke's six panels, describes the earliest days of the church at Jerusalem and covers the first three to five years of the new messianic movement, from about AD 30 to the mid-30s. Luke deals with the events of this period by means of a thesis paragraph, which is then followed by a series of vignettes illustrating that paragraph. In 1:1–2:41 he dealt in some detail with the constitutive events of the Christian mission. Had he continued on at that rate, his second book would have been inordinately long. So in depicting the early apostolic missions to Jews and Gentiles, Luke uses illustrative vignettes and portrayals of representative situations drawn from many experiences within the early church to present his material more succinctly. The purpose in all he presents was, it appears, to enable his readers to experience something of what God was doing by his Spirit through the witness of the apostles.

A. Thesis Paragraph on the State of the Early Church (2:42–47)

OVERVIEW

In addition to the six summary statements found at 6:7; 9:31; 12:24; 16:5; 19:20; and 28:31, each of which concludes one of the six panels, Acts also has in its first panel three short, introductory paragraphs: 2:42–47; 4:32–35; and 5:12–16. The latter two introduce blocks of material that follow them, with the specific details of those materials directly related to their respective introductory paragraphs. The first of these paragraphs (2:42–47), however, is longer than the other two and introduces the entire first panel.

Rather than credit this paragraph to some supposed "Recension B" of a Jerusalem-Caesarean source (so Harnack), or partly to an older body of source material and partly to Luke's redaction (so J. Jeremias, L. Cerfaux, P. Benoit, though variously), I take vv.42–47 to be Luke's own thesis paragraph on the state of the church in its earliest days at Jerusalem. And I take the rest of the first panel to be explicating by means of a series of vignettes the various points made in this first thesis paragraph.

> [42]They devoted themselves to the apostles' teaching and to the fellowship, to the breaking of bread and to prayer. [43]Everyone was filled with awe, and many wonders and miraculous signs were done by the apostles. [44]All the believers were together and had everything in common. [45]Selling their possessions and goods, they gave to anyone as he had need. [46]Every day they continued to meet together in the temple courts. They broke bread in their homes and ate together with glad and sincere hearts, [47]praising God and enjoying the favor of all the people. And the Lord added to their number daily those who were being saved.

COMMENTARY

42 In his description of the early church, Luke begins by observing that believers were distinguished by their devotion to (1) "the apostles' teaching," (2) "the fellowship," (3) "the breaking of bread," and (4) "prayer." The verb translated "devoted" (*proskartereō*, GK *4674*) connotes a steadfast and single-minded fidelity to a certain course of action. Luke uses it elsewhere in Acts to characterize the devotion of the 120 in the upper room to prayer (1:14) and the apostles' resolve in the matter of the Hellenistic widows to focus their attention on prayer and the ministry of the word (6:4).

"The apostles' teaching" refers to material considered authoritative because it was the message about Jesus of Nazareth that was proclaimed by accredited apostles. It seems to have included an account of Jesus' earthly ministry, passion, and resurrection (cf. 2:22–24), a compilation of his teachings (cf. 20:35), and a declaration of what all this meant for human redemption (cf. 1Co 15:3–5)—all of which was viewed as a Christian "tradition" (*paradosis*, GK *4142*) that could be passed on to others (cf. 1Co 11:2; 1Th 2:13; 2Th 2:15; 3:6). The number of references to teachers, teaching, and tradition within Acts and the letters to the churches (here, as well as in Ro 6:17; 12:7; 16:17; 1Co 11:2; 14:26; 2Th 2:15; 3:6; Jas 3:1), together with the frequent

linking of prophets and teachers in the NT (cf. Ac 13:1; 1Co 12:28; 14:6; Eph 4:11), suggests that the creative role of prophecy in the early church was balanced by the conserving role of teaching. The early congregation at Jerusalem, along with its lively eschatological expectation and amid its differences of perspective, had a general "sense of center" that was provided by the historical and doctrinal teaching of the apostles. And this teaching, Luke tells us, was the raison d'être and focus of the early Christian community.

The definite article in the expression "the fellowship" (*tē koinōnia*, GK *3126*) implies that there was something distinctive in the gatherings of the early believers. With the influx of three thousand on the day of Pentecost and daily increases to their number after that (cf. 2:47), they must have had some externally recognizable identity. Perhaps in those early days others thought of them as simply a "synagogue of Nazarenes" (cf. the accusation of Tertullus in 24:5, which links them to "the Nazarene sect") and accorded them a place among other such groups within the mosaic that made up Second Temple Judaism. But the Christian community was not just a sect of Judaism, even though they continued to observe Jewish rites and customs and had no intention of breaking with the nation or its institutions. They held to the centrality of Jesus of Nazareth in the redemptive program of God and in their worship. Their proclamation of Jesus as Israel's promised Messiah and humanity's Lord set them apart in Jerusalem as a distinguishable entity.

Just what is meant by "the breaking of bread" has been often debated. Is Luke here referring to some type of Jewish fellowship meal, like the Haburah meals of the Pharisees, which expressed the believers' mutual love and recalled their earlier association with Jesus—but was devoid of any paschal significance, as Paul later (rather illegitimately) saw in it (so Hans Lietzmann)? Or was it even in these early years a commemoration of Christ's death, in line with Paul's later elaboration (so J. Jeremias)? Or was it at first an *agapē* feast that emphasized the joy of communion with the risen Lord and of fellowship with one another—which Paul later (quite legitimately) understood also to have paschal significance, in line with the intention of Jesus (so Oscar Cullmann)? The matter is somewhat difficult to determine. For while 2:42 and 20:7 may relate to the full Pauline understanding as expressed in 1 Corinthians 10:16 and 11:24, and while Luke referred to "the breaking of bread" in that way in his passion narrative at Luke 22:19, elsewhere Luke uses "breaking bread" for an ordinary meal (cf. Lk 24:30, 35; Ac 20:11; 27:35) and he seems to have in mind an ordinary meal in 2:46.

Yet it is difficult to believe that Luke meant only an ordinary meal in 2:42, placing the expression, as he does, between two such religiously loaded terms as "the fellowship" and "prayer." Every meal among Jews, of course, would have had something of a sacred character. And in a Christian setting, where hearts were warmed by devotion, it would have been an occasion for joy, love, and praise, with all such devotion inevitably connected with Jesus' ministry and death on behalf of his people. Probably, therefore, "the breaking of bread" should be under-

stood here in v.42 not only as denoting joyful devotion to Jesus but also as connoting the passion of Christ, although there may well have been a deepening of understanding with regard to Christ's passion as the church's theology came more into focus, in accord with Paul's later elaboration of it.

References to "prayer" are frequent in Acts, both in the summary statements and the narrative (in addition to 2:42, see 1:14, 24; 4:24–31; 6:4, 6; 9:40; 10:2, 4, 9, 31; 11:5; 12:5; 13:3; 14:23; 16:25; 22:17; 28:8). For just as in Luke-Acts there appears the parallelism of the Spirit's work in the ministry of Jesus and the Spirit's work in the mission of the church, so there appears the parallelism between prayer in the life of Jesus and prayer in the life of the church. Luke's use of the definite article and the plural in speaking of "the prayers" (*tais proseuchais*, GK *4666*) suggests formal prayers, probably both Jewish and Christian. It seems, therefore, that the earliest believers not only viewed the old forms as having been filled with new content but also fashioned new vehicles for their praise. In addition, it is not difficult to envision them as praying extemporaneously, with those more informal prayers being built on past models—such as can be seen in Mary's Magnificat (Lk 1:46–55), Zechariah's Benedictus (Lk 1:67–79), and Simeon's Nunc Dimittis (Lk 2:28–32).

43 Luke notes that a lingering sense of awe rested on many who did not take their stand with the Christians and that miraculous things were done by the apostles. "Everyone" (*pasē psychē*, lit., "every soul"), in contradistinction to "all the believers" (*pantes hoi pisteuontes*) of v.44, refers hyperbolically to nonbelievers in Jerusalem who knew of the events of Pentecost and were observing the life of the early congregation in the months that followed. In the expression "wonders and miraculous signs" (*terata kai sēmeia*; GK *5469*, *4956*), Luke picks up the phraseology of Joel's prophecy (cf. 2:19) and Peter's characterization of Jesus' ministry (cf. 2:22). Luke probably used it to suggest that the miracles done by the apostles should be taken as evidences of the presence of God with his people, just as in the ministry of Jesus the miracles done by him showed that God was with him. The use of the verb *ginomai* in the imperfect tense ("were done") denotes that such awe and miracles were no momentary phenomena but continued to be features associated with the church during those early days.

44–45 Within the Christian congregation at Jerusalem, the believers' sense of spiritual unity expressed itself in communal living and sharing with the needy members of their group. While Acts implies that overt persecution of Christians came somewhat later, it may be assumed that in certain instances various economic and social sanctions were imposed on the early believers. In fact, the communal life described in vv.44–45 should probably be understood, at least in part, as a response to these pressures, for such treatment of minority groups is not uncommon, as, sadly, both ancient and contemporary history show. In addition, analogies between the early Jewish Christians and the Dead Sea covenanters at Qumran suggest that the early believers in Jesus, while stressing the primacy of spiritual community, also reflected a practice common to various Jewish sects—a practice especially prominent in the Qumran community—of holding possessions and goods in common. The repeated use of the imperfect tense in these two verses (five times) shows that this was the early Christians' established practice, which involved both their real estate ("possessions," *ktēmata*, GK *3228*) and their personal possessions ("goods," *hyparxeis*, GK *5638*).

46 Here Luke shows that the early Jerusalem believers expressed their faith through daily adherence to the accustomed forms of their Jewish heritage. They not only ate together in their homes in a spirit of gladness and sincerity; they also found a large measure of favor among the people. "Every

day" (*kath' hēmeran*) applies to the whole sentence (which the NIV breaks into two sentences) as far as the words "all the people" in the middle of v.47 and ties together a number of complementary ideas.

The favorite meeting place of the early believers was in the temple (cf. Lk 24:53) at the eastern edge of the outer court called Solomon's Colonnade (cf. 3:11; 5:12). There, in typically Semitic fashion, they carried on their discussions and offered praise to God. As Jews who were Christians and Christians who were Jews, they not only considered Jerusalem to be their city but continued to regard the temple as their sanctuary and the Mosaic law as their law. Evidently they thought of themselves as the faithful remnant within Israel—those for whom all the institutions and customs of the nation existed. As such, their refocused eschatological hopes (cf. Mal 3:1) and all their desires to influence their own people were associated with the city of Jerusalem, with the Jerusalem temple, and with the Mosaic law. For both theological and practical reasons, therefore, as well as because of the inevitable tug of the traditional, the early Christians in Jerusalem sought to retain their hold on the religious forms they had inherited and to express their new faith through the categories of the old.

But while they met formally for discussion and worship in the temple precincts, they took their meals in their own homes (*kat' oikon*, lit., "by households," GK *3875*). The noun *trophē* ("food," "nourishment," GK *5575*) in the Greek statement "they were sharing in the food" (*metelambanon trophēs*; NIV, "ate together"; NASB, "were taking their meals together") implies a substantial meal (cf. 9:19; 27:33–34), which they ate with gladness and sincerity of heart.

47a In Luke's writings, "the people" (*ho laos*, GK *3295*) usually refers to Israel as the elect nation to whom the message of redemption was initially directed and for whom (together with the Gentiles) it is ultimately intended (e.g., 3:9; 4:10; 5:13). Later in the narrative of Acts the attitude of "the people" becomes more and more antagonistic to the Christian gospel and its missionaries. But in this first panel we have a response of the people that is largely favorable toward the early Christians and their manner of life. This cannot be said for the attitude of the Sadducees as depicted in 4:1–22 and 5:17–40. Later in the commentary, reasons will be given for the change of attitude on the part of the people—a change that begins with Acts' second panel and worsens as the narrative develops. What can be said here is that Luke in this panel of material attempts to show, both by his emphasis on the early Christians' meeting in the temple courts and by his highlighting of the favor accorded them by the people, that early Christianity is the fulfillment of all that is truly Jewish and that it directed its mission first to the Jewish world. And Luke continues throughout Acts to stress these themes.

47b Luke's thesis paragraph on the state of the early church at Jerusalem concludes with the triumphant note, "And the Lord added to their number daily those who were being saved"—a note that runs throughout this first panel but is not confined to it. It is the Lord himself who adds to his church, and thus the title *ho kyrios* ("the Lord") appears first in the sentence not only for grammatical reasons but also for emphasis. The force of the present participle *tous sōzomenous* ("those being saved," GK *5392*) is iterative, thus suggesting that they were added as they were being saved. For a discussion of the expression "to their number" (*epi to auto*), see Notes, v.41 above and v.47 below.

NOTES

42 The Greek text of Codex Bezae (D) adds ἐν Ἰερουσαλήμ (*en Ierousalēm*, "in Jerusalem") after τῶν ἀποστόλων (*tōn apostolōn*, "of the apostles"), which is a needless Western expansion. The Latin text of bilingual Bezae, together with the Vulgate, Syriac Peshitta, and Coptic Sahidic and Bohairic versions, reads, "in the fellowship of the breaking of bread."

44 Luke uses the substantival participle οἱ πιστεύοντες (*hoi pisteuontes*, "those who were believing"; NIV, "the believers"; NASB, "who had believed") as a designation for Christians. It may be debated whether the participle is to be read in the present tense (οἱ πιστεύοντες, *hoi pisteuontes*, as in A C D E P and most of the minuscules), thereby highlighting their present state of believing, or in the aorist tense (οἱ πιστεύσαντες, *hoi pisteusantes*, as in ℵ B and some minuscules; also 4:32), thus suggesting their acceptance of the Christian faith at some time in the past, whether recent or remote.

The phrase ἐπὶ τὸ αὐτό (*epi to auto*), which appears here and in v.47, is difficult to translate (NIV, NASB, "were together"). It probably parallels the use of the Hebrew term *yaḥad*, "the gathered fellowship" (GK 3480) at Qumran.

45 Codex Bezae (D), as reflected also in the Syriac Peshitta version, reads καὶ ὅσοι κτήματα εἶχον ἢ ὑπάρξεις (*kai hosoi ktēmata eichon ē hyparxeis*, "and as many as had possessions and goods"), which is a needless qualifying of πάντες (*pantes*, "all") in v.44.

The word κτῆμα (*ktēma*, GK *3228*) literally means a possession of any kind but came to be restricted to "landed property," "a field," or "a piece of ground." Its synonym ὕπαρξις (*hyparxis*, GK *5638*), when used in tandem with *ktēma*, likely signifies more what would be called personal possessions apart from real estate.

46 This is the only occurrence of ἀφελότης (*aphelotēs*, GK *911*; NIV, "sincere"; NASB, "sincerity") in the NT, though it appears in second-century AD writings of Vettius Valens (153.30; 240.15) to mean "simplicity" or "generosity."

47 Codex Bezae (D) reads ὅλον τὸν κόσμον (*holon ton kosmon*, "all the whole") for ὅλον τὸν λαόν (*holon ton laon*, "all the people"), but such an expansion, while laudatory, misses the point Luke is making.

Codex Bezae (D) reads ἐν τῇ ἐκκλησίᾳ (*en tē ekklēsia*, "in" or "to the church"), which Erasmus incorporated into the TR and so is translated by the KJV. But such a reading domesticates the idiom "the gathered fellowship" (see note at v.44b). The word ἐκκλησία (*ekklēsia*, "church") first appears in the more reliable texts of Acts at 5:11.

B. A Crippled Beggar Healed (3:1–26)

OVERVIEW

Luke has spoken in 2:42–47 of the early Christians' continued attendance at the temple, the wonders and miracles that the apostles did, the awe that many of the Jews felt, and the apostles' teaching. Now he sets out a vignette that illustrates these things. Much like the Synoptic Gospels, which selected the healing of a leper as "exhibit A" to represent the nature of Jesus' early ministry in Galilee (cf. Mk 1:40–45 par.), or John's gospel, which used the healing of a Capernaum official's son for the same purpose (cf. Jn 4:46–54), Luke now singles out this episode in the history of the early Jerusalem congregation to "bring the reader into the picture." No doubt the episode at the time was well known and frequently recounted in the early church long before Luke wrote of it.

1. The Healing (3:1–10)

¹One day Peter and John were going up to the temple at the time of prayer—at three in the afternoon. ²Now a man crippled from birth was being carried to the temple gate called Beautiful, where he was put every day to beg from those going into the temple courts. ³When he saw Peter and John about to enter, he asked them for money. ⁴Peter looked straight at him, as did John. Then Peter said, "Look at us!" ⁵So the man gave them his attention, expecting to get something from them.

⁶Then Peter said, "Silver or gold I do not have, but what I have I give you. In the name of Jesus Christ of Nazareth, walk." ⁷Taking him by the right hand, he helped him up, and instantly the man's feet and ankles became strong. ⁸He jumped to his feet and began to walk. Then he went with them into the temple courts, walking and jumping, and praising God. ⁹When all the people saw him walking and praising God, ¹⁰they recognized him as the same man who used to sit begging at the temple gate called Beautiful, and they were filled with wonder and amazement at what had happened to him.

COMMENTARY

1 The story of the healing of the crippled beggar begins with the rather straightforward statement that Peter and John went up to the temple at the time of prayer. In the better Greek MSS the pericope begins without a clear connective, using only the post-positive, mildly adversative *de* ("but" or "and"; NASB, "now"). Codex Bezae (D), however, apparently felt the need for a stronger connective and so began the episode with *en de tais hēmerais tautais* ("in those days"). Likewise, for purely stylistic reasons, the NIV and NRSV begin with "one day." Such sensitivity on the part of translators, both ancient and modern, suggests that the story may have originally circulated among Christians separately and for its own sake.

That the apostles were living in Jerusalem immediately after Jesus' ascension is in accord with his instructions to "stay in the city until you have been clothed with power from on high" (Lk 24:49), "not [to] leave Jerusalem, but wait for the gift my Father promised" (Ac 1:4), and to begin their missionary activity there (Ac 1:8, cf. Lk 24:47). But what kept these Galilean disciples in Jerusalem after Pentecost, and, why did Jewish Christianity become centered in Jerusalem rather than Galilee? Ernst Lohmeyer's thesis (*Galiläa und Jerusalem* [Göttingen: Vandenhoeck & Ruprecht, 1936]) that there were really two centers of Christianity in Palestine from the earliest days—a Galilean center and a Jerusalemite center, and that Acts has blurred that early situation by locating Galilean apostles in Judean Jerusalem—is not convincing (cf. L. E. Elliott-Binns, *Galilean Christianity* [London: SCM, 1956]). While there were certainly Christians "throughout Judea, Galilee and Samaria" who formed themselves into congregations in those provinces (cf. 9:31), Paul's letters, which are the earliest extant Christian writings, highlight the church at Jerusalem and associate the Galilean apostles directly with that church (cf. Gal 1:18–2:10; 1Th 2:14).

The early Christians looked to Jerusalem and to the church of that city as being of central importance. As God's righteous remnant within Israel and as members of the Messiah's eschatological community, the apostles, even though originally from Galilee, centered their activities in Jerusalem. Along with that went their continued adherence to Israel's institutions and forms of worship. So Peter and John are presented as "going up to the temple at the time of prayer—at three in the afternoon" (lit., "at the ninth hour").

The stated times for prayer in Judaism were (1) early in the morning, in connection with the morning sacrifice; (2) at the ninth hour of the day, in connection with the evening (or afternoon) sacrifice; and (3) at sunset (cf. Str-B, 2.696–98). The imperfect verb *anebainon* ("they were going up," GK *326*) conveys a vivid visual impression of the apostles' movement toward the Jerusalem temple. Going to the temple is always spoken of in terms of "going up" (e.g., Lk 18:10; Jn 7:14; cf. also Ac 11:2; 15:2; 18:22), principally out of reverential respect, though also because of geographical elevation.

2–3 The man is described as "crippled [NASB, lame] from his mother's womb" (*chōlos ek koilias mētros autou*; NIV, "crippled from birth") and having to be carried daily "to the temple gate called Beautiful" to beg for his living. Almsgiving was classed in Judaism as a meritorious act (cf. Str-B, 1.387–88). He was therefore placed at the gate so that those coming to the temple could gain merit by giving him a coin.

Just which temple gate is referred to as "the gate called Beautiful" is not easy to determine. Neither Josephus nor the Talmud refers to such a gate. And while Hellenistic Jews commonly called the entire temple complex "the temple" (*to hieron*, GK *2639*) and reserved for the temple proper, with its porch, the names "Holy Place" and "Holy of Holies" (*ho naos*, GK *3724*; cf. Str-B, 1.150–51), Luke does not always maintain this distinction in Luke-Acts. We cannot, therefore, depend on his use of *to hieron* as a guide to whether "the gate called Beautiful" had to do with the outer court or one of the inner courts.

Since the fifth century AD, the Eastern Gate (or Shushan Gate, so called because it portrays the palace of Shushan, or Susa), which is on the eastern side of the outer court and remained standing after the destruction of Jerusalem, has been identified by many as the Beautiful Gate. The weight of evidence from Josephus (*Ant.* 15.410–25; *J.W.* 5.190–221) and the Mishnah (*m. Mid.* 1:3–4; 2:3), however, favors identifying the Beautiful Gate with the Nicanor Gate, which was named for someone named "Nicanor," who in a perilous storm desired to be thrown overboard with the gate during its transport from Alexandria to Jerusalem and for whose sake a miracle occurred that preserved both the gate and Nicanor (cf. *m. Yoma* 3:10). This gate led from the eastern part of the outer court (court of the Gentiles) into the first of the inner courts (court of the women). Josephus (*J.W.* 5.201) describes it as having been overlaid with Corinthian bronze and says that it "far exceeded in value those plated with silver and set in gold."

4–6 In response to the beggar's request for money, Peter fixed his eyes on him and said, "Look at us!" Thinking he had a benefactor, the beggar looked up expectantly. To his astonishment he heard the words, "In the name of Jesus Christ of Nazareth, walk." In Semitic thought a name does not just identify or distinguish a person; it expresses the very nature of his being. Hence the power of the person is present and available in the name of that person. Peter, therefore, does not just ask the risen Jesus to heal the crippled beggar but pronounces over him the name of Jesus, thereby releasing the power of Jesus (cf. 3:16; 4:10). And the power of the risen Jesus, coupled with the man's response of faith (cf. 3:16), effects the healing.

7–10 The healing is described as instantaneous, accomplishing in a moment what God in his providence, through normal healing processes, usually takes months to do. The effect on the man was traumatic.

Some commentators have complained that v.8 is structurally overloaded in comparison with the rest of the narrative, what with all the walking about and jumping and praising God going on. Such a comment only reflects our jaded sensibilities in the presence of divine grace. Certainly it would have been hard to convince the man himself that his response was excessive. As for the people, they were "filled with wonder and amazement." What was taking place was but a token, to those who had eyes to see, of the presence of the messianic age, of which the prophet had long ago predicted: "Then will the lame leap like a deer" (Isa 35:6).

NOTES

1 The inclusion of John along with Peter has often been credited to Luke's redactional activity alone, since (1) John seems to be somewhat tacked on in v.4, (2) Peter speaks in the singular in v.6, and (3) John remains very much the silent partner throughout. But while Luke is obviously interested in developing his two-witness motif wherever possible, it was not unusual in the church's traditions for Peter to take the lead and overshadow his colleagues. Luke could not very well have had them address the crippled beggar in unison, particularly if the miracle occurred principally in response to Peter's invocation of Jesus' name.

Codex Bezae (D) adds τὸ δειλινόν (*to deilinon*, "toward evening") after "going up to the temple" and before "at the time of prayer," which is a needless expansion.

2 The noun κοιλία (*koilia*, GK *3120*) means both "stomach" and "womb" and appears in the NT with both meanings. Luke always uses it in the latter sense (cf. Lk 1:15, 42; Ac 14:8).

6 The shorter command περιπάτει (*peripatei*, "walk," GK *4344*) is better attested externally (א B D and the Coptic Sahidic version), though ἔγειρε καὶ περιπάτει (*egeire kai peripatei*, "arise and walk") also appears widely in the textual sources (A C and many of the Fathers). The longer version may have been influenced by such well-known passages as Matthew 9:5; Mark 2:9; Luke 5:23; and John 5:8. It may, however, have been omitted as superfluous, since Peter in v.7 raises up the crippled man.

7 The adverb παραχρῆμα (*parachrēma*, "instantly") is a favorite expression of Luke that appears in Luke 1:64; 4:39; 5:25; 8:44, 47, 55; 13:13; 18:43; 19:11; 22:60; Acts 3:7 (here); 5:10; 12:23; 13:11; 16:26, 33 (D has it also at Ac 14:10). Elsewhere in the NT it is used only in Matthew 21:19–20.

9 On Luke's use of ὁ λαός (*ho laos*, "the people"), see comments at 2:47a.

2. Peter's Sermon in Solomon's Colonnade (3:11–26)

OVERVIEW

Peter's sermon in Solomon's Colonnade is in many ways similar to his sermon at Pentecost (2:14–41). Structurally, both move from proclamation to a call for repentance. The Pentecost sermon, however, is finished and polished, whereas the Colonnade sermon is rather rough-hewn. Thematically, both focus on the denial and vindication of Jesus of Nazareth, but the Colonnade sermon expresses more of a remnant theology than the sermon at Pentecost. Furthermore, it reflects a more generous attitude toward Israel, though coupled with a greater stress on the nation's responsibility for the Messiah's death, and it makes explicit the necessity of receiving God's grace by faith. Christologically, Peter's sermon here, like his defense in 4:8–12, incorporates a number of archaic and primitive titles used of Jesus within early Jewish Christianity.

It may seem strange for Luke to place two similar sermons of Peter so close together in his narrative. But his putting the Pentecost sermon in the introductory section of Acts was evidently meant to be a kind of paradigm of early apostolic preaching—a paradigm that Luke seems to have polished for greater literary effectiveness. As for the Colonnade sermon, Luke seems to have included it as an example of how the early congregation in Jerusalem proclaimed the message of Jesus to the people of Israel as a whole. Moreover, the material containing both the story of the miracle and Peter's sermon probably came to Luke as something of a self-contained unit, which he evidently was willing, for the most part, to leave in the form he found it.

> [11]While the beggar held on to Peter and John, all the people were astonished and came running to them in the place called Solomon's Colonnade. [12]When Peter saw this, he said to them: "Men of Israel, why does this surprise you? Why do you stare at us as if by our own power or godliness we had made this man walk? [13]The God of Abraham, Isaac and Jacob, the God of our fathers, has glorified his servant Jesus. You handed him over to be killed, and you disowned him before Pilate, though he had decided to let him go. [14]You disowned the Holy and Righteous One and asked that a murderer be released to you. [15]You killed the author of life, but God raised him from the dead. We are witnesses of this. [16]By faith in the name of Jesus, this man whom you see and know was made strong. It is Jesus' name and the faith that comes through him that has given this complete healing to him, as you can all see.
>
> [17]"Now, brothers, I know that you acted in ignorance, as did your leaders. [18]But this is how God fulfilled what he had foretold through all the prophets, saying that his Christ would suffer. [19]Repent, then, and turn to God, so that your sins may be wiped out, that times of refreshing may come from the Lord, [20]and that he may send the Christ, who has been appointed for you—even Jesus. [21]He must remain in heaven until the time comes for God to restore everything, as he promised long ago through his holy prophets. [22]For Moses said, 'The Lord your God will raise up for you a prophet like me from among your own people; you must listen to everything he tells you. [23]Anyone who does not listen to him will be completely cut off from among his people.'
>
> [24]"Indeed, all the prophets from Samuel on, as many as have spoken, have foretold these days. [25]And you are heirs of the prophets and of the covenant God made with your fathers. He said to Abraham, 'Through your offspring all peoples on earth will be blessed.' [26]When God raised up his servant, he sent him first to you to bless you by turning each of you from your wicked ways."

COMMENTARY

11 We are not given many of the stage directions for Peter's Colonnade sermon. What we are told, however, is significant: (1) that the healed cripple "held on to" (*kratountos*, GK *3195*) Peter and John so as to not let them get away (*krateō* is also used to describe a police arrest, as in Mt 14:3; 21:46; 26:4, 48, 50, 55, 57); (2) that "the people" came running to them in Solomon's Colonnade; and (3) that they were all "astonished" at what had happened. Solomon's Colonnade was a covered portico that ran the entire length of the eastern portion of the outer court of the temple precincts, along and just inside the eastern wall of the temple area (cf. 5:12; Jn 10:23).

12–16 The proclamation section of the sermon is an exposition on "the name of Jesus," which is twice repeated in v.16. Structurally and syntactically, v.16 is the most difficult verse in the chapter, probably because Luke chose to do less editorial polishing on this verse since he saw that it contained the statement of Peter's theme.

The sermon begins by denying that it was through the apostles' "own power or godliness" that the crippled man was healed. Rather, "the God of Abraham, Isaac and Jacob" brought about the healing and, through doing so, glorified Jesus. Just as Peter earlier spoke of God as the true author of Jesus' miracles (cf. 2:22), so here he attributes solely to God such wonders as occurred in the apostles' ministries. And just as Jesus' miracles were done by God to accredit him before the people (cf. again 2:22), so miracles continued to be done through the apostles in order for God to glorify Jesus.

The sermon focuses on God's "servant Jesus," whom Israel had disowned and killed, but whom God raised from the dead. It is through his name and the faith that comes through him that the healing of the crippled beggar occurred. In speaking of Jesus, Peter uses a number of primitive and archaic christological titles, whose concentration in these few verses has often been rightly considered by scholars as highly significant.

The sermon begins and ends by ascribing to Jesus the title "God's Servant" (ho pais [GK 4090] autou, vv.13, 26), which echoes the Servant theme of Isaiah 42–53 (cf. "[God] has glorified his servant Jesus" of v.13 with "my servant . . . will be raised and lifted up and highly exalted" of Isa 52:13) and the theme of Moses as prophet of Deuteronomy 18:15, 18–19 (cf. the "raising up" motif of Ac 3:22, 26 with Dt 18:15, 18). It includes the titles "the Holy One" (ho hagios, GK 41, v.14) and "the Righteous One" (ho dikaios, GK 1465, v.14), the ascription "the author of life" (ho archēgos tēs zōēs, v.15), and a reference to Jesus as "a prophet like me [Moses]" (ho prophētēs hōs eme, vv.22–23). And it stresses "the name of Jesus" as the powerful agent in the miracle—a significant fact since "the Name" (to onoma, GK 3950) was a pious Jewish surrogate for God and connoted his divine presence and power.

17–18 What strikes the reader immediately in the call-to-repentance section of Peter's Colonnade sermon is its attitude toward Israel, which in its

hopeful outlook is unmatched in the rest of the NT (except for certain features in Paul's discussion in Ro 9–11). In v.12 Peter addresses his audience as "men of Israel" and in v.13 speaks of God as "the God of our [hymōn] fathers." And though he had emphasized Israel's part in crucifying Jesus (vv.13–15), he now magnanimously says that they had acted "in ignorance" and, somewhat surprisingly, includes their leaders in this characterization. Then he mitigates their guilt still further by saying that God himself had willed it in order to fulfill the words of the prophets.

19–21 Even more positively, Peter goes on to say that if his hearers repent, their repentance will have a part in ushering in the great events of the end-times (cf. the idea of purpose expressed in the conjunction hopōs, "that," which starts v.20). Evidently Luke wants us to understand Peter's call to repentance as being set within the context of a remnant theology and as being quite unlike Stephen's attitude (cf. ch. 7). He also wants us to view the earliest proclamation of the gospel in the Jewish world as a kind of intramural effort, with a self-conscious, righteous remnant issuing prophetic denunciations of Israel's part in the crucifixion of their Messiah and appealing to the people to turn to God in repentance for the remission of their sins.

The call to repentance is tersely stated (v.19a). Then it is elaborated in words unique in the NT and reflective of Jewish remnant theology: "Repent, then, and turn to God," says Peter, "so that your sins may be wiped out"—and, further, so that there may be brought about the promised "times of refreshing," when with the coming of God's "appointed" Messiah (ton prokecheirismenon [GK 4741] Christon, lit., "the foreordained Christ," v.20) God will "restore everything" (v.21). The expressions "times of refreshing" (kairoi anapsyxeōs, GK 2789, 433) and "times to restore everything" (chronōn [GK 5989] apokatastaseōs pantōn, v.21) are without parallel in the

NT, though the verb *apokathistēmi* ("restore," GK 635), the verbal form of *apokatastasis* ("restoration," GK 640), is often used in the LXX of the eschatological restoration of Israel (cf. Jer 15:19; 16:15; 24:6; 50:19 [27:19 LXX]; Eze 16:55; Hos 11:11).

Some see vv. 19b–21 as representing two distinctly different Christologies, based on the supposed chronological ambiguity of these verses—an ambiguity claimed to be found in the words "that times of refreshing may come from the Lord, and that he may send the Christ, who has been appointed for you—even Jesus. He must remain in heaven until the time comes for God to restore everything, as he promised long ago through his holy prophets." J. A. T. Robinson ("The Most Primitive Christology of All?" *JTS* 7 [1956]: 177–89) argued that here we probably have "the most primitive Christology of all" (cf. his *Twelve New Testament Studies* [London: SCM, 1962], 139–53). Taking the expression "the foreordained Christ" to be an affirmation that messiahship was for Jesus a matter *for the future*, he argued (expressing a Bultmannian position) that Jesus was considered by the earliest believers to be the "Messiah-designate" who was awaiting the future coming of the Son of Man, with this latter title referring to a heavenly personage other than Jesus, and not Jesus himself, who would at his coming appoint Jesus to be Israel's Messiah. Robinson believed that in 3:19–21 there appears an outcropping of that earliest stratum of christological speculation, which must have quickly faded away and been replaced by the Christology of Acts 2 and the remainder of Acts 3—as well, of course, by the attribution of present messiahship to Jesus to be found throughout the rest of the NT. In fact, Robinson insisted, Jesus was first considered only Messiah-designate in the earliest congregation at Jerusalem, whereas later he was elevated in the thought of Christians to the actual rank of Messiah.

Robinson's view has had a rather brief shelf life in the dispensary of theological opinion, principally because scholars came to see that it presented two significant exegetical difficulties. First, it imposed on vv. 20–21 a rigid chronological structure unwarranted by the text itself. For while it is clear that Jesus is identified here as "the foreordained Christ" (NIV, "the Christ, who has been appointed for you"; NASB, "the Christ appointed for you"), the question as to when that messianic ordination took place, or would take place, is not anywhere as clear as Robinson assumed. One could just as well read v. 20, "that he may send *again* the foreordained Christ," with the Greek word *palin* ("again") understood to be in mind, as "that he may send the foreordained *and future* Christ," as Robinson assumed.

Second, Robinson's interpretation made Luke appear incredibly naive in placing two distinct and differing Christologies, as Robinson would have it, side by side—one in v. 18, which immediately precedes this passage, where the Messiah of God (*ton Christon autou*, "his Christ") is identified as the one who suffered, and the other in vv. 19–21, which contain a supposedly earlier view that messiahship was to be looked for only in the future. To argue that Luke included vv. 19–21 only to refute them by the preface of v. 18, as Robinson speculates may have been the case, is absurd. Luke could better have refuted such a supposedly earlier and erroneous Christology in vv. 19–21 simply by omitting it. And to say that Luke did not recognize the discrepancy, as Robinson thinks more likely, is to make him astonishingly obtuse.

The fact is that Robinson has detached vv. 19–21 from their context and then played on the looseness of expression that results when those verses are read out of context. He has imposed temporal strictures on the passage at that point where it is ambiguous when detached from its context. But Luke intended it to be read in context. And when read in its context, the passage sets up no contradictory messianology, though it may not be as chronologically precise as one might wish.

22–26 No group within Israel that considered itself to be God's righteous remnant in the inauguration of the final eschatological days could expect to win a hearing among Jews without attempting to define its position vis-à-vis Israel's great leaders of the past—particularly Abraham, Moses, and David. And this is exactly what Luke shows Peter doing as he concludes his call for repentance.

In vv.22–23 Peter does so with respect to Moses by quoting Deuteronomy 18:15, 18–19 ("The LORD your God will raise up for you a prophet like me. . . . You must listen to him. . . ."), to which is coupled Leviticus 23:29 ("Anyone who does not deny himself on that day must be cut off from his people"). These verses were widely accepted messianic proof texts of the time that emphasized the command to "listen to him" and added the injunction to obey "everything he tells you," since disobedience results in being "cut off" from one's people. Peter's argument, though not stated, is implicitly twofold: (1) true belief in Moses will lead to a belief in Jesus, and (2) belief in Jesus places one in true continuity with Moses.

In v.24 Peter also relates faith in Jesus to David by alluding to Samuel and all the prophets who followed him and by insisting that they too "foretold these days." It is, of course, difficult to find any prophecy of Samuel that could be applied to Jesus as explicitly as the words of Moses just quoted. But Samuel was the prophet who anointed David to be king and spoke of the establishment of his kingdom (cf. 1Sa 16:13; see also 13:14; 15:28; 28:17). Furthermore, Nathan's prophecy regarding the establishment of David's descendants, as recorded in 2 Samuel 7:12–16, was accepted in certain quarters within Second Temple Judaism as having messianic relevance (cf. 4Q174) and taken by Christians as having been most completely fulfilled in Jesus (cf. Ac 13:22–23, 34; Heb 1:5).

In v.25 Peter identifies commitment to Jesus as Messiah with the promise God made to Abraham by quoting Genesis 22:18 and 26:4: "Through your offspring [tō spermati sou] all nations on earth will be blessed." What exegetically ties this portion with what has preceded it is the word sperma (GK 5065, lit., "seed," meaning "offspring" or "descendants"), which appears in 2 Samuel 7:12 with reference to David's descendants and in Genesis 22:18 and 26:4 with reference to the descendants of Abraham. On the basis of the Jewish exegetical principle gezerah shawah ("verbal analogy": where the same words are applied to two separate cases it follows that the same considerations apply to both), Peter proclaims that the promise to Abraham has its ultimate fulfillment in Christ.

Peter's call to repentance in this sermon is an expression of the remnant theology of the earliest Christian believers at Jerusalem. He addresses his hearers as "heirs of the prophets and of the covenant." He uses both a pesher approach ("this is that") and midrashic exegesis (gezerah shawah) in his treatment of Scripture. He concludes with an offer of blessing that is extended first to individuals of the nation of Israel: "When God raised up his servant, he sent him first to you to bless you by turning each of you from your wicked ways" (v.26). In the Greek sentence, the expression hymin prōton ("first to you") comes first and so occupies the emphatic position. Many have thought that this stress on Israel "first" is a Pauline import by the hand of Luke (cf. 13:46; Ro 1:16; 2:9–10). But this understanding fails to appreciate the remnant context of the sermon and the remnant perspective expressed throughout it. Luke wants his readers to appreciate something of how the earliest Christian preaching began within a Jewish milieu. From this he will go on to tell how this preaching developed through the various representative sermons he later includes.

NOTES

11 The differences here between the Alexandrian text (ℵ A B C etc.) and the Western text (D) concern principally the location of Solomon's Colonnade. According to the Alexandrian text, Peter and John heal a crippled man at "the gate called Beautiful" and then go into the temple; there in Solomon's Colonnade they draw attention from the gathered crowd. This reading implies that Solomon's Colonnade was within the Jerusalem temple. According to the Western text, however, "As Peter and John came out [of the temple], he [the crippled man] came with them while holding on to them; and others, being amazed, took up their position in Solomon's Colonnade." This reading suggests that Solomon's Colonnade was located outside the temple precincts.

The Western scribe may have been attempting to make explicit what was seen to be implicit in Luke's account. Perhaps the Alexandrian text is correct and the Western text wrong; or, conversely, the Western text is correct and the Alexandrian text wrong. It is likely, however, as noted in the comments at 3:2, that Luke's use of "the temple" should not be used as a guide to whether "the gate called Beautiful" was one of the gates of the outer court or one of the gates of one of the inner courts. It may be that the scribe of Codex Bezae (D) thought he knew the exact location of Solomon's Colonnade and wanted to correct Luke's account.

12 On the address ἄνδρες Ἰσραηλῖται (*andres Israēlitai*, "men of Israel"), see comments at 1:16; 2:14; and 2:22.

13 The designation of God as "the God of Abraham, Isaac and Jacob" stems from God's self-identification in Exodus 3:6. It was a common formula among Second Temple Jews (cf. the opening words of the *Shemoneh Esrei* ("Eighteen Benedictions"))—"Blessed art thou, O Lord our God and God of our fathers, God of Abraham, God of Isaac, and God of Jacob")—and occurs frequently in various forms in the NT (cf. Mk 12:26 par.; Ac 7:32). The Western text here and at 7:32 has the fuller form, "God of Abraham, God of Isaac, and God of Jacob," as do also the MT and most LXX versions of Exodus 3:6, the opening words of the *Shemoneh Esrei*, and the Synoptic Gospels at Matthew 22:32; Mark 12:26; and Luke 20:37. The Alexandrian text may represent a "stylistic pruning," with the Western reading then being preferred (as UBS[4], with "God of" before Isaac and Jacob in brackets, and NRSV). Such a "stylistic pruning," however, may reflect the Christian tradition from which Luke worked or Luke's own redactional hand, and so be original to the text (cf. NIV, NASB).

13–26 On the Jewish and early Christian use of these titles, see my *Christology of Early Jewish Christianity*, 32–47, 53–58, 104–9.

15 The title ἀρχηγὸν τῆς ζωῆς (*archēgon tēs zōēs*, "author/originator of life," GK *795, 2437*) is equivalent to ἡ σωτηρία (*hē sōtēria*, "the salvation, God's salvation," GK *5401*), since both ζωή (*zōē*, "life") and σωτηρία (*sōtēria*, "salvation") are Greek translations of the one Hebrew word *hāyâ* ("be alive," GK *2649*; cf. 5:20).

16 C. C. Torrey, 14–16, declared the awkward syntax of this verse (lit., "and by faith in his name has his name made this man strong, whom you behold and know") to be the result of Luke's mistranslation of his Aramaic source. More likely, however, its structural difficulties are the result of Luke's unwillingness to alter Peter's somewhat cumbersome thesis statement, principally because he could not rework the repetition of the phrase τὸ ὄνομα αὐτοῦ (*to onoma autou,* "the name of him [Jesus]") without losing Peter's emphasis on "the name of Jesus."

17 Peter's stress on the Jews' ignorance is reminiscent of Jesus' words from the cross, recorded only in Luke 23:34: "Father, forgive them, for they do not know what they are doing" (which is certainly a genuine *logion,* despite its omission in ℵ A C D). This emphasis appears also in Paul's preaching (cf. Ac 13:27; 17:30; Ro 10:2; 1Ti 1:13), but Stephen's attitude is quite different (cf. Ac 7:51–53).

22–23 While Deuteronomy 18:15, 18–19 is quoted here, its textual form is not according to either the MT or the LXX. Yet the Greek of v.23 corresponds remarkably well to the Hebrew text of Deuteronomy 18:18–19 in 4Q*Testimonia* (lines 5–8) of the Dead Sea Scrolls, thus suggesting, as de Waard, 79, argues, that "Luke draws here upon a Palestinian Jewish text tradition which is older than the composition of the speech" (see also de Waard, 21–24).

25 On Paul's use of the "promise to Abraham" theme and the motif of Abraham's "seed" (NASB; NIV, "offspring"), see Galatians 3:6–9, 14, 16–18, 29.

26 While in 3:15 the verb ἐγείρω (*egeirō,* "raise up," GK *1586*) is used of the resurrection of Jesus, here ἀνίστημι (*anistēmi,* "raise up," GK *482*) is used with evident reference to the same, in line with Luke's usual practice (cf. 2:24, 32; 7:37; 13:30, 34; 17:31; though with 9:41 and 13:33 as exceptions) and in parallel with the wording of Deuteronomy 18:15, 18—"The LORD your God will raise up [ἀναστήσει, *anastēsei*] for you," and "I will raise up [ἀναστήσω, *anastēsō*] for them"—and perhaps with the wording of 2 Samuel 7:12, which seems also to have been in Peter's mind: "I will raise up [ἀναστήσω, *anastēsō*] your offspring to succeed you."

C. Peter and John before the Sanhedrin (4:1–31)

OVERVIEW

As a direct outcome of the healing of the crippled beggar—and as a further illustration of the thesis paragraph of 2:42–47—Luke now presents a vignette concerning the arrest, trial, and witness of Peter and John. Source criticism, as noted earlier (see Introduction, p. 682), has often taken the two arrests and appearances of the apostles before the Sanhedrin (4:1–22; 5:17–40) as simply two versions of the same event that were somehow brought together prior to Luke's writing to form one of his sources (perhaps "Recension A" of the Jerusalem-Caesarean source, as proposed by Harnack) and of which 4:1–22 was probably the original and 5:17–40 a legendary expansion.

Joachim Jeremias ("Untersuchungen zum Quellenproblem der Apostelgeschichte," *ZNW* 36 [1937]: 208–13) has shown that, far from being repetitious and therefore artificial in their dual inclusion, the two accounts accurately reflect a significant feature in Jewish jurisprudence and complement each other. Jewish law, as Jeremias pointed out, held that a person must be aware of the consequences of his crime before being punished for it. This meant that in noncapital cases the common people—as distinguished from those with rabbinic training, who, presumably, would know the law—had to be given a legal admonition before witnesses and could only be punished for an offense when they relapsed into a crime after due warning. Acts 4:1–22, therefore, presents the Sanhedrin as judging that the apostles were "unschooled, ordinary men" (v.13) and tells how they were given a legal warning not to speak any more in the name of Jesus (v.17). But Acts 5:17–40 tells how the Sanhedrin reminded the apostles of its first warning (v.28) and turned them over to be flogged because they had persisted in their sectarian ways (v.40). Jeremias's explanation has been rightly accepted by most commentators today.

This does not necessarily mean, however, that Luke himself clearly grasped the precise details of Jewish jurisprudence or that he was interested in detailing them for his readers. Likely, he simply found these two accounts in his sources, and, while they reflect the Jewish legal procedures of the day, they appealed to him and he used them because of the development of attitudes that they evidence. Jeremias's explanation refers to the state of the tradition before the composition of Acts, not necessarily to Luke's handling of the material. But it shows that we should not take the historicity of the narratives in Acts lightly just because Luke has used his sources for his own purposes.

1. The Arrest of Peter and John (4:1–7)

¹The priests and the captain of the temple guard and the Sadducees came up to Peter and John while they were speaking to the people. ²They were greatly disturbed because the apostles were teaching the people and proclaiming in Jesus the resurrection of the dead. ³They seized Peter and John, and because it was evening, they put them in jail until the next day. ⁴But many who heard the message believed, and the number of men grew to about five thousand.

⁵The next day the rulers, elders and teachers of the law met in Jerusalem. ⁶Annas the high priest was there, and so were Caiaphas, John, Alexander and the other men of the high priest's family. ⁷They had Peter and John brought before them and began to question them: "By what power or what name did you do this?"

COMMENTARY

1 Luke has so skillfully woven his sources together that vv.1–4 not only conclude the narrative of the crippled beggar's healing but also introduce the first appearance of Peter and John before the Sanhedrin. Linguistically, the adverbial participle *lalountōn* ("while they were speaking," GK *3281*) joins vv.1–4 with what has gone before, with the statement "the next day" (v.5) better taken as beginning a new unit of material. Yet topically vv.1–4 introduce what follows more than they conclude what has preceded.

The early opposition against the preaching of the gospel is shown by Luke as arising chiefly from priestly and Sadducean ranks—from "the priests and the captain of the temple guard and the Sadducees." The captain of the temple guard was the commanding officer of the temple police force. He was considered inferior in rank only to the high priest and had the responsibility of maintaining order in the temple precincts (cf. 5:24, 26; Josephus, *J.W.* 2.409–10; 6.294; *Ant.* 20.131, 208). The Sadducees were descendants of the Hasmoneans, who looked back to Mattathias, Judas, Jonathan, and Simon (168–134 BC) as having inaugurated the messianic age (cf. *Jub.* 23:23–30; 31:9–20; 1 Macc 14:4–15, 41) and who saw themselves as perpetuating what their fathers had begun. As priests from the tribe of Levi, they claimed to represent ancient orthodoxy and were uninterested in innovations. Thus they opposed any developments in biblical law (i.e., the "Oral Law"), speculations about angels or demons, and the doctrine of the resurrection (cf. 23:8; Mk 12:18 par.; Josephus, *J.W.* 2.119, 164–65; *Ant.* 13.171–73; 18.11, 16–17). Likewise, they rejected what they considered to be vain hopes for God's heavenly intervention in the life of the nation and for a coming Messiah, since, as they believed, the age of God's promise had begun with the Maccabean heroes and was continuing on under their supervision. For them, the Messiah was an ideal, not a person, and the messianic age was a process, not a cataclysmic or even datable event. Furthermore, as Israel's political rulers and its dominant landlords, to whom a grateful nation had turned over all political and economic powers during the time of the Maccabean supremacy, they stressed for entirely practical reasons cooperation with Rome and maintenance of the status quo. Most of the priests were of Sadducean persuasion; the temple police force was composed entirely of Levites; and the captain of the temple guard was always a high-caste Sadducee, as was each of the high priests.

2–3 The priests and Sadducees were "greatly disturbed" (*diaponoumenoi*, GK *1387*) about two matters. First, the apostles were "teaching the people," which was an activity the Sadducees saw as a threat to the status quo. Like their Master, Peter and John were rallying popular support and acting unofficially in a way that was viewed as disruptive to established authority—an authority vested in Sadducean hands. Second, Peter and John were annoying the Sadducees by "proclaiming in Jesus the resurrection of the dead." This probably means they were attempting to prove from the fact of Jesus' resurrection (note the phrase *en tō Iēsou*, "in [the case of] Jesus," which suggests that his resurrection was the test case) the doctrine of a general resurrection (cf. 17:31–32; 23:6–8), which the Sadducees denied. So Peter and John were taken into custody by the temple guard (v.3). And since it was evening, they were put in prison until the Sanhedrin could be called together the next morning to judge their case.

4 Not everyone agreed with the Sadducees' view of the activities and message of the apostles. Later in Acts, Luke will speak of (1) the tolerance of the people, (2) the moderation of the Pharisees, and (3) the desire of Rome for peace in the land, with each of these factors having a part in restraining the Sadducees from doing all they might have done to oppose the gospel and its early missionaries. Here, however, he notes that many who heard the message (*ton logon*, lit., "the word," GK *3364*) believed, with the result that the Jerusalem congregation grew to a total of about five thousand.

5 Though the Sadducees had among them the nation's titular rulers, they were actually a minority party and could govern only through the Sanhedrin. Thus on the next day "the rulers" (*hoi archontoi*, GK *807*, a frequent synonym for "the high priests"; cf. 23:5; Josephus, *J.W.* 2.333, 405, 407, 627–28), "the elders" (*hoi presbyteroi*, GK *4565*), and "the teachers of the law" (*hoi grammateis*, GK *1208*, often translated "scribes") came together, with these three groups forming the Sanhedrin.

The Sanhedrin (*to synedrion*, "the council," GK *5284*) was the senate and supreme court of the nation and had jurisdiction in all noncapital cases. It also advised the Roman governors in capital cases. In one situation—that of Gentiles trespassing beyond the posted barriers into the inner courts of the temple—it could on its own inflict a sentence of death, even with respect to a Roman citizen (cf.

21:28–29; Josephus, *J.W.* 6.124–28). The Sanhedrin consisted of the high priest, who by virtue of his office was president, and seventy others, made up of members of the high priestly families, a few influential persons of various formal ideological allegiances or backgrounds within Judaism, and professional experts in the law drawn from both Sadducean and Pharisaic ranks. It was dominated by the Sadducees and probably came together mostly at their request. It met in a hall adjoining the southwestern part of the temple area, probably at the eastern end of a bridge spanning the Tyropean Valley and next to an open-air meeting place called the Xystos (cf. Josephus, *J.W.* 2.344; 5.144; 6.354).

6 In stressing that the early opposition to Christianity arose principally from among the Sadducees, Luke makes the point that the Sadducean element was especially well represented in this first trial of the apostles: "Annas the high priest was there, and so were Caiaphas, John, Alexander and the other men of the high priest's family." Annas was high priest for nine years, from AD 6–15, though he continued to exercise great influence after that and is seen in the NT as the real power behind the throne (cf. Lk 3:2; Jn 18:13–24). Caiaphas, his son-in-law, was high priest for eighteen years, from AD 18–36. Altogether, Annas arranged to have five of his sons, one son-in-law (Caiaphas), and one grandson appointed to the office of high priest. Just who John and Alexander were we do not know, though the Western text suggests that the first was Annas's son Jonathan, who replaced Caiaphas in AD 36.

7 It was before such an assembly, which probably arranged itself in a semicircular fashion, that Peter and John were brought. The man who had been healed was also there (cf. v.14), though Luke does not say whether he had also been imprisoned or just called in as a witness. The apostles were called on to account for their actions, and they used the occasion for an aggressive evangelistic witness.

NOTES

1 Codices B and C read οἱ ἀρχιερεῖς (*hoi archiereis*, "the high priests," GK *797*), probably in an attempt to correlate v.1 with v.6, whereas א A D E read οἱ ἱερεῖς (*hoi hiereis*, "the priests," GK *2636*). The word ἀρχιερεύς (*archiereus*, "high priest") appears 122 times in the NT, whereas ἱερεύς (*hiereus*, "priest") appears only 31 times. It is likely that scribes substituted the more frequently used "high priest" for the less frequent "priest." Evidently, however, the better-attested "priests" has in mind those priests serving in the Jerusalem temple at the time.

2 Codex Bezae (D) reads ἀναγγέλλειν τὸν Ἰησοῦν ἐν τῇ ἀναστάσει τῶν νεκρῶν (*anangellein ton Iēsoun en tē anastasei tōn nekrōn*, "to proclaim Jesus in the resurrection of the dead") instead of the better-attested καταγγέλλειν ἐν τῷ Ἰησοῦ τὴν ἀνάστασιν τὴν ἐκ νεκρῶν (*katangellein en tō Iēsou tēn anastasin tēn ek nekrōn*, "to proclaim in the [case] of Jesus the resurrection of the dead"), which modification fails to understand the expression "in the case of Jesus" as an idiom.

4 Codex Bezae (D) adds the enclitic particle τέ (*te*, "also") after ὁ ἀριθμός (*ho arithmos*, "the number," GK *750*), evidently to heighten the statement but at the expense of good literary style. On the number "five thousand," see Notes, 2:41. The noun ἀριθμός (*arithmos*, "number") probably means here the "total number," as in 6:7 and 16:5 (cf. Dt 26:5; 28:62 [LXX]).

5 The Jewish Sanhedrin (τὸ συνέδριον, *to synedrion*; cf. 4:15; Lk 22:66; Jn 11:47; Josephus, *Ant.* 14.167–81) was also called "the Senate" (ἡ γερουσία, *hē gerousia*, GK *1172*; cf. 5:21; Josephus, *Ant.* 12.138), "the

Body of Elders" (τὸ πρεσβυτέριον, *to presbyterion*; GK *4564*; cf. 22:5; Lk 22:66; Josephus, *Ant.* 13.428), "the Council" (ἡ βουλή, *hē boulē*, GK *1087*; cf. Josephus, *J.W.* 2.331, 336), "the Hall of Hewn Stone" (Heb. *liškâ haggāzît*, which probably refers to the polished stones of the Xystos beside which it stood; cf. *m. Mid.* 5:4)— perhaps also "the Great Sanhedrin" (Heb. *sanhēdrîn gᵉdôlâ*), "the Great Law Court" (Heb. *bêt dîn haggādôl*), and "the Sanhedrin of the Seventy One" (Heb. *sanhēdrîn šel šibᶜîm waᵓeḥād*).

6 The Western text (D, and as represented by recensions of the Old Latin and Vulgate) reads Ἰωναθάς (*Iōnathas*, "Jonathan") for the better-attested Alexandrian text (𝔓⁷⁴ ℵ A B etc.) reading Ἰωάννης (*Iōannēs*, "John"). Josephus (*Ant.* 18.4) says that Jonathan, son of Annas, was appointed high priest in AD 36 in succession to Caiaphas. The translator of D may have been attempting to correct Luke in accord with the tradition recorded by Josephus.

2. Peter's Defense and Witness (4:8–12)

⁸Then Peter, filled with the Holy Spirit, said to them: "Rulers and elders of the people! ⁹If we are being called to account today for an act of kindness shown to a cripple and are asked how he was healed, ¹⁰then know this, you and all the people of Israel: It is by the name of Jesus Christ of Nazareth, whom you crucified but whom God raised from the dead, that this man stands before you healed. ¹¹He is

"'the stone you builders rejected,
    which has become the capstone.'

¹²Salvation is found in no one else, for there is no other name under heaven given to men by which we must be saved."

COMMENTARY

8 In a context of a prophetic description of national calamities and cosmic turmoil, Luke has quoted Jesus as declaring:

But before all this, they [your adversaries] will lay hands on you and persecute you. They will deliver you to synagogues and prisons, and you will be brought before kings and governors, and all on account of my name. . . . But make up your mind not to worry beforehand how you will defend yourselves. For I will give you words and wisdom that none of your adversaries will be able to resist or contradict.

Luke 21:12, 14–15

Luke was undoubtedly thinking of many incidents of opposition to the gospel message when he wrote these words. Indeed, he records a number of such happenings in Acts. But certainly when he wrote about Peter's first defense before the Jewish Sanhedrin—as well as when he wrote about the apostles' second appearance before the Sanhedrin in

5:17–40—these words were ringing in his ears. For almost every item of Jesus' oracle is exemplified in Luke's account of Peter's situation, attitude, and message here in Acts. The use of the aorist passive (*plētheis*, "filled," GK *4437*) in the expression "filled with the Holy Spirit" denotes a special moment of inspiration that complements and brings to a functional focus the presence in every believer's life of the person and ministry of God's Spirit.

9–10 Peter's defense focuses on the healing of the crippled man as being (1) "an act of kindness" that was (2) effected "by the name of Jesus Christ of Nazareth, whom you crucified but whom God raised from the dead." Luke uses the verb *anakrinomai* ("judge," "call to account," GK *373*), which in classical Greek meant "a preliminary inquiry," and so may be seen to reflect in its use here something about the nature of first-century Jewish jurisprudence. However, though Luke found this word *anakrinomai* with its attendant meaning in his sources, his use of the same word in 12:19; 24:8; and 28:18 indicates that he had no great desire to highlight the fact that this first appearance of the apostles before the Sanhedrin was only a preliminary inquiry. Peter's message is specifically addressed to the "rulers and elders of the people" (v.8), though it also has "all the people of Israel" in mind (v.10).

11 The double sense of the verb *sōthēnai* ("to be saved," GK *5392*, v.12) to mean both "restoration to health" physically and "preservation from eternal death" spiritually allows Peter to move easily from the healing of the crippled man to the salvation of all humanity—and therefore from a defensive to an aggressive witness.

In Peter's proclamation two quite early and primitive christological motifs come to the fore. The first is that of "the rejected stone," which has become "the capstone" of the building. There was in Judaism a frequent wordplay between the words for "stone" (*'eben*) and "son" (*bēn*), which was rooted

generally in the OT (cf. Ex 28:9; Jos 4:6–8, 20–21; 1Ki 18:31; Isa 54:11–13; La 4:1–2; Zec 9:16) and attained messianic expression in the combination of "the stone" and "Son of Man" images in Daniel (2:34–35; 7:13–14)—and which continued to be used through the early rabbinic period (cf. *Gen. Rab.* 68.11; *Exod. Rab.* 29; *Tg. Ps-J.* on Ex 39:7). It was for this reason, evidently, that Jesus concluded his parable of the vineyard and the rejected son (Mk 12:1–12 par.) with the quotation of Psalm 118:22–23: "The stone the builders rejected has become the capstone; the LORD has done this, and it is marvelous in our eyes." And it is this motif that Peter, building on the accepted associations of "stone" and "son," picks up in his quotation of Psalm 118:22.

In *Testament of Solomon* 22:7–23:4, which is Jewish material from the first century AD, the expression "the stone at the head of the corner" (*ho lithos* [GK *3345*] *eis kephalēn gōnias* [GK *1224*]) unambiguously refers to the final capstone or copestone placed on the summit of the Jerusalem temple to complete the whole edifice. Peter quotes Psalm 118:22 in this connection. Yet there are also instances within contemporary Jewish writings of "stone imagery" referring to a "foundation stone" that use Isaiah 28:16 for support (cf. 1QS 8.4; *b. Yoma* 54a). Apparently "stone imagery" was used variously in Second Temple Judaism. This same variety is reflected in the NT, for there the three christological stone passages (in addition to Mk 12:10–11 par. and Ac 4:11; cf. Lk 20:18; Ro 9:33; 1Co 3:11; 1Pe 2:4–8) have varying nuances. Here, however, while elsewhere in the NT the ideas of a "foundation stone" and a "stumbling stone" (based respectively on Isaiah 28:16 and 8:14) are present, the thought of Jesus as the rejected stone that becomes the capstone or copestone and so completes the edifice is dominant (cf. Ps 118:22).

12 A second early christological motif in Peter's proclamation is that of "God's Salvation." In the longer Isaiah scroll of the Dead Sea Scrolls, "God's Salvation" and "Salvation" appear as Jewish designations for the expected Davidic Messiah (cf. 1QIsa 51.4–5, which uses the third person masculine suffix and pronoun in connection with the expression "my Salvation"). Likewise, "Salvation" is used as a messianic title in other Qumran texts (cf. CD 9:43, 54; 1QH 7.18–19; 4Q174 on 2Sa 7:14 and in connection with Am 9:11), in various intertestamental writings (cf. *Jub.* 31:19; also *T. Dan* 5:10; *T. Naph.* 8:3; *T. Gad* 8:1; *T. Jos.* 19:11, though the provenance of the Greek version of the *Testaments of the Twelve Patriarchs* is debated), and in the rabbinic materials (cf. *b. Ber.* 56*b*–57*a*).

Luke has already stressed this early christological motif in Zechariah's hymn of praise (Lk 1:69, "a horn of salvation"), in Simeon's prayer (Lk 2:30, "your salvation"), and in introducing the ministry of John the Baptist (Lk 3:6, "God's salvation"). Now in addressing the Sanhedrin, to whom such a messianic designation was doubtless well known, Peter proclaims, "Salvation is found in no one else [i.e., than in "Jesus Christ of Nazareth, whom you crucified but whom God raised from the dead" (v.10)], for there is no other name under heaven given to men by which we must be saved" (v.12). There was nothing of compromise or accommodation in Peter's preaching. As this magnificent declaration shows, he was wholly committed to the uniqueness of Jesus as the only Savior. Peter and the other apostles never watered down the fact that apart from Jesus there is no salvation for anyone.

NOTES

8 Some MSS add τοῦ Ἰσραήλ (*tou Israēl*, "of Israel") after "elders," evidently in the interest of symmetry in order to balance "rulers of the people" with "elders of Israel." The shorter text, however, is supported by such Alexandrian texts as 𝔓74 ℵ A B, as well as the Latin Vulgate, the Coptic Bohairic and Sahidic versions, and a number of church fathers.

10 Some Western texts (E, and as represented by recensions of the Old Latin and the Vulgate, as well as by Cyprian and the Venerable Bede) add καὶ ἐν ἄλλῳ οὐδενί (*kai en allō oudeni*, "and in/by no one else") at the end of the verse. But the words are not supported by the better texts and seem to be influenced by v.12.

11 On the wordplay in Judaism between "stone" and "son," see M. Black, "The Christological Use of the Old Testament in the New Testament," *NTS* 18 (1971): 11–14. On the stone of Psalm 118:22 as a "capstone" or "copestone," see J. Jeremias, "Κεφαλὴ γωνίας—Ἀκρογωνιαῖος," *ZNW* 19 (1930): 264–80; cf. *TDNT* 1.791–93; 4.271–80. See also my *Christology of Early Jewish Christianity*, 50–53.

12 The translators of the Western text seem to have had trouble understanding the expression ἡ σωτηρία (*hē sōtēria*, "the salvation") and have either omitted it (as D and one recension of the Old Latin) or omitted the first clause of this verse in which it is found (as other Old Latin recensions and such church fathers as Irenaeus, Cyprian, and Augustine). On "God's Salvation" as a messianic ascription in early Judaism, the NT, and postapostolic Christianity, see my *Christology of Early Jewish Christianity*, 99–103.

3. The Apostles Warned and Released (4:13–22)

¹³When they saw the courage of Peter and John and realized that they were unschooled, ordinary men, they were astonished and they took note that these men had been with Jesus. ¹⁴But since they could see the man who had been healed standing there with them, there was nothing they could say. ¹⁵So they ordered them to withdraw from the Sanhedrin and then conferred together. ¹⁶"What are we going to do with these men?" they asked. "Everybody living in Jerusalem knows they have done an outstanding miracle, and we cannot deny it. ¹⁷But to stop this thing from spreading any further among the people, we must warn these men to speak no longer to anyone in this name."

¹⁸Then they called them in again and commanded them not to speak or teach at all in the name of Jesus. ¹⁹But Peter and John replied, "Judge for yourselves whether it is right in God's sight to obey you rather than God. ²⁰For we cannot help speaking about what we have seen and heard."

²¹After further threats they let them go. They could not decide how to punish them, because all the people were praising God for what had happened. ²²For the man who was miraculously healed was over forty years old.

COMMENTARY

13–14 While literacy was high among Jews of the first century (cf. Josephus, *Ag. Ap.* 2.178; Philo, *Legat.* 210; *m. ʾAbot* 5:21), theological disputations required rabbinic training. Since the so-called *ʿam haʾāreṣ* ("people of the land") had not had such training, they were thought to be incapable of carrying on sustained theological discussion. But here were Peter and John, whom the council observed to be "unschooled, ordinary men," speaking fearlessly and confidently before the Jewish supreme court and senate. Their judges could not but wonder at such ordinary men having such a mastery of biblical argumentation (cf. Luke's précis of their words in 3:22–26; 4:11–12). So they had to fall back on the only possible explanation: "these men had been with Jesus," who despite his lack of rabbinic training taught "as one who had authority" (Mk 1:22). To this fact they directed their attention

(cf. the use of the intensive verb *epeginōskon*, GK *2105*; NIV, "took note"; NASB, "*began* to recognize") as an important piece of evidence in the case before them.

Furthermore, just as Jesus' teaching was coupled with demonstrations of miraculous powers, which reinforced among the people the impression of authority (e.g., Mk 1:23–28; 2:1–12), Peter and John were now beginning to do the same. There was no denying that the man had been healed. There he stood before them, physically regenerated at an age when regenerative cures do not occur of themselves (cf. v.22, "for the man . . . was over forty years old"). The miraculous, however, apart from an openness of heart and mind, is not self-authenticating. So the Sadducees' preoccupation with protecting their own vested interests shut them off from understanding the significance of what had occurred.

15–17 Just how Luke knew what went on among the members of the Sanhedrin in closed session has often been debated. Was Saul (Paul) a member of the council at the time and later told Luke? Or had Paul heard the gist of the discussion from his teacher Gamaliel and then told it to Luke? Were there secret sympathizers in the council who leaked what was said to the apostles and from whom Luke picked it up? Or was the substance of the discussion inferred from what was said to Peter and John when they were brought back, and so became embedded in Luke's source material? While the latter suggestion seems most probable, we are too far removed from the situation itself to be sure. What is certain about the council's response is that (1) they would have denied the miracle if they could have; (2) they had no disposition to be convinced, either by what had happened or by the apostles' arguments; and (3) they felt the need to stop the apostles' activities and teaching and so resorted to the measures allowed by Jewish law.

18–20 The decision of the council was to impose a ban on the apostles that would both warn them and provide a legal basis for further action should such be needed (cf. 5:28). They therefore called in the apostles and warned them "not to speak or teach at all in the name of Jesus" (*epi tō onomati tou Iēsou*). The prepositions *epi* ("on") and *en* ("in") are often used interchangeably in the NT, and therefore the phrase *epi tō onomati tou Iēsou* should probably be taken as synonymous with *en tō onomati tou Iēsou* ("in the name of Jesus," cf. 2:38; so also the preposition *eis* in 8:16; 19:5).

But the council had before it men whose lives had been transformed by association with Jesus, by God's having raised Jesus from the dead, and by the coming of the Holy Spirit. As with the prophets of old, God's word was in the hearts of Peter and John like a burning fire, and they could neither contain it nor be restrained from speaking it (cf. Jer 20:9). They had been witnesses of Jesus' earthly ministry and resurrection (cf. 10:39–41). They had been commanded by their risen Lord to proclaim his name to the people (cf. 1:8; 10:42). When faced with this ban, their response was never in doubt: "Judge for yourselves whether it is right in God's sight to obey you rather than God. For we cannot help speaking about what we have seen and heard" (vv.19–20).

Established authority per se was not what the apostles believed they must stand against, for Jewish Christianity in its earliest days often accommodated itself to the established forms and functions of Judaism as a baby to its cradle. But where established authority stood in opposition to God's authority—thereby becoming, in effect, demonic—the early believers in Jesus knew where their priorities lay and judged all religious forms and functions from a christocentric perspective.

21–22 The Sanhedrin had given its warning. And after stressing what would happen if it went unheeded (cf. the participial form of the verb *prosapeileō*, "threaten further"; GK *4653*), they let them go. The moderation of the people prevented them from doing more, for "all the people were praising God for what had happened." Yet a legal precedent had been set that would enable the council, if necessary, to take more drastic action in the future. Occasions for such action were soon to be multiplied, as Luke tells us in 5:12–16.

NOTES

13 The word ἀγράμματος (*agrammatos*, GK *63*) is used in the nonliterary Greek papyri in the sense of "illiterate," though it undoubtedly here means "unschooled" or "uneducated" in rabbinic training. The word ἰδιώτης (*idiōtēs*, GK *2626*), while at times signifying "ignorant" (cf. 1Co 14:23–24), is used here in its ordinary

Greek sense of "ordinary person" or "commoner." Codex Bezae (D) omits καὶ ἰδιῶται, probably because the dual attribution of "unschooled" and "ordinary" (NASB, "uneducated and untrained") deprecated the apostles too much.

14–16 The Western text (D, and as represented in recensions of the Old Latin and Coptic versions) has a number of small changes that were evidently meant to enhance the action of the account. For example, it inserts in v.14 ποιῆσαι ἤ (poiēsai ē, "to do or"), so reading "they had nothing *to do or* to say in opposition"; it substitutes in v.15 the more picturesque word ἀπαχθῆναι (apachthēnai, "to be led out," GK 552) for the more prosaic ἀπελθεῖν (apelthein, "to go out" or "withdraw," GK 599); and it uses in v.16 the comparative φανερώτερον (phanerōteron) in the elative sense to mean "it is all too clear" rather than the simple φανερόν (phaneron, GK 5745), "it is clear."

16–17 Haenchen, 218, caustically comments, "The author reports the closed deliberations as if he had been present." His implication is that here Luke clearly reveals the fabricated nature of his work, inserting words on the lips of people when he had no possible knowledge of what was said. But while this may be one way to view the data, it is not the only way.

19 Peter and John had probably never heard of Socrates or read Plato's report (*Apol.* 29d) of how Socrates responded to those who offered him freedom if he would only abandon the pursuit of truth: "I will obey God rather than you." The parallel is probably analogical, not genealogical—i.e., the sort of response any person of principle would give in such a situation.

4. The Church's Praise and Petition (4:23–31)

OVERVIEW

The church's response to the apostles' release was a spontaneous outburst of praise, psalmody, and petition, which begins in v.24 by addressing God as *Despota* ("Despot, Sovereign Lord"). This was a common title in the Greek world for rulers, and it appears occasionally in Jewish circles as a form of address to God (cf. 3 Macc 2:2; Lk 2:29; Rev 6:10). Its use is especially appropriate here in conjunction with the servant language used of David (v.25, *pais sou*, "your servant"), Jesus (vv.27, 30, *ho hagios pais sou*, "your holy servant"), and believers themselves (v.29, *hoi douloi sou*, "your servants"). Structurally, the church's response includes an ascription to God drawn from Hezekiah's prayer in Isaiah 37:16–20 (v.24b), a quotation of Psalm 2:1–2 (vv.25–26), the reference to Jesus' passion in terms of the psalm just cited (vv.27–28), and a petition for divine enablement in the Christians' present circumstances (vv.29–30).

²³On their release, Peter and John went back to their own people and reported all that the chief priests and elders had said to them. ²⁴When they heard this, they raised their voices together in prayer to God. "Sovereign Lord," they said, "you made the heaven and the earth and the sea, and everything in them. ²⁵You spoke by the Holy Spirit through the mouth of your servant, our father David:

> "'Why do the nations rage,
>   and the peoples plot in vain?
> 26 The kings of the earth take their stand
>   and the rulers gather together
> against the Lord
>   and against his Anointed One.'

27 Indeed Herod and Pontius Pilate met together with the Gentiles and the people of Israel in this city to conspire against your holy servant Jesus, whom you anointed. 28 They did what your power and will had decided beforehand should happen. 29 Now, Lord, consider their threats and enable your servants to speak your word with great boldness. 30 Stretch out your hand to heal and perform miraculous signs and wonders through the name of your holy servant Jesus."

31 After they prayed, the place where they were meeting was shaken. And they were all filled with the Holy Spirit and spoke the word of God boldly.

COMMENTARY

25–26 Two matters of theological interest in the prayer of the church stand out. First, there is a pesher treatment of Psalm 2 (see comments at 2:16) in which the groups enumerated in the psalm are equated with the various persons and groups involved in Jesus' crucifixion: "the kings of the earth" with King Herod; "the rulers" with the Roman governor Pontius Pilate; "the nations" with the Gentile authorities; and "the people" with "the people of Israel." The earliest suggestion that Psalm 2 had any messianic import in Jewish thinking appears in *Psalms of Solomon* 17:26, where "the Son of David," who is also spoken of in 17:36 as "the Lord's Anointed" (*ho Christos kyriou*), is presented as acting in terms of Psalm 2:9: "He will destroy the pride of the sinners as a potter's vessel. With a rod of iron he will break in pieces all their substance." More explicitly, Psalm 2:1–2 has been found as a messianic *testimonia* portion in 4Q*Florilegium* (Dead Sea Scrolls, 4Q174) in connection with 2 Samuel 7:10–14 and Psalm 1:1. It seems, therefore, that

sometime prior to the Christian period Psalm 2 was beginning to be used within Jewish nonconformist circles as a messianic psalm and that early Jewish Christians knew of this usage and approved of it—though, of course, with application to Jesus of Nazareth (cf. the use of Ps 2:7 in 13:33; Heb 1:5; 5:5; and Ps 2:9 in Rev 2:27; 12:5; 19:15).

27–28 Second, in the church's prayer the sufferings of Christian believers are related directly to the sufferings of Christ and inferentially to the sufferings of God's righteous servants in the OT. This theme of the union of the sufferings of Christ and those of his own is developed in many ways throughout the NT (cf. esp. Mk 8–10; Ro 8:17; Col 1:24; 1Pe 2:20–25; 3:14–4:2; 4:12–13). It reaches its loftiest expression in the metaphor of the body of Christ in Colossians and Ephesians.

29–30 Most significant is the fact that these early Christians were praying not for relief from oppression or for judgment on their oppressors, but for enablement from God "to speak your word with great boldness" amid opposition and for God to act in mighty power "through the name of your holy servant Jesus" (v.30). Their concern was for God's word to go forth and for Christ's name to be glorified—in effect, for the church's witness—while leaving to God their own circumstances. With such prayer surely God is well pleased. Luke has evidently taken pains to give us this prayer so that it might serve as a pattern for our own praying.

31 As a sign of God's approval, "the place where they were meeting was shaken" (cf. Ex 19:18; Isa 6:4) and "they were all filled with the Holy Spirit" (see comments at v.8). With such motivation and divine enablement, their prayer was answered. And they "spoke the word of God boldly" (*meta parrēsias* [GK *4244*], "with boldness," "confidently," "forthrightly"; cf. *meta pasēs parrēsias*, "with all boldness," at the close of Acts in 28:31).

NOTES

25 The Greek of v.25a is well attested ($\mathfrak{P}^{74}$ ℵ A B E et al.) but almost impossible to translate. C. C. Torrey, 17, called it "an incoherent jumble of words." Various ancient scribes and many modern commentators have tried to delete either τοῦ πατρὸς ἡμῶν (*tou patros hēmōn*, "our father," GK *1609*) or διὰ πνεύματος ἁγίου (*dia pneumatos hagiou*, "by the Holy Spirit"), or both. And many scholars have attempted to reconstruct the Greek syntax of these words in terms of a hypothetical Aramaic source. What we have in v.25a, however, appears to be "a primitive error," as B. F. Westcott and F. J. A. Hort called it, stemming either from the expression of the earliest Christians themselves and/or somehow incorporated into the source Luke used.

31 Codex Bezae (D) and a number of other Western witnesses (E, recensions of the Vulgate and Coptic versions, Ephraem of Syria's commentary on Acts, and such church fathers as Irenaeus and Augustine) add at the end of the verse παντὶ τῷ θέλοντι πιστεύειν (*panti tō thelonti pisteuein*, "to everyone who wished to believe"). But this phrase is not supported by the better MSS and seems to be only a pious accretion to the text.

D. Christian Concern Expressed in Sharing (4:32–5:11)

OVERVIEW

Returning to one of the themes in his thesis paragraph of 2:42–47, Luke now elaborates the nature and extent of the early believers' commitment to one another in social concern. He does this by a summary statement, then by setting out a good example of genuine Christian concern, and finally by a disastrous example of deceit. The topic of Christian social concern, which appears in 2:42–47 quite naturally along with matters of fellowship and worship in the context of the believing community, also appears here in the context of the apostles' proclamation of Jesus' resurrection by its juxtaposition with the vignettes in 3:1–4:31 and the inclusion of v.33. For Luke, as well as for the early Christians, being filled with the Holy Spirit not only entailed proclaiming the Word of God but also sharing possessions with the needy because of the oneness of all believers in Christ.

1. Believers Share Their Possessions (4:32–35)

OVERVIEW

Source-critical analyses of this passage have often concluded that the material is somewhat jumbled, with either vv.32–33 representing one of Luke's sources and vv.34–35 being an editorial insertion, or vv.32, 34–35 stemming from an early source and v.33 being an editorial intruder. Underlying all such analyses is the assumption that v.32 and vv.34–35 speak of the same attitude toward property, and that either vv.34–35 must be a repetitious editorial comment or v.33 an editorial intrusion. In reality, however, v.32 and vv.34–35 express differing views of personal possessions and personal property: in the former, they are retained and shared; in the latter, they are sold and the proceeds distributed to those in need. Likewise, there seems to be a difference between v.32 and vv.34–35 in the attitude of the believers to such practices. In the former they are presented as customary and continuous, whereas in the latter such actions seem to be extraordinary responses to special needs.

In his opening summary statement of vv.32–35, Luke is (1) emphasizing that both continuous and extraordinary acts of Christian social concern were occurring in the early church, and (2) tying these acts into the apostolic proclamation of the resurrection. It was, in fact, because of such acts—and the recognition that they must always be an inextricable part of the Christian ministry—that God's blessing rested on the early church.

> [32]All the believers were one in heart and mind. No one claimed that any of his possessions was his own, but they shared everything they had. [33]With great power the apostles continued to testify to the resurrection of the Lord Jesus, and much grace was upon them all. [34]There were no needy persons among them. For from time to time those who owned lands or houses sold them, brought the money from the sales [35]and put it at the apostles' feet, and it was distributed to anyone as he had need.

COMMENTARY

32 The designation *to plēthos tōn pisteusantōn* (lit., "the multitude of believers"; NIV, "all the believers"; NASB, "the congregation of those who believed") means the whole congregation (cf. 6:2, 5; 15:12, 30), whose allegiance to Jesus and one another is described by the common Hebraic idiom "one in heart and mind" (*kardia kai psychē mia*, lit., "one in heart and soul"; cf., e.g., Dt 6:5; 10:12; 11:13; 26:16; 30:2, 6, 10). This sense of oneness extended to sharing their personal possessions with others in need (cf. 2:45).

Theologically, the early believers considered themselves the righteous remnant within Israel. So Deuteronomy 15:4 would have been in their minds: "There should be no poor among you, for in the land the LORD your God is giving you to possess as your inheritance, he will richly bless you." Other Jewish groups who thought of themselves in terms of a remnant theology expressed their spiritual oneness by sharing their goods, and the Jerusalem church seems to have done likewise. Practically, they had many occasions for such sharing. For with the economic situation in Palestine steadily deteriorating because of famine and political unrest (cf. J. Jeremias, 121–22), employment was limited—not only for Galileans who left their fishing and farming for life in the Judean capital city, but also for the regular residents of Jerusalem who now faced economic and social sanctions because of their new messianic faith. And experientially, the spiritual oneness the believers found to be a living reality through their common allegiance to Jesus must, they realized, be expressed in caring for the physical needs of their Christian brothers and sisters. Indeed, their integrity as a community of faith depended on their acting in this manner.

In v.32 we have Luke's illustration of his thesis statement in 2:44–45 regarding the way the believers practiced communal living. They were not monastics, for the apostles and brothers of Jesus were married (cf. 1Co 9:5), and so were many of the other believers (e.g., Ananias and Sapphira, 5:1–11). Nor did they form a closed society like the covenanters at Qumran. They lived in their own homes (cf. 2:46; 12:12) and had their own possessions, as any household would. But though these early Christians had *personal* possessions, they did not consider them to be *private* possessions (*idion einai*, "to be one's own") to be held exclusively for their own use and enjoyment. Rather,

they shared what they had and so expressed their corporate life.

33 Because of its juxtaposition with v.32, we must understand the "great power" that accompanied the apostles' witness "to the resurrection of the Lord Jesus" as not being just a rhetorical or homiletical expression, or even miraculous power, but the power of a new life in the believing community—a new life that manifested itself in sharing possessions to meet the needs of others. It was this kind of power that Jesus had in mind when he said, "By this everyone will know that you are my disciples, if you love one another" (Jn 13:35 TNIV). In view of such a combination of social concern and proclamation of the word, it is no wonder that Luke concludes this verse by saying, "and much grace was upon them all."

34–35 The insertion of the phrase "from time to time" in the NIV brings out the iterative force of the imperfect verbs in these two verses. The actions alluded to were extraordinary and voluntary acts of Christian concern done in response to special needs among the believers. They involved both sharing possessions and selling real estate. By separating these actions from those described in v.32 and by the way he treats them, Luke suggests that they were exceptional and not meant to be normative for the church. The church at Jerusalem, even in its earliest days, was neither a monastic nor semimonastic community. Nevertheless, such acts were highly regarded as magnanimous expressions of a common social concern, though sadly, as with any noble deed, they could be done either sincerely or hypocritically.

NOTES

32 For πλῆθος (*plēthos*, "crowd, assembly, community," GK *4436*) used of a Jewish group of people, cf. 2:6; 19:9; 23:7; 25:24; for its general sense of "multitude," cf. 14:1; 17:4.

The Western text (D, E, and as represented by Cyprian, Zeno, and Ambrose) add after μία (*mia*, "one") καὶ οὐκ ἦν διάκρισις [or χωρισμός] ἐν αὐτοῖς οὐδεμία (*kai ouk ēn diakrisis* [or *chōrismos*] *en autois oudemia*, "and there was no quarrel [or division] among them at all"). This appears to be an addition made in the interest of emphasizing the unity of the early church.

33 The reading τῆς ἀναστάσεως τοῦ κυρίου Ἰησοῦ (*tēs anastaseōs tou kyriou Iēsou*, "the resurrection of the Lord Jesus"), as found in 𝔓⁸ (fourth century); uncials P and Ψ; some minuscules; and the Old Latin Gigas, Syriac Harclean, and Coptic Sahidic versions, is the simplest and so is usually judged by text critics to account best for the rise of the other variant readings. Codex Vaticanus (B), Codex Bezae (D), and the Byzantine tradition reverse the phrase, perhaps to connect "the Lord Jesus" with "the apostles." Codex Sinaiticus (ℵ) and Codex Alexandrinus (A) read Ἰησοῦ Χριστοῦ τοῦ κυρίου (*Iēsou Christou tou kuriou*, "Jesus Christ the Lord").

34–35 Josephus (*J.W.* 2.122) says of the Essenes, "Riches they despise, and their community of goods [τὸ κοινωνικόν, *to koinōnikon*] is truly admirable. You will not find one among them distinguished by greater opulence than another. They have a law that new members on admission to the sect shall confiscate their property to the order, with the result that you will nowhere see either abject poverty or inordinate wealth; the individual's possessions join the common stock and all, like brothers, enjoy a single patrimony." And with this description Qumran's *Rule of the Community* (1QS 1.11–13) seems to agree: "All who declare their willingness to serve God's truth must bring all of their mind, all of their strength, and all of their wealth into the community of God, so that their minds may be purified by the truth of God's precepts, their strength controlled by his perfect ways, and their wealth disposed of in accordance with his just design."

Many have understood such statements as advocating a complete sharing of possessions and property. Yet the *Rule of the Community* (1QS 7.5–8) assumes some retention of personal property when it speaks of the members paying fines within the community and carrying on business dealings both with one another and with the community itself. Likewise, the *Zadokite Fragments* (or *Damascus Covenant*) suggests that only unjustified or ill-gotten possessions were forbidden and that only a portion of one's income (i.e., at least two working days per month) was to be donated to the fund for the poor (CD 6:15; 8:5; 19:17). It seems, therefore, that we are dealing here with two matters: (1) idealized characterizations (as in the statements of Josephus and 1QS 1.11–13), with further explications serving to clarify more precisely the situation (as in 1QS 7.5–7 and CD 6:15; 8:5; 19:17—and as I suggest is the case in Ac 2:44–45 and 4:34–35); and (2) rules for monastic communities (as in 1QS) and rules seen to be more broadly applicable to life in both encampments and the cities (as in CD). The parallels between the communal sharing of the early Jerusalem Christians and that of the Qumran covenanters are, indeed, close and may legitimately be spelled out. One must also bear in mind, however, (1) the variations that appear between the idealized characterizations and the explanations of actual practice, and (2) the differences that inevitably occurred between the communal life of monastic communities and the sharing of those living in nonmonastic situations.

2. The Generosity of Barnabas (4:36–37)

³⁶Joseph, a Levite from Cyprus, whom the apostles called Barnabas (which means Son of Encouragement), ³⁷sold a field he owned and brought the money and put it at the apostles' feet.

COMMENTARY

36 Luke uses the generosity of Barnabas as "exhibit A" to illustrate the type of extraordinary social concern that was "from time to time" (v.34) expressed by believers at Jerusalem. Joseph was his Hebrew name used at home, in the synagogue, and among Jews generally. To this the apostles added the cognomen or descriptive nickname Barnabas, which means in Hebrew "Son of Encouragement," in order, evidently, to distinguish him from others of the same name (cf. 1:23). His family came from Cyprus, and he evidently had ancestral property there. John Mark was his cousin (*ho anepsios*, GK *463*; Col 4:10), and the home of Mark's mother was in Jerusalem (cf. 12:12).

37 Barnabas is an important figure in Luke's account of the church's expansion from Jerusalem to Rome. He appears a number of times as a kind of hinge between the mission to the Jewish world and that to the Gentiles (cf. 9:27; 11:22–30; 13:1–14:28; 15:2–4, 12, 22, 36–41; see also 1Co 9:6). Here he is introduced as one who "sold a field" (*hyparchontos autō agrou*, lit., "the possession to him of a field") and gave the money to the apostles for distribution among those in need. We are not told whether the property he sold was in Cyprus or Palestine. If his family was from Cyprus but had lived in Palestine, and if he continued to have connections with Cyprus while living in Palestine, he could have inherited or purchased property in Cyprus, Palestine, or both. Nor are we told how the biblical prohibition against Levites owning real estate applied in Barnabas's case (cf. Nu 18:20; Dt 10:9), though such a regulation seems not always to have been observed (cf. Jer 32:7–44; Josephus, *Life* 76). What we are told is that Barnabas gave a practical demonstration of Christian social concern that was under no compulsion of either precedent or rule (cf. 5:4).

NOTES

36 Jews also had alternative Greek names, but evidently because he viewed his ministry as principally within a Jewish milieu, Luke does not give us Barnabas's Greek name. Had he been a Roman citizen, he would also have had three Roman names, of which the third would probably have been identical with his Greek name.

37 Papyrus MSS 𝔓⁵⁷ (fourth–fifth centuries) and 𝔓⁷⁴ (seventh century); codices A (fifth century), B (fourth century), and D (fifth century); most minuscules (ninth century and following); and the TR read παρὰ τοὺς πόδας (*para tous podas*, "at the feet"), whereas codices ℵ (fourth century) and E (sixth century) read πρὸς τοὺς πόδας (*pros tous podas*, "at the feet," GK 4546). Since the former is the more urbane expression and the latter the less elegant, probably the text originally had the latter. This tendency to alter a less elegant expression to the more urbane appears also in 5:10, where πρός, *pros* (as in ℵ A B D), appears in various other textual witnesses as παρά (*para*) or ἐπί (*epi*) or ὑπό (*hypo*).

3. The Deceit of Ananias and Sapphira (5:1–11)

OVERVIEW

The case of Ananias and Sapphira is opposite that of Barnabas, though it was meant to look the same. No doubt the story circulated within the church as a warning of the awfulness of deceit, for in times of great enthusiasm such a warning is especially necessary. And though Luke has taken evident pleasure in reporting the progress of the gospel and the vitality of faith during these early days of the church in Jerusalem, he does not omit this most distressing event. It is a situation that must have lain heavily on the hearts of the early Christians. It is also a message that must be constantly kept in mind by Christians today.

[1]Now a man named Ananias, together with his wife Sapphira, also sold a piece of property. [2]With his wife's full knowledge he kept back part of the money for himself, but brought the rest and put it at the apostles' feet.

[3]Then Peter said, "Ananias, how is it that Satan has so filled your heart that you have lied to the Holy Spirit and have kept for yourself some of the money you received for the land? [4]Didn't it belong to you before it was sold? And after it was sold, wasn't the money at your disposal? What made you think of doing such a thing? You have not lied to men but to God."

[5]When Ananias heard this, he fell down and died. And great fear seized all who heard what had happened. [6]Then the young men came forward, wrapped up his body, and carried him out and buried him.

[7]About three hours later his wife came in, not knowing what had happened. [8]Peter asked her, "Tell me, is this the price you and Ananias got for the land?"

"Yes," she said, "that is the price."

[9]Peter said to her, "How could you agree to test the Spirit of the Lord? Look! The feet of the men who buried your husband are at the door, and they will carry you out also."

[10]At that moment she fell down at his feet and died. Then the young men came in and, finding her dead, carried her out and buried her beside her husband. [11]Great fear seized the whole church and all who heard about these events.

COMMENTARY

1–2 The details of the conspiracy are concisely stated. A certain man named Ananias (Heb. "God is gracious") and his wife, Sapphira (Aram. "beautiful"), both of whom were evidently Christians, apparently wanted to enjoy the acclaim of the church, as Barnabas did, but without making a genuine sacrifice. So they sold some of their real estate (*ktēma*, GK *3228*; NIV, "a piece of property"; cf. 2:45) and pretended to give the full price to the apostles for distribution to the needy, though they agreed to keep back part of the money for themselves. We wish we knew more about their purpose and their expectations so we could better understand what later took place. But not even the apostles knew all about these things, though Peter inferred the substance of what went on between them. Luke's use of the verb *nosphizō* ("put aside for oneself," "keep back," "misappropriate," "purloin," GK *3802*), which in the LXX heads the account in Joshua 7:1–26 of Achan's misappropriation of part of what had been dedicated to God, suggests that Luke meant to draw a parallel between the sin of Achan, as the Israelites began their conquest of Canaan, and the sin of Ananias and Sapphira, as the church began its mission—with both incidents coming under the immediate and drastic judgment of God and teaching a sobering lesson. And this is likely how the early church saw the incident too.

3–4 Peter did not view the action of Ananias and Sapphira as merely incidental. He spoke of it as inspired by Satan and as a lie to both the Holy Spirit and God. It was a case of deceit and was an affront not just on the community level but also and primarily before God. Deceit is spiritually disastrous—a sin, whatever its supposed justification, that sours every personal relationship. Where there is even the suspicion of misrepresentation and deception, trust is completely violated.

5 Psychological explanations for Ananias's sudden death may attribute his fatal collapse to the shock and shame of being found out. The verb Luke uses for his death, however, is *ekpsychō* ("breathe one's last," "die," GK *1775*), which is the same word used in the LXX of Sisera's death in Judges 4:21. It appears in the NT only in contexts where someone is struck down by divine judgment (cf. Ac 5:5, 10; 12:23). Psychological and physical factors may well have been secondary causes in Ananias's death, but Luke's emphasis is on the ultimate causation of God as the agent. It is in this light that he means his readers to understand his further comment: "And great fear seized all who heard what had happened."

6 The expression "the young men" (*hoi neōteroi*, GK *3742*), particularly in parallel construction with its synonym in v.10 (*hoi neaniskoi*, "the young men," GK *3734*), should be understood as simply denoting age and referring to certain younger men in the Christian community, not as designating professional buriers. The verb *systellō* ("cover," "wrap up," "take away," remove," GK *5366*) was frequently used by ancient Greek physicians like Hippocrates, Galen, and Dioscorides to mean "to bandage a limb" or "compress a wound by bandaging," though it was used more widely in the sense of "cover," "wrap up," "fold up," and "take away, remove" (cf. BDAG, 978). Whether the young men covered Ananias with a shroud and carried him away or wrapped him up in some manner and then carried him away—or simply picked him up from the floor and took him off for burial—is impossible to say. It is understandable that burial in hot climates takes place soon after death. But just why Ananias was buried so quickly and why his wife was not told seems strange, though we are not told enough about the circumstances to offer any explanation.

7–10 "About three hours later" the tragic episode was repeated with Sapphira. Just as husband and wife were united in their conspiracy, so they were united in the judgment that came on them. "All this is handled," as Haenchen, 239, says of Luke's account, "without pity, for we are in the presence of the divine punishment which should be witnessed in fear and trembling, but not with Aristotelian fear and pity."

11 It may seem redundant that Luke closes his account of Ananias's and Sapphira's act of deception with the statement, "Great fear seized the whole church and all who heard about these events." But this is a vignette of warning. In concluding it Luke wants to lay stress on this note of reverent fear, as he did earlier in v.5 and as resonates implicitly throughout this sorry account.

This is the first time in Acts that the word "church" (*ekklēsia*, GK *1711*) appears (setting aside its appearance at 2:47 in Codex Bezae), though it is the regular word for both the church universal and local congregations elsewhere in the book (cf. 7:38; 8:1; 9:31; 11:22; 13:1; 14:23; 15:22, 41; 16:5; 19:32, 40; 20:28) and throughout the NT epistles (note that *ekklēsia* occurs three times in the Gospels; cf. Mt 16:18; 18:17 [twice]).

NOTES

3 Codex Bezae (D) inserts πρός (*pros*, "to") between the names Πέτρος (*Petros*) and Ἀνανίας (*Hananias*), either accidentally (a partial dittography of Πέτρος) or deliberately.

"Satan" (Gr. ὁ Σατανᾶς, *ho Satanas*; Heb. *ha śātān*) was originally a common noun that meant "adversary" (cf. 1Ki 11:14; Ps 109:6), but it came to be a personal designation for the angel that accuses people before God (Job 1:6–12; 2:1–7) and tempts them to evil (1Ch 21:1). In the first century, Satan was considered the chief of the evil demons (cf. *Jub.* 10:11; 23:29; 40:9; 50:5), who was also called Asmondeus (Tob 3:8, 17; *b. Giṭ.* 68*b*; *b. Pesaḥ.* 110*a*), Semjaza (*1 En.* 6:3, 7; 8:3; 10:11), Azazel (*1 En.* 8:1; 10:4; 86:1; 88:1), Mastema (*Jub.* 10:5–11; 17:16; 18:4, 12; 48:2), and Beliar or Belial (*Jub.* 1:20; throughout the NT).

"To fill the heart" is a Hebraism that means "to dare to do something" (cf. Est 7:5; Ecc 8:11).

3–4 The association of "the Holy Spirit" and "God" (see also "the Spirit of the Lord" in v.9) is suggestive of the plurality of the Godhead and later doctrinal elaborations on the personality of the Spirit.

5 Codex Bezae (D) inserts παραχρῆμα (*parachrēma*, "immediately," GK *4202*), in parallel with v.10, before πεσών (*pesōn*, "falling down," GK *4406*), evidently to heighten the dramatic effect.

REFLECTIONS

No account in Acts has provoked so much wrath and dismay from critics as this one. Commentators have complained about the impossibility of accepting the death of both a husband and his wife under such circumstances and have questioned Peter's ethics in not giving them an opportunity to repent and in not telling Sapphira about her husband's death. Even more difficult for many is the way the story portrays Peter, who appears to be without the compassion or restraint of his Lord. Jesus' relations with Judas, whose sin was a thousand times more odious, were not on this level. Many, in fact, have found it repugnant to believe that any early ecclesiastical official would have shown such harshness over such a relatively "slight" offense and, furthermore, have doubted that the early church would have wanted to preserve such an account. Some, therefore, have taken this sorry episode to be a fictitious story, which might have arisen within a certain part of the early Christian community to explain why certain members of the community had died before the Parousia.

The Qumran community, however, realized the seriousness of deceit and in a situation somewhat similar to the one here ruled, "If there be found in the community a man who consciously lies in the matter of his wealth, he is to be regarded as outside the state of purity entailed by membership, and he is to be penalized one-fourth of his food ration" (1QS 6.24–25). Of course, the penalty for such deceit at Qumran was not nearly as severe as in Acts 5. But neither were the situations exactly alike.

Ananias and Sapphira were severely dealt with, it seems, (1) because of the voluntary nature of their act of pretended piety (cf. v.4) and (2) because the greater freedom permitted in the church at Jerusalem made individual Christians more responsible to be honest and more culpable when dishonest. In addition, the way Ananias and Sapphira attempted to reach their goals was so diametrically opposed to the whole thrust of the gospel that to allow it to go unchallenged would have set the entire Christian mission off its course. Like the act of Achan, this episode was pivotal in the life and mission of God's people, for the whole enterprise of the church was threatened at its very start. And while we may be thankful that judgment on deceit in the church is not now so swift and drastic, this incident stands as an indelible warning regarding the heinousness in God's sight of deception in spiritual and personal matters.

E. The Apostles Again before the Sanhedrin (5:12–42)

OVERVIEW

Having in his source materials both accounts of the apostles' arraignments before the Sanhedrin, Luke now gives the second account. Whether he clearly grasped or fully appreciated the rationale in Jewish jurisprudence for two such appearances is debatable (see Overview at 4:1–31). Nevertheless, he takes the occasion in telling of the apostles' second appearance before the council to emphasize the development of attitudes in these earliest days of the Christian mission at Jerusalem by highlighting principally (1) the deepening jealousy and antagonism of the Sadducees, (2) the continuing moderation of the Pharisees, and (3) the increasing joy and confidence of the Christians. In so doing, Luke continues the elaboration of his thesis paragraph that appeared in 2:42–47.

1. Miraculous Signs and Wonders (5:12–16)

OVERVIEW

This paragraph, like 2:42–47 and 4:32–35, is a Lukan introduction to the material that follows. It includes some statements (principally vv.12b–14) that reach back to what has been narrated before, recalling the Christians' practice of meeting in Solomon's Colonnade, the reverential fear aroused by the awful end of Ananias and Sapphira, and the increasing number of people who believed. In the main, however, the paragraph introduces the story of the apostles' second appearance before the Sanhedrin by giving a reason for the Sadducees' jealousy and for their second inquisition of the apostles, the reason being the continued success of the Christian mission at Jerusalem.

Source critics have been troubled by the facts that there is no proper connection between vv.14 and 15 and that v.15 links up quite nicely with v.12a, apart from the material of vv.12b–14. Some commentators, therefore, have taken vv.12b–14 as a self-contained unit stemming from an earlier source and vv.15–16 as an awkward editorial addition; others have taken vv.12a and 15–16 as representative of Luke's source material and vv.12b–14 as an editorial intrusion. Luke, however, was probably faced

in his source materials with the juxtaposition of the vignettes about the deceit of Ananias and Sapphira and the apostles' second appearance before the Jewish Sanhedrin, and so felt the need to provide his readers with a summary paragraph as a transition from the one to the other.

We may fault Luke for crowding too much into that paragraph or for arranging it in a somewhat jumbled chronological sequence. But the course he plots in moving from reverential fear on the part of the church and the people (cf. 5:5, 11), to heightened jealousy on the part of the Sadducees (cf. 5:17–33), and then to increased rejoicing on the part of the apostles (cf. 5:41–42) is not difficult to follow. And his purpose in providing such an introductory summary paragraph—which parallels in both motive and pattern what he has done at 4:32–35—is understandable.

¹²The apostles performed many miraculous signs and wonders among the people. And all the believers used to meet together in Solomon's Colonnade. ¹³No one else dared join them, even though they were highly regarded by the people. ¹⁴Nevertheless, more and more men and women believed in the Lord and were added to their number. ¹⁵As a result, people brought the sick into the streets and laid them on beds and mats so that at least Peter's shadow might fall on some of them as he passed by. ¹⁶Crowds gathered also from the towns around Jerusalem, bringing their sick and those tormented by evil spirits, and all of them were healed.

COMMENTARY

12a The reason for the Sadducees' jealousy and the apostles' second appearance before the Jewish Sanhedrin is given quite concisely. In defiance of the council's orders, the apostles continued to carry on their ministry among the people, with "many miraculous signs and wonders" being performed. As with his introductory résumé of 4:32–35, so here

too Luke puts his thesis statement at the very beginning of his portrayal of events.

12b–14 Luke speaks of three groups of people and their response to both the Sanhedrin's warning and the fear engendered by Ananias's and Sapphira's fate: (1) the Christians and their continued meeting together in Solomon's Colonnade; (2) the unbelieving Jews (*hoi loipoi*, "the rest") and their reluctance to associate too closely with the Christians; and (3) the responsive Jews (*ho laos*, "the people," GK *3295*) and their honoring the Christians—with many men and women from this latter group coming to believe in the Lord and being added to the number of Christian believers. Thematically, this résumé serves to support the thesis statement of v.12a; structurally, it relates to its paragraph much as 4:33, with its reference to the apostles' continued preaching, relates to its own paragraph.

15–16 The material in these two verses is structurally like that of 4:34–35, for in both cases there is a logical and linguistic connection with each thesis statement (cf. the *gar*, "for," in 4:34 and the *hōste*

kai, "as a result," in 5:15). In both instances special and extraordinary expressions of the respective thesis statements are detailed. As healing virtue had flowed from Jesus just by touching in faith the edge of his cloak (cf. Mk 5:25–34 par.), so Luke tells us of extraordinary situations where even Peter's shadow was used by God to effect a cure (cf. 19:11–12). And whereas the healing of the crippled beggar had originally aroused the Sadducees' antagonism, now, Luke tells us, such a miracle was being repeated numerous times in the apostles' ministry, and crowds from the outlying districts around Jerusalem thronged the apostles. No wonder the Sadducees' jealousy erupted anew!

NOTES

12 On the compound σημεῖα καὶ τέρατα (*sēmeia kai terata*, "signs and wonders," GK *4956, 5469*), see comments at 2:22. Evidently when Luke was controlled by his sources, he wrote τέρατα καὶ σημεῖα, *terata kai sēmeia* (cf. 2:19, 22, 43; 6:8; 7:36), but when he wrote more freely, he preferred the order σημεῖα καὶ τέρατα, *sēmeia kai terata* (cf. 5:12; 14:3; 15:12).

The Western text (D, minuscule 42, and as represented by the Coptic Sahidic version) adds ἐν τῷ ἱερῷ (*en tō hierō*, "in the temple," GK *2639*) after "to meet together" and before "in Solomon's Colonnade." Solomon's Colonnade, however, was located outside the temple proper (see comments at 3:11).

13 Various other suggestions for understanding οὐδεὶς ἐτόλμα κολλᾶσθαι αὐτοῖς (*oudeis etolma kollasthai autois*, "no one else dared join them" [NIV] or "none of the rest dared to associate with them" [NASB]) have been offered: (1) no one dared to join the believers on his or her own authority, i.e., apart from being received by the apostles and baptized; (2) no one dared to meddle with, i.e., "contend with" or "antagonize" the believers; and (3) no one dared to prevent the believers from meeting in Solomon's Colonnade. Each of these other readings, however, is highly inferential, for the verb κολλάω (*kollaō*, GK *3140*) is best translated "join, associate with on intimate terms," or "come into close contact with" (cf. Lk 15:15, "hired himself out to").

On ὁ λαός (*ho laos*, "the people") in Luke's writings, see the discussion at 2:47a.

2. The Arrest and Trial of the Apostles (5:17–33)

OVERVIEW

Luke's account of the apostles' second appearance before the Sanhedrin is divided into three sections, with a typically Lukan connective beginning each section: *anastas* ("rising up," GK 482; untranslated in NIV) at v.17, which introduces the arrest and trial of the apostles (vv.17–33); *anastas* ("rising up"; NIV, "stood up") at v.34, which introduces Gamaliel's wise counsel of moderation (vv.34–40); and *men oun* (NASB, "so"; untranslated in NIV) at v.41, which begins the statements about the apostles' rejoicing and continued ministry (vv.41–42). The NIV treats *anastas* at the beginning of v.17 and *men oun* at the beginning of v.41 as stylistic connectives and so does not translate them.

¹⁷Then the high priest and all his associates, who were members of the party of the Sadducees, were filled with jealousy. ¹⁸They arrested the apostles and put them in the public jail. ¹⁹But during the night an angel of the Lord opened the doors of the jail and brought them out. ²⁰"Go, stand in the temple courts," he said, "and tell the people the full message of this new life."

²¹At daybreak they entered the temple courts, as they had been told, and began to teach the people.

When the high priest and his associates arrived, they called together the Sanhedrin—the full assembly of the elders of Israel—and sent to the jail for the apostles. ²²But on arriving at the jail, the officers did not find them there. So they went back and reported, ²³"We found the jail securely locked, with the guards standing at the doors; but when we opened them, we found no one inside." ²⁴On hearing this report, the captain of the temple guard and the chief priests were puzzled, wondering what would come of this.

²⁵Then someone came and said, "Look! The men you put in jail are standing in the temple courts teaching the people." ²⁶At that, the captain went with his officers and brought the apostles. They did not use force, because they feared that the people would stone them.

²⁷Having brought the apostles, they made them appear before the Sanhedrin to be questioned by the high priest. ²⁸"We gave you strict orders not to teach in this name," he said. "Yet you have filled Jerusalem with your teaching and are determined to make us guilty of this man's blood."

²⁹Peter and the other apostles replied: "We must obey God rather than men! ³⁰The God of our fathers raised Jesus from the dead—whom you had killed by hanging him on a tree. ³¹God exalted him to his own right hand as Prince and Savior that he might give repentance and forgiveness of sins to Israel. ³²We are witnesses of these things, and so is the Holy Spirit, whom God has given to those who obey him."

³³When they heard this, they were furious and wanted to put them to death.

COMMENTARY

17–18 As in 4:1–31, Luke portrays the early opposition to Christianity as stemming principally from the Sadducees. The Pharisees were undoubtedly represented in the Sanhedrin (see comments on "the full assembly of the elders of Israel" at v.21), but their presence in these early days of the church's existence—i.e., before the "apostasy" of Stephen and the Hellenists—is depicted as exerting a moderating influence on the antagonism of the Sadducees. Thus "the high priest and all his associates, who were members of the party [*hē ousa hairesis*] of the Sadducees," are presented as taking official action a second time against the apostles by arresting them and putting them "in the public jail" (*en tērēsei dēmosia*).

The noun *hairesis* ("party," GK *146*) is used variously in the NT of Sadducees (here), Pharisees (15:5; 26:5), Christians (24:5, 14; 28:22), divisions within the churches (1Co 11:19; Gal 5:20), and outright "heresies" (2Pe 2:1)—either with or without a pejorative nuance. The inclusion of the participle *ousa* ("being") seems to be a Lukan mannerism drawn ultimately from Grecian jurisprudence and usually adds little to the sense (cf. 13:1; 14:13; 28:17). Here, however, it gives the sentence a somewhat official and menacing sound. The word *dēmosia* (GK *1323*) used as an adverb carries the meaning of "publicly" (cf. 16:37; 18:28; 20:20; 2 Macc 6:10; 3 Macc 2:27; 4:7; Josephus, *J.W.* 2.455), and therefore as an adjective with *tērēsis* ("prison," GK *5499*) means "the public prison" or "public jail." *Dēmosion* as a substantive, taking the form of the Hebrew *dîmôs*, passed into the language of the rabbis as the term for "a common jail" (cf. Str-B, 2.635).

19–21a In speaking of the "door-miracles" in the NT, Joachim Jeremias has noted the widespread popularity within the ancient world of legends regarding prison doors that open of themselves under divine instigation. He concludes with the following statement: "The threefold repetition of the motif of the miraculous opening of prison doors in Acts, its distribution between the apostles in Acts 5:19, Peter in 12:6–11, and Paul in 16:26f., and the agreement with ancient parallels in many details, e.g., liberation by night, the role of the guards, the falling off of chains, the bursting open of the doors, the shining of bright light, earthquake, all suggest that in form at least Luke is following an established *topos*" (*TDNT* 3:176). Indeed, the form of such stories may be judged to have influenced Luke, at least to some extent, in the composition of his narrative here, for literary conventions and forms, as well as ideas, were certainly "in the air." Yet as F. F. Bruce, 120 n., observed, "In this as in all form-critical studies it must be remembered that the material is more important than the form; meat-pies and mud-pies may be made in pie-dishes of identical shape, but the identity of shape is the least important consideration in comparing the two kinds of pies."

19 The "angel of the Lord" (*angelos kyriou*, GK *34, 3261*) is the LXX term for the Hebrew "angel of Yahweh" (*malʾāk YHWH*), which denotes God himself in his dealings with people (e.g., Ex 3:2, 4, 7). While the Greek *angelos*, like the Hebrew *malʾāk*, may simply mean "messenger," here it denotes the presence or agency of God himself (cf. 8:26; 12:7, 23 [probably also simply *angelos* in 7:30, 35, 38; 12:11; 27:23]; Mt 1:20, 24; 2:13, 19; 28:2; Lk 1:11; 2:9).

20 By divine intervention, the apostles were released from the public jail and told, "Go, stand in the temple courts . . . and tell the people the full message of this new life." The use of the aorist passive participle *stathentes* ("stand" or, more appropriately, "hold your ground, stand firm," GK *2705*) with the present imperative *poreuesthe* ("go," GK *4513*) suggests that dogged steadfastness on the part of the apostles was required in the face of the Sadducees' opposition.

The apostles' message was to continue to be directed to those who would receive it within Israel (*ho laos*, "the people") and to be proclaimed fully (*panta ta rhēmata*, lit., "all the words"), in spite of the Sanhedrin's attempt to silence it. The focus is on "this new life," with "life" (*zōē*, GK *2437*) and "salvation" (*sōtēria*, GK *5401*) understood in the NT as being synonymous, since both are Greek translations of the Hebrew word "life" (*ḥayyâ*, GK *2652*). And since the apostles had been miraculously released and divinely commissioned, that is exactly what they began to do (v.21a).

21b–27 Having confined (as they thought) the apostles in the public jail for the night, the next morning "the high priest and his associates" again convened the Sanhedrin in order to make a judgment and take some action about the disturbances the Christians had caused. Luke adds, "the full assembly of the elders of Israel" (*pasan tēn gerousian tōn huiōn Israēl*, lit., "all the senate of the sons of Israel"), probably to make clear that the Pharisees were well represented in the council at this time. They may not have been present at the first trial, but they certainly became vocal through Gamaliel at this second trial (cf. vv.34–40).

The Sanhedrin sent to the jail for their prisoners but did not find them. "The captain of the temple guard and the chief priests were puzzled" (v.24), perhaps suspecting that the escape was aided in some way by members of the temple guard. But when they heard that the apostles were teaching the people in the temple courts (v.25), "the captain" took command of his temple police and brought the apostles in before the council to be interrogated (v.26a). Luke states that no violence occurred in their arrest because the captain and his guard feared the reaction of the people (v.26b). This says something about the response of the early Christians to

Jesus' teaching on nonviolence and his example of nonretaliation when he was arrested (cf. Mk 14:43–50 par.), for they might have begun a riot and thus extricated themselves. It also continues the theme of "the favor of all the people" in 2:42–47.

28 The high priest, as president of the Sanhedrin, began the interrogation by reminding the apostles of the council's order for them to be silent, which order had obviously not been complied with. It is uncertain whether Luke had in mind Annas or Caiaphas as leading the interrogation. The latter was officially the high priest at the time. The former, however, is assumed in the NT to be the real power behind the throne and continues to be called the high priest (cf. Lk 3:2; Jn 18:13–24). Formally, the high priest's interrogation contains no question at all but only points up the apostles' refusal to obey the Sanhedrin's order (i.e., a charge of "contempt of court"). He also objects to their insistence on blaming the council for Jesus' death (cf. 4:10, "whom you crucified").

For the Sadducean leadership of the council, the uncontested charge of contempt of court was sufficient legal warrant for taking action against the apostles. The Sadducees only wanted to preserve their own vested authority and put an end to any disturbance among the people. They evidently had no interest in determining the truth or falsity of the Christians' claims. Their hardened attitude is manifest in their refusal to mention the name of Jesus (cf. *epi tō onomati toutō*, "in this name [GK *4047*]," contra *epi tō onomati tou Iēsou*, "in the name of Jesus," 4:18) and their spitting out the epithet "this man" (*tou anthrōpou toutou*; GK *476*) when they had to refer to him.

29 By saying "Peter and the other apostles replied," Luke suggests that Peter was the spokesman for the group of apostles on trial, with the others indicating their agreement. Their response is hardly a reasoned defense, rather, simply a reaffirmation of their position. As at the first trial (4:19), here they voice even more succinctly the noble principle, "We must obey God rather than men."

30 As at the first trial, the focus is on Jesus. "By hanging him on a tree" (*kremasantes epi xylou*) is a locution for crucifixion and stems from Deuteronomy 21:22–23. While the noun *xylou* (GK *3833*) was used in antiquity and the LXX variously for "a tree" or "wood" of any kind, "a pole," and various objects made of wood, including "a gallows," it is also used in the NT for the cross of Jesus (cf. 10:39; 13:29; Gal 3:13 [quoting Dt 21:23]; 1Pe 2:24).

31 "Prince" and "Savior" are christological ascriptions rooted in the confessions of the early church and particularly associated with the NT themes of exaltation and lordship.

33 As far as the Sadducees were concerned, the charge of contempt of court was not only uncontested but repeated. On hearing the apostles reaffirm what to them could only be considered intolerable obstinacy, the Sadducees were furious and wanted to destroy them. While the Sanhedrin did not have authority under Roman jurisdiction to inflict capital punishment, undoubtedly they would have found some pretext for handing these men over to the Romans for such action—as they did with Jesus himself—had it not been for the intervention of the Pharisees, as represented particularly by Gamaliel (v.34).

NOTES

17 On the Sadducees, see comments at 4:1.

18 Codex Bezae (D) adds at the end of the verse καὶ ἐπορεύθη εἰς ἕκαστος εἰς τὰ ἴδια (*kai eporeuthē heis hekastos eis ta idia*, "and each one went to his own home"), which is an extraneous circumstantial detail that parallels John 7:53 and the addition by many scribes to Acts 14:18.

21 The verb ἐδίδασκον (*edidaskon*, GK *1438*) should probably be understood as an inceptive imperfect and so be translated, "they began to teach" (so NIV, NASB).

The epexegetical phrase "the full assembly of the elders of Israel" (*pasan tēn gerousian tōn huiōn Israēl*, lit., "all the senate of the sons of Israel") echoes the LXX wording of Exodus 12:21. On the Sanhedrin, its constitution, and its other names, see comments and note at 4:5.

24–27 On "the captain of the temple guard" (ὁ στρατηγὸς τοῦ ἱεροῦ, *ho stratēgos tou hierou*) and his temple police force, see comments at 4:1.

26 Codex Bezae (D) strangely (perhaps accidentally) omits the negative οὐ (*ou*, "not") in the phrase οὐ μετὰ βίας (*ou meta bias*, "not with force").

27 On Annas and Caiaphas as high priest, see comments at 4:6.

28 Several codices (D E P) and a number of minuscules include the negative οὐ (*ou*, "not") before παραγγελίᾳ (*parangelia*, "strict orders," GK *4132*), whereas Bodmer 𝔓74 and several codices (א A B) omit it. Its inclusion may have been occasioned by the influence of the warning in 4:17 and the verb ἐπηρώτησεν (*epērōtēsen*, "he questioned," GK *2089*) in 5:27; its omission may be due to a copyist's desire to turn the high priest's question into a rebuke.

Perhaps the way in which Jesus is referred to by the high priest as "this man" is an example of the general reluctance of Judaism to pronounce the name of Jesus, as seen particularly in the rabbinic writings (cf. Jacob Jocz, *The Jewish People and Jesus Christ* [London: SPCK, 1949], 111). Codex Bezae (D) somewhat heightens the caustic nature of the high priest's reference to Jesus by substituting the demonstrative pronoun ἐκεῖνος (*ekeinos*, "that") for the demonstrative pronoun τοῦτος (*toutos*, "this").

29 Codex Bezae (D) enhances the role of Peter by omitting "and the apostles answered" and altering εἶπαν (*eipan*, "they said") to εἶπεν (*eipen*, "he said," GK *3306*).

31 On the christological titles ἀρχηγός (*archēgos*, "Prince," GK *795*) and σωτήρ (*sōtēr*, "Savior," GK *5400*), see my *Christology of Early Jewish Christianity*, 53–58, 99–103, 141–44.

3. Gamaliel's Wise Counsel of Moderation (5:34–40)

OVERVIEW

The portrayal of Gamaliel's wise counsel in vv.34–40 is, it seems, the high point of Luke's account of the apostles' second appearance before the Sanhedrin and probably the main reason why he included the whole vignette. Structurally, the aorist participle *anastas* ("rising up") at v.17, used as a connective and introducing the heightened antagonism of the Sadducees to the early Christians in vv.17–33, is balanced by the same connective, *anastas*, at v.34 to introduce the moderation of the Pharisees depicted in vv.34–40 (see Overview, 5:17–33). Apparently Luke's purpose is to contrast the developed antagonism of the Sadducees with the moderation of Gamaliel, who spoke as a significant representative of the Pharisees.

³⁴But a Pharisee named Gamaliel, a teacher of the law, who was honored by all the people, stood up in the Sanhedrin and ordered that the men be put outside for a little while. ³⁵Then he addressed them: "Men of Israel, consider carefully what you intend to do to these men. ³⁶Some time ago Theudas appeared, claiming to be somebody, and about four hundred men rallied to him. He was killed, all his followers were dispersed, and it all came to nothing. ³⁷After him, Judas the Galilean appeared in the days of the census and led a band of people in revolt. He too was killed, and all his followers were scattered. ³⁸Therefore, in the present case I advise you: Leave these men alone! Let them go! For if their purpose or activity is of human origin, it will fail. ³⁹But if it is from God, you will not be able to stop these men; you will only find yourselves fighting against God."

⁴⁰His speech persuaded them. They called the apostles in and had them flogged. Then they ordered them not to speak in the name of Jesus, and let them go.

COMMENTARY

34 The first-century Pharisee Gamaliel I, who was either the son or grandson of the famous Hillel, was himself so highly esteemed among his people that the Mishnah says of him, "Since Rabban Gamaliel the elder died there has been no more reverence for the law; and purity and abstinence died out at the same time" (*m. Soṭah* 9:15). Here in Acts he is portrayed as having taken charge at a certain point in the council meeting and as having gained the acquiescence of those present, not because of any vested authority, but through personal forcefulness and respect for what he represented.

For more on the Pharisees, see Reflections, p. 799.

35 Gamaliel addresses the council members with the traditional designation "men of Israel" (cf. 2:22).

36–37 The most notorious historical blunder in Acts, as many have seen it, is Gamaliel's reference in his speech to the Jewish revolutionaries Theudas and Judas the Galilean. The historical problems are two: (1) the conflict with Josephus as to the chronological order of these rebellions, for Josephus places that of Judas at about AD 6 (*Ant.* 18.4–10) and that of Theudas at about AD 44 (*Ant.* 20.97–98); and, more seriously, (2) that Gamaliel in about AD 34 refers to an uprising of Theudas, which did not, in fact, occur until a decade or so later. Nineteenth-century criticism explained these problems as resulting from Luke's errant dependence on Josephus, arguing that Luke (1) had confused Josephus's later reminiscence (*Ant.* 20.102) of Judas's revolt with Judas's earlier actual revolt and (2) had forgotten some sixty years or more after the event (if indeed he had ever known) that Gamaliel's speech preceded Theudas's rebellion by a decade or so. And many contemporary scholars continue to highlight this problem as being disastrous for any confidence in Luke's historical and chronological accuracy. Haenchen, 257, for example, insists "that Luke should have been capable of transposing Theudas's march to the Jordan—which [on Haenchen's dating of Acts] took place perhaps forty years before the composition of Acts—to the time preceding the census of Quirinius, some eighty years distant from Acts, proves that the traditions reaching him had left him in utter confusion where chronology was concerned."

The arguments for Luke's dependence on Josephus have been fairly well demolished by a number of comparative studies of the two writers. Emil Schürer's dictum still holds true today: "Either Luke had not read Josephus, or he had forgotten all about what he had read" ("Lucas und Josephus," *ZWT* 19 [1876]: 582–83). And despite the caustic comment about "special pleading" usually leveled against the proposal, it remains true that (1) the Theudas whom Gamaliel cites in Acts 5:36 may have been one of the many insurgent leaders who arose in Palestine at the time of Herod the Great's death in 4 BC, and not the Theudas who led the Jewish uprising of AD 44; and (2) Gamaliel's examples of Jewish insurrectionists have in mind a Theudas of about 4 BC and Judas the Galilean of AD 6, whereas Josephus focused on the Judas of AD 6 and another Theudas of AD 44. Our problem with these verses, therefore, may result as much from our own ignorance of the situation as from what we believe we know based on Josephus.

38–39 It has often been claimed that the moderation of Gamaliel portrayed here is "an historical mistake," for such words are not in character with what we know of Pharisaism (J. Weiss, 1.185). Yet in characterizing the respective attitudes of the Pharisees and Sadducees, Josephus (*J.W.* 2.166) notes, "The Pharisees are affectionate to each other and cultivate harmonious relations with the community. The Sadducees, on the contrary, are, even among themselves, rather boorish in their behavior, and in their relations with their compatriots are as rude as to aliens." And later he says, "the Pharisees are naturally lenient in the matter of punishments" (*Ant.* 13.294). Likewise, Rabbi Johanan the sandal maker, a second-century disciple of Rabbi Akiba, taught that "any assembling together that is for the sake of heaven shall in the end be established, but any that is not for the sake of heaven shall not in the end be established" (*m. 'Abot* 4:11)—an instruction expressing a policy of "wait and see the end result of a matter" that exactly parallels the attitude of Gamaliel as Luke reports it here.

Admittedly, both Josephus and Johanan had their own prejudices and purposes in saying what they did (which is true of every writer and teacher, including commentators on Acts). But there are good reasons to believe that such sentiments of tolerance and moderation, with history being viewed as the final judge of whether something is of God, characterized the better Pharisees of the day. So Gamaliel's response to the proclamation and activity of the apostles should not be seen as being out of line for better Hillelian Pharisees.

One major problem with accepting Luke's portrayal of Gamaliel's wise words of moderation is that later in Acts he speaks of Saul of Tarsus, who trained under Gamaliel I (cf. 22:3), as taking a very different attitude toward early believers in Jesus—joining with the Sadducees and obtaining from the high priest authorization to track them down and imprison them (cf. 8:1, 3; 9:1–2). But between Gamaliel's advice in Acts 5 and Saul's action in Acts 8 and 9 there arose from the depths of Christian conviction what the Pharisees as well as the Sadducees could only have considered to be a threat of Jewish apostasy. Before Gamaliel's counsel of moderation, Luke tells us that the central issues of the church's proclamation had been the messiahship, lordship, and saviorhood of Jesus of Nazareth, with

particular emphasis on his heaven-ordained death, his victorious resurrection, and his present status as exalted Redeemer. "The stream of thought," as William Manson (*Jesus the Messiah* [London: Hodder & Stoughton, 1943], 52) observed in characterizing the church's early functional theology, "flowed in an intense but narrow channel, carrying in its flood much that for the time remained in solution in the subconscious rather than in the conscious region of the Christian mentality." To the Sadducees, who instigated the early suppressions, such teaching not only upset orderly rule but, more importantly, impinged on their own vested authority. To the more noble of the Pharisees, however, the Jerusalem Christians were yet within the scope of Judaism and not to be treated as heretics.

The divine claims for Jesus as yet lay in the subconsciousness of the church, and those who were his followers showed no tendency to relax their observance of the Mosaic law because of their new beliefs. Other sects were tolerated within Judaism, and those whom the Pharisees considered to be deluded in their messianic commitment could be countenanced as well. As Arthur Nock (*St. Paul* [New York: Harper, 1938], 35–36) once said, "The Pharisees might wish all men to be even as they were; but that result could be attained only by persuasion."

Between Gamaliel's advice and Saul's action, however, there arose within Christian preaching something that could only be viewed by the Jewish leaders as a real threat of Jewish apostasy. In Acts 6–7 Stephen is portrayed as beginning to apply the doctrines of Jesus' messiahship and lordship to traditional Jewish views regarding the land, the Law, and the temple. Moreover, he is seen as beginning to reach conclusions that related to the primacy of Jesus' messiahship and lordship and the secondary nature of Jewish views about the land, the Law, and the temple. How Stephen got involved in such discussions and how he developed his argument will be dealt with in my comments on Acts 6–7. Suffice it here to note that this was a dangerous path for Stephen to tread, particularly in Jerusalem—a path that even the apostles seemed unwilling to take at that time.

Indeed, Stephen's message was Jewish apostasy! Had Rabbi Gamaliel the Elder faced this feature of Christian proclamation in the second Sanhedrin trial of the apostles, his attitude might well have been different. For with the whole basis of Judaism under attack in Stephen's preaching, as the Pharisees would have viewed it, Saul's persecution of believers in Jesus could have been later undertaken with the full approval of his teacher Gamaliel. As yet, however, that was not the situation. So Gamaliel here urges tolerance and moderation.

40 Gamaliel's wise counsel prevailed to some extent among his Sanhedrin colleagues and held back the worst of Sadducean intentions, though it did not entirely divert their wrath. Thus the apostles were flogged (probably with the severe beating of thirty-nine stripes that is detailed in *m. Mak.* 3:10–15*a*), warned that the ban against teaching in the name of Jesus was still in effect, and then released.

NOTES

34 Codices ℵ A B, together with the Latin Vulgate and Coptic Bohairic versions, have τοὺς ἀνθρώπους (*tous anthrōpous*, "the men"), whereas codices D E H P, together with the Syriac Peshitta and Coptic Sahidic versions and most minuscules, read τοὺς ἀποστόλους (*tous apostolous*, "the apostles"). The expression "the men" was evidently considered by many scribes to be too common for the apostles and too undignified for Luke's narrative, though it appears later in Gamaliel's speech at vv.35 and 38.

On the Pharisees, see L. Finkelstein, "The Pharisees: Their Origin and Their Philosophy," *HTR* 22 (1929): 185–261; Finkelstein, *The Pharisees* (2 vols.; Philadelphia: Jewish Publication Society of America, 1938). For the view that the name "Pharisees" meant "interpreters" (from the idea of "dividing" in the Aramaic verb), see W. O. E. Oesterley, *The Jews and Judaism During the Greek Period* (London: SPCK, 1941), 245ff.; that it originally meant "Persianizers" because of their eschatology and angelology, see T. W. Manson, "Sadducee and Pharisee—the Origin and Significance of the Names," *BJRL* 22 (1938): 153–59.

For the view that Hillel was the father of Gamaliel I, see H. L. Strack, *Introduction to the Talmud and Midrash* (Philadelphia: Jewish Publication Society of America, 1931), 109. Probably, however, Hillel as Gamaliel's grandfather is the more supportable position; cf. W. Bacher, "Gamaliel I," in *Jewish Encyclopedia* (N.Y.: Funk & Wagnalls, 1906), 5.558–59. The title "Rabban" (lit., "our teacher") was an honorific one given to several teachers of the school of Hillel, a title that served to mark them off as being more significant than those designated simply "Rabbi" (lit., "my teacher").

35 Codex Bezae (D) and the Coptic Sahidic version replace αὐτούς (*autous*, "them") by τοὺς ἄρχοντας καὶ τοὺς συνέδριους (*tous archontas kai tous synedrious*, "the rulers and members of the council"), probably because "them" was thought ambiguous and might be taken by a careless reader to refer to "the men" (i.e., "the apostles," as D E H P et al. spell it out) of v.34.

36 The Western text (D, E, minuscule 614, recensions of the Old Latin, Syriac, and Coptic versions, and such church fathers as Origen, Jerome, and Cyril) variously add μέγαν (*megan*, "great") either before or after the reflexive pronoun ἑαυτόν (*heauton*, "himself"), thereby saying explicitly that Theudas claimed to be someone great (cf. Simon's boast in 8:9).

Instead of the simple ἀνηρέθη (anerethē, "he was killed," GK 359), the Greek text of Codex Bezae (D)—but not the corresponding Latin text of Bezae or recensions of the Old Latin—has διελύθη αὐτὸς δι' αὐτοῦ (dielythē autos di' hautou, "he was destroyed by himself"). Metzger, 292, aptly notes in treating this "curious" statement, "Bezae's account of Theudas's suicide is contrary to that of Josephus, who expressly says that Theudas, having been captured alive, was beheaded (Ant., XX.v.1)—or is the disagreement between the two accounts an added argument supporting the theory that Josephus and Acts refer to two different persons with the same name?"

38–39 On the piety of Hebraic Judaism, see my *Paul, Apostle of Liberty*, 65–85. Possibly significant as well for an understanding of Gamaliel's moderate stance is the remembrance in *b. Sanh.* 98b that "Hillel . . . maintained that there will be no Messiah for Israel, since they have already enjoyed him during the reign of Hezekiah," coupled with the rejoinder in *b. Sanh.* 99a: "May God forgive him [i.e., Hillel, for so saying]." Joseph Klausner (*The Messianic Idea in Israel* [London: Allen & Unwin, 1956], 404) believes this remembrance and its rejoinder to refer to someone other than Hillel the Elder, but Sigmund Mowinckel (*He That Cometh* [Oxford: Blackwell, 1956], 284 n. 6) insists that this *is* a reference to the Hillel of Herod the Great's day, the ancestor of Gamaliel. If this is so, then there was in Gamaliel's own family a tragedy of mistaken identity such as would encourage Gamaliel to adopt a policy of moderation toward those who might, in his opinion, have had similarly mistaken views.

REFLECTIONS

The Pharisees represented the continuation of the ancient Hasidim, that group of "pious ones" in Israel who during the Seleucid oppressions joined the Hasmoneans (i.e., the Maccabees) in the struggle for religious freedom but later opposed the Maccabean rulers' political and territorial claims. They came from diverse family, occupational, and economic backgrounds and gave themselves to (1) the study of the Law (Torah) in both its written and oral forms; (2) expounding the Law in terms of its contemporary relevance; and (3) preparing the people for the coming of the messianic age by means of education in Scripture and the oral tradition. The name "Pharisee" probably comes from the Aramaic verb meaning "to separate" (*peras*, GK 10592), which the Pharisees themselves evidently understood in its plural participial form to mean "the separated ones" in the sense of "holy ones dedicated entirely to God." In the period before the destruction of Jerusalem in AD 70 they were in the minority in the Sanhedrin. But their support by the people was so great that all matters of life and ceremony were guided by their interpretations (cf. Josephus, *Ant.* 18.15), and Sadducean magistrates had to profess adherence to their principles in order to hold the formal allegiance of the populace (ibid., 18.17).

Theologically, the Pharisees looked for a messianic age and a personal Messiah. They also believed in the resurrection of the dead, though they understood such a doctrine to mean either the immortality of the soul or the reanimation and resuscitation of the body. Furthermore, they accepted the presence and activity of angels and demons, held in balance the tenets of God's eternal decrees and man's freedom of will, and tried to live lives of simple piety apart from needless wealth and luxury (cf. Josephus, *J. W.* 2.162–63; *Ant.* 13.171–73; 18.11–15).

4. The Apostles' Rejoicing and Continued Ministry (5:41–42)

OVERVIEW

Luke ends his account of the apostles' second appearance before the Sanhedrin with a brief summary that speaks of their rejoicing and continued ministry. It is a statement that has nuances of defiance, confidence, and victory. In many ways it gathers together all that Luke has set forth from 2:42 on.

Dibelius, 124, prefers to think of these chapters as considerably exaggerated throughout and assumes the situation to have been more like the following:

A band of people had been gathered together in a common belief in Jesus Christ and in the expectation of his coming again, and were leading a quiet, and in the Jewish sense, "pious" existence in Jerusalem. It was a modest existence, and nothing but the victorious conviction of the believers betrayed the fact that from this company a movement would go out which was to change the world, that this community was to become the centre of the Church.

Haenchen, 258, agrees, insisting that "in the quiet life of the primitive community there were no mass assemblies such as Luke places at the outset of the Christian mission, therefore no conflicts with the Sadducees arising from them"—and furthermore,

only with the rise of the Hellenists in the church sometime around AD 44 was "this secluded situation, in which the winning of souls for the Lord went on in the quiet personal encounter of man with man" brought to an end.

Ultimately, of course, we are forced to take sides—either with (1) Luke and his claim to have accurate source material that stems from reliable eyewitnesses, or (2) Dibelius and Haenchen and their claims to "expert opinion." The latter would have us believe that it boils down to a choice between tradition and scholarship. In actual fact, however, it is a choice between two quite divergent historical traditions and two quite different philosophical perspectives, each of which has become "orthodox" in its own circle, and two fairly different ways of doing traditio-historical criticism. While Luke's material may, indeed, be selective, styled, fragmentary, and incomplete, it is his understanding of events that leads us much further along the path of truth than the views of Dibelius or Haenchen, despite their many acknowledged excellencies of insight and skill in dealing with various details.

[41]The apostles left the Sanhedrin, rejoicing because they had been counted worthy of suffering disgrace for the Name. [42]Day after day, in the temple courts and from house to house, they never stopped teaching and proclaiming the good news that Jesus is the Christ.

COMMENTARY

41 Luke connects his summary statement with his narrative by the use of the particle *men oun* ("so," "then"), which is one of his favorite connectives. He stresses the fact that just as the apostles performed miracles through the power of the name of Jesus (cf. 3:6) and proclaimed that name before the people and the council (cf. 3:16; 4:10, 12), so they rejoiced when "counted worthy of suffering disgrace for the Name."

42 Furthermore, Luke tells us that "they never stopped teaching and proclaiming the good news that Jesus is the Christ." In this somewhat formal statement, which comes close to concluding our author's whole first panel of material, there is both a correlation with the thesis paragraph of 2:42–47—explicitly in the phrases "in the temple courts and from house to house" (cf. 2:46), though also inferentially in the note of continuance that is sounded—and an anticipation of the final words of Luke's sixth panel at the very end of Acts: "boldly and without hindrance" (28:31).

NOTES

41 On the connective μὲν οὖν (*men oun*, "so," "then") and its appearance elsewhere in Acts, see comments at 1:6.

The textual tradition indicates that scribes often sought to make explicit the referent of τοῦ ὀνόματος (*tou onomatos*, "the name") by adding αὐτοῦ (*autou*, "his"), Ἰησοῦ (*Iēsou*, "of Jesus"), τοῦ κυρίου Ἰησοῦ (*tou kyriou Iēsou*, "of the Lord Jesus"), or τοῦ Χριστοῦ (*tou Christou*, "of the Christ").

Being "counted worthy of suffering disgrace for the Name" was evidently a major theme in early Christian thought (cf. 1Pe 2:21; 4:12–19).

F. The Hellenists' Presence and Problem in the Church (6:1–6)

OVERVIEW

The source or sources at Luke's disposal for his first panel of material on the earliest days of the church in Jerusalem seem to have been fairly well intact for chs. 2–5. Probably Luke added 2:42–47, which serves as the thesis paragraph for the whole panel, and also inserted the two summary paragraphs (4:32–35; 5:12–16) that provide the settings for their corresponding vignettes. Likewise, Luke's literary touch is apparent everywhere in the style and form of his presentation. In the main, it appears he had his sources fairly well in hand for most of this part of his narrative. Furthermore, his source material seems to have contained its own conclusion, which was probably very similar to what we have at 5:41–42.

But in moving on, Luke seems to have been faced with at least two procedural problems. In the first place, his second panel, that of 6:8–9:31, focuses on three individuals—Stephen, Philip, and Saul of Tarsus—whose ministries were essential for his developmental thesis but who have not as yet been mentioned. Lest they be thought of as isolated figures in the development of the early church, Luke must relate them to what has gone on before. Furthermore, since these three men were in some way related to the Hellenists (though, of course, Saul of Tarsus was not himself a Hellenist; cf. Php 3:5b), and since thus far in the narrative there is, aside from 2:5–12, nothing said regarding these Hellenistic Christians, Luke found it necessary to tell his readers something about this element in the church.

Luke might have started his second panel with a discussion of Hellenistic Christians in Jerusalem, for that would have provided an appropriate thematic introduction for the material of that panel. To have done so, however, would have separated them from their roots in the early church and damaged his theme of continuity amid diversity. Instead, he chose to include the portrayal of the Hellenists in the Jerusalem congregation in his first panel and before the summary statement (6:7) that concludes that panel, even though the Jerusalem church itself, for reasons that will be recounted as we proceed, might not have provided him with source material on the Hellenists and he had to ferret it out for himself.

¹In those days when the number of disciples was increasing, the Grecian Jews among them complained against the Hebraic Jews because their widows were being overlooked in the daily distribution of food. ²So the Twelve gathered all the disciples together and said, "It would not be right for us to neglect the ministry of the word of God in order to wait on tables. ³Brothers, choose seven men from among you who are known to be full of the Spirit and wisdom. We will turn this responsibility over to them ⁴and will give our attention to prayer and the ministry of the word."

⁵This proposal pleased the whole group. They chose Stephen, a man full of faith and of the Holy Spirit; also Philip, Procorus, Nicanor, Timon, Parmenas, and Nicolas from Antioch, a convert to Judaism. ⁶They presented these men to the apostles, who prayed and laid their hands on them.

COMMENTARY

1 This verse is one of the most important verses in Acts. It is, in fact, also one of the most complicated. What one concludes regarding the identity of the *Hellēnistai* (GK *1821*; lit., "Hellenists"; NIV, "Grecian Jews"; NASB, "Hellenistic *Jews*"), their relation to the *Hebraioi* (GK *1578*; lit., "Hebraists"; NIV, "Hebraic Jews"; NASB, "*native* Hebrews"), and their circumstances within the church largely affects how one understands the material in Luke's second panel of material in 6:8–9:31 and the whole course of events within the Jerusalem church. It is impor-

tant, therefore, to understand as precisely as possible what Luke says and implies in describing this group within the early church—a group he introduces by the phrases "in those days" and "when the number of disciples was increasing."

Most commentators from John Chrysostom (AD 345–407) to the present have identified the *Hellēnistai* by their language and their geographical origin, i.e., as Greek-speaking Jews of the Diaspora who settled in Jerusalem among the native-born and Aramaic-speaking populace (e.g., *Beginnings of*

Christianity [ed. Foakes–Jackson and Lake], 5.59–74). But that such a definition lacks sufficient precision to be useful is pointed up by the fact that Paul classed himself among the *Hebraioi* (cf. 2Co 11:22; Php 3:5), though he was also fluent in Greek and came from a city of the Diaspora. A few interpreters have understood *Hellēnistai* to mean "Jewish proselytes" (so E. C. Blackman, "The Hellenists of Acts vi.1," *ExpTim* 48 [1937]: 524–25), though the fact that only one of the seven men in v.5 is called a proselyte seems fatal to such a view (assuming that the seven chosen to supervise the daily distribution of food are identified with the Hellenists generally). A few others have argued that *Hellēnistēs* means no more than *Hellēn* ("Greek") because of its derivation from the verb *hellēnizein*, which means "to live as a Greek" rather than just "to speak Greek," and have therefore taken it to refer simply to "Gentiles" (so Henry Cadbury, in *Beginnings of Christianity*, 3.106). But it is difficult to visualize Gentile believers, apart from those who were first Jewish proselytes, as accepted members within the Jerusalem church at any time during the first century, much less at the early date that Acts 6 requires. The case of Cornelius is presented in 10:1–11:18 as being quite exceptional, and this prohibits any easy assumption that such instances were common at an earlier time. Moreover, there is no indication that Cornelius actually joined the body of Jewish Christians at Jerusalem, even though they accepted the fact of his conversion.

Some have proposed that the "Hellenists" of Acts 6 were Jews related in some manner to the Essene movement in Palestine (cf. Oscar Cullmann, "The Significance of the Qumran Texts for Research into the Beginnings of Christianity," in *The Scrolls and the New Testament*, ed. K. Stendahl [London: SCM, 1957], 18–32). In his book *The Johannine Circle* (Philadelphia: Westminster, 1976), Cullmann argued that it was just such a group that formed the "Johannine circle" that he saw as being responsible for both the Johannine writings and the Letter to the Hebrews. In *St. Stephen and the Hellenists in the Primitive Church*, Marcel Simon spoke repeatedly of the Hellenists as a radical reforming "gentilistic" party within Essene sectarianism, while Jean Daniélou (*The Theology of Jewish Christianity* [Chicago: Regnery, 1964], 72) raised the possibility that they were a Samaritan branch of Essenism.

To identify the Hellenists with the Essenes is to presuppose a picture of Essene theology that goes much beyond the available evidence. It is difficult to see how Essene obsessions with ritual purity, strict observance of the law, and the eternal significance of the temple cultus—even though in opposition to the Jerusalem priesthood because of its secularization and impurity—can be correlated with what Acts 6 says about the Hellenists or with Stephen's message in Acts 7. And the anti-Samaritanism of the Qumran community, which comes to the fore in a number of unfavorable allusions in the Dead Sea pesher commentaries to "the men of Ephraim and Manasseh" (cf., e.g., 4QpPs37 on Ps 37:14; 4QpNa on Na 2:13; 3:1, 6), is hard to reconcile with the proclamation of the gospel in Samaria by those who were scattered throughout Judea and Samaria because of the persecution that began with Stephen's martyrdom. If the Essenes are to be brought into the discussion of Acts 6 at all, it is more likely (as I'll suggest later) that they are to be identified in some way with the "large number of priests" in 6:7 who "became obedient to the faith."

Nor is it likely that the Hellenists are to be identified with the Samaritans, as Abram Spiro argued on the basis of the linguistic and conceptual parallels he saw between Stephen's speech in Acts 7 on the one hand, and readings in the Samaritan Pentateuch and Samaritan views of history on the other (cf. "Appendix V," in Munck, 285–300). Variants of the Hebrew biblical text, as the Dead Sea Scrolls have revealed, were more widespread than previously appreciated, and the parallels between Stephen and the Samaritans are more analogical than strictly genealogical. Furthermore, since Samaritan theology was so thoroughly dominated by sacerdotal interests, it is hard to believe that anyone brought up with such an orientation could have given the kind of prophetic interpretation of the OT as expressed in Stephen's discourse.

It seems quite inconceivable that Luke would have neglected to mention in his Acts the Samaritan connections of the Hellenists or of Stephen or Philip if such had been the case. He was not hesitant to speak approvingly of certain Samaritans in his gospel (cf. Lk 10:33; 17:16), and in his account of the advance of the gospel into Samaria (Ac 8:4–25) it would have been to his advantage to speak of the connection of the Samaritans with these Hellenists. And if all this does not carry conviction, it seems even more inconceivable that Luke would have a Samaritan addressing the Jewish Sanhedrin as "brothers and fathers" (22:1).

C. F. D. Moule's suggestion ("Once More, Who Were the Hellenists?" *ExpTim* 70 [1959]: 100)—that the *Hellēnistai* of Acts 6 were "simply Jews (whether by birth or as proselytes) who spoke only Greek and no Semitic language, in contrast to *Hebraioi*, which would then mean the Jews who spoke a Semitic language in addition, of course, to Greek"—has much to commend it and seems to be an advance in the explicit meaning of the term. It has a number of advantages: (1) it hurdles the difficulty as to how Paul could call himself a Hebraic Jew when he was from the Diaspora; (2) it provides an explanation as to why Hellenistic synagogues were required in Jerusalem; and (3) it offers an insight into the problem of why two of the seven men chosen in 6:5 (i.e., Stephen and Philip) appear almost immediately thereafter as evangelists within their own circle when they had actually been appointed to supervise more mundane concerns. Yet as Joseph Fitzmyer ("Jewish Christianity in Acts in Light of the Qumran Scrolls," in *Studies in Luke-Acts*, ed. Keck and Martyn, 238) has aptly noted, "It should also be recalled that such a linguistic difference would also bring with it a difference in outlook and attitude"—or at least would give rise within more Hebraic circles to suspicions and accusations of such a difference.

As reflected in the Talmud, Pharisaism made little secret of its contempt for "Grecian Jews" or "Hellenists." Unlike those from Syria or Babylonia, which were areas often considered extensions of the Holy Land, Jews from other Diaspora lands were frequently categorized by native-born and (assumedly) more scrupulous Jews of Jerusalem as second-class Israelites (cf. A. Edersheim, *The Life and Times of Jesus the Messiah* [3rd ed.; Grand Rapids: Eerdmans, 1967], 1:7–9). And judging by the claim of some in the Corinthian church that they were true Hebraic Jews as opposed to being Hellenists (cf. 2Co 11:22a), and by the need for Paul to defend his Hebraic heritage so stoutly and repeatedly (cf. 22:3; 2Co 11:22; Php 3:5, probably in view of his having been born in Tarsus), it appears that this attitude of Hebraic Jewish superiority was rather widespread.

Probably, then, any definition of the *Hellēnistai* of Acts 6 based on linguistic or geographic considerations alone, while not entirely to be set aside, should be subsumed under a more primary understanding that stresses intellectual orientation, whether actual or assumed. In all likelihood, we should think of this group of people within the early church as "hellenized Jewish believers in Jesus" or "Grecian Jewish Christians"—i.e., as Jews living in Jerusalem who had come from the Diaspora and were under some suspicion, because of their place of birth, their speech, or both, of being more Hellenistic than Hebraic in their attitudes and outlook, but who, since coming to Jerusalem, had become Christians. Many of them, no doubt, had originally returned to the homeland out of religious ardor. Perhaps they tended to group together because of their similar backgrounds and common language, as the many Hellenistic synagogues in Jerusalem would seem to indicate (cf. *Jewish Encyclopedia*, 1:371–72, on the Diaspora synagogues in Jerusalem). But since attitudes and prejudices formed before conversion are often carried over into the Christian life—too often, sadly, the unworthy more than the worthy ones—some of the problems between the Hebraic Jewish believers and the Hellenistic Jewish believers in the church must be related to such earlier differences and prejudices.

Luke reports that the Hellenists' "widows were being overlooked in the daily distribution of food" (v.1). Judaism had a system for the distribution of food and supplies to the poor, both to the wandering pauper and to residents of Jerusalem (cf. J. Jeremias, 126–34). There were also special religious communities, such as the Pharisees and the Essenes, that had their own agents in every city to provide their members "a social service somewhere between the private and public services" (Jeremias, 130). The early Christian community at Jerusalem also expressed its spiritual unity in a communal sharing of possessions and charitable acts (cf. 2:44–45, 4:32–5:11).

Apparently with the "increasing" number of believers and the passing of time, the number of Hellenistic widows who were dependent on relief from the church became disproportionately large. Many pious Jews of the Diaspora had moved to Jerusalem in their later years so as to be buried in the Holy Land and near the Holy City, and their widows would have had no relatives near at hand to care for them as would the widows of longtime residents. Nor as they became believers in Messiah Jesus would the resources of the national system of

relief be readily available to them. So the problem facing the church became acute.

The account of the dispute cannot have been invented by Luke. To do so would have been incompatible with the development of his conciliatory purpose. If anything, Luke's desire to emphasize harmonious relations within the early Christian community (cf. his three introductory summary statements of 2:42–47; 4:32–35; 5:12–16) may have led him to downplay the details of the dispute—which is probably why commentators have had difficulty in interpreting the situation.

Nor should we assume that the issue about the distribution of food was all that disrupted the fellowship. William Manson (*The Epistle to the Hebrews* [London: Hodder & Stoughton, 1951], 27–28) notes that "it is possible that the grievance in question was only the symptom of a larger tension between the two groups, arising from broad differences of outlook and sympathy." Earlier prejudices and resentments may have been reasserting themselves in the Jerusalem church. And if the Hellenists spoke mostly in Greek, separate meetings within the Christian community may have been required for them—meetings that may have awakened former prejudices and resentments, both within the church and throughout the Jewish populace.

2–4 The apostles' response was to call the Christians together and suggest a solution. It is significant that they were not prepared simply to ignore the problem. They seem to have realized that spiritual and material concerns are so intimately related in Christian experience that one always affects the other for better or worse. Similarly, there was no attempt either to assign blame or to act in any paternalistic fashion. Rather, the suggestion was that seven men "full of the Spirit and wisdom" be chosen from among the congregation (*ex hymōn*, "from among you," which probably means "from among the Hellenists" alone) who could take responsibility in this matter (v.3). The apostles sought to give their attention exclusively "to prayer and the ministry of the word" (v.4)

The words "full of the Spirit and wisdom" evidently refer to guidance by the Holy Spirit and skill in administration and business, which both singly and together are so necessary in Christian service. While Christian ministers might wish such qualities were more characteristic of their boards and councils, it is only fair to say that church boards and councils often wish their ministers were given more "to prayer and the ministry of the word"! A pattern is set here for both lay leaders and clergy. Undoubtedly, God's work would move ahead more effectively and efficiently were it followed more carefully.

The reference to the apostles as "the Twelve" (*hoi dōdeka*) occurs only here in Acts (cf. 1Co 15:5), though earlier Luke had spoken of "the Eleven" (*hoi hendeka*) in such an absolute and corporate manner (cf. Lk 24:9, 33; Ac 2:14). Likewise, the references to Christians as "the disciples" (*hoi mathētai*, GK *3412*) in vv.1–2 are the first instances of this usage in Acts, though in the remainder of Acts it occurs fairly often. The designation, however, is not found in the Pauline letters or subapostolic writings. In using both of these terms, Luke seems to have gone back to the language of his sources and tried to make idiomatic use of it, though this usage may not have been entirely natural for him.

5–6 The apostles made a proposal, but the church, which is the community of God's Spirit, made the decision. The apostles, therefore, laid their hands on the Seven and appointed them to be responsible for the daily distribution of food. The laying on of hands recalls Moses' commissioning of Joshua (Nu 27:18–23), where through this act some of Moses' authority was conferred to Joshua (cf. Lev 3:2; 16:21, where, conversely, by the laying on of hands there was the symbolic transference of sin). This is evidently what the laying on of hands was meant to symbolize here, with the apostles delegating their authority to the seven men selected by the church (cf. 8:17; 9:17; 13:3; 19:6 for other instances in Acts of this practice).

All the men appointed have Greek names. One of them is singled out as having been a Gentile convert to Judaism—i.e., a "proselyte" (*prosēlytos*, GK *4670*). But it is impossible to be sure from the names themselves whether all seven were Hellenists, for at that time many Palestinian Jews also had Greek names. Nevertheless, the fact that Luke gives only Greek names suggests that all seven were, in fact, from the Hellenistic group of believers within the church. Likewise, the text does not expressly speak of these seven in terms of the ecclesiastical title "deacon" (*diakonos*, GK *1356*), though it does use the cognate noun *diakonia* ("service," "ministry," "distribution") in v.1 and the verb *diakoneō* ("wait on," "serve") in v.2 in describing what they were to do. It also uses *diakonia* ["service" or "ministry"] in v.4 as a synonym for the proclamation of the apostles. Yet the ministry to which the seven were appointed was functionally equivalent to what is spoken of as the office of "deacon" in 1 Timothy 3:8–13—which is but to affirm the maxim that in the NT "ministry was a function long before it became an office."

NOTES

1 The NIV's translation of Ἑλληνισταί (*Hellēnistai*) as "Grecian Jews" is an endeavor to break away from the usual linguistic understanding and to define the term in a manner more sensitive to the cultural and ideological nuances. On the whole, it succeeds admirably. But its translation of Ἑβραῖοι (*Hebraioi*) as "the Aramaic-speaking community" falls back into the old linguistic trap and raises a whole set of other problems. What is needed is some such translation as "the Hellenistic Jewish believers" and "the Hebraic Jewish believers." The renderings "Hellenistic *Jews*" and "*native* Hebrews" in the NASB attempt to strike a middle ground between such a translation and the purely literal renderings of "Hellenists" and "Hebrews" by the NRSV, which leaves nuancing to the commentators.

Codex Bezae (D) adds ἐν τῇ διακονίᾳ τῶν Ἑβραίων (*en tē diakonia tōn Hebraiōn*, "in the service of the Hebrews") at the end of v.1—an addition that at best is superfluous in view of the context and at worst misleading.

Luke has more references to widows and women than any of the other evangelists. The word χήρα (*chēra*, "widow," GK *5939*) occurs in Luke 2:37; 4:25–26; 7:12; 18:3, 5; 20:47–21:3 (= Mk 12:40–43); Acts 6:1 (here); 9:39, 41, while only twelve times more in the rest of the NT; γυνή (*gynē*, "woman," GK *1222*) occurs twenty-nine times in Matthew, sixteen times in Mark, forty-one times in Luke, seventeen times in John, nineteen times in Acts (thus sixty times in Luke-Acts), and eighty-seven times in the rest of the NT.

2 There are linguistic and functional similarities between the use of τὸ πλῆθος (*to plethos*, "the whole number," "entire") in Acts 6:2, 5 and 15:12 (NIV, "all, the whole group," and "the whole assembly"; NASB, "the congregation," "the whole congregation" and "all the people") and the use of the Hebrew *rabbím* ("the many") in 1QS 6:8–13, which deals with the order of public worship among the Qumran covenanters (cf. F. M. Cross Jr., *The Ancient Library of Qumran* [London: Duckworth, 1958], 174). While neither the Essene encampment at Qumran nor the Jerusalem church could be called in a modern sense a democratic assembly, it is clear that in both groups the congregation was involved in the deliberations of its leaders.

The expression οἱ μαθηταί (*hoi mathetai*, "the disciples") is also used absolutely of Christians at 6:7; 9:1 (with τοῦ κυρίου, *tou kyriou*, "of the Lord"), 10, 19, 26, 38; 11:26, 29; 13:52; 14:20, 22, 28; 15:10; 16:1; 18:23, 27; 19:1, 9, 30; 20:1, 30; 21:4, 16. In 9:25 it is used of the followers of Paul.

The word τράπεζα (*trapeza*, "table," GK *5544*) can mean either a moneychanger's table or a table on which a meal is spread. Here the idea is not that of financial exchange or administration but care for the poor.

3 Codex Bezae (D) prefaces the apostle's suggestion with the interrogative phrase τί οὖν ἐστιν (*ti oun estin*, "What, then, shall we do?"), which adds a colloquial touch to the narrative (as in Western readings at 2:37 and 5:8) but seems here to have been taken from 21:22. Codex Vaticanus (B) begins the verse with the first person plural imperative ἐπισκεψώμεθα (*episkepsōmetha*, "let us select" or "let us choose," GK *2170*), rather than the more widely attested second person plural imperative ἐπισκέψασθε (*episkepsasthe*; NIV, "[you] choose"; NASB, "[you] select"), probably to make it clear that the apostles were not excluded in the selection of the Seven.

Many external witnesses add ἁγίου (*hagiou*, "holy," GK *41*) after πνεύματος (*pneumatos*, "Spirit," GK *4460*), which would have been natural for scribes to do. The shorter text, however, is better supported by 𝔓⁸ 𝔓⁷⁴ ℵ B D Chrysostom et al.

5 The Western text (D, and as represented by recensions of the Old Latin and Coptic versions) adds τῶν μαθητῶν (*tōn mathētōn*, "of the disciples") after παντὸς τοῦ πλήθους (*pantos tou plēthous*; NIV, "the whole group"; NASB, "the whole congregation"), evidently so that the proposal wouldn't be thought to have pleased others outside the Christian community.

Munck, 57, has written: "Surely, to assume that the primitive church would choose a committee for social services in which only one of the feuding parties was represented would be to underestimate its efficiency in practical matters. Such a procedure would probably have given rise to complaints from the Hebrews." Munck may be right. But perhaps the early church had a greater reliance on God's Spirit and a greater confidence in God's people than we have today, and so was not interested in merely balancing various concerns in its selection of a committee.

REFLECTIONS

Acts 6:1–6 is particularly instructive as something of a pattern for church life today. First, the early church took very seriously the combination of spiritual and material concerns in carrying out its God-given ministry. In so doing, it stressed prayer and the proclamation of the Word, but never to the exclusion of providing material aid to the poor and correcting injustices. Even when the church found it necessary to assign differing internal responsibilities and allocate different functions, the early believers saw these as varying aspects of one total ministry.

Second, the early church seems to have been prepared to adjust its procedures, alter its organizational structure, and develop new posts of responsibility in response to the existing needs and for the sake of the ongoing proclamation of the word of God. Throughout the years, various "restorationist" movements in the church have attempted to reach back and recapture the explicit forms and practices of the earliest Christians and to reproduce them as far as possible in their pristine forms, believing that in doing so they are more truly biblical than other church groups. But Luke's narrative here suggests that to be fully biblical is to be constantly engaged in adapting traditional methods and structures to meet existing situations, both for the sake of the welfare of the whole church and for the outreach of the gospel.

Finally, Luke's account suggests certain restraining attitudes that could be incorporated into contemporary church life. Among these are (1) refusing to get involved in the practice of assigning blame where things have gone wrong, preferring rather to expend the energies of God's people on correcting injustices, praying, and proclaiming the word; and (2) refusing to become paternalistic in solving problems, which implies a willingness to turn over to others the necessary authority for working out solutions—even, as seems to have been the case here, to those who would have felt the problem most acutely and may therefore have been best able to solve it.

G. Summary Statement (6:7)

⁷So the word of God spread. The number of disciples in Jerusalem increased rapidly, and a large number of priests became obedient to the faith.

COMMENTARY

7 Luke concludes his first panel of material on the earliest days of the church in Jerusalem with this summary statement, which is very much in line with his thesis paragraph of 2:42–47 and his summary paragraphs of 4:32–35 and 5:12–16 that head their respective units of material. His focus in this first panel has been on the advances of the gospel and the responses of the people. Therefore he concludes by saying that "the word of God spread" and "the number of disciples in Jerusalem increased rapidly."

Before he leaves this first panel, however, Luke inserts the comment—almost as something of an afterthought—that "a large number of priests became obedient to the faith." At first glance this statement is perplexing, to say the least, particularly in view of how Luke has depicted the Jewish priests in 4:1–22 and 5:17–40. It seems extremely difficult to believe that many Jewish priests of the various high priestly families would have become Christians. Nevertheless, as J. Jeremias, 198–213, pointed out in great detail, there were perhaps as many as eight thousand "ordinary" priests and ten thousand Levites, who were divided into twenty-four weekly courses and who served at the Jerusalem temple during the span of a year—whose social position was distinctly inferior to that of the high priestly

families and whose piety could well have inclined them to an acceptance of the Christian message. In addition, the Qumran covenanters thought of themselves as the true sons of Zadok, as the *Zadokite Fragments (Damascus Covenant)* from Caves 4 and 6 testify. And many of the common people in Israel undoubtedly respected, even if they could not support, the claim of these Essene covenanters to the priesthood.

Perhaps Luke himself was not aware of the distinctions in Palestine between high priestly families, ordinary priests, and Essene-type priests. What he evidently learned from his sources was that a great number of persons calling themselves priests became believers in Jesus and were numbered with the Christians in the Jerusalem church. He seems to have included that bit of information as something of an appendix to his portrayal of the church's earliest days in the city. He might also have found it a matter either difficult to believe or difficult to elaborate in view of what he had said earlier about the priests of Jerusalem. If he had known about the ordinary priests of the temple and the Essene-type priests at Qumran, however, the response of the priests that he reports in the final words of this panel might not have seemed so amazing and he might have said more.

NOTES

7 Many witnesses, evidently based on Codex Sinaiticus (ℵ), read τῶν Ἰουδαίων (*tōn Ioudaiōn*, "of the Jews") for τῶν ἱερέων (*tōn hiereōn*, "of the priests"), thereby alleviating the problem. But "of the priests" (τῶν ἱερέων, *tōn hiereōn*) is better supported by 𝔓⁷⁴ A B C D et al.

PANEL 2—CRITICAL EVENTS IN THE LIVES OF THREE PIVOTAL FIGURES (6:8–9:31)

In Acts 6:8–9:31, Luke narrates three key events in the advance of the gospel beyond its strictly Jewish confines: (1) the martyrdom of Stephen, (2) the early ministries of Philip, and (3) the conversion of Saul of Tarsus. Luke's presentation is largely biographical, with the first word of each of the three accounts being the name of its central figure: *Stephanos* in 6:8; *Philippos* in 8:5 (after an editorial introduction at 8:4, which contains Luke's favorite connective *men oun*, "so" or "then"); and *Saulos* in 9:1. This is the type of material that would undoubtedly have circulated among the dispossessed Hellenistic Jewish Christians, what with its heavy emphasis on "who said what to whom" and its detailed account of Stephen's argument before the Sanhedrin. It is also the kind of material that one picks up by talking with one or more of the participants. It is not difficult to imagine that, in addition to source materials that may have circulated widely among Hellenistic Jewish believers regarding Stephen's martyrdom, Philip's ministries, and Saul's conversion, Luke may also have heard Philip and Paul talk about these matters, either during Paul's stay for "a number of days" at Philip's home in Caesarea (cf. 21:8–10a) or during Paul's imprisonment at Caesarea (cf. 25:27).

No doubt Stephen's martyrdom was indelibly imprinted on the memories of both Philip and Saul of Tarsus, and accounts of his defense and martyrdom, whether written or oral, had probably become the raison d'être for the Hellenists' continued ministry. Likewise, Philip must have made a lasting impression on Luke as an important figure in the advance of the Christian mission, just as he was an important person in the Christian community at Caesarea (cf. 8:40; 21:8–9). And certainly the apostle Paul was of such immense significance for Luke's narrative that an account of his conversion would have been inevitable, particularly because of its miraculous circumstances.

When the events of Luke's second panel took place depends largely on the dates for Paul's conversion and ministry. Since Stephen's death occurred before the conversion of Saul of Tarsus (cf. 7:58–8:1), and since Luke presents Philip's ministries in Samaria and to the Ethiopian eunuch as following on the heels of the persecution that arose with Stephen's martyrdom, the accounts of these two Hellenistic Jewish Christian spokesmen are historically tied to the conversion of Saul. For the chronological issues associated with Paul, see comments at Acts 9:1–30. As for the events portrayed in the second panel, suffice it to say that Luke presents them as having taken place sometime in the mid-30s, possibly as early as AD 33 and as late as AD 37.

A. The Martyrdom of Stephen (6:8–8:3)

OVERVIEW

Interpreters have varied considerably regarding the significance of Stephen in the history of early Christianity. Most have attempted to understand him as in some manner the forerunner to Paul, proclaiming an elemental form of a law-free and universal gospel. Some, however, have taken him to be a proto-Marcionite (so F. C. Baur), others an early Ebionite (so Hans J. Schoeps), others a nationalistic Zealot (so S. G. F. Brandon), and a few as a thoroughly Jewish member of the Jerusalem church who represented the entire church's stance in opposition to Judaism (so J. Munck). Between these divergent positions there is no lack of varying opinion.

Marcion of Sinope, a village in the region of Pontus in northeastern Asia Minor, published sometime about AD 140 a truncated canon of the NT (his *Apostolicon* or "Apostolic Writings") that contained only ten letters of Paul (minus the Pastorals) and the gospel according to Luke, though with

deletions and alterations to suit his own understanding of Christianity. He rejected everything Jewish and Jewish Christian as being opposed to the Christian gospel. "Ebionites" refers to Jewish Christians who thought of Jesus as the Messiah but not as divine. It literally means "the poor" and connotes piety and humility before God. "Zealots" in a Jewish context signifies those committed to an intense nationalism, which was often militant.

1. Opposition to Stephen's Ministry (6:8–7:1)

[8]Now Stephen, a man full of God's grace and power, did great wonders and miraculous signs among the people. [9]Opposition arose, however, from members of the Synagogue of the Freedmen (as it was called)—Jews of Cyrene and Alexandria as well as the provinces of Cilicia and Asia. These men began to argue with Stephen, [10]but they could not stand up against his wisdom or the Spirit by whom he spoke.

[11]Then they secretly persuaded some men to say, "We have heard Stephen speak words of blasphemy against Moses and against God."

[12]So they stirred up the people and the elders and the teachers of the law. They seized Stephen and brought him before the Sanhedrin. [13]They produced false witnesses, who testified, "This fellow never stops speaking against this holy place and against the law. [14]For we have heard him say that this Jesus of Nazareth will destroy this place and change the customs Moses handed down to us."

[15]All who were sitting in the Sanhedrin looked intently at Stephen, and they saw that his face was like the face of an angel.

[7:1]Then the high priest asked him, "Are these charges true?"

COMMENTARY

8 Stephen has earlier been described as "full of the Spirit and wisdom" (6:3) and "full of faith and of the Holy Spirit" (6:5). Now Luke says he was "full of God's grace and power." The three descriptions are complementary, though Luke may have drawn the precise wording from different sources. The word "grace" (*charis*, GK *5921*) was previously used by Luke to characterize both Jesus (Lk 4:22)

and the early church (Ac 4:33). It connotes "spiritual charm" or "winsomeness." "Power" (*dynamis*, GK *1539*) has already appeared in Acts in conjunction with "wonders and signs" (2:22) and "grace" (4:33), and so should be understood to connote divine power expressed in mighty works.

Like Jesus and the apostles (cf. 2:22, 43; 5:12), Stephen is portrayed as having done "great wonders and miraculous signs among the people." Just what these were, Luke does not say, though undoubtedly we are to think of them as being of the same nature as those done by Jesus and the apostles. Nor does Luke tell us when these manifestations of divine power began in Stephen's ministry. Many have insisted that they were a direct result of the laying on of the apostles' hands (cf. 6:6), though it is possible that such acts characterized Stephen's ministry even before that.

9–10 Stephen soon began preaching among his Hellenistic Jewish compatriots. Many commentators have seen this as a major problem in the narrative, for Stephen was appointed to supervise relief for the poor, not to perform the apostolic function of preaching. Some, therefore, have viewed this as a Lukan discrepancy (so S. G. F. Brandon), whereas others have claimed that Stephen was not really preaching but only uttering the name of Jesus and providing a Christian rationale for his divinely empowered acts (so T. Zahn). Most commentators, however, are prepared to accept the fact of Stephen's preaching (just as Philip, another of the Seven, also preached later on), yet they remain uneasy with Luke's portrayal because of its conflict with the division of labor that is spelled out in 6:3–4 (so E. Haenchen).

But if we posit (1) the continuation to some extent of old tensions between Hebraic Jewish believers and Hellenistic Jewish believers in the Jerusalem church, and (2) separate meetings, at least occasionally, for Aramaic-speaking and Greek-speaking believers (see comments at 6:1), several difficulties in the historical reconstruction of this period are partially explained. While not minimizing the importance of the apostles to the whole church, in some way Stephen, Philip, and perhaps others of the appointed Seven may well have been to the Hellenistic Jewish believers what the apostles were to the native-born Hebraic believers in Jesus.

Philip seems to have performed such a function later on at Caesarea. And in the early church, where "ministry was a function long before it became an office," such preaching was evidently looked on with approval.

Opposition to Stephen arose from certain members within the Hellenistic Jewish community. Opinion differs widely as to just how many Hellenistic synagogues are in view in v.9. Many have insisted that there are five: those of the (1) *Libertinoi* or Freedmen, (2) Cyreneans, (3) Alexandrians, (4) Cilicians, and (5) Asians (so Bernhard Weiss, Emil Schürer). Others have argued that the twofold use of the article *tōn* ("the") groups these five into two: (1) the synagogue of the Freedmen, which was made up of Jews from Cyrene and Alexandria; and (2) another synagogue composed of Jews from Cilicia and Asia (so H. H. Wendt, T. Zahn). Still others, emphasizing the singular form of "synagogue" (*synagōgēs*, GK *5252*) in the passage and the epexegetical nature of the last four designations, posit only one synagogue as being in mind: a synagogue of the Freedmen, which was composed of Jews from Cyrene, Alexandria, Cilicia, and Asia (so K. Lake, H. Cadbury, J. Jeremias, F. F. Bruce, E. Haenchen). The NIV and NASB read the passage in this latter way, and this is probably how it ought to be understood. The name *Libertinoi* ("Freedmen") is a Latin loanword that refers to Jewish freedmen (i.e., former slaves who had been set free) and their families; the adjective *legomenēs* ("so-called"; NIV, "as it was called") probably was included as an apology to Greek sensibilities for the inclusion of a foreign word.

We have no account of the content of Stephen's preaching that so antagonized his Hellenistic Jewish compatriots. Luke labels the accusations against him (vv.11–14) as false—though to judge by Stephen's response in ch. 7, they seem to have been false more in nuance and degree than in kind. From both the accusations and his defense, it is clear that Stephen had begun to apply his Christian convictions regarding the centrality of Jesus of Nazareth in God's redemptive program to such issues as the significance of the land, the law, and the temple for Jewish Christians in view of the advent of the Messiah. This, however, was a dangerous path to tread, particularly for Hellenistic Jewish Christians! It was one that the apostles themselves seem to have been unwilling to explore. And it was a path that those who had lately returned to Jerusalem from various regions of the Jewish Diaspora would undoubtedly have viewed not only with reticence but also with disgust.

Having originally immigrated to the homeland out of a desire to be more faithful Jews, and having come under suspicion of an inbred liberalism by the native-born populace, the Hellenistic Jewish community in Jerusalem had a vested interest in keeping deviations among its members to a minimum—or to expose them as being outside its own commitments, lest its synagogues fall under further suspicion. The Hellenistic members of the Synagogue of the Freedmen, therefore, were probably quite eager to bait Stephen in order to root out such a threat from their midst. And Stephen, it seems, welcomed the challenge. But as Luke tells us, "they could not stand up against his wisdom or the Spirit by whom he spoke" (v.10). This fulfills Jesus' promise of the gift of "words and wisdom" in the time of persecution (cf. Lk 21:15).

11–14 The subject "they" of the verbs of these sentences refers to those members of the Synagogue of the Freedman represented in v.9 by the masculine plural indefinite pronoun *tines* ("some"; NIV, "members"; NASB, "some men"). Four things are said about them: (1) "they secretly persuaded some men to say" that Stephen had spoken blasphemy; (2) "they stirred up the people and the elders and the teachers of the law" on their trumped-up charge

against Stephen; (3) "they seized Stephen and brought him before the Sanhedrin"; and (4) "they produced false witnesses" at his trial. Their charge against Stephen was that he had blasphemed "against Moses and against God," i.e., (1) "against Moses" because his arguments seemed to challenge the eternal validity of the Mosaic law, and (2) "against God" because he appeared to be setting aside what was taken to be the foundation and focus of the nation's worship, the Jerusalem temple.

These accusations of blasphemy against the Mosaic law and the Jerusalem temple struck at the heart of both Pharisaic and Sadducean interests. Later rabbinic law held that "the blasphemer is not culpable [and thus not subject to the penalty of death] unless he pronounces the Name itself" (*m. Sanh.* 7:5, based on Lev 24:10–23). But in the first century AD, the definition of blasphemy was more broadly interpreted along the lines of Numbers 15:30: "Anyone who sins defiantly, whether native-born or alien, blasphemes the LORD, and that person must be cut off from his people" (cf. Gustaf H. Dalman, *The Words of Jesus* [Edinburgh: T&T Clark, 1909], 314).

The testimony of witnesses who repeated what they had heard a defendant say was part of Jewish court procedure in a trial for blasphemy (cf. *m. Sanh.* 7:59). But this testimony against Stephen, Luke tells us, was false. "We have heard him say," they claimed, "that this Jesus of Nazareth will destroy this place and change the customs Moses handed down to us" (v.14). Like the similar charge against Jesus (Mt 26:61; Mk 14:58; cf. Jn 2:19–22), its falseness lay not so much in its wholesale fabrication but in its subtle and deadly misrepresentation of what was intended. Undoubtedly Stephen spoke about a recasting of Jewish life in terms of the supremacy of Jesus the Messiah. And it cannot be doubted that Stephen expressed in his manner and message something of the subsidiary significance of the

Jerusalem temple and the Mosaic law, as did Jesus before him (cf., e.g., Mk 2:23–28; 3:1–6; 7:14–15; 10:5–9). But this is not the same as advocating the destruction of the temple or the changing of the law (though on these matters we must allow Stephen to speak for himself in Ac 7).

6:15–7:1 The members of the council "looked intently" at Stephen as he was brought before them and saw one whose appearance was "like the face of an angel." In Judaism very devout men were often spoken of as resembling angels. Here, however, Luke probably only wants his readers to understand that Stephen, being filled with the Holy Spirit (cf. 6:3, 5) and possessing a genuine spiritual winsomeness (cf. 6:8), radiated a presence marked by confidence, serenity, and courage. And with the question of the high priest, "Are these charges true?" the stage is set for Stephen's defense.

NOTES

8 On the compound τέρατα καὶ σημεῖα (terata kai sēmeia, "wonders and signs"), see comments at 2:22; note at 5:12. On Luke's use of ὁ λαός (ho laos, "the people"), see comments at 2:47a.

The Western text (D, and as reflected in the Coptic Sahidic version and Augustine) adds at the end of the verse διὰ τοῦ ὀνόματος τοῦ κυρίου Ἰησοῦ Χριστοῦ (dia tou onomatos tou kyriou Iēsou Christou, "through the name of the Lord Jesus Christ"), which is probably an interpolation carried over from 4:30.

9 Codices Alexandrinus (A) and Bezae (D) omit καὶ Ἀσίας (kai Asias, "and Asia"). This is probably a case of homoioteleuton (i.e., when the eye of a copyist passes from one word to another with the same ending), here accidentally skipping from the immediately preceding similar ending of Κιλικίας (Kilikias, "Cilicia").

10 The Western text (D, E, Vulgate, and various Syriac and Coptic recensions) expands this verse, in slightly different forms, to read, "But they could not stand up against the wisdom that was in him and the Holy Spirit by whom he spoke, for they were confuted before him with all boldness of speech. Being unable, therefore, to face up to the truth . . ."

13 The TR reads ῥήματα βλάσφημα λαλῶν (rhēmata blasphēma lalōn, "speaking blasphemous words") for the better-supported λαλῶν ῥήματα (lalōn rhēmata, "speaking words"; NIV, "speaking"; NASB, "speaks"), which wording, though expressing the sense of the sentence, is probably carried over from 6:11.

14 The demonstrative pronoun οὗτος (houtos, "this") in "this Jesus of Nazareth" likely carries a note of contempt.

15 Luke often uses the verb ἀτενίζω (atenizō, "look intently," GK 867) to heighten the dramatic effect of the narrative (cf. also Lk 4:20; 22:56; Ac 1:10; 3:4, 12; 7:55; 10:4; 11:6; 13:9; 14:9; 23:1). See comments at 1:10.

7:1 The Western text (D, E, as reflected in various Latin and Coptic recensions) adds τῷ Στεφάνῳ (tō Stephanō, "to Stephen") after εἶπεν ὁ ἀρχιερεύς (eipen ho archiereus, "the high priest said"), which is comparable to the quite natural addition of "him" in the NIV, "the high priest asked him."

2. Stephen's Defense before the Sanhedrin (7:2–53)

OVERVIEW

Stephen's defense before the Sanhedrin is hardly a defense in the sense of an explanation or apology calculated to win an acquittal. Rather, it is a proclamation of the Christian message in terms of the popular Judaism of the day and an indictment of the Jewish leaders for their failure to recognize Jesus of Nazareth as their Messiah or to appreciate the salvation God has provided in him. Before the destruction of Jerusalem in AD 70, the three great pillars of popular Jewish piety were (1) the land, (2) the law, and (3) the temple—or, to put it more alliteratively, territory, Torah, and temple. The Talmud shows that rabbinic Judaism was later able to exist apart from the Jerusalem temple and without any overriding stress on the land. And undoubtedly there were individual teachers even before the nation's calamities of AD 66–70 and 132–35 who thought in somewhat similar fashion. But before such a time, the land, the law, and the temple were the cardinal postulates in the religious faith of the vast majority of Jews. It is this type of thought that Stephen confronts here, as did the writer of Hebrews. Dibelius, 167, has argued:

> The irrelevance of most of [Stephen's] speech has for long been the real problem of exegesis.

It is, indeed, impossible to find a connection between the account of the history of Israel to the time of Moses (7:2–19) and the accusation against Stephen; nor is any accusation against the Jews, which would furnish the historical foundation for the attack at the end of the speech, found at all in this section. Even in that section of the speech which deals with Moses, the speaker does not defend himself; nor does he make any positive countercharge against his enemies, for the words *hoi de ou synēkan* in 7:25 do not constitute such an attack any more than does the report of the gainsaying of Moses by a Jew in 7:27. It is not until 7:35 that we sense any polemic interest. From 7:2–34 the point of the speech is not obvious at all; we are simply given an account of the history of Israel.

Dibelius adds such statements as the following: "The major part of the speech (7:2–34) shows no purpose whatever, but contains a unique, compressed reproduction of the story of the patriarchs and Moses" (p. 168); "The most striking feature of this speech is the irrelevance of its main section" (p. 169). Just how wrong Dibelius was, however, will become evident as we proceed.

a. On the land (7:2–36)

OVERVIEW

Declarations of faith within a Jewish milieu were often based on a recital of God's intervention in the life of Israel, for God is the God who is known by his redemptive activity on behalf of his people in history. So by beginning his defense with a résumé of Israel's history, Stephen is speaking in accord with Jewish form. But while Jewish in form, the content of his address runs counter to much of the popular piety of the day. For Stephen argues that (1) God's significant activity has usually taken place outside the confines of Palestine; (2) wherever God meets his people can be called "holy ground"; (3) God is the God who calls his own to move forward in their religious experience; and therefore (4) dwelling in the land of promise requires a pilgrim lifestyle in which the land may be appreciated but never venerated.

The important concepts of "rest" and "remnant" in the OT are often associated closely with the land. Deuteronomy 12:9–10, for example, reads: "You have not yet reached the resting place and the inheritance the LORD your God is giving you. But you will cross the Jordan and settle in the land the LORD your God is giving you as an inheritance, and he will give you rest from all your enemies around you so that you will live in safety" (see also Dt 3:20; Jos 1:13;

Joel 2:32b; Mic 4:6–7). And the linking of God's righteous remnant with the Holy Land is common in the literature of Second Temple Judaism (cf. 2 Esd 9:7–8; 12:31–34; 13:48; *2 Bar.* 40:2). Facing much the same problem—and with much the same purpose as the writer of Hebrews (cf. Heb 4:1–13; 11:8–16), though with a difference of method and structure in his argument—Stephen argues against a veneration of the Holy Land that would leave no room for God's further saving activity in Jesus of Nazareth, Israel's Messiah. Stephen does not renounce Israel's possession of the land; nor does he set aside or deny God's promise that Abraham's descendants would inherit Palestine. Rather, he is delivering a polemic against such a veneration of the land as would miss God's further redemptive work.

²To this he replied: "Brothers and fathers, listen to me! The God of glory appeared to our father Abraham while he was still in Mesopotamia, before he lived in Haran. ³'Leave your country and your people,' God said, 'and go to the land I will show you.'

⁴"So he left the land of the Chaldeans and settled in Haran. After the death of his father, God sent him to this land where you are now living. ⁵He gave him no inheritance here, not even a foot of ground. But God promised him that he and his descendants after him would possess the land, even though at that time Abraham had no child. ⁶God spoke to him in this way: 'Your descendants will be strangers in a country not their own, and they will be enslaved and mistreated four hundred years. ⁷But I will punish the nation they serve as slaves,' God said, 'and afterward they will come out of that country and worship me in this place.' ⁸Then he gave Abraham the covenant of circumcision. And Abraham became the father of Isaac and circumcised him eight days after his birth. Later Isaac became the father of Jacob, and Jacob became the father of the twelve patriarchs.

⁹"Because the patriarchs were jealous of Joseph, they sold him as a slave into Egypt. But God was with him ¹⁰and rescued him from all his troubles. He gave Joseph wisdom and enabled him to gain the goodwill of Pharaoh king of Egypt; so he made him ruler over Egypt and all his palace.

¹¹"Then a famine struck all Egypt and Canaan, bringing great suffering, and our fathers could not find food. ¹²When Jacob heard that there was grain in Egypt, he sent our fathers on their first visit. ¹³On their second visit, Joseph told his brothers who he was, and Pharaoh learned about Joseph's family. ¹⁴After this, Joseph sent for his father Jacob and his whole family, seventy-five in all. ¹⁵Then Jacob went down to Egypt, where he and our

fathers died. [16]Their bodies were brought back to Shechem and placed in the tomb that Abraham had bought from the sons of Hamor at Shechem for a certain sum of money.

[17]"As the time drew near for God to fulfill his promise to Abraham, the number of our people in Egypt greatly increased. [18]Then another king, who knew nothing about Joseph, became ruler of Egypt. [19]He dealt treacherously with our people and oppressed our forefathers by forcing them to throw out their newborn babies so that they would die.

[20]"At that time Moses was born, and he was no ordinary child. For three months he was cared for in his father's house. [21]When he was placed outside, Pharaoh's daughter took him and brought him up as her own son. [22]Moses was educated in all the wisdom of the Egyptians and was powerful in speech and action.

[23]"When Moses was forty years old, he decided to visit his fellow Israelites. [24]He saw one of them being mistreated by an Egyptian, so he went to his defense and avenged him by killing the Egyptian. [25]Moses thought that his own people would realize that God was using him to rescue them, but they did not. [26]The next day Moses came upon two Israelites who were fighting. He tried to reconcile them by saying, 'Men, you are brothers; why do you want to hurt each other?'

[27]"But the man who was mistreating the other pushed Moses aside and said, 'Who made you ruler and judge over us? [28]Do you want to kill me as you killed the Egyptian yesterday?' [29]When Moses heard this, he fled to Midian, where he settled as a foreigner and had two sons.

[30]"After forty years had passed, an angel appeared to Moses in the flames of a burning bush in the desert near Mount Sinai. [31]When he saw this, he was amazed at the sight. As he went over to look more closely, he heard the Lord's voice: [32]'I am the God of your fathers, the God of Abraham, Isaac and Jacob.' Moses trembled with fear and did not dare to look.

[33]"Then the Lord said to him, 'Take off your sandals; the place where you are standing is holy ground. [34]I have indeed seen the oppression of my people in Egypt. I have heard their groaning and have come down to set them free. Now come, I will send you back to Egypt.'

[35]"This is the same Moses whom they had rejected with the words, 'Who made you ruler and judge?' He was sent to be their ruler and deliverer by God himself, through the angel who appeared to him in the bush. [36]He led them out of Egypt and did wonders and miraculous signs in Egypt, at the Red Sea and for forty years in the desert."

COMMENTARY

2–8 Stephen begins by addressing the council in a somewhat formal yet fraternal manner: "men, brothers and fathers" (*andres adelphoi kai pateres*; NIV, "brothers and fathers"; NASB, "brethren and fathers"; cf. 22:1). Then he launches into his message, taking up first the story of Abraham. "The God of glory," Stephen says, "appeared to our father Abraham *while he was still in Mesopotamia, before he* *lived in Haran*" (italics mine, so attempting to highlight Stephen's emphasis). God's word to Abraham was to move forward into the possession of a land that was promised to him and his descendants. But though he entered into his promised inheritance, he did not live in it as though living in it was the consummation of God's purposes for him. Rather, he cherished as most important the covenantal and personal relationship that God had established with him, whatever his place of residence—a relationship of which circumcision was the God-given sign.

There are a number of difficulties as to chronological sequence, historical numbers, and the use of biblical quotations in Stephen's address, which difficulties have led to the most strenuous exercise of ingenuity on the part of commentators in their attempts to reconcile them. Four of these difficulties appear in vv.2–6. The first is in v.3, which quotes the words of God to Abraham given in Genesis 12:1 and implies by its juxtaposition with v.2 that this message came to Abraham "while he was still in Mesopotamia, before he lived in Haran," whereas the context of Genesis 12:1 suggests that it came to him in Haran. The second is to be found in v.4, where it is said that Abraham left Haran after the death of his father, whereas the chronological data of Genesis 11:26–12:4 suggests that Terah's death took place after Abraham's departure from Haran. The third is in v.5, which uses the words of Deuteronomy 2:5 as a suitable description of Abraham's situation in Palestine, whereas their OT context relates to God's prohibition to Israel not to dwell in Mount Seir because it had been given to Esau. And the fourth is in v.6, which speaks of four hundred years of slavery in Egypt, whereas Exodus 12:40 reads "430 years."

We need not get overly disturbed about such difficulties. Some pounce on them to disprove a "high view" of biblical inspiration, while others attempt to harmonize them. But these matters relate to the conflations and inexactitude of popular religious piety, not necessarily to any then-extant scholastic tradition or variant texts. In large measure they can be paralleled in other popular writings of the day, whether overtly Hellenistic Jewish or simply more nonconformist in the broadest sense of that term. Philo, for example, also explained Abraham's departure from Ur of the Chaldees by reference to Genesis 12:1 (cf. *Abraham* 62–67), even though he knew that Genesis 12:1–5 was set in the context of Abraham's leaving Haran (cf. *Migr.* 176). Josephus (*Ant.* 1.154) spoke of Abraham's being seventy-five years old when he left Chaldea (contra Ge 12:4, which says he was seventy-five when he left Haran) and of leaving Chaldea because God told him go to Canaan, with evident allusion to Genesis 12:1. Likewise, Philo (*Migr.* 177) placed the departure of Abraham from Haran after his father's death. And undoubtedly the number "four hundred" for the years of Israel's slavery in Egypt, which was a rounded figure that stemmed from the statement credited to God in Genesis 15:13, was often used in popular expressions of religious piety in the period of Second Temple Judaism—as were also the transpositions of meaningful and usable phrases from one context to another.

There is, in fact, a remarkable degree of reality in Luke's portrayal of Stephen's address. With his life at stake, Stephen was speaking under intense emotion—and Luke vividly presents him as both eloquently and with commonly understood language speaking about Israel's history. Stephen's speech was not a scholarly exposition but a powerful portrayal of God's dealing with his own people Israel, which mounted inexorably to a climax in unmasking the obstinacy and disobedience of the nation and its leaders in Stephen's time. History knows few greater displays of moral courage than Stephen showed in this speech. And to dissect it on precisionist grounds evidences a lack of appreciation for its circumstances or an understanding of its basic truth.

9–16 Stephen's address next turns to the sons of Jacob, or the "twelve patriarchs" as they were popularly known (cf. 4 Macc 16:25; see also 4 Macc 7:19 and *Testaments of the Twelve Patriarchs*). Stephen's point here is that God was with Joseph and his brothers *in Egypt* (the name "Egypt" is repeated six times in vv.9–16). The only portion of the Holy Land they then possessed was the family tomb in Palestine, to which their bones were later brought for final burial.

Two further difficulties of the type noted in vv.2–6 that seem to appear somewhat regularly in Stephen's speech are (1) the number "seventy-five" in v.14 for the total number who originally went down to Egypt, whereas Genesis 46:27 (MT) sets the figure at "seventy" (i.e., sixty-six plus Jacob, Joseph, and Joseph's two sons); and (2) the confusion in v.16 between Abraham's tomb at Hebron in the cave of Machpelah, which Abraham bought from Ephron the Hittite (cf. Ge 23:3–20) and wherein Abraham, Isaac, and Jacob were buried (cf. Ge 49:29–33; 50:13), and the burial plot purchased by Jacob at Shechem from the sons of Hamor, wherein Joseph and his descendants were buried (cf. Jos 24:32). These are, however, just further examples of the conflations and inexactitudes of Jewish popular religion, which, it seems, Luke simply recorded from his sources in his attempt to be faithful to what Stephen actually said.

Such inexactitudes of popular expression can in large measure be paralleled elsewhere in Jewish writings. Genesis 46:27 in the Septuagint (LXX), for example, does not include Jacob and Joseph but does include nine sons of Joseph in the reckoning ("the sons of Joseph, who were born to him in the land of Egypt, were nine souls"), thereby arriving at a total of "seventy-five souls" who went down to Egypt. And this number "seventy-five" is found in both Exodus 1:5 (LXX) and 4QExodᵃ 1:5, whereas Exodus 1:5 in the Hebrew text (MT) reads "sev-

enty." Likewise, the telescoping of the two burial grounds in v.16 of Stephen's address can be compared to the similar phenomenon with regard to his speaking about Abraham's two calls in vv.2–3. Interestingly, while the tradition in popular circles of Second Temple Judaism was rather strong that the other eleven sons of Jacob were buried at Hebron (cf. *Jub.* 46:8; Josephus, *Ant.* 2.199; Str-B, 2.672–78), Josephus seems somewhat vague as to just where Joseph's bones were finally laid to rest—apart, of course, from his rather general statement that "they conveyed them to Canaan" (*Ant.* 2.200).

17–36 Still on the subject of "the land," Stephen recounts the life of Moses. Incorporated into this section, largely by way of anticipation, is a "rejection of Moses" theme in vv.23–29 and 35—a theme that will later be highlighted in vv.39–43 and then driven home in the scathing indictment of vv.51–53. But here Stephen's primary emphasis is on God's providential and redemptive action for his people that occurred apart from and outside the land of Palestine, of which Stephen's hearers made so much: (1) God's raising up of the deliverer Moses *in Egypt* (vv.17–22); (2) his provision for the rejected Moses *in Midian* (v.29); (3) his commissioning of Moses *in the desert near Mount Sinai*—which was the place that God himself identified as being "holy ground," for wherever God meets with his people is holy ground, even though it may possess no sanctity of its own (vv.30–34); and (4) Moses' resultant action in delivering God's people and doing "wonders and miraculous signs" (v.36) for forty years *in Egypt, at the Red Sea, and in the desert*.

This narration of events in Moses' life is not given just to introduce the Second Moses theme that follows in vv.37–43, though it certainly does that. Rather, its primary purpose seems to be that of making the vital point, contrary to the popular piety of the day in its veneration of "the Holy Land," that no place on earth—even though given as an inheritance by God himself—can be claimed to possess such sanctity or be esteemed in such a way as to preempt God's further working on behalf of his people. By this method Stephen was attempting to clear the way, apart from the dominance of any territorial claims, for the proclamation of the centrality of Jesus in the nation's worship, life, and thought.

NOTES

2 On the address ἄνδρες ἀδελφοί (andres adelphoi, "men, brothers"), see comments at 1:16.

4 The Western text includes several minor expansions, including (1) the addition of Ἀβραάμ (Abraam, "Abraam") after τότε (tote, "then"), (2) the insertion of κἀκεῖ ἦν (kakei ēn, "and there it was") instead of κἀκεῖθεν (kakeithen, "and from there"), (3) the addition of καί (kai, "and") before μετῴκισεν (metōkisen, "removed/sent"), and (4) the addition at the end of the verse of καὶ οἱ πατέρες ὑμῶν (kai hoi pateres hymōn, "and your fathers"). All of these expansions, as Metzger, 300, notes, represent "the kind of superfluity that is characteristic of the Western text."

12 Two peculiarities of Koine Greek usage may be noted here, which also appear elsewhere in Acts: (1) the use of πρῶτος (prōtos, "first") for πρότερος (proteros, "former"; cf. 1:1), and (2) the use of εἰς (eis, "into") for ἐν (en, "in"; cf. 8:16; 19:5). Codex Bezae (D), following the LXX, reads ἐν rather than εἰς.

21 The Western text (D, E, and as reflected in certain Syriac and Coptic recensions) adds the detail that Pharaoh's daughter found the infant Moses "after he had been cast out into the river."

26 Codex Bezae (D) reads ἄνδρες ἀδελφοί (andres adelphoi, "men, brothers"), rather than ἄνδρες ἀδελφοί ἐστε (andres adelphoi este, "men, you are brothers"), evidently attempting to be in harmony with the form of address at 1:16; 2:29, 37; 7:2; 13:15, 26, 38; 15:7, 13; 22:1; 23:1, 6; 28:17.

33 Codex Bezae (D) reads καὶ ἐγένετο φωνὴ πρὸς αὐτόν (kai egeneto phōnē pros auton, "and there came a voice to him") for the better-attested and more common introductory clause εἶπεν δὲ αὐτῷ ὁ κύριος (eipen de autō ho kyrios, "then the Lord said to him").

36 On the compound τέρατα καὶ σημεῖα (terata kai sēmeia, "wonders and signs"), see comments at 2:22; see also Notes, 5:12.

REFLECTIONS

Stephen's message, of course, relates specifically to his particular time and situation. But it also has great relevance for us today. For we as Christians are constantly tempted to assert that our nation and our possessions are God-given rather than to confess our dependence on God, who is not limited by anything he has bestowed, and to affirm our readiness to move forward with him at all cost.

b. On the law (7:37–43)

OVERVIEW

Inevitably, the Jewish exaltation of the law also involved (1) the veneration of Moses the lawgiver and (2) the idealization of Israel's wilderness days. All the parties within Second Temple Judaism—whether Sadducees, Pharisees, Essenes, Zealots, apocalyptic speculators, Hellenists, Samaritans, or the so-called "people of the land"—were united in this veneration and idealization. So in meeting the accusation that he was speaking blasphemous words "against Moses" (6:11) and "against the law" (6:13), Stephen argues two points explicitly and a third point more inferentially: (1) that Moses himself spoke of God's later raising up "a prophet like me" from among his people and for his people, which means that Israel cannot limit the revelation and redemption of God to Moses' precepts (vv.37–38); (2) that Moses had been rejected by his own people, even though he was God's appointed redeemer, which rejection parallels the way Jesus of Nazareth was treated and explains why the majority within the nation refused him, even though he was God's promised Messiah (vv.39–40); and (3) that even though Moses was with them and they had the living words of the law and the sacrificial system, the people fell into gross idolatry and actually opposed God (vv.41–43).

37"This is that Moses who told the Israelites, 'God will send you a prophet like me from your own people.' 38He was in the assembly in the desert, with the angel who spoke to him on Mount Sinai, and with our fathers; and he received living words to pass on to us.

39"But our fathers refused to obey him. Instead, they rejected him and in their hearts turned back to Egypt. 40They told Aaron, 'Make us gods who will go before us. As for this fellow Moses who led us out of Egypt—we don't know what has happened to him!' 41That was the time they made an idol in the form of a calf. They brought sacrifices to it and held a celebration in honor of what their hands had made. 42But God turned away and gave them over to the worship of the heavenly bodies. This agrees with what is written in the book of the prophets:

"'Did you bring me sacrifices and offerings
    forty years in the desert, O house of Israel?
43You have lifted up the shrine of Molech
    and the star of your god Rephan,
    the idols you made to worship.
Therefore I will send you into exile beyond Babylon.'"

COMMENTARY

37–38 The twofold use of *houtos estin* ("this is that"), together with the articular adjectival participle *ho eipas* ("the one who said"), represents an intensification of the demonstrative pronouns *touton* ("that") and *houtos* ("this") with reference to Moses in vv.35–36. This suggests a buildup of tension in Stephen's speech—a tension that starts from a rather placid historical narrative (vv.2–34), moves on to a strident conclusion (vv.35–36), and peaks with passion about the Moses *testimonium* in Deuteronomy 18:15 and the significance of Moses in that passage (vv.37–38). All of this probably reflects a pesher exegesis of Scripture that was common among nonconformist Jews during the period of Second Temple Judaism (see comments at 2:16). More important, it likely points to the crux of Stephen's argument.

Stephen in no way disparages Moses. Indeed, when he refers to Moses as being "in the assembly in the desert, with the angel who spoke to him on Mount Sinai, and with our fathers," he is speaking in a complimentary way. Likewise, in Stephen's statement that "[Moses] received living words to pass on to us," the expression "living words" (*logia zōnta*, GK *3359, 2409*) suggests exactly the opposite of any disparagement of the Mosaic law. Rather, Stephen's point is that in Deuteronomy 18:15 Moses pointed beyond himself and beyond the instruction that came through him to another whom God would raise up in the future and to whom Israel must give heed, and that therefore Israel cannot limit divine revelation and redemption to the confines of the Mosaic law.

Jews in the first century AD generally looked for a Messiah who would in some way be "like Moses." The inclusion of Deuteronomy 18:18–19 as the second *testimonium* passage in the five Qumran texts of 4Q *Testimonia* (4Q175) highlights this for us. The degree to which a Mosaic understanding of messiahship was embedded in Jewish expectations is further illustrated by the many claimants to messiahship who attempted to validate their claims by reenacting the experiences of Moses (cf. *TDNT* 4:862). The Samaritans talked about a Moses redivivus ("restored," "reborn") and (as did the Dead Sea sectarians) used Deuteronomy 18:15–18 to support this notion. And though later rabbis, in what may have been a conscious reaction to Christian usage, used Deuteronomy 18:15–18 in a decidedly noneschatological and nonmessianic fashion by applying the passage to Samuel (cf. *Midr. Ps.* 1.3), to Jeremiah (cf. *Pesiq. Rab Kah.* 13.6), and to the whole line of prophets (cf. *Sifre Deuteronomy* [175–76]), a number of talmudic passages explicitly parallel Israel's first redeemer Moses with Israel's expected Messiah-Redeemer, who will be like Moses (cf. the "like the first redeemer, so the last Redeemer" theme of the Jerusalem Targum on Ex 12:42; *Deut. Rab.* 2.9; *Ruth Rab.* 5.6; *Pesiq. Rab.* 15.10; *Pesiq. Rab Kah.* 5.8). Stephen's argument, therefore, as based on Moses' prophecy in Deuteronomy 18:15–18, was generally in accord with Jewish eschatological expectations. Expecting it to be convincing, he evidently used it as Peter did before him (cf. 3:22–23).

39–40 While Peter and Stephen agree in seeing christological significance in Deuteronomy 18:15–18, with both considering it an important *testimonium* passage for a Jewish audience, their respective attitudes toward Israel are portrayed by Luke as being very different. For Peter, his hearers are the legitimate children of the prophets who should hear the new Moses (cf. 3:22–26); for Stephen, his hearers are simply those who rejected Moses and killed the prophets (cf. 7:35–40, 51–53). Stephen specifically applies this "rejection of Moses" theme to his hearers by picking up the awful words of Numbers 14:3 and applying those words to them: "their hearts turned back to Egypt" (v.39). Furthermore, he cites almost verbatim, and with evident reference to his tormentors, Israel's ancient defiance as given in Exodus 32:1: "Make us gods who will go before us. As for this fellow Moses who led us out of Egypt—we don't know what has happened to him!" (v.40).

The Talmud also speaks of the people's rebellion in making the golden calf and generally views it as Israel's ultimate and most heinous sin (e.g., *b. Šabb. 17a*; *b. Meg. 25b*; *b. ʿAbod. Zar. 5a*; *Exod. Rab. 48.2*; *Lev. Rab. 2.15*; *5.3*; *9.49*; *27.3*; *Deut. Rab. 3.10, 12*). Some rabbis, however, tried to shift the blame onto the proselytes who came out of Egypt with the people (cf. *Exod. Rab. 42.6*; *Lev. Rab. 27.8*; *Pesiq. Rab Kah. 9.8*), or even onto God himself because he blessed Israel with all the gold with which they constructed the idol (cf. *b. Sanh. 102a*). But while the rabbis have much to say about the awfulness of the incident in Israel's history, calling it by such euphemisms as "that unspeakable deed" (cf. *Pesiq. Rab. 33.3*; *Num. Rab. 5.3*) and forbidding a translation of the account into the vernacular in the synagogue services (cf. *b. Meg. 25b*), there is a decided difference between the way they treat the people's rebellion and the way Stephen does. For the rabbis did not take the golden calf episode as the people's rejection of Moses (though Korah's later rebellion was so considered), but they laid emphasis on Moses' successful intercession for Israel (cf. esp. *b. Soṭah 14a*); whereas Stephen lays all of his emphasis on Israel's rejection of their deliverer and implicitly draws a parallel between their treatment of Moses and Israel's treatment of Jesus—a parallel he

will broaden and drive home in his scathing indictment of vv.51–53.

41–43 "In those days" (*en tais hēmerais ekeinais*; NIV, "that was the time"; NASB, "at that time"), says Stephen, "they made an idol in the form of a calf. They brought sacrifices to it and held a celebration in honor of what their hands had made." So detestable to God was this episode in Israel's wilderness experience that Stephen calls it a time when "God turned away and gave them over [*ho theos paredōken autous*] to the worship of the heavenly bodies" (v.42; cf. Ro 1:24, where *ho theos paredōken autous*, "God gave them over," also occurs, though there the giving over was from idolatry to immorality). The inescapable inference from Stephen's words is that Israel's shameful behavior and God's drastic response find their counterparts in the nation's rejection of Jesus.

To support his assertion that Israel's idolatry caused God to give them over to the worship of heavenly bodies, Stephen quotes Amos 5:25–27. The form of the Greek in Stephen's quotation is fairly close to that of the LXX, which (1) understands "Sikkuth your king" (MT) to be "the shrine of Moloch" (deriving *skēnē*, "shrine" [GK *5008*], from vocalizing the Hebrew *sikkût* to read *sukkoth*, "booths," and "Moloch" from a misreading of the Hebrew *malʿkkem*, "your king"; cf. LXX at 4 Kgdms 23:10 [MT = 2Ki 23:10] and Jer 31:35 [MT = Jer 32:35]) and (2) transliterates the Hebrew name *Kiyyûn* as *Raiphan* (probably originally transliterated *Kaipan*). But Stephen's use of Amos 5:25–27 is very much like that found among the Qumran covenanters (cf. CD 7:14–15), where the rejection of God's redemptive activity in the eschatological day of salvation is the cause for God's judgment despite all the sacrifices and offerings that may be offered, just as Israel's idolatry of the golden calf eventuated in Israel's exile "beyond Babylon" (or, as the LXX has it, "beyond Damascus").

NOTES

38 In Deuteronomy 4:10; 9:10; and 18:16 (LXX), ἡ ἡμέρα τῆς ἐκκλησίας (*hē hēmera tēs ekklēsias*, "the day of the assembly") means the day when the people gathered to receive the law at Mount Sinai. This is probably what Stephen had in mind in speaking of "the assembly in the desert" (NASB, "the congregation in the wilderness"), particularly in view of the immediately following clauses: "with the angel who spoke to him on Mount Sinai" and "with our ancestors [fathers]."

The view that angels were involved in the giving of the law at Mount Sinai was widely held in Second Temple Judaism (cf. Dt 33:2 [LXX]; *Jub.* 1:29; Philo, *Somn.* 1.141ff.; Josephus, *Ant.* 15.136; *T. Dan* 6:2; Ac 7:53; Gal 3:19; Heb 2:2).

The expression λόγια ζῶντα (*logia zōnta*, "living words") stems from αὕτη ἡ ζωὴ ὑμῶν (*hautē hē zōē hymōn*, "it is your life") in Deuteronomy 32:47. Codices Sinaiticus (ℵ) and Vaticanus (B), together with 𝔓74 and a number of minuscules, read ὑμῖν (*hymin*, "to you"; so NASB) rather than ἡμῖν (*hēmin*, "to us"; so NIV). These plural pronouns were pronounced alike and so were frequently confused by scribes. Probably ἡμῖν (*hēmin*, "to us") was the original reading, for as Metzger, 307, observes, "Stephen does not wish to disassociate himself from those who received God's revelation in the past, but only from those who misinterpreted and disobeyed that revelation."

43 On the relation between Acts 7:43 and CD 7:14–15 in the use of Amos 5:26–27, see de Waard, 41–47.

c. On the temple (7:44–50)

OVERVIEW

In the preceding section of his defense, Stephen met the accusation of blasphemy against the law by (1) reassessing Moses' place in redemptive history and (2) countercharging his accusers with rejecting the One whom Moses spoke of and turning to idolatry in their refusal of Jesus the Messiah. In this section he proceeds to meet the charge of blasphemy against the temple in the same way. In form, this section recalls the more placid manner of vv.2–34; in tone and content, however, it carries on the strident and passionate appeal of vv.35–43, which amounts to a vigorous denunciation of the Jerusalem temple and the type of mentality that would hold to it as the apex of revealed religion.

44"Our forefathers had the tabernacle of the Testimony with them in the desert. It had been made as God directed Moses, according to the pattern he had seen. 45Having received the tabernacle, our fathers under Joshua brought it with them when they took the land from the nations God drove out before them. It remained in the land until the time of David, 46who enjoyed God's favor and asked that he might provide a dwelling place for the God of Jacob. 47But it was Solomon who built the house for him.

⁴⁸"However, the Most High does not live in houses made by men. As the prophet says:

⁴⁹"'Heaven is my throne,
    and the earth is my footstool.
What kind of house will you build for me?
                                    says the Lord.

    Or where will my resting place be?
⁵⁰Has not my hand made all these things?'"

COMMENTARY

44–46 Stephen's assessment of Israel's worship experience lays all the emphasis on the tabernacle, which he eulogistically calls "the tent [or tabernacle] of the Testimony" (*hē skēnē tou martyriou*, GK *5008, 3457*). It was with our forefathers, he says, during that period in the desert which so many in his day considered exemplary. It was made according to the exact pattern that God gave Moses. It was central in the life of the nation during the conquest of Canaan under the leadership of Joshua. And it was the focus of national worship through the time of David, who found favor in God's sight. So significant was it in Israel's experience, in fact, that David asked to be allowed to provide a permanent "dwelling place" for God in Jerusalem (v.46). (Here Ps 132:5 is quoted, with 2Sa 6:17 and 1Ch 15:1 being alluded to.)

Like the covenanters at Qumran (cf. 1QS 8.7–8) and the writer to the Hebrews (cf. Heb 8:2, 5; 9:1–5, 11, 24)—and probably like many other nonconformist Jews of his time—Stephen seems to have viewed the epitome of Jewish worship in terms of the tabernacle, not the temple. Very likely it was because he felt the mobility of the tabernacle was a restraint on the status quo mentality that had grown up around the Jerusalem temple. But unlike the Qumranites, who desired a restoration of that classical ideal, Stephen, as well as the writer to the

Hebrews, was attempting to lift his compatriots' vision to something far superior to even the wilderness tabernacle, i.e., to the dwelling of God with men and women in Jesus of Nazareth, as expressed through the new covenant.

47 "But it was Solomon," Stephen says rather tersely, "who built the house for him." This brevity suggests something of Stephen's pejorative attitude toward the Jerusalem temple. And his contrast between the tabernacle (vv.44–46) and the temple (v.47) shows his disapproval. Probably Stephen had in mind 2 Samuel 7:5–16 (cf. 1Ch 17:4–14). There God speaks through the prophet Nathan of his satisfaction with his "nomadic" situation and declines David's offer to build a house for his divine presence, but then goes on to announce that David's son would build such a house and promises to build a "house," i.e., a lineage, for David. Certainly 2 Samuel 7:5–16 was a foundational passage at Qumran (cf. 4Q174 on 2Sa 7:10–14) and for much of early Christian thought (cf. Lk 1:32–33 alluding to 2Sa 7:12–16; Ac 13:17–22 on 2Sa 7:6:16; Heb 1:5b on 2Sa 7:14; and, possibly, 2Co 6:18 on 2Sa 7:14). But obviously Stephen did not consider Solomon's temple to be the final fulfillment of God's words to David in 2 Samuel 7. Probably he understood the announcement of a temple to be a concession on

God's part and laid greater emphasis on the promise of the establishment of David's seed and kingdom (cf. 2Sa 7:12–16).

48–50 Stephen reaches the climax of his antitemple polemic by insisting that "the Most High does not live in houses made by men"—a concept he supports by citing Isaiah 66:1–2a. Judaism never taught that God actually lived in the Jerusalem temple or was confined to its environs, but spoke of his "Name" and presence as being there. In practice, however, this concept was often denied. This would especially appear so to Stephen, when further divine activity was refused by the people in their preference for God's past revelation and redemption, as symbolized in the existence of the temple.

As a Hellenistic Jew, Stephen may have had a tendency to view things in a more "spiritual" manner, i.e., in more inward and nonmaterial terms. This was a tendency with both good and bad features. As a Christian, he could have been aware of the contrast in the primitive Christian catechesis (the oral instruction of new converts) between what is "made with hands" and what is "not made with hands" (cf. esp. Mk 14:58; Heb 8:2; 9:24). But whatever its source, Stephen's assertion is that neither the tabernacle nor the temple was meant to be such an institutionalized feature in Israel's religion as to prohibit God's further redemptive activity or to halt the advance of God's plan for his people. The response Stephen evidently wanted from his hearers was what God declared to be his desire for his people in the strophe that immediately follows the Isaiah passage just cited (Isa 66:2b):

> This is the one I esteem:
>> he who is humble and contrite in spirit,
>> and trembles at my word.

To those who desired to localize God's presence and confine his working, Stephen repeated the denunciation of Isaiah 66:1–2a and left this appeal in 66:2b to be inferred.

NOTES

46 Codices Sinaiticus (ℵ), Vaticanus (B), Bezae (D), and Bodmer 𝔓⁷⁴ read τῷ οἴκῳ Ἰακώβ (*tō oikō Iakōb*, "for the house of Jacob"), whereas A, C, and the TR read τῷ θεῷ Ἰακώβ (*tō theō Iakōb*, "for the God of Jacob"). Choosing between the two readings is not easy. For while "the house of Jacob" is more strongly supported by the textual tradition (both Alexandrian and Western witnesses) and was common among the Jews (so NRSV), the parallel with Psalm 132:5 and the contrast set up between David's desire in v.46 and Solomon's action in v.47 seem to require "the God of Jacob" here (so NIV, NASB). Evidently there has arisen a primitive corruption in the usually better textual sources (ℵ B 𝔓⁷⁴).

49–50 Isaiah 66:1 is quoted in the *Epistle of Barnabas* 16:2 with reference to the destruction of the Jerusalem temple in AD 70, with the same variation in text form from the LXX as here (ἢ τίς τόπος, *ē tis topos*; NIV, "or where"; NASB, "or what place")—and Isaiah 66:1–2, together with Amos 5:25–27, is quoted by Justin (*Dial.* 22). This has raised the possibility that there existed within early Christian circles a *testimonia* collection in which Isaiah 66:1–2 and Amos 5:25–27 were brought together. But it is also possible that the writer of the *Epistle of Barnabas* and Justin Martyr were dependent on Acts.

d. The indictment (7:51–53)

OVERVIEW

The most striking feature of Stephen's speech—the one that sets it off most sharply from Peter's temple sermon of Acts 3—is its strong polemical stance toward Israel. As Stephen recounts the history of Israel, it is a litany of sin, rebellion, and rejection of God's purposes that emphasizes, as Simon, 41, has rightly said, "the unworthiness and perpetual rebelliousness of the Jews who, in the long run, exhaust the immense riches of God's mercy."

Some have supposed that the suddenness and harshness of the indictment were occasioned by an angry outburst in the court, to which vv.51–53 are a kind of knee-jerk response. But there is little reason to assume this is the case. Stephen's address has led naturally up to the invective. After his quotation of Isaiah 66:1–2a, there was really nothing to add.

[51]"You stiff-necked people, with uncircumcised hearts and ears! You are just like your fathers: You always resist the Holy Spirit! [52]Was there ever a prophet your fathers did not persecute? They even killed those who predicted the coming of the Righteous One. And now you have betrayed and murdered him—[53]you who have received the law that was put into effect through angels but have not obeyed it."

COMMENTARY

51 Stephen's description of his accusers is loaded with pejorative theological nuances. The phrase "stiff-necked" was fixed in Israel's memory as God's own characterization of the nation when it rebelled against Moses and worshiped the golden calf (cf. Ex 33:5; Dt 9:13). The expression "with uncircumcised hearts and ears" recalls God's judgment on the apostates among his people as being "uncircumcised in heart" (cf. Lev 26:41; Dt 10:16; Jer 4:4; 9:26). And now, says Stephen, speaking like a prophet of old, God's indictment rests on you, just as it did on your idolatrous and apostate ancestors.

52 Israel's persecution and killing of her prophets is a recurrent theme in Jewish writings. The OT not only speaks of the sufferings of individual prophets but also has a number of statements about how the nation had persecuted and killed God's prophets (cf.

2Ch 36:15–16; Ne 9:26; Jer 2:30). Various compositions from the period of Second Temple Judaism elaborated this theme, particularly as a result of the idealization of martyrdom that arose in Maccabean times (cf. Sir 49:7; *Jub.* 1:12; *1 En.* 89:51–53). In the Talmud, while there are scattered references to the prophets being wealthy (cf. *b. Ned.* 38*a*) and/or living to a great age (cf. *b. Pesaḥ.* 87*b*), there are also a great many statements about Israel persecuting and killing her prophets (cf. *b. Giṭ.* 57*b*; *b. Sanh.* 96*b*; *Exod. Rab.* 31.16; *Pesiq. Rab.* 26.1–2). All of these were for the council well-learned lessons from the past. Stephen's accusation, however, was that nothing had been learned from the past, since an even more horrendous crime had been committed in the present by those who were so smug about Israel's past failures: the betrayal and murder of "the Righteous One."

NOTES

52 On the christological title "the Righteous One," see comments at 3:14.

53 On the law as mediated by angels, see Notes, 7:38.

REFLECTIONS

Stephen's address began in v.2 with the fraternal greeting "men, brothers and fathers" (*andres adelphoi kai pateres*; NIV, "brothers and fathers"; NASB, "brethren and fathers"; cf. 22:1). It affirmed throughout his deep respect for such distinctly Jewish phenomena as the Abrahamic covenant (vv.3–8), circumcision (v.8), and the tabernacle (vv.44–46). It also repeatedly referred to "our father Abraham" and "our fathers" in such a way as to stress his ready acceptance of his Israelite heritage (vv.2, 11–12, 15, 19, 39, 44–45). Yet his repeated use of the second person plural pronoun in vv.51–53 shows his desire to disassociate himself from the nation in its constantly recurring refusal of God throughout its history. Therefore, taking the offensive, Stephen drives home his point: "*Your* fathers always resisted the Holy Spirit. . . . *Your* fathers persecuted the prophets. . . . *You* received the law put into effect through angels, but *you* have not obeyed it." Perhaps he reinforced his statements by gesticulating with an extended index finger at his accusers, though even a blind man would have felt his verbal blows.

3. The Stoning of Stephen (7:54–8:1a)

OVERVIEW

To interpret Stephen's address as an absolute renunciation of the land, the law, and the temple and its sacrificial system is an exaggeration. Indeed, like the Qumran covenanters (though for different reasons), Stephen saw worship in terms of the tabernacle, not the temple, to be the ideal of Israel's worship. But this is not to say he rejected the worship of the temple, particularly as it continued the pattern of worship instituted by God in the giving of the tabernacle. Nor can it be said that Stephen was proclaiming a law-free and universal gospel or suggesting the futility of a Christian mission to Israel. Rather, his desire, it seems, was to raise a prophetic voice *within* Israel by pleading, as Filson, 103, summed up his message, for "a radical recasting of Jewish life to make Jesus, rather than these traditionally holy things, the center of Jewish faith, worship, and thought." Certainly Stephen was more daring than the Jerusalem apostles, more ready to explore the logical consequences of commitment to Jesus than they were, and more ready to attribute Israel's rejection of its Messiah to a perpetual callousness of heart. Adolf Harnack, however, was probably right (at least in the main) to insist that "when Stephen was stoned, he died . . . for a cause whose issues he probably did not foresee" (*The Mission and Expansion of Christianity* [London: Williams & Norgate, 1908], 1:50).

⁵⁴When they heard this, they were furious and gnashed their teeth at him. ⁵⁵But Stephen, full of the Holy Spirit, looked up to heaven and saw the glory of God, and Jesus standing at the right hand of God. ⁵⁶"Look," he said, "I see heaven open and the Son of Man standing at the right hand of God."

⁵⁷At this they covered their ears and, yelling at the top of their voices, they all rushed at him, ⁵⁸dragged him out of the city and began to stone him. Meanwhile, the witnesses laid their clothes at the feet of a young man named Saul.

⁵⁹While they were stoning him, Stephen prayed, "Lord Jesus, receive my spirit." ⁶⁰Then he fell on his knees and cried out, "Lord, do not hold this sin against them." When he had said this, he fell asleep.

^{8:1}And Saul was there, giving approval to his death.

COMMENTARY

54 Stephen's message was for his Jewish hearers flagrant apostasy, both in its content and in its tone. While his purpose was to denounce the status quo mentality that had grown up around the land, the law, and the temple, thereby clearing a path for a positive response to Jesus as Israel's Messiah, this was undoubtedly taken as a frontal attack against the Jewish religion in its official and popular forms. And in the council's eyes the assumed prophetic stance of Stephen's address, together with what appeared to be its obnoxious liberal spirit, must have represented the worst of both Jewish Hellenism and the infant Christian movement. So, Luke tells us, "they were furious and gnashed their teeth at him."

55–56 While the content and tone of his address infuriated the council, Stephen's solemn pronouncement as he was dying raised again the specter of blasphemy and brought his hearers to a frenzied pitch: "Look," he announced, "I see heaven open and the Son of Man standing at the right hand of God" (v.56). Only a few years before, Jesus had stood before this same tribunal and was condemned for answering affirmatively the high priest's question about his being Israel's Messiah and for saying

of himself, "You will see the Son of Man sitting at the right hand of the Mighty One and coming on the clouds of heaven" (Mk 14:62). Now Stephen was saying, in effect, that his vision confirmed Jesus' claim and condemned the council for having rejected him. Unless the council members were prepared to repent and admit their awful error, they had no option but to find Stephen also guilty of blasphemy. Had he been judged only an impertinent apostate (cf. 5:40), the thirty-nine lashes of Jewish punishment would have been appropriate (cf. *m. Mak.* 3:10–15a). To be openly blasphemous before the council, however, was a matter that demanded his death.

Luke's description of Stephen as "full of the Holy Spirit" (v.55) is in line with his characterizations of him in ch. 6 (vv.3, 5, 8, 15). The identification of Jesus as "the Son of Man" is used outside the Gospels only here and at Revelation 1:13; 14:14 (cf. Heb 2:6, though probably not as a christological title but as a locution for "man" in line with Ps 8:4). In the canonical gospels Jesus alone is portrayed as having used "Son of Man" with reference to himself (the apparent exceptions in Lk 24:7 and Jn

12:34 are, in actuality, only echoes of Jesus' usage). Jesus used the expression both as a locution for the pronoun "I" and as a titular image reflecting the usage in Daniel 7:13–28 (esp. vv.13–14). As a title it carries the ideas of (1) identification with mankind and suffering and (2) vindication by God and glory. The title was generally not attributed to Jesus by the church between the time when his sufferings were completed and when he would assume his full glory. Here, however, an anticipation of Jesus' full glory is set within a martyr context (as also at Rev 1:13; 14:14); and so the use of "Son of Man" as a title for Jesus is fully appropriate.

The juxtaposition of "the glory of God" and the name of Jesus in Stephen's vision, together with his saying that he sees "heaven open and the Son of Man standing at the right hand of God," are christologically significant. Unlike the Greek understanding of *doxa* ("glory") as akin to "opinion," the Hebrew OT and Greek LXX viewed "the glory of God" (Heb. *kᵉbôd YHWH*; Gr. *doxa theou*) as "the manifestation or revelation of the divine nature" and even as "the divine mode of being" itself (cf. *TDNT* 2.233–47). The bringing together of "the glory of God" and the name of Jesus, therefore, suggests something about Jesus' person as the manifestation of the divine nature and the divine mode of being. Likewise, inasmuch as God dwells in the highest heaven, the open heaven with Jesus at God's right hand suggests something about his work as providing access into the very presence of God.

Stephen's reference to Jesus "standing" at the right hand of God, which differs from the "sitting" of Psalm 110:1 (the passage alluded to here), has been variously understood. Dalman (*Words of Jesus*, 311) argued that it is merely "a verbal change," for both the perfect infinitive *estanai* ("to stand," GK 2705) and the present infinitive *kathēsthai* ("to sit," GK 2767) connote the idea "to be situated" (Heb. *ᶜamād*), without any necessary implication for the

configuration of posture. The majority of commentators, however, have interpreted "standing" to suggest Jesus' welcome of his martyred follower, who like the repentant criminal of Luke 23:43 was received into heaven the moment he died. Dispensational commentators have taken Stephen's reference to Jesus' "standing" as supporting their view that the distinctive redemptive message for this age was not proclaimed until the Pauline gospel (either at its inauguration, its close, or somewhere in between), and so in the transitional period between Israel and the church Jesus is represented as not yet having taken his seat at God's right hand. Others speak of Jesus as "standing" in order to enter his messianic office on earth or as "standing" in the presence of God, in line with the common representation of angels in God's presence.

More likely, however, the concept of "witness" is what is primarily highlighted in the portrayal of Jesus as "standing" at Stephen's martyrdom. F. F. Bruce, 168, has aptly noted that "Stephen has been confessing Christ before men, and now he sees Christ confessing His servant before God. The proper posture for a witness is the standing posture. Stephen, condemned by an earthly court, appeals for vindication to a heavenly court, and his vindicator in that supreme court is Jesus, who stands at God's right hand as Stephen's advocate, his 'paraclete.'" Yet in accepting such an interpretation, one does well to keep Bruce's further comment, 168–69, in mind:

> When we are faced with words so wealthy in association as these words of Stephen, it is unwise to suppose that any single interpretation exhausts their significance. All the meaning that had attached to Psalm 110:1 and Daniel 7:13f. is present here, including especially the meaning that springs from their combination on the lips of Jesus when He appeared before the Sanhedrin; but the replacement of "sitting" by

"standing" probably makes its own contribution to the total meaning of the words in this context—a contribution distinctively appropriate to Stephen's present role as martyr-witness.

57–58 Haenchen, 274, has noted the progression in Luke's portrayals of the trial scenes of 4:1–22; 5:17–40; and here—the first ending with threatenings (4:17, 21), the second with flogging (5:40), and the third with stoning (7:58–60). He observes from that pattern the following: "It goes without saying that in the circumstances the moderating Gamaliel and the Pharisees who (according to Luke!) to some extent sympathized with the Christians do not make themselves heard," and he concludes from this account that "Luke possessed the happy gift of forgetting people when they might interfere with his literary designs." But while Haenchen has rightly noted Luke's developmental theme in the three trial scenes, he fails to appreciate the historical interplay of divergent ideological factors that gave rise to Judaism's united stance against the Hellenistic Jewish believers in Jesus.

The message of Stephen served as a catalyst to unite the Sadducees, the Pharisees, and the common people (Heb. ʿam haʾāreṣ, "people of the land"; Gk. ho laos, "the people") in opposition to the early believers in Jesus. Had Gamaliel been confronted by this type of preaching earlier, his attitude as reported in 5:34–39 would surely have been different. The Pharisees could tolerate Palestinian Jewish believers in Jesus because their messianic beliefs, though judged by them as terribly misguided, effected no change in their practice of the Mosaic law. Those early converts to Jesus "the Messiah" who had been raised as scrupulous Jews continued their scrupulous observance of the law, and those raised as "people of the land" continued to live in accordance with at least the law's minimal requirements. But Hellenistic Jewish believers in Jesus, who had probably originally entered the Holy Land avowing their desire to become stricter in their religious practice, were now beginning to question the centrality of Israel's traditional forms of religious expression and to propagate within Jerusalem a type of religious liberalism that, from a Pharisaic perspective, would eventually undercut the basis for the Jewish religion. The Jewish leaders might have been able to do little about such liberalism in the Diaspora and certain quarters within Palestine, but they were determined to preserve the Holy City from further contamination by such "foreign" ways of thinking—and so, as they believed, best prepare the way for the coming of the messianic age.

It is not easy to determine whether the stoning of Stephen was only the result of mob action or was carried out by the Sanhedrin in excess of its jurisdiction. Josephus (*Ant.* 20.200) recounts a somewhat parallel instance when the high priest Ananus killed James the Just during the procuratorial interregnum between Festus's death and Albinus's arrival in AD 61. The reference in v. 58 to "the witnesses" (*hoi martyres*, GK *3457*), whose grisly duty it was to knock the offender down and throw the first stones, suggests an official execution. This hardly corresponds with the stipulation in the Mishnah that "in capital cases a verdict of acquittal may be reached on the same day [as the trial], but a verdict of conviction not until the following day" (*m. Sanh.* 4:1). Nor is it in accord with the Roman regulation that death sentences in the provinces could not be carried out unless confirmed by the Roman governor. But if (as I believe) Stephen's martyrdom occurred sometime in the mid-30s AD, during the final years of Pilate's governorship over Judea (AD 26–36), and if (as I have argued) the Pharisees were not prepared to come to his defense in the council, conditions may well have been at a stage where the Sanhedrin felt free to overstep its legal authority. Pontius Pilate normally resided at Caesarea, and the later years of his governorship were beset by increasing troubles that tended to divert his attention (e.g., the Samaritan affair where he killed a number of Samaritan fanatics in an action that ultimately resulted in his removal from office).

"The witnesses," Luke tells us, in preparing for their onerous work of knocking Stephen down and throwing the first stones, "laid their clothes at the feet of a young man named Saul" (v.58). This suggests that Saul had some official part in the execution. The term *neanias* (GK *3733*), which is translated "young man," was used in Greek writings of the day for a male of about twenty-four to forty years old (cf. BDAG, 667; see 20:9; 23:17–18, 22). Some have argued from the action of the witnesses and Saul's age that he was a member of the Jewish Sanhedrin at the time, though he may have been exercising only delegated authority.

59–60 As Stephen was being stoned (note the imperfect verb *elithoboloun*, "they were stoning" [GK *3344*], which suggests a process), he cried out, "Lord Jesus, receive my spirit," and, "Lord, do not hold this sin against them." The cries are reminiscent of Jesus' words from the cross (Lk 23:34, 46), though the sequence and wording are not exactly the same. It is probably going too far to say that Luke meant Stephen's execution to be a reenactment of the first great martyrdom, that of Jesus, as many commentators have proposed (so C. H. Talbert, *Luke and the Gnostics* [Nashville: Abingdon, 1966], 76). The parallelism, however, can hardly be seen as simply inadvertent. It was probably included to show that the same spirit of commitment and forgiveness that characterized Jesus' life and death was true as well of his earliest followers.

The expression "fall asleep" (*koimaō*, GK *3121*) is a common biblical way of referring to the death of God's own (cf. Ge 47:30 [LXX]; Dt 31:16 [LXX]; Jn 11:11; Ac 13:36; 1Co 7:39; 11:30; 15:6, 51; 2Pe 3:4). While the nuances of a doctrine of "soul sleep" are incompatible with the biblical message, the word "sleep" suggests something as to the nature of the believer's personal existence during that period of time theologians call "the intermediate state."

In comparing Stephen's death to that of a Stoic philosopher, Oscar Cullmann (*Immortality of the Soul or Resurrection of the Dead?* [London: Epworth, 1958], 60) made this apt observation:

> The Stoic departed this life dispassionately; the Christian martyr on the other hand died with spirited passion for the cause of Christ, because he knew that by doing so he stood within a powerful redemptive process. The first Christian martyr, Stephen, shows us how very differently death is bested by him who dies in Christ than by the ancient philosopher: he sees, it is said, "the heavens open and Christ standing at the right hand of God!" He sees Christ, the Conqueror of Death. With this faith that the death he must undergo is already conquered by Him who has Himself endured it, Stephen lets himself be stoned.

8:1a Again, as in 7:58, Luke makes the point that Saul was present at Stephen's death and approved of it. Because of the use of the verb *syneudokeō* ("agree with," "approve of," "consent to," GK *5306*) and its parallel usage in 26:10, some have taken the reference here to be to Saul's official vote as a member of the Sanhedrin. But this is not necessarily implied. Nor is it possible to argue from v.1a that the seeds of Saul's later Christian teaching on the law were implanted either through the force of Stephen's preaching or the sublimity of his death. Paul himself credits his conversion and theology to entirely other factors. All Luke wants to do here is to provide a transition in his portrayal of the developing Christian mission.

NOTES

55 The Western text (D, and as represented by various Old Latin and Coptic recensions) characteristically adds τὸν κύριον (*ton kyrion*, "the Lord") after Ἰησοῦν (*Iēsoun*, "Jesus").

56 Bodmer 𝔓⁷⁴ reads τὸν υἱὸν τοῦ θεοῦ (*ton huion tou theou*, "the Son of God") for the better-supported τὸν υἱὸν τοῦ ἀνθρώπου (*ton huion tou anthrōpou*, "the Son of Man"). On the christological title "Son of Man," see my *Christology of Early Jewish Christianity*, 82–93.

58 Some later MSS (H P and many minuscules) omit αὐτῶν (*autōn*, "their"), suggesting that Stephen's clothes were laid at the feet of Saul. But Acts 22:20 confirms that it was the clothes of the executioners ("the witnesses") that were entrusted to Saul for safekeeping.

The Qumran covenanters (cf. CD 10:4–10) speak of a complement of ten men to act as judges in the community and stipulates that "their minimum age shall be twenty-five and their maximum sixty," with no one over sixty eligible to hold a judicial office—which is an interesting parallel.

4. The Immediate Aftermath (8:1b–3)

¹ᵇOn that day a great persecution broke out against the church at Jerusalem, and all except the apostles were scattered throughout Judea and Samaria. ²Godly men buried Stephen and mourned deeply for him. ³But Saul began to destroy the church. Going from house to house, he dragged off men and women and put them in prison.

COMMENTARY

1b Taken in the broader context of Luke's presentation, we should probably understand the "great persecution" (*diōgmos megas*, GK *1501, 3489*) that broke out "against the church at Jerusalem" as directed primarily against the Hellenistic Jewish Christians rather than against the whole church (so Hans Lietzmann, *A History of the Early Church* [New York: World, 1967], 1:90; Filson, 62–64, though roundly denied by Geoffrey W. H. Lampe, *St. Luke and the Church of Jerusalem* [London: Athlone, 1969], 20–21). A certain stigma must also have fallen on the native-born, more scrupulous Jewish believers in Jesus, and they probably became as inconspicuous as possible in the countryside and towns around Jerusalem. The Hellenistic Jews of the city had been able to disassociate themselves from the Hellenistic Jewish Christians among them. And Jewish officials probably made a similar distinction between the Hellenistic Jewish believers and the more Hebraic believers within the Jerusalem church.

In a somewhat sweeping statement, Luke reports that "all" (*pantes*) the Christians of Jerusalem "except the apostles were scattered throughout Judea and Samaria." But only the Hellenistic believers in Jesus, it seems, felt it inadvisable to return. So while we should not minimize the protecting power of God or the courage of the earliest Christian leaders, it might not have been impossible, even within such difficult circumstances, for the apostles to have remained in Jerusalem in order to preserve the continuity of the community.

As a result of the persecution that began with Stephen's martyrdom, the gospel was carried beyond the confines of Jerusalem, in initial fulfillment of Jesus' directive in 1:8: "And you will be my witnesses in Jerusalem, and in all Judea and Samaria, and to the ends of the earth." From this time onward—i.e., until AD 135, when the Roman emperor Hadrian banished all Jews from Jerusalem and refounded the city as the Roman colony Aelia Capitolina—the church at Jerusalem seems to have been largely, if not entirely, devoid of Hellenistic Jewish Christians. With the martyrdom of Stephen, believers in Jesus at Jerusalem had learned the bitter lesson that to espouse a changed relationship to the land, the law, and the temple was (1) to give up the peace of the church and (2) to abandon the Christian mission to Israel (cf. Walter Schmithals, *Paul and James* [London: SCM, 1965], 44–45). The issues and events connected with Stephen's death, together with the expulsion of those who shared his concerns, would stand as a warning to the Jerusalem congregation throughout its brief and turbulent history and exert mental pressure on believers in the city to be more circumspect in their future activities within Judea.

2 Luke has already used the expression "godly men" (*andres eulabeis*, GK *467, 2327*) of the Jews at Pentecost who were receptive to the working of God's Spirit (cf. 2:5). He has also used the adjective "devout" (*eulabēs*, GK *2327*) of the aged Simeon in the temple (cf. Lk 2:25), and he will later use it of Ananias of Damascus (cf. Ac 22:12). Therefore, when Luke says that "godly men [*andres eulabeis*]

buried Stephen," he apparently means that certain devout Jews who were open to the Christian message asked for Stephen's body and buried him, much as Joseph of Arimathea did for Jesus (cf. Lk 23:50–53). The Mishnah speaks of "open lamentation" as inappropriate for anyone who has been stoned, burned, beheaded, or strangled under Sanhedrin judgment, but does allow "mourning" in such cases, "for mourning has place in the heart alone" (*m. Sanh.* 6:6). Luke tells us that those who buried Stephen "mourned deeply for him," which may be Luke's way of suggesting their repentance toward God as well as their sorrow for Stephen.

3 Haenchen, 294, takes the occasion here to mock Luke's portrayal: "The transformation in the picture of Saul is breathtaking, to say the least. A moment ago he was a youth looking on with approval at the execution. Now he is the arch-persecutor, invading Christian homes to seize men and women and fling them into gaol." But as noted, the Greek word for "young man" in 7:58 signifies a man between the ages of twenty-four and forty—hardly a youth in our modern sense. Furthermore, the description of Saul's presence at the execution suggests some kind of official capacity, even though it may have been only a delegated authority. Saul in 7:58 and 8:1 hardly appears to have been a casual onlooker. And while Luke reserves the fuller account of Saul's persecuting activities and his conversion for the narrative in 9:1–30 and the speeches in 22:1–21 and 26:2–23, here he introduces these accounts and ties them in with Stephen's martyrdom—using, in particular, the inceptive imperfect verb *elymaineto* ("he began to destroy," GK *3381*)—to tell us that at this time "Saul began to destroy the church."

NOTES

1b The Western text (D, and as reflected in the Coptic Sahidic version) adds καὶ θλῖψις (*kai thlipsis*, "and affliction," GK *2568*) either after (so D) or before (so Cop^sa) διωγμὸς μέγας (*diōgmos megas*, "great persecution"), which addition only underlines the obvious. For a similar Western expansion, see Notes, 13:50. Nor do we need to be told regarding the apostles, as Codex Bezae (D), some Latin and Coptic versions, and Augustine have it, that οἳ ἔμειναν ἐν Ἰερουσαλήμ (*hoi emeinan en Ierousalēm*, "they remained in Jerusalem").

On the use of πάντες (*pantes*, "all") in Luke's writings and the NT, see comments at 1:1. Barnabas of Cyprus (4:36) and Mnason of Cyprus (21:16) may be seen as exceptions to the expulsion of the Hellenistic Jewish believers from the city, though only if we define a "Hellenist" exclusively along geographic lines. Barnabas, however, is also spoken of as a Levite. Mnason, who lived in Jerusalem and to whose home Paul and his Gentile companions were brought on the occasion of Paul's final visit to Jerusalem, is referred to as ἀρχαίῳ μαθητῇ (*archaiō mathētē*, "a disciple from the beginning"; NIV, "one of the early disciples"; NASB, "a disciple of long standing").

B. The Early Ministries of Philip (8:4–40)

OVERVIEW

The accounts of Philip's ministries in Samaria and to the Ethiopian minister of finance are placed in Acts between the Hellenistic Jewish Christians' expulsion from Jerusalem and the outreach of the gospel to the Gentiles—an outreach prepared for by Saul's conversion and first effected through the preaching of Peter to Cornelius. As such, Luke uses these accounts of Philip's ministries as a kind of bridge in depicting the advance of the church. Each account represents a further development in the proclamation of the gospel within a Jewish milieu: the first, an outreach to a dispossessed group within Palestine often considered by Jerusalem Jews as half-breeds, both racially and religiously; the second, an outreach to a proselyte or near-proselyte from another land.

1. The Evangelization of Samaria (8:4–25)

OVERVIEW

Historically, the movement of the gospel into Samaria—following directly on the heels of the persecution of Hellenistic Jewish Christians in Jerusalem—makes a great deal of sense. Doubtless a feeling of kinship would easily have been established between the formerly dispossessed Samaritans and the recently dispossessed Hellenistic Jewish Christians. Stephen's opposition to the mentality of mainstream Judaism and its veneration of the Jerusalem temple would have facilitated a favorable response to Philip and his message in Samaria. Redactionally, the thrust of the church into its mission after the persecution of the Christian community at Jerusalem is parallel to Luke's portrayal in his gospel of the spread of Jesus' fame after the devil's assault in the wilderness (cf. Lk 4:1–15).

The Tübingen school of "tendency criticism" focused on this account of a Christian mission to Samaria as a prime example of the "tendentiousness" of Acts, arguing that the sources used by Luke must have viewed Simon Magus as a cover figure for Paul, who was bested by Peter (as set out in the Pseudo-Clementine *Homilies and Recognitions*), and that Luke recast Simon as an entirely different person with an entirely different history in an endeavor to protect his hero Paul. Modern source criticism tends to see two or three separate stories intertwined here, which Luke has somewhat confusedly worked together: one of Philip in Samaria; another of Peter and John in Samaria; and yet another account of the early "Christian" experience of the arch-Gnostic Simon Magus. Earlier source critics, however, following the hypothesis of Adolf Harnack, viewed the intermeshing of these stories as the type of thing that results from an oral recounting of experiences on the part of an enthusiastic storyteller and even suggested that Philip himself may have been the source of Luke's narrative here. I believe there is much in the narrative to support this latter suggestion, whether from an account given to him orally or one that came to him in some written form.

The equation of the Hellenists of Acts 6–7 with the Samaritans of ch. 8 has little to commend it (see comments at 6:1). Likewise, Oscar Cullmann's thesis (*The Johannine Circle* [Philadelphia: Westminster, 1976]) of a "triangular relationship" existing between (1) his "Johannine Circle" (which includes John, the Hellenists of Ac 6–7, and the writer of Hebrews), (2) the Samaritans, and (3) the Qumranites is far too specific for the data presently available. Nonetheless, it remains true that in the highly fluid and syncretistic atmosphere of first-century Palestine a number of analogical parallels of outlook and ideology existed between various Jewish nonconformist groups. Stephen, the covenanters of Qumran, and the Samaritans, for example, all had an antitemple polemic, which at least superficially could have drawn them together, though in reality their respective positions were based on different rationales. In addition, as the antagonism of the Jerusalem Jews became focused on the Hellenistic Jewish believers in Jesus, these lately dispossessed Jewish believers undoubtedly found a welcome among the Samaritans, who had for so long felt themselves the objects of a similar animosity.

[4] Those who had been scattered preached the word wherever they went. [5] Philip went down to a city in Samaria and proclaimed the Christ there. [6] When the crowds heard Philip and saw the miraculous signs he did, they all paid close attention to what he said. [7] With shrieks, evil spirits came out of many, and many paralytics and cripples were healed. [8] So there was great joy in that city.

[9] Now for some time a man named Simon had practiced sorcery in the city and amazed all the people of Samaria. He boasted that he was someone great, [10] and all the people, both high and low, gave him their attention and exclaimed, "This man is the divine power known as the Great Power." [11] They followed him because he had amazed them for a long time with his magic. [12] But when they believed Philip as he preached the good news of the

kingdom of God and the name of Jesus Christ, they were baptized, both men and women. [13]Simon himself believed and was baptized. And he followed Philip everywhere, astonished by the great signs and miracles he saw.

[14]When the apostles in Jerusalem heard that Samaria had accepted the word of God, they sent Peter and John to them. [15]When they arrived, they prayed for them that they might receive the Holy Spirit, [16]because the Holy Spirit had not yet come upon any of them; they had simply been baptized into the name of the Lord Jesus. [17]Then Peter and John placed their hands on them, and they received the Holy Spirit.

[18]When Simon saw that the Spirit was given at the laying on of the apostles' hands, he offered them money [19]and said, "Give me also this ability so that everyone on whom I lay my hands may receive the Holy Spirit."

[20]Peter answered: "May your money perish with you, because you thought you could buy the gift of God with money! [21]You have no part or share in this ministry, because your heart is not right before God. [22]Repent of this wickedness and pray to the Lord. Perhaps he will forgive you for having such a thought in your heart. [23]For I see that you are full of bitterness and captive to sin."

[24]Then Simon answered, "Pray to the Lord for me so that nothing you have said may happen to me."

[25]When they had testified and proclaimed the word of the Lord, Peter and John returned to Jerusalem, preaching the gospel in many Samaritan villages.

COMMENTARY

4 Luke connects his account of the evangelization of Samaria by his favorite connective *men oun* ("then," "so"; untranslated in NIV; NASB, "therefore"), which he uses also in v.25 to conclude the narrative (NIV, "when"; NASB, "so"). Between this twofold use of the connective he inserts the mission to Samaria, which was begun by Philip and carried on by Peter and John, as "Exhibit A" in the explication of his thesis that "those who had been scattered preached the word wherever they went." Luke does this because in the mission to Samaria he sees, in retrospect, a significant advance in the outreach of the gospel.

5 Philip, the second of the Seven enumerated in 6:5 (cf. 21:8) and one of the Hellenistic Jewish

Christians expelled from Jerusalem, traveled to the north and proclaimed "the Christ" (*ton Christon*, i.e., "the Messiah") to Samaritans. The text is uncertain as to which city of Samaria Philip preached in, for every direction from Jerusalem is "down" (note the adverbial participle *katelthōn*, GK *2982*, "went down"). The MS evidence varies regarding the inclusion of the article *tēn* ("the"), reading "the city of Samaria" ($\mathfrak{P}^{74}$ ℵ A B etc.), or simply "a city of Samaria" (C D E etc.). Some commentators, following the better-attested reading, insist that "the city of Samaria" can mean only the capital city of the province, which in OT times bore the name "Samaria." Herod the Great, however, rebuilt ancient Samaria as a Greek city and renamed it

"Sebaste" in honor of Caesar Augustus (*Sebastos* is the Greek equivalent of the Latin *Augustus*). But Sebaste was a wholly pagan city in NT times, and it seems somewhat strange for it to be referred to here by its archaic name. Other commentators, either accepting the articular reading (so NASB, NRSV) or preferring the less-well-attested "a city in Samaria" (so RSV, NEB, NIV), believe that Shechem, the religious headquarters of the Samaritans, is the city in mind, because during the Greek period it was the leading Samaritan city (cf. Josephus, *Ant.* 11.340) and was brought within the Jewish orbit of influence by the conquest of John Hyrcanus (ibid., 13.255).

Others prefer to think of the Samaritan city of Gitta as in view here, because Justin Martyr (*1 Apol.* 1.26) says that Simon Magus was a native of Gitta. Still others think of Sychar, for it was near (even at times identified with) Shechem and is the principal Samaritan city in the gospel tradition (cf. Jn 4:5). But Luke, while he probably had some particular city in mind when he wrote, was evidently not interested in giving us a precise geographical identification, as his general reference to "many Samaritan villages" in v.25b also suggests. So we will have to leave it at that.

Animosity between Judeans and Samaritans stemmed from very early times and fed on a number of incidents in their respective histories. The cleavage began in the tenth century BC with the separation of the ten northern tribes from Judah, Benjamin, and the city of Jerusalem in the disruption of the Hebrew monarchy after Solomon's death. It became racially fixed with Sargon's destruction of the city of Samaria in 722 BC and the Assyrians' policy of deportation and mixing of populations. It was intensified in Judean eyes by (1) the Samaritans' opposition to the rebuilding of the Jerusalem temple in the fifth century (cf. Ne 2:10–6:14; 13:28; Josephus, *Ant.* 11.84–103, 114, 174);

(2) the Samaritans' erection of a schismatic temple on Mount Gerizim sometime around the time of Alexander the Great (cf. Josephus, *Ant.* 11.310–11, 322–24; 13.255–56); and (3) the Samaritans' identification of themselves as Sidonians and joining with the Seleucids against the Jews in the conflict of 167–164 BC (cf. ibid., 12.257–64). On the other hand, it was sealed for the Samaritans by John Hyrcanus's destruction in 127 BC of the Gerizim temple (cf. ibid., 13.256) and the city of Samaria itself (ibid., 13.275–77).

The intensity of Samaritan feelings against Jerusalem is shown by the Samaritans' refusal of Herod's offer in 25 BC to rebuild their temple on Mount Gerizim when it was known that he also proposed to rebuild the Jerusalem temple—a rebuilding that began about 20–19 BC (ibid., 15.280–425). The Judean antagonism to Samaria is evident as early as Sirach 50:25–26, which lumps the Samaritans with the Idumeans and the Philistines as Israel's three detested nations and then goes on to disparage them further by the epithets "no nation" and "that foolish people that dwell in Shechem." Many such pejorative references to the Samaritans also appear elsewhere in writings reflecting or reporting a Judean stance (e.g., 4QpPs37 on Ps 37:14; 4QpNa on Na 3:6; Jn 8:48). Nevertheless, Jeremiah and Ezekiel treated the northern tribes as an integral part of Israel, and, conversely, there were always a few in Samaria who viewed Judean worship with respect (cf. 2Ch 30:11; 34:9). Furthermore, Samaritans accepted the Pentateuch as Holy Writ and looked for a coming messianic Restorer (the *Taeb*), who would be Moses redivivus.

6–8 Philip's preaching was defined in v.5 as a proclamation of "the Messiah" (*ton Christon*), with its content further specified in v.12 as "the kingdom of God and the name of Jesus Christ." Undoubtedly he used Deuteronomy 18:15, 18–19 as a major *testimonium* passage in his preaching, as Peter and

Stephen had done before him. With the Pentateuch as their Scriptures, and looking for the coming of a Mosaic Messiah, the Samaritans were open to Philip's message. Furthermore, God backed up Philip's preaching by various "miraculous signs" (*ta sēmeia*, GK *4956*), with many demoniacs, paralytics, and lame people being healed (vv.6–7). Thus Luke summarizes the response of the Samaritans to Philip's ministry by writing, "So there was great joy in that city" (v.8).

9 Simon the sorcerer, or Simon Magus as he is called in postapostolic Christian writings, was a leading heretic in the early church. Justin Martyr (d. ca. 165), who was himself a Samaritan, says that nearly all his countrymen revered Simon as the highest god (*1 Apol.* 1.26; *Dial.* 120). Irenaeus (*Haer.* 1.23; writing ca. 180) speaks of him as the father of Gnosticism and identifies the sect of the Simonians as being derived from him. The second-century *Acts of Peter* has extensive descriptions of how Simon Magus corrupted Christians in Rome by his teachings and how he was repeatedly bested by Peter in their displays of magical powers. These themes were picked up by the Pseudo-Clementine *Homilies* and *Recognitions* of the third and fourth centuries, though in them Simon was used as a cover figure for Paul in a radically Ebionite manner. Hippolytus (d. ca. 236) outlines Simon's system, which he avers was contained in a Gnostic tractate titled "The Great Disclosure," and tells how he allowed himself to be buried alive in Rome with the prediction that he would rise on the third day (*Refutation of All Heresies* 6.2–15). Justin Martyr (*1 Apol.* 1.26) tells of Simon being honored with a statue in Rome on which was written, "To Simon the Holy God"— which was probably a misreading either by Justin or the Simonians of an inscription beginning SEMONI SANCO DEO ("To the God Semo Sancus," an ancient Sabine deity) that either he or they read as SIMONI SANCTO DEO.

Just how Simon of Acts 8 is related to Simon Magus of later legend is not clear. They may have been different men, though the church fathers regularly equated them. Luke's statement about the Samaritans' veneration of Simon—that they said, "This man is the divine power known as the Great Power"—seems to support the Fathers' identification. Likewise, what exactly is meant by the title "the Great Power" (v.10) is uncertain. It may mean that Simon was acclaimed to be God Almighty (so Dalman, *Words of Jesus*, 200), or the Grand Vizier of God Almighty (so J. de Zwaan, in *Beginnings of Christianity* [ed. Foakes-Jackson and Lake], 2:58). At any rate, he claimed to be an exceedingly great person and supported his claim by many acts of magic.

13 Nevertheless, as the gospel advanced into Samaria, Simon believed and was baptized. His conversion must have been a momentous event that greatly impressed the Samaritans. Philip, too, who was their evangelist, must have long remembered it. But Simon himself, to judge by the narrative that follows, was more interested in the great acts of power that accompanied Philip's preaching than God's reign in his life or the proclamation of Jesus' messiahship. Simon's belief in Jesus seems to have been like that spoken of in John 2:23–25—a belief based only on miraculous signs, and therefore inferior to true commitment to Jesus.

14 For the early church the evangelization of Samaria was not just a matter of an evangelist's proclamation and a people's response; it also involved the acceptance of these new converts by the mother church at Jerusalem. Thus Luke takes pains to point out that the Jerusalem church sought to satisfy itself as to the genuineness of the Samaritans' conversion (as it did later with regard to Cornelius's conversion in 10:1–11:18) and that they did this by sending Peter and John to investigate. Concomitant with his interest in development and advances in the outreach of the gospel, Luke is also interested in establishing lines of continuity and highlighting features of unity within the church. So in his account of Philip's mission in Samaria, he tells also of the visit of Peter and John. Instead of minimizing Philip's success in Samaria, as some have proposed, it is more likely that Luke wants us to understand the ministry of Peter and John in Samaria as confirming and extending Philip's ministry. And just as in Romans 15:26 and 2 Corinthians 9:2, where a whole province is regarded as acting in a Christian manner when represented by only one or two congregations located there, so Luke here speaks sweepingly of the Jerusalem church's hearing "that Samaria had accepted the word of God," even though in v.25 he refers to further evangelistic activity in other Samaritan villages.

15–17 When Peter and John arrived (lit., "went down," *katabantes*, GK *2849*), they prayed for the Samaritan converts, laid their hands on them, and "they received the Holy Spirit" (v.17). Before this, Luke tells us, "the Holy Spirit had not yet come upon any of them; they had simply been baptized into the name of the Lord Jesus" (v.16). We are not told how the coming of the Holy Spirit on these new converts was expressed in their lives. But the context suggests that his presence was attended by such external signs as marked his coming on the earliest believers at Pentecost, and so, probably, by some form of glossolalia.

The temporal separation of the baptism of the Spirit from commitment to Jesus and water baptism in this passage has been of perennial theological interest. Catholic sacramentalists take this as a biblical basis for the separation between baptism and confirmation. Charismatics of various denominational persuasions see in it a justification for their doctrine of the baptism of the Spirit as a second work of grace following conversion. But before making too much of this separation theologically,

one does well, as noted earlier (see comments at 2:38), to look at the circumstances and ask an elementary question, yet one of immense importance: What if both the logical and the chronological relationships of conversion, water baptism, and the baptism of the Spirit, as proclaimed in Peter's call to repentance at Pentecost (cf. 2:38; see also Ro 8:9; 1Co 6:11), had been fully expressed in this case?

The Jerusalem Jews considered the Samaritans to be second-class residents of Palestine and kept them at arm's length religiously. For their part, the Samaritans returned the compliment. It is not too difficult, therefore, to imagine what would have happened had the apostles at Jerusalem been the first missionaries to Samaria. They may well have been rebuffed, just as they were rebuffed earlier in their travels with Jesus when the Samaritans associated them with the city of Jerusalem (cf. Lk 9:51–56). But God in his providence used as their evangelist the Hellenistic Jewish Christian Philip, who shared their fate (though for different reasons) of being rejected at Jerusalem—and the Samaritans received him and accepted his message.

But what if the Spirit had come on them at their baptism, which was administrated by Philip? Undoubtedly, whatever feelings there were against Philip and the Hellenists generally would have carried over to them, and they would then have been doubly under suspicion. But God in his providence withheld the gift of the Holy Spirit until Peter and John laid their hands on the Samaritans—these two leading apostles, who were highly thought of in the mother church at Jerusalem and who would have been accepted as brothers in Christ by the new converts in Samaria. In effect, therefore, in this first advance of the gospel outside the confines of Jerusalem, God worked in ways conducive not only to the reception of the good news in Samaria but also to the acceptance of these new converts by believers at Jerusalem.

The further question as to how far the Jerusalem church's acceptance would have been extended had Samaritan believers in Jesus actually traveled to Jerusalem to meet and worship with the Jerusalem believers is left unanswered. Nor does Luke tell us anything about how these Samaritan believers expressed their commitment to Jesus in their cultural and religious milieu. These are matters of interest to us today, but they seem not to have concerned Luke. What Luke does tell us is that in such a manner as this vignette shows, God was working in ways that promoted both the outreach of the gospel and the unity of the church. Rather than try to extract from the account further theological nuances of a deeper kind, it would be better to expend our energies in trying to work out in theory and practice the implications of such a divine interest in "outreach" and "unity" for the church today.

18–19 Simon's response to the presence of God's Spirit and evidences of God's power is one of those tragic stories that accompany every advance of the gospel. Whenever and wherever God is at work, there are not only genuine responses but also counterfeit ones. Simon "believed" and "was baptized," Luke has reported (v.13). Evidently Simon was included among those on whom Peter and John laid their hands (v.17). But the NT frequently reports incidents and events from a phenomenal perspective without always giving the divine or heavenly perspective. For this reason the verb "believe" (*pisteuō*, GK *4409*) is used in the NT to cover a wide range of responses to God and to Christ (e.g., Jn 2:23; Jas 2:19). Neither baptism nor the laying on of hands conveys any status or power of itself, though Simon with his shallow spiritual perception thought they could.

20–24 Simon's offer to pay for the ability to confer the Holy Spirit through the laying on of hands evoked Peter's consignment of Simon and his money to hell. Simon regarded the bestowal of the Spirit as a specially effective bit of magic, and he had, it seems, no idea of the spiritual issues at stake. Peter's analysis of the situation, however, is that Simon's heart was "not right before God" (v.21)—it was still "full of bitterness and captive to sin" (v.23). So Peter urges him, "Repent of this wickedness and pray to the Lord. Perhaps he will forgive you for having such a thought in your heart" (v.22). But Simon, preoccupied with external consequences and physical effects, asks only, and rather lamely, "Pray to the Lord for me so that nothing you have said may happen to me" (v.24).

We would like to know more from this narrative. Did Simon later become the heretic Simon Magus of ecclesiastical legend? Or did he repent and genuinely respond to God, thereby becoming a true Christian? How did the Samaritan Christians respond to Simon's perverse request and to his possible later heretical activity? Beyond what Luke tells us, we can only speculate. Instead of such speculations, it is better to allow the sobering truth of what Luke does tell us to penetrate into our consciousness, namely, that it is all too often possible to make a counterfeit response to the presence and activity of God's Spirit.

25 Luke closes his account of the evangelization of Samaria with a transitional sentence that uses the same connective he began with: *men oun* (NIV, "when"; NASB, "so"). Here he tells us that on the apostles' return journey to Jerusalem further evangelization of Samaria took place. The "they" of the third person pronominal suffix in the verb *hypestrephon* ("they returned," GK *5715*) refers primarily to Peter and John, though it may also include Philip for part of the journey as he and the two Jerusalem apostles evangelized together in the southern regions of Samaria.

NOTES

4 On the use of μὲν οὖν (*men oun*, "so," "then") in Acts, see comments at 1:6.

Several Western texts (e.g., E and Augustine) add τοῦ θεοῦ (*tou theou*, "of God") after τὸν λόγον (*ton logon*, "the word"). Some Latin translations of the Western text (e.g., certain recensions of the Old Latin and Vulgate) add at the end of the verse *circa ciuitates et castella Iudee* ("all around the cities and regions of Judea"). Both additions are unnecessary interpolations.

5 For other references in Acts that speak of "going down" from Jerusalem, see the verbs κατέρχομαι (*katerchomai*, GK *2982*) in 9:32; 11:27; 15:1, 30; 21:10 and καταβαίνω (*katabainō*, GK *2849*) in 7:15; 8:26; 18:22; 24:1, 22; 25:6–7. On "going up" to Jerusalem, see ἀναβαίνω (*anabainō*, GK *326*) in 11:2; 21:12, 15; 24:11; 25:1, 9.

7 This verse has a syntactical anacoluthon, i.e., an inconsistency or incoherence, which is attested in all the most reliable MSS (𝔓⁷⁴ ℵ A B C), particularly in its use of πολλοί (*polloi*, "many") as the subject of the sentence. Codex Bezae (D) attempted to correct this by reading πολλοῖς (*pollois*, "to the many"), and codices H and P, the Coptic Boharic version, and Chrysostom read πολλῶν (*pollōn*, "of the many"). Some scholars have argued that the anacoluthon represents a conjectural Aramaic original, where such a suspended construction is not an unusual phenomenon. Probably, however, we should view what we have here as "'one of those tricks of mental "telescoping" to which all writers are liable,' and that, as such, 'it is one of several indications in the text that it was never finally revised'" (Metzger, 313, quoting K. Lake and alluding to H. Cadbury).

9–11 While Simon of Acts 8 is likely the same as "Simon Magus," who is referred to by the church fathers, he need not be thought of as a full-blown Gnostic. Much of Simon's Gnosticism was probably attributed to him by later adherents (cf. R. McL. Wilson, *Gnosis and the New Testament* [Philadelphia: Fortress, 1968], 49, 141).

10 The present passive participle καλουμένη (*kaloumenē*, "the one called"; NIV, "known as"; NASB, "what is called") is syntactically awkward but textually well supported (𝔓⁷⁴ ℵ A B C D E etc.). It is omitted by later Byzantine texts and replaced by λεγομένη (*legomenē*, "the so-called") in several minuscules.

12 On the use of ἡ βασιλεία τοῦ θεοῦ (*hē basileia tou theou*, "the kingdom of God") in Acts, see comments at 1:3.

15 On the use of καταβαίνω (*katabainō*) in Acts in contexts of "going down" from Jerusalem, see note above at v.5.

16 On the use of εἰς (*eis*, "into") for ἐν (*en*, "in") in the expression "baptized in [or into] the name of the Lord Jesus," see comments and note at 2:38. The prepositions were frequently used synonymously (cf. 7:4, 12), and probably should be taken in that way here and at 19:5.

17 For other instances in Acts of the practice of laying hands on someone, see 6:6; 9:17; 13:3; 19:6.

18 Most textual witnesses, both early and late (e.g., 𝔓⁴⁵ 𝔓⁷⁴ A C D E etc.), read τὸ πνεῦμα τὸ ἅγιον (*to pneuma to hagion*, "the Holy Spirit"). Only Sinaiticus (ℵ) and Vaticanus (B), as well as the Coptic Sahidic version and the *Apostolic Constitutions*, omit τὸ ἅγιον (*to hagion*, "holy"). The shorter version, however, is preferable (so NIV, NASB), since "the addition of τὸ ἅγιον was as natural for Christian scribes to make as its deletion would be inexplicable" (Metzger, 314).

19 Codex Bezae (D) adds παρακαλῶν καί (*parakalōn kai*, "answering and") before λέγων (*legōn*, "saying"), which is a combination of verbs often found elsewhere in the NT and probably inserted here to parallel v.24, but is unnecessary.

24 Codex Bezae (D) adds at the end of the sentence ὅς πολλὰ κλαίων οὐ διελίμπανεν (*hos polla klaiōn ou dielimpanen*, "who did not stop weeping profusely"), evidently attempting to suggest Simon's repentance (though in the Clementine *Homilies* 20:21 and *Recognitions* 10:63 his tears are portrayed as tears of rage and disappointment). The verb διαλιμπάνω (*dialimpanō*, "stop," GK *1366*) appears again in Codex Bezae at Acts 17:13 but nowhere else in the NT.

2. An Ethiopian Eunuch Converted (8:26–40)

OVERVIEW

This account of Philip's ministry to a high-ranking Ethiopian government official represents a further step in the advance of the gospel from its strictly Jewish confines to a full-fledged Gentile mission. Though a Gentile, the official was probably a Jewish proselyte or near-proselyte (a "Proselyte of the Gate") and was therefore viewed by Luke as still within a Jewish religious milieu. He had been to Jerusalem to worship, was studying the prophecy of Isaiah, and was open to further instruction from a Jew. The "enthusiastic historiography" that many have detected in the narrative may well reflect Philip's enthusiasm in telling the story, which Luke may have captured either directly or from a written source. In any event, here was a notable instance of providential working that carried the development of the gospel proclamation even beyond Samaria.

²⁶Now an angel of the Lord said to Philip, "Go south to the road—the desert road—that goes down from Jerusalem to Gaza." ²⁷So he started out, and on his way he met an Ethiopian eunuch, an important official in charge of all the treasury of Candace, queen of the Ethiopians. This man had gone to Jerusalem to worship, ²⁸and on his way home was sitting in his chariot reading the book of Isaiah the prophet. ²⁹The Spirit told Philip, "Go to that chariot and stay near it."

³⁰Then Philip ran up to the chariot and heard the man reading Isaiah the prophet. "Do you understand what you are reading?" Philip asked.

³¹"How can I," he said, "unless someone explains it to me?" So he invited Philip to come up and sit with him.

³²The eunuch was reading this passage of Scripture:

"He was led like a sheep to the slaughter,
    and as a lamb before the shearer is silent,
    so he did not open his mouth.
³³In his humiliation he was deprived of justice.

> Who can speak of his descendants?
> For his life was taken from the earth."

³⁴The eunuch asked Philip, "Tell me, please, who is the prophet talking about, himself or someone else?" ³⁵Then Philip began with that very passage of Scripture and told him the good news about Jesus.

³⁶As they traveled along the road, they came to some water and the eunuch said, "Look, here is water. Why shouldn't I be baptized?" ³⁸And he gave orders to stop the chariot. Then both Philip and the eunuch went down into the water and Philip baptized him. ³⁹When they came up out of the water, the Spirit of the Lord suddenly took Philip away, and the eunuch did not see him again, but went on his way rejoicing. ⁴⁰Philip, however, appeared at Azotus and traveled about, preaching the gospel in all the towns until he reached Caesarea.

COMMENTARY

26 We are not told just where Philip was when he received his divine directive to "go south to the road . . . from Jerusalem to Gaza." Most have assumed he was at the Samaritan city referred to in v.5—whether Sebaste, Samaria, Gitta, or Sychar. Some have seen him at Jerusalem because of the *eis Hierosolyma—apo Ierousalēm* ("into Jerusalem—from Jerusalem") couplet in vv.25–26, while others think of him as already at Caesarea. It is also possible that Philip was in one of the Samaritan villages alluded to in v.25, if he is included in the pronominal suffix "they" of that verse. But Luke is not interested in the specifics of geography, and it is idle to speculate further. What our author is interested in is highlighting the fact that Philip's ministry to the Ethiopian eunuch was especially arranged by God and providentially worked out in all its details.

When Luke wants to stress the special presence and activity of God, he often uses the expression the "angel of the Lord" (*angelos kyriou*) for the more normal reference to "the spirit of the Lord" (*pneuma kyriou*), as he does in Luke 1:11; 2:9; Acts 8:26; 12:7, 23 (cf. also *angelos tou theou*, "angel of God," in 10:3,

and simply *angelos*, "angel," in 7:30, 35, 38; 10:7, 22; 11:13; 12:11; 27:23). Here he begins in just such a way and with such a purpose, telling us that "an angel of the Lord" began the action by giving instructions to Philip—also, of course, he sustained it throughout, but with the more usual "the Spirit" and "the Spirit of the Lord" being used in vv.29 and 39.

In the LXX the word *mesēmbria* (GK *3540*) usually means "midday" or "noon," and it is used that way in Acts 22:6. Here, however, as in Daniel 8:4, 9 (LXX), *mesēmbria* probably means "south," with *kata mesēmbrian* (lit., "according to the south") meaning "toward the south" or "southward." The clarifying phrase *hautē estin erēmos* ("this is desert") can refer grammatically either to "the road" (*tēn hodon*, as RSV, NEB, JB, NIV, NASB) or to the area of the city of Gaza itself (see NASB text note). Gaza was the southernmost of the five chief Philistine cities in southwestern Palestine and the last settlement before the desert that stretched on to Egypt. The fifty-mile journey from Jerusalem to Gaza trailed off at its southwestern terminus into patches of desert, and most commentators think that the expression "this is desert" has reference to that southernmost portion of the road.

Sometime around 100–96 BC, however, Gaza was destroyed by the Maccabean priest-king Alexander Jannaeus and literally laid waste (cf. Josephus, *Ant.* 13.358–64). A new city was built under Pompey's orders by Gabinius in 57 BC (ibid., 14.76, 88). Strabo and Diodorus of Sicily seem to refer to this new Gaza as located a bit to the south of the old site and to distinguish it from a "Desert Gaza" or "Old Gaza" (cf. Schürer, 2.1:71). So some commentators understand "this is desert" to be specifying the old city of Gaza ("Desert Gaza") rather than the new city.

27–28 It is difficult to determine from the text how Luke wanted his readers to understand the Ethiopian eunuch's relation to Judaism. Furthermore, it is uncertain how first-century Judaism would have viewed a eunuch coming to worship at Jerusalem. While Deuteronomy 23:1 explicitly stipulates that no emasculated male could be included within the Jewish religious community, Isaiah 56:3–5 speaks of eunuchs being accepted by the God of boundless loving-kindness. Likewise, it is not at all as clear as it might appear what was the Ethiopian official's physical condition, for the word "eunuch" (*eunouchos*, GK *2336*) frequently appears in the LXX and Greek vernacular writings "for high military and political officials; it does not have to imply emasculation" (*TDNT* 2.766). We are probably justified in taking "eunuch" here to be a governmental title in an Oriental kingdom. Rather than focusing on his physical condition, two facts are to be emphasized when considering the Ethiopian's relation to Judaism: (1) he had been on a religious pilgrimage to Jerusalem, and (2) he was returning with a copy of the prophecy of Isaiah in his possession, which would have been difficult for a non-Jew to get.

Admittedly, Luke leaves us in some doubt when he might well have used some such expression as *prosēlytos* ("proselyte," "Jewish convert," GK *4670*; cf. 6:5; 13:43), *sebomenos ton theon* ("God-fearer," "Proselyte of the Gate," "near-convert"; cf. 13:50; 16:14; 17:4, 17; 18:7), *phoboumenos ton theon* ("reverent," GK *5828*, which is used in 13:16, 26 as equivalent to *sebomenos ton theon*, though in 10:2, 22, 35 with no necessary relation to Judaism involved), or even *eusebēs* ("pious," GK *2356*, with no necessary relation to Judaism involved; cf. 10:2, 7). Nevertheless, judging by what Luke does tell us and by the placement of this vignette in his overall plan, we are probably to understand that this Ethiopian government official was a proselyte or near-proselyte to Judaism.

The ancient kingdom of Ethiopia lay between Aswan and Khartoum and corresponds to modern Nubia. It was ruled by a queen mother who had the dynastic title Candace and who ruled on behalf of her son the king, since the king was regarded as the child of the sun and so was too holy to be involved in the merely secular functions of the state (cf. Strabo, *Geogr.* 17.1.54; Pliny, *Nat.* 6.186; Cassius Dio, *Hist.* 54.5.4; Eusebius, *Hist. eccl.* 2.1.13). One of the ministers of the Ethiopian government, the minister of finance, having become either a full proselyte or a Proselyte of the Gate, had gone to Jerusalem to worship at one of the Jewish festivals and was now returning home, reading Isaiah on the way. It might even have been Isaiah 56:3–5 that first caught his attention and caused him to return to Isaiah again and again:

> Let no foreigner who has bound himself
>> to the LORD say,
>> "The LORD will surely exclude me
>> from his people."
> And let not any eunuch complain,
>> "I am only a dry tree."

For this is what the LORD says:

"To the eunuchs who keep my Sabbaths,

who choose what pleases me
and hold fast to my covenant—
to them I will give within my temple
and its walls
a memorial and a name
better than sons and daughters;
I will give them an everlasting name
that will not be cut off."

If he had begun reading here, he would doubtless have gone on to read what immediately follows (56:6–8):

"And foreigners who bind themselves
to the LORD
to serve him,
to love the name of the LORD,
and to worship him,
all who keep the Sabbath without desecrating it
and who hold fast to my covenant—
these I will bring to my holy mountain
and give them joy in my house of prayer.
Their burnt offerings and sacrifices
will be accepted on my altar;
for my house will be called
a house of prayer for all nations."
The Sovereign LORD declares—
he who gathers the exiles of Israel:
"I will gather still others to them
besides those already gathered."

But whatever got him into Isaiah's prophecy, the interpretation of the Servant passage of Isaiah 52:13–53:12 troubled him.

29–30 Having been directed to the desert road on the way to Gaza, Philip is again directed by the Spirit to the carriage in which the Ethiopian minister of finance is traveling. As Philip approaches, he hears the minister reading from Isaiah, for reading aloud to oneself was "the universal practice in the ancient world" (Cadbury, 18). So while running along beside the Ethiopian's carriage Philip asks, "Do you understand what you are reading?"

(*ginōskeis ha anaginōskeis*—which is in Greek a play on words).

31–34 The Ethiopian, being open to instruction from a Jew, invites Philip into his carriage to explain Isaiah 53:7–8 to him. His problem, it seems, concerns the suffering and humiliation references, and his question is, "Who is the prophet talking about, himself or someone else?" (v.34). Perhaps he had heard an official explanation of this passage at Jerusalem but still had questions about its meaning.

While in Second Temple Judaism the concept of "God's Servant" carried messianic connotations in certain contexts and among certain groups, there is no evidence that any pre-Christian Jew ever thought of the Messiah in terms of a "Suffering Servant." The Talmud speaks of suffering sent by God as having atoning efficacy (cf. W. D. Davies, *Paul and Rabbinic Judaism* [4th ed.; Philadelphia: Fortress, 1980], 262–65). And there are many indications that "humility and self-humiliation, or acceptance of humiliation from God's hand, were expected of a pious man and thought to be highly praiseworthy" (E. Schweizer, *Lordship and Discipleship* [London: SCM, 1960], 23; see the fuller discussion in 23–31). But there is no explicit evidence that this general attitude toward suffering was ever consciously carried over to ideas regarding the Messiah, God's Servant par excellence. Joseph Klausner's dictum still holds true: "In the whole Jewish Messianic literature of the Tannaitic period there is no trace of the 'suffering Messiah'" (*The Messianic Idea in Israel* [New York: Macmillan, 1955], 405).

The Targum on the earlier and later prophets, the so-called *Pseudo-Jonathan*, which stems from a Palestinian milieu, consistently applies all mention of suffering and humiliation in Isaiah 52:13–53:12 either to the nation Israel (at 52:14; 53:2, 4, 10) or to the wicked Gentile nations (at 53:3, 7–9, 11). Nor can it be said that the Dead Sea Scrolls have a suffering messianology. The *Thanksgiving Hymns* or *Hodayot*, it is true, bring us somewhat closer to such a concept than anything extant from the world of Judaism—chiefly in their association of suffering and the Servant of God with ideas about the coming Messiah(s): (1) that the psalmist (the Teacher of Righteousness himself?) was conscious of being God's servant (cf. 1QH 13.18–19; 14.25; 17.26); (2) that persecution and suffering were the lot of both the Teacher and the community in following God's will (cf. 1QH 5.15–16; 8.26–27, 35–36); and (3) that the group at times expressed itself in language drawn from the Servant Songs of Isaiah (cf. 1QH 4.5–6, which is an expanded paraphrase of Isa 42:6). But that these ideas were ever brought together at Qumran to form a Suffering Servant messianology is at best highly uncertain. It may be that rabbinic Judaism later purged a Suffering Servant messianology based on Isaiah's Servant Songs from its own traditions because of the use made of such a doctrine and these passages by Christians, as Joachim Jeremias has argued (cf. *TDNT* 5.695–700). More likely, however, the lack of clarity regarding such a connection of concepts at Qumran—from whence we might have expected greater precision on this point, had it existed in early Judaism—points to the conclusion that, while the individual elements for a suffering conception of the Messiah may have been in the process of being formed in certain quarters, a doctrine of a suffering Messiah was unheard of and considered unthinkable in first-century Jewish religious circles generally.

35 At a time when only what Christians call the OT was Scripture, what better book to use in proclaiming the nature of divine redemption than Isaiah—and what better passage could be found than Isaiah 52:13–53:12? Thus Philip began with the very passage the Ethiopian was reading and proclaimed to him "the good news about Jesus" by explaining from Isaiah 53:7–8 and its context a suffering messianology. Of the evangelists, Matthew and John apply Isaiah 53 to Jesus' ministry of healing (cf. Mt 8:17 on 53:4; Jn 12:38 on 53:1; see also Mt 12:18–21 on 42:1–4). Luke, however, alone among the evangelists portrays Jesus as quoting Isaiah 53 as being fulfilled in his passion (cf. Lk 22:37 on 53:12). In his two volumes, therefore, Luke sets up a parallel between Jesus' use of Isaiah 53 and Philip's preaching based on that same passage, and he implies in that parallel that the latter was dependent on the former (cf. also 1Pe 2:22–25 on 53:4–6, 9, 12). But Philip, we are told, only began his preaching about Jesus with Isaiah 53. Probably he went on to include other passages from that early Christian block of *testimonium* material that has been dubbed "Scriptures of the Servant of the Lord and the Righteous Sufferer," which also probably included Isaiah 42:1–44:5; 49:1–13; 50:4–11; and Psalms 22; 34; 69; 118 (cf. C. H. Dodd, *According to the Scriptures* [London: Nisbet, 1952], 61–108).

36–38 The eunuch responded to Philip by asking for baptism. As a Jewish proselyte or near-proselyte, the eunuch probably knew that water baptism was the expected external symbol for a Gentile's repentance and conversion to the religion of Israel. Therefore, it would have been quite natural for him to view baptism as the appropriate expression for his commitment to Jesus, whom he had come to accept as the fulfillment of Israel's hope and promised Messiah. Or perhaps Philip closed his exposition with an appeal similar to Peter's at Pentecost (cf. 2:38) and his own in Samaria (cf. 8:12). But however the subject of baptism arose, "both Philip and the eunuch went down into the water and Philip baptized him." Traditionally the Wadi el-Hesi, located northeast of Gaza, has been identified as the place of the eunuch's baptism. But Luke's interest is not geography but the fact that in baptism the Ethiopian minister of finance proclaims his commitment to Jesus. This is the climax Luke has been building up to.

39–40 The account of the Ethiopian's conversion ends as it began—with a stress on the special presence of God and his direct intervention. We are told that the Spirit of the Lord "suddenly took away" (*hērpasen*; NASB, "snatched away") Philip from the scene. The verb *harpazō* ("take" or "snatch away," GK 773) connotes both a forceful and sudden action by the Spirit and a lack of resistance from Philip.

With our Western interest in cause-and-effect relations and our modern-day understanding of historiography, we would like to know more about what took place between the eunuch and Philip and more about their subsequent lives. Irenaeus (*Haer.* 3.12), writing sometime during AD 182–188, says that the eunuch on his return became a missionary to the Ethiopians, though we do not know whether he only inferred that from this account in Acts or had independent knowledge about it. All Luke tells us about the eunuch is that his conversion was a significant episode in the advance of the gospel and that he "went on his way rejoicing."

Likewise, all Luke tells us about Philip is that his early ministries in Samaria and to the eunuch were important features in the development of the Christian mission from its strictly Jewish confines to its Gentile outreach. He refers to further evangelistic activity on the part of Philip in the maritime plain of Palestine and to a final ministry at Caesarea (v.40). Later he mentions Philip and his four prophetess daughters at Caesarea in connection with Paul's last visit to Jerusalem (cf. 21:8–9). Beyond these meager references, Luke tells us nothing, because his interest was in the advances of the gospel proclamation and not in what happened after that.

NOTES

28 The designation τὸ ἅρμα (*to harma*, GK 761) was commonly used of a war chariot, though here it refers more to a traveling chariot or carriage (see also v.38).

33 The better MS evidence (𝔓⁷⁴ ℵ A B) omits the possessive pronoun αὐτοῦ (*autou*, "his"), which is present in most other MSS. The LXX reading of Isaiah 53:8 also lacks the pronoun, though it is included in the MT. While such external testimony in support of the omission usually carries conviction as to its originality (since the Hebrew text, from which the LXX was translated, evidently included this third person singular possessive pronoun, and since the sense of the quotation in this verse demands it), most translations (so NIV, NASB) and commentators have also included it, though sometimes in brackets.

34 The earliest messianic use in the Talmud of the suffering element in an Isaian Servant passage is in *b. Sanh.* 98*b*, where the Hebrew *nāgûaʿ* ("stricken") led some rabbis to speak of the Messiah as "the leprous one" or "the sick one." The attribution, however, can be dated no earlier than AD 200.

37 The better MSS omit v.37. Codex Bezae (D) is lacking for 8:26–10:14, but E, a number of minor texts, and such church fathers as Irenaeus, Tertullian, Cyprian, Ambrose, Ambrosiaster, and Augustine add (with minor variations), "Philip said, 'If you believe with your whole heart, you may.' He answered and said, 'I believe that Jesus Christ is the Son of God.'" The Byzantine text (H L P and most minuscules) also omits this reading. But Erasmus included it in his critical editions because he judged that it had been "omitted by the carelessness of scribes," and so it became embedded in the TR and resultant KJV. There is, however, no reason why scribes would have omitted this verse if it had originally been in the text. Furthermore, (1) the construction τὸν Ἰησοῦν Χριστόν (*ton Iēsoun Christon*) and its use as a proper name breaks a Lukan pattern in the first half of Acts (see comments at 2:36); (2) the wording πιστεύω . . . Χριστόν (*pisteuō . . . Christon*, "I believe . . . the Christ") was a formula used by the early church in baptismal ceremonies; and (3) the verse adds nothing to the narrative except to make explicit what is already implied, i.e., that the eunuch confessed his faith in Jesus Christ before being baptized.

39 The Western text (though D is lacking here) reads, "The Holy Spirit fell upon the eunuch, and the angel of the Lord suddenly took Philip away," thereby setting up a parallel of expression with the Spirit's coming on believers at Pentecost and in Samaria, as well as picking up the expression "the angel of the Lord" from v.26.

Luke's gospel is aptly described as "the Gospel of Messianic Joy," with words of joy, rejoicing, and exultation occurring with notable frequency: χαίρω (*chairō*, "rejoice," "be glad," GK *5897*) twelve times in Luke (six times in Matthew, twice in Mark); χαρά (*chara*, "joy," GK *5915*) eight times in Luke (six times in Matthew, once in Mark); ἀγαλλίασις (*agalliasis*, "exultation," GK *21*) twice in Luke (not at all in Matthew or Mark); ἀγαλλιάω (*agalliaō*, "exult," "be glad," GK *22*) twice in Luke (once in Matthew, not at all in Mark); σκιρτάω (*skirtaō*, "leap," "spring about" as a sign of joy, GK *5015*) three times in Luke (not at all in Matthew or Mark). Here in Acts this emphasis is continued in recounting that the eunuch "went on his way rejoicing."

C. The Conversion of Saul of Tarsus (9:1–30)

OVERVIEW

There are three accounts of Paul's conversion in Acts: the first here in ch. 9 and two more in Paul's defenses in chs. 22 and 26. Source criticism has had a field day with these accounts, often attributing the repetitions to a plurality of sources and the differences to divergent perspectives among the sources. Haenchen, 327, however, has rightly pointed out that "Luke employs such repetitions only when he considers something to be extraordinarily important and wishes to impress it unforgettably on the reader. That is the case here."

The major charges against Paul were his willingness to carry the gospel directly to Gentiles and his refusal to be confined to a mission to Israel. His defense before the people of Jerusalem in ch. 22 ends with him quoting his divinely given commission to go to the Gentiles and the people's fervent objection to it (cf. 22:21–22). Paul's defense before Agrippa II in ch. 26 also ends on this same note and is followed by Festus's comment that he was mad (cf. 26:23–24).

Paul would have had no great problem with either Judaism or Rome had he contented himself with a mission to Jews, and Christianity would have been spared the head-on collision with both Judaism and Rome. But Luke's point in ch. 9—one he will make twice more in chs. 22 and 26—is that Christ himself brought about this change in the strategy of divine redemption. It was not a strategy Paul thought up or a program given to him by another. Rather, it was a compelling call that came directly from Christ himself. Nor can it be explained psychologically or as an evolution of ideas whose time was ripe. It came to him by revelation and he had no choice but to obey.

Luke, therefore, climaxes his portrayals of three pivotal figures in the advance of the gospel to the Gentile world with an account of the conversion of Saul of Tarsus that emphasizes the supernatural nature of the call and the miraculous circumstances of the conversion. With these emphases, though with inevitable variations in detail, Paul himself was in full agreement (cf. Gal 1:1–24).

1. The Christ-Encounter on the Damascus Road (9:1–9)

¹Meanwhile, Saul was still breathing out murderous threats against the Lord's disciples. He went to the high priest ²and asked him for letters to the synagogues in Damascus, so that if he found any there who belonged to the Way, whether men or women, he might take them as prisoners to Jerusalem. ³As he neared Damascus on his journey, suddenly a light from heaven flashed around him. ⁴He fell to the ground and heard a voice say to him, "Saul, Saul, why do you persecute me?"

⁵"Who are you, Lord?" Saul asked.

"I am Jesus, whom you are persecuting," he replied. ⁶"Now get up and go into the city, and you will be told what you must do."

⁷The men traveling with Saul stood there speechless; they heard the sound but did not see anyone. ⁸Saul got up from the ground, but when he opened his eyes he could see nothing. So they led him by the hand into Damascus. ⁹For three days he was blind, and did not eat or drink anything.

COMMENTARY

1–2 The account of Saul's conversion opens with the picture of him "still breathing out murderous threats against the Lord's disciples." The adverb *eti* ("still") ties the narrative into what has gone before (cf. 8:3). It also suggests that, even after the death of Stephen and the expulsion of the Hellenistic Jewish Christians from Jerusalem, Saul saw that it was necessary to continue the persecution of Hellenistic Jewish believers in Jesus in localities outside the Sanhedrin's immediate jurisdiction. The expression *apeilēs kai phonou*—which the NIV, together with a number of other translations (e.g., NEB), treats as a hendiadys (i.e., one idea expressed through the use of two independent words connected by the conjunction "and") and translates as "murderous threats" (though the NASB translates it as "threats and murder")—may have connoted in Luke's source material the dual ideas of a legal warning (*apeilē*, GK 581) and a judicial punishment (*phonos*, GK 5840), as was inherent in Jewish jurisprudence (cf. Introduction, p. 682; Overview at 4:1–31; see also Dupont, 44 n. 43), though it seems that Luke himself took it to be simply a hendiadys and so made no effort to spell out the exact nuances of Jewish legal procedure.

Past generations of commentators, particularly those of the English-speaking world, often read into such passages as Romans 7:14–25; Galatians 1:13–

14; Philippians 3:4–6; and the portrayals of Acts 9, 22, and 26 a mental and spiritual struggle on the part of Saul that was—either consciously or unconsciously—fighting fervently against the logic of the early Christians' preaching, the dynamic quality of their lives, and/or their fortitude under oppression. Therefore Saul's "breathing out murderous threats" was taken as his attempt to slay externally the dragons of doubt that he could not silence within his own heart and to repress "all humaner tendencies in the interests of his legal absolutism" (C. H. Dodd, *The Mind of Paul: Change and Development* [Manchester: John Rylands Library, 1934], 36; cf. Dodd's companion lecture of the same year titled *The Mind of Paul: A Psychological Approach*, esp. 12–13). But the day of the psychological interpretation of Paul's conversion experience appears to be over, and deservedly so. Indeed, Luke connects historically the martyrdom of Stephen, the persecution of the Hellenistic Jewish Christians, and the conversion of Saul. But the argument for a logical connection among these events is far from certain.

It is, of course, impossible today to speak with certainty about what was going on in Saul's subconscious mind, for psychoanalysis nearly two millennia later is hardly a fruitful exercise. His own references as a Christian to this earlier time in his life, however, do not require us to view him as struggling with uncertainty, doubt, or guilt before becoming a Christian. Rather, they suggest that, humanly speaking, he was immune to the Christian proclamation and immensely satisfied with his own ancestral faith (cf. my *Paul, Apostle of Liberty*, 65–105). While he looked forward to the full realization of the hope of Israel, Paul seems from his reminiscences of those earlier days to have been thoroughly satisfied with the revelation of God given through Moses and to have counted it his chief delight to worship God through those revealed forms. Nor need we suppose that the logic

of the early Christian preachers greatly affected the Pharisee Saul. His later references to "the offense of the cross" in 1 Corinthians 1:23 and Galatians 5:11 (cf. also Justin Martyr, *Dial.* 32, 89) suggest that for him the cross was the great stumbling block to any acknowledgment of Jesus of Nazareth as Israel's Messiah—a stumbling block that no amount of logic or verbal gymnastics could remove.

It is probable that Saul took up his brutal task of persecution with full knowledge of the earnestness of his opponents, the stamina of the martyrs, and the agony he would necessarily cause. Fanaticism was not so foreign to Palestine in his day as to leave him unaware of such factors. And it is quite possible he was prepared for the emotional strain involved in persecuting those whom he believed to be dangerous schismatics within Israel.

More important, however, in days when the rabbis viewed the keeping of the Mosaic law as the vitally important prerequisite for the coming of the messianic age (cf. *b. Sanh.* 97b–98a; *b. B. Bat.* 10a; *b. Yoma* 86b), Paul could validate his actions against the Christians by reference to such godly precedents as (1) Moses' slaying of the immoral Israelites at Shittim (cf. Nu 25:1–5); (2) Phinehas's killing of the Israelite man and Midianite woman (cf. Nu 25:6–15); and (3) the actions of Mattathias and the Hasidim in rooting out apostasy among the people (cf. 1 Macc 2:23–28, 42–48). Perhaps even the divine commendation of Phinehas's action in Numbers 25:11–13 rang in his ears:

Phinehas son of Eleazar, the son of Aaron, the priest, has turned my anger away from the Israelites; for he was as zealous as I am for my honor among them, so that in my zeal I did not put an end to them. Therefore tell him I am making my covenant of peace with him. He and his descendants will have a covenant of a lasting priesthood, because he was zealous for the honor of his God and made atonement for the Israelites.

And 2 Maccabees 6:13 counsels that "it is a mark of great kindness when the impious are not let alone for a long time, but punished at once."

The Dead Sea Scrolls define a righteous man as one who "bears unremitting hatred toward all men of ill repute" (1QS 9.22). Furthermore, they speak of unswerving allegiance to God and his laws as alone providing a firm foundation for the Holy Spirit, truth, and the arrival of Israel's hope (cf. 1QS 9.3–4, 20–21), and they call for volunteers who are blameless in spirit and body to root out apostasy in the final eschatological days (cf. 1QM 7.5; 10.2–5). The Qumran psalmist (1QH 14.13–15), in fact, directly associates commitment to God and his laws with zeal against apostates and perverters of the law: "The nearer I draw to you, the more am I filled with zeal against all who do wickedness and against all men of deceit. For they who draw near to you cannot see your commandments defiled, and they who have knowledge of you can brook no change of your words, seeing that you are the essence of right, and all your elect are the proof of your truth."

With such precedents and parallels, coupled with the rising tide of messianic expectation within Israel, Saul may well have felt justified in mounting a further persecution against the early Christians. He probably felt that, in light of Israel's rising messianic hopes, the nation must be united and faithful in its obedience to the law and kept from schism or going astray. And in his task, he doubtless expected to receive God's commendation.

According to 1 Maccabees, the three great Hasmonean rulers—Judah, Jonathan, and Simeon—established friendly relations with Rome (cf. 1 Macc 8:17–32; 12:1–4; 14:16–24), with a reciprocal extradition clause included in Rome's reply to Simeon (cf. 1 Macc 15:15–24). And the decrees of the Roman senate recorded by Josephus (*Ant.* 13.259–66; 14.145–48) seem to indicate that the treaties of friendship between Rome and the Jew-

ish people were renewed in the time of John Hyrcanus. While the Sadducean high priests of Jerusalem no longer exercised the civil authority of their predecessors, they were recognized by Rome as the titular rulers of their people in most internal matters—including, it seems, the right of extradition in strictly religious situations. Saul, therefore, seeking the return and punishment of the Hellenistic Jewish Christians, "went to the high priest and asked him for letters to the synagogues in Damascus, so that if he found any there who belonged to the Way, whether men or women, he might take them as prisoners to Jerusalem" (cf. 22:5; 26:12).

Damascus was a large and thriving commercial center at the foot of the Anti-Lebanon mountain range. Since 64 BC it had been part of the Roman province of Syria and was granted certain civic rights by Rome as one of the ten cities of eastern Syria and the Transjordan called the Decapolis (cf. Mk 5:20; 7:31). It had a large Nabatean Arab population and may have been ruled by the Nabatean king Aretas IV (9 BC–AD 40) at some time during this period (cf. 2Co 11:32). It also had a large Jewish population, 10,500 of whom Josephus reports were killed by the people of Damascus at the outbreak of Jewish-Roman hostilities in AD 66 (cf. *J.W.* 2.561, though in *J.W.* 7.368 the number given is 18,000). It was to this city that Saul went with the authority of the Jewish Sanhedrin, seeking to return to Jerusalem those Christians who had fled the city in order to contain the spread of what he considered to be a pernicious and deadly contagion within Israel.

While I have spoken repeatedly of the early believers in Jesus as Christians, the name "Christian" (*Christianos*) was first coined at Antioch of Syria (cf. 11:26) and appears only three times in the entire NT (11:26; 26:28; 1Pe 4:16). It was probably first given by others in derisive mocking of the early believers as "Those Who Belong to Christ" or "Christ's People." But before being so identified at Syrian

Antioch, and before accepting what was originally meant as a taunting nickname, those who accepted Jesus as Messiah and claimed him as their Lord called themselves those of "the Way" (*hē hodos*, GK *3847*, cf. 19:9, 23; 22:4; 24:14, 22; see also 16:17; 18:25–26), while their opponents spoke of them as members of "the sect of the Nazarenes" (*hē hairesis tōn Nazōraiōn*; cf. 24:5, 14; 28:22). The origin of the absolute use of "the Way" for the early believers is uncertain, though it surely had something to do with their consciousness of walking in the true path of God's salvation and moving forward to accomplish his purposes. In the vignette of 9:1–30, it is synonymous with such self-designations as "the Lord's disciples" (vv. 1, 10, 19), "saints" (v.13), "all who call on [Jesus'] name" (v.14), and "brothers" (vv. 17, 30).

3 As he approached Damascus, Saul saw "a light from heaven" (v.3) and heard a voice (v.4). In 22:6 it is "a bright light from heaven," and in 26:13 it is "a light from heaven, brighter than the sun." Here in v.3 and in 22:6 the light is spoken of as shining around Saul alone, whereas in 26:13 it includes his companions as well. But these are matters that can be paralleled in the portrayals of Jesus in the Synoptic Gospels and are of small consequence in any repeated telling of an event. As Haenchen, 321 n.3, rightly notes, "It is open to a narrator [whether here Paul himself or Luke] to counter the lulling effect of repetition by reinforcing the emphasis of salient features."

4 Likewise, in v.4 it is reported that Saul heard the voice (*ēkousen phōnēn*, GK *201*, *5889*) and in v.7 that his companions also heard the voice (*akouontes men tēs phōnēs*), whereas in 22:9 it is said that his companions did not hear the voice (*tēn phōnēn ouk ēkousan*) and in 26:14 that only Saul heard the voice speaking to him (*ēkousa phōnēn legousan pros me*). Some commentators have seen here a flagrant contradiction in Luke's source materials, which he unwittingly incorporated into his finished product. But since the noun *phōnē* means both "sound" in

the sense of any noise, tone, or voice and "articulated speech" in the sense of language, undoubtedly it was understood by all concerned (as the respective contexts suggest) to mean that while the whole group traveling to Damascus heard the sound from heaven, only Saul understood the spoken words.

As Saul fell to the ground, the voice from heaven intoned his name in solemn repetition: "Saul, Saul." It was common in antiquity for a person in a formal setting to be addressed by the repetition of his name (cf., e.g., Ge 22:11; 46:2; Ex 3:4; 1Sa 3:10; Lk 10:41; 22:31; 2 Esd 14:1; *2 Bar.* 22:2). The fact that the transliterated form *Saoul* (from Heb. and Aram. *šāʾul*) was used in addressing Saul, rather than the Greek vocative *Saule*, suggests that the words came to him in either Hebrew or Aramaic (cf. 26:14). Of more significance is the fact that Saul understood the voice to be a message from God himself, for in the rabbinic thought of the day to hear a voice from heaven (a *bat qôl*, lit., "a daughter of the [divine] voice") never meant to hear a lower deity in the pantheon of gods speaking, as in Greek religious speculations, or some psychological disturbance, as many would presume today. Rather, it always connoted a rebuke or a word of instruction from the one true God himself. So when the voice went on to ask, "Why do you persecute me?" Saul was undoubtedly thoroughly confused. As he saw it, he had not been persecuting God; he was defending God and his laws!

5 Some have translated Saul's reply as, "Who are you, sir?" since the Greek word *kyrios* was used in the ancient world not only as an ascription of worshipful acclaim but also as a form of polite address. Furthermore, the context suggests that Saul did not know to whom he was speaking. But he did know that he had been struck down by a light from heaven and addressed by a voice from heaven, both of which would have signaled the divine presence. So his use of "Lord," even when first uttered, was probably meant in a worshipful manner, though he was thoroughly confused as to how he could be rebuked by God for doing the will and service of God. Unable to articulate his confusion, yet realizing the need for some response in the presence of the divine, he cries out in stumbling fashion, "Who are you, Lord?"

In what must have been for Saul almost total disbelief, he hears the reply, "I am Jesus, whom you are persecuting." Then in a manner that throws Saul entirely on the guidance of Jesus apart from anything he could do or work out for himself, the voice continues: "Now get up and go into the city, and you will be told what you must do."

Such a confrontation and such a rebuke must have been exceedingly traumatic for Saul. Time would be needed to heal his emotions and to work out the implications of this experience. Both Saul's later Christian letters and Luke's second volume reveal something of the process of that development as it went on throughout the rest of his life. But in this supreme revelational encounter, Saul received a new perspective on divine redemption, a new agenda for his life, and the embryonic elements of his new Christian theology.

Once Saul had been encountered by Jesus on the Damascus road, a number of realizations must have begun to press in on his consciousness—each of which would receive further explication in his life and thought as time went on, though here in their elemental forms they could not be evaded. These realizations may be enumerated as follows:

1. Saul began to understand that despite his zeal and sense of doing God's will, his previous life and activities in Judaism lay under divine rebuke. A voice from heaven had corrected him, and there was nothing more to be said.

2. He could not escape the fact that Jesus of Nazareth, whose followers he had been persecuting, was alive, exalted, and in some manner to be associated with God the Father, whom Israel worshiped. Therefore, he had to revise his whole estimate of the life, teaching, and death of the Nazarene, because God had vindicated him. Thus he came to agree with the Christians that Jesus' death on the cross, rather than discrediting him as an impostor, fulfilled prophecy and was really God's provision for humanity's sin, and that Jesus' resurrection confirmed him as being the nation's Messiah and humanity's Lord.

3. He came to appreciate that if Jesus is Israel's Messiah and the fulfillment of the nation's ancient hope, then traditional eschatology, rather than merely dwelling on the future, must be restructured to emphasize the realized and inaugurated factors associated with Jesus of Nazareth and to focus on the personal and transcendent dimensions instead of just the legal and historical.

4. In the question "Why do you persecute me?" Saul came to realize something of the organic and indissoluble unity that exists between Christ and those who belong to Christ. For though he believed he was only persecuting the followers of Jesus, the heavenly interpretation was that he was persecuting the risen Christ himself.

5. He came to understand that he had a mission to carry out for Christ. Its details, to be sure, were first given in general terms by Ananias (vv. 15–16), and only later were they set forth more fully by various providential circumstances and visions. But though it was not until later that Saul understood his mission as involving the equality of both Jews and Gentiles before God and the legitimacy of a direct approach to the Gentile world, it was his constant habit to relate his Gentile commission firmly and directly to Christ's encounter of him on the Damascus road.

7–9 The effect on Saul's traveling companions of this encounter with Jesus was dramatic. Acts 26 says that they fell to the ground at the flash of heavenly light. Here we are told that after getting up they "stood there speechless" (v.7). Evidently they were able to regain a semblance of composure and so lead Saul into Damascus (v.8). For Saul, for whom the spoken message was even more traumatic than the light and the sound, the experience was overpowering. Physically, as his system reacted to the emotional shock, he became blind for three days, during which time he neither ate nor drank as he waited in Damascus for further instructions (v.9).

NOTES

2 Some have noted that in 9:1–2, 14 and 26:10, 12 it is the high priest (or "chief priests") from whom Saul received letters of delegated authority, whereas in 22:5 he is depicted as saying that he obtained such letters from the whole council (i.e., "the high priest and all the Council"). The difference, however, is merely verbal.

3–4 Though the apparition of 2 Maccabees 3 of the great horse, its frightful rider, and the two accompanying youths who attacked Heliodorus has been compared to Luke's portrayal here, the resemblances are superficial.

4–5 The Western text adds σκληρόν σοι πρὸς κέντρα λακτίζειν (*sklēron soi pros kentra laktizein*, "it is hard for you to kick against the goads") at one of two places: either after διώκεις (*diōkeis*, "persecute," GK *1503*) in v.4 (so E, some Syriac and Latin recensions, Jerome, and Augustine) or after the same verb διώκεις (*diōkeis*, "persecute") in v.5 (so other Latin recensions, Lucifer, and Ambrose). The most reliable MSS (𝔓[74] ℵ A B C etc.) do not include the clause, though through Erasmus it found its way into the TR and therefore the KJV. Most scholars consider the clause to be an interpolation taken from 26:14.

6 The TR deletes the adversative ἀλλά (*alla*) and begins the verse: τρέμων τε καὶ θαμβῶν εἶπε, Κύριε, τί με θέλεις ποιῆσαι; καὶ ὁ κύριος πρὸς αὐτόν (*tremōn te kai thambōn eipe, Kurie, ti me theleis poiēsai; kai ho kurios pros auton*, "Trembling and astonished he said, 'Lord, what will you have me to do?' And the Lord said to him"). No extant Greek MS has these words at this place. They have evidently been taken from 26:14 and 22:10. They were, however, included here in the Latin Vulgate (also some Syriac and Coptic versions) and inserted by Erasmus from the Vulgate into his Greek New Testament of 1516, and so found their place in the KJV.

2. Ananias's Ministry to Saul (9:10–19a)

¹⁰In Damascus there was a disciple named Ananias. The Lord called to him in a vision, "Ananias!"

"Yes, Lord," he answered.

¹¹The Lord told him, "Go to the house of Judas on Straight Street and ask for a man from Tarsus named Saul, for he is praying. ¹²In a vision he has seen a man named Ananias come and place his hands on him to restore his sight."

> ¹³"Lord," Ananias answered, "I have heard many reports about this man and all the harm he has done to your saints in Jerusalem. ¹⁴And he has come here with authority from the chief priests to arrest all who call on your name."
>
> ¹⁵But the Lord said to Ananias, "Go! This man is my chosen instrument to carry my name before the Gentiles and their kings and before the people of Israel. ¹⁶I will show him how much he must suffer for my name."
>
> ¹⁷Then Ananias went to the house and entered it. Placing his hands on Saul, he said, "Brother Saul, the Lord—Jesus, who appeared to you on the road as you were coming here—has sent me so that you may see again and be filled with the Holy Spirit." ¹⁸Immediately, something like scales fell from Saul's eyes, and he could see again. He got up and was baptized, ^{19a}and after taking some food, he regained his strength.

COMMENTARY

10 Ananias was a Jew of Damascus and a believer in Jesus. Here he is called a "disciple" and portrayed as one who immediately recognized the Lord Christ, who speaks to him in a vision; in 22:12 he is called "a devout observer of the law and highly respected by all the Jews." From Ananias's statement that he had heard reports about Saul's persecutions in Jerusalem (v.13), it may be inferred that he was not one of the Hellenistic Jewish Christians who had formerly lived in Jerusalem but that he lived in Damascus. We are not told anything about how he became a believer in Jesus or about the Jewish Christian community of Damascus.

11 The Lord Jesus directed Ananias, "Go to the house of Judas on Straight Street and ask for a man from Tarsus named Saul, for he is praying." The street called Straight was an east-west street, which is still one of the main thoroughfares of Damascus, the *Derb el-Mustaqim*. It had colonnaded halls on both sides and imposing gates at each end (cf. *Beginnings of Christianity* [ed. Foakes-Jackson and Lake], 4:102). Presumably, it was as well known in antiquity as Regent Street in London or Fifth Avenue in New York today. The directions included not only

the name of the street but also the house where Saul could be found.

More significantly, Jesus' words to Ananias identified Saul as one who was praying. For Luke, his hero Paul was a man of prayer (cf. 16:25; 20:36; 22:17), as was also Jesus in his earthly ministry (cf. Lk 3:21; 6:12; 9:18, 28; 11:1; 22:41). Probably in the religious experience of Paul, as David M. Stanley (*Boasting in the Lord: The Phenomenon of Prayer in Saint Paul* [New York: Paulist, 1973], 42) suggests, "the most important link between his Christian life and Pharisaism was that devotion to prayer for which the Pharisees were rightly celebrated and held in esteem among their people" (cf. my "Prayer in the Pauline Letters," in *Into God's Presence: Prayer in the New Testament*, ed. R. N. Longenecker [Grand Rapids: Eerdmans, 2001], 203–27). Stanley goes on to say, "If one may conjecture about Paul's preparation for the overpowering event which changed his life, surely the chief element was prayer" (p. 42).

13–16 It takes no great imaginative power to appreciate the reasons for Ananias's hesitation in going to meet Saul. It is, in fact, not at all difficult to sympathize with Ananias. Even the prophets of old had doubts about the appropriateness of what they understood to be God's will, particularly when it seemed so contrary to what might be expected. But Luke lays emphasis on Ananias's hesitancy not just to humanize his narrative, but also to impress on his readers the magnitude of the change in Saul's life and to highlight the heaven-ordained nature of his later Christian mission: (1) that instead of a persecutor, he is Christ's "chosen instrument" (v.15); (2) that instead of a concern for Israel alone, his mission is "to carry [Jesus'] name before the Gentiles and their kings and before the people of Israel" (v.15); and (3) that instead of prominence and glory, it is necessary for him to "suffer for [Jesus'] name" (v.16). In highlighting these features of being a "chosen instrument" sent to "the Gentiles" to "suffer for [Jesus'] name," Luke has, in effect, given a theological précis of all that he will portray historically in chs. 13–28—a précis that also summarizes the self-consciousness of Paul himself as reflected in his own letters.

17–19a Ananias was obedient to his Lord and followed the directions given in the vision. He was undoubtedly comforted by knowing that Saul, too, had been given a vision about his coming (v.12), though still he must have proceeded with some trepidation. Going to the house of Judas on Straight Street, he went in and laid his hands on Saul. Ananias greeted him, evidently in Hebrew or Aramaic (note the transliterated *Saoul*; see comments at v.4), with the fraternal greeting "brother" (*adelphe*, GK 81)—believing, it seems, (1) that whoever Jesus had accepted was his brother, whatever he might think about such a person himself, and (2) that all further relationships between them must be built on that basis. He spoke about Jesus, who had appeared to Saul on the Damascus road, and about the restoration of Saul's sight and his being filled with the Holy Spirit. And "immediately," Luke tells us, "something like scales fell from Saul's eyes, and he could see again. He got up and was baptized, and after taking some food, he regained his strength" (vv.18–19).

NOTES

12 The inclusion and positioning of the phrase ἐν ὁράματι (*en horamati*, "in a vision," GK 3969) varies in the MSS, thus suggesting that it is an explanatory gloss introduced to complete the sense of εἶδεν (*eiden*, "he has seen"). Inattentive scribes, however, may have either (1) thought this "vision" of v.12 was the same as the "vision" referred to in v.10 and so left out what they considered to be a redundancy, or (2) confused the word ὁράματι (*horamati*, "in a vision") with the following word ὀνόματι (*onomati*, "by the name of," GK 3950), and so omitted it.

This entire verse is omitted in one recension of the Old Latin (it[h]). But there is no parallel passage that might have influenced its inclusion, and so there is no apparent reason why it should have been inserted. Probably, as Metzger, 319, says, its omission was "due to an accident in transcription, occasioned perhaps by the presence of the name Ananias early in both ver. 12 and ver. 13."

17 On Ananias's laying of his hands on Paul (cf. v.12), see comments at 6:6 and the other instances in Acts at 8:17; 13:3; 19:6.

Codices H L P Ψ (all eighth- to ninth-century uncials), the Coptic Sahidic version, and many minuscules omit the name Ἰησοῦς (*Iēsous*, "Jesus"), perhaps because it was already used in v.5. But the more reliable textual witness, both early and diverse (𝔓[45] 𝔓[74] ℵ A B C E, the Latin Vulgate, and most minuscules), include it.

On being baptized and filled with the Holy Spirit, see comments on 2:38.

18 The term λεπίς (*lepis*, "scale," "scaly substance," GK *3318*) is used in Tobit 3:17 and 11:13 for that which covered Tobit's eyes and blinded him.

Corrected Codex C, E L, many minuscules, the Syriac Peshitta and Coptic Sahidic versions, and Chrysostom add a second "immediately" (παραχρῆμα, *parachrēma*, GK *4202*) to the account of the restoration of Paul's eyesight, which serves to supplement the "immediately" (εὐθέως, *eutheōs*, GK *2311*) at the beginning of the verse. This second "immediately" is not included in the better MSS but was evidently added to heighten and intensify the account.

On baptism and the gospel, see comments at 2:38.

19a Chester Beatty 𝔓⁴⁵ includes ἡμέρας ἱκανάς (*hēmeras hikanas*, "after many days"), which is reflected also in an Old Latin recension. But this inclusion is not found elsewhere in the textual tradition. It was probably introduced under the influence of the similar phrase in v.23.

REFLECTIONS

There is much more we would like to know about the persons and details of this event. What was the Jewish Christian community of Damascus like? What was Ananias's background, and what happened to him after this incident? When did Saul receive his vision regarding Ananias's coming, and how? What was the scaly substance that fell from Saul's eyes? Where and how was Saul baptized? Were there any immediate evidences in Saul's life of his being filled with the Holy Spirit such as appeared among believers at Jerusalem and in Samaria? On some of these matters (e.g., water baptism and the baptism of the Spirit), Luke probably means us to understand his presentation here in terms already given in his earlier portrayals and so felt no need to repeat himself. On other matters, though, he seems to have had no interest, and so we should not seek to distill anything more from the text.

What Luke does tell us, however, is significant. In the advance of the gospel to the Gentiles, the main missionary in that advance was converted to Jesus Christ and given his commission in a manner that fully expressed the heaven-ordained nature of his conversion and call. Furthermore, the way in which he was converted and commissioned did not make him dependent on the Jerusalem church, yet it brought him into essential unity with all those who are Christ's and who call themselves people of "the Way."

3. Saul's Conversion Evidenced in Damascus (9:19b–25)

OVERVIEW

It may seem strange for Luke to include in his account of Saul's conversion a rather sketchy report of his preaching Christ in Damascus and his rather unceremonious exit from the city that it brought about. The material is so undeveloped that it raises more historical problems than it answers. Therefore, many source critics have viewed it as extraneous to the substance of vv. 1–19a, and many commentators have treated it apart from the story of Saul's conversion.

On closer inspection, however, we can discern a distinctly Lukan rationale for the inclusion of this material, namely, to emphasize the unprecedented nature of Saul's about-face and the genuineness of his conversion. In clarifying his purpose, Luke (1) presents Saul as proclaiming Jesus as both "the Son of God" and "the Messiah," (2) depicts his hearers as being so astonished that they had to ask themselves whether this was indeed the same man who had been persecuting Christians, and (3) highlights the fact that the persecution he once headed was now directed against him.

---

^{19b}Saul spent several days with the disciples in Damascus. ²⁰At once he began to preach in the synagogues that Jesus is the Son of God. ²¹All those who heard him were astonished and asked, "Isn't he the man who raised havoc in Jerusalem among those who call on this name? And hasn't he come here to take them as prisoners to the chief priests?" ²²Yet Saul grew more and more powerful and baffled the Jews living in Damascus by proving that Jesus is the Christ.

²³After many days had gone by, the Jews conspired to kill him, ²⁴but Saul learned of their plan. Day and night they kept close watch on the city gates in order to kill him. ²⁵But his followers took him by night and lowered him in a basket through an opening in the wall.

COMMENTARY

19b–22 Luke's references to Saul after his conversion—his being "several days with the disciples in Damascus" (*meta tōn en Damaskō mathētōn hēmeras tinas*) and his preaching "at once" (*eutheōs*) in the synagogues of the city—are, when compared with Paul's own account of his conversion, so general and ambiguous as to set up all sorts of historical problems for commentators today. No one familiar with Paul's delineation of chronology and personal relationships in Galatians 1:15–24 could have written the narrative here with such disregard for the emphases laid out there. No later admirer of Paul would have written these verses, which disregard the most important autobiographical statements in Galatians about Paul's conversion and commission and give a portrayal that could be taken as ambiguous at best and contradictory at worst. But if we are correct in holding to Luke's authorship of Acts and in understanding the "we" sections as reflecting his times of personal association with Paul (see Introduction, pp. 701–3)—and further, if we postulate an early date for the composition of Paul's letter to the Galatians (as I do), namely, at a time before Luke became a Christian and joined Paul's missionary team (cf. my *Galatians* [Dallas: Word, 1990])—then it may well have been the case that Luke was unfamiliar with the specific contents of Paul's earlier Galatian letter.

Of more importance is the fact that the purposes of Paul in Galatians 1:15–24 and those of Luke in Acts 9:1–30 are different, with these purposes affecting the selection and shaping of each writer's presentation. Thus with his desire to assert the revelational nature of his Gentile ministry, Paul emphasized in Galatians that he was not dependent on "any man" (*sarki kai haimati*, lit., "flesh and blood," GK *4922, 135*) for his distinctive gospel—particularly not on the Jerusalem apostles (Gal 1:16b–17)—whereas Luke, while also interested in depicting the heaven-ordained nature of Paul's conversion and commission, is concerned in 9:19b–25 to stress the genuineness of Saul's conversion and call. This he does by speaking of the new convert's distinctly Christian proclamation in the synagogues of Damascus and of his being persecuted by the Jews of the city because of his preaching. Neither this preaching nor its resultant persecution is necessarily ruled out by Galatians 1:15–24, though the intermeshing of historical details between the two accounts may be lacking. But such a failure of synchronization is fairly common between two narratives of the same set of circumstances where neither author seems to have read the other and where both have their own distinctive purposes.

It is not going beyond a reasonable historical reconstruction to suggest that the actual order of events was probably as follows: (1) Saul's conversion and commission (9:1–19a); (2) his preaching in the synagogues of Damascus for a time immediately following his conversion (9:19b–22); (3) his prolonged residence in Arabia (Gal 1:17); (4) his return to Damascus (9:23–25); and (5) his first visit to Jerusalem as a Christian some three years after his conversion, with his subsequent travel to Caesarea, Syria, and Cilicia (9:26–30; Gal 1:18–24).

The content of Saul's preaching in the Damascus synagogues focused on Jesus: "Jesus is the Son of God" (v.20) and "Jesus is the Christ [Messiah]" (v.22). That Saul could preach such a message immediately after his conversion is not impossible, for the certainty of Jesus' messiahship was deeply implanted in his soul by his experience on the Damascus road. While he had much to understand and appreciate about the implications of commit-

ment to Jesus as Israel's Messiah, he was certainly in a position to proclaim with conviction and enthusiasm the "thatness" of Jesus' messianic status.

Nor is it surprising that Saul spoke of Jesus as "the Son of God," though this is the only occurrence in Acts of this christological title. In a number of NT passages, the titles "Messiah" and "Son of God" are brought together (cf. Mt 16:16; 26:63; Lk 4:41; Jn 11:27; 20:31), for the "Anointed One" par excellence (which is the meaning of the title "Messiah") expressed in a unique fashion the loving obedience inherent in a Jewish understanding of sonship. This is how the concepts of Messiah and Son are used in 4Q*Florilegium* (4Q174) on 2 Samuel 7:14 and in 2 Esdras 7:28–29; 13:32, 37, 52; 14:9, and it is how Paul used the titles "Son" and "Son of God" some fifteen times in his letters (cf. Ro 1:3–4, 9; 5:10; 8:3, 29, 32; 1Co 1:9; 15:28; 2Co 1:19; Gal 1:16; 2:20; 4:4, 6; 1Th 1:10).

Those who heard Saul preach, Luke says, were "astonished" (v.21; NASB, "amazed") and "baffled" (v.22; NASB, "confounded"). But with his interest in advance and growth (cf. Lk 2:52), Luke also says that "Saul grew more and more powerful"—phraseology that suggests (1) a growth in his understanding of the meaning of commitment to Jesus as Messiah and Son of God, and (2) an increasing ability to demonstrate the validity of his proclamation.

23–24 Luke's expression "after many days had gone by" must be taken with Paul's statement in Galatians 1:18 that his first visit to Jerusalem as a Christian was three years after his conversion. Also, the description here of the plot against him and his escape from Damascus must be compared with Paul's words in 2 Corinthians 11:32–33: "In Damascus the governor under King Aretas had the city of the Damascenes guarded in order to arrest me. But I was lowered in a basket from a window in the wall and slipped through his hands." A number of details in the accounts are unclear to us. What is clear, however, is that Saul's preaching stirred such opposition that plans were laid to kill him. Rather ingeniously, though also somewhat ignominiously, he was able to elude his opponents' designs. What is also clear is that Luke recounts this episode in order to emphasize the genuineness of Saul's conversion, for now Saul, too, has become the object of persecution directed against believers in Jesus.

Luke credits the Jews of Damascus as being the perpetrators of the plot to kill Saul (v.23), whereas in 2 Corinthians 11:32 that honor is given to "the governor [*ho ethnarchēs*, lit., "the ethnarch," GK *1617*] under King Aretas." The situation presupposed in the narrative is somewhat unclear chiefly because the status of the governor is uncertain. Did he have jurisdiction over the city of Damascus as the viceroy of the Nabatean king Aretas? This has often been argued on the ground that Damascus was at this time ruled by Aretas IV (9 BC–AD 40) and considered part of Nabatean Arabia (so Schürer, 2.1:98). Or did the governor, serving as Aretas's representative to Arabs living under Roman rule, have jurisdiction to some extent over the Damascus suburbs, where many Nabateans would have lived (so *Beginnings of Christianity* [ed. Foakes-Jackson and Lake], 5.193)? In either case, the city gates would have been strategic locations for an ambush of the

Christian preacher and would have been closely watched (v.24). Also, certain Jews and an Arab governor might have seen fit to join in common cause against Saul—particularly if Saul had preached in Nabatean Arabia during this three-year period and stirred up opposition there as well, as some commentators have proposed. Luke does not tell us enough of the situation to enable us to piece the story together historically. But then his purpose was not to enlighten us about the political and historical circumstances of the day, but rather to support his portrayal of the genuineness of Saul's encounter with Christ on the Damascus road.

25 Acts uses "disciple" (*mathētēs*, GK *3412*) almost exclusively to denote the members of the Christian community (e.g., 6:1–2, 7; 9:19; 11:26, 29; 13:52; 15:10). The one exception to this usage is here in v.25 (NIV, "followers"), where it is used of those who responded favorably to Saul's new proclamation about Christ and wanted to help him. One of these converts, it seems, had a home situated on the city wall (or perhaps was able to arrange for the use of such a home for a night) from whose window Saul was let down in a basket outside the wall and so was able to elude his opponents. From there, evidently, he made his way directly back to Jerusalem.

NOTES

20 The reading Ἰησοῦν (*Iēsoun*, "Jesus") is strongly attested (𝔓⁴⁵ 𝔓⁷⁴ ℵ A B D E etc.) and not to be displaced by Χριστόν (*Christon*, "Christ"), which appears in the later Byzantine tradition (H L P and many minuscules). This later reading was incorporated by Erasmus into the TR and so into the KJV.

On the christological title "Son of God," see my *Christology of Early Jewish Christianity*, 93–99.

22 Codices C and E, together with some Latin and Coptic recensions, added the words ἐν τῷ λόγῳ (*en tō logō*, "in the word") after the first clause, probably to make sure that readers focused on his increasing ability in preaching and not just his recovery of physical strength (as in v.19).

The Western text, as preserved in recensions of the Old Latin, may have read ἐν ᾧ [or εἰς ὃν] εὐδόκησεν ὁ θεός (*en hō* [or *eis hon*] *eudokēsen ho theos*, "with whom God was well-pleased") after Χριστός

(*Christos*, "Christ"). But this inclusion appears nowhere in any of the extant Greek MSS and so should probably be regarded as an interpolation derived from either Matthew 3:17 or Luke 3:22 (cf. 2Pe 1:17).

25 The manuscript evidence for οἱ μαθηταὶ αὐτοῦ (*hoi mathētai autou*, "his disciples")—i.e., "[Saul's] followers" (NIV; NASB, "disciples")—is very strong ($\mathfrak{P}^{74}$ ℵ A B C etc.). It is, indeed, somewhat strange to speak of "disciples of Saul," who himself was a new convert to Christ. But it is hardly an appropriate expression for converts to Christianity at Damascus generally. Nor can it be made to apply to Saul's companions who accompanied him on his way to Damascus.

Luke uses the rather nondescript word σπυρίς (*spyris*, "basket, hamper," GK *5083*) for the means of conveyance in lowering Saul to the ground, whereas 2 Corinthians 11:33 has the more specific term σαργάνη (*sarganē*, GK *4914*), which connotes a "braided rope basket" or a "netting."

4. Saul's Reception at Jerusalem (9:26–30)

OVERVIEW

As in his earlier narrative concerning the evangelization of Samaria (8:4–25)—as well as in his later accounts of the conversion of Cornelius (10:1–11:18) and the founding of the church at Antioch of Syria (11:19–30), where he not only stresses features of advance and development but also shows continuity with the mother church at Jerusalem—Luke ends his account of the conversion of Saul by telling of his reception by Christians at Jerusalem. And as in Luke's depiction of Saul's preaching in Damascus (vv.19b–25), here the material, when compared with Paul's account in Galatians 1:18–24 of his first visit to Jerusalem as a Christian, entails a number of problems relating to historical correlations. These problems arise probably for much the same reasons as in vv.9b–25, though there they seem to parallel Paul's purpose in Galatians to stress his lack of dependence on the Jerusalem church, whereas here Luke's purpose is to trace out lines of continuity.

> ²⁶When he came to Jerusalem, he tried to join the disciples, but they were all afraid of him, not believing that he really was a disciple. ²⁷But Barnabas took him and brought him to the apostles. He told them how Saul on his journey had seen the Lord and that the Lord had spoken to him, and how in Damascus he had preached fearlessly in the name of Jesus. ²⁸So Saul stayed with them and moved about freely in Jerusalem, speaking boldly in the name of the Lord. ²⁹He talked and debated with the Grecian Jews, but they tried to kill him. ³⁰When the brothers learned of this, they took him down to Caesarea and sent him off to Tarsus.

COMMENTARY

26 Saul's arrival at Jerusalem as a Christian, according to his own reckoning in Galatians 1:18, was three years after his conversion. Being persona non grata among his former associates and suspected by the Christians of Jerusalem, he probably stayed at his sister's home in the city (cf. 23:16). We can understand why his reception by his former Jewish colleagues might have been less than welcome. But the fact that the apostles and other Christians at Jerusalem were leery of him does raise questions, for certainly they must have heard of his conversion and his preaching in Damascus.

It may be postulated that the Christians of Jerusalem had never known Saul personally, either as a persecutor or as a Christian. Stories about his motives and activities during the three-year period between his conversion and his return to Jerusalem might well have become distorted. Many might have asked why, if Saul had really become a Christian, he remained aloof from the Twelve and the Jerusalem congregation for such a long time. We may wish—might even have expected—that there had been more openness toward Saul the convert on the part of the Jerusalem Christians. History, however, has shown that minority movements under persecution frequently become defensive and suspicious of news that sounds too good.

27–28 It was Barnabas who was willing to risk accepting Saul as a genuine believer and who built a bridge of trust between him and the Jerusalem apostles. Just why Barnabas alone showed such magnanimity we are not told, though such action is in character with what is said about him elsewhere in Acts (cf. 4:36–37; 11:22–30; 13:1–14:28; 15:2–4, 12, 22). In presenting Saul to the apostles, Barnabas told of what Saul had seen and heard on the Damascus road and of his preaching "in the name of Jesus" in the city of Damascus, thereby summarizing what we have learned from Luke's account of Saul's conversion and explicitly using his activity in Damascus to support the genuineness of his conversion. So with Barnabas's help, Saul and the Jerusalem apostles were brought into fellowship.

In the light of Paul's own insistence in Galatians 1:18–20 that he saw only Peter and James on this first visit to Jerusalem, Luke's use of the term "apostles" must be considered a generalizing plural for the Jerusalem church's leadership. Likewise, in view of Paul's statement in Galatians 1:18 that he stayed with Peter for fifteen days, Luke's claim that he "stayed with them and moved about freely in Jerusalem" (v.28) must be seen as somewhat overstated. Probably we are not far wrong in reconstructing the situation as follows: Saul resided with his sister's family on his first visit to Jerusalem as a Christian; through the aid of Barnabas he came to visit with Peter for fifteen days and to meet James as well; and his reception by the Christians he met was cordial—even though (1) there might still have existed some fears about him within the Jerusalem congregation, which after the expulsion of the Hellenistic Jewish believers in Jesus was made up entirely of native-born and more Hebraic Jewish believers, and (2) his own activity within the city was largely within the Hellenistic Jewish synagogues.

29–30 At Jerusalem Saul took up a ministry to Jews in the Hellenistic synagogues there. It was a ministry that had been neglected, it appears, since Stephen's death and the expulsion of the Hellenistic Jewish Christians. But it was one Saul may have felt himself particularly suited for, coming as he did from Tarsus in Cilicia and having probably carried on such a ministry at Damascus—and perhaps in Nabatean Arabia (though of such a ministry there is no record). In so doing, however, he soon faced the same opposition that Stephen had faced, and he seems to have gotten into the same difficulty Stephen did. The Jerusalem church apparently did not care to go again through the same kind of disruption that followed Stephen's preaching. So when they realized what was taking place in Saul's newly begun ministry in Jerusalem, "they took him down to Caesarea and sent him off to Tarsus" (v.30).

Saul might have taken such an enforced departure as a personal rebuff. Rather, he seems to have accepted it as by divine approval. In his defense in Acts 22 he speaks of having received in that early postconversion visit to Jerusalem a vision in the temple that not only confirmed his apostleship to the Gentiles but also warned him to flee Jerusalem (22:17–21).

NOTES

26 The Western text (E) and Byzantine text (H L P and most minuscules), and as later picked up in the TR, have the classical verb ἐπειρᾶτο (*epeirato*, "he tried" or "attempted," GK *4281*), whereas the earlier Alexandrian text (𝔓74 ℵ A B C) has the more colloquial form of the same verb: ἐπείραζεν (*epeirazen*, "he tried" or "attempted"). The more common form is undoubtedly original, even though it could also be taken in the sense of "to tempt" or "to make trial of."

REFLECTIONS

Luke does not refer to Saul again between his early experiences as a Christian in Jerusalem and his later ministry at Antioch (11:25–30). From Galatians 1:21–24, however, it seems fairly certain that he continued to proclaim his new message to Diaspora Jews in Caesarea and his hometown of Tarsus. The cordiality of Christian believers in Caesarea at the end of his third missionary journey may imply that Saul had an earlier association with Philip and the believers there. Many of the hardships and trials he enumerates in 2 Corinthians 11:23–27 may stem from situations in Caesarea and Tarsus during those days, for they find no place in the records of the later missionary journeys in Acts. Perhaps the ecstatic experience of 2 Corinthians 12:1–4 also comes from this period in his life.

D. Summary Statement (9:31)

³¹Then the church throughout Judea, Galilee and Samaria enjoyed a time of peace. It was strengthened; and encouraged by the Holy Spirit, it grew in numbers, living in the fear of the Lord.

COMMENTARY

31 Luke's second panel of material on the martyrdom of Stephen, the early ministries of Philip, and the conversion of Saul ends with a summary statement that speaks of the church throughout Judea, Galilee, and Samaria enjoying a time of peace after the turbulence resulting from what happened to Stephen, Philip, and Saul. Though in the first two panels there has been nothing about any advance of the Christian mission into Galilee, Luke's gospel, in line with the synoptic tradition, has emphasized Galilee. It cannot be doubted, therefore, that there were believers in Jesus who lived in Galilee. Here, however, Luke's reference to Judea, Galilee, and Samaria probably means only "all the Jewish homeland of Palestine." And here he insists that instead of being torn apart by what God was doing in the advance of the gospel through these three pivotal figures, the church in the homeland "was strengthened" and "encouraged by the Holy Spirit, it grew in numbers, living in the fear of the Lord," despite a certain lack of discernment and openness that may seem to have been present in the thought and actions of the Jerusalem believers.

PANEL 3—ADVANCES OF THE GOSPEL IN PALESTINE-SYRIA (9:32–12:24)

In his portrayal of the widening of the Christian mission from its Jewish beginnings to its ultimate Gentile outreach, Luke sets out in 9:32–12:24, which comprises the third panel of material in Acts, three episodes of the gospel's advance, two vignettes that give further glimpses of the Spirit's working in behalf of his people in Jerusalem, and a summary statement. The three episodes of advance concern (1) the ministry of Peter in the maritime plain of Palestine (9:32–43), (2) the conversion of a Roman centurion and his friends at Caesarea (10:1–11:18), and (3) the founding of the church at Antioch of Syria (11:19–30). Two notes are sounded in these episodes of advance: the first has to do with geography and stresses the spread of the gospel into areas more distant from Jerusalem than before; the second, and undoubtedly more important, has to do with the attitudes of the converts and the missionaries.

Then, before moving on to speak of the distinctive advances of the gospel within the Gentile world through the ministry of his hero Paul, Luke returns to an account of the circumstances at Jerusalem and God's continued working on behalf of his people there (12:1–23). In returning to Jerusalem at this stage in his overall picture, Luke seems to be making the point that, though his interest is in tracing the movement of the early Christian mission from Jerusalem to Rome, his readers are not to assume that God was finished with Jerusalem Christianity or that his divine activity within the Jewish world had come to an end—which is a point all too often ignored by Christians since then. Finally, in summation of all he has presented in this third panel, Luke appends this statement: "But the word of God continued to increase and spread" (12:24).

A. The Ministry of Peter in the Maritime Plain (9:32–43)

OVERVIEW

Luke's rationale for including Peter's miracles at Lydda and Joppa has often been debated. Did Luke use the vignettes of the healing of Aeneas and the raising of Dorcas to shift the focus of his narrative from Jerusalem to the west country of Palestine, thereby setting the stage for the conversion of Cornelius at Caesarea? Or did he include them to suggest that with Peter's ministry in the maritime plain the evangelization of Palestine was completed and that it was now time to look farther afield? Or since the maritime plain was populated by both Jews and Gentiles, was Luke here depicting a further ideological widening of the range of the Christian mission—one that had to do with (1) an outreach of the gospel to Jews living in a not entirely Jewish area and (2) the nonlegalistic attitude of Peter their Christian missionary? All three explanations can be supported from the text. From the developing presentation in Acts, however, we should probably judge that geographical and ideological concerns were uppermost in Luke's mind.

1. Aeneas Healed at Lydda (9:32–35)

³²As Peter traveled about the country, he went to visit the saints in Lydda. ³³There he found a man named Aeneas, a paralytic who had been bedridden for eight years. ³⁴"Aeneas," Peter said to him, "Jesus Christ heals you. Get up and take care of your mat." Immediately Aeneas got up. ³⁵All those who lived in Lydda and Sharon saw him and turned to the Lord.

COMMENTARY

32 Lydda (Lod in the OT; cf. 1Ch 8:12; Ezr 2:33; Ne 11:35) was located twenty-five miles northwest of Jerusalem at the intersection of the highways from Egypt to Syria and from coastal Joppa to Jerusalem. Josephus (*Ant.* 20.130) calls it "a village that was in size not inferior to a city." It had been restored to the Jews in the time of John Hyrcanus by Julius Caesar (cf. *Ant.* 14.208), and later it became a center for both Pharisaic studies (prior to Jamnia) and Christian activity. Lydda was the legendary locale for Saint George's slaying of the dragon and his later martyrdom in AD 303. In the fourth century, Lydda was the seat of episcopal authority for the Syrian church. The council that tried Pelagius for heresy in AD 415 met there. It appears in the NT only here.

Peter was engaged in an itinerant ministry in the western part of Palestine—a ministry somewhat like his earlier preaching in Samaria (cf. 8:25). In the course of his travels, he visited "the saints" (*tous hagious*, GK *41*) in the important commercial center of Lydda. We are not told how they had become believers. Perhaps they received the gospel from some of those who were originally at Pentecost (cf. 2:5–41) or perhaps from some who were forced to flee Jerusalem during the persecution of the Hellenistic Jewish Christians (cf. 8:1, 4, 40). However they came to believe in Jesus as God's Messiah, Peter viewed them as within the sphere of his ministry, even though many of them were probably less scrupulous in keeping the Mosaic law than Jews of Jerusalem.

33 At Lydda Peter came upon Aeneas, a paralytic who had been bedridden for eight years. Luke does not say that Aeneas was a Jew nationally or a Christian by profession, though presumably, despite his thoroughly Greek name, he was both. It would hardly have been consistent with Luke's purpose to show Peter ministering to a Gentile before his encounter with Cornelius. Furthermore, the adverb "there" (*ekei*) at the beginning of the sentence has as its antecedent the community of believers at Lydda, which was composed of Jewish believers in Jesus, and not just the city itself.

34 Peter's words, "Jesus Christ heals you. Get up and take care of your mat" (*strōson seautō*; NASB, "make your bed"), are recorded in the present tense by Luke. The third person singular verb *iatai* (from *iaomai*, "heal" or "cure," GK *2615*) may be accented so as to be understood as a consummative perfect ("Jesus Christ has healed you") or as a durative pres-

ent ("Jesus Christ is engaged in healing you"), but probably should be read here as an aoristic present ("this moment Jesus Christ heals you"). The expression *strōson seautō* (lit., "prepare yourself"), which is usually used with the noun *klinē* ("sleeping mat," "bed," or "cushion used at mealtimes"), is an idiom that may mean "take care of your mat," "make up your bed," or "prepare a meal for yourself" (cf. Mk 14:15). The latter would go well with the interest shown elsewhere by the evangelists in nourishment for convalescents (cf. Mk 5:43; Lk 8:55). In the case of a paralytic, however, for whom immobility and not nourishment was the problem, getting up and taking care of one's mat is probably in view.

35 News of Aeneas's healing spread throughout Lydda and into the plain of Sharon to the north. Rather hyperbolically, Luke says that "all those who lived in Lydda and Sharon saw him and turned to the Lord." The plain of Sharon is the largest of the maritime plains of northern Palestine, stretching along the coast from Joppa to Mount Carmel and with Caesarea at its center. So, Luke tells us, there was a further widening of the Christian mission within the Jewish nation that prepared the way both geographically and ideologically for the accounts of Peter's ministry at Joppa (9:36–43) and at Caesarea (10:1–48).

NOTES

33 The clause ἐξ ἐτῶν ὀκτώ (*ex etōn oktō*) could be translated "since he was eight years old," but "for eight years" is more probable (so NIV, NASB, though the latter omits "for").

34 Codex Vaticanus (B) has εἴαται (*eiatai*), which indicates that the scribe understood the word to be in the perfect tense (as B has also at Mk 5:29, where there is no question that the perfect tense was intended).

Codices A E H L P and most minuscules read Ἰησους ὁ Χριστός (*Iēsous ho Christos*, "Jesus the Christ"), which seems to have a certain ring of originality. Nevertheless, the better manuscript evidence (𝔓74 ℵ B C) has simply the name without the article. Codex Alexandrinus (A), the Vulgate and Coptic Sahidic versions, and a number of minuscules prefix the name with ὁ κύριος (*ho kyrios*, "the Lord"), which is most likely a later, pious addition.

2. Dorcas Raised at Joppa (9:36–43)

³⁶In Joppa there was a disciple named Tabitha (which, when translated, is Dorcas), who was always doing good and helping the poor. ³⁷About that time she became sick and died, and her body was washed and placed in an upstairs room. ³⁸Lydda was near Joppa; so when the disciples heard that Peter was in Lydda, they sent two men to him and urged him, "Please come at once!"

³⁹Peter went with them, and when he arrived he was taken upstairs to the room. All the widows stood around him, crying and showing him the robes and other clothing that Dorcas had made while she was still with them.

⁴⁰Peter sent them all out of the room; then he got down on his knees and prayed. Turning toward the dead woman, he said, "Tabitha, get up." She opened her eyes, and seeing Peter she sat up. ⁴¹He took her by the hand and helped her to her feet. Then he called the believers and the widows and presented her to them alive. ⁴²This became known all over Joppa, and many people believed in the Lord. ⁴³Peter stayed in Joppa for some time with a tanner named Simon.

COMMENTARY

36–39 Joppa (modern Jaffa; Heb. *yāpô*, cf. Jos 19:46) was the ancient seaport for Jerusalem. Situated on the coast thirty-five miles northwest of the capital city and ten miles beyond Lydda, it possesses the only natural harbor on the Mediterranean between Egypt and Ptolemais (the OT city of Acco). Through Joppa Solomon brought cedar beams from Lebanon to build the temple (2Ch 2:16); from it Jonah sailed for Tarshish (Jnh 1:3). Its rival in NT times was Caesarea, thirty miles to the north, which Herod the Great, because the people of Joppa hated him, built into a magnificent new port city and provincial capital.

At Joppa lived a woman called Tabitha (her Hebrew name) or Dorcas (her Greek name). Both names mean "gazelle." She was a "disciple" (*mathētria*, GK *3413*, the only instance in the NT of the feminine form of the word) and "was always doing good and helping the poor." Her energies, we are told in v.39, were devoted chiefly to helping destitute widows.

When she died the Christians at Joppa sent this message to Peter at Lydda: "Please come at once!" (v.38). Luke does not say what they expected from him or asked him to do. But since (1) Tabitha's body was washed but not anointed for burial (cf. *m. Šabb.* 23:5) and (2) her good deeds were told to Peter when he arrived, they apparently wanted him to restore her to life. Having heard of Aeneas's healing, they seem to have thought it only a slight extension of divine power to raise the dead.

40–42 Peter had been instrumental in a number of physical healings (cf. 3:1–10; 5:12–16; 9:32–35) and even pronounced the death sentence on Ananias and Sapphira (cf. 5:1–11). Raising people from the dead, however, was hardly a common feature of his ministry. Nevertheless, knowing himself to be an apostle of Jesus empowered by the Holy Spirit—and probably remembering the incident of his Lord's having raised Jairus's daughter (cf. Mk 5:21–24, 35–43 par.)—Peter responded to the urgent call. Just as he had seen Jesus do in raising Jairus's daughter, he ordered the mourners out of the room and prayed. Then he spoke these words: "Tabitha, get up" (the Aramaic form *Tabitha koum* would have differed in only one letter from Jesus' command *talitha koum*, "Little girl, get up," in Mk 5:41). When she opened her eyes and sat up, Peter took her by the hand, helped her to her feet, and presented her alive to the Christians who stood by (v.41). It was an exceptional exhibit of God's mercy and the Spirit's power, and "many people believed in the Lord" (v.42).

43 This verse serves as a geographical and ideological hinge between the accounts of Peter's miracles in the maritime plain and the account of Cornelius's conversion at Caesarea. Instead of returning 10 miles to Lydda, Peter "for some time" (cf. 8:11) remained at Joppa, where the messengers from Cornelius later found him. Of greater significance, however, is the fact that Peter stayed with a man called Simon, a tanner who presumably was working in his own home. The rabbis considered tanning an unclean trade (cf. Str-B, 2.695). Thus the fact that Peter lodged with such a man suggests that Peter himself was not overly scrupulous in his observance of Jewish ceremonial traditions (cf. Gal 2:14). This may not tell us anything more about Peter than can be easily inferred from the evangelists' representations of him in their gospels. But Luke's stress on this feature of Peter's lifestyle provides a significant preface to the events recorded in 10:1–11:18.

NOTES

38 The sending of "two men" (δύο ἄνδρας, *dyo andras*, as in 𝔓⁴⁵ 𝔓⁷⁴ ℵ A B C E and most minuscules) is in accord with Near Eastern custom and a common feature of Luke's narrative (cf. 10:7; 11:30). The omission of the words in some MSS (H L P Ψ and other minuscules) is probably due to the influence of 10:19, where the number of messengers was debated by the scribes.

40 Several Western witnesses (Old Latin, Vulgate, Syriac and Coptic versions, Cyprian, and Ambrose) add the words ἐν τῷ ὀνόματι τοῦ κυρίου ἡμῶν Ἰησοῦ Χριστοῦ (*en tō onomati tou kyriou hēmōn Iēsou Christou*, "in the name of our Lord Jesus Christ") after ἀνάστηθι (*anastēthi*, "arise," "get up," GK 482). Another Western reading (E and Old Latin and Coptic versions) is the addition of παραχρῆμα (*parachrēma*, "immediately") before ἤνοιξεν (*ēnoixen*, "she opened," GK 487).

Perhaps it was the name Tabitha itself that triggered in Peter's mind the incident of Jesus' raising of Jairus's daughter with the command ταλιθα κουμ (*talitha koum*, "Little girl, get up," Mk 5:41). But from Luke's recounting of Jesus' words in that incident (ἡ παῖς, ἔγειρε, *hē pais, egeire*, "My child [fem.], get up," Lk 8:54), it seems that Luke himself was not conscious of such a parallel.

B. The Conversion of Cornelius at Caesarea (10:1–11:18)

OVERVIEW

With the range of the Christian mission steadily broadening, the time had come for the gospel to cross the barrier that separated Jews from Gentiles and to be presented directly to Gentiles. Thus Luke takes up the story of the conversion of Cornelius. That this story of a Gentile's conversion was of great importance to Luke can be judged, in part, by the amount of space he devotes to it—sixty-six verses in all.

Four matters in the account of Cornelius's conversion receive special emphasis, and, in turn, they provide insight into Luke's purpose for presenting this material. The first has to do with the early church's resistance to the idea of Gentiles' being either directly evangelized or accepted into the Christian fellowship apart from any relationship to Judaism (cf. 10:14, 28; 11:2–3, 8). The second is the demonstration that it was God himself who introduced Gentiles into the church and miraculously showed his approval (cf. 10:3, 11–16, 19–20, 22b, 30–33, 44–46; 11:5–10, 13, 15–17). The third is that it was not Paul but Peter, the leader of the Jerusalem apostles, who was the human instrument in opening the door to the Gentiles (cf. 10:23, 34–43, 47–48; 11:15–17). The fourth has to do with the Jerusalem church's subsequent acceptance of a Gentile's conversion to Jesus the Messiah apart from any allegiance to Judaism, for God had so obviously validated it (cf. 11:18).

Many earlier commentators, under the spell of the old Tübingen school (see Introduction, pp. 666–68), declared the Cornelius episode to be an unhistorical fabrication because it gives to Peter the honor of having begun the Gentile mission. But though Peter is presented as the first to go directly to a Gentile, he is not depicted in any way as an "apostle to the Gentiles." In fact, as Bernhard Weiss (*A Manual of Introduction to the New Testament* [London: Hodder & Stoughton, 1887], 1.169–70; 2.329) observed, "the story in no way settles the issue of whether the mission to the Gentiles is either lawful or obligatory, as it was considered to be a quite exceptional divine intervention that compelled Peter to preach the gospel to Cornelius."

Other commentators, influenced by Martin Dibelius, have treated the account of Peter's converting a "God-fearing Gentile" by the name of Cornelius as a pious "conversion legend," which must have sprung from some traditional story preserved in some Hellenistic Christian community, but which by its use in 15:7–11, 14 is manifestly a Lukan creation in its present form (cf. Dibelius, 109–22). But such a verdict confuses the issues faced by the Jerusalem church in chs. 11 and 15, which, of course, are related but still distinguishable (see comments at those passages). And as Charles S. C. Williams, 134, observed, "Behind Dibelius's analysis there seems to lie a desire to reduce the supernatural element in Acts to nothing."

1. Cornelius's Vision (10:1–8)

¹At Caesarea there was a man named Cornelius, a centurion in what was known as the Italian Regiment. ²He and all his family were devout and God-fearing; he gave generously to those in need and prayed to God regularly. ³One day at about three in the afternoon he had a vision. He distinctly saw an angel of God, who came to him and said, "Cornelius!"

⁴Cornelius stared at him in fear. "What is it, Lord?" he asked.

The angel answered, "Your prayers and gifts to the poor have come up as a memorial offering before God. ⁵Now send men to Joppa to bring back a man named Simon who is called Peter. ⁶He is staying with Simon the tanner, whose house is by the sea."

⁷When the angel who spoke to him had gone, Cornelius called two of his servants and a devout soldier who was one of his attendants. ⁸He told them everything that had happened and sent them to Joppa.

COMMENTARY

1 Caesarea is on the shore of the Mediterranean in the center of the coastal plain of Sharon in northern Palestine, some sixty-five miles northwest of Jerusalem. It was named in honor of Augustus Caesar (Caius Octavianus, who was later called Augustus), the adopted heir of Julius Caesar. Formerly it was called Strato's Tower and considered a second-class harbor because of its shallow entrance and vulnerability to the strong southern winds. But in carrying out his pro-Roman policy, Herod the Great changed all that by making the harbor into a magnificent seaport and the village into a provincial capital. He deepened the harbor, built a breakwater against the southern gales, constructed an imposing city with an amphitheater and a temple in honor of Rome and Augustus, brought in fresh water through an aqueduct that ran over stately brick arches, and established a garrison of soldiers to protect not only the harbor and city but also the freshwater supply. The magnificence of the port dwarfed the splendor of the city, which is probably why a Neronian coin bears the inscription "Caesarea by Augustus's Harbor." Nevertheless, in the NT period the city was the Roman capital of the province of Judea. Here Rome had a safe haven for its administration of Palestine, though after Roman times the city fell into decay.

"Cornelius" was a common name in the Roman world from 82 BC, when Cornelius Sulla liberated ten thousand slaves, all of whom took their patron's name as they established themselves in Roman society. Probably, therefore, the Cornelius of Acts 10–11 was a descendant of one of the freedmen of Cornelius Sulla's day. He is identified as a centurion of "the Italian Regiment" (NASB, "cohort"). A centurion was a noncommissioned officer who had worked his way up through the ranks to take command of a group of soldiers within a Roman legion,

and therefore would be roughly equivalent to a captain today. A regiment or cohort was a tenth of a Roman legion and numbered anywhere from three hundred to six hundred men, with the official count always being the latter.

Commentators have frequently proposed that the regiment mentioned here was probably the *Cohors II Miliaria Italica Civium Romanorum*. This consisted of archers who were freedmen originally from Italy on whom citizenship had been conferred. It was known to have been transferred to Syria sometime before AD 69 and to have been in Palestine-Syria during the troublesome times associated with the two destructions of Jerusalem in AD 70 and 135 (cf. T. R. S. Broughton, "The Roman Army," in *Beginnings of Christianity* [ed. Foakes-Jackson and Lake], 5.427–45). On the basis of this identification, together with the suggestion that during the administration of Herod Agrippa I over Judea in AD 41–44 there would have been no need for a Roman occupying force in Palestine, Luke is frequently charged with error in speaking of a Roman regiment or cohort and its captain in Caesarea during the early or mid-40s AD. But surely the objection is unwarranted, for throughout Caesarea's history there was always the need for protection—not only for the port and city, which were strategic for Roman rule, but particularly for Caesarea's elegant but extremely vulnerable water supply. While in times of nationalistic tumult a much larger garrison was required, this does not minimize the need for Rome's continual protection of Caesarea as its bridgehead of authority on alien soil.

2 Luke describes Cornelius as "devout and God-fearing" (*eusebēs* [GK 2356] *kai phoboumenos* [GK 5828] *ton theon*). These characteristics are also attributed to "all his household" (*panti tō oikō autou*), which likely refers not only to his immediate family but also to his servants. Perhaps we are to understand by *phoboumenos ton theon* (lit., "one who fears God") that Cornelius was a near-proselyte to Judaism or a "Proselyte of the Gate" (see comments at 8:27–28). For while *sebomenos ton theon* (lit., "one who worships God," GK *4933*) is Luke's usual way of identifying this special class of Gentile followers in Acts (cf. 13:50; 16:14; 17:4, 17; 18:7), at times he uses *phoboumenos ton theon* synonymously (cf. 13:16, 26).

Here in Acts 10, however, we should probably understand *phoboumenos ton theon* not as a technical term for this special class associated somewhat loosely with Judaism but more broadly as meaning something like "devout" (NIV), "a devout man" (NASB), "a religious man" (NEB, TEV), or "a deeply religious man" (Phillips). The fact that Luke adds *eusebēs* ("pious," "devout," GK *2356*) to his assessment of Cornelius here in v.2 and *dikaios* ("just," "righteous," GK *1465*) in repeating his spiritual qualities in v.22 suggests that he meant *phoboumenos ton theon* to be taken not technically but generally. And from his report of Peter's use of this expression for Cornelius in v.35 ("men from every nation who fear [God] and do what is right"), it seems we must understand Cornelius to have been a Gentile who, having realized the bankruptcy of paganism, sought to worship a monotheistic God, practice a form of prayer, and lead a moral life, apart from any necessary association with Judaism. Probably we should view him as a pious, devout, and intensely religious man who might have known very little about the Jewish religion but who in his own way "gave generously to those in need" (*tō laō*, lit., "to the people," which phrase suggests "the Jewish people") and "prayed to God regularly."

In sum, Cornelius was a noble and spiritually sensitive Roman army officer who seems to fit Virgil's picture of the Gentile world as one that "stretched out its hands in longing for the other shore" (*Aeneid* 6.314). It was, then, to such a spiritually minded Gentile, Luke tells us, that God first reached out his hand in the advance of the Christian mission.

3 "One day at about three in the afternoon" (lit., "about the ninth hour of the day"), an angel of God appeared to Cornelius in a vision and called him by name. While the ninth hour was the second of the set times during the day for prayer in Judaism (see comments at 3:1), here the expression is used with the adverb *phanerōs* ("plainly," "distinctly," GK *5747*) to emphasize that the vision happened in broad daylight.

4 Cornelius's response was that he "stared at [the angel] in fear" (NASB, "being much alarmed") and could only blurt out the words, "What is it, Lord?" (*Ti estin, kyrie?*). While the Greek title *kyrios* (GK *3261*) was used in antiquity for everything from polite address to worshipful acclamation, Cornelius undoubtedly meant it in some sense of worshipful acclaim, even though it seems he had no firm idea who he was addressing (cf. 9:5). He would hardly have been so blasé in the face of this heavenly vision as to have meant by the title only "sir." In his consternation he heard the reassuring words that his prayers and alms had arisen as "a memorial" or "remembrance before God" (*eis mnēmosynon* [GK *3649*] *emprosthen tou theou*)—which is a biblical and traditional way of saying that he was commended before God and that God was attentive to his situation (cf. Lev 2:2; Php 4:18; Heb 13:15–16; see also Tob 12:12).

5–6 Cornelius was told to send to Joppa for Simon Peter. The surname "Peter" distinguishes the apostle from his host Simon the tanner, whose house was by the sea (probably so that he could use the seawater in his tanning process). No indication is given as to why Peter was to be summoned. Rather, the emphasis is entirely on the fact that Cornelius was prepared to respond to God.

7–8 Cornelius's response was immediate. Calling two household servants and a soldier and telling them what had occurred and what he had been told to do, he sent them to Joppa to bring back Peter. The servants were probably two of those already mentioned in v.2 as part of Cornelius's household. The soldier is identified as being also "pious" or "devout" (*eusebēs*), one to whom the full characterization of v.2 (also vv.22 and 35) applied as well.

NOTES

2 Because of their personal qualities, centurions were considered the salt of the Roman legions. Polybius (*Hist.* 6.24) describes their character thus: "Centurions are desired not to be bold and adventurous so much as good leaders, of steady and prudent mind, not prone to take the offensive or start fighting wantonly, but able when overwhelmed and hard-pressed to stand fast and die at their post."

3 The TR, following L P Ψ and most minuscules, omits περί (*peri*, "about"), probably because it was considered superfluous. The preposition, however, is strongly supported by 𝔓74 ℵ A B C E etc.

4 The verb ἀτενίζω (*atenizō*, "stare," GK 867) is a favorite expression of Luke, who uses it for twelve of its fourteen appearances in the NT (Lk 4:20; 22:56; Ac 1:10; 3:4, 12; 6:15; 7:55; 10:4 [here]; 11:6; 13:9; 14:9; 23:1).

6 Several minuscule MSS at the end of this verse add the words ὃς λαλήσει ῥήματα πρός σε, ἐν οἷς σωθήσῃ σὺ καὶ πᾶς ὁ οἶκός σου (*hos lalēsei rhēmata pros se, en hois sōthēsē sy kai pas ho oikos sou*, "who will speak words to you, in which you will be saved and all your house"). Other minuscules, as reflected in some Latin versions as well, have a similar phrase—ὗτος λαλήσε σοι τί σε δεῖ ποιεῖν (*houtos lalēse soi ti se dei poiein*, "he will tell you what you ought to do")—which is carried on in the KJV.

2. Peter's Vision (10:9–16)

OVERVIEW

Though Peter was not by training or inclination an overly scrupulous Jew—and though as a Christian his inherited prejudices seem to have been gradually wearing thin—he was not prepared to go so far as to minister directly to Gentiles. A special revelation was necessary for that, and Luke now tells how God took the initiative in overcoming Peter's reluctance.

⁹About noon the following day as they were on their journey and approaching the city, Peter went up on the roof to pray. ¹⁰He became hungry and wanted something to eat, and while the meal was being prepared, he fell into a trance. ¹¹He saw heaven opened and something like a large sheet being let down to earth by its four corners. ¹²It contained all kinds of four-footed animals, as well as reptiles of the earth and birds of the air. ¹³Then a voice told him, "Get up, Peter. Kill and eat."

> ¹⁴"Surely not, Lord!" Peter replied. "I have never eaten anything impure or unclean."
> ¹⁵The voice spoke to him a second time, "Do not call anything impure that God has made clean."
> ¹⁶This happened three times, and immediately the sheet was taken back to heaven.

COMMENTARY

9 The revelation came to Peter on the day following Cornelius's vision (or perhaps the day after the messengers' start, if that was later), as the three from Caesarea were approaching Joppa. About noon Peter went to the roof of the tanner's house to pray, apparently looking not only for solitude but also for shade under an awning and a cool breeze from the sea. Noon was not one of the stated times for prayer among the Jews, and some have viewed Peter as engaging in a belated morning prayer or an early evening (i.e., a "ninth hour" in the afternoon) prayer. Yet pious Jews, on the basis of Psalm 55:17 (cf. Da 6:10; *Did.* 8:3), often also prayed at noon. Moreover, the stated hours for prayer, while prescriptive, were not restrictive.

10–13 While in prayer, Peter became very hungry and, it seems, somewhat drowsy. As he was waiting for food, he "fell into a trance" (*ekstasis*, GK *1749*) and saw a vision (cf. *horama*, GK *3969*, "vision," in 10:17, 19; 11:5) of "something like [*skeuos ti hōs*, lit., "a certain object like"] a large sheet being let down to earth by its four corners," on which were "all kinds of four-footed animals, as well as reptiles of the earth and birds of the air." Then he heard a voice say, "Get up, Peter. Kill and eat." Psychologically, the details of the vision may be explained in terms of (1) Peter's increasing perplexity about Jewish-Gentile relations within various Christian congregations of the maritime plain; (2) the flapping awning over him—or perhaps the full sail of a boat out on the sea; and (3) his gnawing hunger. God frequently reveals himself

not only in but also by means of our human situations. Peter took what the voice said as a message from God—a message in the form of an almost inscrutable riddle, but one soon to be clarified by both word and event.

14 Peter's shock and repugnance are expressed in his words: "Surely not, Lord!" This response is in word and content like that of the prophet Ezekiel when called on by God to eat unclean food among the Gentiles (Eze 4:14). While not overly scrupulous, Peter nonetheless had always observed the basic dietary restrictions of Leviticus 11, which distinguished the clean quadrupeds fit for food (those that chewed the cud and had split hooves) from animals considered unclean. While clean animals were represented in the sheet, Peter was scandalized by the unholy mixture of clean and unclean and by the fact that no distinctions were made in the command to "kill and eat." Indeed, it was a command given by one he acclaimed as "Lord"—perhaps the voice was even recognizable to him as the voice of Jesus (cf. F. F. Bruce, *The Acts of the Apostles* [3d ed.; Grand Rapids: Eerdmans, 1990], 220). But that did not leave him any less repelled by the idea.

15–16 The voice told Peter, "Do not call anything impure [*koinos*, lit., "common," a synecdoche for the dual expression *koinos kai akathartos*, v. 14; NIV, "impure or unclean"; NASB, "unholy and unclean"] that God has made clean." The particular application had to do with nullifying Jewish dietary laws for Jewish believers in accord with Jesus' remarks on the subject in Mark 7:17–23. But Peter was soon to learn that the range of the vision's message extended much more widely—touching directly on Jewish-Gentile relations as he had known them and explicating those relations in ways

he could never have anticipated. Three times this interchange took place, with the message being three times indelibly impressed on Peter's subconscious. Luke then says, "The sheet [*to skeuos*, lit., "the object"] was taken back to heaven."

NOTES

9 Codex Sinaiticus (א) in a corrected form reads "ninth hour" rather than "sixth hour" (so NIV: "about noon"; NASB: "about the sixth hour"), thereby making Peter's prayer coincide with Cornelius's prayer (cf. v.30).

10 The Greek πρόσπεινος (*prospeinos*, "very hungry"; NIV, "hungry," GK *4698*) is a rare word used only here and by Demosthenes Ophthalmicus, a famous first-century eye doctor of Laodicea (as quoted by the sixth-century medical writer Aëtius; cf. F. W. Dillistone, "πρόσπεινος (Acts 10:10)," *ExpTim* 46 [1934–35]: 380). Peter's hunger is not explained, and he may not have been waiting for a noon meal. While Greeks and Romans usually had noon meals, among the Jews breakfast was eaten in the forenoon and the main meal in late afternoon (cf. Str-B, 2.204–7).

11 The verbs θεωρεῖ (*theōrei*, "he sees," GK *2555*) here and εὑρίσκει (*heuriskei*, "he finds," GK *2351*) in v.27 are among the few cases of a historic present in Luke-Acts, perhaps reflecting the style of Luke's source material more than his own.

13 The omission of Πέτρε (*Petre*, "Peter") from Chester Beatty 𝔓⁴⁵ seems simply to be a scribal accident. It is included in all other texts.

3. Messengers from Cornelius Arrive at Joppa (10:17–23a)

¹⁷While Peter was wondering about the meaning of the vision, the men sent by Cornelius found out where Simon's house was and stopped at the gate. ¹⁸They called out, asking if Simon who was known as Peter was staying there.

¹⁹While Peter was still thinking about the vision, the Spirit said to him, "Simon, three men are looking for you. ²⁰So get up and go downstairs. Do not hesitate to go with them, for I have sent them."

²¹Peter went down and said to the men, "I'm the one you're looking for. Why have you come?"

²²The men replied, "We have come from Cornelius the centurion. He is a righteous and God-fearing man, who is respected by all the Jewish people. A holy angel told him to have you come to his house so that he could hear what you have to say." ²³ªThen Peter invited the men into the house to be his guests.

COMMENTARY

17–18 While Peter was recovering from the shock of the vision and its message, the men from Cornelius had found the tanner's house. It was nothing like a patrician's home, with a gatehouse and courtyard separating the living quarters from the street, but rather a craftsman's quarters, with immediate access from the street through a gateway or vestibule (*ton pylōna*, "the gate," GK 4784). Thus at the gate the messengers shouted out their inquiry for anyone within earshot to hear: "Is Simon who is known as Peter staying here?"

19–20 On the roof of the tanner's house, Peter was still so deep in thought about the vision that even the messengers' shouting and calling out his name failed to rouse him. Rather, the Spirit told him of their presence and urged him to go with them. "For I have sent them," he said. A question naturally arises about the relation of "the angel of God" who appeared to Cornelius (10:3–6, 22, 30; 11:13), "the voice" that spoke to Peter (10:13–15; 11:7–9), and "the Spirit" here who urged him to go with the messengers from Cornelius. But the question, though legitimate, is almost unanswerable, since it is by the Holy Spirit that the ascended Christ manifests his presence to his own. Thus it is both exegetically and experientially difficult, if not impossible, to draw any sharp lines between an "angel of God," the Holy Spirit, and the ascended

Christ. This is the same situation that appeared in 8:26, 29, and 39 ("an angel of the Lord" and "the Spirit" directing Philip, with "the Spirit of the Lord" taking him away) and that will appear again in 16:6–7 ("the Holy Spirit" and "the Spirit of Jesus" forbidding Paul). It crops out in even such closely reasoned didactic statements on the relation of Christ and the Spirit as Romans 8:9–11 and 2 Corinthians 3:17–18.

21–23a In response to the Spirit's urging, and probably by means of an outside stairway, Peter went down to meet the messengers. After he identified himself and asked why they had come, they told him of their master (Cornelius), of the angel's visitation, and of their mission to bring Peter back so that he might tell their master what he had to say. In so doing they characterized Cornelius not only as "an upright ["just," "righteous"] and God-fearing man" (see comments at 10:2) but also as one whose personal qualities were witnessed to "by all the Jewish people" (*hypo holou tou ethnous tōn Ioudaiōn*; NASB, "the entire nation of the Jews"; here non-Jews are portrayed by Luke as referring to Jews by the term *ethnos*, "nation" [GK 1620], rather than *laos*, "people" [GK 3295]). Peter, in obedience to the command of the vision, received these Gentiles into the house as his guests—acting, no doubt with the tanner's permission, more as a host than a lodger.

NOTES

17 Codices C D E L P and most minuscules (and as incorporated into the TR) read καὶ ἰδού (*kai idou*; "and behold"), but 𝔓⁴⁵ 𝔓⁷⁴ ℵ A and B have only the demonstrative particle ἰδού (*idou*, "behold"). Since "and behold" is a Hebraism, it may be considered to have been in Luke's source material. But the better textual tradition of the Alexandrian papyri and MSS represents Luke as not carrying it on, and modern translations have also had trouble with it (NIV, untranslated; NASB, "behold").

Codices A C D L P and many minuscules (and as incorporated into the TR) read the preposition ἀπό (*apo*, "from") rather than ὑπό (*hypo*, "by"), as in 𝔓⁷⁴ B E etc.—probably being influenced by the preposition in the substantival participle οἱ ἀπεσταλμένοι (*hoi apestalmenoi*, "those who were sent," or "the men sent," GK *690*).

19 Codex Vaticanus (B) deletes the dative pronoun αὐτῷ (*autō*, "to him"), either accidentally or as being unnecessary. But it is widely attested in the MSS.

Codices ℵ A C E, along with 𝔓⁷⁴ and various other textual traditions, read that Peter was told by the Spirit, "Three [*treis*] men are looking for you"; but Codex Vaticanus (B) has "two [*dyo*] men." The reading "three" is supported by the majority of early MSS and conforms nicely with the description in 10:7 and Peter's words in 11:11. The reading "two," however, is supported by the very important fourth-century witness Codex B and is the "harder reading," and so on internal grounds is probably to be preferred, understanding 10:7 to be referring to the two servants as the messengers and the soldier as their guard. Either reading would allow Peter in 11:11 to refer later to three men coming from Caesarea for him. But determination of the exact number is extremely difficult and probably beyond final resolution.

It is not too difficult to appreciate why Codex Bezae (D) and its Western associates decided to cut the Gordian knot by omitting any reference to a specific number rather than to try to untie it. For whereas Bezae (D) is lacking for 8:26–10:14, here in 10:19 it adds its testimony to a number of the church fathers (e.g., Cyril, Ambrose, Chrysostom, Augustine) and various Western uncial and minuscule texts for the omission of any number—i.e., neither "two" nor "three."

4. Peter's Reception by Cornelius (10:23b–33)

23bThe next day Peter started out with them, and some of the brothers from Joppa went along. 24The following day he arrived in Caesarea. Cornelius was expecting them and had called together his relatives and close friends. 25As Peter entered the house, Cornelius met him and fell at his feet in reverence. 26But Peter made him get up. "Stand up," he said, "I am only a man myself."

27Talking with him, Peter went inside and found a large gathering of people. 28He said to them: "You are well aware that it is against our law for a Jew to associate with a Gentile or visit him. But God has shown me that I should not call any man impure or unclean. 29So when I was sent for, I came without raising any objection. May I ask why you sent for me?"

30Cornelius answered: "Four days ago I was in my house praying at this hour, at three in the afternoon. Suddenly a man in shining clothes stood before me 31and said, 'Cornelius, God has heard your prayer and remembered your gifts to the poor. 32Send to Joppa for Simon who is called Peter. He is a guest in the home of Simon the tanner, who lives by the sea.' 33So I sent for you immediately, and it was good of you to come. Now we are all here in the presence of God to listen to everything the Lord has commanded you to tell us."

COMMENTARY

23b The conversation in Simon the tanner's home that evening must have been a lively one, with many of the Joppa believers joining in the discussion of the strange visions. Six believers from Joppa accompanied Peter to Caesarea the next day (cf. 11:12)—which was surely a wise action, especially in view of questions that would later be raised at Jerusalem. So the party of ten set out for Caesarea.

24 It apparently took the group longer to cover the thirty miles than the messengers had taken earlier, because they did not get to Caesarea until the following day. Cornelius was expecting them and had drawn together a group of relatives and close friends to hear Peter.

25–26 As Peter was brought into the centurion's home past the gatehouse and then into the courtyard, Cornelius came from his living quarters to meet him. Cornelius fell at Peter's feet and offered him "reverence" (*proskyneō*, "worship," "reverence," "do obeisance to," "welcome respectfully," GK 4686—a word used for homage to deity, to angels, and to men). It seems that Cornelius believed there was something supernatural about Peter. Peter, however, who was not only unaccustomed to such honors but brought up to consider them blasphemous, ordered him to stand up and assured him, "I am only a man myself" (cf. 14:14–15; Rev 19:10; 22:8–9).

27–29 In Cornelius's living quarters Peter found a large group waiting to hear what he had to say. Perhaps he was self-conscious and so began by saying that Jewish law prohibited a Jew from associating with Gentiles. Admittedly, this was an ideal representation of the Jewish position (as so often happens in the Talmud), for Jewish ethical law contains a number of provisions for Jewish-Gentile business partnerships (e.g., *b. Šabb.* 150*a*) and even for Jews' bathing with Gentiles (ibid., 151*a*). But such contacts made a Jew ceremonially unclean, as did entering the buildings of Gentiles or touching their possessions. Above all, it was forbidden to accept the hospitality of Gentiles and eat with them, particularly because Gentiles did not tithe. Scrupulous Jews were not even permitted to be guests of a Jewish commoner (cf. *m. Demai* 2:2–3), much less of a Gentile (ibid., 3:4). But God in a vision, Peter said, had taught him not to call anyone impure or unclean; so now he was associating with them without traditional scruples.

30–33 Cornelius told Peter all about his vision and described how he sent for him, and he invited him to relate "everything the Lord has commanded you to tell us" (v.33). Few preachers ever had a more receptive audience than Peter had on this occasion.

The reference to the "ninth hour" (NASB; NIV, "three in the afternoon") is probably not meant to specify the time of evening prayer in Judaism (see comments at v.3), but to highlight a feature that was of great importance to Cornelius, i.e., that the vision happened "at this hour" (*mechri tautēs tēs hōras*). Also significant are Luke's repetitions of the circumstances of Cornelius's vision and the details of Peter's vision (11:4–10), for they serve an important function in the doublet structure of his whole presentation (see Overview, pp. 754–55).

NOTES

24 Codices Vaticanus (B) and Bezae (D) have the singular verb εἰσῆλθεν (*eisēlthen*, "he arrived," GK 1656), though ℵ A C E and P have the plural εἰσῆλθον (*eisēlthon*, "they arrived"). External evidence is difficult to evaluate, for equally good MSS support each option (so NIV, "he arrived," and NASB, "he entered";

cf. NRSV, "they came"). Probably the singular was original, for scribes would have been tempted to assimilate a singular verb to the plural verb that precedes it and the plural pronoun that follows it, rather than the opposite.

Codex Bezae (D) inserts καί (*kai*, "and") before the aorist participle συγκαλεσάμενος (*synkalesamenos*, "called together," GK *5157*) and adds περιέμεινεν (*periemeinen*, "he was waiting for them," GK *4338*) at the end of the sentence.

25 Codex Bezae (D) and some of its Western associates (various Latin, Syriac, and Coptic recensions) add, "And as Peter was drawing near to Caesarea, one of the servants ran ahead and announced that he had arrived. And Cornelius sprang up and went out to meet him." Whether this servant should be understood as someone stationed at the city gate to bring Cornelius word of Peter's coming or one of the original messengers in the party who ran ahead to tell his master of Peter's soon arrival, the words appear to be a gloss inserted to answer the question of how Cornelius knew when to go out to meet Peter and summon his relatives and close friends to his home.

30 Codex Bezae (D) reads ἀπὸ τῆς τρίτης ἡμέρας (*apo tēs tritēs hēmeras*, "three days ago," lit., "from the third day"), which shortens the journey by one day. Bezae (D) with its Western associates also adds νηστεύων (*nēsteuōn*, "fasting," GK *3764*): "I was in my house fasting and praying"—which is a pietistic addition typical of this family of MSS.

32 The Western text (D E and Old Latin and Syriac recensions) and the Byzantine tradition (H L P and many minuscules), and so the TR and KJV, add ὃς παραγενόμενος λαλήσει σοι (*hos paragenomenos lalēsei soi*, "who, when he arrives, will speak to you," evidently seeking to parallel 11:14.

33 The Western text modifies this verse in several respects, most notably by adding παρακαλῶν ἐλθεῖν πρὸς ἡμᾶς (*parakalōn elthein pros hēmas*, "asking [you] to come to us") in the first clause and ἐν τάχει (*en tachei*, "so quickly") in the second.

Chester Beatty 𝔓45 omits πάντες (*pantes*, "all") and ἐνώπιον τοῦ θεοῦ (*enōpion tou theou*, "in the presence of God"), though they are otherwise well supported.

5. Peter's Sermon in Cornelius's House (10:34–43)

OVERVIEW

Peter's sermon in Cornelius's house is a précis of the apostolic *kerygma*. It is similar in structure and content to his earlier sermons in 2:14–40 and 3:11–26, though it contains more information about Jesus' earthly ministry than those two sermons (cf. 4:8–12; 5:29–32). Dibelius, 110, complained that "a speech which is so long, relatively speaking, cannot have had any place in a legend told among Christians about the conversion of a centurion." But surely a Gentile audience, even though it may have known something about Jesus of Nazareth from living in Palestine, would require more details about Jesus' life and work than a Jewish-Palestinian audience would. Peter's more lengthy account of Jesus' ministry here must, therefore, be considered particularly appropriate, considering his audience. Furthermore, the sermon is sprinkled with Semitisms, which show its rooting in history (see the discussion of Semitisms, pp. 682–84) and is comparable in both scope and emphasis to Mark's gospel, which may very well reflect Peter's preaching in Rome (cf. C. H. Dodd, "The Framework of the Gospel Narrative," *Exp Tim* 43 [1931–32]: 396–400).

> [34]Then Peter began to speak:"I now realize how true it is that God does not show favoritism [35]but accepts men from every nation who fear him and do what is right. [36]You know the message God sent to the people of Israel, telling the good news of peace through Jesus Christ, who is Lord of all. [37]You know what has happened throughout Judea, beginning in Galilee after the baptism that John preached—[38]how God anointed Jesus of Nazareth with the Holy Spirit and power, and how he went around doing good and healing all who were under the power of the devil, because God was with him.
>
> [39]"We are witnesses of everything he did in the country of the Jews and in Jerusalem. They killed him by hanging him on a tree, [40]but God raised him from the dead on the third day and caused him to be seen. [41]He was not seen by all the people, but by witnesses whom God had already chosen by us who ate and drank with him after he rose from the dead. [42]He commanded us to preach to the people and to testify that he is the one whom God appointed as judge of the living and the dead. [43]All the prophets testify about him that everyone who believes in him receives forgiveness of sins through his name."

COMMENTARY

34–35 The sermon is prefaced by the words "opening his mouth, Peter said" (*anoixas de Petros to stoma eipen*). This was one way to introduce a weighty utterance (cf. Mt 5:2; 13:35 [quoting Ps 78:2]; Ac 8:35). In Luke's eyes, what Peter was about to say was indeed momentous in sweeping away centuries of racial prejudice. It begins by Peter's statement that God does not show "favoritism" or "partiality" (*prosōpolēmptēs* [GK 4720], which appears only here in the NT but whose synonym *prosōpolēmpsia* is found in Ro 2:11; Eph 6:9; Col 3:25; Jas 2:1; 1Pe 1:17), "but accepts [people] from every nation who fear him and do what is right." While some consciousness of this may be implicit in Israel's history and at times have been expressed by her prophets (cf. Am 9:7; Mic 6:8), it was only by means of a revelational clarification—i.e., a "pesher" interpretation of what was earlier consid-

ered to be a highly enigmatic "mystery" (cf. Eph 3:4–6)—that Peter came to appreciate the racial challenge of the gospel.

36 Peter captions his sermon, "The message God sent to the people of Israel, telling the good news of peace through Jesus Christ, who is Lord of all." The Greek of vv.36–38 is syntactically awkward, thus suggesting either a translation from an earlier Semitic source (as C. C. Torrey argued), a Septuagintal "archaizing" on Luke's part (as H. F. D. Sparks proposed), or the reproduction of speech patterns of one who thought in Semitic fashion even while speaking Greek. Interestingly (and I believe significantly), Raymond Martin's 1974 study (*Syntactical Evidence of Semitic Sources in Greek Documents*) does not credit the syntax of Peter's sermon here either to Semitic sources or to Lukan ingenuity, though he includes Peter's defense of Cornelius's conversion in

11:1–18 among those portions that reflect an earlier Semitic source. We may reasonably conclude that the awkwardness of the syntax in the account of this sermon probably stems from Peter himself as he spoke before his Gentile audience in somewhat "broken" Greek. Had it been Luke's own composition, it would have been much clearer.

The caption of Peter's sermon contains three emphases that set the tone for all that follows. First, there is a revelational emphasis. For while the caption begins in somewhat elliptical fashion by omitting the understood subject and verb "this is" (*touto estin*), it nonetheless expresses in form and content a pesher type of revelational understanding that was common in early apostolic Christianity (cf. the *touto estin* of 2:16). Second, there is an emphasis on the proclamation of the gospel "to the people of Israel," its immediate recipients. Joined with this is a third emphasis related to bringing that gospel to the Gentile world in terms that would be comprehensible to Gentiles—an emphasis characterized by the expression "Lord of all." This title was properly a pagan title for deity (cf. H. Cadbury, *Beginnings of Christianity* [ed. Foakes-Jackson and Lake], 5.361–62), but it was rebaptized by the early believers in Jesus to become an appropriate christological title (cf. Col 1:15–20). So Peter's sermon in Cornelius's house concerns (1) a new revelational understanding of God's message of peace, (2) which is given to the sons of Israel as its primary recipients, but (3) which also includes Gentiles under the rubric of Christ as "Lord of all"—with "all" understood as connoting Christ's lordship over both Jews and Gentiles.

37–41 Peter begins his sermon with a résumé of Jesus' life and work during his earthly ministry. Though Peter assumes his hearers, because they lived in Palestine, already knew something about Jesus' ministry, he proceeds to summarize it in greater detail than anywhere else in his recorded preaching. In scope and emphasis, the account is much like the portrayal of Jesus' ministry in Mark's gospel: It begins with John the Baptist, moves on to Jesus' anointing with the Holy Spirit, refers to Jesus' many acts of divine power in Galilee, alludes to his continued ministry throughout Palestine and in Jerusalem, stresses his crucifixion, and concludes with a declaration of his resurrection and its verification by his appearances to chosen followers.

As it stands before us, the sermon is only a summary of what Peter actually said at the time. Originally, it may have contained a number of examples of Jesus' acts of kindness and healing, such as those recorded in the Synoptic Gospels. In addition, as a précis of what Peter said, it shows the interests of Luke, who put the sermon into its present form— i.e., the influence in v.38 of Isaiah 61:1, which is an OT passage that Luke highlighted in his theme paragraph of Luke 4:14–30 at the start of his two-volume writing (see Introduction, pp. 693–96). Also, the importance of the apostolic witness in establishing the Christian tradition comes to the fore in vv.39–41, as it does elsewhere throughout Luke-Acts. Furthermore, Luke's interest in Jesus' post-resurrection eating and drinking with his disciples is evident in v.41. Only Luke records this occasion (cf. Lk 24:41–43) as a convincing proof of Jesus' physical presence—evidently reflecting a Jewish understanding that angels and apparitions, being without digestive tracts, are unable to eat or drink.

42–43 Peter ends his sermon by stating that the risen Christ has commanded his apostles to preach "to the people" (*tō laō*) and to testify about his divine appointment as "judge of the living and the dead." By his use of *ho laos* ("the people"), Peter probably had in mind "the Jewish people." Until then, the early church knew no other mission. But then Peter went on to speak of the OT prophets' testifying about this risen Lord and saying that "everyone who believes in him [*panta ton pisteuonta* eis auton] receives forgiveness of sins through his name" (v.43). It was this reference to "everyone who believes in him" that seems to have broken through the traditional barrier between Jews and Gentiles and to have encouraged Cornelius and those in his house to be bold enough to think that they, together with Jews, could receive the blessings promised to Israel.

NOTES

34–36 On pesher interpretation at Qumran and in the NT, see my *Biblical Exegesis in the Apostolic Period*, 24–30.

36–38 The Greek syntax of the Alexandrian text ($\mathfrak{P}^{45}$ $\mathfrak{P}^{50}$ $\mathfrak{P}^{74}$ $\aleph$ A B C etc.) is in several respects awkward and broken. Some have argued that an Aramaic original has been rather ungrammatically translated into Greek, and others that these verses evidence an unrevised conflation of sources. Perhaps, however, this was simply how Peter himself spoke. The Western text (D and its associates), evidently embarrassed by the awkward syntax, recasts these verses to read, "For you know the message that he sent to the sons of Israel, which was published throughout all Judea, when he preached the good news of peace through Jesus Christ, who is Lord of all. For beginning in Galilee, after the baptism that John preached, Jesus of Nazareth, whom God anointed with the Holy Spirit and power, went about doing good."

37 Codex Vaticanus (B) reads κήρυγμα (*kērygma*, "proclamation," GK *3060*) for βάπτισμα (*baptisma*, "baptism," GK *967*).

38 Ἰησοῦν τὸν ἀπὸ Ναζαρέθ (*Iēsoun ton apo Nazareth*, "Jesus of Nazareth"), which is in the accusative case, is grammatically the object of the verb ἔχρισεν (*echrisen*, "he anointed," GK *5987*), but it appears at the beginning of its clause for emphasis and is caught up later by the pronoun αὐτόν (*auton*, "him").

40 Codex Bezae (D) adds at the end of the first clause μετὰ τὴν τρίτην ἡμέραν (*meta tēn tritēn hēmeran*, "after the third day"), evidently to attempt a harmony with Matthew 27:63 et al.

41 The Western text (D E and various recensions of Latin, Syriac, and Coptic versions) adds συνανεστράφημεν or συνεστράφημεν (*synanestraphēmen* or *synestraphēmen*, "we accompanied [him]," GK *5266*) ...ἡμέρας τεσσεράκοντα (*hēmeras tesserakonta*, "forty days") after "who ate and drank with him," evidently to attempt a harmony with 1:3.

6. Gentiles Receive the Holy Spirit (10:44–48)

⁴⁴While Peter was still speaking these words, the Holy Spirit came on all who heard the message. ⁴⁵The circumcised believers who had come with Peter were astonished that the gift of the Holy Spirit had been poured out even on the Gentiles. ⁴⁶For they heard them speaking in tongues and praising God.

Then Peter said, ⁴⁷"Can anyone keep these people from being baptized with water? They have received the Holy Spirit just as we have." ⁴⁸So he ordered that they be baptized in the name of Jesus Christ. Then they asked Peter to stay with them for a few days.

COMMENTARY

44 As Peter was "speaking these words [*ta rhēmata tauta*], the Holy Spirit came on all who heard the message [*ton logon*, GK *3364*]." The expression "these words" may refer to the entire sermon just delivered, as epitomized by the term "the message" in the predicate of the sentence. Probably, however, "these words" have in mind the statement "everyone who believes in him receives forgiveness of sins through his name" of v.43—with special attention being directed to the clause "everyone who believes in him" (*panta ton pisteuonta eis auton*), which appears at the end of v.43 in the Greek probably for emphasis. If this is true, then Luke is saying that it was this phrase that struck like a thunderbolt into the consciousness of the assembled Gentiles, thus releasing their pent-up emotions and emboldening them to respond by faith. With the promise of forgiveness offered "through his name" and to "everyone who believes in him," they were given a reason for hope beyond their fondest expectations. And with their reception of that inclusive message, the Holy Spirit came on the Gentile congregation there gathered just as he had come on the disciples at Pentecost. In fact, this was, as Frederic Chase long ago called it, "the Pentecost of the Gentile world" (*The Credibility of the Book of the Acts of the Apostles* [New York: Macmillan, 1902], 79).

45–46 The six Jewish believers (*hoi ek peritomēs pistoi*, "the circumcised believers," GK *4364, 4412*) who had come with Peter were astonished at what they saw and heard. For in accepting these Gentiles and bestowing his Holy Spirit on them, God had providentially attested his action by the same sign of tongues as at Pentecost. The gift of tongues at Pentecost is probably to be understood as distinguishable languages, because they were immediately recognized as dialects then current (see comments at

2:4). Here, however, an outburst of foreign languages would have fallen on deaf ears and failed to be convincing. So we should probably view what was expressed here as ecstatic utterances, such as Paul later described in 1 Corinthians 12–14. Undoubtedly the sign of tongues was given primarily for the sake of the Jewish believers who were present at that time in Cornelius's house. But it was also given for the sake of the Jerusalem believers who would later hear of what happened, so that all would recognize the conversion of these Gentiles as being entirely of God and none would revert to their old prejudices and relegate these new converts to a role of second-class Christians.

47–48 Peter may not have been much of an abstract thinker, but to his great credit he was ready to follow the divine initiative—if only he could be sure that God was really at work. So, convinced by God and consistent with his conviction about the logical connections between Christian conversion, the baptism of the Holy Spirit, and water baptism (see comments at 2:38), Peter calls for the Gentiles who have received the baptism of the Spirit to be baptized with water "in the name of Jesus Christ" (v.48). While Acts 2 and 8 indicate that water baptism does not take the place of the Spirit's baptism but that the two go hand-in-hand with conversion, so vv.47–48 speak of the baptism of the Holy Spirit as not supplanting baptism with water but as being the spiritual reality to which water baptism testifies. Thus the baptism of these Gentile converts pointed to a new spiritual reality in their lives. But it also had immense significance for Peter and his six companions. For in baptizing these Gentiles, Peter and those with him confessed that God in his sovereignty does bring Gentiles directly into relationship with Jesus Christ apart from any prior relationship with Judaism.

Peter may have been somewhat uncertain as to (1) how Cornelius's new commitment to Jesus of Nazareth as Messiah and Lord should be expressed in worship and service and (2) how it should be related to the Roman social order and to Judaism. But these were matters yet to be worked out. For now it was sufficient that God had broken down the traditional barriers between Jews and Gentiles. So Peter was content to stay in Caesarea with these new Gentile converts "for a few days."

NOTES

46 Several Latin Western witnesses (Old Latin, Vulgate, and several Latin church fathers) qualify "tongues" with readings that presuppose one or another of the following Greek adjectives: ποίκιλαις (*poikilais*, "various kinds of," GK 4476), καίναις (*kainais*, "new," GK 2785), or ἑτέραις (*heterais*, "different," GK 2283), thereby suggesting foreign languages rather than ecstatic utterances.

48 On the synonymous use of the prepositions ἐπί (*epi*, "on"), ἐν (*en*, "in"), and εἰς (*eis*, "into") with Christian baptism, see comments and note at 2:38.

The Western text adds τοῦ κυρίου (*tou kyriou*, "of the Lord") before Ἰησοῦ Χριστοῦ (*Iēsou Christou*, "Jesus Christ"), as it does also in 2:38 in harmony with 8:16 and 19:5.

7. The Response of the Jerusalem Church (11:1–18)

OVERVIEW

The conversion of Cornelius was a landmark in the history of the gospel's advance from its strictly Jewish beginnings to its penetration of the Roman Empire. True, it did not settle any of the issues relating to Jewish-Gentile relations within the church. Nor did Jewish believers take it as a precedent for a direct outreach to Gentiles. But it did show that the sovereign God was not confined to the traditional forms of Judaism and that he could bring a Gentile directly into relationship with himself through Jesus Christ apart from any prior commitment to distinctive Jewish beliefs or lifestyle.

Cornelius's conversion was important to Luke not only because of the gospel's advance but also because of the response of believers in the Jerusalem church to it. Amid his portrayals of development and advance, Luke also wanted to highlight lines of continuity and areas of agreement within the early church. So he takes pains to point out here—as he did in his account of the conversion of the Samaritans in 8:14–25—that, despite objections raised, the leadership of the Jerusalem church accepted the validity of Cornelius's conversion apart from any prior affiliation with Judaism. And that acceptance was of as great importance in validating a later Gentile mission as was the event itself.

¹The apostles and the brothers throughout Judea heard that the Gentiles also had received the word of God. ²So when Peter went up to Jerusalem, the circumcised believers criticized him ³and said, "You went into the house of uncircumcised men and ate with them."

⁴Peter began and explained everything to them precisely as it had happened: ⁵"I was in the city of Joppa praying, and in a trance I saw a vision. I saw something like a large sheet being let down from heaven by its four corners, and it came down to where I was. ⁶I looked into it and saw four-footed animals of the earth, wild beasts, reptiles, and birds of the air. ⁷Then I heard a voice telling me, 'Get up, Peter. Kill and eat.'

⁸"I replied, 'Surely not, Lord! Nothing impure or unclean has ever entered my mouth.'

⁹"The voice spoke from heaven a second time, 'Do not call anything impure that God has made clean.' ¹⁰This happened three times, and then it was all pulled up to heaven again.

¹¹"Right then three men who had been sent to me from Caesarea stopped at the house where I was staying. ¹²The Spirit told me to have no hesitation about going with them. These six brothers also went with me, and we entered the man's house. ¹³He told us how he had seen an angel appear in his house and say, 'Send to Joppa for Simon who is called Peter. ¹⁴He will bring you a message through which you and all your household will be saved.'

¹⁵"As I began to speak, the Holy Spirit came on them as he had come on us at the beginning. ¹⁶Then I remembered what the Lord had said: 'John baptized with water, but you will be baptized with the Holy Spirit.' ¹⁷So if God gave them the same gift as he gave us, who believed in the Lord Jesus Christ, who was I to think that I could oppose God?"

¹⁸When they heard this, they had no further objections and praised God, saying, "So then, God has granted even the Gentiles repentance unto life."

COMMENTARY

1–3 News of Peter's activity at Caesarea reached Jerusalem and believers of the Jewish capital city before Peter did. Codex Bezae (D) and its Western associates expand v.2 to read that he stayed in Caesarea "for a considerable time" and that "he did a great deal of preaching throughout the regions" around Caesarea (see Notes, v.2). But however long it took Peter to return to Jerusalem, news of his direct approach to Gentiles and acceptance of them apart from the strictures of Judaism caused great alarm both within the Jerusalem church and among the Jewish populace generally. The Hellenistic-Jewish Christians had stirred up a great deal of antagonism by their liberal attitudes toward the tenets of popular Jewish piety (cf. 6:8–7:56). The immediate consequences were the martyrdom of Stephen and the expulsion of those believers from areas under Sanhedrin control (cf. 7:57–8:3). Now if it were really true that Peter, the leading member of the apostolic band, had gone further in disregarding the traditional laws of Judaism in favor of a direct association with Gentiles, whatever goodwill still remained toward believers in Jerusalem would be quickly dissipated. The practical implications for the existence and the mission of the Christian church in Jerusalem were grave. Undoubtedly, such practical considerations led to basic theological questions.

Peter's return to Jerusalem, therefore, was hardly a return to a more comfortable situation after a strenuous journey. It was more like lighting a match in highly combustible air. "The circumcised believers" (*hoi ek peritomēs*, lit., "those of the circumcision," which usually means only "the Jews" but in context certainly connotes Jewish "believers") immediately confronted Peter and charged, "You went into the house of uncircumcised men and ate with them." This charge, while traditionally worded, was tantamount to saying that Peter had set aside Christianity's Jewish features and thereby seriously endangered relations between the church and the nation.

4–17 Peter defended his actions by recounting his experiences at Joppa and Caesarea, with an emphasis on (1) the divine initiative in all that transpired and (2) his inability to withstand God. He recounted the details of the vision that came to him at Joppa (vv.5–10), his reception by Cornelius (vv.11–14), and the Spirit's coming on the people who gathered in Cornelius's house (vv.15–17). It was the Lord, insisted Peter, who gave him the vision and who explained its meaning. It was the Spirit who told him to "have no hesitation" (v.12, *mēden diakrinanta*, lit., "making no distinction"; NASB, "without misgivings" [see NASB text note]) to go with the messengers to Caesarea and enter Cornelius's house. And it was God who took the initiative by baptizing Cornelius and his companions with the Holy Spirit. Therefore, concluded Peter, "Who was I to think that I could oppose God?" (v.17).

Of interest in this account are the many Semitic features incorporated into the Greek of Peter's defense—features that have led a number of scholars to postulate a written Aramaic source drawn on by Luke for his depiction in ch. 11 of what Peter said. While Peter's sermon in Cornelius's house was probably delivered in a broken, "Semitized" Greek (see comments and note at 10:36–38), his defense at Jerusalem may well have been delivered in Aramaic and circulated among the Hebraic believers in that form. Likewise of interest is the vividness of Peter's address here in ch. 11, as compared with the rather colorless third-person style in ch. 10. While in structure and content the two accounts are very similar, the retelling of Peter's experiences in ch. 11 has a freshness and vitality that make it more than a mere résumé of events as related in ch. 10. This may only reflect the literary genius of Luke. Probably, however, it points to a use of differing sources for chs. 10 and 11—the one of Caesarean origin and narrating the events in Greek; the other of Jerusalem origin and containing Peter's defense in Aramaic. With his stress on a twofold witness to truth (see Overview, p. 754), Luke probably viewed these two sets of material as providing greater support for his presentation and so brought them together in the manner presently before us.

18 On hearing about Peter's experiences, the Christians at Jerusalem "remained silent" (*hēsychasan*, GK 2483; NIV, "had no further objections"; NASB, "quieted down") and "praised God." This probably means that his critics, at least for the moment, were silenced, while those more receptive to God's working acknowledged that Peter was right and credited God rather than human ingenuity for what had happened. In view of what Peter reported, the Jerusalem church could come to no other conclusion than that "God has granted even the Gentiles repentance unto life."

This was a response of momentous importance for the church at Jerusalem, and undoubtedly Luke meant his readers to appreciate it as being as significant in validating a later Gentile mission as was the conversion of Cornelius itself. But while the acceptance of Gentiles was of vital significance for the course of redemptive history, it said nothing about the many related questions that were bound to arise soon: What lifestyle was appropriate for Gentiles coming to Christ directly out of paganism? How should they relate themselves as Christians to Jewish Christians and to Jews, both of whom followed a Jewish lifestyle? How should the Jerusalem church relate itself in practice to these new Gentile believers that it had in theory accepted? These are matters the Jerusalem church did not address when it acknowledged God's working and approval, as recorded in v.18. Yet such matters were logically involved in its response and were to be taken up again later, particularly in the Jerusalem Council of 15:1–35.

Just as there were ideological issues left unresolved in the response of the church in ch. 11, so there are also a number of historical matters about which Luke gives us no information, though we would like very much to know: Whatever happened, for example, to Cornelius and his fellow Gentile Christians after Peter left them? Did they troop en masse to Jerusalem to worship with the Jewish believers there? (For a number of reasons, this hardly seems likely.) Or did they join with Philip and his converts in Caesarea (cf. 8:40) to form a worshiping community there? Or did they somehow inaugurate a distinctive form of Gentile-Christian worship? Or, being doubtless all associated in one way or another with the Roman army and the Roman administration in Palestine, were these Gentile believers in Jesus transferred to other posts in the empire by Rome, either through due course or because of their recent alignment with a minority group within Palestine? Luke does not tell us.

Neither does Luke tell us how such a response affected the Jerusalem church: Did it lose a measure of goodwill among its Jewish compatriots because of its acceptance of Cornelius's conversion? Were there believers within its ranks who felt bad about the decision and expressed their dissatisfaction, either then or later, in ways that would be disruptive to a further Gentile outreach? Was this one of the reasons why the Jerusalem church soon found it appropriate to have as its leader the Pharisaically trained and legally scrupulous James the Just, rather than one or more of the apostles (see comments at 12:2)? Again, Luke does not tell us, though some of these matters will come to the fore later in Acts.

NOTES

2 On going "up to" and "down from" Jerusalem, see comments and note at 8:5.

Codex Bezae (D) differs widely from the text preserved in the other Greek MSS, for it reads, "Peter, therefore, for a considerable time wished to journey to Jerusalem; and having called to him the brothers and strengthening them, he departed. Speaking much throughout the country and teaching, he also went to meet them [i.e., those of the church at Jerusalem] and reported to them the grace of God. But the brothers of the circumcision disputed with him, saying . . . ." The scribe of Bezae seems to have wanted to avoid putting Peter in a bad light—i.e., to avoid any impression that Peter had to break off his mission work and go to Jerusalem in order to justify himself. So he has Peter continuing his missionary activity "for a considerable time," and finally, on his own initiative and without any sense of having to give account of himself, voluntarily going to Jerusalem simply to report to the home church about his mission.

4–17 On the Semitisms of Peter's defense, see Raymond A. Martin, *Syntactical Evidence of Semitic Sources in Greek Documents*.

9 Codex Bezae (D) reads ἐγένετο φωνὴ ἐκ τοῦ οὐρανοῦ πρός με (*egeneto phōnē ek tou ouranou pros me*, "there came a voice from heaven to me").

11 The first person plural ἦμεν (*ēmen*, "we were [staying]") is supported by Bodmer 𝔓⁷⁴ (seventh century), ℵ A B D and some minuscules; the first person singular ἤμην (*ēmēn*, "I was [staying]") is supported by Chester Beatty 𝔓⁴⁵ (third century), E P and most minuscules. The "harder reading" is ἦμεν (*ēmen*) simply because of its apparent irrelevancy (so NASB); ἤμην (*ēmēn*) is more appropriate to the context (so NIV).

12 The Western text omits μηδὲν διακρίναντα (*mēden diakrinanta*, lit., "making no distinction"; NIV, "have no hesitation"; NASB, "without misgivings").

15 The use of the verb ἄρχω (*archō*, "begin," GK *806*) in the expression "as I began to speak" should probably be viewed as a redundant auxiliary (cf. 11:4; also 2:4; 18:26; 24:2; 27:35) and its temporal or chronological significance not unduly pressed.

17 Codex Bezae (D) omits ὁ θεός (*ho theos*, "God"), probably because the Western scribe viewed the Holy Spirit as the gift of Christ, who is God the Son.

C. The Church at Antioch of Syria (11:19–30)

OVERVIEW

Antioch of Syria was founded about 300 BC by Seleucus I Nicator, who named it after either his father or his son, both of whom bore the name Antiochus. It was situated on the Orontes River, about three hundred miles north of Jerusalem and twenty miles east of the Mediterranean, at the joining of the Lebanon and Taurus mountain ranges where the Orontes breaks through and flows down to the sea. To distinguish it from some fifteen other Asiatic cities built by Seleucus and also named Antioch, it was frequently called "Antioch-on-the-Orontes," "Antioch-by-Daphne" (Daphne, the celebrated temple of Apollo, was nearby), "Antioch the Great," "Antioch the Beautiful," and "The Queen of the East." During the first Christian century it

was, after Rome and Alexandria, the third largest city in the empire, with a population of more than five hundred thousand. In AD 540 Antioch was sacked by the Persians—a calamity from which it never recovered. Today Antakiyeh (ancient Antioch) is a poor place of about thirty-five thousand inhabitants.

First-century Antioch was a melting pot of Western and Eastern cultures, a city where Greek and Roman traditions mingled with Semitic, Arab, and Persian influences. The Jewish population is estimated to have been about one-seventh of the total population and had vested rights to follow its own laws within its three or more settlements in and around the city. During the reign of Caligula (AD

37-41), however, many Jews were killed; and during the tumultuous period of the middle and late 60s AD, Jewish acceptance and prosperity in Antioch came to an end. The city was known not only for its sophistication and culture but also for its vices. The beautiful pleasure park of Daphne was a center for moral depravity of every kind, and the expression *Daphnici mores* became a proverb for depraved living. The Roman satirist Juvenal (AD 60-140) aimed one of his sharpest gibes at his own decadent Rome when he said that the Orontes River had flowed into the Tiber (*Sat.* 3.62), thus flooding the imperial city with the superstition and immorality of the East. (For an extensive discussion of Antioch-on-the-Orontes, see my article "Antioch of Syria," in *Major Cities of the Biblical World*, ed. R. K. Harrison [Nashville: Nelson, 1985], 8-21.)

In Christian history, apart from Jerusalem no other city of the Roman Empire played as large a part in the early life and fortunes of the church as Antioch of Syria. It was the birthplace of foreign missions (13:2) and the home base for Paul's outreach to the eastern half of the empire. It was the place where those of "the Way" (9:2) were first called "Christians" (11:26) and where the question as to the necessity for Gentile converts to submit to the rite of circumcision first arose (15:1-2; cf. Gal 2:11-21). It had among its teachers such illustrious persons as Barnabas, Paul, and Peter in the first century (cf. Gal 2:11-13); Ignatius and Theophilus in the second century; and Lucian, Theodore, Chrysostom, and Theodoret—as well as a host of others, including Nestorius—at the end of the third and throughout the fourth centuries.

In the light of its great importance for both the empire and the early church, it is somewhat surprising that Luke's account of the founding of the church at Syrian Antioch and of the progress of the gospel there is so compressed. Adolf Harnack proposed that 11:19-30 was part of a Jerusalem-Antiochene source that included 12:25-15:35 and was related to the source for 6:1-8:4 (see Introduction, pp. 681-82). But the narrative here clearly differs in style from that which Luke has already used in his account of Stephen and the Hellenists—likewise, from that which he will use in writing about Paul and his first missionary journey. It is devoid of Semitisms, whereas 6:1-8:4 and 12:25-15:35 contain many (cf. Martin, *Syntactical Evidence for Semitic Sources in Greek Documents*). And it has a number of favorite Lukan expressions (e.g., *lalountes ton logon*, "speaking the word" [v.19]; *polys arithmos*, "a great number" [v.21]; *anēr agathos*, "a good man" [v.24; GK 467, 19]; *prosetethē ochlos hikanos*, lit., "a great crowd was added" [v.24; NIV, "a great number of people were brought"; cf. v.26]), as well as the repeated use of Luke's favorite christological title "Lord" (which appears five times in vv.20-24). Probably, therefore, we should view 11:19-30 as a free Lukan summary of certain items of information known to him—perhaps, in fact, as the way that Luke wrote when not having written source material at his disposal (as seems to underlie much of the first half of Acts) or when not himself an eyewitness of the events (as seems to be the rationale for the "we" sections of the last half of Acts).

1. Founding of the Church at Antioch (11:19–26)

¹⁹Now those who had been scattered by the persecution in connection with Stephen traveled as far as Phoenicia, Cyprus and Antioch, telling the message only to Jews. ²⁰Some of them, however, men from Cyprus and Cyrene, went to Antioch and began to speak to Greeks also, telling them the good news about the Lord Jesus. ²¹The Lord's hand was with them, and a great number of people believed and turned to the Lord.

²²News of this reached the ears of the church at Jerusalem, and they sent Barnabas to Antioch. ²³When he arrived and saw the evidence of the grace of God, he was glad and encouraged them all to remain true to the Lord with all their hearts. ²⁴He was a good man, full of the Holy Spirit and faith, and a great number of people were brought to the Lord.

²⁵Then Barnabas went to Tarsus to look for Saul, ²⁶and when he found him, he brought him to Antioch. So for a whole year Barnabas and Saul met with the church and taught great numbers of people. The disciples were called Christians first at Antioch.

COMMENTARY

19 Luke opens his account of the gospel's proclamation at Antioch with the same words with which he began the story of the mission to Samaria in 8:4—a fact that suggests he wanted to reach behind his accounts of Peter's ministries at Lydda, Joppa, and Caesarea to start a new strand of history beginning with the death of Stephen. From such an opening we should probably understand that the Hellenistic-Jewish Christians' mission to Phoenicia, Cyprus, and Antioch was (1) logically similar to that in Samaria, and not a continuation of Peter's mission at Lydda, Joppa, and Caesarea; and (2) chronologically parallel, at least in its early stages, to the accounts in 8:4–11:18. Phoenicia, Cyprus, and the city of Antioch-on-the-Orontes had large Jewish populations. Syria, like Babylonia, was often considered, in fact, an integral part of the Jewish homeland because of the many scrupulous Jews living there. Thus since this mission to the north was (1) carried on within areas roughly considered to be Jewish territory; (2) mounted by Hellenistic-Jewish believers in Jesus; and (3) directed, at least at first, "only to Jews," Luke

presents it here as still being part of the Christian witness to the Jewish world, even though the account speaks of a time when the categories "Jew" and "Gentile" were beginning to break down.

20–21 At Antioch some of the Hellenistic Jewish Christians "began to speak to Greeks also." Some MSS read *Hellēnas* ("Greeks"), while others read *Hellēnistas* ("Hellenists," possibly "Grecian Jews"). The external evidence for the text is inconclusive and difficult to evaluate (see Notes). But certainly the contrast drawn between the "Jews" of v.19 and those who receive the gospel here in v.20 makes it all but impossible to understand those referred to in v.20 as anything other than Gentiles. It is necessary, therefore, to read the text as having in mind "Greeks" or Gentiles (so NIV, NASB), not "Hellenists" or Hellenistic Jews (so NRSV).

But reading "Greeks" (*Hellēnas*) here raises other problems: Did Luke have in mind Gentiles who had no affiliation whatever with Judaism? Or did he have in mind Gentiles who had some kind of relationship with Judaism, perhaps "Proselytes of the

Gate" or something like that? Usually Luke speaks of such near-proselytes as "God-fearers" (*sebomenoi ton theon*, 13:50; 16:14; 17:4, 17; 18:7; see also *phoboumenoi ton theon* in 13:16, 26), which is not his expression here. Yet judging by his evident purpose in Acts to present Paul as the first to inaugurate a deliberate policy of direct approach to Gentiles, it is extremely difficult to view these Greeks as being apart from the ministrations of Judaism. Peter's activity in Caesarea was, indeed, a direct approach to Gentiles, but it set no precedent and established no policy for such an outreach. If this is what Luke is saying happened at Antioch of Syria, he has nullified the point he makes later in chs. 13–15.

On the other hand, by the way Luke treats these Greeks as being both a part of the mission to Jews and yet distinct from the Jews, probably we are to view them as having become Christians "through the door of the synagogue" (Ramsay, *St. Paul the Traveller*, 41) and thought of by the early church as an adjunct in its ministry to the Jewish nation. With the merging of cultures and blurring of distinctives taking place in Antioch generally, perhaps even Judaism faced some problems in drawing a sharp line between Gentiles who had some minimal relationship with the synagogue and those considered to be near-proselytes. But whatever their status, it seems fair to say (1) that Luke did not look on the Greeks in v.20 as simply Gentiles unaffected by the influence of Judaism, and (2) that he did not view the Hellenistic-Jewish Christians' approach to them as preempting the uniqueness of Paul's later Gentile policy.

All we are told about the identity of the Jewish-Christian missionaries to Antioch is that they were from Cyprus and Cyrene. Perhaps Simeon Niger and Lucius of Cyrene were two of them (cf. 13:1), though Barnabas of Cyprus was not. But Luke does say that to the missionaries' proclamation of "the good news about the Lord Jesus" there was a significant response, so that "a great number of people

believed and turned to the Lord." And since among that "great number" were both Jews and Gentiles, the Antioch church, though born within the synagogue, took on a decidedly different complexion from that of other early Christian congregations spoken of thus far. For it was a mixed body of Jews and uncircumcised Gentiles who met together for worship and fellowship in common allegiance to Jesus of Nazareth (cf. Gal 2:12).

22 News of the situation in Antioch was of definite concern to believers at Jerusalem. With the conversion of Samaritans and of some Gentiles in Caesarea, and now the report of a mixed congregation in Syrian Antioch, many of the believers in the Jerusalem congregation were doubtless fearful that the Christian mission was moving ahead so rapidly as to be out of control. The Jerusalem church, therefore, as in the case of the Samaritan conversions, decided to send a delegate to Antioch—probably in order to regularize whatever had gone awry and report back to the mother church. The man chosen for this task was Joseph, a Levite from Cyprus, who was residing in Jerusalem and who had gained an outstanding reputation for piety and generosity among the Christians there—and so was called by them "Barnabas," which means "Son of Encouragement" (*huios parakleseōs*; cf. 4:36–37). In all likelihood, it was the fact that he was a "Zionistic" Jew, coupled with his well-known piety and generosity, that qualified him in the eyes of the Jerusalem church for this mission to Antioch. In addition, the high esteem in which he was held made it certain that both his counsel and his report would be received with all seriousness.

23–24 The Jerusalem church could hardly have selected a better delegate, particularly from Luke's point of view. His generous spirit was gladdened by what he saw of the grace of God at work among the believers at Antioch, and true to his nickname ("Son of Encouragement"), he "encouraged them all to remain true to the Lord with all their hearts." Here was a crisis point in the history of the early church, for much depended on Barnabas's reaction, counsel, and report—not only for the life of the church at Syrian Antioch itself but also for the health of the church at Jerusalem and for the success of the later advances of the gospel through Paul's missions. With evident feeling, Luke says of him: "He was a good man, full of the Holy Spirit and faith" (v.24). And as a result of his response, the work that was started at Antioch was enabled to go on, with many brought to Christ.

25 Sometime after reaching Antioch, Barnabas went to Tarsus to find Saul to help him in the ministry back in Syria. We have no record of what Saul was doing between the time he left Jerusalem (cf. 9:30) and the time Barnabas found him in Tarsus. From Galatians 1:21–24 (cf. also Gal 2:2, 7), it is certain that in some way Saul continued preaching after leaving Jerusalem and that this was known back in Jerusalem. Perhaps the five lashings he received at the hands of the synagogue authorities (2Co 11:24), together with some of his other afflictions and hardships (cf. 2Co 11:23–27), occurred during those days in Tarsus, for they find no place in the records of his later missionary endeavors. If so, it might indicate that in Tarsus and its environs he was trying to carry on a Gentile ministry within the Cilician synagogues and was getting into trouble for it. It may also have been during this period that he began to experience the loss of all things for Christ's sake (Php 3:8), perhaps by being disinherited by his family. Perhaps the ecstatic experience he speaks about in 2 Corinthians 12:1–4 should be also associated with this period of his life.

26 It was Barnabas who had supported Saul when there was suspicion among the Christians at Jerusalem about his conversion (cf. 9:27). And now, knowing of Saul's God-given commission to minister to the Gentiles, recalling his testimony at Jerusalem, and needing help in ministering to Gentiles at Antioch, Barnabas sought out Saul to help him, and so they served together at Antioch "for a whole year" and taught "great numbers of people." Barnabas may also have heard of Saul's growing interest in the Gentiles and known of his work with them in Cilicia.

In joining Barnabas at Antioch, Saul may have thought he was carrying out the mandate received at his conversion to take the message of the risen Christ to Gentiles. Probably, however, the Antioch mission in those days was confined to the synagogue, the Antiochene Jews being more tolerant of Saul's activities than possibly the Jews at Tarsus. It may also have been viewed as part of the ministry to Jews, without any thought of the propriety of appealing more widely and directly to Gentiles. All the early believers at Antioch, whether Jews or Gentiles, may well have been related in some way to the synagogue. Thus in the eyes of many Jewish Christians, the conversion of Gentiles who had to some extent come under the ministry of Judaism before they believed in Jesus would not have been thought too exceptional.

But others within the city—evidently nonbelievers who were more perceptive in this matter than the church itself—nicknamed this group of Jewish and Gentile believers "Christians" (*Christianoi*, GK *5985*, i.e., "Christ followers" or "those of the household of Christ"). They saw that the ministry to Gentiles and the fellowship of Jews with Gentiles went beyond the bounds of what was usually permitted within Judaism. They also voiced an insight that the Christians themselves only saw clearly later on, namely, that Christianity was no mere conventicle or sect of Judaism. The new name doubtless helped develop the self-consciousness of the early Christians, despite its having been first given in derision. Later, the early Christians accepted it and used it of themselves (cf. 26:28; 1Pe 4:16; see Josephus, *Ant.* 18.64), along with their earlier self-designation, those "who belonged to the Way" (9:2; cf. 19:9, 23).

The use of the name "Christian," however, posed two great problems for the church. For one thing, Christians risked losing the protection that Rome gave to a *religio licita*, a "legal religion" officially recognized within the Roman empire (see Introduction, pp. 678–80), which status they had enjoyed when viewed by Roman authorities as only a sect within Judaism. Furthermore, being now in some way differentiated from Judaism, Christians were faced with how to understand their continuity with the hope of Israel, their acceptance of the promises of the Jewish Scriptures, and their relations with the Jewish nation. As we will see, these problems were to loom large as the Christian mission moved onto Gentile soil.

NOTES

19 On the use of μὲν οὖν (*men oun*; NIV, "now"; NASB, "so then") in Acts, see comments and note at 1:6.

20 The textual evidence for Ἕλληνας (*Hellēnas*, "Greeks") or Ἑλληνιστάς (*Hellēnistas*, "Hellenists" or "Grecian Jews") is inconclusive, the former being supported by 𝔓⁷⁴ ℵ² A D etc.; the latter by B D² E Ψ and most minuscules. In one sense, Ἑλληνιστάς (*Hellēnistas*) could be considered the "harder reading" and so more internally supportable, for the contrast with Ἰουδαίοις (*Ioudaiois*, "Jews") in v.19 clearly implies that the people spoken of here were Gentiles and not Jews—which, indeed, makes Ἑλλήνιστάς (*Hellēnistas*) the more difficult reading. On the other hand, if Ἕλληνας (*Hellēnas*) and Ἑλληνιστάς (*Hellēnistas*) were understood as roughly equivalent, as seems was the case within the ante-Nicene and post-Nicene churches (cf. the versions), it is not too hard to imagine that an original Ἕλληνας (*Hellēnas*) was replaced by Ἑλληνιστάς (*Hellēnistas*) in some texts in order to parallel the appearance of Ἑλληνιστάς (*Hellēnistas*) in 6:1 and 9:29.

On the "Hellenists" as distinguished from "Hebraic Jews" and "Greeks," see comments at 6:1 and 9:29.

25–26 Codex Bezae (D), together with some of its Western associates, expands these verses to read: "And having heard that Saul was at Tarsus, he went out to seek him; and when he met him, he entreated him to come to Antioch. When they had come, for a whole year a large company of people were stirred up, and then for the first time the disciples in Antioch were called 'Christians.'" This appears to be a rewriting of the Alexandrian text (𝔓⁴⁵ ℵ A B etc.) in order to portray more clearly why Barnabas went to Tarsus and to argue that Saul was not "brought" to Antioch but "entreated" to come.

2. Famine Relief for Jerusalem (11:27–30)

²⁷During this time some prophets came down from Jerusalem to Antioch. ²⁸One of them, named Agabus, stood up and through the Spirit predicted that a severe famine would spread over the entire Roman world. (This happened during the reign of Claudius.) ²⁹The disciples, each according to his ability, decided to provide help for the brothers living in Judea. ³⁰This they did, sending their gift to the elders by Barnabas and Saul.

COMMENTARY

27–28 Luke uses the connective "in those days" (*en tautais de tais hēmerais*; NIV, "during this time"; NASB, "at this time"), just as he did at 1:15 and 6:1 to link parts of his narrative. Now he tells of certain "prophets" who "came down from Jerusalem to Antioch." Among them was Agabus, with his dire prediction of impending famine in Jerusalem (cf. 21:10). The Jews believed that with the last of the writing prophets the spirit of prophecy had ceased in Israel, but that with the coming messianic age there would be an outpouring of God's Spirit, and prophecy would again flourish. The early Christians, having experienced the inauguration of the messianic age, not only proclaimed Jesus to be the Mosaic eschatological prophet (cf. 3:22; 7:37) but also viewed prophecy as a living phenomenon within the church (cf. 13:1; 15:32; 21:9–10) and ranked it among God's gifts to his people; they even classified it next to that of being an apostle (cf. 1Co 12:28; Eph 4:11).

Agabus's prediction was of a "severe famine" that would affect "the entire Roman world" (*holēn tēn oikoumenēn*), which took place, Luke notes, during the reign of the emperor Claudius (AD 41–54). The word *oikoumenē* (GK 3876; lit., "inhabited world") was commonly used in exaggerated fashion by Romans to refer to the empire (Lat., *orbis terrarum*) and probably has that meaning here—"the entire Roman world" (so NIV) rather than "all over the world" (so NASB). Although there is no record of a single famine that ravaged the whole empire in the time of Claudius, various Roman historians referred to a series of bad harvests and famine conditions during his reign (cf. Suetonius, *Claud.* 18:2; Tacitus, *Ann.* 12.43; Cassius Dio, *Hist.* 60.11; Orosius, *History* 7.6.17). And Josephus tells of a particularly severe famine in Palestine about AD 45–47 (*Ant.* 20.51–53; perhaps also 3.320–21, if the reference to Claudius is not in error).

Josephus's reference (*Ant.* 20.51–52) to a famine is in his account of the conversion to Judaism of Helena and Izates, the queen mother and the king of Adiabene in northern Mesopotamia, who provided food and money for the people of Jerusalem. As Josephus tells it, Helena's coming to Jerusalem as a pilgrim sometime around AD 46

> was advantageous for the people of Jerusalem, for at that time the city was hard-pressed by famine and many were perishing from want of money. . . . Queen Helena sent some of her attendants to Alexandria to buy grain for large sums and others to Cyprus to bring back a cargo of dried figs. Her attendants speedily returned with these provisions, which she thereupon distributed among the needy. She has thus left a very great name that will be famous forever among our whole people for her benefaction.

Josephus goes on to say, "When her son Izates learned of the famine, he likewise sent a great sum of money to the leaders of the Jerusalemites [*tois prōtois tōn Hierosolymitōn*]. The distribution of this fund to the needy delivered many from the extremely severe pressure of famine" (*Ant.* 20.53; cf. *b. B. Bat.* 11*a*, which refers to Izates's successor Monobazus as later on also supplying such famine relief, probably also to Jerusalem, "in years of scarcity").

29 Similarly, though certainly not as extravagantly, the Christians (*hoi mathētai*, lit., "the disciples," GK 3412) at Antioch, in response to Agabus's prophecy, decided to provide help for their fellow believers at Jerusalem, whose plight as a minority group within the nation would be particularly difficult at such a time. Ramsay (*St. Paul the Traveller*, 50) speculated that arrangements for such a mission must have taken a good deal of time and that the relief would only have been given as the famine worsened, because "the manner of relief must, of course, have been by purchasing and distributing corn, for it would have shown criminal incapacity to send gold to a starving city; and the corn would not be given by any rational person until the famine was at its height." But the text does not demand such a reading, nor does the analogy of the action of Helena and Izates require it.

30 We are not given any details as to how the relief was collected, how it was administered, or when it was delivered. All we know from the text is that it was an expression of Christian concern by the church at Antioch "for the brothers and sisters (*tē adelphois*, GK *81*) living in Judea" and was taken by Barnabas and Saul "to the elders" (*pros tous presbyterous*) of the Jerusalem church. While the term "elders" (*presbyteroi*, GK *4565*) may indicate that at that time the Jerusalem church had a structured presbyterate, here we should probably understand it as somewhat parallel to Josephus's "leaders" (*prōtoi*; *Ant.* 20.53) and in line with Luke's nontechnical use of "disciples" (*mathētai*) in v.29.

This "famine visit" of Barnabas and Saul to Jerusalem should probably be dated about AD 46. That date, even though somewhat tentative and general, presents commentators with their first real date for working out a Pauline chronology—although a chronology is probably better and more easily constructed from references to the reign of Herod Agrippa I at 12:1–23, the Edict of Claudius at 18:2, and Gallio's proconsulate at 18:12 (see comments at those verses). But how we are to reconcile this date with what Paul tells us in his letters and

how we are to fit that date into an overall chronology depend largely on the answer to the conundrum of the relation of Paul's two Jerusalem visits mentioned in Galatians to his three Jerusalem visits reported in Acts. While most accept the correlation of Galatians 1:18–20 with Acts 9:26–29 and count that as the first visit, many believe that Galatians 2:1–10 should be identified with the Jerusalem Council of Acts 15. But this makes Acts 11:27–30 either a fabrication on Luke's part or a doublet of the Acts 15 material placed here by Luke for his own purposes.

The issues are complex and have far-reaching consequences. (For a brief analysis, see comments at ch. 15 in the context of 12:25–16:5; for an extensive discussion, see my *Galatians* [Dallas: Word, 1990], lxxii–lxxxviii.) Suffice it to say that the simplest solution which provides the most satisfactory and convincing reconstruction—one leaving the fewest loose ends—is that Galatians 2:1–10 corresponds to the famine visit of Acts 11:27–30. On such an understanding, and taking the temporal conjunctions "then" (*epeita*) of Galatians 1:18 and 2:1 as referring back to Saul's conversion (ca. AD 33, allowing some flexibility in rounding off the years), the apostle's first visit to Jerusalem can be dated to about AD 36 and his famine visit to about AD 46, some fourteen years after his conversion. If this is true, then the reference in Galatians 2:2 to the Christian Saul having gone to Jerusalem "in response to a revelation" (*kata apokalypsin*, GK *637*) should probably be related to Agabus's prophecy of 11:28.

NOTES

27 On "going down from" Jerusalem, see comments and note at 8:5.

28 Codex Bezae (D) and its Western associates (as reflected in some Old Latin and Coptic recensions, and Augustine) begin this verse with, "And there was much rejoicing. And when we were gathered together [συνεστραμμένων δὲ ἡμῶν, *synestrammenōn de hēmōn*], one of them named Agabus spoke, signifying . . ."

This is the first "we" passage of any text of Acts and seems to be due either to the tradition that Luke was a native of Syrian Antioch (see Introduction, p. 702) or to the identification of our author with Lucius of Cyrene in 13:1.

On the cessation and revival of prophecy in Jewish thought, see comments and note at 2:4.

C. C. Torrey conjectured that ὅλην τὴν οἰκουμένην (*holēn tēn oikoumenēn*, "the whole inhabited world") mistakenly translates the Aramaic expression *kōl ʾarʿaʾ* ("all the land"), and so the famine should be understood as having been restricted to the land of Palestine. But as noted above, 11:19–30 appears in other respects not to be based on a Semitic source.

The Byzantine text (H L P and most minuscules), and so the TR and KJV, reads Κλαυδίου Καίσαρος (*Klaudiou Kaisaros*, "Claudius Caesar").

D. Divine Intervention on Behalf of the Jerusalem Church (12:1–23)

OVERVIEW

With its acceptance of the conversions of (1) "half Jews" in Samaria; (2) a Gentile Roman centurion, his household, and his friends at Caesarea; and (3) Gentiles only loosely associated with the synagogue at Antioch of Syria, the Jerusalem church was straining the forms and commitments of Judaism almost to the breaking point. There was hardly any further room for expansion within the traditions of Judaism, and soon the Christian mission would break out of those limits to embrace a direct mission to the Gentile world. Preparations for such an expansion, in fact, had been put into place with Saul's conversion and his early attempts to carry on a Christian ministry in such places as Damascus, Jerusalem, and Antioch (perhaps also Arabia and Tarsus), even though it would not be until later that he would formally espouse and explicitly carry out a direct Christian mission to Gentiles.

Before Luke turns to his portrayal of the Christian mission to the Gentile world, he takes the opportunity of presenting two further glimpses of God's working on behalf of believers in Jesus at Jerusalem. Just as his mentor Paul, while arguing for the legitimacy of a direct outreach to Gentiles, continued to characterize Jewish Christianity as "the church of God" (Gal 1:13; cf. 1Th 2:14) and to respect God's ongoing activity within the Jewish world (cf. Ro 9–11), so Luke seems desirous of making the point that, though he is about to portray the advances of the gospel within the Gentile world, it should not be assumed that God was finished with Jerusalem Christianity or that his activity within the Jewish world was finished. Luke has portrayed the Christian mission to the Jewish world that had its center at Jerusalem; now he prepares to present the Christian mission to the Gentiles as a kind of ellipse emanating from that same center. Before doing so, however, he gives us two further vignettes regarding God's intervention on behalf of the Jerusalem church.

It may be hypothesized that these two vignettes of God's working on behalf of the Jerusalem church were set out by Luke so that his readers would appreciate that while the Christian mission within the Jewish world and the Christian mission to Gentiles in many ways differed, they possessed a common focus and had many similarities. Like the analogy of a circle and an ellipse, which share a common center but extend to somewhat different areas (cf. Henry Chadwick's characterization of relations between Jewish and Gentile Christianity [*The Circle and the Ellipse* (Oxford: Clarendon, 1959)]), Luke's point is that they should be seen as complementary and not contradictory. Divine activity in behalf of the Gentiles, Luke seems to be insisting, does not mean divine inactivity with respect to Jewish Christians or unconcern for Jews—which is a heresy that has frequently afflicted Gentile Christians and has all too often resulted in horrendous calamities.

1. Deliverance of Peter (12:1–19a)

OVERVIEW

The account of Peter's miraculous deliverance from prison and death really begins at v.5, with Luke's favorite connecting phrase *men oun* signifying its start (see comments and note at 1:6). Probably Luke's source material for his narrative covered what we now have in vv.5–19, to which he has added an historical introduction in vv.1–4.

¹It was about this time that King Herod arrested some who belonged to the church, intending to persecute them. ²He had James, the brother of John, put to death with the sword. ³When he saw that this pleased the Jews, he proceeded to seize Peter also. This happened during the Feast of Unleavened Bread. ⁴After arresting him, he put him in prison, handing him over to be guarded by four squads of four soldiers each. Herod intended to bring him out for public trial after the Passover.

⁵So Peter was kept in prison, but the church was earnestly praying to God for him.

⁶The night before Herod was to bring him to trial, Peter was sleeping between two soldiers, bound with two chains, and sentries stood guard at the entrance. ⁷Suddenly an angel of the Lord appeared and a light shone in the cell. He struck Peter on the side and woke him up. "Quick, get up!" he said, and the chains fell off Peter's wrists.

⁸Then the angel said to him, "Put on your clothes and sandals." And Peter did so. "Wrap your cloak around you and follow me," the angel told him. ⁹Peter followed him out of the prison, but he had no idea that what the angel was doing was really happening; he thought he was seeing a vision. ¹⁰They passed the first and second guards and came to the iron gate leading to the city. It opened for them by itself, and they went through it. When they had walked the length of one street, suddenly the angel left him.

¹¹Then Peter came to himself and said, "Now I know without a doubt that the Lord sent his angel and rescued me from Herod's clutches and from everything the Jewish people were anticipating."

> [12]When this had dawned on him, he went to the house of Mary the mother of John, also called Mark, where many people had gathered and were praying. [13]Peter knocked at the outer entrance, and a servant girl named Rhoda came to answer the door. [14]When she recognized Peter's voice, she was so overjoyed she ran back without opening it and exclaimed, "Peter is at the door!"
>
> [15]"You're out of your mind," they told her. When she kept insisting that it was so, they said, "It must be his angel."
>
> [16]But Peter kept on knocking, and when they opened the door and saw him, they were astonished. [17]Peter motioned with his hand for them to be quiet and described how the Lord had brought him out of prison. "Tell James and the brothers about this," he said, and then he left for another place.
>
> [18]In the morning, there was no small commotion among the soldiers as to what had become of Peter. [19]After Herod had a thorough search made for him and did not find him, he cross-examined the guards and ordered that they be executed.

COMMENTARY

1 The story is introduced very generally as having taken place "about this time" (*kat' ekeinon ton kairon*; NASB, "about that time"), which probably refers to events connected with the famine visit to Jerusalem of 11:27–30. But if the famine visit occurred about AD 46 and Herod Agrippa I died in AD 44 (see below), the materials of 11:27–30 and 12:1–23 are chronologically reversed. We must remember that ancient historians frequently grouped their materials *per species*, without always being concerned about chronology (see Introduction, p. 672). So Luke, having begun his account of Christianity in Antioch by speaking of the founding of the church, seems to tie into that narrative a further vignette about the famine relief that Antiochene believers sent to Jerusalem. As a result, his full account of the church at Antioch of Syria (11:19–30) reaches back behind Peter's ministries at Lydda, Joppa, and Caesarea at its start (cf. 11:19) and goes beyond the accounts of Peter's deliverance

(12:6–19a) and Herod Agrippa I's death at its close (cf. 12:19b–23).

It is because he is working *per species* within a broad chronological framework that Luke begins the narrative of Peter's deliverance with such a general temporal statement. If we were to seek to be more chronologically precise, we might say that the events of ch. 12 occurred between those of 11:19–26 and 11:27–30. But Luke seems to have wanted to close his portrayals of the Christian mission within the Jewish world (2:42–12:24) with two vignettes having to do with God's continued activity in behalf of the Jerusalem church. Therefore he closes with ch. 12 and uses the expression "about this [that] time" to connect it with what has already been presented.

The Herod of Acts 12 is Agrippa I, who was born in 10 BC. He was the son of Aristobulus and the grandson of Herod the Great. After his father's execution in 7 BC, he was sent as a very young boy with his mother Bernice to Rome, where he grew up on intimate terms with the imperial family. He became something of a playboy and in AD 23 was so heavily in debt that he had to flee to Idumea to escape his creditors. Later he received asylum at Tiberias and a pension from his uncle Herod Antipas, with whom he eventually quarreled. In AD 36 he returned to Rome but offended the emperor Tiberius and was imprisoned. After the death of Tiberius in AD 37, he was released by the new emperor, Caligula, and received from him the northernmost Palestinian tetrarchies of Philip and Lysanias (cf. Lk 3:1) and the title of "king." When Herod Antipas was banished in AD 39, Agrippa received his tetrarchy as well. And at the death of Caligula in AD 41, Claudius, who succeeded Caligula and was Agrippa's friend from youth, added Judea and Samaria to his territory, thereby reconstituting for him the entire kingdom of his grandfather Herod the Great, over which Agrippa ruled till his death in AD 44.

Knowing how profoundly the masses hated his family, Herod Agrippa I took every opportunity during his administration in Palestine to win their affection. When in Rome, he was a cosmopolitan Roman—but when in Jerusalem, he acted the part of an observant Jew. So careful were both he and his wife Cypros regarding Jewish traditions that a Jewish Gemara says of them, "The King is guided by the Queen, and the Queen is guided by Gamaliel" (b. Pesaḥ. 88b). The Mishnah records that in the pilgrim processions bearing baskets of firstfruits into the temple, "when [they] reached the Temple Mount even Agrippa the king would take his basket on his shoulder and enter in as far as the Temple Court" (m. Bik. 3:4). On the Festival of Tabernacles (Sukkoth) in AD 41, when Agrippa was given Deuteronomy 17:14–20 ("the law of the kingdom") to read in public to the pilgrims assembled, the Mishnah says of him, "King Agrippa received it standing and read it standing [which were signs of respect, contrary to the practice of previous Roman rulers], and for this the Sages praised him. And when he reached, 'Thou mayest not put a foreigner over thee which is not thy brother' [Dt 17:15], his eyes flowed with tears [because of his Edomite ancestry]; but they called out to him, 'Our brother art thou! Our brother art thou! Our brother art thou!'" (m. Soṭah 7:8).

Such a show of Jewish affection for a Herodian may seem inconceivable. In reality, however, it was the response of a grateful nation for benefits received. For in AD 40 Agrippa had cajoled Caligula not to carry out his insane plan of erecting a statue to himself as a god in the Jerusalem temple and had intervened on behalf of the Jews in Alexandria for their more humane treatment. Furthermore, when Judea came under his jurisdiction, he moved the seat of government from Caesarea to Jerusalem. This established the Holy City in Jewish eyes as the political capital of the country. He also began to rebuild the city's northern wall and fortifications, thereby enhancing both its security and its prestige (cf. Josephus, Ant. 19.326–27; J.W. 2.218; 5.151–62). Many Jews viewed these days as the inauguration of a better era—perhaps even the beginning of the messianic age—as their grief and prayers during Agrippa's fatal illness at Caesarea suggest (cf. Josephus, Ant. 19.349). Agrippa himself, however, seems to have been primarily interested in a successful reign through the cooperation of loyal subjects, and his expressions of concern for the people and their religion were probably more pragmatically based than sincere.

2–4 Agrippa's policy was the Pax Romana through the preservation of the status quo. He supported the majority within the land and ruthlessly suppressed minorities when they became disruptive. He viewed Jewish Christians as divisive and felt their activities could only disturb the people and inflame antagonisms. So he arrested some of the believers and had James, one of Jesus' original disciples, beheaded by the sword. According to the Mishnah (*m. Sanh.* 9:1), murderers and apostates ("people of an apostate city") were to be beheaded—a form of execution probably ordered by Agrippa to show his Jewish subjects his evaluation of the embryonic Christian movement. Finding that this pleased the Jewish leaders, he took Peter during Passover Week ("Feast of Unleavened Bread") and imprisoned him till he could bring him out for public trial after the Jewish holy days. While in prison, the apostle was guarded by "four squads of four soldiers each," probably on shifts of three hours each (cf. Vegetius, *De Re Mili* 3.8), with two soldiers chained to him on either side and two standing guard at the inner entrance to the prison (cf. v.6). Evidently Agrippa planned to make of Peter something of a warning and a spectacle at a forthcoming show trial and did not want to be embarrassed by Peter's escape.

5 Most commentators speculate that the place of Peter's imprisonment was somewhere within the Fortress of Antonia, which overlooked the temple area to the north and had entrances to both the temple courts and the city. Of greater importance to Luke, for whom prayer is the natural atmosphere of God's people and the normal context for divine activity (cf. 1:14, 24; 2:42; 4:24–31; 6:4, 6; 9:40; 10:2, 4, 9, 31; 11:5; 13:3; 14:23; 16:25; 22:17; 28:8), is the fact that "the church was earnestly praying to God for [Peter]."

6–9 On the night before Agrippa's show trial, "an angel of the Lord" appeared in Peter's cell and began to take charge of affairs. The expression "angel of the Lord" (*angelos kyriou*) stems from the LXX and signifies God himself in his dealings with men (e.g., Ex 3:2, 4, 7; Mt 1:20, 24; 2:13, 19; 28:2; Lk 1:11; 2:9; Ac 5:19; 8:26; 12:23; see also *angelos* in 7:30, 35, 38; 12:11; 27:23). The angel awoke Peter,

and the chains by which he was bound fell from Peter's wrists. Then the angel, like a parent with a child awakened from a sound sleep, carefully instructed the groggy apostle to get dressed. He ordered Peter to follow him, and they left the cell. But Peter, too sleepy to grasp the reality of what was happening, thought he was dreaming.

Herod Agrippa I had planned to try Peter as the leader of the divisive minority in Palestine that identified itself with the crucified Jesus of Nazareth and then execute him as a warning to other followers of Jesus to stop their activities. Usually a prisoner was chained to only one guard (cf. Seneca, *Ep.* 5.7), but in view of Agrippa's intentions, the guard was doubled. The Christians of Jerusalem well understood Agrippa's intentions because he had earlier imprisoned some of them and killed James the son of Zebedee (v.2). Neither Peter nor his fellow believers were in any doubt about what the king had in mind. It was a crisis of great magnitude for the life of the early Christian church at Jerusalem. But while God does not promise deliverance from persecution and death, at crucial times he often steps in to act for the honor of his name and the benefit of his people. In fact, Luke insists, this was what now happened: God acted directly in delivering Peter from Agrippa's designs. Peter's deliverance must be ascribed entirely to God, for it was in no way due to the apostle's own efforts or those of the Christian community—apart, of course, from their prayers.

10–11 Passing the two guards at the inner entrance to the prison, Peter and the angel came to the main iron gate, which opened automatically (*automatē*; NIV, "by itself") as they approached. Then the angel left Peter a block away from the prison. Stories about prison doors opening of their own accord and of miraculous escapes from imprisonment were popular in the ancient world, and the form of such legends undoubtedly influenced to some extent Luke's narrative here (see comments at 5:19). But as Charles S. C. Williams, 148, noted, "The 'form' of an escape story cannot of course decide the problem of its historicity." Some may prefer to believe, as did F. C. Burkitt, 103–4, "that Peter's escape was contrived by human means"— "that some human sympathizer [unbeknown to Peter himself or the early church] was at work, who had drugged the guards and bribed the turnkey." That the story is not told in much detail may lead to such a conjecture. God certainly has acted in history on behalf of his people through human agents. Yet for Peter, standing alone in the street and brought to his senses by the cool night air, there was no doubt that "the Lord sent his angel and rescued [him] from Herod's clutches and from everything the Jewish people were anticipating" (v.11). Apart from an ingrained philosophical skepticism, there is no reason to doubt that his deliverance was miraculous and not arranged by human means.

12 Realizing where he was and the danger he faced if Herod's soldiers should find him there, Peter went to one of the meeting places of the early Jerusalem Christians—to the home of Mary, John Mark's mother. A number of people were praying there. Luke's identification of Mary by her son implies that her son's name was better known to his readers than hers (cf. Mk 15:21, 40). It also suggests that this John Mark was the one who was with Paul and Barnabas on a portion of the first missionary journey (Ac 13:5, 13)—a cousin of Barnabas (Col 4:10) who returned with him to Cyprus after the falling out with Paul (Ac 15:37–39), a later companion of both Paul (Col 4:10; Phm 24) and Peter (1Pe 5:13), and the writer of the second gospel.

13–14 Mary's house must have been of some size, with a vestibule opening onto the street, an intervening court, and rear living quarters. Not only were "many people gathered" there (v.12), but Luke says that Peter was knocking at the door of the vestibule (*tēn thyran tou pylōnos*, GK *2598*, *4784*; NIV, "the outer entrance"; NASB, "the door of the gate") and Rhoda the servant girl was rushing back and forth for joy.

15–16 The unfolding scene is one of utter confusion and bewilderment tinged with humor and embarrassment, which must have led to hilarity every time it was repeated among the early believers. There was Peter knocking more and more urgently on the door; Rhoda losing her wits for joy and forgetting to open the door; the Christians refusing to believe it was Peter, even though they had just been praying for him; their belittling of Rhoda for her report ("you're out of your mind") and for saying she had heard Peter's voice at the door ("it must be his angel"); Rhoda's frantic persistence; and their utter astonishment when they finally opened the door and let Peter in.

17 On entering, Peter "motioned with his hand for them to be quiet." This was not a time for celebration, what with Herod's soldiers prowling about the streets in search of their prisoner and the city silent in sleep. Peter had to be moving on in order to escape being recaptured. So he gave them a quick summary of "how the Lord had brought him out of prison" and instructed them to tell James and the other brothers what had happened. And with that, Luke tells us, Peter left "for another place."

The James mentioned here is, of course, James the Lord's brother, not James the brother of John and son of Zebedee who had earlier been beheaded by Herod Agrippa I (cf. v.2). Undoubtedly, Peter was the leader of the first Christian community at Jerusalem, as the early chapters of Acts presuppose. But from the mid-30s through the mid-40s, James seems to have exercised some form of administrative leadership along with Peter and the apostles (cf. Gal 1:19; 2:9), and he presided at the Jerusalem Council of AD 49 (cf. 15:13–21). Later still Luke refers to him as head of the Jerusalem church (cf. 21:18).

In AD 62 he was martyred by the younger Ananus (cf. Josephus, *Ant.* 20.200). Luke does not state how or why the shift in leadership of the church from Peter to James came about or what qualified James for such a position. Apparently it had to do with (1) external pressures on the Jerusalem congregation to demonstrate its Jewishness and (2) the need within the church for someone who could lead the growing number of scrupulously minded converts drawn from Pharisaic and priestly backgrounds (perhaps Essene; see comments at 6:7).

After the expulsion of the Hellenistic-Jewish Christians, both the Jews and the Hebraic-Jewish Christians in Jerusalem felt the need for the community of believers in Jesus to demonstrate more actively their continued respect for the traditions of Israel. Peter and his fellow apostles, all being *ʿam hā ʾāreṣ* (lit., "people of the land") Jewish Christians, would hardly have been the best ones to head up such an endeavor. In fact, Peter's associations with "half-breed" Samaritans and the Roman centurion Cornelius may have made him particularly suspect in certain quarters. It is not improbable, then, that as the pressures mounted the Jerusalem church found it advantageous to be represented in its leadership by one whose legal and spiritual qualifications were above reproach. Such a person, it seems, was James the Lord's brother, whom Hegesippus (a second-century Christian of Aelia, the renamed Gentile Jerusalem) described as a Pharisee and ascetic, who was so pious that his knees were like camels' knees from his frequent praying in the temple on behalf of the people (cf. Eusebius, *Hist. eccl.* 2.1.23; 23.4–7) and who was not only physically related to Jesus but also had seen the risen Jesus (1Co 15:7).

Furthermore, the missionary activities of Peter and the apostles would require some kind of arrangement for the continuance of administrative authority at Jerusalem. That the apostles considered themselves to be something other than ecclesiastical functionaries has already been shown in Acts 6:2–6. It is not too difficult, therefore, to imagine that with the dispersion of the Hellenistic-Jewish believers and their seven leaders who were appointed to supervise the distribution of food within the community, the church turned to James for administrative leadership—not only, as has been suggested, to demonstrate its Jewishness but also to free the apostles for their "ministry of the word." The writings of postapostolic Jewish Christianity speak of Peter and his fellow apostles remaining in Jerusalem for twelve (or seven) years and then engaging in missionary activity throughout the Jewish Diaspora (cf. Clement of Alexandria, *Strom.* 6.5.43, citing an earlier but now extinct work called *The Preaching of Peter*; *Acts of Peter* 5; *Clementine Recognitions* 1.43; 9.29; note also 1Co 9:5; *1 Clem.* 5; Justin, *Dial.* 53.5; 109.1; 110.2). Many of the details of this tradition are undoubtedly apocryphal. Yet the fact that the apostles carried on missionary activities away from Jerusalem and outside Palestine cannot be doubted. For these reasons administrative leadership within the Jerusalem church seems to have gradually shifted to James the Lord's brother.

The mention of "another place" to which Peter went after his miraculous deliverance has led to all kinds of comments. Roman Catholicism has frequently asserted that this place was Rome, where, on the basis of the apocryphal *Acts of Peter*, the *Clementine Recognitions*, and the *Clementine Homilies*, it has been claimed that Peter arrived in AD 42 and remained for twenty-five years. This assertion is improbable and has rightly been abandoned by many Roman Catholic scholars today. If 12:1–19 precedes 9:32–11:18 chronologically, as some insist (see comments at 12:1), this other place may refer to the maritime plain of Palestine, with its cities of Lydda, Joppa, and Caesarea. But such a region, though geographically removed from Jerusalem, would hardly be separated from Herod Agrippa's jurisdiction. More likely, Antioch of Syria is the other place Luke had in mind—a city where Peter had fellowship with a mixed body of Jewish and Gentile believers until "certain men came from James," and where he was the brunt of the rebuke by Paul (cf. Gal 2:11–21). Later on Peter appears at Jerusalem in connection with the Jerusalem Council (cf. 15:7–11, 14), though presumably he was only in transit.

18–19a In Roman law a guard who allowed his prisoner to escape was subject to the same penalty the escaped prisoner would have suffered (cf. *Code of Justinian* 9.4.4). No wonder, then, that in the morning when Peter's escape was discovered "there was no small [*ouk oligos*, lit., "not a little"] commotion among the soldiers." When Herod heard of Peter's escape, he instituted a search and cross-examined the guards. Frustrated by his lack of success, he ordered the guards "to be led away" (*apachthēnai*, GK 552)—which is likely an idiom for being taken out to be executed (NIV, "that they be executed"; NASB, "that they be led away *to execution*"; cf. Lk 23:26).

NOTES

1 The Western text (D, and as represented in various recensions of the Old Latin, Syriac, and Coptic versions) adds at the end of this verse, after ἐκκλησίας (*ekklēsias*, "church," GK 1711), the words ἐν τῇ Ἰουδαίᾳ (*en tē Ioudaia*, "in Judea"), evidently in order to bring the account of 12:1–19a into closer relation with that of 11:29–30.

3 The Western text (D, and as represented in certain recensions of the Old Latin and Syriac versions) adds ἡ ἐπιχείρησις αὐτοῦ ἐπὶ τοὺς ἁγίους καὶ πιστούς (*hē epicheirēsis autou epi tous hagious kai pistous*, "his attack on the saints and faithful") after τοῖς Ἰουδαίοις (*tois Ioudaiois*, "the Jews"), evidently to specify more exactly what it was that Herod did to please the Jews.

3–4 Passover was celebrated on the fourteenth day of the Jewish month Nisan and continued into the early hours of the fifteenth (cf. Josephus, *Ant.* 3.248–49. This was followed immediately by the Feast of Unleavened Bread on the fifteenth through the twenty-first of Nisan. Popular usage merged the two festivals and treated them as one (τὸ πάσχα, *to pascha*, "the Passover"), as in fact they were for all practical purposes.

6 Commentators' statements to the effect that Peter slept "like a baby" or "calmly from a good conscience and with confidence in God" reflect a pious imagination but nothing in the text. Nor does the text warrant speculation about the mental or psychological state of the guards.

10 The Western text (D, and as reflected in recensions of the Old Latin and Coptic versions) adds κατέβησαν τοὺς ἑπτὰ βαθμοὺς καί (*katebēsan tous hepta bathmous kai*, "they went down the seven steps and") after the participle ἐξελθόντες (*exelthontes*, "went through," GK 2002) and before the verb προῆλθον (*proēlthon*, "walked," GK 4601)—which may seem to be an original note of local color but probably only reflects a later tradition (perhaps an attempt to parallel the seven and eight steps of Ezekiel's vision of the temple [Eze 40:22, 26, 31] or Luke's reference to the steps that led from the Fortress of Antonia into the temple area [Ac 21:40]).

13 Codex Vaticanus (א) and a few other witnesses (a corrected B and recensions of the Old Latin and Vulgate versions) have προῆλθεν (*proēlthen*, "she came forward," GK 4601), rather than the much more widely supported reading προσῆλθεν (*prosēlthen*, "she came," GK *4665*) attested by 𝔓⁴⁵ 𝔓⁷⁴ A uncorrected B C D E etc. The dropping of the letter sigma was probably inadvertent.

15 Codex Bezae (D) prefixes ὁ ἄγγελός ἐστιν αὐτοῦ (*ho angelos estin autou*, "it is his angel") with the adverb τυχόν (*tychon*, "perhaps"), thereby softening the definiteness of the explanation offered: "Perhaps it is his angel." Elsewhere in the NT the adverb τυχόν (*tychon*, "perhaps") appears only in 1 Corinthians 16:6 (though also in D at Lk 20:13).

17 The Western text (D, and as represented in certain recensions of the Old Latin, Vulgate, and Syriac versions) add εἰσῆλθεν καί (*eisēlthen kai*, "he came in and"), evidently to prevent readers from thinking that Peter made his explanation while standing at the outer gate or entrance of the outer vestibule.

18 The Western text generally omits οὐκ ὀλίγος (*ouk oligos*, lit., "not a little"; NIV, "no small"), probably due to homoioteleuton (i.e., when the eye of a scribe passes from one word to another with the same ending—here from the preceding word τάραχος [*tarachos*]), or perhaps because of failing to appreciate the rhetorical use of litotes (i.e., expressing an affirmative by the negative of its opposite).

19a Codex Bezae (D) spells out the idiom by substituting ἀποκτανθῆναι (*apoktanthēnai*, "to be put to death," GK *650*) for ἀπαχθῆναι (*apachthēnai*, "to be led away").

2. Death of Herod Agrippa I (12:19b–23)

OVERVIEW

Peter had been miraculously delivered from prison and death. But the tyrant Herod Agrippa was still at large and continuing his oppression of the church. Therefore Luke gives us a second scene in his account of God's intervention on behalf of the Jerusalem church. He does this not only to show how far-reaching this intervention was, but also to reinforce by a second witness the theme of God's continued interest in Jewish Christianity (see comments at Overview, 2:42–12:24).

¹⁹ᵇThen Herod went from Judea to Caesarea and stayed there a while. ²⁰He had been quarreling with the people of Tyre and Sidon; they now joined together and sought an audience with him. Having secured the support of Blastus, a trusted personal servant of the king, they asked for peace, because they depended on the king's country for their food supply.

²¹On the appointed day Herod, wearing his royal robes, sat on his throne and delivered a public address to the people. ²²They shouted, "This is the voice of a god, not of a man." ²³Immediately, because Herod did not give praise to God, an angel of the Lord struck him down, and he was eaten by worms and died.

COMMENTARY

19b–20 The situation Luke describes here is not entirely clear. Caesarea, with its excellently constructed harbor (see comments at 10:1), was still nominally the provincial capital of Palestine. Tyre and Sidon were important Phoenician seaport cities incorporated into the Roman Empire about 20 BC. There is nothing in Josephus about any trouble between Caesarea and the seaports to the north at this time, though competition for trade was fierce and the cities of the Phoenician seaboard were always heavily dependent on Galilee for much of their food supply. Nevertheless, for whatever reason, Herod became enraged with the people of Tyre and Sidon; they, in turn, sent a delegation to ask for peace, using in some way the good offices of Blastus, King Agrippa's personal servant, for their purposes. By his use of the coordinate *kai* ("and"; NIV, "then") and the participle *katelthōn* ("he went [down]"; GK *2982*) in v.19b, Luke implies that Agrippa left Jerusalem for Caesarea shortly after the Jewish Passover, perhaps because of frustration over Peter's escape.

21–23 Luke's account of Agrippa's death is paralleled by Josephus:

> After the completion of the third year of his reign over the whole of Judea, Agrippa came to the city of Caesarea, . . . [where] he celebrated spectacles in honor of Caesar. On the second day of the spectacles, clad in a garment woven completely of silver . . . , he entered the theater at daybreak. There the silver, illumined by the touch of the first rays of the sun, was wondrously radiant and by its glitter inspired fear and awe in those who gazed intently upon it. Straightway his flatterers raised their voices from various directions—though hardly for his good—addressing him as a god. "May you be propitious to us," they added, "and if we have hitherto feared you as a man, yet henceforth we

> agree that you are more than mortal in your being." The king did not rebuke them nor did he reject their flattery as impious. But shortly thereafter he looked up and saw an owl perched on a rope over his head. At once, recognizing this as a harbinger of woes just as it had once been of good tidings [cf. *Ant.* 18.195, 200], he felt a stab of pain in his heart. He was also gripped in his stomach by an ache that he felt everywhere at once and that was intense from the start. Leaping up he said to his friends: "I, a god in your eyes, am now bidden to lay down my life, for fate brings immediate refutation of the lying words lately addressed to me. I, who was called immortal by you, am now under sentence of death. But I must accept my lot as God wills it. In fact I have lived in no ordinary fashion but in the grand style that is hailed as true bliss." Even as he was speaking these words, he was overcome by more intense pain. They hastened, therefore, to convey him to the palace; and the word flashed about to everyone that he was on the very verge of death. . . . Exhausted after five straight days by the pain in [his] abdomen, he departed this life in the fifty-fourth year of his life and the seventh of his reign [*Ant.* 19.343–50].

These two accounts of Herod Agrippa's death, that of Luke and that of Josephus, differ enough from one another that neither can be dependent on the other. Luke sets the scene by referring to a quarrel between the king and the people of Tyre and Sidon, whereas Josephus speaks of a festival in honor of Caesar—either the quinquennial games inaugurated by Herod the Great at the founding of Caesarea to honor Augustus (cf. Josephus, *J.W.* 1.415) or a festival instituted by Agrippa to honor his patron Claudius. Josephus makes no mention of a delegation from Tyre and Sidon. Furthermore, Luke's account, though more concise, gives us the physical cause of Agrippa's death—"eaten by worms." On the other hand, the two accounts are so similar in outline that we may assume we know in general how and when Herod Agrippa I died.

Agrippa I's death occurred in AD 44, "after the completion of the third year of his reign over the whole of Judea" (Josephus, *Ant.* 19.343; *J.W.* 2.219) and in the fourth year of the emperor Claudius (Josephus, *Ant.* 19.351). Luke's reference to worms suggests an infection by intestinal roundworms (*Ascaris lumbricoides*), which grow as long as ten to sixteen inches and feed on the nutrient fluids in the intestines. Bunches of roundworms can obstruct the intestines, causing severe pain, copious vomiting (including vomiting of the intestinal worms), and death. But whatever the physical details, both Luke and Josephus attribute Agrippa's death to the king's impiety and God's judgment. Moreover, Luke sees it as part of God's activity on behalf of the Jerusalem church.

NOTES

19b Caesarea, though the titular provincial capital, was distinguished from Judea, the territory of the Jews, as Jerusalem was also distinguished from Judea by some Jews. One significant difference between the two is that one "goes down" (κατελθών, *katelthōn*; NIV, "went"; NASB, "went down") to Caesarea from Judea, whereas one always "goes up" to Jerusalem (see comments and note at 8:5).

20 Codex Bezae (D), by its use of γάρ (*gar*, "for") rather than δέ (*de*, "now," "and," or "but"), more clearly suggests the reason why Herod "went from Judea to Caesarea" (v.19).

The Western text also refines the adverb ὁμοθυμαδόν (*homothymadon*, "with one mind or purpose"; NIV, "joined together"; NASB, "with one accord") by reading: οἱ δὲ ὁμοθυμαδὸν ἐξ ἀμφοτέρων τῶν πόλεων παρῆσαν πρὸς τὸν βασιλέα (*hoi de homothymadon ex amphoterōn tōn poleōn parēsan pros ton basilea*, "So they came with one mind [i.e., one purpose] out of all the districts of the cities related to the kingdom").

21 If the festival Josephus refers to was the one established by Herod the Great to be celebrated every five years on the anniversary of the founding of Caesarea, it probably occurred on March 5 (cf. Eusebius, *Martyrs of Palestine* 11.30), a month or two before the Jewish Passover. This would place Agrippa's death ten or eleven months after Peter's deliverance—which is possible, but not the impression one receives from Acts by the juxtaposition of these two events. It may be that the festival was specially instituted by Agrippa I to honor Claudius on his birthday on August 5 (cf. Suetonius, *Claud.* 2.1).

21–22 Between vv.21–22 the Western text (D, as reflected also in various Latin, Syriac, and Coptic recensions) inserts καταλλαγέντος δὲ αὐτοῦ τοῖς Τυρίοις (*katallagentos de autou tois Tyriois*, "and on the occasion of his reconciliation with the Tyrians")—with the Old Latin and Vulgate continuing with the words *et Sidoniis* ("and the Sidonians"): "And the Sidonians shouted [or "kept shouting"]."

23 Codex Bezae (D) rewords the final clause of the verse to read καὶ καταβὰς ἀπὸ τοῦ βήματος, γενόμενος σκωληκόβρωτος ἔτι ζῶν καὶ οὕτως ἐξέψυξεν (*kai katabas apo tou bēmatos, genomenos skōlēkobrōtos eti zōn kai houtōs exepsyxen*, "and he came down from the platform, and while he was still living he was eaten by worms and so died"), evidently to inform the reader that, while the angel of the Lord smote him immediately after his address, Agrippa did not expire at once but was able to descend from his throne.

E. Summary Statement (12:24)

²⁴But the word of God continued to increase and spread.

COMMENTARY

24 Luke's third panel on the Christian mission within the Jewish world ends with a summary statement comparable to the summaries that concluded the two preceding panels at 6:7 and 9:31. In its immediate context, v.24 contrasts the progress of the gospel to the awful end of the church's persecutor Herod Agrippa I. More broadly, it implies that though Luke's attention throughout the remainder of Acts will be focused on the advances of the gospel to Gentiles, within the Jewish world "the word of God continued to increase and spread." In other words, God was still at work in behalf of the Jerusalem church and its ministry and was still concerned for his ancient people Israel.

NOTES

24 Codex Vaticanus (B), also represented by the Latin Vulgate, reads τοῦ κυρίου (*tou kyriou*, "of the Lord") rather than τοῦ θεοῦ (*tou theou*, "of God"), probably having been influenced by the expression ἄγγελος κυρίου (*angelos kyriou*, "angel of the Lord") in v.23.

IV. PART II: THE CHRISTIAN MISSION TO THE GENTILE WORLD (12:25–28:31)

OVERVIEW

In recording Jesus' sermon in his hometown synagogue at Nazareth, Luke in his gospel (4:14–30) has highlighted the main themes for all that will follow in his two volumes (see Introduction, pp. 693–96). In the Nazareth pericope, which functions in Luke's writings as the "programmatic prologue," "frontispiece," or "prelude" to both the ministry of Jesus (in his gospel) and the ministry of the early church (in his Acts), two features of particular relevance for the advance of the "good news" and the outreach of the Christian mission to the Gentile world stand out:

1. That in reading Isaiah 61, Jesus ended his reading in midsentence at 61:2a, thereby emphasizing the note of divine grace ("to proclaim the year of the Lord's favor") without also sounding the corollary theme of judgment present in the passage ("and the day of vengeance of our God"). Jesus' omission of

the reference to judgment underscores a fact that Luke wants to emphasize: the period of the Christian gospel is a time characterized by God's grace, when the offer of deliverance is freely extended. To such a message of salvation, as they understood it, the residents of Nazareth responded positively. They failed to see any other implication in a message of free grace than that of God's messianic blessings being poured out on the nation of Israel. So they spoke well of Jesus and commented favorably about his "gracious words" (4:22).

2. That in his sermon, Jesus indicated that the blessings of the messianic age were not only for Israel but also for Gentiles, as illustrated by the fact that God's grace in the past had been extended to a Phoenician widow who was destitute and a Syrian army general who was a leper (4:26–27). Here, however, was a repudiation of the Jewish concept of exclusive election. So when Jesus made this point and used these illustrations in support, his Nazareth neighbors were so furious that they drove him out of the synagogue and tried to do away with him (4:28–29).

Jesus' own earthly ministry was limited almost entirely to Jews. Luke's gospel portrays only one healing of a Gentile, that of the Roman centurion's servant (7:1–10), and two very brief contacts with Samaritans (9:52–55; 17:11–19). Moreover, it even omits the pericope of the Syrophoenician woman contained in Mark 7:24–30 (cf. also Mt 15:21–28), though it includes several intimations of a later inclusion of Gentiles (cf. Lk 2:30–32; 3:6; 11:31; 13:29; 14:16–24). In the first half of Acts, as well, Luke depicts the ministry of the Jerusalem church as having been focused primarily on the Jewish world, with outreaches of the gospel to Samaria, Caesarea, and Syrian Antioch viewed as being in some ways exceptional but still within a Jewish Christian mission.

Luke's hero is Paul, and he has reserved for him the missionary outreach to the Gentile world that Jesus saw as inherent in the Servant theology of Isaiah 61. And now as he turns in the latter half of Acts to portrayals of the "good news" to the Gentile world, Luke is, in effect, concluding his two volumes by explicating Jesus' promise of the universal extension of God's grace. The author's portrayals in this latter portion of Acts are presented as advances in the proclamation of the Christian gospel. But evidently he also wanted these advances to be seen as in continuity with God's redemptive activities in the past, for they are presented as being (1) founded on what Jesus accomplished in his earthly ministry, death, and resurrection (as presented in his gospel); (2) parallel at many points to what transpired in the Christian mission to the Jewish world (as presented in the first half of Acts); and (3) fuller explications of certain crucial passages and central themes of the OT (as seen in Paul's sermons and defenses and as alluded to in Luke's editorial comments).

PANEL 4—FIRST MISSIONARY JOURNEY AND JERUSALEM COUNCIL (12:25–16:5)

OVERVIEW

Luke's fourth panel of material, which is the first of his three panels on the Christian mission to the Gentile world, embodies both Paul's first missionary journey and the Jerusalem Council. It concludes in the final verse by telling us how believers in Syria, Cilicia, and Galatia received the decisions of "the apostles and elders" at that first church council.

Luke presents his material in this panel more thematically than geographically. Therefore, before closing with the summary in 16:5 he draws together several matters: (1) a report of events on the first missionary journey that led up to the Jerusalem Council; (2) an account of the debate and decisions reached at the council; and (3) a précis of how those decisions were received in areas of Gentile outreach. Most commentators have tended to treat these topics as practically separate and distinguishable. But to judge by the way Luke groups his material thematically within his various panels, he evidently meant these matters to be taken together and understood as having some integral relation to one another.

Chapters 13 and 14 are sometimes viewed as something of a "filler" inserted by Luke to get from the situation of the church under Agrippa I to the Jerusalem Council—or worse, relegated to the status of either a Lukan invention or some misplaced aspect of the Pauline mission that probably occurred later (cf., e.g., Haenchen, 400–404, 438–39). But to look on these chapters as being rather inconsequential in the overall scheme of things is to miss Luke's point about an important advance in the Christian mission and to be left without an adequate rationale for the Jerusalem Council.

In reality, Paul's first missionary journey began a radically new policy for Christian missions, for proclaiming the gospel, and for making converts, namely, (1) the legitimacy of a direct approach to the Gentile world, apart from any prior commitments to Judaism on the part of the converts or any Jewish stance on the part of the missionaries; and (2) the legitimacy of Gentile Christians' expression of their faith in Jesus apart from a Jewish lifestyle or any distinctive Jewish practices (cf. 14:27b; 15:3). For the early church, with its Jewish roots, such a policy was revolutionary. It had, in fact, enormous significance and many implications for the Christian movement that, not having been foreseen, required a full discussion and decision at the Jerusalem Council.

A. The Missionaries Sent Out (12:25–13:3)

²⁵When Barnabas and Saul had finished their mission, they returned from Jerusalem, taking with them John, also called Mark.

¹³:¹In the church at Antioch there were prophets and teachers: Barnabas, Simeon called Niger, Lucius of Cyrene, Manaen (who had been brought up with Herod the tetrarch) and Saul. ²While they were worshiping the Lord and fasting, the Holy Spirit said, "Set apart for me Barnabas and Saul for the work to which I have called them." ³So after they had fasted and prayed, they placed their hands on them and sent them off.

COMMENTARY

25 This verse reaches back behind the events of ch. 12 to connect 13:1–3 with the account of the Antioch church in 11:19–30. Indeed, 12:25–13:3 exhibits the same terse and somewhat colorless style of 11:19–30, thus suggesting both a topical and literary connection. So Luke uses v.25 as a kind of bridge statement before turning to whatever source materials he has for the missionary journey itself (cf. the connective *men oun* of 13:4). In so doing, he shifts his readers' attention from Jerusalem to Antioch of Syria by telling of John Mark's being brought by Barnabas (his cousin, cf. Col 4:10) and Saul from Jerusalem to Antioch.

A notoriously difficult textual problem having to do with the prepositions "to" (*eis*) or "from" (*ex* or *apo*) appears in this verse (see Notes).

13:1 At Antioch there were five "prophets and teachers" in the church. The Greek particle *te* (untranslatable) was used in antiquity to connect word pairs, coordinate clauses, and identify similar sentences. Often it also functioned to set off one set of coordinates from another. Probably, therefore, we should understand the first three of those listed—Barnabas, Simeon, and Lucius, who are introduced by the first *te*—as the "prophets," and the last two—Manaen and Saul, who are grouped by the second *te*—as the "teachers," with prophecy being understood to include "forthtelling" as well as "foretelling" and teaching having to do with identifying logical and thematic relationships, explicating OT foundations, and spelling out practical implications.

Earlier in Acts, Barnabas was presented as a Levite from Cyprus who resided in Jerusalem and became a leading figure in the Jerusalem church (4:36–37; 9:27; 11:22–30). He was, as Luke tells us, "a good man, full of the Holy Spirit and faith" (11:24). Having come from the Jerusalem church, he undoubtedly served in some manner as a channel for and authorization of the truth of the gospel. Simeon Niger (his surname is a Latin loanword that means "black") may have come from Africa. He was possibly the Simon from Cyrene of Luke 23:26, whose sons Alexander and Rufus were later known to be among the Christians at Rome (cf. Mk 15:21; also possibly Ro 16:13). If he was made to carry Jesus' cross on the way to Golgotha, what a story he would have had to tell! Lucius of Cyrene was frequently identified in the postapostolic period with Luke the evangelist and author of Acts. But the Roman praenomen Lucius (Luke) was common in the empire. And if Luke refrained from identifying himself as being with Paul on his missionary journeys—except, as has been often postulated, through the occasional use of the pronoun "we"—it is hardly likely that he would identify himself here by name. Nor should Luke be equated with the Lucius of Romans 16:21.

As for Manaen, we know nothing about him except from this verse. His name is the Greek form of the Hebrew name Menahem, and he is identified here as a *syntrophos* (GK *5343*), i.e., a "foster brother" or "intimate friend" of Herod the tetrarch. This identification suggests that he had been raised as an adopted brother or close companion of Herod Antipas. As for Saul, we know him from 7:58–8:3; 9:1–30; 11:25–30; and his many later letters.

2–3 While Barnabas and Saul were carrying out their activities at Antioch, the Holy Spirit directed that they should be set apart for a special ministry. Luke says, "After they had fasted and prayed, they placed their hands on them and sent them off [*apelysan*, GK *668*; lit., "they released them"]" from their duties at Antioch. Luke's literary style in these verses is somewhat clipped, and we could wish he had given us more details. He does not tell us, for example, how the Spirit made his will known, though we may assume it was through a revelation given to one of the believers. Neither does he tell us the nature of the special ministry that the two were set apart for, though from what follows it is obvious we are meant to understand it was to be a mission to Gentiles. Nor does he give us the precise antecedent of the third person verbal suffix "they" (*apelysan*). Still, we may infer from (1) the parallel usage in 15:2 (*etaxan*, "appointed," GK *5435*), where the antecedent is relatively clear from the context, and (2) the descriptions of early church government in 6:2–6 and 15:4–30 (see Notes, 6:2, on *to plēthos*, "the

whole number") that the whole church at Antioch, together with its leaders, was involved in attesting the validity of the revelation received, laid hands on the newly designated missionaries, and sent them out. This is further confirmed by the reference to the whole church in 14:27. For just as in that latter case it was the whole church that sent out the missionaries, so it was the whole church that they reported to on returning to Antioch. Nevertheless, however we may view the details of their call and commission, ultimately Luke insists that Barnabas and Saul were "sent on their way by the Holy Spirit" (13:4).

NOTES

12:25 Codices ℵ B L P and a number of minuscules have it that, having "finished their mission," Barnabas and Saul returned "to [εἰς, *eis*] Jerusalem" (so NRSV), whereas 𝔓⁷⁴ A and other minuscules read that they returned "from [ἐξ, *ex*] Jerusalem" (so NIV, NASB)—and in substantial agreement with the latter, though with a different preposition, D and Ψ together with still other minuscules read "from [ἀπό, *apo*] Jerusalem." The impression one gets when reading 11:27–13:1 is that 11:30 refers to the arrival of Paul and Barnabas at Jerusalem, and that, therefore, 12:25 ought to tell of their departure *from* Jerusalem. Furthermore, John Mark presumably grew up in Jerusalem, so he did not need to be taken by Barnabas and Saul to Jerusalem. Yet the earliest and best attested MS evidence supports "to [εἰς, *eis*] Jerusalem," with the reading "from Jerusalem" being divided against itself in the use of ἐξ, *ex*, in 𝔓⁷⁴ A etc., and ἀπό, *apo*, in D Ψ etc. "To [εἰς, *eis*] Jerusalem" is, in fact, the "harder reading."

In context, however, the reading "to [εἰς, *eis*] Jerusalem" makes no sense with the verb "they returned" (ὑπέστρεψαν, *hypestrepsan*, GK *5715*), leaves obscure the clause "[having] finished their mission" (πληρώσαντες τὴν διακονίαν, *plērōsantes tēn diakonian*, GK *4444, 1355*), and does not explain why Barnabas and Saul needed to take John Mark with them "to Jerusalem" when he was presumably already there. Furthermore, the fact that Luke begins his fourth panel of material with this verse—which panel deals with the beginning of the Christian mission to the Gentile world, with the headquarters of that mission being in Syrian Antioch—the text reads much better as a telling of Barnabas and Saul having finished their mission in Jerusalem (i.e., the famine relief they brought from Antioch to Jerusalem, cf. 11:29–30) and now returning "from Jerusalem" back to the church at Antioch. It seems best, therefore, to assume (1) that εἰς, *eis* ("to"), came into the text at an early date, either through a slip of a scribe's pen or a marginal gloss; (2) that as a primitive error it has infected many of the early witnesses, as Westcott and Hort long ago concluded; and (3) that ἐξ, *ex* ("from"), or possibly ἀπό, *apo* ("from"), was the original preposition.

13:1 Codex Bezae (D), as reflected in the Latin Vulgate, replaces the relative pronoun ὅ (*ho*) and the particle τε (*te*) by the expression ἐν τοῖς (*en tois*, "among whom [were]"), thereby implying that the five mentioned were not the only "prophets and teachers" in the church at Antioch. Codices E H L P and the

TR add τινες (*tines*, "certain") after ἦσαν δέ (*ēsan de*, "now there were"), evidently for much the same reason.

3 Codex Bezae (D) adds πάντες (*pantes*, "all") after the participle προσευξάμενοι (*proseuxamenoi*, "praying," GK 4667)—which is a typical Western expansion. D also omits at the end of the verse the verb ἀπέλυσαν (*apelysan*, lit., "they released them" or "sent them off"). This omission was probably a scribal error, for the absence of the verb ruins the syntax of the verse.

B. The Mission on Cyprus and John Mark's Departure (13:4–13)

OVERVIEW

The first major outreach of the gospel from Antioch-on-the-Orontes encountered the false prophet Bar-Jesus in Cyprus, just as the first major outreach from Jerusalem ran afoul in the case of Simon the sorcerer in Samaria (cf. 8:9–24). By the manner in which these two events are narrated, it seems evident that Luke wanted his readers to appreciate the parallel. Moreover, not only does Luke seem to have been interested in drawing the parallel between these two episodes; he was also interested in showing how great a step forward the mission to Cyprus really was. For in the Cyprus mission of Barnabas and Saul, with John Mark as their helper, revolutionary implications came to light for the Christian mission to the Gentile world, with these implications also having radical effects on the missionaries themselves.

[4]The two of them, sent on their way by the Holy Spirit, went down to Seleucia and sailed from there to Cyprus. [5]When they arrived at Salamis, they proclaimed the word of God in the Jewish synagogues. John was with them as their helper.

[6]They traveled through the whole island until they came to Paphos. There they met a Jewish sorcerer and false prophet named Bar-Jesus, [7]who was an attendant of the proconsul, Sergius Paulus. The proconsul, an intelligent man, sent for Barnabas and Saul because he wanted to hear the word of God. [8]But Elymas the sorcerer (for that is what his name means) opposed them and tried to turn the proconsul from the faith. [9]Then Saul, who was also called Paul, filled with the Holy Spirit, looked straight at Elymas and said, [10]"You are a child of the devil and an enemy of everything that is right! You are full of all kinds of deceit and trickery. Will you never stop perverting the right ways of the Lord? [11]Now the hand of the Lord is against you. You are going to be blind, and for a time you will be unable to see the light of the sun."

Immediately mist and darkness came over him, and he groped about, seeking someone to lead him by the hand. [12]When the proconsul saw what had happened, he believed, for he was amazed at the teaching about the Lord.

[13]From Paphos, Paul and his companions sailed to Perga in Pamphylia, where John left them to return to Jerusalem.

COMMENTARY

4 Having brought his readers back to Syrian Antioch and shown how Barnabas and Saul were directed to undertake a mission to Gentiles, Luke now begins the account of the gospel's outreach to Cyprus, Pamphylia, and the southern portion of Galatia. That his descriptions of events on the Christian evangelists' first missionary journey are fuller and more detailed than the description of the church at Antioch (cf. 11:19–30; 12:25–13:3) seems to suggest that in setting out the events of that first journey Luke was working from written source materials. His linking of the portrayal of this first missionary journey in 13:4–14:28 to the introduction in 12:25–13:3 by his favorite connective *men oun* ("so," "then"), which appears at the beginning of this verse (NIV, untranslated; NASB, "so"), seems also to support the hypothesis of his working from source materials in what immediately follows. Furthermore, his use of the personal pronoun "they" (*autoi*) at the beginning of vv. 4 (here) and 14 may be seen as signaling some distinction in his source materials concerning the ministry on Cyprus in 13:4–12 and the ministry at Antioch of Pisidia in 13:14–52.

While the church (1) confirms in its own experience the divine will, (2) identifies itself with God's purposes and those he has called for specific tasks, and (3) releases them from their duties for wider service (cf. v.3), it is God who by his Spirit is in charge of events and sends out his missionaries. Thus being "sent on their way by the Holy Spirit," they went down to Seleucia on the Mediterranean and sailed from there to the island of Cyprus. Just why they thought of going to Cyprus first in carrying out their mandate we do not know. But Barnabas was from Cyprus (cf. 4:36), and evidently knowing generally the will of God he and Saul were ready to move from the known at Cyprus to the unknown in the larger Greco-Roman world.

Seleucia was the port city of Antioch of Syria, some sixteen miles west of Antioch and four or five miles northeast of the mouth of the Orontes River. It was founded by Seleucus I Nicator, the first king of the Seleucid dynasty, about 300 BC in conjunction with the founding of Antioch. Cyprus was an island of great importance from very early times, being situated on the shipping lanes between Syria, Asia Minor, and Greece. In 57 BC it was annexed by Rome from Egypt and in 55 BC incorporated into the province of Cilicia. In 27 BC it became a separate province governed on behalf of the emperor Augustus by an imperial legate. In 22 BC Augustus relinquished control of the island to the senate, and like other senatorial provinces it was administered by a proconsul.

5 Leaving the mainland of Syria, the missionary party sailed to Salamis on the eastern coast of Cyprus, about 130 miles west of Seleucia. Salamis was the most important city of the island and the administrative center for its eastern half, though the provincial capital was 90 miles southwest at Paphos. The population of Cyprus was predominantly Greek, but many Jews lived there as well (cf. Philo, *Legat.* 282; Josephus, *Ant.* 13. 284, 287). Thus Barnabas and Saul began their mission in the synagogues of the city, and John Mark was with them as their helper (*hypēretēs*, "servant," "helper," "assistant," GK 5677). Jewish grave inscriptions and various papyri use the word *hypēretēs* in the sense of a synagogue attendant, as does Luke also in his gospel (cf. 4:20). This has caused many to view John Mark's responsibilities as related to caring for the scrolls—probably the OT Scriptures; perhaps also a passion narrative, an Olivet discourse, a "Sayings of Jesus" collection, and certain confessional materials of the early church—and serving as a catechist for new converts. In Luke 1:2 and Acts 26:16, however, Luke also uses the term more broadly to mean a servant of Christ and in Acts 5:22, 26 to designate members of the temple guard. Here it should probably be understood in its broader sense.

6–8 From Salamis, Barnabas and Saul traveled throughout the island of Cyprus. They continued to preach within the Jewish synagogues to both Jews and "God-fearing" Gentiles. But when they reached the city of Paphos—or, more exactly, New Paphos, the Roman provincial capital seven miles northwest of the old Phoenician city of Paphos—their ministry dramatically and decisively changed. For at Paphos the Roman proconsul Sergius Paulus asked them to present their message before him (v.7). This was probably meant to be an official inquiry into the nature of what these traveling evangelists were preaching in the Jewish synagogues, so that the proconsul might know how to deal with the charges already laid against them and be able to head off any further disruptions within the Jewish communities. It was something like a "command performance," and so the invitation could not have been refused. But neither the proconsul nor the missionaries themselves could have anticipated what actually happened at that inquiry.

Luke describes Sergius Paulus as a man of discernment (*anēr synetos*, "an intelligent, sagacious, understanding man," or "wise man," GK *467, 5305*), as he proved to be in accepting the Christian message. Possibly he was the Lucius Sergius Paulus known to have been one of the curators of the Tiber during the reign of Claudius (cf. *CIL* 6.4.2, No. 31545). If so, he probably went to Cyprus as proconsul after his curatorship in Rome. Within his court at Paphos was a certain Jewish sorcerer and false prophet named Bar-Jesus (*Bariēsou*, which is a Greek transliteration of the Aramaic *bar Yeshua*, "son of Jeshua," and comes from a Semitic root meaning "to be worthy"). In assuming to be the Jewish spokesman in opposition to these Jewish-Christian

evangelists, this man probably wanted to enhance his own reputation. While sorcery and magic were officially banned in Judaism, there were still Jews who practiced it, both under the guise of Jewish orthodoxy and as renegades (cf. Lk 11:19; Ac 19:13–16). Bar-Jesus is also called Elymas ("sorcerer," "magician," "fortune-teller"), which cannot be a translation of the name Bar-Jesus. There is some evidence in the Western text for the spellings "Etymas" or "Hetoimas," both of which mean something like "to be ready" and are therefore partly parallel to the root meaning of Bar-Jesus ("to be worthy"). If either Etymas or Hetoimas was originally in his text, Luke may have been referring to a Jewish magician of Cyprus named Atomos, who according to Josephus (*Ant.* 20.142) helped the procurator Felix to win Drusilla (cf. Ac 24:24), formerly married to Aziz of Emesa, for himself as his wife.

9 In all of Saul's activities thus far, nothing had happened to suggest that he was anything but "a Hebrew born of Hebrew parents" (cf. Php 3:5). He had been called to proclaim the message of Jesus to Gentiles but so far had made no special appeal to them directly. Nor did he approach them as being on an equal footing with Jews or apart from the synagogue. Though his preaching had aroused strong feelings within certain Jewish communities, it engendered no more ill will than had been directed against the other apostles before him. Here in the hall of the proconsul, however, Saul was in new surroundings as he presented his message before a leading member of the Roman world—a world he himself was a member of and well knew. As a Jew, he proudly bore the name of Israel's first king, Saul. As a Roman citizen (cf. 16:37–38; 25:10–12), he undoubtedly had two Roman names, a praenomen and a nomen, though neither is used of him in the NT. But as a Jew of the Diaspora, who must necessarily rub shoulders with the Gentile world at large, he also bore the Greek name "Paul"

(*Paulos*, meaning "little"), which became his cognomen in the empire and was used in Gentile contexts. So at this point in his narrative Luke speaks of "Saul, who was also called Paul," and hereafter refers to him only by this name.

10–11 As the gospel was being proclaimed to Sergius Paulus, Bar-Jesus tried to divert the proconsul from the faith (v.8). But Paul turned on the sorcerer and pronounced a curse on him. In thoroughly biblical language—which was used for solemn adjurations and curses—he denounced Bar-Jesus as "a child of the devil," "an enemy of everything that is right," one who was "full of all kinds of deceit and trickery," one who was always "perverting the right ways of the Lord" (v.10), and he pronounced a curse of temporary blindness on him (v.11). "Immediately," Luke tells us, "mist and darkness came over him, and he groped about, seeking someone to lead him by the hand."

12 The nature of the proconsul's response has often been debated, chiefly because the text says nothing about his being baptized when he believed. William M. Ramsay (*Bearing of Recent Discovery on the Trustworthiness of the New Testament*, 165) suggested that for Luke "belief" was only the first step in a process of conversion, with the second being "turning to the Lord," and therefore our author's statement that "he believed" (*episteusen*, GK *4409*) should not be taken to mean that at this time he became a Christian. On the other hand, Kirsopp Lake and Henry Cadbury proposed that the missionaries "may have mistaken courtesy for conversion" and warned their readers not to take Luke's words here in v.12 too seriously (cf. *Beginnings of Christianity* [ed. Foakes-Jackson and Lake], 4.147). But the statement that Sergius Paulus believed can hardly be read with any less significance than Luke's use of the same verb in 14:1; 17:34; and 19:18, where baptism also goes unmentioned and yet where we may well assume that it was performed.

13 Pamphylia was a geographically small and economically poor province on the southern coast of Asia Minor, with the mountains of Lycia to the west, the foothills of Pisidia to the north, and the Taurus range to the east. It contained a mixed population and seems to have been as open to the gospel as any other province. Yet Luke gives us no account of evangelization in Perga or its environs at this time, though he expressly states that Paul and Barnabas "preached the word in Perga" on their return to Syrian Antioch (14:25). More puzzling still is the fact that it was at Perga that John Mark left the group to return to Jerusalem.

The usual explanation for initially bypassing Perga and moving on to Antioch of Pisidia is that Paul may have been ill with a case of malaria and that his sickness forced redirecting the mission to gain the healthier, higher ground to the north. As for John Mark's departure, it is usually explained as a combination of homesickness, the rigors of travel, dissatisfaction with Paul's assumption of leadership over his cousin Barnabas, and/or being unhappy about leaving Cyprus so soon. But discussion among the missionaries after Paphos and during their stay at Perga may well have focused on the implications of Sergius Paulus's conversion for their ministry. And it can plausibly be argued (1) that their lack of preaching in Perga at this time was due primarily to uncertainty within the missionary party itself about the validity of a direct approach to and full acceptance of Gentiles, and (2) that John Mark's departure occurred because he disagreed with Paul.

John Mark may have been concerned about the effect that such news of a direct Christian mission to Gentiles would have in Jerusalem and on the church there—and it may be that he wanted no part in it. It may even have been his return to the Christian community in Jerusalem, coupled with an account of his disagreement with Paul about a direct approach to Gentiles, that originally stirred the

"Judaizers" in the church to action. Other explanations for Mark's defection are at best only partial and at worst rather thin. They fail to account for Paul's vehement opposition to Mark recorded in 15:37–39—an opposition that suggests that Mark's departure on this first missionary journey may have been for reasons that hurt Paul deeply and were more than merely personal.

NOTES

4 On Luke's use of μὲν οὖν (*men oun*, "so," "then"), see comments at 1:6. In this fourth panel of material, note the pattern that develops here at 13:4 (after four verses of introduction), at 14:3 (after a two-verse introduction), at 15:3 (after another two-verse introduction), and in summary at 15:30 and 16:5.

5 Codex Bezae (D), and as represented in recensions of the Old Latin and Syriac, reads τὸν λόγον τοῦ κυρίου (*ton logon tou kyriou*, "the word of the Lord"), instead of the more widely supported τὸν λόγον τοῦ θεοῦ (*ton logon tou theou*, "the word of God"). "The word of God" is the more usual expression in Luke-Acts and is the only form used in Luke's gospel (5:1; 8:11, 21; 11:28), though both forms appear in Acts.

6 The name Bar-Jesus appears in the textual evidence in various forms: (1) in the genitive as Βαριη-σοῦ (*Bariēsou*) in 𝔓[74] ℵ and a number of minuscules, as well as reflected in various recensions of the Old Latin, Vulgate, Coptic, and Syriac; (2) in the nominative as Βαριησοῦς (*Bariēsous*) in B C E and many minuscules, as well as the Coptic Sahidic; (3) in the accusative as Βαριησοῦν (*Bariēsoun*) in A, a corrected recension of D, H L P, many other minuscules, and some recensions of the Syriac. Uncorrected D has Βαριησοῦαν (*Bariēsouan*), evidently attempting a more exact transliteration of "Bar-Yeshua." The genitival form is the "harder reading" and probably best accounts for the others, with the nominative attempting to improve the grammar and the accusative being influenced by the attribution ψευδοπροφήτην (*pseudoprophētēn*, "false prophet," GK *6021*) that precedes it.

8 Codex Bezae (D), as supported by E and recensions of the Syriac and Coptic, adds at the end of the verse ἐπειδὴ ἥδιστα ἤκουεν αὐτῶν (*epeidē hēdista ēkouen autōn*, "because he was listening with great pleasure to them"), thereby stating the obvious as to why Elymas tried to turn the proconsul from the faith.

11 The textual evidence is almost equally divided between παραχρῆμά τε (*parachrēma te*, "and immediately"), as in 𝔓[45] ℵ C etc., and παραχρῆμα δέ (*parachrēma de*, "and immediately"), as in 𝔓[74] A B E H L P etc. Codex Bezae (D) goes its own way in reading καὶ εὐθέως (*kai eutheōs*, "and immediately"). Luke's fondness for the expression παραχρῆμα (*parachrēma*; sixteen of its eighteen NT occurrences appear in Luke-Acts) and the particle τε (*te*) suggest that παραχρῆμά τε (*parachrēma te*) was probably the original reading.

REFLECTIONS

The conversion of Sergius Paulus was a turning point in Paul's whole ministry. In fact, it inaugurated a new policy in the Christian mission to Gentiles, namely, the legitimacy of a direct approach to and acceptance of Gentiles apart from any distinctive Jewish stance. This is what Luke clearly sets forth as the great innovative development of this first missionary journey in 14:27 (cf. 15:3). Cornelius had been earlier converted to Christ apart from any prior commitment to Judaism, and the Jerusalem church had accepted his conversion. But the Jerusalem church seems not to have taken Cornelius's conversion as a precedent for the Christian mission—and apparently it preferred not to dwell on its ramifications. Paul, however, whose mandate was to proclaim Jesus Christ among the Gentiles, saw in the conversion of Sergius Paulus further aspects of what a mission to the Gentile world involved, and he seems to have been prepared to take this conversion as a precedent fraught with far-reaching implications for his ministry. It is significant that from this point on Luke (1) always calls Saul of Tarsus by his Greek name Paul, and (2) always emphasizes Paul's leadership in the missionary team by listing him first— except in 14:14; 15:12; and 15:25, which depict situations where Barnabas was looked on by others as being more prominent or more important. After this event of the conversion of Sergius Paulus, it was Paul's insight and understanding that set the tone for the church's outreach to the Gentile world.

C. At Antioch of Pisidia (13:14–52)

OVERVIEW

At Pisidian Antioch the typical pattern of Paul's ministry was established: an initial proclamation in the synagogue to Jews and Gentile adherents and then, when refused an audience in the synagogue, a direct ministry to Gentiles. This pattern is reproduced in every city with a sizable Jewish population visited by Paul except Athens. As he later declares in his letter to the Romans, there is no difference between Jews and Gentiles in condemnation (Ro 2:1–3:20) or in access to God (Ro 3:21–31). And it was at Pisidian Antioch that the Christian mission to the Gentile world began to express this equality.

Historically, Israel had been tremendously advantaged (Ro 3:1–2; 9:4–5). Paul himself had a great desire to see his nation respond positively to Christ (Ro 9:1–3; 10:1). But while the Jewish synagogue was an appropriate venue for beginning his ministry in each of the cities of the Roman Empire, inasmuch as the synagogue offered an audience of Jews and "God-fearing" Gentiles who were theologically prepared for his message, the traditional Jewish meeting place was not the exclusive sphere of Paul's missionary activity. For since Jews and Gentiles stood before God on an equal footing, they could be appealed to equally and, if need be, even separately.

This understanding of the validity of a direct approach to Gentiles and their full acceptance as Christians is what Paul speaks of as "my gospel" (Ro 2:1b; 16:25; cf. Gal 1:11–2:10). It was not a gospel different in content from the earliest gospel (1Co 15:1–11), but a gospel distinct in strategy and broader in scope. By revelation, the nature of Paul's Christian ministry had been given; by providential action at the beginning of this first missionary journey, its specifics were spelled out. This was, as Paul reflects some time later, "the mystery made known to me by revelation, . . . which was not made known to men in other generations as it has now been revealed by the Spirit to God's holy apostles and prophets. This mystery is that through the gospel the Gentiles are heirs together with Israel, members together of one body, and sharers together in the promise in Christ Jesus" (Eph 3:3–6).

1. A Welcome Extended at Antioch (13:14-15)

¹⁴From Perga they went on to Pisidian Antioch. On the Sabbath they entered the synagogue and sat down. ¹⁵After the reading from the Law and the Prophets, the synagogue rulers sent word to them, saying, "Brothers, if you have a message of encouragement for the people, please speak."

COMMENTARY

14-15 Pisidian Antioch was in reality not in Pisidia but in Phrygia near Pisidia (cf. Strabo, *Geogr.* 12.577). To distinguish it from the other Antioch in Phrygia, however, the city was popularly called "Antioch of Pisidia." It was founded by Seleucus I Nicator about 281 BC as one of the sixteen cities he named in honor of either his father or his son, both of whom bore the name Antiochus. It was situated 100 miles north of Perga on a lake-studded plateau, some 3,600 feet above sea level. The foothills between Perga and Pisidian Antioch largely ruled out any extensive east-west traffic until one reached the plateau area, though following the river valleys one could move northward from the area of Pamphylia. On the plateau Antioch stood astride the Via Sebaste, the Roman road from Ephesus to the Euphrates. The city had been incorporated into the expanded Roman province of Galatia in 25 BC by Augustus, who imported into it some three thousand army veterans and their families from Italy and bestowed on it the title "Colonia Caesarea." Antioch was the most important city of southern Galatia and included within its population a rich amalgam of Greek, Roman, Oriental, and Phrygian traditions. Acts tells us that it also had a sizable Jewish population.

Arriving at Pisidian Antioch, Paul and Barnabas entered the synagogue on the Sabbath. A typical first-century synagogue service would have included the *Shema* (Dt 6:4-9; 11:13-21; cf. Nu 15:37-41), the *Shemoneh Esreh* ("Eighteen Benedictions," "Blessings," or "Prayers"), a reading from the Law, a reading from one of the prophets, a free address given by any competent Jew in attendance, and a closing blessing (cf. Str-B, 4.1.153-249; see also descriptions of Jewish prayers in my "Prayer in the Pauline Letters," in *Into God's Presence*, ed. R. N. Longenecker [Grand Rapids: Eerdmans, 2001], 207-12). The leader of the synagogue (the *archisynagōgos* [GK *801*], which is equivalent to the Hebrew *rō'š hakᵉnēset*, "head of the synagogue") took charge of the building and made arrangements for the services (Lk 8:41, 49). He was usually one of the elders of the congregation. Generally there was only one such leader in each synagogue (cf. 18:8, 17), but at times two or more made up the synagogue chapter. The office was sometimes held for life and passed on within a family. Occasionally, the title was even given honorifically to women and children. Perhaps Paul's clothes or manner of attire identified him as a Pharisee and so opened the way for an invitation to speak.

NOTES

14 Though τῶν σαββάτων (*tōn sabbatōn*, "the Sabbaths") is a neuter plural, its meaning was singular (cf. 16:13; 20:7; see also Mk 16:2 par.; Jn 20:1, 19; 1Co 16:2). Speculation that the missionaries were asked to speak only on their second visit to the synagogue, therefore, is without warrant.

15 On the address ἄνδρες ἀδελφοί (*andres adelphoi*, "men, brothers") as a type of formal address used within first-century synagogues and among congregated Jews, see comments at 1:16.

2. Paul's Sermon in the Synagogue at Antioch (13:16–41)

OVERVIEW

Three missionary sermons of Paul are presented in Acts: the first here in 13:16–41 in the synagogue at Antioch of Pisidia; the second in 14:15–17 to Lystrans assembled outside the city gates; the third in 17:22–31 before the Council of Ares at Athens. Each sermon as we have it is only a précis of what was said, for the longest in its present form would take no more than three minutes to deliver and the shortest can be read in thirty seconds or less. But there is enough in each account to suggest that whereas Paul preached the same gospel wherever he went, he altered the form of his message according to the circumstances he encountered.

¹⁶Standing up, Paul motioned with his hand and said:"Men of Israel and you Gentiles who worship God, listen to me! ¹⁷The God of the people of Israel chose our fathers; he made the people prosper during their stay in Egypt, with mighty power he led them out of that country, ¹⁸he endured their conduct for about forty years in the desert, ¹⁹he overthrew seven nations in Canaan and gave their land to his people as their inheritance. ²⁰All this took about 450 years.

"After this, God gave them judges until the time of Samuel the prophet. ²¹Then the people asked for a king, and he gave them Saul son of Kish, of the tribe of Benjamin, who ruled forty years. ²²After removing Saul, he made David their king. He testified concerning him:'I have found David son of Jesse a man after my own heart; he will do everything I want him to do.'

²³"From this man's descendants God has brought to Israel the Savior Jesus, as he promised. ²⁴Before the coming of Jesus, John preached repentance and baptism to all the people of Israel. ²⁵As John was completing his work, he said:'Who do you think I am? I am not that one. No, but he is coming after me, whose sandals I am not worthy to untie.'

²⁶"Brothers, children of Abraham, and you God-fearing Gentiles, it is to us that this message of salvation has been sent. ²⁷The people of Jerusalem and their rulers did not

recognize Jesus, yet in condemning him they fulfilled the words of the prophets that are read every Sabbath. 28Though they found no proper ground for a death sentence, they asked Pilate to have him executed. 29When they had carried out all that was written about him, they took him down from the tree and laid him in a tomb. 30But God raised him from the dead, 31and for many days he was seen by those who had traveled with him from Galilee to Jerusalem. They are now his witnesses to our people.

32"We tell you the good news: What God promised our fathers 33he has fulfilled for us, their children, by raising up Jesus. As it is written in the second Psalm:

"'You are my Son;
today I have become your Father.'

34The fact that God raised him from the dead, never to decay, is stated in these words:

"'I will give you the holy and sure blessings promised to David.'

35So it is stated elsewhere:

"'You will not let your Holy One see decay.'

36"For when David had served God's purpose in his own generation, he fell asleep; he was buried with his fathers and his body decayed. 37But the one whom God raised from the dead did not see decay.

38"Therefore, my brothers, I want you to know that through Jesus the forgiveness of sins is proclaimed to you. 39Through him everyone who believes is justified from everything you could not be justified from by the law of Moses. 40Take care that what the prophets have said does not happen to you:

41"'Look, you scoffers,
wonder and perish,
for I am going to do something in your days
that you would never believe,
even if someone told you.'"

COMMENTARY

16 When Jesus addressed the congregation at Nazareth, he read the lesson standing and then sat down to speak (cf. Lk 4:16, 20). Luke, however, portrays Paul as "standing" (*anastas*, GK *2705*) to address the worshipers at Pisidian Antioch. Indeed, Philo (*Spec.* 2.62) speaks of members of the synagogue as standing (*anastas*) to address the congregation. Greek orators also stood to speak. Probably the difference between Jesus and Paul in addressing their respective synagogue audiences is best explained by postulating that Jesus' address at Nazareth was an exposition of Isaiah 61, whereas Paul's at Pisidian Antioch was an exhortation that did not arise from the biblical passages read that day from the Law or the Prophets (cf. I. Abrahams, *Studies in Pharisaism and the Gospels* [Cambridge: Cambridge Univ. Press, 1917], 1.9). In Paul's audience there were both Jews and "God-fearing" Gentiles. So he addressed them, "Men of Israel" (*andres Israēlitai*) and "you Gentiles who worship God" (*hoi phoboumenoi* [GK *5828*] *ton theon*; see also v.26). With a wave of his hand—a typically Jewish gesture, though some commentators prefer to see it only as a Greek affectation inserted by Luke—and with his words he invites them to listen to him.

17-22 Paul's exhortation begins with a résumé of Israel's history that emphasizes the pattern of God's redemptive activity from Abraham to David. It is an approach in line with Jewish interests and practices, and it can be paralleled by Stephen's defense before the Sanhedrin, by the argument of the letter to the Hebrews, and by the underlying structure of Matthew's gospel.

Highlighted in this résumé is a four-point confessional summary that for Jews epitomized the essence of their faith: (1) God is the God of the people of Israel; (2) he chose the patriarchs for himself; (3) he redeemed his people from Egypt and led them through the wilderness; and (4) he gave them the land of Palestine as an inheritance (cf. G. E. Wright, *The God Who Acts* [London: SCM, 1952], 76). To such a confessional recital, Jews often added God's choice of David to be king and the promises made to him and his descendants (cf. Pss 78:67-72; 89:3-4, 19-37). Paul also proclaims these great confessional truths of Israel's faith, for they speak of God's redemptive concern for his people and undergird the Christian message.

Also of importance is the fact that underlying Paul's treatment of David is 2 Samuel 7:6-16 (cf.

J. W. Doeve, *Jewish Hermeneutics in the Synoptic Gospels and Acts* [Assen:Van Gorcum, 1954], 172; E. Lövestam, *Son and Saviour:A Study of Acts 13:32-37* [Lund: Gleerup, 1961], 6-15). This is a passage that speaks of David's descendant as being God's "son" (cf.2Sa 7:14,"I will be his father, and he will be my son") and was understood in at least one Jewish community during the period of Second Temple Judaism to have messianic significance (cf. 4Q174 on 2Sa 7:10-14). By anchoring Israel's kerygma in the messianically relevant "son" passage of 2 Samuel 7, Paul has begun to build a textual bridge for the Christian kerygma, which in v.33 he will also root in the messianic "son" passage of Psalm 2:7. And by drawing together 2 Samuel 7:6-16 (a Jewish *testimonium* passage) and Psalm 2:7 (which may have had some currency among the Qumran covenanters [cf. 4Q174 on Ps 2:1-2; also 3Q2, which includes Ps 2:7] and is used of Christ elsewhere in the NT [cf. Heb 1:5; 5:5]) on a *gezerah shawah* ("verbal analogy") basis, he will draw together Israel's confession and the church's confession, thereby demonstrating both continuity and fulfillment.

23 Paul's Christian proclamation begins by announcing that God has brought forth the messianic Deliverer from David's line in the person of Jesus. The promise Paul alludes to is in Isaiah 11:1-16, which is a messianic passage of special import for Judaism because it speaks of the Messiah's descent from David ("A shoot will come up from the stump of Jesse; from his roots a Branch will bear fruit"), of his righteous rule, of his victories, and of the establishment of his kingdom.

24-25 The announcement of Jesus as the Messiah is put in the usual form of the apostolic proclamation beginning with John the Baptist and his ministry (cf. Mk 1:2-8). John's preaching and baptism of repentance paved the way for the public ministry of Jesus. John was the forerunner of the

Messiah, as he himself confessed: "I am not that one. No, but he is coming after me, whose sandals I am not worthy to untie" (cf. Lk 3:15–18).

26–31 As Paul comes to the heart of his sermon, he appeals respectfully and urgently for a hearing. "[Men,] Brothers [*andres adelphoi*], children of Abraham [*huioi genous Abraam*], and you God-fearing Gentiles [*hoi en hymin phoboumenoi ton theon*]," he says, "it is to us that this message of salvation has been sent." Then he sets out a four-point Christian confession, which is closely parallel to the early Christian confession incorporated in 1 Corinthians 15:3b–5a : (1) that Jesus was crucified, with "the people of Jerusalem and their rulers" in their condemnation of him having "fulfilled the words of the prophets that are read every Sabbath" (vv.27–29a; cf. 1Co 15:3b: "that Christ died for our sins according to the Scriptures"); (2) that "they took him down from the tree and laid him in a tomb" (v.29b; cf. 1Co 15:4a: "that he was buried"); (3) that "God raised him from the dead" (v.30; 1Co 15:4b: "that he was raised on the third day according to the Scriptures"); and (4) that "for many days he was seen by those who had traveled with him from Galilee to Jerusalem," who are "now his witnesses to our people" (v.31; cf. 1Co 15:5a: "that he appeared to Peter, and then to the Twelve"). Particularly significant here is the clear note of fulfillment sounded in v.27 ("in condemning him they fulfilled the words of the prophets that are read every Sabbath") and implied throughout the whole presentation.

32–33 To support this four-point confession and to demonstrate the fulfillment of what God has promised, Paul cites three OT passages fraught with messianic meaning for the early Christians and also for some Jews (vv.33–35). The first in v.33 is Psalm 2:7 ("You are my Son; today I have become your Father"), which Paul uses to bind together the confessions of Judaism and Christianity by juxtaposing it with 2 Samuel 7:6–16, which passage (as noted

above) underlies vv.17–22. Both 2 Samuel 7:14 and Psalm 2:7 portray God as speaking of his "son," and it was undoubtedly this feature that brought these two passages together. Linking passages on the basis of their verbal analogies was common in early Judaism. Furthermore, the evidence from Qumran suggests that these two passages may also have been brought together by the Dead Sea covenanters even before the rise of Christianity and understood to have messianic relevance. For the Qumran text 4Q*Florilegium* (4Q174) is a pesher commentary on 2 Samuel 7:10–14; Psalm 1:1; and Psalm 2:1–2 (with the remainder of the scroll being unfortunately broken off), and Psalm 2:7 has been found in the Qumran material designated 3Q2 (without, however, an accompanying commentary). Knowledge of how Judaism viewed these two passages is not as full as one might desire, though their union and treatment at Qumran is suggestive. But whatever is concluded as to the pre-Christian union and usage of these two passages, it seems clear (1) that Paul is bringing these two "son" passages together as the textual substructure of his argument in the synagogue at Pisidian Antioch; (2) that in so doing he is joining OT redemptive history and the history of Jesus and understanding both as having messianic significance; and (3) that his approach and method were highly appropriate to his synagogue audience.

34–37 In addition to his use of 2 Samuel 7:6–16 and Psalm 2:7, in vv.34–35 Paul quotes Isaiah 55:3 ("I will give you the holy and sure blessings promised to David") and Psalm 16:10 ("You will not let your Holy One see decay") and again joins these two passages on a *gezerah shawah* ("verbal analogy") hermeneutical principle, which draws attention to the verbal similarities between *ta hosia* ("the holy blessings," GK 4008) and *ton hosion* ("the Holy One"). The promises made to David are understood to have been extended in Isaiah 55:3 to include not only God's righteous people but also the Messiah, while the messianic treatment of Psalm 16:10 stemmed from the earliest Christian preaching at Pentecost (cf. 2:27), if not also from pre-Christian Second Temple Judaism. And it was the fact that God raised Jesus from the dead—whereas David both died and decayed—that confirms, Paul declares, the messianic intent of these two biblical passages.

38–40 Having begun his sermon by addressing his audience as "men of Israel and you Gentiles who worship God" (v.16), and having focused it by his appeal to "[men,] brothers, children of Abraham, and you God-fearing Gentiles" (v.26), Paul now uses the simpler and broader appellation "men, brothers" (*andres adelphoi*, v.38; NIV, "my brothers"; NASB, "brethren") in his application and call to repentance. Through Jesus, Paul declares, are such important redemptive features as (1) "forgiveness of sins" (*aphesis hamartiōn*, GK *912, 281*) and (2) "justification" or "righteousness" (*dikaiosynē*, GK *1466*), which are (3) for "everyone who believes" (*pas ho pisteuōn*). The awkward sentence construction of vv.38b–39 in the Greek has led some interpreters (e.g., B. W. Bacon, *The Story of St. Paul* [Boston: Houghton Mifflin, 1904], 103) to read Paul as saying here that the Mosaic law could set a person free from some sins, while belief in Jesus would do so for the rest. Such an interpretation, however, is not only incompatible with Paul's teaching in Galatians and Romans, it would also be inconceivable for Luke—or any other Pauline disciple, for that matter, who might be viewed as having drawn up a précis of his preaching—to put it on his lips. Haenchen, 412 n. 4, is quite right to insist that "anyone who . . . makes the author here develop a doctrine that an incomplete justification through the law is completed by a justification through faith imputes to him a venture into problems which were foreign to him." What we have in the application of Paul's message, despite its somewhat cumbersome expression in its present précis form, are the apostle's distinctive themes of "forgiveness of sins," "justification" or "righteousness," and "faith," which resound in this first address ascribed to him in Acts, just as they do throughout his extant letters.

41 The call to repentance is cast in terms of Habakkuk 1:5, a passage we now know was accepted at Qumran as having messianic significance (cf. 1QHab) and that may also have been so considered more widely in other circles of Second Temple Judaism. In effect, then, Paul concludes by warning the congregation that Habakkuk's words apply to all who reject God's working in Jesus' ministry and who refuse Jesus as the divinely appointed Messiah: "Look, you scoffers, wonder and perish, for I am going to do something in your days that you would never believe, even if someone told you" (v.41).

NOTES

16 On the appellation ἄνδρες Ἰσραηλῖται (*andres Israēlitai*, "men of Israel") and its synonymous relation to ἄνδρες ἀδελφοί (*andres adelphoi*, "men, brothers") of vv.15, 26, and 38, see comments at 1:16 and note at 2:14.

On οἱ φοβούμενοι τὸν θεόν (*hoi phoboumenoi ton theon*) as used both here and at v.26 (though not of Cornelius) as a synonym of οἱ σεβόμενοι τὸν θεόν (*hoi sebomenoi ton theon*) to mean "God-fearers" or "Proselytes of the Gate," see comments at 10:2.

18 Codices ℵ B and D read ἐτροποφόρησεν (*etropophorēsen*, "he put up with [them]," "he bore with [them]," "he endured [their conduct]"), whereas 𝔓⁷⁴ A and C read ἐτροφοφόρησεν (*etrophophorēsen*, "he cared for [them]," "he bore [them]," "he carried [them]"). The Hebrew word *nāśā'* may mean either "to endure" or "to care for," and both meanings appear almost equally in the various LXX translations of Deuteronomy 1:31—the passage to which Paul is undoubtedly alluding. The textual evidence here is almost evenly balanced. Probably, however, ἐτροποφόρησεν (*etropophorēsen*, "he put up with [them]") is to be preferred, for it is supported by both the Alexandrian and Western families of texts and is the "harder" reading (so NIV, "he endured their conduct"; NASB, "He put up with them").

20 The Western text (D E P Ψ), most minuscules, and as incorporated into the TR (so also KJV) read "about 450 years" after "gave them judges," thereby suggesting that the judges reigned for 450 years rather than that 450 years was the time between the exodus and the possession of the land, as is preferable from codices ℵ A B and C. But in accepting the better Alexandrian reading an exegetical issue arises. When modern translators break up the one Greek sentence of vv.17–19, they tend to make the clause "about 450 years" in v.20 refer only to the final sentence. The NIV attempts to correct this by translating v.20a, "All this took about 450 years."

23 Codices ℵ A B E and P, together with 𝔓74, strongly support the reading ἤγαγεν (*ēgagen*, "he has brought," GK *149*), whereas C and D read ἤγειρε (*ēgeire*, "he has raised up," GK *1586*), evidently attempting to parallel ἀναστήσας Ἰησοῦν (*anastēsas Iēsoun*, "having raised up Jesus," GK *482*) in v.33.

𝔓74 H L and a number of minuscules read "God has brought to Israel salvation [σωτηρίαν, *sōtērian*, GK *5401*]" rather than the better-attested "God has brought to Israel the Savior Jesus (σωτῆρα Ἰησοῦν, *sōtēra Iēsoun*)." This later reading is probably a scribal error that came about through the conflation of σωτῆρα Ἰησοῦν, *sōtēra Iēsoun*.

26 On the appellation ἄνδρες ἀδελφοί (*andres adelphoi*, "men, brothers") and the designation οἱ φοβούμενοι τὸν θεόν (*hoi phoboumenoi ton theon*, "God-fearing Gentiles"), see v.16 above.

Codices ℵ A B and D, together with 𝔓74, support the first person plural pronoun ἡμῖν (*hēmin*, "to us"), whereas 𝔓45 C E and P have the second person plural pronoun ὑμῖν (*hymin*, "to you"). The exchange of the vowels ὑ (*hy*) and ἡ (*hē*) was a common blunder among scribes, for the two were pronounced alike.

27–29 The Western text seems to have circulated in a number of versions, with Codex Bezae (D) being ungrammatical and obviously corrupt. All these additions to the shorter readings of the Alexandrian text (𝔓45 ℵ B C etc.) attempt to provide in summary fashion a more complete account of Jesus' trial and death.

33 Codices ℵ A B and C, together with 𝔓74, read τοῖς τέκνοις ἡμῶν (*tois teknois hēmōn*, "to our children" [so NASB]), which produces an awkward sense. For internal reasons Codex Bezae (D), which reads τοῖς τεκνοῖς ἡμῖν (*tois teknois hēmin*, "for us, their children"), is probably to be preferred (so NIV).

Several Western texts expand "Jesus" to "the Lord Jesus Christ" (D, also Coptic Sahidic, and Ambrose) or "our Lord Jesus" (the Syriac Harclean version and Hilary), evidently influenced by ecclesiastical habit and as an expression of reverence.

The Western text (D, and as reflected in recensions of the Vulgate, Syriac, and Coptic versions) continues the quotation of Psalm 2:7 with the words of Psalm 2:8: "Ask of me and I will give you Gentiles for your inheritance, and for your possession the ends of the earth."

33–35 On Hillel's seven exegetical rules and their development, see my *Biblical Exegesis in the Apostolic Period*, 18–24.

34–35 For a similar citing of Scripture in support of Jesus' resurrection and using similar exegetical methods, see 2:25–35.

38 On the appellation ἄνδρες ἀδελφοί (*andres adelphoi*), see vv.16 and 26 above.

Codices ℵ A C D L P and many minuscules read διὰ τούτου (*dia toutou*, "through this [man]"), whereas 𝔓⁷⁴ B and a number of minuscules read διὰ τοῦτο (*dia touto*, "on account of this" or "for this [reason]"). The latter reading probably arose accidentally when the upsilon was omitted by haplography.

41 The second instance of ἔργον (*ergon*, "a work," GK *2240*), thereby reading "a work that you will never believe," is supported by the better textual tradition (𝔓⁷⁴ ℵ A B C etc.) but omitted in Western readings (D E L P, the Vulgate and Syriac versions, and many minuscules). Probably it was omitted because it was thought to be redundant or in order to assimilate the text to the LXX of Habakkuk 1:5, as seem to have been the reasons for its omission also from the NIV, though it is included in the NASB.

J. de Waard, 17–19, 78–80, points out that the quotation of Habakkuk 1:5 shows affinity to the Dead Sea sectarians' text and usage in 1QpHab. See also 3:22–23 on Deuteronomy 18:15, 18–19; 7:43 on Amos 5:26–27; and 15:16–17 on Amos 9:11–12.

3. Varying Responses to Paul's Sermon (13:42–45)

⁴²As Paul and Barnabas were leaving the synagogue, the people invited them to speak further about these things on the next Sabbath. ⁴³When the congregation was dismissed, many of the Jews and devout converts to Judaism followed Paul and Barnabas, who talked with them and urged them to continue in the grace of God.

⁴⁴On the next Sabbath almost the whole city gathered to hear the word of the Lord. ⁴⁵When the Jews saw the crowds, they were filled with jealousy and talked abusively against what Paul was saying.

COMMENTARY

42–43 The brevity of Luke's report of the responses to Paul's sermon has raised some questions in the minds of modern interpreters: Who are the "they" (*autōn*; NIV translates "Paul and Barnabas") and the "they" (in the suffix of the verb *parekaloun*, GK *4151*; "invited") of v.42? Where did the action take place—inside or outside the synagogue? How was it that the apostles were first favorably received but later rejected? And what does our author mean by the expression "devout converts to Judaism" (*hoi sebomenoi prosēlytoi*, GK *4933, 4670*; NASB, "God-fearing proselytes") in v.43? Many commentators have expressed perplexity about these matters and

proposed various source-critical explanations or deleted what appear to be the more difficult statements. But if we take the account to be an abbreviated summary of what happened and allow for the generalizations that invariably appear in any such summary, Luke's comments about the varying responses to Paul's sermon are not too difficult to understand.

Evidently the pronouns in v.42 refer to "Paul and Barnabas," who were requested by "the people" who heard Paul's sermon "to speak further about these things on the next Sabbath." More than likely, the synagogue authorities took a less favorable view of the sermon. But many of the Jews and "devout converts to Judaism" were interested and after the service followed the apostles to hear more. And "some" (*hoitines*, here used as a sweeping relative pronoun; NIV, "who") of those who heard more of the Christian proclamation were "persuaded" (*epeithon*; NIV, "urged"; NASB, "were urging") by the apostles to continue "in the grace of God," which, to judge by Paul's usual understanding of grace, must connote their reception of and continuance in the good news about salvation through Jesus.

44–45 "Almost the whole city," as Luke says rather hyperbolically, gathered on the following Sabbath to hear "the word of the Lord" (*ton logon tou kyriou*)—an expression suggesting the christological content of Paul's preaching. But "when the Jews saw the crowds," their initial interest turned to antagonism. Not only was the synagogue being flooded by Gentiles as though it were a common theater or town hall, but even more it became clear that Paul and Barnabas were ready to speak directly to Gentiles without first relating them in some way to Judaism. The Jews, it seems, were unwilling to countenance a salvation as open to Gentiles as it was to Jews. So in their opposition they not only "talked abusively" (NIV) but also were actually "blaspheming" (*blasphēmountes* [GK 1059], as the NASB translates the present participle). From Luke's perspective, opposition to the gospel was directed not so much against the messengers, Paul and Barnabas, as against the content of the message—i.e., against Jesus himself (cf. the use of *blasphēmeō* in 26:11).

NOTES

42–43 The brevity of these two verses, coupled with a certain amount of repetition and various ambiguities, have given rise to a rather large number of variant readings in the textual tradition. None of these, however, add significantly to the implied sense of these verses, and so the variants need not be detailed here.

43 The expression οἱ σεβόμενοι προσήλυτοι (*hoi sebomenoi prosēlytoi*) makes sense only if σεβόμενος (*sebomenos*) does not here denote a "God-fearing Gentile," as in 13:50; 16:14; 17:4, 17; and 18:7, but rather a "devout Gentile convert" (NIV; NASB, "God-fearing proselytes") to Judaism who had accepted circumcision and obligation to the entire Jewish law (see NASB text note).

On the use of the verbs πείθω (*peithō*, "persuade" or "urge," GK 4275), διαλέγομαι (*dialegomai*, "reason," GK 1363), διανοίγω (*dianoigō*, "explain," GK 1380), and παρατίθημι (*paratithēmi*, "prove," GK 4192) as being characteristic of Paul's manner of preaching and teaching, see comments at 17:2–4, 17; 18:4, 19; 19:8–10; 20:9; 24:25; 26:28; and 28:23.

45 Codex Bezae (D) adds ἀντιλέγοντες καί (*antilegontes kai*) before βλασφημοῦντες (*blasphēmountes*), thereby reading, "they were contradicting and blaspheming"—which is simply a tautological expansion of the obvious.

4. To the Jews First, but Also to the Gentiles (13:46–52)

46Then Paul and Barnabas answered them boldly: "We had to speak the word of God to you first. Since you reject it and do not consider yourselves worthy of eternal life, we now turn to the Gentiles. 47For this is what the Lord has commanded us:

> "'I have made you a light for the Gentiles,
>   that you may bring salvation to the ends of the earth.'"
>
> ⁴⁸When the Gentiles heard this, they were glad and honored the word of the Lord; and all who were appointed for eternal life believed.
>
> ⁴⁹The word of the Lord spread through the whole region. ⁵⁰But the Jews incited the God-fearing women of high standing and the leading men of the city. They stirred up persecution against Paul and Barnabas, and expelled them from their region. ⁵¹So they shook the dust from their feet in protest against them and went to Iconium. ⁵²And the disciples were filled with joy and with the Holy Spirit.

COMMENTARY

46–47 In response to the Jews' abuse and blasphemy, Paul and Barnabas asserted their new policy: "To the Jews first but also to the Gentiles." This was a policy that evidently (1) began to take form with the conversion of Sergius Paulus and (2) was discussed both fervently and extensively by the missionaries on their way from Paphos to Pisidian Antioch. It is significant that Jerome in his commentary on Isaiah (written ca. AD 403) refers five times to an interpretation of Isaiah 9:1–2 (the regions of Zebulun and Naphtali "have seen a great light") that he found among the Nazoreans of Syria, who were Jewish believers in Jesus—an interpretation, Jerome tells us, that went beyond the use of Isaiah 9:1–2 in Matthew 4:13–16 in establishing the priority of the gospel outreach as being "first to Jews and then to Gentiles." Therefore, since according to Jerome the Nazoreans had an uninterrupted tradition stretching back to the very beginning of the Christian church, it may be fairly claimed that the policy of preaching "first to Jews and then to Gentiles" was acknowledged very early even among certain Jewish Christians at Jerusalem, although, it seems, the first part of that axiom was more important to the early Jewish believers in Jesus, whereas the second

part became vitally important to Paul on his first missionary journey.

As Paul and Barnabas saw it, in their exclusiveness the Jews of Pisidian Antioch had rejected the very thing they were earnestly looking for—"the life of the age to come" (Heb. *ḥayyê haʿolām habbāʾ*), or "eternal life" (Gr. *hē aiōnios zōē*, GK *173, 2437*). Now, however, the gospel must be directed to the Gentiles, for included in its mandate was the promise of Isaiah 49:6 that God's servant will be "a light for the Gentiles" and a bringer of salvation "to the ends of the earth" (cf. Lk 2:28–32). It was, of course, Jesus of Nazareth, who is uniquely God's Servant and is at work through his Spirit in the church, completing what he had begun. But in that redemptive work of Jesus through his Spirit in the church, Paul and Barnabas were also made God's servants and inheritors of the promise in Isaiah 49:6.

48 Many of the Gentiles responded with thankfulness for the apostles' ministry and openness to their message, which is characterized as "the word of the Lord" (*ton logon tou kyriou*). The statement "all who were appointed for eternal life believed" suggests that belief in Christ is not just a matter of one's own response of faith but primarily involves divine

927

appointment (cf. Str-B, 2.726, on Jewish concepts of predestination).

49 Through the conversion of many of the Gentiles, who brought the message of salvation to others, "the word of the Lord spread through the whole region." This spreading of the Christian proclamation (*ho logos tou kyriou*, "the word of the Lord"), along with the apostles' own outreach to the various cities named in chs. 13 and 14, probably led to the agitation of the "Judaizers," which resulted in the problem that Paul had to deal with in his letter to converts in the province of Galatia.

50 Unable to confine the ministry of Paul and Barnabas to the synagogue, the Jews stirred up trouble against them and brought pressure on the city's magistrates (*tous prōtous tēs poleōs*, lit., "the leading men of the city") through their "God-fearing" wives (*tas sebomenas gynaikas tas euschēmonas*, lit., "the God-fearing women of high standing"). Since Luke speaks of this persecution as an official expulsion rather than a mob action, it probably took the form of a charge that Christianity, being disowned by the local Jewish community, was not an officially sanctioned religion (*religio licita*) and so must be viewed a disturbance to the "Peace of Rome" (Pax Romana). Later in Acts, Luke will show how agitations against the gospel usually arose from within the Jewish communities, not from Roman authorities, and that the charge against Paul was that he was preaching an illegal religion (cf. 16:20–21; 17:7; 18:13)—a charge Luke takes pains to insist was unfounded. This is part of the overall fabric of Luke's apologetic argument (see Introduction, pp. 678–80), and he probably meant to suggest it here as well.

51 Having been expelled from Pisidian Antioch, Paul and Barnabas "shook the dust from their feet in protest against them"—a Jewish gesture of scorn and disassociation, which here was directed against the city's magistrates and the Jewish leaders. Then they went southeast on the Via Sebaste and headed for Iconium, some eighty miles away.

52 The new "disciples" (*hoi mathētai*) left behind at Pisidian Antioch and its environs, far from being discouraged at this turn of events, were "filled with joy and with the Holy Spirit."

NOTES

48 Codex Bezae (D) reads ἐδέξαντο (*edexanto*, "they accepted," GK *1312*) rather than the better established ἐδόξαζον (*edoxazon*, "they glorified," GK *1519*; NIV, "they . . . honored"; NASB, "they *began* . . . glorifying").

𝔓⁴⁵ 𝔓⁷⁴ ℵ A C, most minuscules, the Old Latin, Vulgate, and Coptic versions, and Chrysostom read τὸν λόγον τοῦ κυρίου (*ton logon tou kyriou*, "the word of the Lord"), whereas B D E, some minuscules, and sometimes Augustine have it as τὸν λόγον τοῦ θεοῦ (*ton logon tou theou*, "the word of God"). "The word of the Lord" seems better supported externally, while internally its parallel in v.49 makes such a judgment almost certain.

50 The Western text (D, partly supported by E) reads θλίψιν μεγαλὴν καὶ διωγμόν (*thlipsin megalēn kai diōgmon*, "great tribulation and persecution")—which is a redundant expansion of διωγμόν (*diōgmon*, "persecution"). For a similar Western expansion, see note at 8:1.

D. At Iconium, Lystra, and Derbe, and Back to Antioch (14:1–28)

OVERVIEW

The great Roman road from Ephesus to the Euphrates, which was extended into the heart of the south Galatian plateau by Augustus's engineers in 6 BC and named Via Sebaste in his honor (Sebastos being the Greek equivalent of Augustus), became two roads at Pisidian Antioch. One went north through mountainous terrain to the Roman colony of Comana, about 122 miles away. The other moved southeast across rolling plains and past the snow-capped peaks of Sultan Dag to terminate at the important Greek city of Iconium, some 80 miles distant from Antioch. A few years later, this road was extended another 24 miles southwest to reach the Roman colony of Lystra. As Paul and Barnabas left Pisidian Antioch, they were, therefore, faced with a choice as to the future direction of their mission. Choosing the southeastern route, they headed off to what would become a ministry to people of three very different types of cities in the southern portion of the Roman province of Galatia.

1. The Ministry at Iconium (14:1–7)

¹At Iconium Paul and Barnabas went as usual into the Jewish synagogue. There they spoke so effectively that a great number of Jews and Gentiles believed. ²But the Jews who refused to believe stirred up the Gentiles and poisoned their minds against the brothers. ³So Paul and Barnabas spent considerable time there, speaking boldly for the Lord, who confirmed the message of his grace by enabling them to do miraculous signs and wonders. ⁴The people of the city were divided; some sided with the Jews, others with the apostles. ⁵There was a plot afoot among the Gentiles and Jews, together with their leaders, to mistreat them and stone them. ⁶But they found out about it and fled to the Lycaonian cities of Lystra and Derbe and to the surrounding country, ⁷where they continued to preach the good news.

COMMENTARY

1 Iconium, an ancient Phrygian town, had been transformed by the Greeks into a city-state. Situated in the heart of the high and healthy plateau of south-central Asia Minor, it was surrounded by fertile plains and verdant forests, with mountains to its north and east. With Augustus's reorganization of provinces in 25 BC, Iconium became part of Galatia. But while Rome chose Antioch of Pisidia and Lystra as bastions of its authority in the area, Iconium remained largely Greek in temperament and somewhat resistant to Roman influence, though later Hadrian made it a Roman colony. As a Greek city, it was governed by its assembly of citizens (the *Dēmos*) and held itself aloof from interference by the Roman praetorian legate. Greek was the language of its public documents, and during the NT period it attempted to retain the ethos of the old city-state.

"Iconium" is probably a Phrygian name, but a myth was invented to give it a Greek meaning. According to the myth, Prometheus and Athena re-created mankind in the area after a devastating flood by making images of people from the mud and breathing life into them. The Greek word for "image" is *eikōn* (GK *1635; ikon* in modern Greek), hence the name Iconium. William M. Ramsay (*Cities of St. Paul*, 317–19) called Iconium "the Damascus of Asia Minor," for like Damascus it was blessed with abundant water, a genial climate, rich vegetation, and great prosperity. It was a place of beauty and a natural center of activity, as its survival into modern times as the thriving town of Konya shows.

Entering Iconium, Paul and Barnabas went to the Jewish synagogue. The phrase *kata to auto* literally suggests that the apostles went into the synagogue "together" (so NASB, KJV, RSV). But since to say that the apostles entered the synagogue together belabors the obvious, many commentators prefer to understand it as meaning "after the same manner" (i.e., as at Pisidian Antioch) and so translate it with some such expression as "as usual" (NIV), "the same thing occurred" (NRSV), "similarly" (NEB), or "as they had at Antioch" (JB). At Iconium, as Paul and Barnabas proclaimed the same gospel in the same way as they had at Pisidian Antioch, a great number believed—both Jews and Gentiles.

2 Opposition to the gospel, however, soon arose. The Western text recasts this verse to read, "But the leaders of the synagogue and the rulers [of Iconium] brought persecution against the righteous and made the minds of the Gentiles hostile against the brothers, though the Lord soon gave peace." The Western text presupposes that opposition against Christianity in Iconium followed the usual pattern in Acts of Jewish agitation and local Roman action against a *religio illicita*, whereas Iconium was a Greek city governed by its assembly of citizens. Furthermore, it appears that Western scribes had trouble seeing how the apostles could continue an extensive ministry in the city, as v.3 presents, after such an official judgment, and so they added the clause "though the Lord soon gave peace." But if we recognize that opposition to the gospel arose within a city governed by Greek jurisprudence, and if we take the aorist verbs of v.2 to be ingressive, Luke's portrayal of Jews "stirring up" the Gentiles and "poisoning their minds" may be both appropriate and meaningful without the addition of a qualifying clause (as Codex D and its associates inserted) or reversing the order of vv.2 and 3 (as some commentators think necessary).

3 To judge by his use of the connective *men oun*, Luke is here returning to some written source for his account of the ministries of Paul and Barnabas in southern Galatia. He tells us that the apostles ministered for a "considerable time" in the city and preached boldly "for the Lord," with God confirming "the message of his grace" by "miraculous signs and wonders" (*sēmeia kai terata*, GK *4956, 5469*). The reference to "the Lord" undoubtedly has in mind the Lord Jesus, thereby suggesting the christocentric nature of the missionaries' preaching. The couplet "miraculous signs and wonders" places the ministry of Paul and Barnabas directly in line with that of Jesus (cf. 2:22) and the early church (cf. 2:43; 4:30; 5:12; 6:8; 7:36) in fulfillment of prophecy (cf. 2:19), as it does also in 15:12. Later when writing to his Galatian converts (assuming an early "South Galatian" origin for the letter), Paul appeals to these mighty works performed by the Spirit as evidence that the gospel as he preached it and as they received it was fully approved by God (cf. Gal 3:4–5).

4–5 Luke tells us that there was a division among "the people" (*to plēthos*, "the population" or "the assembly," GK *4436*) of the city regarding the apostles and their message, with some siding with the Jews and others with the apostles. Interpreted broadly, the term *to plēthos* denotes no more than the populace or residents of a city (so KJV, NIV, NASB, NRSV, NEB, JB et al.). Yet the word was also used of a stated assembly (cf. 23:7) and so may denote "the assembly" of prominent citizens that met to conduct the business of a Greek city-state. If this is its meaning here, then Luke is telling us that the official response to Paul and Barnabas at Iconium was mixed—that while there might not have been any official action taken against them, there was a "plot" (*hormē*, GK *3995*) brewing among some of the Gentiles and Jews to mistreat and stone them. The Greek word *hormē* connotes impulsiveness and suggests an action not controlled by reason—which is exactly how Luke viewed the opposition at Iconium against the gospel and its evangelists.

Also significant is the fact that Luke here calls Barnabas an apostle by lumping him with Paul in the phrase "with the apostles" (*syn tois apostolois*, GK *693*), as he does also in v.14. While Barnabas was neither one of the Twelve nor a claimant to any special revelation, he was probably one of the 120 referred to in Acts 1:15. He may also have been one of the 500 to whom the resurrected Jesus appeared, as mentioned in 1 Corinthians 15:6. Yet as with such other titles as "disciple," "prophet," "teacher," and "elder," Luke, like Paul himself (cf. 2Co 8:23; Gal 1:19; Php 2:25), used "apostle" not only in the restricted sense of a small group of highly honored believers who had a special function within the church, but also in the broader sense of messengers of the gospel.

6–7 The opposition to the ministry of Paul and Barnabas must have grown to sizable proportions, for they took it seriously enough to leave Iconium and travel to Lystra and Derbe. By referring to Lystra and Derbe as "Lycaonian cities," Luke implies that Iconium belonged to a different region from Lystra and Derbe. All three cities, of course, were part of the Roman province of Galatia. But in the administration of such a large province, the Romans subdivided Galatia into various regions (*regiones* or *chōrai*), four of which have come down to us by name: Isauria, Pisidia, Phrygia, and Lycaonia. The fourth-century BC Greek general and writer Xenophon called Iconium "the last city of Phrygia" (*Anab.* 1.2.19), though later Roman authors frequently referred to it as a Lycaonian city (e.g., Cicero, *Fam.* 15.4.2; Pliny, *Nat.* 5.25). However, William M. Ramsay (*Bearing of Recent Discovery*, 39–114) has shown that between AD 37 and 72—and at no other time under Roman rule—Iconium was on the Phrygian side of the regional border between Phrygia and Lycaonia, not only linguistically but also politically (cf. W. M. Ramsay, *St. Paul the Traveller*, 110–12). In fleeing to Lystra and Derbe, therefore, Paul and Barnabas were leaving one political region to start afresh in another. Thus in that Lycaonian region they continued preaching the gospel, both in the cities of Lystra and Derbe and in the surrounding countryside, as Luke now tells us in a general way and as he will explain in the following verses.

NOTES

2–7 The Western text adds a number of small details in these verses, which were evidently meant to smooth over any seeming lack of coherence and to clarify ambiguities. Metzger's comment, 371, is appropriate (crediting F. F. Bruce for the first part and H. J. Cadbury and K. Lake for the second): "The greater smoothness of the Western text is probably a mark of its secondary character, for all the additions seem to be comments calculated to remedy difficulties of the ordinary text."

3 On Luke's use of μὲν οὖν (*men oun*, "so," "then"), see comments at 1:6. In this fourth panel of Luke's presentation, note the pattern that develops at 13:4 (after four verses of introduction), here (after a two-verse introduction), at 15:3 (after another two-verse introduction), and in summary at 15:30 and 16:5.

Codices ℵ and A, followed by the Syriac Peshitta and Coptic Bohairic versions, include the preposition ἐπί (*epi*, with the dative: "on," "in," "to") before the clause τῷ λόγῳ τῆς χάριτος αὐτοῦ (*tō logō tēs charitos autou*, "the word [or "message"] of his grace"). The weight of external evidence ($\mathfrak{P}^{74}$ B C D E L P Ψ and all the minuscules), however, omits the preposition (so NIV, though NASB includes it: "to the word of His grace").

6 Luke's use of τὴν περίχωρον (*tēn perichōron*, "the surrounding country," GK *4369*) probably has in mind the "large Lycaonian territory which contained no constitutionally organised city [as Lystra and Derbe], but only villages of the Anatolian type" (W. M. Ramsay, *Cities of St. Paul*, 409).

2. The Ministry at Lystra (14:8–20)

⁸In Lystra there sat a man crippled in his feet, who was lame from birth and had never walked. ⁹He listened to Paul as he was speaking. Paul looked directly at him, saw that he had faith to be healed ¹⁰and called out, "Stand up on your feet!" At that, the man jumped up and began to walk.

¹¹When the crowd saw what Paul had done, they shouted in the Lycaonian language, "The gods have come down to us in human form!" ¹²Barnabas they called Zeus, and Paul they called Hermes because he was the chief speaker. ¹³The priest of Zeus, whose temple was just outside the city, brought bulls and wreaths to the city gates because he and the crowd wanted to offer sacrifices to them.

¹⁴But when the apostles Barnabas and Paul heard of this, they tore their clothes and rushed out into the crowd, shouting: ¹⁵"Men, why are you doing this? We too are only men, human like you. We are bringing you good news, telling you to turn from these worthless things to the living God, who made heaven and earth and sea and everything in them. ¹⁶In the past, he let all nations go their own way. ¹⁷Yet he has not left himself without testimony: He has shown kindness by giving you rain from heaven and crops in their seasons; he provides you with plenty of food and fills your hearts with joy." ¹⁸Even with these words, they had difficulty keeping the crowd from sacrificing to them.

¹⁹Then some Jews came from Antioch and Iconium and won the crowd over. They stoned Paul and dragged him outside the city, thinking he was dead. ²⁰But after the disciples had gathered around him, he got up and went back into the city. The next day he and Barnabas left for Derbe.

COMMENTARY

8 Lystra was an ancient Lycaonian village whose origins are unknown. Caesar Augustus turned it into a Roman colony in 6 BC and brought army veterans and their families into it. He made it the most eastern of the fortified cities of Galatia. Its population was mostly uneducated Lycaonians who came from a small Anatolian tribe and spoke their own language. The ruling class was made up of Roman army veterans, while education and commerce were controlled by a few Greeks. Jews also lived there (16:1–3), but their influence seems to have been minimal. A secondary military road was built between Lystra and its more powerful sister colony Pisidian Antioch in 6 BC, and a few years later an extension of the Via Sebaste also joined Lystra to Iconium.

9–10 That Paul began the ministry at Lystra by preaching to a crowd probably implies that there was no synagogue available for him to preach in. While he was speaking, Paul saw "a man crippled in his feet, who was lame from birth and had never walked" (the triple stress on his condition may reflect the pattern of a frequently told story) and who was listening to him attentively. Seeing "that he had faith to be healed," Paul commanded him to stand up, and the man jumped up and walked around. Luke undoubtedly wanted his readers to recognize the parallel between the healing of this crippled man and the healing of another one by Peter (cf. 3:1–8), for the expressions "lame from birth" (*chōlos ek koilias mētros autou*, lit., "lame from his mother's womb"), "looked directly at him" (*atenisas* [GK 867] *autō*), and "walk about" (*periepatei*, GK 4344; NIV, "began to walk") are common to both accounts. The Western text heightens the parallel by adding the words "I say to you in the name of the Lord Jesus" before Paul's command (cf. 3:6) and the statement "immediately he leaped up and

walked" after it (cf. 3:7–8). But the sequel to the healing of the crippled man here differs from that of Peter's miracle, and it is narrated by Luke with much local color.

11–12 The healing amazed and excited the crowd, and they shouted out in the Lycaonian dialect, "The gods have come down to us in human form!" (cf. 28:6). Barnabas they identified as Zeus, the chief of the Greek pantheon, probably because of his more dignified bearing. It was evidently because Luke wanted to reflect this esteem by the people that he lists Barnabas first in his pairing of the apostles here, as he does also in another context at 15:12, 25. Paul they identified as Hermes, Zeus's son by Maia and the spokesman for the gods, since "he was the chief speaker" (*ho hēgoumenos tou logou*, GK 2451, 3364; cf. the description of Hermes by Iamblichus, the Syrian Neoplatonic philosopher [ca. AD 250–325], as "the god who leads in speaking" [*ho theos tōn logōn hēgemōn*] in his *On the Egyptian Mysteries* 1). Two inscriptions discovered at Sedasa, near Lystra (dating from the middle of the third century AD), identify the Greek gods Zeus and Hermes as being worshiped at Lycaonian Galatia. On one inscription, which records the dedication to Zeus of a statue of Hermes along with a sundial, the names of the dedicators are Lycaonian; the other inscription mentions "priests of Zeus" (cf. W. M. Calder, "Acts 14:12," *ExpTim* 37 [1926]: 528). Also found near Lystra was a stone altar dedicated to "the Hearer of Prayer [presumably Zeus] and Hermes" (ibid.).

Approximately half a century before Paul's first missionary journey, the Roman poet Ovid (ca. 43 BC–AD 17) in his *Metamorphoses* (8.626–724) retold an ancient legend that may have been well known in southern Galatia and may in part explain the wildly emotional response of the people to Paul and Barnabas. According to the legend, Zeus and Hermes once came to "the Phrygian hill country" disguised as mortals seeking lodging. Though they asked at a thousand homes, none took them in. Finally, at a humble cottage of straw and reeds, an elderly couple bearing the names Philemon and Baucis welcomed them with a lavish banquet that strained the hosts' meager resources. In appreciation, the gods transformed their cottage into a temple with a golden roof and marble columns and appointed Philemon and Baucis priest and priestess of the temple, who instead of dying became an oak and a linden tree. As for the inhospitable people of the region, the gods destroyed their houses. Just where in "the Phrygian hill country" this was supposed to have taken place, Ovid does not say. But it appears that, seeing the healing of the crippled man and remembering the legend, the people of Lystra believed Zeus and Hermes had returned and wanted to pay them homage, lest they again incur the gods' wrath.

13 The fact that the people shouted in Lycaonian probably explains why the apostles were so slow to understand what was afoot until the preparations to honor them as gods were well underway. But when the priest of Zeus—whether himself believing in their deity or for entirely pragmatic reasons—joined the crowd and began to pay them homage, Paul and Barnabas realized what was about to happen. Temples situated outside city gates were common in the ancient world, and therefore Luke's reference to "Zeus . . . just outside the city" (*Dios . . . pro tēs poleōs*) probably had in mind a temple of Zeus located just outside the gates of Lystra. We can visualize the priest of Zeus bringing out sacrificial oxen (*taurous*, "bulls," GK *5436*) draped in woolen "wreaths" (*stemmata*, GK *5098*) and beginning to sacrifice at an altar that stood in front of the temple of Zeus, which was right by the city gates. As the idolatrous worship proceeded, Paul and Barnabas

looked on with a combination of disgust and horror, particularly as they began to realize that they were in some way the object of it all.

14 When they finally realized what was going on, Paul and Barnabas tore their clothes in horror at such blasphemy and rushed into the crowd shouting out their objections and trying to make the people understand them. There is no reason to think that the people of Lystra knew anything about Jewish history or the Jewish Scriptures. Nor would they have been vitally affected by any of the philosophies of Athens. Culturally, they were probably peasants living in the hinterlands of Greco-Roman civilization, with all of the lack of advantages of people in their situation. Such is the context of Paul's second missionary sermon. By far the briefest of his three sermons in Acts (cf. 13:16–41; 17:22–31), its brevity reflects its confused setting.

15–18 Negatively, Paul's sermon at Lystra has to do with the futility of idolatry; positively, it is a proclamation of the one true and living God. Its language, particularly in its denunciation of paganism, is biblical. Indeed, Paul knows no other kind of language (cf. 13:10). But its argument is suited to its hearers. And despite the brevity with which Luke reports it, two features stand out in the development of Paul's argument. First, his demonstration of the interest and goodness of God is drawn neither from Scripture (as at Pisidian Antioch) nor from philosophy (as later at Athens) but from nature: "He has shown kindness by giving you rain from heaven and crops in their seasons; he provides you with plenty of food and fills your hearts with joy" (v.17). It is an approach to theism that peasants would understand, and here at Lystra Paul used it for all it was worth.

A second feature is the claim that "in the past, [God] let all nations go their own way" (v.16), which suggests that at Lystra Paul spoke of a progressive unfolding of divine redemption. While the sermon does not explicitly refer to salvation through Christ, it is hard to believe that it was not meant to point to Jesus Christ and his work as the divine climax of history. "We too are only men, human like you," Paul and Barnabas insisted (v.15). But we are men with a message from God, they went on to say, "bringing you good news"—in fact, the best news possible—that has to do with (1) the unity and character of the one true God, for it would hardly have been good news in the Christian sense apart from such a theocentric emphasis; and (2) redemption through the person and work of Jesus his Son. Yet for most of the Lystrans the message fell on deaf ears and they tried to carry on the sacrifices in honor of the visitors (v.18).

19–20 Later on, certain Jews from Pisidian Antioch and Iconium, disaffected with Paul and Barnabas, came to Lystra to disseminate their views. Complaining first among the Jewish residents of the city, they managed to gain a hearing with the people. The fickle Lystrans, thinking that if the apostles were not gods then they must be impostors, stoned Paul and dragged him outside the city, leaving him for dead. But with the aid of those who had accepted the gospel he revived; and showing great courage, that evening he returned to the city where he had almost been killed. The next day, Paul and Barnabas left for the border town of Derbe.

Some months later, when Paul wrote to his Gentile converts in Galatia (assuming a "South Galatian" destination for the letter), he closed by saying, "Finally, let no one cause me trouble, for I bear on my body the marks [*ta stigmata*, GK *5116*] of Jesus" (Gal 6:17). Apparently he interpreted these marks as showing that he belonged to Jesus and as protecting him from unjust accusations. Some of these marks may well have been scars caused by the stoning at Lystra. And when still later he wrote to the Corinthians of his having been stoned (2Co 11:25), it was Lystra that he had in mind (cf. also 2Ti 3:11). Perhaps also, as Chrysostom proposed, we should see in Paul's reference to his "thorn in [the] flesh" (2Co 12:7) an allusion to the persecutions he suffered and their lingering effects, of which those at Lystra were by no means least.

NOTES

9 Codex Bezae (D) adds ὑπάρχων ἐν φόβῳ (*hyparchōn en phobō* [GK *5832*], "being in fear" or "despair") after the participle λαλοῦντος (*lalountos*, "speaking," GK *3281*).

10 Several Western texts add at the end of this verse a statement to the effect that the cure was instantaneous (as at 3:7). Codex D inserts εὐθέως παραχρῆμα (*eutheōs parachrēma*, "immediately at once"); Codex E adds παραχρῆμα (*parachrēma*, "at once"); and a marginal reading of the Syriac Harclean version reads "at once that same hour."

12–13 The inclusion of the names of the Greek gods suggests that the hellenization of the local Lycaonian gods had already taken place rather than that Luke interpreted the Lycaonian gods in Greek terms (cf. Charles S. C. Williams, 170; contra *Beginnings of Christianity* [ed. Foakes-Jackson and Lake], 4.164 n.).

13 Codex Bezae (D) has the plural οἱ ἱερεῖς (*hoi hiereis*, "the priests," GK *2636*) rather than the better-supported singular ὁ ἱερεύς (*ho hiereus*, "the priest"), evidently reflecting the fact that great temples usually had a college of priests in attendance. But the temple of Zeus at Lystra was probably more modest.

14 The Western text (D, and as reflected in the Old Latin and Syriac Peshitta) omits οἱ ἀπόστολοι (*hoi apostoloi*, "the apostles," GK *693*), evidently desiring to parallel 15:12, 25—perhaps also not wanting to extend the title to Barnabas, particularly in a case where Barnabas is mentioned before Paul.

The Byzantine text reads εἰσεπήδησαν εἰς τὸν ὄχλον (*eisepēdēsan eis ton ochlon*, "they rushed into the crowd") rather than the better-supported Alexandrian and Western readings ἐξεπήδησαν εἰς τὸν ὄχλον (*exepēdēsan eis ton ochlon*, "they . . . rushed out into the crowd"; so NIV, NASB).

15 Chester Beatty 𝔓⁴⁵ omits the conjunction καί (*kai*, "and," "also," "too").

18 A number of scribes, as represented in 𝔓⁴⁵ C and many Western texts, added at the end of the sentence "but that they should each go home," probably to round off the section for lectionary purposes (cf. the reading of D at Ac 5:18 and the text of Jn 7:53).

19 The Western text considerably expands this verse to read, "And as they spent some time there and taught, there came certain Jews from Iconium and Antioch, and while they were discoursing with boldness they persuaded the people to revolt against them, saying, 'Nothing they say is true; it is all lies.' And having stirred up the people and having stoned Paul, they dragged him out of the city, thinking he was dead."

20 Codex Bezae (D), together with 𝔓⁴⁵ and E, add the possessive pronoun αὐτοῦ (*autou*, "his"), thereby reading "his disciples."

3. The Ministry at Derbe and Return to Antioch (14:21–28)

²¹They preached the good news in that city and won a large number of disciples. Then they returned to Lystra, Iconium and Antioch, ²²strengthening the disciples and encouraging them to remain true to the faith. "We must go through many hardships to enter the kingdom of God," they said. ²³Paul and Barnabas appointed elders for them in each church and, with prayer and fasting, committed them to the Lord, in whom they had put their trust. ²⁴After going through Pisidia, they came into Pamphylia, ²⁵and when they had preached the word in Perga, they went down to Attalia.

²⁶From Attalia they sailed back to Antioch, where they had been committed to the grace of God for the work they had now completed. ²⁷On arriving there, they gathered the church together and reported all that God had done through them and how he had opened the door of faith to the Gentiles. ²⁸And they stayed there a long time with the disciples.

COMMENTARY

21a Derbe was situated in the southeastern part of the Lycaonian region of Galatia about sixty miles southeast of Lystra. According to the lexicographer Stephen of Byzantium, its name in the Lycaonian dialect meant "juniper tree." In 25 BC Augustus incorporated it into the province of Galatia, thus making it a provincial border town on the eastern edge of the southern Galatian plateau. During AD 41–72 it bore the prefix "Claudia" in recognition of its strategic position as a frontier town. For some time its exact location was disputed by archaeologists, but it has now been established as being at Kerti Huyuk (cf. M. Ballance, *The Site of Derbe: A New Inscription* [London: British Institute of Archaeology at Ankora, 1957]).

Luke's account of the ministry at Derbe is very brief. All he says is that the apostles "preached the good news" there and "won a large number of disciples." Evidently Luke was more interested in the illustrious Phrygian cities of Antioch and Iconium than he was in the smaller Lycaonian towns of Lystra and Derbe. Probably, as well, the larger and more influential churches were in Antioch and Iconium, though, it seems, congregations in the smaller and more rural towns contributed more candidates for the Christian missionary endeavor (e.g., Timothy from Lystra [16:1–3; 20:4]; Gaius from Derbe [20:4])—which is a pattern not altogether different from today, as large churches often capture the headlines and small congregations provide much of the personnel.

21b Having preached at Derbe, Paul and Barnabas returned to Lystra, Iconium, and Pisidian Antioch. Why they did not push farther eastward through the passes of the Taurus range into Cilicia Luke does not tell us. Perhaps Cilicia was considered already evangelized through Paul's earlier efforts (see comments at 9:30; 11:25), which would also explain why the apostles began their missionary outreach on Cyprus and not in Cilicia (cf. 13:4). Undoubtedly their concern for the new converts in the Galatian cities led them to return by the same road. But this raises questions about how they could gain entrance into these cities after having been recently forced to leave them. Here again Luke is silent. William M. Ramsay (*St. Paul the Traveller*, 120) suggested that "new magistrates had now come into office in all the cities whence they had been driven; and it was therefore possible to go back." In each of these cities, however, the particular circumstances of their forced departure differed, and even with an annual change of administrators it would have taken considerable courage to return. Probably in returning to Lystra, Iconium, and Pisidian Antioch the apostles confined their ministries to those who had

been already converted, and so did not stir up any further opposition (cf. 16:6; 18:23; 20:3–6).

22 Returning through the Galatian cities, Paul and Barnabas tried to strengthen their converts, both personally and corporately. They encouraged them to remain in the faith and told them that many persecutions must necessarily (*dei*) be the lot of Christians in order to enter into the kingdom of God—i.e., that the same pattern of suffering and glory exemplified in Jesus' life and ministry must also be theirs if they are to know the full measure of the reign of God in their lives (cf. Mk 8:31–10:52; Ro 8:17; Php 3:10–11; Col 1:24).

23 Paul and Barnabas "appointed [*cheirotonēsantes*, GK *5936*] elders for them in each church," thus leaving them with suitable spiritual guides and an embryonic ecclesiastical administration. In the early Gentile churches—as also, undoubtedly, in the church at Jerusalem—the terms "elders" (*presbyteroi*, GK *4565*) and "bishops" or "overseers" (*episkopoi*, GK *2176*) were used somewhat interchangeably and functionally rather than as titles (cf., e.g., Ac 20, where Paul calls for the "elders" of the Ephesian church [v.17] and exhorts them: "Keep watch over yourselves and all the flock of which the Holy Spirit has made you overseers" [v.28]). The elders were the "rulers" (*proistamenoi*, GK *4613*) at Thessalonica (1Th 5:12) and at Rome (Ro 12:8). They were not only associated with the "bishops" or "overseers" but also with the "deacons" (*diakonoi*, GK *1356*) as the constituted leaders in the churches (Php 1:1; 1Ti 3:1–13; Tit 1:5–9).

24–25 Directly south of Phrygia was the region of Pisidia, and south of that the province of Pamphylia. In Pamphylia the apostles preached at Perga, the chief city of the province, thereby beginning the kind of witness in Perga they had been unable to begin on their first visit (see comments at 13:13). Of its results we know nothing. Nor do we know the nature of their visit to the port of Attalia (modern

Antalya), some eight miles farther south on the Mediterranean coast at the mouth of the Cataractes (modern Ak Su) River. Ports in antiquity were often satellite towns of larger and more important cities situated some distance inland for protection from pirates. So Luke's mention of Attalia here probably has no more significance than his mention of Seleucia (13:4), the port of Syrian Antioch, and merely identifies the place of embarkation for the voyage back to Syria.

26–28 On returning to Antioch of Syria and to the congregation that had sent them out, Paul and Barnabas "reported all that God had done through them and how he had opened the door of faith to the Gentiles" (v.27). They had gone out under divine ordination. Now their report stressed the fact that God himself had brought about a revolutionary new policy for the evangelization of the Gentiles— a policy that, while entirely unexpected, had been inaugurated by divine sanction at Paphos and thereafter was followed throughout the cities of southern Galatia. It was a claim called into question by some believers at Jerusalem, and it was a claim soon to be tested at the Jerusalem Council. So having returned from a missionary journey that occupied the better part of a year, the apostles remained at Syrian Antioch, ministering for approximately another year in the church there.

NOTES

22 On the note of divine necessity implied in the word δεῖ (*dei*, "it is necessary," "one must or has to"), see comments at 1:16.

On the phrase ἡ βασιλεία τοῦ θεοῦ (*hē basileia tou theou*, "the kingdom of God") in Christian usage, see comments at 1:4.

23 The verb χειροτονέω (*cheirotoneō*) means "to choose" or "select by raising hands" (cf. 2Co 8:19; see also Ignatius, *Phld.* 10:1; *Smyr.* 11:2; *Pol.* 7:2; and *Did.* 15:1), but can also mean "to appoint" or "install" (cf. Ac 10:41; see also Philo, *Joseph* 248; *Moses* 1.198; Josephus, *Ant.* 6.312; 13.45). Here in the Galatian cities the initiative was taken by the apostles in the appointment of elders, but undoubtedly with the concurrence of the congregations (cf. Ac 6:2–6; 13:2–3; 15:3–30).

25 The shorter λαλήσαντες τὸν λόγον (*lalēsantes ton logon*, "when they had spoken [i.e., "preached"] the word") is well supported by B D H L P, most minuscules, and the Coptic Sahidic and Bohairic versions. Other excellent textual witnesses add either τοῦ κυρίου (*tou kyriou*, "of the Lord"), as do ℵ A C, Vulgate, Syriac Peshitta, etc., or τοῦ θεοῦ (*tou theou*, "of God"), as 𝔓74 E and a recension of the Old Latin. But as Metzger, 425, rightly notes, "no one would have omitted either of the qualifying genitives if it had been present originally."

The Western text (D, some minuscules, and some recensions of the Syriac and Coptic versions) adds at the end of the verse εὐαγγελιζόμενοι αὐτούς or αὐτοῖς (*euangelizomenoi autous* or *autois*, "and they were preaching the gospel to them"), thereby stating that Paul and Barnabas evangelized in the port of Attalia. But this is not supported in the better texts or from the context in Acts.

27 Codex Bezae (D) reads μετὰ τῶν ψυχῶν αὐτῶν (*meta tōn psychōn autōn*, "with their souls") rather than the better-attested μετ' αὐτῶν (*meta autōn*, "with them" or "through them").

E. The Jerusalem Council (15:1–29)

OVERVIEW

The convening of the Jerusalem Council in approximately AD 49 was an event of great importance for the early church. There can be no doubt that Gentiles were always meant by God to share in the promises to Israel. This is a recurring theme of the OT (cf. Ge 22:18; 26:4; 28:14; Isa 49:6; 55:5–7; Zep 3:9–10; Zec 8:22). It was the underlying presupposition for all Jewish proselytizing (cf. *m. ʾAbot* 1:12; Mt 23:15). And it is implicit in the sermons of Peter at Pentecost (2:39) and in the house of Cornelius (10:35). But the correlative conviction of Judaism was that Israel was God's appointed agent for the administration of these blessings—that only through the nation and its institutions could Gentiles have a part in God's redemption and share in his favor. And there seems to have been no expectation on the part of Christian believers at Jerusalem that this program would be materially altered.

In the experience of the church, all Gentiles who had come to acknowledge Jesus as Messiah had been, with only one exception, either full proselytes or near-proselytes (i.e., "God-fearers"). Only Cornelius's conversion did not fit the pattern (cf. 10:1–11:18). But his conversion was viewed as exceptional and certainly not a precedent for any change of policy. The practice of preaching to Gentiles directly, however, which was begun by Paul in his mission on Cyprus and throughout southern Asia

Minor, was a matter of far-reaching concern at Jerusalem, especially in view of the tensions arising within Palestine after the death of Herod Agrippa I in AD 44.

As the faithful remnant, believers in the Jerusalem church naturally expected the Christian mission to proceed along the lines that God had set out long ago. They could point to the fact that, with few exceptions, commitment to Jesus as Israel's Messiah did not make Jews any less Jewish. Furthermore, sometimes it even brought Gentiles who were only loosely associated with the synagogues into greater conformity with Jewish ethics. The Christian movement had always insisted on its integral relation to the religion and nation of Israel, even though this relation contained a number of unresolved ambiguities and may have been defined in various ways within the movement. But Paul's new policy for reaching Gentiles, despite his claims of divine sanction, seemed to many Jewish believers in Jesus to undercut the basis and thrust of the ministry of the Jerusalem church. It undoubtedly stirred up serious questions among Jewish Christians, for it seemed to give the lie to the basic stance of Jerusalem Christianity. And it would have brought believers at Jerusalem under grave suspicion by their Jewish compatriots, particularly if they appeared to be condoning what Paul was doing.

REFLECTIONS

Any discussion of the Jerusalem church's attitude toward the Pauline mission that seeks to go beyond generalities is immediately faced with the thorny question of the relation of Paul's "second visit" to

Jerusalem (Gal 2:1–10) to the Jerusalem Council (Ac 15:1–29). The literary and historical issues are complex (see comments at 11:29–30). But one point drawn from the polemic in Galatians needs to be made here, namely, that Paul's silence in that letter to his converts in Galatia as to the decision of the Jerusalem Council forces the irreconcilable dilemma of saying either (1) that Luke's account in Acts 15 of a decision reached in Paul's favor at Jerusalem is pure fabrication, or (2) that Galatians was written before the Jerusalem Council.

That Paul felt it necessary in Galatians 1:18–2:10 to explain his two visits to Jerusalem as a Christian shows that his adversaries had been using one or both of those visits in a manner detrimental to his position and authority. But that he should recount his contacts with the Jerusalem leaders yet fail to mention the decision reached at the Jerusalem Council regarding his mission (accepting for the moment the veracity of Ac 15 and a late date for Galatians) is entirely inconceivable. His lack of reference to the idolatry clause of the "decrees" when writing to his converts at Corinth (cf. 1Co 8:1–11:1) may be explainable on other grounds (see comments at 15:31). But in the context of the Judaizing problem at Galatia, the decision of the Jerusalem Council would have been the coup de grâce to the whole conflict.

Many commentators argue that Galatians 2:1–10 is the account of the Jerusalem Council from Paul's perspective. But if this is true, it is exceedingly strange that the decision of the council is so muted in Paul's account. One would have expected him to have driven the decision home more forcefully in his debate with the Judaizers had he known about the council's decision when writing Galatians. He certainly pulled no punches when speaking elsewhere in that letter.

Others suggest that since there is a possibility of the "decrees" being promulgated apart from Paul's knowledge (a possibility I consider highly improbable), there is a similar possibility of an early formulation of the council's primary decision without Paul's being aware of it, thereby allowing Paul to write to his Galatian converts at a later time without any mention of the Jerusalem decision yet retaining the basic veracity of the account in Acts 15. But whatever is said of the decrees, the major decision of the Jerusalem Council was so overwhelmingly in Paul's favor that there is little likelihood of his not knowing about it and no reason for it having been kept from him. We cannot get out of the problem so easily. We are still faced with the dilemma that either (1) Paul did not know of the council's decision when he wrote to his converts in Galatia because he wrote before such a decision had been reached, or (2) the decision in question has no basis in fact. And while others have often asserted the latter hypothesis, I do not believe our only recourse is to discredit Luke's account in Acts.

Furthermore, if one assumes that Paul's clash with Peter at Syrian Antioch took place after the Jerusalem Council, then Paul's account of the clash between Peter and himself at the arrival of "certain men . . . from James" (Gal 2:12) undercuts his whole argument and turns to the advantage of his Judaizing opponents. Indeed, it would reveal Paul's recognition of a deep chasm between himself and the Jerusalem apostles, which had only been rather superficially bridged at the Jerusalem Council. Including the incident in his argument at a time before the council is understandable, but to use it in support of his polemic after the decision at Jerusalem, and without reference to that decision, casts doubt on Paul's powers of logic. One might, of course, try to support Paul's rationality by reversing the order of events in Galatians 2, thereby making vv. 11–21 refer to a time before the Jerusalem Council and vv. 1–10 reflect Paul's version of the council itself. But "the most natural interpretation of the biographical statements in Galatians i and ii," as F. C. Burkitt, 116, and others have insisted, "is that they were written before the 'Council' of Jerusalem." And while there are difficulties in an early dating of the

Galatian letter, Philip Carrington (*The Early Christian Church* [Cambridge: Cambridge Univ. Press, 1957], 1.91) was likely correct in asserting that "the arguments which perplexed the older theologians and still go on in the schools were due in no small degree to the fact that they accepted the late date of Galatians, which was traditional in their time."

Accepting, then, that Galatians was written before the Jerusalem Council, we have some idea from Paul himself concerning repercussions in Jerusalem regarding his Gentile ministry, both as it was carried on in the synagogues at Antioch of Syria and as it was further developed in Cyprus and southern Asia Minor. On his second visit to Jerusalem after his conversion, which I have proposed was the "famine visit" of AD 46 (cf. 11:27–30 and comments on those verses), the issue came to a head in the case of the Gentile Christian Titus, who was uncircumcised and who accompanied Paul and Barnabas on that visit. Paul says in Galatians 2:1–10 that there were two responses to Titus's presence at Jerusalem: (1) that of "some false brothers" who "had infiltrated our ranks to spy on the freedom we have in Christ Jesus and to make us slaves" (v.4); and (2) that of James, Peter, and John, the so-called pillar apostles (v.9).

It is somewhat difficult to identify those whom Paul calls "some false brothers"—i.e., to determine whether they were either Jewish spies sent to see what treachery the Christians were planning next in conjunction with Gentiles, or simply angry Jewish believers who threatened to publish what was happening in the church unless Titus was circumcised. Nor can it be exactly determined whether Paul brought Titus to Jerusalem as a test case, or whether, having included him in the group from Antioch for some other reason, Paul underestimated the pressures a certain segment in the Jerusalem congregation would put on him. But the crucial point here is that, in spite of real pressures and perhaps

some uncertainty, the Jerusalem apostles stood with Paul on the validity of a Gentile mission and on the inappropriateness of making circumcision a requirement for Gentile believers in Jesus—though probably neither they nor Paul himself then saw that a direct ministry to Gentiles was in the offing.

From Galatians 2:1–10, therefore, we learn that as early as the mid-40s (1) there was concern among Jerusalem Christians regarding the ministry to "God-fearing" Gentiles at Antioch of Syria, and (2) there were pressures exerted by some in the Jerusalem church to bring it more in line with strict Jewish practice.

Likewise, the account of the Antioch episode in Galatians 2:11–21 clearly indicates that Paul's Gentile ministry was causing repercussions at Jerusalem and that pressures were being exerted on the Jerusalem congregation because of it. Just who were "those who belonged to the circumcision group" (v.12) and whom Peter feared is difficult to say. And just why Peter, together with the Jewish Christians of Antioch and "even Barnabas" (v.13), separated themselves from Gentile believers is difficult to determine. It may be that they viewed such an action as a necessary, temporary expediency in order to avoid any dangerous, practical consequences for Jewish believers at Jerusalem. Or perhaps they considered such a separation as necessary in order to quell the rising demands by believers at Jerusalem for the circumcision of Gentile believers at Antioch, thereby preserving both the Jewish mission of the church and Gentile freedom (cf. Dix, 44).

Whatever rationale might be proposed for what happened at Antioch, Galatians 2:11–21 highlights the fact that there were rising pressures at Jerusalem against a direct outreach to Gentiles and that these pressures were felt at Syrian Antioch. The passage also suggests that a separation of Jewish and Gentile believers in the church at Antioch was, at least once in its early history, based on expediency rather than on a clear theological principle. And it was this issue of expediency versus theological principle that required clarification in the early church and lent urgency to the Jerusalem Council. (For a detailed and nuanced discussion of these issues, see my *Galatians* [Dallas: Word, 1990], lxi–lxxxviii, 35–80.)

1. The Delegation from Syrian Antioch (15:1–4)

¹Some men came down from Judea to Antioch and were teaching the brothers: "Unless you are circumcised, according to the custom taught by Moses, you cannot be saved." ²This brought Paul and Barnabas into sharp dispute and debate with them. So Paul and Barnabas were appointed, along with some other believers, to go up to Jerusalem to see the apostles and elders about this question. ³The church sent them on their way, and as they traveled through Phoenicia and Samaria, they told how the Gentiles had been converted. This news made all the brothers very glad. ⁴When they came to Jerusalem, they were welcomed by the church and the apostles and elders, to whom they reported everything God had done through them.

COMMENTARY

1 The immediate occasion for the Jerusalem Council was the visit to Syrian Antioch of some Jewish Christians from Jerusalem and their teaching that circumcision was essential for salvation. These have become known as "Judaizers," and their comrades promoted a similar teaching among Paul's converts in the Roman province of Galatia. They may have been incited by the return of John Mark and his unfavorable report (see comments at 13:13). That James and Peter stood behind these Judaizers, however, is a fiction without factual support (contra F. C. Baur and the "Tübingen School"), though the other extreme—namely, that the Jerusalem church was devoid of any Judaizing element—is just as erroneous (contra Munck, *Acts of the Apostles*).

Both James and Peter were interested in minimizing conflicts between Judaism and Jewish Christianity. Yet neither was prepared to sacrifice the principles of the gospel to expediency when the implications of doing so became plain. The Judaiz-

ers, on the other hand, while probably first justifying their legalism on practical grounds, were arguing as a matter of principle for the necessity of circumcision and a Jewish lifestyle. In 1 Thessalonians 2:14–16, Paul recognizes unbelieving Jews as the ultimate source of opposition to the mission among the Gentiles. Therefore, when he says in Galatians 6:13 that the Judaizers "want you to be circumcised that they may boast about your flesh," he probably means so that they could "point out to *non*-Christian Jews that conversion to Christianity does in fact *transfer Gentiles from the 'Greek' to the 'Jewish' cause*, in that wider conflict of the Two Cultures which is daily growing more intense" (Dix, 41–42 [italics his]). Undoubtedly the Judaizers thought of themselves as acting conscientiously and on sound theological principles (see comments at v.5 below). But as Paul saw it, they sought "a good impression outwardly . . . to avoid being persecuted for the cross of Christ" (Gal 6:12).

2 With the issues highlighted by the "sharp dispute and debate" that followed, Paul and Barnabas were appointed, along with certain others from the Antiochene congregation, to go up to Jerusalem to meet with "the apostles and elders" about the matter. The antecedent of the third person plural verb *etaxan* ("they appointed," GK *5435*) is not specified. Codex Bezae (D) assumes the hierarchical authority of the mother church at Jerusalem in reading "those who had come from Jerusalem ordered Paul and Barnabas and certain others to go up to the apostles and elders at Jerusalem that they might be judged before them about this question." But this Western reading reflects a later ecclesiastical situation. Probably the reference in v.3 to being sent "by the church" (*hypo tēs ekklēsias*) gives the context for Luke's use of *etaxan*, so we should understand the third person plural "they" as signifying the involvement of the entire congregation at Antioch and its leaders in the appointment (cf. 13:3).

The church at Antioch was concerned with the Judaizers' challenge to the legitimacy of a direct ministry to Gentiles and to the validity of the conversion of Gentiles to Christ apart from any commitment to Judaism. The Jerusalem leaders undoubtedly had practical concerns about Paul's new policy, but they seem to have been prepared to let some measure of expediency affect their relations with the Jewish world generally and the nation of Israel in particular. The Judaizers, however, had shifted these practical concerns into the area of theological principle. Believers at Antioch, therefore, sought clarity with regard to the relation between the Jerusalem church's policy of cautious expediency and the Judaizers' argument founded on theo-

logical principle. Outside Judea there was growing confusion because of the Judaizers' equation of expediency with theological principle and their claim to be supported by the church's leaders at Jerusalem. The Jerusalem Christians, for their part, probably welcomed an opportunity to air their concerns, particularly those regarding the impasse created by Paul and Barnabas through their Gentile policy. For while there may have been earlier agreement on the validity of evangelizing Gentiles (cf. Gal 2:7–10), recent events involving a direct approach to Gentiles and no necessary relation of Gentile believers to the rites or customs of Judaism reopened that agreement for reconsideration.

3–4 The connection *men oun* (NIV, untranslated; NASB, "therefore") may simply mark off Luke's source material from his own introduction. As the delegation from Antioch journeyed to Jerusalem, they told Christian believers in the regions of Phoenicia and Samaria the news of "the conversion of the Gentiles" (*tēn epistrophēn* [GK *2189*] *tōn ethnōn*; NIV, "how the Gentiles had been converted"). Since the presence of proselytes and "God-fearing" Gentiles in the church was hardly newsworthy in AD 49, this report of Gentile conversions undoubtedly meant that Gentiles were converted on a direct basis apart from any necessary commitment to Judaism. The Phoenician and Samaritan Christians, being themselves converts of the Hellenistic Jewish Christian mission after Stephen's martyrdom (cf. 8:4–25; 11:19), probably took a broader view than that which prevailed at Jerusalem, and so they rejoiced at the news. Believers at Jerusalem also were interested, but their interest by no means involved wholehearted approval.

NOTES

1–4 The Western text expands these verses considerably. For example, in v.1 it expands "some men" by adding "of the party of the Pharisees who believed"; it also inserts καὶ περιπατῆτε (*kai peripatēte* [GK 4344], "and you walk") in the statement "unless you are circumcised [and walk] according to the custom taught by Moses, you cannot be saved." In v.2, after referring to the debate between Paul and Barnabas and those from Judea, it inserts, "for Paul spoke, maintaining firmly that they [the Gentile converts] should stay as they were when converted; but those who had come from Jerusalem ordered them, Paul and Barnabas and certain others, to go up to Jerusalem to the apostles and elders that they might be judged before them about this question." And in v.4 it adds the adverb μεγάλως (*megalōs*, "greatly," "heartily," GK 3487), thereby reading, "they were welcomed heartily by the church."

2 On the expression "to go up [ἀναβαίνειν, *anabainein*, GK 326] to Jerusalem," see comments at 3:1.

3 On Luke's use of μὲν οὖν (*men oun*, "so," "then"), see comments and note at 1:6.

In this fourth panel, note the pattern that develops at 13:4; 14:3; and here, with summary uses at 15:30 and 16:5.

2. The Nature and Course of the Debate (15:5–12)

⁵Then some of the believers who belonged to the party of the Pharisees stood up and said, "The Gentiles must be circumcised and required to obey the law of Moses."

⁶The apostles and elders met to consider this question. ⁷After much discussion, Peter got up and addressed them: "Brothers, you know that some time ago God made a choice among you that the Gentiles might hear from my lips the message of the gospel and believe. ⁸God, who knows the heart, showed that he accepted them by giving the Holy Spirit to them, just as he did to us. ⁹He made no distinction between us and them, for he purified their hearts by faith. ¹⁰Now then, why do you try to test God by putting on the necks of the disciples a yoke that neither we nor our fathers have been able to bear? ¹¹No! We believe it is through the grace of our Lord Jesus that we are saved, just as they are."

¹²The whole assembly became silent as they listened to Barnabas and Paul telling about the miraculous signs and wonders God had done among the Gentiles through them.

COMMENTARY

5 In the ensuing debate among believers in general and within the council itself, some Christian Pharisees, in support of the Judaizers, insisted that it was absolutely necessary for Gentile Christians to "be circumcised and required to obey the law of Moses." By their emphasis on "necessary" (*dei*), these overscrupulous Jewish believers at Jerusalem evidently meant that these things were not only matters of expedience but were also theologically required by the revealed will of God. Indeed, the prophets spoke of the salvation of the Gentiles as an event of the "last days" (cf. Isa 2:2; 11:10; 25:8–9; Zec 8:23), but they also visualized the Gentiles as being brought to God through the witness of a restored Israel (cf. Isa 2:3; 60:2–3; Zec 8:23). Any Christian believer, therefore, could hardly oppose reaching Gentiles through the ministry of the Jewish-Christian church at Jerusalem, which represented "the true remnant" of the nation Israel. But that outreach to Gentiles, so these overscrupulous Jewish Christians argued, was meant to come from within their group and to follow a proselyte model—not from outside their group or expressed in any way apart from the Mosaic law and Jewish customs. In the "last days," all nations are to flow to the house of the Lord at Jerusalem (cf. Isa 2:2–3; 25:6–8; 56:7; 60:3–22; Zec 8:21–23), but not to depart from it.

6 While Luke says only that the apostles and elders met to consider these questions, his mention of "the whole assembly" (*pan to plēthos* [GK 4436]) in v.12 and "the whole church" (*holē tē ekklēsia* [GK 3910]) in v.22 shows that other members of the church, if not the entire congregation, were also present. The discussion was undoubtedly extensive and heated. But Luke focuses only on the arguments of Peter (vv.7–11), then Barnabas and Paul (v.12), and finally James (vv.13–21).

7–8 Peter was no longer the chief figure of the Jerusalem church. James had at some earlier time assumed that role (see comments at 12:17). But Peter was dominant in the Jewish-Christian mission and responsible to the Jerusalem church. And it was

as a missionary, not an administrator, that Peter spoke up and reminded the council that God had chosen to have the Gentiles hear and accept the gospel first from him. He argued that since God had established such a precedent within the Jewish-Christian mission some ten years earlier—though it had not, it seems, been recognized by the church as a precedent at that time—God has already indicated his approval of a direct mission to Gentiles. Thus Paul's direct approach to Gentiles could not be branded as a deviation from the divine will.

9–10 Peter had evidently completely recovered from his temporary lapse at Syrian Antioch. Now he saw matters more clearly and so was prepared to agree with Paul (1) that there is "no distinction" between Jews and Gentiles, and (2) that the Mosaic law is an unnecessary "yoke" for Gentile believers in Jesus.

12 Luke's reference to the silence of the assembly after Peter spoke implies that the turning point had come. Though resisted at Jerusalem for almost a decade, the precedent of Cornelius's conversion opened the way for the report of Barnabas and Paul regarding God's validation of their missionary policy through "miraculous signs and wonders" (*sēmeia kai terata*, GK 4956, 5469). It was a report not of their successes but of how God had acted, and its implication was that by his acts God had revealed his will. As at Lystra, where Barnabas was taken to be the greater of the two (cf. 14:12, 14), so here Barnabas is mentioned first (cf. also v.25), probably because he enjoyed greater confidence among believers at Jerusalem.

NOTES

5 On δεῖ (*dei*) as connoting divine necessity, see comments at 1:16.

The Western text reads, "But those who ordered them to go up to the elders stood up and said," in line with its expansion of v.2.

7 The Western text (D, several minuscules, and as represented in the Syriac version, Ephraem of Syria's commentary on Acts, and Tertullian) adds ἐν (ἁγίῳ) πνεύματι (*en [hagiō] pneumati*, "in the [Holy] Spirit") either before or after Πέτρος (*Petros*, "Peter"), evidently to enhance the solemnity of the occasion and the authority of Peter.

Chester Beatty 𝔓45 reads τοὺς ἀποστόλους (*tous apostolous*, "the apostles," GK *693*) for the better-supported and simple αὐτούς (*autous*, "them").

12 Several Western texts (D, and as represented by the Syriac version, Ephraem's commentary on Acts, etc.) add at the beginning of the verse συνκατατεθεμένων δὲ τῶν πρεσβυτέρων τοῖς ὑπὸ τοῦ Πέτρου εἰρημένοις (*synkatatethemenōn de tōn presbyterōn tois hypo tou Petrou eirēmenois*: "And when the elders had consented to the words spoken by Peter"), thereby again enhancing the authority and prestige of Peter— which is a common feature in the Western readings.

On the use of τὸ πλῆθος (*to plēthos*) to signal the involvement of "the whole assembly," see note at 6:2.

On σημεῖα καὶ τέρατα (*sēmeia kai terata*, "miraculous signs and wonders") as characterizing the Pauline mission, thereby putting it in line with OT prophecy, the ministry of Jesus, and the ministry of the early church, see comments at 2:22 and 14:3.

3. The Summing Up of the Debate by James (15:13–21)

¹³When they finished, James spoke up: "Brothers, listen to me. ¹⁴Simon has described to us how God at first showed his concern by taking from the Gentiles a people for himself. ¹⁵The words of the prophets are in agreement with this, as it is written:

¹⁶"'After this I will return
and rebuild David's fallen tent.
Its ruins I will rebuild,
and I will restore it,
¹⁷that the remnant of men may seek the Lord,
and all the Gentiles who bear my name,
says the Lord, who does these things'
¹⁸   that have been known for ages.

¹⁹"It is my judgment, therefore, that we should not make it difficult for the Gentiles who are turning to God. ²⁰Instead we should write to them, telling them to abstain from food polluted by idols, from sexual immorality, from the meat of strangled animals and from blood. ²¹For Moses has been preached in every city from the earliest times and is read in the synagogues on every Sabbath."

COMMENTARY

13 James the Lord's brother presided at the Jerusalem Council. He was known as "James the Just" because of his piety. He was also an ascetic who scrupulously kept the Mosaic law. The more scrupulously minded and the Judaizers within the Jerusalem church undoubtedly looked to him for support, since they knew both his legal qualifications and his personal qualities (see comments at 12:17). But while he was rigorous and scrupulous in his personal practices, James was more broadminded than many of his followers. After calling the council to order by using the formal mode of address "[men,] brothers" (*andres adelphoi*), he went on to sum up the emerging view of the council in a way that linked it to what had already been said.

14 If, as Luke's account implies, James in his summation made no reference to the report of Barnabas and Paul (referring instead only to the argument of Peter), he probably did so more for political and practical reasons than any matter of principle. After all, it was the work of Paul and his associate Barnabas that was on trial, and James wanted to win his audience to the position he believed to be right without causing needless offense. So he began by reminding the council of the testimony of Peter, whom he called by his Hebrew name "Simon" (cf. 2Pe 1:1). And he showed how he felt about the question at issue by speaking of believing Gentiles as a "people" (*laos*, GK 3295) whom God has taken "for himself" (*tō onomati* [GK 3950] *autou*, lit., "for his name"), thereby (1) applying to Gentile believers in Jesus a designation formerly used of Israel alone, and (2) agreeing with Peter that in the conversion of Cornelius God himself had taken the initiative for a direct Gentile ministry.

15-17 James's major contribution to the Jerusalem Council was to shift the discussion of the conversion of Gentiles from a strictly proselyte model, with its centripetal action and inward movement, to an eschatological and missionary model, with its centrifugal action and outward movement. Isaiah had indeed spoken of Gentiles coming to Jerusalem to learn God's ways so that they might walk in them, but the prophet also spoke of Gentiles continuing as national entities whose salvation did not negate their national identities (cf. Isa 2:4; 25:6–7). Likewise, James cites Amos, who spoke of "the remnant of men" (LXX, Dead Sea Scrolls) in the last days when "David's fallen tent" would be rebuilt as being "all the Gentiles who bear my name" and whose continuance as Gentiles was understood (cf. Am 9:11–12). In the end-times, James seems to be saying, God's people will consist of two concentric groups: (1) at the core will be a restored Israel (i.e., "David's rebuilt tent"); and (2) gathered around them will be a group of Gentiles (i.e., "the remnant of men") who will share in the messianic blessings but who will continue as Gentiles without necessarily becoming Jewish proselytes. It is this understanding of Amos's message, James insisted, that Peter's testimony has affirmed. Therefore, the conversion of Gentiles in these last days should be seen not on a proselyte model of bringing Gentiles into the institutions, temple, and laws of Judaism (a centripetal emphasis) but on an eschatological missionary model that reaches out to the Gentile world without necessarily relating Gentile believers to the forms and practices of Judaism (a centrifugal emphasis).

James's quotation of Amos 9:11–12 is both textually and exegetically difficult. Textually, his rendering of v.12 deviates from the MT and agrees with the LXX in (1) reading "they will seek" (*ekzētēsōsin*, GK 1699) for "they will possess" (Heb. *yîrĕšû*), (2) in treating "the remnant" (*hoi kataloipoi*,

GK *2905*) as the subject of the sentence rather than its object, and (3) in reading "of men" (*tōn anthrōpon*, GK *476*) for "of Edom." It would have been impossible, in fact, for James to have derived his point from the text had he worked from the MT. On the other hand, the text of Amos 9:11 in James's quotation differs from the LXX in (1) reading "after this" (*meta tauta*) for "in that day" (*en tē hēmera ekeinē*), (2) reading "I will return and rebuild" (*anastrepsō kai anoikodomēsō*, GK *418, 488*) for "I will raise up" (*anastēsō*, GK *482*), (3) reading "I will restore" (*anorthōsō*, GK *494*) for "I will raise up" (*anastēsō*), and (4) omitting the clause "and I will rebuild it as in the days of old" (*kai anoikodomēsō autēn kathōs hai hēmerai tou aiōnos*).

Focusing on the quotation's difference from the MT and essential agreement with the LXX, many commentators have complained that "the Jewish Christian James would not in Jerusalem have used a Septuagint text, differing from the Hebrew original, as scriptural proof," and so have concluded, "It is not James but Luke who is speaking here" (Haenchen, 448). But while the text of Amos 9:11–12 differs from the MT in meaning and the LXX in form, "it is exactly identical with that of 4QFlor [*Florilegium*]," as de Waard, 24–26, 47, 78–79, has shown. And it is not too difficult to visualize James as using a then current Hebrew variant of Amos 9:11–12, as incorporated in 4Q*Florilegium* (4Q174 1.12), in arguing his point with the scrupulous Jewish Christians in the council—particularly if among those most concerned for Jewish legalities were some drawn from an Essene background (see comments at 6:7).

18 Textually and exegetically, the interpretation of v.18 is also difficult. Codices ℵ B and C (as reflected also in Coptic and Armenian versions) read "that have been known for ages" (*gnōsta ap' aiōnos*). To accept this reading is to understand the clause as part of a conflated biblical citation that extends from

v.16 through to the end of v.18 (so NIV, NASB, NRSV, NEB, JB, TEV et al.), probably alluding to Isaiah 45:21. But Codices A and D, together with Bodmer 𝔓⁷⁴ and the major Latin and Syriac versions, read "known to the Lord from eternity is his work" (*gnōsta ap' aiōnos estin tō kyriō panta ta erga autou*; see NIV text note); and codices E and P, together with the Byzantine text, read "known from eternity to God are all his works" (*gnōsta ap' aiōnos estin tō theō panta ta erga autou*). To read the text in either of these latter two ways tends to separate the clause from the preceding biblical quotation, thereby viewing it as a comment by James himself.

It was not unusual in the Jewish world to express such a sentiment when one is confronted with a difficult passage or some remarkable event that seemed almost beyond any human explanation—especially when the passage or event seem to point in a rather obvious direction but its logical connections are obscure. So it is perhaps best to interpret the words of v.18 not as part of a conflated biblical quotation (as is usually done) but as a comment added by James to this effect: We cannot be in opposition to the express will of God, as evidenced by Peter's testimony (v.14) and as predicted by Amos's prophecy (vv.16–17)—but only God himself knows how everything fits together and is to be fully understood! In so concluding, James, it appears, voiced one of the greatest of all theological judgments, which at this point in God's dealing with humanity was one of the great turning points of redemptive history.

19 On the basic issue that brought together that first ecumenical council of Christendom—i.e., the necessity of relating Gentiles to Judaism in the Christian mission—James refused to side with the Judaizers. He may not have been prepared to endorse openly all the details of Paul's Gentile policy. Certainly there is no indication that he expected the Jerusalem church to reach out to or receive

Gentiles directly itself. But he could not be in opposition to the express will of God, and therefore his advice was that Jewish Christianity should not take any stance against the promotion of the Gentile mission. In so concluding, he swept aside the obstacles that had arisen to Paul's Gentile mission among believers at Jerusalem and left it free for further advances within the empire.

It is significant that, while many insist that "what circumcision meant under the old dispensation, that and no less, is the meaning of baptism for those living in the new age" (so W. F. Flemington, *The New Testament Doctrine of Baptism* [London: SPCK, 1948], 62), James made no mention at the council of Christian baptism as superseding the Jewish rite of circumcision. If, indeed, the early church understood circumcision and baptism as being analogous, James's pointing to the Christian baptism of pagan Gentiles would have silenced forever the Jewish-Christian critics of Gentile salvation. Nor does Paul make any such connection in either Galatians or Romans, where it might have been expected had baptism been seen as the replacement of circumcision. Moreover, had Paul believed that Christian baptism superseded Jewish circumcision, his circumcision of Timothy would have been nonsense (cf. 16:3).

20 On the practical questions that troubled many Christians at Jerusalem and originally gave rise to the Judaizers' assertion—i.e., questions of relations between Jewish and Gentile believers in the church and tolerance for the scruples of others—James's advice was that a letter be written to the Gentile Christians requesting them to abstain (1) "from food polluted by idols" (*tōn alisgēmatōn tōn eidōlōn*, lit., "from pollutions of idols," GK *246, 1631*), (2) "from sexual immorality" (*tēs porneias*, GK *4518*, which probably means here "from marriage in prohibited degrees of relationship"; cf. Str-B, 2.729), (3) "from the meat of strangled animals" (*tou pniktou*, lit., "from things strangled," GK *4465*), and (4) "from blood" (*tou haimatos*, i.e., "from eating blood," GK *135*).

21 These prohibitions have often been viewed as a compromise between two warring parties that in effect nullified James's earlier words and made the decision of the Jerusalem Council unacceptable to Paul. In reality, however, they are to be seen not as dealing with the central issue of the council but as meeting certain practical concerns—i.e., not as primarily theological in nature but more sociological. Seen in this light, they were meant not as divine ordinances for acceptance before God but as concessions to the scruples of others for the sake of harmony within the church and the continuance of the Jewish-Christian mission. So James adds the rationale of v.21: "For Moses has been preached in every city from the earliest times and is read in the synagogues on every Sabbath"—that is to say, since Jewish communities are to be found in every city, their scruples are to be respected by Gentile believers.

NOTES

13 On the address ἄνδρες ἀδελφοί (*andres adelphoi*, "men, brothers"), see comments at 1:16.

16–17 On other quotations in Acts that evidence an affinity to biblical quotations and uses in the Dead Sea Scrolls, see 3:22–23 on Deuteronomy 18:15, 18–19; 7:43 on Amos 5:26–27; and 13:41 on Habakkuk 1:5.

17 The conjunction καί (*kai*) is probably here explicative, and so should be rendered "even all the Gentiles."

18 Metzger, 379, makes this relevant comment: "Since the quotation from Am 9:12 ends with ταῦτα [*tauta*], the concluding words are James's comment. The reading γνωστὰ ἀπ' αἰῶνος [*gnōsta ap' aiōnos*], however, is so elliptical an expression that copyists made various attempts to recast the phrase, rounding it out as an independent sentence."

20 The Western text omits καὶ τοῦ πνικτοῦ (*kai tou pniktou*, "from things strangled") and adds the negative Golden Rule, thereby turning the four prohibitions into three ethical maxims having to do with idolatry, immorality, and murder, with an appended injunction. Chester Beatty 𝔓⁴⁵, together with Origen (*Cels.* 8.29) and the Ethiopic version, omits τῆς πορνείας (*tēs porneias*, "from sexual immorality"). The originality of the four prohibitions, however, is well attested by codices ℵ A B C and with Bodmer 𝔓⁷⁴. These four prohibitions were widely known within Judaism as the Noachian precepts (cf. *b. Sanh.* 56*b*, based on Lev 17:1–18:30) and were viewed by some rabbis as the essential requirements for Gentiles in the eschatological age (cf. *Gen. Rab.* 98.9).

For a fuller treatment of the Jerusalem decree and Paul's acceptance of it, see my *Paul, Apostle of Liberty*, 254–60.

21 Some commentators see this verse as a justification for the exegesis of vv.16–17, while others as a justification for the judgment of v.19. But the γάρ (*gar*, "for") does not easily reach back to either.

REFLECTIONS

Two types of "necessary" and vitally important matters were raised at the Jerusalem Council. The first had to do with the theological necessity of circumcision and the Jewish law for salvation, and that was rejected; the second had to do with the practical necessity for Gentile Christians to abstain from certain practices for the sake of Jewish-Gentile fellowship within the church and for the sake of the Jewish-Christian mission throughout the Diaspora, and that was approved. The major work of the council had to do with the vindication of Gentile freedom, while a secondary matter concerned the expression of that freedom with regard to the scruples of others. (Compare Martin Luther's interpretation of these two concerns, one theological and one practical, in his important Reformation tractate "On the Councils and the Churches," in *Works of Martin Luther* [Philadelphia: Holman, 1915–32], esp. 5.150–54, 188, 193–95).

4. The Decision and Letter of the Council (15:22–29)

²²Then the apostles and elders, with the whole church, decided to choose some of their own men and send them to Antioch with Paul and Barnabas. They chose Judas (called Barsabbas) and Silas, two men who were leaders among the brothers. ²³With them they sent the following letter:

The apostles and elders, your brothers,
To the Gentile believers in Antioch, Syria and Cilicia:
Greetings.

²⁴We have heard that some went out from us without our authorization and disturbed you, troubling your minds by what they said. ²⁵So we all agreed to choose some men and send them to you with our dear friends Barnabas and Paul—²⁶men who have risked their

lives for the name of our Lord Jesus Christ. [27]Therefore we are sending Judas and Silas to confirm by word of mouth what we are writing. [28]It seemed good to the Holy Spirit and to us not to burden you with anything beyond the following requirements: [29]You are to abstain from food sacrificed to idols, from blood, from the meat of strangled animals and from sexual immorality. You will do well to avoid these things.
Farewell.

COMMENTARY

22 With James's judgment "the apostles and elders, with the whole church," agreed. They decided to send their decision back to Antioch of Syria not only with Paul and Barnabas but also with two leaders of the Jerusalem congregation, Judas Barsabbas and Silas, whose presence would assure reception of the decision and who could interpret the feelings of the council from a Jerusalem perspective. The multiunit reference to "the apostles" (*hoi apostoloi*, GK 693), "the elders" (*hoi presbyteroi*, GK 4565), and "the whole church" (*holē hē ekklēsia*, GK 3910, 1711) is comparable to the Qumran structure of authority in which executive action for religious matters was in the hands of the priests; administrative and financial matters were in the hands of an "overseer" or "guardian"; an advisory council of twelve to fifteen persons was apparently active; and all the mature members of the community (i.e., "the many," Heb. *hārabbîm*) gave their approval to the decisions of the priests, overseer, and council. Other models of organization were undoubtedly used among other groups within Palestine, and the lines of demarcation between various officials and their functions were evidently quite flexible. But it seems clear that at Qumran and within the Jerusalem church the congregation, while not equivalent to the Greek assembly (*dēmos*, GK 1322) in its governmental powers, was involved in the deliberations of its leaders.

23–29 With Paul and Barnabas the Jerusalem church sent Judas (called Barsabbas) and Silas back to the church at Syrian Antioch with a letter. At the end of the second century, Clement of Alexandria (*Strom.* 4.15) spoke of this letter as "the Catholic epistle of all the Apostles" that was "conveyed to all the faithful by the hands of Paul himself" and was later incorporated into the book of Acts. By the appearance of such expressions as "the apostles and elders, your brothers" (*hoi apostoloi kai hoi presbyteroi adelphoi*, v.23), "our dear friends Barnabas and Paul" (*tois agapētois hēmōn Barnaba kai Paulō*, v.25), and "it seemed good to the Holy Spirit and to us" (*edoxen tō pneumati tō hagiō kai hēmin*, v.28)—all phrases apparently more characteristic of the Jewish-Christian leadership at Jerusalem than of Luke—it may be postulated that here "we are dealing with an original document copied by Luke more or less verbatim" (Wilfred L. Knox, *The Acts of the Apostles* [Cambridge: Cambridge Univ. Press], 50).

23 The placing of "brothers" in the salutation in apposition to "the apostles and elders"—or perhaps to the "elders" alone—is somewhat unusual. Some commentators have attempted to read it as "the apostles and elders and brothers" (adding an "and"), or as "the apostles and elders" (deleting "brothers"), or as "the brothers" (deleting "apostles and elders"). But it should probably be understood as reflecting a form of expression used within the Jerusalem congregation, similar to "men, brothers" (*andres adelphoi*) of 1:16; 2:29, 37; 7:2; 13:15, 26, 38; 15:7, 13; 22:1; 23:1, 6; and 28:17, and almost as untranslatable. Likewise, the address "to the Gentile believers in Antioch, Syria and Cilicia" is surprising. For though Paul refers to spending some time in Syria and Cilicia, Luke has not spoken of any mission outside Antioch in these areas. Yet 15:36, 41 assume that churches were established in these areas with Paul's assistance. And 16:4 shows that the content of the letter from the Jerusalem Council was meant not only for congregations in the areas listed in 15:23 but also applied to Gentile believers generally (cf. 15:19; 21:25).

24–29 The body of the letter speaks of the problem faced by the churches because of the Judaizers' claims and sets out the Jerusalem Council's response to it. It also commends to the churches Barnabas and Paul (see comments at 14:14 and 15:12 for this order) and the Jerusalem emissaries Judas and Silas.

On the fundamental matter that brought the council together—i.e., the theological necessity of circumcision and a Jewish lifestyle for Gentile Christians—the letter rebukes the Judaizers for going beyond their authority and assures the churches that there are no such requirements for salvation. On the practical issues of (1) relations between Jewish and Gentile believers in the churches and (2) preventing needless offense to Jews throughout the empire, the letter asks Gentile Christians to abstain from "idolatry" (*eidōlothytōn*), "blood" (*haimatos*), "things strangled" (*pniktōn*), and "sexual immorality" (*porneias*), which four prohibitions are given in a slightly different order and more abbreviated fashion than in v.20 but with the same sense. In closing there is the perfect passive imperative "Farewell" (*errōsthe*, GK 4874)—which is a typical way of ending a Greek letter, as so many of the ancient nonliterary papyri indicate.

NOTES

22 Nothing further is known of Judas Barsabbas. He could be the brother of Joseph Barsabbas of 1:23, but the surname Barsabbas ("Son of the Sabbath," which means "one born on the Sabbath") was common. Rather than Βαρσαββᾶν (*Barsabban*), Codex Bezae (D) reads Βαραββᾶν (*Barabban*) here at 15:22 and Βαρνάβαν (*Barnaban*) at 1:23.

24 Many Western texts (though not D) add "you must be circumcised and keep the law" after "troubling your minds," which is an interpolation derived from vv.1 and 5 that is inserted here to specify in what particulars the Judaizers had sought to trouble Gentile believers in Antioch, Syria, and Cilicia. The interpolation was picked up by Erasmus and so found a place in the TR and KJV.

26 The Western text (D E and a number of minuscules) adds at the end of the verse εἰς πάντα πειρασμόν (*eis panta peirasmon*, "in every trial"), perhaps in anticipation of Paul's words in 20:19 or as an echo of Sirach 2:1.

29 The Western text treats these four prohibitions as a three-clause ethical maxim with appended negative Golden Rule, as it does at v.20. Chester Beatty 𝔓⁴⁵, Origen, and the Ethiopic version omit τῆς πορνείας (*tēs porneias*, "from sexual immorality"), as they do also at v.20.

The Western text adds at the end of the letter, before the "Farewell," the words φερόμενοι ἐν τῷ ἁγίῳ πνεύματι (*pheromenoi en tō hagiō pneumati*, "being carried along by the Holy Spirit"), which probably is merely a pious expansion that gives to an otherwise rather common "you will do well" a specifically Christian turn.

REFLECTIONS

When one considers the situation of the Jerusalem church in AD 49, the decision reached by the Jerusalem Christians must be considered one of the boldest and most magnanimous in the annals of church history. While still attempting to minister exclusively to the nation, the council refused to impede the progress of that other branch of the Christian mission whose every success meant further difficulty for them from within their own nation. Undoubtedly there was uncertainty among the council's leaders about details of the decision. Certainly they reached it only after much agonizing. Likewise, there probably remained in the Jerusalem church a recalcitrant group that continued to predict ominous consequences. But the decision was made and the malcontents silenced—at least for a time.

The effects of the decision were far-reaching. In the first place, it freed the gospel from any necessary entanglement with Judaism, whether expressed as Jewish rites or Jewish customs. Nevertheless, it did not renounce the legitimacy of a continued Jewish expression for Jewish believers in Jesus. Thus both Paul's mission to the Gentiles and the Jewish-Christian mission to Jews were enabled to progress side by side without conflict. Second, attitudes toward Paul within Jewish Christianity were clarified. While some of the Jewish believers probably became even more opposed to Paul, others (e.g., John Mark; cf. 15:37–39) seem to have become more accepting of his position. Also, as a result of the council some felt happier in a Gentile ministry than at Jerusalem (e.g., Silas; cf. 15:40). Third, the decision of the council had the effect of permanently antagonizing many Jews. From this time onward, the Christian mission within the nation, particularly in and around the city of Jerusalem itself, faced very rough sledding (cf. Ro 11:28). And when coupled with the zealotism within the nation during the next two decades, this antagonism proved fatal to the life and ministry of the Jerusalem church.

F. The Reception of the Council's Decision and Letter (15:30–16:4)

OVERVIEW

Luke describes the aftermath of the Jerusalem Council in three vignettes that all relate to the reception of the council's decision and letter in three localities of earlier Gentile outreach: Antioch of Syria (15:30–35), the regions of Syria and Cilicia (15:36–41), and the southern part of Galatia (16:4). Other items of information are also included, for Luke uses these final scenes of his fourth panel to prepare for the extensive outreach of the gospel through Paul's second and third missionary journeys.

1. At Antioch of Syria (15:30–35)

30The men were sent off and went down to Antioch, where they gathered the church together and delivered the letter. 31The people read it and were glad for its encouraging message. 32Judas and Silas, who themselves were prophets, said much to encourage and strengthen the brothers. 33After spending some time there, they were sent off by the brothers with the blessing of peace to return to those who had sent them. ³⁵But Paul and Barnabas remained in Antioch, where they and many others taught and preached the word of the Lord.

COMMENTARY

30–32 The connective *men oun* (NIV, untranslated; NASB, "so") opens this new section on the reception of the council's decision and letter. At Antioch of Syria the delegation, on returning from Jerusalem, "gathered the church [*to plēthos*, "assembly" or "congregation"] together and delivered the letter," with Judas and Silas saying "much to encourage and strengthen the brothers [*tous adelphous*, here meant inclusively for all "the believers"]." The Gentile believers, Luke tells us, "were glad" (NIV; NASB, "rejoiced") in reading the letter.

Some commentators have complained that Luke's account of the reception of the letter by Gentile believers is a pure idealization, for such a fourfold decree, as Hans Lietzmann (*The Beginnings of the Christian Church* [London: Nicholson & Watson, 1937], 142) expressed it, "was by no means an insignificant requirement" and cannot be seen as acceptable to Paul, who "undisturbedly . . . pushed along the straight road of freedom from the law." But if we understand the council as dealing with two matters—the first, a matter of theological principle; the second, a matter of practical expediency (as did Luther in his tractate "On the Councils and the Churches"; see Reflections, p. 950)—it is not too difficult to believe that, having gained a decided victory in the first matter, Paul and the existing Gentile churches were prepared to accept the so-called decrees as a modus operandi for reducing friction between two groups of people drawn from two different ways of life. Such an attitude is quite in accord with an apostle who could proclaim:

Though I am free and belong to no man, I make myself a slave to everyone, to win as many as possible. To the Jews I became like a Jew, to win the Jews. To those under the law I became like one under the law (though I myself am not under the law), so as to win those under the law. To those not having the law I became like one not having the law (though I am not free from God's law but am under Christ's law), so as to win those not having the law. To the weak I became weak, to win the weak. I have become all things to all men so that by all possible means I might save some. I do all this for the sake of the gospel, that I may share in its blessings (1Co 9:19–23).

James's later reference to the decree in 21:25 appears not because it was then first promulgated, but probably because James was reminding Paul of their agreed-on basis of fellowship and because Luke was reminding his readers of what they had already read. The fact that nothing is said of the decree in either Galatians or 1 and 2 Corinthians is no proof that Paul knew nothing about it or could not have wholeheartedly accepted it. If Galatians was written before the Jerusalem Council, reference to such a decree in that letter could hardly be expected—indeed, any mention of it would have been miraculous. And while "food sacrificed to idols" (*eidōlothytōn*, v.29) exactly fits the problem dealt with at Corinth (cf. 1Co 8:1–11:1), Paul may not have been able to quote any type of ecclesiastical pronouncement to his supraspiritual Gentile converts at Corinth, especially if he wanted to win them over to a truer understanding and expression of their Christian freedom. In fact, as many have suggested, it could just as well be argued (1) that Paul's problems with the supraspiritual faction within the Corinthian church arose, at least in part, because he had originally delivered the Jerusalem letter to them; and (2) that in seeking to correct them, he was forced to argue on different grounds. Paul's silence with respect to the Jerusalem decree in his letters, therefore, can be explained just as reasonably on other grounds than that it must be seen as being historically incriminating.

33 After some time, Judas and Silas returned to Jerusalem with the commendation of the believers in Antioch. The Western and Byzantine texts add material that was later versified as v.34: "But it seemed good to Silas to remain there, and Judas journeyed alone." No doubt this sentence was inserted by scribes to explain why Silas appears again at Antioch in v.40. But the addition contradicts the plain sense of v.33 and fails to take into account the fact that Paul could have sent for Silas after the latter's return to Jerusalem. Paul and Barnabas, however, remained at Syrian Antioch and joined others in carrying on the ministry there (v.35).

NOTES

30 On Luke's use of μὲν οὖν (*men oun*, "so," "then"), see comments and note at 1:6. Note especially his use of this connective in his fourth panel of material at 13:4; 14:3; 15:3; and 16:5.

On "going down" (κατῆλθον, *katēlthon*) from Jerusalem, see comments and note at 8:5.

On the term τὸ πλῆθος (*to plēthos*, "the assembly"), see note at 6:2 (also v.12 above).

31 On Paul's manner of dealing with the issues in the church at Corinth—which is a discussion relevant for understanding his acceptance of the Jerusalem decree—see my *Paul, Apostle of Liberty*, 232–44.

32 Codex Bezae (D) adds in the middle of the verse (after ὄντες, *ontes*, "being") the words πλήρεις πνεύματος ἁγίου (*plēreis pneumatos hagiou*, "filled with the Holy Spirit"), thereby reading "who were themselves prophets filled with the Holy Spirit," which reflects D's characteristic interest in the Holy Spirit (cf. esp. 15:7, 29; 19:1; 20:3).

33 Instead of the widely supported (𝔓⁷⁴ ℵ A B C D and as reflected in the Latin Vulgate and Syriac versions) reading πρὸς τοὺς ἀποστείλαντας αὐτούς (*pros tous aposteilantas autous*, "to those who sent them"), many later textual witnesses (H L P S, many minuscules, and as reflected in recensions of the Syriac and Coptic versions) read πρὸς τοὺς ἀποστόλους (*pros tous apostolous*, "to the apostles"), which seems to be a deliberate alteration in order to bring the apostolate into greater prominence.

2. Disagreement and Two Missionary Teams (15:36–41)

³⁶Some time later Paul said to Barnabas, "Let us go back and visit the brothers in all the towns where we preached the word of the Lord and see how they are doing." ³⁷Barnabas wanted to take John, also called Mark, with them, ³⁸but Paul did not think it wise to take him, because he had deserted them in Pamphylia and had not continued with them in the work. ³⁹They had such a sharp disagreement that they parted company. Barnabas took Mark and sailed for Cyprus, ⁴⁰but Paul chose Silas and left, commended by the brothers to the grace of the Lord. ⁴¹He went through Syria and Cilicia, strengthening the churches.

COMMENTARY

36 Beginning at this point in Acts, the preposition *meta* with a time designation—*meta tinas hēmeras*, "after some days"; *meta tauta*, "after these things"; or *meta tas hēmeras tauta*, "after these days"—vies somewhat with the connective *men oun* to mark off the beginning of a new section and to join that section with what has gone before it. So Luke now presents Paul as taking the initiative for another missionary journey. In Paul's mind, it appears, such a proposed journey would involve no new outreach, but only a revisiting of believers who had been converted on the first journey. Nonetheless, God in his providence was to bring about out of it a further extension of the gospel to the Gentile world—an extension that in Acts can be spoken of as "the second missionary journey" of Paul. Actually, vv.36–41 provide something of a bridge between the completion of the gospel's advances reported in the fourth panel and the beginning of those advances reported in the fifth panel.

37–38 John Mark, who was Barnabas's cousin (cf. Col 4:10), probably became convinced about the appropriateness of Paul's Gentile policy as a result of the debate and action of the Jerusalem Council, despite his earlier qualms (see comments at 13:1–3). Barnabas had evidently called him back to Syrian Antioch to minister in the church there. Barnabas's earlier involvement in the dispute at Antioch evidenced that his sympathies lay principally with Jewish Christians (cf. Gal 2:13), and it was also natural for him to want to take Mark with them in revisiting the churches. Paul, however, for what seem to have been reasons of principle rather than merely personal ones, did not want to have so unreliable a man with them day after day (note the intensive present infinitive *mē symparalabanein*, "not to take along with," GK *5221*). The scar tissue of the wounds that Paul suffered in establishing his missionary policy was still too tender for him to look favorably on Mark's being with them—particularly if, as I have proposed, Mark was in some way responsible for inciting the Judaizers to action.

39 The fact that Luke does not gloss over the quarrel between Paul and Barnabas shows his honesty. The Greek word for "disagreement" (*paroxysmos*, GK *4237*) is so neutral as not to touch on the question of responsibility, and it is idle for us to try to apportion blame. Yet far from letting the disagreement harm the outreach of the gospel, God providentially used it to double the missionary force—with Barnabas taking Mark and returning to Cyprus, which was home territory for Barnabas and where Mark had been before (cf. 13:4–12). Acts tells us nothing more about their further mission to Cyprus or these two missionaries themselves, though Paul's later letters refer in cordial terms to both Barnabas (cf. 1Co 9:6; perhaps also, as Martin Luther and John Calvin suggested, 2Co 8:18–19) and John Mark (cf. Col 4:10; 2Ti 4:11; Phm 24).

40–41 Paul's selection of Silas (or "Silvanus," as he is referred to more formally by his Latinized name in 2Co 1:19; 1Th 1:1; 2Th 1:1; 1Pe 5:12) to accompany him on his return visit to the churches was wise. He had evidently come to appreciate Silas in their contacts at Jerusalem and Syrian Antioch, and he evidently concluded that he would make a congenial colleague. More than that, Silas was a leader in the Jerusalem church (15:22) and was explicitly identified in the Jerusalem letter as one who could speak with authority on the attitude of that church (15:27). He was also, it seems, a Roman citizen who could claim, if need be, the privileges of Roman citizenship along with Paul (16:37). This was not true of Barnabas. Likewise, Silas was a prophet (15:32), who appears to have been fluent in

Greek (15:22, 32), and a helpful amanuensis (cf. 1 Th 1:1; 2 Th 1:1; 1 Pe 5:12). Thus Paul and Silas set out with the blessing of the church at Antioch. The churches in the regions of Syria and Cilicia that they revisited and strengthened were presumably founded through the efforts of Paul (15:23, 36). As such, they would be receptive to the decision and letter of the Jerusalem Council.

NOTES

36 On μετά (*meta*) with a time designation as a connection in Acts, see also 18:1; 21:15; 24:1, 24; 25:1; 28:11, 17. On μὲν οὖν (*men oun*) in the remainder of Acts, see 16:5; 17:12, 17, 30; 19:32, 38; 23:18, 22, 31; 25:4, 11; 26:4, 9; 28:5.

38 Codex Bezae (D) expands the sentence by spelling out what is implied: "But Paul was not willing, saying that one who had withdrawn from them in Pamphylia, and had not gone with them to the work for which they had been sent, should not be with them."

40 The reading τῇ χάριτι τοῦ κυρίου (*tē chariti tou kyriou*, "to the grace of the Lord") is strongly supported by both Alexandrian and Western witnesses ($\mathfrak{P}^{74}$ ℵ A B D, Vulgate, Coptic Sahidic). Others, however, some of them ancient ($\mathfrak{P}^{45}$ C H I P, most minuscules, Syriac Peshitta, Coptic Bohairic), read τῇ χάριτι τοῦ θεοῦ (*tē chariti tou theou*, "to the grace of God"). The latter is probably a scribal assimilation to 14:26.

41 Codex Bezae (D) expands the end of this verse to read παραδιδοὺς τὰς ἐντολὰς τῶν πρεσβυτέρων (*paradidous tas entolas tōn presbyterōn*, "delivering [to the churches] the commands of the elders"), with this being expanded still further by the Syriac Harclean version and several recensions of the Vulgate to read "the commands of the apostles and elders." But these additions only make explicit what is implicit in the narrative, probably assimilating the text here to 16:4.

3. Paul Adds Timothy to the Team in Galatia (16:1–4)

> ¹He came to Derbe and then to Lystra, where a disciple named Timothy lived, whose mother was a Jewess and a believer, but whose father was a Greek. ²The brothers at Lystra and Iconium spoke well of him. ³Paul wanted to take him along on the journey, so he circumcised him because of the Jews who lived in that area, for they all knew that his father was a Greek. ⁴As they traveled from town to town, they delivered the decisions reached by the apostles and elders in Jerusalem for the people to obey.

COMMENTARY

1–2 Pushing on through the Cilician Gates (modern Gulek Bogaz) in the Taurus mountains, Paul and Silas came to the Galatian border town of Derbe and then moved on to Lystra. There at Lystra (note the adverb *ekei*, "there," "at that place") he found a young man who was highly spoken of by believers in both Lystra and the neighboring city of Iconium. The Jewish community at Lystra seems to have been small and without influence (see comments at 14:8−10). Probably for that reason Timothy's mother, who was a Jewess, was allowed to marry a Greek. Timothy, however, had never been circumcised. In Jewish law, a child takes the religion of its mother; so Timothy should have been circumcised and raised as a Jew. But in Greek law the father dominates in the home. Apparently the Jewish community at Lystra was too weak or lax to interfere with the prevalent Greek customs.

Second Timothy 1:5 speaks of the sincere Jewish faith of Timothy's grandmother Lois and of his mother Eunice, and 2 Timothy 3:15 speaks of his early instruction in the Jewish Scriptures. Here Eunice is identified as a Jewess as well as a Christian believer, and so she had probably been converted during the first visit of Paul and Barnabas to Lystra. From the use of the imperfect verb *hypērchen* ("[his father] was") in v.3, it may reasonably be conjectured that her husband was now dead. Likewise, from Paul's reference to Timothy in 1 Corinthians 4:17 as his son we may assume that Timothy's conversion to Christ also dates from the proclamation of the gospel on that first missionary journey.

3−4 Most scholars accept at face value the statement in v.3a about Paul's desire to take Timothy along with him on his journey. Many, however, question what is said in vv.3b−4 about Paul circumcising Timothy and delivering the Jerusalem decisions to the Galatian churches. The hand of a redactor has often been seen in this latter portion. Furthermore, Luke has often been accused of perpetuating a gross confusion in either (1) attributing to Paul's relations with Timothy an erroneous tradition concerning Titus (cf. *Beginnings of Christianity* [ed. Foakes-Jackson and Lake], 4.184, citing Gal 2:3), or (2) taking over some slanderous rumor that Paul did on occasion circumcise his converts (cf. Haenchen, 482, citing Gal 5:11). But while Paul stoutly resisted any imposition of circumcision and the Jewish law on his Gentile converts, he himself continued to live as an observant Jew and urged his converts to express their Christian faith through the cultural forms they had inherited (cf. 1Co 7:17−24).

As for Timothy, because of his Jewish mother he was a Jew in the eyes of the Jewish world. Therefore, it was both proper and expedient for Paul to circumcise him. As Paul saw it, being a good Christian did not mean being a bad Jew. Rather, it meant being a fulfilled Jew. Paul had no desire to flout Jewish scruples in his endeavor to bring both Jews and Gentiles to salvation in Christ.

Similarly, there is no reason to think he would have refused to deliver the decision of the Jerusalem Council to his Galatian converts, but every reason to believe he would have wanted to deliver the decision—particularly if he had written what we know as the letter to the Galatians to them earlier and was now able to say that the Jerusalem leaders supported his position.

NOTES

1 The Western text (D, and as reflected in recensions of the Old Latin, Vulgate, and Syriac versions) begins this verse "And having passed through these nations, he came to Derbe and Lystra," thereby making it clear that Derbe and Lystra were not located in the regions of either Syria or Cilicia.

3 On Paul's own expression of his Christian faith through the traditional forms of Judaism, see my *Paul, Apostle of Liberty*, esp. 245−63.

4 Some Western texts (D, and as represented by the Syriac Harclean version and Ephraem in his Acts commentary) expand the first part of this verse to read "While going through the cities, they preached [and delivered to them], with all boldness, the Lord Jesus Christ, delivering at the same time also the commands of the apostles and elders . . . ." Evidently these words were included to explain the growth of the church described in v.5.

G. Summary Statement (16:5)

⁵So the churches were strengthened in the faith and grew daily in numbers.

COMMENTARY

5 This summary statement concludes what F. F. Bruce, 324, has called "perhaps the most crucial phase of Luke's narrative." It is comparable to the summary statements of 6:7; 9:31; and 12:24, which culminate their respective panels (cf. also 19:20 and 28:31 later). Introduced by Luke's favorite connective *men oun* (see comments at 1:6), it stresses the strengthening and growth of the churches as a result of Paul's new missionary policy and the response of the Jerusalem church to it. And, indeed, in spelling out the nature of Paul's new policy of outreach to the Gentile world—a policy unexpectedly inaugurated under divine sanction on his first missionary journey—and of the Jerusalem church's response to it—a response also unexpectedly and providentially worked out at the Jerusalem Council, this fourth panel of material in Acts 12:25–16:5 can rightly be called "the most crucial phase of Luke's narrative."

PANEL 5—WIDE OUTREACH THROUGH TWO MISSIONARY JOURNEYS (16:6–19:20)

Acts 16:6–19:20, the fifth panel of Luke's material, presents the wide outreach of the Christian message through two further missionary journeys of Paul in the eastern part of the Roman Empire. Having described the gradual extension of the gospel to new groups of people and through a new missionary policy, Luke now shows how the Christian mission entered rapidly and widely into new areas of the Greco-Roman world.

Notable in this panel are Luke's emphases on (1) God's direction in and supervision of the gospel's outreach, (2) Christianity's right to be considered a *religio licita*, and (3) Paul's circumstantial preaching in terms of proclamation and persuasion. Also of interest is the fact that the missionary outreach was confined to the major cities of the Aegean coastline, which were connected by the main Roman roads, and that at the beginning of this fifth panel we have our first "we" section (16:10–17) of the latter half of Acts (cf. 20:5–15; 21:1–18; 27:1–28:16).

Temporal references in the panel are fairly general, even when datable; for example, Luke's references to the Edict of Claudius (18:2) and Gallio's proconsulate (18:12) leave some margin for dispute. Generally, however, the material given here covers the years AD 49–56, with the first journey into Macedonia and Achaia taking place about 49–52 and the second centered in Ephesus during 53–56.

A. Providential Direction for the Mission (16:6–10)

OVERVIEW

The missionary journeys of Paul reveal an extraordinary combination of strategic planning and sensitivity to the guidance of the Holy Spirit in working out the specific details. This is especially noticeable here. For having revisited the churches at Derbe, Lystra, Iconium, and Pisidian Antioch, Paul evidently expected to follow the Via Sebaste westward to Ephesus, the important coastal city and capital of the Roman province of Asia. But he was "kept by the Holy Spirit" from entering Asia and so continued to travel throughout "the region of Phrygia and Galatia" (v.6).

> 6Paul and his companions traveled throughout the region of Phrygia and Galatia, having been kept by the Holy Spirit from preaching the word in the province of Asia. 7When they came to the border of Mysia, they tried to enter Bithynia, but the Spirit of Jesus would not allow them to. 8So they passed by Mysia and went down to Troas. 9During the night Paul had a vision of a man of Macedonia standing and begging him, "Come over to Macedonia and help us." 10After Paul had seen the vision, we got ready at once to leave for Macedonia, concluding that God had called us to preach the gospel to them.

COMMENTARY

6 The heightening of terminology from "the Holy Spirit" (v.6) to "the Spirit of Jesus" (v.7) to "God" (v.10) is more than stylistic—it is an unconscious expression of the early church's embryonic Trinitarian faith. All three terms refer to God by his Spirit's giving of direction to the mission. But just how the Holy Spirit revealed his will we are not told. Perhaps in one or more instances Silas had a part, for he was a prophet (15:32).

Likewise, we are left somewhat uncertain as to what Luke meant by "the region of Phrygia and Galatia" (*tēn Phrygian kai Galatikēn chōran*). Many are of the opinion that the reference to the "region of Galatia" (*Galatikēn chōran*) must be taken to mean that Galatia is "a second country named beside Phrygia" (Haenchen, 483 n. 2), and that therefore Galatia cannot here be equated with Phrygia, thus ruling out a continued ministry around Iconium and Pisidian Antioch and suggesting a journey into northern Galatia (cf. also 18:23). But Ernest DeWitt Burton (*A Critical and Exegetical Commentary on the Epistle to the Galatians* [Edinburgh: T&T Clark, 1921], xxxi–xxxii) has aptly noted that "the most obvious and, indeed, only natural explanation of the phrase *tēn Phrygian kai Galatikēn chōran* in v. 6 is that *Phrygian* and *Galatikēn* are both adjectives and both limit *chōran*"; and, further, that "the joining of the words *Phrygian* and *Galatikēn* by *kai*, with the article before the first one only, implies that the region designated by *chōran* is one, Phrygian and Galatian." There is no linguistic support here for a so-called North Galatian theory. Rather, we are left to explain this juxtaposition of adjectives either (1) politically, meaning not the entire province of Galatia but only the Phrygic region of Galatia, or possibly (2) ethnologically and popularly, meaning a district adjoining the region of Phrygia in the southern portion of the Roman province of Galatia where both Phrygian and Celtic (Galatic or Gaulish) dialects could be heard.

7–8 Mysia was a region in northwest Asia Minor that lacked precise boundaries because it was never an independent political entity. It was generally considered to be bounded by the Aegean Sea on the west; the Hellespont (or Dardanelles), Propontis (or Sea of Marmara), and Bithynia along its northern extremities from west to east; Galatia on the east and southeast; Phrygia to the south; and the area of Lydia to the southwest. It included the historic Aegean seaport of Troas and the site of ancient Troy some ten miles inland.

As Paul and his missionary party moved northwest along the borders of Mysian territory, they decided to go on into the Thracian area of Bithynia in order to evangelize the strategic cities and important Black Sea ports there, all of which were interconnected by an elaborate Roman road system. But, Luke tells us, "the Spirit of Jesus would not allow them to" (v.7). Later, Christians in Bithynia were included in the salutation of 1 Peter (1:1). Also, Pliny the Younger, who was governor of Bithynia under Trajan in AD 110–12, spoke of Christians in the province who, though a minority, had to be taken into account (cf. Pliny, *Epist.* 10.96–97). But Paul was not directed by God to evangelize in Bithynia. Instead, he and his associates turned westward again, traveling through Mysia until they reached Troas on the Aegean coast (v.8). The participle *parelthontes* (GK *4216*) literally means "passing by" (i.e., "they passed by" the region of Mysia). At first glance it seems to be somewhat out of place, since one could not get to Troas without passing through Mysia. Probably, however, Luke used the word *parelthontes* ("they passed by") instead of *dielthontes* ("they passed

through," GK *1451*) to indicate that they did not stay in Mysia to evangelize.

9–10 Troas became an important Greek port about 300 BC and was named Alexandria Troas. After the breakup of Alexander the Great's short-lived empire, Troas was ruled for a time by the Seleucids from Syrian Antioch, but it soon became an independent city-state. To the Greeks, mountains protected but also separated people, whereas the sea, while frightening, united people. Therefore Troas, at the mouth of the Dardenelles, was the pivotal port between the landmasses of Europe and Asia Minor and the great waterways of the Aegean and Black seas. When Rome annexed Anatolia, Julius Caesar seriously considered making Troas the governmental center of the entire area (cf. Suetonius, *Divus Julius* 79; Horace, *Odes* 3.3).

At Troas Paul had a vision of a man from Macedonia asking for help. He took this as a divine call to evangelize Macedonia. Many commentators have suggested that when Paul met Luke at Troas, perhaps initially for medical reasons, Luke had impressed on him during their conversations the need for the proclamation of the gospel in Macedonia—and that it was this encounter that God used in a vision to direct Paul and his colleagues to cross over the Aegean Sea to the region of Macedonia. Perhaps, indeed, that is how it happened. Luke gives us none of the psychological details, though it must be said that Paul's recognition of the man in his vision as being a Macedonian could as easily have been gained from the nature of his request as from any prior acquaintance or knowledge. But whatever secondary means God may have used in formulating the vision, Paul and his party responded to it at once (*eutheos*, "immediately") and so began to make preparations to leave for Macedonia (v.10). Such preparations would have required finding passage on a ship sailing for Neapolis.

Authentic turning points in history are few. But surely among them this Macedonian vision ranks high. Because of Paul's obedience at this point, the gospel went westward, and ultimately Europe and the Western world were evangelized. Christian response to the call of God is never a trivial thing. Indeed, as in this instance, great issues and untold blessings may depend on it.

It is at Troas that the first of the "we" sections of Acts appears in 16:10–17. Since (1) this "we" section stops at Philippi, (2) the second "we" section of 20:5–15 begins when the missionaries revisit Philippi after the third missionary journey, and (3) the ministry at Philippi receives the greatest attention (some thirty verses) in this fifth panel, we may reasonably suppose that the use of the first person plural pronoun "we" points to a resident of Philippi who traveled from Troas to Philippi with Paul and Silas and that this person was Luke himself (see Introduction, pp. 684–85).

NOTES

6 The Western text (D, and as represented in recensions of the Old Latin, Syriac, and Coptic versions) adds τοῦ θεοῦ (*tou theou*, "of God") after τὸν λόγον (*ton logon*, "the word"), which is an obvious secondary modification.

7 The expression τὸ πνεῦμα Ἰησοῦ (*to pneuma Iēsou*, "the spirit of Jesus") appears nowhere else in the NT but is well supported here ($\mathfrak{P}^{74}$ ℵ A B D E, and as reflected in the Vulgate, Syriac Peshitta, and Coptic Bohairic versions). A few witnesses (C and a recension of the Old Latin), evidently because the expression is unusual, replace it with τὸ πνεῦμα τοῦ κυρίου (*to pneuma tou kyriou*, "the spirit of the Lord"). Other witnesses have only τὸ πνεῦμα (*to pneuma*, "the Spirit"), omitting altogether any reference to either "Jesus" or "the Lord" (H L P, most minuscules, and the Coptic Sahidic version), as does the TR and so the KJV.

8 The Western text (D, and as represented by recensions of the Old Latin, Vulgate, and Syriac versions) reads διελθόντες (*dielthontes*, "passing through" or "they passed through"), which is more geographically correct but ignores Luke's point. It seems unlikely that a common word such as διελθόντες (*dielthontes*, "they passed through") would have been changed to the less common word παρελθόντες (*parelthontes*, "they passed by"). That Codex Bezae (D) changed a less common word to one more common is far more probable.

9 Codex Bezae (D) and a number of its Western Latin associates recast this verse to include such clarifying matters as (1) the particle ὡσεί (*hōsei*, "as it were," thus, "as it were a man of Macedonia") and (2) the expression κατὰ πρόσωπον αὐτοῦ (*kata prosōpon autou*, "before his face," thus, "standing before his face").

10 Codex Bezae (D), supported in part by the Coptic Sahidic version, recasts this verse to read "Then awakening, he related the vision to us, and we recognized that the Lord had called us to evangelize those in Macedonia," evidently to make sure that readers understood how it was that Paul's companions knew what he had seen in the vision—i.e., because he told them. But the more reliable text ($\mathfrak{P}^{74}$ ℵ A B C etc.) can easily be understood without such a recasting.

B. At Philippi (16:11–40)

OVERVIEW

Despite the missionary party's brief stay, Luke devotes more space to the Christian mission at Philippi than he does to any other city on Paul's second and third missionary journeys. Philippi is the only city Luke describes as a Roman colony. And when he calls it "the leading [or first] city of that district of Macedonia" (v.12; see comments there), he seems to be reflecting local pride. To judge by the way the "we" sections in 16:10–17 and 20:5–15 focus on Paul's visits to Philippi, it may be that Luke had some part in the founding and growth of the church there.

1. Arrival in the City (16:11–12)

¹¹From Troas we put out to sea and sailed straight for Samothrace, and the next day on to Neapolis. ¹²From there we traveled to Philippi, a Roman colony and the leading city of that district of Macedonia. And we stayed there several days.

COMMENTARY

11 Samothrace is an island in the northeastern part of the Aegean Sea and lies between the cities of Troas (in northwest Asia Minor) and Philippi (in eastern Europe). The most conspicuous landmark in the North Aegean, it is a mountainous island. It was called Poseidon's Island because from the top of Mount Fengari (5,577 feet above sea level) the Greek god Poseidon, who was god of the waters, earthquakes, and horses, was said to have surveyed the plains of ancient Troy (cf. Homer, *Iliad* 13.12). It became a stopover for ships plying their trade in the North Aegean, as captains preferred to anchor there rather than face the hazards of the sea at night (cf. Pliny, *Nat.* 4.23). Neapolis on the northern coast of the Aegean Sea was the port for the commercial center of Philippi, which lay ten miles farther inland. Neapolis was on the Via Egnatia, which ran east to Byzantium and west to Philippi, then to Thessalonica, and finally across the Balkan penin-

sula to the city of Dyrrhachium and its port Egnatia (from which the great Roman road may have been named) on the Adriatic coast.

The narrator on board (note the use of "we" in this section) gives a port-by-port description of the voyage, with specific mention of the time it took (as appears also in the other "we" sections; cf. 20:5, 13–15; 21:1–8; 27:1–28:16). The wind on this first crossing must have favored the travelers, for it took only two days to sail the 156 miles to Neapolis, though the trip in the other direction after the third missionary journey took five days (cf. 20:5).

12 Philippi was situated 10 miles northwest of Neapolis on a plain bounded by Mount Pangaeus to the north and northeast, with the rivers Strymon and Nestos on either side. Shielded from the sea by a very rocky ridge, it lay astride the Via Egnatia and near the Gangites River, a tributary of the Strymon. Its fame in earlier days came from its fertile plain and gold in the mountains to the north. Philip II of Macedon recognized the city's importance, so in 356 BC he established a large Greek colony there and changed its name from Krenides ("springs") to Philippi (cf. Diodorus, *Bibl. hist.* 7.6.7). With the subjugation of the Macedonians by Rome in 167 BC, Philippi became part of the Roman Empire. In 146 BC, it was included within the reorganized province of Macedonia, whose capital was at Thessalonica. Shortly thereafter it was connected to other important Roman cities by the Via Egnatia.

The fame of Philippi during Roman times stemmed from its having been the site of the decisive battle of the second civil war in 42 BC, when Mark Anthony and Caius Octavius (the heir of Julius Caesar, who after 27 BC was properly known as Augustus) defeated Marcus Junius Brutus and Longinus Cassius. After the war many Roman army veterans were settled at Philippi and the city was designated a Roman colony. Its government was responsible directly to the emperor and not made subservient to provincial administration. Philippi's importance during the NT period, therefore, resulted from its agriculture, its strategic commercial location on both sea and land routes, its still functioning gold mines, and its status as a Roman colony. In addition, it had a famous school of medicine with graduates throughout the then-known world.

NOTES

11 Several early textual witnesses ($\mathfrak{P}^{74}$ ℵ A D etc.) begin this verse with the postpositive conjunction δέ (*de*, "but," "and"), whereas others (B C H L etc.) begin with the postpositive particle οὖν (*oun*, "when," "then"). Codex Bezae (D) also adds at the beginning of the verse the phrase τῇ ἐπαύριον ἀναχθέντες (*tē epaurion anachthentes*, "on the next day when we got up"), evidently to assure its readers that the missionary party responded quickly to the Macedonian call. Whereas δέ (*de*) is probably to be preferred over οὖν (*oun*), neither is necessarily to be translated (so NIV; NASB, "so").

12 Luke's reference to Philippi as "the leading [or "first"] city of that district of Macedonia" (πρώτη τῆς μερίδος Μακεδονίας πόλις, *prōtē tēs meridos Makedonias polis*, according to $\mathfrak{P}^{74}$ ℵ A and C, with Codex Vaticanus [B] basically in agreement, though placing the article τῆς, *tēs*, before Μακεδονίας, *Makedonias*) is somewhat confusing. Actually Amphipolis, the early district capital between 167–146 BC, and Thessalonica, the provincial capital after that, had a more valid claim to that title. Some Alexandrian MSS read πρώτης, *prōtēs* ("of the first"), for πρώτη, *prōtē* ("the first"), thereby suggesting that Philippi was "a city of the first district of Macedonia," i.e., a city of the first of the four administrative districts that Macedonia was divided into by the Romans in 167 BC, before the whole area was reorganized into the province of Macedonia in 146 BC. Codex Bezae (D) reads κεφαλή, *kephalē* ("the head" or "capital," GK *3051*), which wrongly asserts its status as the provincial capital.

Commentators have differed widely in interpreting the textual evidence here. We should probably accept the better-attested reading of ℵ A C and $\mathfrak{P}^{74}$, together with B, and translate the ascription as "the leading city of the district of Macedonia" (NIV, "the leading city of that district of Macedonia; NASB, "a leading city of the district of Macedonia"). As such, it is probably to be understood as an expression of Luke's pride in his city, much as a resident of Pergamum, Smyrna, or Ephesus might claim his or her city to be "the leading city of Asia," for other than merely governmental reasons.

2. The Conversion of Lydia (16:13–15)

¹³On the Sabbath we went outside the city gate to the river, where we expected to find a place of prayer. We sat down and began to speak to the women who had gathered there. ¹⁴One of those listening was a woman named Lydia, a dealer in purple cloth from the city of Thyatira, who was a worshiper of God. The Lord opened her heart to respond to Paul's message. ¹⁵When she and the members of her household were baptized, she invited us to her home. "If you consider me a believer in the Lord," she said, "come and stay at my house." And she persuaded us.

COMMENTARY

13 A Jewish congregation was made up of ten men who were heads of their households. Wherever there were ten male heads of households who could be in regular attendance, a synagogue was to be formed (cf. *m. Sanh.* 1:6; *m. 'Abot* 3:6). Failing this, a place of prayer (*proseuchē*, GK 4666) under the open sky and near a river or the sea was to be arranged (cf. Philo, *Flacc.* 14; Josephus, *Ant.* 14.258, though rabbinic sources do not explicitly say that the place of prayer must be by water, cf. Str-B 2.742). But Philippi apparently did not have such a male quorum and so was without a synagogue. On the Sabbath, therefore, Paul and his associates walked outside the city in search of a Jewish place of prayer; they probably headed toward the Gangites River about a mile and a half west of the city. There they found some women gathered to recite the Shema, pray the *Shemoneh Esreh*, read from the Law and the Prophets, discuss what they had read, and, if possible, hear from a traveling Jewish teacher an exposition or exhortation and receive a blessing (see comments at 13:15). Paul and his companions sat down with these women and began to speak to them.

14–15 One of the women was from Thyatira, a city in western Asia Minor. Thyatira, which was formerly in the ancient kingdom of Lydia before its incorporation into the Roman province of Asia, continued to be considered a city in the region of Lydia. Hence the woman was called Lydia (or perhaps "the Lydian lady"). Thyatira was famous for making purple dyes and for dyeing clothes—industries mostly carried on by women in their homes (cf. Homer, *Iliad* 4.141–42). As an artisan specializing in purple dyes, Lydia had come to Philippi to carry on her trade. She is spoken of as a "God-fearer" (*sebomenē ton theon*; NIV, "worshiper of God") and had doubtless received instruction at a synagogue in her native Thyatira before carrying her interest in Judaism to Philippi. We may surmise that she was either a widow or unmarried and that some of the women gathered for worship were relatives and servants living in her home. As she listened, God opened her heart to the Christian message, and "she and the members of her household were baptized" (v.15). Then she urged the missionary party to stay at her home, which they did.

From such small beginnings the church at Philippi began. To judge from his letter to the Philippians, it was one of Paul's most-loved congregations. Luke, as has been suggested, may have been involved in the establishment and growth of this church. Lydia was also probably prominent in it. Some commentators have suggested that the real name of this "Lydian lady" was either Euodia or Syntyche (cf. Php 4:2) and that the other was the wife of the converted jailer. Other commentators think that Paul had Lydia in mind when he referred to a "loyal yokefellow" (Php 4:3), and a few even suppose that Paul married Lydia. But all this is mere conjecture. All we really know from the text is that Lydia and the members of her household responded to the gospel and that she opened her house to Paul and his colleagues. Soon, it seems, her home became the center for Christian outreach and worship in Philippi (cf. 16:40).

NOTES

13 The MS evidence for "we expected to find a place of prayer" (NIV) or "we were supposing that there would be a place of prayer" (NASB) is mixed and somewhat baffling. The better-attested Alexandrian text ($\mathfrak{P}^{45}$ $\mathfrak{P}^{74}$ ℵ A B C) has the verb as either ἐνομίζομεν (enomizomen) or ἐνομίζαμεν (enomizamen), both of which can be translated "we thought, expected," or "supposed," and construes the word for "prayer" as either the subject (προσευχή, proseuchē) or the object (προσευχήν, proseuchēn) of the verb. The Byzantine text (H L P) has ἐνομίζετο προσευχή (enomizeto proseuchē; KJV, "prayer was wont"), and the Western text (D and its Latin associates) has ἐδόκει προσευχή (edokei proseuchē, "prayer seemed").

The use of προσευχή (proseuchē, "prayer") is also a bit confusing, for the term among Greek-speaking Jews was nearly always equivalent to συναγωγή (synagōgē, "synagogue," GK 5252). Thus some have argued that an actual synagogue is here in view (cf. Schürer, 2.4.499–500, 517–18). But probably "the place of prayer" (vv.13, 16) was not a synagogue, since (1) only women are spoken of as being present, and (2) Luke is not adverse to using the term "synagogue" when one actually existed (cf., e.g., 17:1, 10, 17).

15 The Western text (D, and as reflected in the Old Latin) adds πᾶς (pas, "all") before ὁ οἶκος αὐτῆς (ho oikos autēs, "her house")—which is a characteristic Western expansion.

3. A Demon-possessed Girl (16:16–18)

> [16]Once when we were going to the place of prayer, we were met by a slave girl who had a spirit by which she predicted the future. She earned a great deal of money for her owners by fortune-telling. [17]This girl followed Paul and the rest of us, shouting, "These men are servants of the Most High God, who are telling you the way to be saved." [18]She kept this up for many days. Finally Paul became so troubled that he turned around and said to the spirit, "In the name of Jesus Christ I command you to come out of her!" At that moment the spirit left her.

COMMENTARY

16 While on their way to the Jewish place of prayer (note the present participle *poreuomenōn*, GK *4513*), Paul and his associates were met by a slave girl whom Luke describes as having a "Python spirit" (*pneuma pythōna*; NIV, "a spirit by which she predicted the future"; NASB, "a spirit of divination"). The Python was a mythical serpent or dragon that guarded the temple and oracle of Apollo, located on the southern slope of Mount Parnassus to the north of the Gulf of Corinth. It was supposed to have lived at the foot of Mount Parnassus and to have eventually been killed by Apollo (cf. Strabo, *Geogr.* 9.3.12). Later the word "python" came to mean a demon-possessed person through whom the Python spoke. Even a ventriloquist was thought to have such a spirit living in his or her belly (cf. Plutarch, *Def. orac.* 9.414). Undoubtedly, all who knew the girl regarded her as neither fraudulent nor insane but as demon-possessed and able to foretell the future. And by her fortune-telling, Luke tells us, she earned her masters a great deal of money.

17 As the girl followed Paul and his associates around, she kept on screaming out (note the imperfect *ekrazen*, GK *3189*) to the crowd, "These men are servants of the Most High God, who are telling you [*hymin*] the way to be saved." Her screaming recalls that of the demons during Jesus' ministry (cf. Mk 1:24; 3:11; 5:7; Lk 4:34, 41; 8:28). In both instances there was a compulsive acknowledgment of the true character of those confronted. Here this acknowledgment is stated in terms acceptable to the Jewish world and readily understandable to Gentiles. For while the title "Most High God" (*ho theos ho hypsistos*) was originally a Phoenician ascription for deity (*ʾĒl ʿElyôn*), it was used by Jews of Yahweh (cf. Nu 24:16; Ps 78:35; Isa 14:14; Da 3:26; 4:32; 5:18, 21; 1 Esd 2:3) and by Greeks of Zeus (cf. C. Roberts, T. C. Skeat, and A. D. Nock, "The Guild of Zeus *Hypsistos*," HTR 29 [1936]: 39–88). The announcement of "salvation" (*sōtēria*, GK *5401*)—which for Paul and the Jews referred to deliverance from sin—would have connoted for Gentiles release from the powers governing the fate of humans and of the material world. It was an acknowledgment, therefore, cast in terms that Gentiles could understand but that Paul could build on.

18 While the demon-inspired words provided some free publicity for Paul and his associates and helped gather an audience, when continued for many days it became a nuisance. The demon's words were getting more of a hearing than the proclamation of the gospel! So Paul commanded the evil spirit "in the name of Jesus Christ" to come out of the girl, and the demon left her. Presumably, having been delivered by the power of God, she became a Christian and—along with Lydia the businesswoman, members of Lydia's household, Luke the physician (notice that the "we" section stops at v.17), and an unnamed army veteran and jailer (vv. 27–36)—was a member of the embryonic church at Philippi.

NOTES

17 Chester Beatty 𝔓⁴⁵ omits δοῦλοι (*douloi*, "servants," GK *1528*). Codices A C and P, together with a number of minuscules and church fathers, read ἡμῖν (*hēmin*, "to us"). But Bodmer 𝔓⁷⁴, codices ℵ B D and E, and most versions include δοῦλοι (*douloi*, "servants") and read ὑμῖν (*hymin*, "to you").

4. Paul and Silas in Prison (16:19–34)

¹⁹When the owners of the slave girl realized that their hope of making money was gone, they seized Paul and Silas and dragged them into the marketplace to face the authorities. ²⁰They brought them before the magistrates and said, "These men are Jews, and are throwing our city into an uproar ²¹by advocating customs unlawful for us Romans to accept or practice."

²²The crowd joined in the attack against Paul and Silas, and the magistrates ordered them to be stripped and beaten. ²³After they had been severely flogged, they were thrown into prison, and the jailer was commanded to guard them carefully. ²⁴Upon receiving such orders, he put them in the inner cell and fastened their feet in the stocks.

²⁵About midnight Paul and Silas were praying and singing hymns to God, and the other prisoners were listening to them. ²⁶Suddenly there was such a violent earthquake that the foundations of the prison were shaken. At once all the prison doors flew open, and everybody's chains came loose. ²⁷The jailer woke up, and when he saw the prison doors open, he drew his sword and was about to kill himself because he thought the prisoners had escaped. ²⁸But Paul shouted, "Don't harm yourself! We are all here!"

²⁹The jailer called for lights, rushed in and fell trembling before Paul and Silas. ³⁰He then brought them out and asked, "Sirs, what must I do to be saved?"

³¹They replied, "Believe in the Lord Jesus, and you will be saved—you and your household." ³²Then they spoke the word of the Lord to him and to all the others in his house. ³³At that hour of the night the jailer took them and washed their wounds; then immediately he and all his family were baptized. ³⁴The jailer brought them into his house and set a meal before them; he was filled with joy because he had come to believe in God—he and his whole family.

COMMENTARY

19–21 What Paul did for the slave girl was not appreciated by her masters. In exorcising the demon, he had exorcised their source of income. Because of interference with what they claimed as their property rights and with callous disregard for the girl's welfare, they seized Paul and Silas and dragged them into the marketplace (*tēn agoran*, "the agora," GK *59*) to face the city's authorities. The charge was that Paul and Silas were advocating a *religio illicita* and so were disturbing the Pax Romana. But the charge, couched in terms that appealed to

the latent anti-Semitism of the people ("these men are Jews") and their racial pride ("us Romans"), ignited the flames of bigotry and prevented any reasoned, dispassionate discussion of the issues.

Many have asked why only Paul and Silas were singled out for persecution, with Timothy and Luke left free. Of course, Paul and Silas were the leaders of the missionary party and therefore most open to attack. But we must also remember that Paul and Silas were Jews and probably looked very much like Jews (see comments at 14:3 on the tradition of

Paul's appearance). Timothy and Luke, however, being respectively half-Jewish and fully Gentile (cf. Col 4:14, where Luke is grouped by Paul with his Gentile friends), probably looked Greek in both their features and their dress, and so were left alone. Anti-Semitism lay very near the surface throughout the Roman Empire. Here it seems to have taken over not only in laying the charge but also in identifying the defendants.

22-24 As a Roman colony, Philippi had a form of government that was independent of the provincial administration headquartered at Thessalonica. There were two chief magistrates who were called *duoviri* in most Roman colonies, though in certain colonies they were referred to by the honorary title *praetores* (cf. Cicero, *Agr.* 2.93), which translates into Greek as *stratēgoi* (vv.20, 22, 35-36, 38). At Philippi the magistrates were given this honorary title. Functioning under the magistrates were two lictors, which translates into Greek as *rhabdouchoi* (vv.35, 38), who carried bundles of rods with axes attached (*fasces et secures*) as a sign of their judicial authority and whose job it was to carry out the orders of the magistrates. Jailers commonly were retired army veterans who could be expected to follow orders and use their military skills as required.

Incited to anti-Semitic fury by the slave girl's owners, the crowd turned on Paul and Silas. The magistrates had them stripped and severely flogged as disturbers of the peace and then ordered them jailed. The jailer put them into the innermost cell (the comparative *tēn esōteran* [NIV, "the inner"; NRSV, "the innermost"] used here as a superlative) and fastened their feet in stocks. Though both Paul and Silas were Roman citizens and politically exempt from such treatment (see comments at v.37), the frenzy of the mob and the rough justice of the colonial magistrates overrode their protestations. Later, when writing to the Christians at Corinth, Paul looked back on this experience as one of the afflictions he suffered as a servant of Christ. He reminded the boasters in the church at Corinth that for the sake of the gospel he had "been in prison more frequently, been flogged more severely" than they had, and had "been exposed to death again and again"—indeed, "three times . . . beaten with rods" (2Co 11:23, 25).

25-26 One would expect that after such brutal treatment Paul and Silas would be bemoaning their plight. Certainly they were suffering pain and shock from the flogging they had received. But about midnight, as Paul and Silas were "praying and singing hymns to God," an earthquake suddenly shook the prison, opened its doors, and loosened the chains of all the prisoners.

27-28 When the awakened jailer saw the doors open, he presumed the worst. Under Roman law, a guard who allowed his prisoner to escape was liable to the same penalty the prisoner would have suffered (cf. *Code of Justinian* 9.4.4). Thus the jailer, believing the prisoners had all escaped, drew his sword to kill himself. But Paul saw him in the doorway and shouted out from within the prison, "Don't harm yourself! We are all here!"

Form criticism has pointed out (1) that stories regarding prison doors opening of their own accord and miraculous escapes from confinement were popular in the ancient world (cf. Euripides, *Bacchae* 443ff., 586ff., as early cited by Celsus [see Origen, *Cels.* 2.34]; Ac 5:19-24; 12:7-10; *Acts of Thomas* 154) and (2) that v.35 can be read immediately following v.24 without any noticeable break in the story. Various form critics have concluded, therefore, that vv.25-34 should be viewed as some "independent legend" inserted by Luke into a more original narrative. But the fact that a story resembles other accounts of a similar type provides very little basis for impugning its historicity. And to conclude that because one portion of a story follows nicely another portion, which is separated from it by an intervening block of material, the intervening material must be a later insertion is a precarious critical procedure.

As a matter of fact, there is no escape from prison in vv.25–28, so the appeal to parallels is vain. Paul and Silas, together with all the other prisoners, remained in their cells. Their praying and singing, the earthquake, the opening of the doors, and the loosing of the chains all have special significance as vindicating God's servants Paul and Silas and preparing for the jailer's conversion. Thus while we may not be able to piece together each detail of the story according to strict logic, we cannot say that vv.25–34 constitute some independent miracle story Luke has inserted into his narrative for effect. The account of the imprisonment of Paul and Silas has meaning only in the context of the whole presentation in vv.16–40.

29–30 Since it was midnight, the jailer called for torches to dispel the darkness of the prison. Rushing in, he fell trembling before Paul and Silas—doubtless taking them to be some kind of divine messengers. If he had not heard the demon-possessed slave girl shouting out, "These men are servants of the Most High God, who are telling you the way to be saved" (v.17), he undoubtedly heard from others what she was saying. And now what had happened

confirmed her words about Paul and Silas. So he cried out, "Sirs, [*kyrioi*, which certainly carries a note of adoration here], what must I do to be saved?" His question showed recognition of his spiritual need and opened the way for Paul and Silas to give him the good news about Jesus Christ.

31–32 What Paul and Silas proclaimed to the Philippian jailer was the same Christ-centered gospel that had been proclaimed since Pentecost: "Believe in the Lord Jesus, and you will be saved—you and your household" (cf. 2:38–39; 3:19–26; 4:12; 8:12, 35; 10:43; 13:38–39). But since it was all new to the jailer, the missionaries took time to explain to him and the others of his household "the word of the Lord" (*ton logon tou kyriou*) and to set the gospel message of redemption in Jesus before them in terms they could understand.

33–34 To judge by their actions, the jailer and his family believed in Christ and received the Holy Spirit. The jailer washed the wounds of Paul and Silas, probably at a well in the prison courtyard—and probably there, too, he and all his family were baptized. Then he brought the missionaries into his home and fed them. And the "whole family," Luke tells us, "was filled with joy, because [they] had come to believe in God."

NOTES

22 The phrase περιρήξαντες αὐτῶν τὰ ἱμάτια (*perirēxantes autōn ta himatia*, "tearing off their clothes") could be read to mean that the magistrates tore off their own clothes (cf. 14:14), but that is hardly likely here.

26 Codex Vaticanus (B) omits παραχρῆμα (*parachrēma*, "at once"), but probably only accidentally. The adverb is a favorite of Luke's (cf. Lk 1:64; 4:39; 5:25; 8:44, 47, 55; 13:13; 18:43; 19:11; 22:60; Ac 3:7; 5:10; 12:23; 13:11; 16:33). It appears elsewhere in the NT only in Matthew 21:19–20 (twice).

27 Several minuscules add ὁ πιστὸς Στεφανᾶς (*ho pistos Stephanas*, "faithful Stephanas") after ὁ δεσμοφύλαξ (*ho desmophylax*, "the jailer," GK *1302*)—an identification that seems to date from the eighth century.

28 The first part of this verse reads ἐφώνησεν δὲ μεγάλῃ φωνῇ ὁ Παῦλος λέγων (*ephōnēsen de megalē phōnē ho Paulos legōn*, lit., "but Paul shouted in a loud voice, saying"). The repetition of ἐφώνησεν (*ephō-*

nēsen, "he shouted," GK *5888*), μεγάλη φωνῆ (*megalē phōnē*, "in a loud voice," GK *3489, 5889*), and λέγων (*legōn*, "saying," GK *3306*) is a typical Semitic-type construction supported by 𝔓⁷⁴ A Ψ etc. It seems, though, not to have been always understood, as witness the wide variety of deletions and rearrangements in other MSS.

29 The Western text (D, and as represented by recensions of the Old Latin, Vulgate, Syriac, and Coptic versions) adds πρὸς τοὺς πόδας (*pros tous podas*, "to their feet") after the verb προσέπεσεν (*prosepesen*, "he fell down before")—which is an obvious and extraneous detail.

30 The Western text (D, and as represented in the Syriac Harclean version) adds τοὺς λοιποὺς ἀσφαλισάμενος (*tous loipous asphalisamenos*, "having secured the others") after the statement προαγαγὼν αὐτοὺς ἔξω (*proagagōn autous exō*, "he brought them out"), evidently to satisfy readers' curiosity about what happened to the other prisoners.

31 The Western and Byzantine texts characteristically add Χριστόν (*Christon*, "Christ"), thereby reading "the Lord Jesus Christ."

31–34 For other instances of the conversion of members of a household with the head of the household, see 10:2–48; 11:14; 16:15; 18:8; 1 Corinthians 16:15.

32 The Byzantine text (E H L P and most minuscules), followed by TR, replaces the preposition σύν (*syn*, "with") of 𝔓⁷⁴ A B C D etc. with the conjunction καί (*kai*, "and"), thereby conforming to v.31.

5. Paul and Silas Leave the City (16:35–40)

³⁵When it was daylight, the magistrates sent their officers to the jailer with the order: "Release those men." ³⁶The jailer told Paul, "The magistrates have ordered that you and Silas be released. Now you can leave. Go in peace."

³⁷But Paul said to the officers: "They beat us publicly without a trial, even though we are Roman citizens, and threw us into prison. And now do they want to get rid of us quietly? No! Let them come themselves and escort us out."

³⁸The officers reported this to the magistrates, and when they heard that Paul and Silas were Roman citizens, they were alarmed. ³⁹They came to appease them and escorted them from the prison, requesting them to leave the city. ⁴⁰After Paul and Silas came out of the prison, they went to Lydia's house, where they met with the brothers and encouraged them. Then they left.

COMMENTARY

35–36 In the morning the magistrates sent the lictors ("officers") to the prison with an order to release the two vagabond Jews. Since they make no mention of an earthquake during the night, apparently they did not relate it to the situation of Paul and Silas. They had probably only wanted to teach Paul and Silas a lesson about the peril of disturbing the peace in a Roman colony and felt that a public flogging and a night in the city's jail would be sufficient to do that. So they ordered the jailer to release the two Jewish Christian evangelists (v.36).

37 Paul refused to be dealt with so summarily. Claiming the rights of Roman citizenship for himself and Silas, he demanded that they be shown the courtesy due a citizen and be escorted out of the prison by the magistrates themselves. According to the Valerian and Porcian laws, which were passed at various times between 509 BC (the time of the founding of the Roman Republic) and 195 BC, a Roman citizen could travel anywhere within Roman territory under the protection of Rome. He was not subject to local legislation, unless he consented (which was usually the case in business and personal relations); and he could appeal to be tried by Rome, not by local authorities, when in difficulty. As a citizen he owed allegiance directly to Rome, and Rome would protect him. Even Roman governors in the provinces were forbidden, as Arnold H. M. Jones (*Studies in Roman Government and Law* [Oxford: Blackwell, 1960], 54) has pointed out, "to kill, scourge, torture, condemn or put in bonds a Roman citizen who appealed to the people, or to prevent a defendant from presenting himself in Rome within a certain time," with the situation being that "under the principate, appeal to the people was converted into appeal to Caesar, perhaps by the law of 30 BC."

Evidence regarding the exercise of this right of appeal is scanty. Nor do we know how a person who made the claim "I am a Roman citizen" (*civis Romanus sum*) supported that claim. The Roman orator, philosopher, lawyer, and statesman Cicero (106–43 BC), in his second prosecution of Caius Verres in 70 BC, tells of a citizen who was beaten in the marketplace of Messina in Sicily and speaks of it as a disgraceful and illegal procedure (*Verr.* 2.5.161–62). But other than that, most of our information about the Roman right of appeal is supplied

from Acts itself (here in v.37 and at 22:25–29; 25:9–12; 26:32; 27:1; 28:16). Nonetheless, on the basis of the extant evidence, "it would seem that a Roman citizen was protected against arbitrary flogging without trial, and if accused could refuse to submit to trial by appealing to Caesar" (ibid., 54–55).

Paul took pride in his Roman citizenship and valued it highly (cf. 22:25–28)—a stance doubtless shared by Silas. Just why they did not assert their rights earlier we can only conjecture. Perhaps the uproar of the mob and the hubbub of the beating kept their protestations from being heard. But now they claimed their rights as Roman citizens—an action probably not only for their own sakes but also to provide some measure of protection for the few believers who were meeting at Lydia's home.

38–39 To beat and imprison a Roman citizen without a trial was a serious offense. So when the magistrates heard that Paul and Silas were citizens, they came to apologize for their illegal actions and to escort them out of prison. To avoid any further embarrassment or opposition from the crowd, they asked Paul and Silas to leave Philippi. Here was a case where Roman officials took action against the gospel and its messengers. As such, the narrative seems to run counter to Luke's apologetic purpose in Acts (see Introduction, pp. 678–80). But Luke's point is that the magistrates at Philippi had acted in ignorance—and that when they came to understand matters more fully, they apologized and did what they could to avoid repetition of the blunder.

40 After leaving the prison, Paul and Silas met with the small body of Christians (*tous adelphous*, "the brothers," used broadly for "the believers"; cf. 18:18, 27) at the house of Lydia and encouraged them in their new faith. Then they left with Timothy to go westward toward Thessalonica. Apparently, however, Luke stayed at Philippi, for only later in 20:5 does the second "we" section commence—i.e., when Paul and his associates return again to

Philippi at the end of their third missionary journey. By that time, it seems, the little congregation—which had begun so modestly with Lydia and her household, Luke, the slave girl, and the jailer and his family—had grown in size and spirituality. For in the letter Paul later wrote them, he speaks of their "overseers and deacons" (Php 1:1), counsels them as believers growing in maturity, and commends them for their continuing concern for him (cf. Php 2:25–30; 4:10–19).

NOTES

35 The Western text (D, and as reflected in the Syriac Harclean version) expands this verse to read, "But when it was day, the magistrates came into the marketplace [*agora*] and, calling to mind the earthquake that had taken place, they were afraid and they sent the lectors," apparently to explain the magistrates' change of attitude.

36 The Western text (D and a recension of the Old Latin) omits ἐν εἰρήνῃ (*en eirēnē*, "in peace").

37 The Western text (D, and as reflected in the Syriac Peshitta) has ἀναιτίους (*anaitious*, "innocent," GK *360*) instead of the better-supported ἀκατακρίτους (*akatakritous*, "without being guilty," GK *185*; NIV, "without a trial"; NASB, "without trial").

39–40 The Western text (D, and as supported in part by the Syriac Harclean version and Ephraem in his Acts commentary) recasts these verses to read, "And arriving with many friends at the prison, they requested them to go out, saying: 'We did not know the truth about you, that you are righteous men.' And leading them out, they requested them, saying: 'Depart from this city, lest they come together again to us and cry out against you.' So they went out from the prison and visited Lydia. And when they had seen the brothers, they reported the things that the Lord had done for them; and having exhorted them, they departed."

C. At Thessalonica (17:1–9)

¹When they had passed through Amphipolis and Apollonia, they came to Thessalonica, where there was a Jewish synagogue. ²As his custom was, Paul went into the synagogue, and on three Sabbath days he reasoned with them from the Scriptures, ³explaining and proving that the Christ had to suffer and rise from the dead. "This Jesus I am proclaiming to you is the Christ," he said. ⁴Some of the Jews were persuaded and joined Paul and Silas, as did a large number of God-fearing Greeks and not a few prominent women.

⁵But the Jews were jealous; so they rounded up some bad characters from the marketplace, formed a mob and started a riot in the city. They rushed to Jason's house in search of Paul and Silas in order to bring them out to the crowd. ⁶But when they did not find them, they dragged Jason and some other brothers before the city officials, shouting: "These men who have caused trouble all over the world have now come here, ⁷and Jason has welcomed them into his house. They are all defying Caesar's decrees, saying that there is another king, one called Jesus." ⁸When they heard this, the crowd and the city officials were thrown into turmoil. ⁹Then they made Jason and the others post bond and let them go.

COMMENTARY

1 Thirty-three miles southwest of Philippi was Amphipolis, the capital of the northern district of Macedonia between 167–146 BC. Situated on the eastern bank of the Strymon River, it straddled the Via Egnatia. Though it was larger and more important than Philippi, Paul and his companions "passed through" it. As they continued west-southwest on the Via Egnatia, they also passed through Apollonia, some twenty-seven miles beyond Amphipolis. Their desire was to reach Thessalonica, the capital of the province of Macedonia and the largest and most prosperous city in Macedonia, lying another forty miles southwest of Apollonia.

Thessalonica (modern Salonika) was strategically located on the Thermaic Gulf. It too straddled the Via Egnatia. It linked the rich agricultural plains of the Macedonian interior with the land and sea routes to the east. Cicero (*Planc.* 41) in 54 BC described it as "situated in the bosom of our domain." It was probably founded by Cassander in 315 BC and named for his wife, the daughter of Philip II (cf. Strabo, *Geogr.* 7.21), though other traditions trace its foundation to Philip himself and say that it was named either for his daughter or in honor of his victory over the Thessalonians. When Rome conquered Macedonia in 167 BC, Thessalonica became the capital of the second of the four administrative districts of the province. With the reorganization of Macedonia into one province in 142 BC, Thessalonica became its capital. In the second civil war it sided with Mark Anthony and Caius Octavius (later Augustus) against Marcus Junius Brutus and Longinus Cassius, and because of its loyalty it was declared at the close of that war in 42 BC a free city (cf. Plutarch, *Brutus* 46).

As a large city of perhaps two hundred thousand, and one that dominated Macedonian government and commerce, Thessalonica naturally attracted diverse groups of people, including a substantial Jewish contingent (1Th 2:14–16). Paul seems to have viewed it as a strategic center for the spread of the gospel throughout the Balkan peninsula (1Th 1:7–8). Therefore, Paul and Silas, though doubtless in some pain from their recent beating and time in the stocks, pushed on resolutely to travel the 100 miles from Philippi to Thessalonica.

2–3 In portraying the extension of the gospel to the main cities bordering the Aegean Sea, Luke lays emphasis on the fact that Paul's preaching consisted of both proclamation and persuasion—interlocking elements of the one act of preaching. He had struck such a note earlier (cf. 13:43), and it will continue to be heard in 20:9; 24:25; 26:28; and 28:23. Here in panel 5 these features of proclamation and persuasion sound with unmistakable clarity throughout the portrayals of the ministries at Thessalonica (17:2–4), Athens (17:17), Corinth (18:4), and Ephesus (18:19; 19:8–10).

At Thessalonica, the missionaries, true to their policy of "to the Jews first, but also to the Gentiles" (see comments at 13:46–52), sought out the local synagogue, certain of finding there a prepared audience of both Jews and "God-fearing" Gentiles. During the span of three Sabbath days, Paul "reasoned [*dielexato*, GK *1363*] with them from the Scriptures, explaining [*dianoigōn*, GK *1380*] and proving [*paratithemenos*, GK *4192*] that the Christ had to suffer and rise from the dead." "This Jesus I am proclaiming [*katangellō*, GK *2859*] to you is the Christ," he said. Furthermore, Luke tells us in v.4 that some "were persuaded [*epeisthēsan*, GK *4275*] and joined Paul and Silas." The preaching of Paul in the book of Acts in general and at Thessalonica in particular took the form of a "proclaimed witness," i.e., a witness to the facts (1) that Jesus of Nazareth is the Christ, (2) that his suffering and resurrection were in accord with the Scriptures, and (3) that through his earthly ministry and living presence men and women can experience the reign of God in their lives. At times, the proclamation was accompanied by miracles. But though miracles brought quick results, "reason," "explain," "prove," and "persuade" are the operative words to describe Paul's method of preaching—which words also imply his careful dealing with his hearers' questions and doubts.

4 "Some of the Jews were persuaded," but the greater number of those who responded positively to Paul's preaching in the synagogue at Thessalonica were "God-fearing Greeks" (*hoi sebomenoi Hellēnōn*) and "prominent women" (*gynaikes tōn prōtōn*, which probably denotes women of high standing who were the wives of the principal citizens). Jason (the Greek form of the Jewish name Joshua), who is mentioned in v.5 as Paul's host, was probably one of the Jewish converts. Aristarchus and Secundus, who are identified as Thessalonians in 20:4, may have also been converted at this time.

5–7 Just as at Antioch, Iconium, and Lystra, the Jews who did not believe the gospel were incensed at Paul's direct approach to the Gentiles and their response to his preaching. So they stirred up a riot. Their plan was to bring Paul and Silas before "the assembly of citizens" (*ton dēmon*, GK *1322*; NIV, "the crowd"; NASB, "the people") and "the politarchs" (*tous politarchas*, GK *4485*; NIV, "the city officials"; NASB, "the city authorities") on a charge of disturbing the Pax Romana by preaching a *religio illicita* and by advocating another king in opposition to Caesar. But when they could not find Paul and his associates at Jason's house—evidently because Jason and others who believed their message had hidden them—they dragged Jason and some other Christian brothers before the politarchs. Jason was probably a Diaspora Jew (see comment at v.4) who became one of Paul's first converts at Thessalonica. He need not be identified

with the Jason of Romans 16:21, for the name was fairly common.

As a free city, Thessalonica had its governing assembly of citizens, which is probably what Luke had in mind by the use of the term *dēmos* in v.5 (though v.8 speaks of the "crowd" [*ochlos*] somewhat synonymously). The magistrates of Thessalonica were called "politarchs" (*politarchēs*), a title found in inscriptions ranging from the second century BC through the third century AD and applied almost exclusively to Macedonian cities. From five inscriptions referring to Thessalonica, it appears that a body of five politarchs ruled the city during the first century AD—a group that was expanded to a board of six politarchs in the second century (cf. E. D. Burton, "The Politarchs," *American Journal of Theology* 2 [1898]: 598ff.).

The assembly of citizens and the politarchs at Thessalonica would certainly have known of troubles within the Jewish community at Rome in connection with Christianity and of Claudius's edict of AD 49–50 for all Jews to leave that city (cf. Suetonius, *Claud.* 25.4, who speaks of "constant riots at the instigation of *Chrestus*" and tells of the emperor's order of expulsion; see also 18:2). Probably the Jewish opponents of the Christian missionaries played on the fear that such a situation might be duplicated at Thessalonica unless Paul and Silas were expelled. In addition, from their charge that the missionaries proclaimed "another king" (v.7), it may be inferred that they tried to use Paul's preaching of "the kingdom of God" (cf. 14:22; 19:8; 20:25; 28:23, 31) to arouse suspicion that he was involved in an anti-imperial sedition. Indeed, it may be for this reason that Paul avoided the use of "kingdom" and "king" in his latter letters to his converts, lest Gentile imperial authorities misconstrue them to connote opposition to the empire and emperor.

8–9 The charges against Paul and Silas and their companions naturally alarmed the Thessalonian politarchs. They certainly did not want riots like those at Rome in their city. Apparently, however, they found the evidence for the charges scanty. Furthermore, Paul and Silas, against whom the charges were directed, could not be found. So the politarchs took what they thought to be a moderate and reasonable course of action. They made Jason and those with him post a bond, thereby giving assurance that there would be no repetition of the trouble. This probably meant that Paul and Silas had to leave the city and that their friends promised they would not come back—at least not during the term of office of the present politarchs.

When writing his Thessalonian converts a few months later, Paul speaks of desiring to visit them again but of being unable to do so because "Satan stopped us" (1 Th 2:18). Likely Paul had in mind the fact that a bond had been posted assuring his non-return, and therefore his hands were tied. But though he was unable to return, that did not stop either the spread of the gospel or the opposition of the Jews (cf. 1 Th 1:2–10). Amid all the persecutions and difficulties, believers at Thessalonica maintained their faith and witness in a manner that filled Paul with joy when he heard of it (cf. 1 Th 3:6–10).

NOTES

1 Codex Bezae (D) reads κατῆλθον εἰς Ἀπολλωνίδα κἀκεῖθεν εἰς Θεσσαλονίκην (*katelthon eis Apollonida kakeithen eis Thessaloniken*, "they went down to Apollonia, and thence to Thessalonica"), thereby implying that while Paul and his associates "passed through" Amphipolis, they ministered in Apollonia before going on to Thessalonica.

3 Codex Vaticanus (B) is the only textual witness that reads ὁ Χριστός ὁ Ἰησοῦς (*ho Christos ho Iesous*, "the Christ, the Jesus"). This unusual construction has given rise to a number of variant readings: Ἰησοῦς Χριστός (א etc.); Χριστὸς Ἰησοῦς (𝔓[74] A D etc.); Ἰησοῦς ὁ Χριστός (E etc.); ὁ Χριστὸς Ἰησοῦς (Ψ L P Byz); and ὁ Χηριστός (some minuscules). It has also affected modern translations (e.g., NIV, NASB, "This Jesus . . . is the Christ"; NRSV, "this is the Messiah, Jesus").

4 Codex Bezae (D) reads, "And many of the God-fearers adhered to the teaching, and a large number of Greeks and not a few prominent women," thereby including pagan Greeks as well as Gentile "God-fearers" as having responded favorably.

5 Codex Bezae (D) reads οἱ δὲ ἀπειθοῦντες Ἰουδαῖοι συνστρέψαντες τινας ἄνδρας τῶν ἀγοραίων πονηρούς (*hoi de apeithountes Ioudaioi synstrepsantes tinas andras ton agoraion ponerous*, "but the Jews who disbelieved assembled some wicked men of the markets [i.e., the rabble]"), and this reading appears also in the later Byzantine text (H L P and most minuscules) and the TR.

D. At Berea (17:10–15)

¹⁰As soon as it was night, the brothers sent Paul and Silas away to Berea. On arriving there, they went to the Jewish synagogue. ¹¹Now the Bereans were of more noble character than the Thessalonians, for they received the message with great eagerness and examined the

Scriptures every day to see if what Paul said was true. [12]Many of the Jews believed, as did also a number of prominent Greek women and many Greek men.

[13]When the Jews in Thessalonica learned that Paul was preaching the word of God at Berea, they went there too, agitating the crowds and stirring them up. [14]The brothers immediately sent Paul to the coast, but Silas and Timothy stayed at Berea. [15]The men who escorted Paul brought him to Athens and then left with instructions for Silas and Timothy to join him as soon as possible.

COMMENTARY

10 The bail bond that Jason and his friends posted would have been forfeited were Paul and Silas found in their homes. So they sent them on, together with Timothy, to Berea (modern Verria), some fifty miles southwest of Thessalonica by way of Pella. Berea was located in the foothills of the Olympian range south of the Macedonian plain. It was a city of little importance historically or politically, though it had a large population in NT times. It lay south of the Via Egnatia, but with access to the eastern coastal road that ran down to Achaia and Athens. Cicero in 55 BC, in a speech against Lucius Piso, spoke of how the Roman authorities at Thessalonica were so unpopular with the people that when he was on government business he found it wise to sneak into the provincial capital at night and at times withdraw from the storm of complaints to Berea because it was "off the beaten track" (*In Pisonem* 36). On arriving at Berea, Paul and his companions went as usual to the synagogue to proclaim the good news of salvation in Jesus the Christ.

11–12 Luke gave the Jews at Berea undying fame by characterizing them as being "more noble" (*eugenesteroi*, GK *2302*) than the Thessalonian Jews because they tested the truth of Paul's message by the touchstone of Scripture rather than judging it by political and cultural considerations. So they examined the Scriptures daily (*kath' hēmeran*) to see

whether what Paul proclaimed was really true. And many believed (v.12). Among them was probably Sopater, the son of Pyrrhus, who is identified in 20:4 as being from Berea (cf. Ro 16:21). Included among the Berean believers were not only "a number of prominent Greek women" but also "many Greek men" (*tōn Hellēnidōn . . . andrōn ouk oligoi*, lit., "of the Greeks . . . not a few men")—i.e., not just converts from among Gentile "God-fearers" but also converts who were pagan Gentiles.

13–15 The Thessalonian Jews, on hearing that "the word of God" was being preached at Berea, sent a delegation there to stir up the same opposition as at Thessalonica. The believers at Berea recognized that Paul was safe neither at Thessalonica nor anywhere else in the region, evidently because the Thessalonian Jews had the ear of the provincial authorities. So they acted "immediately" (*eutheōs*). Some of them accompanied Paul to a coastal town (e.g., Methone or Dium), as though to sail to some other country. Having thrown their opponents off the track, they then escorted Paul down to the province of Achaia and into the city of Athens, apparently to have him reside there with some of their relatives. As for Silas and Timothy, they remained in Berea since they were not in such danger as was Paul. But when the men who accompanied Paul to Athens returned to Berea, they brought with them a message from Paul telling Silas and Timothy to "join him as soon as possible," doubtless because he saw that Athens was another strategic center for proclaiming the gospel and wanted Silas and Timothy with him when he began.

The movements of Silas and Timothy after Paul left them at Berea are rather difficult to trace, principally because Luke was not always concerned with details of the minor characters in his Acts, but also because Paul's references in his letters to their activities are somewhat incidental and allusive. What can

be reconstructed is that, in accord with Paul's instructions, they both rejoined Paul at Athens (cf. 1 Th 3:1). Then Timothy was sent back to Thessalonica (cf. 1 Th 3:2), but Silas seems to have gone back to Macedonia (cf. 18:5)—probably to Philippi, where he received from the young congregation there a gift of money for the support of Paul and his associates (cf. Php 4:15). In the meantime, Paul had moved from Athens to Corinth (cf. 18:1) and was joined there by Silas and Timothy on their return from Macedonia (cf. 18:5; 1 Th 3:6).

NOTES

11 The Western text (as represented by some minuscules and reflected by various recensions of the Old Latin, Vulgate, and Syriac versions) adds καθὼς Παῦλος ἀπαγγέλλει (kathōs Paulos apangellei, "even as Paul was proclaiming") at the end of the verse after οὕτως (houtōs, "so").

12 On the use of μὲν οὖν (men oun, "so," "then"), see comments and note at 1:6.

Codex Bezae (D) smoothes out the grammar of the generally received text in reading καὶ τῶν Ἑλλήνων καὶ τῶν εὐσχημόνων ἄνδρες καὶ γυναῖκες ἱκανοὶ ἐπίστευσαν (kai tōn Hellēnōn kai tōn euschēmonōn andres kai gynaikes hikanoi episteusan, "and many of the Greeks and men and women of high standing believed"). Not only, however, is this reading better Greek; it also has the effect of toning down the prominence of women by its reversal of order—which is characteristic of the antifeminist tendency of Codex Bezae (see Notes, 17:34; 18:26).

13 Chester Beatty 𝔓⁴⁵ and the Byzantine text (E P and many minuscules), followed by the TR, lack the words καὶ ταράσσοντες (kai tarassontes, "and stirring them up," GK 5429), reading only σαλεύοντες τοὺς ὄχλους (saleuontes tous ochlous, "agitating the crowds," GK 4888, 4063). The omission is probably accidental, i.e., a homoioteleuton (where the eye of a copyist passes from one word to another with the same ending) in reading σαλεύοντες καὶ ταράσσοντες (saleuontes kai tarassontes). Codex Bezae (D) adds at the end of the verse the phrase οὐ διελίμπανον (ou dielimpanon, "they did not stop"), which is a vernacular expression that occurs only in D (here and at 8:24).

14 Whereas the Alexandrian text (𝔓⁷⁴ ℵ A B E etc.) reads ἕως ἐπὶ τὴν θάλασσαν (heōs epi tēn thalassan, "as far as the sea"), the Western text (D, and as reflected in recensions of the Old Latin) reads ἐπὶ τὴν θάλασσαν (epi tēn thalassan, "to the sea") and the Byzantine text (H L P and most minuscules) adds ὡς (hōs, "as it were") to read "as it were to the sea." The Alexandrian text suggests something of a ruse to foil the Jews, and the Byzantine text seems to make this suggestion explicit.

15 Codex Bezae (D) recasts this verse after "Athens" to read, "But he passed by Thessaly [τὴν Θεσσαλίαν, tēn Thessalian], for he was prevented from preaching the word to them. And having received a command from Paul to Silas and Timothy to come to him speedily, they departed." This recasting seems to be an attempt to explain why nothing happened on Paul's journey through Thessaly.

E. At Athens (17:16–34)

OVERVIEW

Paul's coming to Athens appears to have been intended primarily to escape persecution in the province of Macedonia. It seems to have been no part of his original plan to preach at Athens. When called to Macedonia, he had apparently planned to follow the Via Egnatia all the way to the city of Dyrrhachium, then cross the Adriatic to Italy and on to Rome. When writing to the Christians at Rome some six or seven years later, Paul speaks of having often planned to visit them but having been unable to do so (Ro 1:13; 15:22–23). The action of the magistrates at Thessalonica, which was the capital of Macedonia, had effectively thwarted Paul's plans for a continued mission in Macedonia. Fur-

thermore, news of Claudius's expulsion of the Jewish community at Rome (AD 49–50) might very well have caused him to change his plans.

Now Paul was in Athens under circumstances not altogether in accord with what he would have planned. He was waiting for Silas and Timothy to come before beginning any mission in Athens. But the rampant idolatry he saw around him compelled him to present the claims of Christ to Jews and "God-fearing" Gentiles in the synagogue on the Sabbath and to anyone who would listen in the agora or marketplace on weekdays (v.17). As with Jeremiah, God's word burned within him like a fire in his bones (cf. Jer 20:9), and he could not keep silent.

1. Inauguration of a Ministry (17:16–21)

[16]While Paul was waiting for them in Athens, he was greatly distressed to see that the city was full of idols. [17]So he reasoned in the synagogue with the Jews and the God-fearing Greeks, as well as in the marketplace day by day with those who happened to be there. [18]A group of Epicurean and Stoic philosophers began to dispute with him. Some of them asked, "What is this babbler trying to say?" Others remarked, "He seems to be advocating foreign gods." They said this because Paul was preaching the good news about Jesus and the resurrection. [19]Then they took him and brought him to a meeting of the Areopagus, where they said to him, "May we know what this new teaching is that you are presenting? [20]You are bringing some strange ideas to our ears, and we want to know what they mean." [21](All the Athenians and the foreigners who lived there spent their time doing nothing but talking about and listening to the latest ideas.)

COMMENTARY

16 Athens is five miles inland from its port of Piraeus, which is on the Saronic Gulf, an arm of the Aegean Sea that stretches fifty miles between Attica and the Peloponnesus. It is situated on a narrow plain between Mount Parnes to the north, Mount Pentelicus to the east, and Mount Hymettus to the southeast. The city was said to have been founded by Theseus, the hero of Attica who slew the Minotaur and conquered the Amazons, and to have been named in honor of the goddess Athena.

When the Persians tried to conquer Greece in the fifth century BC, Athens played a prominent role in resisting them. Though completely destroyed by the Persians, it quickly recovered. Its fleet, which contributed decisively to the defeat of the Persians, became the basis of a maritime empire. Athens reached its zenith under Pericles (495–429 BC), and during the last fifteen years of Pericles's life the Partheon, numerous temples, and other splendid buildings were built. Literature, philosophy, science, and rhetoric flourished, and Athens attracted intellectuals from all over the world. Politically it became a democracy.

Athens had attained its eminence, however, at the expense of its allies in the Delian Confederacy. In dissatisfaction, many of them began turning to its rival Sparta, with the Peloponnesian War of 431–404 BC finally putting an end to its political supremacy and greatness. Intellectually and culturally, Athens retained its superiority for centuries, with such philosophers as Socrates (ca. 470–399 BC), Plato (ca. 428–348 BC), Aristotle (ca. 384–322 BC), Epicurus (ca. 342–270 BC), and Zeno (ca. 340–263 BC) living and teaching there. In 338 BC, Philip II of Macedonia conquered Athens, but the conquest only served to spread Athenian culture and learning into Asia and Egypt through his son Alexander the Great. The Romans conquered Athens in 146 BC. They were lovers of everything Greek, and under their rule Athens continued as the intellectual and cultural center of the world. Politically, Rome also left the city to carry on her own institutions as a free city within the empire.

When Paul came to Athens, it had long since lost its political importance and wealth. Its population probably numbered no more than ten thousand. Yet it had a glorious past on which it continued to live. Its temples and statuary were related to the worship of the Greek pantheon, and its culture was pagan. So Paul, with his Jewish abhorrence of idolatry, could not but find the culture of Athens spiritually repulsive.

17 The connective *men oun* ("so") introduces a new scene, perhaps tying together Luke's introduction in v.16 with his source material in vv.17–21. Though apparently not wanting to begin a mission in Athens until Silas and Timothy came from Macedonia, Paul could not keep from proclaiming the good news about Jesus the Messiah when he attended the synagogue on the Sabbath. In the synagogue he "reasoned" (*dielegeto*, GK *1363*) with the Jews and "God-fearing" Gentiles. He also continued to proclaim his message in the agora (*tē agora*, GK *59*) every day (*kata pasan hēmeran*) to all who would listen.

The agora lay west of the Acropolis. It was the forum and marketplace of the city, and therefore the center of Athenian life. The commercial sections included the large Stoa of Attalus, which stretched along the eastern side and was flanked by a number of smaller colonnades on the northern and southern sides. The western side consisted of a number of important public buildings and monuments: the circular Tholos, or office and dining room of the Prytaneum; the Bouleuterion, or senate house; the Metroon, or official archives; the temple of Ares;

statues of the eponymous heroes of the city; the temple of Apollo Patroon; and the Stoa Basileios.

18 Athens was the home of the rival Epicurean and Stoic schools of philosophy. Epicurus (342–270 BC) held that pleasure was the chief goal of life, with the pleasure most worth enjoying being a life of tranquillity free from pain, disturbing passions, superstitious fears, and anxiety about death. He did not deny the existence of the gods but argued in deistic fashion that they took no interest in the lives of people. Zeno (340–263 BC) was the founder of Stoicism, which took its name from the "painted Stoa" (i.e., the colonnade or portico) where he habitually taught in the Athenian agora. His teaching focused on living harmoniously with nature and emphasized humanity's rational abilities and individual self-sufficiency. Theologically, he was essentially pantheistic and thought of God as "the World-soul."

Epicureanism and Stoicism represented the popular Gentile alternatives for dealing with the plight of humanity and for coming to terms with life apart from biblical revelation and God's salvific work in Jesus Christ. (Post-Christian paganism in our day has been unable to come up with anything better.) When the followers of Epicurus and Zeno heard Paul speaking in the agora, they began "to dispute with [*syneballon*, GK *5202*; lit., "to converse with," but also "to engage in argument with"] him." Some declared him to be a "babbler" (*spermologos*, GK *5066*)—a word originally used of birds picking up grain, then of scrap collectors searching for junk, then extended to those who snapped up ideas of others and peddled them as their own without any understanding of them, and finally of any ne'er-do-well. Others thought he was advocating foreign gods, probably misunderstanding *anastasis* ("resurrection," GK *414*) as the name of the goddess consort of some god named Jesus.

19–20 The Areopagus (*Areios Pagos*, lit., "Court" or "Council of Ares," the Greek god of thunder and war) reaches back to legendary antiquity. Presumably it first met at Athens on the Hill of Ares (Latin equivalent: "Mars Hill"), northwest of the Acropolis, for murder trials. Early descriptions of processions in ancient Greek city-states depict the Areopagus of the cities as always heading the column of dignitaries, which suggests that the "Court" or "Council of Ares" was the senate or city council of a Greek city-state. At Athens, therefore, while the earlier powers of the Council of Ares were greatly reduced with the demise of the maritime empire, during Roman times it was still the chief judicial body of the city and exercised jurisdiction in such matters as religion and education. The name "Areopagus" survives as the title of the present-day Greek Supreme Court. In Paul's time, its membership consisted of all city administrators ("Archons") who after their term of office were free of official misconduct. Since the fifth century BC, it met in the Stoa Basileios ("the Royal Portico") at the northwest corner of the agora.

It was before this council that the followers of Epicurus and Zeno brought Paul—probably half in jest and half in derision, but certainly not seeking an impartial inquiry after truth. The city fathers, however, took their task seriously, for the fame of Athens rested on its intellectual ferment and the interplay of competing philosophies. So we should doubtless understand Paul's appearance before the Athenian Council of Ares as having the purpose of explaining his message before those in control of affairs in the city so that he might either receive the freedom of the city to preach or be censored and silenced.

21 Luke's comment about the Athenians "doing nothing but talking about and listening to the latest ideas" is paralleled in the evaluation of his fellow Athenians by Cleon, a fifth-century BC politician and general: "You are the best people at being deceived by something new that is said" (Thucydides,

Hist. 2.38.5). The Athenian orator Demosthenes (384–322 BC) also reproached his people for continually asking for new ideas in a day when Philip II of Macedon's rise to power presented the city with a threat calling for actions, not merely words (*Philip* 1.10). And evidently this characterization of the Athenians was widespread, particularly in Macedonia.

NOTES

17 On the use of μὲν οὖν (*men oun*, "so," "then"), see comments and note on 1:6; also vv. 12 and 30 of this chapter. On Luke's emphasis on persuasion in Paul's preaching, particularly in this fifth panel of material, see comments at 17:2–3.

18 The Western text (D, and as represented in a recension of the Old Latin) omits the final explanatory clause ὅτι τὸν Ἰησοῦν καὶ τὴν ἀνάστασιν εὐηγγελίζετο (*hoti ton Iēsoun kai tēn anastasin euēngelizeto*, "because he was preaching about Jesus and the resurrection"), probably because it might be taken by some to class Jesus among the "gods" (δαιμόνια, *daimonia*, GK *1228*) just referred to.

19 Codex Bezae (D) enhances the verse by prefixing it with μετὰ δὲ ἡμέρας τινάς ἐπιλαβόμενοι αὐτοῦ (*meta de hēmeras tinas epilabomenoi autou*, "after some days they took hold of him") and adding πυνθανόμενοι καὶ (*pynthanomenoi kai*, "inquiring and") before ἤγαγον λέγοντες (*ēgagon legontes*, "they were saying").

2. Paul's Address before the Council of Ares (17:22–31)

²²Paul then stood up in the meeting of the Areopagus and said: "Men of Athens! I see that in every way you are very religious. ²³For as I walked around and looked carefully at your objects of worship, I even found an altar with this inscription: TO AN UNKNOWN GOD. Now what you worship as something unknown I am going to proclaim to you.

²⁴"The God who made the world and everything in it is the Lord of heaven and earth and does not live in temples built by hands. ²⁵And he is not served by human hands, as if he needed anything, because he himself gives all men life and breath and everything else. ²⁶From one man he made every nation of men, that they should inhabit the whole earth; and he determined the times set for them and the exact places where they should live. ²⁷God did this so that men would seek him and perhaps reach out for him and find him, though he is not far from each one of us. ²⁸'For in him we live and move and have our being.' As some of your own poets have said, 'We are his offspring.'

²⁹"Therefore since we are God's offspring, we should not think that the divine being is like gold or silver or stone—an image made by man's design and skill. ³⁰In the past God overlooked such ignorance, but now he commands all people everywhere to repent. ³¹For he has set a day when he will judge the world with justice by the man he has appointed. He has given proof of this to all men by raising him from the dead."

COMMENTARY

22–23 Paul does not begin his address before the council by referring to Jewish history or by quoting the Jewish Scriptures, as he did in the synagogue at Pisidian Antioch (cf. 13:16–41). He knew it would be futile to refer to a history that no one knew, or to argue from the fulfillment of a prophecy that no one was interested in, or to quote from a book that no one read or accepted as authoritative. Nor did he develop his argument from the God who gives rain and crops in their season and who provides food for the stomach and joy for the heart, as he did at Lystra (cf. 14:15–17). Rather, he took as his point of departure and his feature of contact an altar he had seen in the city with the inscription *Agnōstō Theō* ("To an Unknown God"). Later, the second-century geographer Pausanias (*Description of Greece* 1.1.4) and the third-century philosopher Philostratus (*Vit. Apoll.* 6.3.5) spoke of altars to unknown gods at Athens, by which they meant either (1) altars to unknown deities generally or (2) altars to individual unknown gods. But while there is insufficient evidence for us to know the nature or number of such altars at Athens or what their dedicatory inscriptions were, it is not surprising that Paul came across such an altar in walking about the city. And Paul used the words of the inscription to introduce his call to repentance.

Many critics have asserted that all of the speeches in Acts—particularly Paul's speech to the Council of Ares—are free compositions by Luke that set out what Luke himself thought Paul would have said. Admittedly, as with every précis, Luke must be seen to have edited the missionary sermons of Paul in Acts. Furthermore, he must be credited with some genius for having highlighted their suitability to their respective audiences (see Introduction, p. 685). But for one who elsewhere said he was willing to be "all things to all men" for the sake of the gospel (1Co 9:22), Paul's approach to his audience in this address is by no means out of character. On the contrary, in his report of Paul's speech to the Council of Ares, Luke gives another illustration of how Paul began on common ground with his hearers and sought to lead them on from that to accept the work and person of Jesus as the apex of God's redemptive work for humanity.

24–25 The substance of Paul's Athenian address concerns the nature of God and the responsibility of people to God. Contrary to all pantheistic and polytheistic notions, God is the one, Paul says, who has created the world and everything in it: he is "the Lord of heaven and earth" (v.24; cf. Ge 14:19, 22). He does not live in temples "built by hands" (*en cheiropoiētois*); nor is he dependent for his existence on anything he has created. Rather, he is the source of life and breath and everything else that humanity possesses (v.25). Earlier in the fifth century BC, Euripides asked, "What house built by craftsmen could enclose the form divine within enfolding walls?" (*Fragments* 968); and in the first century BC, Cicero (*Verr.* 2.5.187) considered the image of Ceres worshiped in Sicily worthy of honor because it was not made with hands but had fallen from the sky. While Paul's argument can be paralleled at some points by the higher paganism of the day, its content is decidedly biblical (cf. 1Ki 8:27; Isa 66:1–2) and its forms of expression are Jewish as well as Greek (cf. Isa 2:18; 19:1; 31:7 [LXX]; *Sib Or.* 4.8–12; Ac 7:41, 48; Heb 8:2; 9:24 on the pejorative use of "built with hands" for idols and temples).

26–27 Contrary to the Athenians' boast that they had originated from the soil of their Attic homeland and therefore were not like other men, Paul affirms the oneness of all people in their creation by one God and their descent from a common ancestor. And contrary to the primitive "deism" that permeated the philosophies of the day, he proclaimed that this God has determined specific times (*prostetagmenous kairous*) for humanity and "the exact places where they should live" (*tas horothesias tēs katoikias*, lit., "the boundaries of their habitation"), so that men and women "would seek him . . . and find him" (v.27).

28 In support of this teaching about the nature and condition of humans, Paul quotes two maxims from the Greek poets. The first comes from a quatrain attributed to the Cretan poet Epimenides (ca. 600 BC), which appeared first in his poem *Cretica* and is put on the lips of Minos, Zeus's son, in honor of his father:

> They fashioned a tomb for thee, O holy and
> high one—
> The Cretans, always liars, evil beasts, idle bellies!
> But thou art not dead; thou livest and abidest
> for ever,
> *For in thee we live and move and have our being.*
> Cited in M. D. Gibson, ed., *Horae Semiticae X*
> (Cambridge: Cambridge Univ. Press, 1913), 40;
> italics mine.

The second is from the Cilician poet Aratus (ca. 315–240 BC): "It is with Zeus that every one of us in every way has to do, *for we are also his offspring*" (*Phaenomena* 5; italics mine). The allusion is also found in Cleanthes's (331–233 BC) earlier *Hymn to Zeus*, line 4.

Paul is not suggesting by the use of such maxims that God is to be thought of in terms of the god Zeus of Greek polytheism or Stoic pantheism. Rather, he is arguing that the poets whom his hearers recognized as authorities have at least to some extent corroborated his message. In his search for a measure of common ground with his hearers, he is, so to speak, disinfecting and rebaptizing the words of two Greek poets for his own purposes. Quoting these Greek poets in support of his teaching sharpened his message for his particular audience. But despite its form, Paul's address was thoroughly biblical and Christian in its content. It is perhaps too strong to say that "the remarkable thing about this famous speech is that for all its wealth of pagan illustration its message is simply the Galilean gospel, 'The kingdom of God is at hand; repent and believe the tidings'" (Charles S. C. Williams, 206). Nonetheless, there is nothing in the speech that militates against Paul's having delivered it or that is in genuine opposition to his letters.

29–31 The climax of the address focuses on the progressive unfolding of divine redemption and the apex of that redemption in Jesus Christ. Being "God's offspring"—not, of course, in a pantheistic sense, but in the biblical sense of being created by God in his image—we should not, Paul insists, think of deity in terms of gold, silver, or stone (v.29). All that idolatrous ignorance was in the past overlooked by God (v.30; cf. 14:16; Ro 3:25), for God has always been more interested in repentance than judgment (cf. Wis 11:23: "But you have mercy on all men, because you have power to do all things, and you overlook the sins of men to the end that they may repent"). Nevertheless, God has now acted in the person and work of Jesus in such a manner as to make idolatry particularly heinous. To reject Jesus, therefore, is to reject the personal and vicarious intervention of God on behalf of humanity and to open oneself up to divine judgment, which will be meted out in the future by the very one who is being rejected in the present (v.31). For God himself has authenticated the person and redemptive work of Jesus by raising him from the dead.

NOTES

26 The Western text (D E) and Byzantine text (L P), together with a number of early versions (e.g., recensions of the Old Latin and Syriac) and church fathers (e.g., Irenaeus, Chrysostom, Theodoret), read ἐξ ἑνὸς αἵματος (*ex henos haimatos*, "from one blood") rather than the shorter Alexandrian text (𝔓74 ℵ A B and Vulgate and Coptic Sahidic versions) reading ἐξ ἑνός (*ex henos*, "from one [man]"). The Western and Byzantine readings were incorporated into the TR and so appear in the KJV. Most text critics, however, prefer the Alexandrian reading and view the inclusion of αἵματος (*haimatos*, "blood") as a pious expansion.

27 Codex Bezae (D), and as reflected in recensions of the Old Latin and by such church fathers as Irenaeus, Clement, and Ambrose, reads μάλιστα ζητεῖν τὸ θεῖόν ἐστιν (*malista zētein to theion estin*, "especially to seek the divine being") rather than the better-supported (𝔓74 ℵ A B L Ψ etc.) reading ζητεῖν τὸν θεόν (*zētein ton theon*, "to seek God"). Evidently the scribe of D sought to bring this verse into agreement with τὸ θεῖον (*to theion*, "the divine being") in v.29, with the use of the superlative μάλιστα (*malista*, "most of all, above all, especially") also suggesting its secondary character. Codex E (sixth-century Western text) and Codex P (ninth-century Byzantine text) read ζητεῖν τὸν κύριον (*zētein ton kyrion*, "to seek the Lord").

28 Clement of Alexandria (*Strom.* 1.14.59) attributed "the Cretans, always liars, evil beasts, idle bellies!" of Titus 1:12 to Epimenides. The Syriac version of this quatrain comes to us from the Syrian church father Isho'dad of Mero (probably based on the work of Theodore of Mopsuestia), which J. R. Harris (*Expositor* 7 [1907]: 336) translated back into Greek.

Codex Vaticanus (B) and Bodmer 𝔓74 read ἡμᾶς ποιητῶν (*hēmas poiētōn*, "our poets"), which seems strange since it appears to have Paul identify himself as a Greek. Perhaps ἡμᾶς (*hēmas*, "our") was included to take into account the fact that both Aratus and Paul were from Cilicia. Or perhaps it resulted from a scribal confusion between ὑμᾶς (*hymas*, "your") and ἡμᾶς (*hēmas*, "our"), which were pronounced alike.

Some Western witnesses (Syriac Peshitta, Armenian and Ethiopic versions) omit ποιητῶν (*poiētōn*, "poets"), evidently because of an aversion to quoting Greek poets.

30 On the use of the connective μὲν οὖν (*men oun*, "so," "then"), see comments and note at 1:6; also vv.12 and 17 of this chapter.

31 The Western text (D, and as represented by some recensions of the Old Latin and Irenaeus) adds Ἰησοῦ (*Iēsou*, "Jesus") after ἐν ἀνδρί (*en andri*, "by the man")—which is a typical Western expansion.

3. The Response to Paul's Address (17:32–34)

³²When they heard about the resurrection of the dead, some of them sneered, but others said, "We want to hear you again on this subject." ³³At that, Paul left the Council. ³⁴A few men became followers of Paul and believed. Among them was Dionysius, a member of the Areopagus, also a woman named Damaris, and a number of others.

COMMENTARY

32 While the resurrection of Jesus from the dead was the convincing proof to the early Christians and Paul that "God was reconciling the world to himself in Christ" (2Co 5:19), to the majority of Athenians it was the height of folly. Five hundred years earlier, the tragic poet Aeschylus (525–456 BC), when describing the institution of the Athenian Council of Ares, represented the god Apollo as saying, "When the dust has soaked up a man's blood, once he is dead, there is no resurrection" (*Eumenides* 647–48). If Paul had only talked about the immortality of the soul, he would have gained the assent of most of his audience—except, of course, the Epicureans. But the idea of resurrection was to most Greeks simply absurd. Outright scorn was the response of some of his hearers. Others, probably expressing more politeness than any real curiosity or conviction, suggested that they would like to hear Paul on the subject at another time.

33–34 Paul obviously failed to convince the council of the truth of his message—and so, it seems, failed to gain the right to propagate his views. The official response of the council was to hold the matter in abeyance for a time. But Paul could tell from this first meeting that sentiment was against him. Some, of course, did believe, for God always has his few in even the most difficult of situations. Among them were Dionysius, who was himself a member of the Council of Ares, and a woman named Damaris. But because no action had been taken to approve Paul's right to continue teaching in the city, his hands were legally tied. All he could do was either (1) wait in Athens until the council gave him the right to teach there or (2) move on to some other place where his message would be more favorably received. With a vast territory yet to be entered and a great number of people yet to be reached, Paul chose the latter. We hear of no church at Athens in the apostolic age. And when Paul speaks of "the first converts [*aparchē*, lit., "the firstfruits," GK *569*] in Achaia," it is to "the household of Stephanas" in the city of Corinth that he refers (1Co 16:15).

NOTES

34 Dionysius of Corinth (ca. AD 171) is cited by Eusebius (*Hist. eccl.* 3.4.11; 4.23.3) as saying that Dionysius, who was a member of the Council of Ares and the first named convert at Athens, was the first bishop of the church at Athens. But that is probably only an inference drawn a century later from the text itself.

Codex Bezae (D) adds εὐσχήμων (*euschēmōn*, "prominent," "of high standing") after "a member of the Council of Ares." Elsewhere in Acts, however, that identification is used only of women (cf. 13:50; 17:12). Codex Bezae (D) also omits καὶ γυνὴ ὀνόματι Δάμαρις (*kai gynē onomati Damaris*, "also a woman named Damaris"), which omission reflects the antifeminist attitude of the scribe of D (cf. 17:12; 18:26).

REFLECTIONS

Many have claimed that Paul's failure at Athens stemmed largely from a change in his preaching (as seen in his address before the Council of Ares), and that later at Corinth he repudiated such an approach (as witnessed by his words in 1Co 1:18–2:5). He spoke, they charge, (1) about providence and being "in God," but forgot the message of grace and being "in Christ"; (2) about creation and appealed to the Greek poets, but did not refer to redemption or revelation; (3) about world history, but not salvation history; and (4) about resurrection, but not the cross. We should remember, however, that going to Athens was not part of Paul's original missionary strategy, nor did he expect to begin work there until Silas and Timothy joined him from Macedonia. Moreover, there were, in fact, some converts at Athens, and we should not minimize the working of God's Spirit or Paul's message simply because only a few responded or because we do not know what happened to them afterward. Admittedly, the outreach of the gospel at Athens was cut off before it really began, and in overall terms the Christian mission in the city must be judged a failure. But the reason the gospel did not take root there probably lay more in the attitude of the Athenians themselves than in Paul's approach or in what he said.

F. At Corinth (18:1–17)

OVERVIEW

Paul's coming to Corinth was "in weakness and fear, and with much trembling" (1Co 2:3). Though he had been directed through a vision to minister in Macedonia (cf. Ac 16:9–10), the mission had not gone at all as he had expected. Nor had his initial attempt to minister in the province of Achaia provided him with any reason to hope for a change of fortunes. In fact, matters seemed to have gone from bad to worse at Athens, where he was dismissed with polite contempt rather than being either welcomed or violently driven out. So he must have traveled from Athens to Corinth in a somewhat dejected mood, wondering what worse could happen and why God had allowed matters to fall out so badly. Furthermore, he was almost sick with anxiety over the state of his Thessalonian converts, whom he had been forced to leave with the threat of persecution hanging over them (cf. 1Th 2:17–3:5).

This anxiety probably played a part in preventing Paul, while at Athens, from fully grasping the opportunities at hand. (Compare 2Co 2:12–13, where in a parallel situation he speaks of intense concern for the Corinthians as having prevented him from starting a mission at Troas.) Anxiety, in fact, seems to have weighed on him and driven him into a state of depression. Paul was only human, and he found that his emotions affected his spiritual well-being and his work. Furthermore, he may have been ill during much of this period from the effects of the beating at Philippi, which would undoubtedly have contributed further to his emotional depression. Perhaps it was at this time that he prayed repeatedly for deliverance from his "thorn in [the] flesh" (cf. 2Co 12:7–10) but God said to him, "My grace is sufficient for you, for my power is made perfect in weakness" (2Co 12:9).

As we read Luke's account of Paul's ministry at Corinth in the light of the apostle's own Corinthian letters, we cannot help but conclude that Luke has provided his readers with only a brief summary of what occurred there. More than anywhere else in the accounts of Paul's missionary activities the situation at Corinth is difficult to ascertain, simply because in his letters Paul provides so much allusive material about his relations with believers at Corinth and Luke gives so little data in Acts. Consequently, theories are rampant regarding historical, personal, and literary relationships between Paul and the church at Corinth. Furthermore, there are wide differences of purpose between Paul and Luke in their Corinthian materials because Paul's concern was principally pastoral and Luke's mainly apologetic. Here in Acts 18 Luke is chiefly interested in the proceedings before Gallio (vv.12–17). He presents that situation (1) to demonstrate that one of the wisest of the Roman proconsuls declared Christianity to be a *religio licita* and (2) to warn that if Rome began to persecute the church, it would be acting contrary to Gallio, a Roman official renowned for his judgment, urbanity, and wit.

1. Arrival at Corinth (18:1–4)

¹After this, Paul left Athens and went to Corinth. ²There he met a Jew named Aquila, a native of Pontus, who had recently come from Italy with his wife Priscilla, because Claudius had ordered all the Jews to leave Rome. Paul went to see them, ³and because he was a tentmaker as they were, he stayed and worked with them. ⁴Every Sabbath he reasoned in the synagogue, trying to persuade Jews and Greeks.

COMMENTARY

1 Corinth was on a plateau overlooking the isthmus connecting central Greece to the north with the Peloponnesus to the south. It was built on the northern side of the Acrocorinth, which was an acropolis that rose precipitously to 1,886 feet and provided an almost impregnable fortress for the city. To the east was the port of Cenchrea on the Saronic Gulf, which led to the Aegean Sea; to the west the port of Lechaeum on the Gulf of Corinth, which opened to the Adriatic Sea. In order to avoid the long and dangerous trip around Cape Malea at the southern tip of the Peloponnesus, small ships were actually dragged over wooden rollers across the isthmus for the 3 1/2 miles between the port cities of Cenchrea and Lechaeum. The cargoes of large ships were carried overland from port to port.

Because of its strategic land and sea location, Corinth became a prosperous city-state in the eighth century BC. During the seventh and sixth centuries BC, it reached the zenith of its prestige and power, with a population numbering approximately two hundred thousand free men and five hundred thousand slaves. In the fifth century BC, however, because of the imperialism of Athens, it declined in importance and size—though the Peloponnesian War of 431–404 BC, which was won by Sparta and her associates, was disastrous for both. In 338 BC, the city was captured by Philip II of Macedon, who made it the center of his Hellenic League, and from the death of Alexander the Great to the rise of Roman influence in Greece, it became a leading member of the Achaian League of Greek city-states. For a time it was the chief city of that league. In 196 BC, Corinth was captured by the Romans and declared a free city. In 146 BC, however, as retribution for the leading part it played in the revolt of the Achaian League against Rome, it was leveled to the ground by the general Lucius Mummius and its population sold into slavery. For one hundred years, the city lay in ruins until Julius Caesar decreed in 46 BC that it should be rebuilt. It was refounded as a Roman colony in 44 BC, and in 27 BC it became the capital of the Roman province of Achaia.

The population of Corinth in NT times was probably over two hundred thousand—at least twenty times the population of Athens—and was made up of local Greeks, freedmen from Italy, Roman army veterans, businessmen and governmental officials, and Orientals from the Levant. Counted among its Orientals was a large number of Jews. Thanks to its commercial advantages at the convergence of land and sea trade routes, the city greatly prospered. But along with its wealth and luxury there was immorality of every kind. Beginning in the fifth century BC, the verb "to Corinthianize" (*korinthiazesthai*) meant to be sexually immoral—a reputation that continued to be well deserved by Corinth in Paul's day.

Corinth was the center for the worship of the goddess Aphrodite, whose temple with its one thousand sacred prostitutes crowned the Acrocorinth. At the foot of the Acrocorinth stood the temple of Melicertes (the Greek name for Melkart, the principal god of Tyre), who was considered the god of sailors. Temples to Apollo and to Asclepius, the god of healing, have also been found in the ruins of the first-century city, and there were undoubtedly many more such pagan shrines at Corinth. The city became a favorite of the Roman emperors. Every two years the pan-Hellenic Isthmian Games were held in the city and presided over by its administrators.

2–3 Entering this large and thriving city, Paul may have asked a passerby where he could find a master tentmaker or leatherworker (*skēnopoios*, GK *5010*) from whom he could seek a job so that he could support himself by his trade. Jewish law directed that young theological students be taught a trade (cf. *m.* ʾ*Abot* 2:2; see Str-B, 2.745–46), and on his various missionary journeys Paul frequently earned his living as a tentmaker and leatherworker (cf. 20:34; 1Co 9:1–18; 2Co 11:7–12; 1Th 2:9; 2Th 3:7–10). So he came in contact with the Jewish-Christian couple Aquila and Priscilla, with whom he lived and worked—presumably alongside other journeymen in their shop.

Aquila was a native of Pontus, a region in northern Asia Minor on the southern shore of the Black Sea. Priscilla is the diminutive of the more formal name Prisca. Luke's habit is to use the colloquial, diminutive form of names (e.g., Silas, Sopater, Priscilla, Apollos), whereas Paul usually refers to his friends by their more formal names (e.g., Silvanus, Sosipater, Prisca, Epaphroditus), though in certain situations Paul also speaks of some of his friends more popularly (e.g., Apollos, Epaphras). Since Priscilla is often listed before her husband (18:18–19, 26; Ro 16:3; 2Ti 4:19), we may conclude that she came from a higher social class than her husband or was in some way considered more important. Perhaps Aquila was a former Jewish slave who became a freedman in Rome and married a Jewess connected with the Roman family Prisca (*gens Prisca*), which had citizenship rights. Together, perhaps through Aquila's craftsmanship and Priscilla's money and contacts, they seem to have established a tentmaking and leatherworking firm with branches of the business at Rome, Corinth, and Ephesus (cf. 18:2, 18–19, 26; Ro 16:3; 1Co 16:19; 2Ti 4:19).

Aquila and his wife, Priscilla, had been forced to leave Rome, evidently because of the Edict of Claudius—an expulsion order proclaimed during the ninth year of Emperor Claudius's reign (i.e., January 25, AD 49, to January 24, AD 50) and directed against Jews in Rome in order to put down the riots arising within the Jewish community there (cf. Suetonius, *Claud.* 25.4: "As the Jews were indulging in constant riots at the instigation of Chrestus, he banished them from Rome"). The "Chrestus" of whom Suetonius speaks may have been an otherwise unknown agitator who was active in Jewish circles within Rome in the 40s (the Greek name *Chrestos* means "useful" or "kindly" and was a common name for slaves in the Greco-Roman world). Probably, however, the Roman biographer and historian Suetonius, writing seventy years after the event, had no clear idea of who this "Chrestus" really was and assumed him to be a local troublemaker, whereas the dispute in the Jewish community was really about Jesus Christ and between those who favored his messiahship and those who rejected it.

We do not know whether Aquila and Priscilla had any part in the riots either as agitators or victims. They are not identified as Paul's converts either in Acts or in Paul's letters. Probably they had been converted to Christianity at Rome. If Priscilla herself was from a family with Roman citizenship, she might not have been included under Claudius's expulsion order. But her husband, if a former Jewish slave and now a freedman, would have been—and Priscilla had cast her lot with him.

Luke's hero, however, is Paul, and he treats minor characters only as they come into contact with Paul.

As for Paul, he calls Priscilla and Aquila his "fellow workers in Christ Jesus"; speaks of their having "risked their lives for me" (probably at Ephesus, cf. 19:23–41); and says of them, "Not only I but all the churches of the Gentiles are grateful to them" (Ro 16:3–4). All of this suggests that he considered them close and loyal friends and that their services to the Christian cause far exceeded their assistance to him.

4 While working with Aquila and Priscilla, Paul attended the local synagogue every Sabbath. There, Luke tells us, "he reasoned" (*dielegeto*, GK *1363*) with those gathered, "trying to persuade" (*epeithen*, GK *4275*) both Jews and Gentiles. But his ministry during those weeks seems to have been relatively unobtrusive, probably conforming to the kind of witness Aquila and Priscilla were already carrying on among their Jewish compatriots. As was his intention at Athens—though he was unable to hold to it there—Paul may have wanted to refrain from a more aggressive ministry at Corinth until Silas and Timothy could join him.

NOTES

1 On μετὰ ταῦτα (*meta tauta*, "after these things" [NASB]; NIV, "after this") as vying with μὲν οὖν (*men oun*, "so," "then") in the latter half of Acts to designate the beginning of a new section and connect it with what has gone before, see comments at 15:36.

Codices A E P, many minuscules, and a number of versions add ὁ Παῦλος (*ho Paulos*, "Paul") to clarify the subject of the verb. "The insertion of the subject," as Metzger, 408, notes, "was apparently made in the interest of clarifying the passage when it was read as the opening sentence of an ecclesiastical lesson. Certainly if the words ὁ Παῦλος [*ho Paulos*] were present originally, no one would have deleted them." Modern translations, which work with chapter and verse designations, also begin this section with "Paul" for much the same reason (so NIV, NRSV).

3 On σκηνοποιός (*skēnopoios*) as meaning both "tentmaker" (etymology) and "leatherworker" (usage), see J. Jeremias, "Zöllner und Sünder," *ZNW* 30 (1931): 299.

Codices Sinaiticus (א) and Vaticanus (B), evidently followed by the Coptic Sahidic and Bohairic versions, has the third person plural aorist intransitive verb ἠργάζοντο (*ērgazonto*, "they worked," GK *2237*), which is probably an accommodation to the plural forms that immediately precede and follow.

4 On Luke's emphasis throughout panel 5 on persuasion in Paul's preaching—which appears here in his use of the verbs διαλέγομαι (*dialegomai*, "reason") and πείθω (*peithō*, "persuade")—see comments at 17:2–3.

The Western text (D, and as represented by recensions of the Old Latin and Syriac versions) adds καὶ ἐντιθεὶς τὸ ὄνομα τοῦ κυρίου Ἰησοῦ (*kai entitheis to onoma tou kyriou Iēsou*, "and he inserted the name of the Lord Jesus") after διελέγετο (*dielegeto*, "he reasoned"), thereby suggesting that as Paul read the OT Scriptures he would insert the name of Jesus where appropriate.

2. An Eighteen-Month Ministry (18:5–11)

⁵When Silas and Timothy came from Macedonia, Paul devoted himself exclusively to preaching, testifying to the Jews that Jesus was the Christ. ⁶But when the Jews opposed Paul and became abusive, he shook out his clothes in protest and said to them, "Your blood be on your own heads! I am clear of my responsibility. From now on I will go to the Gentiles."

⁷Then Paul left the synagogue and went next door to the house of Titius Justus, a worshiper of God. ⁸Crispus, the synagogue ruler, and his entire household believed in the Lord; and many of the Corinthians who heard him believed and were baptized.

⁹One night the Lord spoke to Paul in a vision: "Do not be afraid; keep on speaking, do not be silent. ¹⁰For I am with you, and no one is going to attack and harm you, because I have many people in this city." ¹¹So Paul stayed for a year and a half, teaching them the word of God.

COMMENTARY

5 The coming of Silas and Timothy to Corinth altered the situation for Paul. They brought good news about the believers at Thessalonica (cf. 1Th 3:6) and a gift of money from the congregation at Philippi (cf. 2Co 11:9; Php 4:14–15). The news from Thessalonica was better than Paul dared to expect, and it greatly comforted and encouraged him (cf. 1Th 3:7–10)—though it evidently also told of a slanderous campaign that had been mounted against him from those outside of the congregation (1Th 2:3–6) and of some perplexity within the church concerning the return of Christ (1Th 4:13–5:11).

The money from Philippi was especially welcome at this time. Therefore, with his spirits lifted by the report of his Thessalonian converts' spiritual well-being and the gift from Philippi providing him freedom from earning a living, "Paul devoted himself exclusively to preaching" (*syneicheto tō logō ho Paulos*, lit., "Paul held himself to the word"). That the verb *syneicheto* (GK *5309*) is reflexive (middle voice), durative (imperfect tense), and inchoative (a function of the imperfect) suggests that with the coming of Silas and Timothy, Paul began to devote himself exclusively to the ministry of the word and that he continued to do so throughout his stay at Corinth. His initial purpose was to proclaim the good news to the Jews of the synagogue, and his message to them was that Jesus is "the Christ" (*ton Christon*, lit., "the Messiah").

It was in response to the report of Silas and Timothy that Paul wrote the letter now identified as

1 Thessalonians, in which are interwoven (1) commendation for growth, zeal, and fidelity; (2) encouragement in the face of local persecution; (3) defense of his motives against hostile attack; (4) instruction regarding holiness of life; (5) instruction about the coming of the Lord; and (6) exhortation to steadfastness and patience. Some weeks later, on learning of continued confusion at Thessalonica regarding the return of Christ and the believers' relation to it, he wrote 2 Thessalonians. In that second letter, while acknowledging that believers live in eager expectation of the Lord's return, Paul insists that imminency must not be construed to mean immediacy but is rather the basis for dogged persistence in doing right.

6 The ministry at Corinth followed the pattern set at Pisidian Antioch (cf. 13:46–52) of initial proclamation in the synagogue, rejection by the majority of Jews, and then a direct outreach to Gentiles. In solemn biblical style (cf. Ne 5:13), Paul "shook out his clothes"—an act that symbolized repudiation of the Jews' opposition, exemption from further responsibility for them (cf. 13:51), and protest against what he considered their "blasphemy" (*blasphēmountōn*, GK *1059*; NASB, "blasphemed"; NIV, "became abusive"; NRSV, "reviled him"; cf. 13:45; 26:11).

7 Leaving the synagogue (*metabas ekeithen*, lit., "leaving from there"), Paul went next door to the house of Titius Justus, a "God-fearing" Gentile ("worshiper of God") who had been receiving instruction at the synagogue (i.e., a *sebomenos ton theon*; cf. 13:50; 16:14; 17:4, 17). He invited Paul to make his home the headquarters for his work in Corinth, presumably because he believed Paul's message. The house of Titius Justus thus became the first meeting place of the Corinthian church.

Though the textual tradition varies as to the form of the name of Paul's host (see Notes), we should probably read it in line with the better MSS as "Titius Justus." With two names, he was doubtless

a Roman citizen and may have been from a family brought in by Julius Caesar to colonize Corinth. Many have plausibly argued that while his Roman nomen was Titius and his cognomen Justus, his praenomen was probably Gaius, and so he should be identified with the Gaius of Romans 16:23 of whom Paul says, "whose hospitality I and the whole church here [at Corinth] enjoy" (cf. William M. Ramsay, *Pictures of the Apostolic Church* [London: Hodder & Stoughton, 1910], 205 n. 2; E. J. Goodspeed, "Gaius Titius Justus," *JBL* 69 [1950]: 382–83). In 1 Corinthians 1:14, Paul speaks of a Gaius he personally baptized at the inauguration of his Christian ministry in Corinth. Presumably he was referring to this man, who after being expelled from the synagogue hosted the Christian mission when it needed a center.

8 One of the first to accept Paul's message at Corinth was Crispus, the leader or ruler of the synagogue (*ho archisynagōgos*, GK *801*), who together with his whole household "believed in the Lord." He was not the first believer at Corinth (Stephanas and his family were; cf. 1Co 16:15). But he was certainly one of the most prominent believers, and his conversion must have made a great impression and led to other conversions. Paul lists him first in 1 Corinthians 1:14–16 among the few whom he had personally baptized.

9–10 Paul had come to Corinth in a dejected mood, burdened by the problems in Macedonia and his dismissal at Athens. He had, of course, been encouraged by the reports and the gift brought by Silas and Timothy, and he was beginning to witness a significant response to his ministry. But a pattern had developed in his Galatian and Macedonian missions of a promising start, which was followed by opposition strong enough to force him to leave. Undoubtedly he was beginning to wonder whether such a pattern would be repeated at Corinth. So one night God graciously gave Paul a vision in which "the Lord" (*ho kyrios*—evidently Jesus, as in 23:11) encouraged him not to be afraid but to keep on, assured him of his presence, promised him that he would suffer no harm, and told him that "many people" in the city were to be Christ's own. Here was one of those critical periods in Paul's life when he received a vision strengthening him for what lay ahead (cf. 23:11; 27:23–24). In this case, it was confirmed by the Gallio incident that followed it.

11 With such a promising start and encouraged by the vision, Paul continued to minister at Corinth for "a year and a half" (*eniauton kai mēnas hex*)—a figure that should be understood to indicate the entire length of his stay. This period probably stretched from the fall of 50 to the spring of 52, as can be determined from the pericope about Gallio in vv.12–17. So Luke summarizes the whole of Paul's original mission at Corinth by telling us that for eighteen months he taught in the city "the word of God" (*ton logon tou theou*), i.e., the message about Jesus, belief in whom brings forgiveness of sins, salvation, and reconciliation with God.

NOTES

5–6 The Western text (D, and as represented by recensions of the Old Latin and Syriac versions) characteristically inserts at the end of v.5 the title κύριον (*kyrion*, "the Lord") before the name Ἰησοῦν (*Iēsoun*, "Jesus") and at the beginning of v.6 adds πολλοῦ δὲ λόγου γινομένου καὶ γραφῶν διερμηνευομένων (*pollou de logou ginomenou kai graphōn diermēneuomenōn*, "but when there had been much discussion and the Scriptures had been interpreted").

7 Codex Bezae (D), as reflected also in some recensions of the Old Latin, reads ἀπὸ Ἀκύλα (*apo Akyla*, "from Aquila") rather than ἐκεῖθεν (*ekeithen*, "from there"), suggesting that Paul moved his personal lodgings as well as the venue for his mission to the home of Titius Justus. Probably, however, all Luke means is the latter, and we should visualize Paul and his associates as still residing with Aquila and Priscilla.

B and 𝔓⁷⁴ read Τιτίου Ἰούστου (*Titiou Ioustou*, "Titius Justus"); ℵ and E read Τίτου Ἰούστου (*Titou Ioustou*, "Titus Justus"); A and D read only Ἰούστου (*Ioustou*, "Justus"); and various Latin and Coptic recensions read only Τίτου (*Titou*, "Titus"). The argument that "Titius" arose by dittography from the last two letters of ὀνόματι (*onomati*, "by the name of"), which appears immediately before, is weakened by the fact that ὀνόματι (*onomati*) does not appear in A, which is the chief support for the omission of both "Titius" and "Titus." It is more probable to suppose that later scribes changed Titius to the easier Titus (as ℵ and E) or omitted it altogether (as A and D).

8 On the office and function of ὁ ἀρχισυνάγωγος (*ho archisynagōgos*, "the ruler of the synagogue"), see comments at 13:15 (cf. Lk 8:41, 49; Ac 18:17).

For other instances of the conversion of members of a household with the head of the household, cf. 10:2–48; 11:14; 16:15, 31–34; 1Co 16:15.

10 On ὁ λαός (*ho laos*, "the people," GK *3295*) in Luke-Acts as usually referring to Israel as the elect nation to whom the message of redemption is initially directed and for whom it is ultimately intended, see 2:47; 3:9; 4:10; 5:13. Here however, as in 15:14, it is used of "the new people of God," which includes Gentiles (cf. Tit 2:14; 1Pe 2:9–10).

3. Before the Proconsul Gallio (18:12–17)

¹²While Gallio was proconsul of Achaia, the Jews made a united attack on Paul and brought him into court. ¹³"This man," they charged, "is persuading the people to worship God in ways contrary to the law."

¹⁴Just as Paul was about to speak, Gallio said to the Jews, "If you Jews were making a complaint about some misdemeanor or serious crime, it would be reasonable for me to listen to you. ¹⁵But since it involves questions about words and names and your own law—settle the matter yourselves. I will not be a judge of such things." ¹⁶So he had them ejected from the court. ¹⁷Then they all turned on Sosthenes the synagogue ruler and beat him in front of the court. But Gallio showed no concern whatever.

COMMENTARY

12 The promise given Paul in the vision (v.10) was that he would be protected from harm at Corinth, not that he would be free from all difficulties or any attack. The statement *oudeis epithēsetai soi tou kakōsai* of v.10 is probably best understood as, "You will not be harmed by anyone's attacks" (NEB text note), or, "No one will be able to harm you" (TEV). As more and more people responded to Paul's preaching, his Jewish opponents attacked him and laid a charge against him (v.12). This occurred, Luke says, "while Gallio was proconsul of Achaia" (see Notes).

The facts that Luke (1) distinguishes correctly between senatorial and imperial provinces, and (2) speaks of the former as governed by a proconsul on behalf of the senate and the latter by a propraetor representing the emperor says much for his accuracy, for the status of provinces changed with the times. Achaia was a senatorial province from 27 BC to AD 15 and then again from AD 44 onwards, as were Cyprus from 22 BC and Asia from 84 BC (see comments at 13:4; 19:1). Achaia, therefore, was governed by a proconsul, as were also Cyprus and Asia during this time (see comments at 13:7; 19:38). Macedonia, however, was an imperial province, and

Luke rightly calls the magistrates at Philippi "praetors" (Latin, *praetores*; Greek, *stratēgoi* [GK *5130*]; see comments at 16:12, 22–24), while he identifies the rulers at Thessalonica by the special designation of "politarchs" (see comments at 17:6).

Gallio was the son of Marcus Annaeus Seneca (50 BC–AD 40), a distinguished Spanish rhetorician. He was also a younger brother of Lucius Annaeus Seneca (4 BC–AD 65), the Stoic philosopher, politician, and dramatist. He was born in Cordova at the beginning of the Christian era and named Marcus Annaeus Novatus. On coming to Rome with his father during the reign of Claudius (AD 41–54), he was adopted by the Roman rhetorician Lucius Junius Gallio and thereafter bore the name of his adoptive father. He was renowned for his personal charm. His brother Seneca once said of him, "No mortal is so pleasant to any person as Gallio is to everyone" (*Naturales quaestiones* 4a, Preface 11), and Cassius Dio spoke of his wit (*Hist.* 61.35).

An inscription at Delphi recording a reply from the emperor Claudius to the people of Delphi mentions Gallio as being proconsul of Achaia during the period of Claudius's twenty-sixth acclamation as imperator—a period known from other inscriptions to have covered the first seven months of AD 52. Proconsuls entered office in the senatorial provinces on July 1, and so it is reasonable to assume that Gallio became proconsul of Achaia on July 1, 51. He was not, however, proconsul of Achaia for very long. Seneca (*Ep.* 104.1) tells us that soon after becoming proconsul Gallio went on a cruise to rid himself of a recurring fever; and Pliny the Elder (*Nat.* 31.33) speaks of him as later (probably in AD 55 or 56) taking another cruise from Rome to Egypt to relieve his asthma. In AD 65, along with his brother Mela (the father of the poet Lucan) and after the enforced suicide of his older brother Seneca, he became a victim of Nero's suspicions and was killed (Cassius Dio, *Hist.* 62.25.3).

13 Paul seems to have been preaching in Corinth for eight or nine months—from the fall of 50 to July 1, 51—before Gallio came to Achaia as proconsul. When Gallio took office, the Jews decided to test the new proconsul. So they brought Paul before him on a charge that he was "persuading the people to worship God in ways contrary to the law." In the context of a trial before a Roman proconsul, such a charge meant acting contrary to Roman law by proclaiming a *religio illicita*. The Greek text says that they brought Paul *epi to bēma* (GK *1037*), which has been variously translated as "before the judgment seat" (NASB), "to the judgment seat" (KJV), "before the tribunal" (NRSV, JB), or "into court" (NEB, TEV, NIV), all of which are attempts to translate the expression into a form suitable to modern ears. "The Bema" (*to bēma*) at Corinth, however, was a large, raised platform that stood in the agora or marketplace in front of the residence of the proconsul and served as a forum where he tried cases.

The word "law" (*nomos*, GK *3795*) in the Jewish accusation against Paul is used somewhat ambiguously. When used by Paul's antagonists in their synagogue it would have referred to God's law, against which they were convinced Paul was speaking. But at the proconsul's forum they undoubtedly meant "law" to be understood as Roman law, which they charged Paul was breaking.

15–16 After hearing the charges, Gallio was not at all convinced that Paul had broken Roman law. For him the squabble was an intramural one having to do with questions *peri logou kai onomatōn kai nomou tou kath' hymas* ("about a word [NIV, NASB, "words"] and names and your own law"), which undoubtedly means disputes about (1) "a message" (*logos*, GK *3364*) being proclaimed by Jews, not some political action disruptive to Roman society; (2) "names" (*onomata*, GK *3950*) having to do with an expected Jewish Messiah; and (3) particular interpretations of the Jewish law. Gallio's responsibility, as he saw it, was to judge civil and criminal cases, not to become the arbitrator of intramural Jewish religious disputes. What Paul was preaching, in his view, was simply a variety of Judaism that did not happen to suit the leaders of the Jewish community at Corinth, but which was not for that reason to be declared *religio illicita*. Thus he did not need to hear Paul's defense but ejected the plaintiffs from the forum as not having a case worth being heard by a proconsul (v.16).

17 Taking their cue from the snub Gallio gave the leaders of the Jewish community, the crowd—in an outbreak of the anti-Semitism that always lay near the surface in the Greco-Roman world—took Sosthenes, the synagogue ruler, and beat him in the marketplace "before the forum" (*emprosthen tou bēmatos*; NIV, "in front of the court"). Gallio turned a blind eye to what was going on, evidently because he wanted to teach a lesson to those who would waste his time with such trivialities. Large Jewish synagogues sometimes had more than one leader or ruler (see comments at 13:15), and Sosthenes may have served jointly with Crispus (before his conversion) in the local synagogue chapter at Corinth.

Or perhaps he took Crispus's place after the latter's conversion. Perhaps he became a Christian and is the Sosthenes of 1 Corinthians 1:1 who served as Paul's amanuensis or secretary in writing the Corinthian believers from Ephesus, though that is only conjecture.

NOTES

12 The Western text (D, and as represented by recensions of the Old Latin and Syriac versions) inserts after οἱ Ἰουδαῖοι (*hoi Ioudaioi*, "the Jews") the words συνλαλήσαντες μεθ' ἑαυτῶν ἐπὶ τὸν Παῦλον, καὶ ἐπιθέντες τὰς χεῖρας ἤγαγον αὐτόν (*synlalēsantes meth' heautōn epi ton Paulon, kai epithentes tas cheiras ēgagon auton*, "having talked together among themselves against Paul, and having laid hands on him")— which is a typical Western expansion. The Western text (though not D here) also reads ἤγαγον αὐτὸν πρὸς τὸν ἀνθύπατον (*ēgagon auton pros ton anthypaton*, "they brought him to the proconsul"), evidently unable to understand the expression ἐπὶ τὸ βῆμα (*epi to bēma*, "to the Bema").

13 The Western text (D, and as reflected in recensions of the Old Latin and Syriac versions) expands λέγοντες (*legontes*, "saying"; NIV, "they charged"; NASB, "saying") to read καταβοῶντες καὶ λέγοντες (*kataboōntes kai legontes*, "shouting and saying").

14 The Western text expands the vocative ὦ Ἰουδαῖοι (*ō Ioudaioi*, "O Jews") to read ὦ ἄνδρες Ἰουδαῖοι (*ō andres Ioudaioi*, "O men, Jews").

17 The Western and Byzantine texts read πάντες οἱ Ἕλληνες (*pantes hoi Hellēnes*, "all the Greeks"), thereby making explicit the subject (as does TR and so KJV). The tenth- and eleventh-century minuscules 307 and 431 read πάντες οἱ Ἰουδαῖοι (*pantes hoi Ioudaioi*, "all the Jews"), which is surely an error of interpretation.

The Latin text of bilingual Bezae (D)—the Greek text being erased and not now legible, though it may be assumed it corresponded to the Latin—has the last sentence of this verse as follows: "Then Gallio pretended not to see."

REFLECTIONS

The importance of Gallio's decision for the outreach of the gospel to the Gentile world was profound. Luke highlights it in his account of Paul's ministry at Corinth and makes it the apex from an apologetic perspective of all that took place on Paul's second missionary journey. Earlier in Macedonia, there had been no vindication by Roman authorities of Christianity's claim to share in the *religio licita* status of Judaism. At Athens as well, the issue had been left entirely unresolved. Now at Corinth, if Gallio had accepted the Jewish charge and found Paul guilty of the alleged offense, provincial governors everywhere would have had a precedent and Paul's ministry would have been severely restricted. But Gallio's refusal to act in the matter was tantamount to Rome's recognition of Christianity as a *religio licita*, and the decision of so eminent a Roman proconsul would carry weight wherever the issue arose again and give pause to those who might want to oppose the Christian movement. Later, in the 60s, Rome's policy toward both Judaism and Christianity would be reversed. But for the coming decade or so, the Christian message could be proclaimed in the provinces of the empire without the threat of coming into conflict with Roman law, thanks largely to Gallio's decision.

G. An Interlude between the Journeys (18:18–28)

OVERVIEW

The ministry at Corinth proceeded without any legal hindrance and with considerable success for some nine months after Gallio's important decision. In the spring of 52, however, Paul left Corinth to return to Jerusalem and then to Syrian Antioch, principally, it seems, to complete a vow at Jerusalem that he had taken earlier (probably while at Corinth). In vv.18–23, Luke summarizes Paul's travel and activities while en route. And in vv.24–28, he uses this interlude in his portrayal of the advance of the good news to the Gentile world to introduce Apollos (cf. 1Co 3:5–9; 4:6–7; 16:12).

1. Paul's Return to Palestine-Syria (18:18–23)

[18]Paul stayed on in Corinth for some time. Then he left the brothers and sailed for Syria, accompanied by Priscilla and Aquila. Before he sailed, he had his hair cut off at Cenchrea because of a vow he had taken. [19]They arrived at Ephesus, where Paul left Priscilla and Aquila. He himself went into the synagogue and reasoned with the Jews. [20]When they asked him to spend more time with them, he declined. [21]But as he left, he promised, "I will come back if it is God's will." Then he set sail from Ephesus. [22]When he landed at Caesarea, he went up and greeted the church and then went down to Antioch.

[23]After spending some time in Antioch, Paul set out from there and traveled from place to place throughout the region of Galatia and Phrygia, strengthening all the disciples.

COMMENTARY

18 Luke's brevity in this part of Acts has left open to many the reason for Paul's leaving Corinth and sailing for Jerusalem and then returning to the church at Syrian Antioch. The reading of the Western and Byzantine texts at v.21, "I must by all means keep the coming festival at Jerusalem," assumes that Paul wanted to be in Jerusalem for either the Passover or Pentecost. John Knox, on the other hand, supposes that Paul returned to Jerusalem at this time to attend the Jerusalem Council—which he dates to AD 51 and finds depicted in Galatians 2:1–10—and that Luke plays down this purpose here because he had already (and mistakenly) depicted the Jerusalem Council in 15:1–29 (cf. J. Knox, *Chapters in a Life of Paul* [New York: Abingdon, 1950], 68–69; see also J. C. Hurd Jr., "Pauline Chronology and Pauline Theology," in *Christian History and Interpretation*, ed. W. R. Farmer, C. F. D. Moule, and R. R. Niebuhr [Cambridge: Cambridge Univ. Press, 1967], 225–48). A large part of Knox's rationale is that he cannot believe that the issue of Gentile freedom was only finally settled so late in Paul's ministry. But Luke himself may well suggest the real reason for Paul's present travel to Jerusalem when he tells his readers that Paul "had his hair cut off at Cenchrea because of a vow he had taken"—though as a Gentile writing to Gentiles, he probably felt no need to expand on such a distinctly Jewish practice.

The fact that Paul had cut his hair at Cenchrea suggests that he had earlier taken a Nazirite vow for a particular period of time that was now ended. Such a vow had to be fulfilled at Jerusalem, where the hair would be presented to God and sacrifices offered (cf. Nu 6:1–21; *m. Naz.* 1:1–9:5; Josephus, *J.W.* 2.313). Some have proposed that Paul cut off his hair at the beginning of his vow. But there is no evidence for this, and much of the literature about Nazirite vows speaks directly against it. Others have called this a "Nazirite-like" vow, feeling somewhat uneasy with Paul at any time in his Christian ministry taking a Jewish vow. But for one who thought of himself as a Jewish Christian (2Co 11:22; cf. Ro 9–11) and who at the conclusion of three missionary journeys to the Gentile world could still insist that he was "a Pharisee, the son of a Pharisee" (Ac 23:6; cf. 26:5), such an action should not be thought strange.

Evidently, it may be conjectured, at some time during his residence at Corinth—perhaps at its beginning when he was depressed—Paul had taken a Nazirite vow to God as he asked for his intervention. And now, having seen God's hand at work in Corinth and a thriving church established there, Paul was determined to return to Jerusalem to fulfill his vow by presenting his hair as a burnt offering and by offering sacrifices in the temple (cf. 21:26). The vow could only be fulfilled after a thirty-day period of purification in the Holy City (cf. *m. Naz.* 3:6, according to the more lenient ruling of the school of Shammai).

19 Boarding a ship at Cenchrea, Paul crossed to Ephesus, the major commercial center and capital of the Roman province of Asia. With him were Priscilla and Aquila, his hosts at Corinth, who were now either transferring their business from Corinth to Ephesus or leaving their Corinthian operation in charge of a manager (as possibly they did earlier at Rome) in order to open a new branch at Ephesus. Perhaps Priscilla and Aquila, who seem to have been fairly well-to-do, paid Paul's passage as they joined him on board the ship for Ephesus. Perhaps they also paid his passage on to Jerusalem. Being themselves Jewish Christians, they would have appreciated Paul's desire to fulfill his vow at Jerusalem.

What happened to Silas and Timothy during this time we do not know. They may have remained at Corinth to carry on the ministry there. Or perhaps they went with Paul to Jerusalem, then to Antioch in Syria, and later came back to Ephesus. Less likely is the suggestion that they sailed to Ephesus with Paul and then stayed with Priscilla and Aquila while awaiting his return.

On arriving at Ephesus, Priscilla and Aquila set about their business in the city. There they were to remain for four or five years, during which time they hosted a congregation of believers in their home and sent their greetings back to their Corinthian friends in one of Paul's letters (cf. 1Co 16:19). They were probably there during Demetrius's riot (cf. Ac 19:23–41) and even risked their lives to protect Paul (cf. Ro 16:4). Sometime after Claudius's death in AD 54 (perhaps 56), they probably returned to Rome (cf. Ro 16:3). Paul, however, having wanted earlier to minister at Ephesus (cf. Ac 16:6), went to the synagogue and "reasoned" (*dielexato*, GK *1363*) with the Jews gathered there. Though it was not the Sabbath, he knew he could find an audience in the synagogue and probably desired to test the waters in anticipation of his later return.

20–21 Paul found a receptive audience in the synagogue at Ephesus. But though they encouraged him to stay, he seems to have felt that fulfilling his vow at Jerusalem took priority over everything else. Nevertheless, he promised to return if it were in the will of God. So with a heart lightened by the prospect of a future ministry at Ephesus, he sailed for Jerusalem.

22 Some have suggested that the ship Paul sailed on was really trying to make harbor at Seleucia, the port of Syrian Antioch, but under a heavy north-northeastern spring gale found it easier to land at Caesarea, some 250 miles farther south. But this assumes Paul wanted only to return to Syrian Antioch, and it discredits the capability of ancient navigation for the sake of a theory. Paul, however, probably booked passage for Caesarea, the port city of Jerusalem since the time of Herod the Great (see comments at 10:1). It was there that he finally disembarked.

From Caesarea, Paul "went up" to Jerusalem, some sixty-five miles southeast. Since the name "Jerusalem" does not appear in the text, some have supposed that Luke only meant that Paul went up from the harbor at Caesarea into the city to greet the congregation there. But Jerusalem is certainly implied by the expressions "went up" (*anabas*, GK *326*) and "went down" (*katebē*, GK *2849*), as well as by the absolute use of the term "the church" (*hē ekklēsia*, GK *1711*). At Jerusalem, he met with the mother church, from which the gospel had spread to both Jews of the Diaspora and Gentiles in the Greco-Roman world. In addition, and in accord with fulfilling his aim in

coming, he entered into a thirty-day program of purification (cf. *m. Naz.* 3:6), after which he presented his shorn hair to God in thanksgiving and offered sacrifices. Then he "went down" to Antioch of Syria, some 300 miles north, reporting to and ministering within the church that had originally commissioned him to reach the Gentiles.

23 Luke tells us that Paul remained at Syrian Antioch for "some time," probably from the summer of AD 52 through the spring of AD 53. Then, on what was to be his third missionary journey, he set out for Ephesus, some 1,500 miles to the west, and revisited on the way the churches "throughout the region of Galatia and Phrygia, strengthening all the disciples." The readings "the region of Phrygia and Galatia" (16:6) and "the region of Galatia and Phrygia" (as here) seem to be only stylistic variations for the same locality. Here, as in 16:6, the expression probably means the Phrygian region of Galatia or some district in southern Galatia where both Phrygian and Celtic (Galatic or Gaulish) dialects could be heard (see comments at 16:6). There is no warrant in this verse for supposing that Paul entered the country around Ancyra, Pessinus, or Tavium. It is also most reasonable to assume that the expression "strengthening all the disciples" refers to converts made at Pisidian Antioch, Iconium, Lystra, and Derbe.

NOTES

18 A fifth-century recension of the Old Latin (it^h) has Aquila as the one who made a vow and cut his hair at Cenchrea, whereas many MSS of the Vulgate have Aquila and Priscilla, obviously not wanting to attribute to Paul such an action. But while the Greek word order may allow for either Aquila alone or Aquila and Priscilla together to be the subject(s), Luke usually does not provide such details regarding a secondary figure in his portrayals. For a fuller treatment of "The Problem Practices of Acts," see my *Paul, Apostle of Liberty*, 245–63.

19 Bodmer 𝔓^74, codices P and Ψ, and most minuscules read κατήντησεν (*katēntēsen*, "he arrived" or "came"), which was picked up by the TR and incorporated into the KJV, evidently to conform to the other verbs in the context. The better textual tradition (‭א‬ A B E etc.) has κατήντησαν (katēntēsan, "they arrived" or "came").

Codex Bezae (D), followed in part by various Western witnesses, inserts τῷ ἐπιόντι σαββάτῳ (tō epionti sabbatō, "on the following Sabbath") between καί (kai, "and") and the pronoun ἐκείνους (ekeinous, "they") of the conflated κἀκείνους (kakeinous, "and they"). But Paul did not visit synagogues only on the Sabbath.

On Luke's emphasis in panel 5 on persuasion in Paul's preaching, here by the use of the verb διαλέγομαι (dialegomai, "to reason"), see comments at 17:2–3.

21 Codex Bezae (D), as well as a fifth-century recension of the Old Latin and the eighth-ninth-century Codex Ψ, add δεῖ δὲ [or με] πάντως τὴν ἑορτὴν τὴν ἡμέραν ἐρχομένην ποιῆσαι εἰς Ἱεροσόλυμα (dei de [or me] pantōs tēn heortēn tēn hēmeran erchomenēn poiēsai eis Hierosolyma, "I must by all means keep this feast that comes today in Jerusalem"). The addition is undoubtedly an interpolation, for it is not supported by the earlier and better textual tradition (𝔓⁴⁵ ‭א‬ A B E etc.). Nonetheless, it is paralleled by a similar statement in 20:16 and so likely captures the real reason for Paul's desire to go to Jerusalem and his hasty departure from Ephesus.

22 On the reverential use of the verbs ἀναβαίνω (anabainō, "go up") and καταβαίνω (katabainō, "go down") in connection with Jerusalem, see comments at 3:1 and 8:5 (also note); cf. also 11:27.

2. Apollos at Ephesus and Corinth (18:24–28)

²⁴Meanwhile a Jew named Apollos, a native of Alexandria, came to Ephesus. He was a learned man, with a thorough knowledge of the Scriptures. ²⁵He had been instructed in the way of the Lord, and he spoke with great fervor and taught about Jesus accurately, though he knew only the baptism of John. ²⁶He began to speak boldly in the synagogue. When Priscilla and Aquila heard him, they invited him to their home and explained to him the way of God more adequately.

²⁷When Apollos wanted to go to Achaia, the brothers encouraged him and wrote to the disciples there to welcome him. On arriving, he was a great help to those who by grace had believed. ²⁸For he vigorously refuted the Jews in public debate, proving from the Scriptures that Jesus was the Christ.

COMMENTARY

24 Between the time of Paul's stopover at Ephesus (18:19–21) and his return to the city on his third missionary journey (19:1–20), Apollos came to Ephesus. A native of Alexandria, he was an educated man (anēr logios, which came also to connote "an eloquent man"; NIV, "a learned man"; NASB, "an eloquent man") who possessed a thorough knowledge of the Jewish Scriptures.

25–26 Somewhere and somehow Apollos had received instruction about Jesus, and up to a point he knew the gospel "accurately" (*akribōs*, GK 209). What he knew he accepted. And he spoke about Jesus "with great fervor" (NIV) or "fervent in spirit" (NASB, taking *tō pneumati*, "in the spirit" [GK 4460], to refer to Apollos's own spirit). Yet when Priscilla and Aquila heard Apollos in the synagogue, they recognized some deficiencies in his understanding of the Christian message. So they invited him to their home and explained "the way of God [*tēn hodon tou theou*] more accurately" (the comparative *akribesteron*; so NASB; NIV, "more adequately").

Apollos's knowledge of Jesus seems to have come through disciples of John the Baptist ("he knew only the baptism of John," v.25), either when he was in Alexandria or somewhere else in the empire (perhaps even at Ephesus). Presumably he knew that Jesus of Nazareth was the Messiah and something of Jesus' earthly ministry, but he may have known nothing more. When instructed further by Priscilla and Aquila, Apollos readily accepted all that God had done in the death and resurrection of Jesus and in sending the Holy Spirit at Pentecost. There is no suggestion that he was then baptized—or, as some might expect, rebaptized. As with Jesus' disciples, probably Apollos's earlier baptism of repentance was considered Christian baptism when viewed as pointing to Jesus, and so was not redone every time there was a growth in understanding. Nothing is said about his having received the Holy Spirit, though the nature of his later ministry leads to that assumption.

27–28 A number of people who identified themselves in some way with the gospel were at Ephesus before Paul began his ministry there—people such as Priscilla and Aquila, who understood clearly; Apollos, whose understanding was growing; or those mentioned in 19:1–7, 13–16, whose faith was to some extent deviant. So when Apollos desired to visit Achaia, apparently on behalf of the gospel, the believers at Ephesus (*hoi adelphoi*, lit., "the brothers"; cf. 16:40; 18:18) encouraged him and sent a letter of commendation, probably written by Priscilla and Aquila, to the believers at Corinth. There Apollos vigorously debated with the Jews and showed from the OT that Jesus was the Messiah (*ton Christon*). Chapters 1–4 of 1 Corinthians indicate how highly Apollos was thought of in the Corinthian church and also how highly he was respected by Paul. Perhaps, as Martin Luther first suggested (*Luther's Works*, ed. J. Pelikan and H. T. Lehman [Saint Louis: Concordia, 1958–67], 29.109–241), the letter to the Hebrews is an example of Apollos's biblical argumentation to a group of Jewish Christians who were in danger of lapsing back to their former Jewish commitments.

NOTES

24 Codex Sinaiticus (א), a number of minuscules, and such church fathers as Didymus and Ammonius call him Ἀπελλῆς (*Apellēs*, "Apelles"); Codex Bezae (D) has Ἀπολλώνιος (*Apollōnios*, "Apollonius"); and the Vulgate has "Apollo." The name "Apelles" seems to have been an Egyptian preference, "Apollonius" the more formal name, and "Apollo" the Latinized version. See the note at 19:1.

25 The Western text (D, and as represented by a recension of the Old Latin) adds ἐν τῇ πατρίδι (*en tē patridi*, "in his native land") after the participle κατηχημένος (*katēchēmenos*, "he had been instructed"), thereby specifying that his conversion through the agency of disciples of John the Baptist had taken place in Alexandria.

26 The Western text (D, and as represented by recensions of the Old Latin, Syriac, Coptic, and Armenian versions) reverses the names Priscilla and Aquila to read "Aquila and Priscilla," in line with its antifeminist attitude reflected in 17:12, 34 (see notes at those verses). Though unusual in antiquity to refer to a wife before her husband, it was customary in the early church to refer to Priscilla before Aquila (cf. Ro 16:3; 2Ti 4:19; see comments at 18:2–3).

27 Codex Bezae (D), supported in large part by a Syriac marginal reading, recasts this verse to read, "And certain Corinthians who were residing at Ephesus heard him [Apollos] and requested him to cross over with them to their native land. And when he consented, the Ephesians wrote to the disciples at Corinth to receive the man. And when he took up residence in Achaia, he was of great help to the churches." Such a recasting was apparently felt necessary in order to clarify certain perceived ambiguities in Luke's more concise account. But textual support for this reading is meager. Furthermore, Metzger, 415, has observed, "If Apollos's visit is made at his own initiative, an introductory letter recommending him to the Corinthians is appropriate; if, on the other hand, he goes at the invitation of members of the Corinthian church, why is it necessary that the Ephesians supply such a letter?"

28 The Western text ($\mathfrak{P}^{38}$ D, a number of minuscules, and a recension of the Old Latin) characteristically expands ἐπιδεικνύς (*epideiknys*, "proving") to read διαλεγόμενος καὶ ἐπιδεικνύς (*dialegomenos kai epideiknys*, "reasoning and proving").

H. At Ephesus (19:1–19)

OVERVIEW

The third missionary journey of Paul was chiefly devoted to an extended ministry at Ephesus, which was the city he had earlier hoped to reach at the start of his second journey. On his brief visit there less than a year before, the people of Ephesus had shown a real response to Paul's Christian proclamation. In all, the apostle's Ephesian ministry lasted about three years, from approximately AD 53 through AD 56. Luke's account of this ministry, however, is much abbreviated, with only a short summary of five verses (vv.8–12) sandwiched between two rather striking vignettes of a deviant kind of faith (vv.1–7, 13–19).

1. Twelve Men without the Spirit (19:1–7)

¹While Apollos was at Corinth, Paul took the road through the interior and arrived at Ephesus. There he found some disciples ²and asked them, "Did you receive the Holy Spirit when you believed?"

They answered, "No, we have not even heard that there is a Holy Spirit."

³So Paul asked, "Then what baptism did you receive?"

"John's baptism," they replied.

[4]Paul said, "John's baptism was a baptism of repentance. He told the people to believe in the one coming after him, that is, in Jesus." [5]On hearing this, they were baptized into the name of the Lord Jesus. [6]When Paul placed his hands on them, the Holy Spirit came on them, and they spoke in tongues and prophesied. [7]There were about twelve men in all.

COMMENTARY

1 Ephesus was on the western coast of Asia Minor at the mouth of the Cayster (or Little Meander) River and between the Koressos mountain range and the Aegean Sea. It was founded in the twelfth or eleventh century BC by Ionian colonists from Athens as a gateway to the vast resources of the Asian steppes. In its early days it was a secondary port to Miletus thirty miles south at the mouth of the Meander River. But when Miletus's harbor became clogged with silt and Miletus itself was destroyed by the Persians, commerce and power shifted to Ephesus. In 334 BC Alexander the Great captured Ephesus at the start of his "drive to the East." From Alexander's death to 133 BC it was ruled by the Pergamum kings, the most dynamic and powerful of the lesser rulers of Alexander's divided empire. With the looming inevitability of a Roman takeover, Attalus III, the last of the kings of Pergamum, willed the city to Rome at his death, and Ephesus was made the capital of the newly formed Roman province of Asia.

Ephesus relied on two important assets for its wealth and vitality. The first was its position as a center of trade, linking the Greco-Roman world with the rich hinterland of western Asia Minor. But because of excessive lumbering, charcoal burning, and overgrazing, the topsoil slipped into streams, streams were turned into marshes, and storm waters raced to the sea laden with silt that choked the river's mouth. The Pergamum kings promoted the maintenance of the harbor facilities at Ephesus, and Rome followed suit. But it was a losing battle against the unchecked erosion of the hinterland. In Paul's day, the zenith of the city's commercial power had long since past. Deepening economic decline had cast a long shadow over the city. Efforts were repeatedly made to improve the harbor, with a large-scale attempt being undertaken in AD 65, but such efforts either failed or provided only temporary relief. Domitian at the end of the first century AD was the last ruler to attempt to repair the harbor's facilities and to enlarge its dwindling capacities. Today the mouth of the Cayster River is so choked with silt that the ancient harbor works of Ephesus sit back behind a swamp some seven miles from the sea.

The second factor that the life of Ephesus depended on was the worship of Artemis (the Roman goddess Diana), the multibreasted goddess of fertility whose temple was one of the Seven Wonders of the ancient world. The relation of Artemis of Ephesus to the Greek goddess Artemis is somewhat difficult to determine. Though quite different in their distinctive characteristics, in the popular mind they were often equated. King Croesus of nearby Lydia (reigned 564–546 BC) built the first temple to Artemis 1.5 miles northeast of Ephesus. It was rebuilt on the same site in the fourth century BC after having been set on fire in 356 BC. This temple was almost four times the size of the

Parthenon at Athens and stood until the Goths sacked Ephesus in AD 263. With the decline of its commerce, the prosperity of Ephesus became more and more dependent on tourism and the pilgrim trade associated with the temple and cult of Artemis. At the time of Paul's arrival, the people of Ephesus—while surrounded by evidences of past wealth and still enjoying many of its fruits—were becoming increasingly conscious of the precariousness of their position as a commercial and political center, and so were turning more toward the temple of Artemis in support of their economy.

After revisiting the churches of Galatia (cf. 18:23), Paul "took the road through the interior" (NIV; NASB, "passed through the upper country" [*dielthonta ta anōterika merē*, lit., "going through the interior districts"]) and came to Ephesus. He arrived after Apollos had left for Corinth and entered the city probably in the summer of AD 53. There he found "about twelve men" (v.7) who professed to be Christian "disciples" (*mathētai*, GK *3412*) but in whom Paul discerned something amiss.

2–3 The question Paul put to the twelve, "Did you receive the Holy Spirit when you believed?" suggests two things: (1) that he assumed they were truly Christians, since they professed to believe; and (2) that he held that true belief and the reception of the Holy Spirit went together, being unable to be separated either logically or chronologically. These two assumptions caused Paul some difficulty when he met these twelve men, for something in their lives indicated that one or the other was wrong. When they answered, "We have not even heard that there is a Holy Spirit," Paul knew the second assumption was not in error. So he asked further about the first one and found that they claimed to have been baptized only with "John's baptism" (v.3).

The account is extremely difficult to interpret, principally because it is so brief. Probably we should assume that these twelve men, while considering themselves Jewish-Christian "disciples" in some sense, thought of John the Baptist as the apex of divine revelation—perhaps even as the Messiah himself. John 1:19–34 and 2:22–36 are directed against anyone thinking of the Baptist as superior to Jesus. Together with an emphasis on "one Lord, one faith, one baptism" in Ephesians 4:5, these passages suggest that a John the Baptist sect existed within Jewish-Christian circles in Asia in the first century (assuming, of course, Ephesian connections for both the fourth gospel and the letter to the Ephesians). As in any such group, particularly before issues became defined and positions solidified, some would have appreciated John the Baptist and yet looked forward to the greater fulfillment of which he spoke, whereas others would have gone no further in their devotion than the Baptist himself—honoring him as an equal with Jesus or perhaps even considering him greater than Jesus.

Apollos seems to have been among those of the first category. Though he became a convert to Jesus through the ministry of disciples of John the Baptist, he had been taught "accurately" and needed only that Priscilla and Aquila teach him "more accurately" (18:25–26 NASB). Though, as Luke says, he knew "only the baptism of John," he evidently considered John's message as a prolegomenon to the reception of God's Messiah. Thus when he was taught about Jesus' redemptive ministry and its resultant implications, he readily accepted such further teaching.

The twelve men Paul met, however, apparently made the Baptist the focus of their devotion. Luke calls them "disciples," just as he speaks of Simon of Samaria as having "believed" (8:13), of the Judaizers at Jerusalem as "believers" (15:5), of the seven sons of Sceva at Ephesus as exorcising demons "in the name of Jesus" (19:13), and of Sceva their father as "a Jewish chief priest" (19:14)—i.e., he describes them phenomenally as to how they represented themselves, not analytically or by means of hypotheses with respect to their true condition. Luke's practice, it seems, was to portray the spiritual condition of his characters by their actions without always evaluating it. Here it seems—both from their own statements and from how Paul deals with them—that we should consider these twelve so-called Christian "disciples" as sectarians who thought highly of John the Baptist but had no real commitment to Jesus.

4–6 Despite their being known as disciples, Paul preached Jesus to these twelve men as he would to any Jew or Gentile. "John's baptism," he said, "was a baptism of repentance," which pointed beyond itself and the Baptist to "the one coming after him"—to Jesus (v.4). So on acceptance of Jesus as the focus of their religious experience, they were baptized "into the name of the Lord Jesus" (*eis to onoma tou kyriou*

Iēsou, v.5). Then Paul laid his hands on them and they received the Holy Spirit, as evidenced by the same signs of the Spirit's presence as at Pentecost, namely, tongues and prophecy (v.6). In Paul's mind, it seems, these former devotees of John the Baptist, whatever they might have called themselves, were not now being "rebaptized" but were simply being baptized once and for all into Christ. When baptism by John the Baptist was seen as pointing beyond itself to Jesus (as with Apollos), it was apparently accepted as Christian baptism by the early church and not repeated whenever a believer learned or experienced more of the Christian faith. But when John's baptism was understood as rivaling commitment to Jesus, then, on profession of faith in Jesus, Christian baptism "into the name of the Lord Jesus" was administered.

NOTES

1 The Western text ($\mathfrak{P}^{38}$ D, with partial support from recensions of the Old Latin and Syriac versions) deletes the first clause of the verse, ἐγένετο δὲ ἐν τῷ τὸν Ἀπολλῶ εἶναι ἐν Κορίνθῳ (*egeneto de en tō ton Apollō einai en Korinthō*, "while Apollos was at Corinth"), and reads instead, θέλοντος δὲ τοῦ Παύλου κατὰ τὴν ἰδίαν βουλὴν πορεύεσθαι εἰς Ἱερουσόλυμα εἶπεν αὐτῷ τὸ πνεῦμα ὑποστρέφειν εἰς τὴν Ἀσίαν, διελθὼν δὲ τὰ ἀνωτέρικα μέρη ἔρχεται εἰς Ἔφεσον (*thelontos de tou Paulou kata tēn idian boulēn poreuesthai eis Hierousolyma eipen autō to pneuma hypostrephein eis tēn Asian, dielthōn de ta anōterika merē erchetai eis Epheson*: "Although Paul wished, according to his own plan, to go to Jerusalem, the Spirit told him to return to Asia, and having passed through the upper country he comes to Ephesus"). Evidently the Western reviser took "the church" of 18:22 to be the Caesarean church and so rewrote 19:1 to explain why Paul did not carry out his plans, as per the Western reading, of 18:21 (cf. 16:6–7).

Instead of Ἀπολλῶ (*Apollō*, "Apollos" in the dative), Codex Sinaiticus (ℵ), a number of minuscules, and such church fathers as Didymus and Ammonius have Ἀπελλῆν (*Apellēn*, "Apelles" in the dative; see note at 18:24); $\mathfrak{P}^{74}$, corrected Alexandrinus (A), and some minuscules read Ἀπολλῶν (*Apollōn*).

5 On the synonymous use of the prepositions ἐπί (*epi*, "on"), ἐν (*en*, "in"), and εἰς (*eis*, "into") with Christian baptism, see note at 2:38.

The Western text (D, some minuscules, and as reflected in a recension of the Syriac version) expands εἰς τὸ ὄνομα τοῦ κυρίου Ἰησοῦ (*eis to onoma tou kyriou Iēsou*, "into the name of the Lord Jesus") by adding Χριστοῦ (*Christou*, "Christ") and then continuing with the clause εἰς ἄφεσιν ἁμαρτιῶν (*eis aphesin hamartiōn*, "so that your sins may be forgiven"), evidently in an attempt to parallel the wording of 2:38.

6 For other instances of the laying on of hands in a variety of circumstances, see 6:6; 8:17; 9:17; 13:3.

Codex Bezae (D), as represented also in the Latin Vulgate, has the more dramatic reading εὐθέως ἐπέπεσεν (*eutheōs epepesen*, "immediately he [the Holy Spirit] fell [on them]"), rather than simply ἦλθε (*ēlthe*, "he [the Holy Spirit] came [on them]") of the better textual tradition.

Some Western texts (i.e., recensions of the Old Latin, Vulgate, and Syriac versions) reflect the Greek reading ἑτέραις γλώσσαις (*heterais glōssais*, "other tongues"), rather than simply γλώσσαις (*glōssais*, "tongues"), in an evident attempt to parallel the wording of 2:4. On tongues and prophecy as signs of the Spirit's presence at Pentecost, see 2:3–4.

2. A Summary of Paul's Ministry in the City (19:8–12)

OVERVIEW

Paul's ministry at Ephesus lasted approximately three years (cf. 20:31). It is remarkable how concisely Luke summarizes this extensive period, though perhaps not so remarkable if we assume from the absence of the pronoun "we" that Luke was not himself an eyewitness of the events narrated. The conciseness of this passage is especially notable when compared with Luke's expansive anecdotal treatments of events at Philippi in 16:10–40 and the return journey of Paul and his associates to Jerusalem in 20:5–21:19, where to judge by the presence of the pronoun "we" the author was an eyewitness. Yet though we would like to know much more than Luke gives us here, we cannot for that reason fault what we have.

> ⁸Paul entered the synagogue and spoke boldly there for three months, arguing persuasively about the kingdom of God. ⁹But some of them became obstinate; they refused to believe and publicly maligned the Way. So Paul left them. He took the disciples with him and had discussions daily in the lecture hall of Tyrannus. ¹⁰This went on for two years, so that all the Jews and Greeks who lived in the province of Asia heard the word of the Lord.
>
> ¹¹God did extraordinary miracles through Paul, ¹²so that even handkerchiefs and aprons that had touched him were taken to the sick, and their illnesses were cured and the evil spirits left them.

COMMENTARY

8–10 In the synagogue at Ephesus, Paul was "arguing persuasively [*dialegomenos kai peithōn*] about the kingdom of God." He was speaking to those who had earlier received him favorably (cf. 18:19–21). And the three-month hearing they gave him was one of the longest he had in any synagogue.

When opposition to "the Way" (*tē hodos*, GK 3847) arose, he withdrew from the synagogue and continued to minister for two more years in "the lecture hall of Tyrannus," which may have been the lecture hall of a local philosopher named Tyrannus ("Tyrant") or a hall rented out to traveling philosophers by a landlord of that name. Since it is extremely difficult (except perhaps in certain bleak moments of parenthood) to think of any parent naming his or her child "Tyrant," the name must have been a nickname given by students of the philosopher or tenants of the landlord.

As for the money needed to rent the hall, perhaps Priscilla and Aquila provided it or the growing congregation underwrote the cost. Following the Western text, which adds at the end of v.9 the interesting detail that Paul discussed every day in Tyrannus's lecture hall "from the fifth to the tenth hour" (*apo hōras e heōs dekatēs*, though Codex Bezae reads "to the ninth and tenth hours" and the Vulgate "to the ninth hour"), we might picture the apostle as using the hall between the hours of 11:00 a.m. and 3:00 or 4:00 p.m.—i.e., the time of the usual midday rest and after Tyrannus had dismissed his students and Paul had completed his morning's work (cf. 20:34). It may be, as many have thought, that this piece of information was derived from some bit of reliable oral tradition, but that is only a conjecture. All we really know is (1) that for two years in Tyrannus's lecture hall Paul "reasoned daily" (*kath' hēmeran dialegomenos*; NIV, "had discussions daily"; NASB, "reasoning daily") about the claims of Christ, and (2) that during this time through Paul's converts the gospel radiated out from Ephesus to the outlying cities and villages of Asia Minor, so that "all the Jews and Greeks who lived in the province of Asia heard the word of the Lord" (v.10) and many churches were founded (cf. Col 1:7; 2:1; 4:16; perhaps also Rev 2–3 and five of the seven letters of Ignatius: *To the Ephesians*; *To the Magnesians*; *To the Trallians*; *To the Philadelphians*; and *To the Smyrneans*). Then after sending Timothy and Erastus as his envoys to Macedonia and Achaia, Paul stayed for a while longer at Ephesus (cf. 19:21–22).

11–12 From his Corinthian correspondence we learn that Paul had his difficulties while at Ephesus, which arose chiefly from conditions at Corinth (see Reflections, pp. 1008–9). But Luke does not speak of them or mention any further difficulties at Ephesus beyond his general reference to Jewish opposition (v.9) and the Demetrius incident (vv.23–41). Instead he rounds off his summary of Paul's Ephesian ministry by speaking of "extraordinary miracles" (*dynameis te ou tas tychousas*, lit., "miracles not of the ordinary kind"—a somewhat strange way to talk about the miraculous, which by definition is hardly "ordinary") being effected by Paul directly and through his handkerchiefs and aprons indirectly when they were taken to the sick and the demon-possessed.

The particle *te* and the adverbial use of the conjunction *kai* in the Greek sentence indicate that Luke had two types of "extraordinary miracles" in mind: (1) direct healings through the laying on of Paul's hands (note the phrase *dia tōn cheirōn Paulou*, "through [NASB, "by"] the hands of Paul," which the NIV does not explicitly pick up), and (2) indirect healings through the application of Paul's handkerchiefs and aprons. The Greek word *soudarion* (GK 5051), which is a loanword from the Latin *sudarium*, refers to a facecloth used for wiping perspiration and corresponds somewhat to our handkerchief—though, of course, the garments of antiquity had no pockets. And the Greek word *simikinthion* (GK 4980), which is a loanword from the Latin *semicinctium*, refers to a workman's apron. So prominent was the divine presence in Paul's ministry at Ephesus, Luke tells his readers, that even such personal items as Paul's sweat cloths and work aprons were taken out to the sick and demon-possessed, and through their application cures were effected.

It is certainly strange to read of healings occurring through sweat cloths and work aprons. Most commentators are uneasy with the narrative here, and so either explain it away as a pious legend or downplay it as verging on the bizarre. Even when the account is accepted as factual, some would prefer to take it as having been done apart from Paul's knowledge or approval. But Ephesus was the home of all sorts of magic and superstition, with the expression "Ephesian writings" (*Ephesia grammata*) being common in antiquity for documents that contained spells and magical formulas (cf. Athenaeus, *Deipn.* 12.548; Clement of Alexandria, *Strom.* 5.242). So it need not be thought too strange that just as Paul met his audiences logically and ideologically at a point of common ground in order to

lead them on to the good news of salvation in Christ, so at Ephesus he acted in the way here depicted. The virtue, of course, lay not in the materials themselves but in the power of God and the faith of the recipients.

Luke's interest throughout this chapter is in emphasizing the supernatural power of the gospel. Therefore he has highlighted these "extraordinary miracles." Undoubtedly, as well, he included reference to miracles done through Paul's sweat cloths and work aprons in order to set up a further parallel with the ministries of Jesus and Peter, where healings took place by touching Jesus' cloak (Lk 8:44) and by simply coming under Peter's shadow (Ac 5:15).

NOTES

8 The Western text (D, and as represented by a recension of the Syriac version) adds ἐν δυνάμει μεγάλῃ (*en dynamei megalē*, "with great power") before the verb ἐπαρρησιάζετο (*eparrēsiazeto*, "he spoke boldly," GK *4245*).

On Luke's emphasis in panel 5 on persuasion in Paul's preaching—here by the use of διαλεγόμενος καὶ πείθων (*dialegomenos kai peithōn* [GK *1363, 4275*], which is probably a hendiadys and so to be translated "arguing persuasively"), and in v.9 by the verb διαλέγομαι (*dialegomai*, "reason" or "discuss")—see comments at 17:2–3.

On ἡ βασιλεία τοῦ θεοῦ (*hē basileia tou theou*, "the kingdom of God") in Acts (cf. 1:3; 8:12; 20:25; 28:23, 31), see comments at 1:3.

9 On believers in Jesus as those of "the Way" (ἡ ὁδός, *hē hodos*; cf. 9:2; 19:23; 22:4; 24:14, 22; also 16:17; 18:25–26; 2Pe 2:2), see comments at 9:2.

REFLECTIONS

While at Ephesus, Paul wrote a letter to the Corinthian church on the subject of separation from the ungodly (cf. 1Co 5:9–10), which letter is either not now extant or partially preserved (as is often suggested) in 2 Corinthians 6:14–7:1. In reply he received a letter from certain members of the Corinthian church (cf. 1Co 7:1) asking for his advice about existing marital problems at Corinth, food pre-

viously dedicated to idols, the decorum of women in worship, the observance of the Lord's Supper, and spiritual gifts—perhaps also about the nature and significance of the resurrection. At about the same time, he had some visitors from Corinth, whom he identifies as "Chloe's household" (1Co 1:11), who told him about deep and bitter divisions within the church. And from rumors widely circulating (cf. 1Co

5:1) he knew that there existed among the Corinthian believers rather blatant cases of immorality and litigation in the public law courts. To deal with all these matters the apostle wrote a second pastoral letter—what we know as 1 Corinthians.

The problems at Corinth seem to have taken the course of opposition to Paul's authority and criticism of his doctrine, and he was forced to make a "painful visit" back to the city in an attempt to settle matters within the church (cf. 2Co 2:1; 12:14; 13:1). This visit is extremely difficult to place historically because Luke's summary of events during this time is so brief and Paul's references are so allusive. It may even have been conducted on his behalf by Timothy and Erastus (cf. 19:22) or by Titus (cf. 2Co 12:17–18; see also 2:13; 7:6, 13–14; 8:6, 16, 23). Nevertheless, the fact that Paul speaks of it as a painful visit and that he found it necessary to continue to rebuke his Corinthian converts suggests that it was not entirely successful. His opponents even taunted him, it seems, with being humble in their presence but bold when away (cf. 2Co 10:1).

3. The Seven Sons of Sceva (19:13–19)

OVERVIEW

Most commentators are convinced that at this point Luke completely set aside his sources for some popular Oriental legend, which he then attempted to recast into an edifying Christian story. Even so staunch a defender of the historical reliability of Acts as William M. Ramsay, after squirming through an account of "rebaptism" (as he interpreted it) in vv.1–7 and of healings by means of sweat cloths and work aprons in vv.11–12, found this section to be the proverbial "last straw" and declared, "In this Ephesian description one feels the character, not of weighed and reasoned history, but of popular fancy; and I cannot explain it on the level of most of the narrative" (*St. Paul the Traveller*, 273).

13Some Jews who went around driving out evil spirits tried to invoke the name of the Lord Jesus over those who were demon-possessed. They would say, "In the name of Jesus, whom Paul preaches, I command you to come out." 14Seven sons of Sceva, a Jewish chief priest, were doing this. 15⌊One day⌋ the evil spirit answered them, "Jesus I know, and I know about Paul, but who are you?" 16Then the man who had the evil spirit jumped on them and overpowered them all. He gave them such a beating that they ran out of the house naked and bleeding.

17When this became known to the Jews and Greeks living in Ephesus, they were all seized with fear, and the name of the Lord Jesus was held in high honor. 18Many of those who believed now came and openly confessed their evil deeds. 19A number who had practiced sorcery brought their scrolls together and burned them publicly. When they calculated the value of the scrolls, the total came to fifty thousand drachmas.

COMMENTARY

13 The use of magical names in incantations to exorcise evil spirits was common in the ancient world, and it seems to have been especially prominent at Ephesus. In addition, Jewish practitioners of magic were highly esteemed in antiquity, for they were believed to have command of particularly effective spells. The great reluctance of Jews to pronounce the divine name was known among the ancients and often misinterpreted according to magical principles. Moreover, those connected with the Jewish priesthood would have enjoyed great prestige in magical circles, since they were the most likely ones to know the true pronunciation of the Ineffable Name and so most able to release its power (cf. Bruce M. Metzger, "St. Paul and the Magicians," *Princeton Seminary Bulletin* 38 [1944]: 27–30).

14 Some Jewish exorcists, on coming into contact with Paul and his preaching, tried to make magical use of this new name "Jesus" they had heard (v.13). Luke identifies them as "seven sons of Sceva, a Jewish chief priest" (*Skeua Ioudaiou archiereōs hepta huioi*). Perhaps they did belong to one of the high priestly families of Jerusalem (even the best families have their deviants), and probably the title "Jewish chief priest" was a self-designation manufactured to impress their clients. That title is reported by Luke without evaluation and simply depicts these Jewish exorcists phenomenally in terms of how they represented themselves, much as Luke does in speaking of Simon of Samaria (cf. 8:13) and the Judaizers of the Jerusalem church (cf. 15:5). Perhaps these seven even professed to accept Paul's message and to be committed to Jesus personally, much as Simon of Samaria did (cf. 8:9–24). But if they thought of themselves as in some sense Jewish Christians, it was primarily for the benefits they could derive for their magical arts from the power of the name of Jesus. So, it seems, they simply continued in their old ways with a new twist.

15–16 When, however, the seven sons of Sceva tried to use this more powerful name in their exorcisms, they soon found they were dealing with realities far beyond their ability to control. The demon they were trying to exorcise turned violently on them, and they fled from the house "naked and bleeding" (v.16). The name of Jesus, like an unfamiliar and misused weapon, exploded in their hands, and they were quite dramatically taught a lesson about the danger of using the name of Jesus indiscriminately in their dabbling in the realm of the supernatural.

17–19 News of what happened spread quickly throughout Ephesus. All who heard were overcome by reverential "fear" (*phobos*, GK *5832*) and held the name of Jesus in high honor. Negatively, they learned not to misuse the name of Jesus or treat it lightly, for it is a powerful name (v.17). Positively, many Christians renounced their secret acts of magic and several magicians were converted (v.18). Openly demonstrating the change in their lives, they gathered their magical scrolls and burned them in the presence of the whole congregation (*enōpion pantōn*, "in the presence of them all"; NIV, "publicly"; NASB, "in the sight of everyone," v.19). The value of the papyrus scrolls, Luke adds, was estimated at fifty thousand pieces of silver (*argyriou myriadas pente*; NIV, "fifty thousand drachmas"; NASB, "fifty thousand pieces of silver" [see NASB text note]).

NOTES

13 A parallel use of the name of Jesus in exorcism appears in the Paris Magical Papyrus (no. 574, lines 3018–19): "I adjure you by Jesus the god of the Hebrews" (cf. Karl Preisendanz, *Papyri Graecae Magicae* [Leipzig: Teubner, 1928, 1931], vol. 1, plate IV). Rabbinic writings denounce the invoking of the name of Jesus in healings (cf. *t. Ḥul.* 2:22–23; *y. Šabb.* 14.4.14*d*; *y. ʿAbod. Zar.* 2.2.40*d*–41*a*; *b. ʿAbod. Zar.* 27*b*), which suggests that some Jewish exorcists and healers were doing just that.

14 The Western text (D, in part 𝔓³⁸, and as reflected in recensions of the Old Latin and Syriac versions) recasts this verse to read, "Among whom also the sons of Sceva, a priest, desired to do the same (it was their practice to exorcise such people); and coming before the demon-possessed man, they began to invoke the Name, saying: 'We command you by Jesus, whom Paul proclaims, to come out'"—thereby toning down Sceva's priestly title and omitting reference to the sons as being seven in number (see note at v.16). The thirteenth-century Old Latin recension Gigas reflects the reading "two [δύο, *duo*] sons" (see note at v.16).

15 Two verbs for "know" are used in this verse: γινώσκω (*ginōskō*, GK *1182*) for the demon's knowledge of Jesus and ἐπίσταμαι (*epistamai*, GK *2179*) for the demon's knowledge of Paul. It is doubtful that they should be understood here as denoting differing types or degrees of knowledge, as though the demon knew Jesus in some intimate fashion but had only heard about Paul.

16 The word ἀμφότεροι (*amphoteroi*) means "both" (cf. Mt 9:17; 15:14; Eph 2:14, 16, 18) but was also used more loosely to mean "all" (so NIV, NASB; cf. 23:8). The Western scribe evidently read it as "both" and so omitted "seven" in v.14 (see note above), as did the Gigas recension of the Old Latin in its reading of "two sons of Sceva" (see note above).

I. Summary Statement (19:20)

²⁰In this way the word of the Lord spread widely and grew in power.

COMMENTARY

20 The advances of the gospel into Macedonia, Achaia, and Asia did not come about without great difficulty and several periods of discouragement. At times, in fact, matters looked very bleak. Viewed externally, one may even be tempted to agree with Wilfred L. Knox (*St. Paul and the Church of the Gentiles* [Cambridge: Cambridge Univ. Press, 1939], 85) that Paul's "journey into Macedonia had been the height of unwisdom and its results negligible." Perhaps Paul felt that way himself when forced to leave

the province. But such a view forgets that at Philippi, Thessalonica, and Berea a flame had been lit that was to spread throughout the area. Furthermore, it is to ignore the fact that, to judge by Paul's own extant letters, the churches founded in these cities—certainly at Philippi and Thessalonica but probably also at Berea—were among his best and most loyal ones.

At Athens Paul faced the snobbery and polite refusal of self-satisfied people, and it seems evident that their lack of response on top of his difficulties in Macedonia almost drove him to despair. But at Corinth, in spite of his own feelings of "weakness," "fear," and "much trembling" (1Co 2:3), God worked remarkably by giving Paul an open door and a successful ministry. Of course with success also came problems, which at Corinth arose from within the congregation. Nonetheless, Paul had much to thank God for when he called to mind his experiences at Corinth, and he evidently returned to Jerusalem to fulfill his Nazirite vow with much joy. At Ephesus, after revisiting his Galatian converts, his ministry continued in ways that evidenced God's presence and power.

Paul's second and third missionary journeys read like a slice of life. Having set out in his earlier panels episodes depicting the gradual widening of the gospel to new groups of people and the establishment of a new missionary policy to the Gentiles, Luke in panel 5 presents for his readers a graphic account of the gospel's entrance into new regions. It is the story of the church's dedicated service under the guidance and power of the Holy Spirit in proclaiming the good news to those who desperately needed to hear it. It is a story not without opposition and not without times of depression and soul-searching. But it is also a story of divine blessing, times of elation, and periods of confidence. Through it all God was at work. And in looking back on those days Luke says simply, "In this way the word of the Lord spread widely and grew in power."

NOTES

20 Codex Bezae (D) reads οὕτως κατὰ κράτος ἐνίσχυσεν καὶ ἡ πίστις τοῦ θεοῦ ηὔξανε καὶ ἐπλήθυνε (*houtōs kata kratos enischysen kai hē pistis tou theou ēuxane kai eplēthyne*, "So mightily it prevailed, and the faith of God grew and multiplied"), thereby conflating the verse, changing its order, and substituting ἡ πίστις τοῦ θεοῦ (*hē pistis tou theou*, "the faith of God") for τοῦ κυρίου ὁ λόγος (*tou kyriou ho logos*, "the word of the Lord").

PANEL 6—TO JERUSALEM AND FROM THERE TO ROME (19:21–28:31)

OVERVIEW

Acts 19:21–28:31, the sixth and last panel of material in Acts, sets out Paul's somewhat circuitous journey to Jerusalem, his arrest and defenses at Jerusalem, his imprisonment and defenses at Caesarea, his voyage to Rome, and his entrance into and ministry at Rome. The panel is introduced by the programmatic statement of 19:21–22 and concludes with the summary statement of 28:31. Three features immediately strike the reader in this panel: (1) the disproportionate length of the material presented, for it includes one-third of the total material in Acts; (2) the prominence given the speeches of Paul in his defense (22:1–21; 23:1–6; 24:10–21; 25:8–11; 26:1–29); and (3) the dominance of the "we" sections in the narrative portions (cf. 20:5–15; 21:1–18; 27:1–28:16).

There are many matters of theological interest that appear in this sixth panel. Yet it cannot be said that its length is related to the theological significance of the material presented. Rather, its length seems to be related primarily to (1) the apologetic purpose of Luke, particularly in the five defenses of chs. 22–26, and (2) the eyewitness character of the narrative, with the inevitable elaboration of details in such an eyewitness report. In particular, starting at 20:5 and going throughout the rest of Acts to 28:31,

Luke's narrative gives considerable attention to ports of call, stopovers, and time spent on Paul's travels. Furthermore, it includes a number of revealing anecdotes and detailed accounts of the various events narrated. It contains, in fact, the kind of detail found in a travel journal. And the use of "we" in 20:5–15; 21:1–18; and 28:16 suggests its eyewitness character—as seen earlier in the treatment of Paul's ministry at Philippi in the "we" section of 16:10–17 and the further events of 16:18–40. The material of this final panel spans the time from about AD 56 through AD 62.

A. Programmatic Statement (19:21–22)

21After all this had happened, Paul decided to go to Jerusalem, passing through Macedonia and Achaia. "After I have been there," he said, "I must visit Rome also." 22He sent two of his helpers, Timothy and Erastus, to Macedonia, while he stayed in the province of Asia a little longer.

COMMENTARY

21 "After all this had happened" (*hōs de eplērōthē tauta*, lit., "when these things were fulfilled") refers to the events bracketed by the participle *plērōsantes* ("having fulfilled"; NIV, "when Barnabas and Saul had finished"; NASB, "when they had fulfilled") of 12:25 and the verb *eplērōthē* ("they were fulfilled"; NIV, "had happened"; NASB, "were finished") of 19:21—i.e., to the events of the first, second, and third missionary journeys of Paul as recorded in 12:25–19:20 (the two preceding panels, which depict the extension of the Christian proclamation to Gentiles in the Greco-Roman world). Some have conjectured that "after all this had happened" has reference only to the two-year ministry of v.10. But for Luke the fulfillment of the Gentile mission came in (1) the inauguration of the new missionary pol-

icy for reaching Gentiles, which was established on Paul's first missionary journey and confirmed at the Jerusalem Council (i.e., panel 4), and (2) the extensive outreach of the gospel to the Gentile world, which took place during Paul's second and third missionary journeys (i.e., panel 5). All that took place earlier (i.e., panels 1–3) was for Luke a preparation for the Gentile mission, and all that happened afterwards (i.e., panel 6) was its aftermath and extension into Rome.

With the eastern part of the Roman Empire evangelized (cf. Ro 15:23, "now that there is no more place for me to work in these regions"), Paul decided to return to Jerusalem and then go on to Rome. On the way he would revisit the churches of Macedonia and Achaia, ministering to them and gathering from them a collection for the Jewish believers at Jerusalem (cf. 1Co 16:1–4). After Jerusalem and Rome, he planned to take up a Gentile mission in the western part of the empire, using the Roman church as the base for that western outreach, just as the church at Syrian Antioch had been his base for evangelizing the eastern part of the empire (cf. Ro 15:24–29). Now, however, he must return to Jerusalem, knowing full well that serious difficulties would befall him there (cf. Ro 15:30–32).

Luke says that Paul's decision to go to Jerusalem and then on to Rome was *en tō pneumati*, which may mean "by his human spirit" (so NASB, "in the spirit") and be translated he "decided" or "resolved" (so NEB, JB, TEV, NIV), or may refer to direction "by the Holy Spirit" and be translated "in the Spirit" (so NRSV). This same expression is used in 18:25 to refer to Apollos's own spirit (NIV, "with great fervor"; NASB, "fervent in spirit"). But in 20:22, *tō pneumati* probably has reference to the Holy Spirit (NIV, "by the Spirit"; NRSV, "captive to the Spirit"), and in 21:4, *dia tou pneumatos* (NIV and NASB, "through the Spirit") certainly refers to the Holy Spirit—with both references having to do with Paul's travel plans. So we should probably understand the statement *etheto ho Paulos en tō pneumati* of this verse to mean that "Paul decided [lit., made up his mind] by the direction of the Spirit" to go to Jerusalem and then on to Rome. This seems to be supported by the use of the impersonal verb *dei* ("must"), which in Luke's writings usually connotes the divine will. Thus by the combination of the expression *en tō pneumati* and the verb *dei*, Luke appears to be making the point in this programmatic statement that the aftermath of the Gentile mission and its extension into Rome were likewise under the Spirit's direction, just as the Gentile mission itself had been.

22 Before going to Jerusalem, Paul sent Timothy and Erastus into Macedonia while he remained "in Asia" (*eis tēn Asian*; NIV, "in the province of Asia"), which probably means that he stayed on at Ephesus a while longer, not that he went on a further mission elsewhere in the Roman province of Asia. Luke has not mentioned Timothy since his return from Macedonia to rejoin Paul at Corinth (cf. 18:5). But he was with Paul at Ephesus and served at some time during Paul's Ephesian ministry as his emissary to Corinth (cf. 1Co 4:17; 16:10–11). This is, however, the first time we hear of Erastus, though in 2 Timothy 4:20 he is spoken of as a well-known companion of Paul who had a special interest in the church at Corinth. That he was the "director of public works" (NIV) or "city treasurer" (NASB) of Corinth referred to in Romans 16:23 is not at all likely. Nor can he easily be identified with the Erastus mentioned in a Latin inscription found at Corinth in 1929 that reads, "Erastus, commissioner of public works [*aedile*], laid this pavement at his own expense" (H. J. Cadbury, "Erastus of Corinth," *JBL* 50 [1931]: 42–58). Erastus was a common Greek name, and it is unlikely that Luke would mention so casually such a significant person as the "director of public works" or "treasurer" of the city of Corinth.

As for Silas, though Luke speaks of him repeatedly in his accounts of Paul's second missionary journey (nine times in 15:40–18:5), he makes no reference to him in the rest of Acts. Luke's interest in these last chapters of Acts is focused solely on his hero Paul. Nonetheless, that is no reason to assume that others were no longer with Paul. Titus, for example, is not mentioned at all by Luke in Acts, but Paul refers to him in his letters as having been extensively involved at various times during the Gentile mission (cf. 2Co 2:13; 7:6, 13–14; 8:6, 16, 23; 12:18; Gal 2:1, 3; 2Ti 4:10; Tit 1:4).

NOTES

21 On the use of δεῖ (*dei*, "it is necessary," "one must") in Luke-Acts, see comments and note at 1:16.

22 Codex Bezae (D) adds ὀλίγον (*oligon*, "little," "short") after the word χρόνον (*chronon*, "time," GK *5989*), thereby making it clear that Paul only stayed at Ephesus a "short time" longer (NIV, "a little longer"; NASB, "for a while").

On the synonymous use of the preposition εἰς (*eis*, "into") and ἐν (*en*, "in")—here with respect to the expression εἰς τὴν Ἀσίαν (*eis tēn Asian*)—see comments and note at 2:38 (cf. 7:4, 12 [also note]; 8:16 [note]; 19:5 [note]).

B. The Journey to Jerusalem (19:23–21:16)

1. A Riot at Ephesus (19:23–41)

OVERVIEW

Before Paul left Ephesus, a riot threatened his life and could have put an end to the outreach of the gospel in the Roman province of Asia. The situation was undoubtedly more dangerous than Luke's account suggests. In what may well be allusions to this riot, Paul in his letters speaks of having "fought wild beasts at Ephesus" (1Co 15:32), of having "despaired even of life" in the face of "a deadly peril" in Asia (2Co 1:8, 10), and of Priscilla and Aquila having "risked their lives" for him (Ro 16:4). Luke's purpose in presenting this vignette is clearly apologetic, in line with his argument for the *religio licita* status of Christianity in panel 5 (16:6–19:20)

and in anticipation of the themes stressed in Paul's speeches of defense in panel 6 (chs. 22–26). Politically, Luke's reports of (1) the friendliness of *hoi Asiarchoi* (NASB, "the Asiarchs"; NIV, "officials of the province [of Asia]") toward Paul (v.31) and (2) the city clerk's intervention on his behalf (vv.35–41) comprise the best defense imaginable against the charge that Paul and Christianity were any threat to the empire. Religiously, Luke's description of the Ephesian riot makes the point that, as Haenchen, 578, aptly expressed it, "in the final analysis the only thing heathenism can do against Paul is to shout itself hoarse."

²³About that time there arose a great disturbance about the Way. ²⁴A silversmith named Demetrius, who made silver shrines of Artemis, brought in no little business for the craftsmen. ²⁵He called them together, along with the workmen in related trades, and said: "Men, you know we receive a good income from this business. ²⁶And you see and hear how this fellow Paul has convinced and led astray large numbers of people here in Ephesus and in practically the whole province of Asia. He says that man-made gods are no gods at all. ²⁷There is danger not only that our trade will lose its good name, but also that

the temple of the great goddess Artemis will be discredited, and the goddess herself, who is worshiped throughout the province of Asia and the world, will be robbed of her divine majesty."

28When they heard this, they were furious and began shouting: "Great is Artemis of the Ephesians!" 29Soon the whole city was in an uproar. The people seized Gaius and Aristarchus, Paul's traveling companions from Macedonia, and rushed as one man into the theater. 30Paul wanted to appear before the crowd, but the disciples would not let him. 31Even some of the officials of the province, friends of Paul, sent him a message begging him not to venture into the theater.

32The assembly was in confusion: Some were shouting one thing, some another. Most of the people did not even know why they were there. 33The Jews pushed Alexander to the front, and some of the crowd shouted instructions to him. He motioned for silence in order to make a defense before the people. 34But when they realized he was a Jew, they all shouted in unison for about two hours: "Great is Artemis of the Ephesians!"

35The city clerk quieted the crowd and said: "Men of Ephesus, doesn't all the world know that the city of Ephesus is the guardian of the temple of the great Artemis and of her image, which fell from heaven? 36Therefore, since these facts are undeniable, you ought to be quiet and not do anything rash. 37You have brought these men here, though they have neither robbed temples nor blasphemed our goddess. 38If, then, Demetrius and his fellow craftsmen have a grievance against anybody, the courts are open and there are proconsuls. They can press charges. 39If there is anything further you want to bring up, it must be settled in a legal assembly. 40As it is, we are in danger of being charged with rioting because of today's events. In that case we would not be able to account for this commotion, since there is no reason for it." 41After he had said this, he dismissed the assembly.

COMMENTARY

23 The temporal notation "about that time" (*kata ton kairon*) is indefinite (cf. 12:1). By itself, it does not necessarily place the riot at the end of Paul's Ephesian ministry. Nevertheless, by the separation of this pericope from the account of Paul's mission in Ephesus in 19:1–19, which closes the fifth panel of material, and by the temporal reference in 20:1 ("when the uproar had ended"), Luke certainly wanted his readers to understand that the riot set off by Demetrius took place at the close of Paul's min-

istry there. Also, by the absolute use of "the Way" (*hē hodos*, cf. v.9), it seems evident he wanted them to understand that what happened was not simply against Paul personally but was primarily a threat to the continued outreach of the gospel.

24–27 The goddess "Artemis of Ephesus" was not the fair and chaste huntress of Greek mythology but a Near-Eastern mother-goddess of fertility. Her image at Ephesus, which was believed to have been fashioned in heaven and fallen from the sky (cf. v.35), depicted her as a grotesque, multibreasted woman. Probably the Ephesian Artemis was originally a meteorite that resembled a multibreasted woman and so became an object of worship, just as other meteorites that had fallen at or near Troy, Pessinus, Enna, and Emesa became sacred cult objects. Her worship incorporated the traditional features of nature worship. Her high priest was a eunuch with the Persian title "Megabyzos," and under him served other eunuch priests and three classes of priestesses (cf. L. R. Taylor, "Artemis of Ephesus," *Beginnings of Christianity* [ed. Foakes-Jackson and Lake], 5.251–56).

With the silting up of the harbor, the temple of Artemis became the primary basis for the wealth and continued prosperity of the city of Ephesus (see comments at 19:1). This temple was situated 1.5 miles northeast of the city, measured about 400 by 200 feet in size, and was considered by the ancients as one of the Seven Wonders of the World. Thousands of pilgrims and tourists came to it from far and near. Around it swarmed all sorts of tradesmen and hucksters who made their living by supplying visitors with food and lodging, dedicatory offerings, and souvenirs. The temple of Artemis was also a major treasury and bank where merchants, kings, and even cities made deposits and where their money could be kept safe under the protection of a deity.

Paul's preaching turned many away from the idolatry of the Artemis cult, with the result that the economy of Ephesus was being affected. One profitable business was the making of "silver shrines of Artemis" (*naous argyrous Artemidos*, v.24), which probably denotes not just souvenirs of the Artemis temple but miniature silver statuettes of Artemis herself to be used as votive offerings, amulets, and replicas of the goddess to be venerated in people's homes. When the gospel began to touch their income, the silversmiths led by their guildmaster, Demetrius, instigated a disturbance that they hoped would turn the people against the missionaries and stir up greater devotion for the goddess Artemis—a greater devotion that would, of course, bring about greater profits for them.

28–29 The silversmiths began shouting out the ceremonial chant "Great is Artemis of the Ephesians!" (cf. Bel 18: "Great is Bel"; also 41: "Great are you, O Lord, the God of Daniel"), in hope of stirring up the city on a pretext of religious devotion. Codex Bezae (D), together with some minuscule MSS, inserts "and running into the street" after the reference to their being "furious" (*thymou*, GK 2596) and before the verb "[began] shouting" (*ekrazon*, GK 3189) and so adds a note of local color that may well fit the situation. A magnificent boulevard, the so-called Arcadian Way, ran through the heart of Ephesus from its harbor to its great theater at the foot of Mount Pion. Lined with fine buildings and columned porticoes, it was the main artery of Ephesian life. Into this boulevard Demetrius and his fellow craftsmen poured, sweeping along with them in noisy procession all the residents and visitors within earshot. Their destination was the large open-air theater on the eastern side of the city—a theater whose ruins show it could have held some twenty-four thousand people. In it the city assembly probably met.

On their way the crowd laid hold of Gaius and Aristarchus, two traveling companions of Paul from Derbe and Thessalonica respectively (cf. 20:4; 27:2; the genitive "from Macedonia" [*Makedonas*] probably refers not to both men but only to Aristarchus, contra NIV and NASB), and dragged them into the theater. And there, much to the delight of Demetrius and his fellow silversmiths, the procession became a fanatical mob.

30–31 While there is no evidence that Paul was ever tried by a kangaroo court or imprisoned at Ephesus, as some have maintained, the riot presented him with an extremely serious situation. He wanted to appear before "the assembly" (*ho dēmos*, GK *1322*; NIV, "the crowd"; NASB, "the assembly"), doubtless in the belief that because of his Roman citizenship and his earlier successful appearances before governmental officials he could quiet the mob, free his companions, and turn the whole affair to the advantage of the gospel. But his converts in the city would not let him enter the theater. And even some of *hoi Asiarchoi* (NASB, "the Asiarchs"; NIV, "officials of the province [of Asia]") who were his friends sent an urgent message for him not to go there.

The Asiarchs were members of the noblest and wealthiest families of the province of Asia and were bound together in a league to promote the cult of the emperor and of Rome. Their headquarters were at Pergamum, where their chief temple had been erected about 29 BC. Other temples in honor of the ruling emperor had been erected at Smyrna and Ephesus. Every year an Asiarch was elected for the entire province, with additional Asiarchs elected for each city that had a temple honoring the emperor. The title was borne for life by officers in the league, and so in Paul's day there would have been a number of Asiarchs at Ephesus. Like similar leagues in the other Roman provinces—for example, the Lyciarch of Lycia or the Galatarch of Galatia—the Asiarch was a quasi-religious organization with certain political functions. While it did not have political authority, it served Rome's interests by securing loyalty to Roman rule. That some of these men were friendly to Paul and gave him advice in such an explosive situation suggests that imperial policy at this time was not hostile to Christianity. Luke had an apologetic purpose in stressing their action, for as Haenchen, 578, observed, "A sect whose leader had Asiarchs for friends cannot be dangerous to the state."

32 The crowd had been worked up into a frenzy. "Some," Luke says, "were shouting one thing, some another. Most of the people did not even know why

they were there"—which is a remark that reveals Luke's Greek sense of ironical humor. What united them was a common resentment against those who paid no honor to the goddess Artemis. Yet there appears to have been widespread confusion among the people as to the focus of their resentment.

33-34 The Jewish community at Ephesus was large and enjoyed a number of special exemptions granted by past provincial proconsuls (cf. Josephus, *Ant.* 14.227, 263-64). But it also suffered from the latent anti-Semitism that lay just beneath the surface of Greco-Roman society. In an endeavor to disassociate themselves from the Christians in such an explosive situation, the Jews sent one of their number, Alexander, to the podium. This may be the same Alexander of 1 Timothy 1:19-20 or 2 Timothy 4:14, but it is difficult to prove because the name Alexander was common among both Gentiles and Jews (cf. Josephus, *Ant.* 14.226). To the idolatrous mob, however, Jews were as insufferable as Christians on the point at issue, because both worshiped an invisible deity and rejected all idols. So Alexander was shouted down with the chant, "Great is Artemis of the Ephesians!" (v.34). And this shouting kept on for about two hours.

35-37 The "city clerk" (*ho grammateus*, GK *1208*) of Ephesus was the scribe of "the assembly" and its chief executive officer. He came to his position from within the assembly and was not appointed by Rome. As the most important native official of the city, he was held responsible for disturbances within it. He argued with the crowd that a riot would hardly enhance the prestige of the city in the eyes of Rome, and therefore any complaint raised by Demetrius and his guild of silversmiths should be brought before the legally constituted authorities. Gaius and Aristarchus, Paul's two companions who stood before them, were, he pointed out, neither robbers of temples nor blasphemers of other gods—which were the common accusations made by Gentiles against Jews generally (including Jewish Christians) in antiquity (cf. Josephus, *Ant.* 4.207; *Ag. Ap.* 2.237).

38–40 "The courts [*agoraioi*, GK *61*] are open and there are proconsuls [*anthypatoi*, GK *478*]," the clerk insisted. "Courts" and "proconsuls" are probably generic references and should not be taken to mean that Ephesus had two agora courts (see comments at 18:12) or two provincial proconsuls—as some argue occurred in late AD 54 when two assassins of the proconsul Junius Silanus usurped power in Asia (cf. Tacitus, *Ann.* 13.1). The clerk continued by saying that anything further that could not be brought before the courts and the proconsuls could be presented "in the regular assembly" (*en tē ennomō*

ekklēsia [GK *1711*]; NIV, "in a legal assembly"; NASB, "in the lawful assembly"), which according to Chrysostom (*Hom. Acts* 42:2) met three times a month. Otherwise, the clerk concluded, the city risked being called to account by Rome and losing its favorable status because of a riot for which there was no reason (v.40).

41 So the city clerk dismissed the crowd. His arguments are highlighted by Luke in the previous six verses because they are important elements in the author's apologetic motif in Acts. And it is these kinds of arguments that Luke will emphasize further in reporting Paul's five speeches in his own defense in chs. 22–26.

NOTES

24 Codex Vaticanus (B) omits ἀργυροῦς (*argyrous*, "silver") and simply reads "shrines of Artemis."

25 The Western text (D, and as possibly reflected in the Syriac Harclean version) expands the vocative ἄνδρες (*andres*, "men") to ἄνδρες συντεχνῖται (*andres syntechnitai*, "men, fellow craftsmen").

26 Codex Bezae (D) inserts ἕως (*heōs*, "as far as") before "Ephesus." D also adds τίς τοτε (*tis tote*, "whoever he may be") after ὁ Παῦλος οὗτος (*ho Paulos houtos*, "this [fellow] Paul"), thereby heightening the pejorative nature of the clerk's identification.

29 Probably the final sigma of Μακεδόνας (*Makedonas*, "Macedonia") came about because of a scribal dittography with the following word συνεκδήμους (*synekdēmous*, "traveling companions").

32 On the use of the connective μὲν οὖν (*men oun*, "so," "then") in Acts, see comments at 1:6 (also at v.38).

32, 39–40 The term ἡ ἐκκλησία (*hē ekklēsia*, "the assembly," GK *1711*) is used in these verses in its purely secular sense of a duly summoned gathering of people. Its use here is more specific than σύλλογος (*syllogos*, "a gathering"), being synonymous with ὁ δῆμος (*ho dēmos*, "the assembly"; NIV, "the people") of v.33 (cf. 12:22). Elsewhere in Acts the word is used in its distinctive biblical sense of "the people of God" or "the church"—both universally and locally (e.g., 5:11; 7:38; 8:1, 3; 9:31; 11:22, 26; 12:1, 5; 14:23, 27; 15:3–4, 22, 41; 16:5; 18:22; 20:17, 28).

33 Codex Bezae (D) reads κατεβίβασαν (*katebibasan*, "they pulled [him] down") rather than συνεβίβσαν (*synebibsan*, "they instructed [him]"; NIV, "shouted instructions"; NRSV, "gave instructions"), so depicting the crowd as pulling Alexander, the Jewish spokesman, down from the podium.

35 On the address ἄνδρες Ἐφέσιοι (*andres Ephesioi*, "men, Ephesians"; NIV, "men of Ephesus"), cf. 1:16; 2:14, 22; 17:22.

37 The Byzantine text (L P and most minuscules) and a number of Western texts (E and many minuscules, though not D), followed by the TR and so incorporated into the KJV, have the pronoun ὑμῶν (*hymōn*, "your," so reading "your goddess"), which Byzantine and Western scribes evidently thought suited better the second person plural ἠγάγετε (*hēgagete*, "you have brought"), rather than ἡμῶν (*hēmōn*, "our," so reading "our goddess") of the Alexandrian text (𝔓⁷⁴ ℵ A B etc.) and Codex Bezae (D).

40 The negative οὐ (*ou*, "not") is omitted in Bodmer 𝔓⁷⁴, codices D and E, a number of minuscules, and various recensions of the Old Latin, Vulgate, and Coptic versions. It is, however, included in the major Alexandrian uncials (ℵ A B Ψ etc.) and the major Byzantine uncials (L P), other minuscules, and other recensions of the Old Latin, Vulgate, Syriac, and Coptic versions. Conjectures are numerous regarding its inclusion or omission, but probably its inclusion in the major Alexandrian texts calls for its acceptance.

2. Return Visit to Macedonia and Achaia (20:1–6)

OVERVIEW

The report of Paul's return visit to Macedonia and Achaia is the briefest account of an extended ministry in all of Acts—even more so than the summary of the ministry at Ephesus in 19:8–12. Nonetheless, it can be supplemented to some extent by various personal references and historical allusions in 2 Corinthians and Romans, which are letters of Paul written during this time.

¹When the uproar had ended, Paul sent for the disciples and, after encouraging them, said good-by and set out for Macedonia. ²He traveled through that area, speaking many words of encouragement to the people, and finally arrived in Greece, ³where he stayed three months. Because the Jews made a plot against him just as he was about to sail for Syria, he decided to go back through Macedonia. ⁴He was accompanied by Sopater son of Pyrrhus from Berea, Aristarchus and Secundus from Thessalonica, Gaius from Derbe, Timothy also, and Tychicus and Trophimus from the province of Asia. ⁵These men went on ahead and waited for us at Troas. ⁶But we sailed from Philippi after the Feast of Unleavened Bread, and five days later joined the others at Troas, where we stayed seven days.

COMMENTARY

1 Leaving Ephesus, Paul moved north to Troas, probably following the Roman coastal road that connected Ephesus with the Hellespont or perhaps going by ship. At Troas he hoped to find Titus, whom he had earlier sent to Corinth to deal with and report on the situation in the church there. Not finding him and being disturbed about conditions at Corinth, he went on to Macedonia without any further preaching in either Troas itself or the surrounding region (cf. 2Co 2:12–13). As at Athens and Corinth when his concern for believers at Thessalonica prevented him from giving full attention to an evangelistic outreach (see Overview at 18:1–17), so at Troas Paul seems to have been consumed with concern about the believers at Corinth and unable to launch out into any new missionary venture.

2 In Macedonia (probably at Philippi) Paul met Titus, who brought him reassuring news about the church at Corinth (cf. 2Co 7:5–16). In response to the triumphs and continuing problems that Titus told him about, Paul sent back to the church the letter known as 2 Corinthians. Many have proposed that 2 Corinthians 10–13, the so-called "Severe Letter," preceded the writing of 2 Corinthians 1–9 (with or without 6:14–7:1), the so-called "Conciliatory Letter." That is possible, though there is nothing to require it.

Just how long Paul stayed in Macedonia we do not know. Luke's words seem to suggest a fairly prolonged period. It was probably during this time that the gospel entered the province of Illyricum in the northwestern corner of the Balkan peninsula (cf. Ro 15:19; see also 2Ti 4:10, where Titus is mentioned as returning to Dalmatia, the southern district of the province of Illyricum). Perhaps Paul himself traveled across the Balkan peninsula on the Via Egnatia to the city of Dyrrhachium, from which the southern district of Illyricum (i.e., Dalmatia) would have been readily accessible. Or perhaps one or more of his traveling companions (e.g., Titus) were the missionaries to this area. But however we visualize the movements of Paul and his colleagues during this time, we are doubtless not far wrong in concluding that this ministry in Macedonia lasted for a year or more, probably from the summer of AD 56 through the latter part of AD 57.

One activity that especially concerned Paul at this time was collecting money for the relief of impoverished believers at Jerusalem. He instructed the churches in Galatia, Asia, Macedonia, and Achaia about this (cf. Ro 15:25–32; 1Co 16:1–4; 2Co 8:1–9:15). The collection was an act of love—like that undertaken earlier by the church at Syrian Antioch (cf. 11:27–30). More than that, Paul viewed it as a symbol of unity that would (1) help his Gentile converts realize their debt to the mother church at Jerusalem and (2) give Jewish believers an appreciation of the vitality of the Christian faith in the Gentile churches.

3 After spending some time in Macedonia, Paul went to Corinth, where he stayed for three months, probably during the winter of AD 57–58. While there, and before his final trip to Jerusalem, Paul wrote his letter to the church at Rome (cf. Ro 15:17–33). The Greek world in the eastern part of the empire had been evangelized (cf. Ro 15:19, 23)—the flame had been kindled; the fire was spreading—and he desired to transfer his ministry to the Latin world, as far west as Spain (cf. Ro 15:24). He wanted to use the Roman church as his base of operations, much as he had previously used the church at Antioch in Syria. Earlier he had hoped to go directly to Rome from Macedonia. When that proved impossible, he then wanted to go to Rome from Achaia. But now it became necessary for him to go to Jerusalem if the collection from the Gentile Christians was to have the meaning that he earnestly desired it to have (cf. Ro 15:25–32). So in place of a visit at this time and in preparation for his future coming to them—and in order to set before believers there the nature of what he was proclaiming to Gentiles in the Greco-Roman world (cf. Ro 1:11)—Paul sent a letter of introduction and exposition to Christians at Rome.

The letter to the Romans is the longest and most systematic of Paul's writings and more a comprehensive exposition of the gospel than a letter as such. Some have suggested that the body of the letter was composed earlier in Paul's ministry and circulated among his Gentile churches as a kind of missionary tractate that presented a résumé of his message and, when directed to Rome, was supplemented by an epistolary introduction (Ro 1:1–12; 1–15; or 1–17) and the personal elements of chs. 15 and 16 (esp. 15:14–16:23, with the doxology of 16:25–27 being part of the original tractate). Or the four major sections of Romans that appear in 1:16–15:13 may be understood as Paul's "message of exhortation" (paralleling an ancient form of rhetoric called a *logos protreptikos*) set within an epistolary framework. Either view would do much to explain the uncertainties within the early church regarding the relation of the final two chapters to the rest of the writing, the absence of "in Rome" at 1:7 and 15 in some minor MSS, and the presence of two doxologies at 15:33 and 16:25–27.

At the end of a three-month ministry in Corinth, Paul sought to sail for Palestine-Syria with the intent of reaching Jerusalem in time for the great pilgrim festival of Passover (held in conjunction with the Feast of Unleavened Bread) and the expectation of taking passage on a Jewish pilgrim ship. But a plot to kill him at sea was uncovered, and he decided instead to travel overland through Macedonia. Attacks by robbers were endemic on the ancient roads, and inns were not always safe. With Paul carrying a substantial amount of money collected from the Gentile churches, he undoubtedly wanted to get to Jerusalem as quickly and safely as possible. Nevertheless, he felt it best to spend extra time on the longer land route, preferring its possible dangers to the known perils of the sea voyage. So he began to retrace his steps through Macedonia.

4 Gathered at Corinth for the return journey to Jerusalem with Paul were representatives from his Gentile churches: Sopater of Berea, Aristarchus and Secundus of Thessalonica, Gaius of Derbe, Timothy of Lystra, and Tychicus and Trophimus from Asia. With the change in travel plans, they accompanied him (together with Silas and perhaps others) into Macedonia. Almost all the main centers of the Gentile mission were represented, with the notable exception of the Corinthian church. Perhaps Paul himself had been delegated by the Corinthians to represent them. On the other hand, the lack of mention of Corinth may suggest continuing strained relations within the church there. Luke, who appears to have joined the group at Philippi (cf. v.5), may have done so to represent Philippi.

5–6 Having been unable to get to Jerusalem for Passover, Paul remained at Philippi to celebrate the festival and the weeklong Feast of Unleavened Bread (for the conjunction of the two festivals in the first century, see Josephus, *Ant.* 14.21; *J.W.* 6.421–27). He sent his Gentile companions to Troas and stayed on at Philippi, apparently with Silas and Timothy. Then after the Feast of Unleavened Bread, the missionary party—accompanied by Luke (note the "we" section of vv.5–15; cf. also 16:10–17; 21:1–18; 27:1–28:16)—went down to Neapolis, the port city of Philippi, and crossed the Aegean to Troas. It was evidently a difficult crossing because it took five days instead of two days as earlier (cf. 16:11).

NOTES

2 Ἑλλάδα (*Hellada*, "Greece") is the popular title for the Roman province of Achaia (cf. 18:12). Luke prefers the popular territorial names; Paul prefers the official Roman provincial names (cf. Ro 15:26; 1Co 16:15; 2Co 1:1; 9:2).

3 On Συρία (*Syria*, "Syria") as a broad designation for "Palestine-Syria," see 18:18.

The Western text (D, and as represented by the Syriac Harclean version and Ephraem of Syria in his Acts commentary) recasts the last part of this verse to read εἶπεν δὲ τὸ πνεῦμα αὐτῷ ὑποστρέφειν (*eipen de to pneuma autō hypostrephein*, "but the Spirit told him to return") before διὰ Μακεδονίας (*dia Makedonias*, "through Macedonia").

4 The Byzantine text (A E L P and most minuscules) reads συνείπετο δὲ αὐτῷ ἄχρι τῆς Ἀσίας (*syneipeto de autō achri tēs Asias*, "they accompanied him as far as Asia"), whereas the Western text (D, and as represented by a recension of the Old Latin) reads μέλλοντος οὖν ἐξιέναι αὐτοῦ μέχρι τῆς Ασίας (*mellontos oun exienai autou mechri tēs Asias*, "when he was about to go, they accompanied him to Asia"). The shorter Alexandrian text ($\mathfrak{P}^{74}$ ℵ B etc.) reads simply συνείπετο δὲ αὐτῷ (*syneipeto de autō*, "they accompanied him"), which is to be preferred.

The Byzantine text (L P and as reflected in the Syriac Peshitta and Harclean versions and by Chrysostom) omits Πύρρου (*Pyrrou*, "son of Pyrrhus").

The Western text (D, and as represented by recensions of the Old Latin) calls Gaius Δουβήριος (*Doubērios*, "a Doberian"), thereby identifying him as a native of Doberus in Macedonia, located twenty-six miles from Philippi, evidently in agreement with the plural genitive Μακεδόνας (*Makedonas*, "Macedonia") of 19:29, which probably resulted from dittography (see note there).

Codex Bezae (D) explicitly calls Tychicus and Trophimus Ἐφέσιοι (*Ephesioi*, "Ephesians"), not Ἀσιανοί (*Asianoi*, "Asians"). This change may suggest, as has been proposed, that the scribe of D came from or was closely associated with Ephesus. It also has Εὔτυχος (*Eutychos*, "Eutychus"), not Τυχικός (*Tychikos*, "Tychicus"), probably by confusion with v.9.

5 Codices ℵ E P etc. read οὗτοι δὲ προσελθόντες (*houtoi de proselthontes*, "these men had come," GK 4047, 4665), whereas $\mathfrak{P}^{74}$ B D et al. read οὗτοι δὲ προελθόντες (*houtoi de proelthontes*, "these men went on ahead"). The external textual evidence is about evenly divided, though with slightly more weight to be given to the latter. And the latter fits the context better (so NIV, NASB).

3. The Raising of Eutychus at Troas (20:7–12)

OVERVIEW

From 20:5 through to 28:31 (the end of Acts), as noted earlier in introducing panel 6, Luke's narrative gives considerable attention to ports of call, stopovers, and time spent on Paul's travels. And it includes a number of revealing anecdotes and detailed accounts of events. It contains, in fact, the kind of detail found in a travel journal. And the use of "we" in 20:5–15; 21:1–18; and 28:16 suggests its eyewitness character.

⁷On the first day of the week we came together to break bread. Paul spoke to the people and, because he intended to leave the next day, kept on talking until midnight. ⁸There were many lamps in the upstairs room where we were meeting. ⁹Seated in a window was a young man named Eutychus, who was sinking into a deep sleep as Paul

talked on and on. When he was sound asleep, he fell to the ground from the third story and was picked up dead. ¹⁰Paul went down, threw himself on the young man and put his arms around him. "Don't be alarmed," he said. "He's alive!" ¹¹Then he went upstairs again and broke bread and ate. After talking until daylight, he left. ¹²The people took the young man home alive and were greatly comforted.

COMMENTARY

7 Though Paul himself had not undertaken a mission at Troas (cf. 2Co 2:12–13), the gospel radiated out from many centers of influence in the Roman provinces of Galatia, Asia, Macedonia, and Achaia, and so penetrated the entire Gentile world of the eastern part of the empire. Thus at Troas, Paul and his colleagues found a group of believers and met with them "to break bread" and to give instruction regarding the Christian life. The mention of their meeting "on the first day of the week" (*en tē mia tōn sabbatōn*) is the earliest unambiguous evidence we have for believers in Jesus gathering together for worship on that day (cf. Jn 20:19, 26; 1Co 16:2; Rev 1:10). The Christians met in the evening, which because of the necessity of working during the day was probably the most convenient time. They met, Luke tells us, "to break bread" (*klasai arton*, GK *3089, 788*), which, especially after Paul's teaching in 1 Corinthians 10:16–17 and 11:17–34, must surely mean "to celebrate the Lord's Supper" (see comments at 2:42). At this time Paul "spoke to" (*dielegeto*, lit., "reasoned" or "discussed with"; NASB, "*began* talking to") the believers and continued doing so until midnight.

8–9 "As Paul talked on and on" (*dialegomenou tou Paulou*, lit., "during the course of the discussion by Paul," v.9), a young man named Eutychus, who was seated on a windowsill of the third-story room where the people were meeting, went to sleep and fell to his death. Just why he was seated there and why he went to sleep we are not told. He may sim-

ply have been bored by Paul's long discussion. Luke's reference to "many lamps" or "torches" (*lampades hikanai*, v.8) in that upstairs room may be taken to suggest that a lack of oxygen and the hypnotic effect of flickering flames may have caused Eutychus's drowsiness—thereby perhaps clearing Luke's hero Paul of any blame. Whatever its cause, Eutychus's fall from that third-story windowsill brought the meeting to a sudden and shocking halt. The people dashed down and found him dead.

10–11 Paul also ran down, and in an action reminiscent of Elijah's and Elisha's actions (cf. 1Ki 17:21; 2Ki 4:34–35), he "threw himself on the young man and put his arms around him" and declared to the troubled group, "Don't be alarmed! He's alive!" Indeed, Eutychus was restored to life. Then everyone returned to the third-story room, where they had a midnight snack—here certainly the compound "broke bread and ate" (*klasas ton arton kai geusamenos*) signifying an ordinary meal, not the Lord's Supper—and Paul continued to talk till dawn.

12 There is no hint that Paul took Eutychus's fall as a rebuke for long-windedness. Nor were the people troubled by the meeting's length. They were eager to learn and only had Paul with them a short time. It was an evening of great significance for the church at Troas! For Paul had taught them, they had fellowship in the Lord's Supper, and they had witnessed a dramatic sign of God's presence and power. No wonder Luke says they "were greatly comforted" (*pareklēthēsan ou metriōs*, lit., "were comforted not a little").

NOTES

7 On Luke's emphasis on persuasion in Paul's preaching—here by the use of the verb διαλέγομαι (*dialeg-omai,* "to reason" or "discuss") and in v.9 by the adverbial participle διαλεγόμενος (*dialegomenos*)—see comments at 17:2–3.

8 Codex Bezae (D) reads ὑπολαμπάδες (*hypolampades,* "small windows" or "lookout holes") instead of λαμπάδες (*lampades,* "lamps" or "torches," GK *3286*), though the Latin translation in that bilingual codex has *faculae* ("little torches").

12 Codex Bezae (D) reads ἀσπαζομένων αὐτῶν ἤγαγεν τὸν νεανίσκον ζῶντα (*aspazomenōn autōn ēgagen ton neaniskon zōnta,* "as they were saying farewell, he [Paul] brought the young man [to the people] alive") rather than the better-supported reading ἤγαγον δὲ τὸν παῖδα ζῶντα (*ēgagon de ton paida zōnta,* "they [the people] brought the boy [home] alive").

4. From Troas to Miletus (20:13–16)

> ¹³We went on ahead to the ship and sailed for Assos, where we were going to take Paul aboard. He had made this arrangement because he was going there on foot. ¹⁴When he met us at Assos, we took him aboard and went on to Mitylene. ¹⁵The next day we set sail from there and arrived off Kios. The day after that we crossed over to Samos, and on the following day arrived at Miletus. ¹⁶Paul had decided to sail past Ephesus to avoid spending time in the province of Asia, for he was in a hurry to reach Jerusalem, if possible, by the day of Pentecost.

COMMENTARY

13 Leaving Troas, Paul's companions took passage on a coastal vessel that was to stop at various ports along the western coast of Asia Minor. Paul waited a while longer at Troas. Then while the boat went around Cape Lectum, he took the direct route to Assos on the Roman coastal road and got there in time to join his colleagues on board. He may have wanted to wait at Troas in order to make sure that Eutychus was all right. Or he may have wanted to avoid the northeastern winds that blew around Cape Lectum. Or perhaps he just wanted to be alone with God on the walk to Assos.

14 Assos (modern Bahram Koi) was twenty miles south of Troas on the Gulf of Adramyttium. It was on the Roman coastal road and faced south toward the island of Lesbos. The boat sailed on to Mitylene, a splendid port on the southeastern coast of Lesbos and the chief city of this largest of the islands of western Asia Minor.

15 From there the contingent sailed to Kios, the major city of the island of Kios and an early free port—at least until Vespasian suspended its rights and brought it under Roman authority. Then they "passed through" (*parebalomen;* NIV, "we crossed over," GK *4125*) the channel separating Kios from the mainland of Asia Minor to come to Samos, an island directly west of Ephesus. So the boat arrived at Miletus, the ancient port at the mouth of the Meander River, some thirty miles south of Ephesus (see comments at 19:1).

16 Because of the extra time involved in his circuitous route of travel, Paul had to miss Passover at Jerusalem (see comments at vv.3, 5–6). But if at all possible he wanted at least to get to Jerusalem for Pentecost, on the fiftieth day after Passover (see comments at 2:1). This was the second of the great pilgrim festivals of Judaism. (The Festival of Sukkoth or Tabernacles, some four months after Pentecost, was the third.) Paul had previously decided not to take a boat that would stop at Ephesus, for he evidently preferred to forgo the emotional strain of another parting with the Ephesian church—possibly also to avoid some local danger. Furthermore, (1) the Aegean crossing had taken five days, (2) Paul and his companions had remained at Troas seven days, (3) the trip along the western coast of Asia Minor would take at least another ten days, and (4) they had yet to sail across the Mediterranean and then travel by land from Caesarea up to Jerusalem. So Paul was content to sail past Ephesus.

NOTES

13 The Old Syriac text, which is preserved in an Armenian translation of Ephraem of Syria's commentary on Acts, seems to reflect a Greek reading, ἐγὼ δὲ Λουκᾶς καὶ οἱ μετ' ἐμοῦ (*egō de Loukas kai hoi met' emou*, "and I, Luke, and those with me"), instead of the better-supported ἡμεῖς (*hēmeis*, "we"). Evidently this reading stems from a Western text.

A E P (and a corrected B) read προσελθόντες ἐπὶ τὸ πλοῖον (*proselthontes epi to ploion*, "when [we] had come to the ship"), and D reads κατελθόντες ἐπὶ τὸ πλοῖον (*katelthontes epi to ploion*, "when [we] went down to the ship"). But the Alexandrian text (𝔓⁷⁴ ℵ uncorrected B C etc.), which has προελθόντες ἐπὶ τὸ πλοῖον (*proelthontes epi to ploion*, "[we] went on ahead to the ship"), is better attested and fits the context better (cf. v.5).

Some Byzantine texts (L P, a number of minuscules, and certain recensions of the Syriac and Coptic versions), together with 𝔓⁴¹ (eighth century), read Θάσον (*Thason*, "Thasos") for the earlier and better-supported Ἄσσον (*Asson*, "Assos"). Thasos, an island east of Amphipolis, is a geographically impossible reading. It is a puzzle how it found its way into these texts here.

15 Codex Vaticanus (B) reads τῇ ἑσπέρᾳ (*tē hespera*, "in the evening") for τῇ ἑτέρᾳ (*tē hetera*, "on the following [day]"), which is probably a scribal error.

Several Western and Byzantine texts add καὶ μείναντες ἐν Τρωγυλλίᾳ [–ίῳ] (*kai meinantes en Trōgyllia* [*–iō*], "and having remained at Trogyllia" or "Trogyllium") after Σάμον (*Samon*, "Samos").

5. Farewell Address to the Ephesian Elders (20:17–38)

OVERVIEW

Paul's farewell address to the Ephesian elders is the closest approximation to a Pauline letter in Acts. Its general content recalls how in his letters Paul encouraged, warned, and exhorted his converts. Moreover, its theological themes and vocabulary are distinctly Pauline. In his three missionary sermons (13:16–41; 14:15–17; 17:22–31) and five defenses (chs. 22–26) Paul addressed non-Christian audiences. But here he is depicted as speaking in a pastoral manner to his own converts. It is significant that, in a situation similar to many of those faced in his letters, this farewell to the Ephesian elders reads like a miniature Pauline letter. This becomes all the more significant when we recall that nowhere else in Acts is there any evidence of a close knowledge of Paul's letters on the part of Luke.

The address is constructed in a way familiar to all readers of Paul's letters. The body of the letter has three parts, which deal with (1) Paul's past ministry at Ephesus (vv.18–21), (2) Paul's present plans in going to Jerusalem (vv.22–24), and (3) the future of Paul himself and of the church at Ephesus (vv.25–31). It concludes with a blessing (v.32) and then adds further words of exhortation that point the hearers to Paul's example and the teachings of Jesus (vv.33–35). Heading each section is an introductory formula, "you know" (*hymeis epistasthe*) at v.18; "and now, behold" (*kai nyn idou*; NASB) at v.22; "and now, behold, I know" (*kai nyn idou egō oida*; NASB) at v.25; and "and now" (*kai ta nyn*; NASB) at v.32.

17From Miletus, Paul sent to Ephesus for the elders of the church. 18When they arrived, he said to them: "You know how I lived the whole time I was with you, from the first day I came into the province of Asia. 19I served the Lord with great humility and with tears, although I was severely tested by the plots of the Jews. 20You know that I have not hesitated to preach anything that would be helpful to you but have taught you publicly and from house to house. 21I have declared to both Jews and Greeks that they must turn to God in repentance and have faith in our Lord Jesus.

22"And now, compelled by the Spirit, I am going to Jerusalem, not knowing what will happen to me there. 23I only know that in every city the Holy Spirit warns me that prison and hardships are facing me. 24However, I consider my life worth nothing to me, if only I may finish the race and complete the task the Lord Jesus has given me—the task of testifying to the gospel of God's grace.

25"Now I know that none of you among whom I have gone about preaching the kingdom will ever see me again. 26Therefore, I declare to you today that I am innocent of the blood of all men. 27For I have not hesitated to proclaim to you the whole will of God. 28Keep watch over yourselves and all the flock of which the Holy Spirit has made you overseers. Be shepherds of the church of God, which he bought with his own blood. 29I know that after I leave, savage wolves will come in among you and will not spare the flock. ³⁰ Even from your own number men will arise and distort the truth in order to draw away disciples after them. ³¹So be on your guard! Remember that for three years I never stopped warning each of you night and day with tears.

³²"Now I commit you to God and to the word of his grace, which can build you up and give you an inheritance among all those who are sanctified. ³³I have not coveted anyone's silver or gold or clothing. ³⁴You yourselves know that these hands of mine have supplied my own needs and the needs of my companions. ³⁵In everything I did, I showed you that by this kind of hard work we must help the weak, remembering the words the Lord Jesus himself said: 'It is more blessed to give than to receive.'"

³⁶When he had said this, he knelt down with all of them and prayed. ³⁷They all wept as they embraced him and kissed him. ³⁸What grieved them most was his statement that they would never see his face again. Then they accompanied him to the ship.

COMMENTARY

17 At Miletus the coastal boat docked for a number of days to load and unload cargo. So Paul took the opportunity to send for the elders of the Ephesian church to join him at Miletus. The road back to Ephesus around the gulf was considerably longer than the thirty miles directly between Ephesus and Miletus. It would have taken some time to engage a messenger and summon the elders, who could hardly have made the return trip as quickly as a single runner. Probably, therefore, we should think of the elders as arriving at Miletus, at the earliest, on the third day of Paul's stay there.

18–21 Paul's address to the Ephesian elders begins with an apologia closely paralleling that of 1 Thessalonians 2:1–12. As at Thessalonica, Paul's Ephesian opponents seem to have been prejudicing his converts against him during his absence, and so he found it necessary to defend his conduct and teaching by appealing to his hearers' knowledge of him. The opponents at Ephesus, like those at Thessalonica, seem to have been chiefly Jewish (v.19) and to have been asserting that full acceptance by God could

only come about by means of a faithful observance of the traditional forms of Judaism. Therefore Paul declares, "I have not hesitated to preach anything that would be helpful to you" (v.20). His preaching to both Jews and Gentiles focused on "repentance toward God" (*tēn eis theon metanoian* [GK *3567*]; NIV, "that they must turn to God") and "faith in the Lord Jesus" (*pistin* [GK *4411*] *eis ton kyrion hēmōn Iēsoun*; NIV, "faith in our Lord Jesus" [NASB adds "Christ" at the end of this phrase], v.21)—a content that is wholly sufficient for salvation (cf. Ro 10:9–10; 2Co 5:20–6:2; also Ac 26:20–23).

22–24 The second section of Paul's address concerns his plans to go to Jerusalem. Many have claimed a discrepancy between his being "compelled by the Spirit" to go to Jerusalem in 20:22–24 and his being warned by the Spirit not to go to Jerusalem in 21:4, 10–14. Furthermore, some have questioned Luke's account here in light of their understanding of the situations at Tyre and Caesarea. But Luke opened panel 6 of Acts with the statement that Paul's decision to go to Jerusalem was "by the

Spirit" (see comments at 19:21), and nothing here is incompatible with that programmatic statement. Both compulsion and warning were evidently involved in the Spirit's direction, with both being impressed on Paul by the Spirit at various times as he journeyed—probably through Christian prophets he met along the way. So he considered it necessary to complete his ministry of testifying to the grace of God throughout the eastern part of the empire by taking to believers at Jerusalem the money sent by Gentile believers in Galatia, Macedonia, Achaia, and Asia—a contribution he viewed as a tangible symbol of the faith of these Gentiles and of the unity of Jews and Gentiles in Christ.

25-27 In the third section of his address, Paul begins by speaking of his own future expectations after visiting Jerusalem. He tells the Ephesian elders that (1) neither they nor any of those he has ministered to in the eastern part of the empire would ever see him again, and (2) he felt free from any further responsibility in the East because he had done all that he could in proclaiming "the whole will of God" (v.27). Adolf Harnack, who accepted the hypothesis of two Roman imprisonments, concluded from 2 Timothy 4 that Paul did in fact return later to Asia after being released from imprisonment at Rome and that, therefore, for Luke to record the premonition expressed in v.25, which was falsified by later events, meant that he wrote before Paul's release and further ministry (cf. his *Date of the Acts and of the Synoptic Gospels*, 103). On the other hand, Martin Dibelius, who denied such an early date for Acts, used this passage to dismiss a two-imprisonment theory, for as Haenchen (who was probably Dibelius's closest disciple), 592, argued, "Anyone who writes thus knows nothing of Paul's deliverance and return to the East, but rather of his death in Rome."

In accord with my own acceptance of an early date for the writing of Acts (see Introduction,

pp. 699-701) and my belief that two Roman imprisonments can be inferred from the data, I judge Harnack's opinion in this matter to be closer to the truth. Romans 15:23-29 clearly indicates that at this time Paul intended to leave his ministry in the East and after visiting Jerusalem to move on to evangelize in the western part of the empire with Rome as his base. But it is not impossible that later his plans changed—as they did at various times throughout his eastern campaign—and that Luke wrote at a time when the remembrance of Paul's purpose not to return to the East was still fresh and his modification of it still in the future.

28-31 The third section of Paul's address continues with an exhortation to the Ephesian elders in the light of what Paul sees as soon taking place in the church. He warns regarding persecution from outside and apostasy within (vv.29-30; cf. 1Ti 1:19-20; 4:1-5; 2Ti 1:15; 2:17-18; 3:1-9, which tell of a later widespread revolt against Paul's teaching in Asia, and Rev 2:1-7, which speaks of the Ephesian church as having abandoned its first love). So he gives the elders the solemn exhortation of v.28: "Keep watch over yourselves and all the flock of which the Holy Spirit has made you overseers. Be shepherds of the church of God, which he bought with his own blood."

Theologically, much in Luke's précis of Paul's address reflects Paul's thought and expression at this stage in his life, as these are revealed in the letters he wrote at Ephesus (i.e., 1 Corinthians), in Macedonia (i.e., 2 Corinthians), and at Corinth (i.e., Romans), all of which were composed shortly before this time. Paul's use of the word for "church" (*ekklēsia*, GK *1711*), for example, is an interesting case in point. For while in the salutations of his Galatian and Thessalonian letters he used *ekklēsia* in a local sense (cf. Gal 1:2, "to the churches in Galatia"; 1Th 1:1 and 2Th 1:1, "to the church of the Thessalonians"), in addressing his converts at Corinth he used the word in a more universal way: "to the church of God in Corinth" (1Co 1:2; 2Co 1:1). And thereafter in his writings *ekklēsia* or "church" appears always in a universal sense (cf. esp. Ephesians and Colossians). Likewise, his easy association of "God" with the one who obtained the church for himself "with his own blood"—i.e., Jesus—corresponds closely in expression to the doxology of Romans 9:5, which speaks of "Christ, who is God over all, forever praised!" In addition, reference to the blood of Jesus (*hē haima tou idiou*, "his own blood," GK *135*) as being instrumental in humanity's redemption appears first in Paul's writings at Romans 3:25 and 5:9 (and thereafter in Eph 1:7; 2:13; Col 1:20).

32 Paul concludes his address with a blessing committing them "to God and to the word of his grace." Though Paul must leave them, God was with them and so was his word—the word of grace that was able to build them up, give them an inheritance, and sanctify them. Again, the expressions used in Luke's précis of Paul's blessing comprise a catena of Pauline terms: "grace" (which appears in almost all of his salutations and benedictions, as well as being at the heart of his expositions); "build up" (cf. 1Co 8:1; 10:23; 14:4, 17; 1Th 5:11); "inheritance" (cf. Ro 8:17; Gal 3:18; Eph 1:14; 5:5; Col 3:24); and "sanctified" (cf. Ro 15:16; 1Co 1:2; 6:11; 7:14; Eph 5:26; 1Th 5:23).

33–35 Following his blessing, Paul adds—as he does in his own letters—a few further words of exhortation, which urge the elders of the church to

care for the needs of God's people without thought of material reward. He asks them to follow his example (cf. Php 3:17) and calls on them to remember the words of Jesus applicable here: "It is more blessed to give than to receive" (v.35). Paul often related his ethical exhortations to the teachings of Jesus (cf. Ro 12–14; 1Th 4:1–12), as well as to the personal example of Jesus (cf. Php 2:5–11), and he does so here. These express words, of course, do not explicitly appear in any of the canonical gospels. But they can be approximately paralleled by Luke 6:38, and the spirit they express certainly permeates the portrayals of Jesus in all four gospels. While some believe the words themselves to have come through a post-ascension revelatory oracle by a Christian prophet that was attributed to Jesus, it is probably truer to ascribe them to an original Logia or "Sayings" collection of Jesus' teachings (so-called "Q") that circulated within the early Christian communities, whether in written or oral form.

36–38 When Paul had finished speaking he knelt down with the Ephesian elders and prayed with them. On the basis of the parallels between this farewell address and Paul's own letters, the substance of what he prayed for can be found in such places as Ephesians 1:15–23; Philippians 1:3–11; Colossians 1:3–14; and 1 Thessalonians 1:2–3; 3:11–13; 5:23–24. Then after a deeply moving, affectionate, and sorrowful farewell with tears on both sides, Paul and his traveling companions boarded the ship.

NOTES

18 Codex Bezae (D) has a number of characteristic additions in this verse: (1) it adds ὁμόσε ὄντων αὐτῶν (*homose ontōn autōn*, "while they were together") after ὡς δὲ παρεγένοντο (*hōs de paregenonto*, "when they [the Ephesian elders] arrived"), which is decidedly superfluous; (2) it inserts ἀδελφοί (*adelphoi*, "brothers") after ἐπίστασθε (*epistasthe*, "you know"), which is understandable but unnecessary; and (3) it reads ὡς τριετίαν ἢ καὶ πλεῖον ποταπῶς μεθ᾽ ὑμῶν ἦν παντὸς χρόνου (*hōs trietian ē kai pleion potapōs meth' hymōn ēn pantos chronou*, "for about three years or even more") after Ἀσίαν (*Asian*, "Asia"), which is probably derived from v.31.

21 The Alexandrian text ($\mathfrak{P}^{74}$ ℵ A B C E Ψ) and Byzantine text (L P and most minuscules) read εἰς τὸν κύριον ἡμῶν Ἰησοῦν Χριστόν (*eis ton kyrion hēmōn Iēsoun Christon*, "in our Lord Jesus Christ"), though B Ψ L and some recensions of the Old Latin, Syriac, and Coptic versions omit Χριστόν (*Christon*, "Christ"). There is, however, as Metzger, 424, comments, "no good reason why Χριστόν [*Christon*] should have been omitted if it were present originally, whereas scribal expansion of the names of the Lord is of frequent occurrence." The Western text (D, and as represented in a recension of the Old Latin) has the preposition διά (*dia*, "through") rather than εἰς (*eis*, "in").

24 The Alexandrian text ($\mathfrak{P}^{74}$ ℵ B C etc.) reads ἀλλ' οὐδενὸς λόγου ποιοῦμαι τὴν ψυχὴν τιμίαν ἐμαυτῷ (*all' oudenos logou poioumai tēn psychēn timian emautō*, "but I consider my life worth nothing to me"), which is a somewhat awkward Greek construction. Codex Bezae (D) rephrases and expands that better-supported reading as follows: ἀλλ' οὐδενὸς λόγον ἔχω μοι οὐδὲ ποιοῦμαι τὴν ψυχήν μου τιμίαν ἐμαυτοῦ (*all' oudenos logon echō moi oude poioumai tēn psychēn mou timian emautou*, "but I take no account regarding myself, nor do I value my life as being precious to me"). The Byzantine text (E H L P and most minuscules) has the same expansion as the Western text but reverses the verbs ἔχω (*echō*) and ποιοῦμαι (*poioumai*).

The Byzantine text (E H L P and most minuscules) adds μετὰ χαρᾶς (*meta charas*, "with joy") after τὸν δρόμον μου (*ton dromon mou*, "my race"; NIV, "the race"; NASB, "my course"); so also the TR, which was picked up by the KJV.

Codex Bezae (D) adds τοῦ λόγου (*tou logou*, "of the word") after τὴν διακονίαν (*tēn diakonian*, "the ministry"; NIV, "the task"). It also adds Ἰουδαίοις καὶ Ἕλλησιν (*Ioudaiois kai Hellēsin*, "to Jews and Greeks") after διαμαρτύρασθαι (*diamartyrasthai*, "to testify"; NIV, "testifying"), evidently attempting to parallel v.21.

25 The Western text (D, and as reflected in recensions of the Old Latin and Coptic versions) adds τοῦ [κυρίου] Ἰησοῦ (*tou [kyriou] Iēsou*, "of [the Lord] Jesus") after τὴν βασιλείαν (*tēn basileian*, "the kingdom"), while the Byzantine text (E H L P and most minuscules) add τοῦ θεοῦ (*tou theou*, "of God"), as does the TR and thus the KJV. The text without either of these additions is well supported by the Alexandrian text ($\mathfrak{P}^{74}$ ℵ A B C etc.).

28 Codices Sinaiticus (ℵ) and Vaticanus (B), together with a number of minuscules and many church fathers, read τὴν ἐκκλησίαν τοῦ θεοῦ (*tēn ekklēsian tou theou*, "the church of God"), whereas $\mathfrak{P}^{74}$ A C E Ψ, together with a number of other minuscules and many other church fathers, read τὴν ἐκκλησίαν τοῦ κυρίου (*tēn ekklēsian tou kyriou*, "the church of the Lord"). The external textual evidence seems almost evenly balanced, though because of the combined testimony of the major Alexandrian uncial MSS ℵ and B it is probably best to read "the church of God."

On the early use of the christological title "God" in Romans 9:5, see my *Christology of Early Jewish Christianity*, 138–39.

32 The reading τῷ θεῷ (*tō theō*, "to God") is well supported by $\mathfrak{P}^{74}$ ℵ A C D E Ψ L P, most minuscules, and most versions, though Codex Vaticanus (B), supported by some minuscules and some Old Latin and Coptic versions, reads τῷ κυρίῳ (*tō kyriō*, "to the Lord").

Several Western texts (though D is here corrupt) add at the end of this verse the doxology, "To him be the glory for ever and ever. Amen."

6. On to Jerusalem (21:1–16)

OVERVIEW

The narrative of Paul's journey to Jerusalem is of particular literary and historical interest because it comprises most of the third of Luke's four "we" sections (21:1–18; cf. 16:10–17; 20:5–15; 27:1–28:16). The material in this section seems to be based on a travel journal of one of Paul's companions (see Introduction, p. 684), for it includes numerous details about the trip and various anecdotes. The section is also significant theologically because Luke appears to be describing Paul's trip to Jerusalem in terms of Jesus' journey to Jerusalem to die. Luke knows, of course, that Paul did not die at Jerusalem. Yet he seems to sketch out Paul's journey to Jerusalem in terms that roughly parallel Jesus' journey: (1) a similar plot by the Jews; (2) a handing over to the Gentiles (cf. v.11); (3) a triple prediction of coming suffering (cf. 20:22–24; 21:4, 10–11; see also Lk 9:22, 44; 18:31–34); (4) a steadfast resolution (cf. v.13); and (5) a resignation to God's will (cf. v.14). As Luke has reserved for Paul the mission to the Gentiles, which Jesus saw as inherent in the Servant theology of Isaiah 61 (cf. Lk 4:16–21; see Overview, pp. 907–8), so he describes Paul's journey to Jerusalem in terms reminiscent of the Suffering Servant.

¹After we had torn ourselves away from them, we put out to sea and sailed straight to Cos. The next day we went to Rhodes and from there to Patara. ²We found a ship crossing over to Phoenicia, went on board and set sail. ³After sighting Cyprus and passing to the south of it, we sailed on to Syria. We landed at Tyre, where our ship was to unload its cargo. ⁴Finding the disciples there, we stayed with them seven days. Through the Spirit they urged Paul not to go on to Jerusalem. ⁵But when our time was up, we left and continued on our way. All the disciples and their wives and children accompanied us out of the city, and there on the beach we knelt to pray. ⁶After saying good-by to each other, we went aboard the ship, and they returned home.

⁷We continued our voyage from Tyre and landed at Ptolemais, where we greeted the brothers and stayed with them for a day. ⁸Leaving the next day, we reached Caesarea and stayed at the house of Philip the evangelist, one of the Seven. ⁹He had four unmarried daughters who prophesied.

¹⁰After we had been there a number of days, a prophet named Agabus came down from Judea. ¹¹Coming over to us, he took Paul's belt, tied his own hands and feet with it and said, "The Holy Spirit says, 'In this way the Jews of Jerusalem will bind the owner of this belt and will hand him over to the Gentiles.'"

¹²When we heard this, we and the people there pleaded with Paul not to go up to Jerusalem. ¹³Then Paul answered, "Why are you weeping and breaking my heart? I am ready not only to be bound, but also to die in Jerusalem for the name of the Lord Jesus." ¹⁴When he would not be dissuaded, we gave up and said, "The Lord's will be done."

¹⁵After this, we got ready and went up to Jerusalem. ¹⁶Some of the disciples from Caesarea accompanied us and brought us to the home of Mnason, where we were to stay. He was a man from Cyprus and one of the early disciples.

COMMENTARY

1–2 "After we had torn ourselves away" (the passive participle *apospasthentas*, GK *685*, offering the suggestion of emotional violence in the parting), Luke says that "we"—i.e., Paul and his associates—continued by boat to Cos. Cos was a small island of the Dodecanese group of islands and a free state within the province of Asia in NT times. The next day, they sailed to Rhodes, the capital of the large Dodecanese island of Rhodes just twelve miles off the mainland of Asia Minor. In the Greek period, Rhodes had been a rich and powerful city-state. In Paul's day, however, it was little more than a beautiful port with an aura of past glory, which still lingers on in the Rhodes of today. The next stop was Patara, a Lycian city on the southwestern coast of Asia Minor. Patara was a fairly large commercial city with a fine harbor. It served as a favorite port of call for large ships traveling between the eastern Mediterranean ports in Syria, Palestine, and Egypt and the Aegean ports in Asia, Macedonia, and Achaia. There Paul and his associates boarded a large merchant ship bound nonstop for Tyre, the famous Phoenician seaport of Syria, for they desired to travel quickly (v.2).

3 Sailing the 400 miles from Patara to Tyre, they passed by Cyprus to the south. John Chrysostom (*Hom. Acts* 45.2) of Syrian Antioch said that the voyage took five days, which is as intelligent an approximation as any.

4 A church had been established at Tyre through the witness of the Christian Hellenists, or hellenized Jewish believers in Jesus (see comments and note at 6:1), who were forced to leave Jerusalem at the time of Stephen's martyrdom (cf. 11:19). Paul had fellowship with the Christians at Tyre while the ship was unloading. Their attempt to dissuade him "through the Spirit" (*dia tou pneumatos*) from going on to Jerusalem may mean that the Spirit was ordering Paul not to continue on with his plans. In that case, his determination to proceed was in disobedience to the Holy Spirit. Or it may be, as Kirsopp Lake proposed, that Paul doubted the inspiration of these Tyrian believers (*Beginnings of Christianity* [ed. Foakes-Jackson and Lake], 4.266). In all likelihood, however, it is probably best to understand the Greek preposition *dia* ("through") as meaning that it was the Spirit's message that was the occasion for the Christians' concern rather than that their trying to dissuade Paul was directly inspired by the Spirit. So in line with 19:21 and 20:22–24, we should treat this not as Paul's rejection of a prophetic oracle but as another case of the Spirit's revelation to Christian prophets of what lay in store for Paul at Jerusalem—and, of course, of his new friends' natural desire to dissuade him (cf. vv.10–15).

5–6 After a scene reminiscent of Paul's parting with the Ephesian elders (cf. 20:36–37), the apostle and his companions sailed from Tyre.

7 The ship went on to Ptolemais (Acco, or modern Acre on the northern cove of Haifa bay), which was another ancient Phoenician seaport some twenty-five miles south of Tyre. There it made harbor for a day, undoubtedly again to unload cargo. Once more, Paul met with the Christians of the city. Like the origin of the church at Tyre, probably

Christianity at Ptolemais also stemmed from the witness of the Hellenistic Jewish believers who had to flee Jerusalem earlier (cf. 11:19).

8 Paul and his party came to Caesarea, the magnificent harbor and city built by Herod the Great as the port of Jerusalem and the Roman provincial capital of Judea (see comments at 10:1). Caesarea is thirty-two miles south of Ptolemais. Luke does not say so, but Paul and his companions probably reached it by the ship on which they had crossed the Mediterranean instead of by disembarking at Ptolemais and walking to Caesarea.

There they stayed with Philip the evangelist (not the apostle Philip), one of the Seven who had been appointed in the early days of the Jerusalem church to take care of the daily distribution of food (cf. 6:1–6). He had evangelized in Samaria and the maritime plain of Palestine (cf. 8:4–40) and then apparently settled at Caesarea for some twenty years. Paul stayed at Philip's home for "a number of days" (*hēmeras pleious*, v.10). The timing of Paul's stopovers from Troas to Caesarea had been largely dependent on the shipping schedules. But having disembarked at Caesarea, he could now arrange his own schedule. For a man in a hurry to get to Jerusalem, this delay of several days—perhaps, as has often been supposed, up to two weeks—seems somewhat strange and leads us to ask why he broke his journey here. Of course, he might simply have wanted to rest after his strenuous trip from Corinth to Philippi by land and from Philippi to Caesarea by sea. Certainly he would have been warmly welcomed by the Caesarean believers, and they would undoubtedly have wanted him to rest after such a strenuous journey. More to the point, however, is the fact that he wanted to be in Jerusalem on the day of Pentecost (cf. 20:16)—not just to get there as early as possible, but to arrive at what he believed was a strategic moment. So Paul's stay at Caesarea was probably a deliberate matter of timing.

9 Luke speaks of Philip as having four unmarried daughters who were prophetesses (*prophēteuousai*, GK *4736*), yet says nothing about what they prophesied. Had he been in the habit of making up speeches for the various characters he portrays in Acts, this would have been a prime opportunity for doing so. Perhaps these prophesying maidens and their father gave Luke source material for his two volumes—possibly, it may be conjectured, on women for the writing of his gospel and on Philip's mission in Samaria and ministry to the Ethiopian eunuch for his Acts. He could have received such information from them either during this visit or during the two-year period of his imprisonment in the city, or perhaps at both times (so Harnack, *Luke the Physician*, 155–57). Eusebius (*Hist. eccl.* 3.39) tells us that Philip and his daughters eventually moved to Hierapolis in the province of Asia—probably in flight from Roman antagonism toward Jews in Palestine from the mid-60s on—and that his daughters provided information on the early days of the Jerusalem church to Papias, the author of five books (which are not extant) on "Our Lord's Sayings."

10–11 While Paul was at Caesarea, the Jerusalemite prophet Agabus (cf. 11:27–28) came to the city. With the belt that held together Paul's outer cloak, he tied his own feet and hands in an act of prophetic symbolism (cf. 1Ki 11:29–39; Isa 20:2–6; Eze 4:1–5:17) and announced, "In this way the Jews of Jerusalem will bind the owner of this belt and will hand him over to the Gentiles" (v.11).

12–13 In response to this dramatic prophecy, the Caesarean believers, together with Paul's own traveling companions (note the "we" of v.12), begged him not to go. But Paul's determination to go to Jerusalem came from an inner spiritual constraint that could not be set aside. It had come to Paul by the Spirit's direction (cf. 19:21; 20:22) and was in response to a growing conviction that he must present the gift of money from the Gentile churches personally for it to be understood as the symbol of unity he intended it to be (cf. 1Co 16:4 with Ro 15:31). Paul well knew that his reception at Jerusalem might be less than cordial (cf. Ro 15:30–32). And when his friends learned of the dangers ahead of him, they naturally tried to dissuade him.

15–16 Paul and his colleagues, accompanied by some Caesarean Christians, took the road up to Jerusalem, some sixty-five miles to the southeast. At Jerusalem they brought him to the home of Mnason, a Cypriot and one of the "early disciples" (*archaiō mathētē*)—i.e., a disciple of Jesus from the beginning of the Jerusalem church. Not everyone in the Jerusalem church, of course, would have been prepared to have Paul and his company of Jewish and Gentile associates as houseguests during the festival of Pentecost. But the Caesarean Christians knew their man.

NOTES

1 The Western text (D, and as represented in recensions of the Old Latin, Vulgate, and Syriac versions) reads εἰς Πάταρα καὶ Μύρα (*eis Patara kai Myra*, "to Patara and Myra"), while 𝔓⁴¹ (eighth century) apparently reads only εἰς Μύρα (*eis Myra*, "to Myra"). Myra was a Lycian port farther east of Patara on the south coast of Asia Minor. Probably it was added here under the influence of 27:5 ("we landed at Myra in Lycia") or possibly assimilated to the narrative of the apocryphal *Acts of Paul and Thecla*, ch. 4 (Paul preaching at Myra).

8 The Byzantine text (H L P and most minuscules) inserts οἱ περὶ τὸν Παῦλον (*hoi peri ton Paulon*, "those with Paul" or "those of Paul's party") before ἤλθομεν (*ēlthomen*, "we came" or "reached," GK *2262*), which was incorporated into the TR and so into the KJV.

12 The Western text (D, and as represented by a recension of the Old Latin) adds the name τὸν Παῦλον (*ton Paulon*, "Paul"), evidently for stylistic reasons (as does the NIV, though not the NASB).

On "going up" (ἀναβαίνω, *anabainō*, GK *326*) to Jerusalem, see 11:2; 21:15; 24:11; 25:1, 9. On the reverential use of the expressions "to go up" and "to go down," see comments at 3:1 and 8:5.

13 Codex Bezae (D) adds πρὸς ἡμᾶς (*pros hēmas*, "to us") before ὁ Παῦλος (*ho Paulos*, "Paul"), thereby picking up the first person plural ἡμεῖς (*hēmeis*, "we") of v.12. It also adds βούλομαι (*boulomai*, "I am resolved") after δεθῆναι (*dethēnai*, "to be bound"), which only strengthens the adverb ἑτοίμως (*hetoimōs*, "ready," "willing"). And D, together with C and recensions of the Old Latin and Syriac versions, adds Χριστοῦ (*Christou*, "Christ") after τοῦ κυρίου Ἰησοῦ (*tou kyriou Iēsou*, "of the Lord Jesus"), which is a fairly typical expansion of many ancient scribes.

14 Codex Bezae (D) adds πρὸς ἀλλήλους (*pros allēlous*, "to one another") after εἰπόντες (*eipontes*, "saying" or "we said"), which in context is superfluous.

15 On the preposition μετά (*meta*) with a temporal designation (here μετὰ τὰς ἡμέρας ταύτας, *meta tas hēmeras tautas*, "on the next day"; NIV, "after this"; NASB, "after these days") as vying with μὲν οὖν (*men oun*, "so," "then") as a Lukan connective in the latter half of Acts, see comments at 15:36.

Codex Bezae (D) recasts the first part of this verse to read μετὰ δέ τινας ἡμέρας ἀποταξάμενοι (*meta de tinas hēmeras apotaxamenoi*, "and after some days we bade them farewell").

The participle ἐπισκευασάμενοι (*episkeuasamenoi*; NIV and NASB, "we got ready") is without parallel in the middle voice. Its general meaning seems to be "having furnished ourselves for the journey" and so may suggest anything from "packed our baggage" (NEB, JB)—which is a refinement on "took up our baggage" (RSV, ASV), and which, in turn, was a modernization of "took up our carriages" (KJV)—to "saddled our horses" (cf. W. M. Ramsay, in *A Dictionary of the Bible*, ed. James Hastings [Edinburgh: T&T Clark, 1898], 5:398).

16 The Western text (D, and as represented in a recension of the Syriac version) recasts the last half of this verse to read, "And these [the Caesarean believers] brought us to those with whom we were to lodge. And when we arrived at a certain village, we stayed with Mnason of Cyprus, an early disciple." Such a reading suggests that Paul and his associates stayed with Mnason in "a certain village" outside Jerusalem, not in Jerusalem, which is wholly unnecessary to postulate.

C. Arrival, Arrest, and Defenses at Jerusalem (21:17–23:22)

1. Arrival at Jerusalem (21:17–26)

¹⁷When we arrived at Jerusalem, the brothers received us warmly. ¹⁸The next day Paul and the rest of us went to see James, and all the elders were present. ¹⁹Paul greeted them and reported in detail what God had done among the Gentiles through his ministry.

²⁰When they heard this, they praised God. Then they said to Paul: "You see, brother, how many thousands of Jews have believed, and all of them are zealous for the law. ²¹They have been informed that you teach all the Jews who live among the Gentiles to turn away from Moses, telling them not to circumcise their children or live according to our customs. ²²What shall we do? They will certainly hear that you have come, ²³so do what we tell you. There are four men with us who have made a vow. ²⁴Take these men, join in their purification rites and pay their expenses, so that they can have their heads shaved. Then everybody will know there is no truth in these reports about you, but that you yourself are living in obedience to the law. ²⁵As for the Gentile believers, we have written to them our decision that they should abstain from food sacrificed to idols, from blood, from the meat of strangled animals and from sexual immorality."

²⁶The next day Paul took the men and purified himself along with them. Then he went to the temple to give notice of the date when the days of purification would end and the offering would be made for each of them.

COMMENTARY

17–18 With these two verses the third "we" section of Acts concludes (cf. 16:10–17; 20:5–15; 21:1–18; 27:1–28:16). It is likely, however, that the pronoun "we" is dropped in 21:19–26:32 for purely literary reasons and that we should assume Luke's presence in Palestine for a longer time than vv.17–18 themselves imply. Where Paul is the focus of the narrative—particularly in his discussion with the leaders of the Jerusalem church, his arrest in the temple precincts, and his five speeches of defense at Jerusalem and Caesarea—Luke speaks only of him, though it may be assumed that Luke himself was also somewhere in the background.

It was probably at Mnason's house in Jerusalem that the believers gathered to receive Paul and his associates "warmly." Then on the next day, "Paul and the rest of us," as Luke has it (v.18), called on James. In all likelihood, Peter, John, and some of the other apostles had been in the city fifty days earlier for Passover. But from the fact that Luke does not mention them when Paul arrived for the festival of Pentecost, we may assume they were away from Jerusalem at the time. James was the resident leader of the Jerusalem church (see comments at 12:17; 15:13). Sharing with him in the administration of the church was a body of "elders" (*hoi presbyteroi*, GK *4565*)—perhaps, as many have surmised, a group of seventy leaders patterned after the Sanhedrin—who were also there to meet Paul and his colleagues.

19 On this occasion, Paul "reported in detail what God had done among the Gentiles through his ministry." Undoubtedly he also presented the collection of money from the Gentile churches to James and the elders. Nowhere in Acts does Luke himself refer to this collection for believers at Jerusalem, except later at 24:17 in reporting Paul's speech before Felix. This omission is probably because he did not know how to explain to his Gentile readers (1) the significance of such a gift of money as being anything more than a way of currying favor, and (2) Paul's fears that the Jerusalem Christians might not accept it. But the presentation of this gift from his Gentile churches was the chief motive for Paul wanting to go to Jerusalem (cf. 1Co 16:1–4; Ro 15:25–27). In fact, he felt it absolutely necessary to present the gift personally to the Jerusalem church so that it would be viewed as a true symbol of Christian unity and not as a bribe,

though he feared both opposition from the Jews and rejection by the Jewish Christians of the city (cf. Ro 15:30–31).

To understand Paul's fears we must realize that the Jerusalem church was increasingly caught between its allegiance to the nation and its fraternal relation to Paul's Gentile mission. In such a bind, to accept a contribution from the Gentile churches was to be identified further with that mission, and so to drive another wedge between themselves and their Jewish compatriots. True, believers at Jerusalem had accepted such a contribution earlier (cf. 11:27–30) and had declared their fraternity with Paul in previous meetings (cf. Gal 2:6–10; also Ac 15:13–29). But with the rising tide of Jewish nationalism and a growing body of scrupulous believers in the Jerusalem church—perhaps as a result of a large number of Essenes becoming "obedient to the faith" (see comments at 6:7b)—Jewish-Christian solidarity with the Gentile mission was becoming more and more difficult to affirm. For if the Jerusalem church's relations with the nation were to be maintained and opportunities for an outreach to Israel kept open, Jewish Christians could hardly be seen to be fraternizing with Gentiles.

Undoubtedly, Paul recognized the increased tensions at Jerusalem. No wonder he feared that James and the elders, for the sake of their Jewish relations and mission, might feel constrained to reject the contribution, thereby severing, in effect, the connection between the Pauline churches and the Jerusalem church—which, at least in his eyes, would have been a disaster in many ways. Luke, however, seems to have found all this exceedingly difficult to explain to his Gentile readers. Thus it may be postulated that he excluded (except in 24:17 when reporting Paul's words in his defense before Felix) any mention of this collection in his Acts.

20–24 James and the elders responded to Paul's report about "what God had done among the

Gentiles" (v.19) by praising God (v.20). Yet they also urged Paul to join with four Jewish Christians who were fulfilling their Nazirite vows and to pay for their required offerings (v.24). In effect they were saying to Paul, "We can identify ourselves more openly with your Gentile mission if you will join with these men and identify yourself openly with the Jewish nation." Thus they were protecting themselves against Jewish recriminations while at the same time affirming their connection with Paul and his mission. As they saw it, they were providing Paul with a way of protecting himself against any accusation that he was teaching Jews to apostatize from Judaism. In view of his having come earlier to Jerusalem in more placid circumstances to fulfill a Nazirite vow of his own (cf. 18:18–19:22), Paul seems not to have viewed such a suggestion as particularly onerous (cf. v.26). Such an action was evidently considered by all concerned to be a happy solution to the vexing practical and political problems facing both Paul and the Jerusalem church.

25 Many commentators have argued that the fourfold Jerusalem decree (cf. 15:20, 29) has no relevance to this situation but was only brought in to inform Paul for the first time of something drawn up behind his back at Jerusalem after the Jerusalem Council. Yet the reference to the decree here is closely connected with what has gone before and should be viewed as a reminder of that agreed-on basis for fellowship between Jewish and Gentile believers. So having urged Paul to follow their proposed course of action, the leaders of the Jerusalem church go on to assure him that such action would in no way rescind their earlier decision to impose nothing further on Gentile converts than these four injunctions, which were given for the sake of harmony within the church and in order not to impede the progress of the Jewish-Christian mission.

26 Coming from abroad, Paul would have had to regain ceremonial purity by a seven-day ritual of purification before he could be present at the absolution ceremony of the four Jewish Christians in the Jerusalem temple. This ritual included reporting to one of the priests and being sprinkled with water of atonement on the third and seventh days. To imagine that Paul was here taking on himself a seven-day Nazirite vow conflicts with Jewish law because thirty days were considered the shortest period for such a vow (cf. *m. Naz.* 3:6). What Paul did was to report to the priest at the start of his seven days of purification, inform him that he was providing the funds for the offerings of the four impoverished men who had taken Nazirite vows, and return to the temple at regular intervals during the week for the appropriate rites. He would have also informed the priest of the date when the Nazirite vows of the four would be completed (or perhaps they were already completed and the four had only to make the offerings and present the hair) and when he planned to be with them (either with all of them together or with each individually) for the absolution ceremony. To pay the charges for Nazirite offerings was considered an act of piety and a symbol of identification with the Jewish people (cf. Josephus, *Ant.* 19.294, on Herod Agrippa I's underwriting of the expenses for a number of poor Nazirites).

NOTES

17 Codex Bezae (D), as supported by the Syriac Harclean version, reads κακεῖθεν δὲ ἐξιόντες ἤλθομεν (*kakeithen de exiontes ēlthomen,* "when we had departed thence we came [to Jerusalem]") rather than the better-supported γενομένων δὲ ἡμῶν (*genomenōn de hēmōn,* "when we arrived [at Jerusalem]"). The Western reading assumes that Mnason lived in a village outside Jerusalem (see note at v.16) and so has Paul and his associates leaving Mnason's home in that village and coming to Jerusalem.

20 Codex Sinaiticus (ℵ) omits the phrase ἐν τοῖς Ἰουδαίοις (*en tois Ioudaiois*, "among the Jews"), probably accidentally. The Western text interprets the phrase to mean simply Ἰουδαίων (*Ioudaiōn*, "of Jews"), as does the NIV. The Byzantine text (H L P and several minuscules) omits any reference to "the Jews," probably as the result of homoioteleuton, where the eye of the scribe passed from one word to another with the same ending (Ἰουδαίων καὶ πεπιστευκότων, *Ioudaiōn kai pepisteukotōn*).

21 The word πάντας (*pantas*, "all") is omitted by A D E and by the Vulgate and the Coptic Bohairic version. It is otherwise well attested ($\mathfrak{P}^{45}$ ℵ B etc.). Furthermore, its awkwardness in the sentence suggests that it would hardly have been inserted by a later scribe.

23 For εὐχή (*euchē*, "oath" or "vow," GK *2376*) as meaning a Nazirite vow, see *TDNT* 2.777 (cf. 18:18).

24 The Greek verb ξυράω (*xyraō*, "to shave," GK *3834*) is the equivalent of the Hebrew verb *gillaḥ*, which appears several times in *m. Naz.* 2:5–6 to mean "to bring the offerings of a Nazirite"—i.e., a male lamb, a female lamb, a ram, and their associated meal and drink offerings as stated in Numbers 6:14–15.

25 The Western text treats the Jerusalem decree as a three-clause ethical maxim, as it does at 15:20 and 29 (though here without the appended negative Golden Rule).

2. Arrest in the Temple (21:27–36)

27When the seven days were nearly over, some Jews from the province of Asia saw Paul at the temple. They stirred up the whole crowd and seized him, 28shouting, "Men of Israel, help us! This is the man who teaches all men everywhere against our people and our law and this place. And besides, he has brought Greeks into the temple area and defiled this holy place." 29(They had previously seen Trophimus the Ephesian in the city with Paul and assumed that Paul had brought him into the temple area.)

30The whole city was aroused, and the people came running from all directions. Seizing Paul, they dragged him from the temple, and immediately the gates were shut. 31While they were trying to kill him, news reached the commander of the Roman troops that the whole city of Jerusalem was in an uproar. 32He at once took some officers and soldiers and ran down to the crowd. When the rioters saw the commander and his soldiers, they stopped beating Paul.

33The commander came up and arrested him and ordered him to be bound with two chains. Then he asked who he was and what he had done. 34Some in the crowd shouted one thing and some another, and since the commander could not get at the truth because of the uproar, he ordered that Paul be taken into the barracks. 35When Paul reached the steps, the violence of the mob was so great he had to be carried by the soldiers. 36The crowd that followed kept shouting, "Away with him!"

COMMENTARY

27–29 The strategy of Paul's taking a vow and paying for the Nazirite offerings hardly proved successful. Probably nothing could have conciliated those whose minds were already prejudiced against Paul. Jews from Asia who had come to Jerusalem for the festival of Pentecost determined to take more effective action against him than they had at Ephesus. So toward the end of Paul's seven-day purification—possibly when he came to receive the water of atonement on the seventh day—they instigated a riot under the pretense that he had brought Trophimus, the Gentile representative from Ephesus, beyond the barrier (the *soreg*) that separated the court of the Gentiles from the temple courts reserved for Jews alone.

Josephus (*J.W.* 5.193) described the wall separating the court of the Gentiles from the Holy Place, or inner courts reserved for Jews alone, as "a stone balustrade, three cubits high [ca. four and one-half feet high; though *m. Mid.* 2:3 says it was "ten handbreadths high," ca. two and one-half feet high] and of excellent workmanship." "In this at regular intervals," he goes on to say, "stood slabs giving warning, some in Greek, others in Latin characters, of the law of purification, to wit that no foreigner was permitted to enter the Holy Place, for so the second enclosure of the temple was called" (ibid. 5.194; cf. 6.124–26; *Ant.* 15.417). One of these Greek notices was found by C. S. Clermont-Ganneau in 1871, and two Greek fragments of another were found in 1935. The complete notice reads, "No foreigner is to enter within the balustrade and embankment around the sanctuary. Whoever is caught will have himself to blame for his death which follows" (cf. C. S. Clermont-Ganneau, "New Discoveries," *PEQ* 3 [1871]: 132). Roman authorities were so conciliatory of Jewish scruples about this matter that they ratified the death penalty for any Gentile—even a

Roman citizen—who was caught going beyond the balustrade (cf. Josephus, *J.W.* 6.126).

The charge against Paul resulted from the fact that he and Trophimus were seen together in the city, which led to the assumption that they went together into the Holy Place in the temple (v.29). But as F. F. Bruce, 434 n. 46, has rightly observed, "It is absurd to think that Paul, who on this very occasion was going out of his way to appease Jewish susceptibilities, should have thus wantonly flouted Jewish law and run his own head into danger."

30 "The whole city [*hē polis holē*]," Luke says in rather hyperbolic fashion, "was aroused." The crime Paul was alleged to have committed was a capital offense—and one that could easily ignite the fanatical zeal of many pilgrims who had come to Jerusalem for this important Jewish festival. So they seized Paul in one of the inner courts of the temple and dragged him out to the court of the Gentiles. Then the temple police, who patrolled the area and stood guard at the gates leading into the inner courts, closed the gates so as to prevent the inner courts from being defiled by the tumult and possible bloodshed (cf. J. Jeremias, 209–10).

31–32 Word of the riot came to "the commander of the cohort" (*tō chiliarchō tēs speirēs*; NIV, "the commander of the Roman troops"; NASB, "the commander of the *Roman* cohort") garrisoned in the Fortress of Antonia, and with some soldiers (*stratiōtas*, GK *5132*) and centurions (*hekatontarchas*, GK *1672*) he rushed into the mob and prevented the people from beating Paul further. While the temple police were drawn from the ranks of the Levites (see comments at 4:1), the commander of the fortress was a Roman military officer whose responsibility it was to keep peace in the city. The Fortress of Antonia was built by Herod the Great to overlook the temple area immediately to the south and the city to the north and west, with exits to both the court of the Gentiles and the city proper. The commander was not a chief priest (contra Str-B, 2.631; 4.644) and had nothing to do with the priests and officials of the temple (contra Schürer, 2.1.267). Rather, he represented Rome's interests and was commissioned to intervene in the affairs of the people on behalf of those interests (cf. J. Jeremias, 211–12).

33–36 The commander formally arrested Paul and ordered him bound with two chains. Undoubtedly he thought him to be a criminal and was prepared to treat him as such. But when he asked the mob about his crime, he got no clear answer. Therefore he ordered Paul to be taken into the fortress where he could be questioned directly and a confession extracted from him (v.34). But the mob continued to press hard after its quarry—so hard, in fact, that the soldiers had to carry Paul up the steps to the fortress (though probably they dragged him more than carried him). All the while the mob was crying out, "Away with him!" (*Aire auton!* v.36)—a cry that, on the basis of its other occurrences in Luke's writings and Christian literature (cf. Lk 23:18; Ac 22:22; see also Jn 19:15; *Martyrdom of Polycarp* 3.2; 9.2), meant, "Kill him!"

NOTES

31 At the end of this verse, a marginal reading in the Syriac Harclean version (which represents a Western reading) adds with an asterisk the words, "See, therefore, that they do not make an uprising."

3. Defense before the People (21:37–22:22)

OVERVIEW

The account of Paul's defense before the people consists of three parts: (1) Paul's request to address the people (21:37–40), (2) his speech in defense (22:1–21), and (3) the people's response (22:22). In this first of Paul's five defenses, Luke's apologetic interests come to the fore in highlighting the nonpolitical character of Christianity (contrary to other messianic movements of the day, cf. 21:38) and presenting Paul's mandate to the Gentiles as being the major reason for Jewish opposition to the gospel (cf. 22:10–22).

37As the soldiers were about to take Paul into the barracks, he asked the commander, "May I say something to you?"

"Do you speak Greek?" he replied. 38"Aren't you the Egyptian who started a revolt and led four thousand terrorists out into the desert some time ago?"

39Paul answered, "I am a Jew, from Tarsus in Cilicia, a citizen of no ordinary city. Please let me speak to the people."

40Having received the commander's permission, Paul stood on the steps and motioned to the crowd. When they were all silent, he said to them in Aramaic: 22:1"Brothers and fathers, listen now to my defense."

²When they heard him speak to them in Aramaic, they became very quiet.

Then Paul said: ³"I am a Jew, born in Tarsus of Cilicia, but brought up in this city. Under Gamaliel I was thoroughly trained in the law of our fathers and was just as zealous for God as any of you are today. ⁴I persecuted the followers of this Way to their death, arresting both men and women and throwing them into prison, ⁵as also the high priest and all the Council can testify. I even obtained letters from them to their brothers in Damascus, and went there to bring these people as prisoners to Jerusalem to be punished.

⁶"About noon as I came near Damascus, suddenly a bright light from heaven flashed around me. ⁷I fell to the ground and heard a voice say to me, 'Saul! Saul! Why do you persecute me?'

⁸"'Who are you, Lord?' I asked.

"'I am Jesus of Nazareth, whom you are persecuting,' he replied. ⁹My companions saw the light, but they did not understand the voice of him who was speaking to me.

¹⁰"'What shall I do, Lord?' I asked.

"'Get up,' the Lord said, 'and go into Damascus. There you will be told all that you have been assigned to do.' ¹¹My companions led me by the hand into Damascus, because the brilliance of the light had blinded me.

¹²"A man named Ananias came to see me. He was a devout observer of the law and highly respected by all the Jews living there. ¹³He stood beside me and said, 'Brother Saul, receive your sight!' And at that very moment I was able to see him.

¹⁴"Then he said: 'The God of our fathers has chosen you to know his will and to see the Righteous One and to hear words from his mouth. ¹⁵You will be his witness to all men of what you have seen and heard. ¹⁶And now what are you waiting for? Get up, be baptized and wash your sins away, calling on his name.'

¹⁷"When I returned to Jerusalem and was praying at the temple, I fell into a trance ¹⁸and saw the Lord speaking. 'Quick!' he said to me. 'Leave Jerusalem immediately, because they will not accept your testimony about me.'

¹⁹"'Lord,' I replied, 'these men know that I went from one synagogue to another to imprison and beat those who believe in you. ²⁰And when the blood of your martyr Stephen was shed, I stood there giving my approval and guarding the clothes of those who were killing him.'

²¹"Then the Lord said to me, 'Go; I will send you far away to the Gentiles.'"

²²The crowd listened to Paul until he said this. Then they raised their voices and shouted, "Rid the earth of him! He's not fit to live!"

COMMENTARY

37–38 At the head of the stone stairway leading into the Fortress of Antonia, Paul asked for permission to say something to Claudius Lysias, the garrison commander (cf. 23:26). The commander was startled to hear his charge speaking in fluent Greek and surmised (note the inferential particle *ara* in the commander's question) that perhaps the prisoner was the Egyptian Jew who three years earlier had appeared at Jerusalem claiming to be a prophet, had led a large band of followers into the wilderness, and then marched to the Mount of Olives in preparation for the messianic overthrow of Jerusalem (cf. Josephus, *J.W.* 2.261–63; *Ant.* 20.169–72). Most people considered him a charlatan, and Felix and his soldiers drove him away.

39 Paul assured the commander that he was not the Egyptian revolutionary. The epithet "no ordinary city" (*ouk asēmou poleōs*), by which Paul referred to Tarsus, had been used by various cities to publicize their greatness (cf. Euripides' reference [*Ion* 8] some five hundred years earlier to Athens as "no ordinary city of the Greeks" [*ouk asēmos Hellenōn polis*]). Paul's use of the epithet here reflects his pride in the city of his birth. Jerome (*On Illustrious Men* 5; *Commentary on Philemon* 23) records a tradition that Paul's parents originally came from Gischala in Galilee and migrated to Tarsus after the Roman devastation of northern Palestine in the first century BC.

40 Paul spoke to the crowd in Aramaic (lit., "in the Hebrew dialect," which elsewhere in the NT means "in Aramaic," except at Rev 9:11 and 16:16). Haenchen, 620–21, claimed that the record here is clearly unhistorical for three reasons: (1) Paul would have been physically unable to make such a speech after having been mauled by the mob; (2) the commander would not have allowed him to speak just because he asked to; and (3) the crowd would not

have honored Paul's request for silence. But these objections are certainly quite pedantic. We need not think that the rioters had beaten Paul into insensibility. The Roman commander may well have been impressed by Paul's composure under such a trying circumstance and may also have thought that by letting him speak he might gain some insight into the cause of the riot. As for the crowd, they may also have been momentarily impressed by Paul's composure—probably, as well, their attentiveness was encouraged by gestures of the commander and rough proddings by his soldiers for them to be quiet. Moreover, Paul's use of Aramaic (the lingua franca of Palestine), though probably frustrating for the commander, may have been appreciated by some of the crowd and elicited a temporary measure of goodwill.

22:1–2 Paul opens his defense with the formal Jewish address "men, brothers" (*andres adelphoi*), to which he adds "and fathers" (*kai pateres*, GK *4252*), as did Stephen before the Sanhedrin (cf. 7:2). Some have thought that this form of address, particularly with its addition of "and fathers," implies that members of the Sanhedrin were in the crowd. But that need not follow either from the parallel with Stephen's defense or from the way Paul addresses the Sanhedrin later on (cf. 23:1). Many commentators have objected that this defense does not fit the occasion, for it makes no mention of the people's charge that Paul had defiled the temple by taking Trophimus, a Gentile, into its inner courts (cf. 21:28b–29). In reality, however, Paul's speech from the steps of the Fortress of Antonia deals eloquently with the major charge against him—that of being a Jewish apostate (cf. 21:28a). It does this by setting all that had happened in his Christian life in a Jewish context and by insisting that what others might consider apostasy really came to him as a revelation from heaven. Indeed, the speech parallels much of what Luke has already given us about Paul's conversion in 9:1–19 and what he will set out again in 26:2–23. These repetitions are given, it seems, to impress indelibly on his readers' minds something of the exceptional importance of what Paul says in defense (see Overview, 9:1–30). Yet it is remarkable how Luke fits the variations in each of these three accounts so closely to their respective contexts and purposes.

3 The triad of "birth" (*gennēsis*, GK *1167*), "upbringing" (*trophē*, GK *5575*, lit., "nourishment"), and "training" (*paideia*, GK *4082*) was a conventional way in antiquity of describing the stages of a man's youth (cf. W. C. van Unnik, *Tarsus or Jerusalem: The City of Paul's Youth* [London: Epworth, 1962], 9, 28). Alternative ways of punctuating this verse leave open the question as to whether (1) Paul's early childhood was spent in Jerusalem (as van Unnik proposed) or (2) his coming to Jerusalem was related to his studying under Gamaliel I some time later in his teens (as I argue in *Paul, Apostle of Liberty*, 25–27). If each participle of this triad is taken as heading its respective clause (so KJV, NASB, NRSV, TEV; contra JB, NEB, NIV), Paul is here saying: "I am a Jew, born [*gegennēmenos*, GK *1164*] in Tarsus of Cilicia, brought up [*anatethrammenos*, GK *427*] in this city at the feet of Gamaliel, and instructed [*pepaideumenos*, GK *4084*] in the strict manner of the law of our fathers." From this he argues that his Jewishness cannot be disputed. And he goes on to insist that with such a background he was as zealous for all that Judaism stands for as any of those in the crowd before him (cf. Gal 1:14).

Needless to say, not everyone has accepted these biographical claims. Many have taken the fact of Paul's birth at Tarsus as sufficient grounds for consigning him to the ranks of Hellenistic Judaism. Others have cited certain of the apostle's attitudes, actions, and teachings, as well as various phrases he uses, as negating any real knowledge on his part of Judaism as it existed in the orthodox circles of Jerusalem. Theologically, the assertion has often been made that Paul's doctrine of the law is so gross a caricature of Pharisaic teaching and his understanding of repentance so deficient as to prohibit his having had any real association with the famed rabbi Gamaliel I (cf., e.g., *Beginnings of Christianity* [ed. Foakes-Jackson and Lake], 4.279). Methodologically, the claim has sometimes been made that Paul's exegetical procedures do not correspond to rabbinic practices (cf., e.g., Haenchen, 625). But these assertions and claims must be judged from the evidence to be very wide of the mark (cf. my *Paul, Apostle of Liberty*, 21–64 [on Paul's biographical claims], and my *Biblical Exegesis in the Apostolic Period* [2d ed.], 6–35, 88–116 [on rabbinic and Pauline exegetical procedures]). Paul himself claims to be "a Hebrew of Hebrews" (2Co 11:22; Php 3:5), and the evidence is almost overwhelming in support of this claim in his own letters and in the portrayal of him by Luke in Acts.

4–5 As evidence of his zeal for God and the Jewish religion, Paul cites his earlier persecution of Christians (see comments at 9:1–2). The ascription "the Way" (*hē hodos*, GK *3847*) picks up what was the earliest self-designation of the first believers in Jesus at Jerusalem, i.e., "those of the Way" (see comments at 9:1–2; also 19:9, 23; 24:14, 22).

6–9 This description of Christ's encounter with Paul on the road to Damascus, except for some stylistic differences, closely parallels the earlier description in 9:3–6 (see comments there). As in Acts 9, here both Paul and Luke describe Paul's conversion to Jesus as God's Messiah as the result of a heavenly confrontation, not something that Paul himself originated or others imposed on him. It was, indeed, "Jesus of Nazareth" who confronted him (v.8), and this places his messianology in the matrix of the Jewish homeland. But it was the risen and ascended

Jesus, the heavenly Christ, who rebuked him and turned him about spiritually, and this alone explains his new understanding of life and his new outlook on all things Jewish.

10–11 In response to the heavenly confrontation—and as a good Jew who thought first in terms of how he should act in obedience to divine revelation—Paul's immediate question was "What shall I do, Lord?" He was told to go into Damascus, where the divine will would be revealed to him. So in his blindness he was led into Damascus by his companions to await instructions as to God's purposes for him (v.11).

12–16 At Damascus Paul was visited by Ananias, God's messenger to bring about renewal of Paul's sight and announce God's purpose for him as a witness "to all men" (*pros pantas anthrōpous*, v.15). The Jewish matrix of Paul's commission is highlighted by the description of Ananias as "a devout observer of the law and highly respected by all the Jews living there" (v.12), and the Jewish flavor of the episode is strengthened by the expression "the God of our fathers" and the messianic title "the Righteous One" (v.14; cf. 3:14). The words "Brother Saul, receive your sight!" (v.13) are a summary of the fuller statement reported in 9:17. What was important in the present circumstance was not to reproduce the exact words of Ananias but to emphasize that the commission Paul received from the risen Christ was communicated by a pious Jew who spoke in distinctly Jewish terms. Later on, when Paul defends himself before Agrippa II (ch. 26), there will be no need for this particular emphasis, and so the substance of what Ananias said in the name of the Lord Jesus is there included in the words spoken by the heavenly voice on the Damascus Road (cf. 26:16–18). Having thus delivered the Lord's message, Ananias called on Paul to respond: "Get up, be baptized and wash your sins away, calling on his name" (v.16)—an exhortation

reminiscent of Peter's invitation at Pentecost in 2:38.

17–21 Paul's commission at Damascus to be God's witness to all people was reaffirmed and amplified in a vision he received as he was praying in the temple. Most likely the visit to the temple and the vision referred to here occurred on Paul's return to Jerusalem three years after his conversion (cf. 9:26–29; Gal 1:18–19). At that time, Luke tells us, Paul faced opposition from the city's Hellenistic Jews, who viewed him as a renegade and sought to kill him (cf. 9:29). It was evidently at that time—during a period in his life when he most needed divine direction and support—that the same heavenly personage he met on the road to Damascus, the risen and exalted Jesus, directed him to "leave Jerusalem immediately, because they will not accept your testimony about me" (v.18). More important, it was at that time that the same exalted Jesus also ordered him, "Go, I will send you far away to the Gentiles" (v.21). Therefore Jerusalem, Paul says, was his intended place of witness and the temple God's place of revelation. But his testimony was refused there. And by revelation he learned that his commission to all people was to have explicit reference to Gentiles who are "far away" (*makran*, lit., "far off," GK *3426*; see comments at 2:39).

22 During most of Paul's defense the crowd listened with a certain degree of respect, for he had spoken mostly of Israel's messianic hope and had done so in a thoroughly Jewish manner. Even his identification of Jesus of Nazareth as Israel's Messiah and the one who spoke to him from heaven, while undoubtedly straining his credibility for many in the crowd, could have been tolerated by a people given more to orthopraxis (i.e., correct practice) than orthodoxy (i.e., correct belief). When, however, Paul spoke of being directed by divine revelation to leave Jerusalem and go far away to the Gentiles, who had no relation to Judaism, it was "the last straw." In effect, Paul was saying that Gentiles can be approached directly with God's message of salvation without first being related to the nation and its institutions, which was tantamount to placing Jews and Gentiles on an equal footing before God. For Judaism, that was the height of apostasy indeed! When he made such an assertion, Paul was shouted down by the crowd, who called for his death: "Rid the earth of him! He's not fit to live!" In reporting this incident, Luke highlights the major reason for the Jewish opposition to Paul, namely, his universal outlook, which was willing to include Gentiles in God's redemptive plan on the same basis as Jews.

NOTES

21:38 The number "thirty thousand" in Josephus (*J. W.* 2.261) for the followers of the Egyptian self-styled prophet possibly derives from a misreading by Josephus or his secretary of the Greek capital letter Δ (D), which means four thousand (as Luke has it here), for the Greek capital letter Λ (L), which means thirty thousand.

22:1 On the address ἄνδρες ἀδελφοί (*andres adelphoi*, "men, brothers"), see comments at 1:16.

3 Instead of the well-supported phrase ζηλωτὴς ὑπάρχων τοῦ θεοῦ (*zēlōtēs hyparchōn tou theou*, "being zealous for God"), several Western witnesses offer other readings; e.g., the Vulgate reads "being zealous for the law" (*legis*); the Syriac Harclean version reads "being zealous for the traditions of my ancestors" (cf. Gal 1:14).

5 Some minor Western witnesses (minuscule 614 and the Syriac Harclean recension) add the name Ἀνανίας (*Hananias*, "Ananias") after ὁ ἀρχιερεύς (*ho archiereus*, "the high priest," GK 797), evidently influenced by 23:2.

7 Some Western texts (represented by the Old Latin Gigas and the Syriac Harclean recensions) add "in the Hebrew language," evidently influenced by 26:14.

Likewise, several Western texts (E, some minuscules, and as represented by the Old Latin Gigas, Vulgate, and Syriac Harclean recensions) add σκληρόν σοι πρὸς κέντρα λακτίζειν (*sklēron soi pros kentra laktizein*, "It is hard for you to kick against the goads"), also influenced it seems by 26:14.

9 The Western text (D E etc.) and Byzantine text (L P and most minuscules) add καὶ ἔμφοβοι ἐγένοντο (*kai emphoboi egenonto*, "and they were afraid") after τὸ μὲν φῶς ἐθεάσαντο (*to men phōs etheasanto*, "they saw [indeed] the light")—a phrase incorporated by Erasmus into the TR and so translated by the KJV.

11 Several Western witnesses (recensions of the Old Latin, Syriac, and Coptic versions) add at the beginning of this verse, "And rising up I could not see."

Codex Vaticanus (B) reads οὐδὲν ἔβλεπον (*ouden eblepon*, "I saw nothing") instead of the more widely supported οὐκ ἐνέβλεπον (*ouk eneblepon*, "I could not see"; NIV, "had blinded me"), probably influenced by 9:8.

4. Claim of Roman Citizenship (22:23–29)

²³As they were shouting and throwing off their cloaks and flinging dust into the air, ²⁴the commander ordered Paul to be taken into the barracks. He directed that he be flogged and questioned in order to find out why the people were shouting at him like this. ²⁵As they stretched him out to flog him, Paul said to the centurion standing there, "Is it legal for you to flog a Roman citizen who hasn't even been found guilty?"

²⁶When the centurion heard this, he went to the commander and reported it. "What are you going to do?" he asked. "This man is a Roman citizen."

²⁷The commander went to Paul and asked, "Tell me, are you a Roman citizen?"

"Yes, I am," he answered.

²⁸Then the commander said, "I had to pay a big price for my citizenship."

"But I was born a citizen," Paul replied.

²⁹Those who were about to question him withdrew immediately. The commander himself was alarmed when he realized that he had put Paul, a Roman citizen, in chains.

COMMENTARY

23–24 The garrison commander—evidently at a loss to ascertain from the people why they were rioting and probably unable to understand Paul's defense in Aramaic—decided to find out the truth of the matter by torturing Paul. His earlier friendliness toward Paul had soured, and the brutal part of his nature and job came to the fore.

The scourge (Lat. *flagellum*), an instrument of Roman inquisition and punishment, consisted of leather thongs studded with pieces of metal or bone and fastened to a wooden handle. Its use often crippled for life and sometimes killed. Earlier in his ministry, Paul had five times received thirty-nine lashes at the hands of Jewish authorities and three times been beaten with rods by the order of Roman magistrates (cf. 2Co 11:24–25; also comments at Ac 9:30; 11:25; 16:22–24). But being flogged with a scourge was a far more brutal penalty than any of these. Here Paul was on the brink of receiving the kind of unjust punishment that Jesus had endured when Pilate, in a travesty of justice, had him flogged after declaring him innocent (cf. Jn 18:38–19:1).

25 Roman citizens were exempt from examination under torture. The Valerian and Porcian laws, confirmed and amplified by the Edicts of Augustus, prescribed that in trials of Roman citizens there must first be a formulation of charges and penalties, then a formal accusation laid, and then a hearing before a Roman magistrate and his advisory cabinet. So as the soldiers "stretched him out to flog him"—i.e., stretched Paul out on the stone floor or at a pillar or post, or perhaps by suspension from the ceiling or a hook—he said to the centurion in charge, "Is it legal for you to flog a Roman citizen who hasn't even been found guilty?"

26–28 Roman citizenship in Paul's day was a highly prized right conferred only on those of high social or governmental standing, on those who had done some exceptional service for Rome, or on those able to bribe an imperial or provincial administrator to have their names included on a list of candidates for enfranchisement. In the second and third centuries AD, bribery in order to gain citizenship rights became increasingly common. Earlier, however, it accounted for only a small minority of citizens. New citizens received a *diploma civitatis Romanae* or *instrumentum*, and their names were recorded on one of the thirty-five tribal lists at Rome and also on their local municipal register. Succeeding generations of a citizen's family possessed a *professio* or registration of birth recording their Roman status and were registered as citizens on the taxation tables of their respective cities.

No article of apparel distinguished a Roman citizen from the rest of the people except the toga, which only Roman citizens could wear. But even at Rome the toga was unpopular because of its cumbersomeness and was worn only on state occasions. Papers validating citizenship were kept in family archives and not usually carried on one's person. The verbal claim to Roman citizenship was accepted at face value. Penalties for falsifying documents and making false claims of citizenship were exceedingly stiff—in fact, the Greek Stoic philosopher Epictetus (ca. AD 55–135) speaks of death for such acts (*Diatr.* 3.24, 41; see also Suetonius, *Claud.* 25).

We do not know how, why, or when Paul's family acquired Roman citizenship. William M. Ramsay (*Cities of St. Paul*, 185) argued that it stemmed from 171 BC, when Tarsus received its constitution as a Greek city and many of its socially elite were made citizens. Cadbury, 73–74, proposed that Pompey, in settling the eastern provinces during the 60s BC, transferred a number of Jewish prisoners to Tarsus, set them free, and bestowed Roman citizenship on them. But Roman citizenship was not a corollary of citizenship in a Greek city-state, nor were former prisoners or slaves considered fit subjects for enfranchisement. Most likely one of Paul's ancestors received Roman citizenship for some valuable service rendered to a Roman administrator or general (perhaps Pompey), whether in the Gischala region of northern Palestine or at Tarsus.

When Paul claimed Roman citizenship, the centurion immediately stopped the proceedings and reported to the commander, "This man is a Roman citizen" (v.26). This news brought the commander posthaste to question Paul, who convinced him that he was indeed a Roman citizen (v.27). His own citizenship, the commander said, was purchased by a large sum of money—probably, since his name was Claudius Lysias (23:26), during the reign of Claudius by paying a bribe to one of the members of Claudius's court. Paul's response, "But I was born a citizen" (v.28), suggests his high estimate of his citizenship.

29 The fact that Paul was a Roman citizen put the situation in an entirely different light (cf. 16:37–39). Examination under torture, while suitable for ordinary men in the empire, had to be abandoned and some other way of determining the nature of the charge had to be found. Undoubtedly the commander shuddered as he realized how close he had come to perpetrating a serious offense against a Roman citizen.

NOTES

26 The Western text (D, and as represented in recensions of the Old Latin and Vulgate) adds ὅτι Ῥωμαῖον ἑαυτὸν λέγει (*hoti Rhōmaion heauton legei*, "that he calls himself a Roman") after ἀκούσας (*akousas*, "when he heard"), thereby leaving nothing unclarified about Paul's claim.

27 Codex Bezae (D) has εἶπεν εἰμί (*eipen eimi*, "'I am,' he said") in place of the better-supported ἔφη ναί (*ephē nai*, "'Yes,' he answered"; NIV, "'Yes, I am,' he answered"; NASB, "And he said, 'Yes'").

29 The Greek text of Codex Bezae (D) ends with εὐθέως οὖν ἀπέστησαν ἀπ' αὐτοῦ (*eutheōs oun apestēsan ap' autou*, "immediately then they withdrew from him"), which sentence begins this verse. (The Latin text of bilingual D ended earlier in the middle of 22:20.) Hereafter the Western text of Acts is represented by other Greek uncial and minuscule MSS; recensions of the Latin, Syriac, Coptic, and Armenian versions; and various Latin and Syrian church fathers.

The Western text (some minuscules, and as represented by recensions of the Syriac Harclean and Coptic Sahidic versions) adds at the end of the verse καὶ παραχρῆμα ἔλυσεν αὐτόν (*kai parachrēma elysen auton*, "and at once he released him"), which again is an attempt to clarify matters for the reader.

5. Defense before the Sanhedrin (22:30–23:11)

OVERVIEW

The structure of Luke's account of Paul's defense before the Sanhedrin is somewhat irregular, which probably reflects the tumultuous nature of the session itself. Three matters pertaining to Luke's apologetic purpose quite clearly come to the fore: (1) Christianity is rooted in the Jewish doctrine of the resurrection of the dead (cf. 23:6); (2) the debate Paul was engaged in regarding Christianity's claims must be viewed as first of all a Jewish intramural affair (cf. 23:7–10); and (3) the ongoing proclamation of the gospel in the Gentile world stems from a divine mandate (cf. 23:11).

³⁰The next day, since the commander wanted to find out exactly why Paul was being accused by the Jews, he released him and ordered the chief priests and all the Sanhedrin to assemble. Then he brought Paul and had him stand before them.

²³:¹Paul looked straight at the Sanhedrin and said, "My brothers, I have fulfilled my duty to God in all good conscience to this day." ²At this the high priest Ananias ordered those standing near Paul to strike him on the mouth. ³Then Paul said to him, "God will strike you, you whitewashed wall! You sit there to judge me according to the law, yet you yourself violate the law by commanding that I be struck!"

⁴Those who were standing near Paul said, "You dare to insult God's high priest?"

⁵Paul replied, "Brothers, I did not realize that he was the high priest; for it is written: 'Do not speak evil about the ruler of your people.'"

⁶Then Paul, knowing that some of them were Sadducees and the others Pharisees, called out in the Sanhedrin, "My brothers, I am a Pharisee, the son of a Pharisee. I stand on trial because of my hope in the resurrection of the dead." ⁷When he said this, a dispute broke out between the Pharisees and the Sadducees, and the assembly was divided. ⁸(The Sadducees say that there is no resurrection, and that there are neither angels nor spirits, but the Pharisees acknowledge them all.)

⁹There was a great uproar, and some of the teachers of the law who were Pharisees stood up and argued vigorously. "We find nothing wrong with this man," they said. "What if a spirit or an angel has spoken to him?" ¹⁰The dispute became so violent that the commander was afraid Paul would be torn to pieces by them. He ordered the troops to go down and take him away from them by force and bring him into the barracks.

¹¹The following night the Lord stood near Paul and said, "Take courage! As you have testified about me in Jerusalem, so you must also testify in Rome."

COMMENTARY

30 Still unsuccessful in ascertaining why the people were so angry with Paul, the commander ordered the Jewish Sanhedrin (see comments at 4:5) to come together to interrogate his captive. As a Roman citizen, Paul had a right to know the nature of the charges against him and the penalties involved before formal accusations were laid. The commander also needed to know these things in order to decide what else should be done. Perhaps he had talked with Paul after releasing him from his chains (cf. 21:33). Since this was a religious matter, however, he decided to have it clarified before the highest judicial body of Judaism. As a Roman military commander, he had no right to participate in the Sanhedrin's deliberations. But as the Roman official charged with keeping peace in Jerusalem, he could order the Sanhedrin to meet to determine the cause of the riot.

23:1 Paul began his defense by addressing the members of the Sanhedrin as "men, brothers" (*andres adelphoi*; NIV, "my brothers"; NASB, "brethren"), the common formal address used among assembled Jews. Then he asserted, "I have fulfilled my duty to God in all good conscience to this day"—which was certainly a bold claim, but not without parallel on Paul's part in other situations (cf. 20:18–21, 26–27; 24:16; Ro 15:19b, 23; Php 3:6b; 2Ti 4:7).

2 Such a claim so enraged the high priest that, in violation of the law, he ordered those near Paul to strike him on the mouth. Ananias, the son of Nedebaeus, reigned as high priest from AD 48 to 58 or 59 and was known for his avarice and liberal use of violence. Josephus (*Ant.* 20.205–7, 213) says that he confiscated for himself the tithes given to the ordinary priests and gave lavish bribes to Roman and Jewish officials. In a parody on Psalm 24:7, the Talmud lampoons Ananias's plundering and greed:

> The temple court cried out, "Lift up your heads, O you gates, and let Yohanan [mixing the letters in his Hebrew name Hananiah, which is Ananias in Greek], the son of Narbai [a textual corruption that confuses the similarly formed Hebrew letters ד and ר and reads Narbai for Nadbai, a title meaning "generous one" and used ironically] and disciple of Pinqai [a satirical wordplay on the Hebrew verb *pānaq*, "to pamper"], enter and fill his stomach with the divine sacrifices" (*b. Pesah.* 57a).

Ananias was a brutal and scheming man who was hated by Jewish nationalists for his pro-Roman policies. When the war with Rome began in AD 66, the nationalists burned his house (cf. Josephus, *J.W.* 2.426), and he was forced to flee to the palace of Herod the Great in the northern part of Jerusalem (ibid., 2.429). He was finally trapped while hiding in an aqueduct on the palace grounds and killed along with his brother Hezekiah (ibid., 2.441–42).

3 Indignant at the affront, Paul lashed out at Ananias and accused him of breaking the Jewish law, which safeguarded the rights of defendants and presumed them innocent until proven guilty. Paul had not even been charged with a crime, let alone tried and found guilty. Anyone who behaved as Ananias did, Paul knew, was bound to come under God's judgment. Paul's words, however, were more prophetic than he realized. For Ananias's final days, despite all of his scheming and his bribes, were lived as a hunted animal and ended in death at the hands of his own people.

Ananias's order to strike the defendant was in character. But Paul's retort seems quite out of character for a follower of the one who "when they hurled their insults at him, . . . did not retaliate; [and] when he suffered, . . . made no threats" (1Pe 2:23). Paul, it seems, momentarily lost his composure—as, evidently, Ananias hoped he would—and put himself at a disadvantage before the council. We cannot excuse Paul's burst of anger, though we must not view it self-righteously. We are made of the same stuff as Paul, and his provocation was greater than most of us will ever face. Yet his quickness in acknowledging his wrongdoing (v.5) was more than many of us are willing to emulate.

4–5 In his apology Paul cites Exodus 22:28. Theodor Zahn (*Die Urausgabe der Apostelgeschichte des Lucas* [Leipzig: Deichert, 1916], 763) supposed that, in disclaiming knowledge of Ananias's being the high priest, Paul was speaking ironically. But the tone of the statement (cf. the use of *adelphoi*, "brothers," in v.5) and the reference to Exodus 22:28 suggest that the words were meant quite seriously. William M. Ramsay (*Bearing of Recent Discovery*, 90ff.) proposed that a meeting convened by a Roman officer would have been run like a Roman assembly, with Paul on one side, the Sanhedrin (including the high priest) on the other, and the commander himself presiding. But while Rome's chief administrative officer in the city could order the Sanhedrin to meet, he was not a member of the council—nor would he have wanted to offend Jewish sensibilities by taking part in the session.

It is frequently claimed that Paul's failure to recognize the high priest suggests that he had an eye affliction that would have obscured his vision. This is a doubtful inference drawn from the juxtaposition of Paul's mention of an illness in Galatians 4:13–14 and his colloquial idiom of concern ("you would have torn out your eyes and given them to me") in Galatians 4:15. Luke was not averse to excusing his hero from blame wherever possible (see comments at 20:8), and it may be assumed that he would have made some reference to Paul's failing eyesight if that were the case and was relevant here.

The high priest presided at regular meetings of the Sanhedrin and so would have been easily identifiable. But this was not a regular meeting, and the high priest may not have occupied his usual place or worn his robes of office. Furthermore, since he had visited Jerusalem only sporadically during the past twenty years, and since the office of high priest passed from one to another within certain priestly families (see comments at 4:6), Paul might very well not have known who held the office of high priest in AD 58—whether Ananias, who had reigned since AD 48, or Ishmael ben Phabi, who took the office in AD 58–59 (see comments at 25:2). Nor would he have known any of the current high priestly claimants by sight.

All Paul could do when told that he was speaking to the high priest was apologize—though he did so, it seems, more to the office than to the man—and acknowledge by his citation of Scripture that, while he did not accept the view that laws provide the supreme direction for life (cf. 1Co 2:15; 9:20–21), he had no intention in being guided by Christ and the Holy Spirit to act in a way contrary to the law or to do less than the law commanded.

6 Ananias's interruption changed the entire course of the meeting, but not as he had evidently expected. For instead of being cowed into submission, Paul began again (note the resumptive use of the formal address "men, brothers" [*andres adelphoi*; NIV, "my brothers"; NASB, "brethren"]). This time he took the offensive. "I am a Pharisee, the son of a Pharisee," he declared; "I stand on trial because of my hope in the resurrection of the dead" (cf. 24:21; 26:6–8; 28:20b).

Many have agreed with Johannes Weiss, 1.148, that "we must be on our guard against spoiling the portrait of Paul by the impressions we receive from the speeches of the Apostle which have been interpolated, especially the speeches in the defence during his trial." Adjectives such as "improbable," "incomprehensible," and "unhistorical" have, in fact, been frequently used of the narrative here. And even when Luke's account is accepted as being at least basically reliable, Paul is often interpreted as having played the *enfant terrible* before rather unworthy opponents and engaged in an adroit maneuver that was not really sincere. But Pharisaism in Paul's day was not as stereotyped as it later became under rabbinic development. He could still have been considered a Pharisee because of his personal observance of the law and his belief in the resurrection, even though he did not separate himself from Gentiles.

And as for saying he was tried "because of my hope in the resurrection of the dead," we must realize, as Harnack (*Date of the Acts and of the Synoptic Gospels*, 87) has aptly pointed out, that "whenever the Resurrection was spoken of, our Lord, as a matter of course, formed for St Paul, for St Luke, and for the listeners the efficient cause." The phrase "the resurrection of the dead" seems to have been used by Paul and by Luke to refer to the whole doctrine of resurrection as that doctrine was validated and amplified by the resurrection of Jesus (cf. 17:32 in the context of 17:31)—even before members of the Jewish Sanhedrin. We need not, therefore, attribute deceit to Paul in this matter. Luke may have been condensing Paul's speech by leaving out the obvious, as seems to have been done in 17:32. And as Harnack (ibid.) went on to argue, "We may even believe that St Paul, at the beginning of his discourse, said roundly, 'Touching the Resurrection of the dead I stand here called in question'; for Luther also declared a hundred times that he was called in question touching the merits and honour of Jesus Christ, while his opponents asserted that these things did not come at all into the question."

7–10 Paul's declaration served to divide the council, with Sadducees on the one side (see comments at 4:1) and Pharisees on the other (see comments at 5:34). Some of the Pharisees may have viewed the inquisition of Paul as an attempt by the Sadducees to discredit Pharisaism generally (i.e., to make Paul and his message the reductio ad absurdum of a Pharisaic position) and so rose to his defense (v.9). The Sadducees, however, kept pressing their objections, and the debate soon got out of hand. So violent, in fact, did it become that the commander had to bring in soldiers and rescue Paul (v.10). Once more the commander was frustrated in his effort to learn exactly why the Jews were so adamantly opposed to his prisoner.

11 Paul had feared such a reception at Jerusalem (cf. 20:22–23; 21:13; Ro 15:31), and now his worst fears were being realized. He had planned to go to Rome and minister throughout the western part of the empire after his visit to Jerusalem (cf. Ro 15:24–29). But developments at Jerusalem were building up to a point where it appeared his life could come to an end through any number of circumstances beyond his control. Undoubtedly he was despondent as he awaited the next turn of events in his cell at the Fortress of Antonia. "On the following night" (*tē de epiousē nykti*, lit., "the night of the next day"), however, the risen and exalted Jesus appeared to Paul—as he had done at other critical moments in his ministry (e.g., 18:9–10; 22:17–21)—and encouraged him by his presence. The Lord said, "Take courage!" He assured Paul that he would yet testify in Rome as he had done in Jerusalem. Certainly, as F. F. Bruce, 455, has observed, "this assurance meant much to Paul during the delays and anxieties of the next two years, and goes far to account for the calm and dignified bearing which seemed to mark him out as a master of events rather than their victim."

NOTES

1 On the address ἄνδρες ἀδελφοί (*andres adelphoi*, "men, brothers") here and in v.6, see comments at 1:16.

Some have difficulty squaring Paul's claim to a good conscience here with their interpretation of his words in Romans 7:7–25. On Romans 7:7–25 as (1) a preconversion autobiographical statement, (2) a postconversion autobiographical statement, or (3) a gnomic (i.e., a timeless or widely applicable) statement that expresses a more general truth (as I argue), see my *Paul, Apostle of Liberty*, 86–127.

9 The Byzantine text (H L P and most minuscules), as incorporated into TR and so included by the KJV, adds at the end of the verse μὴ θεομαχῶμεν (*mē theomachōmen*, "let us not fight against God"), evidently to balance the protasis (εἰ δὲ . . . , *ei de* . . .) of the previous statement, and so reads: "What if a spirit or an angel has spoken to him? Let us not fight against God."

6. A Plot to Kill Paul (23:12–22)

¹²The next morning the Jews formed a conspiracy and bound themselves with an oath not to eat or drink until they had killed Paul. ¹³More than forty men were involved in this plot. ¹⁴They went to the chief priests and elders and said, "We have taken a solemn oath not to eat anything until we have killed Paul. ¹⁵Now then, you and the Sanhedrin petition the commander to bring him before you on the pretext of wanting more accurate information about his case. We are ready to kill him before he gets here."

¹⁶But when the son of Paul's sister heard of this plot, he went into the barracks and told Paul.

¹⁷Then Paul called one of the centurions and said, "Take this young man to the commander; he has something to tell him." ¹⁸So he took him to the commander.

The centurion said, "Paul, the prisoner, sent for me and asked me to bring this young man to you because he has something to tell you."

¹⁹The commander took the young man by the hand, drew him aside and asked, "What is it you want to tell me?"

²⁰He said: "The Jews have agreed to ask you to bring Paul before the Sanhedrin tomorrow on the pretext of wanting more accurate information about him. ²¹Don't give in

to them, because more than forty of them are waiting in ambush for him. They have taken an oath not to eat or drink until they have killed him. They are ready now, waiting for your consent to their request."

²²The commander dismissed the young man and cautioned him, "Don't tell anyone that you have reported this to me."

COMMENTARY

12-15 Failing in their earlier plot to kill Paul in the temple precincts, more than forty Jews—probably many of them Asian Jews who had instigated the earlier plot (cf. 21:27-29)—resolved to do away with him by ambushing him in the narrow streets of Jerusalem. For this, however, they needed a pretext to lure him out of the fortress. So they arranged with "the chief priest and elders" (evidently Ananias, together with some of his Sadducean cohorts) to ask for Paul's return before the Sanhedrin for further questioning (vv.14-15). They pledged that they would kill him as he was brought from the Fortress of Antonia north of the temple to the hall of the Sanhedrin southwest of the temple area (see comments at 4:5). To show their determination, they vowed not to eat or drink until they had accomplished their purpose (v.12). That did not mean, however, that they would necessarily face starvation if they failed. The rabbis allowed four types of vows to be broken: "vows of incitement, vows of exaggeration, vows made in error, and vows that cannot be fulfilled by reason of constraint" (*m. Ned.* 3:1-3), which exclusions allow for almost any contingency. The conspirators' plan, though violating both the letter and the spirit of Jewish law pertaining to the Sanhedrin (cf. *b. Sanh.* 82a), was in keeping with the character of the high priest Ananias (see comments at 23:2).

16 We have no knowledge about Paul's sister and his nephew. Nor do we know anything about how the young man learned of the plot. In his letters Paul says nothing of his immediate family, and this is Luke's only reference to any of Paul's relatives. Perhaps Paul had stayed with his sister and her family when he studied under Gamaliel I at Jerusalem (cf. 22:3) and then when he returned from Damascus as a Christian (cf. 9:26-28)—though probably not on his later visits to the city, and certainly not on his last visit (cf. 21:16). From Philippians 3:8, where Paul speaks of having "lost all things" for the sake of Christ, many have supposed that he was disinherited by his family for accepting and proclaiming Jesus as the Messiah. Such a supposition seems likely. Yet family ties are not easily broken. So when his uncle was in mortal danger, Paul's nephew could not stand by without warning him. After all, the saving and preservation of life takes precedence in Judaism over everything else.

17 As a Roman citizen under protective custody Paul could receive visitors. Without doubt he could be visited by his nephew. And when Paul heard his nephew's warning, he asked one of the centurions to take his nephew to the commander.

18-22 This pericope is set off as almost a separate unit of material by Luke's favorite connecting phrase *men oun* ("so," "then"), which appears at both its beginning and its end. Luke may have inferred from the commander's action what was said between him and Paul's nephew. But the use of *men oun* suggests a separate and distinguishable source for his information here, which may very well have been the nephew himself. The seriousness with which the commander took the warning suggests that (1) he knew Ananias to be the kind of man who would fall in with such a plot, and (2) he realized that Jewish feeling against Paul was strong enough to nurture it.

NOTES

12 The Western and Byzantine texts read τινὲς τῶν Ἰουδαίων (*tines tōn Ioudaiōn*, "some of the Jews" or "certain of the Jews"), as do also the TR and KJV, rather than simply οἱ Ἰουδαῖοι (*hoi Ioudaioi*, "the Jews") of the Alexandrian text, but v.13 sufficiently explains the general statement without the addition.

15 The Western text (as reflected in recensions of the Old Latin, Syriac, and Coptic versions) expands the first part of this verse to read, "Now, therefore, we ask you to grant us this: gather the Sanhedrin together and notify the commander in order that he might bring him down to you."

The Western text (some Greek minuscules, and as represented by various recensions of the Old Latin and Syriac versions) also closes this verse with the words "even if we must die for it."

18 On Luke's use of the connective μὲν οὖν (*men oun*) here and at v.22, see comments at 1:6.

20 The Byzantine text (H L P and most minuscules), and probably also the original Western text (to judge by various recensions of the Latin and Syriac versions), reads μέλλοντες (*mellontes*, "as though they would"), with the plural of the masculine nominative participle referring to "the Jews" (so the TR, KJV, NIV, NASB, NRSV, JB). Most Alexandrian texts (𝔓⁷⁴ A B E etc.) read μέλλων (*mellōn*, "as though he would"), with the singular of the masculine nominative participle evidently referring to the high priest. Codex Sinaiticus (א), however, reads μέλλον (*mellon*, "as though it would"), with the singular of the neuter accusative participle agreeing with its immediate antecedent τὸ συνέδριον (*to synedrion*, "the Sanhedrin," GK *5284*). The reading of Codex Sinaiticus, though early, is not as well supported externally as are the others. Nonetheless, it is probably to be preferred (so UBS⁴, TEV), for μέλλοντες (*mellontes*, "as though they would") seems to be influenced by v.15 and μέλλων (*mellōn*, "as though he would") is a somewhat common misspelling of μέλλον (*mellon*, "as though it would"). Furthermore, it fits the context better.

D. Imprisonment and Defenses at Caesarea (23:23–26:32)

1. Imprisonment (23:23–35)

²³Then he called two of his centurions and ordered them, "Get ready a detachment of two hundred soldiers, seventy horsemen and two hundred spearmen to go to Caesarea at nine tonight. ²⁴Provide mounts for Paul so that he may be taken safely to Governor Felix."

²⁵He wrote a letter as follows:

²⁶Claudius Lysias,

To His Excellency, Governor Felix:

Greetings.

²⁷This man was seized by the Jews and they were about to kill him, but I came with my troops and rescued him, for I had learned that he is a Roman citizen. ²⁸I wanted to know why they were accusing him, so I brought him to their Sanhedrin. ²⁹I found that the accusation had to do with questions about their law, but there was no charge against him that deserved death or imprisonment. ³⁰When I was informed of a plot to be carried out against the man, I sent him to you at once. I also ordered his accusers to present to you their case against him.

³¹So the soldiers, carrying out their orders, took Paul with them during the night and brought him as far as Antipatris. ³²The next day they let the cavalry go on with him, while they returned to the barracks. ³³When the cavalry arrived in Caesarea, they delivered the letter to the governor and handed Paul over to him. ³⁴The governor read the letter and asked what province he was from. Learning that he was from Cilicia, ³⁵he said, "I will hear your case when your accusers get here." Then he ordered that Paul be kept under guard in Herod's palace.

COMMENTARY

23–24 Since the commander could not risk having a Roman citizen assassinated while in his custody, he took steps to transfer Paul to the jurisdiction of Felix, the governor (*ho hēgemōn*, "the procurator," GK 2450) of the province of Judea. He wanted to get Paul to Caesarea, the provincial capital (see comments at 10:1), as quickly as possible—before the conspirators got wind of it. So the commander ordered two centurions to ready two hundred infantry and seventy cavalry, together with two hundred "spearmen" (*dexiolaboi*), for escort duty, who would leave for Caesarea at nine that evening (lit., "the third hour of the night"). In addition, he ordered that "mounts" (*ktēnē*, GK 3229) be provided for Paul (v.24)—which probably means not only a horse for Paul but also another one for either riding or carrying his baggage, or both, since the word *ktēnos* is a collective term for both "a riding animal" and "a pack animal."

The word *dexiolaboi* appears only here in the NT and nowhere else in extant Greek literature until the sixth century AD. All that can be said for certain is that it is a Greek term translating some Latin title used in the Roman army. Most translators have guessed that it means "spearmen," since *dexios* (GK 1288) means "right-handed" and spears were usually thrown with the right hand (cf. KJV, ASV, NASB, TEV, NRSV, NIV). Others prefer not to infer its meaning from its etymology and translate it as either "light-armed troops" (NEB) or "auxiliaries" (JB). Perhaps, however, the *dexiolaboi* were not another kind of soldier but "led horses" that were included within the cavalry contingent as additional mounts and pack animals (cf. *Beginnings of Christianity* [ed. Foakes-Jackson and Lake], 4.293).

The purpose of the detachment was security and speed. So we should probably visualize the first (i.e., security) as provided by the two hundred infantry and the second (i.e., speed) by the seventy cavalry with their two hundred extra mounts and pack animals, many of which may also have been used to carry infantry during the night. Luke has repeatedly called the commander a *chiliarchos* (GK 5941; cf. 21:31–33, 37; 22:24, 26–29; 23:10, 15, 17–19, 22), literally, "commander of a thousand," though usually he would command about six hundred soldiers. If, therefore, we surmise that the garrison at the Fortress of Antonia consisted of about six hundred men in all—and, further, that the term *dexiolaboi* refers not to infantry soldiers but to additional mounts or pack animals—then the commander had considered the plot against Paul serious enough to commit almost half his troops to escort Paul, with most of them due to return in a day or two (cf. v.32).

25 In saying that the commander wrote a letter "of this type" (*echousan ton typon touton*, lit., "having this pattern"; NIV, "as follows"; NASB, "having this form"), Luke is acknowledging that what follows is only the general purport of the letter. He would hardly have been in a position to have read a letter sent by a Roman commander and to a Roman provincial governor. What he knew of the letter probably came from Paul, who himself would only have known about its contents as the governor used it in the initial questioning of his prisoner.

26 To have begun the letter with a salutation that (1) named the sender, (2) named the recipient, and (3) sent greetings would hardly have taxed Luke's ingenuity. This is standard form for a letter of antiquity and is common to every letter of the NT except Hebrews and 1 John.

For the first time in Acts the commander's name is given. He was evidently a freeborn Greek who had worked his way up through the ranks of the Roman army and at some time had paid an official of Claudius's government to receive Roman citizenship (see comments at 22:28). His Greek name Lysias then became his Roman cognomen and he took the nomen Claudius in honor of the emperor.

Felix was the governor of the Roman province of Judea from AD 52–59 (on Felix, see comments at 24:1). The title "Excellency" (*kratistos*) originally denoted a member of the Roman equestrian order (Lat. *egregius*), like that of knights in Britain. Later it became an honorific title for highly placed officials

in the Roman government (as here; 24:3; 26:25). But it was also used as a form of polite address (cf. 1:1).

27–30 The body of the letter summarizes the events from the riot in the temple precincts to the commander's discovery of a plot against Paul's life. Paul may very well have smiled to himself when he heard how Lysias stretched the truth to his own benefit in claiming to have rescued Paul from the mob because "I had learned that he is a Roman citizen" and in omitting any reference to the near flogging. But the most important part of the letter concerning Lysias's evaluation of the Jewish opposition to Paul was clear: "I found that the accusation had to do with questions about their law, but there was no charge against him that deserved death or imprisonment" (v.29). And that was of great significance not only for Paul's fortunes but also for Luke's apologetic purpose.

31–32 "So" (*men oun*), Luke says, completing his account of the transfer of Paul from Jerusalem to Caesarea with a note of evident relief, the soldiers carried out their orders and brought Paul during the night to Antipatris. The town of Antipatris was built by Herod the Great in honor of his father Antipater, but its exact location is today unknown. Most identify it with modern Kulat Ras el Ain some thirty-five miles northwest of Jerusalem, at the foot of the Judean hills. Having left Jerusalem at nine in the evening (cf. v.23), the detachment would have lost no time in covering the distance by morning. If the cavalry contingent included two hundred extra mounts and packhorses (see comments at v.23), perhaps the infantry soldiers were allowed to ride and jog alternately. At any rate, the purpose of the mission was both safety and speed. And when the conspirators were left far behind and ambush was less likely, the infantry turned back to Jerusalem and the cavalry took Paul to Caesarea, some forty miles distant.

33–35 At Caesarea the prisoner and Lysias's letter were turned over to Felix, the governor. On reading the letter he questioned Paul on the basis of its contents. Had Paul been from one of the client kingdoms in Syria or Asia Minor, Felix would probably have wanted to consult the ruler of that kingdom. But on learning that Paul was from the Roman province of Cilicia, he felt competent as a provincial governor to hear the case himself, and so he ordered the case to be held over until Paul's accusers arrived from Jerusalem (v.34). In the meantime, Paul was kept under guard in the palace that Herod the Great had built for himself at Caesarea. It now served as the governor's headquarters and also had cells for prisoners.

NOTES

23 Codex Alexandrinus (A) reads δεξιοβόλους (*dexiobolous*, "javelin-throwers," lit., "those throwing with the right hand") instead of δεξιολάβους (*dexiolabous*; NIV, "spearmen"), which appears to be only an inadvertent confusion of letters.

23–24 The Western text (eighth-century minuscule 614, and as represented by recensions of the Old Latin, Vulgate, and Syriac versions) recasts these verses to read, "'Get ready soldiers to go to Caesarea, a hundred horsemen and two hundred spearmen [δεξιολάβους, *dexiolabous*].' And they said, 'They are ready.' And he ordered the centurions also to provide mounts that they might set Paul on them and bring him safely by night to Caesarea to Felix the governor. For he was afraid that the Jews might seize and kill him [Paul] and that afterwards he himself should be blamed for having taken bribes."

25 Some Western texts read περιέχουσαν τάδε (*periechousan tade*, "containing these things") instead of the better-attested ἔχουσαν τὸν τύπον τοῦτον (*echousan ton typon touton*, "having this pattern" or "to this effect"), evidently wanting to be more precise regarding the contents of the letter. For other instances of τύπος (*typos*, GK *5596*) used in this fashion, see 1 Maccabees 11:29; 2 Maccabees 1:24; 3 Maccabees 3:30.

29 The Western text (minuscules 614 and 2147, and as represented by the Syriac Harclean version) adds Μωϋσέως καὶ Ἰησοῦ τινος (*Mōyseōs kai Iēsou tinos*, "of Moses and a certain Jesus") after the possessive pronoun αὐτῶν (*autōn*, "their"), thereby reading, "questions about their law of Moses and a certain Jesus." The same Western witnesses, with the addition of the Old Latin Gigas version, adds at the end of the verse ἐξήγαγον αὐτὸν μόλις τῇ βίᾳ (*exēgagon auton molis tē bia*, "I brought him out with difficulty by force").

30 On a classical model, the Greek of the first part of this verse is confused, for it has a genitive absolute passing into an indirect statement. But Koine Greek is not adverse to such a construction.

Codex Sinaiticus (ℵ) and the Byzantine text (E and many minuscules), and so incorporated into the TR and translated by the KJV, add a final "Farewell" (either ἔρρωσο, *errōso*, or ἔρρωσθε, *errōsthe*, GK *4874*)—in agreement with the close of the letter of the Jerusalem Council in 15:29 and numerous nonliterary papyrus letters. But it is difficult to account for the absence of "Farewell" in 𝔓74 A B and the better Old Latin and Syriac recensions if, indeed, it had been original.

31 On Luke's use of μὲν οὖν (*men oun*, "so," "then"), see comments at 1:6.

34 The Western text (minuscules 383 and 614, and as represented by recensions of the Old Latin, Syriac, and Coptic versions) recasts the indirect discourse of the better-attested reading into direct discourse: "And when he had read the letter, he asked Paul: 'From what province are you?' He said: 'A Cilician.' And when he understood this, he said . . ."

2. Defense before Felix (24:1–27)

OVERVIEW

In his account of Paul's defense before Felix, Luke gives almost equal space to (1) the Jewish charges against Paul (vv.1–9), (2) Paul's reply to these charges (vv.10–21), and (3) Felix's response (vv.22–27). He does this, it seems, because he wants to show that despite the devious skill of his Jewish opponents and the notorious cruelty and corrupt-ibility of the Roman governor Felix, no other conclusions can be drawn from Paul's appearance before the governor than that (1) Christianity had nothing to do with political sedition, and (2) Jewish opposition to Christianity sprang from the claim that the person and work of Jesus was the legitimate fulfillment of the hopes of Judaism.

¹Five days later the high priest Ananias went down to Caesarea with some of the elders and a lawyer named Tertullus, and they brought their charges against Paul before the governor. ²When Paul was called in, Tertullus presented his case before Felix: "We have enjoyed a long period of peace under you, and your foresight has brought about reforms in this nation. ³Everywhere and in every way, most excellent Felix, we acknowledge this with profound gratitude. ⁴But in order not to weary you further, I would request that you be kind enough to hear us briefly.

⁵"We have found this man to be a troublemaker, stirring up riots among the Jews all over the world. He is a ringleader of the Nazarene sect ⁶and even tried to desecrate the temple; so we seized him. ⁸By examining him yourself you will be able to learn the truth about all these charges we are bringing against him."

⁹The Jews joined in the accusation, asserting that these things were true.

¹⁰When the governor motioned for him to speak, Paul replied: "I know that for a number of years you have been a judge over this nation; so I gladly make my defense. ¹¹You can easily verify that no more than twelve days ago I went up to Jerusalem to worship. ¹²My accusers did not find me arguing with anyone at the temple, or stirring up a crowd in the synagogues or anywhere else in the city. ¹³And they cannot prove to you the charges they are now making against me. ¹⁴However, I admit that I worship the God of our fathers as a follower of the Way, which they call a sect. I believe everything that agrees with the Law and that is written in the Prophets, ¹⁵and I have the same hope in God as these men, that there will be a resurrection of both the righteous and the wicked. ¹⁶So I strive always to keep my conscience clear before God and man.

¹⁷"After an absence of several years, I came to Jerusalem to bring my people gifts for the poor and to present offerings. ¹⁸I was ceremonially clean when they found me in the temple courts doing this. There was no crowd with me, nor was I involved in any

disturbance. [19]But there are some Jews from the province of Asia, who ought to be here before you and bring charges if they have anything against me. [20]Or these who are here should state what crime they found in me when I stood before the Sanhedrin—[21]unless it was this one thing I shouted as I stood in their presence: 'It is concerning the resurrection of the dead that I am on trial before you today.'"

[22]Then Felix, who was well acquainted with the Way, adjourned the proceedings. "When Lysias the commander comes," he said, "I will decide your case." [23]He ordered the centurion to keep Paul under guard but to give him some freedom and permit his friends to take care of his needs.

[24]Several days later Felix came with his wife Drusilla, who was a Jewess. He sent for Paul and listened to him as he spoke about faith in Christ Jesus. [25]As Paul discoursed on righteousness, self-control and the judgment to come, Felix was afraid and said, "That's enough for now! You may leave. When I find it convenient, I will send for you." [26]At the same time he was hoping that Paul would offer him a bribe, so he sent for him frequently and talked with him.

[27]When two years had passed, Felix was succeeded by Porcius Festus, but because Felix wanted to grant a favor to the Jews, he left Paul in prison.

COMMENTARY

1 There are a number of time notations in the narrative covering the period from Paul's arrival at Jerusalem to his being brought to Caesarea (cf. 21:17–18, 26–27; 22:30; 23:11–12, 23, 32). Yet helpful as they are, it is difficult to correlate Luke's temporal connective "five days later" (*meta pente hēmeras*) with any of them. One could suppose that "five days later" meant five days after Paul's arrival at Caesarea. But in view of his quoting of Paul's remark that "no more than twelve days ago I went up to Jerusalem to worship" (v.11), Luke evidently meant the five days to be reckoned from Paul's arrest in the temple—whether his arrest occurred on the last day of the seven-day purification period (see comments at 21:26) or a day or two before its end (cf. "when the seven days were nearly over," 21:27).

With the notations of time ("five days later") and place ("Caesarea"), the names of Paul's adversaries ("the high priest Ananias . . . with some of the eld-

ers and a lawyer named Tertullus"), and the identification of the judge ("the procurator/governor" Felix), the stage is set for Paul's defense. It was within Ananias's character to prosecute Paul as quickly as possible (see comments at 23:2); so to present his trumped-up charges as effectively as possible, he employed a lawyer named Tertullus. Tertullus was a common Greek name in the Roman world, and all we know of this particular Tertullus comes from this passage. Probably he was a Hellenistic Jew chosen by Ananias because of his expertise in affairs of the empire and his allegiance to Judaism. Perhaps Ananias also felt confident that in Felix he had a governor he could manipulate for his own purposes.

Antonius Felix was born a slave but freed by Antonia, the mother of the emperor Claudius. He was a brother of Pallas, who was also a freedman of Antonia and became a good friend of the young prince Claudius in the imperial household. Through the influence of Pallas, in AD 48 Felix was appointed to a subordinate governmental post in Samaria under the provincial governor Ventidius Cumanus. In AD 52 Claudius appointed him "procurator" or governor of Judea when Cumanus was deposed—an office usually reserved for freemen of the Roman equestrian order, but which Felix obtained through intrigue and the support of Quadratus, the procurator or governor of Syria (cf. Tacitus, *Ann.* 12.54; Josephus, *J.W.* 2.247; *Ant.* 20.137). During his governorship, insurrections and anarchy increased throughout Palestine. Try as he would to put down the uprisings and regain control, his brutal methods alienated the Jewish population more and more and served, in fact, only to foster further disturbances (cf. Josephus, *J.W.* 2.253–70; *Ant.* 20.160–81). The Roman historian Tacitus (ca. AD 55–117) described him as "a master of cruelty and lust who exercised the powers of a king with the spirit of a slave" (*Hist.* 5.9).

Despite his lowly birth, Felix had a succession of three highborn wives, each of whom in her own right was a princess (cf. Suetonius, *Claud.* 28). His first wife was the granddaughter of Mark Anthony and Cleopatra, thereby making him a grandson-in-law of Anthony. His third wife was Drusilla, the youngest daughter of Agrippa I. She was unhappy as the wife of Azizus, king of Emesa. Felix desired her because of her beauty, and she was persuaded through the intervention of a Cyprian magician named Atomus (see comments at 13:6–8) to leave her husband for him (cf. Josephus, *Ant.* 20.141–44). Nero recalled Felix to Rome sometime during AD 59–60, and he was saved from the consequences of his tyranny and misrule by the intercession of his brother Pallas with the emperor. Nothing is known of his subsequent fate.

2–4 Tertullus began the case for the prosecution with the customary flattery of the judge in words chosen for his purpose. Many Jews would undoubt-

edly have been shocked to hear the high priest's mouthpiece attributing "a long period of peace" and "reforms" to Felix's administration (v.2). Certainly few would have joined in any expression of "profound gratitude" for the governor's frequent displays of ferocity, cruelty, and greed (v.3). But Tertullus knew how to appeal to Felix's vanity. It was also customary to promise brevity (v.4; cf. Lucian, *Bis Accusatus* 26: "But in order not to make a long speech, since much time has elapsed already, I will begin with the accusation")—though such is human nature that the promise was (and still is) rarely kept.

5–9 The three charges laid against Paul are probably only a précis of the entire case, which Tertullus had gone on to elaborate. But this précis makes it clear that Tertullus intended to create the impression of political sedition against Rome in his first two charges—disturbing the peace among the Jews and being a ringleader of the Nazarenes—and, even more important, to argue for the right of Judaism to impose the death penalty in his third charge—attempting to desecrate the temple (v.8; see comments at 21:28–29). During his reign over Judea, Felix had repeatedly crucified leaders of various uprisings and killed many of their followers for disturbing the Pax Romana (cf. Josephus, *J.W.* 2.253–63). Tertullus's endeavor, therefore, as supported by the high priest and the Jewish elders with him (v.9), was to put Paul on the same level as these brigands, with the hope that in his insensitivity to the issues Felix would act in his usual manner simply on the basis of their testimony. As in Jesus' trial before Pilate, their accusations were framed mainly in terms of political sedition (cf. Lk 23:2, 5), though all along their grievance was principally religious.

10 Invited to respond, Paul also began with a complimentary statement—but a briefer and truer one. Felix had been in contact with the Jewish nation in Palestine for over a decade, first in Samaria and then as governor over the entire province of Judea. Therefore Paul was pleased to make his defense before one who was in a position to know the situation as it was and to understand his words in their context.

11–13 In refuting the charges against him, Paul dealt with each in turn. First, it was "no more than twelve days ago" that he came to Jerusalem, not for political agitation, but for worship (v.11). Such a short time, he implied, hardly provided sufficient opportunity to foment a revolt. Second, his accusers could hardly charge him with being a ringleader of any sedition, for he was alone when they arrested him in the temple and they could not cite any time when he was stirring up a crowd anywhere in the city (v.12). Third, their claim that he desecrated the temple was unproved because it was entirely without foundation (v.13).

14–16 The real reason Ananias and the Jewish elders opposed him, Paul insisted, was a religious one: "I worship the God of our fathers as a follower of the Way, which they call a sect. I believe [understanding *pisteuōn*, GK *4409*, to be a concessive adverbial participle] everything that agrees with the Law and that is written in the Prophets, and I have the same hope in God as these men, that there will be a resurrection of both the righteous and the wicked" (vv.14–15). And while he differed from Ananias and the elders in his acceptance of "the Way," his conscience in the matter was "clear before God and man" (v.16; cf. 23:1) because his position was in agreement with the Law and the Prophets.

Paul's statements about having "the same hope in God as these men" and believing in "a resurrection of both the righteous and the wicked" have led to a great deal of comment, since Ananias himself would not have accepted the doctrine of a resurrection (see comments at 4:1 regarding Sadducean beliefs) and Paul in his letters speaks only of a resurrection of the righteous (cf. 1Co 15:12–58; 1Th 4:13–5:11; 2Th 2:1–12). But evidently there were some Pharisees among the Jewish elders who came down to Caesarea with Ananias (cf. v.1). And while Sadducees did not share with the Pharisees the hope of a resurrection, Paul as a Pharisee was probably sufficiently self-confident to believe that it was the Pharisaic hope that characterized—or at least should characterize—all true representations of the Jewish faith. Furthermore, while Paul in his letters speaks only of a resurrection of the righteous (as also Jesus in Lk 14:14; 20:35–36), this is probably because his treatment of the resurrection in his letters is pastoral in nature and so deals only with the future of the righteous. We should not assume from Luke's portrayal here, however, that Pharisaic Judaism or Paul never spoke of a twofold resurrection (as in Da 12:2; Jn 5:28–29; Rev 20:12–15).

17 Reconstructing for Felix what happened in Jerusalem, Paul spoke of coming to Jerusalem "to bring my people (*eis to ethnos mou*, lit., "for my nation") gifts for the poor and to present offerings" (i.e., "to worship," cf. v.11). This is the only time Luke mentions the collection for the poor at Jerusalem, which was so dear to Paul's own heart (cf. Ro 15:25–27, 31; 1Co 16:1–4). Some have complained that for Paul to say that the gift was "for my nation" adds a note of insincerity that should be discounted, for Paul's efforts were directed toward relieving the plight of poor believers in the Jerusalem church, not that of Jews generally. Yet it need not be thought strange for the man who said in Romans 15:31 that the collection he was taking for Jewish Christians was "my service *for Jerusalem* [*eis Ierousalēm*; NASB; NIV, in Jerusalem]" also said, "I came to Jerusalem to bring *for my nation* [*eis to ethnos mou*; NIV, my people] gifts for the poor" (emphasis added). What he did, he did not only for the relief of Jewish believers in Jesus and as a symbol of unity between Gentile and Jewish Christians but also, as Harnack long ago insisted, "for all Israel;

he had ever before his eyes the nation *in its entirety.* . . . The conversion of the whole nation was the ultimate aim of all his exertions" (*Date of the Acts and of the Synoptic Gospels,* 74 [italics his]). By aiding that branch of the church whose mission it was to call the nation to its Messiah, he was indirectly engaged in a mission to his own nation (cf. Ro 11:13b–14).

18–21 Continuing the summary of what took place at Jerusalem, Paul spoke of his arrest in the temple (v.18) and his arraignment before the Sanhedrin (v.20). But, he insisted, there was no crowd to incite nor was there any attempt on his part to create a disturbance; rather, he was taken by the crowd while worshiping in a ceremonially clean condition. If the Asian Jews who instigated the riot had any serious charge against him, they should have been present to accuse him before the governor (v.19). Roman law imposed heavy penalties on accusers who abandoned their charges (*destitutio*). The absence of accusers, in fact, often meant the withdrawal of a charge; and their absence, Paul implies, suggests that they had nothing against him that would stand up in a Roman court of law. Nor did the Sanhedrin, Paul went on, find any crime in him—only the complaint that he believed in the resurrection of the dead. Therefore, Paul declared, he was on trial because of his belief in "the resurrection of the dead" (v.21).

22–23 Felix seems to have summed up the situation accurately. After a decade among the Jewish populace in Palestine (see comments at v.1), he was, in his own way, "well acquainted with the Way" (v.22). While certainly not a Christian, he could see that the charges against Paul were entirely religious in nature, even though they were presented in the guise of political sedition. He therefore sought to preserve the Pax Romana simply by removing the possibility of confrontation between the disputants and by delays in judicial procedure. So Paul was placed under protective custody in the palace of Herod the Great (v.23) and Ananias was given the deceptive promise of a decision being reached when the commander Lysias came down to Caesarea and presented his testimony (v.22), which, of course, he had already given in his letter (cf. 23:25–30). As a Roman citizen, Paul was allowed some freedom and permitted visits from friends to care for his needs. But both he and Ananias seem to have realized that Felix had no intention of bringing the case to a decision in the near future. And they evidently decided, each for his own reasons, to await the appointment of a new provincial governor before pressing for a resolution—an appointment they expected soon, given the recent course of Felix's reign.

24–26 Added to the description of Felix's response is this vignette about the interaction between the Roman governor, his Jewish wife, and the Christian apostle, which elaborates further the nature of Felix's response and highlights one aspect of Paul's continued though restricted ministry while under protective custody at Caesarea. The vignette is joined to the rest of the narrative by a favorite Lukan connective—the preposition *meta* with a time designation (*meta hēmeras tinas*, "after certain days"; NIV, "several days later"; NASB, "some days later"). While it may be tempting to see in the expression a chronological note of significance, Luke's earlier use of the same temporal designation (see comments at 9:19b) prohibits it.

Drusilla, Felix's third wife and the youngest daughter of Herod Agrippa I, had broken off her marriage to Azizus, the king of Emesa, because of Felix (see comments at v.1). Emesa was a small kingdom in Syria (modern Homs), and Azizus had agreed to become a convert to Judaism in order to marry her. But the teenage Drusilla was unhappy with Azizus and was captivated by Felix's ruthlessness and power, just as he was captivated with her beauty. So she accepted his offer of marriage. Neither his birth as a slave, his Roman paganism, nor her Jewish scruples deterred her from what she considered a higher station in life. The relationship between Felix and his young wife seems to have been based on greed, lust, and expectations of grandeur. Yet they apparently still had some qualms of conscience and therefore took the opportunity to send for Paul and hear his message.

Paul spoke to Felix and his wife about the necessity of "faith in Christ Jesus" (v.24). He also made it plain that this involved leading an ethical life, for he spoke of "righteousness, self-control and the judgment to come" (v.25)—three subjects that Felix and Drusilla particularly needed to learn about! His preaching touched the very heart of their kind of living, and so Felix ordered him to stop. Apparently Drusilla was offended by what she considered Paul's moralistic ranting, for though we are told that Felix later frequently talked with Paul (but for other reasons), Luke makes no mention of her ever having listened to him again. Felix also seems to have been unhappy at the shift in the discussion from divergent religious views to personal morality and responsibility. In fact, Luke tells us that he was "terrified" (*emphobos*, GK *1873*, with the preposition strengthening the noun for "fear, alarm, fright"; NIV, "afraid"; NASB, "frightened") in the presence of such preaching. Yet his greed and corruption led him to call for Paul to appear before him often in the hope of getting a bribe for his release (v.26). Felix must have believed that Paul had access to some money, either from an inheritance from his parents (as William M. Ramsay postulated) or through Christian friends who visited him (cf. 24:23; 27:3), and he hoped to get his hands on some of it.

27 After two years Festus succeeded Felix as governor of Judea. Felix's downfall came through an outbreak of hostilities between Jews and Greeks at Caesarea, with both claiming dominant civil rights in the city. The Jews based their claim on their greater numbers and wealth, and because Herod the Great, a Jew, had rebuilt the city; the Greeks based theirs on the support of the military and the assertion that the city was always meant to be a Gentile city (cf. Josephus, *J.W.* 2.266–70; *Ant.* 20.173–78). Using the Syrian troops under his command, Felix's intervention took the form of military retaliation on the Jews. Many were killed, taken prisoner, or plundered of their wealth. A delegation of Jews went to Rome to complain, and Felix was recalled by Nero to Rome. He would have suffered severe punishment had not his brother Pallas interceded for him before the emperor (cf. Josephus, *Ant.* 20.182). Felix was replaced with Festus in AD 60.

During this time Paul remained in Herod's palace at Caesarea—with Felix undoubtedly rationalizing his imprisonment as a protection for Paul and a favor to the Jews, though in reality it was an expression of Felix's cupidity. It must have been an extremely tedious time for Paul. Luke, however, seems to have made full use of the two years to investigate "everything from the beginning" about Christianity (Lk 1:3). And while we cannot say whether at this time he produced either a preliminary draft of his gospel (perhaps something like a "proto-Luke") or any portion of Acts, it is probable that during this time he became quite familiar with (1) the traditions comprising Mark's gospel (whenever Mark's gospel was written); (2) other materials having to do with the story of Jesus, which he would also incorporate into his gospel (so-called "Q" and "L" materials); (3) accounts circulating in Palestine of events and circumstances within the early church, which he would include in the first half of Acts; and (4) recollections and interpretations of Paul as to his activities before Luke joined him. Undoubtedly during this time he also began to sketch out the structure and scope of his two-volume work known as Luke-Acts.

NOTES

1 On the preposition μετά (*meta*, "after" [NASB]; NIV, "later") with a time designation (here πέντε ἡμέρας, *pente hēmeras*, "five days") as a Lukan connective in the latter half of Acts, see comments at 15:36.

3 On κράτιστε (*kratiste*, "most excellent") as a title and a polite form of address, see comments at 23:26.

6b–8a The Western text, which was incorporated into the TR and so translated by the KJV, reads: " . . . and wanted to judge him according to our law. ⁷But the commander, Lysias, came and with the use of much force snatched him from our hands ⁸and ordered his accusers to come before you." The Western scribe evidently felt it unlikely that παρ' οὗ (*par' hou*, "from whom") of v.8 referred to Paul, thinking that Felix would hardly have gotten the whole story only "by examining him," and so he recast vv.6b and 8a and inserted v.7 in order to bring the commander Lysias into the account as the antecedent of the relative pronoun. Yet while the Western version of these verses is in Lukan style—and while some have thought it necessary to make sense of the account—the reading of the more reliable texts is quite straightforward and understandable.

10 A marginal reading of the Syriac Harclean version reads, "And when the governor had motioned for him to make a defense for himself, Paul answered; and having assumed a godlike bearing, he said . . . ." This rather curious reference to Paul's posturing may be typical of the Western scribe but is not supported by other texts.

14 On the self-designation of early Christians as those of "the Way" (ἡ ὁδός, *hē hodos*), see comments at 9:2. See also 19:9, 23; 22:4; and v.22 below (also 16:17; 18:25–26; 2Pe 2:2).

15 The Western and Byzantine texts, together with various Latin and Syriac recensions, the TR, and the KJV, add νεκρῶν (*nekrōn*, "of the dead") after ἀνάστασιν (*anastasin*, "resurrection," GK *414*), and so read: "There will be a resurrection *of the dead* of both the righteous and the wicked"—a natural supplement found elsewhere in the NT but not here in the more reliable textual tradition.

17 Six years had passed since Paul's brief visit to Jerusalem to fulfill his Nazirite vow (cf. 18:22), and nine since his coming to the city for the Jerusalem Council (cf. 15:1–29).

20 The Alexandrian text (𝔓⁷⁴ ℵ A B et al.) reads τί εὗρον ἀδίκημα (*ti heuron adikēma*, "what crime they found"), whereas the Western text (C E Ψ et al.) and Byzantine text (L P et al.) read τί εὗρον ἐν ἐμοί ἀδίκημα (*ti heuron en emoi adikēma*, "what crime they found in me")—a natural expansion that rounds out the phrase and makes it explicit (so the TR, KJV, NIV but not UBS⁴ or NASB) but is not represented by the more reliable textual tradition.

22 On the self-designation "those of the Way," see note at v.14.

24 The weight of the external textual evidence (𝔓⁷⁴ ℵ B E Ψ, together with many minuscules and versions) supports the longer reading of the name Χριστὸν Ἰησοῦν (*Christon Iēsoun*, "Christ Jesus"; so NIV, NASB); Codex Alexandrinus (A) and the Byzantine text (P, together with other minuscules), however, read the name as only Χριστόν (*Christon*, "Christ"), as incorporated into the TR and translated by KJV.

On μετά (*meta*, "after"; NIV and NASB, "later") with a time designation as a Lukan connective in the latter half of Acts, see note at v.1.

26 The Byzantine text (H L P and most minuscules), followed by the TR and KJV, add ὅπως λύσῃ αὐτόν (*hopōs lysē auton*, "that he might release him")—which is an unnecessary addition that leaves nothing to the imagination of the readers.

27 The Western text (minuscules 614 and 2147, and as reflected in a marginal reading of the Syriac Harclean version) recasts the latter portion of this verse after Πόρκιον Φῆστον (*Porkion Phēston*, "Porcius Festus") to read τὸν δὲ Παῦλον εἴασεν ἐν τηρήσει διὰ Δρούσιλλαν (*ton de Paulon eiasen en tērēsei dia Drousillan*, "but Paul he kept in prison on account of Drusilla"), evidently wanting to justify Drusilla's presence by ascribing to her a part in the action.

3. Defense before Festus (25:1–12)

OVERVIEW

The account of Paul's defense before Festus is the briefest of his five defenses. Most of it parallels in summary fashion the account of Paul's defense before Felix. The new element is Paul's appeal to Caesar, which sets the stage for his journey to Rome.

In this pericope Luke's apologetic purpose is to show that only when Roman administrators were largely ignorant of the facts of the case were concessions made to Jewish opposition—which concessions could prove disastrous for the Christian movement.

¹Three days after arriving in the province, Festus went up from Caesarea to Jerusalem, ²where the chief priests and Jewish leaders appeared before him and presented the charges against Paul. ³They urgently requested Festus, as a favor to them, to have Paul transferred to Jerusalem, for they were preparing an ambush to kill him along the way. ⁴Festus answered, "Paul is being held at Caesarea, and I myself am going there soon. ⁵Let some of your leaders come with me and press charges against the man there, if he has done anything wrong."

⁶After spending eight or ten days with them, he went down to Caesarea, and the next day he convened the court and ordered that Paul be brought before him. ⁷When Paul appeared, the Jews who had come down from Jerusalem stood around him, bringing many serious charges against him, which they could not prove.

⁸Then Paul made his defense: "I have done nothing wrong against the law of the Jews or against the temple or against Caesar."

⁹Festus, wishing to do the Jews a favor, said to Paul, "Are you willing to go up to Jerusalem and stand trial before me there on these charges?"

¹⁰Paul answered: "I am now standing before Caesar's court, where I ought to be tried. I have not done any wrong to the Jews, as you yourself know very well. ¹¹If, however, I am guilty of doing anything deserving death, I do not refuse to die. But if the charges brought against me by these Jews are not true, no one has the right to hand me over to them. I appeal to Caesar!"

¹²After Festus had conferred with his council, he declared: "You have appealed to Caesar. To Caesar you will go!"

COMMENTARY

1 For the Jewish population of Palestine, Porcius Festus was a welcome successor to Felix (cf. Josephus, *J.W.* 2.271; *Ant.* 20.185–88)—and, it may be noted by way of anticipation, immeasurably better than the villainous Lucceius Albinus (AD 62–64) and the totally corrupt Gessius Florus (AD 64–66) who succeeded him in office (cf. Josephus, *J.W.* 2.272–83). Nothing is known of Festus before he was the procurator or governor of Judea. Nor can the time of his nomination for the post or his arrival in Palestine be precisely fixed. Probably Festus began to rule in Judea in AD 60 and continued to AD 62. He inherited all the troubles and tensions that were mounting during the period of Felix's maladministration—troubles and tensions that culminated in the disastrous war of AD 66–70, when the Roman Tenth Legion marched against the Jewish nation and both the city of Jerusalem and its temple were destroyed (cf. Josephus, *J.W.* 2.271; *Ant.* 20.185–96). His term of office was cut short by his death in AD 62.

The situation in Palestine demanded immediate action to bring together opposing factions within the Jewish nation. Therefore on arriving in Palestine, Festus took only three days to settle in at Caesarea before going up to Jerusalem to meet with the leaders of the nation.

2 The high priest at Jerusalem when Festus took office was Ishmael, the son of Phabi, whom Herod Agrippa II had appointed to succeed Ananias during the final days of Felix's governorship (cf. Josephus, *Ant.* 20.179, 194, 196). The Talmud says that Ishmael served as high priest for ten years (*b. Yoma* 9a), though Josephus reports that Agrippa II replaced him with Joseph the son of Simeon during Festus's rule because of a dispute over a wall erected to block the king's view of the temple and during the time Ishmael was detained at Rome (cf. Josephus,

Ant. 20.189–96). Ananias, however, continued to exercise a dominant role in Jerusalem's affairs right up to his death in AD 66 at the hands of Jewish nationalists (cf. Josephus, *Ant.* 20.205, 209). It is probably for this reason that Luke speaks in the plural of "the chief priests" (*hoi archiereis*), not just the high priest Ishmael, as appearing with the elders before Festus when he came to Jerusalem (cf. 4:23; 9:14; 22:30; 23:14; 25:15).

3 Counting on the new governor's inexperience, the Jewish authorities urged Festus to transfer Paul's case to Jerusalem for trial. Luke says they did this in order to ambush and murder him on the way (cf. 23:12–15). Perhaps also they hoped that with such a change of venue, should their plans for an ambush again be frustrated, they could arrange to have Paul tried before the Sanhedrin on the single charge of profaning the temple—for which, of course, they had the right to impose the death penalty (see comments at 21:27–29)—without having to sustain the charade of claiming political sedition, as was required for the death penalty in a Roman court.

4–5 Unwittingly, Festus overturned their plans by inviting the Jewish leaders to return with him to Caesarea and press charges against Paul there. Evidently he desired to carry out only such business as was absolutely necessary on his first visit to Jerusalem and preferred to preside over any extended trial back at Caesarea, particularly since the prisoner was already there.

6–8 Festus convened the court and ordered Paul brought before him, thereby reopening the whole case against Paul, and the Jewish accusers restated their charges against him (cf. 24:5–6). But again they produced no witnesses; nor could they prove their charges. As for Paul, he stoutly continued to insist on his innocence (v.8). So the impasse remained.

9 Festus was at a loss to know what to make of the Jewish charges and Paul's denials (cf. vv.18–20a). Yet the Sanhedrin plainly wanted the case transferred to Jerusalem for trial. And as the new governor of Judea, who evidently wanted to gain the goodwill of those he governed, Festus saw no reason why he could not concede to their request. Festus seems not to have fully appreciated what lay behind their request and apparently thought it would be expedient to gain their goodwill by a change of venue.

10–11 Paul understood that to return to Jerusalem was to place himself in serious jeopardy. It would be tantamount to being turned over to the Sanhedrin, for once he was in Jerusalem the Jewish authorities would exert every pressure on Festus to have him turned over to them for trial on the charge of profaning the temple. "I am now standing before Caesar's court, where I ought to be tried," he asserted (v.10). But being unsure as to just what action Festus might take in the matter if left at that, Paul went on to claim one final right he had as a Roman citizen: "I appeal to Caesar!" (v.11)

Roman law in the Julio-Claudian period (the *lex Iulia*) protected Roman citizens who invoked the right of *provocatio ad Caesarem* ("appeal to the emperor") from violent coercion and capital trials by provincial administrators. By the beginning of the second century AD, Roman citizens were automatically sent off to Rome by provincial governors for trial for a variety of offenses (cf. Pliny the Younger, *Epist.* 6.31.3; 10.96.4; Tacitus, *Ann.* 16.10.2). And in the third century AD, when everyone except a slave was considered a citizen, the right of *appellatio ad Caesarem* ("appeal to the emperor") in two or three days after a civil or criminal conviction was universally allowed. But in the Julio-Claudian period when Roman citizenship was not widely diffused, a citizen of Rome living outside Italy could appeal to Caesar for trial by an imperial court at Rome only in cases that went beyond the normal civil and criminal jurisdiction (i.e., beyond the *ordo* to the *extra ordinem*) of a governor—particularly where the threat of violent coercion or capital punishment was present.

As many have noted, the texts that speak of Paul's appeal to Caesar (25:11–12, 21, 25–26; 26:32; 28:19) do not connect it explicitly to the fact of his Roman citizenship. "But there was no necessity," as Adrian Sherwin-White has pointed out, "to reassert what had been established very circumstantially at the beginning of the inquiry" (*Roman Society and Roman Law in the New Testament* [1963; repr., Grand Rapids: Baker, 1978], 66). Likewise, it may seem somewhat strange that Paul would prefer to appeal to the emperor Nero (AD 54–68), who became renowned as the persecutor of Christians at Rome, rather than continue to entrust his case to Festus, whether at Caesarea or Jerusalem. But the early years of Nero's rule during AD 54–62, under the influence of the Stoic philosopher Seneca and the prefect of the praetorian guard Afranius Burrus, were something of a Golden Age in the history of the Roman Empire. And there was little in the year AD 60 to be feared from Nero or that would have warned regarding his later character and relations with Christianity during the last five years of his life.

12 Festus's discussion with his advisers was probably not whether a *provocatio ad Caesarem* should be allowed. The *lex Iulia* required that such an appeal by a Roman citizen be honored if the charges against him were judged to be *extra ordinem*. What Festus had to determine was (1) whether the charges against his prisoner fell into the category of normal provincial jurisdiction (the *ordo*) or went beyond that jurisdiction (the *extra ordinem*), and (2) whether it was either just or feasible to acquit the prisoner so as to make such an appeal unnecessary. Since the charges against Paul concerned political sedition, which in Roman law could be punished by death, and profanation of the Jerusalem temple, which in Jewish law called for death, Festus had no choice but to acknowledge the *extra ordinem* character of the charge and accept Paul's appeal. But Festus still could pronounce an acquittal after the act of appeal. Legally he had the right. Yet politically no newly arrived governor would have dreamed of antago-nizing the leaders of the people he sought to govern by acquitting one against whom they were so vehemently opposed. It was thus more a political than a legal decision that Festus had to make, and he was probably only too glad to have this way out of a very sticky situation. So he agreed to Paul's appeal to the emperor, evidently happy to rid himself of the prisoner and the problem.

NOTES

1 On μετὰ (*meta*, "after") with a time designation (here τρεῖς ἡμέρας, *treis hēmeras*, "three days") as a Lukan connective in the latter half of Acts, see comments at 15:36 (though here its connective force is less obvious).

On "going up" (ἀναβαίνω, *anabainō*, GK *326*) to Jerusalem, see note at 8:5.

4 On μὲν οὖν (*men oun*, "so," "then") as a favorite Lukan connective, see comments at 1:6. See also v.11 below.

6–7 On "going down" (καταβαίνω, *katabainō*, GK *2849*) from Jerusalem to Caesarea, see note at 8:5.

10 Codex Vaticanus (B) adds a second ἑστώς (*hestōs*, "standing," GK *2705*), thereby reading, "Standing before Caesar's court, I am standing where I ought to be tried"—which is an attractive reading, whose flavor seems to be captured by the NIV with the inclusion of "now."

11 On μὲν οὖν (*men oun*, "so," "then") as a favorite Lukan connective, see comments at 1:6. See also note on v.4 above.

4. Festus Consults with Herod Agrippa II (25:13–22)

OVERVIEW

Although ridding himself of one problem, Festus now took on another, though it seems for him a much more minor one than the first. What would he write in his report to the imperial court at Rome about the charges against Paul and the issues in the case (cf. v.26)? Undoubtedly, Luke had no direct knowledge of what was said in private between a Roman governor and the king of a neighboring principality. But the gist of what was discussed would certainly have been evident from their result-ant actions. So Luke here fleshes out the details of that conversation in order to prepare the way for Paul's last great defense before Herod Agrippa II.

¹³A few days later King Agrippa and Bernice arrived at Caesarea to pay their respects to Festus. ¹⁴Since they were spending many days there, Festus discussed Paul's case with the king. He said: "There is a man here whom Felix left as a prisoner. ¹⁵When I went to Jerusalem, the chief priests and elders of the Jews brought charges against him and asked that he be condemned.

¹⁶"I told them that it is not the Roman custom to hand over any man before he has faced his accusers and has had an opportunity to defend himself against their charges. ¹⁷When they came here with me, I did not delay the case, but convened the court the next day and ordered the man to be brought in. ¹⁸When his accusers got up to speak, they did not charge him with any of the crimes I had expected. ¹⁹Instead, they had some points of dispute with him about their own religion and about a dead man named Jesus who Paul claimed was alive. ²⁰I was at a loss how to investigate such matters; so I asked if he would be willing to go to Jerusalem and stand trial there on these charges. ²¹When Paul made his appeal to be held over for the Emperor's decision, I ordered him held until I could send him to Caesar."

²²Then Agrippa said to Festus, "I would like to hear this man myself."

He replied, "Tomorrow you will hear him."

COMMENTARY

13 Marcus Julius Agrippa II (AD 27–93) was the son of Agrippa I, the grandson of Aristobulus, and the great-grandson of Herod the Great. He was brought up at Rome in the court of Claudius and like his father was a favorite of the emperor. At his father's death in AD 44 he was only seventeen years old—and too young to rule over his father's extensive domains (see comments at 12:1). Therefore Palestine became a Roman province administered by a provincial governor. In AD 49 or 50, however, following the death of his uncle Herod [Philip?] of Chalcis in AD 48, Claudius appointed Agrippa II king of Chalcis, a petty kingdom to the northeast of Judea. In AD 53 Claudius gave him the tetrarchy of Philip, Abilene (or Abila), Trachonitis, and Acra (the tetrarchy of Varus) in exchange for the kingdom of Chalcis. And in AD 56 Nero added to his kingdom the Galilean cities of Tarichea and Tiberias with their surrounding lands and the Perean city of Julias (or Betharamphtha) with fourteen villages

belonging to it (cf. Josephus, *J.W.* 2.220–23, 247, 252; *Ant.* 20.104, 138, 159). As ruler of the adjoining kingdom to the north, Herod Agrippa II came to pay his respects to Festus, the new governor of Judea.

Later Agrippa II would try to prevent the Jews from revolting against Rome (cf. Josephus, *J.W.* 2.343–404), but his efforts were in vain (ibid., 405–7). During the war of AD 66–70 he was firmly on the side of Rome, and after the war Vespasian confirmed him as king in the territory he previously governed and added new areas to his domain. The Talmud implies that he had two wives (cf. *b. Sukkah* 27a). But Josephus gives no indication of his being married or having children, and his death marked the end of the Herodian dynasty.

With Agrippa II was Bernice (properly Berenice or Pherenika; Veronica in Latin), who was his sister one year younger than himself. She had been engaged to Marcus, a nephew of the philosopher

Philo. Then she was married to her uncle Herod [Philip?], king of Chalcis. But at his death in AD 48 she came to live with her brother Agrippa. Rumors of their incestuous relationship flourished in both Rome and Palestine (cf. Juvenal, *Sat.* 6. 156–60; Josephus, *Ant.* 20.145–47), and in an effort to silence them she married King Polemo of Cilicia in AD 63. In AD 66, however, she returned to live with her brother. She became Titus's mistress at the close of the Roman war in Palestine and in AD 75 went to Rome to live with him. Her relationship with Titus became a public scandal, and he was forced to send her away (cf. Tacitus, *Hist.* 2.2). When Titus became emperor in AD 79, Bernice returned once more to Rome. But Titus was obliged to have nothing to do with her, and she returned to Palestine (cf. Cassius Dio, *Hist.* 56.18).

14 Though Agrippa II did not rule over Judea, he had been appointed by Claudius—as was his uncle Herod [Philip?], king of Chalcis, before him (Josephus, *Ant.* 20.103)—to be "the curator of the temple" (*hē epimeleia tou hierou*), with power to depose and appoint the high priest and responsibility for preserving the temple's treasury and priestly vestments (Josephus, *Ant.* 20.213, 222). The Talmud reports that his mother, Cypros, took a profound interest in the Jewish religion (see comments at 12:1, citing *b. Pesaḥ.* 88*b*), and some of this interest may have rubbed off on him. Agrippa II, in fact, was viewed by Rome as an authority on the Jewish religion. And it was for this reason that Festus broached the subject of Paul's case when Agrippa visited him.

15–21 Festus told Agrippa how the Jewish leaders confronted him with Paul's case when he first went to Jerusalem and that they had asked for Paul's death (v.15), but how he had acted in accordance with Roman law in demanding that charges be properly laid and the defendant allowed his day in court (v.16). Furthermore, he insisted, he acted with due dispatch, for on the day after he and the Jewish leaders returned to Caesarea he convened the court in order to try the case (v.17). To his surprise, however, as he continued to point out, he found that the charges did not concern real offenses punishable under Roman law but instead consisted of theological differences of a Jewish intramural nature (vv.18–19a) and a debate "about a dead man named Jesus who Paul claimed was alive" (v.19b). Such matters were plainly incomprehensible and pointless to a Roman administrator. With a shrug of his shoulders Festus confessed his total inadequacy to deal with them (v.20a). In an endeavor to resolve the impasse, Festus told Agrippa that he was prepared to accede to the Sanhedrin's request for a change of venue to Jerusalem (v.20b), but Paul had objected and appealed to Caesar, and Festus had granted Paul's appeal (v.21). Now then, what in the world was he to write in sending Paul to the imperial court regarding the charges against the prisoner and the issues of the case (cf. v.26)?

22 All this stirred Agrippa's interest. So instead of merely giving his advice, he asked to hear Paul himself. The Greek expression *kai autos* ("also myself"; NIV and NASB, "myself") makes the "I" emphatic and lays stress on Agrippa's real desire to meet Paul. Festus was only too happy to arrange a meeting for the very next day.

Paul's meeting with Herod Agrippa II has often been paralleled with that of Jesus before Herod Antipas in Luke 23:6–12. For not only was each arraigned before a Roman governor, but each was also brought before a Jewish king who wanted very much to meet him (cf. Lk 23:8). Paul's time with Agrippa II, however, turned out far more harmoniously than that of Jesus before Antipas. While Luke may have had the parallels in mind (only Luke among the evangelists includes the pericope of Jesus' appearance before Antipas), the differences of purpose and detail are too great to class the accounts of the two meetings as doublets.

NOTES

13 The Byzantine text has the future participle ἀσπασόμενοι (*aspasomenoi*, GK *832*, "greet," "pay respects to," "welcome") instead of the Alexandrian text's aorist participle ἀσπασάμενοι (*aspasamenoi*), evidently believing that the future participle better expresses intent. But on occasion the aorist participle functions in this manner, if not to highlight future action, at least to signal intended coincident action.

18 Bodmer 𝔓⁷⁴ and codices ℵ A C Ψ, together with a number of minuscules and as reflected in recensions of the Old Latin, Vulgate, and Syriac versions, read either πονηράν (*ponēran*, "evil," GK *4505*) or πονηρά (*ponēra*, "evil") instead of πονηρῶν (*ponērōn*, "of the wickedness"; NIV, "of the crimes"; NASB, "of such crimes") that appears in B E and some minuscules and is reflected in recensions of the Old Latin and Syriac versions. The textual evidence is almost evenly balanced. But because of the witness of Codex Vaticanius (B), most text critics are prepared to opt for πονηρῶν (*ponērōn*, "of the wickedness" or "crimes"). The Byzantine text (L P and most minuscules), and as incorporated into the TR and KJV, omits the word, thereby reading, "They did not charge him with what I had expected."

5. Defense before Herod Agrippa II (25:23–26:32)

OVERVIEW

For Luke, the most important of Paul's five defenses was his defense before Herod Agrippa II. It is the longest and most carefully constructed of the five, which in and of itself should give notice as to something of its importance in Luke's eyes. Perhaps Luke, through the courtesy of an officer of the guard, was in the audience chamber. Or perhaps he heard Paul's account of the event and what was said some time later. But however he got his materials, he chose to conclude his narrative of Paul's five defenses with this speech—a speech that has quite properly been called the apostle's *Apologia Pro Vita Sua* (so F. F. Bruce, 488).

All the attention in the account is focused on Paul himself and the gospel—not on the charges brought forward by the Jews, and certainly not on any rumored incest between Agrippa and Bernice. Inherent in Luke's narrative are at least three apologetic themes: (1) Paul's relations with the Roman provincial government in Judea did not end in dissonance but instead with an acknowledgment of his innocence (cf. 25:25; 26:31); (2) even though the Jewish high priests and Sanhedrin opposed Paul, the Jewish king, who in the eyes of the Greco-Roman world outranked them, agreed with a verdict of innocence (cf. 26:32); and (3) Paul's innocence was demonstrated not only before Roman and Jewish rulers but also publicly before "the high ranking officers and the leading men of the city" (25:23).

Yet Paul's speech before Agrippa II is not just an apologia in the narrow sense of the word. It is also a positive presentation of the gospel with an evangelistic appeal. At least the following four emphases are prominent in it: (1) the prophets and Moses predicted that Christ would suffer, rise from the dead, and proclaim light to both Jews and Gentiles (26:22–23); (2) what God did in and through Jesus the Christ was done openly, "not ... in a corner" (v.26); (3) believing the prophets leads to acceptance of Christ (v.27); and (4) Paul's prayer for all who hear is that they "may become what I am, except for these chains" (v.29). It is with such a kerygmatic purpose that Luke penned his two volumes (see Introduction, pp. 676–78). And this account of Paul's final defense is a fitting climax to that purpose. All that remains is to sketch out the apostle's journey to Rome and his ministry there, thus completing the geographical framework of Luke's presentation and concluding it on a note of triumph (cf. 28:31).

²³The next day Agrippa and Bernice came with great pomp and entered the audience room with the high ranking officers and the leading men of the city. At the command of Festus, Paul was brought in. ²⁴Festus said: "King Agrippa, and all who are present with us, you see this man! The whole Jewish community has petitioned me about him in Jerusalem and here in Caesarea, shouting that he ought not to live any longer. ²⁵I found he had done nothing deserving of death, but because he made his appeal to the Emperor I decided to send him to Rome. ²⁶But I have nothing definite to write to His Majesty about him. Therefore I have brought him before all of you, and especially before you, King Agrippa, so that as a result of this investigation I may have something to write. ²⁷For I think it is unreasonable to send on a prisoner without specifying the charges against him."

²⁶:¹Then Agrippa said to Paul, "You have permission to speak for yourself."

So Paul motioned with his hand and began his defense: ²"King Agrippa, I consider myself fortunate to stand before you today as I make my defense against all the accusations of the Jews, ³and especially so because you are well acquainted with all the Jewish customs and controversies. Therefore, I beg you to listen to me patiently.

⁴"The Jews all know the way I have lived ever since I was a child, from the beginning of my life in my own country, and also in Jerusalem. ⁵They have known me for a long time and can testify, if they are willing, that according to the strictest sect of our religion, I lived as a Pharisee. ⁶And now it is because of my hope in what God has promised our fathers that I am on trial today. ⁷This is the promise our twelve tribes are hoping to see fulfilled as they earnestly serve God day and night. O king, it is because of this hope that the Jews are accusing me. ⁸Why should any of you consider it incredible that God raises the dead?

⁹"I too was convinced that I ought to do all that was possible to oppose the name of Jesus of Nazareth. ¹⁰And that is just what I did in Jerusalem. On the authority of the chief priests I put many of the saints in prison, and when they were put to death, I cast my vote against them. ¹¹Many a time I went from one synagogue to another to have them punished, and I tried to force them to blaspheme. In my obsession against them, I even went to foreign cities to persecute them.

¹²"On one of these journeys I was going to Damascus with the authority and commission of the chief priests. ¹³About noon, O king, as I was on the road, I saw a light from heaven, brighter than the sun, blazing around me and my companions. ¹⁴We all fell to the ground, and I heard a voice saying to me in Aramaic, 'Saul, Saul, why do you persecute me? It is hard for you to kick against the goads.'

¹⁵"Then I asked, 'Who are you, Lord?'

"'I am Jesus, whom you are persecuting,' the Lord replied. ¹⁶'Now get up and stand on your feet. I have appeared to you to appoint you as a servant and as a witness of what you have seen of me and what I will show you. ¹⁷I will rescue you from your own people and from the Gentiles. I am sending you to them ¹⁸to open their eyes and turn them from darkness to light, and from the power of Satan to God, so that they may receive forgiveness of sins and a place among those who are sanctified by faith in me.'

¹⁹"So then, King Agrippa, I was not disobedient to the vision from heaven. ²⁰First to those in Damascus, then to those in Jerusalem and in all Judea, and to the Gentiles also, I preached that they should repent and turn to God and prove their repentance by their deeds. ²¹That is why the Jews seized me in the temple courts and tried to kill me. ²²But I have had God's help to this very day, and so I stand here and testify to small and great alike. I am saying nothing beyond what the prophets and Moses said would happen—²³that the Christ would suffer and, as the first to rise from the dead, would proclaim light to his own people and to the Gentiles."

²⁴At this point Festus interrupted Paul's defense. "You are out of your mind, Paul!" he shouted. "Your great learning is driving you insane."

²⁵"I am not insane, most excellent Festus," Paul replied. "What I am saying is true and reasonable. ²⁶The king is familiar with these things, and I can speak freely to him. I am convinced that none of this has escaped his notice, because it was not done in a corner. ²⁷King Agrippa, do you believe the prophets? I know you do."

²⁸Then Agrippa said to Paul, "Do you think that in such a short time you can persuade me to be a Christian?"

²⁹Paul replied, "Short time or long—I pray God that not only you but all who are listening to me today may become what I am, except for these chains."

³⁰The king rose, and with him the governor and Bernice and those sitting with them. ³¹They left the room, and while talking with one another, they said, "This man is not doing anything that deserves death or imprisonment."

³²Agrippa said to Festus, "This man could have been set free if he had not appealed to Caesar."

COMMENTARY

23 Luke describes Agrippa and Bernice as entering the audience chamber of Herod the Great's Caesarean palace "with great pomp" (*meta pollēs phantasias*), accompanied by a procession of "high ranking officers" (*chiliarchoi*, lit., "commanders of a thousand men") and "the leading men of the city." The Romans always knew how to process well! The sight of Agrippa's royal robes, Bernice's finery, and the military and civil dignitaries decked out in their official attire doubtless overwhelmed those unaccustomed to such displays, which, of course, was the effect the whole affair was calculated to produce. After the procession, Paul the prisoner was brought in. But though the situation was contrived to assert the importance of Roman officialdom and the inferiority of anyone who stood before it, Luke's divinely inspired insight penetrated the trappings and saw that the situation was really reversed. And his evaluation has prevailed in history.

24–27 Festus opened the proceedings by turning the dignitaries' attention to Paul with the words "you see this man!" (*theōreite touton*). After acknowledging that he could not substantiate the charges brought against Paul, he told how Paul had appealed to Caesar. Then asking for help with what he should write in sending Paul to the imperial court at Rome, Festus turned the conduct of the inquiry over to King Agrippa.

A number of subtle touches in these verses are particularly appropriate for the situation. The title *Sebastos* ("Emperor") of v.25, found in the NT only here and at v.21, is the Greek equivalent of the Latin title "Augustus." It was first conferred on Octavian, the adopted heir of Julius Caesar, by the senate in 27 BC to denote "one who is augmented" or "august"—i.e., one lifted above other mortals in dignity and grandeur. It was reserved solely for the reigning emperor (though at times also used for his wife). The addition of *Kyrios* ("Lord" or "Majesty") to the imperial title began in the time of Nero (AD 54–68), with its usage steadily increasing until it became a common appellation for the emperor during the reign of Trajan (AD 98–117). Despite its associations with deity in the eastern realms of the empire, the growth of the imperial cult, and the pretensions to divinity of such emperors as Nero and Domitian, *Kyrios* did not by itself signal to Romans the idea of deity. Rather, it connoted that of majesty (cf. *TDNT* 3.1054–58). Likewise, Festus's statement that he thought it "unreasonable" (*alogos*, GK *263*)

to send on a prisoner without specifying charges against him (v.27) is typical of the face-saving language used among officials when what is really meant is that the failure to specify charges would be a dereliction of duty.

26:1 At Agrippa's invitation to speak, Paul, though manacled by chains (v.29), motioned with his hand for attention (cf. 21:40) and began speaking. While we have only a précis of what was said, it is the longest précis of Paul's five defenses. And that length undoubtedly reflects the relative length of the address itself. Agrippa II was considered by the Romans to be something of an authority on the Jewish religion. So he might have been expected to listen closely to Paul's lengthy explanation of the relation of his message and ministry to the hope of Israel.

2–3 This was just the kind of situation Paul had longed for during two bleak years in prison—a knowledgeable judge and a not inherently antagonistic audience before whom he could not only make his defense but also proclaim his message. Therefore he began with unusual fervor in expressing appreciation for the opportunity to speak, complimenting the judge, and asking for patience in hearing him out. Since Festus had already said that Paul had not committed a capital crime (cf. 25:25), Paul chose to defend himself only against the charge that he had transgressed against Judaism.

4–8 It was not in spite of his Jewish heritage, Paul insisted, but because of it that he believed and proclaimed what he did. So he began the body of his address (note the connective *men oun* at the start of v.4) by drawing together his Pharisaic background and his Christian commitment, arguing that the Jewish hope and the Christian message are inseparably related. His life had been spent among his people in his own country and in Jerusalem (v.4; cf. 22:3). He had lived as a Pharisee, "the strictest sect" (*tēn akribestatēn hairesin*) of the Jewish religion (v.5; cf. Php 3:5–6). It was because of the Jewish hope in the resurrection of the dead that he was being tried (v.6). And the ironic thing was that the charges against him were brought by, of all people, the Jews themselves (note that the phrase *hypo Ioudaiōn*, "by the Jews," is in the place of emphasis at the end of v.7). Yet why should any of his audience (note the plural *hymin*, "you") think it "incredible that God raises the dead" (v.8), particularly when God has validated the truth of the resurrection by raising Jesus from the dead (see comments at 23:6)?

9–11 Speaking retrospectively, Paul went on (note the resumptive use of *men oun*) to acknowledge that he too had once thought that the Christian proclamation about the resurrection of Jesus was incredible. Pharisee though he was, he too had denounced belief in the resurrection of Jesus and persecuted those who claimed to have seen Jesus alive after his crucifixion. He put Christians in prison, agreed with the death penalty for their "heresy" (cf. 8:1), and went from synagogue to synagogue seeking them out in order to punish them for apostasy (cf. *m. Mak.* 3:10–15a on synagogue whippings) and force them to recant. He did this not only in Jerusalem but also in cities outside Judea (*kai eis tas exō poleis*, lit., "even to the outside cities"; NIV, "even . . . to foreign cities," v.11).

12–14 While Paul was trying to stamp out nascent Christianity, the encounter that changed his life took place. The fact that Paul's account of his experience on the road to Damascus appears three times in Acts (chs. 9; 22; 26) undoubtedly shows how important this event was not only for Paul but also for Luke (see Overview at 9:1–30). And it is in this third account that Luke's kerygmatic purpose in Luke-Acts—to proclaim the gospel of Christ—reaches its climax. Yet the threefold repetition of what happened is more than a simple retelling of the same details. Each account fits its own special context in Paul's life and in Luke's purpose.

Here there is an intensification and explication of the details such as are not found in the earlier accounts: (1) the heavenly light was "brighter than the sun" (v.13; cf. 9:3; 22:6); (2) it blazed around both "me and my companions" (v.13; cf. 9:3; 22:6); (3) "we all fell to the ground" (v.14; cf. 9:4; 22:7); and (4) the voice from heaven spoke "in Aramaic" (lit., "in the Hebrew dialect," v.14). None of these matters necessarily contradict details narrated in the other two accounts, but each seems here to have been intended to clarify for Paul's hearers and Luke's readers the significance of the events.

Likewise, in v.14b we have the only place in the three Acts accounts—if we reject (as I do) the Western addition at 22:7, incorporated by Erasmus into the TR—where the statement "it is hard for you to kick against the goads" (*sklēron soi pros kentra laktizein*) appears. In the Greek world, this was a well-known expression for opposition to deity (cf. Euripides, *Bacchanals* 794–95; Aeschylus, *Prom.* 324–25; *Ag.* 1624; Pindar, *Pyth.* 2.94–95; Terence, *Phorm.* 1.2.27). Paul may have picked it up in Tarsus or during his missionary journeys. He uses it here, it seems, to suggest to his Greek-oriented audience the implications of the question, "Saul, Saul, why do you persecute me?" For lest he be misunderstood to be proclaiming only a Galilean prophet whom he had formerly opposed, he points out to his hearers what would have been obvious to any Jew, namely, that correction by a voice from heaven meant opposition to God himself. So he uses an expression that was widely familiar throughout the Greco-Roman world to explicate to Herod Agrippa II and his associates the real significance of what he realized in that encounter with Christ on the Damascus road (cf. my *Paul, Apostle of Liberty*, 98–101).

15–18 On the other hand, this third account leaves out certain features we might have come to expect from the other two: (1) the heavenly speaker identifies himself only as Jesus and not "Jesus of Nazareth" (v.15; cf. 22:8); (2) there is no mention of Ananias (cf. 9:10–19; 22:12–16); and (3) there is no mention of Paul's blindness and subsequent healing (cf. 9:8–9; 18–19; 22:11, 13). There was, however, no need to refer to Nazareth (particularly having mentioned it in v.9) or to refer to the devout Ananias, as when addressing the Jewish crowd from the steps of the Fortress of Antonia in Jerusalem (see comments at 22:8, 12). Nor was it necessary for Paul to refer to his blindness and healing, which might have been confusing to a pagan audience. Rather, in his address before Agrippa and the others, Paul merged the words of Jesus as spoken on the road to Damascus (cf. 9:5–6; 22:8, 10), as given through Ananias of Damascus (cf. 22:14–15), and as received in a vision at Jerusalem (cf. 22:18–21). The result was that Paul did not emphasize details of time or human aid in this third account of his conversion; rather, what he emphasized was the lordship of Christ and the divine commission Christ gave him.

The words of the risen Jesus calling Paul to his mission (vv.16–17) recall God's words in commissioning the prophets Ezekiel and Jeremiah: "Stand up on your feet and I will speak to you. . . . I am sending you . . . to a rebellious nation that has rebelled against me" (Eze 2:1, 3); "You must go to everyone I send you to and say whatever I command you. Do not be afraid of them, for I am with you and will rescue you" (Jer 1:7–8). The commission itself (v.18) echoes that of the Servant of the Lord in Isaiah 42:6b–7: "I . . . will make you . . . a light for the Gentiles, to open eyes that are blind, to free captives from prison and to release from the dungeon those who sit in darkness." Indeed, Paul's mission was to be a prophetic one that perpetuated the commission originally given to God's Righteous Servant, Jesus Christ. And Christians today, as God's servants and prophets, are called to this same kind of ministry.

19–21 Having been confronted by the risen and glorified Jesus, Paul henceforth knew but one Master and found it impossible to resist his commands. So Paul told Agrippa how he began preaching about Jesus "first to those in Damascus" and "then to those in Jerusalem," but more particularly how he proclaimed "to the Gentiles" the message "that they should repent and turn to God and prove their repentance by their deeds" (v.20). The emphasis in his defense is on the fact that it was because he preached such a message of repentance and conversion to Gentiles that the Jews were so aggressively opposed to him (v.21).

A major problem of grammar and context arises in v.20 with the inclusion of the words "all the region of Judea" (*pasan te tēn chōran tēs Ioudaias*; NIV, "in all Judea"; NASB, "throughout all the region of Judea"). Grammatically these words are rather strange, for they appear in an accusative construction in the midst of datives and are without the preposition *eis* ("in") necessary for such a construction. Contextually they conflict with the evidence of Acts 9:20–30 and Galatians 1:18–24 that Paul did not preach the gospel throughout "all the region of Judea." It may be that the preposition *eis* was accidentally omitted by an early scribe, as such diverse scholars as Frederick Blass, William M. Ramsay, and Martin Dibelius have postulated. Codex E of the sixth century and the Byzantine text generally (codices H L and P of the eighth-ninth centuries and most minuscules) add the preposition in order to justify the phrase's dative construction, but that is probably only a later correction and conjecture. More likely, we should probably judge the phrase "all the region of Judea" to be an early gloss, which may have entered the text through a false reading of Romans 15:19. If that be so, then it should be discounted as part of the original text.

22–23 In fulfillment of Christ's promise (v.17), God stood by Paul, protecting him and enabling him to proclaim "to small and great alike" a message thoroughly in accord with Israel's faith and in harmony with all that the prophets and Moses said would happen (v.22): "that [*ei*, here in v.23, as in v.8, being equivalent to a *hoti-recitativum*, which introduces direct discourse] the Christ would suffer and, as the first to rise from the dead, would proclaim light to his own people and to the Gentiles."

Despite occasional claims to the contrary, there is no evidence that pre-Christian Judaism ever thought of the Messiah in terms of suffering. Of course, many of the building blocks for a later doctrine of a suffering Messiah were present in the Jewish consciousness during the period of Second Temple Judaism, and there is some indication that these elements were later brought together at times into either an inchoate (cf. *4 Ezra* 7:29–30) or a distorted (cf. the Sabbati Svi sect of the Middle Ages) suffering Messiah doctrine. But the proclamation of both a suffering Messiah and the resurrection of Jesus was distinctive to early Christianity. And to these foundational tenets of the early Christian faith Paul, by revelation (cf. Gal 1:11–12; Eph 3:1–6), added the legitimacy of a direct outreach to Gentiles.

Indeed, these features of the early Christian proclamation and Paul's understanding went beyond the explicit beliefs and expectations of Judaism. Paul's claims, however, were that they were (1) developments brought about by God himself to show the true intent of Israelite religion, and (2) in continuity with all that the prophets and Moses had said would happen.

24 At this point Festus broke in, unable to endure Paul's address any longer. Festus may not have been speaking for the Jews, to whom a suffering Messiah and a direct ministry to Gentiles were outrageous. But no sensible Roman could believe in the resurrection of a dead person. Even if he did privately accept such a strange view, he would not allow it to interfere with his practical living or bring him into

danger of death. Paul, Festus concluded, was so learned in his Jewish traditions that he had become utterly impractical. Such talk was the height of insanity. And down through the centuries Festus's response has been echoed by men and women too trapped by the natural to be open to the supernatural and too confined by practical concerns to care about life everlasting.

25–27 But what Festus declared to be madness Paul insisted was "true and reasonable" (*alētheias kai sōphrosynēs rhēmata*, lit., "of true and reasonable words"). Then he turned to Agrippa for support. The ministry of Jesus was widely known in Palestine, and Agrippa would have heard of it. Jesus' death and resurrection were amply attested, and the Christian gospel had now been proclaimed for three decades. Certainly the king knew of these things, "because it was not done in a corner" (*ou gar estin en gōnia pepragmenon touto*)—which is another (cf. v.14b) Greek idiom of the day (cf. Plato, *Gorg.* 485D; Epictetus, *Diatr.* 2.12.17; Terence, *Ad.* 5.2.10). And certainly the king believed the prophets—a belief, as Paul saw it, that would inevitably bring a person to belief in Christ. So the prisoner became the questioner and asked directly, "King Agrippa, do you believe the prophets?"

28 Paul's direct question embarrassed Agrippa. He had his reputation to maintain before Festus and the other dignitaries. Whatever he may have thought about Paul's message personally, he was too worldly-wise to commit himself in public to what others thought was madness. So he parried Paul's question with his own clever though rather inane question: "Do you think that in such a short time you can persuade me to be a Christian?" The adjective *oligos* (GK 3900) often has reference to quantity and here could mean "with such few words" or "with such a brief argument." But it is also used with the preposition *en* ("in"), as it is here, to denote duration (cf. BDAG, 703). And this is how it should be translated here (so

NIV, "in such a short time"; NASB, "in a short time";
NRSV, "so quickly"). The KJV's translation of
Agrippa's reply to Paul, "Almost thou persuadest me
to be a Christian," has become one of the famous
quotations in history. Countless sermons have been
preached on it and gospel songs inspired by it. Nevertheless, it is not what Agrippa said (nor, for that matter, is the KJV's translation of v.29 what Paul replied).

29 Addressing the king with extreme politeness
(note the use of the optative *euxaimēn an*, "I could
wish" or "I pray", which in Paul's day had become
rare) and taking up Agrippa's own word *oligos* ("such
a short time"), Paul replied, "Short time or long—I
pray God that not only you but all who are listening
to me today may become what I am." Undoubtedly
he spoke with evangelistic fervor and directed his
appeal not only to the king but also to the other dignitaries. Then in a lighter vein, evidently recognizing
the apparent incongruity of appealing for their
acceptance of spiritual freedom while he himself
stood chained before them, he raised his hands and
added, "except for these chains."

30–32 Paul had had the last word, and his light
touch at the end of his response evidently broke up
the meeting. With it, Agrippa dismissed the proceedings and with Festus and Bernice strode out of
the audience chamber. We need not visualize them
as gathering in some adjoining room to render an
official judgment. In appealing to Caesar, Paul had
removed the case from their jurisdiction. Yet
Agrippa had presumably heard enough to instruct
Festus what he should write in his report to Rome.
Their conclusion was that Paul had done nothing
that in Rome's eyes merited death or imprisonment
(v.31). And Agrippa was heard to comment, "This
man could have been set free if he had not appealed
to Caesar" (v.32).

Agrippa's comment should not be taken to mean
that a king appointed by Rome or a Roman
provincial governor could not free a prisoner after
an appeal to Caesar. In this situation, however, Paul's
status was not only a question of law but also of politics (see comments at 25:12). Luke has picked up
these words of Agrippa II and concludes his
accounts of Paul's five defenses with them. In fact,
they conclude Luke's apologetic motif in Acts and
are used by him to vindicate both Paul and Christianity from any suspicion of sedition.

NOTES

24–25 The Western text (as preserved in the margin of the Syriac Harclean version and possibly supported by a few other recensions) adds and recasts after the adverb ἐνθάδε (*enthade*, "here, in this place")
at the close of v.24 the following: "that I should hand him over to them for punishment without any defense.
[25]But I could not hand him over, because of the commands that we have from the emperor. But if anyone
was going to accuse him, I said he should follow me to Caesarea, where he was in custody. And when they
came, they insisted that he should be put to death."

26:1 The Western text (as found in the margin of the Syriac Harclean version) adds "confident and
encouraged by the Holy Spirit," thereby reading, "So Paul, confident and encouraged by the Holy Spirit,
motioned with his hand . . . ."

4 On Luke's use of μὲν οὖν (*men oun*), both here and at v.9, see comments at 1:6.

8 One early Western text (the third century 𝔓[29]) omits τί ἄπιστον κρίνεται παρ' ὑμῖν (*ti apiston krin-
etai par' hymin*, "Why should any of you consider it incredible?").

14 The Western text (minuscules 614, 1611, 2147, and as represented by recensions of the Old Latin and Syriac versions) adds διὰ τὸν φόβον ἐγὼ μόνος (*dia ton phobon egō monos*, "because of fear, only I") after εἰς τὴν γῆν (*eis tēn gēn*, "to the ground"), thereby reading, "When we had all fallen to the ground on account of fear, only I heard . . ."

15 The Western text (minuscules 181, 614, and recensions of the Vulgate and Syriac versions) adds ὁ Ναζωραῖος (*ho Nazōraios*, "the Nazarene" or "of Nazareth") after the name Ἰησοῦς (*Iēsous*, "Jesus"), evidently influenced by 22:8.

16 Codex Vaticanus (B) omits καὶ στῆθι (*kai stēthi*, "and stand") after ἀνάστηθι (*anastēthi*, "get up"), probably inadvertently.

A number of reliable texts ($\mathfrak{P}^{74}$ ℵ A E Ψ), together with the Byzantine text (L P and many minuscules) omit με (*me*, "me") and read, "What you have seen and what I will show you," whereas other reliable texts (B C and a number of other minuscules) include it and read, "What you have seen [of] me and what I will show you." The evidence is almost equally balanced, but most text critics prefer to include the pronoun because of its support by Codex Vaticanus (B).

20 The addition of εἰς (*eis*, "in") in codices E H L and P is probably a later correction and conjecture attempting to improve the grammar of the dative construction, which is hardly tolerable as Greek without the preposition (see comments at vv.19–21).

24 One Western text (the fifth-century Old Latin recension "h") reads *insanisti, Paule; insanisti* ("You are out of your mind, Paul! You are out of your mind!").

25 The Western and Byzantine texts omit Παῦλος (*Paulos*, "Paul").

On κράτιστε (*kratiste*, "most excellent") as a title and/or a polite form of address, see comments at 23:26.

28 Capturing the exact nuance of Agrippa's reply is notoriously difficult. Part of the difficulty consists in whether to accept the reading πείθεις (*peitheis*, "you persuade") of the Alexandrian text ($\mathfrak{P}^{74}$ ℵ B etc.) or the reading πείθῃ (*peithē*, "you trust") of Codex Alexandrinus (A). The Alexandrian reading of $\mathfrak{P}^{74}$ ℵ B et al. is probably to be preferred (so NIV, NASB).

On the designation Χριστιανός (*Christianos*, "Christian"), which appears only three times in the NT (Ac 11:26; here at 26:28; 1Pe 4:16), see comments at 11:26.

30 The Western and Byzantine texts begin this verse with the words καὶ ταῦτα εἰπόντος αὐτοῦ (*kai tauta eipontos autou*, "And when he said these things").

E. The Journey to Rome (27:1–28:16)

OVERVIEW

There are many things we would like to know about Paul's two-year imprisonment at Caesarea. For instance, how was he supported during this time?

Felix thought he was a man who had access to some money (cf. 24:26). But why did he think so? How cordial were Paul's relations with the Jerusalem

Christians and their leaders during the time of his imprisonment? How cordial were his contacts with the Caesarean believers or with other groups of Christians in the vicinity? What happened to Silas, who was originally a member of the Jerusalem congregation (cf. 15:22)? What were Timothy and Luke doing during these two years? What happened to the rest of those who represented the Gentile churches at the time of Paul's last visit to Jerusalem (cf. 20:4)? Aristarchus is mentioned in 27:2 as embarking with Paul for Rome, and this implies that he remained in the area during Paul's imprisonment. But what did he and the others do during that time? And a host of other questions arise as well.

Such matters, however, were evidently not of interest to Luke in writing Acts or to Paul when writing his letters. In an endeavor to fill these gaps in Luke's account of Paul's stay at Caesarea, some have proposed that several of the Pauline letters—notably Ephesians, Colossians, and Philemon—were written while Paul was a prisoner at Caesarea. But internal evidence, while not conclusive, suggests their composition during his subsequent imprisonment at Rome.

Luke's account of Paul's voyage to Rome stands out as one of the most vivid pieces of descriptive writing in the whole Bible. Its details of first-century seamanship are so precise and its portrayal of conditions on the eastern Mediterranean so accurate (cf. the almost classic work by James Smith, *The Voyage and Shipwreck of St. Paul* [London: Longmans, Green, 1856] that even the most skeptical have conceded that it probably rests on a journal of some such voyage as Luke describes. Critical discussion, therefore, has focused not so much on the trip itself as on Luke's portrayal of Paul on the trip—i.e., on Paul (1) as a prisoner receiving special favors (cf. 27:3, 43; 28:7), (2) as a speaker giving advice (cf. 27:10, 21–26, 33–34), and (3) as a miracle worker honored by all (cf. 28:3–6, 8–10). Haenchen, 709, speaks for many when he says of the author, "He certainly possessed a journal of this voyage. Yet Paul was no noble traveller with special authority, but a prisoner accused of inciting to riot. He therefore had no say in any of the decisions. Just those edifying supplements which extol Paul are additions by the author to a journal of reminiscences which could not report anything special about Paul, but only described the voyage, the danger and the rescue."

But such a judgment is far too extreme. Clearly Luke viewed Paul as his hero and so may be suspected of having minimized Paul's fears during the voyage and of having cast him in a more heroic mold than was justified. Nevertheless, Paul was a Roman citizen who still retained rights until proven guilty. In addition, he was a man of powerful personality who commanded respect in various situations. Most of all, he was an apostle of Jesus Christ who had been promised divine protection and assured that he would reach Rome (cf. 23:11) and one through whom God by his Spirit worked in an extraordinary fashion (cf. 19:11–12; 20:10–12). Historians may criticize Luke for his preoccupation with Paul and his enthusiastic portrayal of his hero's nobility under great difficulties. But criticism such as Haenchen's reflects more theological skepticism than perceptive scholarship—and more philosophical naturalism than Christian testimony to God's supernatural activity.

1. From Palestine to Crete (27:1–12)

¹When it was decided that we would sail for Italy, Paul and some other prisoners were handed over to a centurion named Julius, who belonged to the Imperial Regiment. ²We boarded a ship from Adramyttium about to sail for ports along the coast of the province of Asia, and we put out to sea. Aristarchus, a Macedonian from Thessalonica, was with us.

³The next day we landed at Sidon; and Julius, in kindness to Paul, allowed him to go to his friends so they might provide for his needs. ⁴From there we put out to sea again and passed to the lee of Cyprus because the winds were against us. ⁵When we had sailed across the open sea off the coast of Cilicia and Pamphylia, we landed at Myra in Lycia. ⁶There the centurion found an Alexandrian ship sailing for Italy and put us on board. ⁷We made slow headway for many days and had difficulty arriving off Cnidus. When the wind did not allow us to hold our course, we sailed to the lee of Crete, opposite Salmone. ⁸We moved along the coast with difficulty and came to a place called Fair Havens, near the town of Lasea.

⁹Much time had been lost, and sailing had already become dangerous because by now it was after the Fast. So Paul warned them, ¹⁰"Men, I can see that our voyage is going to be disastrous and bring great loss to ship and cargo, and to our own lives also." ¹¹But the centurion, instead of listening to what Paul said, followed the advice of the pilot and of the owner of the ship. ¹²Since the harbor was unsuitable to winter in, the majority decided that we should sail on, hoping to reach Phoenix and winter there. This was a harbor in Crete, facing both southwest and northwest.

COMMENTARY

1 The account of Paul's journey to Rome is the longest of Luke's four "we" sections (27:1–28:16; cf. 16:10–17; 20:5–15; 21:1–18). And the vividness and precision of the narrative confirm what the use of "we" implies, namely, that it is an eyewitness report.

Luke says that the centurion Julius, who was to take Paul to Rome, was a member of "the Imperial Regiment" (*speirēs Sebastēs*, lit., "the Sebastan [Lat., "Augustan"] Cohort"). Many commentators, following Theodore Mommsen and William M. Ramsay, have seen this as a reference to a group of imperial officials called the *frumentarii* who not only organized the transportation of grain to Rome but

also had police duties and performed escort services on their travels throughout the empire. But Aurelius Victor (*Liber de Caesaribus* 13.5–6) seems to attribute the organization of the *frumentarii* later to the emperor Trajan (AD 98–117), and there is nothing to indicate that even if there were *frumentarii* earlier, they had police or escort responsibilities. The soldiers who performed these services in Paul's day were the *speculatores*, a special body of imperial guards who were particularly prominent in times of military intrigue (cf. Tacitus, *Hist.* 1.24–25; 2.73). These *speculatores* belonged to no particular division of a Roman army legion, though there was a *Cohors Augusta I* in Syria during the reign of Augustus and there is evidence of a *Cohors Augusta III* at Rome. Rather, they formed a special unit of their own and were assigned various police and judicial functions.

2 While it is not stated explicitly, the port of embarkation was undoubtedly Caesarea. If it had been any other, Luke, in accord with his usual practice, would have mentioned it. The boat was a coastal vessel from the city of Adramyttium, a seaport of Mysia on the northwestern coast of Asia Minor opposite the island of Lesbos. Embarking with Paul were Luke (cf. "we") and Aristarchus, who were possibly entered on the passenger list as Paul's personal doctor and servant, respectively. As a Roman citizen who had appealed to the emperor, Paul would naturally have had a more favored position than the other prisoners, and the centurion would have recognized his superiority as a gentleman with attendants. That Aristarchus is included in Colossians 4:10 and Philemon 24 as sending greetings from Rome (assuming a Roman provenance for these letters) suggests that he traveled with Paul all the way to Rome and remained with him there during his imprisonment rather than returning to his home at Thessalonica.

3 At Sidon, the ancient Phoenician port some seventy miles north of Caesarea and twenty-five miles north of Tyre, the boat took on cargo. Here Paul was permitted to visit the Christians of the city, who like those at Tyre (see comments at 21:4) had probably become believers through the witness of the Hellenistic-Jewish Christians who were forced to leave Jerusalem at the time of Stephen's martyrdom (cf. 11:19). The centurion Julius had probably been advised by Festus to be lenient with Paul, and doubtless Paul had already made a good impression on Julius. Yet a soldier would have always accompanied him during his visit with the believers of Sidon.

4-5 From Sidon the boat sailed northwest toward Cyprus, hugging the long eastern coast of the island ("the lee of Cyprus") because of the westerly winds that blow from spring through fall on the eastern Mediterranean. Two and one-half years earlier Paul and his companions had sailed with that westerly wind from Patara to Tyre and had passed Cyprus on the south, perhaps making the entire voyage in only five days (see comments at 21:3). Now, however, their voyage from Sidon to Myra was considerably slower as their boat had to run against the winds and try to stay in the lee of sheltering land masses. Crossing the open sea between Cyprus and Cilicia to the north, the vessel worked its way westward to Myra in Lycia, on the southwestern coast of Asia Minor, helped along by local land breezes and a westward current that ran along that coast.

6 Myra was 2.5 miles inland to the north of its port of Andriaca. In Paul's day it was the most illustrious city in Lycia, with distinguished public buildings, a very large theater, and many evidences of wealth (cf. Strabo, *Geogr.* 14.3.7). Its port became the natural port of call for grain ships bound for Rome from Egypt, and it overshadowed in commercial importance its rival Patara to the west (see comments at 21:1). At Myra, Julius arranged with the owner of a larger Alexandrian grain ship to take the soldiers and prisoners on board for the longer voyage to Italy.

7-8 Leaving Myra, the grain ship moved slowly along the peninsula that thrusts seaward between the islands of Cos and Rhodes to the port of Cnidus, located at the southwestern tip of Asia Minor. Cnidus was a free city in the province of Asia and the last port of call before sailing westward across the Aegean for the Greek mainland. But the northern winds that blew down the length of the Aegean at this time of year pushed the ship off course and forced the pilot to seek protection along the southern coast ("the lee") of Crete, the 160-mile-long island southeast of Greece. Passing Cape Salmone on the eastern tip of Crete, the ship entered the small bay of Fair Havens (modern Limeonas Kalous), near the town of Lasea and about five miles east of Cape Matala.

9–10 Navigation in this part of the Mediterranean was always dangerous after September 14 and was considered impossible after November 11 (cf. Vegetius, *De Re Militari* 4.39). The ship had lost valuable time since leaving Myra, and it was obvious that there was no hope of reaching Italy before winter. Yom Kippur ("Day of Atonement"), the chief festival of Judaism celebrated on the tenth day of the lunar month Tishri (between the latter part of September and the first part of October in a solar calendar), was already past. So Paul warned that disaster would befall them if they tried to go farther.

11–12 The pilot and the ship's owner, reluctant to seek quarters for themselves and their passengers in the small town of Lasea, preferred not to winter in the small, open bay of Fair Havens. They hoped to winter at the larger and safer port of Phoenix (modern Phineka), some forty miles west of Fair Havens. Between Fair Havens and Phoenix, however, west of Cape Matala, the southern coast of Crete turns suddenly to the north and exposes a ship to the northern gales before it regains the protection of the coast just before Phoenix. Nevertheless, the centurion agreed with the pilot and the ship's owner that it would be best, if at all possible, to winter at Phoenix, whose harbor looked toward the southwest and northwest (*bleponta kata liba kai kata chōron*; NIV, "facing [both] southwest and northwest").

NOTES

1 The Western text (as represented in part by minuscules 97, 421, and more completely by the Syriac Peshitta and Harclean versions) expands these verses to read, "So then the governor decided to send him to Caesar. And the next day he called a centurion named Julius, who belonged to the Sebastan [i.e., "Augustan"] Cohort, and handed Paul over to him along with other prisoners."

2 At the close of the verse, the Western text (minuscules 614, 1518, and as represented by the Syriac Harclean version) adds καὶ Σεκοῦνδος (*kai Sekoundos*, "and Secundus") after Θεσσαλονικέων δὲ Ἀρίσταρχος (*Thessalonikeōn de Aristarchos*, "Aristarchus from Thessalonica"), evidently influenced by 20:4, where "Aristarchus and Secundus from Thessalonica" are included among Paul's traveling companions.

5 The Western text (minuscules 614, 1518, 2138, and as represented by recensions of the Old Latin, Vulgate, and Syriac versions) adds δι' ἡμερῶν δεκάπεντε (*di' hēmerōn dekapente*, "for fifteen days"), thereby reading, "When we had sailed across the open sea for fifteen days." But as Metzger, 440, remarks, "Neither the general character of the witnesses that include the longer reading, nor the variation of location where it appears in the text, inspires confidence in its originality."

2. Storm and Shipwreck (27:13–44)

13When a gentle south wind began to blow, they thought they had obtained what they wanted; so they weighed anchor and sailed along the shore of Crete. **14**Before very long, a wind of hurricane force, called the "northeaster," swept down from the island. **15**The ship was caught by the storm and could not head into the wind; so we gave way to it and were driven along. ¹⁶As we passed to the lee of a small island called Cauda, we were hardly able to make the lifeboat secure. ¹⁷When the men had hoisted it aboard, they passed ropes under the ship itself to hold it together. Fearing that they would run aground on the sandbars of Syrtis, they lowered the sea anchor and let the ship be driven along. ¹⁸We took such a violent battering from the storm that the next day they began to throw the cargo overboard. ¹⁹On the third day, they threw the ship's tackle overboard with their own hands. ²⁰When neither sun nor stars appeared for many days and the storm continued raging, we finally gave up all hope of being saved.

²¹After the men had gone a long time without food, Paul stood up before them and said: "Men, you should have taken my advice not to sail from Crete; then you would have spared yourselves this damage and loss. ²²But now I urge you to keep up your courage, because not one of you will be lost; only the ship will be destroyed. ²³Last night an angel of the God whose I am and whom I serve stood beside me ²⁴and said, 'Do not be afraid, Paul. You must stand trial before Caesar; and God has graciously given you the lives of all who sail with you.' ²⁵So keep up your courage, men, for I have faith in God that it will happen just as he told me. ²⁶Nevertheless, we must run aground on some island."

²⁷On the fourteenth night we were still being driven across the Adriatic Sea, when about midnight the sailors sensed they were approaching land. ²⁸They took soundings and found that the water was a hundred and twenty feet deep. A short time later they took soundings again and found it was ninety feet deep. ²⁹Fearing that we would be dashed against the rocks, they dropped four anchors from the stern and prayed for daylight. ³⁰In an attempt to escape from the ship, the sailors let the lifeboat down into the sea, pretending they were going to lower some anchors from the bow. ³¹Then Paul said to the centurion and the soldiers, "Unless these men stay with the ship, you cannot be saved." ³²So the soldiers cut the ropes that held the lifeboat and let it fall away.

³³Just before dawn Paul urged them all to eat. "For the last fourteen days," he said, "you have been in constant suspense and have gone without food—you haven't eaten anything. ³⁴Now I urge you to take some food. You need it to survive. Not one of you will lose a single hair from his head." ³⁵After he said this, he took some bread and gave thanks to God in front of them all. Then he broke it and began to eat. ³⁶They were all encouraged and ate some food themselves. ³⁷Altogether there were 276 of us on board. ³⁸When they had eaten as much as they wanted, they lightened the ship by throwing the grain into the sea.

³⁹When daylight came, they did not recognize the land, but they saw a bay with a sandy beach, where they decided to run the ship aground if they could. ⁴⁰Cutting loose the anchors, they left them in the sea and at the same time untied the ropes that held the rudders. Then they hoisted the foresail to the wind and made for the beach. ⁴¹But the ship struck a sandbar and ran aground. The bow stuck fast and would not move, and the stern was broken to pieces by the pounding of the surf.

42The soldiers planned to kill the prisoners to prevent any of them from swimming away and escaping. 43But the centurion wanted to spare Paul's life and kept them from carrying out their plan. He ordered those who could swim to jump overboard first and get to land. 44The rest were to get there on planks or on pieces of the ship. In this way everyone reached land in safety.

COMMENTARY

13–15 Shortly after the decision to winter at Phoenix was made, a gentle southern breeze began to blow, and it appeared that they would have no trouble in crossing the Gulf of Messara, which began west of Cape Matala on the southern coast of Crete. But no sooner had they rounded the cape and entered the gulf than they were caught in a hurricane coming from Mount Ida to the north. Sailors called this "the Euroquilon" (*Eurakylōn*), a hybrid compound of the Greek word *euros*, which means "east wind," and the Latin word *aquilo*, which means "north wind" (so NIV, "the 'northeaster'"; on NASB's "Euraquilo," see NASB text note). Before this cyclone wind, with its torrential rain accompanied by peels of thunder and flashes of lightning, they were helpless.

16–17 Driven southwest some twenty-three miles to the small island of Cauda (modern Gavdos or Gozzo), the ship managed to gain the lee of the island. The sailors pulled in the dinghy, which was full of water, reinforced the ship with ropes to keep it from breaking up, and put out the sea anchor to keep the ship from running onto the sandbars of Syrtis, off the African coast west of Cyrene.

The statement *echrōnto hypozōnnyntes to ploion* (NIV, "they tied ropes around the ship"; NASB, "they used supporting cables in undergirding the ship") is difficult to translate precisely because the verb *hypozōnnymi* ("undergird, brace," GK *5690*) seems to have been an ancient nautical term that could have signified any one of a number of proce-

dures: (1) passing ropes under a ship and securing them above deck in order to reinforce the hull in a heavy sea (so KJV, NEB, NIV, NRSV); (2) tying ropes around a ship's hull above water for the same purpose (so JB, TEV); or (3) frapping or hogging a vessel by tying the stem and stern tightly together with ropes above the deck in order to keep it from breaking its back in a heavy sea (so Cadbury, 10, with his argument based on an Egyptian drawing of boats in Queen Hatseput's naval expedition some eighteen and a half centuries before Luke).

18–20 For fourteen days and nights (cf. v.27) the ship was in the grip of the hurricane. The crew tried to lighten the ship by throwing overboard all the deck cargo (v.18) and then by disposing of the ship's tackle (v.19). In the darkness of the storm they could not take their bearings from the sun or stars. All hope of being saved had vanished (v.20).

21–26 Undoubtedly, Paul shared the general pessimism on board the ship (cf. the inclusive use of "we" in v.20). But one night toward the close of the fourteen-day storm, "an angel of . . . God" stood by Paul and reassured him (v.24) with a message of comfort for this time of crisis (cf. 23:11). The next morning, when Paul shared the angel's message with his companions on board, he was human enough to say, in effect, "I told you so" to those who had not taken his advice at Fair Havens (v.21). Moreover, ever one to give advice, he added that in his opinion they would not be saved without running aground on some island (v.26).

27–29 During the fourteenth night after leaving Crete it became clear—probably from the running swell and the roar of the surf—that they were close to shore. And soundings indicated that they had come into shallower water. So to keep the ship from being wrecked in the darkness against the rocks of some unknown coast, they dropped four anchors and waited for dawn. Luke tells us that they were in the Adrian Sea (*en tō Adria*), which many (including NIV, NASB, JB [though not KJV, NEB, TEV, NRSV]) have confused with the Adriatic Sea (though see the footnote in JB). The Greek geographer Strabo (63 BC–AD 24), however, indicated that "the Ionian Sea is part of what is now [in AD 19] called the Sea of Hadria" (*Geogr.* 2.5.20). Josephus (*Life* 15) reports that in AD 63 he suffered shipwreck, together with six hundred others bound for Rome, in the central Mediterranean "in the midst of the sea of Adria" (*kata meson tō Adrian*), with only eighty being plucked from the waters to continue their journey. Such references suggest that the name "Adria[n]" or "Hadria[n]" was used for the entire portion of the Mediterranean Sea between Greece, Italy, and Africa.

30–32 Contrary to the best tradition of the sea, the sailors schemed to save themselves by lowering the dinghy (cf. vv.16–17) under cover of lowering more anchors from the bow. But Paul saw through the ruse, doubtless realizing that no sailor would drop anchors from the bow under such conditions. He knew that to try to make shore in the morning without a full crew would be disastrous. So Paul warned Julius that all would be lost if the sailors deserted the ship (v.31). Though he had not listened to Paul earlier (cf. vv.11–12), Julius now took his advice and ordered his men to cut the lines holding the dinghy and let it fall away (v.32).

33–38 The storm had been so fierce that preparing food had been impossible. At this time of crisis, Paul's qualities of leadership came to the fore. Urging all on board to eat, he took some bread, gave thanks to God, and ate it (v.35). The others on board also ate (v.36). Then, strengthened by the food, they threw the cargo of grain overboard to give the ship a shallower draft as they beached her (v.38).

Only at v.37 does Luke tell us how many were on board. Probably an accurate count became necessary when distributing the food. Perhaps Luke himself had some part in distributing the food and so would have had it fixed in his mind that "altogether there were 276 of us on board." Though there is some manuscript evidence for reading 76, there is nothing improbable in the larger and better-attested number 276. Josephus tells of making a Mediterranean crossing to Rome in a ship with 600 people on board that was also wrecked (see comments at vv.27–29).

39–41 Here Luke tells with a profusion of nautical detail that makes this chapter unique how the ship was beached amid the pounding surf on a sandbar (*eis topon dithalasson*, lit., "on a place of two seas" with deep water on both sides) some distance from land and began to break apart. From then on it was every man for himself.

42–44 Roman military law decreed that a guard who allowed his prisoner to escape was subject to the same penalty the escaped prisoner would have suffered (see comments at 12:18–19a; 16:25–28). Thus the soldiers wanted to kill the prisoners, lest they escape while getting to land. Julius, however, determined to protect Paul, prevented the killing of the prisoners on board. He ordered everyone to get to land either by swimming or by holding on to pieces of the wreckage. So God in his providence brought them all safely to shore, as he had promised Paul he would (cf. v.24). Many, like Luke, undoubtedly saw the relation between the promise and their safety and in their own ways praised the God Paul served.

NOTES

14 The Alexandrian and Western textual traditions most commonly have for this torrential wind the name Εὐρακύλων (*Eurakylōn*), which suffered a number of minor emendations by the ancient scribes. The Byzantine text rather consistently calls the wind Εὐροκλύδων (*Euroklydōn*), which was incorporated by Erasmus into the TR and transliterated "Euroclydon" in the KJV.

15 The Western text (minuscules 82, 614, 1518, 2125, and as represented by the Syriac Harclean version) expands the last portion of this verse to read (with some variation of wording), "We gave way to the wind that was blowing; and having shortened the sail, we were, as chance would have it, driven before it."

16 Codex Sinaiticus (ℵ) has Κλαῦδα (*Klauda*, "Clauda") as the name of the island, whereas most Alexandrian and Western texts read Καῦδα (*Kauda*, "Cauda"). Most likely "Clauda" was the Greek form of its name and "Cauda" the Latin form. The Byzantine text (H L P and most minuscules), as followed by the TR, has Κλαύδην (*Klaudēn*, "Claudan").

19 The Byzantine text (H L P, most minuscules, and as represented by a number of versions), as incorporated into the TR and translated by the KJV, has the first person plural verb ἐρρίψαμεν (*erripsamen*, "we threw out") rather than the better-supported third person plural ἔρριψαν (*erripsan*, "they threw out"; NIV and NASB, "they threw . . . overboard").

The Western text (minuscule 614, and as represented by recensions of the Old Latin, Vulgate, Syriac, and Coptic versions) adds at the end of the verse εἰς τὴν θάλασσαν (*eis tēn thalassan*, "into the sea"), which is rather obvious.

27 Codex Vaticanus (B) reads προσαχεῖν (*prosachein*, "to resound") rather than the more widely supported προσάγειν (*prosagein*, "to approach [the land]"). The use of προσάγειν (*prosagein*) in its context is somewhat difficult, for literally it should be read, "land was approaching them." So it may have given rise to other readings. Perhaps, however, as many have suggested, the verb προσαχεῖν (*prosachein*) was a nautical expression used by sailors to signal a "resounding surf," which is suggested also by the Latin translation *resonare* in the Old Latin recensions "g" and "s" of the ninth and sixth centuries respectively.

29–30 The Old Latin Gigas version and the Vulgate add typical Western expansions at the end of each of these verses: at the end of v.29, *ut sciremus an salvi esse possimus* ("that we might know whether we could be saved"); and at the end of v.30, *ut tutius navis staret* ("that the ship might ride more safely").

35 The Western text (minuscules 614, 1611, 2147, and as represented by the Coptic Sahidic and Syriac Harclean versions) adds at the end of the verse the words ἐπιδιδοὺς καὶ ἡμῖν (*epididous kai hēmin*, "having given also to us"), evidently attempting to include Luke and Aristarchus in the original eating of the food (also Secundus if the Western reading of v.2 above is accepted).

37 Codex Vaticanus (B), supported by the Coptic Sahidic and Ethiopic versions, reads ὡς ἑβδομήκοντα ἕξ (*hōs hebdomēkonta hex*, "about 76"). That Luke's usual use of ὡς (*hōs*, "about"; see note at 1:15) seems somewhat out of place with so exact a number probably explains why Epiphanius has ὡς ἑβδομήκοντα (*hōs hebdomēkonta*, "about 70"), thereby bringing it into line with Luke's usual practice. Codex Alexandrinus (A) reads 275; minuscule 69 and Ephraem in his commentary on Acts read 270; Coptic Bohairic recensions read either 176 or 876.

39 Codices B and C, supported by recensions of the Coptic and Armenian versions, read ἐκσῶσαι τὸ πλοῖον (*eksōsai to ploion*, "to bring the ship [to shore]") rather than the more widely supported ἐξῶσαι τὸ πλοῖον (*exōsai to ploion*; NIV, "to run the ship aground"), which is a more prosaic way to express good nautical language.

41 This is the only instance of ναῦς (*naus*, "ship") in the NT and may reflect Homeric usage. Codices ℵ A and B omit τῶν κυμάτων (*tōn kymatōn*, "of the surf" or "waves") after ὑπὸ τῆς βίας (*hypo tēs bias*, "by the pounding, violence," or "force"), but other Alexandrian texts (𝔓⁷⁴, corrected ℵ, C Ψ) and the Byzantine text (L P and most minuscules) include them. The textual evidence is almost evenly balanced. Most translators, even though the brevity of the Alexandrian text is usually regarded highly, accept them as a logical extension of thought (so, e.g., NIV, "the pounding of the surf"; NASB, "the force of the waves").

3. Ashore at Malta (28:1–10)

¹Once safely on shore, we found out that the island was called Malta. ²The islanders showed us unusual kindness. They built a fire and welcomed us all because it was raining and cold. ³Paul gathered a pile of brushwood and, as he put it on the fire, a viper, driven out by the heat, fastened itself on his hand. ⁴When the islanders saw the snake hanging from his hand, they said to each other, "This man must be a murderer; for though he escaped from the sea, Justice has not allowed him to live." ⁵But Paul shook the snake off into the fire and suffered no ill effects. ⁶The people expected him to swell up or suddenly fall dead, but after waiting a long time and seeing nothing unusual happen to him, they changed their minds and said he was a god.

⁷There was an estate nearby that belonged to Publius, the chief official of the island. He welcomed us to his home and for three days entertained us hospitably. ⁸His father was sick in bed, suffering from fever and dysentery. Paul went in to see him and, after prayer, placed his hands on him and healed him. ⁹When this had happened, the rest of the sick on the island came and were cured. ¹⁰They honored us in many ways and when we were ready to sail, they furnished us with the supplies we needed.

COMMENTARY

1 Malta (*Melitē*), on which the ship was wrecked, is an island about 18 miles long and 8 miles wide. It lies 58 miles south of Sicily and 180 miles north and east of the African coast. It was colonized about 1000 BC by the Phoenicians, and its people in Paul's day spoke a Punic (Carthaginian) dialect. In 218 BC, it was captured by Rome at the start of the Second Punic War waged against Carthage and granted the status of a *municipium*, which allowed a large measure of local autonomy. Augustus established on the island a Roman governor, who bore the title *municipi Melitesium primus omnium*, "the chief man over all in the municipality of Malta" (*CIL* 10.7495; cf. *CIG* 5754), or as more colloquially expressed in v.7, *ho protos tes nēsou*, "the first man of the island." He also settled a number of army veterans and their families there. In Paul's day, the island was known for its prosperity and residential architecture, and its native population must have spoken not only a Punic dialect of Phoenician but also some Latin and Greek.

Melitē has at times been identified with Meleda or Mljet off the Dalmatian coast in the northeastern part of the Adriatic Sea, far to the northeast of Malta. But that is linked to the confusion of "Adria[n]" with "Adriatic" (see comments at 27:27). In all likelihood, the ship was blown westward from Crete to the eastern coast of Malta rather than northwestward into the Adriatic. So the traditional location of Saint Paul's Bay on Malta should continue to be considered the most probable site for Paul's landing. The island was first named by Phoenicians, in whose language *melita* meant "a place of refuge"—a name that fits it quite naturally.

2 Luke calls the natives who welcomed them *hoi barbaroi* (GK *975*), i.e., "barbarians" (cf. also v.4), which the NIV well translates unpejoratively as "islanders" and the NASB as "natives." *Barbaroi* is an onomatopoetic word (i.e., a word whose sound suggests its sense). To the Greeks and Romans strange languages sounded like a jumble of sounds such as "bar-bar-bar"; thus the word "barbarian" (Lat., *barbarus*). Today "barbarian" connotes a savage or primitive person or a crude, uneducated one. But that was not always what the Greeks and Romans meant by it. As for the Maltese, though their language sounded strange, they were hardly savages. They built a fire, Luke says, to welcome "us all" (*pantas hēmas*), which was just what was needed in the cold and rain.

3–4 When Paul was bitten by the snake, the islanders concluded he was a murderer whom the

goddess Dike (*hē dikē*, the Greek word for "justice," GK *1472*) had at last caught up with since he hadn't died at sea. The Greek goddess Dike, or her Phoenician counterpart, was apparently venerated by the Maltese. Had Paul died, they might have written an epitaph like the one Statyllius Flaccus wrote for a shipwrecked sailor who was killed by snakebite:

> O, he escaped the storm and the raging of the murderous sea. But as he lay stranded in the Libyan sand, not far from the beach and heavy with sleep, at last, naked and destitute, weary as he was from the terrible shipwreck, the viper struck him dead. Why did he struggle against the waves? He did not escape the lot which was destined for him on land. (*Palatine Anthology* 7.290)

Today Malta has no venomous snakes. But as William M. Ramsay (*St. Paul the Traveller*, 343) once noted, "Such changes [in animal life] are natural and probable in a small island, populous and long civilized."

6 Seeing that Paul was unaffected by the snakebite, the islanders decided he must be a god or perhaps a favorite of the gods (cf. Plutarch's statement [*Cleomenes* 39.3] that Cleomenes, who was miraculously protected by a snake, was a *theophilēs*, a "favorite of the gods"). Nothing is said about Paul's rebuking of the Maltese islanders as he had rebuked the people at Lystra (cf. 14:15–18), for evidently there was no attempt at Malta to worship Paul.

Luke gives us such a vividly detailed account of the incident because he wants his readers to appreciate that Paul was not only a heavenly directed man with a God-given message but also a heavenly protected man. The powerful account of the storm and shipwreck has shown this to be so, and now this vignette stresses it once more.

7 Though Paul spent three months on Malta (cf. v.11), Luke sets out only one further incident from his stay there, namely, the healing of Publius's father. It is an account much like that of Peter and the crippled beggar in its purpose (cf. 3:1–10), though not in its length. Luke seems to have included the account to illustrate the continuing power of Paul's ministry, despite his being on Malta as a prisoner destined for a hearing before Caesar. For no matter what the circumstances are, the true servant of Christ is, like Paul, never off duty for his Lord.

As the Roman governor of Malta, Publius had the title "the first man of the island" (see comments at v.1). As an act of official courtesy, he brought the survivors of the wreck to his estate and entertained them for three days while their respective situations were sorted out and arrangements were made for their lodgings over the winter on the island. Luke's reference to the governor only by his praenomen, though remarkable, would not have been exceptional in the ancient world. Perhaps the islanders regularly spoke of the governor simply by his first name, and Luke, who had no great sympathy for Roman nomenclature, simply reported the name as he heard it in common use. Or perhaps his use of the first name reflects the friendly relationship that had developed between Publius and Paul (and perhaps Luke also) during those three months.

8–9 The malady the father of Publius was suffering from may have been what has been called "Malta fever," which was a sickness long common at Malta, Gibraltar, and other Mediterranean locales. In 1887, its cause—the microorganism *Micrococcus melitensis*—was discovered and traced to the milk of Maltese goats. A vaccine for its treatment has been developed. Cases of Malta fever are long-lasting—an average of four months, but in some cases lasting two or three years. Luke uses the plural *pyretois* ("fevers," GK *4790*) in his description, probably with reference to the way it affects its victims with intermittent attacks.

After Paul had healed Publius's father through prayer and the laying on of hands, "the rest of the sick on the island" came to him and were healed (v.9). Luke's use of "the rest" (*hoi loipoi*), which suggests that all who were sick on the island flocked to Paul and he healed them all, is doubtless somewhat hyperbolic. What Luke is telling us is that Paul's ministry to those he met consisted in both proclaiming the good news of Jesus Christ and healing them physically.

Luke's inclusion of this vignette prepares for the climax of his book: Paul's entrance into Rome and the triumphant note, "without hindrance" (the adverb *akōlutōs*, GK *219*), with which he ended his two volumes (cf. v.31).

10 As a result of Paul's ministry during his three months on Malta, the islanders honored him and his party in many ways (*hoi kai pollais timais etimēsan hēmas*, lit., "they honored us with many honors"). Paul was no god, as they had soon learned. But he was a messenger of the one true God, with good news of life and wholeness in Christ. In carrying out his God-given commission, Paul gave of himself unstintingly in behalf of people. That they appreciated his selfless ministry is evidenced by their giving to him and his colleagues supplies for the rest of their journey.

From what Luke tells us, it seems that Paul may have looked on his stay on the island of Malta as a high point in his ministry—a time of blessing when God worked in marvelous ways despite the shipwreck and his still being a prisoner. Through the experiences at Malta, God seems to have been refreshing Paul's spirit after the two relatively bleak years at Caesarea and the disastrous time at sea and to have been preparing him for his witness at Rome.

NOTES

1 Codex Vaticanus (B) reads Μελιτήνη (*Melitēnē*) instead of the better-supported Μελίτη (*Melitē*) of the other Alexandrian texts (ℵ A C etc.), the Byzantine text (L P and most minuscules), together with the Byzantine uncial MSS L P, most minuscules, and recensions of the Vulgate, Syriac, and Coptic versions. The reading Μελιτήνη (*Melitēnē*) probably arose through dittography of some of the letters in Μελίτη ἡ νῆσος καλεῖται (*Melitē hē nēsos kaleitai*, "the island called Malta"). Bodmer 𝔓⁷⁴ spells the name Μιλήτη (*Milētē*), which is only a variant spelling. Some recensions of the Old Latin and Vulgate reflect the spelling Μυτιλήνη (*Mytilēnē*), which seems to be a translation or transcriptional error of the Greek name (perhaps from B) into Latin.

5 On Luke's use of μὲν οὖν (*men oun*), see comments at 1:6. Here the connective is used to join two parts of one account (as is more common in the second half of Acts) rather than to tie together source material, editorial introductions, and editorial conclusions (as in the first half of Acts).

4. Arrival at Rome (28:11–16)

¹¹After three months we put out to sea in a ship that had wintered in the island. It was an Alexandrian ship with the figurehead of the twin gods Castor and Pollux. ¹²We put in at Syracuse and stayed there three days. ¹³From there we set sail and arrived at Rhegium. The next day the south wind came up, and on the following day we reached Puteoli. ¹⁴There we found some brothers who invited us to spend a week with them. And so we came to Rome. ¹⁵The brothers there had heard that we were coming, and they traveled as far as the Forum of Appius and the Three Taverns to meet us. At the sight of these men Paul thanked God and was encouraged. ¹⁶When we got to Rome, Paul was allowed to live by himself, with a soldier to guard him.

COMMENTARY

11 Luke tells us that "after three months" (*meta de treis mēnas*) the centurion Julius arranged for another ship to take his group of prisoners and contingent of soldiers on to Italy. Pliny the Elder (AD 23–79), the Roman naturalist, speaks of navigation on the Mediterranean as beginning each spring on February 8, when the westerly winds started to blow (*Nat.* 2.122), though Vegetius (*De Re Militari* 4.39) seems to imply that the seas were closed until March 10, by which he probably meant travel on the high seas and not coastal shipping. It may therefore be postulated that sometime in early or mid-February of AD 61 Paul and his colleagues boarded ship again for the last leg of their voyage to Italy after their shipwreck on Malta, which occurred perhaps in late October of the previous year (see comments at 27:9). The ship was another Alexandrian vessel—probably another grain ship from Egypt that had been able to harbor at Malta before winter set in and the hurricane struck.

Ships, like inns, took their names from their figureheads. And this one, Luke tells us, was "distinguished by the Dioscuroi" (*parasēmō Dioskourois*; NIV, "the twin gods Castor and Pollux"; NASB, "the Twin Brothers"), i.e., the painted carving at its prow of Castor and Pollux (the sons of Leda, queen of Sparta), who in Greek mythology were transformed by Zeus into twin gods represented by the constellation Gemini. The cult of the Dioscuroi (lit., "sons of Zeus") was especially widespread in Egypt, and the Gemini were considered by sailors a sign of good fortune in a storm. For an Alexandrian ship, the figurehead was an appropriate one.

12 Sailing north-northeast, the ship reached the harbor of Syracuse, on the east coast of Sicily. There at the most important city of Sicily it remained for three days, probably loading and unloading cargo and waiting for better weather conditions.

13 From Syracuse the ship "set sail" (*perielontes*, lit., "weighed anchor") for Rhegium (modern Reggio di Calabria), an important harbor at the toe of Italy and on the Italian side of the Strait of Messina. There it docked to await a more favorable breeze. On the next day, a southerly wind began to blow, and they were able to make the 180 miles up the coast of Italy to Puteoli (modern Pozzuoli) in only two days. Puteoli was a resort city on the Bay of Naples, the port city for Neapolis (modern Naples), and the principal port of southern Italy. It vied with Ostia, the port of Rome at the mouth of the Tiber, as a terminus for grain ships from Egypt. There Paul and his associates, who were still prisoners guarded by the centurion Julius and his contingent of soldiers, disembarked.

14 There are two rather surprising statements in this verse. At Puteoli Paul and his companions "found some brothers [*adelphoi*, GK *81*] who invited us to spend a week with them." It was not, of course, unusual for Christians to be found in such an important city as Puteoli. There was a Jewish

colony there (cf. Josephus, *J.W.* 2.104; *Ant.* 17.328), from which some may have become Christians on their travels or through the witness of believers who visited Puteoli. What is surprising is that Paul as a prisoner was at liberty to seek out the Christians of the city and accept their invitation to spend seven days with them. Nevertheless, it is possible that for some reason Julius found it necessary to stop at Puteoli for a week after disembarking and that during that time he allowed Paul the freedom (though undoubtedly accompanied by a guard) to seek out the believers of that city and enjoy their hospitality, as he did at Sidon when the journey to Rome began (cf. 27:3). As Luke presses toward the end of his story, his account becomes more and more concise—so much so that the reader feels some measure of surprise.

A second surprising feature of v.14 is its forthright conclusion: "And so we came to Rome" (*kai houtōs eis tēn Rhōmēn ēlthamen*), which the KJV toned down to "and so we went toward Rome" by treating the verb as an imperfect rather than an aorist. It is not surprising that they came to Rome. That had for some time been the goal of Paul's journey and Luke's narrative. But that the mention of their arrival appears here before v.15—and not as the opening statement of v.16, where it would seem to have been more appropriate—is somewhat surprising. William M. Ramsay (*St. Paul the Traveller*, 346–47) argued that this double mention of Rome was probably due to "the double sense that every name of a city-state bears in Greek," i.e., the whole administrative district of Rome (*ager Romanus*) and the actual city itself. But the adverb *kakeithen* ("and from there"; NIV, "there"; NASB, "from there") that begins v.15 shows that in view is the actual city of Rome, not just an administrative district. The problem, therefore, is not so easy to explain away either by treating the verb as an imperfect (so KJV) or by understanding "Rome" here as the surrounding administrative district of Rome and not the city itself (so W. M. Ramsay).

All things considered, probably the best explanation for the appearance of the statement "and so we came to Rome" in v.14 is that it reflects Luke's eagerness to get to the climax of his story—i.e., his eagerness to get Paul and his associates to Rome led him to anticipate their arrival at Rome, even though he must yet include another detail of the last stage of their journey before actually reaching that climax. It seems, therefore, that the solution to the conundrum lies more along psychological lines than linguistic or administrative lines.

15 Taking the Via Domitiana from Puteoli to Neapolis, Paul would have passed the tomb of the poet Virgil (Publius Vergilius Maro [70–19 BC]). In the Mass of Saint Paul celebrated until the fifteenth century at Mantua (Virgil's birthplace), this Latin poem about Paul at Virgil's tomb was included:

> Virgil's tomb the saint stood viewing,
> And his aged cheek bedewing,
> Fell the sympathetic tear;
> "Ah, had I but found thee living,
> What new music wert thou giving,
> Best of poets and most dear."
>
> T. R. Glover's free translation

Imaginary though the encounter may be, this poem points to the link between Virgil's vibrant humanity and intense longing for a savior on the one hand and Paul's dynamic gospel with its answer to that longing on the other.

At Neapolis, Julius, his contingent of soldiers, and his group of prisoners turned northwest to travel to Rome on the Via Appia—the oldest, straightest, and most perfectly made of all the Roman roads, which was named after the censor Appius Claudius, who

started its construction in 312 BC. During the seven-day stopover at Puteoli, news of Paul's arrival in Italy reached Rome. So a number of Christians there set out to meet him and escort him back to Rome. Some of them got as far as the Forum of Appius (*Forum Appii*), one of the "halting stations" built every ten to fifteen miles along the entire length of the Roman road system. It was forty-three miles from Rome in the Pontine marshland, and a market town had grown up around it. Others only got as far as the Inn of the Three Taverns (*Tres Tabernae*), another halting station about thirty-three miles from Rome. Paul's gratitude to God for the delegation that met him must have been unusually fervent, for Luke pauses in his travel narration to make special mention of it. In his letters Paul often urges his readers to be thankful, and here he spontaneously puts into effect his own advice.

16 At Rome Paul was allowed to live in his own rented quarters, though a soldier guarded him at all times. The "chain" he wore, which he refers to in v.20, was probably attached to his wrists. Yet in Luke's eyes Paul entered Rome in triumph. By his coming the gospel was able to penetrate official circles in the capital of the empire. Furthermore, God used his detention for two years at Rome to spread the proclamation of "the kingdom of God" and "the Lord Jesus Christ" throughout the city (cf. vv.30–31).

With this verse, the last "we" section in Acts comes to an end. To judge by the greetings in Colossians 4:10–14 and Philemon 23–24 (assuming a Roman provenance for these letters), Luke and Aristarchus must have remained with Paul through most, if not all, of his detention at Rome and been joined from time to time by such friends as Epaphras, John Mark, Demas, and Jesus (surnamed "Justus").

NOTES

11 On μετά (*meta*, "after") with time designation (here τρεῖς μῆνας, *treis mēnas*, "three months") as a Lukan connective in the latter half of Acts, see comments at 15:36 (see also v.17 below).

13 The better MSS of the Alexandrian text (ℵ B Ψ) read περιελόντες (*perielontes*, lit., "take away" or "weigh anchor," GK *4311*), whereas Bodmer 𝔓74, a corrected Codex Sinaiticus (ℵ2), and Codex Alexandrinus (A), together with the Byzantine text (L P and most minuscules), read περιελθόντες (*perielthontes*, lit., "sailed around" or "made a circuit," GK *4320*). Perhaps the reading περιελόντες (*perielontes*) was simply a scribal error that dropped the letter θ—an error that was later corrected to read περιελθόντες (*perielthontes*). Probably, however, περιελόντες (*perielontes*) was a nautical term that meant something like "set sail" (NIV) or "sailed" (NASB).

14 The NIV, NASB, NRSV, JB, and TEV treat the verb ἤλθαμεν (*ēlthamen*) as an aorist and translate it, "and so [or thus] we came to Rome." The NEB tries to sidestep the issue with its reading, "and so to Rome," but ends up in agreement with the KJV in wrongly understanding the verb as an imperfect.

Contra William M. Ramsay, since the Forum of Appius and the Three Taverns Inn were both within the administrative district of Rome (*ager Romanus*), Luke would hardly have distinguished them from the *ager Romanus* by the use of the adverb κἀκεῖθεν (*kakeithen*, "and from there"), for one would not go "from there" (i.e., according to Ramsay's view, from the administrative district governed by the city of Rome) to the halting stations of the Forum of Appius and the Three Taverns Inn if they lay within the same district.

16 The Western text (minuscules 614, 1611, 2147, and as represented by recensions of the Old Latin, Vulgate, and Syriac versions), followed in part by the Byzantine text, expands this verse to read, "When we got to Rome, the centurion turned over his prisoners to the *stratopedarch* (τῷ στρατοπεδάρχῳ, *tō stratopedarchō*), but Paul was allowed . . ." What the Western and Byzantine editors had in mind by *stratopedarch* has been surmised to be either (1) the commander of the *castra peregrinorum* on the Caelian Hill (i.e., the headquarters of the legionary officers on furlough at Rome) or (2) the prefect or "captain" of the praetorian guard (who was the noble Afranius Burrus during AD 51–62). This reading was incorporated into the TR and so passed into the KJV.

The Western text also adds ἔξω τῆς παρεμβολῆς (*exō tēs parembolēs*, "outside the barracks") after καθ' ἑαυτόν (*kath' heauton*, "by himself").

F. Rome at Last (28:17–30)

OVERVIEW

At last, Paul's great desire to visit the capital of the empire (cf. Ro 15:22–24, 28–29) was fulfilled. Despite his house arrest, guards, and manacles, he was free to receive visitors. Among them, Luke tells us, were (1) the leading Jews of the city, whom he asked to visit him when he first arrived (vv.17–28), and (2) others, evidently both Jews and Gentiles, who came to his quarters at various times during his two-year detention (v.30).

1. Meetings with the Jewish Leaders (28:17–28)

OVERVIEW

Three days after (*meta hēmeras treis*) arriving at Rome, Paul invited the leaders of the Jewish community to meet with him in his quarters. He wanted to learn what they had heard from Jerusalem about him and find out their attitude toward him, for through their contacts with the imperial court and their money they could, if they desired, support the Jewish charges against him. Since they undoubtedly knew something about his case, he wanted to defend himself before them. He also hoped the occasion would be an opportunity to proclaim the message about Jesus the Messiah and that some would respond favorably to that message.

¹⁷Three days later he called together the leaders of the Jews. When they had assembled, Paul said to them: "My brothers, although I have done nothing against our people or against the customs of our ancestors, I was arrested in Jerusalem and handed over to the Romans. ¹⁸They examined me and wanted to release me, because I was not guilty of any crime deserving death. ¹⁹But when the Jews objected, I was compelled to appeal to Caesar—not that I had any charge to bring against my own people. ²⁰For this reason I have asked to see you and talk with you. It is because of the hope of Israel that I am bound with this chain."

²¹They replied, "We have not received any letters from Judea concerning you, and none of the brothers who have come from there has reported or said anything bad about you. ²²But we want to hear what your views are, for we know that people everywhere are talking against this sect."

²³They arranged to meet Paul on a certain day, and came in even larger numbers to the place where he was staying. From morning till evening he explained and declared to them the kingdom of God and tried to convince them about Jesus from the Law of Moses and from the Prophets. ²⁴Some were convinced by what he said, but others would not believe. ²⁵They disagreed among themselves and began to leave after Paul had made this final statement: "The Holy Spirit spoke the truth to your forefathers when he said through Isaiah the prophet:

²⁶ "'Go to this people and say,
  "You will be ever hearing but never understanding;
    you will be ever seeing but never perceiving."
²⁷ For this people's heart has become calloused;
    they hardly hear with their ears,
    and they have closed their eyes.

> Otherwise they might see with their eyes,
>   hear with their ears,
>   understand with their hearts
> and turn, and I would heal them.'
>
> ²⁸"Therefore I want you to know that God's salvation has been sent to the Gentiles, and they will listen!"

COMMENTARY

17–20 Paul began with the formal salutation used at Jewish gatherings: "men, brothers" (*andres adelphoi*; NIV, "my brothers"; NASB, "brethren"). The very first word of his address—the first person pronoun "I" (*egō*), which in his précis Luke places even before the salutation—clearly shows that Paul was about to deliver a personal apologia. He had done nothing, he insisted, against the Jewish people or against the customs of the fathers. Furthermore, the Roman authorities had judged that he had not committed any capital crime and were willing to release him (v.18). But objections from Jerusalem forced him to appeal to Caesar—not to accuse his own people but to save his life (v.19). The point of contention between him and his accusers had to do with the messianic hope of Israel, which Paul believed was fulfilled in Jesus of Nazareth and they did not. So he concluded, "It is because of the hope of Israel that I am bound with this chain" (v.20; cf. 23:6; 24:21; 26:6–8).

21–22 The immediate response of the Jewish leaders at Rome to Paul's address is somewhat surprising. Apparently they did not want to get involved. They disclaimed having received any letters about him from the Jewish authorities at Jerusalem, and they said that they had heard nothing, officially or unofficially, against him from any Jew who had come to them from Judea (v.21). Yet Christianity had been known within the Jewish

community at Rome for some time (see comments at 2:10). In fact, in the late 40s AD, Jews at Rome had been so sharply divided about Christianity that the emperor Claudius banished them—whether all of them or only the most prominent of their leaders—from the city to stop the riots there (see comments at 18:2). Certainly the Jewish leaders at Rome knew a great deal about Christianity generally and at least something about Paul, and their claim to know only "that people everywhere are talking against this sect" (v.22) seems much too "diplomatic" in light of their knowledge.

It is probably in the light of their recent experiences that we should judge the Jewish leaders' response to Paul's words. For having been expelled from Rome in AD 49 or 50 because of riots about Christianity in their community, and having only recently returned to their city after Claudius's death in AD 54, they were simply not prepared in AD 61 to become involved in Paul's case one way or another. They doubtless had their own opinions about Paul and his message. But (1) the Jerusalem authorities had not requested them to get involved; (2) Paul was a Roman citizen who had had essentially favorable hearings before two Roman governors, Felix and Festus, and before a Jewish king appointed by Rome, Agrippa II; and (3) his case was now to be tried in Caesar's court before the emperor himself. Though they were naturally curious, and as leaders in the Jewish community they needed to know about Paul and his message, they evidently wanted to have as little as possible to do with him or the Christian movement. But they did say that they were willing at some future time to hear his views on "this sect" (*tēs haireseōs* [GK *146*] *tautēs*, with the noun *hairesis* being the word from which our word "heresy" is derived).

23-24 So the leaders arranged a second meeting, and at that meeting an even larger delegation of Jewish leaders came to Paul's quarters. Luke tells us only that it lasted "from morning until evening" and that Paul proclaimed "the kingdom of God" (see comments at 1:3), focusing on Jesus, to whom the Law and the Prophets bore witness (v.23; cf. v.31). For the content of what he said, we should probably think of his sermon in the synagogue at Pisidian Antioch (13:17-41) and/or the substance of his letter sent to the Romans. As for his method, Luke only says that he "tried to convince them" (*peithōn autous*), which implies that Paul combined proclamation with persuasion (see comments at 17:2-4) and that there was a good deal of impassioned debate. The daylong session indeed proved profitable, for "some were convinced by what he said"—though, sadly, "others would not believe" (v.24).

25-28 The points at which many of the Jewish leaders disagreed with Paul, Luke says, were two: (1) Paul's attempt to prove the obduracy of Israel from the Scriptures by arguing that the prophet Isaiah had foretold the Jews' rejection of Jesus as Messiah, and (2) his insistence that because of Israel's hardened attitude the message of "God's salvation" has been sent directly to Gentiles, where it was finding a positive response. He documented the first point by quoting Isaiah 6:9-10. The LXX had already turned the imperatives of vv.9b-10a into finite verbs, with

the result that the entire blame for Israel's estrangement from God is placed on the stubbornness of the people themselves. This is how Jesus is also reported as having used the passage in the "Sayings" or "Logia" collection later incorporated into the Synoptic Gospels (cf. Mt 13:13-15; Lk 8:10; see also the use of the passage in Mk 4:12 and Jn 12:40, though not with quite the same thrust), and how Paul explained Israel's predicament in Romans 9-11. But Paul quotes prophecy here not just to explain Israel's stubbornness but to set the stage for his second point, namely, that in the providence of God redemption was now being offered directly to Gentiles, and they were responding (v.28).

A revolutionary new policy for proclaiming the gospel and making converts had been providentially worked out during Paul's first missionary journey and at the Jerusalem Council (cf. 12:25-16:5 and comments). That policy was then carried out through two more missionary journeys extending into Macedonia, Achaia, and Asia (cf. 16:6-19:20). It was a policy that advocated the proclamation of the gospel "first for the Jew, then for the Gentile" (Ro 1:16; cf. Ac 13:46-52). Luke has taken pains to show how everything that happened in the ministry of the early church at Jerusalem essentially looked forward to the inauguration of this policy and how this policy lay at the heart of Paul's missionary purpose. Now having traced the story of the advance of the gospel to Rome, Luke reports how that same pattern was followed at Rome. And his account of the gospel's advance from Jerusalem to Rome in terms of the distinctive policy of "first for the Jew, then for the Gentile" comes to a fitting conclusion with the quotation of Isaiah 6:9-10, which was one of the oldest Christian *testimonia* portions drawn from the OT.

NOTES

17 On μετά (*meta*, "after" [NASB]; NIV, "later") with a time designation (here ἡμέρας τρεῖς, *hēmeras treis*, "three days") as a Lukan connective in the latter half of Acts, see comments at 15:36 (see also note at v.11 above).

18 The Western text (minuscules 614, 2147, and as represented by the Syriac Harclean version) adds πολλά (*polla*, "much," "for a long time," or "about many things"), thereby reading, "they examined me for a long time [or "about many things"]," in line with its expansion at 24:6b–8a (see notes at those verses).

19 The Western text (minuscule 614, and as represented by the Syriac Harclean version) adds καὶ ἐπικραζόντων, Αἶρε τὸν ἐχθρὸν ἡμῶν (*kai epikrazontōn, Aire ton echthron hēmōn*, "and cried out, 'Away with our enemy!'") after τῶν Ἰουδαίων (*tōn Ioudaiōn*, "of the Jews"), thereby reading, "But when the Jews objected and cried out, 'Away with our enemy!', I was compelled to appeal to Caesar."

The Western text (the same texts as above, as well as other minuscules and recensions of the Old Latin and Vulgate) also adds at the end of the verse, ἀλλ᾽ ἵνα λυτρώσωμαι τὴν ψυχήν μου ἐκ θανάτου (*all' hina lytrōsōmai tēn psychēn mou ek thanatou*, "but in order that I might deliver my soul from death").

25 The Byzantine text (L P and many minuscules), together with various recensions of the Old Latin, Vulgate, and Coptic versions and a number of church fathers, have the first person plural possessive pronoun ἡμῶν (*hēmōn*, "our [ancestors]"), whereas the Alexandrian text (𝔓74 ℵ A B Ψ and many other minuscules), together with other recensions of the Old Latin, Vulgate, and Coptic versions and a number of other church fathers, have the second person plural possessive pronoun ὑμῶν (*hymōn*, "your [ancestors]"). Not only the better-attested Alexandrian text but also the tone and content of Paul's address—which convey nuances of censure and rejection—suggest not "our [fathers]" (so KJV) but "your [forefathers]" (so NIV, NASB).

29 The Alexandrian text (𝔓74 ℵ A B E Ψ etc.) does not include what has traditionally been identified as v.29. Western and Byzantine texts, however, with minor variations, have v.29: "And when he said these things, the Jews departed, and they had a great deal of controversy among themselves." The verse was probably added because of the seemingly abrupt transition from v.28 to v.30. It was incorporated into the TR and so appears in the KJV.

2. Continued Ministry for Two Years (28:30)

³⁰For two whole years Paul stayed there in his own rented house and welcomed all who came to see him.

COMMENTARY

30 Luke has accomplished his purpose in showing how the gospel that Paul proclaimed entered Rome and in depicting the initial response to that message in the capital city of the Roman Empire. Now he gives this terse reference to Paul's two years of house arrest.

Luke does not give us details about Paul's two-year detention at Rome because he is not writing a biography of his hero. Some argue that Paul was executed at the end of his imprisonment and that Luke did not speak of his execution because to do so would have ruined his portrayal of the triumphant advance of the gospel. Others propose that Paul's case never came to trial because his accusers failed to appear within the statutory eighteen-month period and that Luke expected his readers to understand that because a two-year period of detainment went beyond the statutory period for prosecution, Paul was released. But during the storm at sea an angel of the Lord had assured Paul that he would stand trial before Caesar (cf. 27:24). Therefore, it seems proper to assume that Luke intended his readers to infer that Paul's case—whatever its outcome—did in some manner come before the imperial court for judgment.

Henry Cadbury, as noted in the introduction (p. 666), speaks of "the extraordinary darkness which comes over us as students of history when rather abruptly this guide leaves us with Paul a prisoner in Rome." Indeed, we are forced to look elsewhere for further information about Paul's Roman imprisonment, his trial in Caesar's court, and its aftermath. Accepting the so-called Prison Epistles as having been written during Paul's Roman imprisonment, we may surmise that Paul fully expected to stand before Caesar's court and that, while he could not be certain, he also expected to be released (cf. Php 1:19–26; Phm 22). There is little reason to doubt his intuition. Therefore we may date such a release to somewhere around AD 63.

Furthermore, accepting the Pastoral Epistles as genuine—whether written directly by Paul himself, penned by an amanuensis at Paul's direction, or coauthored by someone such as Silas—we may believe that after Paul's release from this Roman imprisonment, he continued his evangelistic work in the eastern portion of the empire, at least in lands surrounding the Aegean Sea. Perhaps after that he even fulfilled his long-cherished desire to visit Spain (Ro 15:23–24, cf. *1 Clem.* 5). And since 2 Timothy 4:6–18 speaks of an approaching second trial in a tone of resignation, we may conclude that Paul was rearrested around AD 67 and, according to tradition, beheaded at Rome by order of Emperor Nero.

NOTES

30 The Western text (minuscules 614, 1518, and as represented by the Old Latin Gigas and Syriac Harclean versions, as well as by Ephraem of Syria in his Acts commentary) adds at the end of the verse, Ἰουδαίους τε καὶ Ἕλληνας (*Ioudaious te kai Hellēnas,* "both Jews and Greeks"), evidently in explication of "all [πάντας, *pantas*] who came to see him."

For a discussion of the major stylistic issues pertaining to the authorship of the Prison and Pastoral Epistles, see my "Ancient Amanuenses and the Pauline Epistles," in *New Dimensions in New Testament Study,* ed. R. N. Longenecker and M. C. Tenney (Grand Rapids: Zondervan, 1974), 281–97.

G. Summary Statement (28:31)

OVERVIEW

Luke's instinct in closing the second volume of his work as he did was completely correct. He was not writing a biography of Paul, even though he included many biographical details about his hero. Rather, he was setting out how the good news of humanity's redemption had swept out from Jerusalem, across Palestine, into Asia Minor, then on throughout Macedonia and Achaia, and how it finally entered Rome, the capital of the Roman Empire. The gospel Jesus had effected in his min- istry from Galilee to Jerusalem (as told in Luke's gospel) had reached its culmination in its extension from Jerusalem to Rome (as told in Luke's Acts). So when the story was told, his writing was finished. Nonetheless, it may be said that in seeming to leave his book open-ended, Luke may also be implying, under divine direction, that the apostolic proclama- tion of the gospel in the first century began a story that will continue until the final consummation of the kingdom in Christ (Ac 1:11).

> ³¹Boldly and without hindrance he preached the kingdom of God and taught about the Lord Jesus Christ.

COMMENTARY

31 This summary statement has often been viewed as only an amplification of v.30 that indi- cates the nature of Paul's ministry during his two years of detention at Rome. But to judge by Luke's practice in his other five summary statements in Acts (6:7; 9:31; 12:24; 16:5; 19:20), we are evidently meant to take it as the summary statement for the whole of panel 6 (19:21–28:31). In all of his prison experiences at Jerusalem, Caesarea, and Rome, Luke is saying that Paul "boldly [*meta pasēs parrēsias*, lit., "with all boldness"—which connotes "publicly," "candidly," and "forcefully"] . . . preached the king- dom of God and taught about the Lord Jesus Christ." And he did this, Luke goes on to insist, "without hindrance" (*akōlytōs*, GK *219*). By so say- ing, Luke suggests something of the tolerance of Rome at that time toward Christianity and the proclamation of the gospel—a tolerance that Luke passionately desired would continue and hoped to promote through his writing of these last chapters. Furthermore, since the final word of Acts is the crisp adverb *akōlytōs*, we may say with reasonable confi- dence that it was Luke's desire to close his two-volume work on this victorious note, namely, that the apos- tolic proclamation of the kingdom of God and the Lord Jesus Christ, despite all difficulties and misun- derstandings, had moved forward throughout the Jewish homeland and into the Roman Empire "without hindrance."

NOTES

31 The Western text, as represented with variations in recensions of the Old Latin, Vulgate, and Syriac versions, adds the following words to the end of this verse: "because this is the Messiah, Jesus the Son of God, by whom the whole world is to be judged." But while this addition was evidently intended to round off Luke's apparent abruptness, it only weakens his point and spoils his unique ending. As Metzger, 444, has aptly expressed it, "The artistic literary cadence of the concluding phrase of the book of Acts and the powerful note of triumph expressed by *akōlytōs* are greatly weakened by the pious Western addition."